~ *Families in the U.S.*

To Kate
Happy Women's History Month!
Anita Garey

In the series *Women in the Political Economy,* edited by Ronnie J. Steinberg

~ Families in the U.S.

Kinship and Domestic Politics

EDITED BY

Karen V. Hansen

AND

Anita Ilta Garey

TEMPLE UNIVERSITY PRESS

Philadelphia

Temple University Press, Philadelphia 19122
Copyright © 1998 by Karen V. Hansen and Anita Ilta Garey
All rights reserved
Published 1998
Printed in the United States of America

♾ The paper used in this publication meets the requirements of the American National Standard for Information Sciences—Permanence of Paper for Printed Library
Materials, ANSI Z39.48-1984

Text design by Erin Kirk New

Library of Congress Cataloging-in-Publication Data
Families in the U.S. : kinship and domestic politics /
    [edited by] Karen V. Hansen, Anita Ilta Garey.
        p.   cm. — (Women in the political economy)
    Includes bibliographical references.
    ISBN 1-56639-589-5 (cloth : alk. paper). — ISBN
1-56639-590-9 (pbk. : alk. paper)
    1. Family—United States. 2. Family policy—
United States. 3. Social structure—United States.
4. Social classes—United States. 5. Interracial marriage—United States. 6. Gay parents—United
States. 7. Family violence—United States. 8. Work
and family—United States. I. Hansen, Karen V. II.
Garey, Anita Ilta, 1947–
HQ536.F3337   1998
306.85′0973—dc21   97-49223

TO OUR FAMILIES

Sasha Garey Friedman, Aaron Garey, Ann Kovach Garey, Jason Garey, Jordyn Garey, Kelley Garey, Margot Garey, Shaaron Garey, Susan Houston Garey, TyAnn Garey, Hyam Glickman, Nicholas Houston, Margaret Weiss Kovach, Ernest Kovach (Paul Feldman), Hannah Laurence, Michael Laurence, Benjamin McFadden, Don McFadden, Donald McFadden, Paul McFadden, Janet Townsend, Nicholas Townsend, Charlotte Townsend-Gault, Emma Townsend-Gault, Ian Townsend-Gault, Sophie Townsend-Gault, Eric Bagai, Jeremy Bagai, Judy Bagai, Annika Bloch, Debbie Brennan, Mabel Chalker, Eilleen Clavere, Karen Frederick, Stanford Garey, Audrey Goodfriend, Barbara Kovach, Kandi Kovach, Kim Kovach, Kitt Kovach, Jacquelyn Marie, Jean Pauline, Pina Piccolo, Janet Roberts, Bob Scofield, Jeff Scofield, Margie Scofield, Cathy Townsend, Dominic Townsend, Margaret Townsend, Mary Baxter Townsend, Sally Townsend, William Townsend, Mary Zinkin,

Walter Benjamin, Alty Bolton, Andrew Bundy, Emma Bundy, James Bundy, Marion Abbott Bundy, Mary Lothrop Bundy, Mary Payton Bundy, McGeorge Bundy, Nora Bundy, Stephen Bundy, Will Bundy, William Bundy, Twilla Douglass, Sonya Haney, Augusta Hansen, Edwin Hansen, Eleanor Hansen, Esther Hansen, Eva Hansen, Gilbert Hansen, Harold Hansen, Jacob Hansen, Jens Christian Hansen, Lena Rosenbeck Hansen, Mabel Hansen, Maren Jensen Hansen, Rod Hansen, Benjy Hansen-Bundy, Evan Hansen-Bundy, Katherine Hippe, Sylvia Horning, Patty Jacobsen, Andrew Kanten, Buzz Kanten, Carmen Kanten, Dwayne Kanten, Ervin Kanten, Fager Kanten, Gilbert Kanten, Glen Kanten, Helena Haugen Kanten, Ivy Kanten, Ken Kanten, Leonard Kanten, Matia Borgerson Kanten, Nigel Kanten, Oscar Kanten, Phyllis Kanten, Sydney Kanten, Toots Kanten, Walter Kanten, Adrienne Kem, Michael Kem, Debbie Kobza, Elsie Little, Jessica Martin, Sandra Motze, Betty Nicholson, George O'Brien, Grant O'Brien, Florence O'Brien, Sharon O'Brien, Ronda Price, Carol Ross, Shannon Rubenstein, Charlene Russell, Health Russell, Candice Spencer, Gwen Thalheimer, Anne Tofflemire, Charles Wangerin, Bill Williams, Evelyn Williams,

. . . and to those who are yet to join us.

∾ *Contents*

III. *Webs of Family Relationships*

❧ Preface

This book was born of necessity, inspiration, and friendship. We both have taught various courses on the sociology of families and have been frustrated by the lack of adequate course materials available to teach from a critical feminist perspective. We typically assign monographs of original research and an anthology or two and then assemble numerous articles to fill in content and perspectives that would otherwise be missing.

After years of frustration, we decided to seize the opportunity and design an anthology that reflected upon and debated the complex intersections of structural forces and micro processes that together shape family life in the United States. We set out to compile and edit a collection that would meet our need for teaching state-of-the-art courses for undergraduate sociology majors, nonmajors, feminists, postfeminists, and nonfeminists alike.

Over the past several years we have read hundreds of articles in a variety of disciplines,

learned more about recent innovations (primarily by feminists) in the study of families, clarified our own perspectives on how to analyze families, and had a wonderful time working together. We have also spent some time wondering about the significance of the fact that our spell-checking software does not recognize the words "parenting," "gendered," "caregiving," or "ethnographic." As in any project, we were assisted along the way by many people. We would like to thank the friends and colleagues who helped us enormously through the process of compiling this volume.

Several colleagues and students read earlier drafts of the Introduction, sometimes on short notice, usually at the most inconvenient of times. Our thanks to Karen Barone, Andrew Bundy, Karla Hackstaff, Cameron Macdonald, Monica Roberts, Nicholas Townsend, Latasha Treger, and Lynet Uttal, and to our writing group who did not flinch at the prospect of reading work-in-progress: Paul Aymer, Carol

Brown, Nazli Kibria, JoAnne Preston, and Shelley Tenebaum. Many colleagues along the way suggested articles to include, titles to avoid, and ingenious marketing strategies. To those people, too numerous to mention, we offer our thanks.

Research assistants and graduate students helped us at various moments by searching the literature on elder care and on family violence, for example, or by running to the library to obtain and photocopy yet another new article, and by doing a myriad of supportive and intellectual tasks. We wish to thank Jody Grimes, Anne Pollock, Robyn Whipple, and Carrie Yodanis for their careful work and good humor. The reference librarians, especially Leslie Stebbins, at the Goldfarb Library at Brandeis have been unstinting in their time and energy, hunting down articles in obscure journals or finding phone numbers or e-mail addresses for authors we desperately sought.

The world of "permissions" is a mysterious and often frustrating place. In requesting from publishers the rights to reprint previously published material, we sometimes felt as if we had wandered into enemy territory. But they enabled us to compile this anthology and for that we thank them. We want particularly to thank Jim Henson of Sage Publication's Permissions Department for his assistance throughout this process, and we wish all permissions departments ran as smoothly as his does. But most of all, we appreciate his wonderful sense of humor, which made working with him fun as well as productive.

It has been deeply satisfying to work with the authors whose writings are included in this collection. We thank them for their enthusiasm about this project and for their collegial responses to our editing. But most of all we thank them for research and writing that

contributes to analyzing families with a feminist sociological imagination.

It has been our great pleasure to work with Michael Ames, who regularly offers us the best tradition of editorship—one that combines intellectualism and sage advice—and who has exercised a supportive, noninterventionist strategy toward the book.

In addition to those who have contributed directly to the completion of this book, we wish to acknowledge those who have provided emotional and material support through and beyond the journey of this joint project. Megan King good naturedly played "Civil War" and Parcheesi with Benjy and Evan even when her senior thesis beckoned. When we encountered a setback early on and considered abandoning the project, Andrew Bundy encouraged us to move forward. He and Nicholas Townsend have covered our share of daily life responsibilities during periods of intense work on the book, have joined us in celebrating each milestone in the book's preparation, and have, throughout it all, kept us laughing. And our children—Kelley, Sasha, Benjy, and Evan—have kept us mindful of the satisfactions of daily life, the importance of playing, and the reasons for writing this book.

We especially wish to thank Arlie Russell Hochschild. Not only has she been influential as a teacher, a mentor, and a role model risk-taker, but it was as graduate students in her class on gender at the University of California at Berkeley, that we first met.

The work of producing this collection was shared equally. We have listed our names in alphabetical order in the Introduction and we have reversed the order on the volume itself, but the editorship was a joint effort in every respect. We brought different expertise and interests to the project—for example, one of us had edited an anthology before, and one of us has the proclivities of a tenacious lawyer. But we both compulsively meet deadlines, indulge our cats, honor our working-class and immigrant heritage (Hungarian-Jewish and Scandinavian-Peasant, respectively), and share the joyful and sometimes frustrating experience of being mothers of sons. Through the past several years we have weathered our respective professional roller coaster rides while taking turns managing family crises. And despite a difference of opinion about the role of the state in our visions of utopia, we have had remarkably few disagreements about politics, methodology, or which articles to include. The postpartum depression we anticipate will not be about publishing the book but about no longer sharing a collaborative project.

Introduction

Analyzing Families with a Feminist Sociological Imagination

ANITA ILTA GAREY AND KAREN V. HANSEN

Imagine a family photo—of a wedding, of a holiday gathering, of a picnic at the beach. Who are these people? What is their relationship to one another? How do they feel about one another? Where were they the day before the photo was taken? Although a snapshot may provide a lot of information, the "Big Family Picture" lies outside the frame. What is the income of this family? How does their income influence the size of the wedding? Or where and how do they spend their summer vacation, if indeed they have one at all? We need to know the immediate circumstances in which the photograph was taken as well as the larger political, economic, and cultural worlds in which these people live. What would we see if we turned a page in the family album? Do some people disappear from the photographs? Has divorce, death, or separation removed someone from the family constellation? What new faces appear? Births, deaths, weddings, and family feuds change the particular picture of family but are evident only when looking at the collectivity of photographs over time. And we can only understand that visual collection

by placing it within a historical moment, an economic system, a political process that shape what is possible in family life.

Sociologist C. Wright Mills (1959:3) once wrote: "Neither the life of an individual, nor the history of a society, can be understood without understanding both." In this collection of readings, we apply Mills's insight to the study of families in the United States. To understand families we place them in their social and historical context—and to understand this society, we study the families within it. This moves us toward answers to the questions we posed about the snapshot. Mills called this approach "the sociological imagination." We expand his approach by analyzing the differing relationship of men and women to work, privilege, and power both inside and outside the family. We posit a feminist sociological imagination as the most illuminating way to study families.

Using rich ethnographic field work, in-depth interviews, historical analyses, and nuanced quantitative analyses, the authors in this book trace the interconnections of families and social structure. Our collective analysis begins with the knowledge that the organization of work influences the possibilities for finding employment, for earning a living wage, for advancing in a career, for affording education, and in turn, for making a satisfying family life. But despite the power of economic processes and social institutions to shape the parameters of what is possible, individuals engage in relationships and take action. They strategize to find resources for their families; they seek satisfaction for their souls; they make decisions that have consequences in the marketplace and in the political arena. In addition to anchoring families in a larger context, the articles in this reader analyze the complexity of kin relationships and chart the peaks and valleys of emotional life.

This collection is about families in the United States. While there is much to be learned from looking at families internationally, we have chosen to concentrate on presenting a textured portrait of family life in one country. There are three advantages to our focus on families in the United States: (1) we investigate fully the influence of the dominant *culture and social structure* within shared geographical, political, and social boundaries; (2) we explore the direct relationship between the *privileged circumstances* of some families and the *disadvantaged positions* of other families; and (3) we deepen our understanding of the *experiences of individuals* within families as they differ by race-ethnicity, sexual orientation, class, gender, or culture.

To study families with a feminist sociological imagination, we integrate the following analyses: (1) of structural inequality within society, (2) of power within the family, (3) of the connections between families and kinship systems, and (4) of change over time. These four analytic fields run through each of the six parts of the book. Below, we briefly elaborate on each of these areas of analysis.

Structural Inequalities

All families do not share equal opportunities or equal conditions of living. Families, like individuals, occupy particular social locations in regard to race-ethnicity,[1] social class, and place in the life cycle. Therefore, the structure of everyday life within families, the meaning of relationships, and the effect of economic and social changes will vary with a family's social location.

The belief that the United States is a relatively class-less society and that most people are "middle class" camouflages a system of structural inequities that shapes family life. The assumption that upward mobility is possible for everyone in the "land of opportunity" leads some people to claim that those who do not succeed are not trying—they must be lazy, or stupid, or in some way unworthy. The ideology of equal opportunity portrays children who are born into poverty and those who are born into affluence as if they competed on a level playing field. A structure of opportunity in which children from poor families receive less education and African Americans earn a lower income than whites with the same education affects their respective families differently (U.S. Bureau of Census 1995). The ideology of equal opportunity ignores Mills's (1959) distinction between "private problems" and "public issues of social structure" because it locates social issues and their solutions *within* families. So, for example, poverty gets framed as a private problem caused by teenage mothers, divorce, or "dead-beat dads" rather than as a public issue caused by changes in government tax policies to favor the wealthy, or shifts in the economy, such as the export of jobs, corporate downsizing, and massive unemployment in some sectors of the population. Attention to patterned structural inequalities makes visible the connection between families and the society as a whole.

For this reason, we must also link structures of racial inequality to those of economic opportunity. Attempts to represent the racial-ethnic and class diversity of families in this country have often taken a pluralistic approach. Studies of Korean American, African American, Mexican American, and immigrant families, to name a few, are often represented as alternatives to "The Family," which is presented as white, Euro-American, middle-class. In the best instances, they are celebrated as "different." In the worst instances, they are judged inadequate by the standards set for "The Family."

This pluralist approach to the racial-ethnic and class diversity of families has several key limitations. First, consistent with American pluralist politics, it is presented as a smorgasbord of different experiences and cultures. This focus on "difference" obscures the relationships between the social locations of families and ignores the problem of race and class privilege. The economically and socially privileged position of the upper-middle-class dual-earner couple is linked to the economic and social disadvantages of the immigrant woman who is paid to care for their children.

Second, the pluralist approach does not question the importance of middle-class status or whiteness in defining the "normative" family. White middle-class families are not just the norm from which all others depart. They too have a racial identity and occupy a class position.

Third, it does not challenge the idea that the most typical family form is a "breadwinning father" and "stay-at-home mother." All other families are then seen as somehow lacking and less than adequate when compared to this "norm."

Looking at all families with attention to their race-ethnicity and class emphasizes the connection between social structure and the organization of everyday life.

Domestic Politics: Power Within Families

Feminist scholarship launched a renaissance in family studies. Since the 1970s, scholars have taken a critical stance in investigating families, questioning the taken-for-granted and sparing no relationship from assessment. They have uncovered the painful underside of an institution popularly regarded as a "haven in a heartless world" (Lasch 1977). An inquiry into American history reveals that the greatest culprits of the mistreatment of children are their parents. And according to several authors in this volume (Barrett and McIntosh, Chapter 16; Demos, Chapter 49; and Straus, Chapter 48), this abuse and its toleration result from the misconception that children are private property. In heated debates about the nature of family violence, researchers may disagree about whether physical violence in the family amounts to "mutual combat," but they do not debate the statistics that show women, not men, as the vast majority of those who end up in emergency rooms with broken bones, lacerations, and serious injuries.

Feminist scholarship has explored the many ways that family life is gendered. That is, family processes often have asymmetrical outcomes for women and for men. Jessie Bernard writes that there are two marriages within every marriage: "his marriage" and "her marriage" (see Chapter 33). For example, no surprise to any working mother, studies have found that even women who work full time outside the home continue to do most of the housework. Arlie Russell Hochschild (1989) says this means that women work an extra month of twenty-four hour days every year.

In terms of parents and children, there may be a "child's family," a "mother's family," and a "father's family." Even siblings in the same household may experience and interpret their upbringing in very different ways. These differences are not simply products of individual variation. They are patterned differences, related both to power and authority within families and to larger economic, legal, and social structures.

The insight that families are gendered leads feminist scholars to examine women's and men's concrete experiences in families. In so doing, researchers have shifted the focus away from seeing women's family activities as the result of their "natural" expressiveness and nurturance. Instead, scholars investigate child rearing, feeding the family, organizing holiday celebrations, and the like, using the analytical category of "work." To describe these activities as "work" does not imply that they are necessarily unrewarding chores. On the contrary, people can take great pride in and reap meaningful rewards from their work. What the concept of "work" does imply is that women expend a great deal of effort in thinking about and executing these tasks. Further, analyzing what women do within the family as "work" enables scholars to conceptualize men's family activities also as "work." Men's labor force participation has been portrayed as the only thing men do for their families, overshadowing their other contributions.

Much is gained from applying the concept of "work" to family members' activities. The focus shifts from a description of activities to an analysis of the product of those activities. Much of this family "work" reproduces the family as a social institution. As di Leonardo illustrates in Chapter 31, keeping in touch with relatives by making telephone calls, sending birthday cards, visiting, and planning holiday gatherings constitutes "kin work," which reinforces family ties and maintains family networks. Monitoring one's marriage and "working" to keep the relationship strong is "marital work," as Hackstaff argues in Chapter 34. Approaching women's and men's family activities as "work" makes visible the connections between individual actions and social institutions.

While it is important to analyze a family as a group, with its own identity and interests, it is also necessary to understand that families are made up of individuals. Within a family, individuals occupy distinct positions and may want dissimilar things. Not only do positions vary by gender, but they also vary by generation. As a result, the interests of various family members often conflict. For example, if a young woman born to a farming family in the mid-nineteenth century wanted to continue her education beyond the sixth grade, her desires may have conflicted with the household imperative. Her parents could see her labor as essential to the family economy and therefore deny her further schooling. The existence of conflict points to an important issue in our analysis: family life is not the same for each member of a family.

Families and Larger Kinship Systems

Families are not isolated units but exist as part of webs of kinship relations. "Kinship" is a system of rights and responsibilities between particular categories of people, for example, fathers and children, wives and husbands, and maternal aunts and their nephews and nieces. It is important to note that "kinship" refers not only to biological or legal connections between people but also to particular positions in a network of relationships.

Anthropologists distinguish between two kinds of kin: consanguineal kin, who are related by descent or "blood" (children, grandparents, siblings), and affinal kin, who are related by marriage (husband and wife, parents-in-law). Families and cultures differ in the importance they give to these different kinds of kin. Some families are organized around relationships of descent: for instance, a man, his sons, and their sons; or adult sisters and brothers living together. Others organize kinship around relationships of marriage, a husband and a wife.

Most adults will eventually belong to both the families they were born into and the families they create as adults. Cultural groups vary, however, by how they organize the rights and responsibilities of family members along these two lines. In many African cultures, for example, the rights and responsibilities between generations are more central than those between wives and husbands (see Sudarkasa, Chapter 8).

Different cultures have various implicit and explicit rules and understandings about the rights and obligations between members of kinship groups. All cultures recognize that each person must have a place within a network of kin relations (see Stack and Burton, Chapter 30). In some cultures, for example, a woman's brother has important obligations toward his nieces and nephews. If the mother has no brother, someone else must step into that kinship position and take on the rights and obligations that come with it. The term "fictive kin" refers to the practice of including nonbiologically related people as kin in the web of rights and responsibilities (Stack 1974). For example, people in the United States often refer to friends of their parents as "uncles" and "aunts."

In the United States, however, the dominant cultural image of "The Family" is of a conjugal unit organized around the husband and wife and of a nuclear family in which husband, wife, and their children live together in their own household. Even our terminology reflects the centrality of the conjugal unit: Calling some relationships "premarital" implies that marriage is the inevitable end point; and calling some children "illegitimate" implies that the only "legitimate" children (those that count) are those born of a legal marriage. The nuclear family is the image pre-

sented in the popular media, the ideal embedded in most discussions of family policy, and the starting point in the majority of textbooks on the subject of families in the United States. But the increase in single-parent households, people living alone, and multiple-generation households makes the nuclear family household one form among many. And although many families may pass through a nuclear phase, households expand and contract with life-course changes and economic fluctuations. Individual families change over time; and the structure and content of families has changed historically. It is therefore inaccurate to limit research and discussion to nuclear family forms.

Because the conjugal nuclear family has been used as the social norm for describing "The Family," other family forms and other ways of organizing familial rights and responsibilities are described as failing to meet this norm and are often labeled as "deviant." Therefore, family stability has become equated with marital stability; adult children who live with their parents are described as having failed in the transition to adulthood; and in most states same-sex parents, unlike heterosexual couples, are denied the legal right to adopt.

Historical Context: Change over Time

While the family must be understood in the context of kinship, structures of inequality, and internal inequities, none of these intersecting forces is static. The family is not universal; nor is it unchanging. The family must be culturally situated and placed within a historical moment. All societies and cultures have webs of kinship relationships, and the design of these webs changes over time and differs across cultures. And even if, looking backward in time, we see dimensions of eighteenth-century family life that seem familiar, we cannot assume that those features held the same meaning in 1776 as they do at the turn of the twenty-first century.

Studying change over time within a culture can uncover striking differences in human kinship arrangements. The meaning of childhood, even the ages that define childhood, has profoundly changed in the past two hundred years. Farm families of the early nineteenth century constituted an economic unit whose members were expected to work. Children made economic contributions to their household. An eight-year-old child was expected to gather eggs or weed in the garden or take care of an infant while his or her parents worked in the field. In a dramatic transformation from the economically productive child, the twentieth century witnessed the arrival of the "priceless child," who elicits deep emotional satisfaction and "costs" a great deal (Zelizer 1985). While the priceless child may occasionally take out the garbage, family well-being does not rise or fall on his or her reliability in doing chores. When we read about children in the eighteenth century, we must remember that their experience was very different from that of children today. Sensitivity to historical change challenges many assumptions about what seems "natural" or inevitable. Historical studies have taught us about changes over time in household composition, sexual behavior, the organization of motherhood, the rights and responsibilities of fatherhood, and the roles of siblings, aunts, uncles, grandparents, and cousins. Families and kinship networks exist in a historical and social context; that is, they exist in a constant state of flux.

Defining a Critical Feminist Perspective

This anthology celebrates the renaissance of scholarship on families and embraces an ex-

plicitly feminist perspective on families. It does not intend to incorporate all feminist perspectives, but, rather, feminisms that recognize structural inequalities and that situate their analyses in historical context. Our feminist approach does not accept existing inequalities as inevitable. We apply a critical analysis to racial hierarchies and the unequal distribution of wealth and income, and to how these shape families.

Scholars and citizens alike have reacted to feminist criticism: "The Family," they say angrily, "Love it or leave it." But our critical perspective on the family does not translate into a rejection of the family. Despite some popular misconceptions, feminists neither hate men nor reject out-of-hand those characteristics—nurturing, caretaking, kinkeeping—associated with traditional femininity. Feminists care passionately about families. We believe that families can be satisfying places for people to live, grow, and love. But we acknowledge that families can simultaneously be arenas of conflict and exploitation. In the quest to overturn oppression and eliminate inequality, the goals of feminism include developing a full range of emotional capacities in all people and sharing the work of family life.

Not all the authors in *Families in the U.S.* subscribe to this kind of critical feminist perspective. In our judgment, however, their scholarship contributes to an important reconceptualizing of families and significantly advances the analysis of kinship and domestic politics.

NOTE

1. According to Baca Zinn, Chapter 3 in this volume, the use of race and ethnicity together points to the ways that groups of people are "labeled as races in the context of certain historical, social, and material conditions. Blacks, Latinos, and Asian Americans are racial groups that are formed, defined, and given meaning by a variety of

social forces in the wider society, most notably distinctive forms of labor exploitation. Each group is also bound together by ethnicity, that is, common ancestry and emergent cultural characteristics that are often used for coping with racial oppression. The concept racial-ethnic underscores the social construction of race and ethnicity for people of color in the United States" (note 1).

REFERENCES

Hochschild, Arlie Russell, with Anne Machung. 1989. *The Second Shift: Working Parents and the Revolution at Home.* New York: Viking.

Lasch, Christopher. 1977. *Haven in a Heartless World: The Family Besieged.* New York: Basic Books.

Mills, C. Wright. 1959. *The Sociological Imagination.* New York: Oxford University Press.

Stack, Carol. 1974. *All Our Kin: Strategies for Survival in a Black Community.* New York: Harper & Row.

U.S. Bureau of the Census. 1995. *Statistical Abstract of the United States: 1995.* 115th edition. Washington, D.C.: G.P.O.

Zelizer, Viviana. 1985. *Pricing the Priceless Child: The Changing Social Value of Children.* New York: Basic Books.

Organization of the Book

With this anthology, we intend to prompt readers to rethink the conventional social science approaches to studying families. *Families in the U.S.* does not begin with the assumption that the heterosexual two-parent nuclear family is the basic family form. Such an assumption posits "intact" families to be only those with two biological parents and their children living in the same household. Even the term "extended family" implies that in all cases there is some smaller unit that forms the "basic" or "core" or "real" unit of the family. Instead, we have de-centered "the breadwinning-father, stay-at-home mother" family by treating it as one family form among many, and by placing families into the wider context of kinship relations. *Families in the U.S.* incorporates some of the most outstanding and thoughtful writing on families. We have included classic writings as well as new, cutting-edge scholarship. Our selections exhibit the best of interdisciplinary thinking, drawing from anthropology, sociology, history, economics, and social policy.

The book is organized into six parts:

- Family Composition
- Families Within Society
- Webs of Family Relationships
- Complexities and Contradictions of Family Bonds
- Labor and Family Intersections
- Social Policy and Family Values

Each part includes a brief introduction that situates the chapters in relation to one another, to the themes of the part, and to the study of families.

These parts approach each topic with a feminist sociological imagination. Chapters are not arranged by "type of family"—whether by family form, the class status, or race-ethnicity—or by stages of the life course. Instead, chapters are arranged by analytical topics, such as "families and the economy" or "kin networks," and each article contributes to an overall and interconnected understanding of an issue. This creative reordering provokes a new way of thinking about families.

So, for example, chapters on marriage can be found in the part titled "Webs of Family Relationships" along with articles on fathering, mothering, and divorce. Similarly, chapters on care giving and nurturance are juxtaposed with chapters on violence and power in the part titled "Complexities and Contradictions of Family Bonds." We chose to pair these two sections in order to call attention to the contradictions of an ideology that constructs the family as universally nurturant and "the irony that in our society the place where nuturance and noncontingent affection are supposed to be located is simultaneously the place where violence is most tolerated" (Collier, Rosaldo, and Yanagisako 1992, 44).

We realize there are many ways to study families. We have tried several of them in our own teaching and have struggled with issues of organization. Because we have organized the book in a way that cuts across the traditional structure of family courses, we have created the Guide to Topics for locating chapters. For example, someone taking a life-course approach to teaching about families could turn to the Guide to Topics to find all the selections that deal with children and childhood or aging/elder adults. Or one could use it to identify the chapters on immigration or on historical perspectives on families. The Guide to Topics provides instructors with a user-friendly way to incorporate the articles in this collection into their own course organization.

REFERENCE

Collier, Jane, Michelle Z. Rosaldo, and Sylvia Yanagisako. 1992. "Is There a Family? New Anthropological Views." In *Rethinking the Family: Some Feminist Questions,* revised edition. Edited by Barrie Thorne with Marilyn Yalom. Boston: Northeastern University Press.

～ Guide to Topics

Part I

Family Composition

At the heart of contemporary debates about family is the very basic question of how to define it—"Who's In and Who's Out?" as Martha Minow puts it. Minow poses the question of whether the legal definition of the family, which currently specifies that a "family" must be related by birth, marriage, or adoption, should become, instead, a functional definition, one that considers care taking and the lived realities of who nurtures whom. Families "by choice" are increasingly frustrated by the courts' unwillingness to broaden the legal definition to reflect the many ways people raise children at the end of the twentieth century.

Virtually all of the chapters in the first section, "Defining and Analyzing Families," render the legal definition of family problematic. The host of new reproductive technologies make even the biological relationships difficult to decipher, as Barbara Katz Rothman makes clear in "Motherhood Under Patriarchy." In a culture where bio-genetic ties are increasingly revered, the social stigma of adoption further complicates matters for adoptive parents and children. Katarina Wegar explores, in "Adoption and Kinship," the sociological meanings and consequences of adoption in a society that sensationalizes adoptees' quests for their "true" parents. This returns us to Minow's question about how to define the family. Who is the rightful mother? Who is the "real" father? Who gets credit for raising a child—the person who donates the sperm? The "gestational surrogate" who provided the womb? The nanny who raised the child for five years? The father who fled before birth? And why?

Definitions change, in part, because the subject of definition changes. Families and households transform in relation to structural factors that shape family experiences and opportunities. As Maxine Baca Zinn argues in "Family, Feminism, and Race in America," racial hierarchies and economic systems affect family formation as well as definition. She recommends that theories of gender inequality and racial inequality be combined to better understand the complexity of these intersecting forces. Many of the chapters in the section "Family Structure and Accordion Households" reflect how much the parameters of families and households fluctuate over time and over the life cycle. Households, as distinct from families, can expand and contract in various ways, much like an accordion, throughout the family life cycle—folding in children, taking in boarders, emptying of a divorced partner, and the like (Stacey 1990).

Kinship systems can be organized many ways, varying by culture and economic system, among other things. Nazli Kibria finds that Vietnamese refugees blur the distinction between household and kin as they devise collectivist strategies to survive in the U.S. economy. In "Household Structure and Family Ideologies," she reveals the complex systems Vietnamese refugees develop to survive. Not only do they live together, they share resources—"patchworking" sources of income—a practice consistent with their family ideology, if not with the circumstances of their home culture. Niara Sudarkasa, in her investigation of the influence of African culture in African American families, finds continuity and adaptation. She argues that African American family patterns are products of both the socioeconomic environments in which they exist and the West African cultural contexts from which they originated. Both class and culture affect the organization of kinship.

Large-scale demographic changes over the century have similarly changed family size and the pool of potential kin members, if not expectations for what constitutes kin. In Anita Ilta Garey's chapter, "Fertility on the Frontier," diaries and letters between women on the frontier in the first half of the nineteenth century reveal deep and compelling motivation on the part of women for limiting family size. The chapter contributes a key missing dimension to the analysis of the decline in the average number of children born to women from 7 children in 1800 to 3.5 children in 1900. Peter Uhlenberg extends demographic analyses of family size through the year 2000 in "Mortality Decline in the Twentieth Century and Supply of Kin over the Life Course." By examining the pool of *potential* extended kin, he finds that mortality rates have declined dramatically in the past one hundred years, although marital stability has not correspondingly increased. In effect, divorce has replaced death as the primary source of family disruption.

These chapters illustrate the various ways in which the definition, size, structure, and organization of families change over time and vary by race-ethnicity, class, and culture.

REFERENCE

Stacey, Judith. 1990. *Brave New Families: Stories of Domestic Upheaval in Late Twentieth Century America.* New York: Basic Books.

Section A

Defining and Analyzing Families

∾ *Chapter 1*

Redefining Families: Who's In and Who's Out?

MARTHA MINOW

My remarks here are partly inspired by that distinguished scholar, Lily Tomlin. You see, I am going to discuss a series of worries, and no one is more acute or perceptive about worry than Lily Tomlin (and her collaborator, Jane Wagner). Lily Tomlin says she worries because *what if* the inventor of Muzak thinks up something else. She says, "I worry about reflective flea collars. Oh, sure, drivers can see them glow in the dark, but so can the fleas."[1] And "I worry if peanut oil comes from peanuts and olive oil comes from olives, where *does* baby oil come from?"[2] "I worry no matter how cynical you become, it's never enough to keep up."[3]

I worry because I worked on a lawsuit recently presented to the highest court in New York. I'm not just worried about losing; I am worried about the whole thing being in court in the first place.

The case is called *Alison D. v. Virginia M.*[4]

From *University of Colorado Law Review* 62, no. 2 (1991): 269–85. Reprinted by permission.

The facts, briefly, are these: two unmarried people who lived together for several years decided to have a child. Because the two people are both women, they turned to artificial insemination. Virginia became pregnant and had a child; she agreed to raise the child together with her partner, Alison, and for two years they all lived together. Alison participated in the care of the child. Then, Alison and Virginia separated. The child remained with Virginia but spent regular weekly visits—overnight visits—with Alison for the next two years. The child also stayed in close contact with Alison's parents, known to the child as his grandparents. During this time, Alison continued to pay child support and mortgage payments to Virginia, but after two years had passed, Virginia started to place limits on such visits. When Virginia foreclosed all contact between Alison and the child, Alison went to court and sought a judicial declaration that she could continue her visits with the child.

I worry that this case should never have come to court. I worry that a judge could be so disapproving of the entire situation that the child will be taken away from both adults. I worry that we may see here the fulfillment of the lawyer's adage: hard cases make bad law.

I also worry that some of you will find the whole situation unacceptable, and I am not sure how to convince you that it's not. I will tell you about the argument I made in favor of a functional notion of family—and I will tell you about my worries about that argument. If you want to count how many times I say *worry*, you may do so, but then I will worry about that as well.

A. Functional Family

I worry that neither you nor the courts will buy the argument that I and other lawyers working on the side of Alison have made: that it is not important here whether a group of people fit the formal legal definition of a family (created by marriage or adoption). Instead, what is important is whether the group of people function as a family: do they share affection and resources, think of one another as family members, and present themselves as such to neighbors and others?

The tension between official legal forms and functional families has created issues for centuries. The contrast between official, formal marriage and informal but still ultimately lawful marital unions is a good example. In medieval Europe, the practice of clandestine marriage, entered into with only the participation and knowledge of the two parties and without banns or public ceremony, persisted despite opposition by church and other leaders.[5] Similarly, in places like the frontier in the early United States where people lived scattered from one another, the requisites of a formal marriage were often difficult to fulfill: finding a minister, recording the marriage officially. Therefore, many people—and many

courts—concluded that a man and a woman could acquire the legal status of being married if they lived as husband and wife long enough to be functionally like a marriage.[6]

Like most lawyers, I get nervous—I grow worried—when we start to imagine the law being whatever anyone says it is rather than what the rules say it is. But I am equally worried about preserving a set of legal rules that have little relationship to how people actually live. That's not law: that's ideology; that's the production of a set of beliefs used to distribute status and value rather than effectively guide behavior.

Sticking to the rules that define marriage has proved a real problem in Sweden; cohabitation without marriage grew so widespread that the lawmakers changed the tax code to treat cohabiting couples as if they too were married. Because this meant paying more taxes, many cohabiting couples started to obtain separate apartments next to one another—so the lawmakers changed the tax code again to treat people involved with one another and living in adjoining apartments as if they were cohabiting and thus as if they were married.[7] What a mess!

But unless we start to make family law connect with how people really live, the law is either largely irrelevant or merely ideology: merely statements of the kinds of human arrangements the lawmakers do and do not endorse. The gap between law and practice is especially pronounced in the face of revolutionary scientific and technological changes. With the wonders of modern technology— indeed, not even that modern—people can have children with the help of an absent and even anonymous sperm donor. With the wonders of modern technology, a doctor today implants an embryo made with the genetic material of two people into the womb of a third person. This is a feat not only of science but also law, because this act also bypasses the usual legal rules of adoption.[8]

And with the wonders of modern technology, I can dip into the database of thousands if not millions of court cases just by sitting at my computer. When I plug in the terms: nonparent within 10 words of visitation, out pop a pile of cases. Some are like the Alison D. case, same-sex couples that have raised a child together. Many more are different family constellations: a boyfriend of the mother[9] who lived with her and her children by another man; an aunt who cared for a child; a grandparent; a foster parent who cared for the child for years before the child returned to the biological parent. A related case involves a woman who belongs to the Navajo tribe; the tribe gave this woman custody of the three children of her cousin because the tribe concluded the children were neglected. When the woman applied for Aid to Families with Dependent Children (AFDC) benefits to support the children, she was denied on the ground that she did not fit the requisite definitions of kin used by the regulations in New Mexico.[10]

These cases are windows into the home lives of people who do not fit the legal definition of parent—but who may well have lived in the kinds of relationships we signify by saying "parent-and-child." Getting behind words, legal formalities, and even blood ties to see how people really live and who cares for whom I think should bear on the question, who should be treated like family?

The trial judge in the case of *In re Alison D.* did not think about things this way. Instead, that court reasoned that Alison is not a parent and thus cannot even be heard in her argument for visitation. The governing law[11] only empowers the courts to hear petitions for visitation brought by parents. Alison is not a biological or adoptive parent, reasoned the court, so she cannot be heard. Case dismissed. And it is that dismissal we appealed. The majority on review agreed with the trial court.

I worry about court decisions like this one.

The court assumed that it knew what a "parent" is—the notion that a parent must be biological or adoptive is not set out in the statute; the court supplied it on its own.

The court there was not irrational; the dictionary might provide some support. So might popular cultural images—so even might statistical predictions about the likelihood that people without a biological or adoptive tie take on parental roles. But I worry about all these things. Turning to the dictionary as if it gave answers about how people do or should live is simply submitting important social—and judicial—choices to another group of people, the people who write dictionaries. And those people are not too with it. It takes a long time for a new word to get in, or for an old word to reflect its current meanings. Current dictionaries define "yo" to mean warning; feminism as "the state of being feminine";[12] and bush as a "shrub." (The *Oxford English Dictionary* also defines bush-fighting as guerilla warfare in the bush,[13] which is close but missing a little sand and U.N. diplomacy.) But most worrisome to me is the way a dictionary can be used to foreclose discussion, as in one case in which a judge rejected two women's argument that the clerk wrongly denied them a marriage license. The judge reasoned that the dictionary defines marriage as the union of a man and a woman, so these applicants themselves were to blame for their ineligibility for the license.[14] They could easily obtain licenses if they came in with the right kind of partners. End of discussion. I think that this "dictionary" approach is bad legal reasoning, whatever the result. If there are arguments for gay and lesbian marriage, the court should address them; if the court concludes that these issues belong in the legislature, the court should say that. Let's not, instead, simply open Webster's and shut the case.

Relying on popular cultural images also

troubles me. With whom, exactly, are the images popular? Why would those images that are popular be right? Mass media saturation once gave us the *Leave It to Beaver* family and also *My Mother the Car*; more recently television has blessed us with *Maude*, on her fourth husband;[15] *Kate and Allie*—two divorced women living together with their children;[16] *My Two Dads*—an all-male household;[17] and *The Cosby Show*, which seems to discover new cute kids for the household as soon as the last batch grows up. These days, if a judge relies consciously or subconsciously on images created by television writers and advertisers in evaluating who is a family, there is a wide array to pick from, but it is not clear that any of these mirror much of actual human life.

A conscientious judge may seek empirical information, then, about actual family living patterns. Statistical predictions have their own problems, but if forced to use that form of argument, I bet we'd see an intriguing challenge to prevailing popular images of parent/child relationships and of families more generally. Perhaps this too reflects a lag in reconciling images with changing realities. Thus, according to the U.S. Census, in 1970, 40 percent of the nation's households were composed of a married couple with one or more children under the age of 18; in 1980, that proportion dropped to 31 percent; and in 1990, it dropped again to 26 percent.[18]

Here's where I start to worry about how to read and use statistics. Another source suggests that the percentage is even smaller—23.9 percent—if you look at two parents living with children *of their own* rather than [with] stepchildren under 18. This source also limits this group to families in which the mother is not in the paid work force.[19] Yet another group claims that the percentage of American homes consisting of a married couple with one or more children under 18 where the husband is employed and the wife does not work

outside the home is only 8 percent of current households.[20] . . . It all becomes even more complicated if we focus on stepparents, including those who have not adopted the children of their spouses.[21]

In the face of statistical complexity, how should lawyers make arguments on behalf of clients with real problems? As I worked with my colleagues on behalf of Alison, we asked, what if instead of dictionaries, or social images, or statistics, the judge could turn to a functional definition? What if the Court were to ask, is Alison someone who has filled the functions of a parent? Of course, then we need to define the functions of a parent. We could try one out, like, someone who has taken care of the child on a daily basis, is known to the child as a parent, and has provided love and financial support.[22] Interestingly, kids themselves seem to identify who is a family based on who lives together and has daily contact.[23]

It is not absolutely incredible that a court would turn to something like this. In fact, the very court that heard Alison D.'s case, the New York Court of Appeals (which happens to be New York's highest court), turned to a functional definition of *family* to resolve another case, called *Braschi v. Stahl Associates*.[24] The question in that case was whether a man could inherit a rent-controlled apartment after the death of his lover, whose name was on the lease. The governing law called for protecting family members after the death of the named tenant; it said that a landlord cannot evict "either the surviving spouse or some other member of the deceased tenant's family who has been living with the tenant"[25] after the tenant of record dies thereby letting the apartment go back on the market—and importantly—off rent control.

The court ruled[26] that a homosexual man could claim membership in the family because of the "reality" of family life.[27] The court found that these two men had emotional and financial commitments and interdependence: they lived together as a couple for over ten years. They also were known to other family members and neighbors as a couple; they exchanged bracelets to symbolize their relationship; they were faithful to one another. They had joint credit cards and safe deposit boxes.[28] They also had joint bank accounts. This is the one that amazes me: my sister's advice is that the secret to a happy marriage is separate checking accounts. The court here didn't make shared banking the key: it looked to the totality of the circumstances and found that these two men functioned like a family.[29] Our hope was that this same reviewing court would adopt a functional approach to defining "parent" and give Alison simply the chance to be heard in her request for visitation. But we lost.

B. Problems with the Functional Approach

I did not tell the New York Court of Appeals my worries about the functional approach. I saved them for you. First, a functional approach can be messy. That's law talk for unpredictable. Which factor or combination of factors ends up being enough? Isn't this simply a more direct invitation for judges to express their own ideas about what should count as a family? Decision-making in light of a list of varied factors is decision-making in light of discretion. That the results in a given case are unpredictable may be all that we can predict.

We could guide or limit that unpredictable discretion if we legislated more specific rules— and more specific rules could be drafted that still use the idea of a functional family. Already, different legislative rules rely on uniquely tailored definitions of family status for each possible legal purpose. I have some favorites: the immigration service's rule recognizing stepfamily relationships, but not if the marriage creating the step-relationship was itself a sham, and the tax law specifying that a family corporation can actually be formed through the joint efforts of several families. The problem is, if we proliferate specific and allegedly functional notions of family, domestic partnership, parent, and child for each distinctive social context, we will expose real people to enormously varied rules that create their own kind of unpredictability.[30]

One emerging effort to devise a general and still functional definition of "family" through legislative means seeks to establish domestic partnership registries. Under this scheme, anyone who wants to be treated as a married couple can sign up at city hall or a similarly gray and bureaucratic place. Several cities have adopted this route; others have rejected it or not even considered it.[31] And no place that has debated it has actually asserted that this would answer the question of family status for all federal, state, and local legal purposes. And it is not clear to me how such a general statement could answer the myriad questions of family status for public and private programs if we want to take a functional approach seriously. Some functions may well be present in one household setting and not in others, and this difference could well be germane to a disputed legal question.

Perhaps the longest unit of time—other than when you are late and waiting for the elevator—is what we call "in the meantime." And we are here in the meantime until we answer these problems of unpredictability and inadequacy of generalized definitions. Certainly nothing in the meantime exists to help someone like Alison who is claiming parental status. I find myself returning to the functional approach—only to find new worries about it.

Besides its unpredictability, I have a second

set of worries about a functional approach. Using a functional test rather than a formal, legal definition may open the system up to manipulation by people who want to take advantage of certain benefits from family status but not take on certain obligations or burdens. For example, if the legal consequences of being treated like a married couple are desirable because of benefits that accrue, we might get into another mess, such as the one depicted in the movie *Green Card*. There, a noncitizen and a citizen of this country marry and claim that theirs is a genuine marriage although it is really a sham, arranged solely to deceive the Immigration and Naturalization Service and designed to get advantageous immigration status for the noncitizen.

As the movie suggests, suspicion about such uses of marriage has led the Immigration and Naturalization Service to investigate whether asserted marriages are "real" or "sham" and produced massive invasions of the privacy of many people. By tolerating this kind of invasion, society may be jeopardizing the security of anyone's family relations. At the same time, without some kind of check, there is a genuine concern that some people can manipulate the system by arranging for a sham marriage and thereby leapfrog ahead of other immigrants waiting in line for the nation's approval. Flexible definitions, especially when chosen by their users, can be abused. Both that abuse and the likely bureaucratic response can hurt people.

Unpredictability and manipulability are a lot to worry about, and not just because they are tongue twisters. But I have two more worries. One I will mention only briefly: functional approaches have a suspicious pedigree. The first element to be suspicious of is that functionalists are themselves often quick to deny that there *is* a pedigree, or a history, to functional approaches; they like to think this is just truth or realism. But in fact historians have

pointed out the rise of functional analysis in several fields of social science in the late nineteenth century just as the academics sought to separate themselves from social reformers.[32] A history of family sociology I have read emphasizes the connection between analyses of family functions and evolutionary thought, a notion of progressive development from the more primitive to the more civilized.[33] It is this kind of intellectual work that also brought us Social Darwinism, eugenics, and programs of governmental intervention into and control over the lives of immigrants, racial minorities, and poor people. Perhaps put more gently, talk of functions has tended to be pushed by people with little sensitivity to cultural variation or to their own biases. But just because some functionalists did it badly does not seem to be enough of a reason to abandon this kind of analysis. Why not just try to do it better? Still, the failure to see one's own biases is a real risk in any approach to family law matters, and I feel cautioned by the history of functionalism.

My final worry is my biggest worry. My biggest worry is that even inclined as I am in the cases of *Alison D.* and *Braschi* to support functional definitions of parent and family, in other cases I have contrary intuitions. Now, I can handle inconsistency when I have to, and I know about hobgoblins and little minds. But this kind of inconsistency makes me think I have to think some more. And after reflecting about those instances where I favor less expansive, functional definitions, I think this: I favor functional definitions of families that expand beyond reference to biological or formal marriage or adoptive relationship because the people involved have chosen family-like roles. But I worry when the government assigns family-like status in order to punish people or deny them benefits for which they would otherwise be eligible. Thus I think there is an important difference between the expanded family chosen by its participants and the expanded family used by the government to achieve its own ends.

Let me give you some examples. These are contrasting situations that lead me at times to oppose expansive, functional definitions of family because the government is using those definitions for its own purposes.

The Department of Housing and Urban Development has adopted a regulation that allows the eviction—or forfeiture of subsidized housing eligibility—of any family member of an individual suspected of engaging in criminal drug-related or violent activity.[34] "Family" is treated quite expansively here and basically includes any member of the same household. Certainly it is important to try to assure safety in housing settings, but I worry that this expansive reading could permit the eviction of a child due to drug-related activities of one parent. I worry about the government using an expansive reading to evict a grandmother due to the drug related activities of a grandchild.

Now, it is true that in other contexts, I would support an interpretation that would treat a grandmother as a member of a family. One such context is when the question is whether a grandmother living with her child and grandchildren form a single family for purposes of satisfying a zoning restriction.[35] Recognizing this as a family seems to match the traditional functions that the family serves. But treating the grandmother as "family" in an extended household in which another person is suspected of engaging in criminal activity seems largely punitive without cause or else predicated on an unrealistic view that the grandmother has the ability to prevent the criminal activity.

In announcing its eviction policy, the Department of Housing and Urban Development declared that "The purpose of this rule is not to punish families for past behavior, but rather to discourage such behavior by impos-ing an obligation on the family to not engage in the proscribed activities as a condition for receiving the housing assistance."[36] Nonetheless the effect could be punitive towards innocent or helpless people. The rule seems to assume that people in the household have control over others or else that they have a kind of guilt by association that our system of justice otherwise rejects.

Another worrisome example arises when the state seeks to reduce its own obligation to pay financial benefits by finding someone else on whom to pin the financial responsibility—or on whom to blame the ineligibility decision. Until the Supreme Court rejected such a practice, the administrators of AFDC denied benefits to single mothers who were found to have paramours. This "man-in-the-house" rule was officially justified on the theory that the presence of another adult even occasionally in a household implied the availability of his income to support the children; it clearly was also used to express disapproval of the single mothers found to have lovers.[37] The Supreme Court ultimately did reject this rule by relying on a strict and formal definition: the Court held that Congress specified the presence of another "parent" would make that income presumed available to the children, and a paramour is not a legal parent and has no legal duty to support the child.[38] Here, then, is an instance in which insistence on the narrow, formal definition of parent helped families avoid the state's effort to deny them public benefits.[39]

States continue to try to assert family or familylike relationships in order to avoid or reduce public responsibility for a family's economic dependency.[40] In one case, an agency drastically reduced the amount of food stamps available to a mother and two minor daughters because a disabled adult son lived in the household and received his own Supplemental Security Income Benefits, even though these benefits were deemed under the Social Security Act for *his* exclusive use.[41]

Sometimes even the presence of a sibling who receives child support can threaten a family's eligibility for public benefits. States often treat child support not as the entitlement of the child who receives it but instead as income to the family household if that household applies for food stamps or welfare. The state governments clearly prefer this view because it will reduce the benefit awards or even make the household ineligible. But one consequence may be to make the absent father less inclined to pay the child support after learning it is going to people besides his child, including other children he did not father. And this could also impair his visiting relationship with the child. Another consequence may be to lead the mother to relinquish custody of this child in order to avoid the reduction of benefits for the rest of her household. In the face of considerable evidence about these negative effects, the Supreme Court nonetheless rejected a challenge to such an approach and approved the deeming of sibling income to the household in its application for public benefits.[42]

Similarly, the states routinely deny AFDC benefits to a person who refuses to name the father of her child and to someone who names as the father of her child someone excluded by a blood test.[43] Yet there may be many reasons why a woman would decline to name the father of her child—reasons that include seeking to protect herself against physical violence or other intrusion by that individual.[44] An oddly different kind of threat can arise if an absent father makes one child support payment—for the government may then terminate the mother's public benefits even if the father never pays child support again.[45]

My objection is not to enforcing the child support obligation: it is to treating the absent parent as a member of the household that is applying for public benefits—the effects of this treatment may punish the individuals only to help the state.

There are punitive uses of family status under way even with narrow or traditional definitions of family, as with the Wisconsin law that terminates a parent's welfare benefits if the minor child is truant from school, or the California law that applies criminal penalties against a parent who fails to supervise a child—a law adopted specifically to try to reduce gang activity.[46] Another example arises in the Medicaid rules that require a spouse to deplete all of her or his own assets before the ailing spouse may become eligible for public medical benefits. This last rule is prompting divorces simply to allow individuals to avoid losing all their goods while trying to assure care for an ailing wife or husband.[47]

Again, my objection is not to the notion that being a family member entails obligations. Indeed, I may occupy a somewhat unusual position in that I favor what might be called a liberal approach to family membership but a strict view of family obligations. I would favor legal recognition of a wide variety of personal groupings and would urge the state to permit a range of voluntary, chosen relationships. I oppose state appropriation of these relationships to achieve governmental ends such as budget cutting. Yet I do not favor leaving the content of family obligations to the private choices of those individuals. I think people should be able to choose to enter family relationships but not be free to rewrite the terms of those relationships.[48]

You see, I worry—see, I worry a lot—about unequal bargaining power and faulty judgments that may lead people to sign agreements foregoing any rights to financial support from their families. I don't think that a husband should be able to avoid sharing his income and wealth with a wife just because he was a better negotiator of the premarital contract. I don't think in particular that after a lengthy marriage in which one party became a major earner and the other raised children that the marriage should be subject to a termination that excuses the earner from an obligation to share those earnings or help prevent the economic vulnerability of the partner.[49] Granted, the duration of the marriage may affect the scope of the obligation to pay support after it ends. Perhaps the sharing obligation should be minimal for a short-term marriage. And I don't mean to impose by law the relationship of wife-in-law I recently saw described: an ongoing and painful emotional relationship between a man's current wife and his past wife. But a long-term relationship of mutual support means something more than what appears when a partner walks out with a disproportional share of the economic returns on the couple's lifetime work in building a family and home.

The danger of an expansive, functional voluntarist view of family—in which people can pick and choose what kinds of family ties that they want to have—is that people will choose to walk out when it gets tough and to avoid responsibilities when it is no longer fun.[50] I am against this. I am interested in exploring ways to lead people to adhere to their obligations, to understand that life is not just about fun or self-interest.

At the same time, I worry about governmental uses of relationships to serve governmental ends, like reducing governmental financial obligations. And I worry that by advocating expansive, functional definitions of family in some contexts, I may be fueling this kind of governmental control in others.

A vivid illustration of this dilemma arises as states debate how to treat stepparent relationships. In almost every state, stepparents who have not adopted the children do not have a financial support obligation, nor indeed do they have legal rights to control the health, education, or religious training of the children of their spouses. This is especially important where the biological parent retains an involvement with the children. Functionally, however, in many contexts, stepparents *are* parents: they provide emotional and financial support and help to make the fast-growing household type—the blended family. Moreover, some states do treat stepparent income as a factor in determining eligibility for public benefits, one of life's many inconsistencies. Should the law treat such stepparents as *in the family* and if so, for what purposes? Might such a conclusion deter some adults from being willing to join a new household—given obligations they already have to a prior family? Up until recently, stepfamily relationships, like friendships, were blessedly free of governmental regulation, free to develop however they would. If, however, we seek the benefits of governmental recognition for these relationships, what negative consequences could also follow?

C. Children's Interests

Perhaps we can resolve dilemmas raised by legal adoption of a functional definition of family by leaving it to the parties; let them choose: do you want to be a family for legal purposes? But the dangers of unpredictability and manipulability surely return with a vengeance in that scenario.

In part because of the tension between arguments for expansive family definitions and arguments for more restrictive ones, I felt in the case of *Alison D.* a need to search for an alternative approach. It is compatible with a functional approach but I think it adds an important difference. With my colleagues in law and in human development, I developed an argument that emphasizes not any particular definition of family, but instead, the interests of the child. We defended the functional test as a way of achieving the child's interests—but those interests, above all, are what must take center stage. Neither the government's interests nor the interests of the adults supply the justification for regulating otherwise private and intimate concerns. The needs of vulnerable and developing children supply that justification.

Thus, in our brief, we argued that, based on psychological evidence and theories, children form strong attachments to not only one primary parenting figure but to more than one caretaker if they have sustained contact in the home. From the child's point of view, the marital status, biological or nonbiological connection, and also the sexual orientation of such adults is irrelevant. Children form strong attachments without asking about such things; indeed, children from strong attachments before they even know what it is to ask about such things. Nonetheless, at very early ages, children perceive the differences between parents and others of significance in their lives.[51] Based on a concern for the child's interests we argued that the reviewing court should at least order a hearing to determine whether visits with Alison would indeed serve the child's needs. Our brief also argued that this psychological evidence supports a functional test for parenthood and that this evidence also helps to limit the number of people who could seek such visitation hearings.[52]

To talk of children's interests hardly simplifies matters. Just think about emphasizing children's interests in the regulation of in vitro fertilization. Or think of new problems for property law posed by unborn widows and fertile octogenarians, brought to you courtesy of new reproductive technologies.

Calling for inquiry into any person's interests is hardly an easy task; it may be even more difficult than deciding who should be treated as a parent or as a family member.[53] But at least this inquiry is addressed to what matters most. If we are going to worry, let's worry about something that is worth it!

NOTES

Acknowledgments: My thanks to Joe Singer, Sarah Jeffries, Tracy Merwise, Sally Merry, Emily Shulman, Susan Silbey, and Vicky Spelman.

1. J. WAGNER, THE SEARCH FOR INTELLIGENT LIFE IN THE UNIVERSE 25 (1985).

2. *Id.*

3. *Id.* at 26.

4. Alison D. v. Virginia M. LEXIS 634 (N.Y. 1991).

5. *See* F. & J. GIES, MARRIAGE AND THE FAMILY IN THE MIDDLE AGES 243–44, 266–67, 299–300 (1987) (clandestine marriage permitted despite criticism until 1563 Council of Trent repudiation); L. STONE, THE ROAD TO DIVORCE 96–120 (1991).

6. *See* J. AREEN, *Should Common Law Marriage Be Abolished?* in CASES AND MATERIALS ON FAMILY LAW 61 (2d ed. 1985).

7. Swedish statistics about family types count married couples and cohabitants together. Sorrentino, *The Changing Family in International Perspective*, 113 MONTHLY LAB. REV. 41, 47 n.1 (Mar. 1990). At the same time it is possible to measure increases in nonmarital cohabitation: the proportion of such unions rose from 1 percent of all couples in 1960 to 19 percent in 1985. *Id.* at 48. A growing number of such couples never marry. *Id.*

8. Remarks of Professor Betsy Bartholet at Harvard Law School, Feb. 8, 1991.

9. Mark V. v. Gale P., 143 Misc. 2d 487, 540 N.Y.S.2d 966 (N.Y. Fam. Ct. 1989).

10. Monte v. New Mexico Dep't of Human Services (N.M. Human Services Dep't Fair Hearings Bureau, June 22, 1990).

11. N.Y. DOM. REL. LAW § 70(a) (McKinney 1988).

12. OED, vol. 1, 982 (compact ed. 1977).

13. *Id.* at 301.

14. Jones v. Hallahan, 501 S.W.2d 588 (Ky. Ct. App. 1973).

15. E. TAYLOR, PRIME TIME FAMILIES: TELEVISION CULTURE IN POST-WAR AMERICA 86 (1989).

16. *Id.* at 158.

17. *Id.*

18. *Only One U.S. Family in Four Is 'Traditional,'* N.Y. Times, Jan. 30, 1991, at A19 col. 1.

19. Paul Smith of Children's Defense Fund (CDF) explained this result as a conclusion of an unpublished report by the research department of CDF. Telephone conversation with Paul Smith (Feb. 12, 1991).

20. The Census Bureau's figure differs because the denominator—total households—is much larger than that used in the CDF calculation, which used a survey of 57,400 housing units.

Note that the Ford Foundation offers 10% as the figure of families fitting the "Leave It to Beaver" mold. L.A. Times, Aug. 12, 1990, at A1, A26 col. 3.

21. For example, one estimate is that only 1/3 of the children born in the early 1980s will be living with both natural parents by the age of 14; 1/4 will be living with a stepparent, and 40% will be living in one-parent families. F. K. GOLDSCHEIDER & L. WAITE, NEW FAMILIES, NO FAMILIES? THE TRANSFORMATION OF THE AMERICAN HOME 27 (1991).

22. This definition of parental functions is founded on psychological theories about children's needs. *See* J. GOLDSTEIN, A. SOLNIT & A. FREUD, BEYOND THE BEST INTERESTS OF THE CHILD (1973). This differs from descriptions of family functions, which vary from theory to theory. One recent list of family functions identifies these six (1) procreation; (2) socialization of children; (3) affection, caring and nurturing; (4) regulating sexuality; (5) sharing resources and cooperating economically; and (6) providing a precondition for cultural diversity, free economics, and democratic institutions. Blankenhorn, *Introduction,* in REBUILDING THE NEST: A NEW COMMITMENT TO THE AMERICAN FAMILY, at xiii (1990). Other lists identify similar and also diverging functions. *See, e.g.,* F. ENGELS, THE ORIGIN OF THE FAMILY, PRIVATE PROPERTY AND THE STATE IN LIGHT OF THE RESEARCHES OF LEWIS H. MORGAN (1885) (monogamous marriage and gender roles developed to serve the interests of those who own property); T. PARSONS, THE SOCIAL SYSTEM (1964) (families function as places in which people can be known as individuals rather than as occupants of social and economic positions).

23. Until, that is, the children grow older and

learn legal definitions. *See* Gilby & Pederson, *The Development of the Child's Concept of the Family* 14 CANAD. J. BEHAV. SCI. 110, 117–18 (1982).

24. 74 N.Y.2d 206, 543 N.E.2d 44 (1989).

25. N.Y. City Rent and Eviction Regulations, 9 NYCRR § 2204.6(d) (1984).

26. The ruling was through a plurality, not a majority; the concurring opinion by Judge Bellacosa agreed only about the equities in the particular case. 74 N.Y.2d at 214, 543 N.E.2d at 55 (Bellacosa, J., concurring).

27. *Id.* at 211, 543 N.E.2d at 53.

28. Blanchard also gave Braschi power of attorney regarding medical, personal, and financial decisions and named Braschi beneficiary of the life insurance policy and principal legatee of the estate. *Id.* at 212–14, 543 N.E.2d at 55.

29. *Id.* Other courts, too, have at times considered functional definitions rather than formal and usually more restrictive definitions of "family" or "parent"—and sometimes the functional and sometimes the formal wins. *See* Curry v. Dempsey, 520 F. Supp. 70 (W.D. Mich. 1981) (legal guardians eligible for AFDC application despite statute requiring applicant be a "relative"). This was reversed by the 6th Circuit Court of Appeals, 701 F.2d 580 (6th Cir. 1983).

30. Compare: the tax code uses lineal descent for some purposes, thus excluding son-in-law, daughter-in-law, 26 U.S.C. § 267(c)(4) (1988), while other sections include the spouse of a lineal descendent, 26 U.S.C. § 4975(e)(6) (1988); it also defines dependent to include relatives of household members except if those persons are not U.S. citizens, nationals, unless they are legalized residents of the U.S. or a country contiguous to the U.S., 26 U.S.C. § 152(b) (1988); members of two or three families may join together as a family corporation for some tax purposes, Cal-Maine Foods Inc., 93 TC 181 (1981) (discussing § 447(a) and 447(h)); family may be a single person if that person is handicapped for some legislative purposes, 12 U.S.C. § 1701(q)(d)(4) (1988); *see also* 50 U.S.C. App. § 31 (1988) (defining member of the former ruling family of sovereignties in the German Empire). The Immigration and Nationality Act excludes from a step-relationship an actual family relationship between stepchild and stepparent where

the marriage creating the step-relationship itself was a sham. Matter of AWWAL, In Rescission Proceedings under Section 246 of the Immigration and Nationality Act, Board, April 4, 1988 (citing Matter of Teng, 15 I & N Dec. 516 (BIA 1975)). *See also* NB Hutcheson v. Califano, 638 F.2d 96, 99 (9th Cir. 1981) ("There is no general federal common law relating to family relationships. . . . [In the absence of a statutory definition, 'stepchild' is defined by reference to applicable state law.]").

31. *See* Madison, Wis. General Ordinances §§ 3.36, 28.03 (1988); West Hollywood, Cal., Ordinance No. 22 (Feb. 26, 1985). A similar recent proposal in Boston received support from a broad cross-section of religious leaders and lesbian and gay leaders. Boston Globe, May 16, 1991, at 83, col. 1.

32. *See* R. HOWARD & L. VAN LEEUWEN, A SOCIAL HISTORY OF AMERICAN FAMILY SOCIOLOGY, 1865–1940, 13–14 (J. Mogey ed. 1981).

33. *Id.* at 12–13.

34. Section 8 Certificate Program, Moderate Rehabilitation Program and Housing Voucher Program, 55 Fed. Reg. 28,538 (1990) (to be codified at 24 CFR Parts 882 and 887).

35. *See* Moore v. City of East Cleveland, 431 U.S. 494 (1977). But perhaps I come out differently when the question is application by the mother for income support benefits: why should the grandmother be financially responsible here, and who is helped if such a rule leads the mother to ask the grandmother to leave the household? *See* Carpozzi v. N.Y. State Dept. of Social Services, 520 N.Y.S. 2d 471 (1987). *See infra* Section C of this chapter (regarding analysis of people's interests).

36. 55 Fed. Reg. 28,540 (1990).

37. *See* Sugerman, Roe v. Norton; *Coerced Material Cooperation,* in In the Interests of Children: Advocacy, Law Reform, and Public Policy 365, 376–77 (R. H. Mnookin, ed. 1985).

38. King v. Smith, 392 U.S. 309 (1968).

39. The Supreme Court's ruling has been followed up by regulations; *see, e.g.,* McCoog by and through Ferguson v. Hegstrom, 690 F.2d 1280 (9th Cir. 1982) (enforcing HHS regulations prohibiting the state from assuming the presence in the home of "any individual" other than a parent or stepparent would make income available to the child).

40. *See* Gurley v. Wolgemuth, 421 F. Supp. 1337 (D.C.Pa. 1976) (state regulation treated two adult sisters living together with their three children as a single assistance unit, subject to an economies-of-scale declining benefits formula, rather than as two assistance units; the court found this regulation in conflict with a federal regulation providing that the income of a parent can only be considered available for children in the household). In *Gurley,* an expansive definition of "parent" would have hurt this group of people by reducing their benefits. Other courts, addressing similar situations, have reached opposite conclusions. *See* Sherrod v. Hegstrom, 629 F. Supp. 150 (D. Or. 1985) (rational to presume that family unit shared expenses and thus fair for AFDC to treat family unit to include all siblings and half-siblings).

41. Moody v. Lung, No. 86 Civ. 3088 (SDNY, filed March 24, 1986) described in Billings, *The Choice Between Living with Family Members and Eligibility for Government Benefits Based on Need: A Constitutional Dilemma,* 1986 UTAH L. REV. 695, 703 (interpreting 7 U.S.C. § 2012(i)(2) (1988), which provides that "parents and children, or siblings, who live together shall be treated as a group of individuals who customarily purchase and prepare meals together for home consumption even if they do not do so.").

42. Bowen v. Guillard, 483 U.S. 587 (1987).

43. Doston v. Duffy, 732 F. Supp. 857 (N.D. Ill. 1988); French v. Mansour, 834 F.2d 115 (6th Cir. 1987).

44. *See* Sugerman, *supra* n.37, at 389.

45. Yelder v. Hornsby, Civ. No. 84-1271 (MD Ala. July 20, 1987) (Clearinghouse No. 38, 551). There the AFDC benefits were indeed terminated based on receipt of one child support payment. In the face of a challenge to this action, the court held that the federal regulations require the state to make a "best guess" as to the family income in future months before terminating the family from public assistance. Similarly, joint custody or even active visitation by an absent parent can jeopardize the custodial parent's eligibility for AFDC. *See* Johnson, *Joint Custody Arrangements and AFDC Eligibility,* 18 CLEARINGHOUSE REV. 3 (1984).

46. California Street Terrorism Enforcement and Prevention Act (1988) (codified at CAL. PENAL CODE §§ 186.20–27). *See* Los Angeles Times, *ACLU*

Sues to Overturn Law Targeting Parents of Gang Members, July 20, 1989.

47. See Comment, *Medicaid's Unhealthy Side Effect: The Financial Burdens on At-Home Spouses of Institutionalized Recipients,* 18 LOY. U. CHI. L.J. 1031, 1051 (1987).

48. At the same time, laws designed to enforce obligations of adult children to support their parents or other family members besides their own children may be counterproductive or ineffective. For a thoughtful and empirical exploration of these issues in Great Britain, see J. FINCH, FAMILY OBLIGATIONS AND SOCIAL CHANGE (1989). A sense of obligations develops between real people, not from abstract statements of values or roles. *Id.* at 242. Therefore, restrictions on state support in the name of family support is a thinly veiled policy of restricting access to state programs. *Id.* at 237. At the same time, it is noteworthy that in the United States, many African Americans demonstrate a sense of commitment to aid relatives in an extended family—even if this means jeopardizing their own at times tenuous economic status. *See* Wilkerson, *Middle-Class Blacks Try to Grip a Ladder While Lending a Hand,* N.Y. Times, Nov. 26, 1990, at A1, col. 1.

49. *See generally* L. WEITZMAN, THE DIVORCE REVOLUTION: THE UNEXPECTED SOCIAL AND ECONOMIC CONSEQUENCES FOR WOMEN AND CHILDREN IN AMERICA (1985).

50. I worry about parents abandoning their children, refusing to pay for college, and more troubling, refusing to pay for any child support. I am not the only one to worry about these things: the massive failures of absent parents to pay child support has spurred dramatic legal changes, involving the federal government in what had been traditionally matters of state law, and authorizing courts to order automatic deductions from parents' wages to insure the payment of child support.

So far these obligations have only been assigned to biological parents; if we took the functional parent idea seriously, perhaps stepparents too should have support obligations. But this might deter some people from being willing to take on the commitment.

51. In the Matter of Application of Alison D., Brief of Amicus Curiae Eleven Concerned Academics (Jane A. Levine, David Chambers, Martha Minow on brief), No. 692-88 (New York Court of Appeals).

52. We proposed that the term "parent" in Section 70(a) of the New York Domestic Relations Law mean: (1) a child's biologic or adoptive parent, unless parental rights have been terminated or otherwise unrecognized by applicable law; and (2) "parent" also includes a person who meets the following three criteria: (a) the person has lived with the child for a substantial portion of the child's life; and (b) the person has been regularly involved in the day-to-day care, nurturance, and guidance of the child appropriate to the child's stage of development; and (c) if the child has also been living with a biologic parent, the biologic parent has consented to the assumption of a parental role by the person, and the child has in fact looked to this person as a parent.

Id. at 25. The New York Ct. of Appeals concluded that the legislature would have to articulate such a definition before the courts could use it. In a thoughtful dissenting opinion, Judge Judith Kaye noted that while other state legislatures restrict the definition of parent to biological and adoptive parent, New York as not done so, and instead the legislature left the definitional task to the courts. The dissent also criticized the majority for departing from its traditional commitment to construe family law controversies to advance children's interests. Alison D. v. Virginia M., LEXUS 634, 5, 10–11 (N.Y. 1991).

53. *Cf.* Cruzan v. Dir., Mo. Dept. of Health, 110 S. Ct. 2841 (1990) (debating who can know the interests of a person in a persistent vegetative state).

∾ Chapter 2

Motherhood Under Patriarchy

BARBARA KATZ ROTHMAN

The term "patriarchy" is often used loosely as a synonym for "sexism," or to refer to any social system where men rule. The term technically means "rule of fathers," but in its current practical usage it more often refers to any system of male superiority and female inferiority. But male dominance and patriarchal rule are not quite the same thing, and when the subject is motherhood, the difference is important.

Patriarchal kinship is the core of what is meant by patriarchy: the idea that paternity is the central social relationship. A very clear statement of patriarchal kinship is found in the book of Genesis, in the "begats." Each man, from Adam onward, is described as having "begot a son in his likeness, after his image." After the birth of this firstborn son, the men are described as having lived so many years and begot sons and daughters. The text then turns

From Barbara Katz Rothman, *Recreating Motherhood: Ideology and Technology in a Patriarchal Society*, pp. 29–47, copyright © 1989 by W. W. Norton & Company. Reprinted by permission.

to that firstborn son, and in turn his firstborn son after him. Women appear as the "daughters of men who bore them offspring." In a patriarchal kinship system, children are reckoned as being born to men, out of women. Women, in this system, bear the children of men.

The essential concept here is the "seed," the part of men that grows into the children of their likeness within the bodies of women. Such a system is inevitably male dominated, but it is a particular kind of male domination. Men control women as daughters, much as they control their sons, but they also control women as the mothers of men's children. It is women's motherhood that men must control to maintain patriarchy. In a patriarchy, because what is valued is the relationship of a man to his sons, women are a vulnerability that men have: to beget these sons, men must pass their seed through the body of a woman.

While all societies appear to be male dominated to some degree, not all societies are patriarchal. In some, the line of descent is not from father to son, but along the lines of the women. These are called "matrilineal" societies: it is a shared mother that makes for a shared lineage or family group. Men still rule in these groups, but they do not rule as fathers. They rule the women and children who are related to them through their mother's line. Women in such a system are not a vulnerability, but a source of connection. As anthropologist Glenn Petersen says, in a matrilineal system "women, rather than infiltrating and subverting patrilines, are acknowledged to produce and reproduce the body of society itself."[1] People are not men's children coming through the bodies of women, but the children of women.

In one such society, among the Trobriand Islanders, the man who rules or has rights of domination over children is not the father, but the mother's brother. The uncle rules as a man, but not as a father. Women are not the mothers of men's children: men are the children of women. The anthropologist Bronislaw Malinowski looked at this system and seemed to have some difficulty figuring out what was happening. He thought the Trobriand Islanders just didn't understand biological paternity. After all, it seemed to Malinowski, how could a man not have control over the children which are *his* if he knew they were his, and yet have control over those which are his sister's husband's children? For Malinowski, for Western society, what makes a child belong to a man, what makes it *his*, is that it grew from his sperm, from his seed. For the Trobriand Islanders sperm was not all that important. Later anthropologists have shown that the Trobriand Islanders understand the nature of biological paternity but that it does not have the same significance for them as it has for us.[2]

Our society developed out of a patriarchal system in which paternity is a fundamentally important relationship. Some of our social customs and traditions have their roots in this patriarchal system. To maintain the purity of the male kinship line, men had to control the sexuality of women and ensure that no other man's seed entered the body. They had to control her virginity so that she came to the marriage bed unimpregnated. They had to control her in pregnancy, so that she could not destroy the seed of men. The "double standard"—the ideas about virginity for brides, abortion, "illegitimacy," about women's sexual and procreative freedom in all areas—reflects men's concern for maintaining paternity.

Remnants of this patriarchal system can also be seen in the way we name children: children take their "family" name from the line of the father. Half-siblings with the same father share a family name; those with the same mother do not. The name is passed down male lines: children of brothers share a name that came from the brothers' father; children of sisters or of brother and sister do not share a name. They belong to the family line of other men. American children continue to take the name of the father, in spite of changes in the position of women. Even those women who have not taken their husband's family name for themselves almost always give their children the last name of the father.

In spite of all of these signs of patriarchy, the modern American kinship system is not classically patriarchal. It is what anthropologists call a bilateral system, in that individuals are considered to be equally related to their mother's and their father's "sides" of the family. We have in English, for example, no everyday word to distinguish a "paternal" aunt (father's sister) from a "maternal" aunt (mother's sister). We don't even have a common word to distinguish an aunt by birth (or by "blood") from an aunt by marriage: we use the same word, *aunt,* for the father's sister and the father's brother's wife. That is probably because these relationships carry very little weight. There are no legal obligations involved and few firm societally shared expectations, beyond showing up for major rituals like weddings and funerals. In actual practice, people do seem to take these relationships far more seriously than that, though, and the exchange of help, money, love, and social support between members of extended families is an important part of American life.

Underneath this casual, almost sloppy reckoning of kinship, there are certain fixed ideas about family and relatedness. Blood, we say, is thicker than water. Blood ties are the fundamental basis for reckoning kinship and one of the few permanencies left in American life. In a society like ours, where people move every few years, where marriages last as long as they work, where job changes and career changes are expected, the family is a fixed point in a changing landscape. Who knows where they will be living or working, who their friends, neighbors, or colleagues will be in twenty years, but a sister is always a sister. Marriages may end, but children are forever. These relationships may be close or distant, loving or not, easy or tense. But they do not go away. They cannot be divorced, quit, annulled, fired, or dissolved. An estranged sister is still a sister.

So kinship reckoning in America still matters, still counts for something, even if it is a far cry from what it might mean in some tribal society. But this begs the question: *what is kin?* This is one of those commonsensical questions, something that "everybody knows" that shows the force of an ideology in shaping our understanding of the world's workings. Yet kinship and blood ties are reckoned differently in different cultures.

An interesting if bizarre demonstration of how very differently people reckon kin occurred in the 1950s. There was a disease that struck in the Eastern Highlands of Papua New Guinea, among the Fore people. Called kuru, it was a fatal neurological disorder.

Because kuru seemed to run in families and was isolated to a small, interrelated population, a genetic basis for the disease was suspected. By the late 1950's it was proposed that kuru was a hereditary disorder, determined by a single autosomal gene that was dominant in females but recessive in males.[3]

That was a reasonable and very frightening hypothesis. It explained the transmission of the disease within families and made a lot more deaths seem inevitable. The hypothesis was wrong, though, because what the Fore meant by family, by kin, was not at all what the Western physicians meant. The "sisters" dying in a family were often not, according to Western notions of kinships, in any way "related" to each other. It turned out that kuru is a slow virus, one that becomes active only after years of incubation. It is spread by cannibalism: kin ate the bodies of kin among the Fore. The right to eat the body, and the particular body part one ate, was determined by kinship lines—kinship as reckoned by the Fore.

The confusion between genetic kinship and social kinship occurs in our society, too. I've observed genetic-counseling sessions where the counselors tried to take a history using their language of kinship and clients answered using a different way of reckoning. In one case, after a long, involved description of a cousin's stillbirth, it turned out that the cousin was an aunt-by-marriage's child by another marriage. So we may get confused sometimes, this confusion being furthered by the inexactness of our kinship language, but we do have a fixed idea of what kin means: our society's definition of kin is based on genetic relatedness. In this sense, it harks back to the idea of a "seed." As soon as we hear the whole story, we understand the confusion: it's not *really* her cousin; in-laws are not *really* related. American ideas about "really" related people are based on genetic connections. It's a way of reckoning that makes us see adoptive

parents as not the real parents, aunts and uncles by marriage as not real aunts and uncles,
in-laws as not real relatives. Real kin, in our
system, share a genetic tie.

What happens in a matrilineal system,
when the genetic tie between a man and the
children conceived of his sperm does not determine lineage? In this case the most "real"
relatives are the ones that share what is called
a "uterine" relationship: children and grandchildren of the same woman. Among the Nayar of Central Kerala of India, for example,
marriage between half-siblings who share a
father was considered "indelicate" but was
not prohibited, and the children of brothers
(first cousins on their father's side) are not
considered related and might marry or not as
they chose.[4] It was only the experience of a
shared mother that defined "real" kinship.

In a patriarchal system, when people talk
about blood ties, they are talking about a genetic tie, a connection by seed. In a mother-
based system, the blood tie is the mingled blood
of mothers and their children: children grow
out of the blood of their mothers, of their bodies and being. The shared bond of kinship comes
through mothers. The maternal tie is based on
the growing of children. The patriarchal tie is
based on genetics, the act of impregnating.

Each of these ways of thinking leads to different ideas about what a person is. In a
mother-based system, a person is what mothers grow—people are made of the care and
nurturance that bring a baby forth into the
world and turn the baby into a member of the
society. In a patriarchal system, a person is
what grows out of men's seed. The essence of
the person, what the person really is, is there
in the seed when it is planted in the mother.
Early scientists in Western society were so
deeply committed to the patriarchal concept
that it influenced what they saw. One of the
first uses of the microscope was to look at semen and see the little person, the homuncu-

lus, curled up inside the sperm. And in 1987
the director of a California sperm bank distributed T-shirts with a drawing of sperm
swimming on a blue background accompanied by the words "Future People."

The Seeds of Women

Out of the patriarchal focus on the seed as the
source of being, on the male production of
children from men's seed, has grown our current, usually far more sophisticated thinking
about procreation.

Modern procreative technology has been
forced to go beyond the sperm as seed.
"Daddy plants a seed in Mommy" won't work
anymore. Modern science has had to confront the *egg* as seed also. Modern scientific
thinking cannot possibly hold on to old notions of women as nurturers of men's seeds.
The doctor who has spent time "harvesting"
eggs from women's bodies for in vitro fertilization fully understands the significance of
women's seed. but that does not mean we no
longer continue to think of the seed as the
essence of being. It is not the end of the belief
that the seeds, the genes, are everything, that
they are all that really matters in the making
of a baby, that they are what *real* kinship is
based on.

The old patriarchal kinship system had a
clear place for women: they were the nurturers of men's seeds, the soil in which seeds
grew, the daughters who bore men offspring.
When forced to acknowledge that a woman's
genetic contribution is equal to a man's,
Western patriarchy was in trouble. *But the
central concept of patriarchy, the importance of
the seed, was retained by extending the concept
to women.* Valuing the seed of women, the genetic material women too have, extends to
women some of the privileges of patriarchy.
That is, when the significance of women's

seed is acknowledged in her relationship with her children, women, too, have paternity rights in their children. In this modified system based on the older ideology of patriarchy, women, too, can be seen to own their children, just like men do. Unlike what happens in a mother-based system, however, this relationship between women and their children is not based on motherhood per se, not on the unique nurturance, the long months of pregnancy, the intimate connections with the baby as it grows and moves inside her body, passes through her genitals, and sucks at her breasts. Instead, women are said to own their babies, have "rights" to them, just as men do: based on their seed.

This does not end patriarchy, and it does not end the domination of the children of women by men. Instead, by maintaining the centrality of the seed, the ideology maintains the rights of men in their children, even as it recognizes something approaching equal rights of women in their children. Since men's control over women and the children of women is no longer based simply on men's (no longer) unique seed, men's economic superiority and the other privileges of a male-dominated social system become increasingly important. Children are, based on the seed, presumptively "half his, half hers"—and might as well have grown in the backyard. Women do not gain their rights to their children in this society as *mothers,* but as *father equivalents,* as equivalent sources of seed.

The Genetic Tie

What precisely is the physical nature of this highly valued genetic connection between parent and child?

Our bodies are composed of cells. The cells each have in them a nucleus. Within the nucleus are twenty-three pairs of chromosomes.

In each pair, one chromosome came from the genetic mother and one from the genetic father. Located on the chromosomes are the genes, the basic units of heredity, composed of a kind of protein called DNA. Any particular gene of a parent may or may not be passed on to a child. A gene passed on may or may not be "expressed"—that is, a child with the gene may or may not have the characteristic. A child can carry one parent's gene for blue eyes, and yet have brown eyes.

The closest genetic connection a human being can have is an identical twin. Identical twins have the same chromosomes, the same genes. The next closest relations are those between parent and child, and between full siblings, including fraternal twins. If an individual carries a certain gene, the chances that a sibling will carry the same gene are fifty-fifty, the same as the parent-child relationship. Genetically, "there is nothing special about the parent-offspring relationship except its close degree and a certain fundamental asymmetry. The full-sib relationship is just as close."[5]

Using the word "inheritance" for genetic characteristics is misleading. It makes us think of genes as we do of other things that are inherited, such as royal titles, or titles to property. The word far predates modern genetics and carries the older implication of things "passed on," a human chain of giving through generations and time. But that is not the way genetic inheritance works. First off, one doesn't lose the thing passed: more of it is created. Using one cell from the parent, the new being creates its own replicas of the genes.

Second, there is no intention here. Careful planning and good living won't give you a better genetic estate to pass on. There is no separating out of the characteristics you want to pass on and those you want to lose. The characteristics you pass on are not necessarily even the ones you've expressed: it may be your father's or mother's genetic trait, one you did not show, that shows up in your child. The only sibling to have escaped "the family nose" may be the only sibling whose child has it.

Third, there is something strangely ahistoric about these relationships of genetic connection that defies the word "inherit." Looking at two genes, there is no way to tell which came from the parent, which from the offspring. Looking at the genes, parent and child have the same relationship as do siblings: half their genes are shared in common. And half-siblings (only one parent in common, either mother or father because genetically it makes no difference) have the same genetic connection as do grandparents and grandchildren, with one-fourth of their genes shared. Genetic connections exist in these percentages: the 100 percent connection of identical twins; the 50 percent connection of siblings and of parents to children; the 25 percent connection of grandparents to grandchildren and of half-siblings to each other; and the 12.5 percent connection of cousins, and so on. In strictly genetic terms, your sister might as well be your mother. The genetic connection is the same.

But parenthood is not just a genetic connection, a genetic relationship. And it is more than the age difference that distinguishes the parent-child relationship: the social relationship of a seventeen-year-old sibling to a newborn baby is quite different than the relationship of a seventeen-year-old parent to a newborn baby. It may be six of one and half a dozen of the other genetically, but socially these are not interchangeable relationships.

The parent-child relationship is invested with social and legal rights and claims that are not recognized, in this society, in any other genetic relationship. That is because of our social heritage of patriarchy: that genetic connection was the basis for men's control over the children of women. The contemporary modifica-tion of traditional patriarchy has been to recognize the genetic parenthood of women as being equivalent to the genetic parenthood of men. Genetic parenthood replaces paternity in determining who a child is, who it belongs to. I believe it is time to move beyond the patriarchal concern with genetic relationships.

We can recognize and appreciate the genetic tie without making it the determining connection. We do that in most of our genetic relations. American society recognizes no special claims of a sibling on a sibling, or of aunts and uncles for nieces and nephews. We recognize the relationship, we allow people to make what they will of it, but it carries no legal weight. If my brother does not like the way I am raising his niece, so be it. Even though he is closely related to her genetically, even if she were to look more like him than like me, it gives him no legal claim to her. He has no basis to challenge my claim as parent, short of showing me to be unfit—and even then, no assurance that the child would be turned over to him. And if my son doesn't like the way I'm raising my daughter, even though he is just as closely related to her genetically as I am, there is no way he can challenge my custody, and that will still be true when he is over twenty-one. But my husband, as her father, can challenge my custody, without showing me to be unfit, as I can challenge his custody. We are parents, and that gives us special legal rights over the child.

When I argue that we need to value nurturance and caring relationships more than genetic ties, that does not mean that genetics is a dirty word to me. Surely we have these genetic relations, and they can be a source of pleasure. I found myself grinning last week when a new neighbor recognized me as "Leah's mother" because she looks like me. Or I like her. And no one on earth understands like my sister does what it is to go shoe shopping for these absurd feet our father bestowed upon us. I painted my great-grandmother's portrait from a photograph—and my cousin's face emerged from the canvas. This flash of connection, this recognition of genetic relationship—it's powerful. I can understand the adoptee's joy and astonishment to meet a genetic relation and find that "somebody looks like me."

But. Just how much weight do we need to give this tie? How much can it hold? Stripped of all the social supports, is that genetic tie sufficient to define a person? Am I my mother's daughter because of our chromosomes? If a woman donates an egg, or a man turns over to a lab technician a vial of semen, does that make the person a *parent* to a child created with those chromosomes?

Patriarchal Ideology and New Procreative Technology

The new procreative technology being developed is based on the patriarchal focus on the seed. The seed, the genetic material, is the one absolutely irreplaceable part of procreation, as science now approaches it. The procreative technology continues to substitute for one after another of the nurturing tasks but makes no substitute for the seed. Breasts became unnecessary quite some time ago, as artificial formula substituted for human milk. The act of giving birth becomes increasingly unnecessary, as doctors work on surgical removal of babies to the point now where one out of five American babies are born by cesarean section. The nurturance of late pregnancy becomes unnecessary as neonatal intensive-care units develop the skill to maintain ever younger and smaller premature babies or "extrauterine fetuses" in incubation. And the nurturing environment of the fallopian tube becomes replaceable as the nurturance of the glass dish, the in vitro environment, is developed.

None of these techniques of artificial nurturance works as well as the natural mothering experience, though as one or another becomes "faddish" there is a tendency for doctors to proclaim its superiority over the natural mother.

But once a substitute for a thing is possible, the thing itself loses its mystique. By their very existence, substitutes denigrate the original. What is the value of penmanship in a world with typewriters? Who needs to do long division in a world with calculators? What happened to oral history in a world that learned to write? Once a substitute, or just a "manmade" alternative is available, what's so special about the original? Think about how the mystical meaning of flight changed as airplanes streaked over eagles.

That is what is happening to mothering—as a physical and as a psychological experience—as we offer substitute after substitute, surrogate after surrogate. What is so *special* about motherhood?

I recently listened to a group of lawyers trying to figure out if there was anything special or unique about a mother's relationship to her fetus, compared to anyone else's relationship to that fetus. The context was the issue of prenatal torts—the ever-present legal question of who can sue whom for what. If a child can sue someone, say a manufacturer of a chemical, for harm that was done to that child when it was a fetus, then is there any reason the child cannot sue the mother for harm she did to the child when it was a fetus? Is there anything that makes a mother's relationship to her fetus unique? They had a hard time thinking of anything.

We have focused on the seed, on the embryo, and then on the fetus, and reduced all of the nurturance, all of the intimacy, all of the *mothering*, to background environmental factors. And so as we substitute for this and for that environmental factor, substitute for this or for that mothering experience, we wonder what is so special about the original, what is so unique about the mother's relationship.

The problem has been brought to a head with the new procreative technology, which forces us to confront questions about mothering and the mother-child relationship. But these are not new problems or new questions.

People in our society have been substituting for aspects of mothering for a long time, always along the same patterns. Upper-class women have bought the services of lower-class women to provide one or another mothering service for their children. Or, it might more accurately be said in some circumstances, upper-class men have bought the services of lower-class women to supplement the services of their wives. Some societies have let men have mistresses while their wives mothered; some have let men hire servants to do the mothering so that their wives could be more like mistresses.

Wet nurses are the earliest example of this biological substitution of one woman for another in mothering. Sometimes wet nursing has been done in an exchange system between women—two or more women occasionally nursing each other's babies, substituting for one another. "Commercializing" wet nursing meant putting a price tag on that service. When the wet nurses were slave mammies, the price was factored into the cost of the slave. When it was a hired wet nurse, the cost was per feeding, per hour, or per week. In these cash exchanges, the breast-feeding relationship was considered unimportant. Milk became a product to be bought and sold, and not the basis of an intimate relationship. Once one buys the milk, the producer of the milk is reduced in status—her relationship is not a mothering relationship, not a relationship to the child, but a relationship to her product, to her milk. Her value lies in the quality of her milk, not in the quality of her

relationship with the child. And so wet nurses were inspected, like animals, for the quality of their product.

Today we are more familiar with the non-biological services that we hire from mother substitutes. We hire babysitters, day-care workers, nannies, and housekeepers to "watch" our children. The tasks are the traditional tasks of mothering—feeding, tending, caring, the whole bundle of social and psychological and physical tasks involved in the care of young children. When performed by mothers, we call this mothering. When performed by fathers, we have sometimes called it fathering, sometimes parenting, sometimes "helping the mother." When performed by hired hands, we call it unskilled.

We devalue these nurturing tasks when we contract for them. When we do them ourselves because we want to do them, we see them as precious, as special, as treasured moments in life. That is the contradiction that allows us to value our children so highly, to value our special time with them, to speak lovingly of the child's trust, the joys of that small hand placed in ours—and hire someone to take that hand, at minimum wage.

In sum, the ideology of a patriarchal society goes much deeper than male dominance. It means far more than just having men in charge, or men making more decisions than women do. The ideology of patriarchy is a basic worldview, and in a patriarchal system that view permeates all of our thinking. In our society, the ideology of patriarchy provides us with an understanding not only of the relations between men and women but also of the relations between mothers and their children.

In a patriarchal society, men use women to have their children. A man can use this woman or that woman to have *his* children. He can hire this woman or that woman to substitute for one or another aspect (biological, social, or psychological) of the mothering his child needs. From the view of the man, his seed is irreplaceable; the mothering, the nurturance, is substitutable.

And from the woman's point of view? We can use this man's sperm or that one's to have our children. With this or that man as father, our bellies will swell, life will stir, milk will flow. We may prefer one man's seed to another, just as a man may prefer one woman's nurturance to another for his child, but they are substitutable, they are interchangeable. For a man, what makes the child *his* is his seed. For women, what makes the child ours is the nurturance, the work of our bodies. Wherever the sperm came from, it is in our bodies that our babies grow, and our physical presence and nurturance that make our babies ours.

But is that inevitable? Did not some women substitute other women's bodies when they hired wet nurses? Don't some women substitute other women's arms, other women's touch, when they hire housekeepers and babysitters and day-care workers? And now the new procreative technology lets us cut our seeds loose from our bodies and plant them in other women's bodies. Now the seed, the egg, of one woman can be brought to term in the body of another.

We have a technology that takes Susan's egg and puts it in Mary's body. And so we ask, *who* is the mother? Who is the surrogate? Is Mary substituting for Susan's body, growing Susan's baby for Susan? Or is Susan's egg substituting for Mary's, growing into Mary's baby in Mary's body? Our answer depends on where we stand when we ask the questions.

When we accept the patriarchal valuing of the seed, there is no doubt—the real mother, like the real father, is the genetic parent. When we can contract for pregnancy at the present rate of $10,000 we can choose which women to substitute for us in the pregnancy. The workers have books of pictures of women

for potential parents to choose from, to take this woman or that woman to carry the pregnancy, to nurture the seed.

But for which women are these substitutes available? Who can afford to hire substitutes for the various parts of mothering? The situation today is exactly what it has been historically: women of privilege, wealthy or fairly wealthy women, hiring the services of poor, or fairly poor, women. Upper-class women can have some of the privileges of patriarchy. Upper-class women can have, can buy, some of the privileges of their paternity, using the bodies of poorer women to "bear them offspring." And upper-class women can, as they so often have, be bought off with these privileges, and accept men's worldview as their own. And so we have women, right along with men, saying that what makes a child one's own is the seed, the genetic tie, the "blood." And the blood they mean is not the real blood of pregnancy and birth, not the blood of the pulsing cord, the bloody show, the blood of birth, but the metaphorical blood of the genetic tie.

This is the ultimate meaning of patriarchy for mothers: seeds are precious; mothers are fungible.

Baby M: A Parable of Modern Patriarchy

Bill Stern wanted a child. He wanted *his own* child, a child grown of his sperm. Betsy Stern, his wife, was ill and afraid that a pregnancy would worsen her condition. The Sterns went to the Infertility Center of New York, where Noel Keane brokered a contract between Bill Stern and Mary Beth Whitehead. Whitehead agreed to be a "surrogate," substituting for a fee for Stern's wife in bearing him a child. Stern provided semen, a physician inserted it into Mary Beth Whitehead, and she conceived, carried, and gave birth to a daughter. But things did not go as planned. Whitehead changed her mind and refused to give up the baby. For four months she kept that child, hiding from Stern and from the courts.

Stern wanted the baby—obviously he wanted her very much. But until he got a court order and sent the police to take the child from her mother, until the police took the child from her and brought her into Stern's home, until he began to live with her and care for her, what was she to him? Was she really *his*?

How was Stern's situation different from that of any potential adoptive parent who has been promised a child? How was *Bill* Stern's situation different from *Betsy* Stern's situation? She also waited for this child, genuinely prepared to become a mother to her. Like any waiting adopters, they were heartbroken when the birth mother changed her mind.

In her book *With Child: One Couple's Journey to Their Adopted Children*, Susan Viguers describes a similar experience. A young pregnant woman promised Susan and her husband, Ken, her child. She gave birth to a boy. The waiting couple gathered their family around, readied the baby's room, named the child Jonathan. The day, the hour the baby was to be turned over came. And, like Mary Beth Whitehead, the mother changed her mind:

> Our experience with him remains a touchstone for us. We continue to feel that we lost our first child. Many people have indicated, often obliquely, that they cannot understand the intensity of that feeling. "You never saw the baby," they point out. We know that is mercifully true. It could have been much worse, although at the time that did not seem possible. People have also reminded us that the baby did not die. Again, that is literally true. In another sense, our loss was nonetheless a death: a life was taken from us as finally as death takes life. Certainly, we experienced the grief that follows death. Ken and I still regret the decision that Jonathan's biological mother made, because we believe it was

not in his best interest, nor, of course, in ours; nevertheless we feel uneasy condemning her decision to retain her parental rights. Ours, we know, is a one-sided story, but that does not take away our loss.[6]

That loss is very real, that grief is true grief. I believe that is just the loss that the Sterns were experiencing, and it is very serious. But it is the stillbirth Susan Viguers later explicitly compares it to: it is the loss of the *idea* of a baby, not a particular baby held inside, not a baby one has lived with intimately and then birthed. The Viguers, rightly, felt uneasy condemning the birth mother, and had absolutely no legal basis to protest her decision. And neither would *Betsy* Stern have had any legal basis for protesting Mary Beth Whitehead's decision. But Bill Stern claimed paternity: on the basis of his genetic tie, he claimed ownership of the child and was prepared to dismiss the claim of the birth mother.

Ultimately, Bill Stern won. Even though the contract was declared illegal, the socially weighted fact of his paternity made the child *his* in the eyes of the law. Based on his genetic connection, based on that vial of semen, he alone had a legal right to challenge and ultimately to win custody of the child. And now, in the eyes of the law, Betsy Stern is the surrogate mother, raising his child for him.

Is that genetic tie, that chromosomal connection, strong enough to bear the weight we place on it?

NOTES

1. Glenn Petersen, 1982, "Ponepean Matriliny: Production, Exchange and the Ties that Bind," *American Ethnologist*, vol. 9, no. 1, p. 141.

2. Annette Weiner, 1976, *Women of Value, Men of Renown: New Perspectives on Trobriand Exchange* (Austin: University of Texas Press); also Weiner, personal communication.

3. Shirley Lindenbaum, 1979, *Kuru Sorcery: Disease and Danger in the New Guinea Highlands* (Palo

Alto, California: Mayfield Publishing Company), p. 15.

4. Kathleen Gough, 1961, "Nayar: Central Kerala," in David M. Schneider and Kathleen Gough, editors, *Matrilineal Kinship* (Berkeley, and Los Angeles: University of California Press), p. 365.

5. W. D. Hamilton, 1978, "The Genetic Evolution of Social Behavior," in Arthur L. Caplan, editor, *The Sociobiology Debate: Readings on Ethical and Scientific Issues* (New York: Harper and Row), p. 191.

6. Susan Viguers, 1986, *With Child: One Couple's Journey to Their Adopted Children* (New York: Harcourt Brace Jovanovich), p. 207.

Chapter 3

Family, Feminism, and Race in America

MAXINE BACA ZINN

Much of the contemporary crisis in American family life is related to larger socioeconomic changes. Upheavals in the social organization of work have created a massive influx of women into the labor force. At the same time, the removal of certain kinds of work has left millions of workers without jobs. Both kinds of change have affected the well-being of American families.

As debates about the context and consequences of family change reach heightened proportions, the racial-ethnic[1] composition of the United States is undergoing dramatic shifts. Massive waves of immigration from Latin America and Asia are posing difficult issues for a society that clings stubbornly to its self-image of the melting pot. Changes in fertility and immigration patterns are altering the distributions of Whites and people of color and, at the same time, creating a nation

From Susan Farrell and Judith Lorber, *The Social Construction of Gender,* pp. 119–33, copyright © 1991 by Sociologists for Women in Society. Reprinted by permission of Sage Publications, Inc.

of varied racial ethnic groups. In many cities and communities, Blacks, Hispanics, Asians, and Native Americans outnumber the White population. Their families are distinctive not only because of their ethnic heritage but because they reside in a society where racial stratification continues to shape family resources and structures in important ways. The changing demography of race in the United States presents compelling challenges to family sociology.

Questions about what is happening to families in the United States and how this country's racial order is being reshaped are seldom joined. Yet they are more closely related than either popular or scholarly discourse on these topics would suggest. The national discussion about the erosion of inner-city Black and Latino families has not been applied to our understanding of the family in general. Although many sources of this crisis are rooted in new forms of race and class inequality in America, the empirical data can sharpen our theoretical understanding of "the family" and its relationship to wider social forces. Instead of marginalizing minority families as special cultural cases, it is time to bring race into the mainstream of our thinking about family life in America.

In this chapter, I take a step toward incorporating race into the feminist revision of the concept of the family. One of its aims is to show that research on racially and ethnically diverse families can make an essential contribution to the study of the family. The intent is not to provide a theory of racial stratification and family life but to raise issues about the extent to which racial formation is a meaningful category for analyzing family experience.

Assessing the Revisions in Feminist and Race-Relations Scholarship

The feminist revisioning of the family and the revisioning of studies of families in race-relations scholarship have common origins. Both gained momentum as critiques of functionalism by an emergent critical sociology. The family was an important starting point in the development of women's studies, Black studies, and Chicano studies. In each of these areas, study of the family represented a vital thread in the evolution of critical scholarship. Both bodies of scholarship locate family experience in societal arrangements that extend beyond the family and allocate social and economic rewards. Both begin with the assumption that families are social products and then proceed to study their interrelationships with other social structures. Just as feminist theories have reconceptualized the family along a gender axis of power and control, racial-ethnic family scholarship has reconceptualized the family along the axis of race, also a system of power and control that shapes family life in crucial ways.

Because they both locate family experience in societal arrangements extending beyond

the family, these two streams of revisionist scholarship fall within the "radical critical" tradition. Although they are not commonly identified with this framework (see Osmond 1987, p. 119), they do adopt basic assumptions, major premises, and general directions of this approach.

Despite such fundamental similarities in their intellectual roots, the feminist revision and the racial-ethnic studies revision have not been combined, nor have they had the same impact on theories of the family. Feminist scholarship with its gender-as-power theme has had a far greater impact. Especially noteworthy in this regard has been the application of certain feminist insights to studies of minority families. In fact, gender-as-power and the racial division of labor have become key themes of recent studies of racial-ethnic families. Nakano Glenn's study of Japanese families (1986) and Zavella's study of Chicano families (1987) are particularly meaningful because they explore the close connections between the internal dynamics of women's family lives and economic conditions as they are bound up in broader systems of class and race inequality.

Studying the intersection of gender, race, and class in minority families has enormously enhanced family scholarship. Now, in studying racial-ethnic families, we routinely examine race and gender as interacting hierarchies of resources and rewards that condition material and subjective experiences within families.

Interacting race, class, and gender ideologies have shaped prevailing models of minority families, appearing even in the culturally deviant explanations of racial-ethnic families. As Hill Collins (1989) explains, the new version of this argument is that because minority women and men do not follow dominant notions of masculinity and femininity, they are responsible for their subordinate class placement in society. As Bridenthal (1981) has put it:

Black people have been called matriarchal (ruled by the mother) and Chicano families have been called patriarchal (ruled by the father). These supposed opposite family structures and relationships have been blamed for the failure of many members of each group to rise to a higher socioeconomic level. In other words, black and Chicano families have been blamed for the effect of racial discrimination. (p. 85)

While revisionist research on racial-ethnic families has incorporated many feminist insights, the reverse has not occurred. Knowledge about racial stratification has not been incorporated into much feminist research on the family, and race enters the discussion of family life only when minority families are concerned.

To be fair, feminist literature on the family does recognize the societal context of inequality that gives rise to distinctive family forms. Feminist rethinking of the family has dropped the cultural *deviant* perspective. But for the most part, it retains a *cultural* perspective. Most contemporary feminist thought takes great care to underscore class, race, and gender as fundamental categories of social organization, but when it comes to family patterns, race and ethnicity are used as elements of culture, not social structure. Descriptions of cultural diversity do not explain why families exhibit structural variations by race. While it is true that many family lifestyles are differentiated by ethnicity, structural patterns differ because social and economic conditions produce and may even require diverse family arrangements. Although the family nurtures ethnic culture, families are not the product of ethnic culture alone.

Racial Inequality and Family Life

The feminist revision has been reluctant to grapple with race as a power system that affects families throughout society and to apply

that understanding to "the family" writ large. As Nakano Glenn (1987) says, "Systematically incorporating hierarchies of race and class into feminist reconstruction of the family remains a challenge, a necessary next step in the development of theories of family that are inclusive" (p. 368).

In our quest to understand the structural sources of diversity in family life, we must examine all of the "socioeconomic and political arrangements and how they impinge on families" (Mullings 1986a, p. 13). Like class and gender hierarchies, racial stratification is a fundamental axis of American social structure. Racial stratification produces different opportunity structures that shape families in a variety of ways. Marriage patterns, gender relations, kinship networks, and other family characteristics result from the social location of families, that is, where they are situated in relation to societal institutions allocating resources.

Thinking about families in this way shifts the theoretical focus from cultural diversity of "ethnic lifestyles" of particular groups to race as a major element of hierarchical social relations that touches families throughout the social order (Omi and Winant 1986, p. 61). Racial stratification is a basic organizing principle in American society even though the forms of domination and discrimination have changed over time. Omi and Winant use the term "racial formation" to refer to the process by which social, economic, and political forces determine the content and import of racial categories and by which they are in turn shaped by racial meanings (1986, p. 61). As racial categories are formed and transformed over time, the meanings, practices, and institutions associated with race penetrate families throughout the society.

Social categories and groups subordinate in the racial hierarchy are often deprived of access to social institutions that offer supports for family life. Social categories and groups elevated in the racial hierarchy have different and better connections to institutions that can sustain families. Social location and its varied connection with social resources thus have profound consequences for family life.

If families are to be conceptualized in a way that relates them to social, historical, and material conditions, then racial stratification cannot be ignored. We are forced to abandon conventional notions that racial-ethnic diversity is a cultural phenomenon best understood at the microstructural level. Instead of treating diversity as a given, or as a result of traditions alone, we must treat racial stratification as a macrostructural force situating families in ways requiring diverse arrangements. These macrostructural forces can be seen in two periods of economic upheaval in the United States—industrialization and the current shift from manufacture to information and services. In both of these transitions, the relationship between families and other institutions has been altered. Despite important differences, these economic transformations have produced new relations among individuals, families, and labor systems that have had profound effects on family development throughout American society. Industrialization and deindustrialization are not neutral transformations that touch families in uniform ways. Rather, they manifest themselves differently in their interaction with race and gender, and both periods of transition reveal racial patterning in family and household formation. The theme of historical variation has become increasingly accepted in family studies, but theories of the family have largely ignored the new knowledge about race, labor, and family formation.

Industrialization and Family Structure

The past two decades of historical research on the family have revealed that industrialization has had momentous consequences for American families because of massive changes in the way people made a living. The industrial revolution changed the nature of the work performed, the allocation of work responsibilities, and the kind of pay, prestige, and power that resulted from various positions in the economy. The effect of industrialization on American family life was uneven. Instead of a linear pattern of change in which families moved steadily to a more modern level, the pattern of change was checkered (Hareven 1987). Labor force exploitation produced various kinds of family and household adaptations on the part of slaves, agricultural workers, and industrial workers.

Both class and race were basic to the relations of production in the United States in this period. Race was intertwined with class; populations from various parts of the world were brought into the labor force at different levels, and racial differences were utilized to rationalize exploitation of women and men (Mullings 1986b, p. 56). European ethnics were incorporated into low-wage industrial economies of the North, while Blacks, Latinos, Chinese, and Japanese filled labor needs in colonial labor systems of the economically backward regions of the West, Southwest, and the South. These colonial labor systems, while different, created similar hardships for family life.

All these groups had to engage in a constant struggle for both immediate survival and long-term continuation of family and community, but women's and men's work and family patterns varied considerably within different racial labor structures, with fundamentally different social supports for family life. Thornton Dill (1988) has compared patterns of White families in nineteenth-century America with those of racial ethnics and identified important racial differences in the social supports for family life. She finds that greater importance was accorded Euro-American families by the wider society. As primary laborers in the reproduction and maintenance of family life, these women were acknowledged and accorded the privileges and protections deemed socially appropriate to their family roles. Although this emphasis on family roles denied these women many rights and privileges and seriously constrained their individual growth and development, it also revealed public support for White women's family roles. Women's reproductive labor was viewed as an essential building block of the family. Combined with a view of the family as the cornerstone of the nation, this ideology produced experiences within the White dominant culture very different from those of racial ethnics (Dill 1988, p. 418). Because racial-ethnic men were usually unable to earn a "family wage," their women had to engage in subsistence and income-producing activities both in and out of the household. In additions, they had to struggle to keep their families together in the face of outside forces that threatened the integrity of their households (Glenn 1987, pp. 53–4).

During industrialization, class produced some similarities in the family experiences of racial ethnic women and those of White working-class immigrants. As D. E. Smith (1987) has argued, working-class women during this period were often far removed from the domestic ideal. The cults of domesticity and true womanhood that proliferated during this period were ideals attained more frequently by those Euro-American women whose husbands were able to earn enough to support their families (Mullings 1986b, p. 50).

This ideal was not attainable by Blacks, Latinos, and Asian Americans, who were excluded from jobs open to White immigrants. For example, in most cities, the constraints that prevented Black men from earning a family wage forced Black married women into the labor market in much greater proportions than White immigrant women. By 1880, about 50 percent of Black women were in the labor force, compared with 15 percent of White women (Degler 1980, p. 389). Furthermore, the family system of the White working class was not subject to institutional assaults, such as forced separation, directed against Black, Latino, and Chinese families (Glenn 1987, p. 73).

Racial-ethnic women experienced the oppressions of a patriarchal society but were denied the protections and buffering of a patriarchal family. Their families suffered as a direct result of the labor systems in which they participated. Since they were a cheap and exploitable labor force, little attention was given to their family and community life except as it related to their economic productivity. Labor and not the existence or maintenance of families was the critical aspect of their role in building the nation. They were denied the social and structural supports necessary to make their families a vital element in the social order (Dill 1988, p. 418). Nevertheless, people take conditions that have been thrust upon them and out of them create a history and a future (Mullings 1986b, p. 46). Using cultural forms where possible and creating new forms where necessary, racial ethnics adapted their families to the larger social order. These adaptations were not exceptions to the rule; they were instead variations created by mainstream forces. One family type was not standard and the others peripheral. Different forms existed at the same time.

Once we recognize how racial stratification has affected family formation, we can understand why the idealized family was not a lux-ury shared by all. At the same time, we can see how some idealized family patterns were made possible because of the existence of al-ternative family forms and how all of these are products of the social and economic condi-tions of the times. Although Blacks, Mexi-canos, and Asians were excluded from indus-trial work, all three groups helped build the agricultural and industrial base for subse-quent industrial development. New ways of life and new family patterns sprang from in-dustrialization. As Mullings (1986b) says, "It was the working class and enslaved men and women whose labor created the wealth that allowed the middle class and upper middle class domestic life styles to exist" (p. 50).

Deindustrialization and Families

Vast changes in the social organization of work are currently transforming the Ameri-can family across class and race groups. Not only are women and men affected differently by the transformation of the economy from its manufacturing base to service and high technology, but women and men in different racial categories are experiencing distinctive changes in their relationship to the economy. This transformation is profoundly affecting families as it works with and through race and gender hierarchies.

In the current American economy, indus-trial jobs traditionally filled by men are being replaced with service jobs that are increas-ingly filled by women. Married White women are now entering the labor force at a rate that, until recently, was seen exclusively among women of color (J. Smith 1987, p. 416). The most visible consequences of the increased la-bor force participation among White women include declining fertility and changes in marriage patterns. American White women

are delaying marriage and childbearing and are having fewer children over their lifetimes, living alone or as heads of their own house-holds—living with neither parents nor hus-bands (Hartmann 1987, p. 36). The new econ-omy is reshaping families as it propels these women into the labor force.

In minority communities across America, families and households are also being re-shaped through new patterns of work and gender roles. The high level of female-headed families among Blacks and Hispanics (espe-cially Puerto Ricans) is the outgrowth of changes in the larger economy. The long-term decline in employment opportunities for men is the force most responsible for the growth of racial-ethnic families headed by women. Wilson's (1987) compelling work has shown that the shortage of Black men with the ability to support a family makes it necessary for many Black women to leave a marriage or forgo marriage altogether. Adaptation to structural conditions leaves Black women dis-proportionately separated, divorced, and solely responsible for their children.

Families throughout American society are being reshaped by economic and industrial change: "The shifting economy produces and even demands diverse family forms—includ-ing, for example, female headed households, extended kinship units, dual-career couples, and lesbian collectives" (Gerstel and Gross 1987, p. 7). Families mainly headed by women have become permanent in all racial cate-gories in America, with the disproportionate effects of change most visible among Blacks and Latinos. While the chief cause of the in-crease in female-headed households among Whites is the greater economic independence of White women, the longer delay of first marriage and the low rate of remarriage among Black women reflects the labor force problems of Black men (Wilson and Necker-man 1986, p. 256). Thus race creates different routes to female headship, but Whites, Blacks, and Latinos are all increasingly likely to end up in this family form.

Conclusion

Knowing that race creates certain patterns in the way families are located and embedded in different social environments, we should be able to theorize for all racial categories. Billingsley (1988) suggests that the study of Black families can generate important insights for White families: Families may respond in a like manner when impacted by larger social forces. To the extent that White families and Black families experience similar pressures, they may respond in similar ways, including the adaptation of their family structures and other behaviors. With respect to single-parent families, teenage childbirth, working mothers, and a host of other behaviors, Black families serve as barometers of social change and as forerunners of adaptive patterns that will be progressively experienced by the more privileged sectors of American society.

While such insights are pertinent, they should not eclipse the ways in which racial meanings inform our perceptions of family diversity. As social and economic changes produce new family arrangements, alternatives—what is sometimes called "family pluralism"—are granted greater legitimacy. Yet many alternatives that appear new to middle-class White Americans are actually variant family patterns that have been traditional within Black and other minority communities for many generations. Presented as the new lifestyles of the mainstream, they are, in fact, the same lifestyles that have in the past been deemed pathological, deviant, or unacceptable when observed in Black families (Peters and McAdoo 1983, p. 228).

In much popular and scholarly thinking, alternatives are seen as inevitable changes, new ways of living that are part of an advanced society. In other words, they are conceptualized as products of the mainstream. Yet such alternatives, when associated with racial ethnic groups, are judged against a standard model and found to be deviant. Therefore, the notion of family pluralism does not correctly describe the family diversity of the past or the present. Pluralism implies that alternative family forms *coexist* within a society. In reality, racial meanings create a hierarchy in which some family forms are privileged and others are subordinated, even though they are both products of larger social forces.

Treating race as a basic category of social organization can make the feminist reconstruction of the family more inclusive. The implications of this approach are also provocative and uncomfortable because they challenge some of our basic sociological and feminist assumptions about how families in different races (and classes) are related to the larger society, to each other, and how they are all changing as a result of ongoing social and economic changes. These are important issues for social scientists, policymakers, and others to ponder, understand, and solve.

NOTE

1. The term *racial-ethnic* refers to groups labeled as races in the context of certain historical, social, and material conditions. Blacks, Latinos, and Asian Americans are racial groups that are formed, defined, and given meaning by a variety of social forces in the wider society, most notably distinctive forms of labor exploitation. Each group is also bound together by ethnicity, that is, common ancestry and emergent cultural characteristics that are often used for coping with racial oppression. The concept racial-ethnic underscores the social construction of race and ethnicity for people of color in the United States.

REFERENCES

Billingsley, A. 1988. "The Impact of Technology on Afro-American Families." *Family Relations* 7:420–25.

Bridenthal, R. 1981. "The Family Tree: Contemporary Patterns in the United States." Pp. 47–105 in *Household and Kin,* edited by A. Swerdlow, R. Bridenthal, J. Kelly, and P. Vine. Old Westbury, NY: Feminist Press.

Collins, P. Hill. 1989. "A Comparison of Two Works on Black Family Life." *Signs: Journal of Women in Culture and Society* 14:875–84.

Degler, C. 1980. *At Odds: Women and the Family in America from the Revolution to the Present.* New York: Oxford University Press.

Dill, B. Thornton. 1988. "Our Mother's Grief: Racial Ethnic Women and the Maintenance of Families." *Journal of Family History* 13:415–31.

Gerstel, N., and H. E. Gross (eds.). 1987. *Families and Work.* Philadelphia: Temple University Press.

Glenn, E. Nakano. 1986. *Issei, Nisei, War Bride: Three Generations of Japanese American Women in Domestic Service.* Philadelphia: Temple University Press.

———. 1987. "Racial Ethnic Women's Labor: The Intersection of Race, Gender and Class Oppression." Pp. 46–73 in *Hidden Aspects of Women's Work,* edited by C. Bose, R. Feldberg, and N. Sokoloff. New York: Praeger.

Hareven, T. 1987. "Historical Analysis of the Family." Pp. 37–57 in *Handbook of Marriage and the Family,* edited by M. B. Sussman and S. Steinmetz. New York: Plenum.

Hartmann, H. I. 1987. "Changes in Women's Economic and Family Roles in Post World War II United States." Pp. 33–64 in *Women, Households and the Economy,* edited by L. R. Benerfa and C. R. Stimpson. New Brunswick, NJ: Rutgers University Press.

Mullings, L. 1986a. "Anthropological Perspectives on the Afro-American Family." *American Journal of Social Psychiatry* 6:11–16.

———. 1986b. "Uneven Development: Class, Race and Gender in the United States Before 1900." Pp. 41–51 in *Women's Work: Development and Division of Labor by Gender,* edited by E. Leacock, H. I. Safa, and contributors. South Hadley, MA: Bergin & Garvey.

Omi, M., and H. Winant. 1986. *Racial Formation in the United States.* London: Routledge & Kegan Paul.

Osmond, M. Withers. 1987. "Radical-Critical Theories." Pp. 103–24 in *Handbook of Marriage and the Family,* edited by M. B. Sussman and S. Steinmetz. New York: Plenum.

Peters, M., and H. P. McAdoo. 1983. "The Present and Future of Alternative Lifestyles in Ethnic American Cultures." Pp. 288–307 in *Contemporary Families and Alternative Lifestyles,* edited by E. D. Macklin and R. H. Rubin. Beverly Hills, CA: Sage.

Smith, D. E. 1987. "Women's Inequality and the Family." Pp. 23–54 in *Families and Work,* edited by N. Gerstel and H. Engel Gross. Philadelphia: Temple University Press.

Smith, J. 1987. "Transforming Households: Working-Class Women and Economic Crisis." *Social Problems* 34:416–36.

Wilson, W., and K. M. Neckerman. 1986. "Poverty and Family Structure: The Widening Gap Between Evidence and Public Policy Issues." Pp. 232–59 in *Fighting Poverty,* edited by S. H. Danziger and D. Weinberg. Cambridge: Harvard University Press.

Wilson, W. J. 1987. *The Truly Disadvantaged.* Chicago: University of Chicago Press.

Zavella, P. 1987. *Women's Work and Chicano Families.* Ithaca, NY: Cornell University Press.

∼ *Chapter 4*

Adoption and Kinship

The text on a recent Valentine's Day card (Carlton Cards 1997) reads:

> Sis, even if you were adopted,
> I'd still love you . . .
> . . . not that you are, of course.
> At least I don't think so.
> But, come to think of it,
> you don't really look like
> Mom and Dad. Gee, maybe
> you should get a DNA test
> or something. Oh well,
> don't worry about it.
> We all love you, even
> if your real parents don't.
>
> Happy Valentine's Day.

In a society where the "molecular" (that is, genetic) family is viewed as the most central social unit, alternative kinship and family forms tend to be viewed not only as second best but even as threats to the social fabric. It is against this background that we can understand the current focus in American popular culture on the search for unknown relatives and reunions between adoptees and their birth parents. Adoptees' search for blood relatives confirms that blood relations still matter despite the upsurge in divorce rates and single parenthood. The molecular connection still implies a sense of belonging, continuity, and care that makes families—and society—possible (Wegar 1997b).

As Dorothy Nelkin and M. Susan Lindee argue in their recent book *The DNA Mystique: The Gene as a Cultural Icon* (1995), the power of genes is currently heralded to an unprecedented extent not only in the scientific community but in American popular culture as well. More than ever, the belief in the paramount importance of genes in matters of human development, identity, and bonding is at the core of the dominant American family ideology (Nelkin and Lindee 1995, 60). Since the ideology of the "molecular family" tends to render all nongenetic family forms abnormal and pathogenic, we should not be surprised that adoptive kinship and adoptive relations in our culture is considered "second best," unlikely to succeed, and even doomed to failure.

Sociologists are not exempt from these cultural biases. Sociologists view the family as a social construct. Feminist sociologists in particular have questioned the "naturalness" and the universal applicability of the dominant American *family* ideal, that is, the nuclear unit of a heterosexual couple and their biological children (Andersen 1991). Yet feminists and sociologists have had surprisingly little to say about the dominant *kinship* ideal in American society (see Schneider 1980), the assumption that *real* families are constituted by blood and that other family forms are in some ways defective, problematic, and pathogenic. Recently, family sociologists have emphasized the great variety of family forms that exist in today's society, such as step-families, single-parent families, and gay and lesbian families, but their bio-centric bias has led them largely to overlook non-biological family forms such as adoption and foster-parenting. Those few feminist researchers who have taken an interest in adoption issues, have primarily emphasized and criticized the plight of birth mothers who have been forced to surrender their children for adoption.

When sociologists have studied adoption their focus has been mainly problem-oriented (e.g., Modell 1994).[1] To foster a more balanced understanding of adoption, we need to acknowledge its existing *positive* aspects.

At the same time, a critical sociological analysis of adoption must begin with the recognition that adoptive kinship in our society is labeled a deviant family form and that members of adoptive families are frequently forced to manage and negotiate their stigmatized status. From this point of view, many of the psychological patterns, problems, and pathologies that mental health professionals have presented as characteristic of adoptive families should not be viewed as inherent to these families but should instead be seen as, at least partially, symptoms of the stigma of infertility and adoptive kinship (Weger 1995).

Cultural Variations in Kinship Systems

The race and class bias of the current preoccupation with the biological basis of kinship and parenthood must be stressed. White, middle-class adoptees are not the only ones who search for their biological kin. Yet the belief that *individual* family ties rather *group or cultural* ties (as in the search for ethnic roots) are central to one's identity and sense of self seems to be a special white, middle-class preoccupation. According to studies of adoptees who search for their biological parents or belong to search activist groups, the majority are white, middle-class females (Bertocci and Schechter 1991).

Researchers have documented ethnic variations in the views of family and kinship bonds, in particular in the African American community. In *All Our Kin* (1974), Carol Stack notes that in the community she studied the concept of kin was not exclusively reserved for biological relatives but could include close friends as well. In a similar manner, the parenting activities were distributed among several individuals, who might or might not have been biologically related (p. 83). As Ernest J. Gaines explains in his classic short story "Just Like a Tree" (reprinted in Washington 1991, 12–38), families need not necessarily be constituted by blood kin. Instead, "familial relationships are nourished and sustained by the accumulation of thousands of daily acts of support and care" (Washington 1991, 40). More recently, in his research on fathering among African Americans in the inner city, Frank Furstenberg (1995) noted a common distinction between "fathers" and "daddies" that grants the sociological father an equally, if not more important, role than that of the mostly absent biological father (p. 139).

Although this flexible understanding of kinship has been linked to African American communities in particular, it would oversimplify the matter to claim that these communities are the only ones to embrace an inclusive definition of kinship. Kath Weston (1991) notes in *Families We Choose: Lesbians, Gays, Kinship* that gays and lesbians have created new kinds of families that are not based on, or symbolized by, blood or biology (p. 27).

Anthropologists have located numerous non-Western societies in which adoption is a common and nonstigmatized type of family formation (for an overview, see Terrell and Modell 1994). For example, in Pacific Island or Oceanic societies (Carroll 1970), in Inuit societies (Guemple 1979), and in West African societies (Goody 1982), adoption and other forms of child exchange are customary. Even as immigrants, as in the case of West Africans living in London (see Goody 1982), non-Westerners might maintain a view of adoption and kinship that differs from that of the dominant culture.

The meanings of adoption, kinship, and parenting vary historically and culturally, however, and cross-cultural studies of adoption practices cannot therefore be interpreted as being pure cross-cultural comparisons. As Vern Carroll (1970) phrases the argument in his Introduction to *Adoption in Eastern Oceania*, "Any anthropological use of a term like 'marriage' or 'family' or 'kinship' seems destined to prejudge the central issues by introducing unspecified assumptions derived from the anthropologist's culture" (p. 3). In Oceania, for example, adoption is seldom an arrangement between strangers. More often it is an informal arrangement that is primarily intended to serve not the child's interests but the interests of the parents and the community (Terrell and Modell 1994, 156).

Conflicts over definitions of kinship can occur between indigenous peoples and government representatives of dominant cultures. Mary Weismantel's (1995) account of adoption practices in the indigenous community of Zumbagua in highland Ecuador reveals the tensions between indigenous kinship beliefs and the Euro-American belief in the primacy of blood ties:

> But it was only when a sleepy little boy entered the kitchen from his nearby bed that the young Iza really came alive. The man served the child hot soup, and sat back beaming, happily watching him empty the bowl. "He was an orphan, a poor boy, so I brought him here to live with me as my son," he explained. "Where he was living there wasn't enough to eat."
>
> The nurse was horrified; she gestured to him frantically to lower his voice. "Don't talk like that in front of the boy," she whispered. "He's very young; maybe, if he's lucky, he'll forget about his own parents and grow up believing you're his real father." Iza, puzzled and offended, responded by raising his voice instead of lowering it. "I *am* going to be his father," he said irritably. "Aren't I feeding him right now?"

In this instance, the nurse—a government representative—not only failed to recognize that parenthood was defined in terms of specific parenting behaviors rather than in terms of blood ties but also assumed that the boy's knowledge of multiple parents and biological genealogy would harm him, the adoptee. The assumption that adoptees are not capable of several significant attachments and that genealogical information consequently should be hidden and forgotten rather than integrated into the adoptee's identity has until recently been a cornerstone of American adoption practice as well (Sachdev 1989).

In addition to the stigma that stems from the failure to conform to the molecular family model, the experiences of adoptees, birth parents, and adoptive parents have been crucially shaped by the "twin stigmata of infertility and illegitimacy" (Haimes and Timms 1985, 77). As Erving Goffman (1963, 32) phrases the argument, the stigmatized person learns and incorporates through socialization "the standpoint of the normal, acquiring thereby the identity beliefs of the wider society and a general idea of what it would be like to possess a particular stigma." Unfortunately, the extent to which adoption policies and the lives of those most intimately affected by adoption have been shaped by these stigmata has rarely been openly recognized or addressed by sociologists. A review of the research literature on adoption reveals that we know surprisingly little about the effects and experiences of the social labeling of adoption as "second best" or even unworkable.

The Experience of Adoption

Adoptees

Our knowledge of adoptees' experiences is limited in two ways: (1) the existing adoption literature emphasizes only negative experiences of adoption, and (2) these negative experiences are typically attributed to the adoption in and of itself, while the possible impact on stigmatizing community attitudes toward adoption have not been taken into account. Except for the writings of adoption search activists who mostly emphasize the negative effect of the sealed records policy on their lives (e.g., Fisher 1973; Lifton 1994) and who also tend to consider adoption as problematic *in itself*, we know relatively little about what it feels like to grow up adopted in a society that considers adoptive kinship "second best."

Perhaps adoptees who do not experience adoption as a painful or central aspect of their lives have little reason to write about adoption. We do not know their stories because they have

no sad, dramatic, or triumphant stories to tell regarding adoption. What we do know, however, is that only a small minority of adoptees who locate their biological parents will establish a traditional parent-child relationship with their birth parent(s). According to a study by Paul Sachdev (1989, 63), only one-fifth of the adoptees he studied established a parent-child relationship with the birth mother, and only half of the searchers continued to see their birth mothers regularly after the initial meeting. In other words, adoptees who want to successfully search for and then meet their biological parents are likely to continue to regard their adoptive parents as "real." Moreover, in their recent large-scale study of adopted adolescents, Peter Benson, Anu Sharma, and Eugene Roehlkepartain (1994) found that child-parent attachments are very strong in most adoptive families and that adopted adolescents are as deeply attached to their parents as are their nonadopted siblings.

Yet, as noted, most research on adoption has so far been strictly problem-oriented. Our current knowledge of adoption experiences—especially the experiences of adoptees—stems mainly from psychological studies of the detrimental effects of adoption on adoptees' mental well-being.

The link between adoption and emotional disturbance has intrigued psychiatrists, social workers, and other mental health professionals since the 1940s, and the search for pathological symptoms among adoptees has generated more than 150 studies over the past fifty years (Howard 1990). The extent to which adoptees suffer from negative personality traits or mental disorders has been the focus of considerable dispute, however. While most researchers have maintained that adoptees are at greater risk to suffer from psychiatric disorders than nonadoptees (cf. LeVine and Sallee 1990; Hajal and Rosenberg 1991; Berry 1992), some recent studies indicate that adoptees as a group are at no greater risk, or may even be at *lesser* risk, than nonadopted adolescents and adults to suffer from negative personality characteristics such as poor self-image, insecurity, and a sense of lack of control (Marquis and Detweiler 1985; Benson, Sharma, and Roehlkepartain 1994). Again, since the purpose of most adoption research has been to explain problems in adoptive families, researchers have made little effort to explore or explain *positive* personality characteristics. For example, although the experience of adoption may be problematic for many adoptees, adopted adolescents as *a group* have been shown to have higher self-esteem and to be somewhat more optimistic about their futures than nonadopted adolescents (Benson, Sharma, Roehlkepartain 1994, 67).

By neglecting, or by at least downplaying, the impact of social stigmatization, researchers have unwittingly contributed to the pathologization of adoption. By failing to take into account the impact of cultural norms and assumptions regarding infertility, childlessness, femininity, kinship, and the significance of the blood relation, researchers have inadvertently defined adoptive bonds as inferior to biological kinship.

In an interview study with adoptees, adoptive parents, and birth parents, Judith Modell (1994, 120) noted that several of the adoptees said that they felt "different." Unfortunately, she did not in this context explore the social sources of this sense of "difference" but instead attributed it to the adoptive parents' failure to communicate properly about adoption issues.[2] From a sociological point of view, however, it is necessary to ponder *why* the adoptive parents found it so hard to communicate about these issues.

Adoptive Parents

In his work on adoption, *Shared Fate: A Theory of Adoption and Mental Health,* sociologist H. David Kirk (1964) notes that the adoptive

parents he studied reacted to the community's view of them and their children as "different." The primary contribution of Kirk's shared-fate theory consisted of recognizing the social character of the adoptive parents' strategies of coping. He argues that adoptive parents were expected by social workers and other community members to both reject and acknowledge the differences of adoptive parenthood, and they thus were placed in a difficult and ambiguous position. Unfortunately, Kirk's key point—that disparaging social attitudes affect the adoptive parents' behavior—has received scant attention by later researchers.

Recent studies have explained adoptees' mental health problems primarily in terms of the adoptive parents' lack of self-acceptance (DiGuilio 1988), unrealistic expectations (Berry 1992), or latent hostility toward the adoptee (Schneider and Rimmer 1984). DiGuilio (1988, 424), for example, emphasizes that "acceptance of self has been closely linked to acceptance *of* others," she does not consider the importance of acceptance *by* others, that is, the effect of stigmatizing attitudes on the adoptive parents' self-acceptance. Even researchers who have recognized issues concerning disclosure of the adoption outside the family and the adoptee's awareness of the social meaning of adoption (Hajal and Rosenberg 1991; LeVine and Sallee 1990) have not noted the full extent to which adoptive parents are subject to demeaning social attitudes and contradictory agency messages regarding the importance of heredity (cf. Kirk 1964).

Many of the studies that explore the effects of parental behavior also reflect and reinforce cultural stereotypes of women as mothers. First, in particular the early studies (e.g., Deutsch 1945; Schechter 1960; Toussieng 1962) rested upon the assumption that the *adoptive mother* was infertile while little if any attention was given to the possible infertility of the adoptive father. Few of the studies actually clarified which partner was infertile, and very little research (with the notable exception of Sachdev 1989) has so far specifically explored the role of the adoptive father *or* the biological father. For example *The Adoption Reader* (Wadia-Ellis 1995) only includes stories by birth mothers, adoptive mothers, and adoptive daughters. Second, the dilemmas of adoption have been interpreted as the consequences of the psychopathology of individual mothers rather than as social reactions to infertility, as manifestations of, or ways of coping with, a social stigma (Miall 1987; Greil et al. 1989). These studies mirror the enduring popular and medical assumption that women's behavior and mental health is determined by their reproductive biology (Eyer 1992).

Although infertility is a stigmatizing social attribute for both women and men, the representation and treatment of adoptive mothers in particular has reflected the assumption that mature, healthy womanhood is intricately linked to biological motherhood. As Laurie Lisle (1996) phrases the argument in her recent account of the cultural stigma of childlessness in American society, "The specter of the woman without a child can invoke an image of a woman who hates children, the archetypal anti-mother, the non-nurturing female" (p. 30). By assuming that adoptive mothers are inherently less capable of providing "good mothering," researchers have tended to reinforce this cultural stigma in their work.

Birth Parents

This section is really about birth mothers because, as noted, the literature on adoption and relinquishment has focused primarily on the birth mother, while the situation of the birth father has been given comparatively little attention. Nevertheless, the term "birth parent" or "biological parent" has often been misleadingly used interchangeably with "birth mother" or "biological mother" (Wegar 1997a).

Studies of attitudes toward illegitimacy in the United States since the late nineteenth century have traced a transition from a view of the white, unwed mother as a fallen woman to be saved, to a sexual delinquent to be controlled, to a neurotic girl to be cured (Kunzel 1993). During the Progressive era, social workers typically regarded adoptees as children of sin who had inherited the mental and moral weakness of their mothers. In response to the rapidly expanding demand for white, adoptable infants and the rising rate of white, single pregnancy, social workers began after the Second World War to emphasize the psychological instead of the biological causes of illegitimacy. For unwed mothers of color, different rules and assumptions have applied. Rather than explaining illegitimacy as a neurotic symptom and an unresolved psychic conflict, child welfare professionals have explained out-of-wedlock pregnancies among women of color in terms of cultural moral pathology (Solinger 1992; Kunzel 1993).

While white, unwed mothers before the Second World War were expected to keep their babies and thus pay the wages of their "sins," in the period after the war they were encouraged to relinquish their babies for adoption (Solinger 1992). Yet, while the new focus on the psychological cause of illegitimacy "transformed the white unwed mother from a genetically tainted unfortunate into a maladjusted woman who could be cured" (Solinger 1992, 152), she could still be absolved only *after* having relinquished her illegitimate infant. Moreover, she had to adhere to a narrow patriarchal model of feminine maturity that assumed a casual link between women's mental health, their sexual and reproductive behavior, and their capacity to mother. The postwar adoption mandate, moreover, channeled social welfare resources into adoption work, while simultaneously curtailing the resources available for single mothers who kept their babies (Solinger 1992, 155). This trend had a particularly detrimental effect upon the lives of black, single mothers, who mostly chose to keep their children and were encouraged to do so by social workers.

The influence of the women's movement on community attitudes toward single mothers has helped reduce the stigma of unwed motherhood and increase the availability of economic and social supports. This change in attitudes has also prompted adoption and mental health professionals to explore in more depth the birth mother's experience (e.g., Pannor, Baran, and Sorosky 1978; Deykin, Campbell, and Patti 1984; Millen and Roll 1985; Brodzinsky 1990). The psychological issue of grief and survival that Suzanne Arms addresses in her seminal book based on interviews with birth mothers, *To Love and Let Go* (1983), are now at least briefly discussed in most professional guides to adoption work (e.g., Kadushin and Martin 1988). For example, researchers have noted that birth mothers experience long-term depression, alienation, and difficulties in making commitments (Millen and Roll 1985) and that surrendering a child for adoption can have negative effects upon later experiences of marriage and parenting (Deykin, Campbell, and Patti 1984). Nevertheless, empirical research on relinquishment in the United States has still tended to emphasize the risks involved in becoming an unwed mother, to support an optimistic view of relinquishment, and to emphasize the positive social benefits of adoption (Curtis 1990, 245).

Since the very first adoption law was enacted in Massachusetts in 1851, policy makers and legislators have argued that adoption should primarily serve adoptees' best interests (Modell 1994, 20). Yet it is clear that the institution of adoption has served other interests as well. Above all, adoption has provided the state with a means whereby, especially unwed, women's reproductive behavior can be regulated and traditional family ideals upheld. Adoption policies have traditionally reflected disparaging community attitudes toward illegitimacy and have tended to punish women, who have been categorized as bad or unfit mothers (Shalev 1989). The most blatant evidence of disparaging attitudes toward unwed mothers is that, until recently, they have had little say in the adoption process.

Since the 1970s, the shortage of white infants in need of adoption relative to the growing number of couples who want to adopt (National Committee for Adoption 1989) has also increased the say of birth mothers in the adoption process. Today, many mothers choose the option of "open adoption" as opposed to the traditional type of "closed" adoption (cf. Melina and Kaplan Rozia 1993). In the postwar years, only about one-fifth of the unwed mothers who came into contact with social workers ended up raising their babies. Since the mid-1970s, however, over 95 percent of unmarried mothers have chosen to parent their children (Curtis 1990, 245).

Critics have stressed that the adoption system relies upon and reinforces class domination: "To obtain children, the middle and the upper classes are more likely than the working and lower classes to turn to adoption agencies rather than to relatives and informal community contacts. The adopted children come not only from strangers, but frequently from poor strangers and from unmarried mothers, who have a stigmatized social status" (Mandell 1973, 29). Although modern adoption in the United States is officially considered a form of child welfare, access to this resource for couples who want children appears to be unequal. Adoption agencies require no explicitly set minimum income for adoptive parents, but their income is usually above average (Bachrach et al. 1990).

While there are no recent in-depth class analyses of the adoption system, since the 1970s critics of interracial adoptions have continued to argue that adoption in the United States has served the white community predominately and that not enough effort has been made to attract adopters from other ethnic groups (cf. Hayes 1993). Although the underrepresentation of African American and other minority adopters can in part be explained by their preference for informal adoptions, adoption agencies have clearly played an active role in excluding adopters on the basis of economic resources, and thus implicitly on the basis of race (cf. Chimezie 1975). Clearly, class and race—along with gender, age, family structure, and sexual preferences—are major structuring principles in the adoption system.

Furthermore, adoption has generally been viewed as a solution to the dangers of teenage pregnancy and unwed motherhood, dangers that often have been seen as *inherent* to unwed motherhood. Consequently, the larger social context—such as the unavailability of contraceptives and the lack of prenatal care, health care, or welfare benefits—is overlooked. The emphasis on the positive effects of relinquishment among minority mothers is particularly misleading since children of color stand a much lesser chance of being adopted than do white infants (Bowen 1987–1988, 491). Policies that depict the problems of single mothers as dangers inherent to unwed motherhood instead of as problems stemming from systemic inequalities in the distribution of resources based on these assumptions reinforce class and race inequalities *among* women.

Conclusion

In their study of identity formation in adopted children, Elinor Rosenberg and Thomas Horner (1991) note that young adoptees are vulnerable to feeling "different" or "bad" because of comments and actions by peers and others. Marie Balter (Balter and Katz 1991) offers in her autobiography a moving account of the social meaning of adoption:

> My life really begins in Gloucester, Massachusetts, when I was five. Ma and Pa have just adopted me and changed my name to Marie. One hot summer day shortly after I've come to live with Ma and Pa, I hear the shrill, sing-song shouts of the neighbor's children: "We know who you are. . . . We know who you are! You don't have a mother! You're adopted." Angry and frustrated, I run to Ruth, a friend of Ma's. Tears fill my eyes and stream down, wetting my cheeks.
> "Why are you crying?" Ruth asks.
> "The kids . . . the kids say I'm adopted," the words barely escape through my sobs.
> As she gently wipes my face, Ruth asks me what I think "adopted" means.
> All I can say is, "I don't know but it's awful bad!" Age five, I feel unloved. I feel that I belong to no one and deserve the hatred and contempt of others (p. 4).

What is needed in adoption research is an interactionist approach, along the path staked out by George Mead (1934), that takes seriously the fact that adoption has been associated with disparaging attitudes toward illegitimacy and the absence of a blood connection (Triseliotis 1991; cf. Wegar 1997b). As Christa Hoffmann-Riem (1990) demonstrates in her symbolic interactionist study of German adoptive families, families must undergo a process of "emotional normalization" whereby the adoptive parents come to view the adopted child as "their own" (pp. 147–182). This process of emotional normalization is complicated by social factors that are not under the adoptive parents' control, such as the intrusiveness of the adoption procedure and other people's failure to recognize adoptive kinship as *real* kinship. As I have noted throughout this chapter, adoption researchers have contributed to this problem by not recognizing the effects of such social factors on the quality of adoptive family life. In order to bring the social and cultural context back into adoption research, the experience of adopting and being adopted in a culture that mostly defines adoptive kinship as inferior must be accounted for as well. We should also remember that although adoptive kinship is socially *produced*, members of adoptive families are not the only ones who "work" or need to work on kinship—even biological kinds of kinship and family life are socially produced.

NOTES

1. Of five major textbooks in family sociology published or revised in 1996 (Baca Zinn and Eitzen 1996; Benokraitis 1996; Rice 1996; Saxton 1996; Wolf 1996), none includes a discussion of social or community attitudes toward adoption and the special problems adoptive families encounter. Even in her recent book on new and varied "postmodern" family forms, Judith Stacey (1996) discusses adoption only in the context of gay and lesbian families.

2. Elsewhere in her book and in her other works, Modell does recognize adoptive parents' negative experiences of the adoption process and their feelings of not being fully entitled to their children.

REFERENCES

Andersen, Margaret L. 1991. "Feminism and the American Family Ideal." *Journal of Comparative Family Studies* 27:235–246.

Arms, Suzanne. 1990. *Adoption: A Handful of Hope.* Berkeley, Calif.: Celestial Arts. (First edition, *To Love and Let Go,* published 1983.)

Bachrach, Christine, Patricia F. Adams, Soledad Sambrano, and Kathryn A. London. 1990. "Adoption in the 1980s." *Advanced Data from Vital Health Statistics* 18:1–12.

Balter, Marie, and Richard Katz. 1991. *Nobody's Child.* Reading, Mass.: Addison-Wesley.

Benet, Mary K. 1976. *The Politics of Adoption.* New York: Free Press.

Benokraitis, Nijole V. 1996. *Marriages and Families: Changes, Choices, and Constraints.* Upper Saddle River, N.J.: Prentice-Hall.

Benson, Peter L., Anu Sharma, and Eugene C. Roehlkepartain. 1994. *Growing Up Adopted: A Portrait of Adolescents and Their Families.* Minneapolis: Search Institute.

Berry, Marianne. 1992. "Contributors to Adjustment Problems of Adoptees: A Review of the Longitudinal Research." *Child and Adolescent Social Work* 9:525–540.

Bertocci, David, and Marshall D. Schechter. 1991. "Adopted Adults' Perception of Their Need to Search: Implications for Clinical Practice." *Smith College Studies in Social Work* 61:179–196.

Bowen, James S. 1987–1988. "Cultural Convergences and Divergences: The Nexus Between Putative Afro-American Family Values and the Best Interests of the Child." *Journal of Family Law* 26:487–532.

Brodzinsky, Anne. 1990. "Surrendering an Infant for Adoption: The Birthmother's Experience." Pp. 295–315 in *The Psychology of Adoption,* edited by David Brodzinsky and Marshall D. Schechter. New York: Oxford University Press.

Carroll, Vern. 1970. "Introduction: What Does 'Adoption' Mean?" Pp. 3–17 in *Adoption in Eastern Oceania,* edited by Vern Carroll. Honolulu: University of Hawaii Press.

Chimezie, Amuzie. 1975. "Transracial Adoption of Black Children." *Social Work* 20:296–301.

Curtis, Peter A. 1990. "An Ethnographic Study of Pregnancy Counseling." *Clinical Social Work Journal* 18:243–256.

Deutsch, Helene. 1945. *The Psychology of Women.* Vol. 2. New York: Grune & Stratton.

Deykin, Eva Y., Lee Campbell, and Patricia Patti. 1984. "The Postadoption Experience of Surrendering Parents." *American Journal of Orthopsychiatry* 54:271–280.

DiGuilio, John F. 1988. "Self-Acceptance: A Factor in the Adoption Process." *Child Welfare* 117:423–429.

Eyer, Diane E. 1992. *Mother-Infant Bonding: A Sci-*

entific Fiction. New Haven: Yale University Press.

Fisher, Florence. 1973. *The Search for Anna Fisher.* New York: Arthur Field Books.

Furstenberg, Frank. 1995. "Fathering in the Inner City: Paternal Participation and Public Policy." Pp. 119–147 in *Fatherhood: Contemporary Theory, Research, and Social Policy,* edited by William Marsiglio. Thousand Oaks, Calif.: Sage.

Goffman, Erving. 1963. *Stigma: Notes on the Management of Spoiled Identity.* Englewood Cliffs, N.J.: Prentice-Hall.

Goody, Esther. 1982. *Parenthood and Social Reproduction.* New York: Cambridge University Press.

Greil, Arthur L., T. A. Leitko, and K. A. Porter. 1988. "Infertility: His and Hers." *Gender & Society* 2:172–199.

Guemple, D. L. 1979. *Inuit Adoption.* Ottawa: National Museums of Canada.

Haimes, Erica, and Noel Timms. 1985. *Adoption, Identity and Social Policy: The Search for Distant Relatives.* Aldershot, England: Gover.

Hajal, Faye, and Elinor B. Rosenberg. 1991. "The Family Life Cycle in Adoptive Families." *American Journal of Orthopsychiatry* 61:78–85.

Hayes, Peter. 1993. "Transracial Adoption: Politics and Ideology." *Child Welfare* 72:301–310.

Hoffman-Reim, Christa. 1990. *The Adopted Child: Family Life with Double Parenthood.* New Brunswick, N.J.: Transaction Publishers.

Hollinger, Joan H. 1993. "Adoption Law." *The Future of Children* 3:43–61.

Howard, May D. 1990. "The Adoptee's Dilemma: Obstacles in Identity Formation." Pp. 243–258 in *Adoption Resources for Mental Health Professionals,* edited by Pamela V. Grabe. New Brunswick, N.J.: Transaction Publishers.

Kadushin, Alfred, and Judith A. Martin. 1988. *Child Welfare Services.* New York: Macmillan.

Kirk, H. David. 1964. *Shared Fate: A Theory of Adoption and Mental Health.* New York: Free Press.

Kunzel, Regina G. 1993. *Fallen Women, Problem Girls: Unmarried Women and the Professionalization of Social Work, 1890–1945.* New Haven: Yale University Press.

LeVine, Elaine S., and Alvin L. Sallee. 1990. "Critical Phases Among Adoptees and Their Families:

Implications for Therapy." *Child and Adolescent Social Work* 7:217–232.

Lifton, Betty J. 1988. *Lost and Found: The Adoption Experience.* New York: Harper & Row.

———. 1994. *Journey of the Adopted Self: A Quest for Wholeness.* New York: Basic Books.

Lisle, Laurie. 1996. *Without Child: Challenging the Stigma of Childlessness.* New York: Ballantine Books.

Mandell, Betty R. 1973. *Where Are the Children? A Class Analysis of Foster Care and Adoption.* Lexington, Mass.: Lexington Books.

Marquis, Kathlyn S., and Richard A. Detweiler. 1985. "Does Adopted Mean Different? An Attributional Analysis." *Journal of Personality and Social Psychology* 48:1054–1066.

Mead, George H. 1934. *Mind, Self, and Society.* Chicago: University of Chicago Press.

Melina, Lois, and Sharon Kaplan Rozia. 1993. *The Open Adoption Experience.* New York: Guilford.

Miall, Charlene. 1987. "The Stigma of Adoptive Parent Status: Perceptions of Community Attitudes Toward Adoption and the Experience of Informal Sanctioning." *Family Relations* 36:34–39.

Millen, Leverett, and Samuel Roll. 1985. "Solomon's Mothers: A Special Case of Pathological Bereavement." *American Journal of Orthopsychiatry* 55:411–418.

Modell, Judith S. 1994. *Kinship with Strangers: Adoption and Interpretations of Kinship in American Culture.* Berkeley: University of California Press.

———. 1996. "In Search: The Purported Biological Basis of Parenthood." *American Ethnologist* 13:646–661.

National Committee for Adoption. 1989. *1989 Adoption Factbook: United States Data, Issues, Regulations, and Resources.* Washington, D.C.: National Committee for Adoption.

Nelkin, Dorothy, and M. Susan Lindee. 1995. *The DNA Mystique: The Gene as a Cultural Icon.* New York: W. H. Freeman & Company.

Pannor, Reuben, Annette Baran, and Arthur D. Sorosky. 1978. "Birth Parents Who Relinquished Babies for Adoption Revisited." *Family Process* 17:329–337.

Rice, Philip F. 1996. *Intimate Relationships, Marriages, and Families.* Mountain View, Calif.: Mayfield.

Rosenberg, Elinor B., and Thomas M. Horner. 1991. "Birthparent Romances and Identity Formation in Adopted Children." *American Journal of Orthopsychiatry* 61:70–77.

Sachdev, Paul. 1989. *Unlocking the Adoption Files.* Lexington, Mass.: Lexington Books.

———. 1991. "The Birth Father: A Neglected Element in the Adoption Equation. *Families in Society* 72:131–139.

———. 1992. "Adoption Reunion and After: A Study of the Search Process and Experience of Adoptees. *Child Welfare* 71:53–68.

Saxton, Lloyd. 1996. *The Individual, Marriage, and the Family.* Belmont, Calif.: Wadsworth.

Schechter, Marshall D. 1960. "Observations on Adopted Children." *Archives of General Psychiatry* 3:21–32.

Schechter, Marshall D., and David Bertocci. 1990. "The Meaning of the Search." Pp. 62–90 in David M. Brodzinsky and Marshall D. Schechter, eds., *The Psychology of Adoption.* New York: Oxford University Press.

Schneider, David M. 1980. *American Kinship: A Cultural Account.* Chicago: University of Chicago Press.

Schneider, Stanley, and Esti Rimmer. 1994. "Adoptive Parents' Hostility Toward Their Adopted Children." *Children and Youth Services Review* 6:345–352.

Shalev, Carmel. 1989. *Birth Power: The Case for Surrogacy.* New Haven: Yale University Press.

Solinger, Ricki. 1992. *Wake Up Little Susie: Single Pregnancy and Race Before Roe v. Wade.* New York: Routledge.

———. 1993. "Race and 'Value': Black and White Illegitimate Babies, 1945–1965." Pp. 287–310 in *Mothering: Ideology, Experience and Agency,* edited by Evelyn N. Glenn, Grace Chang, and Linda Forcey. New York: Routledge.

Sorosky, Arthur, Annette Baran, and Reuben Pannor. 1975. "Identity Conflicts in Adoptees." *American Journal of Orthopsychiatry* 45:18–27.

Stacey, Judith. 1996. *In the Name of the Family: Rethinking Family Values in a Postmodern Age.* Boston: Beacon Press.

Stack, Carol B. 1974. *All Our Kin: Strategies for Survival in a Black Community.* New York: Harper & Row.

Terrell, John, and Judith Modell. 1994. "Anthropology and Adoption." *American Anthropologist* 96:155–161.

Thorne, Barrie, and Marilyn Yalom. 1992. *Rethinking the Family: Some Feminist Questions.* Boston: Northeastern University Press.

Toussieng, Povl W. 1962. "Thoughts Regarding the Etiology of Psychological Difficulties in Adopted Children." *Child Welfare* 41:59–65.

Triseliotis, John. 1991. "Identity and Genealogy in Adopted People." Pp. 35–44 in *Adoption: International Perspectives,* edited by E. D. Hibbs. Madison, Conn.: International Universities Press.

Wadia-Ellis, Susan. 1995. *The Adoption Reader: Birth Mothers, Adoptive Mothers and Adopted Daughters Tell Their Stories.* Seattle: Seal Press.

Washington, Mary H. 1991. *Memory of Kin: Stories About Family by Black Writers.* New York: Doubleday.

Wegar, Katarina. 1995. "Adoption and Mental Health: A Theoretical Critique of the Psychopathological Model." *American Journal of Orthopsychiatry* 65 (4):540–548.

———. 1997a. "In Search of Bad Mothers: Social Constructions of Birth and Adoptive Motherhood." *Women's Studies International Forum* 20 (1):77–86.

———. 1997b. *Adoption, Identity and Kinship: The Debate over Sealed Birth Records.* New Haven: Yale University Press.

Weismantal, Mary. 1995. "Making Kin: Kinship Theory and Zumbagua Adoptions." *American Ethnologist* 22:685–709.

Weston, Kath. 1991. *Families We Choose: Lesbians, Gays, Kinship.* New York: Columbia University Press.

Wolf, Robin. 1996. *Marriage and Families in a Diverse Society.* New York: HarperColl'ins.

Zinn, Maxine Baca, and Stanley Eitzen. 1996. *Diversity in Families.* New York: HarperCollins.

Section B

Family Structure and Accordion Households

~ *Chapter 5*

Household Structure and Family Ideologies:
The Case of Vietnamese Refugees

NAZLI KIBRIA

Family centered studies of the economic behavior of immigrants often view the family as a strategic arena, a social site where individuals can collectively cope with the economic environment to survive and to reach their goals (Dinerman 1978; Massey et al. 1987; Wood 1981). With its focus on the strategic and flexible character of economic behavior, this emphasis on family strategies appears to offer an opportunity for developing a dynamic understanding of immigrant economic adaptation. I suggest, however, that its potential to do so has been constrained by its inattention to household structure and to family ideologies.[1]

The Effects of Household Composition

One of the most basic ways in which households differ is in their composition—who is included within the boundaries of the household. The potential effects of composition on a household's pool of available resources have not been adequately explored in studies of immigrant economic adjustment. I suggest this is largely due to limited definitions of the resources or assets that are pertinent to the household economy. Wage labor is often seen as the sole economic resource of the household, and household composition has accordingly been assessed for its impact on the household's pool of wage labor (Angel and Tienda 1982; Massey et al. 1987; Perez 1986). But this exclusive concern with wage labor neglects other, equally valuable, types of contributions to the household economy. For example, women and children may contribute to the household economy by providing their unpaid labor to the family businesses that have been an important part of the economic experience of some immigrant groups (Aldrich and Waldinger 1990; Portes and Rumbaut 1990).

Besides wages to the household financial pot or labor to the family business, members may also contribute assets of other kinds to the household economy. As current discus-

From *Social Problems* 41, no. 1 (February 1994): 82–93, copyright © 1994 by the Society for the Study of Social Problems, Inc. Reprinted by permission.

sions of immigrant economic life suggest, we must define the structural environment as not simply the labor market but also in terms of institutions that potentially provide a range of important social and economic resources for the household. State institutions and bureaucracies may provide facilities and services such as assistance with education, job training, legal protection, health care, and resettlement (Pedraza-Bailey 1985). Groups within the household that are clearly disadvantaged in the labor market, such as children, may even have a better ability than adults to bring in resources from state institutions (e.g., college tuition loans).

The immigrant household economy is also affected by its social embeddedness in ongoing social relations and networks. As suggested by the extensive literature on the adaptive role of social networks and ethnic community ties (e.g., Massey et al. 1987; Min 1988; Morawska 1985; Portes and Bach 1985), for the immigrant group, the ethnic community may be a crucial source of loans, jobs, and information. Once again, recognition of the important economic role played by the ethnic community enhances our ability to consider forms of contribution to the household economy that are hidden by focus on wage labor. For example, the work that immigrant women put into cultivating and sustaining the kinship and friendship ties that socially integrate a family into the ethnic community may be seen as an important form of labor, one that facilitates the access of the household economy to ethnic community resources (di Leonardo 1987; Ewen 1985; Seller 1981).

When the definition of household economy includes relevant resources and institutions, household composition must be considered as well. Instead of assuming that a household membership configuration that maximizes the capacity for wage labor (such as one that is dominated by adult men) is advantageous, it becomes important to consider household composition in light of its repercussions for a wider range of household assets. Resources that appear to have little value when viewed individually may prove to be critical in their economic impact on the household economy when combined with other types of assets.

The Impact of Family Ideologies

Another dimension of the household critical to understanding its economic dynamics are the beliefs about family life held by members (Grasmuck and Pessar 1991; Moen and Wethington 1992). These family beliefs or ideologies define norms and expectations about household activities and relations that affect the household economy. For example, beliefs about women's family roles have important implications for the household economy, since they shape women's labor force participation as well as the ability of female household members to control economic resources. In a study comparing the economic activities of single female factory workers in Java and Taiwan, Diane Wolf (1990, 1992) found that the Javanese women, in contrast to their Taiwanese counterparts, often did not contribute their earnings to the family economy. Instead, the Javanese women retained control over their pay, spending it independently of their families. Wolf attributes the Javanese pattern to the relatively high degree of autonomy accorded women in the Javanese kinship system. In this particular case, family ideology concerning women's roles weakened the ability of the household economy to effectively incorporate the financial resources of its young, single female members.

One of the central ways in which family ideology impacts the household economy is through its role in defining normative patterns of economic exchange within the household.

That is, family ideology helps to define the economic relationships of household members. It thus influences the extent to which individual household members view their own economic activities and resources as part of the collective household economy. A household economy in which members view their economic life in collectivist terms will differ in its goals and dynamics from one in which the orientation is individualistic. Analyses of immigrant entrepreneurship, for example, suggest that groups with an ideology that emphasizes a collectivist and familial orientation towards economic achievement are more likely to engage in small business than others (Aldrich and Waldinger 1990; Sibley Butler 1991). However as Aldrich and Waldinger (1990) note, such economic orientations tend to be fluid and responsive to the changing social context, as evidenced by the often radical shifts over the course of a few generations.

In general, family ideology must be seen as not only varied across groups but also as fluid and reactive, constantly shifting in response to changing social contexts. The changing character of family ideology is often downplayed in cultural analyses of immigrant economic adaptation, which tend to portray immigrant cultural traditions as "given" and static (Caplan, Whitmore, and Choy 1989; Glazer and Moynihan 1963; Petersen 1971). The fluidity of familial cultural traditions is highlighted by Geschwender's (1992) analysis of historical changes in women's labor force participation. In brief, structural changes in the economy led to shifts in family ideology concerning women's employment outside the home.

Methods

During 1983–85, I studied newly arrived Vietnamese refugees in Philadelphia through participant-observation and in-depth interviews

(Kibria 1993). I conducted 31 interviews, 15 with women and 16 with men in the ethnic community. The interviews, which were tape-recorded, focused on the respondents' past and current experiences of family life. I also asked my interviewees a series of questions about their employment experiences and household budgeting practices in the United States. Because my knowledge of Vietnamese was minimal, many, but not all, of the interviews took place with the help of Vietnamese language interpreters. I also interviewed 11 Vietnamese American community leaders and social service agency workers in the city about the organizations in which they were involved and the relationship of these organizations to the Vietnamese American population in the city.

I also conducted participant-observation in household and community settings. For more than two years, I regularly visited 12 households in the community. During these visits, I observed and talked informally with household members. I spent time as a participant-observer in the neighborhood of study, in an attempt to gain a better understanding of the informal community life of Vietnamese Americans in the area, and the relationship of community life to household dynamics. Eventually, I focused my time on three popular community gathering places—a restaurant, a grocery store, and a hairdressing shop—all neighborhood businesses run by Vietnamese Americans.

More than 80 percent of the study-participants were from urban middle-class backgrounds in Southern Vietnam. Those men who had been beyond school age in Vietnam had usually been involved in military or government service. Women had worked, often sporadically, in family businesses or in informal, small-scale trading. All had experienced economic and social dislocations following the 1975 political transition to Communist rule in Vietnam. Directly and indirectly, these dislocations were responsible for the decisions of the refugees to undertake the hazardous escape by sea out of Vietnam during the late 1970s and early 1980s. While most of the refugees had been resettled in Philadelphia by social service agencies, others had relocated there from other places in the United States to join with kin or friends, forming households with them. The households in the community tended to be extended in character, containing a variety of kinfolk and friends (cf. Gardner, Bryant, and Smith 1985; Gold 1992).

The Social Context

Critical to understanding the economic dynamics of the Vietnamese refugee households are the conditions they encountered in three social arenas: the labor market, government policies and services, and the Vietnamese ethnic community. These arenas were central axes in the structure of opportunities facing the group, and thus provided the structural parameters for their economic behavior. The discussion shows available resources to be limited and unstable in supply and restricted in availability to certain segments of the community.

Labor Market

Labor market opportunities for Vietnamese Americans were limited, a reflection of both the conditions of the local economy and the job skills of the group. During the study the Philadelphia city economy was highly polarized, composed of a professional high-income sector and a service sector that provided mainly low-paid, semi-skilled or unskilled work. The increasingly limited range of job opportunities, combined with the effects of a nationwide recession, inflated unemployment and poverty rates in the city dur-

ing the early 1980s (Philadelphia City Planning Commission 1984). Further restricting the group's employment opportunities was its minority ethnic status and lack of suitable job skills for the formal economy. It is not surprising, then, that unemployment rates in the community were high; in mid-1984, roughly 35 percent of the adult men in the 12 study households were unemployed.

The jobs that were most easily accessible to the group were low-level service sector positions, such as cleaning and waitressing, which tended to be poorly paid, part-time, unstable, and devoid of benefits and opportunities for advancement. Also available to the group were jobs in the informal economy, particularly in garment assembly, an industry in which the Vietnamese refugee women were far more likely to be involved than the men.

Government Policies and Services

The "political refugee" status of the Vietnamese Americans gave legal legitimacy to their presence in the United States and also provided access to a federal refugee aid and resettlement system (Pedraza-Bailey 1985; Rumbaut 1989). Voluntary social service agencies (VO-LAGS) played a leading role in finding housing for new refugee arrivals and providing information on services available to refugees such as English-language classes, job counseling, and income support. All refugees were eligible for cash assistance and medical benefits through the Refugee Cash Assistance and Refugee Medical Assistance programs. When eligibility (based on length of residence in the United States) for Refugee Cash assistance ran out, those meeting the family composition and income-level requirements continued to receive assistance through programs available to U.S. citizens such as AFDC (Aid to Families with Dependent Children), SSI (Supplemental Security

Income), Medicaid, food stamps, and GA (General Assistance). While all of the Vietnamese refugees had some contact with this system of assistance, a few had more sustained contact with the programs than others. Given the eligibility requirements, it is not surprising that those who were elderly, disabled, under the age of 18, and single parents were more likely to have a long-term relationship with the cash and medical assistance programs.

The cash and medical assistance available to Vietnamese immigrants by virtue of their refugee status has been identified as an important economic boost for the group. What has been less noted, perhaps because it is less visible, is the access provided by the system to valuable social relationships, or "social capital" (cf. Coleman 1988). For example, out of their initial contacts with the resettlement system, some of the refugees developed close relationships with individual social service agency workers or sponsors, relying on them as a source of information about jobs, bank loans, and educational opportunities. In one particular case, members of a church congregation that had collectively sponsored a refugee household helped them to obtain a bank loan that they needed to open a business. Furthermore, sponsors or social service agency officials often provided job referrals for refugees. For some of my respondents, the friends that they had gained through the refugee resettlement system represented their only relationships with persons outside the ethnic community and were thus highly valued as a source of help for dealing with the dominant society's institutions. In some cases these "outside" persons were identified by adults as important role models for their children, who could turn to them for help with homework and other academic matters. In short, the social relationships that households were able to acquire through the resettlement system enhanced the socioeconomic heterogeneity of its social networks.

Households with children under age eighteen had greater access to public education than other households did. Public schools provided the opportunity to gain educational credentials, to learn English, and to acquire other cultural skills important for getting by in the United States. Because of this, households with school-age children had an advantage in dealing with dominant society institutions, since their children could serve as reliable interpreters. In addition, much like the refugee assistance system, the schools were also an arena through which the immigrants were able to develop relationships with teachers and other school officials. Once again, these social relations could be an important source of information and assistance. A high school teacher in the community helped the families of his students fill out home loan mortgage forms, while another teacher provided much-needed information about the complex regulations of the public assistance bureaucracy.

Ethnic Community

Two dimensions of ethnic community life—economic enclaves and ethnic associations—are widely identified by social scientists as important resources for immigrants, at least in the initial process of settlement in the United States. Ethnic economic enclaves are important sources of jobs, training, and opportunities for advancement for immigrant groups (Portes and Bach 1985). Ethnic associations also provide assistance in the form of capital, information about jobs, business ventures, and various aspects of life in the "host" society.

For the Philadelphia Vietnamese community, both ethnic economic enclaves and formal ethnic organizations were underdeveloped, partly due to the recency of Vietnamese settlement in the area. Ethnic ties did, however, play an extremely important role in the group's economic experiences. The immigrants belonged to ethnic social networks that provided a range of important resources, including financial loans and information about jobs, housing, and welfare (cf. Gold 1992; Hein 1993). While these informal social networks were often based on kinship ties and shared neighborhoods, they were also organized around age, gender and social class background. In other words, the social networks of individuals reflected their status along these variables.

Patchworking and Household Composition

In the structure of opportunities that I have described, the resources potentially available from any one source were limited and unreliable. Available jobs tended to be low-paying and unstable. Payments from the Refugee Cash Assistance and other assistance programs were also restricted and viewed by the Vietnamese refugees as highly temporary and unstable assets that could be terminated abruptly. The immigrants saw social relations in the ethnic community as far more reliable sources of economic and social assistance than either the labor market or government assistance programs. But, given both the economically homogeneous and fairly transient character of the community, even these resources were viewed as inherently scarce and unstable.

Like other economically disadvantaged communities (Bolles 1983; Glenn 1991; Stack 1974), Vietnamese Americans responded to these economic conditions by pooling resources within their domestic groups. But the notion of "pooling," which suggests sharing resources, does not adequately convey the

Vietnamese American practice of sharing diverse resources. I suggest that this practice is better conveyed by the notion of "patchworking" because the term conjures up an image of jagged pieces of assorted material stitched together in sometimes haphazard fashion.

Patchworking—the bringing together and sharing of diverse resources—is a practice that helps the Vietnamese American households to protect themselves against economic instability, or fluctuations in the supply of resources. The importance of having access to multiple resources was suggested by the experiences of an informant named Binh,[2] a man in his forties who came to the United States with his two teenage sons. After arriving, the family lived on the government benefits available to newly arrived refugees. Binh also took English language classes while his sons attended high school. Binh described the household as being economically self-sufficient at this time. Although his sister and her husband lived in the city, Binh did not rely on them for assistance. In fact, priding himself in his self-sufficiency, he had forbidden his sons to either "give or take money or anything else from other people." After about two years, Binh began looking for work; however, his job search was cut short by a back injury. Despite what he described as debilitating back pain, he was told by social service agency workers that he was no longer eligible for government aid. At the same time, his oldest son, who had just turned nineteen, was also told that he could no longer receive public assistance. These events created a crisis during which the household relied heavily on Binh's sister for food and other household expenses. Binh said his beliefs regarding the viability of self-sufficiency and survival in the United States had radically changed as a result of this unfortunate period. He came to realize that relations with kin were virtually a necessity in the United States. He also recognized the dangers of having only one source of income.

In Binh's case, access to a diverse resource base provided some degree of stability in a risky economic context. In an environment in which the quantity of assets from any one arena was limited, it was also a strategy that enhanced the scope of a household's resource pool. In a household I observed, one member took courses in machine repair at a local technical institute, while another member worked for a sewing contractor at home, also taking care of the young children in the family, and collecting Refugee Cash Assistance payments. Of the other two household members, one worked in an ethnic business run by friends and the other in a semi-skilled manufacturing job outside the city. Through these various activities, household members brought in wages from the formal and the informal economy, benefits from public assistance programs, and job skills and cultural capital from participation in training programs. Because a member worked in an ethnic business the household also had access to a variety of ethnic community networks and resources.

The ability to access a wide range of resources was enhanced by a high degree of differentiation among household members. The structure of available resources was scarce, unstable, and restricted, since not all household members had equal access to jobs, welfare, or the ethnic community networks. For example, in many informal sector jobs, such as those in the garment industry, women were more favored as employees than men. Furthermore, age clearly affected access to government assistance programs. Households with children and elderly were more likely to have a sustained and long-term relationship with public assistance programs. Membership in social networks and access to the resources embedded in these networks was also determined by age and gender. Thus, a high degree of status differentiation among household members expanded the household's

reach, allowing it to more effectively take advantage of available opportunities and to "patchwork" resources. The economic advantages of internally heterogeneous households were suggested to me by the words of a Vietnamese American man in his thirties who had come to the United States alone:

> After coming to America I realized that my college education from Vietnam doesn't mean anything here. I look around and I see that many of the Vietnamese who do well here are not the ones who have education. If you come here with your family, or maybe your relatives are already here, you're better off because you can live together and save money. The children can go to school and slowly they can help their parents. Maybe they can open a store together, or maybe two people can get jobs and support the family while the rest of the people go to school or the community college.

To further clarify the economic consequences of differentiation in household composition, I will next contrast the economic experiences of three specific households. These three households represent the range of diversity in terms of age and gender composition that I found in my sample. Different degrees of internal diversity resulted in different levels of access to such resources as public assistance and education and to social networks in the community.

Household One: High Diversity

Household One contained members of varied age and gender. It consisted of seven people: a woman named Thanh, in her late fifties, her three adult sons, two daughters, and one son-in-law.

After arriving in the United States, all household members received government aid through refugee assistance programs. But about a year-and-a-half later, the four men in the household were cut off from these programs when social service workers judged them to be capable of economic self-sufficiency. The household economy continued, however, to draw resources from public assistance programs. After receiving Refugee Cash Assistance and Refugee Medical Assistance for more than two years, Thanh and her daughters were transferred into other aid programs. For Thanh and her youngest daughter (who was fourteen), age was a critical factor in their continued eligibility for government assistance. Due to her status as a low-income elderly person, Thanh was eligible for Supplemental Security Income. The youngest daughter could receive General Assistance because she was under age eighteen, attending school, and a member of a low-income household. Following the birth of her baby, Thanh's older daughter became eligible for Aid to Families with Dependent Children, a program that targets low-income families with young children.

The diverse composition of Household One enabled it to have a sustained relationship with government aid programs. The household's age and gender diversity also gave it access to a wide range of community networks. About five years after arriving in the United States, the household opened a Vietnamese-Chinese restaurant. The household's wide-ranging networks were critical to its ability to open the business since small personal loans from friends and contacts provided the household start-up capital. The success with which the household was able to obtain these loans was related to its diversity. For example, Thanh was able to borrow money from her circle of friends, which was composed of elderly Vietnamese refugee men and women. Without Thanh, the household would not have had access to these financial resources. Similarly, Thanh's older daughter was able to prevail on her own group of woman friends for small loans. Thanh's three

sons were also able to obtain funds from their friendship networks of young, single men. In addition, Thanh's son-in-law, who was a member of the household, was able to tap into his own separate kinship networks in New York to obtain loans. In short, the household worked to obtain a large number of small personal loans to open the business. The age and gender diversity of the household contributed to the success of this strategy.

Household Two: Medium Diversity

Household Two represents the middle range in terms of age and diversity of the households in my study. The household consisted of six persons: a married couple named Hung and Lien, Hung's three younger brothers, and a male friend. Not only was the household numerically dominated by men, but it was also marked by age homogeneity. All of the household members were in their late teens or early twenties.

The household's homogeneous composition contributed to its somewhat weaker links to the public assistance system, compared to Household One. Two of Hung's younger brothers collected General Assistance payments, which they were eligible to receive because they were under age eighteen and attending school. Hung and Lien had also attended school and received public assistance for about three years after arriving in the United States. But neither of them had been able to complete high school before turning eighteen. The household's access to public assistance did strengthen, however, after the birth of Hung and Lien's daughter. As a low-income mother, Lien became eligible for Aid to Families with Dependent Children.

Government assistance resources available to the household were crucial to its economic survival. All household members had trouble finding stable jobs. Hung and the two other young men who were not attending school worked sporadically, usually in janitorial jobs in restaurants. Lien often supplemented the household income by sewing garments at home or working as a waitress in one of the area's Chinese or Vietnamese restaurants. Further compounding the paucity of household economic resources was the fact that, unlike the first household, it was not connected to a set of diverse and wide-ranging social networks. The similar age of household members was a critical factor in the household's homogeneous networks. Household members' social circles tended to overlap a great deal since they all socialized with other Vietnamese refugees in the area who were young, unmarried, or newly married.

Household Three: Low Diversity

Household Three was extremely homogeneous in age and gender composition. It consisted of five unrelated men, all single and in their early twenties. All of the men had received Refugee Cash Assistance and Refugee Medical Assistance after arriving in the United States for periods of one to two years. After this, the household was completely cut off from government aid programs. As young, able-bodied, single men, they were unable to meet the programs' core requirement: an inability to financially sustain oneself due to age, illness, or the burden of dependents. All five men had also arrived in the United States at an age (seventeen years or more) preventing them from taking full advantage of public education opportunities.

Like Household Two, the members of Household Three belonged to overlapping social circles. These social circles provided them with referrals and information about jobs as well as other aspects of life in the United States. However, as the young men discovered when they began to investigate the

possibility of opening a car repair shop, their social contacts limited their financial capacity. They were unable to borrow enough money from friends and contacts for the venture. This inability reflected the limited range and diversity of the household's social networks, which were composed almost solely of young, single, recently arrived Vietnamese refugee men. Thus, unlike Household One, this household was unable to turn to a diverse set of acquaintances for financial loans.

Patchworking and Family Ideologies

While composition structured a household's access to societal resources, the manner in which these resources were utilized or "processed" was critically shaped by the family ideology of household members. Here I examine two ideological dimensions of Vietnamese refugee life that help to explain the "patchworking" strategy of households.

The Ideology of Family Collectivism

A tradition of defining kinship in an inclusive and fluid manner encouraged the members of the Vietnamese refugee households to view each other as kin, regardless of whether or not the relationships fulfilled formal kinship criteria (Kibria 1993; Luong 1984). Thus in the households that I observed, familial expectations of economic participation applied to all household members, both kin and non-kin. Underlying these economic expectations was an ideology of family collectivism, a set of beliefs about the nature and significance of family life. The ideology of family collectivism, which drew on Vietnamese kinship traditions, organized and undergirded the economic patchworking of households in several ways. It advanced the view that economic reliance on family ties was an appropriate and judicious response to the economic demands and opportunities of the migration process. It also helped to promote a collective, cooperative approach towards resources and activities among household members by stressing, and indeed, idealizing the unity of family interests.

Central to the ideology of family collectivism is the notion that the kin group is far more significant than the individual. This dimension of family collectivism drew strength from Confucian family traditions, including the practice of ancestor worship. Family altars that were used to perform rites to honor ancestors were a common sight in the Vietnamese American households that I visited. Ancestor worship affirmed the sacredness and essential unity of the kin group, as well as its permanence in comparison to the transience of the individual. It also highlighted obligation as a key feature of a member's relationship to the kin group. The central obligation of the family member was to place the needs and desires of the kin group over and above any personal ones.

Another component of the ideology of family collectivism is the belief that the family is an individual's most reliable source of support—the only institution that could be counted on for help under all circumstances. Among my informants there was a strong belief that kin ties were an economic safety net, a belief that had been cultivated by the long years of social turmoil in contemporary South Vietnam, during which time kin ties had been a source of security for many Vietnamese. Respondents told me several traditional proverbs that stressed the durability and significance of kin over non-kin relations, such as: "A bitter relative is still a relative, a sweet stranger is still a stranger"; and "If your father leaves you, you still have your uncle; if your mother leaves you, you can nurse on your aunt's milk."

In a variety of ways, these family beliefs encouraged individuals to maintain close economic ties to the households in which they lived and to participate in "patchworking." The ideology of family collectivism, for example, could be used as a sanction against rebellious household members who refuse to go along with the decisions made by others. One such situation involved a young man named Doan, who was living in a household with three older brothers and their wives and children. Doan's refusal to contribute money towards the collective household purchase of a family home gave rise to conflict with his older brothers. Doan was planning to use his extra income to sponsor his girlfriend (who was in a refugee camp in Thailand) to the United States. Drawing on notions embedded in the ideology of family collectivism, such as individual obligation to the family, Doan's older brothers interpreted his refusal as evidence of selfishness and lack of concern for the family, as well as lack of respect for his family elders. Doan justified his refusal by arguing that the purchase of a house would serve his brothers' interests far better than his own. Since his brothers were all married and had children (unlike him), it was far more important for them to secure housing that was stable and in a relatively prosperous neighborhood. Unable to resolve the dispute, Doan eventually moved out of the household and into a friend's home.

As this example suggests, households were not always successful in forcing deviant members to conform to established economic decisions. Migration had, in fact, created conditions that made non-compliance to the principles of family collectivism more likely than ever. According to traditional Vietnamese family patterns, authority in the family rested with men and the elderly. But migration to the United States had diminished the power of men and the elderly. This opened opportunities for traditionally less powerful groups to challenge their authority, thus increasing the potential for intra-household conflicts over economic decisions. Doan, for example, told me he probably would not have disagreed with his brothers' decision in Vietnam, because the elder status of his brothers had carried more authority there.

The challenge posed by migration to the authority of men over women was particularly striking. The economic power of men in the community had declined with migration, thus weakening the economic basis for male authority (Kibria 1990). In many households, men were periodically or chronically unemployed, with women contributing a major share of the household finances. This economic power shift challenged the traditional authority of men and generated household environments that were ripe for conflicts between men and women. It is not surprising then, that "patchworking" was often accompanied by dissension and negotiation between men and women, particularly over the ways in which money should be spent. But despite these conflicts, the wholesale defection of men and women from the household economy was rare, because most were dependent on it for economic survival and economic mobility. In this sense, the economic conditions of life in the United States, in their poverty and uncertainty, had reinforced traditional beliefs about the economic significance of kinship ties and how they fulfilled the function of an economic safety net. Thus the conditions of settlement in the United States were simultaneously strengthening and challenging the ability of the ideology of family collectivism to organize the economic life of the Vietnamese American households.

"Making it" Through the Education of the Young

For the Vietnamese Americans, cooperative household economic behavior is also promoted by widely shared goals that helped to generate consensus among members about collective economic investment. One of these goals is the schooling of the young. This is seen as an effective path by which the family as a whole can achieve mobility in the future, a view that encourages the household economy to invest resources in education. This perspective on education reflects the experiences of my informants in pre-1975 South Vietnam, a context in which academic credentials had been deeply valued among the middle class. Education could secure one a high-ranking place in the government bureaucracy or military or in the professions. Historically, education was seen by the group as an effective method by which to achieve economic prosperity and stability (cf. Ogbu 1978). This understanding of education had been reinforced for the Vietnamese Americans by the comparatively greater opportunities in the United States for obtaining higher education.

A child's education was understood as a venture from which the household as a whole would reap rewards in the future. In the short run, the academic achievements of the young were a source of collective familial status and prestige in the ethnic community. In the informal social gatherings that I attended, it was not unusual for parents or other family elders to pass around and compare the report cards of school-aged children. In the long run, household members expected to gain not only status privileges but also material rewards. In accordance with the prescriptions of the ideology of family collectivism, the young were expected to pay back their families after completing their educations. In fact, many parents explicitly identified the children's education as an investment for their future and for the collective future of the kin group. Although not without ambivalence, these expectations of payback were also shared by many young Vietnamese Americans who often focused on fields that would allow them to more effectively meet family financial obligations. Thus a young Vietnamese American who was studying for a degree in pharmacy (although he would have preferred to study art) told me that he planned to buy a house for his sister and brother-in-law, with whom he was living, as soon as he completed college. Similarly, in a study of Southeast Asian refugee youth conducted by Rumbaut and Ima (1988), a Vietnamese refugee said the children in his family were all expected to pay a money "tax" to their mother after completing college.

Expectation of future rewards to motivate households to invest in the schooling of the young was vividly highlighted to me by one case in which a young member was actually dissuaded by kin from continuing his education. Kim's mother and aunt discouraged him from taking courses in college, encouraging him instead to find a job that would help the household to amass the savings necessary to purchase a home. The household preferred to channel its educational aspirations into Kim's younger brother, who was seen as more likely to succeed academically, since he was proficient in English and was receiving much better grades.

The rewards of education are not the only means by which Vietnamese Americans collectively approach schooling. Researchers have noted how studying is organized in Vietnamese refugee households as a collective rather than individual task or activity. Children sit down together to study and assist each other with school-related problems (Caplan, Choy, and Whitmore 1992). Rumbaut and Ima (1988) further describe the Vietnamese refugee family as a "mini-school system," with older siblings playing a major role in mentoring and tutoring their younger brothers and sisters.

The manner in which the Vietnamese immigrants view the education of the young helps to explain the well-publicized educational suc-

cesses of Vietnamese refugee youth as a group (Caplan, Choy, and Whitmore 1992). Perhaps most importantly, the collectivist familial orientation to schooling that I have described results in a situation in which the stakes for doing well at school are extremely high; for the young, it is not only their own future that hinges on their ability to do well at school but also that of the family. However, as with other ideological dimensions of Vietnamese American family life, these ideas about education are being challenged in the United States. Perhaps the most significant challenge stems from the diminishing strength of the ideology of family collectivism among young Vietnamese Americans, who are increasingly likely to favor an individualistic rather than collective familial approach to economic activities. For family elders, the cultural assimilation and potential defection of the young from the cooperative family economy raises questions about the education of the young as a collective goal. The "Americanization" of the young endangers the payback that kin hope to receive in the future from their investments in the education of the young.

NOTES

Acknowledgments: I would like to thank Eun Mee Kim, Barrie Thorne, and Diane Wolf for their comments on earlier drafts.

1. Whereas households are residential units, families may be defined as kinship groups in which the members do not necessarily live together. As in the case of a household in which members do not see themselves as kin, it is possible for the household and the family to be units that are entirely distinct. More commonly, however, the household and family are vitally connected. As Rapp (1992:51) observes, "families organize households." That is, notions of family tend to define the membership of households as well as relations between household members.

2. All names have been changed to maintain anonymity.

REFERENCES

Aldrich, Howard E., and Roger Waldinger. 1990. "Ethnicity and entrepreneurship." *Annual Review of Sociology* 16:111–35.

Angel, Ronald, and Marta Tienda. 1982. "Determinants of extended family structure: Cultural pattern or economic need?" *American Journal of Sociology* 87:1360–83.

Bolles, A. Lynn. 1983. "Kitchens hit by priorities: Employed working-class Jamaican women confront the IMF." In *Women, Men, and the International Division of Labor*, ed. June Nash and M. Patricia Fernandez-Kelly, 138–60. Albany, N.Y.: State University of New York Press.

Caplan, Nathan, John Whitmore, and Marcella Choy. 1989. *The Boat People and Achievement in America: A Study of Family Life, Hard Work, and Cultural Values.* Ann Arbor: University of Michigan Press.

Caplan, Nathan, Marcella Choy, and John Whitmore. 1992. "Indochinese refugee families and academic achievement." *Scientific American* 266:36–42.

Coleman, James. 1988. "Social capital in the creation of human capital." *American Journal of Sociology* 94:S95–S120.

di Leonardo, Micaela. 1987. "The female world of cards and holidays: Women, families, and the work of kinship." *Signs* 12:440–53. (See Chapter 31, this volume.)

Dinerman, Ina R. 1978. "Patterns of adaptation among households of U.S.-bound migrants from Michoacan, Mexico." *International Migration Review* 12:485–501.

Ewen, Elizabeth. 1985. *Immigrant Women in the Land of Dollars: Life and Culture on the Lower East Side, 1890–1925.* New York: Monthly Review Press.

Gardner, Robert W., Robey Bryant, and Peter Smith. 1985. "Asian Americans: Growth, change and diversity." *Population Bulletin* 40.

Geschwender, James A. 1992. "Ethgender, women's waged labor, and economic mobility." *Social Problems* 39:1–16.

Glazer, Nathan, and Daniel P. Moynihan. 1963. *Beyond the Melting Pot.* Cambridge, Mass.: MIT Press.

Glenn, Evelyn Nakano. 1991. "Racial ethnic women's labor: The intersection of race, class and gender oppression." In *Gender, Family, and Economy: The Triple Overlap*, ed. Rae Lesser Blumberg, 173–201. Newbury Park, Calif.: Sage Publications.

Gold, Steven J. 1992. *Refugee Communities: A Comparative Field Study.* Beverly Hills, Calif.: Sage Publications.

Grasmuck, Sherri, and Patricia Pessar. 1991. *Between Two Islands: Dominican International Migration.* Berkeley, Calif.: University of California Press.

Hein, Jeremy. 1993. *States and International Migrants: The Incorporation of Indochinese Refugees in the United States and France.* Boulder, Colo.: Westview Press.

Kibria, Nazli. 1990. "Power, patriarchy and gender conflict in the Vietnamese immigrant community." *Gender & Society* 4:9–24.

———. 1993. *Family Tightrope: The Changing Lives of Vietnamese Americans.* Princeton, N.J.: Princeton University Press.

Luong, Hy Van. 1984. "'Brother' and 'uncle': An analysis of rules, structural contradictions, and meaning in Vietnamese kinship." *American Anthropologist* 86(2):290–313.

Massey, Douglas, R. Alarcon, J. Durand, and H. Gonzalez. 1987. *Return to Aztlan.* Berkeley, Calif.: University of California Press.

Min, Pyong Gap. 1988. *Ethnic Business Enterprise: Korean Small Business in Atlanta.* Staten Island, N.Y.: Center for Migration Studies.

Moen, Phyllis, and Elaine Wethington. 1992. "The concept of family adaptive strategies." *Annual Review of Sociology* 18:233–51.

Morawska, Ewa. 1985. *For Bread with Butter.* New York: Cambridge University Press.

Ogbu, John U. 1978. *Minority Education and Caste.* New York: Academic Press.

Pedraza-Bailey, Silvia. 1985. *Political and Economic Migrants in America: Cubans and Mexicans.* Austin, Tex.: University of Texas Press.

Perez, Lisandro. 1986. "Immigrant economic adjustment and family organization: The Cuban success story reexamined." *International Migration Review* 20:1, 4–20.

Petersen, William. 1971. *Japanese Americans.* New York: Random House.

Philadelphia City Planning Commission. 1984. "Socioeconomic characteristics for Philadelphia census tracts: 1980 and 1970." Technical Information Paper.

Portes, Alejandro, and Robert Bach. 1985. *Latin Journey: Cuban and Mexican Immigrants in the U.S.* Berkeley, Calif.: University of California Press.

Portes, Alejandro, and Ruben Rumbaut. 1990. *Immigrant America: A Portrait.* Berkeley, Calif.: University of California Press.

Rapp, Rayna. 1992. "Family and class in contemporary America." In *Rethinking the Family: Some Feminist Questions,* ed. Barrie Thorne and Marilyn Yalom, 49–70. Boston: Northeastern University Press.

Rumbaut, Ruben G. 1989. "The structure of refuge: Southeast Asian refugees in the U.S., 1975–85." *International Review of Comparative Public Policy* 1:97–129.

Rumbaut, Ruben G., and Kenji Ima. 1988. The Adaptation of Southeast Asian Refugee Youth: A Comparative Study. Washington, D.C.: United States Office of Refugee Resettlement.

Seller, Maxine S. 1981. "Community life." In *Immigrant Women,* ed. Maxine Seller, 157–66. Philadelphia, Pa.: Temple University Press.

Sibley Butler, John. 1991. *Entrepreneurship and Self-Help Among Black Americans.* Albany, N.Y.: State University of New York Press.

Stack, Carol. 1974. *All Our Kin: Strategies for Survival in a Black Community.* New York: Harper & Row.

Wood, Charles H. 1981. "Structural changes and household strategies: A conceptual framework for the study of rural migration." *Human Organization* 40:338–44.

Wolf, Diane L. 1990. "Daughters, decisions and domination: An empirical and conceptual critique of household strategies." *Development and Change* 24:43–74.

———. 1992. *Factory Daughters: Gender, Household Dynamics, and Rural Industrialization in Java.* Berkeley, Calif.: University of California Press.

∽ Chapter 6

Mortality Decline in the Twentieth Century and Supply of Kin over the Life Course

PETER UHLENBERG

Mortality decline over the twentieth century has drastically increased the chances that a newborn will survive to experience old age. Under mortality conditions existing in 1900, only 39% of an initial birth cohort would survive to age 65, and only 12% would survive to age 80. By the end of the twentieth century, mortality rates had fallen to a level where 86% would survive to 65 years of age and 58% would survive to age 80. This remarkable increase in probability of surviving to older ages has implications for the structure of family relationships which involve older persons. An earlier study, "Death and the Family" (Uhlenberg 1980) explores some of the family consequences of declining death rates between 1900 and 1976. This study extends the earlier one in two ways. First, data are updated to show the continuing effects of mortality decline on kinship structures in the last quarter of this century. Second, greater attention is given to kinship implications of changing gender differences in survival to old age.

The twentieth century mortality revolution has altered potential connections with elderly relatives for people at all stages of life. As death rates fall, it becomes more likely that children and young adults will have living grandparents. Delaying death to older ages means that middle-aged persons increasingly will have older parents still living. And, lower death rates increase the odds that those who survive to old age will have elderly spouses and siblings still living. With the concentration of deaths in old age, it also becomes less likely that an older person will have experienced the death of any of his or her own children. The point of this study is to provide a quantitative assessment of changes in the survival of grandparents, parents, spouses, siblings, and children for persons at different stages of the life course.

This brief descriptive report focuses specifically on implications of changing mortality and does not attempt to discuss other important factors that are changing kinship rela-

From *The Gerontologist* 36, no. 5 (1996): 681–85, copyright © by The Gerontological Society of America. Reprinted by permission.

tionships. For example, the effects of declining fertility and changes in marriage patterns are not examined here. This analysis does not explore consequences of changes in family structure (one-parent families, step-kin, fictive kin, etc.) for kin relationships. And, finally, it does not speak to the nature of kin relationships. Different types of data from those utilized here are needed to gain insight into the meaning of grandchild-grandparent, child-parent, sib-sib, husband-wife, and parent-child relationships at different historical time periods.

What is accomplished by focusing on mortality levels as the independent variable? First, it allows a clear statement of the profound effects that mortality changes over the past century have had on the potential for specific kin ties to exist. Second, it demonstrates that recent mortality declines continue to significantly impact kinship structures. And third, this study provides data that may be used in future studies which develop a more complete picture of how kin relationships involving older persons are changing over time.

Assessing Implications of Mortality Levels

Period life tables are used to assess the implications of mortality conditions for the survival of various family and kin relationships. The life tables used here, prepared by the actuaries for the Social Security Administration, cover the entire twentieth century (Social Security Administration 1992). I have selected life tables for 1900, 1920, 1940, 1960, 1980, and 2000 to track the timing of change over the 100 years. These period life tables allow one to focus specifically on the implications of mortality conditions that exist at particular historical time periods. The probability of death disrupting particular relationships by the time a person reaches a particular age are cal-

culated for the situation where women marry at age 22 and men at age 25, where children are born to mothers aged 27 and fathers aged 30, and where siblings are born 3 years apart. (While the distribution of ages at which these events occur varies over time, the ages used here are close to the median ages over this century.) Several comments on interpreting the results reported are in order.

First, the survival patterns of grandparents, parents, siblings, spouses, and children that are obtained from period life tables do not reflect the experiences of actual cohorts. Since death rates change over time, no period table captures the experience of a cohort that ages through time. The experience of actual cohorts could be assessed using appropriate cohort life tables for the experiences of members of different generations. An analysis of this type would be useful for answering some questions, but it would not answer the question addressed here—what are the implications of mortality conditions existing at particular time periods?

Second, this analysis assumes that the risks of death for various family members are independent. This is not a particularly good assumption because family members tend to share certain risk factors, such as genetic makeup and social class. Unfortunately, adequate historical data for a more refined analysis, which takes into account differential mortality risks across family groups, are not available. The findings produced by this study provide rough estimates of change occurring over time, not precise and fully nuanced statements of survival within kin groups.

Third, as noted, changes in fertility are not examined in this study. Changes in family size do not affect the likelihood that individuals have grandparents, parents, or spouses still alive at various stages of life. They do, however, affect the likelihood that siblings or children have died. Thus, it is important to note

that the discussion of siblings refers to survival of particular siblings (not all siblings)
and the discussion of children refers to families with two children (one son and one
daughter). By keeping family size constant
over time, attention is directed to the consequences of mortality change.

Supply of Grandparents

The supply of grandparents for children and
young adults has changed remarkably over
the twentieth century. The steadily increasing
prospects of having grandparents alive at various stages of the life course are shown by data
in Table 1. These calculations were made assuming that in each generation a child is born
when the mother is 27 years of age and the father is 30. With these assumptions, mortality
levels existing in 1900 imply that fewer than
one fourth of all children began life with all
four of their grandparents alive, and by age
30, only 21% had any surviving grandparent.
By the end of the century, on the other hand,
over two thirds will have begun life with all
grandparents still living and more than three
fourths will have at least one grandparent
alive when they reached age 30. In addition to
this overall increase in supply of grandparents, several additional interesting changes
are revealed by data in Table 1.

First, having at least one grandparent alive
during early childhood was usual even in
1900—only 6% did not have a living grandparent at age 10. However, at the beginning of the
century, most persons no longer had any living
grandparents by the time they reached their
mid-twenties. About 80% of all persons would
experience the loss of their last grandparent by
the time they were likely to be rearing young
children (i.e., at age 30). By the end of the century, not only will almost all children (97%) arrive at adulthood with at least one grandparent

living, but 76% will still have a living grandparent when they reach age 30. The growing likelihood of having grandparents alive during one's
childbearing years has implications for the
great-grandparent role in kin groups. In particular, it is only toward the end of the twentieth
century that it was common for young children
to coexist with great-grandparents, thereby
having the potential for a relationship.

Second, throughout this century, it has been
more common to have grandmothers alive
than grandfathers. But a growing gender gap
in mortality rates over much of this time period led to an increasing differential in survival
of grandmothers compared to grandfathers.
More specifically, the excess of grandmothers
compared to grandfathers increased. Consider, for example, the ratio of those with only
a grandmother alive to those with only a
grandfather alive. For those aged 20, this ratio
increased from 1.9 in 1900 to 4.5 in 2000, and
for those aged 30, the ratio increased from 2.8
to 5.5. Among those aged 30 in 2000, 67% will
have a grandmother alive, while only 27% will
have a grandfather alive. And the contrast at
age 40 is even greater (19% vs. 2%). Clearly, a
large majority of the great-grandparents in this
country are female. (Mortality conditions in
2000 imply that about 75% of the living grandparents of 30-year-olds will be grandmothers.)

A final observation concerns the timing of
the growth in supply of grandparents. The
largest increase in life expectancy at birth occurred early in this century (73% of the total
increase that will occur between 1900 and 2000
occurred before 1950). The drop in death rates
leading to the increase in life expectancy before 1950 affected all age groups, but was
greater for infants and children than for
adults. More recent mortality declines have
been greater among the elderly. Over half of
this century's gain in average years lived past
age 60 has occurred since 1960. Consequently,
mortality declines in the past 40 years have

TABLE 1. Percentage of Persons at Various Ages Who Have Grandparents Still Living, Under Mortality Conditions Existing in Selected Years: 1900–2000*

	All Grandparents Alive at Age:				1+ Grandparent Alive at Age:				
Year	0	10	20	30	0	10	20	30	40
1900	23.8	6.4	0.4	0.0	99.2	94.2	69.6	20.6	1.0
1920	31.0	9.8	0.7	0.0	99.6	96.4	75.5	24.6	1.6
1940	41.3	14.0	1.2	0.0	99.9	98.1	82.5	32.5	2.3
1960	54.8	22.6	3.2	0.0	100.0	99.4	92.0	51.3	6.5
1980	62.7	31.0	6.1	0.1	100.0	99.7	95.8	68.3	15.4
2000	67.8	38.9	9.7	0.3	100.0	99.9	97.4	75.8	21.0

	1+ Grandmother Alive at Age:					1+ Grandfather Alive at Age:				
Year	0	10	20	30	40	0	10	20	30	40
1900	92.5	80.1	52.1	15.4	0.8	89.4	71.1	36.5	6.2	0.2
1920	94.5	84.3	57.4	17.9	1.3	92.6	77.3	42.4	8.1	0.2
1940	97.8	91.2	68.9	25.8	2.0	94.2	78.6	44.0	9.0	0.3
1960	99.3	96.2	83.2	43.2	5.7	96.4	83.5	52.3	14.1	0.8
1980	99.6	97.7	89.3	60.2	14.1	97.7	88.5	60.8	20.4	1.6
2000	99.7	98.3	91.3	66.9	19.1	98.3	92.2	69.7	26.8	2.4

*Assuming children are born in each generation to mothers age 27 and fathers age 30.

been especially important in increasing the supply of grandparents for persons in the post-childhood years of life. For example, the proportion of 30-year-olds with a living grandparent will have increased from 51% in 1960 to 76% in 2000 and the proportion of 40-year-olds with a living grandparent will have tripled (from 7% to 21%). If death rates at older ages continue to fall in the future as expected, the supply of grandparents for young adults will continue to grow at a brisk pace.

Survival of Old Parents

A decline in adult mortality rates obviously leads to an increase in the typical ages at which individuals experience the deaths of their parents. Information in Table 2 shows that under 1900 mortality conditions, only 22% of those who survived to age 40 would still have two living parents, and few (4%) who survived to 50 would not have lost at least one parent. By the end of the century, a majority of 40-year-olds will still have both parents alive, and over one fourth of 50-year-olds will. Nevertheless, it will still remain uncommon to reach old age with both parents still alive.

The likelihood of arriving at midlife with at least one parent still alive increased consistently throughout the twentieth century. The proportion who are complete orphans by age 50 will drop from over 60% in 1900 to under 20% by 2000. And by 2000, it will no longer be uncommon to have an old parent alive as one approaches old age—44% will have a parent alive when they reach age 60. The near-doubling between 1960 and 2000 in propor-

TABLE 2. Percentage of Persons at Various Ages Who Have Parents Still Living, Under Mortality Conditions Existing in Selected Years: 1900–2000*

Year	Both Parents Alive at Age:				Neither Parent Alive at Age:			
	40	50	60	70	40	50	60	70
1900	22.1	4.4	0.1	0.0	27.6	61.0	92.5	99.8
1920	26.6	6.0	0.2	0.0	23.3	55.8	90.7	99.7
1940	33.4	8.1	0.3	0.0	16.5	48.2	87.0	99.5
1960	48.5	14.4	1.0	0.0	8.3	33.5	76.4	98.2
1980	51.4	20.7	2.5	0.0	6.5	24.5	63.3	95.0
2000	58.5	26.7	4.0	0.0	4.6	19.8	56.2	92.9

Year	Only Mother Alive at Age:				Only Father Alive at Age:			
	40	50	60	70	40	50	60	70
1900	30.0	22.3	5.6	0.2	20.3	12.2	1.8	0.0
1920	28.2	24.2	6.6	0.3	21.9	13.9	2.5	0.0
1940	33.8	31.1	10.0	0.4	16.3	12.6	2.7	0.1
1960	29.6	40.1	18.5	1.6	13.6	12.0	4.1	0.2
1980	31.4	42.9	28.8	4.6	10.7	11.9	5.4	0.4
2000	26.7	40.4	33.1	6.5	10.1	13.1	6.8	0.6

*Assuming children are born when mothers are age 27 and fathers age 30.

tion of 60-year-old women who have a widowed parent alive (from 23.6% to 43.8%) is clearly related to the growing literature on the burden of caring for aging parents.

Throughout the twentieth century, it has been more common for adults with only one living parent to have a mother alive than a father. The odds of the last parent to die being a mother, however, will be higher at the end of the century than at the beginning. Between 1920 and 1980, death rates declined much more rapidly for adult females than for males. For example, the average years of life remaining at age 30 grew by 11.7 for females over this time period (from 37.5 to 49.2 years) compared with 5.9 for males (from 36.8 to 42.7). Consequently, the ratio of those having only a mother alive at midlife to those with only a father alive rose steeply. Between 1920 and 1980, the proportion

of 50-year-olds with only a mother alive grew from 24% to 43%, while the proportion with a father only declined from 14% to 12%. After 1980, adult death rates declined more for males than for females, leading to a slight reversal of the earlier trend of the gap growing larger. Nevertheless, it is still about five times more likely that a 60-year-old will have a widowed mother than a widowed father.

Survival of Spouses

The story of twentieth century changes in the probability that surviving persons will experience widowhood before they reach various stages of old age is relatively simple. Data in Table 3 show the likelihood of having a first spouse still alive at ages 60, 70, and 80 for men

TABLE 3. Percentage of Persons at Various Ages Whose First Spouse Is Still Living, Under Mortality Conditions Existing in Selected Years: 1900–2000*

Year	Wife Alive for Husband at Age:			Husband Alive for Wife at Age:		
	60	70	80	60	70	80
1900	67.9	50.2	25.8	56.5	33.1	9.8
1920	72.3	55.3	29.3	63.0	38.7	12.1
1940	82.4	66.4	38.8	65.9	40.5	13.1
1960	90.0	77.8	54.3	71.9	46.4	18.0
1980	92.3	82.5	63.4	77.1	53.3	23.6
2000	93.9	85.0	66.9	80.8	60.6	29.7

*Assuming that wife is age 22 and husband is age 25 at marriage.

and women who marry at ages 25 and 22, respectively. Under 1900 mortality conditions, only half of the men and a third of the women who survive to age 70 would still have a living spouse. By 2000, these proportions will increase to 85% and 61%, respectively. In 1900, only 26% of the men who reached age 80 could expect their first spouse to be alive, but by 2000 the proportion in this category will increase to 67%. Similar increases in spouse survival occurred for women who survived to very old ages, although widowhood has always been a more common experience for women than men.

While decreasing death rates created large gains in potential years that men and women could expect to live in uninterrupted marriages, increasing divorce rates have had an opposite effect. Divorce ended approximately 10% of the marriages contracted at the beginning of the twentieth century, compared with 50% of those contracted at the end of century. Because divorces are concentrated in the earlier years of marriage, the rise in divorce rates increased the number of persons whose first marriage ended before midlife. The major impact of decreasing death rates, on the other hand, has been to decrease the rate of marital disruption after midlife. The balancing point of these opposing forces is about 70 years—

that is, the prospects of 70-year-old men and women still living with a first spouse are quite similar under conditions in 1900 and 2000. (At both times, about 45% of the men and 30% of the women would be living with their first spouses.) At ages past 70 years, the prospects of still living with a first spouse are greater now than in the past. For example, the proportion of 80-year-old men still living with their first wives will increase from about 23% in 1900 to 33% in 2000.

Survival of Siblings

Although sibling relationships typically are less intense than husband-wife and parent-child relationships, there is evidence that siblings frequently provide social and instrumental support for each other throughout life. And sibling relationships are unique in their potential longevity. Two siblings who are born within a few years of each other and who both survive into old age can maintain a relationship for 70 or more years. The odds of such long-lasting sibling relationships actually occurring have, of course, changed greatly as mortality has declined over the past 100 years. Table 4 shows how prospects have

TABLE 4. Percentage of Persons at Various Ages Who Have a Particular Sibling Still Living, Under Mortality Conditions Existing in Selected Years: 1900–2000*

	Older Brother Alive at Age:			Older Sister Alive at Age:		
Year	60	70	80	60	70	80
1900	40.3	23.6	7.0	43.9	27.1	8.9
1920	51.2	31.4	9.9	53.6	34.3	11.6
1940	59.5	36.6	11.8	68.7	47.5	18.4
1960	68.0	43.9	17.0	80.9	63.2	32.0
1980	74.2	51.3	25.4	85.6	71.1	47.8
2000	78.9	59.2	29.0	88.5	74.5	49.9

	Younger Brother Alive at Age:			Younger Sister Alive at Age:		
Year	60	70	80	60	70	80
1900	48.0	34.2	14.7	51.3	37.9	17.7
1920	59.4	44.3	22.3	61.4	46.9	24.9
1940	69.7	51.2	26.0	76.6	61.7	36.0
1960	78.2	59.2	33.0	86.9	75.2	52.4
1980	82.7	66.4	39.9	90.5	80.9	62.2
2000	85.3	72.5	47.9	92.8	84.0	66.1

*Assuming a three-year age difference between person and his or her sibling.

changed for a person with a brother or a sister who is either three years older or three years younger than him- or herself.

Given the preceding discussion of changes in other relationships, the changing proportion who have particular siblings still alive at various stages of old age is not surprising (Table 4). First, the magnitude of the historical change is large. For example, consider those who survive to 70 and who had a sister born three years earlier than themselves. In 1990, 27% of these individuals would have their sister still living, but in 2000 the proportion was 75%. Second, because of gender differences in declining mortality, differences in the prospects of a sister surviving, compared with a brother, grew much larger between 1920 and 1980. In 1920, the proportion of 80-year-olds whose older sister would still be living (12%) differed little from the proportion whose older brother would still be living (10%). By 1980, however, this contrast was marked (48% vs. 25%). And third, at older ages, where death rates are high, the difference in probability of an older sibling compared to a younger one being alive are significant. In 2000, the proportion of older brothers of 80-year-olds still living will be 29%, while the proportion of younger brothers still living will be 48%. Combining gender and birth order differentials leads to even larger contrasts in sibling survival. At age 80 in 2000, only 29% could expect an older brother to be alive, while 66% could expect a younger sister to be alive. Under contemporary mortality conditions, most persons will not experience the death of any particular sibling until they are well past 70 years of age.

TABLE 5. Percentage of Women at Various Ages Whose Children Are Still Living, Under Mortality Conditions Existing in Selected Years: 1900–2000*

Year	Both Children Alive at Age:			Neither Child Alive at Age:		
	60	70	80	60	70	80
1900	49.9	41.7	33.1	8.5	12.5	17.9
1920	64.9	55.9	46.6	3.7	6.3	10.0
1940	81.7	75.9	66.2	0.9	1.6	3.3
1960	90.2	87.0	79.6	0.2	0.4	1.0
1980	93.2	90.5	84.5	0.1	0.2	0.5
2000	95.3	91.8	86.6	0.0	0.1	0.4

Year	Daughter Only Alive at Age:			Son Only Alive at Age:		
	60	70	80	60	70	80
1900	22.9	25.2	27.2	18.6	20.7	21.8
1920	17.3	20.4	23.6	14.1	17.4	19.8
1940	10.1	13.2	18.4	7.3	9.3	12.0
1960	6.0	8.1	12.9	3.5	4.5	6.4
1980	4.5	6.5	10.5	2.2	2.8	4.4
2000	3.3	6.0	9.7	1.4	2.2	3.3

*Assuming two children are born, a daughter when the mother is age 27 and a son when the mother is age 30.

Survival of Children

The final set of calculations (Table 5) illustrates the changing likelihood over the twentieth century of women at various stages of old age having their children still living. The conditions shown in the table refer to a situation where a woman has a daughter when she is 27 years old and a son when she is 30. (The statistics would apply equally to men who were these ages when their children were born.) What proportion of these women would have both, neither, or only one child alive as they reach ages 60, 70, or 80? Under contemporary circumstances, it is uncommon for women with this type of childbearing history to experience the death of a child at any stage of their later life. In other words, relatively few children now die before their parents. Mortality

conditions in 2000 imply that 95% would still have both children living when they reach age 60 and 87% would have them still living when they reach age 80. Only four out of 1,000 would have lost both children before reaching age 80. As many have noted, with low mortality, it is not necessary to bear more than a couple of children in order to be relatively certain that you will have a surviving child when you are old. But loss of children was not exceptional for those surviving to old age in past times. Under mortality conditions of 1900, only half of all women surviving to age 60 would have both the son and daughter still alive, and two thirds would have experienced the death of at least one of their two children before reaching 80 years of age. It was more likely that an 80-year-old mother of two in 1900 would have lost both of her children

(18%) than that a similar 80-year-old in 2000 would have lost any child (13%). Over the past century, it has become increasingly likely that when only one child survives, that the child is a daughter. The ratio of 70-year-old women with only a daughter to those with only a son increased from 1.2 in 1900 to 2.7 in 2000. Thus, not only are daughters currently more likely than sons to provide care for their aging parents but they are also less likely to drop out of the relationship completely by dying.

Conclusion

Four rather startling examples illustrate the implications of twentieth century mortality decline for the prevalence of kin relationships involving older persons:

1. It is more likely that 20-year-olds alive now have a grandmother still living (91%) than that 20-year-olds alive in 1900 had a mother still living (83%).

2. It is more likely that 70-year-olds today have a younger sister (one born three years after they were) still living (84%) than that 10-year-olds in 1910 had a younger sister still living (80%).

3. Men age 80 today are about as likely to have their first wives still living (67%) as were men age 60 in 1900 (68%). And more women were widowed by age 45 in 1900 (21%) than by age 60 today (19%).

4. Women who bear sons at age 25 now are more likely to have those sons alive when they are 80 years old (87%) than women in 1900 were to have their sons survive the first two years of life (82%). And if the child is a daughter, a higher proportion are now still living when their mothers reach age 90 (86%) than were surviving for just two years around 1900 (85%).

Clearly, declining mortality has altered the structure of kin relationships involving older persons. Children and young adults have more grandparents living today than in the past. More middle-aged adults have aging parents still living. Fewer persons at all stages of old age are widowed. And more older persons have their siblings still living. Demographic forces have created an unprecedented potential for persons at all stages of life to have kin relationships involving older persons.

While low mortality makes relationships with older kin increasingly possible, the nature of these relationships is primarily determined by social forces. Grandparents may be valued resources, or they may be irrelevant. Old parents may be loved ones, or they may be burdens. Aging first spouses may be intimate companions, or they may be ex-spouses. Elderly siblings may be close friends, or they may be distant relatives. How kin relationships that link the elderly to other persons actually develop is likely to have significant consequences for the social-emotional well-being of older persons.

NOTE

Acknowledgments: The author wishes to thank Vern Bengtson for suggesting that I update my earlier article, "Death and the Family." Also thanks to reviewers of the first draft for their constructive suggestions.

REFERENCES

Social Security Administration. (1992). *Life tables for the United States Social Security Area, 1900–2080* (Actuarial Study No. 107): Washington, DC: U.S. Department of Health and Human Services.

Uhlenberg, P. (1980). "Death and the family." *Journal of Family History, 5*: 313–320.

Chapter 7

Fertility on the Frontier:
Women, Contraception, and Community

ANITA ILTA GAREY

In the nineteenth century, the fertility of the U.S. white population was striking in two ways.[1] First, the late-eighteenth- and early-nineteenth-century crude birthrate was much higher in the United States than it was in Europe. (This differential, however, can be explained largely by differences in age structure and marriage patterns.) Second, the U.S. birthrate began declining by the beginning of the nineteenth century, much earlier than the decline in western Europe, where, with the exception of France, fertility did not begin its consistent decline until well into the second half of the nineteenth century. The Total Fertility Rate (TFR) declined from 7.04 in 1800 to 5.07 in 1860 (Coale and Zelnik 1963, 82). Although regional differences existed in the United States, the downward trend occurred not only at the national level but also within each state and territory. Older, more settled regions exhibited lower levels of fertility than did

the more recently settled frontier regions, but a decline in fertility occurred in both areas.[2]

My purpose in this chapter is to pose an old problem, the reason for the nineteenth-century decline in U.S. frontier fertility, from a different perspective, that of women. I argue that a perspective which focuses on the way in which women experience the world results in an alternative way of posing the question. This viewpoint leads to a reinterpretation of the available data, indicates other sources of relevant data, and points to new, and interdisciplinary, directions of research.

There is no concensus among demographers about what accounted for this decline in fertility when the United States was still a predominantly rural and non-industrialized country or why fertility should have declined among families living on the frontier. While most demographers agree that declining fertility was a product of increasing urbanization, this argument does not apply very well to the United States in the first half of the nineteenth century. The proportion of the population that was urban did not rise above one-tenth until

1840 (Forster and Tucker 1972, 11; Wells 1982, 123), and "if it occurred, the spread of family limitation practices from urban to rural areas must have begun very early in the United States; ... after 1810 the declines in fertility ratios of the rural population more than kept pace with those of the urban population" (Grabill, Kiser, Whelpton 1958, 16).

Although modernization is usually treated as being concomitant with urbanization and industrialization, it need not be, and it may be that the United States experienced modernization before it became very urbanized or industrialized (Vinovskis 1981b, 118). Measures of education, literacy, women's social and economic status, political participation, and secularization have all been used as proxies for modernization. Vinovskis (1981b, 129) found that education and literacy were the best predictors of differentials in fertility in Massachusetts from 1840 to 1860.

The most widely accepted explanation for the decline of fertility on the frontier, however, is based on the strong correlation that has been found between measures of land availability and fertility ratios (or estimates of birth and fertility rates based on those ratios) (Yasuba 1962; Easterlin 1976, 1977). The availability of easily accessible and affordable farmland could affect fertility in two ways: indirectly, through changes in marriage patterns, which were connected to the relative ease or difficulty of acquiring land on which to establish new households; and, directly, through the limitation of marital fertility as a response to changes in the relative value or cost of children.

The argument for the indirect effect of land availability on fertility is that relatively inexpensive, accessible, and farmable land meant economic opportunity and the ability to establish a household and support a family. Children did not have to postpone marriage until they inherited or could afford a farm of their own if new land was widely available.

Economic opportunity of this type might encourage early and universal marriage which, in the absence of marital fertility control, would result in an increase in fertility. On the other hand, for those who remained in older, more settled areas, where land was becoming scarcer and more expensive, age at marriage might increase and incidence of marriage might decrease. The available data support the hypothesis that fertility *differentials* between earlier and more recently settled areas can be accounted for by differences in marriage patterns, but the fertility *decline* cannot be attributed solely to marriages patterns (Yasuba 1962; Forster and Tucker 1972; Vinovskis 1981a, 339). Most demographers agree that the decline in fertility was caused by couples' intentional limitation of fertility.

Richard Easterlin (1976, 1977), the leading proponent of the land availability hypothesis, has posited a "bequest model" explanation of the correlation between measures of available land and measures of fertility. This model states that farm couples wanted to give each child a start in life and so tried to settle each adult child on a nearby farm. As land in the immediate area became less available, couples deliberately limited their fertility rather than have more children than they were able to settle on farmland. Easterlin acknowledges that the bequest model assumes that parents (1) wanted their adult children to be farmers; (2) wanted their adult children to settle near them; (3) wanted or felt obliged to establish their adult children in life; and (4) given 2 and 3 above, did not want to subdivide their property (Easterlin, Alter, and Condran 1978, 72), but he provides no real evidence to support these assumptions. Allan Bogue suggests that if farm couples did limit their fertility in order to keep adult children near, the motivation is less likely to have been a concern for their ability to provide each child with the capital equivalent to that with which the couple started, as Easterlin claims, and more likely to have been one of "values concerning appropriate generational living arrangements" (1976, 80) or "insurance against the uncertainties of old age" (1976, 80 n7).

In the case of the bequest model, the limitations of a purely economic approach lead those who cast the explanation of fertility decline in terms of land availability to construct an *a posteriori* account of frontier life in which motivation is inferred from an observed correlation, but which does not rely on, nor is upheld by, the historical evidence. For instance, if parents wanted their children to have land and wished to avoid subdividing their property, then available land on the frontier must surely have acted as a safety valve. Not only did young couples leave their parents' homes and migrate west, but whole families, in search of greater opportunities, also migrated (Wheeler and Wortman 1977, 28; Wells 1982, 111–16), and parents sometimes followed their adult children who had established households on the frontier (Brown 1975; Hampsten 1982).

What is the impact of looking at frontier fertility decline from an alternative perspective which brings women back in? For example, by focusing on the couple as an economic, decision-making unit, the economic model ignores the motivation of individuals within the household. Long-range concerns with inheritance, and not women's immediate concerns for their own health and well-being, are the motivations reflected in the land availability thesis. But what if one focuses on women's concerns?

Women in the nineteenth century considered childbirth a perilous event. Whether or not most births were uncomplicated, the easy birth and the good health of mother and child were treated as exceptional conditions. What I discovered from reading the letters of nineteenth-century frontier women was that childbirth was feared by both the pregnant

woman and her family and friends. The terminology is revealing: a woman is "unwell" when pregnant; she is "taken ill" when labor begins; she is "confined" during the period of labor and recovery. All of these phrases connote a sense of powerlessness. It was not merely the unknown or the remembrance of pain during previous births that frightened pregnant women; death in childbirth was a very real consideration. We do not have statistics on the number of women on the frontier who died in childbirth, but the letters of nineteenth-century frontier settlers attest to the fact that people were confronted frequently with the personal knowledge or news of such cases. In addition, women often complained of feeling weak or feeble for a prolonged period after childbirth and frequently commented on weaning their children and the improvement in health that they hoped this would bring, as in the following two excerpts from nineteenth-century letters.[3]

> As to my health it is very poor I have been such a great part of the time since I was married, and I am now very lame with the rheumatism so that it is with great difficulty that I walk a great part of the time, but I am in hopes that I shall be better when I wean my third Child, which is more than Eight Months Old, and I have never suckled Either of my Children more than about Nine Months on account of ill Health. (Molly Perkins in Woodbridge to Nabby Hitchcock in Burton, Ohio, 16 January 1812, Peter Hitchcock Family Papers, Western Reserve Historical Society)

> I was sorry to learn by your letter to Father and D. Which we re'cd yesterday that your health was feeble. I expect we shall have to wean our babies before we shall either of us have much strength & perhaps not then. (To Mary Dana Dustin from [her sister?], 21 August 1839, Dana Family Papers, Ohio Historical Society)

I would contend, and the letters of nineteenth-century women support this contention, that women on the United States frontier felt little control over their fertility but that they did have reason to want control over this process and that they were cognizant of this desire. While visiting her mother, Cornelia Brown wrote home to her husband the news, modestly phrased, that she was not again pregnant.

> I do not know whether it is over fatigue and anxiety, or that all is right, but I am *again disarmed* of my *fears* respecting myself which is another great relief. (16 August 1851, Fayette Brown Family Papers, Western Reserve Historical Society)

But within a year she was pregnant again, with her third child, and received the following commiseration from her girlhood friend, Sarah Park.

> I was really sorry dear Neal to hear you were again . . . so—I had hoped you might escape for a while—at least until your other troubles were lighter. They say *misery* loves company, but I assure you I don't want yours in *that*. . . . But you must tell me when *the event* is to take place— and I will try and *not* be there. And I think as I was at both the others—you might excuse me this time, and accept not of my *regret* but I hope of my *congratulations*. (Undated [1852?], Fayette Brown Family Papers, Western Reserve Historical Society)

Not only did women experience discomfort in pregnancy, fear of childbirth, and postpartum fatigue, but they also recognized that children placed a drain on their time and often interfered with or prevented the performance of other activities. This stands in contrast to the idea that frontier women approached childbirth and childrearing with a matter-of-fact and casual attitude, or that children were woven seamlessly into the fabric of household life.

Focusing on what women's concerns might have been also provides an alternative perspective on the traditional picture of the nineteenth-century family as an economic unit to which children added value by their labor power and in which children were productive members of the family unit. According to this view, children were not pulling on their mother's apron strings but were, instead, out pulling weeds, gathering eggs, or collecting firewood. The idea that children helped rather than hindered women in their work is not a recent one, but the letters of nineteenth-century women tell a somewhat different story.

I am not arguing that children were of no value to their parents, although value must be defined more broadly than the contribution of productive labor. Nor would I argue that children did not contribute their labor to economic production and the maintenance of daily life. But the point at which children start contributing their labor and what kind of contribution they make is likely to influence women's attitudes toward childbearing. If during the first four or five years of their lives, the care and attention required by children increases a mother's workload, then the promise of help in the future must be weighted against other factors. For example, if there are already several older children in the family, is there a point beyond which an additional child makes no further contribution? If male children grow up to assist their father in his work, do they ever lighten their mother's work, or do they continue to increase her portion of the family labor? Such a consideration, as well as the companionship a daughter provided, may have prompted this remark from Sarah Park, the mother of two boys and pregnant with her third child:

> If that little daughter only comes after all we will be amply repaid, but I fear it will be the same old tune. (To Cornelia Brown in Cleveland, [1851– 52?], Fayette Brown Family Papers, Western Reserve Historical Society)

And Rachel Metcalf, a Kansas farm woman, wrote to her mother:

I had a letter from Alice a while ago which I must answer soon if she can find [time] to write with her four babys. . . . If her little girls live she will have some help in a few years to pay her for all this care and trouble. Ceals girls are a big help to her now. They have threshed, Had 37 bu of wheat & 125 of oats. (16 September 1885, Evylyn Barber Metcalf Brewster Papers, Center for Archival Collections, Bowling Green State University)

The number of children already in the family, the sex-ratio, and the family's economic base may all influence a woman's perception of how much help another child is likely to be. Women recognized that before children became mother's helpers, and male children may never have become so, babies increased rather than diminished a mother's workload. Comments by women in letters of the period about the burden imposed by children were frequent, and have a depressingly modern ring.

As it is a long time since I wrote to you [and] I have a good opportunity I will try to write a few lines; believing it will be acceptable. The children make such a noise & plague me so that I hardly know what I write. (Lucy Wheeler to her sister, Sally Browning, 5 September 1827, Faxon, Starr, Wheeler Family Papers, Lorain County Historical Society)

Forgive all mistakes in writing and also the writing for I am tired & sick almost and the children they are all around me. (Icebenda Baker to her sister, Eliza Baker Barker, 5 October 1834, Barker Family Papers, Western Reserve Historical Society)

I have to stop every minute or two to make Jane let go the table cover and Sarah leave the ink stand alone. . . . Now Sarah has just gone in the kitchen and is kicking up a fuss with Barbara. (Catharine Gordon to her mother, Jane Barrington, 27 Feb 1845, Barrington Family Papers, Ohio Historical Society)

Mrs O's babe is about the age of Mrs. W's, 10 months old, and is now about as fleshly as she can be. Marian O. is quite wrathy about it. She says she is forever tied to a young one, too bad. (Esther Fuller in Peoria, Illinois, to Jane Keefer in Richmond, Indiana, 26 October 1848, Keefer Papers, Ohio Historical Society)

I am getting so that I hardly know how to write *babies* and home duties occupying most of my thoughts. (Cynthia Tolles in Burton, Ohio, to her sister-in-law, Sarah Marshal Hitchcock in Painesville, 4 February 1859, Peter Hitchcock Family Papers, Western Reserve Historical Society)

When we focus on fertility at the microlevel, the issue becomes one of the impact of pregnancy, childbirth, and additional children on the individual lives of women. Would the circumstances of these events motivate women to limit their fertility or to want to limit their fertility if the means to do so were available? As John Faragher notes:

If . . . population growth and unlimited fertility were "rational" for male expansionists, they may have simultaneously seemed "irrational" to the women who bore the children. Certainly on the basis of cross-cultural evidence, as well as the historical trends in fertility, we know that women would have enjoyed the opportunity to limit the burden of childbirth. (Faragher 1981, 549)

If we turn now to the question of how fertility was controlled, the focus on women's experience sheds further light on the nineteenth-century fertility decline. Although Easterlin (1977, 145) implies that farm couples could determine the number of children they could afford, there is no reason to assume that they had enough control over their fertility to make this a realistic model. The bequest model reflects a view of fertility control which does not take into consideration the probability that imperfect control over fertility would result in different kinds of fertility-control behavior than would highly effective contraception. Demographers characterize the fertility transition (from high mortality and fertility to low mortality and fertility) as a change from a situation in which parents do nothing to stop additional births to a situation in which they choose the number of children they want and control their fertility after that number of children is reached.[4]

The concept of planning for the ideal family size, while endemic in the demographic literature that seeks to correlate deliberate fertility control with socioeconomic variables, would not have been a realistic goal in the first half of the nineteenth century. In contrast, if one tries to define the problem as a nineteenth-century woman might, a more realistic and convincing picture appears.

Unless contraception is almost totally effective, with abortion to back up any failure, it is of little use to plan on a specific or very small number of children. A woman marrying in 1800 realized that if she did nothing to prevent it she might have eight, ten, or more children. Because available methods of contraception were not very effective, if she adopted a practice of avoiding as many pregnancies as possible she would, in most cases, still have several children. She might have been quite satisfied with, or resigned to, simply having a few children less than she might have had if she had done nothing to limit her fertility. She would not reduce her fertility *to* a specific desired level, that is; she would reduce it *from* the maximum number she could potentially have. This distinction is crucial, and it has implications for the way in which data are interpreted and for the choice of variables with which fertility is correlated.

As we have seen, there is an assumption in most socioeconomic explanations of deliberate fertility control that the level of fertility reflects rational responses to immediate socioeconomic factors, and that changing levels correspond to changing socioeconomic factors. But the level of fertility is actually a product of these causal variables in conjunction with the effectiveness of available methods of birth control.

In the first half of the nineteenth century, contraceptives and other methods of avoiding pregnancy were available, but were not highly effective. Until about 1840, early abortion was not distinguished from methods of preventing conception (Mohr 1978; Gordon 1983, 211). Home medical manuals published during the first decades of the nineteenth century, some of which were intended specifically for women in rural areas, listed remedies for "obstructed menses" (Mohr 1978, 6–9). American pennyroyal (*Hedeoma pulegioides*), a purely American plant which is a stimulant and an emmenagogue (Coon 1979, 119), was used and recommended by Indian women, who "believed that if they drank enough of it regularly, it prevented pregnancy" (Wheeler and Wortman 1977, 31). Chemical abortifacients and the equipment and chemicals needed for douching were advertised in newspapers and sold through the mail. Some of these products were worthless, but others appear to have had some degree of efficacy (La Sorte 1976, 167–168; Mohr 1978, 9–19), and some of the chemicals for douching had spermicidal properties. Pessaries (vaginal sponges), which absorbed seminal fluid and may have blocked the cervix to some degree, were also available. The existence of "safe periods" and even of the connections between cervical mucus and ovulation were known and discussed in home medical manuals and marriage guides of the period (La Sorte 1976, 175–178). Although some of the periods designated as safe were not, the fact that the topic was discussed indicates that women were motivated to gain the control such information could give them. Unreliable methods are not totally ineffective methods, and they do have an effect on overall fertility levels (Dawson, Meny, Ridley 1980; Weir 1982).

Easterlin assumes that withdrawal was the type of fertility control used by early-nineteenth-century couples and that withdrawal does not depend on new information, so that it is "highly doubtful . . . that the secular fertility decline can be attributed to the diffusion of new fertility-control knowledge" (1977, 114). There are two obvious objections to Easterlin's premise, both of which confront the assumptions that (1) fertility levels reflect changes in motivation alone, and (2) that the ability to control fertility was fairly constant during this period.

The first objection is that knowledge about the use of withdrawal, or any contraceptive technique, as a method of fertility control may be new to a particular social, historical, or geographical group even if the technique is not a new discovery. A second objection is that withdrawal depends on the cooperation of men for whatever degree of efficacy it has, and stopping a potential birth may have been much less important to a man that it was to his wife. Pessaries, douches, and abortifacients, however, were controlled by women, and as these became available, women gave up other less effective, but woman-controlled, methods such as the post-coital dance, which consisted of violent physical activities, such as dancing, jumping, horseback riding, or forced coughing, performed soon after intercourse (La Sorte 1976). Whether this technique actually helped prevent pregnancies or not, its existence indicates that the women performing it felt motivated to do something to limit their fertility.

If women living on the frontier in 1800 and 1810 were less effective in reducing their fertility than were their daughters and granddaughters, recourse to changes in motivational variables is not necessary to account for the decline in fertility between 1800 and 1860. Did the granddaughter necessarily want or "demand" fewer children than her mother or grandmother? Or did she have more knowledge and better means of contraception?

If we now consider the issues which have emerged from a perspective which focuses on women's experiences, a new explanation of nineteenth-century frontier fertility decline emerges which is consistent with a reinterpretation of the correlation which has been used to support the land availability hypothesis. In their correlations of land and fertility rates, demographers have used population density as a proxy for land availability. While there will always be difficulties when choosing proxies to represent variables, because the proxies are not, of course, the variables themselves, it is nevertheless important to be aware of what is actually being measured and with what fertility is really being correlated.[5] It may be that while population density and birth ratios are inversely correlated, the availability of farms is not the determining aspect in this relationship.

The empirical evidence on which the land availability hypothesis rests is that fertility was declining as population density was increasing (Yasuba 1962; Forster and Tucker 1972; Leet 1975; Easterlin 1976; Lindert 1977; McInnis 1977; Schapiro 1982). An alternative hypothesis, based on the same empirical evidence, suggests that increasing population density meant increased social interaction and communication between women, thus enabling them to exchange knowledge, remedies, and advice on the control of fertility. This hypothesis assumes (1) that women were motivated to limit their fertility prior to the observed correlations between population density and fertility; (2) that women shared personal information with each other; and (3) that increased social density enabled women to share this information more effectively.

Women living on the frontier were extremely isolated (Faragher 1981, 548); the letters and diaries of frontier women are filled with expressions of loneliness (Wheeler and Wortman 1977, 37; Hampsten 1982; Luchetti and Olwell 1982; Motz 1983), and the community of women in which a wife and mother could learn and share information was absent for many frontier women. In 1820, Mary Burton migrated from Vermont to Ohio with her husband and four-year old daughter, Lucy. She was incredibly lonely and wrote to her family begging them to visit her.

> You can form no kind of an idea how much I wish to see you. A journey here in the month of May or June—by water—would be very short but one in September by land would be the most pleasant and beneficial to your health. Please give me some encouragement. (Mary Burton to her mother, 8 August 18 [20?], Mary Hollister Burton Papers, Western Reserve Historical Society)

She appended to this letter to her mother, one to her sister.

> My dear sister:
>   If you have any regard for me I wish you would manifest it by coming to see me. . . . If you ever come you must calculate to enjoy yourself with me and my family, for there is no society, or what there is is worse than none. . . . But do come, for mercy's sake. You must not always seek your own enjoyment but try to promote others'. . . . Elijah is gone from home a great part of the time and I do want your company very much.

Another early settler noted that the lack of community was an inevitable problem of frontier settlement.

> Land at government price is one dollar 25 cents per acre the disadvantages here are the same as in other new countries bad roads not so good for schools and meatings as in old places. (Experience Parsons in Lucas County, Ohio, to her brother, Daniel Herring in Maine, 4 June 1837, Experience Parsons Papers, Toledo-Lucas Public Library)

Some women took in boarders, relatives, or friends in order to have company and some social interaction with others.

I have a young woman boarding with me attending school. I took her to be company for me. Mr. Dustin is gone most of the time and I was so lonely especially at night. . . . I am glad to hear you even *think* of visiting us—but I hope you will act as well as think. Just make a start and the worst of the journey is over. (Mary Dana Gustin to her sister, Grace Dana Ewart, 14 June 1842, Dana Family Papers, Ohio Historical Society)

I Am now living on our farm five miles from Peoria and I am so lonly that I can hardly live and as soon as I heard of you the thout struck me that perhaps you would come and live with me as you are alone in the world you shall have a home as long as I live. I do not want you to understand me that I want you to do my work it is your company that I want. (Sophia Caldwell in Illinois to Jane Keefer in Indiana, 18 December 1851, Keefer Papers, Ohio Historical Society)

And it *was* company, community, and social interaction, that women wanted, and those came with density.

As the area filled up, as population density increased, women became less and less isolated. Higher density was accompanied by more and better roads, mail service, and available supplies (Pred 1973), and women were increasingly exposed to the information, remedies, and advice of other women.

> The isolation experienced by families on Michigan's frontier in the 1830's lessened rapidly in mid-century as the agricultural regions of the state were linked to New York and New England by reliable and regular postal service and convenient transportation. Thus women who moved to Michigan [in mid-century] did not sever ties with their kin. They not only communicated frequently by correspondence but also made extended visits, often of several months' duration, with the relatives they had left behind. (Motz 1983, 14)

That women on the frontier had perhaps been born and raised in the more settled areas before marrying and moving to the frontier does not affect this argument about the absence of community. A woman had no reason to learn about contraception before she needed it. An illustration of this is provided by the case of Allettie Mosher, who was born in 1854 in Michigan. Her first husband died within a year of their marriage, leaving her with one child. Soon after 1875, she moved with her widowed mother to North Dakota to join a sister who had married and moved there earlier. In 1885, at the age of 31, she remarried and wrote a letter to her girlhood friend, Rose Williams, asking for advice on contraception. Rose's reply follows:

Well now I should say & did say "who would have thought it." You better bet I was surprised when I read your leter, you never let a fellow know you even had a fellow. . . . You never sent a piece of your dress as you said you would. You want to know of a sure preventative. Well plague take it. The best way is for you to sleep in one bed and your Man in another & bet you will laugh and say "You goose you think I am going to do that" no and I bet you would for I don't see any one that does. Well now the thing we [use] (when I say *we* I means us girls) is a thing: but it hasn't always been *sure* as you know but that was our own carelessness for it is we have been sure. I do not know whether you can get them out there. They are called Pessairre or female preventative if you don't want to ask for a "pisser" just ask for a female preventative. They cost one dollar when sis got hers it was before any of us went to Dak. She paid five dollars for it. The Directions are with it. . . . Reece just told me to tell you to wear a long night dress with a draw string at the bottom and a lock and key for if you was in separate beds you would crawl over together . . . & would not like to have someone else to get this. It would spook them sick I wouldent wonder . . . let me know if it does. (Hampsten 1982, 104)

Most of what frontier women said to one another is lost: the secrets whispered in confidence, the advice shared. But the hints and evidences left in letters and diaries can help us

better understand the historical context from which the data are derived.

It is through social interaction that issues are raised and information shared. Durkheim uses the term "moral density" to refer to a situation in which people are in enough contact with each other "to be able to act and react upon one another" ([1893] 1964, 257). "But this moral relationship can only produce its effect if the real distance between individuals has itself diminished in some way. Moral density cannot grow unless material density grows at the same time, and the latter can be used to measure the former" (Durkheim [1893] 1964, 257)

The decreasing amount of available land was the product of an increase in population density. The social interaction and material resources necessary for the control of fertility were not really available in sparsely populated areas. For women, density meant community and the support of other women, which may have provided the context in which fertility on the frontier could decline.

There are no simple explanations of fertility decline. The decline in fertility which occurred in the United States in the first half of the nineteenth century was undoubtedly the product of many factors. The Princeton European Fertility Project studies of the fertility decline in Europe (Knodel 1974; Lesthaeghe 1977; Livi-Bacci 1977) have indicated that socioeconomic factors alone cannot explain the decline of fertility in Europe; cultural factors have played a decisive role. "The identification of social and cultural indicators that reflect a receptivity to family limitation has lagged behind the measurement of more readily identifiable socioeconomic characteristics" (van de Walle and Knodel 1980, 36). The interaction between cultural, social, and economic variables has yet to be fully understood, but consideration of the interests and desires of women, and of their changing ability to limit their fertility, will help to diminish this lag and to produce a more realistic picture of fertility decline.

NOTES

Acknowledgments: After reviewing the demographic literature on this topic (Garey 1985), I spent the summer of 1985 doing archival research at various historical societies in Ohio. The research was funded by a University of California Humanities Research Grant, administered through the Graduate Division, University of California, Berkeley. I thank the University of California for its support and the libraries and historical societies for granting me permission to quote from letters in their manuscript collections. I also wish to thank Karen V. Hansen for her perceptive comments on an earlier draft and Nicholas Townsend for his research assistance in Ohio and his help, advice, and support throughout.

1. This chapter is about the white population only. All statistics cited will be for that segment of the population, and any hypotheses or conclusions are intended to apply only to that group.

2. For most of the period 1800–1860, "frontier" refers to the area which is now the states of Ohio, Indiana, and Illinois. These are now populous, industrialized states, but in 1814, Cleveland, Ohio, had a population of less than 100, and in 1830 Chicago had about 50 inhabitants. The frontier was of course being extended throughout the period, but it should be noted that at no time in this chapter does "frontier" refer to the far West.

3. Spelling, punctuation, and capitalization in all the material quoted are represented as they appeared in the original letters and manuscripts.

4. "Natural fertility," as originally defined by the French demographer Louis Henry, is fertility in the absence of parity-specific control. "Family limitation," on the other hand, is "a deliberate effort to terminate childbearing once they [the parents] have reached some particular number of children" (van de Walle and Knodel 1980, 10).

5. It is questionable whether these measures really represent the independent variable on which the economic explanation of fertility decline is based, because "availability of farms" actually refers to the cost of establishing a farm (Vinovskis 1981a, 236). Some studies have used a measure based on the value of the average farm, which the federal census began including in 1850 (Lindert 1978; Vinovskis 1981b), but these studies have found a weaker correlation between this measure and fertility measures than between population density measures and fertility. Potter (1965, 677n) questions whether land was really becoming less available, given improvements in transportation and changes in land policy. Yasuba admits that "such relevant factors as the land-laws, the distribution of land-ownership, and the use to which the land was put, are not reflected in the measures of land availability used" (Yasuba 1962, 168).

REFERENCES

Bogue, Allan G. 1976. "Population Change and Farm Settlement in the Northern United States: Discussion." *Journal of Economic History* 36: 76–81.

Brown, Victoria. 1975. *Uncommon Lives of Common Women: The Missing Half of Wisconsin History.* Madison: Wisconsin Feminists Project Fund.

Coale, A. J., and Melvin Zelnik. 1963. *Estimates of Fertility and Population in the United States: A Study of White Births from 1855 to 1960.* Princeton: Princeton University Press.

Coon, Nelson, 1979. *Using Plants for Healing.* Emmaus, PA: Rodale Press.

Dawson, Deborah A., Denise J. Meny, and Jeanne Clare Ridley. 1980. "Fertility Control in the United States Before the Contraceptive Revolution." *Family Planning Perspectives* 12(2).

Durkheim, Emile. (1893) 1964. *The Division of Labor in Society.* Translated by George Simpson. New York: Free Press.

Easterlin, Richard A. 1976. "Population Change and Farm Settlement in the Northern United States." *Journal of Economic History* 36:45–75.

———. 1977. "Population Issues in American Economic History: a Survey and Critique." Pp. 131–158 in *Recent Developments in the Study of*

Business and Economic History: Essays in Memory of Herman E. Kross, edited by Robert Gallman. Greenwich, CT: Jai Press.

Easterlin, Richard A., George Alter, and Gretchen A. Condran. 1978. "Farms and Farm Families in Old and New Areas: the Northern States in 1860." Pp. 22–84 in *Family and Population in Nineteenth Century America,* edited by Tamara K. Hareven and Maris A. Vinovskis. Princeton: Princeton University Press.

Faragher, John Mack. 1981. "History from the Inside-out: Writing the History of Women in Rural America." *American Quarterly* 33(5): 537–557.

Forster, Colin, and G.S.L. Tucker. 1972. *Economic Opportunity and White American Fertility Ratios, 1800–1860.* New Haven: Yale University Press.

Garey, Anita Ilta. 1985. "An Examination of Explanations for Fertility Decline and Differentials on the United States Frontier, 1800–1860." Program in Population Research Working Paper No. 16, University of California, Berkeley.

Gordon, Linda. 1983. "Malthusianism, Socialism, and Feminism in the United States." *History of European Ideas* 4(2):203–214. (Special issue: Malthus Our Contemporary.)

Grabill, W. H., C. V. Kiser, and P. K. Whelpton. 1958. *The Fertility of American Women.* New York: John Wiley.

Hampsten, Elizabeth. 1982. *Read This Only to Yourself: The Private Writings of Midwestern Women, 1880–1910.* Bloomington, IN: Indiana University Press.

Knodel, John. 1974. *The Decline of Fertility in Germany 1871–1939.* Princeton: Princeton University Press.

La Sorte, Michael A. 1976. "Nineteenth-Century Family Planning Practices." *Journal of Psychohistory* 4:163–183.

Leet, Don R. 1975. "Human Fertility and Agricultural Opportunities in Ohio Counties: From Frontier to Maturity, 1810–1860." Pp. 138–158 in *Essays in Nineteenth-Century Economic History: The Old Northwest,* edited by David C. Klingaman and Richard K. Vedder. Athens, OH: Ohio University Press.

Lesthaeghe, Ron. 1977. *The Decline of Belgian Fertility 1820–1970.* Princeton: Princeton University Press.

Lindert, Peter H. 1977. "American Fertility Patterns Since the Civil War." Pp. 229–276 in *Population Patterns in the Past,* edited by Ronald Demos Lee. New York: Academic Press.

———. 1978. *Fertility and Scarcity in America.* Princeton: Princeton University Press.

Livi-Bacci, Massimo. 1977. *A History of Italian Fertility During the Last Two Centuries.* Princeton: Princeton University Press.

Luchetti, Cathy, and Carol Olwell. 1982. *Women of the West.* St. George, UT: Antelope Island Press.

McInnes, R. M. 1977. "Childbearing and Land Availability: Some Evidence from Individual Household Data." Pp. 201–227 in *Population Patterns in the Past,* edited by Ronald Demos Lee. New York: Academic Press.

Mohr, James C. 1978. *Abortion in America: The Origins and Evolution of National Policy, 1800–1900.* Oxford: Oxford University Press.

Motz, Marilyn Ferris. 1983. *True Sisterhood: Michigan Women and Their Kin.* Albany, N.Y.: State University of New York Press. (SUNY series in American Social History.)

Potter, J. 1965. "The Growth of Population in America, 1700–1860." Pp. 631–688 in *Population in History,* edited by D. V. Glass and D. E. C. Eversley. London: Edward Arnold.

Pred, Allan R. 1973. *Urban Growth and the Circulation of Information: The United States System of Cities, 1790–1840.* Cambridge, MA: Harvard University Press.

Schapiro, Morton Owen. 1982. "Land Availability and Fertility in the United States, 1760–1870." *Journal of Economic History* 42(3):577–600.

van de Walle, Etienne, and John Knodel. 1980. "Europe's Fertility Transition: New Evidence and Lessons for Today's Developing World." *Population Bulletin* 34(6).

Vinovskis, Maris A. 1981a. "The Fertility Decline in the West as a Model for Developing Countries Today: the Case of Nineteenth-Century America." Pp. 229–253 in *Fertility Decline in the Less Developed Countries,* edited by Nick Eberstadt. New York: Praeger.

———. 1981b. *Fertility in Massachusetts from the Revolution to the Civil War.* New York: Academic Press.

Weir, David R. 1982. "Fertility Transition in Rural France, 1740–1829." Ph.D. diss., Stanford University.

Wells, Robert V. 1982. *Revolution in Americans' Lives: A Demographic Perspective on the History of Americans, Their Families, and Their Society.* Westport, CT: Greenwood Press.

Wheeler, Adade Mitchell, and Marlene Stein Wortman. 1977. *The Roads They Made: Women in Illinois History.* Chicago: Charles Kerr.

Yasuba, Yasukichi. 1962. *Birth Rates of the White Population in the United States: An Economic Study.* Baltimore: Johns Hopkins University Press.

~ Chapter 8

Interpreting the African Heritage
in Afro-American Family Organization

NIARA SUDARKASA

Many of the debates concerning explanations of Black family organization are waged around false dichotomies. The experience of slavery in America is juxtaposed to the heritage of Africa as *the* explanation of certain aspects of Black family structure. "Class" versus "culture" becomes the framework for discussing determinants of household structure and role relationships. Black families are characterized either as "alternative institutions" or as groups whose structures reflect their "adaptive strategies," as if the two viewpoints were mutually exclusive.

Just as surely as Black American family patterns are in part an outgrowth of the descent into slavery (Frazier [1939] 1966), so too are they partly a reflection of the archetypical African institutions and values that informed and influenced the behavior of those Africans who were enslaved in America (Herskovits

[1941] 1958). With respect to "class" and "culture," it is indeed the case that the variations in historical and contemporary Black family organization cannot be explained without reference to the socioeconomic contexts in which they developed (Allen 1979). But neither can they be explained without reference to the cultural contexts from which they derived (Nobles, 1974a, 1974b, 1978). Whereas Black families can be analyzed as groups with strategies for coping with wider societal forces (Stack 1974), they must also be understood as institutions with historical traditions that set them apart as "alternative" formations that are not identical to (or pathological variants of) family structures found among other groups in America (Aschenbrenner 1978).

After more than a decade of rethinking Black family structure (see, for example, Billingsley 1968; Staples 1971, 1978; Aschenbrenner 1973; English 1974; Sudarkasa 1975a; Allen 1978; Shimkin et al. 1978), it is still the case that a holistic theory of past and present Black family organization remains to be developed. Such a theory or explanation must rest on the premise that political-economic variables are *always* part of any explanation of family formation and functioning, but that the cultural historical derivation of the formations in question helps to explain the nature of their adaptation to particular political-economic contexts.

Obviously, it is beyond the scope of this chapter to try to set forth such a holistic explanation of Black family organization. Its more modest aim is to take a step in this direction by laying to rest one of the false dichotomies that stand in the way of such an explanation. This review seeks to show how an understanding of African family structure sheds light on the form and functioning of Black American family structure as it developed in *the context of slavery* and later periods. It seeks to elucidate African institutional arrangements and values that were manifest in the family organization of Blacks enslaved in America, and suggests that some of these values and institutional arrangements continue to be recognizable in contemporary formations.

The relationships of causality, correlation, and constraint that exist between the political-economic sphere and that of the family cannot be dealt with here. What the chapter seeks to clarify is why Black familial institutions embrace certain alternatives of behavior and not others. It suggests a cultural historical basis for the fact that Black family organization differs from that of other groups even when political and economic factors are held relatively constant.

Thus, it is suggested that it cannot suffice to look to political and economic factors to explain, for example, the difference between lower-class Anglo- or Italian American families and lower-class Afro-American families. One has to come to grips with the divergent culture histories of the groups concerned. In other words, one is led back to the institu-tional heritage stemming from Western Europe on the one hand and from West Africa on the other. Knowledge of the structure and functioning of kinship and the family in these areas helps to explain the structure and functioning of families formed among their descendants in America.

It might appear that this is too obvious a point to be belabored. However, when it comes to the study of Black American families, the scholarly community has historically taken a different view. Whereas it is generally agreed that the history of the family in Europe is pertinent to an understanding of European derived family organization in America (and throughout the world), many—if not most—scholars working on Black American families have argued or assumed that the African family heritage was all but obliterated by the institution of slavery. This view has retained credence, despite the accumulation of evidence to the contrary, in large measure because E. Franklin Frazier ([1939] 1966), the most prestigious and prolific student of the Black American family, all but discounted the relevance of Africa in his analyses.

This chapter takes its departure from W.E.B. DuBois ([1908] 1969), Carter G. Woodson (1936), and M. J. Herskovits ([1941] 1958), all of whom looked to Africa as well as to the legacy of slavery for explanations of Afro-American social institutions. Herskovits is the best-known advocate of the concept of African survivals in Afro-American family life, but DuBois was the first scholar to stress the need to study the Black American family against the background of its African origins.

In his 1908 study of the Black family, DuBois prefaced his discussions of marriage, household structure, and economic organization with observations concerning the African antecedents of the patterns developed in America. "In each case an attempt has been made to connect present conditions with the

African past. This is not because Negro-Americans are Africans, or can trace an un-broken social history from Africa, but because there is a distinct nexus between Africa and America which, though broken and per-verted, is nevertheless not to be neglected by the careful student" (DuBois [1908] 1969, 9). Having documented the persistence of African family patterns in the Caribbean, and of African derived wedding ceremonies in Al-abama, DuBois noted: "Careful research would doubtless reveal many other traces of the African family in America. They would, however, be traces only, for the effectiveness of the slave system meant the practically com-plete crushing out of the African clan and family life" (p. 21).

With the evidence that has accumulated since DuBois wrote, it is possible to argue that even though the constraints of slavery did prohibit the replication of African lineage ("clan") and family life in America, the prin-ciples on which these kin groups were based, and the values underlying them, led to the emergence of variants of African family life in the form of the extended families which de-veloped among the enslaved Blacks in Amer-ica. Evidence of the Africanity to which DuBois alluded is to be found not only in the relatively few "traces" of direct *institutional transfer* from Africa to America but also in the numerous examples of *institutional transfor-mation* from Africa to America.

No discussion of the relevance of Africa for understanding Afro-American family organi-zation can proceed without confronting the issue of the "diversity" of the backgrounds of "African slaves" (read "enslaved Africans") brought to America. Obviously for certain purposes, each African community or each ethnic group can be described in terms of the linguistic, cultural, and/or social structural features which distinguish it from others. At the same time, however, these communities

or ethnic groups can be analyzed from the point of view of their similarity to other groups.

It has long been established that the Africans enslaved in the United States and the rest of the Americas came from the Western part of the continent where there had been a long history of culture contact and wide-spread similarities in certain institutions (Herskovits [1941] 1958, chs. 2 and 3). For ex-ample, some features of kinship organization were almost universal. Lineages, large co-resident domestic groups, and polygynous marriages are among the recurrent features found in groups speaking different languages, organized into states as well as "segmentary" societies, and living along the coast as well as in the interior (Radcliffe-Brown 1950; Fortes 1953; Onwuejeogwu 1975).

When the concept of "African family struc-ture" is used here, it refers to those organiza-tional principles and patterns which are com-mon to the different ethnic groups whose members were enslaved in America. These features of family organization are known to have existed for centuries on the African con-tinent and are, therefore, legitimately termed a part of the African heritage.

African Family Structure: Understanding the Dynamics of Consanguinity and Conjugality

African families, like those in other parts of the world, embody two contrasting bases for membership: *consanguinity,* which refers to kinship that is commonly assumed or pre-sumed to be biologically based and rooted in "blood ties," and *affinity,* which refers to kin-ship created by law and rooted "in law." *Con-jugality* refers specifically to the affinal kin-ship created between spouses (Marshall 1968). Generally, all kinship entails a dynamic tension between the operation of the contrasting principles of consanguinity and affinity. The comparative study of family organization led Ralph Linton (1936, 159–163) to observe that in different societies families tend to be built either around a conjugal core or around a consanguineal core. In either case, the other principle is subordinate.

According to current historical research on the family in Europe, the principle of conjugality appears to have dominated family organization in the western part of that continent (including Britain) at least since the Middle Ages, when a number of economic and political factors led to the predominance of nuclear and/or stem families built around married couples. Certainly for the past three or four hundred years, the conjugally based family has been the ideal and the norm in Western Europe (Shorter 1975; Stone 1975; Tilly and Scott 1978). Whether or not the European conjugal family was a structural isolate is not the issue here. The point is that European families, whether nuclear or extended, tended to emphasize the conjugal relationship in matters of household formation, decision making, property transmission, and socialization of the young (Goody 1976).

African families, on the other hand, have traditionally been organized around consanguineal cores formed by adult siblings of the same sex or by larger same-sex segments of patri- or matrilineages. The groups which formed around these consanguineally related core members included their spouses and children, and perhaps some of their divorced siblings of the opposite sex. This co-resident *extended family* occupied a group of adjoining or contiguous dwellings known as a compound. Upon marriage, Africans did not normally form new isolated households, but joined a compound in which the extended family of the groom, or that of the bride, was already domiciled (Sudarkasa 1980, 38–49).

African extended families could be subdivided in two ways. From one perspective, there was the division between the nucleus formed by the consanguineal core group and their children and the "outer group" formed by the in-marrying spouses. In many African languages, in-marrying spouses are collectively referred to as "wives" or "husbands" by both females and males of the core group. Thus, for example, in any compound in a patrilineal society, the in-marrying women may be known as the "wives of the house." They are, of course, also the mothers of the children of the compound. Their collective designation as "wives of the house" stresses the fact that their membership in the compound is rooted in law and can be terminated by law, whereas that of the core group is rooted in descent and is presumed to exist in perpetuity.

African extended families may also be divided into their constituent conjugally based family units comprised of parents and children. In the traditional African family, these conjugal units did not have the characteristics of the typical "nuclear family" of the West. In the first place, African conjugal families normally involved polygynous marriages at some stage in their developmental cycle. A number of Western scholars have chosen to characterize the polygynous conjugal family as several distinct nuclear families with one husband/father in common (Rivers 1924, 12; Murdock 1949, 2; Colson 1962). In the African conception, however, whether a man had one wife and children or many wives and children, his was *one* family. In the case of polygynous families, both the husband and the senior co-wife played important roles in integrating the entire group (Fortes 1949, chs. 3 and 4; Sudarkasa 1973, ch. 5; Ware 1979). The very existence of the extended family as an "umbrella" group for the conjugal family meant that the latter group differed from the Western nuclear family. Since, for many purposes and on many occasions, *all* the children of the same generation within the compound regarded themselves as brothers and sisters (rather than dividing into siblings versus "cousins"), and since the adults assumed certain responsibilities toward their "nephews" and "nieces" (whom they term sons and daughters) as well as toward their own offspring. African conjugal families did not have the rigid boundaries characteristic of nuclear families of the West.

The most far-reaching difference between African and European families stems from their differential emphasis on consanguinity and conjugality. This difference becomes clear when one considers extended family organization in the two contexts. The most common type of European extended family consisted of two or more nuclear families joined through the parent-child or sibling tie. It was this model of the stem family and the joint family that was put forth by George P. Murdock (1949, 23, 33, 39–40) as the generic form of the extended family. However, the African data show that on that continent, extended families were built around consanguineal cores, and the conjugal components of these larger families differed significantly from the nuclear families of the West.

In Africa, unlike Europe, in many critical areas of family life the consanguineal core group rather than the conjugal pair was paramount. With respect to household formation, I have already indicated that married couples joined existing compounds. It was the lineage core that owned (or had the right of usufruct over) the land and the compound where families lived, farmed, and/or practiced their crafts. The most important properties in African societies—land, titles, and entitlements—were transmitted through the lineages, and spouses did not inherit from each other (Goody 1976).

Within the extended family residing in a single compound, decision making centered in the consanguineal core group. The oldest male in the compound was usually its head, and all the men in his generation constituted the elders of the group. Together they were ultimately responsible for settling internal disputes, including those that could not be settled within the separate conjugal families or, in some cases, by the female elders among the wives (Sudarkasa 1973, 1976). They also made decisions, such as those involving the allocation of land and other resources, which affected the functioning of the constituent conjugal families.

Given the presence of multiple spouses within the *conjugal* families, it is not surprising that decision making within them also differed from the model associated with nuclear family organization. Separate rather than joint decision making was common. In fact, husbands and wives normally had distinct purviews and responsibilities within the conjugal family (Sudarkasa 1973; Oppong 1974). Excepting those areas where Islamic traditions overshadowed indigenous African traditions, women had a good deal of control over the fruits of their own labor. Even though husbands typically had ultimate authority over wives, this authority did not extend to control over their wives' properties (Oppong 1974; Robertson 1976; Sudarkasa 1976). Moreover, even though women were subordinate in their roles as wives, as mothers and sisters they wielded considerable authority, power, and influence. This distinction in the power attached to women's roles is symbolized by the fact that in the same society where wives knelt before their husbands, sons prostrated before their mothers, and seniority as determined by age, rather than gender, governed relationships among siblings (Sudarkasa 1973, 1976).

Socialization of the young involved the entire extended family, not just the separate conjugal families, even though each conjugal family had special responsibility for the children (theirs or their relatives') living with them. It is important to note that the concept of "living with" a conjugal family took on a different meaning in the context of the African compound. In the first place, husbands, wives, and children did not live in a bounded space, apart from other such units. Wives had their own rooms or small dwellings, and husbands had theirs. These were not necessarily adjacent to one another. (In some matrilineal societies, husbands and wives resided in separate compounds.) Children ordinarily slept in their mothers' rooms until they were of a certain age, after which they customarily slept in communal rooms allocated to boys or girls. Children usually ate their meals with their mothers but they might also eat some of these meals with their fathers' co-wives (assuming that no hostility existed between the women concerned) or with their grandmothers. Children of the same compound played together and shared many learning experiences. They were socialized by all the adults to identify themselves collectively as sons and daughters of a particular lineage and compound, which entailed a kinship, based on descent, with all the lineage ancestors and with generations unborn (Radcliffe-Brown and Forde 1950; Uchendu 1965; Sudarkasa 1980).

The stability of the African extended family did not depend on the stability of the marriage(s) of the individual core group members. Although traditional African marriages (particularly those in patrilineal societies) were more stable than those of most contemporary societies, marital dissolution did not have the ramifications it has in nuclear family systems. When divorces did occur, they were usually followed by remarriage. Normally, all adults other than those who held certain ceremonial offices or who were severely mentally or physically handicapped lived in a marital union (though not necessarily the same one)

throughout their lives (for example, Lloyd 1968). The children of a divorced couple were usually brought up in their natal compound (or by members of their lineage residing elsewhere), even though the in-marrying parent had left that compound.

Several scholars have remarked on the relative ease of divorce in some traditional African societies, particularly those in which matrilineal descent was the rule (for example, Fortes 1950, 283). Jack Goody (1976, 64) has even suggested that the rate of divorce in precolonial Africa was higher than in parts of Europe and Asia in comparable periods as a corollary of contrasting patterns of property transmission, contrasting attitudes toward the remarriage of women (especially widows), and contrasting implications of polygyny and monogamy. If indeed there was a higher incidence of divorce in precolonial Africa, this would not be inconsistent with the wide-ranging emphasis on consanguinity in Africa as opposed to conjugality in Europe.

Marriage in Africa was a contractual union which often involved long-lasting companionate relationships, but it was not expected to be the all-encompassing, exclusive relationship of the Euro-American ideal type. Both men and women relied on their extended families and friends, as well as on their spouses, for emotionally gratifying relationships. Often, too, in the context of polygyny women as well as men had sexual liaisons with more than one partner. A woman's clandestine affairs did not necessarily lead to divorce because, in the absence of publicized information to the contrary, her husband was considered the father of all her children (Radcliffe-Brown 1950). And in the context of the lineage (especially the patrilineage), all men aspired to have as many children as possible.

Interpersonal relationships within African families were governed by principles and values which I have elsewhere summarized under the concepts of respect, restraint, responsibility, and reciprocity. Common to all these principles was a notion of commitment to the collectivity. The family offered a network of security, but it also imposed a burden of obligations (Sudarkasa 1980, 49–50). From the foregoing discussion, it should be understandable that, in their material form, these obligations extended first and foremost to consanguineal kin. Excepting the gifts that were exchanged at the time of marriage, the material obligations entailed in the conjugal relationship and the wider affinal relationships created by marriage were of a lesser magnitude than those associated with "blood" ties.

Afro-American Family Structure: Interpreting the African Connection

Rather than start with the question of what was *African* about the families established by those Africans who were enslaved in America, it would be more appropriate to ask what was *not* African about them. Most of the Africans who were captured and brought to America arrived without any members of their families, but they brought with them the societal codes they had learned regarding family life. To argue that the trans-Atlantic voyage and the trauma of enslavement made them forget, or rendered useless their memories of how they had been brought up or how they had lived before their capture is to argue from premises laden with myths about the Black experience (Elkins [1959] 1963, 101–102; see also Frazier [1939] 1966, ch. 1).

Given the African tradition of multilingualism and the widespread use of lingua francas (Maquet 1972, 18–25)—which in West Africa would include Hausa, Yoruba, Djoula, and Twi—it is probable that many more of the enslaved Africans could communicate among themselves than is implied by those

who remark on the multiplicity of "tribes" represented among the slaves. As Landman (1978, 80) has pointed out: "In many areas of the world, individuals are expected to learn only one language in the ordinary course of their lives. But many Africans have been enculturated in social systems where multiple language or dialect acquisition have been regarded as normal." The fact that Africans typically spoke three to five languages also makes it understandable why they quickly adopted "pidginized" forms of European languages as lingua francas for communicating among themselves and with their captors.

The relationships which the Blacks in America established among themselves would have reflected their own backgrounds *and* the conditions in which they found themselves. It is as erroneous to try to attribute what developed among them solely to slavery as it is to attribute it solely to the African background. Writers such as Herbert Gutman (1976), who emphasize the "adaptive" nature of "slave culture" must ask what it was that was being adapted as well as in what context this adaptation took place. Moreover, they must realize that adaptation does not necessarily imply extensive modification of an institution, especially when its structure is already suited (or "preadapted") to survival in the new context. Such an institution was the African extended family, which had served on that continent, in various environments and different political contexts, as a unit of production and distribution; of socialization, education, and social control; and of emotional and material support for the aged and the infirm as well as the hale and hearty (Kerri 1979; Okediji 1975; Shimkin and Uchendu 1978; Sudarkasa 1975b).

The extended family networks that were formed during slavery by Africans *and their descendants* were based on the institutional heritage which the Africans had brought with them to this continent, and the specific forms they took reflected the influence of European-derived institutions as well as the political and economic circumstances in which the enslaved population found itself.

The picture of Black families during slavery has become clearer over the past decade, particularly as a result of the wealth of data in Gutman's justly heralded study. Individual households were normally comprised of a conjugal pair, their children, and sometimes their grandchildren, other relatives, or nonkin. Marriage was usually monogamous, but polygynous unions where the wives lived in separate households have also been reported (Gutman 1976, 59, 158; Blassingame 1979, 171; Perdue et al. 1980, 209).

Probably only in a few localities did female-headed households constitute as much as one-quarter of all households (Gutman 1976, esp. chs. 1–3). The rarity of this household type was in keeping with the African tradition whereby women normally bore children within the context of marriage and lived in monogamous or polygynous conjugal families that were part of larger extended families. I have tried to show elsewhere why it is inappropriate to apply the term "nuclear family" to the mother-child dyads within African polygynous families (Sudarkasa 1980, 43–46). In some African societies—especially in matrilineal ones—a small percentage of previously married women, or married women living apart from their husbands, might head households that were usually attached to larger compounds. However, in my view, on the question of the origin of female-headed households among Blacks in America, Herskovits was wrong, and Frazier was right in attributing this development to conditions that arose during slavery and in the context of urbanization in later periods (Frazier [1939] 1966; Herskovits [1941] 1958; Furstenberg et al. 1975).

Gutman's data suggest that enslaved women

who had their first children out of wedlock did not normally set up independent households, but rather continued to live with their parents. Most of them subsequently married and set up neolocal residence with their husbands. The data also suggest that female-headed households developed mainly in two situations: (1) a woman whose husband died or was sold off the plantation might head a household comprised of her children and perhaps her grandchildren born to an unmarried daughter; (2) a woman who did not marry after having one or two children out of wedlock but continued to have children (no doubt often for the "master") might have her own cabin built for her (Gutman 1976, chs. 1–3).

It is very important to distinguish these two types of female-headed households, the first being only a phase in the developmental cycle of a conjugally headed household, and the second being a case of neolocal residence by an unmarried female. The pattern of households headed by widows was definitely not typical of family structure in Africa, where normally a widow married another member of her deceased husband's lineage. The pattern of neolocal residence by an unmarried woman with children would have been virtually unheard of in Africa. Indeed, it was also relatively rare among enslaved Blacks and in Black communities in later periods. Before the twentieth-century policy of public assistance for unwed mothers, virtually all young unmarried mothers in Black communities continued to live in households headed by other adults. If in later years they did establish their own households, these tended to be tied into transresidential family networks.

The existence during slavery of long-lasting conjugal unions among Blacks was not a departure from African family tradition. Even with the relative ease of divorce in matrilineal societies, most Africans lived in marital unions that ended only with the death of one of the spouses. In the patrilineal societies from which most American Blacks were taken, a number of factors, including the custom of returning bridewealth payments upon the dissolution of marriage, served to encourage marital stability (Radcliffe-Brown 1950, 43–54). Given that the conditions of slavery did not permit the *replication* of African families, it might be expected that the husband and wife as elders in the household would assume even greater importance than they had in Africa, where the elders within the consanguineal core of the extended family and those among the wives would have had major leadership roles within the compound.

When the distinction is made between family and household—and, following Bender (1967), between the composition of the co-resident group and the domestic functions associated with both households and families—it becomes apparent that the question of who lived with whom during slavery (or later) must be subordinate to the questions of who was doing what for whom and what kin relationships were maintained over space and time. In any case, decisions concerning residence per se were not always in the hands of the enslaved Blacks themselves, and space alone served as a constraint on the size, and consequently to some extent on the composition, of the "slave" cabins.

That each conjugally based household formed a primary unit for food consumption and production among the enslaved Blacks is consistent with domestic organization within the African compound. However, Gutman's data, and those reported by enslaved Blacks themselves, on the strong bonds of obligation among kinsmen suggest that even within the constraints imposed by the slave regime, transresidential cooperation—including that between households in different localities—was the rule rather than the exception (Gutman 1976, esp. 131–138; Perdue et al. 1980, esp.

26, 256, 323). One might hypothesize that on the larger plantations with a number of Black families related through consanguineal and affinal ties, the households of these families might have formed groupings similar to African compounds. Certainly we know that in later times such groupings were found in the South Carolina Sea Islands and other parts of the South (Agbasegbe 1976, 1981; Gutman 1976; Johnson 1934, ch. 2; Powdermaker 1939, ch. 8).

By focusing on extended families (rather than simply on households) among the enslaved Blacks, it becomes apparent that these kin networks had many of the features of continental African extended families. These Afro-American groupings were built around consanguineal kin whose spouses were related to or incorporated into the networks in different degrees. The significance of the consanguineal principle in these networks is indicated by Gutman's statement that "the pull between ties to an immediate family and to an enlarged kin network sometimes strained husbands and wives" (1976, 202; see also Frazier [1939] 1966, pt. 2).

The literature on Black families during slavery provides a wealth of data on the way in which consanguineal kin assisted each other with child rearing, in life crisis events such as birth and death, in work groups, in efforts to obtain freedom, and so on. They maintained their networks against formidable odds and, after slavery, sought out those parents, siblings, aunts, and uncles from whom they had been torn (Blassingame 1979; Genovese 1974; Gutman 1976; Owens 1976). Relationships within these groups were governed by principles and values stemming from the African background. Respect for elders and reciprocity among kinsmen are noted in all discussions of Black families during slavery. The willingness to assume responsibility for relatives beyond the conjugal family and selflessness (a form of restraint) in the face of these responsibilities are also characteristics attributed to the enslaved population.

As would be expected, early Afro-American extended families differed from their African prototypes in ways that reflected the influence of slavery and of Euro-American values, especially their proscriptions, and prescriptions regarding mating, marriage, and the family. No doubt, too, the Euro-American emphasis on the primacy of marriage within the family reinforced conjugality among the Afro-Americans even though the "legal" marriage of enslaved Blacks was prohibited. As DuBois noted at the turn of the century, African corporate lineages could not survive intact during slavery. Hence, the consanguineal core groups of Afro-American extended families differed in some ways from those of their African antecendents. It appears that in some of these Afro-American families membership in the core group was traced bilaterally, whereas in others there was a unilineal emphasis without full-fledged lineages.

Interestingly, after slavery, some of the corporate functions of African lineages reemerged in some extended families which became property-owning collectivities. I have suggested elsewhere that "the disappearance of the lineage principle or its absorption into the concept of extended family" is one of the aspects of the transformation of African family organization in America that requires research (Sudarkasa 1980, 57). Among the various other issues that remain to be studied concerning these extended families are these: (1) Did members belong by virtue of bilateral or unilineal descent from a common ancestor or because of shared kinship with a living person? (2) How were group boundaries established and maintained? (3) What was the nature and extent of the authority of the elder(s)? (4) How long did the group last and what factors determined its span in time and space?

Conclusion

At the outset of this chapter it was suggested that a holistic explanation of Black family organization requires discarding or recasting some of the debates which have framed discussions in the past. I have tried to show why it is time to move beyond the debate over whether it was slavery *or* the African heritage which "determined" Black family organization to a synthesis which looks at institutional transformation as well as institutional transfer for the interplay between Africa and America in shaping the family structures of Afro-Americans.

Obviously, Black families have changed over time, and today one would expect that the evidence for African "retentions" (Herskovits [1941] 1958, xxii–xxiii) in them would be more controvertible than in the past. Nevertheless, the persistence of some features of African family organization among contemporary Black American families has been documented for both rural and urban areas. Although this study cannot attempt a full-scale analysis of these features and the changes they have undergone, it is important to make reference to one of them, precisely because it impacts upon so many other aspects of Black family organization, and because its connection to Africa has not been acknowledged by most contemporary scholars. I refer to the emphasis on consanguinity noted especially among lower-income Black families and those in the rural South. Some writers, including Shimkin and Uchendu (1978), Agbasegbe (1976, 1981), Aschenbrenner (1973, 1975, 1978; Aschenbrenner and Carr 1980) and the present author (1975a, 1980, 1981) have dealt explicitly with this concept in their discussions of Black family organization. However, without labeling it as such, many other scholars have described some aspects of the operation of consaguinity within the Black family in their discussions of "matrifocality" and "female-headed households." Too often, the origin of this consanguineal emphasis in Black families, which can be manifest even in households with both husband and wife present, is left unexplained or is "explained" by labeling it an "adaptive" characteristic.

In my view, historical realities require that the derivation of this aspect of Black family organization be traced to its African antecedents. Such a view does not deny the adaptive significance of consanguineal networks. In fact, it helps to clarify why these networks had the flexibility they had and why they, rather than conjugal relationships, came to be the stabilizing factor in Black families. The significance of this principle of organization is indicated by the list of Black family characteristics derived from it.

Some writers have viewed the consanguineally based extended family as a factor of *instability* in the Black family because it sometimes undermines the conjugal relationships in which its members are involved. I would suggest that historically among Black Americans the concept of "family" meant first and foremost relationships created by "blood" rather than by marriage. (R. T. Smith [1973] has made substantially the same point with respect to West Indian family organization.) Children were socialized to think in terms of obligations to parents (especially mothers), siblings, and others defined as "close kin." Obligations to "outsiders," who would include prospective spouses and in-laws, were definitely less compelling. Once a marriage took place, if the demands of the conjugal relationship came into irreconcilable conflict with consanguineal commitments, the former would often be sacrificed. Instead of interpreting instances of *marital* instability as prima facie evidence of family instability, it should be realized that the fragility of the conjugal relationship could be a consequence or

corollary of the *stability* of the consanguineal family network. Historically, such groups survived by nurturing a strong sense of responsibility among members and by fostering a code of reciprocity which could strain relations with persons not bound by it.

Not all Black families exhibit the same emphasis on consanguineal relationships. Various factors, including education, occupational demands, aspirations toward upward mobility, and acceptance of American ideals concerning marriage and the family, have moved some (mainly middle- and upper-class) Black families toward conjugally focused households and conjugally centered extended family groupings. Even when such households include relatives other than the nuclear family, those relatives tend to be subordinated to the conjugal pair who form the core of the group. This contrasts with some older type Black families where a senior relative (especially the wife's or the husband's mother) could have a position of authority in the household equal to or greater than that of one or both of the spouses. Children in many contemporary Black homes are not socialized to think in terms of the parent-sibling group as the primary kin group, but rather in terms of their future spouses and families of procreation as the main source of their future emotional and material satisfaction and support. Among these Blacks the nuclear household tends to be more isolated in terms of instrumental functions, and such extended family networks as exist tend to be clusters of nuclear families conforming to the model put forth by Murdock (1949, chs. 1 and 2).

For scholars interested in the heritage of Europe as well as the heritage of Africa in Afro-American family organization, a study of the operation of the principles of conjugality and consanguinity in these families would provide considerable insight into the ways in which these two institutional traditions have been interwoven. By looking at the differential impact of these principles in matters of household formation, delegation of authority, maintenance of solidarity and support, acquisition and transmission of property, financial management, and so on (Sudarkasa 1981), and by examining the political and economic variables which favor the predominance of one or the other principle, we will emerge with questions and formulations that can move us beyond debates over "pathology" and "normalcy" in Black family life.

NOTE

Acknowledgments: I wish to thank Tao-Lin Hwang for his assistance with the research for this chapter, and Bamidele Agbasegbe Demerson for his helpful comments.

REFERENCES

Agbasegbe, B. (1976) "The role of wife in the Black extended family: perspectives from a rural community in Southern United States," pp. 124–138 in D. McGuigan (ed.) *New Research on Women and Sex Roles.* Ann Arbor: Center for Continuing Education of Women, University of Michigan.

——— (1981) "Some aspects of contemporary rural Afroamerican family life in the Sea Islands of Southeastern United States." Presented at the Annual Meeting of the Association of Social and Behavioral Scientists, Atlanta, Georgia, March 1981.

Allen, W. R. (1978) "The search for applicable theories of Black family life." *Journal of Marriage and the Family* 40 (February): 117–129.

——— (1979) "Class, culture, and family organization: the effects of class and race on family structure in urban America." *Journal of Comparative Family Studies* 10 (Autumn): 301–313.

Aschenbrenner, J. (1973) "Extended families among Black Americans." *Journal of Comparative Family Studies* 4:257–268.

——— (1975) *Lifelines: Black Families in Chicago.* New York: Holt, Rinehart & Winston.

——— (1978) "Continuities and variations in Black family structure," pp. 181–200 in D. B. Shimkin, E. M. Shimkin, and D. A. Frate (eds.) *The Extended Family in Black Societies.* The Hague: Mouton.

Aschenbrenner, J., and C. H. Carr (1980) "Conjugal relationships in the context of the Black extended family." *Alternative Lifestyles* 3 (November): 463–484.

Bender, D. R. (1967) "A refinement of the concept of household: families, co-residence, and domestic functions." *American Anthropologist* 69 (October): 493–504.

Billingsley, A. (1968) *Black Families in White America.* Englewood Cliffs, NJ: Prentice-Hall.

Blassingame, J. W. (1979) *The Slave Community.* New York: Oxford University Press.

Colson, E. (1962) "Family change in contemporary Africa." *Annals of the New York Academy of Sciences* 96 (January): 641–652.

DuBois, W.E.B. (1969) *The Negro American Family.* New York: New American Library. (Originally published, 1908.)

Elkins, S. (1963) *Slavery: A Problem in American Intellectual Life.* New York: Grosset and Dunlap. (Originally published, 1959.)

English, R. (1974) "Beyond pathology: research and theoretical perspectives on Black families," pp. 39–52 in L. E. Gary (ed.) *Social Research and the Black Community: Selected Issues and Priorities.* Washington, DC: Institute for Urban Affairs and Research, Howard University.

Fortes, M. (1949) *The Web of Kinship among the Tallensi.* London: Oxford University Press.

——— (1950) "Kinship and marriage among the Ashanti," pp. 252–284 in A. R. Radcliffe-Brown and D. Forde (eds.) *African Systems of Kinship and Marriage.* London: Oxford University Press.

——— (1953) "The structure of unilineal descent groups." *American Anthropologist* 55 (January–March): 17–41.

Frazier, E. F. (1966) *The Negro Family in the United States.* Chicago: University of Chicago Press. (Originally published, 1939.)

Furstenberg, F., T. Hershbert, and J. Modell (1975) "The origins of the female-headed Black family: the impact of the urban experience." *Journal of Interdisciplinary History* 6 (Autumn): 211–233.

Genovese, E. D. (1974) *Roll Jordan Roll: The World the Slaves Made.* New York: Random House.

Goody, J. (1976) *Production and Reproduction: A Comparative Study of the Domestic Domain.* Cambridge: Cambridge University Press.

Gutman, H. (1976) *The Black Family in Slavery and Freedom: 1750–1925.* New York: Random House.

Herskovits, M. J. (1958) *The Myth of the Negro Past.* Boston: Beacon. (Originally published, 1941.)

Johnson, C. S. (1934) *Shadow of the Plantation.* Chicago: University of Chicago Press.

Kerri, J. N. (1979) "Understanding the African family: persistence, continuity, and change." *Western Journal of Black Studies* 3 (Spring): 14–17.

Landman, R. H. (1978) "Language policies and their implications for ethnic relations in the newly sovereign states of Sub-Saharan Africa," pp. 69–90 in B. M. duToit (ed.) *Ethnicity in Modern Africa.* Boulder, CO: Westview Press.

Linton, R. (1936) *The Study of Man.* New York: Appleton-Century-Crofts.

Lloyd, P. C. (1968) "Divorce among the Yoruba." *American Anthropologist* 70 (February): 67–81.

Maquet, J. (1972) *Civilizations of Black Africa.* London: Oxford University Press.

Marshall, G. A. (Niara Sudarkasa) (1968) "Marriage: comparative analysis," in *International Encyclopedia of the Social Sciences,* vol. 10. New York: Macmillan/Free Press.

Murdock, G. P. (1949) *Social Structure.* New York: Macmillan.

Nobles, W. (1974a) "African root and American fruit: the Black family." *Journal of Social and Behavioral Sciences* 20:52–64.

———— (1974b) "Africanity: its role in Black families." *The Black Scholar* 9 (June): 10–17.

———— (1978) "Toward an empirical and theoretical framework for defining Black families." *Journal of Marriage and the Family* 40 (November): 679–688.

Okediji, P. A. (1975) "A psychosocial analysis of the extended family: the African case." *African Urban Notes,* Series B, 1 (3):93–99. (African Studies Center, Michigan State University.)

Onwuejeogwu, M. A. (1975) *The Social Anthropology of Africa: An Introduction.* London: Heinemann.

Oppong, C. (1974) *Marriage Among a Matrilineal Elite: A Family Study of Ghanaian Senior Civil Servants,* Cambridge: Cambridge University Press.

Owens, L. H. (1976) *This Species of Property: Slave Life and Culture in the Old South.* New York: Oxford University Press.

Perdue, C. L., Jr., T. E. Barden, and R. K. Phillips (eds.) (1980) *Weevils in the Wheat: Interviews with Virginia Ex-Slaves.* Bloomington: Indiana University Press.

Powdermaker, H. (1939) *After Freedom: A Cultural Study in the Deep South.* New York: Viking.

Radcliffe-Brown, A. R. (1950) "Introduction," pp. 1–85 to A. R. Radcliffe-Brown and D. Forde (eds.) *African Systems of Kinship and Marriage.* London: Oxford University Press.

Radcliffe-Brown, A. R., and D. Forde (eds.) (1950) *African Systems of Kinship and Marriage.* London: Oxford University Press.

Rivers, W.H.R. (1924) *Social Organization.* New York: Alfred Knopf.

Robertson, C. (1976) "Ga women and socioeconomic change in Accra, Ghana," pp. 111–133 in N. J. Hafkin and E. G. Bay (eds.) *Women in Africa: Studies in Social and Economic Change.* Stanford: Stanford University Press.

Shimkin, D., and V. Uchendu (1978) "Persistence, borrowing, and adaptive changes in Black kinship systems: some issues and their significance," pp. 391–406 in D. Shimkin, E. M. Shimkin, and D. A. Frate (eds.) *The Extended Family in Black Societies.* The Hague: Mouton.

Shimkin, D., E. M. Shimkin, and D. A. Frate (eds.) (1978) *The Extended Family in Black Societies.* The Hague: Mouton.

Shorter, E. (1975) *The Making of the Modern Family.* New York: Basic Books.

Smith, R. T. (1973) "The matrifocal family," pp. 121–144 in J. Goody (ed.) *The Character of Kinship.* Cambridge: Cambridge University Press.

Stack, C. (1974) *All Our Kin.* New York: Harper & Row.

Staples, R. (1971) "Toward a sociology of the Black family: a decade of theory and research." *Journal of Marriage and the Family* 33 (February): 19–38.

———— (ed.) (1978) *The Black Family: Essays and Studies.* Belmont, CA: Wadsworth.

Stone, L. (1975) "The rise of the nuclear family in early modern England: the patriarchal stage," pp. 13–57 in C. E. Rosenberg (ed.) *The Family in History.* Philadelphia: University of Pennsylvania Press.

Sudarkasa, N. (1973) "Where women work: a study of Yoruba women in the marketplace and in the home." *Anthropoligical Papers No. 53.* Ann Arbor: Museum of Anthropology, University of Michigan.

———— (1975a) "An exposition on the value premises underlying Black family studies." *Journal of the National Medical Association* 19 (May): 235–239.

———— (1975b) "National development planning for the promotion and protection of the family." *Proceedings of the Conference on Social Research and National Development,* E. Akeredolu-Ale (ed.) Nigerian Institute of Social and Economic Research, Ibadan, Nigeria.

———— (1976) "Female employment and family organization in West Africa," pp. 48–63 in D. G. McGuigan (ed.) *New Research on Women and Sex Roles.* Ann Arbor: Center for Continuing Education of Women, University of Michigan.

———— (1980) "African and Afro-American family structure: a comparison." *The Black Scholar* 11 (November–December): 37–60.

———— (1981) "Understanding the dynamics of consanguinity and conjugality in contemporary Black family organization." Presented at the Seventh Annual Third World Conference, Chicago, March 1981.

Tilly, L. A., and J. W. Scott (1978) *Women, Work, and Family.* New York: Holt, Rinehart & Winston.

Uchendu, V. (1965) *The Igbo of South-Eastern Nigeria.* New York: Holt, Rinehart & Winston.

Ware, H. (1979) "Polygyny: women's views in a transitional society, Nigeria 1975." *Journal of Marriage and the Family* 41 (February): 185–195.

Woodson, C. G. (1936) *The African Background Outlined.* Washington, DC: Association for the Study of Negro Life and History.

 # Part II

Families Within Society

The chapters in this part make a compelling case for why families need to be understood within a larger political and economic context. They illustrate the complex and permeable boundaries of families, tied in various ways to the economy and the local community. The transition to an industrial and then post-industrial economy, for example, has profoundly shaped the resources and opportunities available to individuals and families. As John D'Emilio makes clear in "Capitalism and Gay Identity," industrial capitalism, with its system of wage labor, created, for virtually the first time in history, the ability for nonwealthy individuals to survive outside a formal kin system. For lesbians and gay men who have been defined outside the bounds of the nuclear family, this has created opportunities as well as new forms of oppression.

Families are creative entities that do more than simply react to the forces of the market. Family members strategize in the context of structural forces and negotiate internal dynamics, which in turn influence the economy. For example, in "Bread Before Roses," Martha May documents the historical battles of the working classes to earn a wage sufficient to support an entire family. That struggle in the nineteenth and early twentieth centuries also included successful campaigns to limit the workday—from twelve to ten to eventually eight hours. Economist Juliet B. Schor finds in "Time Squeeze" that during the past several decades there has been an unprecedented reversal away from a shorter work week. She discovers that not only are more people working now but also people are working longer hours and taking shorter vacations. The rise of the standard of living in post–World War II society has been maintained in the 1970s, 1980s, and 1990s only through the addition of the paid labor of wives and mothers in dual-earner households. Even with women's increased labor force participation, median family income went up only 6 percent between 1973 and 1990 (Hernandez, Chapter 15). This family speed-up has resulted in a reduction in leisure time and a corresponding decrease in the amount of time parents spend with children. This prompts the question: how will these changes affect women, men, and children in the long run?

Donald J. Hernandez begins with his eye on children. He reports in "Children's Changing Access to Resources" that with the rise in dual-earner families, the rise in divorce, and the decline in large families, over the course of the twentieth century children have fewer siblings, spend less time with their fathers and mothers, and benefit from few economic resources. And whether children live in poverty is greatly influenced by the kind of family with whom they reside. Hernandez argues that public policy should directly address the development and well-being of children, because children can fall through the cracks of policies targeted to families, workers, or even parents.

Families flexibly (although not painlessly) adapt themselves to the economy. Race-ethnicity and class affect the options that families consider, those that they desire, and the ways that they take action. The effects of culture and class are so fundamental that they fashion mealtimes and affect the kinds of food that families can buy and serve. In a probing investigation of how families feed themselves, titled "Affluence and Poetry in Feeding the Family," Marjorie L. DeVault analyzes the class dimensions of food and the symbolic purposes of eating rituals. Maura I. Toro-Morn presents another example of family adaptability in her investigation of families that migrate to the mainland United States in order to compensate for diminished economic opportunities. Her chapter, "Gender, Class, Family, and Migration," analyzes the process of the transition to U.S. society, to which Puerto Ricans bring kinship systems and cultural ways of managing the contradictory demands of wage labor and intensive child rearing.

The numerous struggles that families mount to fight the negative effects of an ever-powerful economy do not deflect the question of what our society should do as a whole to stem inequalities generated by the market. What is the responsibility of the government in mediating the harsh effects of the economy? Several articles identify the importance of government supports and transfer payments, such as food stamps, nutritional programs for pregnant women, social security, and, for homeowners, mortgage deductibility on income tax. Julianne Malveaux, an economist, investigates the economy-government nexus from a particular vantage point, scrutinizing the conditions of older women living in poverty. In "Race, Poverty, and Women's Aging," she finds that social security diminishes income inequality but does not eliminate poverty. And because of the life-long effects of race and gender inequalities in the structure of employment, poverty is more likely to circumscribe life for women of color than for white women. It is also more likely to affect women than men. The contrast with European countries, which provide better social benefits to families, challenges the wisdom of the public assistance and food stamp cutbacks of the Clinton administration and the 120th Congress. These actions will have an enormous impact on our society's future generations.

The chapter in the section "Families and Community" illustrate how families are deeply intertwined with networks of people and societal institutions. In "The Anti-Social Family," a chapter from their now classic book by the same name, Michèle Barrett and Mary McIntosh criticize the organization of the modern nuclear family and how it privileges privacy. They point to the ways the middle-class nuclear family erects boundaries around itself, inhibiting any interference or assistance from elsewhere, be it nutritional programs for pregnant women or child-rearing advice from neighbors.

While this portrait may capture white middle-class *ideology,* other chapters in this section argue that family *practices* are social. Laurel Thatcher Ulrich's history of early New England reveals the extensive economic interdependence of colonial families who have been characterized in historiography as autonomous, independent farmers. In "Housewife and Gadder," Ulrich traces the daily lives of women—the reciprocal sociability, the care for the sick, and the exchanges of weaving—that created a sustained female "secondary" economy, indistinguishable from the community. Studying the late-twentieth century, Barry Wellman maps individuals' extensive social interdependence with kin and nonkin. In "The Place of Kinfolk in Personal Community Networks," he reports that, in the age of e-mail, telephones, and jets, people maintain very intense ties even with family and friends who reside some distance away.

Some people act "in the name of the family" in the political arena as well (Stacey 1996). Conservative Christian rhetoric has never fallen short of singing the virtues of family life. But as a host of these chapters demonstrate, what constitutes "the family" and "family values" and the family's "best interests" is infinitely malleable. In "Mexican American Women Grassroots Community Activists," Mary Pardo shows how some outspoken Mexican American mothers, in a controversial dispute over toxic-waste dumps and prison construction in East Los Angeles, refuse to confine their domestic concerns solely to their own households. These women consider the best interests of the neighborhood to be indistinguishable from a responsibility to all children, not just to biological offspring. Their broad interpretation of motherhood launches them into the role of civic heroes as they fight city hall and the California legislature. Their efforts beautifully illustrate the ways that family boundaries are continuously reinterpreted.

REFERENCES

Stacey, Judith. 1996. *In the Name of the Family: Rethinking Family Values in the Postmodern Age.* Boston: Beacon Press.

~ Section A

Families and the Economy

∾ *Chapter 9*

Time Squeeze: The Extra Month of Work

JULIET B. SCHOR

Time squeeze has become big news. In summer 1990, the première episode of Jane Pauley's television show, *Real Life,* highlighted a single father whose computer job was so demanding that he found himself at 2:00 A.M. dragging his child into the office. A Boston-area documentary featured the fourteen- to sixteen-hour workdays of a growing army of moonlighters. CBS's *Forty-Eight Hours* warned of the accelerating pace of life for everyone from high-tech business executives (for whom there are only two types of people—"the quick and the dead") to assembly workers at Japanese-owned automobile factories (where a car comes by every sixty seconds). Employees at fast-food restaurants, who serve in twelve seconds, report that the horns start honking if the food hasn't arrived in fifteen. Nineteen-year-olds work seventy-

Chapter 2, "Time Squeeze: The Extra Month of Work," from *The Overworked American: The Unexpected Decline of Leisure,* by Juliet B. Schor, copyright © 1991 by Basic-Books, Inc. Reprinted by permission of BasicBooks, a division of HarperCollins Publishers, Inc.

hour weeks, children are "penciled" into their parents' schedules, and second-graders are given "half an hour a day to unwind" from the pressure to get good grades so they can get into a good college. By the beginning of the 1990s, the time squeeze had become a national focus of attention, appearing in almost all the nation's major media outlets.[1]

The shortage of time has also become a staple of women's magazines and business publications. The subject is covered in major newspapers, such as the *New York Times,* the *Wall Street Journal,* and *USA Today,* as well as in the regional dailies. *Time* magazine devoted a cover story to the fact that "America has run out of time."[2] How-to books on time management have proliferated. Even Madison Avenue has discovered time poverty. In a 1990 commercial, statistics on the decline of leisure time flashed across the screen; then General Motors hawked its wares by promising to get the customer in and out of the showroom faster than the competition.

The time squeeze surfaced with the young urban professional. These high achievers had jobs that required sixty, eighty, even a hundred hours a week. On Wall Street, they would regularly stay at the office until midnight or go months without a single day off. Work consumed their lives. And if they weren't working, they were networking. They power-lunched, power-exercised, and power-married. As the pace of life accelerated, time became an ever-scarcer commodity, so they used their money to buy more of it. Cooking was replaced by gourmet frozen foods from upscale delis. Eventually the "meal" started disappearing, in favor of "grazing." Those who could afford it bought other people's time, hiring surrogates to shop, write their checks, or even just change a light bulb. They cut back on sleep and postponed having children. ("Can you carry a baby in a briefcase?" queried one Wall Street executive when she was asked about having kids.)[3]

High-powered people who spend long hours at their jobs are nothing new. Medical residents, top corporate management, and the self-employed have always had grueling schedules. But financiers used to keep bankers' hours, and lawyers had a leisured life. Now bankers work like doctors, and lawyers do the same. A former Bankers Trust executive remembers that "somebody would call an occasional meeting at 8 A.M. Then it became the regular 8 o'clock meeting. So there was the occasional 7 A.M. meeting. . . . It just kept spreading."[4] On Wall Street, economic warfare replaced the clubhouse atmosphere—and the pressure forced the hours up. As women and new ethnic groups were admitted into the industry, competition for the plum positions heightened—and the hours went along. Twenty-two-year-olds wear beepers as they squeeze in an hour for lunch or jogging at the health club.

What happened on Wall Street was replicated throughout the country in one high-income occupation after another. Associates

in law firms competed over who could log more billable hours. Workaholics set new standards of survival. Even America's sleepiest corporations started waking up; and when they did, the corporate hierarchies found themselves coming in to work a little earlier and leaving for home a little later. As many companies laid off white-collar people during the 1980s, those who remained did more for their monthly paychecks. A study of "downsizings" in auto-related companies in the Midwest found that nearly half of the two thousand managers polled said they were working harder than two years earlier.[5]

At cutting-edge corporations, which emphasize commitment, initiative, and flexibility, the time demands are often the greatest. "People who work for me should have phones in their bathrooms," says the CEO from one aggressive American company. Recent research on managerial habits reveals that work has become positively absorbing. When a deadline approached in one corporation, "people who had been working twelve-hour days and Saturdays started to come in on Sunday, and instead of leaving at midnight, they would stay a few more hours. Some did not go home at all, and others had to look at their watches to remember what day it was." The recent growth in small businesses has also contributed to overwork. When Dolores Kordek started a dental insurance company, her strategy for survival was to work harder than the competition. So the office was open from 7 A.M. to 10 P.M., 365 days a year. And she was virtually always in it.[6]

The combination of retrenchment, economic competition, and innovative business management has raised hours substantially. One poll of senior executives found that weekly hours rose during the 1980s, and vacation time fell. Other surveys have yielded similar results.[7] By the end of the decade, overwork at the upper echelons of the labor market had become endemic—and its scale was virtually unprecedented in living memory.

If the shortage of time had been confined to Wall Street or America's corporate boardrooms, it might have remained just a media curiosity. The number of people who work 80 hours a week and bring home—if they ever get there—a six-figure income is very small. But while the incomes of these rarefied individuals were out of reach, their schedules turned out to be downright common. As Wall Street waxed industrious, the longer schedules penetrated far down the corporate ladder, through middle management, into the secretarial pool, and even onto the factory floor itself.[8] Millions of ordinary Americans fell victim to the shortage of time.

The most visible group has been women, who are coping with a double load—the traditional duties associated with home and children and their growing responsibility for earning a paycheck. With nearly two-thirds of adult women now employed, and a comparable fraction of mothers on the job, it's no surprise that many American women find themselves operating in overdrive.[9] Many working mothers live a life of perpetual motion, effectively holding down two full-time jobs. They rise in the wee hours of the morning to begin the day with a few hours of laundry, cleaning, and other housework. Then they dress and feed the children and send them off to school. They themselves then travel to their jobs. The three-quarters of employed women with full-time positions then spend the next eight and a half hours in the workplace.

At the end of the official workday, it's back to the "second shift"—the duties of housewife and mother. Grocery shopping, picking up the children, and cooking dinner take up the next few hours. After dinner there's clean-up, possibly some additional housework, and, of course, more child care. Women describe themselves as "ragged," "bone-weary," "sink-ing in quicksand," and "busy every waking hour." For many, the workday rivals those for which the "satanic mills" of the Industrial Revolution grew justly infamous: twelve- or fourteen-hour stretches of labor. By the end of the decade, Ann Landers pronounced herself "awestruck at the number of women who work at their jobs and go home to another full-time job. . . . How do you do it?" she asked. Thousands of readers responded, with tales ranging from abandoned careers to near collapse. According to sociologist Arlie Hochschild of the University of California, working mothers are exhausted, even fixated on the topic of sleep. "They talked about how much they could 'get by on': . . . six and a half, seven, seven and a half, less, more . . . These women talked about sleep the way a hungry person talks about food."[10]

By my calculations, the total working time of employed mothers now averages about 65 hours a week. Of course, many do far more than the average—such as mothers with young children, women in professional positions, or those whose wages are so low that they must hold down two jobs just to scrape by. These women will be working 70 to 80 hours a week. And my figures are extremely conservative: they are the lowest among existing studies. A Boston study found that employed mothers *average* over 80 hours of housework, child care, and employment. Two nationwide studies of white, married couples are comparable: in the first, the average week was 87 hours; in the second, it ranged from 76 to 89, depending on the age of the oldest child.[11]

One might think that as women's working hours rose, husbands would compensate by spending less time on the job. But just the opposite has occurred. Men who work are also putting in longer hours. The 5:00 Dads of the 1950s and 1960s (those who were home for dinner and an evening with the family) are becoming an "endangered species." Thirty percent of men with children under fourteen report working fifty or more hours a week. And many of these 8:00 or 9:00 Dads aren't around on the weekends either. Thirty percent of them work Saturdays and/or Sundays at their regular employment. And many others use the weekends for taking on a second job.[12]

A twenty-eight-year-old Massachusetts factory worker explains the bind many fathers are in: "Either I can spend time with my family, or support them—not both." Overtime or a second job is financially compelling: "I can work 8–12 hours overtime a week at time and a half, and that's when the real money just starts to kick in. . . . If I don't work the OT my wife would have to work much longer hours to make up the difference, and our day care bill would double. . . . The trouble is, the little time I'm home I'm too tired to have any fun with them or be any real help around the house."[13] Among white-collar employees the problem isn't paid overtime, but the regular hours. To get ahead, or even just to hold on to a position, long days may be virtually mandatory.

Overwork is also rampant among the nation's poorly paid workers. At $5, $6, or even $7 an hour, annual earnings before taxes and deductions range from $10,000 to $14,000. Soaring rents alone have been enough to put many of these low earners in financial jeopardy. For the more than one-third of all workers now earning hourly wages of $7 and below, the pressure to lengthen hours has been inexorable. Valerie Connor, a nursing-home worker in Hartford, Connecticut, explains that "you just can't make it on one job." She and many of her co-workers have been led to work two eight-hour shifts a day. According to an official of the Service Employees International Union in New England, nearly one-third of their nursing-home employees now hold two full-time jobs. Changes in the low end of the labor market have also played a role. There is less full-time, stable employ-ment. "Twenty hours here, thirty hours there, and twenty hours here. That's what it takes to get a real paycheck," says Domenic Bozzotto, president of Boston's hotel and restaurant workers union, whose members are drowning in a sea of work. Two-job families? Those were the good old days, he says. "We've got four-job families." The recent influx of immigrants has also raised hours. I. N. Yazbek, an arrival from Lebanon, works ninety hours a week at three jobs. It's necessary, he says, for economic success.[14]

This decline of leisure has been reported by the Harris Poll, which has received widespread attention. Harris finds that since 1973 free time has fallen nearly 40 percent—from a median figure of 26 hours a week to slightly under 17. Other surveys, such as the 1989 Decision Research Corporation Poll, also reveal a loss of leisure. Although these polls have serious methodological drawbacks, their findings are not off the mark. A majority of working Americans—professionals, corporate management, "working" mothers, fathers, and lower paid workers—*are* finding themselves with less and less leisure time.[15]

Theories of the Time Squeeze

Although the symptoms of time squeeze are relatively uncontroversial—an acceleration in the pace of life, a rise in time-saving innovations, increasing stress, and role overload—analysts differ sharply in how they understand these phenomena. Social critic Jeremy Rifkin believes that what has changed is our perception of time itself. Everything is speeding up, and the culprit is technology. "The computer introduces . . . a time frame in which the nanosecond is the primary temporal measurement. The nanosecond is a billionth of a second, and though it is possible to conceive theoretically of a nanosecond . . . *it is not possible to experience it.* Never before has time been organized at a speed beyond the realm of consciousness." Once people become acclimated to the speed of the computer, normal human intercourse becomes laborious. Programmers get irritable and impatient. Children complain that their teachers talk too slowly, in comparison with Nintendo or Atari. And even the machines can be too slow. Sue Alstedt, a former AT&T manager, became impatient with the computer she bought to save her time at home: "I couldn't stand to wait for it, even though it was coming out at the rate of speech."[16]

Not everyone blames technology. A second theory is that we are merely victims of our own aspirations. We have become more demanding in terms of activities, goals, and achievements. And today's lifestyles "offer people more options than ever before," according to John P. Robinson, one of the nation's leading chroniclers of how people spend their time. This theme is echoed by another time-use expert: "We have become walking résumés. If you're not doing something, you're not creating and defining who you are." Since the time available to us to do and to define ourselves cannot increase, we are naturally frustrated. While some have suggested that this is merely a "baby-boom" problem, the evidence suggests it is more widespread.[17]

The idea of rising aspirations echoes views put forward more than twenty years ago by economists Gary Becker and Staffan Linder.[18] Becker's work was based on the simple observation that consuming takes time. As people get richer and own more and more consumer goods, there is less and less time to spend with each item. Unavoidably, use of the Walkman, the VCR, the camcorder, and concert tickets gets crammed into the space once occupied by the lone record player. Linder also believed that leisure time would eventually become hectic as people tried to keep up with the use

of an accumulating mountain of possessions. In *The Harried Leisure Class,* he predicted that growing affluence would lead people to switch to those activities that can be done quickly. Long courtships, leisurely walks on the beach, or lingering over the dinner table were destined for extinction. People would do more things at once and do them faster. Even if the amount of leisure time itself did not change, it would become much more harried.

At first blush, events appear to have borne out Linder's ingenious argument. The *New York Times* has already chronicled the quiet death of the dinner party, as he prophesized. ("Most people I know have turned their ovens into planters," notes one professional woman.) Life *has* become more harried—but probably not so much for the reasons Linder and Becker predicted. They anticipated that rising incomes would cause the frenzy. But for many workers, earning power reached a high point just after Linder's book was published, and has been declining since. By this analysis, their lives should have become *less* harried. What Linder did not foresee was that the growing demands of work would lead to a decline in leisure time itself.[19]

There is undoubtedly truth in the ideas that technology and aspirations have led to an accelerated sense of time. But both these explanations have missed a much more obvious force operating in our lives. Time was become more precious because people have less of it to call their own. We have become a harried *working,* rather then leisure, class, as jobs take up an ever larger part of ever more Americans' lives.

Doing More for the Paycheck

Behind the mushrooming of worktime is a convergence of various trends. These include an increase in the number of people who hold paying jobs; a rise in weekly hours and in weeks worked each year; and reductions in paid time off, sick leave, and absences from work.

More People Working

The mythical American family of the 1950s and 1960s was comprised of five people, only one of whom "worked"—or at least did what society called work. Dad went off to his job every morning, while Mom and the three kids stayed at home. Of course, the 1950s-style family was never as common as popular memory has made it out to be. Even in the 1950s and 1960s, about one-fourth of wives with children held paying jobs. The nostalgia surrounding the family is especially inaccurate for African American women, whose rates of job holding have historically been higher than whites'. Even so, in recent years, the steady growth of married women's participation in the labor force has made the "working women" the rule rather than the exception. By 1990, two-thirds of married American women were participating in the paid labor market.[20]

Female employment has justifiably received widespread attention: it is certainly the most significant development afoot. But the expansion of work effort in the American family is not occurring just among women. American youth are also working harder in a reversal of a long decline of teenage job holding, the result of increased schooling and economic prosperity. The likelihood that a teenager would hold a job began to rise in the mid-1960s, just as adult hours began their upward climb. By 1990, the labor force participation rate of teens had reached 53.7 percent, nearly 10 points higher than it had been twenty-five years earlier.

Not only are more of the nation's young people working, but they are working longer hours. A 1989 nationwide sweep by government inspectors uncovered wide-scale abuses

of child labor laws—violations of allowable hours, permissible activities, and ages of employment. Low-wage service sector establishments have been voracious in their appetite for teen labor, especially in regions with shortages of adult workers. In middle-class homes, much of this work is motivated by consumerism: teenagers buy clothes, music, even cars. Some observers are worried that the desire to make money has become a compulsion, with many young Americans now working full time, in addition to full-time school. A New Hampshire study found that 85 percent of the state's tenth- to twelfth-graders hold jobs, and 45 percent of them work more than twenty hours a week. At 10 P.M. on a school night, Carolyn Collignon is just beginning hour eight on her shift at Friendly's restaurant. Teachers report that students are falling asleep in class, getting lower grades, and cannot pursue afterschool activities. Robert Pimentel works five days a week at Wendy's to pay off loans on his car and $5,600 motorcycle, the purchase of which he now describes as a "bad move." Pimentel averages "maybe six hours of sleep a night. If you consider school a job, which it pretty much is, I put in a long day." He wants to go to college, but his grades have suffered.[21]

This is the picture in suburban America. In large urban centers, such as New York and Los Angeles, the problem is more serious. Inspectors have found nineteenth-century-style sweatshops where poor immigrants—young girls of twelve years and above—hold daytime jobs, missing out on school altogether. And a million to a million and a half migrant farmworker children—some as young as three and four years—are at work in the nation's fields. These families cannot survive without the effort of all their members.[22]

There is one ironic exception to the general trend of rising labor force participation: Dad, the mainstay of the 1950s family, is more likely to be out of the labor force than ever before. As women's rates of job holding have risen, men's have fallen. The male decline is somewhat less, from 89 percent in 1948 to 78 percent in 1987, but still substantial. This pattern for men should give us pause. Does it contradict our picture of overwork in America? Does it represent a trend toward increasing leisure, albeit among only half the population?

There can be little doubt that many men, especially the elderly, are experiencing newfound leisure. In 1948, almost half of all men aged sixty-five and above were in the labor force; by 1987, the figure had fallen to 16 percent. Social Security, private pension plans, and prosperity have made possible a longer period of leisure at the end of life than ever before.[23]

Yet it would be a serious mistake to characterize as "at leisure" all the men who are out of the labor force. Among young males, schooling—which counts as productive activity and cannot be properly measured as leisure time—has been a major cause of labor force withdrawal. The underground economy is also a source of unmeasured work for young men. A closer look than the standard statistics provide will reveal that much of the "leisure" of older males is involuntary, particularly for the substantial numbers now leaving the labor force before age sixty-five. According to a 1990 survey of men between the ages of fifty-five and sixty-four who are out of the labor force, almost half (45 percent) would prefer to have jobs, a far larger percentage than has previously been recognized. Mandatory retirement and pressures to take early leave have led many unwillingly out of the world of work. Plant closings, corporate restructuring, and ageism have contributed to their difficulties in finding re-remployment. Among African-American men, the unemployment situation is about twice as bad as for whites, and participation rates have fallen far more.[24]

More Hours of Work

My estimates—the first comprehensive calculations of worktime spanning the last two decades—confirm not only that more people are working but also that they are working more. These statistics solve several problems associated with most measures: These are annual, rather than simply weekly, figures. They account for changes in jobs and hours worked which are made within any one year. They are calculated at comparable points in the business cycle to avoid spurious trends. And perhaps most important, they correct for the growth of unemployment and underemployment, which artificially reduces the uncorrected figures.

According to my estimates, the average employed person is now on the job an additional 163 hours, or the equivalent of an extra month a year (see Table 1). Hours have been increasing throughout the twenty-year period for which we have data. The breakdown for men and women shows lengthening hours for both groups, but there is a "gender gap" in the size of the increase. Men are working nearly one hundred (98) more hours per year, or two and a half extra weeks. Women are doing about three hundred (305) additional hours, which translates to seven and a half weeks, or thirty-eight added days of work each year. The research shows that hours have risen across a wide spectrum of Americans and in

TABLE 1. Annual Hours of Paid Employment, Labor Force Participants*

	1969	1987	Change 1969–87
All participants	1,786	1,949	163
Men	2,054	2,152	98
Women	1,406	1,711	305

Source: Author's estimates.
*Includes only fully employed labor force participants.

all income categories—low, middle, and high. The increase is common to a variety of family patterns—people with and without children, those who are married, and those who are not. And it has been general across industries and, most probably, occupations.[25]

The extra month of work is attributable to both longer weekly schedules and more weeks of work, as Table 2 indicates. As long as work is available, people are on the job more steadily throughout the year. This factor accounts for over two-thirds of the total increase in hours. It has been especially important for women, as they are increasingly working full time and year round. Women now take less time off for the birth of a child and are not as likely to stop working during the summer recess in order to care for children.[26] For better or worse, the pattern of women's employment is getting to look more and more like men's.

Weekly schedules are also getting longer, by about one hour per week (fifty-four min-

TABLE 2

Hours Worked per Week, Labor Force Participants*

	1969	1987
All participants	39.8	40.7
Men	43.0	43.8
Women	35.2	37.0

Weeks Worked per Year, Labor Force Participants*

	1969	1987
All participants	43.9	47.1
Men	47.1	48.5
Women	39.3	45.4

Source: Author's estimates.
*Includes only fully employed labor force participants.

utes, to be exact). This is the first sustained peacetime increase in weekly hours during the twentieth century. What is especially surprising is that it is not just women whose days are getting longer, but men as well. And after twenty years of increase, the proportion of employees on long schedules is substantial. In 1990, one-fourth of all full-time workers spent forty-nine or more hours on the job each week. Of these, almost half were at work sixty hours or more.[27]

Frequently, trends in weekly hours of work are caused by changes in a country's occupational or industrial makeup. Because doctors tend to have longer hours than teachers, an employment shift toward doctors and away from teachers will cause average hours to rise. Surprisingly, recent changes in the relative sizes of industries have on balance had no impact on hours. The growth in "short-hour" service jobs, such as those in retail trade, have been offset by rising numbers in "long-hour" areas, such as those that hire large numbers of professional or managerial workers, all of whom have above-average hours. My analysis shows that the shifts in industries have just about canceled each other out.[28]

So what's pushing up hours? One factor is moonlighting—the practice of holding more than one job at a time. Moonlighting is now more prevalent than at any time during the three decades for which we have statistics. As of May 1989, more than seven million Americans, or slightly over 6 percent of those employed, officially reported having two or more jobs, with extremely high increases occurring among women. The real numbers are higher, perhaps twice as high—as tax evasion, illegal activities, and employer disapproval of second jobs make people reluctant to speak honestly. The main impetus behind this extra work is financial. Close to one-half of those polled say they hold two jobs in order to meet regular household expenses or pay off debts.

As one might expect, this factor has become more compelling during the 1980s, with the disappearance of stable positions that pay a living wage and the increase of casual and temporary service sector employment.[29]

A second factor, operating largely on weekly hours, is that Americans are working more overtime. After the recession of the early 1980s, many companies avoided costly rehiring of workers and, instead, scheduled extra overtime. Among manufacturing employees, paid overtime hours rose substantially after the recession and, by the end of 1987, accounted for the equivalent of an additional five weeks of work per year. One automobile worker noted, "You have to work the hours, because a few months later they'll lay you off for a model changeover and you'll need the extra money when you're out of work. It never rains but it pours—either there's more than you can stand, or there isn't enough." While many welcome the chance to earn premium wages, the added effort can be onerous. Older workers are often compelled to stretch themselves, because many companies calculate pension benefits only on recent earnings. A fifty-nine-year-old male worker explains:

> Just as the point in my life where I was hoping I could ease up a little bit on the job and with the overtime, I find that I have to work harder than ever. If I'm going to have enough money when I retire, I have to put in five good years now with a lot of overtime because that is what they will base my pension on. With all the overtime I have to work to build my pension, I hope I live long enough to collect it.

(Apparently he didn't—he was diagnosed with incurable cancer not long after this interview.)[30]

The Shrinking Vacation

One of the most notable developments of the 1980s is that paid time off is actually shrinking.

European workers have been gaining vacation time—minimum allotments are now in the range of four to five weeks in many countries—but Americans are losing it. In the last decade, U.S. workers have gotten *less* paid time off—on the order of three and a half fewer days each year of vacation time, holidays, sick pay, and other paid absences. This decline is even more striking in that it reverses thirty years of progress in terms of paid time off (see Figure 1).

Part of the shrinkage has been caused by the economic squeeze many companies faced in the 1980s. Cost-cutting measures often included reductions in vacations and holidays. DuPont reduced its top vacation allotment from seven to four weeks and eliminated three holidays a year. Personnel departments also tightened up on benefits such as sick leave and bereavement time. As employees became more fearful about job loss, they spent less time away from the workplace. Days lost to illness fell dramatically. So did unpaid absences—which declined for the first time since 1973.[31]

The other factor reducing vacations has been the restructuring of the labor market. Companies have turned to more "casual" workforces—firing long-term employees and signing on consultants, part-timers, or temporaries. Early retirements among senior workers also reduced vacation time. Because the length of vacations in this country is based on duration of employment, these changes have all contributed to lowering the amount of time off people actually receive. The growth of service sector occupations, where the duration of employment tends to be shortest, has also been a factor.[32]

The Time Squeeze at Home

Along with the work people are paid for—time spent at "regular jobs"—almost an equal amount of work is done every year which is

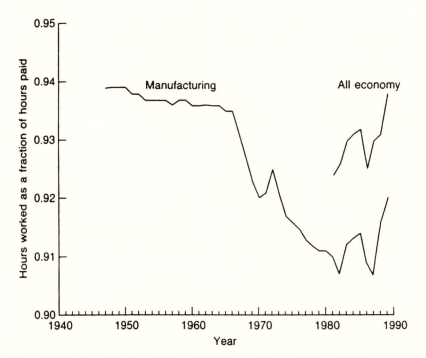

Figure 1. Hours Worked as a Fraction of Hours Paid. Source: Bureau of Labor Statistics.

not paid for—most of it housework, child care, and other "domestic labor." To get the full story on changes in leisure time, we need estimates of this labor, too. However, as one might expect, calculating hours of household work is not a simple matter. The major difficulty is that the government does not provide any information—despite requests from scholars for official household record keeping which date back more than a hundred years. A second problem is that household labor tends to be less regimented than many forms of paid work. There are no time clocks to punch, and schedules can be erratic. Partly for this reason, researchers have found that the most accurate method for measuring household labor is through minute-by-minute records—or diaries—of people's activities. But this procedure is expensive. Because diary surveys have been carried out exclusively by university-based research institutes, the expense has kept their efforts small and spo-

radic; and the data are not always representative of the U.S. population.[33]

To ameliorate these drawbacks, I carried out a statistical procedure that combines the time diaries with the large-scale data set on which my earlier calculations are based. In essence, I have constructed estimates of how much household labor each person in my sample is doing, on the basis of information taken from the diaries. This procedure allows one not only to predict trends in household labor but also to identify those factors that determine how much of this work is done at any point in time. The margin of error with these data is, however, greater than with the earlier figures.

Accounting for household labor does not reverse the upward trend in worktime. On average, employed people are going the same amount of household work they did twenty years ago (I find only a one-hour difference per year!). There have been big changes: women are doing much less at home and men are doing more. But on balance these changes exactly cancel out. *In terms of total hours— that is, market plus household—the extra month of work remains* (see Table 3).

While employed people have maintained their hours of domestic labor, the population as a whole is doing less. The social changes of recent decades—women's employment, reduced marriage rates, lower births, and changes in gender roles—have substantially decreased women's ability, need, and willingness to perform household work. Men are doing more, but they haven't fully compensated for the reduction by women.

To explore these developments, I turn to a second set of estimates—hours worked per adult American (rather than per employed person). This measure (Table 4) allows me to capture work time changes caused by movements in and out of the workforce, as well as what's happening with those who are out of the labor force altogether. The hours-per-person measure has another advantage: it shows, succinctly, the total quantity of work

TABLE 4. Total Hours Worked per Year, Entire Population

	1969	1987	Change 1969–87
Market hours			
All persons	1199	1316	117
Men	1759	1680	−79
Women	723	996	273
Household hours			
All persons	1227	1157	−70
Men	683	834	151
Women	1689	1440	−249
Total hours			
All persons	2426	2473	47
Men	2442	2514	72
Women	2412	2436	24

Source: Author's estimates.

required for a society to sustain its standard of living. On the other hand, it is an average measure, which does not account for the distribution of either work or income among the population. Because it includes those who are not employed, it yields far lower figures than those I have been considering so far.[34]

These figures show that Americans as a whole have also experienced a decline in leisure time. If I correct (once again) for the growth in unemployment and underemployment, leisure time has fallen by 47 hours a year. On average, hours of employment are up, and hours of domestic labor are down. But men and women have had very different experiences. Among women, the labor market has been the driving force. In general, the more work women do for pay, the less work they do without it. A major change has been the disappearance of the full-time housewife and the rise of the "working woman." During this period, the fraction of married women who were housewives fell from 30 percent to 15 percent of the adult female population. This exodus from the home has had a large

TABLE 3. Total Annual Hours, Labor Force Participants*

	1969	1987	Change 1969–87
Market Hours			
All participants	1,786	1,949	163
Men	2,054	2,152	98
Women	1,406	1,711	305
Household Hours			
All participants	889	888	−1
Men	621	689	68
Women	1,268	1,123	−145
Total Hours			
All participants	2,675	2,837	162
Men	2,675	2,841	166
Women	2,674	2,834	160

Source: Author's estimates.
*Includes only fully employed labor force participants.

impact on the quantity of household labor currently being done. Each additional hour a woman puts into her paid job reduces her household work by nearly half an hour. She spends less time with her children, cooks fewer meals, and does less cleaning. There is also a one-time, extra reduction of up to four hours per week when a woman initially joins the labor force. According to my calculations, of the 223-hour decline in women's household labor, slightly over half is due to increased hours of employment.

To some extent, women have been able to substitute commercial services for their own labor, using their newly earned paychecks to pay the bill. Expenditures on precooked food—either at restaurants or from the neighborhood deli—professional child care, and dry cleaning have risen rapidly in recent years. Indeed, there is a self-reinforcing nature to this process, as the growing demand for commercially produced products draws more women into service sector employment. But the buying-out of domestic responsibilities has limits. For both two-earner families and single mothers, the reduction in women's time at home has led to a painful cutback in "household services." Children are left in the care of others or even by themselves, there are shortcuts in cooking and cleaning, and the extras provided by 1950s-type "Moms" disappear. Unless husbands are willing and able to pick up the slack, these changes are virtually inevitable: employed women just do not have the time. Their workloads have already climbed above virtually all other groups.

The changing labor market of the 1970s and 1980s has had just the opposite effect on patterns of men's labor. Their market hours have fallen—by 79—and hours of domestic work have increased—by 151. But men's trends have been slightly more complicated. As I showed earlier, employed men are working more, not less. But for the whole population,

men's market hours have fallen because there are far fewer of them in the labor force (see Table 4). Each man who drops out of the labor force reduces his hours so substantially that this effect has outweighed the longer hours of men who are employed. Overall, a smaller proportion are working longer hours, and a larger proportion are without jobs.

The lower market hours of men have been partially replaced by more work at home, thereby making up for some of women's vanishing labor. The average man is doing just under three additional hours a week. A detailed breakdown of activities shows that men are occupying themselves not only with traditional male tasks such as outdoor work and home repairs but with cooking and cleaning as well. They are also taking on a larger proportion of child care. This combination of more domestic work by men and less by women means that men are now doing almost 60 percent as much as women, up from 40 percent two decades ago.[35]

Despite this rise, it is premature to conclude that we are on the fast track to gender equality with regard to household labor. Most of the increase in men's domestic labor has been caused by the fact that many more men are out of the labor force. Quite naturally, they do more at home (approaching twice as much) than their counterparts with paying jobs. This has been true for decades. Among men who are employed, the increase is far less—amounting to slightly more than one additional hour per week. For the great majority of employed women who also have working husbands, their spouses have provided only partial relief.

The labor market is not the only factor causing a decline in domestic labor. Housewives' hours have finally started to fall. According to my estimates a middle-class, married mother of three is putting in two fewer hours of work a week than she was in 1969. There are also far fewer women who fit this once common de-mographic profile. Women (and men) are having fewer children and are far less likely to be married. Both these factors have further re-duced domestic hours. The influence of chil-dren should be obvious: they require tremen-dous amounts of time, especially when they are young. With marriage, which I define as the presence of a spouse in the household, the ef-fect is more subtle. It turns out that the acqui-sition of a spouse (especially a husband) leads to more work: homecooked meals, and bigger houses and apartments to care for. Married people also try to save more (to buy those houses or raise their children), which cuts down on the purchasing of services. For women, gaining a husband adds about five hours of domestic work per week. (The case of men is a bit ambiguous; not until the 1980s did they do more when they married.)

During the last twenty years, the married proportion of the adult population fell from about 70 percent to 60 percent. At the same time, the average number of children de-clined, from one child per person in 1969 to slightly over one-half child today. By 1987, only one-third of the population had children under eighteen years of age, a 10 percent fall. These factors together reduced domestic la-bor in the neighborhood of one hundred hours a year for women. Of course, declining birth and marriage rates are not independent of the growth of work. Women's employment has also been a cause of fewer births and even later and shorter marriages.[36]

Involuntary Leisure: Underemployment and Unemployment

There is at least one group of Americans for whom time squeeze is not a problem. These are the millions who cannot get enough work or who cannot get any at all. They have plenty of "leisure" but can hardly enjoy it. One of the great ironies of our present situation is that overwork for the majority has been accompa-nied by the growth of enforced idleness for the minority. The proportion of the labor force who cannot work as many hours as they would like has more than doubled in the last twenty years. Just as surely as our economic system is "underproducing" leisure for some, it is "over-producing" it for others.

Declining industries provide poignant il-lustrations of the coexistence of long hours and unemployment. The manufacturing sec-tor lost over a million jobs in the 1980s. At the same time (from 1980 to 1987), overtime hours rose by fifty per year. Many of those on permanent layoff watch their former co-workers put in steady overtime, week after week, year after year. Outside manufacturing, unemployment also rose steadily. At the height of each business expansion (1969, 1973, 1979, and 1987), the proportion of the labor force without a job was higher—rising from only 3.4 percent in 1969 to almost twice that—6.1 percent—in 1987.

Enforced idleness is not just confined to those who have been laid off. Underemploy-ment is also growing. The fraction of the labor force working part-time but desiring full-time work increased more than seven times. The fraction employed only part of the year, but wanting a job year-round, nearly doubled. Those who had neither full-time nor full-year work, but wanted both, rose four times. All told, in the first year of my study, 7 percent of the labor force were unable to obtain the work they wanted or needed. Twenty years later, this category had more than doubled—and stood at almost 17 percent (see Table 5).

The trend toward underemployment and unemployment signals a disturbing failure of the labor market: the U.S. economy is in-creasingly unable to provide work for its pop-

TABLE 5. Percentage of Labor Force Experiencing Unemployment and Underemployment

	1969	1973	1979	1987
Total unemployed and underemployed	7.2	9.8	16.2	16.8
No work all year	0.4	0.7	0.8	1.6
Part year/part-time	1.0	1.8	4.0	4.4
Full year/part-time	0.2	0.3	0.9	1.5
Part year/full-time	5.6	7.0	10.5	9.3

Source: Author's estimates from *Current Population Survey*.

ulation. It is all the more noticeable that growing idleness is occurring at a time when those who are fully employed are at their workplaces for ever longer hours. Like long hours, the growth of unemployment stems from the basic structure of the economy. Capitalist systems such as our own do not operate in order to provide employment. Their guiding principle is the pursuit of profitability. If profitability results in high employment, that is a happy coincidence for those who want jobs. If it does not, bottom-line oriented companies will not take it upon themselves to hire those their plans have left behind. Full employment typically occurs only when government commits itself to the task.

In the past twenty years, full employment has become ever more elusive as a result of high interest rates, declining investment, sluggish productivity, takeovers and mergers, increased market uncertainty, and stiffer foreign competition. At the same time, Washington has abdicated its responsibility for maintaining jobs. The "golden age" of Western capitalism is over, and with it went the promise of high employment. The rise and fall of the golden age is a long story in itself, which I, along with others, have told elsewhere.[37] What is important here is that the pressures on businesses have spurred a search for cost-cutting

measures. Rather than hire new people, and pay the extra benefits they would entail, many firms have just demanded more from their existing workforces. They have sped up the pace of work and lengthened time on the job. In an atmosphere of high unemployment and weak unions, workers have found it difficult to refuse. The result has been a labor market characterized by a glaring inequity.

As unemployment rose in the 1970s, some labor economists and educators began to advocate shorter hours. Harking back to the labor movements's longstanding traditions, they argued that reductions in weekly hours would put millions of people back to work. But despite their obvious appeal, these proposals received little serious attention. Even as the unemployment problem worsened during the 1980s, work sharing continued to be virtually ignored. Yet if "spreading-the-work" is a sensible and humane solution to a clear irrationality of our economic system, why has it failed? The ostensible rationality of workweek reductions fails to come to terms with a "larger" capitalist logic. Employers have strong incentives to keep hours long. And these incentives have been instrumental in raising hours and keeping them high. In retrospect, the reformers underestimated the obstacles within capitalism itself to solving both the nation's shortage of jobs and its shortage of time.[38]

NOTES

1. "All Work, No Play," on *Real Life with Jane Pauley*, NBC, 17 July 1990. "Overworked and Out of Time," on *Our Times*, WHDH–TV, Boston, 14 April 1990. Transcript of "Fast Times," Show 97, *48 Hours*, CBS News, 8 March 1990. All examples are from the script.

2. Nancy Gibbs, "How America Has Run Out of Time," *Time*, 24 April 1989, p. 59.

3. Anne B. Fischer, *Wall Street Women: Women in Power on the Street Today* (New York: Alfred A. Knopf, 1990), 152, 150.

4. Quoted in Brian O'Reilly, "Is Your Company Asking Too Much?" *Fortune,* 12 March 1990, p. 39.

5. See Amanda Bennett, *The Death of the Organization Man* (New York: William Morrow, 1990). On downsizings, see O'Reilly, "Is Your Company," 41.

6. Evidence on the increased commitment in what she calls "post-entrepreneurial" firms can be found in Rosabeth Moss Kanter's *When Giants Learn to Dance* (New York: Simon & Schuster, 1989), chap. 10, p. 275. The quote is from Thomas Bolger, CEO of Bell Atlantic. Kanter, *When Giants Learn,* 273. Dolores A. Kordek, personal interview, 5 January 1991. Kordek followed this schedule for twelve years, rarely seeing her family, eating either in the office or in the car, and eventually "burning out."

7. A poll by Korn/Ferry International in 1985 found that among Fortune 500 and Service 500 companies, senior executives' hours rose from 53 to 56 between 1979 and 1985; vacation days fell from 16 to 14. A poll of CEOs by Heidrick and Struggles found that the percentage who worked more than 60 hours per week rose between 1980 and 1984, from 44 percent to 60 percent. Cited in Ford S. Worthy, "You're Probably Working Too Hard," *Fortune,* 27 April 1987, p. 136. The Harris Poll reports consistent findings for managers. Sixty-two percent of CEOs also report that their subordinates are putting in longer hours. See Sally Solo, "Stop Whining and Get Back to Work," *Fortune,* 12 March 1990, p. 49.

8. See Bennett, *Death,* and Kanter, *When Giants Learn,* for evidence from case-study research on individual companies.

9. Labor force participation rate of adult women from *Current Population Survey,* author's estimates. Rates of labor force participation for mothers (of own children under eighteen) from "Marital and Family Characteristics of the Labor Force from the March 1990 Current Population Survey," unpublished Bureau of Labor Statistics mimeo, October 1990, p. 4, table 15.

10. These quotes are from Ann Landers' column, *Boston Globe,* 26 February 1990. "Busy every waking hour" is from Laurie Sheridan, "Interviews on Working Hours," unpublished mimeo. Arlie Hochschild, *The Second Shift: Working Parents and the Revolution at Home* (New York: Viking Penguin, 1989), 9.

11. The Boston study is by Dianne S. Burden and Bradley Googins, "Boston University Balancing Job and Homelife Study," mimeo (Boston University, 1987), 18, table 10. Shelley Coverman, using the Quality of Employment Survey, found an average workweek of 87.4 hours for white, currently married, employed women. See "Gender, Domestic Labor Time, and Wage Inequality," *American Sociological Review,* 48 (October 1983): 623–37, table 1, p. 629. A second study, based on the Panel Survey of Income Dynamics, found that in white, married couples, mothers who worked full-time had a workweek ranging from 76 hours (if the oldest child was 4 to 13 years old) to 89 (oldest child newborn to 3 years). See Cynthia Rexroat and Constance Shehan, "The Family Life Cycle and Spouses' Time in Housework," *Journal of Marriage and the Family,* 49, 4 (November 1987): 737–50, fig. 1, p. 746. A nationwide magazine survey by the 9 to 5 union found that women respondents had an average workweek of 84.3 hours. *See The 9 to 5 National Survey on Women and Stress* (Cleveland, Ohio: 9 to 5, 1984), estimates calculated from Appendix C; however, this was not a statistically representative survey.

12. Anna Quindlen, "Men at Work" in "Public and Private," *New York Times,* 18 February 1990, p. 19, on "endangered species" and 50-plus hours. Weekend data from Harriet Presser, "Can We Make Time for Children? The Economy, Work Schedules, and Child Care," *Demography,* 26 (November 1989): 523–44, table 1.

13. Sheridan, "Interviews."

14. One-third figure calculated from table 3.5 in Lawrence Mishel and David M. Frankel, *The State of Working America,* 1990–91 ed. (Armonk, N.Y.: M. E. Sharpe); hourly wage figure for 1988, p. 77. Valerie Connor (pseud.), personal interview, 23 December 1990. Bill Meyerson, Service Employees International Union, Hartford, Connecticut, personal interview, 30 November 1990. Dominic Bozzotto, personal interview, December 1990. I. N. Yazbek, personal interview, 11 December 1990.

15. The Harris Poll question on leisure is the following: "About how many hours each week do you estimate you have available to relax, watch TV, take part in sports or hobbies, go swimming or skiing, go to the movies, theater, concerts, or other

forms of entertainment, get together with friends, and so forth?" Louis Harris, *Americans and the Arts,* Study 871009 (New York: Louis Harris and Associates, January 1988), Appendix C. The Decision Research Corporation question is: "Compared to a few years ago do you feel you have more leisure time, less leisure time or the same amount of leisure time?" Decision Research Corporation, *Decision Research Corporation's 1990 Leisure Study: Trends in America's Leisure Time and Activities* (Lexington, Mass.: D. C. Heath, February 1990), 6, table 1.

For the Harris Poll, the most serious problem is that it reportedly has a very low response rate. A second issue, for both the Harris and Decision Research Corporation polls, is the accuracy of estimates that are based on respondent recall. For a critique of this method, see John P. Robinson, "The Validity and Reliability of Diaries Versus Alternative Time Use Measures," in F. Thomas Juster and Frank P. Stafford, eds., *Time, Goods, and Well-Being* (Ann Arbor: Institute for Social Research, University of Michigan, 1985), 63–91. Because time diaries are expensive to administer, most surveys of time use are based on the recall method; therefore, it is difficult to avoid reliance on it altogether.

16. Jeremy Rifkin, *Time Wars* (New York: Henry Holt, 1987), 14–15. On Nintendo, ibid., 26. Alstedt quote from Trish Hall, "Why All Those People Feel They Never Have Enough Time," *New York Times,* 2 January 1988, p. 1.

17. John P. Robinson, "The Time Squeeze," *American Demographics,* 12, 2 (February 1990): 30–33. Results from Robinson's 1985 survey show that rising numbers of people feel rushed in other age groups besides the "baby boomers." The walking résumé quote is from Geoffrey Godbey of Pennsylvania State University, in Hall, "Why All Those People."

18. Gary Becker, "A Theory of the Allocation of Time," *Economic Journal,* 75, 299 (1965): 493–517; and Staffan B. Linder, *The Harried Leisure Class* (New York: Columbia University Press, 1970).

19. Trish Hall, "The Dinner Party Quietly Bows to More Casual Alternatives, " *New York Times,* 24 February 1988, p. C1.

20. The figure one-fourth is from Bureau of Labor Statistics, *Labor Force Statistics Derived from* the *Current Population Survey, 1948–1987* (Washington, D.C.: Government Printing Office, 1988), 801, table C–12, 804, table C–14. The percentage was rising over this period; one-quarter is a rough figure. Bureau of Labor Statistics, "Marital and Family Characteristics," 4, table 15.

21. Bruce D. Butterfield, "Long Hours, Late Nights, Low Grades: In Labor-Short Towns Across America, Teen-agers Are Overworked," *Boston Globe,* Children at Work series, 24 April 1990.

22. Bruce D. Butterfield, "The New Harvest of Shame: For Farm Workers' Children, Cycle of Poverty and Work Unbroken," *Boston Globe,* Children at Work series, 26 April 1990.

23. Bureau of Labor Statistics, *Labor Force Statistics Derived from the Current Population Survey, 1948–1987,* 153, table A–10.

24. One study of older male (aged 45–65) nonparticipants indicates that these men have relatively little income that suggests voluntary retirement—namely, pensions, rental income, interest, or dividends. Instead, their support comes much more from government disability payments, indicating that physical and mental impairments are preventing them from working. The inability to find jobs is also correlated with disability rates. For white men, disability payments alone made up about 30 percent of total family income; for black men, these payments were roughly half. Donald O. Parsons, "The Decline in Male Labor Force Participation," *Journal of Political Economy,* 88, 11 (1980): 117–34. Since these data were collected before the Reagan administration's attack on disability programs, the figures may be lower during the 1980s. The 1990 survey is in The Commonwealth Fund, *Americans Over 50 at Work Program,* Research Reports 1 and 2 (New York: The Commonwealth Fund, 25 January and 8 March 1990).

See Bennett, *Death,* for a discussion of pressures to take early retirement among white-collar workers. For evidence on the effects of plant closings or job loss on older workers, see Paul O. Flaim and Ellen Sehgal, "Displaced Workers of 1979–83: How Well Have They Fared?" *Monthly Labor Review* (June 1985): 3–16. Their figures show that 34 percent of males aged fifty-five and above dropped out of the labor force after being displaced (calculated from table 1, p. 4).

African American men face rates of unemployment more than twice those of white men. They have also been disproportionately hit by plant closings, industrial decline, and suburbanization. Once they suffer job displacement, African Americans have a 42 percent chance of becoming unemployed, nearly twice the rate for whites, and are more likely to drop out of the labor force altogether. Data on job displacement are from a special Bureau of Labor Statistics survey for 1979–83. See Flaim and Sehgal, "Displaced Workers," p. 4, table 1. For a discussion of the long-term picture, see William J. Wilson, *The Truly Disadvantaged: The Inner City, the Underclass, and Public Policy* (Chicago: University of Chicago Press, 1987), 100–101.

25. More information on these categories can be found in Laura Leete-Guy and Juliet B. Schor, "Is There a Time Squeeze? Estimates of Market and Non-Market Hours in the United States, 1969–1987," *HIER Working Paper* 1525, Harvard University, November 1989. The occupational data are difficult to construct due to changes in the occupational codes between 1969 and 1987; however, a rough test confirmed the generality of the rise. The results for industries are also likely to be somewhat correlated with those for occupations.

26. Earl F. Mellor and William Parks II, "A Year's Work: Labor Force Activity from a Different Perspective," *Monthly Labor Review* (September 1988): 13–18.

27. The decline in average weekly hours registered in the establishment data is spurious because it double-counts moonlighters and excludes the informal sector and many of the self-employed. Figures on long schedules are from Bureau of Labor Statistics, *Employment and Earnings,* August 1990, p. 32, table A–27, calculated as a percentage of full-time workers only, all industries (49 + hours are 25 percent, 60 + hours are 11 percent).

28. See Leete-Guy and Schor, "Assessing the Time Squeeze Hypothesis: Estimates of Market and Non-Market Hours in the United States, 1969–1987," unpublished mimeo, Harvard University, June 1990.

29. Bureau of Labor Statistics Press Release, "Multiple Jobholding Reached Record High in May 1989," 89–529, 6 November 1989. See Sar A. Levitan and Richard S. Belous, *Shorter Hours,*

Shorter Weeks: Spreading the Work to Reduce Unemployment (Baltimore: Johns Hopkins University Press, 1977), 12 on under-reporting. See Bureau of Labor Statistics News release, 89–529, 6 November 1989, table 6; and Daniel E. Taylor and Edward S. Sekscenski, "Workers on Long Schedules, Single and Multiple Jobholders," Research Summary, *Monthly Labor Review,* 105, 5 (May 1982): 47–53 for data on reasons for multiple jobholding and the differences between 1980 and 1989.

30. Average annual overtime hours per job were 204.5 in 1987:4, which on the basis of a 40-hour week is equivalent to five weeks. Overtime data are from Ray Fair, of Yale University, whose original source is *Employment and Earnings.* They are the variable HO, as defined in his *Specification, Estimation, and Analysis of Macroeconomic Models* (Cambridge, Mass.: Harvard University Press, 1984), table A–4. Data are not available outside the manufacturing sector. Quotes from Sheridan, "Interviews."

31. Bennett, *Death,* 140–41, on DuPont and other large corporations. Illness data from author's calculations from Current Population Survey data. Absences information from Bruce W. Klein, "Missed Work and Lost Hours, May 1985," *Monthly Labor Review,* 109, 11 (November 1986): 26–30.

32. Max L. Carey, "Occupational Tenure in 1987: Many Workers Have Remained in Their Fields," *Monthly Labor Review,* 111, 10 (October 1988): 3–12.

33. There is no single, convenient term for unpaid work done in the home. Some terms commonly in use are *domestic labor, unpaid labor, household work,* and *work done in the home.* The latter is somewhat confusing because some work for pay is physically located in the home and some domestic labor occurs outside the home (transporting family members, purchasing food, etc.). *Domestic labor* and *unpaid labor* are somewhat arcane. The economist's preferred terminology is *market* and *nonmarket work,* but these have little meaning in common parlance. I try to avoid these terminological minefields by using most of these terms interchangeably. Some readers may have their doubts about whether such household activities as food preparation, child care, and house cleaning should be considered work.

Officers of the Association for the Advancement of Women wrote to the U.S. Congress in 1878, requesting changes in Census procedures that would allow enumeration of household workers. See Nancy Folbre and Marjorie Abel, "Women's Work and Women's Households: Gender Bias in the U.S. Census," *Social Research,* 56, 3 (Autumn 1989): 545–69.

The diary studies originating at the University of Michigan are biased upward in terms of income and the percentage of whites, two factors that raise domestic hours. A second problem is that the Michigan surveys were done during recessions (1975–76 and 1980–81), which distorts their estimates of market work.

34. In the contemporary United States, hours per working-age person is a superior measure to a second, often-cited statistic—namely, hours per capita, which includes children and teenagers. There are at least two reasons for this. First, since child labor has been legally restricted and for some ages prohibited, including children as part of the potential labor force is somewhat suspect. Inclusion of child labor would also be hampered by the lack of adequate data, given that it is often illegal. (As noted earlier, however, child labor is on the rise.) Second, there has been a sharp decline in the number of children per adult during the past twenty years, which artificially inflates the hours-per-capita figure.

The standard of living will also be affected by the extent to which income flows in and out of the country on the basis of assets held abroad by U.S. citizens and domestic assets owned by foreigners. The hours-per-capita measure also does not account for consumption that occurs by running down stocks of previously produced goods and services, or for the labor of children.

35. John P. Robinson, "Who's Doing the Housework?" *American Demographics,* 10, 12 (December 1988): 24–28.

36. See James P. Smith and Michael Ward, "Time-Series Growth in the Labor Force," *Journal of Labor Economics,* 3, 1 (January 1985): S59–S90, and Elaine McCrate, "Trade, Merger, and Employment: Economic Theory on Marriage," *Review of Radical Political Economics,* 19 (1987): 73–89.

37. For a comprehensive discussion of the decline of macroeconomic performance and the resulting unemployment, the reader is referred to Stephen A. Marglin and Juliet B. Schor, eds., *The Golden Age of Capitalism: Reinterpreting the Postwar Experience* (Oxford: Clarendon Press, 1990). For more on changes in unemployment itself, see Jukka Pekkarinen, Matti Pohjola, and Bob Rowthorn, *Social Corporatism: A Superior System?* (Oxford: Clarendon Press, 1991). Both these volumes are produced by the Macroeconomic Policies Project of the World Institute for Development Economics Research.

38. See, among others, Levitan and Belous, *Shorter Hours;* Martin J. Morand and Ramelle Macoy, eds., *Short-Time Compensation: A Formula for Work Sharing* (New York: Pergamon Press, 1984); and William McGaughey, Jr., *A Shorter Workweek in the 1980s* (White Bear Lake, Minn.: Thistlerose Publications, 1981).

These proposals also overestimated the impact workweek reductions were likely to have on the demand for labor. There is strong evidence that workweek reductions are accompanied by rising productivity, which largely negates the positive employment effect. Recent European experience provides strong support for this conclusion. See Wouter van Ginneken, "Employment and the Reduction of the Work Week: A Comparison of Seven European Macro-economic Models," *International Labour Review,* 123, 1 (January/February 1984): 35–52.

Chapter 10

Capitalism and Gay Identity

JOHN D'EMILIO

For gay men and lesbians, the 1970s were years of significant achievement. Gay liberation and women's liberation changed the sexual landscape of the nation. Hundreds of thousands of gay women and men came out and openly affirmed same-sex eroticism. We won repeal of sodomy laws in half the states, a partial lifting of the exclusion of lesbians and gay men from federal employment, civil rights protection in a few dozen cities, the inclusion of gay rights in the platform of the Democratic Party, and the elimination of homosexuality from the psychiatric profession's list of mental illnesses. The gay male subculture expanded and became increasingly visible in large cities, and lesbian feminists pioneered in building alternative institutions and an alternative culture that attempted to embody a liberatory vision of the future.

In the 1980s, however, with the resurgence of an active right wing, gay men and lesbians face the future warily. Our victories appear tenuous and fragile; the relative freedom of the past few years seems too recent to be permanent. In some parts of the lesbian and gay male community, a feeling of doom is growing: analogies with Senator Joseph McCarthy's America, when "sexual perverts" were a special target of the Right, and with Nazi Germany, where gays were shipped to concentration camps, surface with increasing frequency. Everywhere there is the sense that new strategies are in order if we want to preserve our gains and move ahead.

I believe that a new, more accurate theory of gay history must be part of this political enterprise. When the gay liberation movement began at the end of the 1960s, gay men and lesbians had no history that we could use to fashion our goals and strategy. In the ensuing years, in building a movement without a knowledge of our history, we instead invented a mythology. This mythical history drew on personal experience, which we read backward

From Ann Snitow, Christine Stansell, and Sharon Thompson, eds., *Powers of Desire: The Politics of Sexuality* (New York: Monthly Review Press, 1983), 100–113, copyright © 1983 by Snitow, Stansell, and Thompson. Reprinted by permission of Monthly Review Foundation.

in time. For instance, most lesbians and gay men in the 1960s first discovered their homosexual desires in isolation, unaware of others, and without resources for naming and understanding what they felt. From this experience, we constructed a myth of silence, invisibility, and isolation as the essential characteristics of gay life in the past as well as the present. Moreover, because we faced so many oppressive laws, public policies, and cultural beliefs, we projected this into an image of the abysmal past: until gay liberation, lesbians and gay men were always the victims of systematic, undifferentiated, terrible oppression.

These myths have limited our political perspective. They have contributed, for instance, to an overreliance on a strategy of coming out—if every gay man and lesbian in America came out, gay oppression would end—and have allowed us to ignore the institutionalized ways in which homophobia and heterosexism are reproduced. They have encouraged, at times, an incapacitating despair, especially at moments like the present: How can we unravel a gay oppression so pervasive and unchanging?

There is another historical myth that enjoys nearly universal acceptance in the gay movement, the myth of the "eternal homosexual." The argument runs something like this: gay men and lesbians always were and always will be. We are everywhere; not just now, but throughout history, in all societies and all periods. This myth served a positive political function in the first years of gay liberation. In the early 1970s, when we battled an ideology that either denied our existence or defined us as psychopathic individuals or freaks of nature, it was empowering to assert that "we are everywhere." But in recent years it has confined us as surely as the most homophobic medical theories, and locked our movement in place.

Here I wish to challenge this myth. I want to argue that gay men and lesbians have *not* al-

ways existed. Instead, they are a product of history, and have come into existence in a specific historical era. Their emergence is associated with the relations of capitalism; it has been the historical development of capitalism—more specifically, its free labor system—that has allowed large numbers of men and women in the late twentieth century to call themselves gay, to see themselves as part of a community of similar men and women, and to organize politically on the basis of that identity.[1] Finally, I want to suggest some political lessons we can draw from this view of history.

What, then, are the relationships between the free labor system of capitalism and homosexuality? First, let me review some features of capitalism. Under capitalism, workers are "free" laborers in two ways. We have the freedom to look for a job. We own our ability to work and have the freedom to sell our labor power for wages to anyone willing to buy it. We are also freed from the ownership of anything except our labor power. Most of us do not own the land or the tools that produce what we need, but rather have to work for a living in order to survive. So, if we are free to sell our labor power in the positive sense, we are also freed, in the negative sense, from any other alternative. This dialectic—the constant interplay between exploitation and some measure of autonomy—informs all of the history of those who have lived under capitalism.

As capital—money used to make more money—expands, so does this system of free labor. Capital expands in several ways. Usually it expands in the same place, transforming small firms into larger ones, but it also expands by taking over new areas of production: the weaving of cloth, for instance, or the baking of bread. Finally, capital expands geographically. In the United States, capitalism initially took root in the Northeast, at a time when slavery was the dominant system in the South and when noncapitalist Native American societies occupied the western half of the continent. During the nineteenth century, capital spread from the Atlantic to the Pacific, and in the twentieth, U.S. capital has penetrated almost every part of the world.

The expansion of capital and the spread of wage labor have effected a profound transformation in the structure and functions of the nuclear family, the ideology of family life, and the meaning of heterosexual relations. It is these changes in the family that are most directly linked to the appearance of a collective gay life.

The white colonists in seventeenth-century New England established villages structured around a household economy, composed of family units that were basically self-sufficient, independent, and patriarchal. Men, women, and children farmed land owned by the male head of household. Although there was a division of labor between men and women, the family was truly an interdependent unit of production: the survival of each member depended on the cooperation of all. The home was a workplace where women processed raw farm products into food for daily consumption, where they made clothing, soap, and candles, and where husbands, wives, and children worked together to produce the goods they consumed.

By the nineteenth century, this system of household production was in decline. In the Northeast, as merchant capitalists invested the money accumulated through trade in the production of goods, wage labor became more common. Men and women were drawn out of the largely self-sufficient household economy of the colonial era into a capitalist system of free labor. For women in the nineteenth century, working for wages rarely lasted beyond marriage; for men, it became a permanent condition.

The family was thus no longer an independent unit of production. But although no longer independent, the family was still interdependent. Because capitalism had not expanded very far, because it had not yet taken over—or socialized—the production of consumer goods, women still performed necessary productive labor in the home. Many families no longer produced grain, but wives still baked into bread the flour they bought with their husbands' wages; or, when they purchased yarn or cloth, they still made clothing for their families. By the mid-1800s, capitalism had destroyed the economic self-sufficiency of many families, but not the mutual dependence of the members.

This transition away from the household family–based economy to a fully developed capitalist free labor economy occurred very slowly, over almost two centuries. As late as 1920, 50 percent of the U.S. population lived in communities of fewer than 2,500 people. The vast majority of blacks in the early twentieth century lived outside the free labor economy, in a system of sharecropping and tenancy that rested on the family. Not only did independent farming as a way of life still exist for millions of Americans, but even in towns and small cities women continued to grow and process food, make clothing, and engage in other kinds of domestic production.

But for those people who felt the brunt of these changes, the family took on new significance as an affective unit, an institution that produced not goods but emotional satisfaction and happiness. By the 1920s among the white middle class, the ideology surrounding the family described it as the means through which men and women formed satisfying, mutually enhancing relationships and created an environment that nurtured children. The family became the setting for a "personal life," sharply distinguished and disconnected from the public world of work and production.[2]

The meaning of heterosexual relations also changed. In colonial New England, the birthrate averaged over seven children per woman of childbearing age. Men and women needed the labor of children. Producing offspring was as necessary for survival as producing grain. Sex was harnessed to procreation. The Puritans did not celebrate *heterosexuality* but rather marriage; they condemned *all* sexual expression outside the marriage bond and did not differentiate sharply between sodomy and heterosexual fornication.

By the 1970s, however, the birthrate had dropped to under two. With the exception of the post–World War II baby boom, the decline has been continuous for two centuries, paralleling the spread of capitalist relations of production. It occurred even when access to contraceptive devices and abortion was systematically curtailed. The decline has included every segment of the population—urban and rural families, blacks and whites, ethnics and WASPs, the middle class and the working class.

As wage labor spread and production became socialized, then, it became possible to release sexuality from the "imperative" to procreate. Ideologically, heterosexual expression came to be a means of establishing intimacy, promoting happiness, and experiencing pleasure. In divesting the household of its economic independence and fostering the separation of sexuality from procreation, capitalism has created conditions that allow some men and women to organize a personal life around their erotic/emotional attraction to their own sex. It has made possible the formation of urban communities of lesbians and gay men and, more recently, of a politics based on a sexual identity.

Evidence from colonial New England court records and church sermons indicates that male and female homosexual behavior existed in the seventeenth century. Homosexual *behavior,* however, is different from homo-

sexual *identity.* There was, quite simply, no "social space" in the colonial system of production that allowed men and women to be gay. Survival was structured around participation in a nuclear family. There were certain homosexual acts—sodomy among men, "lewdness" among women—in which individuals engaged, but family was so pervasive that colonial society lacked even the category of homosexual or lesbian to describe a person. It is quite possible that some men and women experienced a stronger attraction to their own sex than to the opposite sex—in fact, some colonial court cases refer to men who persisted in their "unnatural" attractions—but one could not fashion out of that preference a way of life. Colonial Massachusetts even had laws prohibiting unmarried adults from living outside family units.[3]

By the second half of the nineteenth century, this situation was noticeably changing as the capitalist system of free labor took hold. Only when *individuals* began to make their living through wage labor, instead of as parts of an interdependent family unit, was it possible for homosexual desire to coalesce into a personal identity—an identity based on the ability to remain outside the heterosexual family and to construct a personal life based on attraction to one's own sex. By the end of the century, a class of men and women existed who recognized their erotic interest in their own sex, saw it as a trait that set them apart from the majority, and sought others like themselves. These early gay lives came from a wide social spectrum: civil servants and business executives, department store clerks and college professors, factory operatives, ministers, lawyers, cooks, domestics, hoboes, and the idle rich: men and women, black and white, immigrant and native born.

In this period, gay men and lesbians began to invent ways of meeting each other and sustaining a group life. Already, in the early twentieth century, large cities contained male homosexual bars. Gay men staked out cruising areas, such as Riverside Drive in New York City and Lafayette Park in Washington, D.C. In St. Louis, Missouri, and the nation's capital, annual drag balls brought together large numbers of black gay men. Public bathhouses and YMCAs became gathering spots for male homosexuals. Lesbians formed literary societies and private social clubs. Some working-class women "passed" as men to obtain better paying jobs and lived with other women—lesbian couples who appeared to the world as husband and wife. Among the faculties of women's colleges, in the settlement houses, and in the professional associations and clubs that women formed one could find lifelong intimate relationships supported by a web of lesbian friends. By the 1920s and 1930s, large cities such as New York and Chicago contained lesbian bars. These patterns of living could evolve because capitalism allowed individuals to survive beyond the confines of the family.[4]

Simultaneously, ideological definitions of homosexual behavior changed. Doctors developed theories about homosexual*ity*, describing it as a condition, something that was inherent in a person, a part of his or her "nature." These theories did not represent scientific breakthroughs, elucidations of previously undiscovered areas of knowledge; rather, they were an ideological response to a new way of organizing one's personal life. The population of the medical model, in turn, affected the consciousness of the women and men who experienced homosexual desire, so that they came to define themselves through their erotic life.[5]

These new forms of gay identity and patterns of group life also reflected the differentiation of people according to gender, race, and class that is so pervasive in capitalist societies. Among whites, for instance, gay men

have traditionally been more visible than lesbians. This partly stems from the division between the public male sphere and the private female sphere. Streets, parks, and bars, especially at night, were "male space." Yet the greater visibility of white gay men also reflected their larger numbers. The Kinsey studies of the 1940s and 1950s found significantly more men than women with predominantly homosexual histories, a situation caused, I would argue, by the fact that capitalism had drawn far more men than women into the labor force, and at higher wages. Men could more easily construct a personal life independent of attachments to the opposite sex, whereas women were more likely to remain economically dependent on men. Kinsey also found a strong positive correlation between years of schooling and lesbian activity. College-educated white women, far more able than their working-class sisters to support themselves, could survive more easily without intimate relationships with men.[6]

Among working-class immigrants in the early twentieth century, closely knit kin networks and an ethic of family solidarity placed constraints on individual autonomy that made gayness a difficult option to pursue. In contrast, for reasons not altogether clear, urban black communities appeared relatively tolerant of homosexuality. The popularity in the 1920s and 1930s of songs with lesbian and gay male themes—"B. D. Woman," "Prove It on Me," "Sissy Man," "Fairey Blues"—suggests an openness about homosexual expression at odds with the mores of whites. Among men in the rural West in the 1940s, Kinsey found extensive incidence of homosexual behavior, but, in contrast with the men in large cities, little consciousness of gay identity. Thus even as capitalism exerted a homogenizing influence by gradually transforming more individuals into wage laborers and separating them from traditional communities, different groups of people were also affected in different ways.[7]

The decisions of particular men and women to act on their erotic/emotional preference for the same sex, along with the new consciousness that this preference made them different, led to the formation of an urban subculture of gay men and lesbians. Yet at least through the 1930s this subculture remained rudimentary, unstable, and difficult to find. How, then, did the complex, well-developed gay community emerge that existed by the time the gay liberation movement exploded? The answer is to be found during World War II, a time when the cumulative changes of several decades coalesced into a qualitatively new shape.

The war severely disrupted traditional patterns of gender relations and sexuality and temporarily created a new erotic situation conducive to homosexual expression. It plucked millions of young men and women, whose sexual identities were just forming, out of their homes, out of towns and small cities, out of the heterosexual environment of the family, and dropped them into sex-segregated situations—as GIs, as WACs and WAVEs, in same-sex rooming houses for women workers who relocated to seek employment. The war freed millions of men and women from the settings where heterosexuality was normally imposed. For men and women already gay, it provided an opportunity to meet people like themselves. Others could become gay because of the temporary freedom to explore sexuality that the war provided.[8]

Lisa Ben, for instance, came out during the war. She left the small California town where she was raised, came to Los Angeles to find work, and lived in a women's boarding house. There she met for the first time lesbians who took her to gay bars and introduced her to other gay women. Donald Vining was a young man with lots of homosexual desire and few gay experiences. He moved to New York City during the war and worked at a large YMCA. His diary reveals numerous erotic adventures with soldiers, sailors, marines, and civilians at the Y where he worked, as well as at the men's residence club where he lived, and in parks, bars, and movie theaters. Many GIs stayed in port cities like New York, at YMCAs like the one where Vining worked. In his oral histories of gay men in San Francisco, focusing on the 1940s, Allan Bérubé has found that the war years were critical in the formation of a gay male *community* in the city. Places as different as San Jose, California, Denver, Colorado, and Kansas City, Missouri, had their first gay bars in the 1940s. Even severe repression could have positive side effects. Pat Bond, a lesbian from Davenport, Iowa, joined the WACs during the 1940s. Caught in a purge of hundreds of lesbians from the WACs in the Pacific, she did not return to Iowa. She stayed in San Francisco and became part of a community of lesbians. How many other women and men had comparable experiences? How many other cities saw a rapid growth of lesbian and gay male communities?[9]

The gay men and women of the 1940s were pioneers. Their decisions to act on their desires formed the underpinnings of an urban subculture of gay men and lesbians. Throughout the 1950s and 1960s, the gay subculture grew and stabilized so that people coming out then could more easily find other gay women and men than in the past. Newspapers and magazines published articles describing gay male life. Literally hundreds of novels with lesbian themes were published.[10] Psychoanalysts complained about the new ease with which their gay male patients found sexual partners. And the gay subculture was not just to be found in the largest cities. Lesbian and gay male bars existed in places like Worcester, Massachusetts, and Buffalo, New York; in Columbia, South Carolina, and Des Moines,

Iowa. Gay life in the 1950s and 1960s became a nationwide phenomenon. By the time of the Stonewall Riots in New York City in 1969—the event that ignited the gay liberation movement—our situation was hardly one of silence, invisibility, and isolation. A massive, grass-roots liberation movement could form almost overnight precisely because communities of lesbians and gay men existed.

Although gay community was a precondition for a mass movement, the oppression of lesbians and gay men was the force that propelled the movement into existence. As the subculture expanded and grew more visible in the post–World War II era, oppression by the state intensified, becoming more systematic and inclusive. The Right scapegoated "sexual perverts" during the McCarthy era. President Dwight Eisenhower imposed a total ban on the employment of gay women and men by the federal government and government contractors. Purges of lesbians and homosexuals from the military rose sharply. The FBI instituted widespread surveillance of gay meeting places and of lesbian and gay organizations, such as the Daughters of Bilitis and the Mattachine Society. The Post Office placed tracers on the correspondence of gay men and passed evidence of homosexual activity on to employers. Urban vice squads invaded private homes, made sweeps of lesbian and gay male bars, entrapped gay men in public places, and fomented local witch hunts. The danger involved in being gay rose even as the possibilities of being gay were enhanced. Gay liberation was a response to this contradiction.

Although lesbians and gay men won significant victories in the 1970s and opened up some safe social space in which to exist, we can hardly claim to have dealt a fatal blow to heterosexism and homophobia. One could even argue that the enforcement of gay oppression has merely changed locales, shifting somewhat from the state to the arena of ex-tralegal violence in the form of increasingly open physical attacks on lesbians and gay men. And, as our movements have grown, they have generated a backlash that threatens to wipe out our gains. Significantly, this New Right opposition has taken shape as a "pro-family" movement. How is it that capitalism, whose structure made possible the emergence of a gay identity and the creation of urban gay communities, appears unable to accept gay men and lesbians in its midst? Why do heterosexism and homophobia appear so resistant to assault?

The answers, I think, can be found in the contradictory relationship of capitalism to the family. On the one hand, as I argued earlier, capitalism has gradually undermined the material basis of the nuclear family by taking away the economic functions that cemented the ties between family members. As more adults have been drawn into the free labor system, and as capital has expanded its sphere until it produces as commodities most goods and services we need for our survival, the forces that propelled men and women into families and kept them there have weakened. On the other hand, the ideology of capitalist society has enshrined the family as the source of love, affection, and emotional security, the place where our need for stable, intimate human relationships is satisfied.

The elevation of the nuclear family to preeminence in the sphere of personal life is not accidental. Every society needs structures for reproduction and childrearing, but the possibilities are not limited to the nuclear family. Yet the privatized family fits well with capitalist relations of production. Capitalism has socialized production while maintaining that the products of socialized labor belong to the owners of private property. In many ways, childrearing has also been progressively socialized over the last two centuries, with schools, the media, peer groups, and employers taking over functions that once belonged to parents. Nevertheless, capitalist society maintains that reproduction and childrearing are private tasks, that children "belong" to parents, who exercise the rights of ownership. Ideologically, capitalism drives people into heterosexual families: each generation comes of age having internalized a heterosexist model of intimacy and personal relationships. Materially, capitalism weakens the bonds that once kept families together so that their members experience a growing instability in the place they have come to expect happiness and emotional security. Thus, while capitalism has knocked the material foundation away from family life, lesbians, gay men, and heterosexual feminists have become the scapegoats for the social instability of the system.

This analysis, if persuasive, has implications for us today. It can affect our perception of our identity, our formulation of political goals, and our decisions about strategy.

I have argued that lesbian and gay identity and communities are historically created, the result of a process of capitalist development that has spanned many generations. A corollary of this argument is that we are *not* a fixed social minority composed for all time of a certain percentage of the population. *There are more of us* than one hundred years ago, more of us than forty years ago. And there may very well be more gay men and lesbians in the future. Claims made by gays and nongays that sexual orientation is fixed at an early age, that large numbers of visible gay men and lesbians in society, the media, and the schools will have no influence on the sexual identities of the young, are wrong. Capitalism has created the material conditions for homosexual desire to express itself as a central component of some individuals' lives; now, our political movements are changing consciousness, creating the ideological conditions that make it easier for people to make that choice.

To be sure, this argument confirms the worst fears and most rabid rhetoric of our political opponents. But our response must be to challenge the underlying belief that homosexual relations are bad, a poor second choice. We must not slip into the opportunistic defense that society need not worry about tolerating us, since only homosexuals become homosexuals. At best, a minority group analysis and a civil rights strategy pertain to those of us who already are gay. It leaves today's youth—tomorrow's lesbians and gay men—to internalize heterosexist models that it can take a lifetime to expunge.

I have also argued that capitalism has led to the separation of sexuality from procreation. Human sexual desire need no longer be harnessed to reproductive imperatives, to procreation; its expression has increasingly entered the realm of choice. Lesbians and homosexuals most clearly embody the potential of this split, since our gay relationships stand entirely outside a procreative framework. The acceptance of our erotic choices ultimately depends on the degree to which society is willing to affirm sexual expression as a form of play, positive and life-enhancing. Our movement may have begun as the struggle of a "minority," but what we should now be trying to "liberate" is an aspect of the personal lives of all people—sexual expression.[11]

Finally, I have suggested that the relationship between capitalism and the family is fundamentally contradictory. On the one hand, capitalism continually weakens the material foundation of family life, making it possible for individuals to live outside the family, and for a lesbian and gay male identity to develop. On the other, it needs to push men and women into families, at least long enough to reproduce the next generation of workers. The elevation of the family to ideological preeminence guarantees that capitalist society will reproduce not just children, but heterosexism and homophobia. In the most profound sense, capitalism is the problem.[12]

How do we avoid remaining the scapegoats, the political victims of the social instability that capitalism generates? How can we take this contradictory relationship and use it to move toward liberation?

Gay men and lesbians exist on social terrain beyond the boundaries of the heterosexual nuclear family. Our communities have formed in that social space. Our survival and liberation depend on our ability to defend and expand that terrain, not just for ourselves but for everyone. That means, in part, support for issues that broaden the opportunities for living outside traditional heterosexual family units: issues like the availability of abortion and the ratification of the Equal Rights Amendment, affirmative action for people of color and for women, publicly funded daycare and other essential social services, decent welfare payments, full employment, the rights of young people—in other words, programs and issues that provide a material basis for personal autonomy.

The rights of young people are especially critical. The acceptance of children as dependents, as belonging to parents, is so deeply ingrained that we can scarcely imagine what it would mean to treat them as autonomous human beings, particularly in the realm of sexual expression and choice. Yet until that happens, gay liberation will remain out of our reach.

But personal autonomy is only half the story. The instability of families and the sense of impermanence and insecurity that people are now experiencing in their personal relationships are real social problems that need to be addressed. We need political solutions for these difficulties of personal life. These solutions should not come in the form of a radical version of the pro-family position, of some left-wing proposals to strengthen the family. Socialists do not generally respond to the ex-

ploitation and economic inequality of industrial capitalism by calling for a return to the family farm and handicraft production. We recognize that the vastly increased productivity that capitalism has made possible by socializing production is one of its progressive features. Similarly, we should not be trying to turn back the clock to some mythic age of the happy family.

We do need, however, structures and programs that will help to dissolve the boundaries that isolate the family, particularly those that privatize childrearing. We need community- or worker-controlled daycare, housing where privacy and community coexist, neighborhood institutions—from medical clinics to performance centers—that enlarge the social unit where each of us has a secure place. As we create structures beyond the nuclear family that provide a sense of belonging, the family will wane in significance. Less and less will it seem to make or break our emotional security.

In this respect gay men and lesbians are well situated to play a special role. Already excluded from families as most of us are, we have had to create, for our survival, networks of support that do not depend on the bonds of blood or the license of the state, but that are freely chosen and nurtured. The building of an "affectional community" must be as much a part of our political movement as are campaigns for civil rights. In this way we may prefigure the shape of personal relationships in a society grounded in equality and justice rather than exploitation and oppression, a society where autonomy and security do not preclude each other but coexist.

NOTES

Acknowledgments. This chapter is a revised version of a lecture given before several audiences in 1979 and 1980. I am grateful to the following groups for giving me a forum in which to talk and get feedback: the Baltimore Gay Alliance, the San Francisco Lesbian and Gay History Project, the organizers of Gay Awareness Week 1980 at San Jose State University and the University of California at Irvine, and the coordinators of the Student Affairs Lectures at the University of California at Irvine.

Lisa Duggan, Estelle Freedman, Jonathan Katz, Carole Vance, Paula Webster, and Bert Hansen, and Ann Snitow, Christine Stansell, and Sharon Thompson provided helpful criticisms of an earlier draft. I especially want to thank Allan Bérubé and Jonathan Katz for generously sharing with me their own research, and Amber Hollibaugh for many exciting hours of nonstop conversation about Marxism and sexuality.

1. I do not mean to suggest that no one has ever proposed that gay identity is a product of historical change. See, for instance, Mary McIntosh, "The Homosexual Role," *Social Problems* 16 (1968): 182–92; Jeffrey Weeks, *Coming Out: Homosexual Politics in Britain* (New York: Quartet Books, 1977). It is also implied in Michel Foucault, *The History of Sexuality*, vol. 1: *An Introduction*, tr. Robert Hurley (New York: Pantheon, 1978). However, this does represent a minority viewpoint and the works cited above have not specified how it is that capitalism as a system of production has allowed for the emergence of a gay male and lesbian identity. As an example of the "eternal homosexual" thesis, see John Boswell, *Christianity, Social Tolerance, and Homosexuality* (Chicago: University of Chicago Press, 1980), where "gay people" remains an unchanging social category through fifteen centuries of Mediterranean and Western European history.

2. See Eli Zaretsky, *Capitalism, the Family, and Personal Life* (New York: Harper & Row, 1976); and Paula Fass, *The Damned and the Beautiful: American Youth in the 1920s* (New York: Oxford University Press, 1977).

3. Robert F. Oaks, "'Things Fearful to Name': Sodomy and Buggery in Seventeenth-Century New England," *Journal of Social History* 12 (1978): 268–81; J. R. Roberts, "The Case of Sarah Norman and Mary Hammond," *Sinister Wisdom* 24 (1980): 57–62; and Jonathan Katz, *Gay American History* (New York: Crowell, 1976), pp. 16–24, 568–71.

4. For the period from 1870 to 1940 see the documents in Katz, *Gay American History*, and *Gay/Lesbian Almanac* (New York: Crowell, 1983). Other sources include Allan Bérubé, "Lesbians and Gay Men in Early San Francisco: Notes Toward a Social History of Lesbians and Gay Men in America," unpublished paper, 1979; Vern Bullough and Bonnie Bullough, "Lesbianism in the 1920s and 1930s: A Newfound Study," *Signs* 2 (Summer 1977): 895–904.

5. On the medical model see Weeks, *Coming Out*, pp. 23–32. The impact of the medical model on the consciousness of men and women can be seen in Louis Hyde, ed., *Rat and the Devil: The Journal Letters of F. O. Matthiessen and Russell Cheney* (Hamden, Conn.: Archon, 1978), p. 47, and in the story of Lucille Hart in Katz, *Gay American History*, pp. 258–79. Radclyffe Hall's classic novel about lesbianism, *The Well of Loneliness*, published in 1928, was perhaps one of the most important vehicles for the popularization of the medical model.

6. See Alfred Kinsey et al., *Sexual Behavior in the Human Male* (Philadelphia: W. B. Saunders, 1948) and *Sexual Behavior in the Human Female* (Philadelphia: W. B. Saunders, 1953).

7. On black music, see "AC/DC Blues: Gay Jazz Reissues," Stash Records, ST–106 (1977), and Chris Albertson, *Bessie* (New York: Stein and Day, 1974); on the persistence of kin networks in white ethnic communities, see Judith Smith, "Our Own Kind: Family and Community Networks in Providence," in *A Heritage of Her Own*, ed. Nancy F. Cott and Elizabeth H. Pleck (New York: Simon and Schuster, 1979), pp. 393–411; on differences between rural and urban male homoeroticism, see Kinsey et al., *Sexual Behavior in the Human Male*, pp. 455–57, 630–31.

8. The argument and the information in this and the following paragraphs come from my book *Sexual Politics, Sexual Communities: The Making of a Homosexual Minority in the United States, 1940–1970* (Chicago: University of Chicago Press, 1983). I have also developed it with reference to San Francisco in "Gay Politics, Gay Community: San Francisco's Experience," *Socialist Review* 55 (January–February 1981): 77–104.

9. Donald Vining, *A Gay Diary, 1933–1946* (New York: Pepys Press, 1979); "Pat Bond," in Nancy

Adair and Casey Adair, *Word Is Out* (New York: New Glide Publications, 1978), pp. 55–65; and Allan Bérubé, "Marching to a Different Drummer: Coming Out During World War II," a slide/talk presented at the annual meeting of the American Historical Association, December 1981, Los Angeles. A shorter version of Bérubé's presentation can be found in *The Advocate*, October 15, 1981, pp. 20–24.

10. On lesbian novels see *The Ladder*, March 1958, p. 18; February 1960, pp. 14–15; April 1961, pp. 12–13; February 1962, pp. 6–11; January 1963, pp. 6–13; February 1964, pp. 12–19; February 1965, pp. 19–23; March 1966, pp. 22–26; and April 1967, pp. 8–13. *The Ladder* was the magazine published by the Daughters of Bilitis.

11. This especially needs to be emphasized to-day. The 1980 annual conference of the National Organization for Women, for instance, passed a lesbian rights resolution that defined the issue as one of "discrimination based on affectional/sexual preference/orientation," and explicitly disassociated the issue from other questions of sexuality such as pornography, sadomasochism, public sex, and pederasty.

12. I do not mean to suggest that homophobia is "caused" by capitalism, or is to be found only in capitalist societies. Severe sanctions against homoeroticism can be found in European feudal society and in contemporary socialist countries. But my focus in this has been the emergence of a gay identity under capitalism, and the mechanisms specific to capitalism that made this possible and that reproduce homophobia as well.

Chapter 11

Bread Before Roses: American Workingmen, Labor Unions, and the Family Wage

MARTHA MAY

"The idea that the worker should be paid a living wage rather than the market rate of wages as determined by the laws of the universe," railed one magazine writer in 1872, "is pure and simple communism."[1] In the late nineteenth century, employers and laissez-faire economists argued strenuously against the living wage capable of supporting a worker and his family. Forcing employers to provide for non-workers through the pay packet, they warned, would mean the demise of American industry. The very spirit of free enterprise was at stake.

In the Progressive era, however, the idea of a living wage won widespread acceptance. By 1918, the authors of a social survey of Philadelphia could state confidently:

> Nowadays very few persons object to the principle of a living wage. It is generally agreed that the humblest worker is entitled to a return for his services that will enable him to support himself and his family in decency and comfort.[2]

From Ruth Milkman, ed., *Women, Work, and Protest: A Century of U.S. Women's Labor History* (London: Routledge, 1985), pp. 1–21. Reprinted by permission.

Once championed only by workingmen and labor unions, now the living-wage ideal was endorsed by Progressive social scientists, and even by some employers—notably Henry Ford, Elbert Gary and John D. Rockefeller—for whom it offered the promise of worker stability and productivity, and a bulwark against radical unionism.[3]

The living wage of labor, Progressives and paternalistic employers was in practice a family wage: the earnings of a male worker which were sufficient to support a dependent family.[4] As an ideal—and, indeed, it was more often a demand than an achievement—the family wage legitimated the division of labor by gender.[5] It encouraged the notion that female participation in the labor force merely supplemented family income, and served to justify unequal wage rates and sex segregation in the labor market.

Contemporary feminists agree on the consequences of the family-wage ideology for women; its historical *purpose*, however, remains ambiguous. Was the family wage a vehicle for male supremacy? Or was it, as Jane

Humphries has argued, primarily an attempt by the working classes to retain autonomy?[6] Or, did the family-wage demand constitute an effort by workers to win better conditions by mobilizing values accepted throughout society in support of their complaints? Exploring these issues may help illuminate the processes through which sex segregation in the labor market is created and maintained, and how it might be overcome. Specifically, analyzing the historical origins of the labor movement's commitment to the family-wage ideal may help to explain the enduring tension between women workers and American labor unions.

This chapter examines the family-wage ideology of organized labor in two periods: the decades of its formation in the nineteenth century, and its operation in the early twentieth century. I will argue that, in the earlier period, the family-wage demand emerged as a working-class cause, which capital opposed but which both working-class men and women supported. Its meaning was transformed in the early twentieth century, however, as the class perspective of labor changed into a more pragmatic unionism. In the Progressive era, the family wage became a cross-class ideology, and now, within that ideology, issues of gender superseded the claims of class autonomy.

The Family Wage as a Working-Class Demand

The family-wage ideology emerged in the first half of the nineteenth century as a response by workingmen to specific industrial and social conditions: the inadequacies of wage rates; the difficulties of securing subsistence; the relative fluidity of the labor market, with its high turnover rates, decreasing skill requirements, and technological innovations; and the presence of a powerful ideology defining gender roles. Fearful of the erosion of customary traditions of craftsmanship, a decline in status and decreasing wages, skilled workmen expressed serious concern about the effects of industrial development on family life. "The name of freedom is but a shadow . . . if we are to be torn from our fireside for endeavoring to obtain a fair and just support for our families," journeymen cordwainers in Philadelphia argued in 1806.[7] Similarly, at a Utica, New York, convention in the 1830s, workers agreed that, "the mechanic with his family . . . has the honest right not only to a livelihood for himself and them, but to save from his earnings the means of education for his children, and comfort for himself in his old age."[8]

The family wage represented a dual claim to subsistence and industrial justice to its early advocates: workingmen, organized in trades' societies and unions, demanded both sufficient wages and the rights due the industrious producer in a republic. Without fair wages, the workingman faced poverty and a diminution in status, as dependency upon industrial wages placed new constraints upon family resources. Under existing wage rates, frequently inadequate for the needs of one person, the working-class family would be unable to maintain a tolerable standard of living or retain its customs or traditions.[9]

Workingmen repeatedly condemned "purse-proud aristocrats" and "tyranny," as labor's demands in the early industrial era centered around regaining status, recouping losses and reaffirming the laborer's basic rights, including the right to maintain a family. In demands for better educational standards, and in attempts to secure consumers' cooperatives, mechanics' lien laws and equitable methods of payment, workingmen recognized the connection between control over working conditions and over home life. The family wage became a first step toward ameliorating the precarious position of the workingman and his family under the new conditions of industrialization, a means to restore their dignity and equality. Male workers claimed that "which the God of nature intended as their right, but which avarice denies them—a comfortable subsistence." The family wage also promised a means to diminish capitalists' control over family life, by allowing workingmen to provide independently for their families. Cordwainers from Lynn, Massachusetts, complained in 1844 about an industrial system which robbed "our families of support, our children of the benefits of the higher branches of education, and ourselves of the many comforts of life," while enriching employers and creating "antirepublican" distinctions.[10]

Through such rhetoric, workingmen expressed the belief that only "producers" and their families faced the dislocations of family life resulting from industrialization. Only their wives and children experienced the pressures to join the labor force; only their children confronted the possibility of a lifetime of poverty and need. Divorced from other sources of income, workers claimed that only a fair wage rate stood between their families and the specter of poverty and starvation. As early as the 1830s, workers argued that if wives and children were forced to enter the labor market to supplement family income, the status of the workingman would be degraded. As labor organizer Seth Luther reasoned, "We know . . . that the *wives* and *daughters* of the rich manufacturers would no more associate with a *factory girl* than they would with a *negro slave.* So much for equality in a republican country."[11] The National Trades' Union asked, "Is not avarice satisfied with a nation of Fathers and Sons, but our Wives and Daughters, the Loved Ones of our hearts and affections, shall be thrown into the spoilers' arms?"[12] One purpose of the family-wage demand was to spare the workingman's wife

and children the degradation of factory labor. And, equally important, it was to insure that the workingman would retain his status within the family, and his right to a family structure resembling that of the more advantaged classes.

Workingmen left little doubt as to the form of family life they sought. William English, a leader in the National Trades' Union, wondered in 1835 if the time would arrive when "our wives, no longer doomed to servile labor, will be the companions of our fireside and the instructors of our children."[13] Without adequate wages, the workingman could not fulfill the normative prescriptions for a "proper" family life. The family-wage demand asserted the social right of the working class to the ideal of family and gender roles embodied in the "cult of true womanhood." Indeed, the family-wage ideology was heavily dependent on arguments about female domesticity and male responsibility. "The physical organization, the natural responsibilities, and the moral sensibilities of woman, prove conclusively that her labor should only be of a domestic nature," declared the National Trades' Union.[14] In a speech delivered in 1867, William Sylvis of the National Labor Union inveighed in similar terms:

> It will be fatal to the cause of labor, when we place the sexes in competition, and jeopardize those social relations which render woman queen of the household. Keep her in the sphere which God designed her to fill, by manly assistance.[15]

The family-wage ideology operated by connecting class issues of subsistence and justice with gender, this defining the relationship between men, women and work. The domestic ideal placed women in the home, while waged work received an increasingly masculine definition. Indeed, the "cult of breadwinning" was featured prominently in the class ideology which developed among industrial workmen.[16] But gender divisions remained subordinate to class claims; the working-class family ideology continued to be qualified by its emphasis on subsistence, justice and the demand for better hours and wages. The similarity between the working-class family and its middle-class counterpart, workingmen argued, ended at the pay packet. Family relationships and idealized roles depended upon material conditions to sustain them: without family wages, the lady became a poor wife and "breadgiver," taking in boarders and laundry, or going out to work; while the industrious male laborer was transformed into an indigent, losing prestige and power not only in the shop but also in society and in the home. In short, while the working-class ideology of family life idealized middle-class gender roles, it did so in the context of an analysis of social and material conditions.[17]

The arguments for the family wage invoked the interests of the entire family, thus going beyond a simple assertion of gender privilege. Workingmen consistently viewed their wage-earning responsibility as beneficial to their dependants. They argued against women's presence in the labor market at lower wage rates because it endangered this wage-earning responsibility and gave rise to a new and undesirable (in their view) type of family structure.

Protest by workingmen over a low-wage population of workers entering a trade was not confined to exclusionism directed at women. Journeymen also opposed the employment of unregulated apprentices, prison labor, unskilled workers and some immigrant groups.[18] But workingmen countered the perceived dangers of women's participation in the labor force with the rhetoric of gender division. Some claimed that women's innate moral virtue would be corrupted by factory employment, while others contended that women were better suited for manual work and should be prohibited as competitors with an unfair

advantage.[19] Occasionally, male unions aided striking female workers. More often, though, male-dominated trades' societies and unions excluded women outright, or admitted them only in the hope of lessening the ill effects of female competition.[20] Prior to 1873, only two among the thirty-plus national unions then in existence admitted women to membership.[21]

The frequency of arguments for female exclusion and their conjunction with the family-wage demand have led a number of historians to theorize that these arguments motivated the family wage itself: job competition between genders led workingmen to use male privilege as a means to achieve access to better wages and conditions.[22] But the history of the family-wage ideology prior to 1890 suggests the need for reevaluation of this interpretation. Nineteenth-century sexual divisions must be understood in the dual context which they had for workingmen themselves: the shop as well as the home. The family wage, as a solution to the threats the workingman perceived to himself and to his family in the new industrial order, appeared *first* as a class demand for industrial justice, and second as a defense of traditional work and family arrangements. As the presence of women wage-earners in the labor market threatened to upset the balance between home and shop, and to diminish further the workingman's ability to have or maintain a family, the family-wage demand took on the additional aspect of female exclusion. The family wage promised to serve the male worker in the shop, by securing his right to better wages; it also maintained the family in the home, allowing women to fulfill their "natural" role as wives and mothers, and allowing children to attain some education. The family wage promised to remedy class injustice by raising the standard of living of workers, and by assuring them family stability and security. "Is it charitable, is it humane, is it honest, to take from the laborer, who is already fed, clothed, and lodged too poorly, a portion of his food and raiment, and deprive his family of the necessities of life?" iron-molders asked in 1859.[23] The family wage promised to resolve this inequity, to sustain family life and to protect family autonomy.

Yet, the family-wage demand ultimately exacted a higher price from its advocates. It worked against the interests of working-class men, women and families, by accepting and deepening a sexual double standard in the labor market. The family-wage ideal gave employers an easy means of undercutting wage rates and fostering competition among workers. It also confined both males and females to gender roles which impeded individual opportunity and expression. Equally important, the family-wage ideology discouraged any attempt to explore new, more egalitarian family arrangements within the context of industrialization. In defending the family through the family wage, working-class men and women placed family interests above individual need. This was especially significant for women, who shared in the advantages accruing to working-class families through the family-wage demand, but who at the same time faced the discrimination it legitimated, both in the shop and at home.

The problems inherent in the family-wage demand gradually became apparent, as the class character of the ideology's supporters underwent a dramatic shift in the Progressive era. Middle-class social reformers and activists came to embrace the family wage as a means of restoring social stability, while some employers recognized its possibilities as a means to control and divide labor. At the same time, within the ranks of organized labor, the family wage increasingly became a defense of gender privilege. Labor's family wage, first predicated on the family, now served fully to rationalize male prerogatives, as women entered the labor market in growing numbers.

The "Modern" Family Wage

As labor struggled for material improvements after 1890, the family wage played a crucial role in its demands. The dominance of the American Federation of Labor (AFL) indicated a new emphasis within labor's ranks on trade union issues of hours, wages and conditions; Samuel Gompers explained the philosophy of the modern trade union as "economic betterment—today, tomorrow, in home and shop"[24] Gompers called for

a minimum wage—a living wage—which when expended in an economic manner, shall be sufficient to maintain an average-sized family in a manner consistent with whatever the contemporary civilization recognized as indispensable to physical and mental health.[25]

Similarly, the family wage demanded by the AFL in 1907 was to be "a constantly growing minimum wage . . . sufficient to maintain [workers] and those dependent upon them in a manner consistent with their responsibilities as *husbands, fathers, men* and *citizens*."[26] The AFL's position remained the same in 1919, when a spokesman summarized it this way:

The workers are tired of having themselves, their wives and children, used as chips for our commercial, financial, and industrial gamblers. . . . What is the price we pay for children free from factory life, for mothers burdened by no duties outside the home, for fathers who have leisure for homes and families? . . . The living wage is the right to be a man and to exercise freely and fully the rights of a free man. That is the living wage, and to realize it is the sure and true destiny of organized labor.[27]

This family-wage idea relied heavily on the male's right to an improved standard of living as the family breadwinner and implied a fundamental difference between the rights of male and female workers. Although the AFL pledged to organize women and joined in the call for female suffrage, affiliates continued to argue that female workers reduced wage rates, and the federation took no action against member-unions prohibiting female membership.[28] Gompers himself contended in 1906, "It is the so-called competition of the unorganized defenseless women workers, the girl and the wife, that often tends to reduce the wages of the father and the husband."[29] As Alice Kessler-Harris has suggested, the AFL tipped the scales balancing female equality and exclusion toward the policy of exclusion—never fully sanctioning gender restrictions, but maintaining barriers against female workers.[30]

Unlike the nineteenth-century labor movement's family-wage argument, which reflected a broad-based response to industrialization, the AFL's family wage shifted the emphasis from the family life to gender privilege. This paralleled the broader shift in the early twentieth century to a pragmatic new unionism seeking material improvements and union strength, rather than a class-based movement for greater equality. As the claim of class justice receded as a motivation for the family-wage demand, the AFL argued for improvements based on the male's primary role as a worker and breadwinner. While rhetorically addressing the interests of a class of producers, the federation pursued a family wage to legitimate higher *male* wages. It implicitly promised the male unionist that only membership in an AFL affiliate would secure for him and his family an "American standard of living." In effect, the family now appeared as one beneficiary of the male worker's claims, and not the reverse, as had been the case in the nineteenth century.

The AFL differentiated between male and female workers in a variety of ways—in its position on minimum wages, for example. The federation opposed wage regulation for males, arguing that legislation interferred

with labor's ability to bargain and negotiate. At the same time, it recognized women, minors and government employees as exceptions requiring special protection. In 1913, the AFL resolved that women workers "constitute a separate and more difficult problem. They are . . . more easily exploited."[31] The federation failed to object to the methods the states used to determine minimum wage levels, which in every case reflected the subsistence needs of single women, not of those supporting dependants. This sharply contrasted with labor's demand that the lowest male earnings should reflect the possibility that the male worker would be supporting a family, whether or not such a family was in fact present. The assumption was that all wage-earning women were single and left the workforce upon marriage; men, by contrast, should always be accorded higher wages because they might, one day, have families to support.

Gender-based wage differentials were also encouraged by the growing use of the family-wage idea in private and governmental budget studies and cost-of-living surveys, which figured minimum standards of "health and decency" on the amount needed by a male breadwinner to support a dependent family. Labor's family-wage demands dovetailed with Progressive reformers' and social activists' insistence upon a male-supported family structure. As social worker Mary Conyngton advised, the "friendly visitor" should "properly use every means to make the wife see her duties as a homemaker, there should be no relaxation in the effort to make the man do his duty as breadwinner."[32] A growing consensus appeared among such middle-class reformers that a family wage would allow working-class families to preserve "proper" social values. Through the inculcation of thrift, sobriety and order, problems of poverty and social upheaval could be eliminated. A family composed of the male breadwinner, home-bound wife and obedient, Americanized children was central to this Progressive outlook. As early as 1904, economist John A. Rayn suggested that the economic vehicle for realizing this form of family life was the family wage.[33]

By World War I, the federal government had become a third advocate of the family wage, along with the Progressive and labor movements. The National War Labor Broad used family-wage-based budget studies in its wage-adjustment determinations.[34] This practice produced debate over what constituted a family standard, and whether the government was encouraging an increase in standards of living. Many employers objected to the use of family wages in wage adjustments; one analyst noted that "the attempt to set a budget-wage on the basis of the family's needs meant . . . the establishment of a family wage for all adult male employees, regardless of family responsibilities."[35] While state support of the family wage did not result in the pernicious effects envisioned by its detractors, nor in the uniform achievement of a family-wage standard, it is significant that sectors of the state accepted its validity and urged its adoption. Once the family-wage ideology became part of a cross-class ideology, it had the status of a truism, an easily accepted statement on the best organization of life.

This cross-class acceptance of the family-wage standard in budget studies and wage determination initially appeared to benefit organized labor. But after World War I, it became a double-edged sword, as government determinations raised some wages while reducing others. The AFL returned to its former position against wage regulations after 1918.[36] Unions discovered that the family wage could be turned against the working-man by employers, as when family-wage rates connected to "welfare" programs served to undercut union organization and divide the

workforce.[37] Under these conditions, the AFL might have qualified or dropped its support of the family-wage notion, now employed to limit earnings and oppose organized labor. That the AFL affiliates continued to cite the male responsibility as family breadwinner to gain access to jobs and higher wages suggests this ideology remained useful in securing short-term goals. If the family wage no longer served to protect labor's family requirements at an optimal level, it still provided an advantage to the male worker in the shop.

Growing public concern over the impact of married women's participation in the labor force provided unionists with new ammunition to protect their jobs and prerogatives. After World War I, the family-wage idea reinforced the notion that most women worked temporarily, supplementing a male's earnings. Few people challenged the single woman's right to work; by the 1920s she was "no longer expected to remain in the household of some related male protector."[38] But the single woman eventually married and began her own family; then, as a Women's Bureau study stated, "It is of manifest importance to know why so large a group of women with home responsibilities should be at work while the usual family providers are in evidence."[39] Observers of the phenomenon of married women's waged work concluded wives' motivation for earning was family need.[40] This perception acknowledged the generally low rate of male earnings while rationalizing women's work, negating the idea of choice. Gwendolyn Hughes noted, "As a rule, even mothers who worked from 'choice' were simply making an effort to raise their families above a mere 'subsistence' level."[41]

Although some commentators hailed married women's work as a sign of a positive, growing independence, most worried about the impact of mothers' absence from their children. Married women's work outside the home represented both a sign of new consumption needs and new household relationships; as Day Monroe viewed it, work for upper-class women was facilitated by the hired help who would assume their household duties. For working-class women, the "problem" was more troublesome: who would ease the double burden they faced, of waged work and family responsibilities? The remedies suggested by analysts included mothers' pensions, family allowances, industry-supported child payments, and the family wage—all geared to ending the necessity for working-class married women to work.[42]

For organized labor, the continued popularity of the family-wage idea afforded male workers an opportunity to further their arguments for higher wage rates. Male unionists could demand first rights to jobs and pay increases because married women's employment only supplemented family income, and single women could expect to marry. Higher male earnings had an ideological legitimacy that women could not claim without asserting equal rights or denying the "natural" organization of the family; the family wage provided a convenient means for male workers to retain their control of jobs and conditions.

The effectiveness of arguments for protection of male positions had a significant impact upon women workers. For example, in Highland Park, Michigan, the city council barred married women from city jobs in 1921, and followed that action by prohibiting all women workers, claiming that women displaced unemployed men.[43] In the 1920s, the Baltimore and Ohio Railroad agreed with the Brotherhood of Railway and Steamship Clerks to prohibit married women's work.[44] In the same decade, other unions simply excluded women entirely; the various unions, representing elastic goring weavers, carpenters and joiners, and pattern-makers all denied women membership. In their twenty-fifth convention, the molders' union resolved that their leaders should "give their best thoughts and effort in opposing the employment of female and child labor in jobs recognized as men's employment."[45] While women workers as a category found themselves relegated to specific sectors of the labor market, married women's employment remained particularly suspect. The married women workers took work away from men who needed to labor. Some social analysts tried to counter such perceptions by arguing that women did not displace male workers; ironically, these advocates of women's expanded roles did not recognize that their defense admitted the importance—and the problems—of a sexually divided workforce.[46]

During the Depression, use of the family-wage argument to limit or prohibit women's employment accelerated. In 1930, the Economy Act's Section 213 mandated the discharge of one spouse in cases where both were federal government employees. This controversial legislation, directly based on the family-wage ideology, was proposed or adopted across the nation. In Kansas, the governor suggested barring women from employment if their husbands could support them. Syracuse, New York, Racine, Wisconsin, and Seattle, Washington, prohibited the employment of women whose husbands earned a "living wage." According to Lois Scharf, a "virtual epidemic" of such legislation infected twenty-six states by 1939, some explicitly labeling the level at which a family income was sufficient to warrant discharge.[47] Despite the position of the national AFL that women workers should receive equal pay for equal work, some state and local federations, such as in Idaho, urged exclusion of married women.[48]

The family-wage ideology remained in full force, promoted by governmental agencies, AFL affiliates and social reformers. For the AFL, tacit support of the family wage was a pragmatic effort to defend falling wage rates, which declined 48 percent between 1929 and 1933.[49] Family-wage arguments continued to defend the male worker's right to a job at decent wages because of his gender and, by implication, his family responsibility. Overall, women's exclusion or lower pay seemed to be in the national interest, for the preservation of the nation's economy. But if the family wage rationalized discrimination against women in the name of the family, it returned ironically few benefits to most working-class households. Instead, it operated to reduce family earnings by reinforcing the exclusion of one family wage-earner or lowering her wage rates, at a time when slightly more than half the families of unskilled workers contained a sole male breadwinner.[50] The family wage continued to serve only one segment of workers: the skilled unionists who could organize to pursue jobs and oppose wage reductions.

Male privilege provided an extra claim to work and wages that unionists would not fully abandon until World War II, when the presence of women workers in jobs previously reserved for men forced them to support equal pay for women in order to protect their own postwar rates. Under these conditions, the family-wage ideology no longer served the interests of unionized men. World War II also brought married women into the labor force in much larger numbers than ever before, a development which became permanent after the war. This change in the composition of the female labor force gradually made the family-wage ideology anachronistic; yet, within the organized labor movement, it dies hard. To this day, one encounters expressions of the family-wage ideology among male unionists, and its resilience is one part of the explanation for the failure of organized labor to bring the ever-increasing number of women workers into its ranks.

Conclusion

The family wage illustrates a complex relationship between gender and class, one that rarely remained static. This wage form, and the ideology defining it, underwent a series of changes through the first 100 years of its operation. During the nineteenth century, it served as one argument for class justice and working-class autonomy. Workingmen perceived themselves denied access to a "proper," traditional family life, and they pressed their grievances about conditions in home and shop by citing family interests. There was little that was revolutionary or reactionary in their calls for family wages. They merely attempted to insure their families would not deviate from prescribed social norms: their demands were remarkably similar to the popular cultural descriptions of family articulated through an ideology of separate spheres. What was crucial in the progress of the nineteenth-century family-wage ideology was the response to these demands outside the working class. No middle-class reformer incorporated the family wage into programs of relief for the poor, which continued to be premised on individual problems of intemperance and moral laxity. In the latter half of the nineteenth century, the family-wage demand also conflicted with employers' and governmental laissez-faire notions that wages should be strictly sufficient for an individual, with no guarantees of family minimums. The class interests of capital and labor were opposed in the family-wage ideology, while the gender interests of working-class men and women appeared to be united in efforts to achieve or maintain particular reproductive structures.[51]

By the turn of the century, organized labor addressed its full efforts to winning economic improvements through trade union strategies. As the class perspective of labor changed into a more pragmatic unionism, Progressive activists and social-reformers took up the issue of the working-class poor. In seeking to reestablish social order, these predominantly middle-class men and women promoted the family wage as a solution to instability within the working-class family. The family wage became a cross-class ideology, with the issues of gender now superseding the claims of class autonomy. Progressive advocacy won widespread support for the family-wage ideology, but in a different form from the family wages pursued by organized labor. The Progressives' family wage, adopted by state and federal government agencies, and by some employers, was calculated at a minimum family level, while labor sought to maximize earnings. Middle-class use of the family wage, and some employers' acceptance of it, effectively limited the long-term economic advantages of the family wage to skilled labor.

Why did the family wage achieve an ideological hegemony? For reformers, this wage form promised to restore the "traditional" family they believed would best provide stability and American values. Without adequate family wages, women and children were forced into the labor market, undermining the foundations of home life so essential to efficient social order. These goals corresponded with the needs of collective capital in several ways. The family-wage ideology reinforced the notion that women worked only to supplement family income, or temporarily as single women. This allowed employers to pay lower female wages without—in popular wisdom—endangering the social structure. But family wages served more subtle interests as well. They divided the workforce between genders, and between high- and low-waged sectors. An employer who awarded the family wage could blunt union activity and increase long-term profitability by reducing high labor turnover. The family wage also decreased

overall working-class earnings by limiting female wages. When families sent several wage-earners into the labor force to earn a joint income sufficient for family needs, their wages together might easily exceed a minimum reasonable family-wage level.[52] In other words, family-wage payments tend to reduce wage costs of collective capital not by securing the unpaid domestic labor of the wife in the home, but by limiting her earnings and the amount paid to a family. Individual employers often failed to recognize this advantage, however, because of their short-term interest in hiring lower-paid females.

For organized labor, the impact of the family wage was, in the long run, detrimental. As unionists themselves occasionally argued, the existence of gender divisions allowed employers to undercut higher rates by using a low-waged workforce. In general, unionists chose to support female exclusion rather than pursue the gender equality which would have resolved the divisions in the interests of the entire working class. Motivated by the short-term goals of job protection and immediate material improvements, unionists maintained a commitment to the family wage to further their specific, limited needs.

The family wage also operated in the long-term interest of male workers, by perpetuating the legitimacy of gender privilege. While women workers struggled to convince employers—and society—of their need for fair wages and jobs, male workers found easier access to positions and power. In the twentieth century, this was facilitated by the abandonment of a class perspective in favor of pragmatism. Unionized workers defended their positions using whatever tools were readily available, including the ideology of sexual division. In the absence of a systematic, feminist class analysis, this probably appeared as the best choice for the trade union movement in the years before World War II. Ultimately, however, this path deepened the problems associated with a sexually divided labor force.

The family-wage ideology retained its power because it promised so much to so many: to reformers, order; to employers, profitability; to unionized male workers, access and job control; to the unskilled, the hope of better conditions. The ideology reinforced class-specific goals while providing social stability. The one group which obviously did not benefit from the family wage was working women. Not only were their wages reduced—or terminated—by the family-wage ideal; there was also pressure from the definition of their work as unfeminine, selfish and detrimental to the social good. It is this legacy of the family wage, as much as its impact on the structure of the labor market and upon wages, which feminist organization still must confront.

NOTES

1. Sidney Fine, *Laissez-Faire and the General Welfare State*, Ann Arbor: University of Michigan Press, 1956, p. 60.

2. Bureau of Municipal Research of Philadelphia, *Workingmen's Standards of Living in Philadelphia*, New York: Macmillan, 1919, p. 1.

3. I do not mean to imply that employers' use of the family wage was widespread; in general, it was the larger corporations with the capital to invest in strategies for long-term productivity which experimented with family-oriented "welfare." See Katherine Stone, "Origins of Job Structures in the Steel Industry," in Richard C. Edwards, Michael Reich, and David M. Gordon, eds., *Labor Market Segmentation*, Lexington, MA: D. C. Heath, 1975, p. 54; Martha May, "The Historical Problem of the Family Wage: The Ford Motor Company and the Five Dollar Day," *Feminist Studies*, vol. 8, no. 2, summer 1982, pp. 399–424.

4. Progressive analysts also estimated the living wage for a single woman worker, and occasionally the single male. Family budget studies predominated, however, indicating both widespread concern about family life and the assumption that most Americans lived in a family unit. Faith M. Williams and Helen Connolly, *Bibliography on Studies and Costs and Standards of Living in the United States*, United States Department of Agriculture, Bureau of Home Economics, 1930; Shelby Harrison, *The Social Survey*, New York: Russell Sage Foundation, 1931; Charles Y. Glock, ed., *Survey Research in the Social Sciences*, New York: Russell Sage Foundation, 1967.

5. While the family-wage ideology promised to end poverty, average wages remained near or beneath estimated subsistence levels in the Progressive era. See, for example, Scott Nearing, *Financing the Wage Earner's Family*, New York: B. W. Huebsch, 1914; and Robert C. Chapin, *The Standard of Living Among Workingmen's Families in New York City*, New York: Russell Sage Foundation, 1909.

6. See Heidi Hartmann, "The Unhappy Marriage of Marxism and Feminism: Towards a More Progressive Union," *Capital and Class*, vol. 8, summer 1979, pp. 1–32, and Jane Humphries, "The Working-Class Family, Women's Liberation and Class Struggle: The Case of Nineteenth-Century British History," *Review of Radical Political Economics*, vol. 9, fall 1977, pp. 25–42.

7. David Saposs, "Colonial and Federal Beginnings," in John R. Commons et al., *History of Labor in the United States*, vol. 1, New York: Macmillan, 1918, pp. 141–42.

8. Mary P. Ryan, *Cradle of the Middle Class: The Family in Oneida County, New York, 1790–1865*, New York: Cambridge University Press, 1981, p. 131.

9. Historians continue to debate the "typical" standard of living of skilled and unskilled working-class families in the nineteenth century. Most argue that unskilled laborers received wages sufficient for the support of a single person, while skilled workers' wages could range from levels beneath poverty to a comfortable family standard. For some members of the working classes, the family wage was obviously a potential means for gaining adequate subsistence. See Clyde Griffen, "Workers Divided: The Effect of Craft and Ethnic Differences in Poughkeepsie, New York, 1850–1880," and Leo F. Schnore and Peter R. Knights, "Residence and Social Structure: Boston in the Antebellum Period," both in Stephan Thernstrom

and Richard Sennett, eds., *Nineteenth-Century Cities: Essays in the New Urban History,* New Haven: Yale University Press, 1969; Norman Ware, *The Industrial Worker, 1840–1860,* Boston: Houghton Mifflin, 1924; Bruce Laurie, *Working People of Philadelphia, 1800–1850,* Philadelphia: Temple University Press, 1980; and Steven Dubnoff, "A Method for Estimating the Economic Welfare of American Families of Any Composition, 1860–1909," *Historical Methods,* vol. 13, no. 3, pp. 171–80.

10. Philip Foner, *History of the Labor Movement in the United States,* vol. 1: *From Colonial Times to the Founding of the American Federation of Labor,* New York: International Publishers, 1947, p. 120; John R. Commons, et al., *A Documentary History of American Industrial Society,* New York: Russell & Russell, 1958, vol. 8, p. 234.

11. Seth Luther, *Address to the Working Men of New England,* pamphlet reprinted in Philip Taft and Leo Stein, eds., *Religion, Reform, and Revolution: Labor Panaceas in the Nineteenth Century,* New York: Arno, 1970, p. 1.

12. Commons, *Documentary,* vol. 5, p. 284.

13. Helen Sumner, *Report on the Condition of Women and Child Wage Earners in the United States,* vol. 9: *History of Women in Industry in the United States.* Washington, DC, 1910, p. 29.

14. Commons, *Documentary,* vol. 6, p. 281.

15. James C. Sylvis, *The Life, Speeches, Labors, and Essays of William H. Sylvis,* Philadelphia: Claxton, Remsen & Haffelfinger, 1872, p. 220.

16. The "cult of breadwinning" has received little attention from historians, and its origins and developments remain sketchy at best. The masculine ideal dates at least to the patriarchal family of colonial America, in which men held legal and economic responsibility for family affairs. See, for example, Philip Greven, *The Protestant Temperament: Patterns in Child Rearing, Religious Experience, and the Self in America,* New York: Alfred A. Knopf, 1977; Mary Beth Norton, *Liberty's Daughters: The Revolutionary Experience of American Women, 1750–1800,* Boston: Little, Brown, 1980. See also Linda Schneider, "The Citizen Striker: Workers' Ideology in the Homestead Strike of 1892," *Labor History,* vol. 22, no. 4, winter 1981, pp. 52–63.

17. An excellent example of this may be found in the speeches of National Labor Union leader William Sylvis. See Sylvis, *Life, Speeches, Labors.*

18. See John Higham, *Strangers in the Land: Patterns of American Nativism, 1860–1925,* New York: Atheneum, 1971; John B. Andrews, "Nationalization," in Commons, *History of Labor,* vol. 2, especially pp. 3–10; Ware, *Industrial Worker.*

19. Ware, *Industrial Worker,* pp. 77–80; Commons, *Documentary,* vol. 8, pp. 134–49.

20. See, for example, Carol Turbin, "And We Are Nothing But Women: Irish Working Women in Troy," in Carol R. Berkin and Mary Beth Norton, eds., *Women of America: A History,* Boston: Houghton Mifflin, 1979, pp. 202–21.

21. Gerald Grob, *Workers and Utopia: A Study of Industrial Conflict in the American Labor Movement, 1865–1900,* Evanston, IL: Northwestern University Press, 1961, p. 55.

22. For example, see Hartmann, "The Unhappy Marriage," and Alice Kessler-Harris, *Out to Work: A History of Wage-earning Women in the United States,* New York: Oxford University Press, 1982, p. 68.

23. Sylvis, *Life, Speeches, Labors,* p. 32.

24. Samuel Gompers, *Seventy Years of Life and Labor,* New York: E. P. Dutton, 1925, p. 286. See also Grob, *Workers and Utopia,* p. 133.

25. James Boyle, *The Minimum Wage and Syndicalism,* Cincinnati: Stewart & Kidd, 1913, p. 73.

26. American Federation of Labor, *History, Encyclopedia, Reference Book,* American Federation of Labor, Washington, DC, 1919, p. 7.

27. David Saposs, *Readings in Trade Unionism,* New York: George H. Doran, 1926, p. 270.

28. Ruth Milkman, "Organizing the Sexual Division of Labor: Historical Perspectives on 'Women's Work' and the American Labor Movement," *Socialist Review,* January–February 1980, pp. 95–144; Women's Bureau, Bulletin no. 12, "The New Position of Women in American Industry," Washington, DC, 1920, p. 157.

29. Alice Kessler-Harris, " 'Where Are the Organized Women Workers?' " *Feminist Studies,* vol. 3, no. 1/2, fall 1975, p. 96.

30. Ibid. See also Ann Schofield, "The Rise of the Pig-Headed Girl: An Analysis of the American Labor Press for Their Attitudes toward Women, 1877–1920," Ph.D. diss., State University of New York, Binghamton, 1980.

31. Taft and Stein, eds., *Religion, Reform and Revolution*, p. 146.

32. See Mary Conyngton, *How to Help: A Manual of Practical Charity*, New York: Macmillan, 1909, p. 131.

33. John A. Ryan, *The Living Wage*, New York: Macmillan, 1906.

34. Selig Perlman and Philip Taft, "Labor Movements," in Commons, *Documentary*, vol. 2, p. 408.

35. Don Lescohier, "Working Conditions," in Commons, *Documentary*, vol. 3, p. 72.

36. Perlman and Taft, "Labor Movements," p. 452.

37. See May, "Historical Problem of the Family Wage."

38. Day Monroe, *Chicago Families: A Study of Unpublished Census Data*, Chicago: University of Chicago Press, 1932, p. 31.

39. Women's Bureau, Bulletin no. 23, "The Family Status of Breadwinning Women," Washington, DC, 1922, p. 42; Women's Bureau, Bulletin no. 30, "The Share of Wage-Earning Women in Family Support," Washington, DC, 1923, p. 1.

40. See Winifred Wandersee, "Past Ideals and Present Pleasures: Women, Work, and the Family, 1920–1940," Ph.D. diss., University of Minnesota, 1976; Robert and Helen M. Lynd, *Middletown: A Study in American Culture*, New York: Harcourt Brace & World, 1929, pp. 26–27; and Lois Scharf, *To Work and to Wed: Female Employment, Feminism, and the Great Depression*, Westport, CT: Greenwood Press, 1980.

41. Gwendolyn S. Hughes, *Mothers in Industry*, New York: New Republic, 1925, p. 25.

42. Ibid., p. 17; Monroe, *Chicago Families*, pp. 1, 185.

43. *New York Times*, November 28, 1921.

44. Scharf, *To Work and to Wed*, p. 44.

45. Women's Bureau, Bulletin no. 12, "The New Position of Women in American Industry," Washington, DC, 1920, p. 57.

46. See Kessler-Harris, *Out to Work*, p. 296.

47. Scharf, *To Work and to Wed*, pp. 42–56; Lorine Pruette and Iva I. Peters, eds., *Women Workers Through the Depression*, New York: Macmillan, 1934, p. 104.

48. Scharf, *To Work and to Wed*, p. 131.

49. Broadus Mitchell, *Depression Decade: From the New Era Through the New Deal*, New York: Holt Rinehart & Winston, 1947, p. 270.

50. In 1930, 78 percent of the employed population was male and 22 percent was female. Lescohier, "Working Conditions," p. 35. Day Monroe discovered that in Chicago in 1920, 57 percent of families of unskilled workers were supported by a sole male breadwinner (Monroe, *Chicago Families*). A later study of Chicago families by Leila Houghteling reported that for over two-thirds of unskilled married wage-earners, a male's earnings were insufficient to provide a standard of living comparable to that awarded by charities (Houghteling, *The Income and Standard of Living of Unskilled Laborers in Chicago*, Chicago: University of Chicago Press, 1927).

51. Fine, *Laissez-Faire*; Robert Bremner, *From the Depths: The Discovery of Poverty in the United States*, New York: New York University Press, 1967, p. 4.

52. A comparison of English and American standards of living as the turn of the century by Peter Shergold illustrates the point: when examined on the basis of male earnings, American working-class incomes appeared higher than those of English laborers. When female earnings were added to family receipts, English families enjoyed a higher family standard. See Peter Shergold, *Working-Class Life: The "American Standard" in Comparative Perspective, 1899–1913*, Pittsburgh: University of Pittsburgh Press, 1982.

~ *Chapter 12*

Race, Poverty, and Women's Aging

JULIANNE MALVEAUX

The woman is almost sixty and it shows. She wears the starched white uniform of a nurse or home health aide and carries herself with the stiff dignity of someone used to working hard for a living. Her cracked knuckles and rough skin suggest that she is not afraid of using elbow grease or of getting down on her knees and scrubbing floors to survive. Her cushioned white shoes suggest that many of her years have been spent standing on her feet. Today, she accompanies a wheelchair-bound woman down a city street, a woman not 15 years older than herself. Women like this pair are often separated by race. They are tenuously connected by their age (one is "old-old," the other "young-old"), bound by their gender, separated by their economic status, connected by their predicament of being old

From Jessie Allen and Alan Pifer, eds., *Women on the Front Lines: Meeting the Challenge of an Aging America* (Washington, D.C.: The Urban Institute Press, 1993), pp. 167–90, copyright © by Southport Institute for Policy Analysis. Reprinted by permission.

and alone, and separated by the way they survive this predicament.

It takes little to establish that the woman navigating the wheelchair has always worked in low-wage jobs like this one, as a home health worker, cleaning service worker, private household worker, or nurse's aide, earning an hourly wage that puts her at the bottom of the pay distribution. At the same time, it is obvious that her charge is protected by her economic past. Perhaps her spouse died recently, leaving her a pension. Perhaps she was a single career woman who put 40 years into the labor market and left having built up a pension history for herself. Even though she is being cared for, her position is far from secure. If the insurance company that invested her pension funds chose junk bonds, her ability to afford the help she gets may be jeopardized. If her certificates of deposit exceed $100,000 and they are held by a bank that faltered, her income is also at risk. For that matter, if her disability persists or worsens so that she requires full-time care, even a generous pension income will not be adequate. She will then be forced to "spend down" her savings to qualify for public assistance with which to pay nursing home fees.

In what years are we observing these women? It could be 1950, when more than half of all black women worked as private household workers, when the typical black woman could be found in some caretaking role. It could also be 1990, when, despite changed occupational status, black and brown women were far more likely to be home health aides and other service workers. Will racial differences in economic status persist until 2030? Will the woman in the wheelchair still be white, her caregiver a woman of color? Will both continue to face an uncertain economic future? The answers depend on policy decisions we make today.

We avert our eyes from the women on the sidewalk because we hope that their fate is one we will be spared—working into old age with no pension to come, or being in faltering health, dependent on a stranger, worrying that the money will run out and poverty will follow. Although most older women have not met this fate—more than two-thirds have incomes of at least 150 percent of poverty level—the possibility of poverty is ever-present for many women who have not contemplated it before.

The economic status of older women is a mirror of their past lives, reflecting their education, employment history, and marital status. The economic problems that older women face are extensions of the problems and choices they faced earlier in their lives. Those who are underemployed as adults have this status reflected by continued underemployment and low retirement incomes in their older years. Those who spent years out of the work force providing family care may be devastated by the loss of pension income when a spouse dies.

Because economic status reflects past expe-

riences, it is difficult to address elder poverty through social policy targeted strictly to the elderly. Poverty is reflective of low pay and occupational segregation during women's working lives, as well as the key assumption society makes about the focus of women's lives—that they will bear responsibility for caregiving in families, whether they are mothers, daughters, sisters, nieces, or wives, without social support for child care or eldercare.

Is this situation likely to change in the future? Today's young and middle-aged women have an advantage that older women do not. They have higher education levels and time before old age to improve their economic histories and, thus, the likelihood that their later years will offer more economic options. Some will not have children, and so will take less time from the paid labor force for caregiving. Others will work at firms whose parental leave policies will not force them to choose between work and family. Does this differ for women of color? In general, the labor market profile of women of color has changed along with that of white women. As is the case with white women, an increasing number of African American women and Latinas are likely to have continuous work histories. But because many minority women still lack opportunities for higher education and fewer will work in high-paying professions and management (Sokoloff 1992), fewer women of color than white women will escape poverty.

If changes in workplace demographics are not accompanied by changes in labor market and family policy, younger women's greater work-force attachment may not be enough to protect them from the plight of today's older women. In some cases, structural changes in the labor market may put some women of color at increasing risk of poverty. In particular, the economic status of African American men, and their lower rates of labor-force participation (than those of white men) suggest differences in family economics between this group and others.

Even the best prepared older women, regardless of race, are often unable to protect themselves from poverty. The high cost of nursing homes, or of continuous home health care, and the requirement of depleting assets before public (Medicaid) assistance is available for long-term care, mean that women whose spouses have had lengthy illnesses face widowhood with few financial resources. Other widows may not inherit their spouse's pensions. Still others have annuities jeopardized by the uncertain financial status (if not outright failure) of some life insurance companies. Despite the best intentions and preparations, for many older women poverty is an accident waiting to happen, a function of the death or disability of a spouse or adult child, or of life's other uncertainties.

Furthermore, the current fiscal and regulatory climate provides older people with less, not more, government protection, and as governments grapple with issues of limited resources, this is likely to get worse. Because the elderly are not the only ones facing economic uncertainty, legislators have begun to question how much health and social insurance should be provided exclusively for older people. But social spending has clearly made a difference in the economic status of this group. Eighty-six percent of those seniors who would be poor without federal programs are lifted out of poverty by government tax and transfer programs (Taylor 1991).

Issues of race and gender equity have dominated political discourse in the latter part of this century and have been pivotal in the life experience of the baby-boom generation. These issues will continue to play themselves out as our population ages and as the members of the baby boom enter retirement in the first decades of the next century. Although women of color have experienced some labor market progress in the past two decades that is likely to pay off in the future, this progress must be balanced by the current, stagnant economy and the social indifference to racial economic gaps. It is entirely possible that the debates about equity and distribution that shaped the adolescence and adulthood of baby-boom women will also affect them in old age.

This chapter discusses the economic status and poverty levels of minority women in the present and future.

Poverty, Income, and the Family Status of Older Women

The elderly poor are not a large group today—in 1990 at about 3.7 million, they were 12 percent of the total elderly population. But poverty is not evenly distributed among the elderly. It hits women harder than men, and people of color harder than whites. In 1990 women were 58 percent of the population aged 65 and over, but almost 74 percent of the poor population for that age group (see Table 1). Among older women, poverty is disproportionately concentrated among women who live alone and women of color. In 1990, black women constituted 8.6 percent of women aged 65 and over, but 21 percent of the female poor in that age group. (In contrast, white women made up 89 percent of all elderly women, and 77 percent of the female elderly poor; Hispanic women[1] constituted about 4 percent of the elderly female population and about 6 percent of poor elderly women) (U.S. Bureau of the Census 1991a.)

Although the majority of older women are not poor, the average older woman is within poverty's reach. In 1990, there were more than 17.5 million women aged 65 and over. These women had a median annual income of $8,044, an amount that was a scant 28 percent

TABLE 1. Elderly (aged 65 and over) Population and Percentage in Poverty in the United States, 1990

	Elderly		Poor Elderly	
	# (thousands)	Percentage of Total Elderly	# (thousands)	Percentage of Poor Elderly
Total	30,093	—	3,658	—
Men	12,547	41.69	959	26.22
Women	17,546	58.31	2,699	73.78
White men	11,235	37.33	634	17.33
White women	15,663	52.05	2,073	56.67
Black men	1,031	3.43	286	7.82
Black women	1,516	5.04	574	15.69
Hispanic men	461	1.53	86	2.35
Hispanic women	631	2.10	159	4.35

Source: U.S. Bureau of the Census (1991a).

above the poverty line of $6,268 for an individual aged 65 and over living alone in that year (U.S. Bureau of Census 1991b). Women of color had lower median incomes than white women—elderly black women had a median annual income of $5,617, which was 66.4 percent of white women's income; Hispanic women had a median annual income of $5,373, or 63.5 percent of white women's income. These income gaps are consistent with income gaps that women of color experience during their working lives, as well as with differences in the labor market status of minority men that affect the pensions women of color receive as widows and survivors.

More than 15 percent of all older women (aged 65 and over), or 2.7 million women, had incomes below the 1990 poverty line (Table 1). In general, older women have a lower incidence of poverty than do young women (aged 18–24) and girls (under age 18), but a higher incidence of poverty than women of other ages (Table 2). Poverty rates rise sharply after age 75: the incidence of poverty among women aged 75 and over is 75 percent higher than that for women aged 65 to 74. The rise is sharpest

among white women, but rates in this oldest group are about 10 percentage points higher for both black and Hispanic women, as well. This sharp increase in poverty among the oldest, most vulnerable women reflects, perhaps, the dwindling resources on which many women rely as they age.

TABLE 2. Poverty Rates for Women in the United States, by Age, Race, and Hispanic Origin, 1989

Age	Total (%)	Black (%)	Hispanic (%)	White (%)
Total	14.4	34.0	28.3	11.3
Under 18	19.8	44.8	35.6	14.7
18–24	18.2	34.5	29.1	15.2
25–34	13.9	31.5	26.0	11.0
35–44	9.6	22.8	23.0	7.6
45–54	8.9	19.0	20.9	7.4
55–59	11.4	33.3	18.9	8.8
60–64	10.5	29.2	21.6	8.4
65 and over	13.9	36.5	22.4	11.8
65–74	10.6	32.7	19.1	8.3
75 and over	18.5	42.0	29.2	16.4

Source: U.S. Bureau of the Census (1991b).

How is this likely to change in the future? The occupational profile of African American and Hispanic women has improved, and more work in jobs that qualify for pensions. Based on current data, it is likely that poverty will continue to be unequally distributed among older women by race; still, some women of color, especially those with continuous work histories, will escape poverty.

The Prevalence of Near Poverty

Poverty data understate the economic predicament of many older women. Although older women's poverty incidence in 1990 was 15.4 percent, nearly a third of all women had incomes within 150 percent of the poverty line (see Table 3). This was the condition for the majority (57.7 percent) of black older women, for nearly half (47.1 percent) of all elderly Latinas, and nearly 3 in 10 (29 percent) white older women. In contrast, just over half (55.2 percent) of all women could be considered "out of the woods" economically, with incomes higher than twice the poverty line. Fewer than a third of all black women

TABLE 3. Poverty and Near Poverty for Older Women (aged 65 and over) in the United States, by Race and Hispanic Origin, 1990

Income[a]	Total (%)	Black (%)	Hispanic (%)	White (%)
Half poverty line	2.4	6.0	2.4	2.0
At the poverty line	15.4	37.9	25.3	13.2
125 percent of poverty	23.4	49.6	38.2	20.9
150 percent of poverty	31.5	57.7	47.1	29.0
175 percent of poverty	38.7	64.2	54.5	36.3
Twice the poverty line	44.8	68.4	61.7	42.6

Source: U.S. Bureau of the Census (1991a).
[a]Each entry represents those who earn that income level or less.

could be so described. Indeed, 6 percent of all older black women had incomes only half as high as the poverty line or less.

In contrast, few women conform to the image of the wealthy elderly. Fewer than 1 in 12 women aged 65 and older had incomes of $25,000 or more in 1990. Fewer than 2 percent of black and Hispanic women had incomes at that level (U.S. Bureau of the Census 1991b). To be sure, some 1.4 million women did have incomes in that range, but depending on their marital status, health, and age, these income levels may not be secure. Far more older women live in poverty (2.7 million), at poverty's periphery as "near poor" (2.8 million), and at risk because their incomes are between 150 percent and 200 percent of the poverty line (2.3 million). Nearly half of all older women fit into one of these three categories.

The Significance of Family Status

When poverty incidence is viewed by family status and living arrangement, the highest concentration of poverty is among older women living alone (i.e., those widowed, separated, divorced, or never married who are not living with other family members). Nearly 1 in 4 elderly women living alone is poor, compared with 1 in 8 older women heading households, and 1 in 20 older women living in married couple families (right-hand column of Table 4). When the composition of poverty by living arrangement is examined, one finds that those living alone represent the vast majority—nearly three-quarters—of older poor women (middle column of Table 4).

The pattern of high concentration of poverty among women living alone cuts across racial lines, though it is less strong among elderly black and Hispanic women than among all elderly women. The slogan often used by women organizers, "a woman is only a hus-

TABLE 4. Poverty Among Women Aged 65 and Over in the United States by Selected Family/Living Status, 1989

Race/Ethnicity Family/Living Status	Poor Women Aged 65 and Over		Poor Women as Percentage of all Women Aged 65 and Over in Family/Living Status Category
	Number (thousands)	Percent Distribution	
All Races			
In all family/living status categories[a]	2,398	100.0	13.9
In married couples	367	15.3	5.4
Household heads	180	7.5	12.2
Living alone	1,698	70.8	23.2
Black			
In all family/living status categories[a]	541	100.0	36.5
In married couples	56	10.4	15.0
Household heads	93	17.2	30.9
Living alone	350	64.7	60.6
Latina			
In all family/living status categories[a]	124	100.0	22.3
In married couples	29	23.4	13.8
Household heads	16	12.9	17.6
Living alone	62	50.0	41.9

Source: U.S. Bureau of the Census (1991b).
[a]Includes women living in household relationships other than those listed separately below.

band away from poverty," is less true for women of color than for white women. Fifteen percent of older black women in married-couple families are poor; 31 percent of all older black women who head households live in poverty (right-hand column of Table 4). But consistent with the overall pattern, the majority of black poor women, 64.7 percent, live alone (middle column of Table 4).

Hispanics have different family patterns than the other groups studied here. Hispanic poor women aged 65 and over are more likely than their black or white counterparts to live in families, especially married-couple families (Table 4). Even so, the overall pattern of single women's poverty prevails among Hispanics, too. The incidence of poverty among Hispanic women living alone is much higher than among those who live in families (right-

hand column of Table 4). And women living alone are the largest group of the elderly Hispanic poor (left-hand column of Table 4).

The information in Table 4 suggests that policy directed toward relieving poverty among older women must focus on women who live alone. This may be as true in the future as in the present, especially for women of color. Demographers project that the proportion of married women aged 65 and older will rise only slightly, from 31 percent to 33 percent, between 1990 and 2030 (Zedlewski et al. 1990), and current life expectancies for black and Hispanic men are lower than those of white men. Further, the projected rise in the proportion of never-married women (from 4.5 percent in 1990 to 8.2 percent in 2030) is likely to be greater among women of color. If current data, which show an increase in the number of black never-married women under age 35, hold, there will be more, not fewer, black women living alone in the future. Cynthia M. Taeuber and Jessie Allen (1993) estimate that there will be 4.4 million black women aged 65 and over by 2030. If present trends hold, 1.7 million of them would be poor and another .9 million would have incomes between 100 percent and 150 percent of the poverty level.

Sources of Income and Policy

The race/gender income gap (which compares the earnings of black, Latina, and white women to those of white men) is more pronounced for women over age 45 than for their younger counterparts. If current income is a proxy for future economic well-being, extrapolating this information might suggest that the disproportionate incidence of minority women in poverty would decline in 20 years.

But the data still do not suggest future parity between men and women. Further, although black and Latina baby boomers (i.e., the 35–44-year-old cohort) earn more than both older and younger minority women, there are continuing gaps between minority women and their white women counterparts at younger ages. The earnings gap is smallest between black and white women aged 35–54. Indeed, black women aged 35–44 have slightly higher earnings (about 3 percent more) than white women of their age group. Much of this difference relates to the greater work effort required of African American women, given differences in family status (Malveaux 1990).

Social Security

Social Security benefits are the major source of income for the elderly. More than 90 percent of all seniors, including 19.4 million women

aged 62 and over, receive Social Security income (Sidel 1986). Social Security contributes about 42.5 percent of the income that individuals aged 65 and over receive, as well as 28.5 percent of the income that families with householders in that age group receive. The contrast between the jobs that the poor and nonpoor hold in their working years results in a different set of opportunities to accumulate wealth and to invest in other income-producing assets. Poor and near-poor individuals and families are far more reliant on Social Security income than are the nonpoor, with the average elderly poor individual receiving nearly 80 percent of her or his total income from Social Security, and the average poor family receiving nearly three-quarters of total income from Social Security. For about a third of older unmarried women, Social Security provides about 90 percent of income (Muller 1983, 23–31), and 60 percent of all older women depend on Social Security as their only source of income (Older Women's League 1991).

There is no direct race bias in the Social Security program. Retirees' benefits are based on the number of quarters they work, earned income, and spousal income. However, differences in work patterns yield differences in Social Security benefits by race, as do differences in life expectancy and family status. These differences have an impact on the poverty status of older women of color today and will continue to do so in the future.

Some of the differences include:

- A higher incidence of female-headed households among blacks
- A lower male life expectancy among minorities (66 years for black men, compared with white men's 73)
- Differences in pension-earning income, women of color are still more likely to be employed "off the books" where benefits do not accrue.

In general, although there have been many reforms to the Social Security system in the past decade, women fare less well than men, and black and Hispanic women fare less well than white women. These differences both reflect lifetime differences in earnings and are a function of ignoring differences in the family responsibilities shouldered by women—differences that are likely to persist in the future.

How could the Social Security system be changed to minimize the amount of older women's poverty? One way would be to allow women credit for caregiving responsibilities. At a minimum, a woman should not be penalized for the time she spends out of the labor force doing family care. Perhaps women's earnings should be calculated on the basis of 25, not 35, years of paid work to allow for the greater number of years a woman spends out of the labor force on her family responsibilities. Indeed, the estimated value of women's unpaid work ranges from $700 billion to $1.4 trillion (Prescod 1991). Crediting that unremunerated work would certainly close the gap between men's and women's Social Security, and thus reduce the prevalence of older women's poverty.

Whatever the flaws in the Social Security system, it is important to note the progressive income redistribution inherent in this program and its effectiveness in moving elderly Americans out of poverty. "If Social Security benefits payments were excluded from after-tax income, the poverty rate in 1986 among the elderly would have been about 45.9% rather than 12.4%" (Hurd 1990, 581). The challenge in changing this progressive income redistribution system is to structure it to allow for differences in family type, so that all benefits are not calculated as though the norm is working husband and stay-at-home wife, a badly outmoded family stereotype that now describes just one-tenth of all American families.

Means-Tested Cash Assistance

The needy elderly qualify for the Supplemental Security Income (SSI) program, a joint federal-state program that guarantees a minimum level of income to financially hard-pressed individuals who are aged 65 and over or blind or disabled. About 2 million elderly individuals and families received SSI in 1989, with slightly more individuals than families receiving the benefit. Seventy-five percent of those receiving SSI aged benefits were women (U.S. Department of Health and Human Services 1990, 33). Although about 10 percent of the elderly received SSI, only 30 percent of all poor elderly individuals and a third of all poor elderly families received this benefit. Why do so few poor seniors qualify for SSI? This low participation is not fully understood, but one factor is the assets test. Seniors must be extremely poor and own few assets to qualify for SSI. Except for the value of a home and car, some personal property, and a small life insurance policy, assets must be worth no more than $3,000 per couple. In addition, monthly income must be less than a minimum, which varies by state, although some types of income (e.g., part of earned income, food stamps, and some gifts) are not counted.

The base SSI benefit amount was $422 a month for an individual in 1992, with a larger amount available for couples. States supplemented the base amount by a variable sum, depending on other income and need—$28 in Washington State and $223 in California in 1991. Many older persons and families receive only a fraction of the SSI amount, because they have income from other sources.

Wages and Salaries

It is tempting to think that though older women's past labor market experiences affect their present economic circumstances, current labor market problems have little impact on them. However, this is not the case. More than 1 in 6 older (aged 65 and over) Americans continue to work. Older white men are most likely to work, followed by black men, black women, and white women (data in this category were not available for Hispanics), and participation rates fall off with age (U.S. Department of Labor 1992). The poor and near poor are much less likely to work, and earnings account for a lower percentage of total income for them.

Where do older women work? Private household workers are among the most likely to stay in the labor market, reflecting both their low income and the fact that such jobs do not provide pensions (Shaw 1988). In addition, private household workers can work "off the books" and receive small amounts of SSI or Social Security income. Note that this income would not be reflected in data showing older people's income sources. It may be that poor and near-poor women work for pay more often than is reported. Unlike many of the white men who stay in the labor market because they enjoy their work, or because their prestigious managerial and professional jobs have no mandatory retirement provisions (in contrast to most manufacturing and clerical jobs), the private household workers in the labor market are there because they need the income. According to Shaw (1988), elderly women with only Social Security or SSI income had poverty rates, in 1984, of 25 percent. But those who were either employed or had a pension in addition to Social Security had poverty rates of 5 percent.

Shaw (1988) also noted that women who work often do so without jeopardizing their Social Security benefits. Social Security recipients face an earnings test; those aged 65–69 must forfeit $1 of every $3 of their earnings above the exempt amount of $9,720 (in 1991). However, that amount is more than half the average earnings ($13,500) of a female clerical worker. In other words, a woman working half time as a secretary would not jeopardize her Social Security income. Thus, although some economists suggest that the structure of the Social Security system dampens the work incentive for those subject to a means test, especially over age 65 (Herz and Rones 1989), women's wages may be so low that the question of work incentive is irrelevant.

Pensions

In 1940, pension coverage was rare, and only 15 percent of all private wage and salary workers were covered by pension plans (Turner and Beller 1989). But private pension coverage grew rapidly in the 20 years that followed 1950, so that by 1970, 46 percent of all workers were covered by pension plans. Until very recently, these numbers have remained steady—in 1988, 46 percent of all private-sector workers were covered by pension plans, as were 83 percent of all public-sector workers (Hurd 1990).

Taeuber and Allen (1993) describe the increasing likelihood that a young minority woman will work in a job covered by a pension. However, pensions have been structured to reflect male employment patterns and to reward continuous employment. Despite some reforms, biases against women in pension policy persist. Women have greater childcare and eldercare responsibilities, which mean that they work fewer years and less continuously than do men. And women's pay is lower than men's pay. When women switch jobs or move because of family responsibilities, it affects their access to pensions (most pensions vest at 5 or 10 years, and the median job tenure for women is 3.7 years, compared with 5.1 years for men) (Older Women's League 1990). Further, women's concentration in part-time work, and as employees of small businesses, means that fewer women than men will, in the future, have access to pensions. Finally, as women have moved into self-employment and business ownership, often to avoid work-family conflicts, they have removed themselves from the very jobs that provide pension coverage.

Private Resources: Interest, Dividends, and Personal Wealth

Although income is a snapshot of monies received during a year, wealth and net worth measure assets accumulated over a lifetime. The way this wealth has been used, in buying a home or in investing in interest-bearing securities, affects the way older people, especially elderly retirees with low incomes, are able to live. Wealth also measures consumption opportunities, flexibility, and mobility. For example, if most net worth is tied up in a home, then the homeowner may have much less choice and flexibility than if wealth is distributed among an array of assets.

Home Equity and "House Poverty"

When the value of home equity is subtracted from the median net worth ($25,088) of the lowest income quintile of households aged 65 and over in 1988, remaining assets are valued at about $3,200, hardly enough to invest in interest-producing assets. Households in the lowest income quintile represented 37 percent of all families with householders aged 65 and over in 1988 (U.S. Bureau of the Census 1990). When home equity is subtracted from net worth, it is easy to see why so many elderly women are house-poor and have little mobility. NBC's situation comedy *The Golden Girls* suggests that this house poverty can be dealt with by finding a few friendly roommates, but in a weak housing market, when the option is unavailable, too many older people, especially older women,

are stuck in homes too large for them and with incomes insufficient to maintain them.

This lack of mobility may be exacerbated for black and Latino seniors by depressed housing values in inner cities. For many, housing appreciation is a key method of wealth accumulation, but those whose property values have been constrained by redlining may be strangled both by high property taxes and urban decay. Stanford (1990, 47) suggests that housing policy is an area with a special impact on the black aged. Since a greater portion of black wealth is concentrated in home value (67 percent, compared with 42 percent for whites and 58 percent for Hispanics), the housing issues that Stanford raises are especially important to blacks.

Wealth data reflect the same pattern of differences among the elderly by race that appears in data on income, unemployment, and poverty. White families in which the householder was aged 65 or over had a median net worth of $81,600, compared with $22,210 for black families with elderly householders and $40,371 for Hispanic families in 1988 (U.S. Bureau of the Census 1990). There may be intergenerational consequences to the low net worth of elderly black and Hispanic households. Those with few assets are likely to depend more on their children who, based on their own occupational options, may have less than others to give.

When aging baby boomers boost the elderly portion of the black population from 8.2 percent in 1990 to 17.5 percent in 2030, the ratio of the black retirement age population (aged 65 and over) to the black working-age population (aged 20 to 64) will rise from about 15 per 100 to about 31 per 100 (U.S. Bureau of the Census 1989). If policy changes are not made to prepare the minority members of the baby boom economically for old age, their children may have to take on more responsibility than the baby boomers are assuming for their own parents.

Wealth, Poverty, and Women of Color

Two factors are important in explaining how private income sources affect the poverty status of older women of color. First, what wealth has a woman amassed during her working lifetime? Second, are her children in a position to contribute to her well-being after she retires? Older women of color today, who earned less in their lifetimes, are likely to have less wealth upon retirement. Depending upon the way the private labor market closes racial wage gaps, the children of these women are also likely to have less to spend on supporting their mothers. The stark difference between the status of middle-income minorities and poor minorities may mean that in the future there will be both a larger group of elderly minority women who are financially secure and a continued high incidence of poverty. In 1990, 14 percent of all black families had earnings that exceeded $50,000, while about a third lived below the poverty line (U.S. Bureau of the Census 1991a, b). Twenty years from now, these differences will be reflected among the black elderly.

Conclusion: Preventing Older Women's Poverty

In the future the over-65 population will be older, and more black and brown than it is today, while continuing to be disproportionately female, especially at the oldest ages. Because elder poverty is concentrated among women and minorities and the very old, these demographic trends suggest that unless corrective policies are instituted, the incidence of poverty will increase in the future. Younger women's educational levels have improved, to be sure, and they are working more continuously. However, the fact that social policy has not been modified to deal with women's dual responsibilities in the workplace and the

household, as well as the fact that there is no family policy in the United States, exacerbates the tendency toward older women's poverty. Educational access and occupational shifts may protect some women, but young minority women still lag behind white women in higher education, and many others will be disadvantaged by their need to take time out of the labor force for caregiving. Older women's poverty, then, is not a cohort effect that only affects today's older women, but a necessary outcome of the absence of social, family, and health policies that would support women's dual roles as family caregivers and members of the work force.

Among older women of color, especially black women, poverty seems less a function of marital status than of past work experience. But in 1990, fewer than 1 percent of black women earned more than $50,000 per year (compared with about 2 percent of white women and 11 percent of white men) (U.S. Bureau of the Census 1991b). By 2030, there will be a much greater minority representation among the aged population. From a policy perspective, this fact should draw our attention to labor market policies that currently affect the employment status of minorities, especially minority women, who are more likely to survive into very old age than are minority men. The poverty of older women— black and white—can be avoided in the future if labor market policies generate access to good jobs and pensions in the present.

The years that women spend outside the labor market for caregiving responsibilities, the unequal pay women receive even when they are working, the peripheral work that many minority women accept that reduces their access to pensions and Social Security, and the likelihood that women will spend part of their old age alone all contribute to high poverty rates among elderly women of color. Certain policy initiatives, affecting both older women and those who are preparing for old age, could help young minority women avoid the predicament of older women's poverty. Included among these initiatives are:

- *Pay equity* and *other equal pay policies* that would assist women in building pension credit for retirement. Women are still heavily concentrated in low-paying occupations, and the long-term consequence of their low pay is low retirement benefits.
- *Enforcement of age* and *race discrimination laws,* which would enable those women who choose to work past age 65 to find employment. It is especially important to note that age discrimination sometimes combines with race discrimination to create a dual hardship for older blacks.
- *More equitable retirement policies,* which could ensure that higher proportions of older women have retirement income from sources other than Social Security. Such policies include those that would reflect women's unpaid work, that would allow workers to begin vesting retirement benefits sooner, and that would make it easier for workers to invest in vehicles like individual retirement accounts (IRAs). As more women work part-time, it also makes sense to mandate that employers allow part-time workers to accumulate retirement credits on a proportional basis.

Older minority women follow many paths to poverty. Following demographic and social trends, some of those paths will narrow or even disappear, but others may widen in the future. Clearly, some women will be protected because of more continuous work histories and improved labor market profiles; but others who have not had the benefit of higher education and good jobs, or who have worked sporadically because of family responsibilities, poor health, and other factors, will face some of the same risks that women face today. It will take some policy intervention to change this outcome, and the challenge will be to create policies that affect not only minority women who are already over age 65 but the women who are approaching their older years with limited means to protect themselves from future economic hardship and dependency.

NOTE

1. The U.S. Bureau of the Census uses the term "Hispanic" to refer to a group of people of diverse cultural backgrounds. Mexican Americans make up the largest segment of this population, followed by Puerto Ricans and Cuban Americans. The Hispanic population also includes people of Central and South American origin or descent.

REFERENCES

Herz, Diane, and Philip L. Rones. 1989. "Institutional Barriers to Employment of Older Workers." *Monthly Labor Review* (April): 14–21.

Hurd, Michael D. 1990. "Research on the Elderly: Economic Status, Retirement, and Consumption and Savings." *Journal of Economic Literature* (June): 565–637.

Malveaux, Julianne. 1990. "Women in the Labour Market: The Choices Women Have." In *Enterprising Women,* edited by Julia Parzen and Sara Gould. Paris: Organization for European Cooperation and Development.

Muller, Charlotte. 1983. "Income Supports for Older Women." *Social Policy* (Fall).

Older Women's League. 1990. *Heading for Hardship: Retirement Income for American Women in the Next Century.* Washington, D.C.: Author.

———. 1991. *Fact Sheet.* San Francisco: Author.

Prescod, Margaret. 1991. "Count Women's Work: Implementing the Action Plans and Strategies of Houston and Nairobi." Los Angeles: International Wages for Housework Campaign.

Shaw, Lois. 1988. "Special Problems of Older Women Workers." In *The Older Worker,* edited by Michael Borus, Herbert Parnes, Steven Sandell, and Bert Seidman. Madison, Wis.: Industrial Relations Research Association.

Sidel, Ruth. 1986. *Women and Children Last.* New York: Penguin Books.

Sokoloff, Natalie. 1992. *Black and White Women in the Professions.* New York: Routledge Press.

Stanford, E. Percil. 1990. "Diverse Black Aged." In *The Black Aged: Understanding Diversity and Service Needs,* edited by Zev Harel, Edward A. McKinney, and Michael Williams. Newbury Park, Calif.: Sage Publications.

Taeuber, Cynthia M., and Jessie Allen. 1993. "Caring Too Much? Women and the Nation's Crisis." In *Women on the Front Lines: Meeting the Challenge of an Aging America,* edited by Jessie Allen and Alan Pifer. Washington, D.C.: Urban Institute Press.

Taylor, Paul. 1991. "Like Taking Money from a Baby." *Washington Post,* National Weekly Edition, March 4, p. 31.

Turner, John A., and Daniel J. Beller. 1989. *Trends in Pension.* Washington, D.C.: U.S. Department of Labor.

U.S. Bureau of the Census. 1989. *Projections of the Population of the United States by Age, Sex, and Race: 1988–2080.* By Gregory Spencer. *Current Population Reports,* ser. P–25, no. 1018. Washington, D.C.: U.S. Government Printing Office.

———. 1990. *Household Wealth and Asset Ownership: 1988. Current Population Reports,* ser. P–70, no. 22. Washington, D.C.: U.S. Government Printing Office.

———. 1991a. *Poverty in the United States: 1990. Current Population Reports,* ser. P–60, no. 175. Washington, D.C.: U.S. Government Printing Office.

———. 1991b. *Money Income of Households, Families, and Persons in the United States: 1990.* By Carmen DeNavas and Edward Welniak. *Current Population Reports,* ser. P–60, no. 174. Washington, D.C.: U.S. Government Printing Office.

U.S. Department of Health and Human Services. 1990. *Fast Facts and Figures and Social Security.* Washington, D.C.: U.S. Government Printing Office.

U.S. Department of Labor, Bureau of Labor Statistics. 1992. *Employment and Earnings* 39(1) (January).

Zedlewski, Sheila R., Roberta O. Barnes, Martha R. Burt, Timothy D. McBride, and Jack A. Meyer. 1990. *The Needs of the Elderly in the 21st Century.* Washington, D.C.: Urban Institute Press.

~ *Chapter 13*

Affluence and Poverty in Feeding the Family

MARJORIE L. DEVAULT

Feeding, like most household work, is performed as a direct service for family members, outside of cash-mediated relations, and is often experienced as freely given, out of "love." But the means for providing a household life are commodities that, for the most part, must be wrested from a cash-mediated market. In the United States, where there is some measure of income protection for most workers and a greatly expanded sphere of "consumption," basic necessities can be obtained more easily than in many societies. However, this observation obscures more disturbing facts: that income differences mean considerable variation in the amounts and kinds of food consumed; that many in the United States must spend a far higher percentage of their income merely to eat; and that a significant group of people continue to experience hunger and malnutrition.[1]

From Marjorie L. DeVault, *Feeding the Family: The Social Organization of Caring as Gendered Work* (Chicago: University of Chicago Press, 1991), copyright © 1991 by The University of Chicago. Reprinted by permission.

The establishment of an official "poverty threshold" recognizes the impossibility of providing for a family without at least a minimal cash income, and social welfare assistance provides minimal cash payments to at least some of those who cannot earn a living wage. The poverty threshold is based on a "household budget" that estimates necessary expenditures. Such a budget, however, says nothing about the kind of work required to translate these minimal sums into household life for a group of people.

In this chapter, I consider how class relations shape and are shaped by distinctive patterns of feeding work and household life. My discussion is based on a conception of social class as a dynamic social process, organizing the activities of individuals and families both in very direct ways—such as through the wages flowing into households, or the demands of particular occupations—and in less direct ways, through locations in particular neighborhoods, schools, and other social groups. My aim is to show how class shapes household life and work, and also to show

how different ways of conducting household life and work are implicated in the reproduction of class relations. I discuss profound differences in the work of "feeding a family," but I also take notice of the ways that these differences are obscured. I will suggest later that cultural discourses abut class-less "wives" and "mothers" are powerful ideological tools that hide the realities of many women and their families.

This analysis is based on a series of semi-structured, taped interviews conducted during 1982–1983 in Chicago, Illinois. I located households in several different neighborhoods and interviewed those household members who shared the work of feeding the family (30 women and three men), asking them to provide accounts of their everyday routines. All of the households included children, and they were ethnically diverse and included single-parent and two-paycheck families, as well as families of different class groups.

Money and the Market

For most people, a general level of spending on food is a settled question, a background assumption that underlies their more specific everyday strategizing about planning and purchasing. But attention to food expense is necessary for some and voluntary for others. Slightly less than half of all of these interviewees (43 percent) talked of having a "budget" for food expenditures, and those who did so were more heavily represented in the lower-income groups. Whether they budget or not, those with very low incomes are most directly aware of economic constraints, and their awareness appears in their talk. In the poorest women's accounts, there are many spontaneous comments about money. When they reported on shopping routines, they often began by mentioning the amounts of money

that structure their decisions: how much money they have each month, and how much they spend on food. These references appeared both earlier in the interviews and more often than in the accounts of more affluent informants. Margaret, a white single mother who works part-time at a low-wage job, offered as an introductory comment in the first few minutes of our interview:

> With cooking and stuff like that, we stick to chicken, hamburger meat, and hot dogs. Because we spend over $100 a week, on food alone.

Like others with limited incomes, she had developed an idiosyncratic but effective system for sticking to an informal "budget":

> Usually if I fill the basket up, it's about [$]130. . . . When the basket is full, that's a little over $100. Because I buy the same amount of stuff. But if it's getting a little over the basket, that's when I have to buy like, deodorant and toilet paper, which I don't buy every week. Or shampoo and toothpaste. And then that makes it 140, 130.

Those in households with more resources often reported a similar result—a generally stable level of expense. They talked of routinizing their purchasing decisions, and of avoiding particularly expensive foods in order to hold their expenditures at a constant level ("He doesn't get filet mignon at home," or somewhat more ambiguously, "I don't buy junk"). In addition, the shopping strategies of some of those in moderate-income households were also tied to specific amounts of money, which came into the household at particular times. But those who had more money to work with talked about these matters more abstractly, and infrequently mentioned how much they spent.

In part, the differences in these accounts seem to arise from differences in attitude, the reticence of more affluent interviewees reflecting a characteristically middle-class "etiquette" of keeping such information within the family. In this study, for instance, the poorest interviewees talked most directly about money, while others were more likely to talk in general terms about whether things were "tight" or "comfortable" (though all except one informant—the wealthiest—were willing to tell me the amount of their household income when asked). This pattern is consistent with other studies of very poor and very wealthy households. Carol Stack's (1974) study of poor families shows that income pooling is an adaptive survival strategy in poor communities and suggests that, as a result, knowledge about the resources available is relatively widely distributed. Rosanna Hertz (1986), by contrast, shows that affluent dual-career couples can afford to use their discretionary money to express individuality and autonomy, and that in some cases, spouses withhold information about their salaries even from each other. But these studies also suggest that such differences arise not only from attitudes toward money but also from material conditions that construct quite different relations to money in poor and affluent households. Those in very poor households must use very small amounts of cash income to maintain their households, and these minimal amounts set narrow limits for expenditures on survival needs. As a result, poor women discussing their food expenses often talked rather specifically about their rent or other household expenses as well, something that others rarely did. When I asked about her income, a black woman caring for six children produced a succinct summary of her monthly budget:

> I do get food stamps—food stamps, I get, uh, $291. And the check [from Aid to Families with Dependent Children, AFDC] is about [$]500. OK. Now my rent's about $300. Then I have the light bill, and the gas bill, and the phone bill. And then I have to figure out ways to get washing done. And somebody's always going to be needing something.

Her account displays the calculus that is ever present in these women's strategizing, the balancing of meager income against fixed expenses, unpredictable needs, and the areas—like food expense—where expenditures can sometimes be reduced through careful purchasing or extra effort. In situations like these, when there is virtually no margin beyond subsistence, even small amounts of money loom large, and particular prices are significant.

Most of the wealthiest interviewees, all from professional/managerial households, made some reference to economizing, though virtually all acknowledged that they did not need to "worry about money." They took for granted a certain kind of attention to money; the underlying assumption, that one should not spend more than necessary on food, seemed not to require elaboration. But these families' incomes—and the security of stable incomes—allow rather generous definitions of what is "necessary." Like others, they sometimes talked about the boundaries to their purchasing decisions—which items they would not buy because of price. But they were less likely than others to rule out particular kinds of food and more likely to report that they decided when to buy things because of price: "If grapes cost more than $1.19, I just don't get them."

These families with more resources can accommodate their preferences more easily; saving money is desirable, but optional. While these people usually refer to the importance of economizing, they also speak without worry about decisions to forego savings for other benefits in particular situations. The voluntary character of economizing is clearest in the account of a relatively affluent white single mother, who reported that she does not worry about saving money on food because time is an even scarcer resource in her life. She explained:

I used to go to the big supermarkets, and try to save a penny here, a penny there, you know. And occasionally I'll look at the, you know, the sale items. But I gave that up. That is the most ridiculous waste of time.

Since her divorce, as she begins a new career and cares for her two children, she chooses to go to a smaller store where she can do her shopping more quickly:

They get you in and out! Oh—it's wonderful. And all of a sudden that became more important to me than any money I was saving or anything.

A final feature that appeared in the talk of a few wealthy women was a concern with the negative implications of economizing, a sense that too much attention to price might be unseemly. For example, one affluent white woman, reporting that she had purchased orange juice on sale rather than squeezing it herself, worried that I would think her "a tightwad." And a white professional woman explained that she clips coupons occasionally because her husband will use them, but that she is uncomfortable with the image of "couponing."

In middle-income, mostly working-class, households, relatively secure but with considerably less income than the most affluent families, typical practices of economy are more limiting. As they describe their routine shopping, these people talk of firmer boundaries to their purchasing, mentioning more items they simply never buy in order to keep their expenditures within relatively predictable limits. Laurel explained:

We don't buy the best cuts of meat, except to entertain, we don't, you know, we buy 39¢ chickens when they're on sale, by the tens, that sort of thing.

Even when the logic of shopping is similar here and for more affluent shoppers, with special items purchased on sale, the resulting

stock of foods is rather different. While those with more money reported watching for bargains on shrimp and scallops, Jean told of making standard purchases of ground beef and chicken and buying pork chops "if they're not too expensive."

Most of the working-class wives I spoke with talked positively about their efforts to use their resources carefully. They constructed economizing in terms of responsibility and virtue, and seemed more anxious than wealthier informants about choices in favor of preference or convenience. Income is less stable in these households than in professional/managerial families, and several interviewees told about times when they suffered losses. Reporting on these episodes, they described minimal meals that became standard fare and allowed them to survive.

Such difficulties inevitably reveal food as one of only a few variable categories of expense. For example, both Robin and Rick were working at the time of the interview, but their expenses for a mortgage, utilities, day care, and transportation to work were so high that food was "very low on a priority list . . . [though] it shouldn't be." Rick explained, "We're hurting right now. So now it's just like, three days—I'll go out and get enough food for three days." Both of them stressed the various ways they save money on purchases: driving to discount stores, comparing prices and saving coupons for items they need. But when they reach the limit of this kind of economizing, sometimes they simply cannot buy adequate food. Robin explained how they make decisions at these times:

If we repeat a meal for three days, it's no big deal to us. To see a nice piece of meat, like a steak or something, is really rare. It's usually the hamburgers and hot dogs and cheese sandwiches and stuff. We just can't afford anything else. . . . If it gets down to it, we buy to feed the kids. . . . And then we'll eat whatever we can scrounge together.

In several ways—including their limited diet and their dissatisfaction with it—this account was similar to those of much poorer families. Ironically, in such cases financial achievements—home ownership and the expenses associated with full-time jobs—have the effect of requiring radically reduced expenditures on food.

In households with incomes near poverty levels, or where food expenditures are especially reduced, another irony appears. Though these families are most in need of any savings produced by economizing, some of the prescribed techniques of "smart" shopping are not always appropriate or even possible. The poorest women I talked with were well aware that the stores in their neighborhoods charged more for many food items than stores in other areas. But few of them had transportation to other shopping areas. One black woman, for example, knew of several stores where she could find bargains, but had to rely on friends or her sister for transportation, or consider whether to spend extra money on a delivery service. In addition, these women often choose to buy more expensive brand-name products simply because they do not have enough cash to experiment with cheaper items and risk wasting money on unsatisfactory purchases. While more affluent shoppers could recite long lists of bargain items they had tried—some acceptable and some not—poor shoppers tended to report more conservative strategies for selecting foods, emphasizing the cost of a single mistake:

> I go for quality. . . . I'd rather go and get Del Monte corn. . . . I have bought some of these—like they had four cans for a dollar. And when you got it, all the husks and stuff was inside it and it was just money wasted, when I could have just took that dollar and bought that one can of Del Monte. . . . To me, it really is a waste of money.

For these women, any waste seems very consequential. Wealthier shoppers seem comfortable thinking of themselves as consumers who freely choose from items on the market, simply rejecting items not up to standard; poor shoppers are more likely to think of the market antagonistically.

Poverty and the Work of Survival

In this section, I consider the work of five women caring for children in households sustained on minimal cash income. This group should not be taken as representative of all poor households, since that group includes more than just single-mother families. However, single-mother families make up a large and significant segment of the poor: in 1986, 60 percent of poor households were headed by single women (U.S. Bureau of the Census 1989). In the group of five I studied, three mothers lived in households of their own, and two thought of themselves and their children as independent "families," but at the time of my interviews resided with parents in what might be described as "subfamily" arrangements.[2] One woman was widowed, two were separated or divorced, and two were never married, though both of these had had relationships of some duration with their children's fathers. One reported that her children's father was often in the household and usually shared their meals.

All of these women were "on their own" in some sense. Though one described herself as engaged and planned to marry soon, the others, like many single mothers, were conscious of their difference from a more accepted form of family life. While the two women in their thirties seemed to take for granted that they would raise their children mostly on their own, the younger women—both in residence with their own parents—seemed to think of their single status as temporary and expressed some worry about living in households that were not "proper" families. Margaret, for example, emphasized that her present living arrangement was a transitional one, and took care to explain how her routine would be different if she were living on her own: the children would set the table, for example, and she would "experiment" more and take more time with the cooking.

All but one of these women were unable, for one reason or another at the time of the interviews, to command a living wage. Two were in their early twenties and had few marketable skills. One of these two and one other of the five reported that they were temporarily unable to hold a paying job owing to recent disturbances in their lives (one was recently widowed and severely depressed; the other was recovering from a bout with drugs). One cared for six children, all younger than ten years old. And the only one who worked at a full-time job received such a low wage that she was able to manage only because she lived in a rent-subsidized apartment.

Accounts of financial arrangements in these households reveal complex relations of adaptation, a process of piecing together enough resources to survive. All received some kind of government assistance, whether in the form of a direct payment, food stamps, or subsidized rent; several received material help from family members; and two held jobs, both of which paid minimum wage or below. These sources of income were interrelated in ways mediated by the bureaucracy of state assistance. For example, the two women who lived with parents thereby forfeited their right to food stamps; a woman working full-time at minimum wage was ineligible for AFDC, while another woman worked only part-time in order to retain her benefits. These "patchwork" combinations of material resources are summarized in Table 1. The information revealed is consistent with what we know of the welfare system: because increments resulting from wage work or family assistance usually mean a reduction in government aid, the total resources of each woman hover at roughly similar levels that barely provide for their subsistence.

Because they depend at least in part on direct government assistance, these women's lives must be understood in the context of the welfare state in the United States. (Government subsidies support wealthier families as well, but less directly, and thus less intrusively.) Mimi Abramovitz (1988) shows that, historically, social welfare policy has included some provision for the support of mothers and children, but has also regulated their lives through restrictive and often moralistic policy. She argues, along with others (e.g., Gough 1980; Dickinson 1986; Corrigan 1977), that the state recognizes the need to reproduce and maintain a healthy labor force and subsidizes women's household labor in order to do so. At the same time, however, welfare provisions are designed to insure that government assistance will not become a preferred alternative to paid employment or traditional family life. The government does this chiefly by limiting eligibility for subsidies to those seen as "deserving," as well as keeping payments at levels below prevailing low-wage employment options. Despite these regulatory effects, most social welfare programs have empowering effects as well, if only limited ones. They do contribute to the subsistence of those outside the labor market, and by doing so they provide a modicum of choice and make possible some resistance to the most severe forms of exploitation.

Aid to Families with Dependent Children, on which several of the women I studied depend, was established in 1935 but was developed in part from earlier Mothers' Pension programs established during the Progressive Era. Abramovitz argues that these programs,

TABLE 1. Sources and Amounts of Income or Subsidy in Five Poor Families, 1982–1983

Household Composition	AFDC	Wages	Housing Assistance	Food Assistance	Estimated Annual Income (including Food Stamps)
Margaret + 2 children 3 in "subfamily," 9 in extended family/household (white)	$302/mo	$260/mo	Lives w/parents	Father buys food	$6,744
Ivy + 2 children 3 in "subfamily," 4 in extended family/household (black)	$302/mo	–	Lives w/mother	Mother buys food	$3,624
DW + 2 children fiancé sometimes in household (black)	–	$500/mo	Rent subsidy	–	$6,000
Annie + 3 children 1 other child lives elsewhere with grandparent (white/Hispanic)	NA[a]	–	–	Food stamps NA[a]	Unknown
LM + 6 children (black)	$500/mo	–	–	Food stamps $291	$9,492

[a]Amounts of subsidies unrecorded.

which provide direct subsidies for poor women raising children alone, have been built around a "family ethic" that assumes the naturalness of gender distinctions and assigns child care and household responsibility exclusively to women. Concern for children has been expressed in terms of the importance of "proper mothering," which has been defined and enforced through education, supervision, and threats of ineligibility for assistance or the removal of children from poor women's homes. The biases in early Mothers' Pension programs had systematic effects: white widows received the most aid, and never-married and black women were seldom on the rolls for assistance. The exclusion of large numbers of women from the programs meant that, despite a rhetoric that supported women's household work, large groups of "undeserving" (especially black) women were channeled into low-paid wage work. Thus, the contradictions in the program helped to mediate conflicting demands for women's household and market labor.

The operation of AFDC has reflected similar dynamics since its inception. Widespread ambivalence toward husbandless women has kept eligibility rules tight and benefit levels low. In the early years of the program, vaguely defined rules about "suitable homes" were used to justify continual scrutiny and harassment of recipients, and these rules kept many women out of the program. During the 1960s, at least partly in response to the growth of a strong grassroots welfare rights movement (Piven and Cloward 1979; West 1981), the mechanisms of regulation shifted somewhat, opening up the program in response to pressure and moving from a coercive to a more paternalistic kind of regulation. A rhetoric of social services to support "proper mothering" began to substitute for some of the harshest program rules, though in practice only limited service was actually provided. As AFDC expanded during the 1960s and 1970s, public and political antagonism toward its recipients grew. In spite of its regulatory agenda, the program did support and in some sense legitimate single mothers living alone with their children. Abramovitz (1988, 352) summarizes:

> Instead of supplying the market with low paid women workers and delegitimizing female-headed households [as program framers intended], AFDC enabled welfare mothers to avoid dangerous marriages and jobs, to prefer public assistance to either wedlock or work, and to accept public aid as a right.

Since it was increasingly seen during the 1970s and 1980s as a challenge to the "family ethic,"

AFDC has been subject to a series of new modifications and restrictions. My interviews with AFDC recipients took place during a period of limitation and cutbacks in the program; inflation during the period worsened their situations as well.

The food stamp program, which supplements AFDC for two of the women I interviewed, has a similar history (DeVault and Pitts 1984). This program—which provides vouchers to be used in purchasing food items—functions chiefly as income supplementation, since it means that recipients can spend their cash income on other needs. However, like AFDC, it incorporates regulatory provisions that control recipients' use of the program: benefits are provided "in kind" (to be used for food only) rather than directly, as additional cash. While this program feature was intended primarily as a subsidy for American agriculture, it also reflects an underlying distrust of recipients and a desire to control the purchases of those in the program. As supplementation to AFDC, it suggests that spending money on food ("wisely," of course) can legitimately be enforced as part of "proper mothering." The more recent Special Supplemental Food Program for Women, Infants and Children (WIC)—which provides in-kind food aid and nutrition education—emphasizes the relation of food and mothering more explicitly and is more restrictive than the food-stamp program.

These social welfare provisions can be seen as part of a transition from private to "public patriarchy" (Brown 1981), with reproduction increasingly subsidized and controlled by the state instead of by individual men as family heads. Johnnie Tillmon, a welfare rights activist (cited in Abramovitz 1988, 313–14), compares welfare to a "supersexist marriage":

> You trade in "a" man for "the" man. But you can't divorce him if he treats you bad. He can di-

vorce you, of course, cut you off anytime he wants. But in that case "he" keeps the kids, not you. "The" man runs everything. In ordinary marriage, sex is supposed to be for your husband. On AFDC you're not supposed to have any sex at all. You give up control over your body. It's a condition of aid. . . . "The" man, the welfare system, controls your money. He tells you what to buy and what not to buy, where to buy it, and how much things cost. If things—rent, for instance—really costs more than he says they do, it's too bad for you.

Many welfare recipients are sharply aware of the punitive restrictions that condition the assistance available to them, especially since the emergence of a welfare rights consciousness during the 1960s. But recipients' perspectives on the system are also conditioned by prevailing cultural ideologies about work and individual achievement, as well as by the ideology built into welfare policy. Most seem to experience a complex mixture of feelings and are subject to dissatisfaction and resentment about their situation, which can be directed both outward and inward. In the following discussion, as I examine the feeding work of the poorest women I interviewed, I will attend to the ways in which the contradictory purposes and consequences of welfare policy intersect with everyday struggles to feed and care for children.

These interviews, as a group, were the most difficult for me to conduct and analyze. I spoke, as a middle-class researcher, with women whose lives were very different from my own. Our conversations were mostly comfortable—the women generously accommodated my curiosity and, in at least some cases, seemed to welcome my listening, perhaps as company. But with some distance from the interview situation, I began to realize how unprepared I was to know their lives and how frightened I could be by their situations. These realizations developed at differ-ent times and in different ways: sometimes unsurprisingly, as when I drove nervously into unfamiliar parts of the city; sometimes much later, as I have studied the transcripts of our conversations, noticing gaps in my understanding and questions I might have asked. Such gaps in understanding present problems for any middle-class researcher talking with those whose lives are quite different from hers (see, for example, Riessman 1987). One approach to a solution involves prolonged immersion in the lives of those studied (e.g., Stack 1974); another involves a more collaborative research strategy (e.g., Mies 1983). In this study, however, I adopted neither of these strategies, but interviewed poor women in the same relatively conventional way as others. An awareness of this problem recommends reading my account here somewhat cautiously, as an attempt to begin to see what is missing from a more middle-class view of feeding work. What we find, I will suggest, is a hint at the dark underside of women's caring work, the most brutal expression of the pitfalls built into women's inexorable responsibility for the well-being of others.

To my knowledge, these households were not visited by hunger and malnutrition, in the clinical senses. However, several comments leave this statement open to some doubt: one woman reported giving her children two meals instead of three during the winter when they slept later and were less active; another's two-year-old daughter had grown so slowly that she had been hospitalized for a time; and a third described one child how "just gobbles . . . down (her food)" and is always "wanting more, wanting seconds." Still, the overall sense of these accounts is one of a skillful management of quite limited resources that makes possible the survival of these household groups. In many ways, these women engage in precisely the same kinds of work activities as mothers with more resources. They pay attention to the needs and preferences of their children, they shop for provisions with which to prepare "proper" meals, and spend time planning such meals, and they work at teaching their children about proper eating, through experience and example as well as direct instruction. But the insufficiency of their cash income adds an additional layer to the web of conditions within which they do this work, and gives the provision of food a different meaning for the household group.

These women talked straightforwardly about the difficulties of their situations. As one black woman explained:

> Being on public aid is a very—well, to me, it's, you know, a hassle. I don't like it. You know, first of all, because the amount of money you receive from public aid is not really enough to, you know, for a person to take care of their family. It's really not enough.

They see quite clearly that their decisions are structured by the restrictive, even punitive regulations that define public aid. The only woman working full-time, for example, explained that since she has started work, she is no longer eligible for enough food assistance to make it worthwhile to apply: "I know the changes I would have to go through downtown with them—it's not worth it, when they're not going to give me, maybe $30." But as they considered their lives within this context, all of these women expressed some pride in their abilities to manage, and especially to care for their children. Some saw themselves as protecting their children in a hostile environment.

For Margaret, pride is tied to a sense that she manages in spite of the difficulties produced by the market:

> I enjoy doing it. Because I know, I can feed—I can get around all these people who think they're going to, you know, BS everybody else. You know, I'm smarter than they are.

With one exception (Ivy, who will be discussed below), these women were active and determined, working to fill in with extra effort for the money resources they lacked. One works at a low-wage telephone job she describes as "a bitch," but "better than sitting home all day"; another cares for six children and also works in a community group; and a third, Annie, reported that she keeps track of all the kids on the street in her area, serves as secretary for a neighborhood organization, and helps Spanish-speaking mothers deal with their children's problems at school.

The lives these women lead can be better understood by examining Annie's in some detail. Annie is a white woman in her late twenties who lived in a predominantly Hispanic neighborhood with three of her four children when I interviewed her. She had been married briefly, to a Puerto Rican man, but her husband had left the family almost a decade earlier when he discovered he was too ill to provide for them. Annie had worked at a variety of low-wage jobs until she became ill herself, and then, as she recovered from surgery, began to use drugs. By the time I interviewed her, she had succeeded in quitting drugs and seemed to have reestablished a relatively stable household life. However, she reported that her health was poor and that she had had "a couple of nervous breakdowns." When I interviewed her, she was not working for pay; she explained, somewhat ruefully, that she was "supposed to be taking it easy." Much of Annie's life was structured by conditions in her neighborhood, an area with a lively and sometimes dangerous street life. Her oldest daughter, who "couldn't handle it," had been sent to live with a relative in a rural area, and Annie spent much of her time keeping an informal watch over the neighborhood's children as well as her own.

Annie acknowledges the help she receives from family and friends, but she also emphasizes her own work and her self-sufficiency: when she told about some workshops offered through her children's Head Start program, she explained, "I figured, 'Well, I'm going to play mother and father, and work, and I've got to learn something.'" She also reported that her sisters are sometimes jealous, and tell her she is "lucky," but she stresses her own effort as the source of whatever comfort she enjoys:

> They don't see how I can make it so good, and not have no money and live on welfare. But I told them, "If you budget yourself, and penny-pinch, you can do it." Because I do. I go to No-Frills, I go to Diamond's, I go to the fruit market. I mean, I don't care, if I have to walk all over the city to get it.

Accounts of "penny-pinching" were prominent in the reports of other poor women as well. Just as they were more likely than others to talk spontaneously about their overall budgets, poor women were more likely than others to include the prices of foods they selected as they talked about their shopping. What is striking in these accounts, and different from others, is the frequent reference to actual sums, the attention to exact prices, which marks these women's necessarily constant concern with the distribution of whatever cash is available.

By "penny-pinching," then, Annie manages to purchase supplies, and works to produce "family meals," as others do. She explained that they all sit down together for dinner:

> The meal is on the table, and I tell them if the steam leaves the bowl before they get to the table, the bowl goes right back in the stove and they don't get any supper. So they make sure they get to the table. And then that's our group discussion, this girlfriend played with that boyfriend at school, and—I hear everything.

As she describes their routines, it is clear that she is conscious, like more affluent mothers,

of using food to construct social relations and mark special events in the week. When she describes a typical meal, we can see the sense of group sociability that arises from having a "house specialty," and also the attention to individual preference that marks the family as "personal":

> Oh, that's our house specialty, macaroni and cheese. And my daughter usually makes that. I guess she's got her way of making it, because when I make it she says I don't make it right. . . . And then plus, the 11-year-old, she doesn't like ground beef in her macaroni and cheese. So hers is made separately. They make the macaroni and cheese, the ground beef, and then before they add the ground beef, my 12-year-old will take out a big bowl and put a separate [gesturing to indicate a separate portion]—for the 11-year-old—and then she'll keep on making the rest of it.

Parents in households with more resources talk about using food, thoughtfully and creatively, to signify love, comfort, and pleasure. They seem rarely to be conscious of the possibility of scarcity, but this spectre is rarely absent from the consciousness of those who live in poverty. Thus, while poor mothers also use food to mean love, comfort, and pleasure, they teach a harsher lesson as well—that survival is never to be taken for granted.

In poor households, children learn early, through direct observation, that their parents are caught up in economic circumstances over which they have little control. In spite of parents' attempts to protect children from the worst consequences of their poverty, children see their parents' frustrating labors, and they typically understand that they must often do without (Stack 1974). Parents face a dilemma: while they would like to let children "enjoy their childhood," they are also concerned to prepare them for independence. Thus, Annie's caring for her children is expressed in part through tough, energetic discipline, and determination and self-sufficiency are part of an attitude toward life that she teaches them quite directly:

> I told them, "You stand up and say 'I am somebody,' because if not, you're just going to be with the rest of them." . . . So my kids, they know, they stand up for themselves. If not, they get stepped on. I tell them, "That's the way it goes."

Poor families like Annie's, and many black families whether poor or not, are in situations requiring that they adapt to hostile environments, and a protective "toughness" emerges as part of the caring work that maintains family members in the present and prepares them for challenges ahead.

Annie relies on her children to help with household work and to begin caring for themselves at an early age. When she worked in the afternoon, they took care of themselves after school and she would leave them a list of chores: "Sometimes I'd forget. . . . So they'd call and say, 'What's there to do today, and what time can we go out?' Very well organized." When she is not working, Annie does most of the housework herself, but she still strategizes about how much help the children should provide, balancing their need to spend time on schoolwork against the importance of learning responsibility and household skills. This general feature of their relationship appears in a specific form in her talk about feeding them:

> Everybody has to do something in order to eat. . . . I don't never let them go without a meal, but I just tell them, "You're not going to eat if the sink is dirty. If I have to start supper with dirty dishes I won't do supper that day."

Children in more affluent households help with chores, too, usually also because their parents want them to learn responsibility and household skills. But in poor families like Annie's, the necessity behind children's independence gives them a distinctive sense of the struggles their parents face. As a result, these children learn that to struggle for physical maintenance is "natural" (as Annie explained, "That's the way it goes."), while more affluent children take survival for granted and learn to feel a sense of entitlement to the pleasures that food can provide.

The gender organization of feeding work is also expressed in a distinctive form in these poor households. Since all of these poor families were headed by single mothers, questions about a division of labor between spouses do not arise. But these mothers' sole responsibility for children can be seen as part of a larger community-level division of labor. The predominance of single-mother families among the poor in the 1980s can be attributed to a variety of factors, including high rates of male unemployment and incarceration among the poor, the relative unavailability of income assistance for two-parent families, and increasing rates of divorce and single childbearing among the population as a whole (Wilson 1987). These trends, together, tend to produce a particular pattern of gender segregation, with poor women more likely than men to be attached to household and children.

Thus, poor women cook at least in part simply because they are more likely than men to live in relatively stable households with children who must be fed. Often, they cook for men who do not live with them, but join their households for meals through kin or "fictive kin" relationships (Stack 1974). Annie, for example, often cooks for a boyfriend, and sometimes for his brother as well. The men usually bring something in exchange—some soda, perhaps—but these exchange relations are delicate ones, and Annie reports that her boyfriend is sometimes embarrassed at how much his brother eats. His worry hints at expectations that surround such relations of service and exchange: they all accept that Annie should provide food for the one man she is attached to, however, informally, but her responsibilities toward others are more ambiguous. Thus, even in the absence of a legal marriage relationship or even cohabitation, the relations of service and entitlement that organize feeding and eating are organized around the heterosexual couple.

Most of the poor women I talked with, like Annie, thought of themselves as managing relatively well, even with their limited resources; indeed, they are probably a more successful group than would be found through random sampling, since those who are managing well are most likely to agree to be interviewed. The kind of maintenance work they do has often been understood as an essential contribution to communities under siege by the wider society; Patricia Hill Collins suggests that black women, for example, "see their unpaid domestic work more as a form of resistance to oppression than as a form of exploitation by men" (1990, 44). The household and feeding work performed by slave women for their families (Davis 1981), by working-class mothers (Caulfield 1974), by Southern black "Mamas" for civil rights workers (Evans 1979; Jones 1985), and by poor women for networks of kin (Stack 1974) has been essential labor that contributes directly to group survival. In groups such as these, women's responsibility for feeding is significantly different from that in more privileged families: rather than a work burden that excludes middle-class, white women from the more remunerative activity and status enjoyed by their male counterparts, feeding others is a work task that also provides an opportunity to promote the survival and well-being of the less privileged community, including men, children, and women themselves. But we will see below that this opportunity, which can bring honor to those women able to fulfill such roles, can also be cruelly demanding for those who are not so gifted or fortunate. One of my informants, Ivy, was in a period of considerable stress and depression, and her story highlights some of the special difficulties of being a poor mother who cannot cope so well with the difficulties of her situation.

Ivy, a black woman in her early twenties, had come to the United States from the Caribbean about ten years before I interviewed her. When we talked, she was recovering from the death of her children's father and a subsequent period of grief and disruption. Despite public assistance and financial help from her mother, she acknowledged that feeding her children was "very hard"; it was a matter of great concern because her young daughter had been hospitalized briefly the year before for failure-to-thrive. Her daughter's hospitalization marked her as a mother in need of help, and since then she had been especially vulnerable to the scrutiny of medical and social welfare professionals. Ivy's situation illustrates the complex reality of troubles with caring work. She had real difficulties managing the care of her children, and she needed and, for the most part, welcomed expert advice. However, her reports about the help she has received reveal significant gaps between what is offered and what she can use. And to some extent, the counseling intended to help Ivy seems to have contributed to her depression and sense of inadequacy.

Though she lives with her mother, who pays for much of their food and often does the shopping, Ivy is responsible for the work at home; her mother, she explains, is tired when she returns home from her very demanding service job. Ivy takes her children to nursery school in the morning and spends most of each day at home alone. Her account hints at the curious contradictions of a state of anxious depression. Though she does not enjoy cooking, she reports that she cleans energetically: "I'm a workaholic. As a matter of fact, I love cleaning up. . . . I'm not used to the type of life sitting and relaxing, it's not me." Yet a few minutes later, when I ask if she usually cleans the dishes after supper:

> No, sometimes I skip that, you know, I watch TV, or try to play with them. I don't do that very often. Or I just sit and watch TV. And you know, you get depressed now and then. You know, I try to play with them. And then after, do the dishes. Sometimes I leave them overnight, because you know, I have to conserve my energy, I'm using up so much trying to get everything done.

This excerpt illustrates a tone that characterized all of Ivy's talk in the interview: an emphasis on things she "tries" or "needs" to do, alongside apologetic accounts of how her actual practice usually falls short.

Because she had been identified as a mother with problems, Ivy had received several kinds of expert advice. She was seeing a psychologist, with whom she talked about her problems with the children; she had talked with doctors (not much help, she reported) and other hospital personnel about nutrition (they had mainly provided "booklets"); and she had discussed her children's eating habits with teachers at their nursery school. She had also participated briefly in a WIC program, and mentioned that the extra food provided was "very helpful," even though she was sometimes unable to make the trip downtown to pick up her coupons at the required time. But when she talked about these relationships, she seemed curiously detached, struck in everyday realities that seldom fit with the information provided. When I asked if the WIC program helped her learn about nutrition, for example, she acknowledged that such teaching was built into the program, but could only talk about it in a vague and general way. Her comment suggests that somehow the instruction offered through the program was only something to "listen to,"

and that she was never able to tell them "her part" or get answers to her own questions:

> Yeah, that was part of it, they had someone to tell you, you know, what you should feed. But I never really did get to tell them, you know, my part. You know, I was just listening to what they had to say. I didn't, like, ask them questions. I didn't take much interest in that.

I do not mean to diminish the importance of information about food and nutrition. But Ivy's problem is not primarily a lack of knowledge. She is severely depressed, with no marketable skills, isolated at home, and responsible for two small children. Given her material and psychological difficulties, the social services emphasis on instruction for homemaking seems primarily to have heightened her anxiety about the work of care.

The depression and discouragement that was so marked in Ivy's case showed up in subtler ways in all of the poor women's accounts, suggesting that however well they manage from day to day, they experience common psychological costs. All of them seemed relatively isolated: they lived in small, crowded apartments, and referred to their difficulties traveling outside their neighborhoods for appointments or to shop. All of them referred to their need sometimes to "just sit," conveying a sense of alternating periods of effort and listlessness. Perhaps most significantly, several of these women referred to their own lack of appetite and indicated that they often simply did not eat. Ivy, for example, complained, "Sometimes the food gets very boring. [Laughing a bit] You know, boring, boring, boring food."

The fact that these poor women were the only ones among these interviewees who spontaneously talked about simply not eating suggests that their loss of appetite is directly related to their poverty. Their comments suggest an alienation from their family work, a distaste for food that arises from the fact that it is always a problem and unavailable as simple pleasure. Further, social welfare policy seems to invade even this intimate physiological aspect of these women's lives. The one woman who was working full-time was the only one of the poor women I interviewed who did not appear to have difficulty with their own eating, or feel guilty about it. This single exception suggests that those receiving assistance are undermined by the public dictum that they are to be valued and assisted only in their roles as "proper mothers." They actually play out this ideology in their everyday lives, working to feed their children as well as possible, but not themselves.

The Illusion of Similarity

In this chapter, I have looked beyond surface similarity to examine the ways that feeding work is organized through access to cash income from different sources. The ideology of a capitalist economy emphasizes similarity in the situations of household/family groups, constructing households as "consumption units" and individuals as consumers who choose freely from what is offered on the market. In this model, each household must garner cash resources, usually by sending some members out to work for a wage. Then, household members decide how to use their resources, allocating them to the necessary expenses of sustenance and other purchases, as desired. Every consumer seems to be doing the same thing: deciding to exchange cash for some desired product. Careful budgeting—shrewd decision making about how much to exchange for what products—seems to determine how well families live.

This simple, ideological model of consumer behavior omits the structural economic factors that determine what kinds of access families have to cash resources, what kinds of products are available on the market, how their cost is determined, and how they are distributed and marketed. But this simple model is the one that underlies discussions of housekeeping in advertising, expert advice for women, and much public policy discussion. The "smart shopper" is the central image in this discourse: she is the woman who carefully tends the family resources, purchasing wisely in order to "make ends meet." This "smart shopper" is class-less: whether she has plenty of money or only a little, she virtuously balances cost and need, spending only what is necessary to provide for her family.

There is, of course, a material base for this image: women (and some men) do budget and calculate as they purchase goods for their families, and many husbands and children would live considerably less comfortable lives but for women's efforts at making ends meet (Luxton 1980). However, the class-neutral character of the image obscures crucial differences in the work of provisioning and in the different kinds of "family" people are able to produce.

Economizing is activity that some people engage in voluntarily; they can make choices about when and how to economize. Others "make do" from necessity, and are rarely able to purchase what they want. Thus, concepts like consumer "choice" and "power" apply to only some consumers. The work of feeding is very different for women of different classes: the woman with plenty of money is able to operate more like a manager, considering the market and making "executive" decisions about purchasing for the family (perhaps this is why more middle-class than working-class men seem interested in shopping for food; see Charles and Kerr 1988, 176), while the woman who does not have enough is more like an unprotected daily laborer, dependent on the local availability of products and unpredictable fluctuations in prices.

Also missing from this picture are those workers in the burgeoning service industries whose labor provides time-saving "conveniences" for those houseworkers who can afford them. For example, Margaret's paid work in a laundry provides essential maintenance work for others, but also limits the time she can spend with her children and renders her too exhausted to eat her own dinner when she returns home late in the evening. Many such workers are members of disadvantaged racial and ethnic groups; and Evelyn Nakano Glenn (1990) suggests that the increasing marketization of household maintenance work reshapes a longstanding racial/ethnic division of labor. Rather than purchasing the labor of women of color directly, as domestic servants, affluent white women increasingly benefit from the labors of others less directly, and perhaps more comfortably because relations of oppression and privilege are less visible.

These differences mean that feeding and eating are experienced quite differently as well. In families with more resources, food becomes an arena for self-expression, providing a chance to experience family as a reward for achievement; in poor families, feeding and eating are themselves the achievement. Since the ability to maintain family members cannot be taken for granted, all family members are recruited into interdependence through necessity. In working-class and poor households, the person who does the work experiences its two sides quite sharply: though she often understands her activity in terms of enabling the pleasures of eating, she also works with more urgency to provide sustenance, and often has the unpleasant task of deciding which desired items must be eliminated from the family's diet.

Finally, it must be clear that, given the market distribution of food, some families enjoy plenty of healthful food, while others do not. The poor have access to such minimal cash re-

sources that they can only obtain an adequate diet through extraordinary effort. They are often blamed for their own deprivation. Social programs are based on calculations that assume that households are managed by "smart shoppers" who will be able to stretch meager resources. Social policy simply assumes that women will do this work, and Ivy's story illustrates how thoroughly mothers are held responsible, whatever their circumstances or individual difficulties. Discourses about such programs emphasize knowledge and skill as a condition for survival and largely ignore the energy, will, and luck that are also necessary. Thus, they help to maintain an illusion—that families share a similar experience of purchasing and preparing foods, and that differences in their diets must indicate that some are at fault, that some "deserve" healthful and satisfying meals, while others do not.

NOTES

1. According to USDA estimates, Americans spent about 12 percent of their disposable personal income on food in 1988. However, those in the 20 percent of households with the lowest incomes spent 42 percent of that income on food while those in the highest 20 percent spent only 9 percent on food (Blaylock, Elitzak, and Manchester 1989).

2. I have adopted the term used by the U.S. Census Bureau, which defines a "subfamily" as a married couple, or parent with one or more children, who live in a larger household and are related to the primary householder or spouse.

REFERENCES

Abramovitz, Mimi. 1988. *Regulating the Lives of Women: Social Welfare Policy from Colonial Times to the Present.* Boston: South End Press.
Blaylock, James, Howard Elitzak, and Alden Manchester. 1989. "Food Expenditures." *National Food Review* (U.S. Department of Agriculture) 12(2): 16–24.
Brown, Carol. 1981. "Mothers, Fathers, and Chil-

dren: From Private to Public Patriarchy." Pp. 239–267 in Lydia Sargent (ed.), *Women and Revolution*. Boston: South End Press.

Caulfield, Mina Davis. 1974. "Imperialism, the Family, and Cultures of Resistance." *Socialist Review* 4(2):67–85.

Charles, Nickie, and Marion Kerr. 1988. *Women, Food and Families*. Manchester: Manchester University Press.

Collins, Patricia Hill. 1990. *Black Feminist Thought: Knowledge, Consciousness, and the Politics of Empowerment*. Boston: Unwin Hyman.

Corrigan, Paul. 1977. "The Welfare State as an Arena of Class Struggle." *Marxism Today*, March: 87–93.

Davis, Angela Y. 1981. *Women, Race, and Class*. New York: Random House.

DeVault, Marjorie L., and James P. Pitts. 1984. "Surplus and Scarcity: Hunger and the Origins of the Food Stamp Program." *Social Problems* 31:545–557.

Dickinson, James. 1986. "From Poor Law to Social Insurance: The Periodization of State Intervention in the Reproduction Process." Pp. 113–149 in James Dickinson and Bob Russell (eds.), *Family, Economy, and State*. New York: St. Martin's Press.

Evans, Sara. 1979. *Personal Politics: The Roots of Women's Liberation in the Civil Rights Movement and the New Left*. New York: Alfred A. Knopf.

Glenn, Evelyn Nakano. 1990. "White Women/ Women of Color: The Racial Division of Social Reproduction." Paper presented at the Henry A. Murray Research Center, Radcliffe College, April, Cambridge, Mass.

Gough, Ian. 1980. *The Political Economy of the Welfare State*. London: Macmillan.

Hertz, Rosanna. 1986. *More Equal Than Others: Women and Men in Dual-Career Marriages*. Berkeley: University of California Press.

Jones, Jacqueline. 1985. *Labor of Love, Labor of Sorrow: Black Women, Work, and the Family from Slavery to the Present*. New York: Basic.

Luxton, Meg. 1980. *More Than a Labour of Love: Three Generations of Women's Work in the Home*. Toronto: The Women's Press.

Mies, Maria. 1983. "Towards a Methodology for Feminist Research." Pp. 117–39 in Gloria Bowles and Renate Duelli Klein (eds.), *Theories of Women's Studies*. London: Routledge and Kegan Paul.

Piven, Frances Fox, and Richard A. Cloward. 1979. *Poor People's Movements*. New York: Vintage.

Riessman, Catherine Kohler. 1987. "When Gender Is Not Enough: Women Interviewing Women." *Gender & Society* 1:172–207.

Stack, Carol. 1974. *All Our Kin: Strategies for Survival in a Black Community*. New York: Harper & Row.

U.S. Bureau of the Census. 1989. *Statistical Abstract of the United States* (109th ed.). Washington, D.C.: U.S. Government Printing Office.

West, Guida. 1981. *The National Welfare Rights Movement: The Social Protest of Poor Women*. New York: Praeger.

Wilson, William Julius. 1987. *The Truly Disadvantaged: The Inner City, the Underclass, and Public Policy*. Chicago: University of Chicago Press.

Chapter 14

Gender, Class, Family, and Migration: Puerto Rican Women in Chicago

MAURA I. TORO-MORN

This chapter examines how Puerto Rican women enter the migration process, how gender relations shape their move, and how women adapt to their new homes in the United States. Specifically, I focus on the experiences of married working-class and middle-class women. My interviews suggest that while both groups migrated to the United States as part of what sociologists have called a "family stage migration," there are important differences between them that challenge our understanding of women's migration.

Methodology

From March 1989 to July 1990, I interviewed women in the Puerto Rican community of Chicago, which covers the areas of West Town, Humboldt Park, and Logan Square. I participated in community activities and at-

From *Gender & Society* 9, no. 6 (December 1995): 712–26, copyright © 1995 by Sociologists for Women in Society. Reprinted by permission of Sage Publications, Inc.

tended cultural events. These activities allowed me to meet the women of the community and, through informal snowball sampling techniques, to select interviewees. The interviews took place in the homes of the informants and lasted between one and three hours. Interviews were conducted in Spanish. The interview questions were organized around a series of themes, ranging from their migration history to family, work, and community experiences.

The sample of married women consisted of 17 informants. Eleven were mostly working class, with little education, who came to Chicago in the early 1950s and 1960s. Generally, at the time of migration, they were married—or were soon to be married—and most had children. The six professional and educated women in the sample had all migrated in the late 1960s and had over 14 years of education at the time of their move. Most educated informants described themselves as predominantly middle class and from urban backgrounds in Puerto Rico. At the time of the interview, two informants had earned doctorate degrees. Ten respondents were in their sixties; seven were in their forties and fifties. Different respondents will be identified by pseudonyms.

Being Puerto Rican and bilingual, I was able to establish rapport with informants. Most of the older migrant women spoke little English, and conducting the interviews in Spanish facilitated the exchange. By the same token, being fluent in English allowed women to use the language with which they felt most comfortable. Sometimes the interview started in Spanish and ended in English. On other occasions, women switched back and forth.

Gender, Class, and Migration

The most significant movement of Puerto Ricans to the United States took place at the end of World War II (Dietz 1986, Falcon 1990; History Task Force 1979; Pantojas-Garcia 1990). In the late 1940s, the impact of U.S. investment and modernization of the economy transformed Puerto Rico from a predominantly agricultural to an industrial economy. Operation Bootstrap, as the development model became popularly known in Puerto Rico, attracted labor intensive light manufacturing industries such as textiles and apparel to Puerto Rico by offering tax incentives, cheap labor, and easy access to U.S. markets (Dietz 1986; Pantojas-Garcia 1990). These changes in Puerto Rico's economy had profound consequences for Puerto Rican families. The development model was unable to create enough jobs, and working-class Puerto Ricans began to leave the island, heading for familiar places like New York City and new places like Chicago. News about jobs spread quickly throughout the island, as informal networks of family members, friends, and relatives told people of opportunities and helped families migrate.

My interviews suggest that working-class women and their families used migration as a strategy for dealing with economic problems. Married working-class women, in particular, talked about migration as a family project. For them, migration took place in stages. Husbands moved first, secured employment and housing arrangements, and then sent for the rest of the family. Even single men frequently left their future brides in Puerto Rico, returning to the island to get married as their employment and economic resources permitted. Some women came as brides-to-be, as they joined their future husbands in Chicago. For example, Rosie's mother came to Indiana in order to join her husband working in the steel mills. He had been recruited earlier, along with other workers in Puerto Rico. Once at the mills in Indiana, these men often found better jobs and moved on. They went back to Puerto Rico, got married, and returned to Indiana. Others arranged for the future brides to join them in Chicago. Alicia's explanation indicates how these decisions took place within the family context.

> My husband I were neighbors in San Lorenzo. Before he left to come to Chicago, he had demonstrated an interest in me. Initially, I did not accept him, because I did not want to get married so young. We started corresponding and I agreed to the relationship. . . . In one letter, he asked me to marry him and come to live with him in Chicago. I told him that he needed to ask my father's permission. . . . He wrote to my father but my father did not agree . . . it took some convincing by my cousins who were coming to Chicago so that he would let me come and get married. My cousin took it upon himself to be responsible for me and that's how I came. Within two weeks of getting here, we got married.

Alicia's experience suggests that even within the constraints of a patriarchal society, single women were active in negotiating their moves to Chicago.

Married working-class women left the island to be with their husbands and families, even though some reported to have been working before leaving. Lucy and Luz were working in apparel factories in Puerto Rico when their unemployed husbands decided to move. Economic opportunities seemed better for their husbands in the United States and they both quit their jobs to move. For others, like Teresa and Agnes, both husband and wife were looking for work, when news about job opportunities came via relatives visiting the island. Similarly, Agnes also came with her husband in the 1970s after a cousin who was visiting from Chicago convinced them that there were better job opportunities for both of them.

Working-class women also talked about the struggles over the decision to move. Fear of the unknown bothered Lucy. In addition, with a baby in her arms and pregnant with a second child, Lucy did not have anyone to help her in Chicago, but accompanied by her sister and her youngest child, Lucy followed her husband. Shortly after her migration, Lucy's mother and her sister-in-law arrived to care for the children while Lucy worked. Asuncion's husband could not find work in Puerto Rico either, so he migrated to Chicago with his relatives. Asuncion took a vacation from work and came to visit. Her family

> started talking about how they were recruiting case workers in the welfare office that could speak Spanish. They all had connections there and could very easily help me get a job. In fact, I went just to try it.

Asuncion gave in to the pressure and started working while still holding her job in Puerto Rico:

> I worked for six months, but I had so many problems, I wanted to go back. Life here [in Chicago] is really different when compared to the Island's. I was really confused. I cried a lot. I had left my children behind and I missed them a lot.

In fact, Asuncion went back to Puerto Rico because she missed her daughters; she was uncertain about what would happen to her marriage. She remembered how she felt when her husband took her to the airport:

> I really did not know whether I was going to see him again. He wanted to stay here and start a new life. I really did not care about what would happen to us and our relationship; I thought about my daughters. I owe it to my mother that my marriage was saved. After I returned to Puerto Rico, she sat me down and told me that my place was to be with my husband. That he was a good man and that my place was next to him. That I had to think about my children growing up without a father, so I returned again.

As Asuncion's case illustrates, she struggled between her husband's needs in Chicago and those of her children on the island. Ultimately, moving to Chicago meant maintaining the family and saving her marriage.

Victoria's story is somewhat similar. She was living in her hometown of Ponce when she fell in love with the son of a family visiting from Chicago. She became pregnant and, in keeping with Puerto Rican culture, she was forced to marry him. Without consulting with Victoria, the young man's parents sent him a ticket so that he could return to Illinois. Once in Chicago, he expected she would follow.

> I did not want to come. . . . One day he sent me a ticket for me and my baby girl. I send it back because I did not want to come. But he send it back again. So I had to come. . . . I had no idea where I was going, I had lived all my life in Ponce and had never left Ponce. I was so scared.

In 1966, she followed her husband to Chicago against her will. The emotional and cultural shock was very strong:

> I cried my eyes out. In Puerto Rico, you are always outside and carefree. Here, we lived in

small apartments, we could not go outside. We could not open the windows. We did not know the language.

When her second child was to be born, Victoria was so intimidated with the city that she asked her mother to send a plane ticket so that she might give birth in Puerto Rico. Within less than a year, she had returned to Puerto Rico. Eventually her husband joined her also, but he was not happy. Soon he began to disappear and neglect his responsibilities as a father. In one of his escapades, he went back to Chicago. Once again, he sent for her. This time, however, Victoria began to analyze the situation in different ways.

> In Puerto Rico, I did not have any money to pay rent, electricity, and other bills or even feed my babies. I recognized it was a difficult situation, but I thought to myself that if I stayed I had less opportunities to do something with my life. So, I thought that if I returned and brought my other brother with me they could help me and eventually even my mother could come and I could get myself a job. I had noticed that there were factories close to where we lived and my sister-in-law had offered to help as well. My brother who had moved with me the first time had gotten married and brought his wife with him.

Victoria had changed; as a married women who followed her husband to Chicago, she began to develop her own agenda and use migration as a way for its realization.

Of the women who followed their husbands to Chicago, only two (Luz and Rita) complained that their husbands failed to fulfill their end of the bargain, forcing them to use migration as a way to assert their claims as wives. Lucy's husband had just returned from the military when he began talking about migrating to Chicago. Initially he went to Indiana, where some relatives helped him find a job. When he was laid off, he learned through other friends that there were job opportuni-

ties in Illinois. He then moved to Chicago, promising to send for the family once he secured employment. But, according to Luz, he had been working for quite a while and had not sent for her and the children. Also, he was not sending any money to support the family. Instead, her husband kept putting off sending for her, and she was forced to confront him. Finally, Lucy left Arecibo in 1951 to join her husband and save her marriage. Rita was also forced to confront her husband by letter, reminding him of his promise to bring the rest of the family to Chicago. Even though it was over 20 years ago, Rita stated with emotion that she

> had to write him a letter. Because it had been over a year and he didn't send for me. I had three babies and I was alone. When he left, he said that he was going to send for me shortly and it had been a year and I was still waiting.

He replied that he did not want her to come, because living in Chicago was hard and she and the children would not be able to get used to the weather. She replied, "either you send the ticket or send me the divorce papers." Apparently, this was a typical problem for Puerto Rican women when their husbands preceded them in migration. Juarbe (1988) reported that Puerto Rican women migrants in New York experienced similar problems. Juarbe's (1988) informant, Anastacia, stated that after her husband had migrated, he did not want her to come. He had been living and working for over three months. He wrote occasionally but did not send any money. Apparently, she had some money saved and was able to buy the ticket without his knowledge. Anastacia wrote him a letter announcing her arrival.

The migration of educated and professional middle-class Puerto Ricans to Chicago remains an unanswered empirical question. Sanchez-Korrol's (1986) study of migration to

New York City hints at the possibility that middle-class Puerto Ricans had been involved in the migration process; furthermore, surveys by the Planning Office in Puerto Rico between 1957 and 1962 found higher literacy levels and English proficiency among migrants than among the population as a whole (Rodriguez 1989). Pantojas-Garcia (1990) comes closest to analyzing the changing political economy in Puerto Rico and its impact on middle-class and educated workers. He points out that skilled and professional workers have increasingly joined semiskilled and unskilled workers in the migration process. As Pedraza (1991) suggests, despite the growing importance of the "brain drain" as a type of migration, from a gender perspective, it remains the least understood.

In contrast to working-class migrants, moving was a joint family project for married middle-class women. In addition, the language this group used to describe the move differs from that of the working-class married woman. Middle-class women came with their husbands and had an agenda of their own. Aurea met her husband while attending the University of Puerto Rico. Initially, the couple moved from San Juan to Boston to enable her husband to take a university position. In 1971, a new job opportunity brought them to Chicago. In fact, Aurea talked about moving as a mutual arrangement between her and her husband. She saw the move to Chicago as an opportunity to join community and political struggles. Shortly after arriving in the city, they bought a house—something that took years for working-class families to accomplish.

Brunilda had just completed her bachelor's degree and was working as a field researcher for the University of Puerto Rico when she was asked to work with a group of American scholars who came to Puerto Rico to conduct research in the 1970s. The researchers were very pleased with her work and offered her a position if she would relocate to Chicago. They promised they would help her to make the transition. She had just been married when the job offer came, and she felt that was a big problem:

> My husband did not want to come, he said that he did not know English. He just did not want to come. I told him that there were no doubts in my mind as to what that job meant for me. It was a great opportunity, and I was not going to let it go. If he did not want to come, then I guess that was it, I knew I was coming with him or without him.

In this case the roles changed. It was the husband who was asked to follow his wife; initially he resisted, but the job meant so much to Brunilda that she was willing to sacrifice her marriage. Brunilda, therefore, moved within a professional rather than a family network. In addition, she did not live close to other Puerto Ricans in Chicago because the research team found her a place to stay closer to the university. After completing her work with the university researchers, Brunilda started graduate studies at a local university. She went to school full time for a year and in 1971 started working as a community organizer in the south side of Chicago.

Vilma had moved from San Juan to Wisconsin to go to graduate school. While in Madison, she met her future husband and they moved in together. They had completed their degrees when he was offered a job in Chicago. In 1986, they both relocated to Chicago. Vilma described her move as

> very traditional in terms that I had just finished my master's and was looking for a job when my "compañero" [live-in boyfriend] got a job offer in Chicago. I followed him to Chicago, but I came not only for him, but also knowing that in Madison there was no professional future for me.

As my interviews suggest, both working-class and middle-class Puerto Rican women found themselves migrating as part of a family migration. Married working-class women came to support their husbands and be with their families. In other words, their roles as mothers and wives compelled them to migrate. The narratives suggest that some women struggled over the decision to move. In contrast, educated married middle-class women were less encumbered by such relations of authority. They shared in the decision making and were less dependent on other family members to make the move. As Vilma's and Brunilda's stories indicate, these middle-class migrants clearly had professional agendas of their own. How does each confront the problem of balancing family and work responsibilities?

Gender, Family, and Work

In Puerto Rican culture, there is a gender-specific division of labor consisting of men's work (*trabajo de hombre*) as the providers and women's work (*trabajo de mujer*) as the caretakers of the home and children. Underlying this gender division of labor is a patriarchal ideology, machismo, emphasizing men's sexual freedom, virility, and aggressiveness, and women's sexual repression and submission (Acosta-Belen 1986). Machismo represents the male ideal and plays an important role in maintaining sexual restrictions and the subordination of women. This ideology rationalizes a double standard where a woman can be seen as *una mujer buena o una mujer de la casa* (a good woman or a good homemaker) or as *una mujer mala o una mujer de la calle* (a bad woman or a woman of the streets). A man has to show that *él lleva los pantalones en la casa* (he is the one who wears the pants in the family) and that he is free to *echar una canita al aire* (literally meaning, blow a gray hair to the wind; culturally, it means to have an affair).

The counterpart of machismo is *marianismo* in which the Virgin Mary is seen as the role model for women (Sanchez-Ayendez 1986, 628). Within this context, a woman's sexual purity and virginity is a cultural imperative. Motherhood, in Puerto Rican culture, lies at the center of such ideology. A woman is viewed in light of her relationship to her children and, as Carmen, one of my informants, put it, in her ability *dar buenos ejemplos* (to provide a good role model).

Among working-class Puerto Ricans, gender roles are very rigid (Safa 1984). Although industrialization and the entrance of women into the labor force completely contradicts this ideal of *la mujer es de la casa* (women belong to the home), in Puerto Rico the domestic role of working class women remains intact. Working mothers are primarily responsible for the care of the home and the children.

In Chicago, in keeping with this ideology surrounding family values, some working-class husbands resisted their wives working. The men would take a double shift so that wives could stay home, take care of the children, and do housework. Carmen stayed home to care for her children and was very proud of her accomplishments as a mother, but economic necessity obliged other husbands to conform to the idea of women working outside the home. Like Lucy said, "I did not come here to work, but I had to." Alicia elaborates, "In those days one paycheck was like nothing. We put together both paychecks and there were times that he had very little or next to nothing left. By that time there were other relatives living with us and there were lots of mouths to feed."

The same network of family and friends that helped in the process of migration helped working wives find employment in Chicago factories. Josefa, Lucy, Luz, Rita, and Teresa all reported working in factories. Chicago's political economy in the 1950s allowed these women to find factory jobs with relative ease; however, most working-class married women viewed employment as a temporary necessity. The way women talked about their work experiences reflected this attitude. Josefa and her husband worked not only to meet the family needs but also to take care of the medical expenses of their child. When her daughter started going to school, Josefa stopped working. Alicia worked in a factory prior to getting pregnant; after having the baby, she stopped working. When the family wanted to buy a house, Alicia went back to work for two years. After her second child, she stopped working altogether. Brunilda started working in a factory immediately upon arriving from Puerto Rico, but when she became pregnant, she stopped. Lucy was the only married respondent who stayed in the factory for a prolonged period of time. Eventually, she stopped working when she got sick.

Although most working-class married women gave in to their husbands' wishes for them to stay home, Rita illustrates how a woman resisted those traditional roles and even sought to change them. Rita's husband did not want her to work. According to Rita:

> After I got to Chicago, my husband didn't want me to work. But I wanted to work. I wanted to work because you can meet people, learn new things, and one can also leave the house for a while. I saw all the women in the family, his sisters and cousins, working and earning some money, and I wanted to work too. They used to tell me that I should be working. But I had four children, and who was going to take care of them?

Rita succumbed to the pressure and started working secretly for about three months. When asked how she managed to work without her husband knowing about it, Rita replied that

> since he left to work very early, I found someone to take care of my smallest child, and the others

went to school. My work hours were from 9:00 to 3:30, so by the time my husband got home, I had everything done. I had the house clean, the children were cleaned and had eaten, and I was all put together. My husband did not like when I was not put together.

Rita eventually told her husband about her work escapades because she did not like doing things *a la escondida* (in hiding); however, her husband's traditionalism prevailed, and Rita was forced to give up working.

> With the money I earned I was able to buy my sewing machine and I felt so proud of myself that I was able to buy it with my own money. We saved a lot of money afterwards. I sew for the family; I felt so proud.

Although she gave in to her husband's traditionalism, Rita found a source of pride and accomplishment even within the confines of the house. Others similarly reported that they stopped working for wages but continued to contribute to the family's income by working in their husbands' neighborhood stores. They used the word "helped," but, in reality, they actually ran the stores while their husbands worked elsewhere.

Puerto Rican men may have accommodated to the wife's employment, but the traditional division of labor within the family did not change. Lucy best articulated the working woman's problem:

> It was very hard work because I had to take care of the house, the children, and the store. Since my husband never learned how to drive, I had to learn to drive. I had to go to the warehouse, do the bookkeeping, everything. In the store, I used to do everything. My husband helped, but I was practically in charge of everything.

Child care first became a problem at the time of migration since families could not afford to travel all at once. A strategy women used to deal with this problem was to leave the children in Puerto Rico in the care of grand-parents. This arrangement was a widespread practice in the island for many years.

Once the family was in Chicago, women developed short-term arrangements to deal with the daily problems of child care. Shift work represented one strategy that couples used to allow these women to stay home with the children. The husband could work the day shift, and the wife worked at night. Haydee's father worked the day shift in a factory, while her mother worked the evening shift as a cook in a hotel. Josefa worked the night shift in a candy store; her husband worked the day shift. I asked Josefa if they ever switched, where he worked nights and she worked days. She replied that working at night allowed her to take care of her daughter during the day.

When children were school age, both hus-band and wife might be able to work during the day. For wives, however, there was always the added responsibility of returning home to care for the children and do the household chores. Here, girls were introduced to the household responsibilities very early and were left to care for younger brothers and sis-ters. When Claudia reached nine years, she acquired household responsibilities. She was given keys to the apartment, and after school she was expected to clean the kitchen, pick up around the house, and start dinner. This was also a way mothers trained their daughters in the traditional gender roles.

Given the ease of migration, other working-class women brought over relatives with them to help care for the children, suggesting that women can get involved in the migration process to do the reproductive work, allowing other women to do work outside the home. Lucy and Daniela brought their mothers, and Teresa brought a younger sister to Chicago to help take care of the children. Teresa's sister stayed home and took care of her children un-til she met a fellow and got married. That was

when Teresa then turned to a woman in her building who took care of them for a small fee. Teresa gave her $12.00 weekly for the care of the two girls and provided their food.

Sanchez-Korrol (1983, 98) found the same kind of informal child care practices in the early "colonias" in New York City in which "childcare tasks previously undertaken by rel-atives defaulted to friends and acquaintances outside the kinship network who provided the services in exchange for a prearranged fee." This grassroots system served both em-ployed women and women who had to stay at home. The arrangement usually consisted of bringing the child, food, and additional cloth-ing to the "mother-substitute" and collecting the child after work. This system provided a practical way to increase family earnings and was an extralegal system with advantages not found in established child care institutions. These informal child care arrangements al-lowed children to be cared for in a familiar en-vironment, where there was mutual trust, agreement between the adults involved, and flexibility. Children were cared for in a family setting where the language, customs, and Puerto Rican traditions were reinforced.

When Teresa stopped working, she became a child care provider for the women in her building. Now, she no longer cares for other people's children but instead cares for her own grandchildren. Teresa's history represents an example of the cycle of care that women pro-vided. Such a cycle may begin when a woman places her children with a neighbor while she works. Then she may care for other neighbor's children while they work and, finally, care for her own children's children.

Middle-class women placed their career goals equally alongside their family responsi-bilities. Rosa talked about how she had man-aged to work full time in Puerto Rico and go to school to acquire an associate's degree be-cause her extended family helped take care of the children and the household chores. In Chicago, since they did not have their extended family, they had to adjust differently. Shortly after arriving in the city, Rosa, who had given birth to her youngest child, opted to stay home with her children until they were of school age. Rosa recognized that she wanted to be with her children, but she also wanted to stay active.

> When I arrived, I saw a lot of possibilities, but I chose to stay home with my baby because I wanted to be with my children. When the baby was three years old, I started thinking what can I do to keep myself busy? In Puerto Rico, I had always worked, and I was not used to be[ing] a full-time mom. I was very independent. I was very active. So I started helping the church. I started just because I wanted to get out of the house.

Eventually it became a full-time job. Then, when she started working full time, her husband took on more household responsibilities:

> Here he has learned all kinds of domestic chores. At times I get home from work and he has everything ready. I don't have to do a thing in the house. Other times, we decide to go out for dinner.

Brunilda could not have made it without her husband, who helped her take care of the children as she pursued both her educational goals and, later, her political activism:

> My husband was very understanding of my goals and political interest. We shared many of the household responsibilities. . . . I have to admit that I spent a lot of time outside of the house during my children's childhood; for that I am a little bit sorry.

Later on she elaborated on her struggles and how she resolved them:

> When you are a professional, you face what Americans call "conflicting priorities." It's like I want to be everywhere at the same time. For me,

community work has always interested me, whereas being a housewife has always been secondary. I feel more gratification in my role as a professional.

At the time of the interview, Brunilda worked as a professor in a local university. Aurea too placed her community activism (which was her professional orientation) alongside her family responsibilities:

> For me, both are part of the same process. I define my family network beyond the nuclear family, or better yet, beyond the traditional American concept of the nuclear family. My family is part of my social activism.

I asked whether this brought about any conflicts. She replied:

> Without doubt, my husband is part of this sexist society and obviously expects privileges that this society accords men, but we have worked and negotiated these roles quite successfully; moreover, we both made a political pact. It worked rather well because he shares the same vision of the world and social change as I do.

Conclusion

Evidence from this research shows how, in the context of a changing political economy, migration emerged as a strategy for families across class backgrounds. Initially, migration was a strategy working-class families used to deal with shrinking economic opportunities for the men in the family, but eventually middle-class better-educated men and women joined working-class Puerto Ricans in the migration process.

Gender relations within the family were a major factor shaping the migration of married working-class women to Chicago. Some married women went willingly, thinking that the moved would improve their families' financial situations. Others resisted, but ultimately their roles as mothers and wives compelled them to follow their husbands to Chicago.

Whether working-class or middle-class, like other immigrant women, Puerto Rican women confronted a basic duality in family and work. Families provided economic and emotional support. They see the family as the only area where people are free to be themselves, and where people come for affection and love, but the family is also an institution that has historically oppressed women (Glenn 1986). When individuals and families confront economic deprivation, legal discrimination, and other threats to their survival, conflict within the context of the family is muted by the pressure of the family to unite against assaults from the outside. The focus on the family as a site of resistance often underestimates how certain family arrangements can be oppressive to women. Often misunderstood by scholars is the reproductive work of women on behalf of the family and the benefits such work brings to the men (Glenn 1987, 192).

Working-class women saw themselves in keeping with Puerto Rican culture as primarily *mujeres de la casa*, but many found themselves working, albeit temporarily, given the family's economic situation. Here, families accommodated to the wives' temporary employment, but in ways that did not challenge the traditional patriarchal structure in the family. Wives were still responsible for cooking, cleaning, and child care. Given this situation, working-class married women developed strategies to accommodate their roles as working wives.

The area of child care best reflects the resourcefulness of working-class Puerto Rican women migrants in developing accommodating strategies. Some women left their children behind in Puerto Rico; others brought relatives from Puerto Rico to help them. Still oth-

ers turned to older daughters as helpers. Some became involved in a cycle of child care similar to the one developed by Puerto Rican women migrants in New York City.

Married working-class Puerto Rican women adapted to life in Chicago in ways that did not disturb traditional family arrangements. They also developed strategies to resist some arrangements. Some sought to change their husband's view about work outside the home and created networks to help accomplish their goals. Others stopped working for wages but continued contributing as mothers, giving them influence and power within the family. In addition, some women remained active in income-generating activities, such as working in the family business. When husbands neglected their responsibilities as fathers, women took charge of the household, providing for their children and family.

Although middle-class women felt differently about work and family obligations, they also struggled over their roles as mothers and wives. They rejected traditional ideologies about women's roles and saw no conflict in doing both. Some husbands supported them, but when husbands resisted, they also negotiated the work and family responsibilities. Their class position afforded them options, such as staying home until they were ready to return to work, hiring help, postponing having children, and organizing their schedule around their children's schooling. Much empirical work needs to be done to fully understand how gender shapes the migration process for other groups of Puerto Rican women in different family arrangements and across class backgrounds.

NOTE

Acknowledgments: I am indebted to Judith Wittner, of Loyola University of Chicago, for her invaluable assistance and suggestions during the early stages of this work and to *las mujeres del barrio* for sharing their experiences with me. I would also like to thank Margaret Andersen and the anonymous reviewers for their comments and suggestions.

REFERENCES

Acosta-Belen, Edna. 1986. *The Puerto Rican woman: Perspectives on culture, history, and society.* New York: Praeger.

Dietz, James L. 1986. *Economic history of Puerto Rico: Institutional change and capitalist development.* Princeton, NJ: Princeton University Press.

Falcon, Luis M. 1990. Migration and development: The case of Puerto Rico. In *Determinants of emigration from Mexico, Central America, and the Caribbean,* edited by S. Diaz-Briquets and S. Weintraub. Boulder, CO: Westview.

Glenn, Evelyn N. 1986. *Issei, Nisei, War Bride: Three generations of Japanese women in domestic service.* Philadelphia: Temple University Press.

———. 1987. Women, labor migration and household work: Japanese American women in the pre-war period. In *Ingredients for women's employment policy,* edited by C. Bose and G. Spitae. Albany: State University of New York Press.

History Task Force. 1979. *Labor migration under capitalism: The Puerto Rican experience.* New York: Monthly Review Press.

Juarbe, Ana. 1988. Anastasia's story: A window into the past, a bridge to the future. *Oral History Review* 16:15–22.

Pantojas-Garcia, Emilio. 1990. *Development strategies as ideology: Puerto Rico's export-led industrialization experience.* Boulder, CO: Lynne Rienner.

Pedraza, Sylvia. 1991. Women and migration: The social consequences of gender. *Annual Review of Sociology* 17:303–25.

Rodriquez, Clara. 1989. *Puerto Ricans: Born in the U.S.A.* Boston: Unwin Hyman.

Safa, Helen. 1984. Female employment and the social reproduction of the Puerto Rican working class. *International Migration Review* 18:1168–87.

Sanchez-Ayendez, Melba. 1986. Puerto Rican elderly women: Shared meanings and informal supportive networks. In *All-American women: Lines that divide, ties that bind,* edited by Johnnetta Cole. New York: Free Press.

Sanchez-Korrol, Virginia. 1983. *From colonia to community: The history of Puerto Ricans in New York City, 1917–1948.* Westport, CT: Greenwood.

———. 1986. The forgotten migrant: Educated Puerto Rican women in New York City, 1920–1940. In *The Puerto Rican woman: Perspectives on culture, history, and society,* edited by E. Acosta-Belen. New York: Praeger.

∾ Chapter 15

Children's Changing Access to Resources:
A Historical Perspective

DONALD J. HERNANDEZ

Children's lives have been completely transformed during the past 150 years by revolutionary changes in the American family, society, and economy. Only within the past two decades, however, have substantial numbers of sociologists, demographers, and economists begun to conduct national studies focusing on children. This chapter discusses results of the first national study using census and survey data to describe the profound changes that have characterized the lives of America's children over the last 50 to 150 years (Hernandez 1993a).

Three Revolutionary Changes

The Rise in Fathers' Nonfarm Work

For hundreds of years, agriculture and the two-parent farm family have represented the primary forms of economic production

From *Social Policy Report* 8, no. 1 (spring 1994): 1–22, copyright © 1994 by the Society for Research in Child Development. Reprinted by permission.

and family organization in Western countries. However, the shift away from farming to the nonfarm father-as-breadwinner, mother-as-homemaker system of family organization was very rapid. A large majority of children, nearly 70%, lived in two-parent farm families in 1830, but by 1930 this proportion had dropped to a minority of less than 30% (Figure 1). During the same 100 years, children living in nonfarm families with breadwinner fathers and homemaker mothers grew from only 15% to a majority of 55%.

This represented a historically unprecedented transformation in the nature of childhood. In two-parent farm families, family members worked side by side to sustain themselves in small communities. In contrast, two-parent urban families consisted of fathers who spent their workday away from home, earning the income required to support the family, and mothers who remained in the home to care for their children and perform domestic functions.

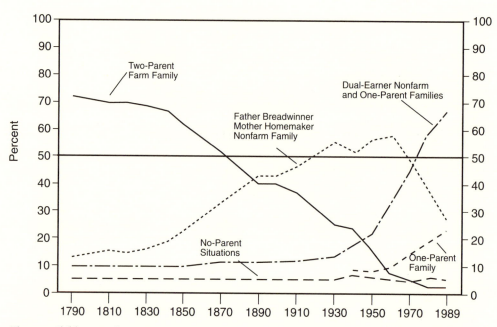

Figure 1. Children Aged 0–17 in Farm Families, Father-as-Breadwinner Families, and Dual-Earner Families: 1790–1989 (estimates are for 10-year intervals to 1980, and for 1989). Source: Hernandez 1993a, p. 103, copyright by Russell Sage Foundation. Reprinted by permission.

The Decline in Large Families

This enormous shift away from farming to an urban life with fathers as the sole family breadwinner was accompanied by a dramatic decline in large families. Among adolescents born in 1865, 82% lived in families with 5 children or more, but this figure fell to only 30% for those born in 1930. During these same 65 years, smaller families with only 1 to 4 children more than tripled, from 18% to 70%. As a result, the median number of siblings in the families of adolescents dropped by almost two-thirds, from 7.3 siblings to only 2.6 siblings per family.

This decline represented a drastic change in the level of competition for resources that children might experience within families. Whereas formerly a majority of children were competing with at least 7 other siblings for their parents' time and economic resources,

by 1930 nearly 60% of children were either only children or had only 1 or 2 siblings in the home.

The Rise in Educational Attainment

A third revolutionary change in children's lives occurred during the same era. School enrollment increased greatly, producing corresponding increases in educational attainments for children and for parents. Between 1870 and 1940, school enrollment rates increased sharply from about 50% for children aged 5–19, to 95% for children aged 7–13, and to 79% for children aged 14–17. During the same time, among enrolled students, the number of days spent in school doubled, expanding from 21% of the total days in the year in 1870 to 42% of the days in the year in 1940. By 1940, then, school days accounted for 59% of all the nonweekend days in the year.

As more and more children 6 years old and older spent larger portions of the year in school—that is, in a formal educational setting—they were also spending less time at home with their parents. By 1940, 95% of children aged 7–13 were spending 5 to 6 hours per day in school, or 59% of all their nonweekend days.

Since the children of today are the parents of tomorrow, this enormous increase in schooling also led, in due course, to large increases in parents' education. For example, comparing adolescents born in the 1920s to those born two decades later, the proportion with fathers completing 8 or more years of schooling increased from 56% to 77%, and the proportion with fathers completing at least 4 years of high school increased from 15% to 39%. Similarly, the proportion of adolescents with mothers completing 8 or more years of schooling increased from 61% to 83%, and with mothers completing at least 4 years of high school, from 17% to 44%. Today, 95% of adolescents have parents who completed at least 8 years of schooling, and more than 80% have parents who completed at least 4 years of high school.

Explaining the Changes

Why did these revolutions in fathers' work, family size, and schooling occur between the mid- to late-1800s and 1940s? The use of children and their parents as the central organizing feature of analysis helps provide an explanation.

A fundamental cause of the massive migration from farms to urban areas was the comparatively favorable economic opportunities in urban areas. The shift from farming to urban occupations was typically necessary to achieve an improved economic status or to keep from losing too much ground compared to others. This shift from farm to urban work also meant that housing, food, clothing, and other necessities had to be purchased with cash, making the costs of supporting each additional child more apparent. At the same time, children's potential economic contribution to their parents and families was sharply reduced by the passage of laws restricting child labor and mandating education.

Economic growth led, moreover, to increases in the quality and quantity of available consumer products and services. Expected standards of consumption rose, and individuals were required to spend more money simply to maintain the new "normal" standard of living. Hence, the costs of supporting each additional child at a "normal" level increased over time.

Finally, newly available goods and services competed with children for parental time and money. Since each additional child in a family requires additional financial support and makes additional demands on parents' time and attention, the birth of each child reduces the time and money parents can devote to their own work or careers, as well as to recreation and to older children. As a result, more and more parents limited their family size to a comparatively small number of children so that available income could be spread less thinly.

When farming gave way to the industrial economy and family size was shrinking, school enrollment increased as labor unions sought to insure jobs for adults (mainly fathers) by limiting child labor, and the child welfare movement obtained the passage of laws protecting children from unsafe and unfair working conditions. These movements also achieved corresponding success in gaining the passage of compulsory education laws, through which the government both mandated and paid for universal schooling.

In addition, as time passed, higher educational attainments became increasingly necessary to obtain jobs that offered higher incomes and greater prestige. Hence, parents encouraged and fostered higher educational attainments among their children as a path to occupational and economic success in adulthood. Once again, their motivation was to improve their children's relative social and economic standing, compared to others in their generation.

The Rise in Mothers' Labor Force Participation

After 1940 two additional revolutions in children's families began. First was the explosion in mothers' employment outside the home. In 1940 only 10% of children lived with a mother who was in the labor force (Figure 2). This figure increased by 6 percentage points during the 1940s, and then by at least 10 percentage points during each of the next four decades. By 1990, nearly 60% of children had a working mother, a six-fold increase in 50 years.

Just as children in an earlier era experienced a massive movement by fathers out of the family home to work at jobs in the urban-industrial economy, children since the Great Depression have experienced a massive movement by mothers into the paid labor force. Both of these revolutions in parents' work brought enormous changes in the day-to-day lives of children. As fathers entered the urban labor force, children aged 6 and over entered schools and spent increasing proportions of their lives in formal educational settings. Now, as mothers are entering the labor force, children under age 6 are spending increasing amounts of time in the care of someone other than their parents.

This revolution is occurring twice as fast in mothers' work as in fathers' work, however. The decline for children in the two-parent farm family from 60% to 10% required the 100 years from 1860 to 1960. But the corre-

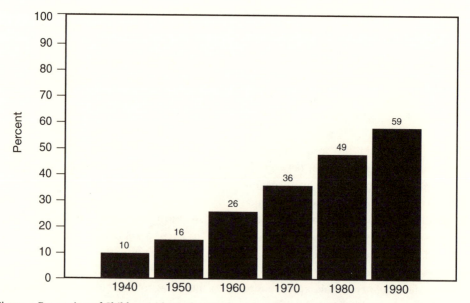

Figure 2. Proportion of Children with Mothers in the Labor Force: 1940–1990. Source: Hernandez 1993a, p. 109; 1993b, p. 9.

sponding rise in the proportion of working mothers from 10% to 60% required only 50 years, from 1940 to 1990.

Why the Increase in Mothers' Labor Force Participation?

What caused this revolutionary increase in mothers' labor force participation? Much of the answer lies in the historic changes that occurred in the family and economy. As suggested earlier, between the early days of the Industrial Revolution and about 1940, many parents had three major avenues for maintaining, improving, or regaining their relative economic standing compared with other families. First, they could move off the farm and have the husband work in comparatively well-paid jobs in the growing urban-industrial economy. Second, they could limit themselves to a smaller number of children, compared to other families, so that available family income could be spread less thinly. Third, they could increase their educational attainments.

By 1940, however, only 23% of Americans lived on farms, and 70% of parents had only 1 or 2 dependent children in the home. Consequently, for many parents, these two historical avenues to altering their relative economic standing had run their course (Elder 1974). Further, since most persons complete their education by age 25, attaining additional schooling beyond age 25 is often difficult or impractical.

With these avenues to improving their family's relative economic status effectively closed for a large majority of parents after age 25, a fourth major avenue to increasing family income emerged between 1940 and 1960, namely, paid work by wives and mothers. The traditional sources of female nonfarm labor, that is, unmarried women, were either stagnant or declining, while the demand for female workers was increasing (Oppenheimer 1970).

Meanwhile, wives and mothers were becoming increasingly available and well-qualified for work outside the home. By 1940 the unprecedented increase in children's school enrollment had effectively released mothers from personal child-care responsibilities for a time period equivalent to about two-thirds of an adult workday for about two-thirds of a full-time adult workyear, except for the few years before children entered elementary school. In addition, many women were highly educated, since the educational attainments of women and mothers had increased along with those of men. By 1940 young women were more likely than young men to graduate from high school, and they were about two-thirds as likely to graduate from college.

Paid work outside the home for mothers was becoming increasingly attractive in our competitive, consumption-oriented society for another reason. Families in which the husband's income was comparatively low could, by virtue of the wife's work, move economically ahead of families in which the husband had the same occupational status but lacked a working wife. This situation placed families with comparatively well-paid husbands at a disadvantage, making their wives' work more attractive (Oppenheimer 1982).

In addition, with the historic rise in the divorce rate, paid work became increasingly attractive to mothers as a hedge against the possible economic disaster of losing most or all of their husbands' income through divorce. This trend is discussed below.

More immediate economic insecurity and need, associated with fathers' lack of access to full-time employment, also made mothers' work attractive. In the Great Depression year of 1940, 40% of children lived with fathers who did not work year round, full time. While this proportion declined after the Great Depression, it has continued at high levels. In 1950 and 1960, 29% to 32% of children lived with fathers who did not work year round, full time.

Even with the subsequent expansion in mother-only families with no father present in the home, discussed below, the proportion of all children living with fathers who did not work year round, full time was 22% to 25% during the past two decades. Throughout the era since the Great Depression, then, at least one-fifth of American children have lived with fathers who, during any given year, experienced part-time work or joblessness. This has been a powerful incentive for many mothers to work for pay. The importance of sheer economic necessity in fostering growth in mothers' employment is reflected in the following fact: in 1988, 1 of every 8 American children in two-parent families was either living in official poverty despite the mother's paid employment or would have been living in official poverty were the mother not working.[1]

Of course, the desire to alter their family's relative social and economic status is not the only reason that wives and mothers enter the labor force. Additional reasons to work include the personal, nonfinancial rewards of the job itself, the opportunity to be productively involved with other adults, and the satisfactions associated with having a career in a high-prestige occupation. Nonetheless, for many mothers it is economic insecurity and need that provide a powerful incentive to work for pay. Finally, all these inducements for mothers to enter the labor force after 1940 existed in the presence of the fact that at age 25 young women still have a potential of about 40 years when they might work for pay in the labor force.

Thus, a revolutionary increase in mothers' labor force participation occurred during the past half century for the following reasons. By 1940 many mothers were potentially available for work, and mothers' work had become the only major avenue available to most couples over age 25 seeking to maintain, improve, or regain their relative social and economic status compared to other families. After 1940, not only did the economic demands on married women increase, but work held a greater attraction.

The Rise in Mother-Only Families

Twenty years after the beginning of the sharp increase in mothers' work, yet another marked change in family life began, namely, an unprecedented increase in mother-only families where the father was not present in the home. Between the 1860s and 1960s, there was a remarkably steady eight-fold increase in the rate of divorce (Figure 3). Three noteworthy, but short-lived interruptions occurred in conjunction with World War I, the Great Depression, and World War II.

Why the Increase in Mother-Only Families?

Why did this sustained increase in divorce occur? Preindustrial farm life compelled the economic interdependence of husbands and wives; fathers and mothers had to work together to maintain the family. But with a nonfarm job, the father could, if he desired, depend on his own work alone for his income. He could leave his family, taking his income with him. Similarly, the post-1940 mother with a job could separate or divorce and keep her own income.

At the same time, in moving to urban areas, husbands and wives left behind the rural small-town social controls that once censured divorce. In addition, economic insecurity and need associated with erratic or limited employment prospects for many men also contributed to the increasing divorce rate, as well as to out-of-wedlock childbearing.

Studies of divorce have shown that insta-

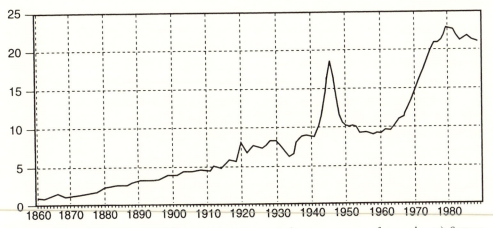

Figure 3. Divorce Rate: 1960–1988 (divorces per 1,000 married women 15 years of age and over). Source: Jacobson 1959; and U.S. National Center for Health Statistics 1991.

bility in husbands' work, declines in family income, and a low ratio of family income-to-needs lead to increased hostility between husbands and wives, decreased marital quality, and increased risk of divorce (Conger et al. 1990; Conger and Elder 1994; Elder et al. 1992; Liker and Elder 1983). In fact, each of the three economic recessions between 1970 and 1982 led to intensified increases in mother-only families compared to each preceding nonrecessionary period.

A rough estimate of the size of this recession effect for children has been developed by assuming that, without each recession, the average annual increase in mother-only families would have been the same during recession years as during the immediately preceding nonrecessionary period. The results suggest that recessions accounted for about 30% of the overall increase in mother-only families between 1968 and 1988, or for about 50% of the increase in mother-only families with separated or divorced mothers (Hernandez 1993a).

Since 70% of the increase in mother-only families for white children between 1960 and 1988 can be accounted for by the rise in separation and divorce, this trend explains much of the rise in mother-only families for white children during these decades. In the case of black children, the explanation is more complicated. Between 1940 and 1960, the proportion of children living in a mother-only family with a divorced or separated mother increased much more for black children than for white children. But, especially since 1970, black children have also experienced markedly large increases in the proportion living in mother-only families with a never-married mother.

In Hernandez 1993a, I argue that those factors which led to increased separation and divorce among whites were also important for blacks. As further explanation, however, the startling drop in the proportion of blacks living on farms between 1940 and 1960 and the extraordinary economic pressures and hardships faced by black families may account for much of the higher proportion of black children living in mother-only families.

In addition, drawing upon the work of Wilson (1987), I calculated that the extent to which joblessness of young black men aged 16–24 exceeded joblessness among young white men expanded from an almost negligible difference in 1955 to 15 to 25 percentage points between 1975 and 1989. Faced with this large and rapid reduction in the availability of black men of family-building age who might provide significant support to a family, many young black women appear to have decided to forego a temporary and unrewarding marriage—a marriage, in some cases, in which a jobless or poorly paid husband might act as a financial drain.

The size of this racial gap in joblessness is at least two-thirds the size of the 23 percentage-point increase that occurred between 1960 and 1988 in the comparative proportions of black and white children living in mother-only families with never-married mothers. Thus, the increasing racial gap in joblessness may well be the major cause of the increasing racial gap in the proportion of children living in mother-only families with never-married mothers.

As a result of sharp rises in divorce and out-of-wedlock childbearing, the proportion of children living with their mother, with no father in the home, about tripled from 6% to 8% between 1940 and 1960, and to 20% by 1990. By 1990, children in mother-only families were about twice as likely to live with a divorced or separated mother as with a never-married mother. Hence separation and divorce account for about two-thirds of children living in mother-only families, and out-of-wedlock childbearing accounts for the remaining third of children living in mother-only families.

The Consequences for Children

Historic Experience with One-Parent Families

It was not until after 1960 that increases in divorce led to increases in children living with one parent. Until then increases in divorce had simply counterbalanced the declining rate at which children formerly lost parents through death. Both historically and today, however, large proportions of children spend, or have spent, at least part of their childhoods with fewer than two parents in the home, because of their parents' death, divorce, or out-of-wedlock childbearing.

Among white children born between 1920 and 1960, for example, a large minority of 28 percent to 34 percent spent part of their childhood living with one parent or no parent in the home (Figure 4). In addition, this proportion was nearly constant for white children born between the late 1800s and 1920, since the historic decline in parental mortality was counterbalanced by the historic increase in divorce during the 100 years spanning the mid-1860s to the mid-1960s. Projections indicate, however, that the proportion of white children born since 1980 ever spending time in a family with fewer than two parents will increase to about 50%.

Among black children born between 1920 and 1950, an enormous 55% to 60% spent part of their childhood living with one parent, and additional evidence indicates that this proportion was roughly the same for black children born since the late 1800s. Projections indicate that this proportion will rise to about 80% for black children born since 1980.

Myth of the "Ozzie and Harriet" Family

In the 1950s the U.S. television program called *Ozzie and Harriet* idealized the urban American family in which the father was a full-time, year-round worker, the mother was a full-time homemaker without a paid job, and all the children were born after the parents' only marriage. In reality, however, never since at least the Great Depression has a majority of children lived in such a family—largely as a consequence of the changing patterns of fathers' and mothers' employment and the instability in parental presence in the home.

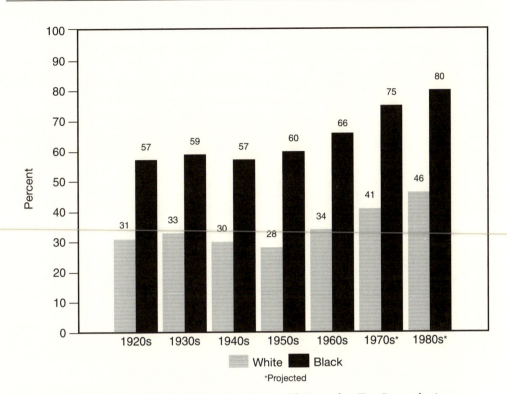

Figure 4. Percent of White and Black Children Ever Living with Fewer than Two Parents by Age 17: 1920s–1980s Cohorts. Source: Hernandez 1993a, p. 86.

This contradiction to the "Ozzie and Harriet" myth holds even for newborns and very young children up to age 1. Since at least the Great Depression, for any single year, more than one-half of children were born into families that did not conform to this ideal, because the father worked less than full time, year round, the mother was engaged in paid employment, or not all of the children were born after the parents' only marriage.

Family Income and Poverty

As the historic changes in fathers' work, family size, and men's educational attainments drew to a close in the early 1970s, and as the post-1940 revolutions in mothers' work and mother-only families proceeded, what were the consequences for family income and poverty rates?

Changes in Income Since World War II. During the 26 years from 1947 to 1973, median family income more than doubled (Figure 5). During the next 17 years, however, between 1973 and 1990, median family income barely increased, by a tiny 6%, despite the enormous growth in mothers' labor force participation.

Defining and Measuring Poverty. Because real income and living standards rose dramatically between 1940 and 1973, social perceptions about what income levels were considered "normal" and "adequate" changed substantially. That such judgments are relative has been noted for at least 200 years. Adam Smith emphasized in the *Wealth of Nations,* for example, that poverty must be defined in comparison to contemporary standards of living. He defined economic hardship as the experience of being unable to consume commodities that "the custom of the country

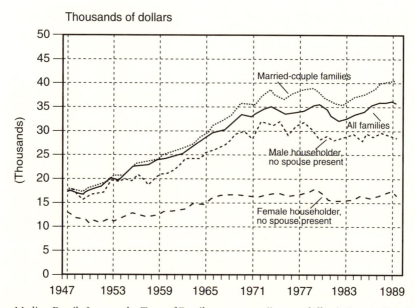

Figure 5. Median Family Income, by Type of Family: 1947–1990 (in 1990 dollars). Source: U.S. Bureau of the Census 1991.

renders it indecent for creditable people, even of the lowest order, to be without" (Smith 1776, cited in U.S. Congress 1989, 10).

More recently, John Kenneth Galbraith also argued that

> people are poverty-stricken when their income, even if adequate for survival, falls markedly behind that of the community. Then they cannot have what the larger community regards as the minimum necessary for decency; and they cannot wholly escape, therefore, the judgment of the larger community that they are indecent. They are degraded, for, in a literal sense, they live outside the grades or categories which the community regards as respectable (1958, 323–324)

Based on these insights, additional literature (Expert Committee on Family Budget Revisions 1980; Fuchs 1965), and a comprehensive review of existing U.S. studies and original research by Rainwater (1974), I developed (Hernandez 1993a) a measure of "relative poverty," relying on poverty thresholds set at 50% of median family income in specific years and adjusted for family size.

The Fall and Rise of Child Poverty. The relative poverty rate among children dropped sharply after the Great Depression, between 1939 and 1949, from 38% to 27%, and the 1950s and 1960s brought an additional decline of 4 percentage points. But by 1988, the rate had returned to the comparatively high level of 27%, a rate that children had experienced in 1949, almost 40 years earlier.

Accounting for Poverty Change. To what extent can these changes in the rate of childhood relative poverty be accounted for by changes in income provided by fathers, mothers, and other family members? To what extent can they be accounted for by changes in income received from government welfare programs?

If, for example, only the income of fathers in the home had been available, the relative poverty rate of children would have fallen sharply during the 1940s, fallen much more slowly or not at all during the 1950s and 1960s, and risen substantially during the 1970s and 1980s.

The addition of mothers' income to that of fathers over the same period acted to speed the decline in child relative poverty that occurred during the 1940s, 1950s, and 1960s, and to slow the subsequent increase in relative poverty that occurred during the 1970s and 1980s. In fact, by 1988, 14% of all children and 11% of children in two-parent families depended on their mother's income to lift them out of relative poverty.

Next, additional income from relatives other than parents in the home—except during the Great Depression year of 1939—served to reduce the relative poverty rate by a nearly constant and comparatively small 4 to 5 percentage points for children overall, and by a nearly constant and even smaller 1 to 2 percentage points for children in two-parent families.

Finally, both for children overall and for children in two-parent families, Aid to Families with Dependent Children (AFDC) and Social Security acted to reduce the relative poverty rate for children by a stable and small 1 to 2 percentage points in any given year. Hence, the role of these welfare programs in reducing child relative poverty—as an addition to all other income sources—has been quite limited throughout the era since the Great Depression.[2]

Children's Economic Status and Public Policy

Children as the Unit of Statistical Analysis

Throughout this chapter children have been used as the unit of analysis. Although it may seem obvious that research on children should be conducted in this fashion, most national statistical studies involving children, until recently, have actually used parents or adults as the unit of analysis. Such an approach can be misleading if children are meant to be the focus.

For example, 27% of children lived in relative poverty, compared to only 18% of parents.[3] For most other adults, the relative poverty rate was still lower, at 13% to 14% for adults aged 18–64 with no children in the home. At the opposite extreme, in 1988, 22% of children lived in luxury (with family income at least 50% greater than the median and adjusted for family size) compared with 30% of parents and 45% to 50% of adults aged 18–64 with no children.

In 1993, 41% of families with children had just one child in the home, but only 22% of children lived in families where they were the only child. At the other extreme, only 20% of families with children had 3 or more children present, but 37% of children lived in families with a total of at least 3 children.

These statistics illustrate that the distribution of children's economic status can be quite different from that of parents and other adults. Thus, whether the unit of analysis is children or an adult-based measure can make a critical difference in measuring and interpreting the actual status of children vis-à-vis the families in which they are living.

International Comparisons

International comparisons serve to demonstrate the importance of public policy for children. It is not only in the U.S. that children's well-being is being jeopardized by social and economic change. Other developed countries have been experiencing similar trends in the growing proportions of children living in single-parent families (Figure 6, see also Burns 1992). The percentage of births occurring to unmarried mothers is also increasing in other countries along with the U.S.—although the rates vary across countries.

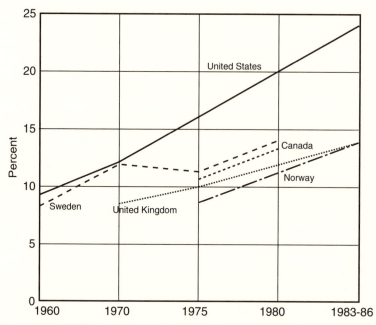

Figure 6. Percentage of Children in Single-Parent Families: 1960–1986. (All data for the United Kingdom refer to Great Britain. Data for 1983 to 1986 refer to 1986 for the United Kingdom, to 1983 for Norway, and to 1985 for the United States. Children are defined as follows: Canada—age 0 to 24 years; Norway—under age 20; Sweden—18 years and under for 1960, 1970, and 1975, and 15 years and under for 1980; United Kingdom—under age 16 or age 16 to 18 and in full-time education; United States—under age 18.) Source: Hobbs and Lippman 1990, p. 35.

There are, however, enormous differences in poverty across countries (Figure 7).[4] For example, children in the United States around 1980 were more than three times as likely as children in Sweden to be living in poverty (17% versus 5%), and U.S. children in single-parent families were more than five times as likely as corresponding Swedish children to be living in poverty (51% versus 9%).

What accounts for these differences in poverty rates? Part of the difference is no doubt due to the low level of support provided by U.S. government transfers (e.g., welfare payments, and housing and child-care subsidies), compared to that provided in Sweden. In the United States, around 1980, the average poor family with children received only about $2,400 per year in government trans-

fers compared to $6,400 in Sweden. In addition, fewer poor families with children in the United States receive any government transfers. Only 73% of poor families in the United States receive government transfers—27% receive none—while in all the other countries shown, 99% to 100% of poor families with children receive government transfers.

Social Policies and Evaluation

These selected comparisons illustrate how crucial social policies can be to the economic welfare of children. It is not difficult to imagine that a wide range of other policies may also have important consequences for children's economic well-being and thereby their intellectual, physical, and socioemotional

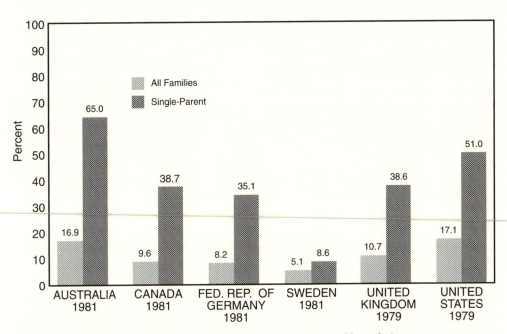

Figure 7. Poverty Among Children by Family Type: c. 1980. Source: Hobbs and Lippman 1990, p. 36.

development and functioning. Tax laws, for example, and the degree to which they are progressive or regressive, have major implications for the economic situation of children. Minimum wage laws and a wide range of other economic policies influence how much parents can earn and how equal or unequal the income distribution is. Still other government policies concerning the quality and cost of housing, the time allowed for parental or family leave, the quality and cost of preschool education, and the quality, cost, and access to health care all affect children's physical and interpersonal living situations.

Such policies can have important consequences for children's well-being and development, but little attention has been devoted to studying their effects on children. Many public policies target families, workers, or parents, with the result that policy analyses typically evaluate consequences not for children but, instead, for families, workers, parents, or the economy as a whole. The living conditions of children may, however, be quite different from those of families, parents, or adults in general. Hence, many public policies designed to enhance the welfare of families, parents, or adults may have quite different effects for children.

To the extent children's needs are not met by policies for families, workers, or parents, it will be necessary to design public policies explicitly directed toward fostering their development and well-being. This suggests that statistics concerning children are essential to both scholars and policymakers who share an interest in tracking the consequences of public policies and understanding how policy interacts with other social and economic change.

A child-centered approach to the design, implementation, and evaluation of public policies can be justified in at least two distinct but important ways. The first justification focuses on humanitarian, moral, human rights, or social equity principles (e.g., Huston 1991).

Here the principle is that children have basic rights because they have inherent value as individual persons. The U.N. Convention on the Rights of the Child (adopted by the General Assembly of the United Nations on November 20, 1989) asserts, for example, the responsibility of national governments to foster the rights of children: to include (1) a standard of living, adequate for physical, mental, spiritual, moral, and social development; (2) education aimed at developing the child's personality, talents, and mental and physical abilities to the fullest extent; and (3) the highest attainable standard of health and health services.

The second justification focuses on children as the human capital upon which rests the future of America (e.g., Hamburg 1992; Lerner 1993; National Commission on Children 1991). Here the tenet is that children are the parents, workers, and citizens of the future. Hence, public investments in children today can yield valuable returns to America's future as an economic power, a democratic nation, and a world leader. But the failure to invest in children can lead to economic inefficiency, loss of productivity, shortages in needed skills, high health care costs, growing prison costs, and a nation that will be less safe, less caring, and less free.

NOTES

Acknowledgments: I am indebted to Edith Reeves and Catherine O'Brien for statistical assistance and the preparation of graphs.

1. The poverty threshold varies with the number of adults and children in a family. It is also adjusted for inflation, in accord with the consumer price index (U.S. Bureau of the Census 1993). In 1992, for example, a family of 4 (with 2 parents and 2 children) was classified as officially poor if its annual income was less than $14,288. A family with a mother and 2 children was classified as officially poor if its annual income was less than $11,304.

2. For a discussion of the additional effects of noncash benefits, health insurance, and taxes, see Hernandez 1993a, 253–259.

3. That children experience higher rates of poverty than parents may seem counterintuitive. However, poverty rates are calculated across all households. If, for example, there are 2 households, the first poor with 2 parents and 4 children, the second nonpoor with 2 parents and 2 children, the poverty rate for parents is 50%, since 2 out of 4 parents are poor, but the poverty rate for children in this instance is 67%, since 4 of 6 children are poor.

4. The method of measuring poverty used here differs somewhat from the official U.S. approach, but the difference is slight.

REFERENCES

Burns, A. (1992). Mother-head families: An international perspective and the case of Australia. *Social Policy Report,* 6(1), 1–X.

Conger, R. D., and Elder, G. H., Jr. (1994). *Families in troubled times: Adapting to change in rural America.* Hawthorne, NY: Aldine de Gruyter.

Conger, R. D., Elder, G. H., Jr., Lorenz, F. O., Conger, K. J., Simons, R. L., Whitbeck, L. B., Huck, J., and Melby, J. N. (1990). Linking economic hardship and marital quality and instability. *Journal of Marriage and the Family,* 52, 643–656.

Elder, G. H. (1974). *Children of the Great Depression: Social change in life experience.* Chicago: University of Chicago Press.

Elder, G. H., Conger, R. D., Foster, E. M., and Ardelt, M. (1992). Families under economic pressure. *Journal of Family Issues,* 13, 5–37.

Expert Committee on Family Budget Revisions. (1980). *New American family budget standards.* Madison, WI: Institute for Research on Poverty.

Fuchs, V. F. (1965). Towards a theory of poverty. In *The concept of poverty* (pp. 79–91). Washington, DC: Chamber of Commerce of the United States.

Galbraith, J. K. (1958). *The affluent society.* Boston: Houghton-Mifflin.

Hamburg, D. A. (1992). *Today's children: Creating a future for a generation in crisis.* New York: Time Books.

Hernandez, D. J. (1993a). *America's children: Resources from family, government, and the economy.* New York: Russell Sage Foundation.

———. (1993b). *We, the American children* (U.S. Bureau of the Census, WE-10). Washington, DC: U.S. Government Printing Office.

Hobbs, F. and Lippman, L. (1990). *Children's well-being: An international comparison* (U.S. Bureau of the Census. International Population Reports, Series P-85, No. 8). Washington, DC: U.S. Government Printing Office.

Huston, A. C. (Ed.). (1991). *Children in poverty: Child development and public policy.* Cambridge, England: Cambridge University Press.

Jacobson, P. H. (1959). *American marriage and divorce.* New York: Rinehart.

Lerner, R. M. (Ed.). (1993). *Early adolescence: Perspectives on research, policy, and intervention.* Hillsdale, NJ: Lawrence Erlbaum Associates.

Liker, J. K, and Elder, G. H. (1983). Economic hardship and marital relations in the 1930s. *American Sociological Review,* 48, 343–359.

National Commission on Children. (1991). *Beyond rhetoric: A new American agenda for children and families* (Final report). Washington, DC: U.S. Government Printing Office.

Oppenheimer V. K. (1970). *The female labor force in the United States* (Population Monograph Series, No. 5, Institute of International Studies). Berkeley: University of California Press.

———. (1982). *Work and the family.* New York: Academic Press.

Rainwater, L. (1974). *What money buys: Inequality and the social meanings of income.* New York: Basic Books.

Smith, A. (1776). *Wealth of nations.* London: Everyman's Library.

U.S. Bureau of the Census. (1991). DeNavas, C., and Welniak, E. J., Jr., *Money income of households, families, and persons in the United States: 1990* (Current Population Reports, Series P-60, No. 174). Washington, DC: U.S. Government Printing Office.

———. (1993). Baugher, E. F., and Shea, M., *Poverty in the United States: 1992* (Current Population Reports, Series P-60, No. 185). Washington, DC: U.S. Government Printing Office.

U.S. Congress. (1989). "Alternative measures of poverty" (Staff study prepared for the Joint Economic Committee). Washington, DC: U.S. Government Printing Office, October 18.

U.S. National Center for Health Statistics. (1991). *Advanced report of final divorce statistics, 1988,* vol. 39, No. 12, supplement 2. Washington, DC: U.S. Government Printing Office.

Wilson, W. J. (1987). *The truly disadvantaged: The inner city, the underclass, and public policy.* Chicago: University of Chicago Press.

∼ Section B

Families and Community

∿ *Chapter 16*

The Anti-Social Family

MICHÈLE BARRETT AND MARY MCINTOSH

1. Inheritance

Almost all of us are born and reared in a family. Those who are not raised by their parents in a private household are brought up in institutions that seek to imitate family life as faithfully as possible. What could be more classless than this universal experience? What could be less divisive? In reality, far from being a social leveler, forging bonds that cut across the barriers of class and sex, the family creates and recreates the very divisions it is often thought to ameliorate.

The family is a class institution and gives us each our initial class position. Each child begins life in the working class or the property-owning class, in the ranks of the professions, or of small business, of the landed aristocracy, or of the lowest group of the insecure and unemployed. Most boys will live out their lives in the same class and even in the same section

From Michèle Barrett and Mary McIntosh, *The Anti-Social Family* (London: Verso, 1982). Reprinted by permission.

of it; most girls will marry a man in a situation very similar to their own father's.

The main way in which social classes reproduce themselves over time is by bearing and rearing children. This is why Engels associated the historical origin of the modern monogamous family (in which a women has only one husband) with the origin of private property and class. "The rule of the man in the family, the procreation of children who could only be his, destined to be the heirs of his wealth—these alone were frankly avowed by the Greeks as the exclusive aims of monogamy."[1]

There have sometimes been classes and social groups that were reproduced by recruitment rather than by birth: the celibate clergy of the Catholic world, slaves in the Americas while the capturing of slaves in Africa continued, and immigrant workers in many parts of Western Europe where settlement is discouraged. Such classes and groups are exceptionally weak and powerless. Even the Catholic Church was weaker than its vast wealth and tenacious ideological grip would have enabled it to be. Indeed, it can be argued that in the heyday of the Church, priestly celibacy was enjoined precisely in order to maintain the access of the great secular families to its highest offices and so to retain the Church as a whole in a position of client. Slave groups and ethnic minorities that reproduce themselves, though exploited and downtrodden, are at least able to develop some forms of accommodation and adaptation over generations. So inheritance of class position serves to establish and to domesticate class divisions.

Of course people's class position is not fixed by their parentage. Some may move from one class to another, and many move up and down the ladder of status and security within the working class and into the ambiguous positions of bureaucrats, accounts clerks, scientists, and managers. In fact, the expansion of these last categories during the twentieth century was achieved largely by recruitment from below and required a large amount of upward mobility. The expansion is now slowing down, and it seems unlikely that such rates of mobility will be seen again. But the experience of social fluidity, the apparent breaking of old class destinies, personified in the career of the grammar-school boy and the success of the working man's son at a redbrick university, has left its mark in popular consciousness. Education has come to be seen as the main road to success in life. It is what you do rather than where you are that counts.

What is deceptive about this social imagery is that it is too strongly colored by the exceptions—those who move—and it ignores what can be taken from granted—that most men follow their fathers. A large-scale survey[2] found that 62 percent of the sons of men who worked as professionals, administrators, managers, supervisors and higher-grade technicians (Class I and II occupations) were in jobs in the same range as their fathers at the time of the study, and only 13 percent had manual jobs. At the other end of the scale 58 percent of the sons of men in manual jobs themselves had manual jobs, and only 18 percent had Class I and II jobs. This was the measure of the extent to which fathers passed on social positions to their sons during a period when expansion at the top of the job hierarchy was producing new opportunities.

It is interesting that families are less effective in passing the father's occupational status on to their daughters. (Unfortunately there is no evidence about how much women follow in their *mother's* footsteps.) Women often marry up or down. "The typical father from Class I is more likely to see his daughter downwardly mobile than his son, or, to be more precise, to have a son-in-law of lower social class than his son. Conversely, the girl from Classes VI or VIII is more likely to be upwardly mobile than her brother."[3] And a woman's own occupation is less determined by her father's than is a man's. (The only exception to this is that it is even more difficult for a woman whose father was not a professional or a manager to become one herself than it is for a man.)

Figures like these give a very gross picture of how social classes are reproduced through the family. They do not tell us much about the processes involved. Perhaps the most important process is the way in which families pass on advantage *and* disadvantage in the chances of educational success.

During the 1950s and 1960s the question of social mobility was a dominant concern among sociologists who studied education. There was socialist concern with equality of opportunity and with showing how the selective system of secondary modern and grammar schools failed in its overt objective of offering such opportunity to pupils from working-class homes. There were some interesting and depressing findings, which in the end were interpreted to place the credit or blame for school success on the child's home, and especially on the mother. A working-class family had to have something unusual about it for its children to do well at school. The mother had to be better educated than average, or the parents interested in reading. What is interesting is how this research showed that parents affected their children's class position even when they did not simply place them in their own class. It is a pity there were not more studies of the way in which parents with professional and managerial jobs so often managed to ensure that their children did not fall too far below them—a task which is becoming increasingly difficult as the expansion of these strata slows down. What is depressing is that the research shows even more clearly how family and class are interwoven. The sociologists who were involved in these studies shrank from their full implications. They were reluctant to see that their work constituted an indictment of the family as an institution—the more so since they would have been tempted to read it in moralistic and individualistic terms as an indictment of the working-class families themselves. The next generation of radical sociologists turned its guns towards a more generally acceptable target and developed a critique of the educational system and school curricula from a class perspective. (Indeed, it is remarkable how the sociology of the family, as a subfield, fell from favor as left-wing and critical perspectives gained strength within sociology; it is only the advent of the new feminism that has brought it back in.)

Another major process in reproducing classes is the inheritance of wealth. "It is difficult to avoid the conclusion that inheritance has been the most important single source of wealth inequality in the fairly recent past in twentieth-century Britain," according to a study by C. D. Harbury and D.M.W.N. Hitchens.[4] They estimate that "something between two-thirds and four-fifths of those who

died rich in the third quarter of the present century owed their wealth to inheritance, and the rest to entrepreneurship and luck."[5] Furthermore, daughters who inherit wealth frequently marry sons who inherit wealth. So both inheritance between generations and patterns of marriage among inheritors serve to reproduce the concentration of wealth in a small class of people.

We have chosen to start at a very general structural level by showing how the family serves to pass on privilege and disadvantage from one generation to the next. We have done this partly because it highlights very clearly how the family embodies the principle of selfishness, exclusion and pursuit of private interest and contravenes those of altruism, community and pursuit of the public good. Society is *divided into* families and the divisions are deep, not merely ones of slight antipathy and mild distrust.

2. Individualism = Familism

Conservative thought is often said to focus on the idea of individualism: self-help, self-support, self-sufficiency, self-respect. It rejects dependence, "scrounging," collectivism, the belief that "the world owes you a living." Yet in practice the unit of self-support is not the individual but the family. In Britain no one nowadays thinks that children, as long as they are being trained or educated, should support themselves. Conservatives think that husbands should support their wives and children and that disabled or old people should be able to turn to their kin for help before they seek help from charity or from the state. Indeed, it has tended to be conservatives who have wished to extend the range of kin among whom mutual aid could be expected and progressives who have made more and more people eligible for public assistance.

This is a boundary that has been contested and shifted many times in the last century and a half. At present, officially speaking, only children under sixteen who live with a parent and wives who live with a husband can have no rights to the basic noninsured state social security payments. And still it is conservatives who resist the socialist demand for an adequate child benefit and reject the feminist demand that husband and wife should have independent rights to social security.

Many of the catch-phrases of conservative politics—individual choice in education or in health-care, freedom of choice for consumers, owner-occupation—thus mask a defense of paternal as against social responsibility and authority. For it is not children who choose their education but their parents who "choose" to give them what education they can afford with the father's income. And so it is with health insurance, with housing and with household consumption. People's standard of living is not determined by their own income but by that of the household they live in and how its income is shared among its members.

In this context children, and to some extent wives, are mere extensions of men. Their needs are defined for them by the head of the family and as part of his needs. A man should not merely be self-supporting but should take care of his dependants as well. He should be expected to be able to earn enough to keep "a family." Indeed, when a wage is said to be so low that it is below the poverty line what is meant is that it is below the level of social security benefit for a family of two adults and two children, not that the worker himself could not live on it.

This idea of the family wage for men is deeply embedded in conservative thought. In part, this is because it helps maintain men's privilege and authority. But it is also because the conflation of the individual and the family is absolutely necessary to sustain the conservative economic fantasy. This is a fantasy of an economy in which the actions of self-seeking "economic men" add up, through the "unseen hand" of the market mechanism, to an optimal pattern of production and consumption. In it, each member is motivated by self-interest to contribute to the wants of others. In order to elevate the morality of the market into an entire social ethic, it is necessary to ignore all those members of society who do not themselves enter the market. For most of them this is done by the sleight of hand of subsuming them as members of families into the individuality of their head of household. He can then be assumed to be an economic agent, complete with income, expenditure, consumer preferences, indifference curves and marginal prospensities to all sorts of economic activity. So it becomes possible to believe that the whole economy is organized on the liberal-individualist model of the free market, with everyone working in order to support themselves, because those who cannot earn a living are subsumed under those who can.

For socialists, it is dangerous to pretend that society is made up entirely of people who can contribute to production. It masks our interdependence and the necessity of a social conception of needs and a social plan for meeting them. Unfortunately, though, there has been a strong tendency in British socialist thought to accept this form of familism. This is largely due to the fact that socialism has been fostered and shaped in a labor movement dominated by the trade unions of the skilled male workers whose own interests lay in privileging those who *could* (or could claim they could) contribute a great deal to production and who could use the idea of the family wage to claim higher wages for themselves and to exclude women, children and young people from the better paid jobs.[6] The idea of being a "provider" for the family has also become a cherished element of male working-class self-esteem.

A broader conception of socialism would recognize that this kind of familism merely papers over some of the cracks in the capitalist system, or protects those lucky enough to be in families with a good wage-earner. It does not solve the fundamental problems of the wage system as a means of meeting the needs of the working class: that some people have no wage-earner to depend on, and some wage-earners have no dependants while others have too many. It is a fantasy solution that would work in reality only if each wage-earner had a household of two adults and 2.4 children to support throughout his working life and the rest of the people were neatly distributed among such households. In other words, it would only work if households were formed on some bureaucratic principle and not, as families, on the basis of kinship.[7]

The confusion of individual and family in conservative thought reflects a close association between the two in everyday life. It is an association that has many pernicious effects. The most marked of these is that children are a private possession. Though they are to join society and be its future members, they are produced by and for their parents. Parents decide how many to have, when to have them, and they try to determine how to bring them up. Often they become extensions of their parent's personalities or a compensation for failings in their lives. They can be a major source of pride, or often of disappointment. During childhood this may be rewarding and apparently successful, but as adolescence wears on and the child becomes more independent a unique kind of problem frequently occurs. The resentment that parents feel about the wrong choices their children make is quite unlike any disagreement between other people about how to live or what to do.

The sort of behavior that provokes the cry of despair, "Why do you treat me like this?" is often not *treating* the parent at all, but simply choosing the wrong lifestyle, the wrong haircut, the wrong job, the wrong partner. What the children do with their own lives necessarily affects the parents. The biblical notion that when fathers have eaten a sour grape the children's teeth are set on edge has little resonance today, but its obverse is part of our daily experience.

In this setting of intimate interdependence, it is not surprising that the explanation of individual troubles should be sought in the constellation of the immediate family. Since the 1950s "family therapy" rather than individual therapy has been the vogue for dealing with difficult or delinquent children, and even to some extent with adults who are mentally ill.[8] In many ways this is more appropriate than the individualism of traditional therapies, though usually the theory has been that a well-organized family with appropriate parental and gender roles would produce adequate personalities and that any problems could be corrected by bringing the family back into line with the good model. R. D. Laing has used a similar vision of family processes to come to the much more disturbing conclusion that in the close-knit emotional tangle of the nuclear "family nexus" the confusions of intersubjectivity and the problems of distinguishing oneself from the attributions imposed by those closest to one could result in schizophrenia. In the nuclear family each member "attempts to regulate the inner life of the other in order to preserve his own."[9] From Laing's accounts of the families of his schizophrenic patients, it is not hard to see how the tight intimacy of nuclear family life may cause acute problems for family members, even when the solutions they seek are less dramatic than schizophrenia.

Another twist of the screw of familialism

and individualism is the way that being reared in an enclosed family, with one parent mainly responsible for the children, tends to produce a highly individualistic personality structure. Critics of more communal forms of childrearing have argued that a close and continuous bond with a single mother-figure during the first few years of life is essential to the development of an adequate personality. There have been many doubts about research that has mostly looked at residential children's institutions in which the inmates are deprived of considerably more than the mother-child bond.[10] But it is often not noticed that even if they were right, the typical personality of the collectively reared child might simply be different, not "inadequate." Indeed, the typical personality of the normal successfully family-reared child may have its undesirable features: a need to form intimate one-to-one ties to the exclusion of a more diffused bond to a wider group, a tendency to go it alone as an individual and a lack of concern for group support and approval or group interests.

Bruno Bettelheim, in *The Children of the Dream,* has provided a balanced study of communal child-rearing in the Israeli kibbutz.[11] He found that the kibbutz-reared generation had more uniform educational attainments, with fewer dramatic successes and fewer "failures," than other Israelis. "The personality of the kibbutz-born generation seems depleted. . . [but] these young people seem much less neurotic than their parents, secure within their limitations, though these are often marked."[12] The most notable feature, though, is the deep peer attachments that they feel and the intensity of group ties. They function and experience the world better in their group than alone; they are reluctant to contemplate a life apart from each other. Bettelheim says: "All these seem to speak more of bondage than attachment"; but he concludes: "If intense group ties discour-

age individuation, neither do they breed human isolation, asocial behaviour or other forms of social disorganizations that plague modern man in competitive society."[13] We might add that even the "successes" of the individual child-rearing system may be less suited to a truly social life than the products of the kibbutz.

Communal societies like the Israeli kibbutzim often discourage an overemphasis on the obligations and attachments of the family. In many kibbutzim, husbands and wives are not allowed to work together and people are expected to refer to their parents, brothers, and sisters and so on by their names rather than in the terminology of kinship.

Similar principles informed many Christian communities in nineteenth-century America. The Oneida community, founded in New York state in 1848, consciously rejected the family and marriage as being inimical to a full communal life. The biblical text, "In heaven they neither marry nor are given in marriage," was taken as justification for "complex marriage" in which all the men and women of the community were joined. Heterosexual relations between any of them were encouraged; long-term pairing was discouraged. Children were cared for in a children's house soon after they were weaned, visiting their own parents only once or twice a week. Their founder, John Humphrey Noyes, saw a very clear contradiction between intense family feelings and community feeling. He believed that "the great problem of socialism now is, whether the existence of the marital family is compatible with that of the universal family, which the term 'community' signifies."[14]

The Oneida community adhered to these principles for little longer than thirty years. The kibbutzim, too, have tended to strengthen family ties and give more time and space to family life as they have moved from the pioneering to a more established phase. In both cases the shift represents a retreat from socialist ideals, in the kibbutz case partly associated with the complexities of Israeli, Middle Eastern and world politics; in the Oneida case—the community actually became a joint stock company in 1881—clearly and directly linked to hostile pressures from the locality and legal action against the community initiated by the Presbyterian Church. The fact that such experiments have not endured, or that they have become weakened and diluted, does not detract from the fact that they illustrate vividly how the strengthening of the community enables and requires the weakening of family ties.

These ideas were the commonplace of an earlier English tradition of socialist thought.[15] They have sadly faded from view. A vigorous critique of marriage was to be found in the writings of many early feminists. Yet it is often thought that the aspects of marriage they inveighed against have now disappeared. Marriage is no longer so obviously the main source of livelihood available to bourgeois women. The campaigns for easier divorce, supported often by socialists and feminists, have meant that marriage is no longer so indissoluble that people are stuck for life in loveless or brutal bonds. The wedding ceremony itself has been modernized so that women no longer need promise to "obey" or men to "worship." Shorn of its more obviously oppressive features, it is often thought that marriage is now a harmless or neutral institution. Yet this is far from being the case. The new marriage is seen as being both romantic and companionate—an impossible fusion, some would say—certainly a less stable form than the older, overtly male-dominated and more prosaic tie. It still produces couples who have a mystic bond, whose relationship is accepted as something special and beyond question. They easily slip into living as a social duo, each the "better half" of the other, each only a half person, and often in a state of hostile dependency, resentful over the failings of a partner who is essential to them. Perhaps all couple relationships have this tendency, but marriage dignifies, privileges and romanticizes the couple.

The marriage relationship becomes protected from criticism, so that people are expected to put up with a great deal more from their spouse than they ever would from anyone else. An extreme example is the fact that there is, in most states, legally, no such thing as rape in marriage. A woman cannot refuse sex to her husband, though she should to every other man. The other side of the coin is that relationships outside the marriage become thinner and less meaningful. Men frequently have no intimate friends apart from their wife. The partners are expected to be loyal to each other if there is any conflict, so much so that a woman's relationship with her best friend or even a sister may be ruptured if their husbands do not get on. When a marriage breaks up—and it is the essence of the new marriage that it may well do so—the partners often find themselves friendless and isolated. A second marriage, replicating the first, is the easiest solution, and so a pattern of serial monogamy is set up.

Such relationships offer a promise of security and a resolution of many tensions and anxieties. Yet we must ask: if people need a long-term couple relationship, why do they get it sanctified by church, state and the most backward-looking elements of society? The cynical answer used to be that it was a good way of binding someone to you (though there was an odds-on chance that *you* would be bound unwilling to *them*). The history of the struggle between state and church for control over marriage is not an edifying one, but it can at least teach us that marriage is a contract controlled not by the partners themselves but by the state. Furthermore it is an unwritten contract, one whose full implications become apparent only when divorce or separation (or, to some extent, death) lay bare its skeleton to public view and make clear that it is a contract not only about the sexual fidelity, cohabitation and mutual support mentioned in the wedding ceremony but also: sexual availability at will, housework, financial support even after marriage breakdown, a relation between a citizen head-of-household and a secondary dependant—and so on to indeterminate terms. We need not be in principle opposed to social control and concern in private household arrangements to believe that marriage is the wrong form for this.

Marriage is a form that is sanctified by tradition, not justified by rational social debate. The tradition is one that carries with it the whole historical baggage of male power and patriarchal authority. One has only to think of the traditional wedding ceremony, with its symbolic "giving away" of the bride by her father to her husband, the white wedding dress symbolizing her claim to virginity (or the cream one admitting that she cannot make this claim—though it will not show up in the photographic record), the striking contrast between men's and women's clothing in the wedding party.[16] But most important, marriage is a form that conflates the sexual with the economic: as Engels so crisply pointed out, monogamous marriage and prostitution were born in the same moment.

Marriage, perhaps, represents a contradiction in the conservative confusion of individualism with familism. For if marriage is the basis of the family, then this supposedly individual and freely chosen form has a state instrument at its heart. Those who defend marriage as what people want and need must explain then why it has to be so massively privileged by social policy, taxation, religious endorsement and the accolade of respectability.

3. Privacy as Imprisonment

The exclusion of outsiders and turning in to the little family group may seem attractive when it works well and when the family does satisfy its members' needs. But the little enclosed group can also be a trap, a prison whose walls and bars are constructed of the ideas of domestic privacy and autonomy. Why is it that when a man is brutally assaulting his wife the police and neighbors—all of us—are so reluctant to intervene? It is thought of as interfering in a private matter. The bond between them is seen as so special that outsiders should not presume to take a stand, even when it is quite clear that what is happening is an extreme form of physical violence. Why is it that the woman in this situation is so reluctant to go to others for help or protection? She often accepts that violence is a normal risk of marriage or that *she* has failed in some way by inviting violence or not managing to stave it off.

The privacy of the family is cast in a new light if we realize that one-quarter of reported violent crime is wife assault,[17] and that a very large proportion of rapes are carried out by men who know their victims well, often husbands, boyfriends, fathers and uncles.[18] If these are reported cases of violence and rape, we can safely assume that there is a huge penumbra of unreported incidents. It is ironical that the very expectations of security and protection in the private family are what make women so vulnerable to victimization within it, and so deprived of any recourse or plausible appeal to anyone outside its walls. Women often avoid going out alone at night for fear of being followed or attacked. Thus they become more ensnared in a home that may itself become a place of danger for them.

The recent public interest in domestic violence, spurred on by feminists, has produced a small increase in official willingness to intervene, and also improved legal procedures enabling a woman to obtain an injunction to exclude a violent man from the home. But it is apparent that for most women in such situations there is no solution other than actually leaving and breaking up the home. For a woman with children this is difficult to accomplish and even to contemplate. The existence now of a network of refuges for battered women, and the fact that local authorities are now obliged to provide accommodation for women with children who have left their home because of domestic violence can help women with some of the most pressing practical problems. The difficulty of finding alternative housing is one of the solid walls of the little family prison, but other less tangible walls will keep many women from escaping.

Violence and rape, it may be thought, are not the everyday experience of family life for most people. This is probably true, though they are much commoner than roseate social images allow. But they do show in a stark way how vulnerable people can be within the family. And they show how women are trapped much more than men. It is true that men sometimes experience the family as a mental prison, but they usually have far more opportunities for steering clear of the house if they want to. It is true that children can be beaten and psychologically confined and mistreated, but they too usually have an escape and another life of school and peers outside the home. It is women, whose work and emotional satisfaction is expected to center around home and family, who are most fully imprisoned there.[19]

It is not the character of the household tasks themselves that is oppressive, but the solitary, continuing and unrelieved nature of the multiplicity of household responsibilities. Many women will push their toddlers miles to a once-a-week play group just in order to have an hour alone without the child's constant questions and demands. The most common complaint of those who have to care for the senile or the severely disabled is that they *never* have any time off. Add to this the fact that the workplace is also the home, so that there is no separate leisure that is not intruded upon by the evidence of uncompleted tasks and the experience of enclosure is total. Of course, most women also work outside the home for much of their lives, and others do manage to form bonds and interests outside it. But even so, they are usually more enmeshed in the family than men and are far more likely to be the ones who take the domestic responsibilities. It is they rather than men who give up their jobs while children are babies or when old people need to be cared for.

4. Family Gains and Social Losses

What happens outside families is much affected by the existence of the family as a privileged institution. Every other aspect of social life is planned on the assumption that people live in families. Those who do not are isolated and deprived. Spinsters, older batchelors and couples who do not have children are frowned upon; people who live by themselves are thought to be abnormal. The popular image of the family—the married couple living with their young children—is constantly projected as the image of normality and of happiness. Yet in fact half the population do not live in this situation. Even those who do get married and have children themselves spend only the first sixteen or so years of their lives and, say twenty years of adulthood living in a family with children. The bulk of their lives is spent living just with adults or on their own.

Yet the family ideal makes everything else seem pale and unsatisfactory. Those who live alone often suffer from loneliness. Families are so wrapped up in their little domestic life that they have no time to spend on visiting; their social lives are with people like themselves. Couples mix with other couples, finding it difficult to fit single people in. The middle-class custom of balancing the sexes at dinner parties is only a formalized version of the endemic exclusion of the single, divorced and widowed. The estrangement of the sexes, outside of specifically sexual relationships, persists at all ages and increases isolation even among the elderly. The cosy image of the family makes all other settings where people can mix and live together seem like second-best. Nurseries, children's homes, student residences, nursing homes, old people's homes, all in their different ways conjure up pictures of bleakness, deprivation, acceptable perhaps for day care or for part of the year or a brief stage in life, but very much *pis-aller,* to be resorted to only if normal family life cannot be provided. Hospital social workers expect a daughter, mother or wife to look after a discharged patient in preference to a convalescent home; nursery nurses are taught to believe a small child is better off spending all day with its mother; old people's homes are only for those who can no long care for themselves and they are expected to give up most of their autonomy on entering. Old people's homes could be a lot more like residential hotels, or else like self-governing communities. A home for the handicapped can be considerably more stimulating for a teenager with Down's syndrome than living alone with her parents. A nursery or children's home can provide positive social experiences of cooperation, companionship and varied activities. It is the overvaluation of family life that devalues these other lives. The family sucks the juice out of everything around it, leaving other institutions stunted and distorted.

Production and all paid work is organized to dovetail with a particular kind of family, one in which the wife is responsible for housekeeping and caring for the family members and can be dependent on the husband's income if need be. Any housewife or parent who has had an ordinary full-time job finds that work is planned at places and times that are incompatible with domestic responsibilities. The hours of work, the distance from shops, the problems of taking time off are all well enough suited to a man who has a wife at home taking care of the house and children, the shopping and cooking, staying in for the gas-meter reader, going out to the school sports day. So it is not surprising that so many women have part-time jobs when they do go out to work. Nor is it surprising that there are probably approaching half a million women who work for money at home, doing machining, assembling, clerical work and child-minding. Because of their home responsibilities many women have a rather marginal relation to the labor market. On the other hand, almost all women are disadvantaged in the labor market from the word go, and it is partly this that makes marriage an attractive option for them. If your chances of earning a good income are small dependence on a man, even if it involves household cares that further reduce your ability to earn, may seem a wise choice.

At first sight, then, there appears to be a neat fit between women's place in the labor market and their place at home. Their part-time or less permanent involvement in paid work frees them to run the home; men's full-time work enables them to earn a "family wage" to support a dependent wife and children. Many would say that women are not disadvantaged in earning a living, but are able to earn in a way appropriate to their family position.

So there is constructed a curious house of cards in which the myth and the reality of the family alternately provide support for ever more ramshackle and unsatisfactory excrescences, each of which in turn serves to shore up the myth and keep the reality more or less intact. The world around the family is not a pre-existing harsh climate against which the family offers protection and warmth. It is as if the family had drawn comfort and security into itself and left the outside world bereft. As a bastion against a bleak society it has made that society bleak. It is indeed a major agency for caring, but in monopolizing care it has made it harder to undertake other forms of care. It is indeed a unit of sharing , but in demanding sharing within it has made other relations tend to become more mercenary. It is indeed a place of intimacy, but in privileging the intimacy of close kin it has made the outside world cold and friendless, and made it harder to sustain relations of security and trust except with kin. Caring, sharing and loving would be more widespread if the family did not claim them for its own.

NOTES

1. "Origin of the Family, Private Property and the State," in *Marx and Engels: Selected Works*, London 1968, p. 502.

2. John H. Goldthorpe, *Social Mobility and Class Structure in Modern Britain*, Oxford 1980, pp. 70, 75. The figures relate to sons born between 1938 and 1947.

3. Anthony Heath, *Social Mobility*, London 1981, p. 113.

4. *Inheritance and Wealth Inequality in Britain*, London 1979, p. 136.

5. Ibid., p. 131.

6. This is discussed more fully in our article "The Family Wage: Some Problems for Socialists and Feminists," *Capital and Class*, no. 11, 1980.

7. See Mary McIntosh, "The Welfare State and the Needs of the Dependent Family," in Sandra Burman, ed., *Fit Work for Women*, London 1979. The impossibility of supporting everyone by paying male workers a uniform "living wage" was first pointed out by Eleanor Rathbone in *The Disinherited Family*, London 1924.

8. There is a useful discussion of this in Mark Poster, *Critical Theory of the Family*, New York 1978.

9. *The Politics of Experience*, London 1967, p. 13.

10. Michael Rutter, ed., *Maternal Deprivation Reassessed*, Harmondsworth 1972.

11. London 1969.

12. Ibid., p. 261.

13. Ibid., p. 262

14. Noyes, *History of American Socialisms*, New York 1870, quoting Charles Lane.

15. Barbara Taylor, "The Woman-Power: Religious Heresy and Feminism in Early English Socialism," in Susan Lipschitz, ed., *Tearing the Veil*, London 1978.

16. Diana Leonard Barker, "A Proper Wedding," in Marie Corbin, ed., *The Couple*, Harmondsworth 1978.

17. R. E. Dobash and R. P. Dobash, "Wives: the 'Appropriate' Victims of Marital Violence," *Victimology*, 2, 1977–78, pp. 426–42.

18. *Rape Crisis Centre Report*, London 1977.

19. See Annike Snäre and Tove Steng-Dahl, "The Coercion of Privacy," in Carol Smart and Barry Smart, eds., *Women, Sex and Social Control*, London 1978.

Chapter 17

The Place of Kinfolk in Personal Community Networks

BARRY WELLMAN

Contemporary Westerners wander freeways and shopping malls surrounded by strangers. The few known faces they encounter are rarely kin. Also, the people whose company they keep are rarely kin—in the neighborhood, at work, or at play.

No wonder that scholars have had to work so hard to assert the persistence and importance of kinship. Yet the closer one looks at personal community networks, the more prominent are kin. Out of their hundreds of relations, people form active ties with almost all of their immediate kin and some of their extended kin. These ties—often dispersed and invisible—make up a large minority of active ties and about half of intimate ties. They loom even larger as reliable, flexible, long-term sources of support.

Family sociologists have usually treated

kinship networks as discrete systems in Western (post)industrial societies. While separate treatment is useful for studying such matters as inheritance and ceremonial obligations, it wrenches out of context an assessment of how ties with kin fit into everyday lives. My purpose in this chapter is to assess the place of kinship ties in *personal community networks: intimate* and *active* ties with friends, neighbors, and workmates as well as with kin.

Social network analysis helps researchers to compare kin with kith. In a tradition started by Bott (1957), network analysts look at how a person (or household) at the center of a network deals with the members of her or his egocentric universe. The network approach treats a community as a set of relationships stretching beyond the household—without a priori limitation on where network members live and how they are related to the person at the center of the network. It allows analysts to compare the characteristics of different kinds of community ties and liberates them from looking only at communities that resemble traditional solidarities of neighbors and kinfolk.

This chapter is an abridged version of "The Place of Kinfolk in Personal Community Networks," *Marriage and Family Review* 15, no. 1/2 (1990): 195–228, copyright © 1990 by Haworth Press, Binghamton, New York. Reprinted by permission.

Network analysts start with a set of all active or intimate relationships and only then ask if the *members* of such networks are kith or kin. They then ask about the *personal characteristics* of the members of their networks (e.g., gender, social class), the characteristics of the *ties* themselves (e.g., frequency of contact, kinship role), and ties among network members (Wellman 1988). Most analyses are concerned with *composition* (e.g., the percentage who are kin, live nearby, or are working class); *structure* (e.g., the density of interconnections among network members); and *contents* (e.g., the supportiveness of network members).

Thus the network approach provides a useful means for seeing how kin fit into personal community networks.

- How prominent are kin in personal community networks in terms of numbers and proportions?
- Do kin form separate clusters within personal community networks? Are their relations densely knit and tightly bounded? Or have kin become just a convenient recruiting area for friendships?
- Do kin differ from kith in the roles they play in such networks? Is kinship and friendship fungible, in the economists' sense of substitutable resources? In particular, does the companionship and social support they provide differ in quality, quantity and reliability?
- How do kinship relations fit into the ways in which personal community networks help people and households deal with problems and opportunities of reproduction and production? Do they provide collective relations that support and control kinfolk, or do they provide resources upon which kin can draw selectively and voluntarily?

In this chapter, I concentrate on describing that mythical category: *people in general.*

Where necessary, I use as a baseline the networks of white, northern-European ethnicity, employed, once-married, North American, forty-year-old (sub)urban women and men with a child in primary school. Although such persons do not constitute a majority of North Americans, they remain a model category.

I focus on the *size, connectivity, contact,* and *supportiveness* of network ties, acknowledging, but not emphasizing the ambivalence, stress, and costs that most relationships experience. Fortunately, the studies of most scholars are comparable enough to permit me to interweave them into one integrated account. Nevertheless, I inevitably gloss over fascinating information about differences between subgroups (e.g., social classes, ethnicities, age strata, women or men, married or not married).

Are Sisters and Cousins Reckoned by the Dozens?

How Many Kin?

Personal community networks have even fuzzier boundaries than kinship networks. Because there are no gates (or gatekeepers) to divide members from nonmembers, analysts must develop a sharp picture from fuzzy reality. Defining personal communities entails the usual kinship dilemmas about including affines, relations that continue after divorces and deaths, and unrecognized kin. In addition, friends, neighbors and workmates come and go, their definition and importance varying by the hour, day, and year. There is the "Bob and Carol and Ted and Alice problem" (Mazursky 1969): Ties to a married couple can function as one relation or two. Indeed, there is no such thing as *the network:* analysts must specify inclusion criteria. For example, our research group studies only those co-workers who are seen socially outside of work.

Available and Actual Ties

The broadest possible personal community network of direct relations contains all those who a person can currently deal with on an informal basis. Yet one rarely acquires relations through random encounters in cafés or on the streets. Instead, social and physical foci—such as kinship groups, churches, workplaces, or neighborhood street corners—bring people together under auspices conducive to interaction (Feld 1982). Weak ties of acquaintanceship far outnumber stronger ties of intimacy, support, companionship, or routine contact.

Active Ties

Just as most kinship studies consider only those kin who have more than trivial relations, community network studies look only at small subsets of personal networks. Researchers have identified a range of fourteen to twenty-three persons who are significant in one's life because of repeated sociable contact, supportiveness, or feelings of connectedness (Fischer 1982a, 1982b; Willmott 1986, 1987; Wellman, Carrington, and Hall 1988; Wellman and Wortley 1989, 1990; Milardo 1989). This score of *active* ties provides people with most of their interpersonal support and companionship.

Kin are substantially represented in most active networks, making up at least 30 percent of the active ties compared with less than 10 percent of all ties and 2 percent of all potentially available ties. Thus a much higher percentage of kin than kith are actively involved in network relations. Preferences for active involvement, however, are bimodal, with most networks containing either few or many kin.

Not all types of kin are equally represented. Most active kin relations come from the small number of available *immediate kin* (parents, adult children, and siblings, including in-laws). By contrast, only a small minority of available *extended kin* (aunts, cousins, grandparents, etc.) are active network members.

Some studies suggest that certain social characteristics foster networks that contain a higher number and proportion of kin:

- Married people who acquire a set of in-laws along with their spouse (Heiskanen 1969; Wellman, Carrington, and Hall 1988).
- Women actively involved in maintaining networks, who bear a triple load of paid work, domestic work, and community networking (Lee 1980; Hammer, Gutwirth, and Phillips 1982; Wellman 1985; Rosenthal 1985).
- Residents of rural areas, perhaps lacking the opportunities of urbanites to make friendships based on shared interests (Fischer 1982b).
- Members of the working class are more reliant on kin for domestic support and less involved with workmates after hours (Willmott 1987).

Most kin who are potentially available do become members of personal community networks. The stronger the relationship used to define a network the higher the proportion of network members who are kin. Indeed, most immediate kin—and some extended kin—have strong ties in these networks as active and even intimate members. Immediate kin tend to be intimates and even confidants. Extended kin tend to be (nonintimate) active network members or have even weaker ties.

Kinship Connections

Kin form both a distinct social network and a part of a broader personal community network. The nature of this kinship system affects the structure and operations of personal community networks. Because kinship is an inherently connected system, the kin who are active or intimate members of personal community networks are usually linked with each other. At least one *kinkeeping* person—usually a mother or daughter—converts normative obligation into high centrality by taking upon herself the task of maintaining ties among kin. As Walker points out, "Family, like community, serves as a euphemism for women" (1986, 7; see also Rosenthal 1985; Wellman 1992a). As a result of kinkeeping, for example, two-thirds of active kin in the Toronto study—compared with only one-quarter of active nonkin—usually get together in group contexts such as dinners, holidays, or picnics. In contrast to those with kinship ties, most of those with friendship ties meet more privately, such as in the relations between individuals or couples.

Kin are usually the most densely connected members of active and intimate networks. Thus they have a unique structural basis for coordinated action: be it supportive, sociable, or controlling. The relative lack of ties between in-laws makes the networks of married persons more sparsely knit than the networks of most unmarried persons. Kinship ties, while densely knit, do not have tight boundaries. Their connectivity provides a more coordinated basis to connect network members to other social circles.

Over the River and Through the Woods

A key message of post–World War II research has been that kinship ties endure over long distances. Densely knit structures and normative obligations encourage people with active kinship ties to maintain contact despite separation. Moreover, kinship ties—even formerly latent ones—often help migrants, for example, to obtain jobs, houses, spouses, and local lore (e.g., Grieco 1987). Community analysts have generalized this message from kinship relations to all community ties. They contend that phones, cars, planes, and the Internet enable people to have relationships that are active and intimate over long distances (Wellman and Leighton 1979; Wellman and Tindall 1993; Wellman and Gulia 1997).

Some have few kin or friends living in the same neighborhood, but many living elsewhere in the same metropolitan area. People are better able to maintain active and intimate kinship ties over greater distances than they are friendship ties, thus they may find that they have more friends than kin living in their own metropolitan area. Although network members who live far apart usually have lower rates of contact, people's contact with kin diminishes less over distance than does their contact with friends.

There is much more contact with immediate kin than with extended kin at the same level of activity or intimacy. Immediate kin usually have more contact with each other than they do with their friends, and extended kin usually have the least contact with each other. Contact between immediate kin is the least affected by distance. Kinship structures keep kin in contact even at a distance, but only immediate kin usually maintain frequent contact.

To be sure, some people—usually from ethnic minorities or low socioeconomic circumstances—have large clusters of kin near at hand for companionship and support. Yet the more common pattern is to maintain intensive relations with a small set of immediate kin: densely connected, but residentially dispersed. Together with approximately equal numbers of friends—also residentially dispersed but less densely connected than immediate kin—these ties make up the core of personal community networks. More latent relations with extended kin remain in place, to be activated for specialized needs, family get-togethers, or during migrations.

Brothers' Keepers

Different network members provide different kinds of supportive resources. Just as general stores have given way to specialized boutiques, people must search their assortment of ties to find specific kinds of support (Lin, Dean, and Ensel 1986; Fischer 1982b; House, Landis, and Umberson 1988; Wellman 1992b). For example, the second Toronto study found that different active network members often supply emotional aid, small services, large services, financial aid, companionship, and job or housing information. Most network members provide zero to two of the six kinds of support. About 60 percent of the members provide some kind of emotional aid, small service, or companionship. Only 10 percent to 16 percent provide some kind of large service, financial aid, or information, however. Less than half of the network members provide both emotional aid and small services (Wellman and Wortley 1990).

To say that kin are supportive and friends are sociable is as much an oversimplification as to say that there is no difference in the content of relations between kin and friends. Kinship significantly affects the nature of ties, but it does so interactively with the strength of a tie, the shared interests of the network members, and their physical access to each other.

At one extreme, parents and children reliably exchange a broad range of support. Their relationship transcends intimacy, different stages in the life course, and physical access. At the other extreme, extended kin are rarely supportive, even if active or living nearby. Between are siblings whose conditionally companionate and supportive relations more closely resemble friends in their dependency on shared intimacy and in their life situations.

W(h)ither Kin in Networks

The Prominence of Kin

The prominence of kin in these networks is greater than current size and contact figures suggest. Because kin usually have known one another at least twice as long as friends have, they have had many more person-years of contact (Wellman et al. 1997). Because kin are densely connected with one another, conversations between two kin often refer to other kin. By contrast, friends are more often likely to engage in separate duets.

The Uniqueness of Kin

The importance of kinship suggests its uniqueness. Why would active and intimate networks have so many kin if they were just like friends? To be sure, quasi-legal norms maintain kinship as systems. Rules and customs emphasize kinship rights to share housing, obtain inheritances, sponsor immigrants, and receive confidential information from bureaucracies. Yet the differences separating kin from kith are neither neat nor simple. Not only do kin differ from friends and neighbors in structure and deed, but also, different types of kin differ from one another. There are no inclusive rules of amity requiring all kin to be supportive, and there are many friends whose ties transcend marketplace reciprocity. *Parents and adult children* are remarkably supportive but often do not enjoy one another's company. *Extended kin* have little content to their relations even when these relations are active; extended kin are bound together only by structure. *Sibling* ties are almost as supportive as parent-child relations and almost as sociable as friendships. *Friendship* ties are the most variable—the term is a residual grab bag for relations that are *non*-kin, *non*-neighbor, and *non*-workmate—yet intimate friends often provide the broad, reliable support characteristic of immediate kin.

Underlying this diversity is the structural connectivity and normative amity of the kinship system. (It would be nice to know if it were the structure or the norms that are doing the job.) It is what keeps extended kin in personal communities, and it is what keeps parents and children supportive even when they do not enjoy each others' company. Friends must reaffirm their ties continually, while neighbors are apt to move away or break relations over petty disputes. By contrast, kinship ties are relatively reliable without needing direct, one-on-one reciprocity. Immediate kin are reliably there for support, and extended kin are reliably available for acquaintanceship, news, and adaptive life changes. Kin are not necessarily expected to reciprocate directly, as long as they remain members in good standing of the kinship network. In their distinctive ways, both immediate and extended kin help people and households to reduce interpersonal uncertainties in making their way through stressful, problematic worlds. As Lyn Lofland has pointed out (1973), we live in "a world of strangers." Yet it is just such circumstances that makes so outstanding the contact, connectivity, and supportive reliability of immediate kin.

Community Saved or Liberated?

For a time, community analysts thought that all communities were densely knit, broadly supportive, local solidarities helping people to endure the ravages of the (post)Industrial Revolution. Such a *Community Saved* model—epitomized by Young and Willmott (1957) and Gans (1962)—celebrated the vitality of kinship and neighboring. As a counterpoise, network analysts have emphasized the diverse, ramified, sparsely-knit nature of most personal communities (e.g., Wellman and Leighton 1979; Fischer 1982b; Wellman 1988). In their view, communities are not merely havens from large-scale social forces but active arrangements by which people and households reproduce. Their *Community Liberated* model has had the virtues of emphasizing the *social* (but not the spatial) basis of community and of showing how networks actively help people to engage with the outside world.

Yet communities are more likely to have mixed compositions and structures than to be purely Saved or Liberated. Within them, kin form a key core cluster efficiently structured for communicating needs and coordinating support. This Saved cluster provides a haven from the demands of the outside world and many of the interpersonal bandages for domestic sores. Complementing this involuted group are strong and weak ties with friends, stretching outwards to connect a focal person to the diverse resources of other groups. These Liberated ties provide companionship in many arenas as well as entry points to new arenas. To the extent to which both types of ties and structures are useful and complementary, both are integral parts of a single personal community network.

Toward a Political Economy of Personal Community Networks

This chapter has reviewed *supportive relations with kin and kith* as one of the three basic ways by which most people obtain resources. The other two are *market exchanges* and access to *institutional resources* as citizenship rights, organizational benefits, or charitable acts.

The uses of these three mechanisms differs substantially between social systems. In the Third World, personal community networks structure important relations of *production*, since there are neither the structures nor the capital to support extensive market eonomies. In those Third World countries where employment is unstable and there are no retirement funds, secure survival is an urgent need. The socially controlled reliability of kinship relations becomes crucial in such situations of competition for scarce survival resources. People develop broadly based ties, expanding them from purely social relationships to key sources of material resources. Marginal groups rely on these ties as a basic survival strategy. Middle-class groups develop informal networks and formal relationships to support upward mobility. In all classes, such networks strongly channel access to such *reproductive* resources distributed by Third World institutions as schools, hospitals, and make-work jobs (Lomnitz 1977; Roberts 1978; Espinoza 1997).

In the Second World of state socialism, personal community networks help people maneuver through bureaucratic obstacles to obtain institutional benefits and provide informal arrangements for production. Among other things, they provide the ties necessary to obtain the resources for getting a job done (Burawoy 1985; Walder 1986). Such networks are even more crucial for reproduction in such bureaucracy-laden societies because they provide informal alternatives to rigid institutional procedures (Sik and Wellman 1997). For example, groups of Hungarian kith and kin take turns building houses for one another. The only way to obtain a telephone in many such countries is to use informal connections; official queues remain dormant window dressing.

By contrast, personal community networks in more prosperous Western, First World milieus are principally relations of *reproduction.* The main difference is in the insecurity that households in each world wish to diminish. This, in turn, affects the type of resources they mobilize through their networks. The low importance of the economic and political aspects

of social support distinguishes the networks of most First Worlders from social systems that are less economically or politically secure. They rely on market exchanges for almost all of their production and much of their consumption. Despite some variation, their institutional benefits, such as schooling and medical care, are available as citizenship rights. Hence they do not pay as much attention as do Second World residents to having network members with skills for fixing things and working with bureaucracies; nor do they have the survival needs of Third World residents to blend domestic ties with employment ties in both the informal and formal sectors.

The networks of First Worlders are therefore often built around achieving companionship, soothing domestic stresses, and obtaining reliable, flexible, low-cost domestic services. These are not trivial pursuits, because few people want to place themselves at the mercy of markets and institutions to deal with such needs.

Although analysts are just starting to calculate the costs and benefits of community network relations, these networks clearly contribute important and central resources that enable people to go about their daily lives, handle chronic stresses, and cope with acute crises.

In this chapter, I have suggested that First Worlders prefer to use personal community networks to meet many needs because they have more control over the workings of network relationships than they do over purchases or beneficences obtained from bureaucracies. They do not yearn to be self-reliant individualists—doing or purchasing all—or dependents of institutions (compare Gans 1988). Yet their dispersed, fragmented networks require constant maintenance. The study of personal community networks should recognize how the different types of relationships divide the labor of providing supportive resources. Reliable relations with immediate kin provide secure stocks of services, emotional aid, and financial aid within these networks. At the same time, friends provide social pleasure, diverse resources, and access to social circles beyond the existing community.

REFERENCES

Bott, Elizabeth. 1957. *Family and Social Network.* London: Tavistock.

Burawoy, Michael. 1985. *The Politics of Production.* London: Verso.

Espinoza, Vicente. 1997. "Social Networks Among the Urban Poor: Inequality and Integration in a Latin American City." In *Networks in the Global Village,* edited by Barry Wellman. Boulder, Colo.: Westview.

Feld, Scott. 1982. "Social Structural Determinants of Similarity Among Associates." *American Sociological Review* 47 (December): 797–801.

Fischer, Claude. 1982a. "The Dispersion of Kinship Ties in Modern Society." *Journal of Family History* 7 (winter): 353–75.

———. 1982b. *To Dwell Among Friends.* Berkeley: University of California Press.

Gans, Herbert. 1962. *The Urban Villagers.* New York: Free Press.

———. 1988. *Middle American Individualism.* New York: Free Press.

Grieco, Margaret. 1987. *Keeping It in the Family: Social Networks and Employment Chance.* London: Tavistock.

Hammer, Muriel, Linda Gutwirth, and Susan Phillips. 1982. "Parenthood and Social Networks." *Social Science and Medicine* 16:2091–100.

Heiskanen, Veronica Stolte. 1969. "Community Structure and Kinship Ties: Extended Family Relations in Three Finnish Communes." *International Journal of Comparative Sociology* 10 (September–December): 251–62.

House, James, Karl Landis, and Debra Umberson. 1988. "Social Relationships and Health." *Science* 241 (July 29): 540–45.

Lee, Gary. 1980. "Kinship in the Seventies: A Decade Review of Research and Theory." *Journal of Marriage and the Family* 42 (4): 923–34.

Lin, Nan, Alfred Dean, and Walter Ensel. 1986. *Social Support, Life Events, and Depression.* Orlando, Fla.: Academic Press.

Lofland, Lyn. 1973. *A World of Strangers.* New York: Basic.

Lomnitz, Larissa Adler. 1977. *Networks and Marginality: Life in a Mexican Shantytown.* Translated by Cinna Lomnitz. New York: Academic Press.

Mazursky, Paul. 1969. *Bob and Carol and Ted and Alice.* Burbank, Calif.: Columbia Pictures.

Milardo, Robert. 1989. "Theoretical and Methodological Issues in the Identification of the Social Networks of Spouses." *Journal of Marriage and the Family* 51:165–74.

Roberts, Bryan. 1978. *Cities of Peasants.* London: Edward Arnold.

Rosenthal, Carolyn. 1985. "Kinkeeping in the Familial Division of Labor." *Journal of Marriage and the Family* 47 (November): 965–74.

Sik, Endre, and Barry Wellman. 1997. "Network Capital in Capitalist, Communist, and Post-Communist Countries: The Case of Hungary." In *Networks in the Global Village,* edited by Barry Wellman. Boulder, Colo.: Westview.

Walder, Andrew. 1986. *Communist Neo-Traditionalism: Work and Authority in Chinese Industry.* Berkeley: University of California Press.

Walker, Alan. 1986. "Communist Care: Fact or Fiction." Pp. 4–15 in *The Debate About Community,* edited by Peter Willmott. London: Policy Studies Institute.

Wellman, Barry. 1985. "Domestic Work, Paid Work, and Net Work." Pp. 159–91 in *Understanding Personal Relationships,* edited by Steve Duck and Daniel Perlman. London: Sage.

———. 1988. "The Community Question Reevaluated." Pp. 81–107 in *Power, Community and the City,* edited by Michael Peter Smith. New Brunswick, N.J.: Transaction Books.

———. 1992a. "Men in Networks: Private Communities, Domestic Friendships." Pp. 74–114 in *Men's Friendships,* edited by Peter Nardi. Newbury Park, Calif.: Sage.

———. 1992b. "Which Types of Ties and Networks Give What Kinds of Social Support?" *Advances in Group Processes* 9:207–35.

Wellman, Barry, Peter Carrington, and Alan Hall. 1988. "Networks as Personal Communities." Pp. 130–84 in *Social Structures: A Network Approach,* edited by Barry Wellman and S. D. Berkowitz. Cambridge: Cambridge University Press.

Wellman, Barry, and Milena Gulia. 1997. "Where Does Social Support Come From? The Social Network Basis of Interpersonal Resources for Coping with Stress." In *Social Conditions, Stress, Resources and Health,* edited by Ann Maney. Rockville, Md.: NIMH Press.

Wellman, Barry, and Barry Leighton. 1979. "Networks, Neighborhoods and Communities." *Urban Affairs Quarterly* 14 (March): 363–90.

Wellman, Barry, and David Tindall. 1993. "Reach Out and Touch Some Bodies: How Social Networks Connect Telephone Networks." Pp.63–93 in *Progress in Communication Sciences,* edited by

William Richards, Jr., and George Barnett. Norwood, N.J.: Ablex.

Wellman, Barry, Renita Wong, David Tindall, and Nancy Nazer. 1997. "A Decade of Network Change: Turnover, Mobility, and Stability." *Social Networks* 19 (January): 27–50.

Wellman, Barry, and Scott Wortley. 1989. "Brothers' Keepers: Situating Kinship Relations in Broader Networks of Social Support." *Sociological Perspectives* 32, no. 3 (July): 273–306.

———. 1990. "Different Strokes from Different Folks: Which Types of Ties Provide Which Kinds of Social Support." Toronto: Centre for Urban and Community Studies, Research Paper.

Willmott, Peter. 1986. *Social Networks, Informal Care, and Public Policy.* London: Policy Studies Institute.

———. 1987. *Friendship Networks and Social Support.* London: Policy Studies Institute.

Young, Michael, and Peter Willmott. 1957. *Family and Kinship in East London.* London: Routledge and Kegan Paul.

~ *Chapter 18*

Housewife and Gadder: Themes of Self-Sufficiency and Community in Eighteenth-Century New England

LAUREL THATCHER ULRICH

In her novel *Northwood,* published in 1827, Sarah Josepha Hale (the future editor of *Godey's Lady's Book*) described a Thanksgiving dinner served in the household of the prosperous New Hampshire farmer she called "Squire Romolee." On two tables pushed together in the parlor were a roasted turkey, a goose, a pair of ducklings, a chicken pie, and a sirloin of beef flanked by a leg of pork and a joint of mutton, all embellished with vegetables, pickles, and preserves. On a side table stood plum pudding, custards, pies of every description, several kinds of rich cake, sweetmeats, fruit and currant wine, cider, and ginger beer. When a visiting Englishman asked Squire Romolee how he could claim temperance after eating such a dinner, the happy farmer replied, "Well, well, I

Laurel Thatcher Ulrich, "Housewife and Gadder: Themes of Self-Sufficiency and Community in Eighteenth-Century New England," in *"To Toil the Livelong Day": America's Women at Work, 1780–1980,* edited by Carol Groneman and Mary Beth Norton, copyright © 1987 by Cornell University. Used by permission of the publisher, Cornell University Press.

may at least recommend industry, for all this variety you have seen before you on the table, excepting the spices and salt, has been furnished from my own farm and procured by our own labor and care."[1]

Although Hale gave the punch line to Squire Romolee, she devoted most of her chapter to the women's "labor and care." Mrs. Romolee and her daughters not only churned, pickled, roasted, and baked with supreme skill; they spun and wove their own linens, raised the geese whose feathers filled their featherbeds, and in spare moment ornamented their house with simple art. Over the mantel in the chamber where the Englishman slept was a "family record" painted and lettered by Sophia.[2]

Hale's description is more than an amusing fantasy. Its essential point, that the early American economy rested on family self-sufficiency, underlies most interpretations of women's work in early America. While Hale and her contemporaries emphasized the character- and body-building virtues of home production, twentieth-century scholars have stressed gender integration through shared responsibility for family support. As mutual labor within self-sufficient rural households declined, so the argument goes, separate spheres were born.[3] Even those historians who reverse the argument, emphasizing the subordination of women in a male-dominated household economy, have not questioned the original model. The essential question has been the relation of husbands and wives within a unified "family economy."[4]

Economic historians, on the other hand, have mounted a formidable attack on the whole notion of self-sufficiency. We now know that few families had the land, the tools, or the labor to produce and process all their own food and clothing. Interdependence rather than independence is the theme of current scholarship, though historians continue to argue over its meaning. Was trade shaped by outside markets or by family need? Did entrepreneurial or communal values predominate?[5] As yet, however, few of these studies have had anything to say about women.

In this regard, a second heroic housewife in Hale's *Northwood* is worth considering. Mrs. Watson, "the gossip of the neighborhood," combined the worst and the best features of neighborliness. She was a charitable soul, always ready to nurse the sick or watch with the dying, but she was also a busybody given to telling fortunes in tea leaves. She was "reputed one of the neatest women and best managers in the village," though Hale cautioned that "those women who have neither her sleight to work, nor constitution to endure fatigue, must not imitate the worst part of her examples—gadding."[6] In Mrs. Romolee the novelist celebrated the virtues of home production, but in Mrs. Watson she remembered the essential and sometimes troubling interdependence that underlay it.

Robert Gross has suggested that increased production in early-nineteenth-century New England was accompanied by growing distrust of communal work. Work exchanges between neighbors now seemed inefficient, while neighborhood work frolics appeared to cost more in refreshment than they gained in productivity.[7] Hale's portraits reflect this anxiety, yet they also convey forgotten details of a world that was passing. She was wrong in thinking the Romolees could achieve such abundance outside the market, but she was right in placing them in the best house in the village.[8] She was also right in making an extravagant (and seemingly wasteful) display of food the mark of their prosperity.

But Hale's portraits are most suggestive in their limning of female roles. Her emphasis on the mother-daughter relationship in the Romolee household, as well as her unforgettable (if somewhat backhanded) acknowledgment of the authority of Mrs. Watson, have the ring of memory. Sarah Hale herself was born in a New Hampshire village in 1788, and she spent the first forty years of her life there before widowhood and the success of *Northwood* propelled her to Boston. Letters and diaries from her mother's generation portray a world in which gentility and industry were indeed compatible, in which the same neighbors who came to drink tea came to nurse the sick and lay out the dead—in short, a world in which self-sufficiency was sustained by neighborliness, and vice versa.

Historians have given far too little attention to the social character of women's work in early New England. In Hale's novel Mrs. Romolee and Mrs. Watson, the housewife and the gadder, stand in splendid isolation. In life they were one, as a quick survey of three eighteenth-century diaries shows.

Martha Ballard, a Hallowell, Maine, midwife, was clearly a gadder. Between 1790 and 1799 she was home less than half the days of the year. Yet she also spun her own linen, grew her own cabbages, and raised enough turkeys to last from August to Thanksgiving.[9] Elizabeth Phelps of Hadley, Massachusetts, the wife of a country squire, was a "good housewife." She made her own sausage and soap, manufactured textiles and candles, and entertained an endless stream of visitors. Yet she also managed to leave home one day in three.[10] Elizabeth Wildes, a young bonnet-maker from Arundel (now Kennebunkport), Maine, also combined housekeeping and gadding. She had three young children at home and a husband at sea, yet she went visiting almost as often as Mrs. Phelps; and when she was confined by illness or work, a host of relatives and neighbors came to her.[11] Given differences of geography, occupation, and age, the evidence of the three diaries is remarkably similar. In 1790 there were only 77 days in the entire year when Martha Ballard neither left home nor received visitors; for Elizabeth Wildes there were 100; Elizabeth Phelps recorded visits or visitors on 200 of the 235 days she wrote in here diary.[12]

Because these women were New Englanders, it is easy to imagine them walking from house to house around a village green. Not so. In 1790, Martha Ballard lived near her husband's sawmill, a third of a mile and across two brooks from here nearest neighbor, a bachelor trader. The meeting house and the handful of houses around it were more than three-quarters of a mile away, by water or land; folks on both sides of the Kennebec River were accounted "neighbors." Elizabeth Phelps lived on a 600-acre estate two miles outside Hadley, while Elizabeth Wildes lived a mile and a half from the meeting house in a sparsely settled area of Arundel.[13] The distances were not impossible, but neither were they inconsequential. In all three towns, interaction with neighbors was the result of intent rather than accident. Women walked; they rode sidesaddle, sometimes carrying a child or neighbor behind them on a pillion;

and they traveled by canoe.[14] Though Mrs. Phelps, the wealthiest of the three, had access to a one-horse vehicle called a chaise, she drove it herself.

Fifty years later, New Englanders found all this coming and going marvelous indeed. Elizabeth Wildes's son, in a family history written in 1855, wondered at his mother's ability to bounce along on horseback. "Men and women in the last century were different from the race of the present," he declared. The theme was repeated in a history of Winthrop, Maine, published in the same year. "The first settlers in a new country cultivate the social affections," the author wrote, following with a long story about a woman who, when invited to visit her neighbor on baking day, was persuaded to carry her dough with her. "What a spectacle it would now present to see a horse, saddled and pillioned, carrying a gentleman and lady on his back, the gentleman having before him a kneading trough, in which was dough for a batch of bread!" he exclaimed.[15] Necessity as much as the "social affections" motivated some such visits; many Maine houses in this period lacked ovens.

There is not space here to explore all the nuances of community interdependence in rural New England, but even a brief survey demonstrates that women were fully involved in at least three forms of economic interaction. They traded goods and services with their neighbors; they engaged in labor transactions; and they joined in communal work.

Family subsistence in early America was achieved by hundreds of transactions with neighbors. Consider again that marvelous Thanksgiving dinner assembled in the home of Squire Romolee. Though few eighteenth-century fireplaces could accommodate the menagerie Hale described, contemporary sources demonstrate that a genuine feast did include more than one kind of meat. Martha Ballard's favorite combination was a "line" (loin) of veal and a leg of pork. The pork was usually the product of the autumn slaughtering, but the veal, killed in spring or early summer, was eaten fresh—and unless the family were large enough to consume a sixty-pound animal at once, they had no choice but to share with neighbors, as Martha Ballard did when she sent a side of veal to one family in May and in June "borrowed" a quarter of veal from another.[16]

This was neighborliness in support of self-sufficiency. Families extended their own supply by sharing with others. Neighborly support also allowed home production of textiles. "Mrs. Peirce put in a piece of overshot," Elizabeth Phelps wrote in June 1778. The neighbor was doing not the weaving but the warping, the difficult preliminary threading of the loom. Once that task was completed, a woman or her daughters could do the weaving. In this way the specialized skills of a few women helped to sustain the general productivity of others.[17]

The interweaving of home production and trade is apparent in a brief entry in Martha Ballard's diary. "Mr. Woodward & his wife here at Evening," she wrote on December 18, 1789. "I let her have 1 lb. of Cotten for Combing worsted." Although the Ballards raised flax, they did not own sheep, nor does cotton grow on the Kennebec. That simple exchange between neighbors involved an elaborate network of barter and trade stretching to the Caribbean. The wool Mrs. Woodward carded probably came from Mrs. Cummings, who paid a medical bill in "sheep's wool" in August, though it may have been part of the wool Martha Ballard's son got "on board Capt. Dana's vessel" in September. The cotton could have come from "Captain Norcross' Lady," who gave Martha Ballard two pounds of cotton and a pound of tea in May, or from Ezra Hodges, who paid his wife's midwifery bill with the same commodity in June.

Thus West Indian cotton and Massachusetts wool helped to sustain a village economy characterized by home production. Once Mrs. Woodward had finished carding the worsted, Martha Ballard's daughter Dolly did the spinning and weaving, though Polly Savage, another neighbor, warped the loom. Meanwhile Martha Ballard was cutting and drying pumpkins that Mrs. Woodward had given her.[18] Not all such transactions made their way into written records, however. On June 21, 1787, for example, Martha Ballard reported that Mrs. Pollard had "sent home 5 lb of poark which shee Borrowed 12 of April 1786," but the entry for April 12 records no such transaction, simply reading, "I went to Mr. Williams'. Mrs. Pollard came home with me."

Jack Larkin has suggested that surviving rural account books were an effort on the part of a few New Englanders "to achieve a greater measure of control over and to have more information about, an economic life still stunningly concrete."[19] The concreteness if not the control is reflected in the diary of Abner Sanger of Dublin, New Hampshire, who on one day noted that Mrs. Ichabod Rowel had received "a brown earthern quart bowl (6 times) full of Indian meal" and on another that Deacon John Knowlton's wife had balanced "13 ounces of good butter" with "9 ounces of tallow" and "a little scoop of rennet bag."[20] Little scoops are hard to quantify and even "quart" bowls must have varied, since Sanger thought it important to specify the "brown earthen" bowl in his entry.

Such accounts are far removed from the double-entry ledgers of merchants with their debits and credits assembled on opposite pages. In rural diaries it is seldom possible to see both sides of a transaction, though an occasional "reckoning" survives. "Mrs. Savage here," Martha Ballard wrote on April 15, 1788. "Shee & I made a settlement on account of her spinning and the wolen wheel, my being with her when sick & 1 pair of shoes & medicine I let her have when her children were sick & we wer Evin in our accounts. I lett her have 4 lb of flax which she has not paid for." The range of products traded, if not the written accounting, was typical. A stream of feathers, ashes, baby chicks, seedlings, and old clothes linked households in rural New England.

Patterns of village trade are so unstudied (and so difficult to study) that many questions remain. Did men and women trade freely with one another, accumulating "family" rather than personal accounts, as in the Sanger diary? Or did women primarily trade with women and men with men, as the Ballard diary suggests? One merchant eager to establish a potash works at Thomaston, Maine, assumed that there were some products that women routinely controlled. "Ashes in general being the women's perquisite certain articles of goods must be kept on hand for payment which will induce them to save as many as they can & often to send them to the works," he wrote.[21] The success of his operation depended upon his ability to divert ashes from household use (in soapmaking) and from neighborhood trade.

The notion of married women trading and reckoning with their neighbors has no place in prevailing models of the preindustrial family economy, yet it conforms well with statistical evidence assembled in recent literature. In a meticulous study of agricultural production in eighteenth-century Massachusetts, Bettye Hobbs Pruitt found that "widows' portions"—those curious passages in early wills which provide allotments of food, fuel, and fiber for a widow's support—typically included far more grain than one woman could consume. Presumably she was expected to trade it to supply other needs. "That such a strategy was not spelled out in wills merely suggests that salable or exchangeable surpluses were so fully incorporated into the notion of subsistence as to be inseparable from it and hence hidden, from our eyes at least," Pruitt writes.[22] Whatever forms it took, female trade was an integral part of economic life.

Women were also involved in exchanges of labor. Again it is not a question of "self-sufficiency" versus "community" but of both. Dependence upon family labor inevitably meant dependence on neighbors. Hale caught the Romolees of *Northwood* in a charmed instant when their daughters were old enough to work but too young to marry. Such richness could not last. Family labor was born helpless and destined to leave. Prosperous households such as the Romolees might keep their daughters at home, but eventually the girls would marry. Nor, given the wide availability of land and the almost universal opportunity to marry, could they fully appropriate the labor of their neighbors' daughters. A bewildering number of young women—Pene, Lucy, Dolly, Polly, Jerusha, Sally, Becca, Fanny, and Submit, in addition to daughters Betsy and Thankful—march though the pages of Elizabeth Phelps's diary. Without surnames or more detailed entries it is difficult to determine which were workers and which were merely visitors. Probably many were both.

Since there were few bound servants in New England, most household workers even in wealthy families were sons or daughters of neighbors. Few stayed long. In 1791, Elizabeth Wildes employed Hannah and Betsy Hutchings, Lydia Kilpatrick, Molly Watson, and Molly Wildes in addition to her sisters, Sally and Abiel Perkins. Between 1785 and 1800 thirty-nine young women lived and worked for some period in Martha Ballard's house; almost all were the daughters of local men in the middle range of the tax list. The social origins of workers helps to explain their comings and goings. Most young women alternated work at home with work "abroad," spending a week or two spinning at a neighbor's house, going home to help with the hay, moving on to a sister's house where there was sickness, going back to the first house or on to another to spin or wash. The promise of self-sufficiency and the reality of insufficiency kept people as well as goods in motion.

A young daughter's labor might be used to balance her mother's accounts, as when Martha Ballard included "2 Days Work of Dolly" when she settled with Mrs. Weston, the wife of a local merchant.[23] Dolly Ballard was then barely fourteen; within three years she had completed an apprenticeship with Mrs. Densmore, a dressmaker, and was working on her own, sometimes in her mother's house, sometimes in the homes of neighbors. Martha Ballard paid most of her helpers directly, occasionally in cash, more often in clothing or credit at a store.[24]

A brief diary kept in Eastport, Maine, in the summer of 1801 explains the system. Mary Yeaton worked at home, helping her mother with the sewing and her father with the reaping, though she longed to return to Portsmouth, New Hampshire, where she had been living with friends. "You speak as tho I ought to stay here," she told her mother. "If you will point out any means for my support I'll thank you. You know very well I can not look to my father for clothing, etc." When her father worried about her becoming dependent on her friends, she insisted she was not. "I told him . . . I was industrious, and endeavored to support myself; that he had not had it in his power to do much for me for some time, and I could sew for my western friends and by this means supply myself."[25]

Since few fathers had the means "to do much" for their daughters, girls balanced obligations to their families (and especially to their mothers) with the necessity of providing for themselves, much as they would do a generation later when they went to the mills. Such a system ensured broad-based but low-level production as well as continuity from one generation to the next but made it difficult even for an unusually energetic woman to sustain specialized work. It is no accident that Elizabeth Wildes was able to weave and market cotton coverlets during the years her daughters were available to help. Nor is it surprising that Martha Ballard's midwifery practice reached its height while her daughters still lived at home. Once the daughters were gone, however, that sort of enterprise depended upon the availability of hired help.[26]

"Lydia went off last night," Elizabeth Phelps reported in a letter to her daughter Betsey, who was visiting in Boston. "Silence Furgunson came last night to tarry . . . & this day we have been hard at it I can tell you, made a cheese—churned—got dinner for between .20. & .30. persons, made between .20. & .30. mince-pies . . . but we shall all be rested by morning I hope."[27] The mistress of the best house in the village parted with her daughters at serious cost to herself. The industrious gentility Sarah Hale so much admired was in large measure a consequence of the instability of servants. In another generation Catharine Beecher would make a virtue of Mrs. Phelps's (and Mrs. Romolee's) necessity. Without servants there was little choice but to "educate" young ladies in their mothers' kitchens.

Communal work was the most picturesque form of economic interdependence in rural New England—and to nineteenth-century moralists the most troubling. Berrying, nutting, breaking wool, fishing, husking, house or barn raising, and quilting joined work with sociability. On February 11, 1792, after a male relative had "drawd some Flowers" on a quilt, Elizabeth Wildes sent him to get "Mrs. Green and Abiel to come here to quilting. We had a frollick." "Frolic" rather than "bee" was the common term. In his single days in Keene, New Hampshire, Abner Sanger reported "quilting frolics," "election frolics," "drunken frolics," and on one summer day, "a cow-tord frolic"—presumably a spontaneous game of tag or toss with two girls who were working near him in a field.[28]

Like other sober citizens, Martha Ballard worried about the behavior of the young folks who frequented the large gatherings. Drinking was a concern and perhaps also, though she never expressed it directly, the high premarital pregnancy rates in the town.[29] On November 10, 1790, she described a quilting that took place at her own house. Fifteen "ladies" arrived about three o'clock in the afternoon and quilted until seven, when twelve "gentlemen" arrived to take tea. The young people danced after supper, "behaved exceeding cleverly," she wrote, and went home by eleven. In contrast, she noted dryly, "Mr. Densmore had a quilting & husking. My young folks there came home late." Her entry for July 7, 1788, after neighbors came to raise a sawmill, reflected both anxiety and relief. "There was a vast concorse of men and children and not many disguised with Licquor."

For women, however, births and illnesses provided the most frequent opportunity for communal work. "Monday morn just at daybreak Mr. Hibbard came here," Elizabeth Phelps wrote on March 21, 1790. "I went there—she had a daughter born about 10. I home directly to help wash." Mrs. Phelps was not a midwife. She was simply responding to one more obligation of neighborliness. In the midwifery accounts of Martha Ballard, "calling the women" usually marked the final stage of labor. "Mrs. Blanchard had her women calld and was delivered at 11 hour Evn of a dagt," she wrote on December 26, 1795, three days after she herself had arrived at the Blanchard house. In midwifery as in textile production, the practiced skills of a few women intersected with the ordinary skills of many.

Watching the sick and laying out the dead were also activities that brought together skilled specialists, such as Martha Ballard, with other friends and neighbors. When Elizabeth Wildes had the measles in 1790, half a dozen women (in addition to a male doctor) appeared by turns at her house. "Mrs. Demsy came here and my Mother and Doc Emerson. Hannah Hutchings Sat up with me," she wrote on March 25. Although Israel Wildes was at home on one of his rare intervals between voyages, it was not he but the women who cared for his wife. When Elizabeth Phelps's mother died, Mrs. Gaylord and Sally Parsons prepared her body for burial.[30] Martha Ballard performed similar services for dozens of Hallowell families, usually with the assistance of one or two other women.

Carroll Smith-Rosenberg has written of a "female world of love and ritual" associated with such events, though her analysis tends to combine and perhaps to confuse two very different kinds of female bonding: one originating in a traditional world that organized work by gender and encouraged communal rather than individual identity, the other in a new, more sentimental hemisphere of intense personal relationships.[31] In the New England I am describing, birth, illness, and death were all group events: friends even accompanied newly married couples on their wedding journeys.[32] "Wedingers here," Elizabeth Phelps wrote when one such party arrived at her house.

The realities of birth and death sometimes bent social and racial barriers. Although paid wet-nursing was unusual in rural New England, even a wealthy woman like Elizabeth Phelps might offer breast milk when a child was in need. Soon after her own baby died in December of 1776, she took in a newborn infant whose mother had died. Apparently there was a marked social distance between the two families: she referred to the father as "one Richmond"; and a week after the baby arrived, she wrote, "We having heard that the mother of those Children had the itch tho't it not safe to keep it," adding, "now Lord I make it my prayer that I may do my duty fully however hard." Whether keeping or giving up the baby was the harder duty is not clear, for Elizabeth Phelps soon reclaimed the child. "We feared it would suffer," she wrote.[33]

Physical need might also bend barriers in the opposite direction, sending privileged women to the homes of social inferiors. "Mrs. Parker had our hors to go & see the Negro woman Docter," Martha Ballard wrote on November 9, 1793. The mysterious black practitioner, never given a name, appeared two or three times in the diary in the 1790s, then disappeared. That Martha Ballard always referred to her as a "Docter" or "doctoress" suggests that she respected the woman's powers as a healer even though she denied her the full dignity of a name.[34]

In early America, of course, blacks and Indians, as well as women, had long been associated with both healing and magic. Jon Butler has suggested that among whites, folk medicine was "the most important depository of occult activity."[35] Unfortunately, the magical practices of New England women have not been studied, though again Hale's *Northwood* contains a tantalizing clue. In her portrait of Mrs. Watson, Hale poked fun at writers who insisted on portraying country fortunetellers as witchlike creatures with "weather beaten, sallow, shrivelled skin" and "grizzled, disheveled" hair. "How I wish the ingenious authors, rich as they are in invention, coud have afforded them a comb!" she wrote. She insisted that her Mrs. Watson was a perfectly respectable woman. Though too fond of tea and gossip, she was nevertheless a tidy woman and a good manager, and she was always ready at a moment's notice to watch with the sick. Clearly, her authority as a fortuneteller was a direct consequence of those errands of mercy and curiosity that took her to the homes of her neighbors.[36]

Again the diaries corroborate Hale's portrait. "The Widow Lassel was here and told our fortunes," Eliza Wilde wrote on January 22, 1790, reporting the widow's visit in the same matter-of-fact way that she noted going to church. For the women of Kennebunk, fortunetelling was apparently just another kind of "frolick." "The Widow Lassel and Sukey Perkins and Sally came here. Had their fortunes told," she wrote on another day; a week later she noted that the girls had repeated the ritual without the help of their neighbor.[37] Although moralists were as hard on female fortunetelling as on male drinking, it may have been as much a part of preindustrial life.[38] In Mrs. Watson, Sarah Hale preserved a forgotten form of neighborliness in early New England.

Most models of the "patriarchal family economy" ill fit the evidence of eighteenth-century diaries, which describe a world in which wives as well as husbands traded with their neighbors, where young women felt themselves responsible for their own support, where matches were made in the tumult of neighborhood frolics, and where outsiders as well as family members were involved in the most intimate events of life. The New England we have explored was a world neither of free-floating individuals nor of self-contained households. It was a world in which some women aspired to the independence of Mrs. Romolee but all were sustained by the running about of Mrs. Watson.

Such material alerts us to a number of undeveloped themes in women's history. First, it invites further exploration of the economic orientation of men and women. Did the barter economy encourage easygoing trade across gender lines, or did patterns of exchange coalesce into two quite different economies, one dominated by men and characterized by developing market transactions, the other devoted to "use exchanges" of the sort increasingly more common to women?

Second, it suggests the importance of relations between women both within and beyond the family economy. If mothers rather than fathers had the chief interest in their daughters' labor, then the central theme in the development of factory employment and of public education for girls may not be increased autonomy for young women but an overall loss by older women of the responsibility to educate and to manage female workers. In this regard, more careful distinctions between elite women and their neighbors, as employers and as workers, are needed.

Third, it shows forms of female association organically related to women's work. One wonders, considering the myriad ways in which ordinary life tied women together, whether the appropriate question for the early nineteenth century is not how some women *developed* bonds of womanhood but how generations of women over time sustained and redefined those that had long existed.

Finally, it encourages closer attention to the concrete details of women's lives at every social level, to patterns of consumption, of production, and of "frolicking." If historians cannot accommodate all of Hale's fanciful feast, we at least may begin to look with new interest at the ashes in Mrs. Romolee's fireplace and the leaves in Mrs. Watson's cup.

NOTES

1. Mrs. S. J. Hale, *Northwood: A Tale of New England* (Boston, 1827), 1:108–16.

2. Hale, *Northwood*, 1:83.

3. E.g., Nancy Cott, *The Bonds of Womanhood: "Women's Sphere" in New England, 1780–1835* (New Haven, Conn., 1978); Ann Douglas, *The Feminization of American Culture* (New York, 1978); and most recently, Ruth Schwartz Cowan, *More Work for Mother: The Ironies of Household Technology from the Open Hearth to the Microwave* (New York, 1983).

4. John Mack Faragher, *Women and Men on the Overland Trail* (New Haven, Conn., 1979), chap. 2.

5. E.g., Carole Shammas, "How Self-Sufficient Was Early America?" *Journal of Interdisciplinary History* 13 (Autumn 1982): 247–72; Joyce Appleby, "Commercial Farming and the 'Agrarian Myth' in the Early Republic," *Journal of American History* 68 (March 1982): 833–49; Michael Merrill, "Cash Is Good to Eat: Self-Sufficiency and Exchange in the Rural Economy of the United States," *Radical History Review* 3 (Winter 1977): 42–71; Winifred B. Rothenberg, "The Market and Massachusetts Farmers, 1750–1855," *Journal of Economic History* 41 (June 1981): 283–314.

6. Hale, *Northwood*, 2:178–90.

7. Robert A. Gross, "Culture and Cultivation: Agriculture and Society in Thoreau's Concord," *Journal of American History* 69 (June 1982): 45–46.

8. As Gross has argued ("Culture and Cultivation," 46), "it was the rich—the large landholders and the men who combined farming with a profitable trade—who could aspire to independence."

9. Martha Moore Ballard Diary, 1785–1812, manuscript, Maine State Library, Augusta (hereafter MMB).

10. "The Diary of Elizabeth (Porter) Phelps," ed. Thomas Eliot Andrews, *New England Historical and Genealogical Register* 118:1–30, 108–27, 217–36, 297–308; 119:43–60, 127–40, 205–23, 289–307; 120:57–63, 123–35, 203–14, 293–304 (hereafter EPP).

11. Elizabeth Perkins Wildes Diary, 1789–93, manuscript, Maine Historical Society, Portland.

12. EPP, 120:62.

13. E. E. Bourne, "The Bourne Family" (1855), typescript, Brick Store Museum, Kennebunk, Maine, 222–24; EPP, 120:61.

14. EPP, 120:60, 118:5; MMB, 24 August 1786.

15. Bourne, "Bourne Family," 222–23; David Thurston, *A Brief History of Winthrop* (Portland, Maine, 1855), 20–21.

16. Darret Rutman and Anita Rutman note the same pattern in seventeenth-century Virginia, in *A Place in Time* (New York, 1984), 36.

17. EPP, 118:305.

18. MMB, 30 May, 5 June, 12 and 23 August, 29 September, 16 and 19 October, 18 December 1789.

19. Jack Larkin, "The World of the Account Book: Some Perspectives on Economic Life in Rural New England in the Early 19th Century," paper presented at the Keene State College Sympo-

sium on Social History, Keene, New Hampshire, 13 October 1984.

20. Abner Sanger Diary, 7 May, 6 October 1794, manuscript, Library of Congress. Lois Stabler of Keene, New Hampshire, allowed me to use her typescript of the original. She has since published *Very Poor and of a Lo Make: The Diary of Abner Sanger* (Portsmouth, N.H., 1986).

21. Thomas Vose to Henry Knox, 14 December 1789, Henry Knox Papers, Massachusetts Historical Society, Boston.

22. Bettye Hobbs Pruitt, "Self-Sufficiency and the Agricultural Economy of Eighteenth-Century Massachusetts," *William & Mary Quarterly*, 3rd ser., 41 (1984): 348.

23. MMB, 16 January 1787.

24. Thomas Dublin notes a similar pattern in nineteenth-century store accounts for hatmaking: "Apparently daughters made hats for the family account for a number of years and then, when they reached a certain age, their parents allowed them to make hats on their own account, perhaps to generate dowries" ("Women and Outwork in a Nineteenth-Century New England Town," in *The Countryside in the Age of Capitalist Transformation*, ed. Steven Hahn and Jonathan Prude [Chapel Hill, N.C., 1985], 57–58).

25. Mary Yeaton Diary, typescript, Maine State Library, Augusta, 29 June and 4 October 1801.

26. Laurel Thatcher Ulrich, "Martha Ballard and Her Girls: Women's Work in Eighteenth-Century Maine," in *Work and Labor in Early America,* edited by Stephen Innes (Chapel Hill, N.C., 1988), pp. 70–105.; Bourne, "Bourne Family," 244–47.

27. Elizabeth Porter Phelps to Elizabeth W. Phelps, 4 November 1797, Phelps Family Papers, Amherst College Library, Amherst, Mass. (I am grateful to Edward McCarron for this reference.)

28. Sanger Diary, 21 May, 18 June 1778; 27 May, 28 December 1779; 7 December, 9 February 1780; 28 November 1782.

29. Marriage dates exist (in Hallowell Town Records, manuscript, Maine State Library, Augusta) for 87 women whose first child was delivered by Martha Ballard between 1785 and 1795. More than one-third of these first births occurred less than 8 1/2 months after marriage. For similar evidence from other parts of New England, see Daniel Scott Smith and Michael Hindus, "Premarital Pregnancy in America, 1640–1971: An Overview and Interpretation," *Journal of Interdisciplinary History* 4 (1975): 537–70; Robert Gross, *The Minutemen and Their World* (New York, 1976), 235; Christopher Jedrey, *The World of John Cleaveland: Family and Community in Eighteenth-Century New England* (New York, 1979), 152; and Laurel Thatcher Ulrich and Lois Stabler, "'Girling of It' in Eighteenth-Century New Hampshire," in *Families and Children,* edited by Peter Benes (Boston, 1987).

30. EPP, 121:67.

31. Caroll Smith-Rosenberg, "The Female World of Love and Ritual: Relations between Women in Nineteenth-Century America," *Signs* 1 (1975): 1–29.

32. Ellen Rothman, *Hands and Hearts: A History of Courtship in America* (New York, 1984), 80–81.

33. EPP, 118:235, 236, 397, 398. The evidence that Elizabeth Phelps breastfed the baby is circumstantial but strong. Having given birth and lost her child, she was capable of nursing another child; since no other "nurse" is mentioned, and since concern about the "itch" implied some sort of physical intimacy, the conclusion seems reasonable.

34. Martha Ballard was usually able to provide a surname even for travelers or strangers in town. Like most diarists of the period, she routinely referred to the black women she knew by first name, regardless of marital status, though she always identified white married women as "Mrs."

35. Jon Butler, "The Dark Ages of American Occultism, 1760–1848," in *The Occult in America: New Historical Perspectives,* ed. Howard Kerr and Charles L. Crow (Urbana, Ill., 1983), 69.

36. Hale, 2:180.

37. Wildes Diary, 31 March, 6 April 1790.

38. For a typical attack on fortunetelling, see *An Explanation of the Ten Commandments . . . by an Aged School-Mistress in the State of Massachusetts* (Keene, N.H., 1794), 17. Also see David Hall, "The Uses of Literacy," in *Printing and Society in Early America,* ed. William Joyce et al. (Worcester, Mass., 1983), 40–41.

Chapter 19

Mexican American Women Grassroots Community Activists: Mothers of East Los Angeles

MARY PARDO

The following case study of Mexican American women activists in "Mothers of East Los Angeles" (MELA) illustrates how these Mexican American women transform "traditional" networks and resources based on family and culture into political assets to defend the quality of urban life. Far from unique, these patterns of activism are repeated in Latin America and elsewhere. Here as in other times and places, the women's activism arises out of seemingly "traditional" roles, addresses wider social and political issues, and capitalizes on informal associations sanctioned by the community.[1] Religion, commonly viewed as a conservative force, is intertwined with politics.[2] Often, women speak of their communities and their activism as extensions of their family and household responsibility. The central role of women in grassroots struggles around quality of life, in the Third World and in the United States, challenges conventional assumptions about the powerlessness of women and static definitions of culture and tradition.

In general, the women in MELA are longtime residents of East Los Angeles; some are bilingual and native born, others Mexican born and Spanish dominant. All the core activists are bilingual and have lived in the community over thirty years. All have been active in parish-sponsored groups and activities; some have had experience working in community-based groups arising from schools, neighborhood watch associations, and labor support groups. To gain an appreciation of the group and the core activists, I used ethnographic field methods. I interviewed six women, using a life history approach focused on their first community activities, current activism, household and family responsibilities, and perceptions of community issues.[3] Also, from December 1987 through October 1989, I attended hearings on the two projects of contention—a proposed state prison and a toxic waste incin-

Originally published in *Frontiers: A Journal of Women's Studies*, vol. xi, no. 1 (1990): 1–7. Reprinted by permission. Another version of this chapter was presented at the 1990 International Sociological Association meetings, held in Madrid, Spain, July 9, 1990.

erator—and participated in community and organizational meetings and demonstrations. The following discussion briefly chronicles an intense and significant five-year segment of community history from which emerged MELA and the women's transformation of "traditional" resources and experiences into political assets for community mobilization, and in the process, the redefinition of motherhood.[4]

The Community Context: East Los Angeles Resisting Siege

Political science theory often guides the political strategies used by local government to select the sites for undesirable projects. In 1984, the state of California commissioned a public relations firm to assess the political difficulties facing the construction of energy-producing waste incinerators. The report provided a "personality profile" of those residents most likely to organize effective opposition to projects:

> middle and upper socioeconomic strata possess better resources to effectuate their opposition. Middle and higher socioeconomic strata neighborhoods should not fall within one-mile and five-mile radii of the proposed site. Conversely, older people, people with a high school education or less are least likely to oppose a facility.[5]

The state accordingly placed the plant in Commerce, a predominantly Mexican American, low-income community. This pattern holds throughout the state and the country: three out of five Afro-American and Latinos live near toxic waste sites, and three of the five largest hazardous waste landfills are in communities with at least 80 percent minority populations.[6]

Similarly, in March 1985, when the state sought a site for the first state prison in Los Angeles County, Governor George Deukme-

jian resolved to place the 1,700-inmate institution in East Los Angeles, within a mile of the long-established Boyle Heights neighborhood and within two miles of thirty-four schools. Furthermore, violating convention, the state bid on the expensive parcel of industrially zoned land without compiling an environmental impact report or providing a public community hearing. According to James Vigil, Jr., a field representative for Assemblywoman Gloria Molina, shortly after the state announced the site selection, Molina's office began informing the community and gauging residents' sentiments about it through direct mailings and calls to leaders of organizations and business groups.

In spring 1986, after much pressure from the 56th assembly district office and the community, the Department of Corrections agreed to hold a public information meeting, which was attended by over 700 Boyle Heights residents. From this moment on, Vigil observed, "the tables turned, the community mobilized, and the residents began calling the political representatives and requesting their presence at hearings and meetings."[7] By summer of 1986, the community was well aware of the prison site proposal. Over two thousand people, carrying placards proclaiming "No prison in ELA," marched from Resurrection Church in Boyle Heights to the 3rd Street bridge linking East Los Angeles with the rapidly expanding downtown Los Angeles.[8] This march marked the beginning of one of the largest grassroots coalitions to emerge from the Latino community in the last decade.

Prominent among the coalition's groups is "Mothers of East Los Angeles," a loosely knit group of over 400 Mexican American women.[9] MELA initially coalesced to oppose the state prison construction but has since organized opposition to several other projects detrimental to the quality of life in the central city.[10] Its second large target is a toxic waste incinerator proposed for Vernon, a small city adjacent to East Los Angeles. This incinerator would worsen the already debilitating air quality of the entire county and set a precedent dangerous for other communities throughout California.[11] When MELA took up the fight against the toxic waste incinerator, it became more than a single-issue group and began working with environmental groups around the state.[12] As a result of the community struggle, AB58 (Roybal-Allard), which provides all Californians with the minimum protection of an environmental impact report before the construction of hazardous waste incinerators, was signed into law. But the law's effectiveness relies on a watchful community network. Since its emergence, "Mothers of East Los Angeles" has become centrally important to just such a network of grassroots activists, including a select number of Catholic priests and two Mexican American political representatives. Furthermore, the group's very formation, and its continued spirit and activism, fly in the face of the conventional political science beliefs regarding political participation.

Predictions by the "experts" attribute the low formal political participation (i.e., voting) of Mexican American people in the United States to a set of cultural "retardants," including primary kinship systems, fatalism, religious traditionalism, traditional cultural values, and mother-country attachment.[13] The core activists in MELA may appear to fit this description, as well as the state-commissioned profile of residents least likely to oppose toxic waste incinerator projects. All the women live in a low-income community. Furthermore, they identify themselves as active and committed participants in the Catholic Church; they claim an ethnic identity—Mexican American; their ages range from forty to sixty; and they have attained at most high school educations. However, these women fail to conform to the predicted political apathy. Instead, they have transformed social identity—ethnic identity, class identity, and gender identity—into an impetus as well as a basis for activism. And, in transforming their existing social networks into grassroots political networks, they have also transformed themselves.

Transformation as a Dominant Theme

From the life histories of the group's core activists and from my own field notes, I have selected excerpts that tell two representative stories. One is a narrative of the events that led to community mobilization in East Los Angeles. The other is a story of transformation, the process of creating new and better relationships that empower people to unite and achieve common goals.[14]

First, women have transformed organizing experiences and social networks arising from gender-related responsibilities into political resources.[15] When I asked the women about the first community, not necessarily "political," involvement they could recall, they discussed experiences that predated the formation of MELA. Juana Gutiérrez explained:

> Well, it didn't start with the prison, you know. It started when my kids went to school. I started by joining the Parents Club and we worked on different problems here in the area. Like the people who come to the parks to sell drugs to the kids. I got the neighbors to have meetings. I would go knock at the doors, house to house. And I told them that we should stick together with the Neighborhood Watch for the community and for the kids.[16]

Erlinda Robles similarly recalled:

> I wanted my kids to go to Catholic school and from the time my oldest one went there, I was there every day. I used to take my two little ones with me and I helped one way or another. I used to question things they did. And the other

mothers would just watch me. Later, they would ask me, "Why do you do that? They are going to take it out on your kids." I'd say, "They better not." And before you knew it, we had a big group of mothers that were very involved.[17]

Part of a mother's "traditional" responsibility includes overseeing her child's progress in school, interacting with school staff, and supporting school activities. In these processes, women meet other mothers and begin developing a network of acquaintanceships and friendships based on mutual concern for the welfare of their children.

Although the women in MELA carried the greatest burden of participating in school activities, Erlinda Robles also spoke of strategies they used to draw men into the enterprise and into the networks:[18]

At the beginning, the priests used to say who the president of the mothers guild would be; they used to pick 'um. But, we wanted elections, so we got elections. Then we wanted the fathers to be involved, and the nuns suggested that a father should be president and a mother would be secretary or be involved there [at the school site].[19]

Of course, this comment piqued my curiosity, so I asked how the mothers agreed on the nuns' suggestion. The answer was simple and instructive:

At the time we thought is was a "natural" way to get the fathers involved because they weren't involved; it was just the mothers. Everybody [the women] agreed on them [the fathers] being president because they worked all day and they couldn't be involved in a lot of daily activities like food sales and whatever. During the week, a steering committee of mothers planned the group's activities. But now that I think about it, a women could have done the job just as well![20]

So women got men into the group by giving them a position they could manage. The men may have held the title of "president," but they were not making day-to-day decisions

about work, nor were they dictating the direction of the group. Erlinda Robles laughed as she recalled an occasion when the president insisted, against the wishes of the women, on scheduling a parents' group fundraiser—a breakfast—on Mother's Day. On that morning, only the president and his wife were present to prepare breakfast. This should alert researchers against measuring power and influence by looking solely at who holds titles.

Each of the cofounders had a history of working with groups arising out of the responsibilities usually assumed by "mothers"—the education of children and the safety of the surrounding community. From these groups, they gained valuable experiences and networks that facilitated the formation of "Mothers of East Los Angeles." Juana Gutiérrez explained how preexisting networks progressively expanded community support:

You know nobody knew about the plan to build a prison in the community until Assemblywoman Gloria Molina told me. Martha Molina called me and said, "You know what is happening in your area? The governor wants to put a prison in Boyle Heights!" So, I called a Neighborhood Watch meeting at my house and we got fifteen people together. Then, Father John started informing his people at the Church and that is when the group of two or three hundred started showing up for every march on the bridge.[21]

MELA effectively linked up preexisting networks into a viable grassroots coalition.

Second, the process of activism also transformed previously "invisible" women, making them not only visible but the center of public attention. From a conventional perspective, political activism assumes a kind of gender neutrality. This means that anyone can participate, but men are the expected key actors. In accordance with this pattern, in winter 1986 an informal group of concerned businessmen in the community began lobbying and testifying against the prison at hearings in Sacramento. Working in conjunction with Assemblywoman Molina, they made many trips to Sacramento at their own expense. Residents who did not have to the income to travel were unable to join them. Finally, Molina, commonly recognized as a forceful advocate for Latinas and the community, asked Frank Villalobos, an urban planner in the group, why there were no women coming up to speak in Sacramento against the prison. As he phrased it, "I was getting some heat from her because no women were going up there."[22]

In response to this comment, Veronica Gutiérrez, a law student who lived in the community, agreed to accompany him on the next trip to Sacramento.[23] He also mentioned the comment to Father John Moretta at Resurrection Catholic Parish. Meanwhile, representatives of the business sector of the community and of the 56th assembly district office were continuing to compile arguments and supportive data against the East Los Angeles prison site. Frank Villalobos stated one of the pressing problems:

We felt that the Senators whom we prepared all this for didn't even acknowledge that we existed. They kept calling it the "downtown" site, and they argued that there was no opposition in the community. So, I told Father Moretta, what we have to do is demonstrate that there is a link (proximity) between the Boyle Heights community and the prison.[24]

The next juncture illustrates how perceptions of gender-specific behavior set in motion a sequence of events that brought women into the political limelight. Father Moretta decided to ask all the women to meet after mass. He told them about the prison site and called for their support. When I asked him about his rationale for selecting the women, he replied:

I felt so strongly about the issue, and I knew in my heart what a terrible offense this was to the people. So, I was afraid that once we got into a demonstration situation we had to be very careful. I thought the women would be cooler and calmer than the men. The bottom line is that the men came anyway. The first times out the majority were women. Then they began to invite their husbands and their children, but originally it was just women.[25]

Father Moretta also named the group. Quite moved by a film, *The Official Story*, about the courageous Argentine women who demonstrated for the return of their children who disappeared during a repressive right-wing military dictatorship, he transformed the name "Las Madres de la Plaza de Mayo" into "Mothers of East Los Angeles."[26]

However, Aurora Castillo, one of the cofounders of the group, modified my emphasis on the predominance of women:

Of course the fathers work. We also have many, many grandmothers. And all this IS with the support of the fathers. They make the placards and the posters; they do the security and carry the signs; and they come to the marches when they can.[27]

Although women played a key role in the mobilization, they emphasized the group's broad base of active supporters as well as the other organizations in the "Coalition Against the Prison." Their intent was to counter any notion that MELA was composed exclusively of women or mothers and to stress the "inclusiveness" of the group. All the women who assumed lead roles in the group had long histories of volunteer work in the Boyle Heights community; but formation of the group brought them out of the "private" margins and into "public" light.

Third, the women in "Mothers of East L.A." have transformed the definition of "mother" to include militant political opposition to state-proposed projects they see as adverse to the quality of life in the community. Explaining how she discovered the issue, Aurora Castillo said,

> You know if one of your children's safety is jeopardized, the mother turns into a lioness. That's why Father John got the mothers. We have to have a well-organized, strong group of mothers to protect the community and oppose things that are detrimental to us. You know the governor is in the wrong and the mothers are in the right. After all, the mothers have to be right. Mothers are for the children's interest, not for self-interest; the governor is for his own political interest.[28]

The women also have expanded the boundaries of "motherhood" to include social and political community activism and have redefined the word to include women who are not biological "mothers." At one meeting a young Latina expressed her solidarity with the group and, almost apologetically, qualified herself as a "resident," not a "mother," of East Los Angeles. Erlinda Robles replied:

> When you are fighting for a better life for children and "doing" for them, isn't that what mothers do? So we're all mothers. You don't have to have children to be a "mother."[29]

At critical points, grassroots community activism requires attending many meetings, phone calling, and door-to-door communications—all very labor-intensive work. In order to keep harmony in the "domestic" sphere, the core activist must creatively integrate family members into their community activities. I asked Erlinda Robles how her husband felt about her activism, and she replied quite openly:

> My husband doesn't like getting involved, but he takes me because he knows I like it. Sometimes we would have two or three meetings a week. And my husband would say, "Why are you going so much? It is really getting out of hand." But he is very supportive. Once he gets

there, he enjoys it and he starts arguing too! See, it's just that he is not used to it. He couldn't believe things happened the way that they do. He was in the Navy twenty years and they brainwashed him that none of the politicians could do wrong. So he had come a long way. Now he comes home and parks the car out front and asks me, "Well, where are we going tonight?"[30]

When women explain their activism, they link family and community as one entity. Juana Gutiérrez, a woman with extensive experience working on community and neighborhood issues, stated:

> Yo como madre de familia, y como residente del Este de Los Angeles, seguiré luchando sin descanso por que se nos respete. Y yo lo hago con bastante cariño hacia mi comunidad. Digo "mi comunidad," porque me siento parte de ella, quiero a mi raza como parte de mi familia, y si Dios me permite seguiré luchando contra todos los gobernadores que quieran abusar de nosotros. (As a mother and a resident of East L.A., I shall continue fighting tirelessly, so we will be respected. And I will do this with much affection for my community. I say, "my community" because I am part of it. I love my "raza" [race] as part of my family; and if God allows, I will keep on fighting against all the governors that want to take advantage of us.)[31]

Like the other activists, she has expanded her responsibilities and legitimated militant opposition to abuse of the community by reprsentatives of the state.

Working-class women activists seldom opt to separate themselves from men and their families. In this particular struggle for community quality of life, they are fighting for the family unit and thus are not competitive with me.[32] Of course, this fact does not preclude different alignments in other contexts and situations.[33]

Fourth, the story of MELA also shows the transformation of class and ethnic identity. Aurora Castillo told of an incident that illustrated her growing knowledge of the relation-ship of East Los Angeles to other communities and the basis necessary for coalition building:

> And do you know we have been approached by other groups? [She lowers her voice in empha-sis.] You know that Pacific Palisades group asked for our backing. But what they did, they sent their powerful lobbyist that they pay thou-sands of dollars to get our support against the drilling in Pacific Palisades. So what we did was tell them to send their grassroots people, not their lobbyist. We're suspicious. We don't want to talk to a high-salaried lobbyist; we are hum-ble people. We did our own lobbying. In one week we went to Sacramento twice.[34]

The contrast between the often tedious and labor-intensive work of mobilizing people at the "grassroots" level and the paid work of a "high salaried lobbyist" represents a point of pride and integrity, not a deficiency or a source of shame. If the two groups were to construct a coalition, they must communi-cate on equal terms.

The women of MELA combine a willing-ness to assert opposition with critical assess-ment of their own weaknesses. At one com-munity meeting, for example, representatives of several oil companies attempted to gain support for placement of an oil pipeline through the center of East Los Angeles. The exchange between the women in the audience and the oil representative was heated, as women alternated asking questions about the chosen route for the pipeline:

> "Is it going through Cielito Lindo [Reagan's ranch]?" The oil representative answered, "No." Another woman stood up and asked, "Why not place it along the coastline?" Without thinking of the implications, the representative re-sponded, "Oh, no! If it burst, it would endanger the marine life." The woman retorted, "You value the marine life more than human beings?" His face reddened with anger and the hearing disintegrated into angry chanting.[35]

The proposal was quickly defeated. But Au-rora Castillo acknowledged that it was not solely their opposition that brought about the defeat:

> We won because the westside was opposed to it, so we united with them. You know there are a lot of attorneys who live there and they also questioned the representative. Believe me, no way is justice blind . . . We just don't want all this garbage thrown at us because we are low-income and Mexican American. We are lucky now that we have good representatives, which we didn't have before.[36]

Throughout their life histories, the women refer to the disruptive effects of land use deci-sions made in the 1950s. As longtime resi-dents, all but one share the experience of los-ing a home and relocating to make way for a freeway. Juana Gutiérrez refers to the com-munity response at that time:

> Una de las cosas que me caen muy mal es la in-justicia y en nuestra comunidad hemos visto mucho de eso. Sobre todo antes, porque creo que nuestra gente estaba mas dormida, nos atrevíamos menos. En los cincuentas hicieron los freeways y así, sin más, nos dieron las noticia de que nos teníamos que mudar. Y eso pasó dos veces. La gente se conformaba porque lo ordeno el gobierno. Recuerdo que yo me enojaba y quería que los demás me secundaran, pero na-dia quería hacer nada. (One of the things that really upsets me is the injustice that we see so much in our community. Above everything else, I believe that our people were less aware; we were less challenging. In the 1950s—they made the freeways and just like that they gave us no-tice that we had to move. That happened twice. The people accepted it because the government ordered it. I remember that I was angry and wanted others to back me but nobody else wanted to do anything.)[37]

The freeways that cut through communi-ties and disrupted neighborhoods are now a concrete reminder of shared injustice, of the vulnerability of the community in the 1950s. The community's social and political history thus informs perceptions of its current predicament; however, today's activists emphasize not the powerlessness of the community but the change in status and progression toward political empowerment.

Fifth, the core activists typically tell stories illustrating personal change and a new sense of entitlement to speak for the community. They have transformed the unspoken sentiments of individuals into a collective community voice. Lucy Ramos related here initial apprehensions:

> I was afraid to get involved. I didn't know what was going to come out of this and I hesitated at first. Right after we started, Father John came up to me and told me, "I want you to be a spokesperson." I said, "Oh no, I don't know what I am going to say." I was nervous. I am surprised I didn't have a nervous breakdown then. Every time we used to get in front of the TV cameras and even interviews like this, I used to sit there and I could feel myself shaking. But as time went on, I started getting used to it.
>
> And this is what I have noticed with a lot of them. They were afraid to speak up and say anything. Now, with this prison issue, a lot of them have come out and come forward and given their opinions. Everybody used to be real "quietlike."[38]

She also related a situation that brought all her fears to a climax, which she confronted and resolved as follows:

> When I first started working with the coalition, Channel 13 called me up and said they wanted to interview me and I said OK. Then I started getting nervous. So I called Father John and told him, "You better get over here right away." He said, "Don't worry, don't worry, you can handle it by yourself." Then Channel 13 called me back and said they were going to interview another person, someone I had never heard of, and asked if it was OK if he came to my house. And

I said OK again. Then I began thinking, what if this guy is for the prison? What am I going to do? And I was so nervous and I thought, I know what I am going to do!

Since the meeting was taking place in her home, she reasoned that she was entitled to order any troublemakers out of her domain:

> If this man tells me anything, I am just going to chase him out of my house. That is what I am going to do! All these thoughts were going through my head. Then Channel 13 walk into my house followed by six men I had never met. And I thought, Oh, my God, what did I get myself into? I kept saying to myself, if they get smart with me I am throwing them ALL out.[39]

At this point her tone expressed a sense of resolve. In fact, the situation turned out to be neither confrontational nor threatening, as the "other men" were also members of the coalition. This woman confronted an anxiety-laden situation by relying on her sense of control within her home and family—a quite "traditional" source of authority for women—and transforming that control into the courage to express a political position before a potential audience all over one of the largest metropolitan areas in the nation.

People living in Third World countries as well as in minority communities in the United States face an increasingly degraded environment.[40] Recognizing the threat to the well-being of their families, residents have mobilized at the neighborhood level to fight for "quality of life" issues. The common notion that environmental well-being is of concern solely to white middle-class and upper-class residents ignores the specific way working-class neighborhoods suffer from the fallout of the city "growth machine" geared for profit.[41]

In Los Angeles, the culmination of postwar urban renewal policies, the growing Pacific Rim trade surplus and investment, and low-wage international labor migration from Third World countries are creating potentially volatile conditions. Literally palatial financial buildings swallow up the space previously occupied by modest, low-cost housing. Increasing density and development not matched by investment in social programs, services, and infrastructure erode the quality of life, beginning in the core of the city.[42] Latinos, the majority of whom live close to the center of the city, must confront the distilled social consequences of development focused solely on profit. The Mexican American community in East Los Angeles, much like other minority working-class communities, has been a repository for prisons instead of new schools, hazardous industries instead of safe work sites, and one of the largest concentrations of freeway interchanges in the country, which transports much wealth past the community. And the concerns of residents in East Los Angeles may provide lessons for other minority as well as middle-class communities. Increasing environmental pollution resulting from inadequate waste disposal plans and out-of-control "need" for penal institutions to contain the casualties created by the growing bipolar distribution of wages may not be limited to the Southwest.[43] These conditions set the stage for new conflicts and new opportunities, to transform old relationships into coalitions that can challenge state agendas and create new community visions.[44]

Mexican American women living east of downtown Los Angeles exemplify the tendency of women to enter into environmental struggles in defense of their community. Women have a rich historical legacy of community activism, partly reconstructed over the last two decades in social histories of women who contested other "quality of life issues," from the price of bread to "Demon Rum" (often representing domestic violence).[45]

But something new is also happening. The issues "traditionally" addressed by women—health, housing, sanitation, and the urban environment—have moved to center stage as capitalist urbanization progresses. Environmental issues now fuel the fires of many political campaigns and drive citizens beyond the rather restricted, perfunctory political act of voting. Instances of political mobilization at the grassroots level, where women play a central role, allow us to "see" abstract concepts like participatory democracy and social change as dynamic processes.

The existence and activities of Mothers of East Los Angeles attest to the dynamic nature of participatory democracy, as well as to the dynamic nature of our gender, class, and ethnic identity. The story of MELA reveals, on the one hand, how individuals and groups can transform a seemingly "traditional" role such as "mother." On the other hand, it illustrates how such a role may also be a social agent drawing members of the community into the "political" arena. Studying women's contributions as well as men's will shed greater light on the networks dynamic of grassroots movements.[46]

The work Mothers of East Los Angeles do to mobilize the community demonstrates that people's political involvement cannot be predicted by their cultural characteristics. These women have defied stereotypes of apathy and used ethnic, gender, and class identity as an impetus, a strength, a vehicle for political activism. They have expanded their—and our—understanding of the complexities of a political system, and understanding of the complexities of a political system, and they have reaffirmed the possibility of "doing something."

They also generously share the lessons they have learned. One of the women in Mothers of East Los Angeles told me, as I hesitated to set up an interview with another women I hadn't yet met in person, "You know, nothing ventured nothing lost. You should have seen how timid we were the first time we went to a public hearing. Now, forget it, I walk right up and make myself heard and that's what you have to do."[47]

NOTES

1. For cases of grassroots activism among women in Latin America, see Sally W. Yudelman, *Hopeful Openings: A Study of Five Women's Development Organizations in Latin American and the Caribbean* (West Hartford, Conn.: Kumarian Press, 1987). For an excellent case analysis of how informal associations enlarge and empower women's world in Third World countries, see Kathryn S. March and Rachelle L. Taqqu, *Women's Informal Associations in Developing Countries: Catalysts for Change?* (Boulder, Colo.: Westview Press, 1986). Also, see Carmen Feijoó, "Women in Neighbourhoods: From Local Issues to Gender Problems," *Canadian Women Studies* 6, no. 1 (Fall 1984) for a concise overview of the patterns of activism.

2. The relationship between Catholicism and political activism is varied and not unitary. In some Mexican American communities, grassroots activism relies on parish networks. See Isidro D. Ortiz, "Chicano Urban Politics and the Politics of Reform in the Seventies," *The Western Political Quarterly* 37, no. 4 (December 1984): 565–77. Also, see Joseph D. Sekul, "Communities Organized for Public Service: Citizen Power and Public Power in San Antonio," in *Latinos and the Political System*, edited by F. Chris Garcia (Notre Dame, Ind.: University of Notre Dame Press, 1988). Sekul tells how COPS members challenged prevailing patterns of power by working for the well-being of families and cites four former presidents who were Mexican American women, but he makes no special point of gender.

3. I also interviewed other members of the Coalition Against the Prison and local political office representatives. For a general reference, see James P. Spradley, *The Ethnographic Interview* (New York: Holt Rinehart and Winston, 1979). For a review essay focused on the relevancy of the

method for examining the diversity of women's experiences, see Susan N. G. Geiger, "Women's Life Histories: Method and Content," *Signs* 11, no. 2 (Winter 1982): 334–51.

4. During the past five years, over 300 newspaper articles have appeared on the issue. Frank Villalobos generously shared his extensive newspaper archives with me. See Leo C. Wolinsky, "L.A. Prison Bill 'Locked Up' in New Clash," *Los Angeles Times*, 16 July 1987, sec. 1, p. 3; Rudy Acuña, "The Fate of East L.A.: One Big Jail," *Los Angeles Herald Examiner*, 28 April 1989, A15; Carolina Serna, "Eastside Residents Oppose Prison," *La Gente UCLA Student Newspaper* 17, no. 1 (October 1986): 5; Daniel M. Weintraub, "10,000 Fee Paid to Lawmaker Who Left Sickbed to Cast Vote," *Los Angeles Times*, 13 March 1988, sec 1, p. 3.

5. Cerrell Associates, Inc., "Political Difficulties Facing Waste-to-Energy Conversion Plant Siting," Report for California Waste Management Board, State of California (Los Angeles, 1984), 43.

6. Jesus Sanchez, "The Environment: Whose Movement?" *California Tomorrow* 3, nos. 3 & 4 (Fall 1988): 13. Also see Rudy Acuña, *A Community Under Siege* (Los Angeles: Chicano Studies Research Center Publications, UCLA, 1984). The book and its title capture the sentiments and the history of a community that bears an unfair burden of city projects deemed undesirable by all residents.

7. James Vigil, Jr., field representative for Assemblywoman Gloria Molina, 1984–1986, Personal Interview, Whittier, Calif., 27 September 1989. Vigil stated that the Department of Corrections used a threefold strategy: political pressure in the legislature, the promise of jobs for residents, and contracts for local business.

8. Edward J. Boyer and Marita Hernandez, "Eastside Seethes over Prison Plan," *Los Angeles Times*, 13 August 1986, sec. 2, p. 1.

9. Martha Molina-Aviles, administrative assistant for Assemblywoman Lucille Roybal-Allard, 56th assembly district, and former field representative for Gloria Molina when she held this assembly seat, Personal Interview, Los Angeles, 5 June 1989. Molina-Aviles, who grew up in East Los Angeles, used her experiences and insights to help forge strong links among the women in

MELA, other members of the coalition, and the assembly office.

10. MELA has also opposed the expansion of a county prison literally across the street from William Mead Housing Projects, home to 2,000 Latinos, Asians, and Afro-Americans, and a chemical treatment plant for toxic wastes.

11. The first of its kind in a metropolitan area, it would burn 125,000 pounds per day of hazardous wastes. For an excellent article that links recent struggles against hazardous waste dumps and incinerators in minority communities and features women in MELA, see Dick Russell, "Environmental Racism: Minority Communities and Their Battle against Toxics," *The Amicus Journal* 11, no. 2 (Spring 1989): 22–32.

12. Miguel G. Mendívil, field representative for Assemblywoman Lucille Roybal-Allard, 56th assembly district, Personal Interview, Los Angeles, 25 April 1989.

13. John Garcia and Rudolfo de la Garza, "Mobilizing the Mexican Immigrant: The Role of Mexican American Organizations," *The Western Political Quarterly* 38, no. 4 (December 1985): 551–64.

14. This concept is discussed in relation to Latino communities in David T. Abalos, *Latinos in the U.S.: The Sacred and the Political* (Indiana: University of Notre Dame Press, 1986). The notion of transformation of traditional culture in struggles against oppression is certainly not a new one. For a brief essay on a longer work, see Frantz Fanon, "Algeria Unveiled," *The New Left Reader,* edited by Carl Oglesby (New York: Grove Press, Inc, 1969): 161–85.

15. Karen Sacke, *Caring by the Hour.*

16. Juana Gutiérrez, Personal Interview, Boyle Heights, East Los Angeles, 15 January 1988.

17. Erlinda Robles, Personal Interview, Boyle Heights, Los Angeles, 14 September 1989.

18. Mina Davis Caulfield, "Imperialism, the Family, and Cultures of Resistance," *Socialist Revolution* 29 (1974): 67–85.

19. Erlinda Robles, Personal Interview.

20. Ibid.

21. Juana Gutiérrez, Personal Interview.

22. Frank Villalobos, architect and urban planner, Personal Interview, Los Angeles, 2 May 1989.

23. The law student, Veronica Gutiérrez, is the daughter of Juana Gutiérrez, one of the cofounders of MELA. Martín Gutiérrez, one of her sons, was a field representative for Assemblywoman Lucille Roybal-Allard and also central to community mobilization. Ricardo Gutiérrez, Juana's husband, and almost all the other family members are community activists. They are a microcosm of the family networks that strengthened community mobilization and the Coalition Against the Prison. See Raymundo Reynoso, "Juana Beatrice Gutiérrez: La incansable luncha de una activista comunitaria," *La Opinion,* 6 August 1989, Acceso, p. 1., and Louis Sahagun, "The Mothers of East L.A. Transform Themselves and Their Community," *Los Angeles Times,* 13 August 1989, sec. 2, p. 1.

24. Frank Villalobos, Personal Interview.

25. Father John Moretta, Resurrection Parish, Personal Interview, Boyle Heights, Los Angeles, 24 May 1989.

26. The Plaza de Mayo mothers organized spontaneously to demand the return of their missing children, in open defiance of the Argentine military dictatorship. For a brief overview of the group and its relationship to other women's organizations in Argentina, and a synopsis of the criticism of the mothers that reveals ideological camps, see Gloria Bonder, "Women's Organizations in Argentina's Transition to Democracy," in *Women and Counter Power,* edited by Yolanda Cohen (New York: Black Rose Books, 1989): 65–85. There is no direct relationship between this group and MELA.

27. Aurora Castillo, Personal Interview, Boyle Heights, Los Angeles, 15 January 1988.

28. Aurora Castillo, Personal Interview.

29. Erlinda Robles, Personal Interview.

30. Ibid.

31. Reynoso, "Juana Beatriz Gutiérrez," p. 1.

32. For historical examples, see Chris Marín, "La Asociación Hispano-Americana de Madres Y Esposas: Tucson's Mexican American Women in World War II," *Renato Rosaldo Lecture Series 1: 1983–1984* (Tucson, Ariz.: Mexican American Studies Center, University of Arizona, Tucson, 1985) and Judy Aulette and Trudy Mills, "Something Old, Something New: Auxiliary Work in the 1983–1986 Copper Strike," *Feminist Studies* 14, no. 2 (Summer 1988): 251–69.

33. Mina Davis Caulfield, "Imperialism, the Family and Cultures of Resistance."

34. Aurora Castillo, Personal Interview.

35. As reconstructed by Juana Gutiérrez, Ricardo Gutiérrez, and Aurora Castillo.

36. Aurora Castillo, Personal Interview.

37. Juana Gutiérrez, Personal Interview.

38. Lucy Ramos, Personal Interview, Boyle Heights, Los Angeles, 3 May 1989.

39. Ibid.

40. For an overview of contemporary Third World struggles against environmental degradation, see Alan B. Durning, "Saving the Planet," *The Progressive* 53, no. 4 (April 1989): 35–59.

41. John Logan and Harvey Molotch, *Urban Fortunes* (Berkeley: University of California Press, 1988). Logan and Molotch use the term in reference to a coalition of business people, local politicians, and the media.

42. Mike Davis, "Chinatown, Part Two? The Internationalization of Downtown Los Angeles," *New Left Review*, no. 164 (July/August 1987): 64–86.

43. Paul Ong, *The Widening Divide: Income Inequality and Poverty in Los Angeles* (Los Angeles: The Research Group on the Los Angeles Economy, 1989). This UCLA-based study documents the growing gap between "haves" and "have nots" in the midst of the economic boom in Los Angeles. According to economists, the study mirrors a national trend in which rising employment levels are failing to lift the poor out of poverty or boost the middle class; see Jill Steward, "Two-Tiered Economy Feared as Dead End of Unskilled," *Los Ange-les Times*, 25 June 1989, sec. 2, p. 1. At the same time, the California prison population will climb to more than twice its designed capacity by 1995. See Carl Ingram, "New Forecast Sees a Worse Jam in Prisons," *Los Angeles Times*, 27 June 1989, sec 1, p. 23.

44. The point that urban land use policies are the products of class struggle—both cause and consequence—is made by Don Parson, "The Development of Redevelopment: Public Housing and Urban Renewal in Los Angeles," *International Journal of Urban and Regional Research* 6, no. 4 (December 1982): 392–413. Parson provides an excellent discussion of the working-class struggle for housing in the 1930s, the counterinitiative of urban renewal in the 1950s, and the inner city revolts of the 1960s.

45. Louise Tilly, "Paths of Proletarianization: Organization of Production, Sexual Division of Labor, and Women's Collective Action," *Signs* 7, no. 2 (1981): 400–417; Alice Kessler-Harris, "Women's Social Mission," *Women Have Always Worked* (Old Westbury, N.Y.: The Feminist Press, 1981): 102–35. For a literature review of women's activism during the Progressive Era, see Marilyn Gittell and Teresa Shtob, "Changing Women's Roles in Political Volunteerism and Reform of the City," in *Women and the American City*, edited by Catharine Stimpson et al. (Chicago: University of Chicago Press, 1981): 64–75.

46. Karen Sacks, *Caring by the Hour*, argues that often the significance of women's contributions is not "seen" because it takes place in networks.

47. Aurora Castillo, Personal Interview.

 *Part III*

Webs of Family Relationships

However "family" is defined, its meaning concerns *relationships*. Family boundaries define who is part of a particular family and who is not. People who are co-members of a family have a very different set of rights and obligations to one another than they do to people outside their family. Within families, people occupy positions *in relation* to other familial positions. Mothers, fathers, and children are mothers, fathers, and children by virtue of their relationship to one another; a child's parents are someone else's children; and, as Nicholas W. Townsend illustrates in his chapter, "Fathers and Sons," when people have children, they transform their own parents into grandparents. Childhood, adolescence, and adulthood are stages in the life course, but people remain the children of their parents regardless of their age, although the rights and responsibilities of these positions change with age and over time. The relationships between families—through marriage, the birth of children, the adoption of fictive kin, or the joining together in community—are threads in webs of family and kinship relationships.

For societies to endure and for humanity to continue, it is not necessary that each woman bear and rear a child. But it is necessary that some members of society bear and rear children and, in a good society, that the group as a whole take some responsibility for the next generation. Mothering and fathering, however, are not contingent upon marriage, heterosexual relationships, or two-parent families. Granted, many people who are parents are married heterosexual couples. What the chapters in this part show us is that this is one of many viable family forms, but it is not a precondition for bearing children or for being a mother or a father. We therefore begin this part with chapters on mothering and on fathering, then moved to chapters on the wider kin networks into which children are born and by which family relationships are organized, and we end with chapters that focus on issues of marriage, as one kind of kinship relation, and divorce, as an event that sometimes strains and sometimes reinforces webs of family relationships.

The chapters on mothers and fathers underscore the point that parenting is gendered—which means that the experience and practice of parenting (mothering and fathering) and the cultural understandings of what it means to be a parent (motherhood and fatherhood) differ for men and women. In "Why Women Mother," Nancy J. Chodorow questions the gendered nature of parenting by asking why *women* are the people responsible for the care and nurturance of children. Parenting is not only gendered but it is also historically contingent and culturally variable. Women and men are mothers and fathers in a particular culture, in interaction with particular social

structures, and at a particular time in history. Therefore, in "Chicana/o Family Structure and Gender Personality," Denise A. Segura and Jennifer L. Pierce examine
Chodorow's thesis on the reproduction of mothering in light of the specific family and
kinship relationships in Chicano families. Families occupy various social locations,
and their differing relationships to the larger society can affect the content and form
of relationships within the family. For example, in "Catching Sense," Suzanne C.
Carothers describes how African American mothers, who have always had high labor-
force participation, transmit lessons to their daughters that enable them to be independent *and* nurturing, while surviving in a racist society.

Mothering is an activity, and motherhood is a social institution and an ideology
(Rich 1976). Mothers, on the other hand, are people who differ by racial-ethnic group,
by class, and by historical circumstance. Ideological beliefs about motherhood determine who is considered an "appropriate" mother. In "Native American Mother,"
Judith K. Witherow pays eloquent tribute to her mother when she discusses why her
mother would not fit the qualifications for a "Mother of the Year" award. In "'I Am
This Child's Mother,'" Claire Reinelt and Mindy Fried illustrate how disabled women
face not only the difficulties of parenting with a disability but also the hurdles presented by the disapproval of those who believe that disabled women cannot be good
mothers. In "Jewish Lesbian Parenting," Linda J. Holtzman presents yet another example of how some women challenge beliefs about who can mother.

As a society, we are also negotiating the meaning of fatherhood and the place of fathers within families. To help us understand the dynamics propelling the transformation of rights and responsibilities of fatherhood, Joseph H. Pleck reviews the sweep
of U.S. history in "American Fathering in Historical Perspective." Cultural definitions
of fatherhood have shifted from fathers as the proprietary owners of property and
household members, the disciplinarians, and the moral guardians in the eighteenth
century; to the economic providers and heads of households in the nineteenth century; to the breadwinners and, more recently, to fathers as nurturant parents who
share the day-to-day work of child rearing in the twentieth century. These transformations have created what Ralph LaRossa in "The Culture and Conduct of Fatherhood" calls an "asynchrony" between our expectations of fatherhood and the actual
practices of fathers.

Although statistics reveal that men, as a group, have an abysmal record of paying
child support and of keeping in contact with their children after divorce (Arendell
1996; Weitzman 1985), some fathers do try to live up to an ideal of involved and nurturant fathers. In "'Best Case Scenarios,'" Terry Arendell reports on a small but significant minority of fathers who, after divorce, immerse themselves in the rhythms of
their children's everyday lives and, in the process, enhance their communication skills

and refigure their understanding of masculinity. Like many of the working-class men that Townsend studies in "Fathers and Sons," they reshape the parameters of fatherhood and creatively explore the boundaries of what is possible.

The chapters in the section "Kin Networks" examine various ways that individuals and familial groups *activate* kinship ties—and the rights and obligations that define those ties. Who will care for young children or frail relatives? Who does an unemployed adolescent or homeless divorced parent have a right to call on for help? And who has the obligation to help them? What is the appropriate time to begin childbearing or to take on the responsibility for other family members? What happens when people do not meet their familial obligations?

The answers to these questions will vary depending on the particular family, the larger culture, and the historical moment, but in "Kinscripts," Carol B. Stack and Linda M. Burton suggest that the framework they developed from their study of African American multigenerational families can be applied to understanding the kin-work performed in all families. In "The Female World of Cards and Holidays," Micaela di Leonardo examines the gendered nature of kin-work in Italian American families and draws attention to the invisibility of much of the labor that maintains and reproduces the links that hold families and kin groups together.

It is important to remember, however, that kin-work occurs in a larger social and economic context. In "Fictive Kin, Paper Sons, and *Compadrazgo*," Bonnie Thornton Dill draws the connection between the place of families in the racial hierarchy of the United States and the structure of family life. Her historical overview of African Americans families in slavery, Chinese sojourner families in the United States, and Chicano families illustrates the role of kinship ties and the kin-work of women of color in the struggle to maintain families in nineteenth-century America.

Marriage is one kind of kinship relation. But, as Jessie Bernard points out in "The Two Marriages," the marriage relationship is experienced differently by men and women. In other words, marriage is a gendered institution. Karla B. Hackstaff examines how the gendered nature of marriage is reflected in the work of keeping a marriage together at a time when divorce is so prevalent. In "Wives' Marital Work in a Culture of Divorce," Hackstaff argues that husbands and wives share a belief in a "marital work ethic"—that is, the idea that good marriages take work—but she finds that they do not share equally in the work itself of maintaining a marriage. When marriages do not work, they often end in divorce. In "Divorced Parents and the Jewish Community," Nathalie Friedman provides a fresh look at how divorce, while disruptive to family life, can sometimes lead single parents toward an increased involvement in social, ethnic, or religious communities.

There is no reason, of course, that marriage must be between only two people (polygyny, polyandry, and group marriage are some alternative forms) or that marriage must be between a man and woman, although that has been the dominant pattern in this country. The question of whether gay and lesbian couples should be able to marry legally is one that is debated within lesbian and gay communities as well as by people outside those communities. In the section "On Marriage and Divorce," we have included three chapters that present different facets of this discussion. Thomas B. Stoddard presents one argument in "Why Gay People Should Seek the Right to Marry," while Paula L. Ettelbrick, in "Since When Is Marriage a Path to Liberation?" argues that marriage for gays and lesbians means assimilation into mainstream life and a retreat from the struggle for recognition of a wide variety of family relationships. Phyllis Burke gives us a first-hand account of the 1991 Valentine's Day ceremony at City Hall in San Francisco when gay, lesbian, and heterosexual couples could, for the first time, register as "domestic partners" in San Francisco. In "Love Demands Everything," Burke conveys the political activism that resulted in the Domestic Partners Law, as well as the meaning and importance to the participants of their public commitment to their partners. The questions raised in these three chapters not only are relevant to same-sex marriages but are applicable to all marriages and to marriage as a social institution.

REFERENCES

Arendell, Terry. 1996. *Fathers and Divorce.* Thousand Oaks, Calif.: Sage.
Rich, Adrienne. 1976. *Of Woman Born: Motherhood as Experience and Institution.* New York: W. W. Norton.
Weitzman, Lenore J. 1985. *The Divorce Revolution: The Unexpected Social and Economic Consequences for Women and Children in America.* New York: Free Press.

Section A

Mothering, Motherhood, and Mothers

Chapter 20

Why Women Mother

NANCY J. CHODOROW

Mothers are women, of course, because a mother is a female parent, and a female who is a parent must be adult, hence must be a woman. Similarly, fathers are male parents, are men. But we mean something different when we say that someone mothered a child than when we say that someone fathered her or him. We can talk about a man "mothering" a child, if he is this child's primary nurturing figure, or is acting in a nurturant manner. But we would never talk about a woman "fathering" a child, even in the rare societies in which a high-ranking woman may take a wife and be the social father of her wife's children. In these cases we call her the child's social father, and do not say that she fathered her child. Being a mother, then, is not only bearing a child—it is being a person who socializes and nurtures. It is being a primary parent or caretaker. So we can ask, why are mothers women? Why is the person who routinely does all those activities that go into parenting not a man?

The question is important. Women's mothering is central to the sexual division of labor. Women's maternal role has profound effects on women's lives, on ideology about women, on the reproduction of masculinity and sexual inequality, and on the reproduction of particular forms of labor power. Women as mothers are pivotal actors in the sphere of social reproduction. As Engels and Marxist feminists, Lévi-Strauss and feminist anthropologists, Parsons and family theorists point out, women find their primary social location within this sphere.

Most sociological theorists have either ignored or taken as unproblematic this sphere of social reproduction, despite its importance and the recognition by some theorists, such as Engels, of its fundamental historical role.[1] As a consequence of ignoring this sphere, most sociological theorists have ignored women, who have been the central figures within it.

Engels helps us to understand this omission through his emphasis on the shift away from kinship-based forms of material production in modern societies. All societies contain both means of producing material subsistence and means of organizing procreation. Earlier societies (and contemporary "primitive" societies) were centered on kinship relations. Production and reproduction were organized according to the rules of kinship. This does not mean that the relations of production were based entirely on actual biological and affinal ties. In contemporary primitive societies, a kinship idiom can come to describe and incorporate whatever productive relations develop.

In modern societies, ties based on kinship no longer function as important links among people in the productive world, which becomes organized more and more in nonkinship market and class relations. Moreover, the relations of material production, and the extended public and political ties and associations—the state, finally—which these relations make possible, dominate and define family relations—the sphere of human reproduction. Many aspects of reproduction are taken over by extrafamiliar institutions like schools. Kinship, then, is progressively stripped of its functions and its ability to organize the social world.[2]

Because of their location within and concern with Western capitalist society, most major social theories have made the recognition of this major historical transformation fundamental to their theories. They have, as a consequence, developed theories which focus on nonfamilial political, economic, and communal ties and have treated familial relations only to point out their declining importance.*

---

*Thus, Durkheim describes the shift from mechanical to organic solidarity. Tönnies distinguishes *gemeinschaft* and *gesellschaft* societies. Weber discusses increasing rationalization and the rise of bureaucracy and market relations. Parsons distinguishes particularistic, ascribed, affective role relationships from those based on universalistic, achieved, and nonaffective criteria. Marx gives an account of the way capitalist market relations increasingly dominate all social life.

This historical transformation also reinforces a tendency in everyday discourse. Social theorists, like societal members, tend to define a society and discuss its social organization in terms of what men do, and where men are located in that society.

It is apparent, however, that familial and kinship ties and family life remain crucial for women. The organization of these ties is certainly shaped in many ways by industrial capitalist development (though the family retains fundamental precapitalist, preindustrial features—that women mother, for instance). However, as production has moved out of the home, reproduction has become even more immediately defining and circumscribing of women's life activities and of women themselves.

Some theorists do investigate the family. Parson's concern with the "problem of order" (what accounts for the persistence of social structures over time) and that of the Frankfurt Institute with the reproduction of capitalist relations of production and ideology have led both, in their attempts to understand social reproductive processes, to turn to the family as an area for sociological inquiry.[3] Feminist theorists, including Engels and Charlotte Perkins Gilman,[4] early recognized the family as a central agent of women's oppression as well as the major institution in women's lives. Anthropological theory also, in its concern with societies in which social ties for both men and women are largely defined through kinship, has developed an extensive and sophisticated analysis of kinship and the organization of gender—of rules of descent, marriage rules, residence arrangements, variations in household and family organization, and so forth. Consequently, anthropological theory has informed much family theory, including some feminist theories.[5]

Most of these theories see women's mothering as central. While understanding the importance of this mothering for social reproduction, however, they do not take it as in need of explanation. They simply assume that it is socially, psychologically, and biologically natural and functional. They do not question and certainly do not explain the reproduction of mothering itself either cross-culturally or within modern societies. They understand how women as mothers currently produce men with particular personalities and orientations, and how women's social location and the sexual division of labor generate other features of the social and economic world and of ideology about women. But they do not inquire about how women themselves are produced, how women continue to find themselves in a particular social and economic location.

The Argument from Nature

Several assumptions underlie this surprising omission. The most prevalent assumption among nonfeminist theorists is that the structure of parenting is biologically self-explanatory. This assumption holds that what seems universal is instinctual, and that what is instinctual, or has instinctual components, is inevitable and unchanging. Women's mothering as a feature of social structure, then, has no reality separate from the biological fact that women bear children and lactate. These social scientists reify the social organization of gender and see it as a natural product rather than a social construct.

Another explanation from nature is bio-evolutionary. This explanation holds that women are primary parents *now* because they always have been. It assumes that the sexual division of labor—for whatever reason—was the earliest division of labor and was simply perpetuated; or that the sexual division of labor was necessary for species survival in the earliest human communities; or that this species survival division of labor is now built

biologically into human sexual dimorphism. In all cases, the implication is that the mode of reproduction of mothering is unchanging and retains the form of its earliest origins. These accounts argue that women's mothering is, or has been, functional—that children, after all, have been reared—and often imply that what is and has been ought to be—that women ought to mother.

Women's mothering, then, is seen as a natural fact. Natural facts, for social scientists, are theoretically uninteresting and do not need explanation. The assumption is questionable, however, given the extent to which human behavior is not instinctually determined but culturally mediated. It is an assumption in conflict with most social scientists' insistence on the social malleability of biological factors, and it also conflicts with the general reluctance of social scientists to explain existing social forms simply as relics of previous epochs.

In contrast to these assumptions, it seems to me that we must always raise as problematic any feature of social structure, even if—and perhaps especially because—it seems universal. In the case at hand, we are confronted with a sexual division of labor in which women parent, which is reproduced in each generation and in all societies. We must understand this reproduction in order to understand women's lives and the sociology of gender. Why men by and large do not do primary parenting, and women do, is a centrally interesting sociological question.

We must question all assumptions which use biological claims to explain social forms, given the recent rise to prominence of sociobiology and the historically extensive uses of explanations allegedly based on biological sex (or race) differences to legitimate oppression and inequality. That there are undeniable genetic, morphological, and hormonal sex differences which affect our physical and social experiences and are (minimally) the criteria according to which a person's participation in the sexual division of labor and membership in a gender-differentiated world are assigned only makes this task more necessary. . . .

Biological sex differences can be found, but these remain hard to define with clarity. Societies, moreover, make of these biological variations two and only two genders. On the basis of presumed biology, they pronounce all infants male or female at birth, assume that the social fact of two and only two genders is isomorphic with biology, and elaborate their social organization of gender on this basis.

Given how difficult it is to articulate exactly what biological sex differences themselves consist in, it is not surprising that claims about the biological bases of sex differences in *behavior* are difficult to substantiate or even to formulate. We are, of course, biological beings, and our embodiment needs accounting for. Women's physiological experiences—pregnancy, menstruation, parturition, menopause, lactation—are certainly powerful (though it is important to bear in mind that either by choice or involuntarily all women do not have all these experiences). In our society, and in many others, they are also given strong meaning socially and psychologically.[6] There is psychological input into these biological experiences, moreover. Menstruation is affected by stress, women have "false pregnancies," and in societies that practice couvade men's bellies may swell as their wife's pregnancy comes to term. Lactation varies not only with individual emotions and attitudes, but in whole societies the lactation rate can change drastically in a short period of time.[7]

I do not question the reality of these biological experiences. Nor do I mean to raise questions about what constitutes "good-enough parenting" (to vary a phrase of psychoanalyst D. W. Winnicott)[8] or whether children need constant, predictable care from people with whom they have a primary relationship (I believe they do). What I wish to question is whether there is a biological basis in women for caretaking capacities specifically and whether *women* must perform whatever parenting children need.

To evaluate arguments that women's mothering is natural, we must distinguish among a number of issues which are often confused in the literature. First, we should separate child *care* from child*bearing*, nurturing *as an activity* from pregnancy and parturition. Most accounts assume that a child's primary parent, or mother, is the woman who has borne that child. Second, we want to know if there is a biological basis for biological mothers to care for their own newborn and what this consists in. If there is a biological or instinctual basis for parenting triggered by pregnancy, parturition, or lactation, what is its actual timespan? Does it extend into an infant's first months, years, throughout its childhood? Third, given that there are sometimes "substitute mothers," we want to know whether it is biologically more natural for a woman who has not borne the child in need of care than for a man to provide this child care. Do women have an instinctual propensity, or biological suitedness, for mothering which is not triggered by the experiences of pregnancy, parturition, or lactation? Finally, we want to evaluate the biological-instinctual basis for claims that women ought to mother. Such claims, again, could argue either that women are harmed by not parenting, or that infants are harmed by not being parented by *women*.

One explanation for women's mothering is a functional-cum-bioevolutionary account of the sexual division of labor put forth mainly by anthropologists, who combine a functionalist account of contemporary gathering and hunting societies (closest to the original human societies) and an evolutionary explanation of the "origins of man." These accounts may argue that men's greater agility, strength, speed, and aggressiveness made it natural for them to hunt, and that women therefore gathered and reared children.[9] Alternately, they rely on the demands of pregnancy and child care itself. They argue that lactating women need to be near their nursing infants for a large part of the time, and that women's pregnancy and lactation made it inefficient and/or dangerous to them, to the children they carried in the womb or on the hip, and to the group at large, for them to hunt.[10]

Most evolutionary-functionalist arguments do not argue that women have greater mothering capacities than men apart from lactation, though they may argue (and this argument is questionable as a generalization about all men as opposed to all women) that men's biology is more appropriate to hunting. Rather, they argue that men's not caring for children was convenient and probably necessary for survival in gathering and hunting bands:

> With the long years that it takes for the human child to develop and learn adult roles and skills, once gathering and hunting had developed as a major adaptive stance, there was no other way for the division to have evolved except between males and females. There is no need to posit special "killer" or "maternal" instincts in males and females to explain the assignment of these roles.[11]

Children and old people, unlike men, played a major part in caring for children. Moreover, these societies probably spaced childbirths to enable women to carry out their other work.

One major bioevolutionary account argues that women have greater maternal capacities than men as a result of the prehistoric division of labor. Sociologist Alice Rossi asserts that the sexual division of labor was not only essential to gatherer-hunter group survival, but that *because* it was essential, it has become built into human physiology.* Reproductive success went to females capable of bearing and rearing the young, gathering and hunting small game. These capacities (not only maternal capacities, but the manual dexterity, endurance, and persistence required for gathering and for hunting small animals) are not built genetically into women: "[We] *are still genetically equipped only with an ancient mammalian primate heritage that evolved largely through adaptations appropriate to much earlier times.*"[12] I discuss the evidence for maternal instincts in women more fully further on, but in order to further evaluate the evolutionary account it is necessary to address some of Rossi's claims here.

There are two major flaws in Rossi's account. One is that she never provides satisfactory evidence for a maternal instinct in the first place. Rossi refers to common "unlearned responses"[13] to infants in mothers, and to studies showing that the earlier and longer the contact between infant and mother, the greater their attachment at the end of the first month, but the studies she cites investigated only mothers and their own infants. They did not investigate whether other women, men, or children have similar or different responses to infants; whether the maternal responses they discuss are found universally—surely a necessary first step toward arguing for innateness; or whether attachment develops between anyone else and infant, given prolonged and early contact. Moreover, Rossi does not provide any evidence or argument that the maternal responses she discusses are unlearned rather than learned. The evidence suggests only that

_____

*I discuss this article at some length, because of the centrality of the issue to feminist research, and because Rossi herself has been an important feminist spokeswoman.

these responses are common to all the women studied. But commonality is not evidence about the origins of such behavior. Rossi also cites studies of monkeys who have been separated from their mothers as evidence of the harm of *mother*-infant separation, without mentioning the difficulties in extrapolating conclusions about humans from studies of monkeys or pointing out that the monkeys were not provided with anything verging on equivalent substitute relationships or care. She asserts, finally, against the anthropological evidence, "that little or no cultural variation can be found in the physical proximity and emotional closeness of the mother and the infant in the early months following birth.[14]

Rossi makes only one claim deriving from maternal hormones. She mentions that infant crying stimulates biological mothers to secrete the hormone ocytocin, leading to uterine contractions and nipple erection preparatory to nursing. However, she neither argues nor provides evidence that this ocytocin stimulation leads to any of the features other than lactation that go into infant care or mother-infant bonding (nor has she looked for studies of ocytocin production in women who are not lactating or in men—a not far-fetched suggestion, since persons of both genders produce some amount of both "male" and "female" hormones).

Second, Rossi's assertion that social arrangements adaptive or necessary for group survival become genetically embedded goes unsupported in her account, and is most probably unsupportable in the unilateral causal form she gives it.[15] If there are genetic bases to particular forms of sociability or human social arrangements, these are of incredible complexity and involve the operation of hundreds of interacting genetic loci. There is no one-to-one correspondence between genes and behavior, as even Rossi herself points out, nor is there evidence that adaptive practices or practices necessary to species survival become genetically programmed simply because some such practices may be so.

Thus, we can safely conclude that the bio-evolutionary argument stands as an argument concerning the division of labor in gatherer-hunter societies, given the specifically incompatible requirements of child care and hunting, and not as an argument concerning maternal instinct or biology in general. . . .

Originally, and in contemporary gathering and hunting societies, the sexual division of labor in which women mother was necessary for group reproduction, for demographic and economic reasons. As long as basic subsistence was problematic, population small, social organization simple, and women spent much of their adult lives bearing or nursing children, it made sense that they should be largely responsible for older children and more associated with the domestic sphere than men.

However, these same conclusions are offered for situations where these conditions do not hold—for horticultural, fishing, or plow-agricultural societies, where men's work is not more dangerous than women's and does not require long periods of travel from home, where women and men are equally near home and work close to each other. The argument is allowed to stand for industrial societies like ours which do not need this division of labor for physical reproduction. In our society women do not spend most of their "childbearing years" bearing children, do not have to nurse, and in any case nurse for only a relatively few months. And work activities in the nonfamilial economy are compatible with the requirements of periodic nursing, even if organized and defined in ways which are not (coffee break, for instance, is excusable time off work, whereas nursing is not). It may even be the case today that this division of labor conflicts with the requirements of production, which in most industrial societies seems to be drawing women of all ages into the paid labor force.

It is not enough today to give an evolutionary-functionalist explanation for women's mothering, then, unless we include in our functional account the reproduction of a particular social *organization,* beyond species survival or unmediated technological requisites. This organization includes male dominance, a particular family system, and women's dependence on men's income. We should see the original sexual division of labor as a once necessary social form used by and modified by other social forms as these have developed and changed. The sexual division of labor in which women mother has new meaning and functions, and is no longer explicable as an outcome of biology or of the requirement of survival. The evolutionary-functionalist account does not provide a convincing argument grounded in biology for why women, or biological mothers, should or must provide parental care.

A second argument for women's mothering, put forth by psychoanalysts and assumed by many others—gynecologists and obstetricians, social scientists, physiologists and physiological psychologists—is that women have a mothering instinct, or maternal instinct, and that therefore it is "natural" that they mother, or even that they therefore *ought* to mother. These accounts sometimes imply that it is instinctual that biological mothers mother, sometimes assume that mothers will parent better than fathers or men for biological reasons, sometimes assume that because children need to be cared for biological mothers naturally care for them, and sometimes argue that women "need" to mother.

Psychoanalysts Alice and Michael Balint, for instance, speak of a "need" or "drive" to

mother following pregnancy—a "biological" or "instinctual" mother-infant mutuality, an "instinctive maternity"[16] and "interdependence of the reciprocal instinctual aims"[17] in which "what is libidinal satisfaction to one must be libidinal satisfaction to the other [and] the mother and child are equally satisfied in this condition."[18] Therese Benedek speaks of women's "primary reproductive drive"[19] and "instinctual need"[20] to fulfill her physiological and emotional preparedness for mothering. Winnicott suggests that holding the infant physically in her uterus leads to a mother's identification with the infant after it is born and therefore to "a very powerful sense of what the baby needs."[21] Rossi argues that women's maternal instinct has been genetically programmed as a result of past adaptive needs. . . .

When we evaluate claims for the instinctual or biological basis for parenting, it turns out that evidence is hard to find.[22] There is little research on humans, and none of it is direct. There is little on animals. Moreover, it is not clear that we can use animal evidence anyway, since human culture and intentional activity have to so large an extent taken over from what is instinctual in other animals.

Chromosomes do not provide a basis either for the wish for a child or for capacities for nurturant parental behavior. Researchers on genetic and hormonal abnormalities find that androgen-insensitive chromosomal males (XY males who will not respond to androgens either prenatally or postnatally, who are born with female-looking genitalia and reared unambiguously as girls) are equally preoccupied with doll play and fantasies about having children, equally want children, and are equally nurturant toward the infants they adopt as chromosally and hormonally normal females.[23] This is also true for females with XO chromosomal pattern (Turner's syndrome), who have no ovaries and therefore cannot bear children.

Hormonal differences may show a greater relation to maternal behavior, but ambiguously. In the case of humans, evidence comes indirectly from hormonal abnormalities. Androgen-insensitive genetic males reared as females, who are without female internal organs but who produce enough estrogen to bring about breast growth and feminization of body contours and bone structure at puberty, are in childhood as nurturant and preoccupied with children as normal females and, when they grow up, as good mothers to adopted children.*

Turner's syndrome females also develop an unambiguous female gender identity, and show no difference or slightly greater "femininity" in measures of maternalism and preoccupation with dolls, babies, and marriage than hormonally and chromosomally normal girls. XO females do not have gonadal hormones. They therefore do not develop a gender dimorphic central nervous system, and they do not have ovaries. But because all fetuses develop a female reproductive anatomy and genitalia in the absence of gonadal hormones, an XO baby looks like a girl; her lack of gonadal hormones is not noticeable until just before puberty. A Turner's syndrome baby is assigned and reared unambiguously as a girl, but she has at most trace elements of either sex's hormone. The maternal behavior and fantasies of marriage and babies in the case of Turner's syndrome girls cannot be a product of female hormones or a prenatally female differentiated brain.

Chromosomally female girls who have received abnormal quantities of androgens prenatally (either because of exogenously introduced progestin or because of endogenous

hormonal malfunction that is only treated after birth) provide a final example of the possible relationship between hormones and maternalism. They tend to be less interested in dolls, more "tomboyish," and less interested in full-time motherhood than hormonally normal girls.** In the case of girls with endogenous hormonal malfunction, they also have fewer fantasies and daydreams about marriage, pregnancy, and motherhood, though they do not exclude possibilities of marriage and children. They simply want other activities in addition. Similarly, adult women whose endogenous androgen production was not treated in childhood tended not to want full-time motherhood and did not fantasize or daydream about motherhood, although they often married and had children whom they breast-fed.

As all reports point out, these data on fetally androgenized females can be read as evidence either for hormonal or cultural determinims. Although they were reared as girls, the genitalia of fetally androgenized females are masculinized at birth. In the case of the adult women studied, their androgen production was never treated. In some of the childhood cases, sex was reassigned from boy to girl in infancy, or they had operations to create more feminized genitalia. In all cases, therefore, parents knew about their daughter's abnormalities. The evidence about them comes from self-report and mothers' reports. In some cases parents were

*They produce the same amount of estrogens (and androgens) as normal males, but because they cannot use the androgens they produce, their bodies develop in response to their much smaller level of estrogens.

**Measures of tomboyism in Money and Ehrhardt are highly culturally specific and sterotypic, and include factors like preference for athletics versus sedentary activity, self-assertion in a childhood dominance hierarchy and preference for playing with boys, as well as childhood disinterest in rehearsals of motherhood and putting marriage and romance second or equal to career achievement. Moreover, none of the girls studied in the controlled comparisons was over sixteen, so we do not know what their adult life outcomes were.

explicitly warned not to discourage tomboy-ishness for fear of counterreaction on their daughters' part, and there is no information provided on what the girls themselves knew or were told about themselves. All these fac-tors weaken the case for hormonal deter-minism, as does the fact that "tomboyism" was defined in culturally and historically specific ways. If fetal androgens are produc-ing "unfeminine" preferences, these prefer-ences are at variance with what would be considered unfeminine in a number of other societies.[24] Still, differences between fetally androgenized and normal females could be a product of hormonal difference or of differ-ence in treatment and socialization.

We can draw no unambiguous conclusions about the relation of hormones to maternal in-stincts or maternalism in humans from these studies. All the girls were reared in a society that socializes particular personalities and preferences in girls and boys. Parents and doc-tors, and perhaps the girls themselves, knew about the abnormalities of many prenatally androgenized girls and androgen-insensitive males reared as females and may well have re-acted to this knowledge in subtle or not-so-subtle ways. As Maccoby and Jacklin point out, however, even if we want to read these studies as supporting or even partially supporting a bi-ological argument, the conclusions we can draw say nothing about the effects of *female* hormones on maternal behavior, feelings or preferences. They suggest only that *male* hor-mones may suppress maternalism. . . .

All researchers on humans as well as on an-imals point out that infants activate maternal behavior in both nonparturient virgin fe-males and in males, as well as in parturient fe-males. Both virgin female and male rats show nurturant behavior to the young after several days of exposure to them, regardless of hor-monal priming (by contrast, a female who has just given birth is responsive immediately).

Similarly, many primate males routinely en-gage in some caretaking behavior. Even those primate males who do not routinely do care-taking often come to care for an infant if left alone with it in an experimental situation.

There have been almost no comparative studies of humans (again, I believe, because of most researchers' assumptions that women's maternal behavior is natural), though all writers assume that men can be nurturant and perform caretaking functions. One ongoing study reports that both men and women react similarly (as measured by pupil dilation) to infant sounds of pain and pleasure.[25] Money and Ehrhardt claim, though without support-ing evidence, that both men and women re-spond to the stimulus of a small infant or child, though women may be quicker to do so than men. Both males and females, they in-sist, can engage in parenting behavior. This behavior is not gender-dimorphic, even if prenatal androgens may partially inhibit it in men. Ehrhardt argues that the most we can conclude is that among mammals it is usually the biological mother who is "most attentive" to her offspring.[26] This conclusion is guarded and does not purport to explain the genesis of this greater attentiveness. Money and Ehrhardt are insistent about the postnatal malleability of dispositions and traits in men and women.

It may be that another basis for women's nurturance comes from exposure to new-borns.[27] Mothers who have been separated from their premature infants for the first few weeks after birth tend to smile less at their in-fants, to hold them less closely, and to touch them affectionately less than mothers of nor-mal infants or mothers of premature infants who were allowed to touch and hold these in-fants. Since fathers have not been studied in this context, we do not know if such contact would establish a similar bond with infants in men. Maccoby and Jacklin conclude,

Extrapolating from what is known about animals much lower than man, it would appear possible that the hormones associated with pregnancy, childbirth and lactation may contribute to a "readiness" to care for a young infant on the part of a woman who has just given birth. The animal studies also suggest, however, that contact with infants is a major factor in developing attachment and caretaking behavior in the juvenile and adult members of a species, and this is true for both individuals that have given birth and individuals (male or female) that have not.[28]

Whatever the hormonal input to human maternal behavior, it is clear that such hormones are neither necessary nor sufficient for it. Studies, and our daily experiences, show that nonparturient females and males can behave in nurturant ways toward infants and children, and can have nurturance called up in them. People who adopt children certainly want them as much as, and perhaps more than, some of those who have their own, and certainly behave in equally nurturant ways toward them. How a person parents, moreover, is to a large extent determined by childhood experiences and conflicts. No psychoanalyst, ethologist, or biologist would claim that instinct or biology *by themselves* generate women's nurturance. If we can extrapolate from Harlow's studies, we can conclude that mothering capacities and behavior in any *individual* higher primate presupposes particular developmental experiences.[29] Harlow studied mothering behavior in "unmothered" monkeys—monkeys who had been raised in a wire cage or with a cloth surrogate, but without their mother. He found them to range from extremely abusive to marginally adequate mothers of their first child. Those who were in the marginally adequate category had had some social experience, either at around one year or as a preadolescent and adolescent. We cannot infer definite conclusions about humans from Harlow's work. But Harlow's studies do imply that even if female hormones are called up during pregnancy and parturition, these are not enough to generate mothering capacities or cause mothering.

We can draw several conclusions concerning the biological basis of mothering. The cross-cultural evidence ties women to primary parenting because of their lactation and pregnancy functions, and not because of instinctual nurturance beyond these functions. This evidence also suggests that there can be a variety of other participants in child care. Children of both sexes, though more often girls, often perform caretaking functions in addition to women. The prehistoric reasons of species or group survival which tied women to children have not held for centuries and certainly no longer hold today. Women in contemporary society do not bear children throughout their childbearing years; there is almost no work incompatible with nursing (and bottle-feeding is available and widespread, either as a total source of food or for occasional feedings). Societies no longer need women's mothering for physical reproduction. The evolutionary-functional account does not explain why women mother today.

When we turn to the more directly biological evidence, we find no direct research on the hormonal basis of nurturance, as opposed to lactation, in humans. Indirect evidence, from persons with chromosomal and hormonal abnormalities, suggests that male hormones may partially inhibit maternal behavior, but the evidence can be read equally to suggest that they do not, whereas masculine socialization does. There is no evidence to show that female hormones or chromosomes make a difference in human maternalness, and there is substantial evidence that nonbiological mothers, children, and men can parent just as adequately as biological mothers and can feel just as nurturant.

The evidence from some animals (and it must be kept in mind that inference from animals to humans is highly problematic) shows that hormones directly connected to pregnancy, parturition, and lactation prime those animals for caretaking. It also shows that this priming lasts only for a certain period after parturition. This could be true in the case of humans as well. That is, there may be physiological processes in human females which in some sense "prepare" a woman for mothering her own newborn, but beyond lactation we have no evidence concerning what these might be. On the other side, the evidence from animals does not suggest that nonparturient females are any more nurturant than males, though they may be less aggressive.

Conclusions about the biological basis of parenting in humans can only be speculative. But the evidence from animals, plus observations of human parenting, allow us to conclude that the hormonal basis of nurturance in parturient females is limited. Even those who argue for physiological components to a woman's tie to her own newborn suggest that these last at most for the first few months of an infant's life. Benedek mentions the six-week period until the termination of the uterine involution, and the somewhat longer period until lactation ceases, and Winnicott suggests that the "projective identification" of the mother with her infant in the womb "lasts for a certain length of time after parturition, and then gradually loses significance."[30] This view accords with the animal evidence.

Even if androgens produce some sort of counterdisposition to parenting, fetally androgenized females become nurturant mothers just as do other females, and men can also be nurturant and respond to infants and children. There is, finally, no evidence to indicate that whatever disposition for parenting parturient women have prepares them for exclusive care of the infant. Nor is there anything to

explain *biologically* why women mother toddlers and older children, though the early exclusive relationship probably produces some *psychological* basis for this later mothering.

Even these conclusions must be qualified. First, and most significant, both experimental research on primates and clinical evidence on humans make clear that individual psychological factors affect the expression of whatever hormonal preparation for caretaking exists. Women who have just borne a child can be completely inadequate mothers, just as adoptive mothers can be completely adequate. We do not know what the hormonal bases of caretaking in humans are, or whether there are any at all. We do know that whatever these are, they are not enough to create nurturance, at least not in all women who give birth.

Second, the evidence from animals suggests that there is no hormonal or instinctual basis for mothering in females other than those who have borne a child. Caretaking behavior can be called up both with hormones and without in both males and nonparturient females. Nor can we argue that biological aggressiveness in human males prevents nurturance, since boys in many societies, and men in our own and elsewhere, can provide anything from occasional to extensive care of young children. It does not seem, if we exclude wet-nursing, that any biological evidence will be forthcoming to support the assumption that women must be "substitute mothers" rather than men.

Arguments from nature, then, are unconvincing as explanations for women's mothering as a feature of a social structure. Beyond the possible hormonal components of a woman's early mothering of her own newborn (and even these do not operate independently), there is nothing in parturient women's physiology which makes them particularly suited to later child care, nor is there any instinctual reason why they should be able to perform it. Nor is there anything biological or hormonal to differentiate a male "substitute mother" from a female one. The biological argument for women's mothering is based on facts that derive, not from our biological knowledge, but from our definition of the natural situation as this grows out of our participation in certain social arrangements. That women have the extensive and nearly exclusive mothering role they have is a product of a social and cultural translation of their childbearing and lactation capacities. It is not guaranteed or entailed by these capacities themselves.

The Role-Training Argument

Nonfeminist theorists do not inquire about the reproduction of mothering or of the social relations of parenting, and seem to assume biological inevitability. This is true whether or not they recognize the sociological significance of the family and women's role in social reproduction. Feminist writers have alternate explanations, sometimes made explicit, sometimes assumed, each pointing to some elements in the process by which women come to mother. Moreover, they do so without relying on biological assumptions. At the same time, they are profoundly limited.

One important tendency in the feminist literature looks (along with social psychologists) at role training or cognitive role learning. It suggests that women's mothering, like other aspects of gender activity, is a product of feminine role training and role identification. Girls are taught to be mothers, trained for nurturance, and told that they ought to mother. They are wrapped in pink blankets, given dolls and have their brothers' trucks taken away, learn that being a girl is not as good as being a boy, are not allowed to get dirty, are discouraged from

achieving in school, and therefore become mothers. They are barraged from early childhood well into adult life with books, magazines, ads, school courses, and television programs which put forth pronatalist and promaternal sex-stereotypes. They "identify" with their own mothers, as they grow up, and this identification produces the girl as a mother. Alternately, as those following cognitive-psychological trends would have it, girls choose to do "girl-things" and, I suppose, eventually "woman-things," like mothering, as a result of learning that they are girls. In this view, girls identify with their mothers as a result of learning that they are girls and wanting to be girl-like.[31]

Margaret Polatnick presents a different view, in specific disagreement with socialization theories. She asks not how women come to mother, but why men do not. Her explanation is in terms of power differences and social control. She takes men's power and women's powerlessness as a given, and suggests that men use their power to enforce the perpetuation of women's mothering: Men don't rear children because they don't *want* to rear children. (This implies, of course, that they're in a position to enforce their preferences)."[32] Her account goes on to show why people in our society who have power over others would choose not to parent. Parenting, as an unpaid occupation outside the world of public power, entails lower status, less power, and less control of resources than paid work. Women's mothering reinforces and perpetuates women's relative powerlessness.

All of these views share the assumption that women's mothering is a product of behavioral conformity and individual intention. An investigation of what mothering consists in helps to explain how it is perpetuated, and indicates the limitations of traditional socialization and social control explanations for the reproduction of mothering.

To begin with, women's mothering does not exist in isolation. It is a fundamental constituting feature of the sexual division of labor. As part of the sexual division of labor, it is structurally and causally related to other institutional arrangements and to ideological formulations which justify the sexual division of labor. Mothering also contributes to the reproduction of sexual inequality through its effects on masculine personality.

Women's mothering is not an unchanging transcultural universal. Although women, and not men, have primary responsibility for children, many features of this responsibility change. Family organization, child-care and child-rearing practices, and the relations between women's child care and other responsibilities change in response particularly to changes in the organization of production. Women's role as we know it is an historical product. The development of industrial capitalism in the West entailed that women's role in the family become increasingly concerned with personal relations and psychological stability. Mothering is most eminently a psychologically based role. It consists in psychological and personal experience of self in relationship to child or children.

As culture and personality research has demonstrated, an important element in the reproduction of social relations and social structure is the socialization of people with psychological capacities and commitments appropriate to participation in these relations and structures. In an industrial late-capitalist society, "socialization" is a particularly psychological affair, since it must lead to the assimilation and internal organization of generalized capacities for participation in a hierarchical and differentiated social world, rather than to training for a specific role.[33] Production, for instance, is more efficient and profitable when workers develop a willing and docile personality. In the last analysis,

however, it is possible to extract labor by coercion (and it is certainly the case that there is some coercive element in needing to enter work relations in the first place).

The use of coercion is not possible in the case of mothering. Clinical research shows that behavioral conformity to the apparent specific physical requirements of infants—keeping them fed and clean—is not enough to enable physiological, let alone psychological, growth in an infant.[34] Studies of infants in understaffed institutions where perfunctory care is given, and of infants whose caretakers do not hold them or interact with them, show that these infants may become mildly depressed, generally withdrawn, psychotically unable to relate, totally apathetic and, in extreme cases, may die. Infants need affective bonds and a diffuse, multifaceted, ongoing personal relationship to caretakers for physical and psychological growth.*

A concern with parenting, then, must direct attention beyond behavior. This is because parenting is not simply a set of behaviors, but participation in an interpersonal, diffuse, affective relationship. Parenting is an eminently psychological role in a way that many other roles and activities are not. "Good-enough mothering" ("good-enough" to socialize a nonpsychotic child) requires certain relational capacities which are embedded in personality and a sense of self-in-relationship.

Given these requirements, it is evident that the mothering that women do is not some-

---

*I am not talking about "maternal deprivation," as it is conventionally labeled, which implies separation from or loss of the biological or social *mother*, or that *she herself* is not providing adequate care. What is at issue is the *quality of care*, and not who provides it: "The notion that the biological mother by virtue of being the biological mother is capable of caring for her child is without foundation";[35] "from the child's point of view, it matters little what sex mother is."[36]

thing that can be taught simply by giving a girl dolls or telling her that she ought to mother. It is not something that a girl can learn by behavioral imitation, or by deciding that she wants to do what girls do. Nor can men's power over women explain women's mothering. Whether or not men in particular or society at large—through media, income distribution, welfare policies, and schools—enforce women's mothering, and expect or require a woman to care for her child, they cannot require or force her to provide adequate parenting unless she, *to some degree* and *on some unconscious or conscious level*, has the capacity and sense of self as maternal to do so.*

Role training, identification, and enforcement certainly have to do with the acquisition of an appropriate gender role. But the conventional feminist view, drawn from social or cognitive psychology, which understands feminine development as explicit ideological instruction or formal coercion, cannot in the case of mothering be sufficient. In addition, explanations relying on behavioral conformity do not account for the tenacity of self-definition, self-concept, and psychological need to maintain aspects of traditional roles which continue even in the face of ideological shifts, counterinstruction, and the lessening of masculine coercion which the women's movement has produced.

*My argument here is extrapolated from clinical findings on the nature of mothering. A good empirical evaluation of the argument could be drawn from investigation of black slave women's mothering of slaveowners' children or from other situations of enforced parenting by slaves, serfs, or servants. (White) folk wisdom has it that slave nurses, although in every fundamental sense coerced, were excellent mothers, whose charges remembered them fondly. Kovel speaks to some outcomes for white men of this situation, but to oedipal-sexual issues rather than to issues concerning the development of self and general relational capacities in white children of both genders.[37]

A second deficiency of role-learning and social control explanations for the reproduction of mothering is that they rely on individual intention—on the part of socializers, of girls who want to do girl-things or be like their mothers, and on the part of men who control women. There is certainly an intentional component to gender role socialization in the family, in schools, in the media. However, social reproduction comes to be independent of individual intention and is not caused by it. There are several aspects to social reproduction, all of which apply in the case of the reproduction of mothering.

Practices become institutionalized in regularized, nonarbitrary ways. Aspects of society—social and economic relations, institutions, values and ideology—develop their own logic and autonomy and come to mutually interact with and maintain one another. Aspects of society are not newly created every day, although they do develop historically through the intended activity of people. The conditions people live in are given as the historical outcome of previous human social activity, which itself has exhibited some regularity and consistency.

In the case of a mother-child relationship, there is an interactive base of expectations of continuity of relationship. This interactive base develops once a woman begins to care for a particular child, and usually includes gratification as well as frustration for both the child and the mother. More generally women's mothering as an organization of parenting is embedded in and fundamental to the social organization of gender. In any historical period, women's mothering and the sexual division of labor are also structurally linked to other institutions and other aspects of social organization. In industrial capitalist societies, women's mothering is central to the links between the organization of gender—in particular the family system—and economic organization. Sexual inequality is itself embedded in and perpetuated by the organization of these institutions, and, is not reproduced according to or solely because of the will of individual actors.

Intentional socialization theories, just as they are generally not sufficient to explain social reproduction, are insufficient to explain the reproduction of the social organization of gender and its major features. The social organization of gender, in its relation to an economic context, has depended on the continuation of the social relations of parenting. The reproduction of these social relations of parenting is not reducible to individual intention but depends on all the arrangements which go into the organization of gender and the organization of the economy.

These institutions create and embody conditions that require people to engage in them. People's participation further guarantees social reproduction. Marx gives an example in the case of capitalism: "Capitalist production, therefore, of itself reproduces the separation between labour-power and the means of labour. It thereby perpetuates the condition for exploiting the labourer. It incessantly forces him to sell his labour-power in order to live, and enables the capitalist to purchase labour-power in order that he may enrich himself. It is no longer a mere accident, that capitalist and labourer confront each other in the market as buyer and seller."[38] Or, for instance, Lévi-Strauss describes a strongly enforced sexual division of labor as a condition for the reproduction of heterosexual marriage:

> Generally speaking it can be said that, among the so-called primitive tribes, there are no bachelors, simply for the reason that they could not survive. One of the strongest field recollections of this writer was his meeting, among the Bororo of central Brazil, a man about thirty years old: unclean, ill-fed, sad, and lonesome.

When asked if the man were seriously ill, the natives' answer came as a shock: what was wrong with him?—nothing at all, he was just a bachelor. And true enough, in a society where labor is systematically shared between man and woman and where only the married status permits the man to benefit from the fruits of woman's work, including delousing, body painting, and hairplucking as well as vegetable food and cooked food (since the Bororo woman tills the soil and makes pots), a bachelor is really only half a human being. . . .[39]

> The sexual division of labor . . . has been explained as a device to make the sexes mutually dependent on social and economic grounds, thus establishing clearly that marriage is better than celibacy. . . . The principle of sexual division of labor establishes a mutual dependency between the sexes compelling them thereby to perpetuate themselves and found a family.[40]

In the case of mothering, the economic system has depended for its reproduction on women's reproduction of particular forms of labor power in the family. At the same time, income inequality between men and women makes it more rational, and even necessary, in any individual conjugal family for fathers, rather than mothers, to be primary wage-earners. Therefore, mothers, rather than fathers, are the primary caretakers of children and the home.

Legitimating ideologies themselves, as well as institutions like schools, the media, and families which perpetuate ideologies, contribute to social reproduction. They create expectations in people about what is normal and appropriate and how they should act. Society's perpetuation requires that *someone* rear children, but our language, science, and popular culture all make it very difficult to separate the need for care from the question of who provides that care. It is hard to separate out parenting activities, usually performed by women and particularly by biological mothers, from women themselves.

Finally, people themselves need to be reproduced both daily and generationally. Most theoretical accounts agree that women as wives and mothers reproduce people—physically in their housework and child care, psychologically in their emotional support of husbands and their maternal relation to sons and daughters. If we accept this view, we have to ask who reproduces wives and mothers. What is hidden in most accounts of the family is that women reproduce *themselves* through their own daily housework. What is also often hidden in generalizations about the family as an emotional refuge is that in the family as it is currently constituted no one supports and reconstitutes women affectively and emotionally—either women working in the home or women working in the paid labor force. This was not always the case. In a previous period, and still in some stable working-class and ethnic communities, women did support themselves emotionally by supporting and reconstituting *one another*.[41] However, in the current period of high mobility and familial isolation, this support is largely removed, and there is little institutionalized daily emotional reconstitution of mothers. What there is depends on the accidents of a particular marriage, and not on the carrying out of an institutionalized support role.[42] There is a fundamental asymmetry in daily reproduction. Men are socially and psychologically reproduced by women, but women are reproduced (or not) largely by themselves.

We also need to understand the intergenerational reproduction of mothers. Parsons and theorists of the Frankfurt Institute have added significantly to our total picture of social reproduction by providing a model of the reproduction of social relations across generations. They argue that in industrial capitalist society, generational reproduction occurs through the creation in the family of men workers with particular personalities and orientations to authority. These social theorists have attempted to integrate a theory of large-scale social-cultural structure and its institutional and ideological reproduction with a theory of the way this structure reproduces itself through everyday interpersonal experiences and personality development in its members. These theorists of social reproduction describe how members of a society come to be (in Parsons's terminology) motivated to comply with role expectations. They describe how the structural organization of that institution in which people grow up, the family, entails that people develop personalities which tend to guarantee that they will get gratification or satisfaction from those activities which are necessary to the reproduction of the larger social structure. In Max Horkheimer's terms, "In so far as the continuance of all social forms goes, the dominant force is not insight but human patterns of reaction which have become stabilized in interaction with a system of cultural formations on the basis of the social life process."[43] And Parsons reiterates his claim: "The integration of a set of common value patterns with the internalized need-disposition structure of the constituent personalities is the core phenomenon of the dynamics of social systems.[44]

Parsons and Frankfurt theorists have investigated the family, and especially the organization of parenting. Furthermore, in their concern to develop a theory of socialization that relies on institutional and structural mechanisms rather than on individual intention, they have turned to psychoanalysis "as a 'psychology of family' pure and simple"[45] for their method of inquiry. They have begun to develop a psychoanalytic sociology of social reproduction.

The empirical efforts of Parsons and the Frankfurt theorists, however, have been directed toward the reproduction of relations of production, and to men as workers. They, as well as Freudian social theorists,[46] and Marxist feminists[47] after them, have been concerned with the way the family and women socialize *men* into capitalist society.* They have developed an extensive and important analysis of the relation of masculine psychological development to capitalist achievement or properly submissive or bureaucratized work behavior, as well as to the relation of masculine attitudes to women and femininity.** But they have not discussed feminine development at all.

The account which follows takes these theories as methodological models and extends their psychoanalytic sociology. I do not mean to deny the basic differences between the theories of Parsons and critical theorists such as Horkheimer. These differences are both methodological and political—but it is their political differences which have often obscured the similarities of their descriptions and their similar use of psychoanalysis. Empirically, both accounts describe how the development of industrial capitalism has affected family structure and personality. This is phrased in critical theory in terms of the decline of paternal authority and the father's role in the home, in Parsons's case in terms of the overwhelming importance of the mother. These changes have in turn affected masculine development: men's orientation to authority and their malleability as labor power have shifted.

Politically, Parsons is basically uncritical of the society he describes. Parsons focuses on the problem of order—so do critical theorists, but in Parsons's case, it always sounds as though he wants to understand order to contribute toward its maintenance. For the critical theorists, the problem of order is posed as the problem of understanding historically specific forms of domination. Parsons's theory, while treating culture, social organization, personality, and biology, tends to define society in terms of its value system, or culture. Critical theorists generally accord primary significance to the social organization of production, and relate values and particular forms of domination to this organization.

Finally, critical theorists like Horkheimer focus on disruptive elements which undermine the smooth reproduction of functional relationships. For Parsons, the family reproduces social and economic organization. For critical theorists, it both reproduces and undermines these forms. While Parsons makes a major contribution to our understanding of social reproduction, and especially to the part played by personality, it is evident that there are contradictions in the contemporary organization of gender and the family—ways in which expectations created in the family cannot be fulfilled, strains in women's and men's and parents' and children's roles and relationships, incompatible needs for women as child-rearers and workers in the labor force.

In *The Reproduction of Mothering* I show how the structure of parenting reproduces itself. Like the psychoanalytic sociologists I discuss, I rely on psychoanalytic theory as an analysis of family structure and social reproduction. Psychoanalysis shows us how the family division of labor in which women mother gives socially and historically specific meaning to gender itself. This engendering of men and women with particular personalities, needs, defenses, and capacities creates the condition for and contributes to the repro-

---

*Social psychological studies of the effect of "father absence" (and consequent maternal ambivalence, seductiveness, or overprotection) on development also focus almost entirely on male development.[48]

**They discuss in this context the oedipus complex, the importance and effects of maternal manipulation of masculine erotism, father absence and the decline of paternal authority, masculine repression and sublimation.

duction of this same division of labor. The sexual division of labor both produces gender differences and is in turn reproduced by them.

The psychoanalytic account shows not only how men come to grow away from their families and to participate in the public sphere. It shows also how women grow up to have both the generalized relational capacities and needs and how women and men come to create the kinds of interpersonal relationships which make it likely that women will remain in the domestic sphere—in the sphere of re-production—and will in turn mother the next generation. Women's mothering as an institutionalized feature of family life and of the sexual division of labor reproduces itself cyclically. In the process, it contributes to the reproduction of those aspects of the sexual sociology of adult life which grow out of and relate to the fact that women mother.

I suggested earlier that women's mothering was reproduced on a number of different levels. Because of the requirements of parenting, and particularly because of its contemporary, largely psychological form, the genesis of psychological mothering capacities and orientations in women is fundamental and conditional to all of these. The capacities and orientations I describe must be built into personality; they are not behavioral acquisitions. Women's capacities for mothering and abilities to get gratification from it are strongly internalized and psychologically enforced and are built developmentally into the feminine psychic structure. Women are prepared psychologically for mothering through the developmental situation in which they grow up, and in which women have mothered them.

Most conventional accounts of gender-role socialization rely on individual intention and behavioral criteria, which do not adequately explain women's mothering. Psychoanalysis, by contrast, provides a systemic, structural account of socialization and social reproduction. It suggests that major features of the social organization of gender are transmitted in and through those personalities produced by the structure of the institution—the family—in which children become gendered members of society.

NOTES

1. See Engels, 1884, *Origin of the Family.*
2. For some empirical elucidation of Engels's theory according to this reading, see Hartmann, 1976, "Capitalism, Patriarchy"; and Reiter, ed., 1975, *Toward an Anthropology of Women.*
3. Parsons, 1942, "Age and Sex"; 1943, "The Kinship System"; 1964, *Social Structure and Personality*; Parsons and Bales, 1955, *Family, Socialization and Interaction Process*; Horkheimer, 1936, "Authority and the Family"; Frankfurt Institute for Social Research, 1972, *Aspects of Sociology*; Mitscherlich, 1963, *Society Without the Father.*
4. Gilman, 1898, *Women and Economics.*
5. On family theory influenced by anthropology, see Coser, ed., 1974, *The Family.* On feminist theory influenced by anthropology, see Mitchell, 1974, *Psychoanalysis and Feminism*; and Hartmann, 1976, "Capitalism, Patriarchy." On feminist theory within anthropology, see Rosaldo and Lamphere, eds., 1974, *Woman, Culture and Society*; and Reiter, ed., 1975, *Toward an Anthropology.*
6. For (very different) readings of the psychological and psychosocial significance of pregnancy and childbirth, see for example Bibring, 1959, "Some Considerations"; Bibring et al., 1961, "Study of the Psychological Processes" and four contributions by Benedek; 1949, "Psychosomatic Implications"; 1952, *Psychosexual Functions in Women*; 1956, "Psychobiological Aspects of Mothering"; and 1959, "Parenthood as a Developmental Phase."
7. Newton and Newton, 1972, "Psychologic Aspects of Lactation."
8. Winnicott, 1965, *Maturational Processes.*
9. Lee and DeVore, eds., 1968, *Man the Hunter*; Tiger, 1969, *Men in Groups*; and Rossi, 1977, "Biosocial Perspective."

10. See Barry, Bacon, and Child, 1957, "A Cross-Cultural Survey"; D'Andrade, 1966, "Sex Differences and Cultural Institutions"; Friedl, 1975, *Women and Men*; Brown, 1970, "Note on the Division of Labor"; and Lancaster, 1976, "Sex Roles."

11. Lancaster, 1976, "Sex Roles," p. 47.

12. Rossi, 1977, "Biosocial Perspective," p. 3.

13. Ibid., p. 6.

14. Ibid., p. 24. See, for the anthropological counterevidence to Rossi's claim, bibliographic listings under Margaret Mead, Beatrice B. Whiting, and John W. M. Whiting.

15. Eileen van Tassell (personal communication); Conner, 1972, "Hormones."

16. Balint, 1939, "Love for the Mother."

17. Ibid., p. 101.

18. Balint, 1961, "Contribution to the Symposium," p. 147.

19. Benedek, 1959, "Parenthood as a Developmental Phase," p. 394.

20. Benedek, 1949, "Psychosomatic Implications," p. 648.

21. Winnicott, 1960, "Theory of the Parent-Infant Relationship."

22. The following discussion comes from my reading and interpretation of Money and Ehrhardt, 1972, *Man and Woman*; Ehrhardt, 1973, "Maternalism"; Maccoby and Jacklin, 1974, *Psychology of Sex Differences*; Martin and Voorhies, 1975, *Female of the Species*; Harlow et al., 1970, "Maternal Behavior of Rhesus Monkeys"; Newton, 1955, *Maternal Emotions*; 1973, "Interrelationships"; Rossi, 1977, "A Biosocial Perspective"; Teitelbaum, ed., 1976, *Sex Differences*; and my review of Clellan S. Ford and Frank A. Beach, 1951, *Patterns of Sexual Behavior*; Beach, 1965, *Sex and Behavior*; Eibl-Eibesfeldt, 1970, *Ethology*; and Bernard, 1974, *The Future of Motherhood*.

23. All the evidence I point to on hormonal and chromosomal abnormalities comes from Money and Ehrhardt, 1972, *Man and Woman,* and Ehrhardt, 1973, "Maternalism."

24. Whiting, ed., 1963, *Six Cultures*; Whiting and Whiting, 1975, *Children of Six Cultures*; Mead, 1935, *Sex and Temperament in Three Primitive Societies*, and 1949, *Male and Female*; Chodorow, 1971, "Being and Doing."

25. Hess and Beck, as reported in Eibl-Eibesfeldt, 1970, *Ethology*, p. 438.

26. Ehrhardt, 1973, "Maternalism," p. 100.

27. See Leifer et al., 1973, "Effects of Mother-Infant Separation."

28. Maccoby and Jacklin, 1974, *Psychology*, p. 220.

29. Harlow et al., 1970, "Maternal Behavior."

30. Winnicott, 1960, "The Theory," p. 594.

31. For good examples of the tendency to explain the reproduction and maintenance of gender-role differentiation through consciously intended socialization and training, see Weitzman, 1975, "Sex-Role Socialization"; Freeman, 1971, "The Social Construction of the Second Sex"; and the journal *Sex Roles*. For investigations of propulsion (and seduction) into motherhood by media and ideology, see Bernard, 1974, *Future of Motherhood*; and Peck and Senderowitz, eds., 1974, *Pronatalism*. For an account of gender-role socialization as a product of a child's learning it is a girl or boy, see Kohlberg, 1966, "A Cognitive Developmental Analysis." For discussions of identification and gender-role learning, see Lynn, 1959, "A Note on Sex Differences," 1962, "Sex Role and Parent Identification"; Parsons and Bales, 1955, *Family*; Parsons, 1942, "Age and Sex"; Winch, 1962, *Identification and Its Familial Determinants*; Mischel, 1966, "A Social-Learning View," and 1970, "Sex Typing and Socialization."

32. Polatnick, 1973, "Why Men Don't Rear Children," p. 60.

33. See Parsons with White, 1961, "The Link Between Character and Society"; Parsons and Bales, 1955, *Family, Socialization*; Frankfurt Institute, 1972, *Aspects*; Reich, 1966, *Sex-Pol*; Slater, 1970, *Pursuit of Loneliness*, and 1974, *Earthwalk*; and Bennis and Slater, 1968, *The Temporary Society*; Bowles and Gintis, 1976, *Schooling in Capitalist America*; Edwards, 1975, "Social Relations of Production."

34. See Bowlby, 1951, *Maternal Care*; Mahler, 1968, *On Human Symbiosis*; Spitz, 1965, *First Year of Life*; and Winnicott, 1965, *Maturational Processes*.

35. Schaffer, 1977, *Mothering*, p. 103.

36. Ibid., p. 105. For another attempt to review research which separates out the various factors in-

volved in "maternal deprivation," see Rutter, 1972, *Maternal Deprivation Reassessed.*

37. Kovel, 1970, *White Racism.*

38. Marx, 1867, *Capital,* vol. 1, p. 577.

39. Lévi-Strauss, 1956, "The Family," p. 269.

40. Ibid., p. 277.

41. See, for example, Stack, 1975, *All Our Kin;* Young and Willmott, 1957, *Family and Kinship in East London.*

42. See Rubin, 1976, *Worlds of Pain,* for discussion of women and men in the contemporary isolated working-class family.

43. Horkheimer, 1936, "Authority," p. 67.

44. Parsons, 1951, *Social System,* p. 42.

45. Frankfurt Institute, 1972, *Aspects,* p. 133.

46. For example, Bakan, 1966, *Duality of Human Existence;* Mitscherlich, 1963, *Society Without the Father;* Slater, 1970, *Pursuit,* and 1974, *Earthwalk.*

47. Especially Morton, 1970, "A Woman's Work Is Never Done." Other Marxist feminist theorists also talk implicitly about the reproduction of male workers, but Morton is the only one to speak to the psychological dynamics I am discussing, rather than to physical reproduction.

48. See, for example, Burton and Whiting, 1961, "The Absent Father"; Whiting, Kluckhohn, and Anthony, 1958, "The Function of Male Initiation Rites at Puberty"; Levy, 1943, *Maternal Overprotection;* Slater, 1968, *The Glory of Hera,* 1970, *Pursuit,* and 1974, *Earthwalk;* Stephens, 1963, *Family in Cross-Cultural Perspective.* For exceptions, see Hetherington, 1972, "Effects of Father Absence," and 1973, "Girls Without Fathers"; Lynn, 1959, "A Note on Sex Differences," and 1962, "Sex Role and Parent Identification"; and Lynn and Sawrey, 1959, "The Effects of Father-Absence on Norwegian Boys and Girls"; and Biller's review (1971) of the literature on "fathering and female personality development"—one short chapter of the book, *Father, Child, and Sex Role.*

REFERENCES

Bakan, David, 1966, *The Duality of Human Existence: Isolation and Communion in Western Man.* Boston, Beacon Press.

Balint, Alice, 1939, "Love for the Mother and Mother-Love," pp. 91–108 in Michael Balint, ed., *Primary Love and Psycho-Analytic Technique.* New York, Liveright Publishing, 1965.

Balint, Michael, 1961, "Contribution to the Symposium on the Theory of the Parent-Infant Relationship," pp. 145–147 in 1965, *Primary Love and Psycho-Analytic Technique.* New York: Liveright Publishing.

Barry, Herbert, III, Margaret K. Bacon, and Irvin L. Child, 1957, "A Cross-Cultural Survey of Some Sex Differences in Socialization," *Journal of Abnormal and Social Psychology,* 55, no. 3, pp. 327–332.

Beach, Frank A., 1965, *Sex and Behavior.* New York, John Wiley.

Benedek, Therese, 1949, "Psychosomatic Implications of the Primary Unit, Mother-Child," *American Journal of Orthopsychiatry,* 19, no. 4, pp. 642–654.

———, 1952, *Psychosexual Functions in Women.* New York, Ronald Press.

———, 1956, "Psychobiological Aspects of Mothering," *American Journal of Orthopsychiatry,* 26, pp. 272–278.

———, 1959, "Parenthood as a Developmental Phase: A Contribution to the Libido Theory," *Journal of the American Psychoanalytic Association,* 7, no. 3, pp. 389–417.

Bennis, Warren G., and Philip E. Slater, 1968, *The Temporary Society.* New York, Harper and Row.

Bernard, Jessie, 1974, *The Future of Motherhood.* New York, Penguin Books.

Bibring, Grete, 1959, "Some Considerations of the Psychological Processes in Pregnancy," *Psychoanalytic Study of the Child,* 14, pp. 113–121.

Bibring, Grete L., Thomas F. Dwyer, Dorothy S. Huntington, and Arthur Valenstein, 1961, "A Study of the Psychological Processes in Pregnancy and of the Earliest Mother-Child Relationship," *Psychoanalytic Study of the Child,* 16, pp. 9–72.

Biller, Henry B., 1971, *Father, Child, and Sex Role.* Lexington, Mass., D.C. Heath.

Bowlby, John, 1951, *Maternal Care and Mental Health.* New York, Schocken Books, 1966.

Bowles, Samuel, and Herbert Gintis, 1976, *Schooling in Capitalist America: Educational Reform and the Contradictions of Economic Life.* New York, Basic Books.

Brown, Judith K., 1970, "A Note on the Division of Labor by Sex," *American Anthropologist*, 72, pp. 1073–1078.

Burton, Roger V., and John W. M. Whiting, 1961, "The Absent Father and Cross-Sex Identity," *Merrill-Palmer Quarterly of Behavior and Development*, 7, no. 2, pp. 85–95.

Chodorow, Nancy, 1971, "Being and Doing: A Cross-Cultural Examination of the Socialization of Males and Females," pp. 173–197 in Vivian Gornick and Barbara K. Moran, eds., *Woman in Sexist Society: Studies in Power and Powerlessness*. New York, Basic Books.

Conner, B. L., 1972, "Hormones, Biogenic Amines and Aggression," in Cymour Levine, ed., *Hormones and Behavior*. New York, Academic Press.

Coser, Rose Laub, ed., 1974, *The Family: Its Structures and Functions*. New York, St. Martin's Press.

D'Andrade, Roy, 1966, "Sex Differences and Cultural Institutions," pp. 173–204 in Eleanor E. Maccoby, ed., *The Development of Sex Differences*. Stanford, Stanford University Press.

Edwards, Richard C., 1975, "The Social Relations of Production in the Firm and Labor Market Structure," in Richard C. Edwards, Michael Reich, and David M. Gordon, eds., *Labor Market Segmentation*. Lexington, Mass., D. C. Heath.

Ehrhardt, Anke, 1973, "Maternalism in Fetal Hormonal and Related Syndromes," in Joseph Zubin and John Money, eds., *Contemporary Sexual Behavior: Critical Issues in the 1970's*. Baltimore, Johns Hopkins University Press.

Eibl-Eibesfeldt, Irenaus, 1970, *Ethology: The Biology of Behavior*. New York, Holt, Rinehart and Winston.

Engels, Frederick, 1884, *The Origin of the Family, Private Property, and the State*. New York, International Publishers, 1967.

Ford, Clellan S., and Frank A. Beach, 1951, *Patterns of Sexual Behavior*. New York, Harper and Row.

Frankfurt Institute for Social Research, 1972, *Aspects of Sociology*. Boston, Beacon Press.

Freeman, Jo, 1971, "The Social Construction of the Second Sex," pp. 123–141 in Michelle Garskof, ed., *Roles Women Play*. Belmont, Calif., Brooks/Cole Publishing.

Friedl, Ernestine, 1975, *Women and Men: An An-thropologist's View*. New York, Holt, Rinehart and Winston.

Gilman, Charlotte Perkins, 1898, *Women and Economics*. New York, Harper and Row, 1966.

Harlow, H. F., M. K. Harlow, R. O. Dodsworth, and G. L. Arling, 1970, "Maternal Behavior of Rhesus Monkeys Deprived of Mothering and Peer Associations in Infants," pp. 88–98 in Freda Rebelsky, ed., *Child Development and Behavior*. New York, Alfred A. Knopf.

Hartmann, Heidi, 1976, "Capitalism, Patriarchy, and Job Segregation by Sex," *Signs*, 1, no. 3, part 2, pp. 137–169.

Hetherington, E. M., 1972, "Effects of Father Absence on Personality Development in Adolescent Daughters," *Developmental Psychology*, 7, pp. 313–326.

———, 1973, "Girls Without Fathers," *Psychology Today*, 6, pp. 46–52.

Horkheimer, Max, 1936, "Authority and the Family," in 1972, *Critical Theory*. New York, Herder and Herder.

Kohlberg, Lawrence, 1966, "A Cognitive Developmental Analysis of Sex-Role Concepts and Attitudes," pp. 82–173 in E. Maccoby, ed., *The Development of Sex Differences*. Stanford, Stanford University Press.

Kovel, Joel, 1970, *White Racism: A Psychohistory*. New York, Vintage Books.

Lancaster, Jane Beckman, 1976, "Sex Roles in Primate Societies," pp. 22–61 in Michael S. Teitelbaum, ed., *Sex Differences*. New York, Anchor Books.

Lee, Richard, and Irven DeVore, eds., 1968, *Man the Hunter*. Chicago, Aldine.

Leifer, A. D., P. H. Leiderman, C. R. Barnett, and J. A. Williams, 1973, "Effects of Mother-Infant Separation on Maternal Attachment Behavior," in F. Rebelsky and L. Dormon, eds., *Child Development and Behavior*, 2nd ed. New York, Alfred A. Knopf.

Lévi-Strauss, Claude, 1956, "The Family," pp. 261–285 in Harry Shapiro, ed., *Man, Culture and Society*. London, Oxford University Press.

Levy, David, 1943, *Maternal Overprotection*. New York, Columbia University Press.

Lynn, David B., 1959, "A Note on Sex Differences in the Development of Masculine and Feminine

Identification," *Psychological Review,* 66, pp. 126–135.

——, 1962, "Sex Role and Parent Identification," *Child Development,* 33, pp. 555–564.

Lynn, David B., and W. L. Sawrey, 1959, "The Effects of Father-Absence on Norwegian Boys and Girls," *Journal of Abnormal and Social Psychology,* 59, pp. 258–262.

Maccoby, Eleanor, and Carol Jacklin, 1974, *The Psychology of Sex Differences.* Stanford, Stanford University Press.

Mahler, Margaret S., 1968, *On Human Symbiosis and the Vicissitudes of Individuation.* Vol. 1, *Infantile Psychosis.* New York, International Universities Press.

Martin, M. Kay, and Barbara Voorhies, 1975, *Female of the Species.* New York, Columbia University Press.

Marx, Karl, 1867, *Capital,* vol. 1. New York, International Publishers.

Mead, Margaret, 1935, *Sex and Temperament in Three Primitive Societies.* New York, William Morrow.

——, 1949, *Male and Female.* New York, Dell Publishing, 1968.

——, 1954, "Some Theoretical Considerations on the Problem of Mother-Child Separation," *American Journal of Orthopsychiatry,* 24, pp. 471–483.

——, 1962, "A Cultural Anthropologist's Approach to Maternal Deprivation," pp. 237–254 in 1966, *Maternal Care and Mental Health/Deprivation of Maternal Care.* New York, Schocken Books.

Mischel, Walter, 1966, "A Social-Learning View of Sex Differences in Behavior," pp. 56–81 in Eleanor E. Maccoby, ed., *The Development of Sex Differences.* Stanford, Stanford University Press.

——, 1970, "Sex Typing and Socialization," pp. 3–72 in Paul Mussen, ed., *Carmichael's Manual of Child Psychology,* 3rd ed., vol. 2.

Mitchell, Juliet, 1974, *Psychoanalysis and Feminism.* New York, Pantheon Books.

Mitscherlich, Alexander, 1963, *Society Without the Father: A Contribution to Social Psychology.* New York, Schocken Books, 1970.

Money, John, and Anke A. Ehrhardt, 1972, *Man and Woman, Boy and Girl.* Baltimore, Johns Hopkins University Press.

Morton, Peggy, 1970, "A Woman's Work Is Never Done," *Leviathan* 2, no. 1, pp. 32–37.

Newton, Niles, 1955, *Maternal Emotions: A Study of Women's Feelings Toward Menstruation, Pregnancy, Childbirth, Breast Feeding, Infant Care, and Other Aspects of Their Femininity.* Psychosomatic Medicine Monograph. New York, Paul Hoeber, Harper and Brothers.

——, 1973, "Interrelationships Between Sexual Responsiveness, Birth, and Breast Feeding," in Joseph Zubin and John Money, eds., *Contemporary Sexual Behavior: Critical Issues in the 1970's.* Baltimore, Johns Hopkins University Press.

Newton, Niles, and Michael Newton, 1972, "Psychologic Aspects of Lactation," pp. 277–284 in Judith M. Bardwick, ed., *Readings on the Psychology of Women.* New York, Harper and Row.

Parsons, Talcott, 1942, "Age and Sex in the Social Structure of the United States," in 1964, *Essays in Sociological Theory.* New York, Free Press.

——, 1943, "The Kinship System of the Contemporary United States," in 1964, *Essays in Sociological Theory.* New York, Free Press.

——, 1951, *The Social System.* New York, Free Press, 1964.

——, 1964, *Social Structure and Personality.* New York, Free Press, 1970.

Parsons, Talcott, and Robert F. Bales, 1955, *Family, Socialization and Interaction Process.* New York, Free Press.

Parsons, Talcott, with Winston White, 1961, "The Link Between Character and Society," in Parsons, 1964, *Social Structure and Personality.*

Peck, Ellen, and Judith Senderowitz, eds., 1974, *Pronatalism: The Myth of Mom and Apple Pie.* New York, Thomas Y. Crowell.

Polatnick, Margaret, 1973, "Why Men Don't Rear Children: A Power Analysis," *Berkeley Journal of Sociology,* 18, pp. 45–86.

Reich, Wilhelm, 1966, *Sex-Pol.* New York, Vintage Books.

Reiter, Reyna, ed., 1975, *Toward an Anthropology of Women.* New York, Monthly Review Press.

Rosaldo, Michelle Z., and Louise Lamphere, eds., 1974, *Woman, Culture and Society.* Stanford, Stanford University Press.

Rossi, Alice, 1977, "A Biosocial Perspective on Parenting," *Daedalus,* 106, no. 2, pp. 1–31.

Rubin, Lillian Breslow, 1976, *Worlds of Pain: Life in the Working Class Family.* New York, Basic Books.

Rutter, Michael, 1972, *Maternal Deprivation Reassessed.* Baltimore, Penguin Books.

Schaffer, H. Rudolph, 1977, *Mothering.* Cambridge, Harvard University Press.

Slater, Philip E., 1968, *The Glory of Hera: Greek Mythology and the Greek Family.* Boston, Beacon Press.

———, 1970, *The Pursuit of Loneliness.* Boston, Beacon Press.

———, 1974, *Earthwalk.* New York, Bantam Books.

Spitz, Rene, 1965, *The First Year of Life: A Psychoanalytic Study of Normal and Deviant Development of Object Relations.* New York, International Universities Press.

Stack, Carol B., 1974, *All Our Kin.* New York, Harper and Row.

Stephens, William N., 1963, *The Family in Cross-Cultural Perspective.* New York, Holt, Rinehart and Winston.

Teitelbaum, Michael S., ed., 1976, *Sex Differences: Social and Biological Perspectives.* New York, Anchor Books.

Tiger, Lionel, 1969, *Men in Groups.* New York, Random House.

Weitzman, Lenore J., 1975, "Sex-Role Socialization," in Jo Freeman, ed., *Women: A Feminist Perspective.* Palo Alto, Mayfield Publishing.

Whiting, Beatrice, ed., 1963, *Six Cultures: Studies of Child-Rearing.* New York, John Wiley.

Whiting, Beatrice B., and John W. M. Whiting, 1975, *Children of Six Cultures.* Cambridge, Harvard University Press.

Whiting, John W. M., Richard Kluckhohn, and Albert Anthony, 1958, "The Function of Male Initiation Rites at Puberty," in Eleanor E. Maccoby, T. M. Newcomb, and E. L. Hartley, eds., *Readings in Social Psychology.* New York, Holt.

Winch, Robert F., 1962, *Identification and Its Familial Determinants.* New York, Bobbs-Merrill.

Winnicott, D. W., 1960, "The Theory of the Parent-Infant Relationship," *International Journal of Psycho-Analysis,* 41, pp. 585–595.

———, 1965, *The Maturational Processes and the Facilitating Environment.* New York, International Universities Press.

Young, Michael, and Peter Willmott, 1957, *Family and Kinship in East London.* London, Penguin Books, 1966.

~ *Chapter 21*

Chicana/o Family Structure and Gender Personality: Chodorow, Familism, and Psychoanalytic Sociology Revisited

DENISE A. SEGURA AND JENNIFER L. PIERCE

The men watched the women—my aunts and mother moving with the grace and speed of girls cooking before they could see the top of the stove. Elvira, my mother, knew she was being watched by the men and loved it. . . . Her thick-lidded eyes never caught theirs as she was swept back into the kitchen by my abuelita's call of "Elvirita," her brown hands deepening in color as they dropped back in the pan of flour.

—Cherríe Moraga, *Loving in the War Years*

In her essay "From a Long Line of Vendidas" Cherríe Moraga not only captures the patriarchal character of the family in which she grew up—the men watching the women cook—but also highlights subtly the presence and significance of women—many women—in her home. Her mother and her aunts work together both to make meals and to nurture the family and each other. Many Chicana/o scholars have characterized the existence of multiple mothering figures as a distinctive feature of

life in Chicana/o families.[1] Yet this feature goes unnoticed in white feminist accounts of "mother-centric" families, most notably in Nancy Chodorow's classic *The Reproduction of Mothering*. Chodorow argues that the development and reproduction of gender identity—that is, of "masculine" and "feminine" personality—arise from a "universal" nuclear family structure in which one heterosexual female parent is primarily responsible for the exclusive mothering of children (1978).

Despite the importance of Chodorow's work to psychoanalytic sociology and particularly to feminist scholarship, theorists have repeatedly criticized her account, as we do, because the family structure that she depicts is not sufficiently particularistic.[2] Gloria Joseph, for example, points out that Chodorow's model does not reflect the experience of black mothers and daughters. "To discuss Black mother/daughter relationships in terms of the patterns of White mother/daughter relationships would be to ignore the explanations and interpretations of Black women regarding their own historical and cultural experiences

From *Signs* 19, no. 1 (autumn 1993): 62–91, published by The University of Chicago Press, copyright © 1993 by The University of Chicago. Reprinted by permission.

as Black women" (1981, 76). Similarly, Judith Lorber et al. contend that class differences reduce the generalizability of Chodorow's model: "American working-class families not only have different relationships, but also instill in their children somewhat different sets of values" (1981, 483). As a result, Lorber finds Chodorow's work to be "culture and time bound" (1981, 483). Indeed, Chodorow's empirical focus is on the structure of European-American middle-class families—a focus that marginalizes non-Western family forms, gay and lesbian families, joint custody arrangements, and single parent households. Elizabeth Spelman speaks specifically to the limitations of the social context described by Chodorow:

> Perhaps the most politically significant part of Chodorow's account is her reminder that mothering occurs in a social context. It is informed, she notes, by the mother's relation to her husband, her economic dependence on him, her experience of male dominance. But why does Chodorow focus on only these elements of the larger social context? After all, most societies—including that of contemporary North America, about which she is concerned—are also characterized by other forms of dominance, other sorts of hierarchies. Women mother in societies that may be racist and classist as well as sexist and heterosexist. (1988, 85)

Such criticism of Chodorow, by now familiar to many feminist scholars, is, in our view, justified. Nevertheless, we take issue with the complete dismissal of Chodorow's theory that often accompanies such critiques. Joseph, for example, rejects Chodorow's model as "dysfunctional" in theorizing the relationship between black mothers and daughters and argues that it would be more "realistic, useful and intellectually astute to speak in terms of roles, positions and functions within Black society and that society's relationship to broader (White) society in America" (1981,

76). The usefulness of Chodorow's theoretical framework, however, should not be obscured by the limitations of her empirical account. Indeed, as Spelman maintains, Chodorow's theory actually provides a useful framework for studying racial and ethnic differences in the acquisition of gender identity because it emphasizes the socially specific context in which mothering takes place (1988).

We argue that Chodorow's theoretical framework is useful in understanding the acquisition of gender identity in Chicana/o families—families characterized by a unique constellation of features derived from their socially and historically specific context. This constellation shapes not only gender identity but also group identity, helping to explain the strong commitment to culture and community that many scholars have noted among Chicanas and Chicanos. A considerable literature has been devoted to differences between Chicana/o families and European-American, middle-class families.[3] Chicana/o families are more likely than European-American families to be from the working class instead of the middle class, to have higher fertility rates, and to value familism—family solidarity—and *compadrazgo*—extended family ties. Finally, Chicana/o families are likely to practice nonexclusive mothering, in contrast to the exclusive approach identified in European-American families. We will show how Chodorow's unique theoretical perspective can be appropriated for studying racial and ethnic differences in the acquisition of a heterosexual gender identity—a social psychological identity as heterosexual and female or heterosexual and male.[4] Considering the unique characterization of "the Chicano family" in the social science literature, we will explore the implications of Chodorow's theoretical model for the reproduction of heterosexual gender personality in Chicana/o families.[5] Our analysis will show that the particular family constellation in which Chicanas mother may have differential consequences for the development of masculine and feminine personality and for the development of group identity, compared with the family structure of the white European-American middle class.

Psychoanalytic Sociology, Chodorow, and Social Specificity

Psychoanalytic sociology embraces work from divergent sociological traditions and political perspectives. Parsonian functionalism or a focus on the function and integration of roles in society (Parsons 1964), psychoanalytic feminist theory (Chodorow 1978; Benjamin 1988; Johnson 1988), and the Marxist work of the Frankfurt School (especially in the writings of Max Horkheimer [(1936) 1972] and Herbert Marcuse [1955]) all fit within this larger theoretical framework. The work that falls within psychoanalytic sociology nevertheless exhibits two common elements: a focus on the relationship between "unconscious mental processes and the organization of conscious social life" (Rabow, Platt, and Goldman 1987, ix) and the assumption that the individual is a complex and active subject rather than an object passively responding to larger social forces (Chodorow 1978; Benjamin 1988; Pierce 1991). The emphasis on unconscious mental processes and behavior renders psychoanalytic sociology a controversial subfield within the broader sociological discipline.

Psychoanalytic sociologists who study gender have been concerned with how the family reproduces in men a personality suited to their role as workers in a capitalist society. While these theorists have contributed to our understanding of the relation between social structure and heterosexual masculine personality, Chodorow (1978) points out that they do not consider the development of heterosexual feminine personality. Chodorow proposes in *The Reproduction of Mothering* (1978) to fill this gap by considering how both feminine and masculine personalities are reproduced in the family, thus preparing women and men for their adult roles in society.

Chodorow's central theoretical question is how and why women come to mother—by which she means to nurture and care for small children. She asks how this pattern is reproduced and how it affects the psychological development of girls and boys. Chodorow sees the family as central in the "sex/gender system."[6] She contends that "the sexual and familial division of labor in which women mother and are more involved in interpersonal, affective relationships than men produces in daughters and sons a division of psychological capacities which leads them to reproduce this sexual and familial division of labor" (1978, 7). Women, as mothers, produce daughters with the capacity and the desire to mother and sons with nurturing capacities and needs that have been systematically curtailed and repressed. "This prepares men for their less affective later family role, and for primary participation in the impersonal extrafamilial world of work and public life" (1978, 7). Indeed, the sexual division of labor in mothering provides a basis for differentiating "public" and "domestic." Yet Chodorow emphasizes that "these spheres are not equal, and since the public sphere dominates the domestic . . . men dominate women" (1978, 10).

Although Chodorow uses a psychoanalytic approach, she rejects the instinctual determinism of the classic Freudian account in favor of a more nuanced, social psychological approach that incorporates recent developments within object relations theory, which focuses on relationships with others. Chodorow emphasizes that pre-oedipal experiences are more pivotal than oedipal ones both for psychological development and for the creation of gender. She argues that because the early social environment differs for and is experienced differently by male and female children, boys and girls develop gender-specific personalities. Mothers tend "to experience their daughters as more like, and more continuous with themselves" (1978, 50). Girls experience themselves as like their mothers, thus fusing their gender identity formation with attachment and relationship to others. In contrast, the mother treats her son quite differently by emphasizing his masculinity in opposition to herself and by pushing him to assume a sexually toned relation to her. Boys begin to separate themselves from their mothers after infancy, thus curtailing "their primary love and sense of empathic tie" (1978, 166). As a result, heterosexual male development involves a "more emphatic individuation and a more defensive firming of ego boundaries" as well as a sense of self as not female (1978, 166).

Differing adult "object-relational capacities" are the psychological consequence for girls and boys of these early asymmetrical relationships with the mother. Each capacity entails a continuing preoccupation with a different set of psychical issues. For men gender identity is the central issue: they experience a constant need to prove their masculinity. Unlike girls, boys must define themselves as not like their mothers and actively strive to acquire the characteristics of their different gender identity. Their repression of their early identification with their mothers engenders a highly ambivalent stance toward women, one characterized by longing and disdain. Men display this ambivalence by seeking out exclusive emotional relationships with women (marriage) and at the same time participating in the denigration of women (male domination).

Girls, in Chodorow's formulation, continue to be preoccupied with relational issues.

Chodorow contends that women fulfill their relational needs by becoming mothers—for heterosexual women, the baby creates a new emotional triangle, that of mother/father/baby, that parallels the woman's inner object relational constellation of daughter/mother/father. Heterosexual women seek men to fulfill their desire for physical and emotional union. Because men cannot satisfy women's emotional needs, women turn to children to recreate the emotional triangle they once experienced as children themselves.[7] Thus, women and men have differing but equally strong unconscious motivations to reproduce the family, gender, male domination, and mothering. For Chodorow, the only way out of this endless cycle is shared parenting wherein women and men actively participate in early child care.

Chodorow is not unaware of the limitations of the family constellation she describes in *The Reproduction of Mothering* (1978). In her most recent book, *Feminism and Psychoanalytic Theory* (1989), she characterizes *The Reproduction of Mothering* as part of the early feminist scholarly effort toward "grand theory"—the search in feminist theorizing for a single cause to account for gender inequality, hierarchy, and male domination of women. She acknowledges that her psychoanalytic model of social relations in *The Reproduction of Mothering* is not attuned to racial and ethnic differences, but contends that feminists should not dismiss psychoanalytic theory altogether. She writes:

> People everywhere form a psyche, self and identity. . . . Historically, this method and theory [psychoanalysis] have not often been applied in a social or culturally specific manner, but there is not a basic antagonism between *psychoanalytic thinking and social specificity.* . . . As factors of race, class, culture or history enter either into a labeled (conscious or unconscious) identity, or as they shape the particular early object-

relational and family patterns and forms of sub-jectivity, psychoanalytic tools should be able to analyze these. (1989, 4; emphasis added)

Spelman supports this view. Although she criticizes Chodorow for neglecting race and class differences "in practice," she argues that Chodorow's emphasis on the social context of mothering in the acquisition of gender iden-tity is useful "in theory" for studying racial and ethnic differences. "If we follow her ad-vice, rather than her own practice, we are led to see that gender identity is not neatly sepa-rable from other aspects of identity such as race and class" (1988, 82).

Chodorow herself demonstrates the versa-tility of her theoretical framework in her ear-liest statement of its premises, in her 1974 essay "Family Structure and Feminine Per-sonality." Focusing here on the acquisition of gender identity in family structures that differ from the traditional structure of the European-American middle class, Chodorow argues that female personality development takes on unique characteristics in societies where the mother is a strong figure in the family con-stellation and social structure, her kin role is positively valued, her status and prestige in-crease with age, and her contribution to the family economic system is important. Provid-ing examples from ethnographies of three matrilocal societies—working-class families in East London and Javanese and Atjehnese families in Indonesia—she writes:

> These social facts [kin role positively valued, etc.] have important positive effects on female psychological development. . . . A mother is not invested in keeping her daughter from individ-uating and becoming less dependent. She has other ongoing contacts and relationships that help fulfill her psychological and social needs. In addition, *the people surrounding a mother while a child is growing up become mediators between mother and daughter with alternative models for personal identification and objects of attachment,*

which contribute to her differentiation from her mother. Finally, a daughter's identification with her mother in this kind of setting is with a strong woman with clear control over important spheres of life, whose sense of self-esteem can reflect this. Acceptance of gender identity in-volves positive valuation of herself, and not an admission of inferiority. (1974, 63; emphasis added)

Chodorow's 1974 essay as well as her more recent work (1989) emphasizing the link be-tween psychoanalytic thinking and "social specificity" suggest that psychoanalytic soci-ology can be used to explore the acquisition of gender identity in a variety of social, cultural, and historical contexts. Even within the United States, patterns of socialization and psychological development differ dramati-cally by socioeconomic class, religion, ethnic-ity, and race. The socially specific psychoana-lytic sociology of Chodorow operates across such differences to explicate the acquisition of gender identity—as we will show by import-ing Chodorow's perspective to the Chicana/o family constellation described in the extant literature.

Chicana/o Family Structure and Gender Personality

Chicanas and Chicanos come to maturity as members of a racial and ethnic minority in a social and historical context in which their political, economic, and cultural uniqueness is constantly undermined, denigrated, and vi-olated. Since the annexation of northern Mexico by the United States in 1848, Chicanas and Chicanos have experienced second-class citizenship both politically and economically. Chicanas and Chicanos have faced discrimi-nation in employment, education, and polit-ical participation. They have been and con-tinue to be concentrated among the poor and the working class in the United States (Barrera 1979; Rochin and Castillo 1991). Furthermore, Chicanas and Chicanos maintain and affirm a distinct culture that emphasizes familism, *compadrazgo*, and a collectivist orientation that is devalued by the dominant culture's emphasis on individualism.

Until quite recently this unique social and historical constellation of features has been ignored in studies on Chicana/o families. Social historian Alex Saragoza argues that the study of Chicana/o families "remains largely unexplored" (1983), an assertion echoed by social scientists Patricia Zavella (1987) and Norma Williams (1990). By this they mean that literature on Chicana/o families tends to be narrow, ahistorical, and atheoretical and that it uses an "idealized" European-American family as the yardstick by which an artificially constructed "homogeneous" Chicano family is measured (Mirandé 1977).

This yardstick, predominant in family sociology until recently, uncritically privileged concepts steeped in modernization theory. That is, the "evolution" of a nuclear family composed of breadwinner husband and stay-at-home wife was postulated as best suited to the socialization of children and to the stabilization of adult personalities in industrial societies (Parsons and Bales 1955). Chicana/o families and other families that did not "fit" this characterization were viewed as "deviant," "backward," and even "pathological."

In her comprehensive review of literature on Chicana/o families (hearkening back to the sixties and early seventies—a period of scholarly "discovery" of such families), Lea Ybarra found that the relevant research could be categorized as pejorative, reactive, or revisionist. Pejorative views emphasize the patriarchal structure (machismo) of Chicana/o families, along with male domination, male sexual obsessions, female submissiveness, and maternal self-sacrifice (1983, 92). Alfredo Mirandé ar-

gued in 1977 that scholarly comparisons between Chicana/o families and middle-class European-American families were insensitive to history, institutional racism, and cultural survival strategies. He repudiated the resultant depiction of Chicana/o families as a "tangle of pathology" that "propagates the subordination of women, impedes individual achievement, engenders passivity and dependency and on occasion can even give rise to incestuous feelings among siblings" (1977, 747–56).

Reactive researchers of Chicana/o families "react against the negative and stereotypical literature about Chicanos" (Ybarra 1983, 98). Miguel Montiel, who coined the phrase "the social science myth of the Mexican-American family," was the first to present a comprehensive and incisive critique of the impressionistic nature of research on Chicana/o families (1970). Montiel, Octavio Romano (1970), and Mirandé (1977), among others, sought to counter the pejorative portrayal of Chicana/o families as dominated by men and by machismo. They exposed such portrayals as inaccurate and racist. Reactive research argues that a variety of Chicana/o family structures exist, ranging from the egalitarian to the patriarchal, and advocates studies that do not judge family forms.

Revisionist research on Chicana/o families questions the nature of families and gender relations and emphasizes historical context, regional variations, and class specificity (Ybarra 1983). It is this approach that we find most useful to our analysis. Research in this tradition seeks to correct past distortions not simply by isolating theoretical contradictions but by offering empirical evidence that points to the heterogeneity among Chicana/o families and that portrays them in more realistic and less evaluative terms.[8]

Much of this research emphasizes the heterogeneity among Chicana/o families by immigrant status, urban/rural residence, household size, acculturation, and class status. Such empirical research also establishes important commonalities. In 1990, nearly 90 percent of Chicana/o families reported income below $50,000 to maintain families significantly larger, on the average, than the societal "norm" (4.03 persons in Chicana/o families compared with 3.12 persons in white families) (U.S. Bureau of the Census 1992, table 1). Half of all Chicana/o families in 1990 were maintained by $23,240 or less for a family of four while 25 percent lived below the poverty level ($13,359 for a family of four) (U.S. Bureau of the Census 1991a, 18, 25). In contrast, 8.1 percent of European-American families and 29.3 percent of black families lived below the poverty rate in 1990 (U.S. Bureau of the Census 1991b, 15). These figures indicate that Chicana/o families are primarily working class and often among the working poor; they provide a key socioeconomic context to the analysis of this community.

Bolstered by empirical data, revisionist researchers often examine features commonly associated with both working-class and middle-class Chicana/o families, including familism (beliefs and behaviors associated with family solidarity), *compadrazgo* (extended family via godparents), *confianza* (a system of trust and intimacy,) high Spanish language loyalty, a gender-specific division of labor, and high fertility. But most such research has focused on working-class families; the degree to which these traits vary by class has not been sufficiently explored. In view of the limited research on middle-class Chicana/o families, we limit our discussion to working-class families and caution that our analysis may be less relevant as income levels rise. Some evidence exists, however, that middle-class Chicana/o families display surprisingly high loyalty to the Spanish language and place a high premium on familism (Keefe and Padilla 1987); our analysis thus may resonate within this

more privileged sector of the Chicana/o community.

Revisionist researchers typically analyze characteristics attributed to Chicana/o families within the context of Chicanas' and Chicanos' historically suppressed social, economic, and political opportunities, their historical clustering within certain geographic areas (the southwestern United States), and their limited political clout (Saragoza 1983; Baca Zinn and Eitzen 1987). This broader social context is important to an analysis of mothering and the reproduction of gendered personalities in Chicana/o families; this context helps to shape and define the unique constellation of features that characterize Chicana/o families. We begin by describing this constellation, which includes features such as familism, *compadrazgo*, and nonexclusive mothering. Then, by extending Chodorow's more recent argument (1989) about social specificity and mothering, we explore the psychological consequences this particular social context poses for the development of gender personality among Chicanas and Chicanos. We argue that in Chicana/o families the blending of gender identity and ethnic identity creates forms of masculine and feminine personality distinct from that of the European-American middle class.

The Constellation of Features in Chicana/o Families

Contemporary sociologists consider familism to be a primary characteristic of Chicana/o families (Griswold del Castillo 1984, 146). Maxine Baca Zinn observes that familism is observable in four ways: by macro-characteristics such as large family size (demographic familism); by the presence of multigenerational households or extended households (structural familism); by the high value placed on family unity and solidarity (normative familism); and by the high level of interaction between family and kin networks (behavioral familism) (Baca Zinn 1982/83, 226–27).

Compadrazgo, another prominent feature of Chicana/o families and one associated with behavioral familism, refers to two sets of relationships with godparents who become "fictive" kin: *padrinos* and *ahiados* (godparents and their godchildren) and *compadres* (godparents and parents who become co-parents) (Falicov 1982). *Compadrazgo* relationships with godparents create connections between families, thereby enlarging Chicana/o family ties. According to Richard Griswold del Castillo, "Godparents [are] required for the celebration of major religious occasions in a person's life: baptism, first communion and marriage" (1984, 42). At these times, godparents enter "into special religious, social and economic relationships with the godchild as well as the parents of the child." They act as co-parents, "providing discipline and emotional and financial support when needed." As *compadres,* they are expected to become the closest friends of the parents and members of the extended family (1984, 40–44). While *compadrazgo* is principally a feature of Roman Catholic Chicana/o families, non-Catholic Chicanas and Chicanos who go through baptism and marriage rituals may also gain *compadres.*

The role and form *compadrazgo* takes in Chicana/o communities is constantly changing. Both Jaime Sena-Rivera (1979) and Norma Williams (1990) argue that *compadrazgo*'s economic functions are declining in importance. Williams's study of two Texas communities found that godparents were less likely than in previous generations to intervene in family affairs or offer economic support—particularly among professional Chicanas and Chicanos. Her study suggests that godparents are more "symbolic" representa-

tions of family unity than they are instrumental ones.

The continuing high fertility rate of Chicanas, for example, enhances their opportunities to acquire *compadres* and to affirm close connections to extended family members. In 1988, Hispanic women had an estimated fertility rate of 94 births per 1,000 women between the ages of 18 and 44, compared with European-American women's 67.5 births per 1,000 women (U.S. Bureau of the Census 1988). High fertility, thus, is one mechanism that reinforces the significance of familism and *compadrazgo* in Chicana/o communities. While *compadrazgo* may be changing, especially in its economic functions, Williams observes it remains an important resource for emotional support and cultural affirmation (Williams 1990, 138, 140).

Extended households and extensive family networks are other important features associated with Chicana/o familism. In their study on extended households or structural familism among whites, blacks, and Hispanics, Marta Tienda and Ronald Angel (1982) found that low-income Chicanas who headed families were more likely than European-Americans to live in households composed of several generations of kin. Charles Mindel (1980) compared European-American, African-American, and Mexican-American families and found that Mexican-Americans had the largest and most socially active extended family networks in several local geographic areas. This study and others emphasize the extensive interaction (behavioral familism) across kinship systems (fictive and real) in Chicana/o families (Horowitz 1983; Zavella 1987).

Behavioral familism reinforces what Zavella terms "the cultural principle of *confianza*" or the belief that "only certain people outside the immediate family are to be trusted with private information" (1987, 28). Mirandé suggests that the mistrust of outsiders to Chicana/o kin networks has developed histori-cally "in response to the oppressive condi-tions of internal colonialism" (1985, 163). "Trust" that resides solely within Chicana/o families serves as an important strategy for cultural survival and resistance in the face of racism and other forms of domination by cre-ating ties within and across kin networks (Bott 1971; Caulfield 1974). Extensive interac-tion across kin networks also enhances the opportunities for relatives other than the mother to become involved in child rearing and providing child care as well as emotional support. In times of crisis, members of the ex-tended family provide physical and affective care for children and emotional and eco-nomic support for the parents (Sotomayor 1971; Keefe 1979; Wagner and Schaffer 1980).

Among Chicanas, mothering and paid em-ployment are not mutually exclusive. In 1990, Chicanas' labor force participation rate was 50.6 percent while that of Chicanos was 79.6 percent (U.S. Bureau of the Census 1991a, table 2). Several researchers have observed that employed Chicanas and Chicanos rely on female kin for child care instead of on institutional arrangements (Zavella 1987; Se-gura 1988). A recent study of Chicana/o and European-American families in the Sunbelt region confirms this finding, but with a twist: Chicano fathers actively parent and care for their children more than Anglo fathers (Lam-phere, Zavella, and Gonzalez 1993, chap. 6). The conditions under which this occurs are quite specific: female kin are not available, and men's work schedules allow them to as-sume child-care duties. It is possible that the higher participation of some Chicano men doing child care reflects their relatively higher representation in shift work (compared with Anglo men). On the other hand, it may also reflect a different cultural orientation. The greater willingness of Chicano fathers to en-gage in expanded parenting flows from their

commitment to their families and familism and lack of *confianza* for nonfamily caretak-ers. While these parenting and childcare strategies used by Chicanas and Chicanos may not be exclusively cultural but may also be economic strategies of a low-income group—shared to some extent by other dis-advantaged groups—they are nevertheless important to consider in analyzing the repro-duction of gender personality.

The practice of nonexclusive mothering, in particular, has critical implications for the de-velopment of feminine and masculine person-alities in Chicana/o families. Multiple mother figures among Chicanas and Chicanos have been reported in numerous accounts. Gris-wold del Castillo (1984) discusses the impor-tant role of godmothers and godfathers in Chi-cana/o communities. Closeness between Chicanas and their grandmothers is described by many social narrators, including Diane Neumaier (1990), Lorna Dee Cervantes (1980), and Tey Diana Rebolledo (1983). Lisa Hernan-dez describes the critical grandmother-mother-daughter triad as a "process of trans-formation" integral to Chicana self-affirmation and empowerment (1988). That is, Chicanas want to affirm themselves "as Chicanas," women with a unique racial and ethnic history, language, and ways of relating to one another through close interaction with women in the kin networks.

Chicanas, Ethnicity, and Gender Identity

Like European-American women, Chicanas are more likely to identify with their daugh-ters than with their sons. Daughters, in turn, identify with their mothers' female role. Be-cause a Chicana's activity as a mother revolves around family and home, Viktor Gecas (1973) argues that these constitute a major arena for the daughter's definition of self. This psycho-logical identification is framed within Chicanas' cultural practices and beliefs. For example, José Límon (1980) discusses the socializing function of a commonly played folk game, La Vieja Inés, which emphasizes Chicana-appropriate mothering roles. This game is usually played by girls and has two major roles: the prized role of *la mamá* and the stigmatized role of *la vieja Inés*. Other child players do not have names, for part of the game is for *La mamá* to assign them names of colors. If *la vieja Inés* can guess the color name of a child, a chase ensues, which ends with a capture of *la vieja Inés* or the safe return to *la mamá* (home). Límon notes that *la mamá* is often selected for her proven proficiency in assigning color names that have successfully eluded the previous guesses of *Inés*. He argues that this game is a "symbolic learning experience" in which Chicanas "learn" and "practice" how "to take responsibility for children by naming them and speaking for them against the world beyond this known kin group" (1980, 92).

Other important differences exist between European-American women and Chicanas. In many poor Chicana/o families, infants often sleep with parents until they are weaned (Johnson 1980). And the larger the family, the more likely young Chicana/o children are to sleep with their parents or with one another. While this theme is not well researched in academic accounts of Chicana/o family life, it shows up in many literary works (Anaya 1972; Elasser, MacKenzie, and Tixier Y Vigil 1980). Chicanas and Chicanos also exhibit a high degree of residential stability by remaining in or close to their community of origin for many years, or several generations (Keefe and Padilla 1987). Moreover, unmarried Chicanas and Chicanos tend to live with their families of origin until they get married. Interaction with primary kin, particularly the mother, intensifies once childbearing begins.

Because many Chicana/o families do not practice exclusive mothering, daughters often have several female attachment figures responsible for the teaching of gender-related cultural behaviors. Chicanas are sometimes as close, if not closer, to grandmothers or godmothers as they are to their own mothers. Marlene Zepeda's research (1979) indicates that grandmothers are important role models for young Chicanas, particularly with respect to culturally specific skills (speaking Spanish, cooking traditional foods, celebrating Mexican holidays), and that they form particularly strong ties to their daughters' children as opposed to the children of their sons.

Norma Alarcón (1985) also discusses the closeness of grandmother/granddaughter relationships, particularly regarding culturally gendered role expectations. Grandmothers, by virtue of their age and long relationship with the family, are honored by others in the kin network. The grandmother/granddaughter relationship is less tense than that of mothers and daughters. Mothers are directly responsible for teaching their daughters how to be Chicanas knowledgeable in cultural traditions and behaviors that signal their gender and ethnicity. Their transmission of a culture overlaid with patriarchal prerogatives can be hotly contested by their daughters, situated generationally in a different social and historical setting. Grandmothers stand one step away from the mother/daughter identity process; they offer granddaughters love and support without dramatically altering cultural messages.

A Chicana may experience herself, thus, not only as an extension of her mother but also of her grandmother. Depending on the extent of behavioral familism, a Chicana may also see herself in relation to her godmother and/or an aunt. Extending Chodorow's theory here suggests that, unlike European-American girls, Chicanas may not develop an inner psychic "triangular object relational constellation" of daughter/mother/father but, rather, a multi-object relational configuration of daughter/mother/aunt/grandmother/godmother/father. To recreate this internal psychic world as an adult, having children may be even more important to Chicanas than to European-American women, and maintaining relationships with other women in the *compadrazgo* system may be particularly crucial for Chicanas to fulfill their relational needs.

Furthermore, for the majority of Chicanas who are working-class, mothers and mothering are enveloped and cast in particular cultural representations, imagery, and symbols (Mirandé and Enríquez 1979; Melville 1980; Baca Zinn 1982). In Chicana/o literature and art and in Catholicism, women, particularly mothers, are represented as essentially sacred and holy. Chicanas are held accountable to *la madre*'s self-sacrificing and pure nature in the image of *La Virgen de Guadalupe* (the Catholic patroness of Mexico whose portrait graces many Mexican immigrant and Chicana/o houses and churches in the Southwest). *La Virgen* as both cultural and religious representation of the good mother frames this gendered/ethnic sense of self. Chicana/o culture identifies several images of "bad" women and mothers, including *La Llorona* (the weeping woman), to dramatically describe the evil fate in store for women who deviate from the norm of the "good" mother. *La Llorona* killed her children and committed suicide. She wanders for eternity, a condemned ghost, in search of her lost children. Both images, *La Virgen* and *La Llorona*, frame a cultural context for mothers and mothering in Chicana/o communities.

Mario García's historical research (1980) on Chicanas highlights women's responsibility to transmit Chicana/o-Mexican cultural values as well as to care for the family unit. Baca Zinn (1975, 1979) argues that Chicana/o families tend to be mother-centered, with women responsible for the majority of household and child-rearing decisions and tasks. These responsibilities form a complementary sphere to the work of men done for the family. Woman's mothering occurs in a patriarchal context and is not a direct challenge to male providers but, rather, an assertion of her culturally gendered role. That is, among Chicanas and Chicanos, women's work in the home is often articulated as part of "doing Chicana" (Segura 1992), a claim legitimized by a shared sense of the Chicana/o culture as under assault by outside social pressures (Baca Zinn 1975, 1982; Segura 1992). The sense that a woman's mothering is part of her Chicana identity is bolstered by interaction across kin networks and the larger ethnic community that can result in Chicanas feeling more strongly motivated to mother than European-American middle-class women whose kinship ties are more dispersed. When Chicanas contest traditional patterns they can become caught between their desire for personal empowerment and their politically charged responsibility for cultural maintenance. Thus, the need or motivation to continue traditional patterns may be more complex for Chicanas inasmuch as it is one potential site for reinforcing Chicana/o culture and ethnicity (Segura 1992; Pesquera 1991).

Chicanos, Ethnicity, and Gender Identity

The psychological consequences the Chicana/o family constellation poses differs for the young Chicano. His early relationship with the mother differs from that of the young Chicana. Although he too may be mothered by more than one primary female caretaker, his maleness means that his female nurturers do not identify with him in the way they identify with their daughters. In *Hunger of Memory: The Education of Richard Rodriguez*,

Rodriguez writes that from the time he was a little boy, his mother would "repeat the old Mexican dictum [to him] that men should be *feo, fuerte y formal*" (1982, 128). Roughly translated, this means rugged, strong, and steady, a man of responsibility and a good provider for the family. The process Rodriguez describes is found in other writings by Chicanos on "becoming masculine" (e.g., Villarreal 1959; Galarza 1971; Acosta 1972). Moreover, Gecas's (1973) research finds that young Chicanos are more likely than their sisters to identify with their fathers and with their potential male occupational roles. In sum, the Chicano boy must learn his gender identity as being not female—or not mother, not grandmother, and not godmother. Extending Chodorow's theoretical formulation, this suggests that the young Chicano must repress his identification and attachment with many women—not just one—and, at the same time, strive to achieve a masculine gender identification with his father and many other men.

Chicanos' personality development is in some ways similar to that of European-American men. Brooks Brennis and Samuel Roll (1975), for example, found that Chicanos tended to organize their internal psychic world around a highly visible, demarcated self that was seen as robust, randomly active, and engaged in contentious interactions with unfamiliar others. Chicanos' repression of several female objects instead of one, however, suggests that they may develop masculine identity differently than do European-American men. Divergent possibilities exist: nonexclusive mothering may make Chicanos more responsive to women—or conversely it may make them more disdainful. The presence of several female caretakers may actually ameliorate male contempt for women because the Chicano child is not completely dependent on any one woman. The opposing view is that nonexclusive mothering makes it much harder for the young Chicano boy than for his European-American counterpart to achieve a masculine identification because the energy involved in repressing feminine identification is greater—a difficulty exacerbated by the disadvantaged structural position of Chicanos. Baca Zinn (1979), for example, argues that machismo may be one response to the structural obstacles Chicano men face in achieving masculinity in a social world that has historically denied them equal participation. In Chodorow's model, boys' repression of their early identification with their mothers engenders a highly ambivalent stance toward women. With more women caring for the Chicano boy, the ambivalence could be greater, suggesting that Chicanos might be even more likely than European-American men to experience strong feelings of longing and disdain for women.

This scenario directly implicates machismo, the politically loaded notion that Chicanos are in some sense more dominating or macho than European-American men. Much of the early pejorative literature on Mexican national character employed psychoanalytic concepts to depict machismo as a problematic psychological component of Mexican men (Bermúdez 1955; Díaz-Guerrero 1955; Gilbert 1959). Early researchers constructed an image cast in the discourse of the "normative" wherein diverse Chicana/o families became the "Chicano family" ruled by "macho-dominated," authoritarian males demanding complete deference, respect, and obedience from wives and children (Humphrey 1944; Jones 1948; Peñalosa 1968).

From the vantage point of the 1990s, the findings of these early and influential studies read like ludicrous stereotypes rather than as valid descriptions of Chicana/o culture and people. As Baca Zinn, Mirandé, and others have concluded, however, the machismo stereotype contains a grain of truth. The most recent research on Chicana/o families confirms patriarchal privilege structurally, ideologically, and interpersonally (Zavella 1987; Williams 1990).

Patriarchy within Chicana/o families does not constitute a culturally unique pathology (or machismo). In Baca Zinn's review of the social science literature on Chicana/o families, she argues that male domination/female subordination transcends any one cultural group. Indeed, the central tenet of feminist theorizing about the family is that the family is not simply a "haven in a heartless world" (Lasch 1977) but the "locus of struggle" and the source of psychological oppression of women (Hartmann 1981; Thorne and Yalom 1982). In this respect, Chicana/o families struggle over the meanings of gender and mothering in the same way that European-American working-class families do. Chicanas and Chicanos are unique, however, insofar as they simultaneously invoke and perceive themselves as reinforcing a distinct Chicana/o and Mexican culture.

Chicanos invoke "family" and "community" in ways that suggest a cultural and political overlap in masculine identity. Accounts of high-achieving Chicanos reveal considerable overlap between their desire to "help the community" and their wish to attain individual excellence. Themes of individual and group identity, family, and community responsibilities inform the autobiographies of prominent Chicanos such as activist-scholar Ernesto Galarza's *Barrio Boy* (1971), Chicano movement leader Rudolfo "Corky" Gonzales's *Yo Soy Joaquín* (1972), and Fred Ross's *Biography of labor leader César Chávez* (1989). Chicano literary critic Ramón Saldívar analyzes what he terms the "themes of transformation and identity" in *Barrio Boy*, asserting that "the motifs of transformation and identity which might have been offered in terms of the individual, are transferred instead to the entire community within which the individuals exist, by which they are created, and which they in turn dialectically transform" (1990, 164). This suggests Chicanos are more likely to affirm their gender identity as masculine by pursuing their interests and affiliations in the immediate ethnic community. For example, Zavella (1989) suggests that Chicano political activists during the turbulent 1960s and 1970s established organizations to reconstruct *familia* and *carnalismo* (Chicano brotherhood).

This blending of gender identity with community also occurs with Chicanas. Writer Helena María Viramontes writes, "I want to do justice to their voices. I want to tell these women, in my own gentle way that I will fight for them, that they provide me with my own sense of humanity" (1990, 292). Similarly, in a personal account of her graduate school experiences, sociologist Gloria Cuádraz characterizes the importance of doing well in school as part of the larger struggle of her community rather than the more individualistic frame of her Anglo counterparts (Cuádraz and Pierce 1993). In a related vein, discussions of Chicana muralists highlight how their works typically express "both personal and collective expression" (Mesa-Baines 1990). Other accounts stress that Chicana political activism (e.g., running for school board, joining the Mothers of East Los Angeles, labor union organizing) is often spurred by Chicanas' desire to better the opportunities for their families and their communities (Pardo 1990; Segura and Pesquera 1992). The ideological commitment in Chicana/o communities to the intertwined notions of *familia* and community is emphasized in recent research on Chicano political activism and political consciousness.[9] What this research suggests is that in the particular constellation of Chicana/o families the development of gender identity and group or ethnic identity are closely intertwined. Chicana mothers do not raise their children to be "independent" or "individualistic," as European-American mothers do (Anderson and Evans 1976). Instead Chicana/o mothers encourage their children to think and act communally—for the good of the family and the community (Ramírez and Castañeda 1974; Trueba and Delgado-Gaitan 1985). This, as well as the constellation of features associated with Chicana/o family structure—working-class status, large family size, familism, *compadrazgo*, nonexclusive mothering—helps explain why Chicanas and Chicanos often realize their interests, skills, and desires in the community and *la familia* instead of the larger public domain. Much of the current research on Chicana feminism highlights the "collective" orientation of Chicanas' struggles against oppression based on gender, race, ethnicity, and class—a struggle distinct from mainstream liberal feminism's focus on gender inequality and individual rights.[10]

Our analysis shows the applicability of Chodorow's theoretical account of gender development to Chicana/o families. The crucial role of women emphasized by Chodorow is evident in Chicana/o families, but as a part of a unique constellation of features that together bear on the acquisition of gender identity and the related development of group identity. In particular, the psychological meaning of other women within the kin network must be taken into account.

Conclusion

In *The Reproduction of Mothering* Nancy Chodorow makes a powerful argument about the reproduction of gender-specific personalities within the European-American middle-class family. Because Chodorow assumes that mothers are the "exclusive" primary caretakers of their children, her empirical account does not explain the reproduction of gender identity in Chicana/o families in which children are mothered by more than one female adult. As Spelman (1988) observes, however, Chodorow's theoretical account emphasizing the social context of mothering may be useful in explaining racial and ethnic differences in the acquisition of gender identity. By extending Chodorow's theoretical argument as well as her recent emphasis on "social specificity," we have posited that a constellation of features related to the Chicana/o family structure—specifically its working-class status, its higher fertility rate, familism, *compadrazgo*, and the practice of nonexclusive mothering—shape the acquisition of Chicana/o gender identities and explain, in part, why Chicanas and Chicanos have channeled their interests into *la familia* and the immediate ethnic community.

To what extent can conclusions about the reproduction of gender personality derive from a secondary review of the literature? Moreover, what questions pertinent to an understanding of gender construction does the literature leave unresolved? The psychological meaning for young Chicanos and Chicanas of multiple female caretakers is one unresolved question. Further, do the biological mother and father remain primary caretakers? Do members of extended kin networks provide alternative models for personal identification and attachment? And how do these arrangements and relationships change through time and place?

While strong agreement about the key features of Chicana/o family structure exists among Chicana/o sociologists, anthropologists, and historians, data about the quality, nuance, and tone of relationships in these families are lacking. Attention to such details lies within the province of clinical work done by practicing analysts and therapists. Unfortunately, as many sociologists and therapists have observed, most of the people who consult analysts are upper middle class and white, which means that people of color from large extended families are not likely to be found in clinical case studies.

Anthropological work in the culture and personality tradition such as Anne Parson's (1964) research on extended families in southern Italy points to one way of addressing this problem. Her work is instructive for future psychoanalytic sociological studies of Chicana/o family life. If we are to understand the complex interplay among family structure, culture, and personality, more clinically guided work grounded in a culturally and historically specific context must be done. Clinical observations and literary works often capture the systematic details of family life largely missing from most sociological and historical studies. By combining the methods of psychoanalysis and sociology, we can place Chicana/o families in their social and historical context. As a result, we can better answer questions about the reproduction of gender personality and group identity in Chicana/o families.

NOTES

Acknowledgments: We would like to thank Denise Bielby, Maxine Baca Zinn, Nancy Chodorow, Arlie Hochschild, Barbara Laslett, Beatríz Pesquera, Eli Sagan, Kate Tyler, Patricia Zavella, and the aonymous reviewers of *Signs* for their comments and suggestions on earlier verions of this article. Please note that we are full coauthors and have listed our names in reverse alphabetical order.

1. Zepeda 1979; Griswold del Castillo 1984; Alarcón 1985; Hernandez 1988. The terms *Chicana* and *Chicano* refer, respectively, to a woman and a man of Mexican descent residing in the United States, without distinguishing immigrant status. They are also political terms. Their usage implicitly recognizes the colonial domination of Mexican Americans follow-

ing the annexation of northern Mexico by the United States after the United States–Mexico war of 1846–48, which limited Chicana/o access to education, employment, and political participation (Almaguer 1971; Barrera, Muñoz, and Ornelas 1972; Blauner 1972; Estrada et al. 1981). During the Chicana movement in the 1960s, the label *Chicano* arose as the symbolic representation of self-determination, conveying a commitment to political struggle for the betterment of the Mexican-American community (Chicano Coordinating Committee on Higher Education 1969; Alvarez 1971; Acuña 1981). *Mexican-American* also refers to people of Mexican descent living in the United States, but it does not bear the same political connotations as *Chicano*. Aware of the sexism implicit in the Spanish language, we use the masculine form *Chicano* only when referring specifically to men; we use *Chicana* when referring to women. For adjectival constructions requiring an inclusive term for both women and men, we prefer to use the more precise and less exclusionary *Chicana/o*.

2. Rich 1980; Flax 1981; Joseph 1981; Lorber et al. 1981; Spelman 1988.

3. Mirandé 1977, 1985; Baca Zinn 1979, 1982/83; Staples and Mirandé 1980; Baca Zinn and Eitzen 1987; Keefe and Padilla 1987; Williams 1990.

4. Chodorow, like the psychoanalytic theory from which she draws, assumes that sexual orientation and gender identity are intimately connected. And, like Freud ([1925] 1963), she conflates the acquisition of gender identity and heterosexual object choice. Feminist scholars, for example, Adrienne Rich 1980, Gayle Rubin 1984, and Miriam Johnson 1988, have criticized Chodorow's conceptualization because it marginalizes the experiences of lesbians and gay men. Further, as Rich observes, gender identity as "feminine" does not automatically lead to the development of a heterosexual object choice (1980). While we agree with this criticism, we are mindful that scholarly work has yet to move beyond a critique of Chodorow's conceptual ambiguity to a more useful analytical distinction between gender identity and sexual orientation. Until a better concept is developed, we adopt—critically and reluctantly—Chodorow's usage of gender identity in this article.

5. It is important to note that social scientists have a long history of overgeneralizing about "the Chicano family" based on findings from small, nonrandom samples. Such research (which we briefly review later in this chapter) does not recognize or analyze diversity among Chicana/o families by immigrant status, generation in the United States, parental sexual orientation, socioeconomic status, or residence. Our article focuses on working-class Chicana/o families, the largest group within the United States Chicana/o or Mexican-origin population. One important limitation of our article is its focus on heterosexual gender identity. While we recognize the importance of analyzing lesbian/gay gender identity and parenting among Chicanas and Chicanos, no social science data are yet available on this topic. Nevertheless, our heterosexual focus has implications for the development of gay/lesbian identity among Chicanas and Chicanos. The significance of the mother-daughter relationship and relationships to other women in Moraga's autobiographical work (1983) is suggestive in this respect.

6. Rubin first introduced the concept of sex/gender system into feminist theory. She defines it as "the set of arrangements by which a society transforms biological sexuality into products of human activity and in which these needs are transformed" (1975, 159).

7. According to Chodorow, another way women may fulfill their relational needs is by developing and maintaining significant friendships with other women (1978, 200).

8. For example, Baca Zinn 1980; Ybarra, 1982; Griswold del Castillo 1984, Zavella 1987; and Williams 1990.

9. González 1982; Muñoz and Barrera 1982; García and Arce 1988; Muñoz 1988; I. García 1989.

10. Cotera 1977; González 1977; Raines 1988; A. García 1989; Zavella 1989; Segura and Pesquera 1992.

REFERENCES

Acosta, Oscar Zeta. 1972. *The Autobiography of a Brown Buffalo.* San Francisco: Straight Arrow.

Acuña, Rodolfo. 1981. *Occupied America: A history of Chicanos.* 2d ed. New York: Harper & Row.

Alarcón, Norma. 1985. "What Kind of Lover Have You Made Me, Mother? Toward a Theory of Chicanas' Feminism and Cultural Identity through Poetry." In *Women of Color Perspectives on Feminism and Identity,* ed. Audrey T. McClusky. Occasional Papers Series 1. Bloomington: University of Indiana Women's Studies Program.

Almaguer, Tomás. 1971. "Toward the Study of Chicano Colonialism." *Aztlán: Chicano Journal of the Social Sciences and Arts* 2:7–22.

Alvarez, Rodolfo. 1971. "The Unique Psycho-Historical Experience of the Mexican American." *Social Science Quarterly* 52:15–29.

Anaya, Rudolfo A. 1972. *Bless Me, Ultima.* Berkeley: Tonatiuh International.

Anderson, James, and Francis B. Evans. 1976. "Family Socialization and Educational Achievement in Two Cultures: Mexican-American and Anglo-American." *Sociometry* 39:209–22.

Baca Zinn, Maxine. 1975. "Chicanas: Power and Control in the Domestic Sphere." *De Colores: Journal of Emerging Raza Philosophies* 2:19–31.

———. 1979. "Chicano Family Research: Conceptual Distortions and Alternative Directions." *Journal of Ethnic Studies* 7:59–71.

———. 1980. "Employment and Education of Mexican-American Women: The Interplay of Modernity and Ethnicity in Eight Families." *Harvard Educational Review* 50:47–62.

———. 1982. "Chicano Men and Masculinity." *Journal of Ethnic Studies* 10:29–44.

———. 1982/83. "Familism Among Chicanos: A Theoretical Review." *Humboldt Journal of Social Relations* 10:224–38.

Baca Zinn, Maxine, and Stanley D. Eitzen. 1987. *Diversity in American Families.* New York: Harper & Row.

Barrera, Mario. 1979. *Race and Class in the Southwest: A Theory of Racial Inequality.* Notre Dame, Ind.: University of Notre Dame Press.

Barrera, Mario, Carlos Muñoz, and Charles Ornelas. 1972. "The Barrio as an Internal Colony." In *People and Politics in Urban Society,* ed. Harlan H. Hahn, 465–99. *Journal of Urban Affairs* annual review, vol. 6. Beverly Hills, Calif.: Sage.

Benjamin, Jessica. 1988. *The Bonds of Love: Psychoanalysis, Feminism and the Problem of Domination.* New York: Pantheon.

Bermúdez, María. 1955. *La Vida del Mexicano.* Mexico City: Antigua Liberia Robredo.

Blauner, Robert. 1972. *Racial Oppression in America.* New York: Harper & Row.

Bott, Elizabeth. 1971. *Family and Social Networks.* 2d ed. New York: Free Press.

Brennis, Brooks, and Samuel Roll. 1975. "Ego Modalities in Manifest Dreams of Male and Female Chicanos." *Psychiatry* 38:172–85.

Caulfield, Mina Davis. 1974. "Imperialism, the Family and Cultures of Resistance," *Socialist Revolution* 2:67–85.

Cervantes, Lorna Dee. 1980. "Beneath the Shadow of the Freeway." In her *Emplumada,* 11–14. Pittsburgh: University of Pittsburgh Press.

Chicano Coordinating Committee on Higher Education. 1969. *El Plan de Santa Barbara: A Chicano Plan for Higher Education.* Santa Barbara, Calif.: La Causa.

Chodorow, Nancy. 1974. "Family Structure and Feminine Personality." In *Woman, Culture and Society,* ed. Michelle Rosaldo and Louise Lamphere, 43–66. Stanford, Calif.: Stanford University Press.

———. 1978. *The Reproduction of Mothering: Psychoanalysis and the Sociology of Gender.* Berkeley: University of California Press.

———. 1989. *Feminism and Psychoanalytic Theory.* New Haven, Conn.: Yale University Press.

Cotera, Marta. 1977. *The Chicana Feminist.* Austin, Tex.: Information Systems Development.

Cuadráz, Gloria, and Jennifer Pierce. 1993. "From Scholarship Girls to Scholarship Women: Race, Class and Gender in Graduate Education." Paper presented at the National Association for Ethnic Studies conference, Salt Lake City, Utah, March 6.

Díaz-Guerrero, Rogelio. 1955. "Neurosis and the Mexican Family Structure." *American Journal of Psychiatry* 112 (December): 411–17.

Elasser, Nan, Kyle MacKenzie, and Yvonne Tixier Y Vigil. 1980. *Las Mujeres: Conversations from a Hispanic Community.* Old Westbury, N.Y.: Feminist Press.

Estrada, Leobardo F., F. Chris García, Reynaldo Flores Macias, and Lionel Maldonado. 1981. "Chicanos in the United States: A History of Exploitation and Resistance." *Daedalus* 110:103–13.

Falicov, Celia Jaes. 1982. "Mexican Families." In *Ethnicity and Family Therapy,* ed. Monica McGoldrick, John K. Pearce, and Joseph Giordano, 134–63. New York: Guilford Press.

Flax, Jane. 1981. "The Family in Contemporary Feminist Thought: A Critical Review." In *The Family in Political Thought,* ed. Jean Bethke Elshtain, 223–53. Amherst: University of Massachusetts Press.

Freud, Sigmund. (1925) 1963. "Some Psychological Consequences of the Anatomical Distinction between the Sexes." In *Sexuality and the Psychology of Love,* ed. Philip Rieff, 183–93. New York: Collier.

Galarza, Ernesto. 1971. *Barrio Boy.* Notre Dame, Ind.: University of Notre Dame Press.

García, Alma M. 1989. "The Development of Chicana Feminist Discourse: 1900–1980." *Gender and Society* 3 (June): 88–98.

García, Ignacio M. 1989. *United We Win: The Rise and Fall of La Raza Unida Party.* Tucson: University of Arizona, Mexican American Studies and Research Center.

García, John A., and Carlos H. Arce. 1988. "Political Orientations and Behaviors of Chicanos: Trying to Make Sense Out of Attitudes and Participation." In *Latinos and the Political System,* ed. F. Chris Garcia, 125–51. Notre Dame, Ind.: University of Notre Dame Press.

García, Mario T. 1980. "The Chicana in American History: The Mexican Women of El Paso, 1880–1920—a Case Study." *Pacific Historical Review* 49:315–37.

Gecas, Viktor. 1973. "Self-Conceptions of Migrant Settled Mexican Americans." *Social Science Quarterly* 54(3):579–95.

Gilbert, G. M. 1959. "Sex Differences in Mental Health in a Mexican Village." *International Journal of Psychiatry* 3 (Winter): 208–13.

Gonzales, Rodolfo. 1972. *I Am Joaquín, Yo Soy Joaquín.* New York: Bantam.

González, César A. 1982. "La Familia de Joaquin Chinas." *De Colores: Journal of Chicano Expression and Thought* 6 (1–2):145–49.

González, Sylvia. 1977. "The White Feminist Movement: The Chicana Perspective." *Social Science Journal* 14 (April): 67–76.

Griswold del Castillo, Richard. 1984. *La Familia:*

Chicano Families in the Urban Southwest. Notre Dame, Ind.: University of Notre Dame Press.

Hartmann, Heidi. 1981. "The Family as the Locus of Gender, Class, and Political Struggle: The Example of Housework." *Signs: Journal of Women in Culture and Society* 6 (3):366–94.

Hernandez, Lisa. 1988. "Canas." In *Palabras Chicanas,* ed. Lisa Hernandez and Tina Benitez, 47–49. Berkeley: University of California, Berkeley, Mujeres in March Press.

Horkheimer, Max. (1936) 1972. "Authority and the Family." In his *Critical Theory.* New York: Herder & Herder.

Horowitz, Ruth. 1983. *Honor and the American Dream: Culture and Identity in a Chicano Community.* New Brunswick, N.J.: Rutgers University Press.

Humphrey, Norman D. 1944. "The Changing Structure of Detroit Mexican Families: An Index of Acculturation." *American Sociological Review* 9 (December): 622–26.

Johnson, Carmen Acosta. 1980. "Breast-feeding and Social Class Mobility: The Case of Mexican Migrant Mothers in Houston, Texas." In *Twice a Minority: Mexican American Women,* ed. Margarita B. Melville, 66–82. St. Louis: Mosby.

Johnson, Miriam. 1988. *Strong Mothers, Weak Wives.* Berkeley and Los Angeles: University of California Press.

Jones, Robert. 1948. "Ethnic Family Patterns: The Mexican-American Family in the U.S." *American Journal of Sociology* 53 (May): 450–52.

Joseph, Gloria. 1981. "Black Mothers and Daughters." In *Common Differences: Conflicts in Black and White Feminist Perspectives,* ed. Gloria Joseph and Jill Lewis, 75–126. New York: Anchor.

Keefe, Susan E. 1979. "Urbanization, Acculturation and Extended Family Ties: Mexican Americans in Cities." *American Ethnologist* 6:349–45.

Keefe, Susan E., and Amado M. Padilla. 1987. *Chicano Ethnicity.* Albuquerque: University of New Mexico Press.

Lamphere, Louise, Patricia Zavella, and Felipe Gonzales, with Peter B. Evans. 1993. *Sunbelt Working Mothers: Reconciling Family and Factory.* Ithaca, N.Y.: Cornell University Press.

Lasch, Christopher. 1977. *Haven in a Heartless World.* New York: Basic.

Limón, José E. 1980. " 'La Vieja Inés,' a Mexican Folk Game: A Research Note." In *Twice a Minority: Mexican American Women,* ed. Margarita B. Melville, 88–94. St. Louis: Mosby.

Lorber, Judith, et al. 1981. "On *The Reproduction of Mothering*: A Methodological Debate." *Signs* 6 (3):482–513.

Marcuse, Herbert. 1955. *Eros and Civilization: A Philosophical Inquiry into Freud.* Boston: Beacon.

Melville, Margarita B. 1980. "Introduction" and "Matresence." In *Twice a Minority: Mexican American Women,* ed. Margarita B. Melville, 1–16. St. Louis: Mosby.

Mesa-Baines, Amalia. 1990. "Quest for Identity: Profile of Two Chicana Muralists: Based on Interviews with Judith F. Baca and Patricia Rodriguez." In *Signs from the Heart: California Chicano Murals,* ed. Eva Sperling Cockroft and Holly Barnet Sanchez, 69–82. Venice, Calif.: Social and Public Art Resource Center.

Mindel, Charles H. 1980. "Extended Familism Among Urban Mexican Americans, Anglos, and Blacks." *Hispanic Journal of Behavioral Sciences* 2:21–34.

Mirandé, Alfredo. 1977. "The Chicano Family: A Reanalysis of Conflicting Views." *Journal of Marriage and the Family* 39:747–56.

———. 1985. *The Chicano Experience: An Alternative Perspective.* Notre Dame, Ind.: University of Notre Dame Press.

Mirandé, Alfredo, and Evangelina Enríquez. 1979. *La Chicana: The Mexican American Woman.* Chicago: University of Chicago Press.

Montiel, Miguel. 1970. "The Social Science Myth of the Mexican American Family." *El Grito: A Journal of Contemporary Mexican American Thought* 3 (Summer): 56–63.

Moraga, Cherríe. 1983. "From a Long Line of Vendidas." In her *Loving in the War Years,* 90–144. Boston: South End.

Muñoz, Carlos, Jr. 1988. *Youth, Identity, Power: The Chicano Movement.* London and New York: Verso.

Muñoz, Carlos, Jr., and Mario Barrera. 1982. "La Raza Unida Party and the Chicano Student Movement in California." *Social Science Journal* 19 (April): 101–20.

Neumaier, Diane. 1990. "Judy Baca: Our People Are the Internal Exiles." In *Making Face, Making Soul—Haciendo Caras,* ed. Gloria Anzaldúa, 256–70. San Francisco: Aunt Lute Foundation.

Pardo, Mary. 1990. "Mexican American Women Grassroots Community Activists (Mothers of East Los Angeles)." *Frontiers: A Journal of Women's Studies* 11(1):1–7.

Parsons, Anne. 1964. "Is the Oedipus Complex Universal?" In *The Psychoanalytic Study of Society,* ed. Warner Muenstenberg and Sidney Axelrod, 278–328. New York: International Universities Press.

Parsons, Talcott. 1964. *Social Structure and Personality.* New York: Free Press.

Parsons, Talcott, and Robert Bales. 1955. *Family, Socialization and Interaction Processes.* New York: Free Press.

Peñalosa, Fernando. 1968. "Mexican-American Family Roles." *Journal of Marriage and the Family* 30(4): 680–88.

Pesquera, Beatríz M. 1991. " 'It Gave Me Confianza': Work Commitment and Identity." *Aztlán: Journal of Chicano Studies Research* 20 (Spring/Fall): 97–118.

Pierce, Jennifer. 1991. "Gender, Legal Workers and Emotional Labor: Women and Men at Work in Corporate Law Firms." Ph.D. dissertation, University of California, Berkeley.

Rabow, Jerome, Gerald Platt, and Marion Goldman. 1987. "Preface." In *Advances in Psychoanalytic Sociology,* ed. Jerome Rabow, Gerald Platt, and Marion Goldman. Malabar, Fla.: Krieger.

Raines, Rosario Torres. 1988. "The Mexican American Women and Work: Intergenerational Perspectives of Comparative Ethnic Groups." In *Mexicanas at Work in the United States,* ed. Margarita B. Melville, 33–46. Houston: University of Houston, Mexican American Studies.

Ramírez, Manuel, III, and Alfredo Castañeda. 1974. *Cultural Democracy, Bicognitive Development, and Education.* New York: Academic Press.

Rebolledo, Tey Diana. 1983. "Abuelitas: Mythology and Integration in Chicano Literature." *Revista Chicano-Riquena* 11 (3–4): 148–58.

Rich, Adrienne. 1980. "Compulsory Heterosexuality and Lesbian Existence." *Signs* 5(4):631–60.

Rochin, Refugio I., and Monica D. Castillo. 1991. "Immigration, *Colonia* Formation and Latino Poor in Rural California: Evolving Immigration." Working Paper no. 91–38. University of California, Davis, Department of Agricultural Economics.

Rodriguez, Richard. 1982. *Hunger of Memory: The Education of Richard Rodriquez.* New York: Bantam.

Romano, Octavio. 1970. "Social Science Objectivity and the Chicanos." *El Grito* 4:4–16.

Ross, Fred. 1989. *Conquering Goliath: Cesar Chavez and the Beginning.* Keene, Calif.: United Farm Workers.

Rubin, Gayle. 1975. "The Traffic in Women: Notes on the Political Economy of Sex." In *Toward an Anthropology of Women,* ed. Rayna Reiter, 157–210. New York: Monthly Review Press.

———. 1984. "Thinking Sex: Notes for a Radical Theory of the Politics of Sexuality." In *Pleasure and Danger,* ed. Carole S. Vance, 267–319. Boston: Routledge & Kegan Paul.

Saldívar, Ramón. 1990. "Ideologies of the Self: Chicano Autobiography." In his *Chicano Narrative: The Dialectics of Difference,* 154–70. Madison: University of Wisconsin Press.

Saragoza, Alex M. 1983. "The Conceptualization of the History of the Chicano Family." In *The State of Chicano Research on Family, Labor, and Migration: Proceedings of the First Stanford Symposium on Chicano Research and Public Policy,* ed. Armando Valdez, Alberto Camarillo, and Tomas Almaguer, 11–38. Stanford, Calif.: Stanford Center for Chicano Research.

Segura, Denise A. 1988. "Familism and Employment Among Chicanas and Mexican Immigrant Women." In *Mexicanas at Work in the United States,* ed. Margarita B. Melville, 24–32. Houston: University of Houston, Mexican-American Studies.

———. 1992. "Chicanas in White-Collar Jobs: 'You Have to Prove Yourself More.'" *Sociological Perspectives* 35:163–82.

Segura, Denise A., and Beatríz M. Pesquera. 1992. "Beyond Indifference and Antipathy: The Chicana Feminist Movement and Chicana Feminist Discourse." *Aztlán: Journal of Chicano Studies Research* 19(2):69–88.

Sena-Rivera, Jaime. 1979. "Extended Kinship in the

United States: Competing Models and the Case of La Familia Chicana." *Journal of Marriage and the Family* 41 (February): 121–29.

Sotomayor, Marta. 1971. "Mexican-American Interaction with Social Systems." In *La Causa Chicana: The Movement for Justice*, ed. Margaret M. Manfold, 148–60. New York: Family Service Association of America.

Spelman, Elizabeth. 1988. *Inessential Woman: The Problem of Exclusion in Feminist Thought*. Boston: Beacon.

Staples, Robert, and Alfredo Mirandé. 1980. "Racial and Cultural Variation Among Americans: A Decennial Review of the Literature on Minority Families." *Journal of Marriage and the Family* 40(4):157–73.

Throne, Barrie, and Marilyn Yalom. 1982. *Rethinking the Family: Some Feminist Questions*. New York: Longman Press.

Tienda, Marta, and Ronald Angel. 1982. "Headship and Household Composition Among Blacks, Hispanics and Other Whites." *Social Forces* 61:508–31.

Trueba, Henry T., and Concha Delgado-Gaitan. 1985. "Specialization of Mexican Children for Cooperation and Competition: Sharing and Copying." *Journal of Educational Equity and Leadership* 5:189–204.

U.S. Bureau of the Census. 1988. "Fertility of American Women." *Current Population Reports*, Series P-20 (June). Washington, D.C.: Government Printing Office.

———. 1991a. "The Hispanic Population in the United States: March 1990." *Current Population Reports*, Series P–20, no. 449 (May). Washington, D.C.: Government Printing Office.

———. 1991b. "Poverty in the United States: 1990." *Current Population Reports*, Series P–60, no. 175. Washington, D.C.: Government Printing Office.

———. 1992. "Household and Family Characteristics: March 1991." *Current Population Reports*, Series P–20, no. 458 (February). Washington, D.C.: Government Printing Office.

Villarreal, José Antonio. 1959. *Pocho*. New York: Doubleday.

Viramontes, Helene María. 1990. "Nopalitos: The Making of Fiction." In *Making Faces, Making Soul—Haciendo Caras: Creative and Critical Perspectives by Women of Color*, ed. Gloria Anzaldúa, 291–94. San Francisco: Aunt Lute Foundation.

Wagner, Roland M., and Diane M. Schaffer. 1980. "Social Networks and Survival Strategies: An Exploratory Study of Mexican-American, Black and Anglo Female Family Heads in San Jose, California." In *Twice a Minority: Mexican American Women*, ed. Margarita B. Melville, 173–90. St. Louis: Mosby.

Williams, Norma. 1990. *The Mexican American Family: Tradition and Change*. New York: General Hall.

Ybarra, Lea. 1982. "When Wives Work: The Impact on Chicano Families." *Journal of Marriage and the Family* 44(1):169–78.

———. 1983. "Empirical and Theoretical Developments in the Study of Chicano Families." In *The State of Chicano Research on Family, Labor, and Migration: Proceedings of the First Stanford Symposium on Chicano, Research and Public Policy*, ed. Armando Valdez, Alberto Camarillo, and Tomas Almaguer, 91–110. Stanford, Calif.: Stanford Center for Chicano Research.

Zavella, Patricia. 1987. *Women's Work and Chicano Families: Cannery Workers of the Santa Clara Valley*. Ithaca, N.Y.: Cornell University Press.

———. 1989. "The Problematic Relationship of Feminism and Chicana Studies." *Women's Studies* 17:25–36.

Zepeda, Marlene. 1979. "Las Abuelitas." *Agenda* 6 (November/December): 10–13.

Chapter 22

Catching Sense: Learning from Our Mothers to Be Black and Female

SUZANNE C. CAROTHERS

My mama was a midwife. She and the other midwives taught each other. Sure, there was a community doctor but, my mama and the other women delivered those babies by themselves. If they had any complications, they'd call the doctor. 'Course, I've never known my mother to lose a case.
—A sixty-four-year-old woman

Black parents are required to prepare their children to understand and live in two cul-

From *Uncertain Terms*, edited by Faye Ginsburg and Anna Lowenhaupt Tsing, copyright © 1990 by Faye Ginsburg and Anna Lowenhaupt Tsing. Reprinted by permission of Beacon Press, Boston.

On the plantations of the St. Helena Island off the coast of South Carolina, one would rarely hear, "Where were you born?" More likely, one would be asked, "Where did you *catch sense?*" The people on this island do not assume that the place where a person was born is the same as the place where that person was raised and socialized. Nor is birthplace viewed as equivalent to the setting, context, or situation in which people begin to make meaning about and understand the world in which they live. "Catching Sense" was discussed in a paper entitled "Black Families on St. Helena Island," by Patricia Guthrie, delivered at The National Council of Negro Women conference *Black Women: An Historical Perspective*, Washington, D.C., November 12–13, 1979.

tures—Black American culture and standard American culture.[1] To confront the bicultural nature of their world, these parents must respond in distinctive ways. In the following essay, I show how this can be seen in the practices and beliefs of several generations of Black women through their descriptions of seemingly ordinary and commonplace activities.

The first setting in which people usually experience role negotiations is the home. Boys and girls will draw from important lessons learned at home during childhood to negotiate their future roles as viable members of society. Distant though the lessons may seem from the perspective of an adult, they were taught directly and indirectly in the context of day-to-day family life. Of the many dyads occurring within families, the interactions between mothers and daughters are a critical source of information on how women perceive what it means to be female. I have been particularly interested in these perceptions among Black mothers and daughters because of the unique socio-economic, political circumstances in which these women find themselves in American culture. During the Fall, Winter, and Spring of 1980–81, I returned to my home town of Hemington, fictitiously named, to collect data for my study. It is the contradiction that emerged between my experience of having grown up in the Black community of Hemington and my graduate school reading of the social science literature on Black family life and mother-daughter relationships that led me to engage in this research.

Background

Prior to the 1960s, studies on Black families in American society characterized them as pathological, dysfunctional, deviant, and matriarchal.[2] These studies emphasized Blacks's difficulties in achieving position, power, and prestige and viewed the family as a major source of weakness.

During the 1960s, new scholarship began to refute these older arguments. This new scholarship identified the strengths, stability and cohesiveness of Black families. Researchers began to re-define Black family life in its own cultural context without expectations of white middle-class nuclear family organization as the model for understanding Black family domestic units. In this research, the positive aspects of Black women's strong position in their families has become more clear.

Yet, the implications of Black women's strength has not been explored fully in the literature on American mother-daughter relationships. Black women have traditionally combined mothering and working roles, while white middle-class women in the United States until recently have not. In Western cultures, mothering is regarded as a role that directly conflicts with women's other societal roles. In response to this condition, many theorists of female status consider the mothering role to be the root cause of female dependence on and subordination to men.[3] Yet, this has not been the experience of Black mothers. As others have argued, "Women have been making culture, political decisions, and babies simultaneously and without structural conflicts in all parts of the world."[4]

During the 1970s, a recurring theme in the United States literature on mother-daughter relationships was the ambivalence and conflict existing between mothers and daughters. The literature describes competition and rivalry and suggests a negative cycle of influences passed from mothers to their daughters. For example, Judith Arcana suggests:

> The oppression of women created a breach among us, especially between mothers and daughters. Women cannot respect their mothers in a society which degrades them; women cannot respect themselves. Mothers socialize their daughters into the narrow role of wife-mother; in frustration and guilt, daughters reject their mothers for their duplicity and incapacity—so the alienation grows in the turning of the generations.[5]

The above quote is generally inapplicable to the relationship between Black mothers and their daughters. The Black cultural tradition assumes women to be working mothers, models of community strength, and skilled women whose competence moves beyond emotional sensitivity. It is through this tradition of a dual role that Black women acquire their identity, develop support systems (networks), and are surrounded by examples of female initiative, support, and mutual respect.

Black mothers do not raise their children in isolation. In contrast, Nancy Chodorow argues:

> The household with children has become an exclusively parent and child realm; infant and child care has become the exclusive domain of

biological mothers who are increasingly isolated from other kin, with fewer social contacts and little routine assistance during their parenting time.[6]

The families to whom Chodorow refers above are child-centered. In the arrangement she describes, the needs of the domestic unit are shaped and determined primarily by those of the children. Scholars of Black family life offer evidence of other arrangements.[7] According to them, Black women raise their children in the context of extended families in which social and domestic relations, as well as kinship and residence structures, offer a great deal of social interaction among adults that includes children. In addition, these researchers have shown that child rearing is only one of many obligations to be performed within Black family households. They agree that child rearing cannot be evaluated in the singular context of an individual but rather in the plural context of the household. The process through which daughters learn from their mothers in Black families, therefore, contradicts the wave of literature on mother-daughter relationships.

In order to appreciate the contrast in orientation of Black mothers, it is necessary to consider the wider social context of Black parenting. Black parents in American society have a unique responsibility. They must prepare their children to understand and live in two cultures—Black American culture and standard American culture.[8] Or as Wade W. Nobles[9] has suggested, Black families must prepare their children to live near and among white people without becoming white. This phenomenon has been referred to as *biculturality* by Ulf Hannerz and by Charles Valentine, an idea derived from W.E.B. Dubois who wrote in the early 1900s about the idea of double consciousness: "that Blacks have to guard their sense of blackness while accepting the rules of the games and cultural consciousness of the dominant white culture."[10] Because Black parents recognize that their children must lean to deal with institutional racism and personal discrimination Black children are encouraged to test absolute rules and absolute authority.[11] It is therefore critical to the socialization of Black children that their parents provide them with ample experiences dealing with procedures of interpersonal interaction rather than rules of conduct. The children are socialized to be part of a Black community rather than just Black families or "a fixed set of consaguinal and affixed members."[12] Beginning early in childhood, the wider social context in which Black children are raised usually involves not only their mothers but also many adults—all performing a variety of roles in relation to the child, the domestic unit, and the larger community. Furthermore, the transmission of knowledge and skills in Black family life is not limited to domestic life but occurs in public life arenas in which Black women are expected to participate. Working outside their homes to contribute to the economic resources of the family has been only one of the many roles of the majority of Black women. As members of the labor market, Black mothers simultaneously manage their personal lives, raise their children, organize their households, participate in community and civic organizations, and create networks to help each other cope with seemingly insurmountable adversities.

Participation in work and community activities broadens the concept and practice of mothering for Black women. How do the women learn these roles? What must they pass on to their female children if they are to one day perform these roles? An exploration of the social interactions between Black working mothers and their daughters, as well as the cultural context and content can extend our knowledge of the cultural variation in mothering roles and mother-daughter relationships and the processes by which mothers shape female identity.

The Study

Several reasons prompted my decision to return to Hemington for this research. Typically, studies of Black family life have been conducted in urban ghetto communities in the north and midwest, some in the deep rural South and most with lower-class or poor people.[13] In developing my research, I wanted to avoid choosing a location where there were vast differences between the Black and white standard of living that so often characterize the research settings in which Blacks are studied. In these settings, the usual distinguishing features for the Black population are poverty, unemployment, underemployment, low wages, and inadequate housing. The white communities are more varied economically, ranging from relatively wealthy managerial elites to welfare recipients living in housing projects. Yet, there are many middle-sized and large southern cities with large, varied and stable Black communities that researchers have not adequately explored. Hemington is such an example.[14]

Prior to 1960 and urban redevelopment, the Black community of Hemington was primarily concentrated in the area closest to the main business district of the city. At the time of the study, most Blacks still lived in predominantly all Black neighborhoods located on the west side of town, where a broad range of housing suggests an economically varied Black community. Blacks in Hemington live in public housing projects, low income hosing (both private homes and apartments), modern apartment complexes, and privately owned homes, ranging from modest to lavish.

Although I had not lived in Hemington for more than ten years, my kinship ties to the community meant that I had access to people, situations, and information that an outsider might not have or would need a considerably longer time to acquire. My experiences of growing up there and then studying and working in educational institutions in northern white society made me sensitive to differences in cultural patterns and more eager to analyze them.

Forty-two women and nine girls between the ages of 11 and 86 from twenty families agreed to participate in the study. I asked them to help me understand the meaning of mothering and working in their lives and how this meaning was passed on from mother to daughter—generation to generation. The stories that the women and girls shared with me about the very ordinary day-to-day activities of their lives became a rich source for understanding how women found and created meaning in the less-than-perfect world in which they lived.[15]

The study was of women whom Alice Walker could call the anonymous Black mothers whose art goes unsigned and whose names are known only by their families.[16] Many of the women in the study have known me all my life. They are great-grandmothers who lived to see their grandchildren's children born and grandmothers who have raised their children. I grew up with some of the mothers who are raising their children. Still others, the young girls, I remember from the time they were born.[17]

Seventy-five years separate the births of the oldest from the youngest participants. According to their ages and the age at which each became a mother, informants fall into five grouping possibilities. I have categorized these groups in Table 1. Identifying these groups helps to locate the women's experiences relative to the challenges each generation confronted in an ever-changing society.

These women perceive themselves as

TABLE 1. Participant Groupings

Group	Name	Ages	Number in Each Group
I	The Rural Born Ladies	68–86	9
II	The First to Pursue Schooling and Technical Training	58–67	6
III	Those Who Received Post-Secondary Education, Most Urban Born	40–57	15
IV	The Young Home Owners, All Urban Born	24–39	12
V	The Children/Unmarried Young Adults	11–23	9

middle-class. All are or have been employed. They are people who share a common system of values, attitudes, sentiments, and beliefs which indicate that an important measure of "class" for these Black Americans is the range of resources available to the extended family unit. This system, then—based on extensive inter-household sharing—is not synonymous with traditional criteria for social class structure, which includes wealth, prestige, and power.[18]

What Black Mothers Teach: Concrete Learnings and Critical Understandings

In order to understand the teaching and learning process taking place between Black mothers and daughters, I observed the women and asked them questions about their seemingly ordinary and commonplace daily activities. When the participants in the study were asked from whom they learned, their answers included their mothers, fathers, stepfathers, stepmothers, grandfathers, grandmothers, great-grandmothers, aunts, the lady next door, an older sister, a brother, a teacher—in short, their community. When asked *what* they had learned from these people, their responses touched a range of possibilities, which can be grouped into two broad categories. Cooking, sewing, cleaning, and ironing are examples of activities that are associated with the daily routines of households that I call "concrete learnings." The regular performance of these leads to what I refer to as "critical understandings," which include such things as achieving independence, taking on responsibility, feeling confident, getting along with others, or being trustworthy. The acquisition of these is not easy to pinpoint and define. They are not taught as directly as the concrete learnings, but they are consistently expected. Their outcomes are not as immediately measurable because they usually take a longer time to develop.

What do mothers do to pass on to their daughters the understandings that are considered critical to a daughter's well-being, and the skills, the learned power of doing a thing competently? Mothers teach their daughters what to take into account in order to figure out how to perform various tasks, recognizing that the individual tasks that they and their daughters are required to perform change over time. Therefore, the preparation that mothers provide includes familiarity with the task itself, as well as a total comprehension of the working of the home or other situations within which the task is being done. The women's interviews reveal that mothers teach by the way that they live their own lives ("example"), by pointing out critical understandings they feel their daughters need ("show-ing"), and by instructing their daughters how to do a task competently. Their teaching is both verbal and nonverbal, direct and indirect. Daughters learn not only from their mothers but also from other members of the family and the community.

The data indicate that concrete learnings teach—in ways that verbal expression alone does not—a route toward mastery and pride that integrates the child into the family and community. Daughters learn competency through a sense of aesthetics, an appreciation for work done beautifully. The women described this notion as follows: "You don't see pretty clothes hanging on the line like you used to"; "Mama could do a beautiful piece of ironing"; "You always iron the back of the collar first. The wrinkles get on the back and it makes the front of the collar smooth"; or "Now if I got in the kitchen and say I saw these pretty biscuits, I might say Mama how did you get your biscuits to look this pretty. . . ." This aesthetic quality becomes one of the measures of competently done work as judged by the women themselves and by other members of their community.

As each generation encountered technological changes in household work, mothers became less rigid about teaching their daughters concrete learnings. However, like previous generations, mothers still teach their daughters responsibility through chores, which gives them opportunities to practice and get better at doing them, both alone and with others. These activities are not contrived but rather they constitute real work and contribute to the daily needs of their households. Participation in these activities encourages mastery of them.

Women across the generations boasted about having mastered chores. Take the comments of the forty-seven-year-old grandmother, Mrs. Edwina Phillips, who said:

By the time I was 11, I could do a lot of stuff, I could do everything in a house. I could iron for people. I started babysitting for people the summer I was seven going on eight. . . . I was seven and I know I did a good job.

Another example can be seen in the statement of Mrs. Queen Ester Washington, a member of the Rural Born Ladies Group, who has one great-granddaughter.

Yea, we had to carry in the night wood. We had to do our night work. We had to milk the cows. We had to feed the horses. We had to do everything. You see, I was raised in the country and you know what country people do? [They] pick cotton, hoe cotton, and you learn to do it all. I know how to do almost anything in the working line.

After I become an expert in farm work in the country, I moved to Hemington and then I become an expert in domestic work.

Sixty-four-year-old Mrs. Odessa Johnson, a grandmother of two, offered these remarks:

I started working when I was in the first grade. This lady who was white lived across the fence from us. My mother used to put me across the fence. I'd wash the dishes. This would give the lady time to spend with her little girl who was sick. Then she'd put me back across the fence and I'd go home. You know people were real proud of me. I know they were because Mama's patients would say, "Jenny you going to let Odessa come and stay with me a while?"

A thirty-two-year-old mother of two said:

Grandmama is a very good cook, and I watched her. Mama is a good cook and I watched her. I'd pick up on things. Gradually they'd let me do little things here and there. If I cooked something, I don't care what it was, they would eat it. I made some dumplings one day that were just like rubber balls! They ate them. They never complained about them. I enjoyed cooking. You know when people act like they enjoy your cooking, even when you know it's bad, you do it, and the more you do, you get better at it. I enjoyed cooking so much that I took over a lot of the cooking from Mama, especially during the week.

Each woman described a certain kind of pride in herself for having learned and accomplished a task well. Such mastery reinforced and established the woman's confidence in her ability to perform well. Having chores to do was the important link bridging concrete learnings to critical understandings germane to a daughter's well-being.

Demands of Double Consciousness or Lessons of Racism

While mothers teach critical understandings through example, maxims, and practical lessons, they use what I am calling "dramatic enactments" as a powerful tool to teach their daughters ways to deal with white people in a racist society. Thus, daughters learn critical understandings that are specific to the Black experience.

When mothers teach by example, they enact before their daughters the particular skills necessary to achieve the task at hand. By contrast, dramatic enactments expose children to conflict or crisis and are often reserved for complex learning situations. "Learning to deal with white people," for example, was viewed by some women in the study as important to their survival, and dramatic enactment was identified as being a powerful technique for acquiring this skill. One thirty-one-year-old woman in group IV explained how she learned this critical understanding through dramatic enactments from her grandmother, who did domestic work.

My sister and I were somewhat awed of white people because when we were growing up, we did not have to deal with them in our little en-

vironment. I mean you just didn't have to because we went to an all-Black school, an all-Black church, and lived in an all-Black neighborhood. We just didn't deal with them. If you did, it was a clerk in a store.

Grandmother was dealing with them. And little by little she showed us how. First, [she taught us that] you do not fear them. I'll always remember that. Just because their color may be different and they may think differently, they are just people.

They way she did it was by taking us back and forth downtown with her. Here she is, a lady who cleans up peoples's kitchens. She comes into a store to spend her money. She could cause complete havoc if she felt she wasn't being treated properly. She'd say things like, "If you don't have it in the store, order it." It was like she had $500,000 to spend. We'd just be standing there and watching. But what she was trying to say [to us] was, they will ignore you if you let them. If you walk in there to spend your 15 cents, and you're not getting proper service, raise hell, carry on, call the manager but don't let them ignore you.

Preparing their daughters to deal with encounters in the world beyond home was a persistent theme in the stories offered by the women in this study. By introducing their daughters and granddaughters to such potentially explosive situations and showing the growing girls how older women could handle the problems spurred by racism, mothers and grandmothers taught the lessons needed for survival, culturally defined as coping with the wider world.

The Community Context

As I suggested earlier, my own and other research shows distinctive patterns according to which mothers and other members of Black families relate and respond to young children. The teaching and learning processes in these families occur in an environment in which a great deal of social interaction among the adults includes children. The present study confirms Young's research[19] and takes her argument further by suggesting how patterns of interaction between Black mothers and daughters within the context of community relationships facilitates teaching and learning.

The concept of Black family units working in concert to achieve the common goals they value arises out of the inherent expectations of helping and assuming responsibility for each other as part of a conscious model of social exchange.[20] Thus, giving and receiving are the understood premises for participating in community life. Different from guilt, this system has been fueled by the racial and economic oppressions that have plagued Black families since their introduction into American society. Women in these family units traditionally assume a critical role in meeting these responsibilities. This does not end when children reach maturity, nor is it hierarchical, from mother to child; it is part of the larger community value that the women believe in and sustain, described by a woman in group II:

> I was raised in a Christian neighborhood. That whole neighborhood was just Christian people. They looked after each other. You know, like if someone was sick in the neighborhood, they didn't have to send out nowhere for people to come in and take care of them. The people in the neighborhood would take care of them. They would iron, cook, do everything. Didn't even go in and say, "Do you need me to do anything." Folk would just come in and take hold.

This community context is especially supportive of the kind of teaching and learning that takes place between Black mothers and daughters.

Given the difficult conditions that racism and economic discrimination have imposed on the Black community (including, of course, the middle-class Black community), it is important for children to know that their parents can survive the difficult situations they encounter. Children need to trust that the world is sufficiently stable to give meaning to what they are learning. *Dependability*— based on elements of character such as hard work, faith, and the belief that their children can live a better life—provides the context for that trust and the daughters' sense of their mothers' competence to deal with the world.

Despite the conflicts that sometimes arose, daughters generally acknowledged the ongoing lessons their mothers had to teach them and that the process of *life-long learning* was central to their relationship, as Mrs. Washington's comments illustrate:

> Kitty and James, either one haven't got to the place today where I couldn't tell them if they were doing something wrong. And people gets on me for that. And I say, well you never get too old to learn. I say, if I know it's right why can't I correct them? They say, "When a child gets up on his own, you ought to let 'em alone." Then I say, well I'm going to bother mine as long as I live if I see 'em doing something wrong. I'm going to speak to them and if they don't do what I say, at least they don't tell me that they aren't. They just go someplace else and do it.

This sense of teaching and learning as an ongoing part of the mother-child relationship adds an impetus to the daughters' frequently expressed belief that they fulfilled their mothers' dreams and in a sense justified their mothers' lives through gaining an education.

> This is what Mama was working toward [my going to college]. This was her ambition. It was just like she was going to college herself. The first summer I finished high school and every summer after that, Mama took sleep-in jobs up in the mountains to earn extra money for my college education. . . . She very much wanted us to take advantage of all the things she never had. This is what she worked for.

Part of what makes increased formal education a continuation, rather than a rupture of the mother-daughter relationship is the daughter's insistence (backed up, of course, by community values) that older women had a kind of wisdom that transcended school-learning. A fifty-year-old woman said:

> Even without a [formal] education, my mother has more common sense than I do. I rely on her because I can say, "Well mother, so and so is going to happen, what do you think about it?" Surprisingly, she has an answer that I would have never thought of. I respect her for that.

Another woman fifty-three years of age agreed:

> Even though my mother did not get much formal education, she knew what was going on the world about her. She could read and write anything that she wanted. That was never a handicap for her. Maybe her language was not up to par, as for correctness of it [grammar], she could communicate her ideas. She knew how to say what she needed to say.

Black domestic units are centered around the needs and work of the household. Because of the necessity of so much work, though the pressures have been reduced over the generations, working together has become one of the major vehicles for learning. Learning is made attractive in this context because it represents access to adulthood and to continued membership in the family and community.

Through *shared work* activities, women give their children substance and sustenance by being available to them and providing an image and structure for them to follow. Their availability cannot be measured in terms of the amount of time mothers spend with their children. These women became skilled in using regular household work as an opportunity to spend time with their children. For example, it was not uncommon for these mothers, in groups I and II especially, not to be home when their children arrived home from school. The women's lives were organized around very demanding paid-work schedules and therefore not geared to making exclusive time for children. As one woman in group IV described it, "Some of the time we spent together was like working . . . working in the yard or I would sew and my mother would clean." Shared activities included going grocery shopping, accompanying a mother to work, cleaning house, hanging clothes on the line, sitting on the porch talking, walking to the bus stop, or, getting up, getting breakfast, and getting out to school. Mothers made the best use of the limited time they had.

These shared activities did not take place in a special world that women designed for their daughters; rather, they took place in the context of the real world of their mothers. And it was these worlds that daughters were expected to understand and eventually manage on their own. As explained by one woman, the activities started early in childhood:

> We bought food, clothes, or whatever we needed. We took great joy in doing it but Mama didn't tax that on us. She just raised us to be thoughtful about the household. If I was working and came home and we were out of bread, I went and bought some. My nine-year-old brother would do the same thing. He'd come from that coal house and if we didn't have any bread, he'd turn right around and go back to get some.

Thus, shared work does not necessarily mean doing the same thing at the same time. Rather, it is an awareness of what is being done by each member of the family or community that contributes to the survival and good of everyone.

Getting work done together requires in turn, a *free flow of information*, which in turn supports the teaching and learning process. It is important for mothers to teach daughters how to cope with the world; therefore, they do not hide the world from their children. Rather, information about what it takes to deal with their reality is readily available to Black daughters, which makes them quite knowledgeable about their mothers' own struggles and sacrifices. A forty-seven-year-old woman illustrated this point when she said:

> Any one of my children could have paid my bills, could have told you how much money I made, how much I was going to pay in church, how much grocery I was going to buy and what week I was suppose to buy what grocery when they were twelve years old. You see, what I did was let them in on the real facts of how we were doing it. I didn't play no games with them. We didn't pretend we had what we did not have. They knew exactly what we had.

The free flow of information creates an atmosphere of problem solving, that problems can and must be solved within the actual limits of the situation.

Black daughters learn their mothers' histories by seeing their mothers in the roles of mamas who nurture as friends, who become confidantes and companions; as teachers, who facilitate and encourage their learning about the world; and as advisors who counsel. For these women, the role of mother is not seen as "a person without further identity, one who can find her chief gratification in being all day with small children, living at a pace tuned to theirs."[21] From early on, the women in the present study see their mothers as complex beings. Knowing her mother's history intensifies the bond between mother and daughter, and helps daughters understand more about the limits under which their mothers have operated.

Getting along, however, is not necessarily dependent on the women always reaching agreement, or daughters following the advice of their mothers. It would not be unusual for a mother and daughter to fall out about an is-

sue one day and speak to each other the next. Such interactions provide continuing opportunities for daughters to practice developing and defending their own points of view, a skill useful in the outside world. These interactions insure the back and forth between Black mothers and daughters, which promotes the teaching and learning process and increases Black daughters' respect for what mothers have done and who they are.

Although respect remains a key value in mother-daughter relationships and helps to foster the teaching and learning process, generational differences between mothers and daughters lead to tensions that threaten the teaching and learning context. Daughters need to *balance* their loyalty to their mothers with their own needs to grow up in accord with the terms of their own generations' realities. Mothers, on the other hand, need to balance their need for their daughters' allegiance with the knowledge that the daughters require a high degree of independence to survive and achieve in the world.

Loyalty is the unspoken but clear message in the words spoken by the mothers and daughters in this study. They describe it in terms of faithfulness and continuing emotional attachment. As loyalty defines what Black mothers and daughters expect from each other, it also is part of the conflict between them—when Black women are unable to separate the tangled threads that bind them so closely. Their obligations to each other and the deep understanding of the plight they share sometimes nurtures a desire to protect, rather than commit what would be seen as an act of desertion.

This conflict was more pronounced between women in groups I and II who are the mothers of women in groups III and IV, respectively. The conflicts experienced by mothers and daughters was tempered by the daughters' desire to protect their mothers, a belief that their mothers wanted what was best for them, and the respect they had for their mothers. A forty-five-year-old woman in group III, describing her mother in group I, explained:

> I would adhere to my mama's wishes because I loved her so. You see, what she believed in got us this far. As these kids say, "if you can't think of something better, don't knock it." That's just the way I feel about it. I might sit down with my husband and get it off my chest but when my Mama says it, I'm going to listen, I'm going to respect her. I'm forty-five and I have never sassed my Mama. I am not trying to change my Mama. She is who she is.

As the quote makes clear, alienation does not characterize the kind of conflicts existing between these Black mothers and daughters. The daughters recognized the web of contradictions in which their mothers' lives were suspended. Women also have respect for their mothers' ability to overcome seemingly insurmountable situations. The women know only too well the odds stacked against them and their mothers. As one women said,

> At my age, I still would not sass my Mama. I don't dispute her because she is so dag gone strong that I don't think I have a right to dispute her. I think that she is entitled to be wrong sometimes. I think she's earned it.

Conclusion

Women in this study routinely have confronted very early on the contradictions between the world in which they were born and raised and the one away from their homes. The result is that the women are not thrown by that which is different or contradictory to their home practices; rather, they can accept, understand, negotiate and deal with the differences in reasonable ways.

A high degree of mutual respect and camaraderie characterize the teaching and learning process taking place between Black mothers and daughters. The community value of mutual responsibility makes this possible. Because of the multiple roles that these mothers play, the interactions between Black mothers and daughters require that mothers balance these roles and determine which one is appropriate in different situations. It also requires that daughters actively consider the context and purpose of the interaction and the mood of her mother to determine the appropriate response. Thus, the issue of authority that is often a major concern and obstacle in school learning for both teacher and students, shifts to mutuality in the teaching and learning process occurring between Black working mothers and their daughters.

The daughters have learned from their mothers by being exposed to the complications, complexities, and contradictions that, as working women, their mothers faced in a society which has traditionally viewed working and mothering as incompatible roles. The recognition of this difference requires that Black women, as a condition of their daily existence, constantly negotiate an alternative understanding of female identity that challenges the dominant gender paradigm in American culture.

NOTES

1. Throughout this chapter, I use the term Black as a proper noun in recognition of a specific cultural group, like Latinos or Asians. To that end, I have chosen to capitalize the "B." For a discussion of the use of an upper case "B" denoting Blacks and the interchangeable use of Blacks with Afro-American consistent with my view, see Kimberle Williams Crenshaw's article "Race, Reform, and Retrenchment: Transformation and Legitimation in Antidiscrimination Law," *Harvard Law Review* 101, no. 7 (May 1988): 1332.

2. The 1930s ushered in a decade of studies on family life in which the *Negro family* became a focal interest. In the 1960s, when social scientists became interested in the question of poverty, the *Negro family* once again became a focus for research. Studies concerning Black family life were conducted in key industrial urban areas. For a discussion of the literature on Black family life in the United States see my unpublished Ph.D. dissertation, "Generation to Generation: The Transmission of Knowledge Skills and Role Models from Black Working Mothers to Their Daughters in a Southern Community," New York University, 1987, pp. 11–19.

3. Nancy Chodorow, *The Reproduction of Mothering: Psychonalysis and the Sociology of Gender* (Berkeley: University of California Press, 1978).

4. Karen Sacks, *Sisters and Wives: The Past and Future of Sexual Equity* (Westport, CT: Greenwood Press, 1979).

5. Judith Arcana, *Our Mothers' Daughters* (Berkeley: Shameless Hussy Press, 1979).

6. Chodorow, p. 5.

7. Joyce Aschenbrenner, *Lifelines: Black Families in Chicago* (New York: Holt, Rinehart & Winston, 1975). Cynthia Epstein, "Positive Effects of the Multiple Negatives: Explaining the Success of Black Professional Women," in *Changing Women in a Changing Society*, ed. J. Huber (Chicago: University of Chicago Press, 1973). T. R. Kennedy, *You Gotta Deal With It: Black Family Relations in a Southern Community* (New York: Oxford University Press, 1980). E. P. Martin and J. M. Martin, *The Black Extended Family* (Chicago: University Press, 1978). Karen Sacks, *Sisters and Wives* (Westport, CT: Greenwood Press, 1979). V. H. Young, "Family and Childhood in a Southern Negro Community," in *American Anthropologist* 72 (1970): 269–88.

8. T. Morgan, "The World Ahead: Black Parents Prepare Their Children for Pride and Prejudice," in *The New York Times Magazine* (1985, October 27), 32. V. H. Young, "A Black American Socialization Pattern," in *American Ethnologist* 1 (1974): 405–513.

9. See Nobles in J. E. Hale, *Black Children: Their Roots, Culture and Learning Styles* (Provo, UT: Brigham Young University Press, 1982).

10. W.E.B. Dubois, *The Gift of Black Folk: The Negroes in the Making of America* (New York: Washington Square Press, 1970), xii. For "biculturality" see Ulf Hannerz, *Soulside: Inquires into Ghetto Culture and Community* (New York: Columbia University Press, 1969), and Charles Valentine, "Deficit, Difference, and Bicultural Models of Afro American Behavior," in *Harvard Educational Review* 41, no. 2 (1971).

11. Young (1974), 405–513.

12. Kennedy, 223.

13. Kennedy, 226. I recognize that one of the reasons that social scientists choose urban settings to study Blacks has to do with the large migration of Black people from the country to the city that began in the early decades of the 1900s. Once in the city, these new arrivals helped to create a new urban metropolis which represented a population vanguard that intrigued social scientists. With the decay of many urban areas, the trend has reversed: Urban dwellers are now returning to southern communities for some of the very reasons people fled the south 70 years ago.

World War II accelerated the growth in industrial areas of job opportunities, which promoted the beginning of the one-way migration from the South to the North. The South lost 1.5 million Blacks between 1940 and 1970. The migration pattern changed in the 1970s. While the majority of Blacks continued to live in the South in the 1920s, by 1970, 53% of the nation's Blacks lived in the South and 81% lived in urban areas. During the 1970–80 decade, the South and West regions which together accounted for 90% of the nation's population also accounted for an estimated 92% growth from April 1980 to July 1982. (United States Department of Commerce, 1979 & 1983).

14. According to the 1980 census approximately one-third of Hemington's population was Black. The population of Hemington County was 404,270. Blacks were 27% of this population. In the City of Hemington Blacks were 32% of the population.

15. The research consisted of 51 taped interviews of two, three, and four generations of mothers and their daughters. In addition, a questionnaire was given to each of the participants on a day other than the interview.

16. Alice Walker, *In Search of Our Mothers' Gardens* (New York: Harcourt Brace and Jovanovich, 1983), 231–243.

17. They represent five different sets of consanguineous generations including: 1) seven grandmothers and mothers; 2) four great grandmothers, grandmothers, and mothers; 3) two great-grandmothers, grandmothers, mothers, and unmarried daughters; 4) three grandmothers, mothers, and unmarried daughters; and 5) four mothers and teenage daughters. The method of selecting the participants was primarily through a snowball sample technique using personal contacts of women in my mother's network of friends, neighbors, and co-workers. The initial source of participants was an older subdivision called Fenbrook Park. Names of participants, when used, have been changed.

18. This study employs the definition of social class as discussed by John F. Cuber and William F. Kenkel in *Social Stratification in the United States* (New York: Appleton-Century-Crofts, 1954). They suggest that "*Social class* has been defined in so many different ways that a systematic treatment would be both time consuming and of doubtful utility. One central core of meaning, however, runs throughout the varied usages, namely, the notion that the hierarchies of differential statuses and of privilege and disprivilege fall into certain clearly distinguishable categories set off from one another. Historically, this conception seems to have much better factual justification than it does in contemporary America. . . . Radical differences, to be sure, do exist in wealth, privilege, and possessions; but the differences *seem to range along a continuum with imperceptible gradation from one per-*son to another, *so that no one can objectively draw 'the line' between the 'haves' and 'the have nots,' the 'privileged' and 'underprivileged,' or for that matter, say who is in the 'working class,' who is 'the common man,' or who is a 'capitalist.' The differences are not categorical, but continuous"* (p. 12). For an in-depth discussion of class see Rayna Rapp's article, "Family and Class in Contemporary America: Notes Toward an Understanding of Ideology," *Science and Society* 42, no. 3 (1978): 278–300.

19. In 1970, Young studied child rearing practices among Black families. She observed southern Black family organization and child rearing systems of household supports. She documented distinctive patterns in which mothers and other members of Black families relate and respond to young children, identifying the value that these families place on children's autonomy, initiative, and ability to fend for themselves. In her 1974 study, Young identified distinctive processes involved in Black parenting. She points out that Black parents must teach their children "techniques of adaptation to persons and situation, while at the same time [they must teach their children how to] maintain . . . a strong sense of [an] independent self" (p. 405). Young's work was concerned with the socialization of young children. The present study has dealt with the socialization of children as they grow older and the interactions between mothers and their daughters.

20. See I. G. Joseph and J. Lewis, *Common Differences: Conflicts in Black and White Feminist Perspectives* (Garden City, NY: Anchor Books/Doubleday, 1981), 76–126.

21. A. Rich, *Of Woman Born* (New York: W. W. Norton, 1976), 22.

~ *Chapter 23*

Jewish Lesbian Parenting

LINDA J. HOLTZMAN

I sat down to start writing about my experiences as a Jewish lesbian mother, thinking that I had a few quiet moments to begin to organize my thoughts. Then Jordan, our two-year-old son, ran in screaming that someone had put his favorite toy too high up for him to reach. Two minutes later, Zachary, our three-week-old son, began crying, demanding to be fed, stopping me from writing for the hundredth time. I realized again that in most ways, life as a Jewish lesbian mother is like life as any mother: chaotic, wonderful, and terribly exhausting. But there are differences, ways in which having a child as a Jewish lesbian is not just like having a child as any other Jew or any other lesbian.

When I first told my mother that I wanted to give birth to a baby, she was outraged. How could I do that to an innocent baby? Me, a rabbi yet, a committed Jew! How could I be so insensitive? We had this conversation months

after my life-partner Betsy had given birth to Jordan, a baby who was (of course) sweet and lovable. Both my parents loved Jordan, but *my* doing the same thing? God forbid!

Betsy and I had spent years debating whether or not we could raise a child together in a world that was far from accepting of lesbian parents. I was then serving a small synagogue near Philadelphia. I had been their rabbi for six years and had decided that I'd like to be there a few more years, even if this meant living a fairly closeted life. When I told the congregation that I would need two weeks of co-parenting leave to "help my housemate when she gave birth" written into my next contract, the board of directors was shocked. One by one they came into my office and let me know that they could never consider the possibility.

Eventually I left the synagogue, promising myself that my next job would be different. Somehow I'd find a way to work for the Jewish community and be open about my relationship and about any children we might have together. I've always hated secrets, and I

knew that young children are generally incapable of keeping them anyway. I couldn't
imagine placing the burden of a large family
secret on our children. In my next job, I'd be
open.

Easy to say—but for me, as a rabbi, this decision meant tackling the Jewish community
head-on. First was my work, but beyond that
was the rest of our life. Could there be a place
for our family in the Jewish community? I
found a job where I could be open at the rabbinical college where I was ordained, so my
short-term career problems were solved, but
other issues remained. I needed to find a way
to sort out the complications involved with
potential parenting.

Betsy and I began our decision-making
process by joining a "baby group." Several
women, mostly lesbian, none in a heterosexual marriage, met monthly to discuss our
thoughts and feelings about having children.
After talking at great length about all the possible means of having children, Betsy and I
decided to use alternative insemination by an
anonymous donor. Our sons will never know
who their fathers are, and we know this is a
great loss. But for us, adding a third adult to
our household seemed impossible, and having a donor who did not share parenting felt
confusing and potentially painful for our children. A man who randomly came and went
would not give very solid parenting. Our hope
is that the men with whom we are close will be
significant people in our sons' lives. We worry
about there not being access to male role
models in our household, but we hope that
our children will have men who are significant in many other aspects of their lives.

Both Betsy and I wanted to give birth to a
child, so we took turns, she having our first
child, I, the second. When Jordan was born,
we consulted a lawyer to determine my legal
rights concerning him. We discovered that I
have virtually no rights, other than the med-

ical power of attorney that we both signed for.
I am named as Jordan's guardian in Betsy's
will, but it is unclear whether a lesbian could
ever gain custody of her partner's child if the
will were contested by the child's biological
grandparents. This is frustrating and frightening, and it is clear that as a community, all
gay and lesbian people, whether parents or
not, need to stand up and fight against such
unjust laws, which undermine the strength of
lesbian parents regardless of whether they're
enforced. It is hard enough to build a household under any circumstances. When there is
constant invalidation by the law, it is even
harder.

Despite the negative laws, despite the fears
underlying our decision, it still seemed possible for us to parent children. We had hoped
for daughters; it seemed easier to raise girls;
we know what girls' lives are like; we could
provide reasonable role models for girls;
somehow, it just seemed safer. How could we
help a boy to find his place in the world? Were
we ready for that challenge? When we found
out that Jordan was going to be a boy
(through amniocentesis), we worried. Could
we overcome the many negative male role
models that he would meet? Could we love
him enough to give him all that he'd need in
life? Would our community of women be an
awkward place to bring a boy?

The minute that Jordan was born, we knew
the answer. Of course we could love him
enough; we adored him instantly. He felt like
so much more than just "a male child"; he was
a marvelously complex being. And there were
so many ways that we could respond to the
full person of Jordan that went far beyond our
femaleness. Blending of male and female roles
has always been important to both of us: in
Jewish life and in all of life. The birth of our
sons convinced us that we could transmit to
the next generation the philosophy that we
both believed. Jordan and Zach see us, two

women, doing everything, "male" and "female" things: women light the Shabbat candles and say the *kiddush*; women do the laundry and mow the lawn. Women cook the dinner and pay the bills. In Jordan and Zach's minds no specific roles belong to either men or women. As much as society tries to invalidate this message, it is at least a clear one in our home life. Hopefully, our sons will incorporate it into their lives.

Before our sons were born we debated at great length what they should call us. We both wanted titles, yet nothing seemed exactly right. Finally, we settled on mommy and *ima*, Hebrew for mommy. I like the sound and feeling of the Hebrew word while Betsy is more comfortable with the English.

The first question for our family arose immediately after Jordan was born. How should we welcome him into the community? Ritual circumcision felt to both of us like an exclusive male initiation rite; we'd be symbolically bringing our son into a world that excluded us and limited his horizons. If we were creating more welcoming rituals for baby boys, they certainly would not include the cutting of the penis. Yet, we were very sensitive to the fact that as the child of lesbians, our son would be different from most other Jewish boys; did he need one more difference?

We reluctantly decided on *brit milah*, ritual circumcision, for our son, and found a very accommodating *mohel*. He assented to our naming our child "son of Esther Miriam (Betsy) and Liba (me)," and he was open to our both saying the blessing after the circumcision traditionally reserved for fathers (or at times both parents). Only immediate family were invited to the *brit*; all of our friends were invited to a second ceremony when Jordan was a month old. This ceremony welcomed him into our community gently and lovingly, with a ritual foot washing, music, poetry, and other soft, warm words of welcome.

We were pleased with what we had done with Jordan, but chose to do it differently for Zachary, who was born in July 1988. We decided to have only one ceremony, since we thought that many people would be away on vacation. The same *model*, the same ritual circumcision, the same anxiety and misgivings were present. But so were at least seventy-five friends and family members, all singing and smiling and helping us relax. The pressure of having a circumcision held in the presence of so many people was great, but so was the outpouring of love and support. We felt the weight of Jewish tradition as the *mohel* performed the rite, and we felt our own ambivalence about *brit milah* very strongly.

The lengthy decision-making process about the *brit* for both our sons was symbolic of the struggles that we knew we would face for the entire length of our parenting careers. The Jewish community is a difficult place for children with a family that is very different from most others. Though divorced parents and blended families are now the norm, two women committed to each other and raising children together is still a rarity. Traditional Judaism is so negative in its teachings about homosexuality that homophobia has found a hospitable environment in the Jewish community. It is not easy to gain legitimacy for a gay or lesbian family in the eyes of the official Jewish world.

Finding a preschool program came next. Relentlessly we quizzed uneasy principals and teachers about how they would accept our son and our family: would they list us both as parents? How would they respond to questions posed by other parents and children? How is "family" taught in their curriculum? Does every book they read have a mommy, daddy, and child?

We wanted to be certain that Jordan's preschool teachers would not only respect our choice of titles but would also help Jordan feel comfortable as perhaps the only one in class with a mommy and an *ima*. Would his teachers use these terms, along with mommy and daddy, when describing families? In as many ways as possible we wanted our son to be fully at peace with himself, with his classmates, with his first plunge into the educational establishment and, as it turned out, the Jewish establishment. Jordan is enrolled in a Jewish preschool program which, much to our pleasant surprise, has met all our criteria.

As we began this process with a preschool program, we both realized that educating our children's teachers and other role models about the special needs of our family will be an ongoing process. Will there possibly be a Jewish day school or a good Hebrew school that does not teach, even in subtle ways, that our family was not formed in an acceptable model? We both want to be acknowledged as parents when our sons become b'nai mitzvah; we both want to *kvel* openly when they have parts in the Purim play or lead a prayer at services. We want their religious educations to be backed up by a solid synagogue base, one that accepts us as women, as feminists, and as lesbians. I had such warm feelings about Jewish life when I was a child because I felt as if I fully belonged in our synagogue. I hope that Jordan and Zachary can have the same warm, comfortable feelings.

There may not be an established synagogue that fully meets our needs, but there certainly are many lesbians, gay men, and others searching along with us for a more inclusive Jewish base. I will not compromise my integrity or values to be part of a Jewish establishment, but I will not give up my Judaism because of an unbending, unaccepting community.

The Jewish community often feels like family, and confronting it often feels as painful as confronting my own biological family. The issues that both "families" raise are linked. My

parents were initially so negative about my decision to have children in part because of their sense of what a "good Jew" did and did not do. Certainly, violating a law that has been expressed so unequivocally throughout Jewish tradition cannot be okay; it is simply not acceptable to be a lesbian. Having children as a lesbian is out of the question. We dare not inflict our own shame on the next generation.

In my parents' eyes a Jewish family looks a certain way and behaves a certain way; there is little room for diversity. Yet a very interesting change has taken place in my parents. When I first told them that I was thinking about having a baby, they planned on moving to Florida to escape the shame that I would heap upon them. Yet my parents were actually present at my son's birth; my mother cut Zachary's umbilical cord. And at his *brit*, they both stood up next to Betsy and Jordan and me. They recited a grandparents' blessing with pride, and I overheard my mother joking about how quickly she'd started "talking like a grandmother" as she declared the new baby "absolutely gorgeous." The change is dramatic, and it is largely based on my parents' realization that this is the only way they'd ever be grandparents (I'm an only child). Yet the change is incomplete.

My parents will accept Zachary as their daughter's son. I'm thirty-six years old, and I am (in their eyes) unmarried and am unlikely to be married soon. It's unusual but certainly understandable that I would want to find a way to parent a child. Insemination by an anonymous donor also seems strange to them but is safer than "sleeping around." This picture is a good one for my parents to present to their friends and relatives.

There's just one problem: in my eyes they already have a grandson, and I am in essence married. I am not, as they present to people, a single parent. When Jordan calls my parents

Grandmom and Pop-pop, it's because he sees them as his second set of grandparents. Yet, as much as my parents seem to love Jordan, he is not quite a grandchild; as much as they like and respect Betsy, she is still my housemate and not my life-partner.

As both of our sons grow up, there will be some confusion and pain as our biological families struggle with questions of how to accept these nonbiological nonlegal relatives. What should Betsy's siblings tell their children when they ask how two mommies can have babies? How do our parents explain these two children who call themselves brothers, who call us parents and who see them as grandparents?

It's hard to resist an adorable baby, but as the babies grow, the questions multiply. We will always be honest with our sons about their biological and nonbiological families. We will tell them whenever they ask about the way that they were conceived. And we will teach them that family does not only mean biologically linked people. They will know that people who love each other and who are committed to supporting and caring for each other are family. (That is also a lesson I hope our biological families are able to learn.)

While the traditional definition of family is exclusive and must be broadened, I still believe that family is at the heart of Judaism. To grow up Jewish, our children need to experience the two: family and Judaism, linked together. We need to celebrate holidays, be together for life-cycle events, share these events with our families. Biological or nonbiological, our families create our Jewish memories and our Jewish life experiences. When I saw our extended families reach out to us during the births of our sons, I knew that if we kept working at building solid nonbiological family relationships, our sons would feel the warmth they deserve.

Facing the Jewish community is not easy and dealing with our biological families is even more difficult, but the most difficult aspect of having children for me has been facing ourselves and each other. Betsy and I began questioning the feasibility of our having children several years ago. We made a formal commitment to spend our lives together with the understanding that we would begin the process of decision making. If we decided to have a child, could we iron out our personal differences so that our children would have a consistent upbringing in a stable home? Could our very different approaches to Judaism and religious observance be life-enhancing and not confusing for a child? Betsy and I are very different people in almost every way. I talk incessantly and she is somewhat quiet; I like taking my time and doing things slowly and Betsy is quick and efficient; I love doing public speaking and sharing my life with groups of people while Betsy is a very private person; I love Judaism and the Jewish community passionately, while living a Jewish life is not one of Betsy's goals. Some of our differences feel healthy when presented to children; after all, two differing role models only expand one's sense of possibilities in life. It's okay to be talkative or quiet, public or private. But it is not possible to have a home that is both kosher and not kosher. Either a child is enrolled in a Hebrew school or not enrolled.

Before Jordan and Zach were born, Betsy and I could experiment with as many Jewish options as we wanted. I could do one thing and she could do another. Our house could be "loosely kosher," and we could vary our Shabbat and holiday observances on the basis of our current needs. Children changed our attitudes and limited our flexibility. I want Jordan and Zach to see candles lit, to taste wine and challah every Shabbat. I want them to know how to observe holidays, how to sing Hebrew songs and to know Jewish stories, to incorporate Jewish values into their lives. Betsy knows how important this is to me and has been willing to compromise in many ways: we have a Shabbat dinner together most weeks; I take our children to shul when it's feasible; we build a *sukkah*, light a menorah, bake *homentashn*, have a seder. Our sons will live Jewish lives. But I also compromise. Our home is only a modified form of kosher; our Shabbat observance is limited; our conversation rarely revolves around Judaism. We have both become more adept at compromise.

As Jordan and Zach grow and develop so do we: together and individually. We bend in ways we didn't know possible and we see new aspects in each other that increase our love and our respect for each other. We also push each other in new directions. Betsy never thought she'd help build a *sukkah* or light Shabbat candles; I never thought I'd be concerned about my astrology chart. We have incorporated respect for each other's values and enriched our own lives in the process. When I see Betsy sitting down with our two-year-old son to discuss his feelings with him, I am impressed and touched. When I hear her singing tunelessly and happily as she puts Jordan to bed, I feel a fresh surge of love for her. And when we argue with each other about the clothes our sons wear or the food they eat or the other ways we express ourselves through them, I feel exasperated, angry and deeply grateful—grateful that our sons have two parents who love them enough to care so passionately about the details of their lives.

Having children as a Jewish lesbian has meant a new closeness with my parents, an ever-deepening relationship with my partner, and a sense of connection to both past and future. It has meant finding strengths I barely knew I had and using them: to struggle with the Jewish community, to assert myself with my parents, to work with Betsy to find ways to raise our sons in a difficult, complex world. It means learning that as a lesbian and a Jew I have much to give my sons. My values and ideas can be a source of strength and nourishment to a new generation. Most of all, having children has meant learning to love deeply and fully and to bind my life to the lives of these members of the next generation. All of us need to find a way of learning just how much we have to offer, how valuable our contribution to the world can be. All of us must feel free to decide whether or not to use our abilities to raise children, and society must open up to let us make honest, clear decisions. Then, whether or not we decide to, our decisions will be worthy of celebration.

Chapter 24

Native American Mother

JUDITH K. WITHEROW

Some months ago I saw an article in the newspaper about a Mother of the Year contest. Fantastic, I thought! Here's my chance to make up for a whole lot of things. Simple, too, because I always figured I had the best mother in the world. Then I started reading the necessary qualifications and found that not one of them applied to her. This woman that I had always loved was a complete failure according to these rules:

"First, that she be a successful mother, as evidenced by the character and the achievements of her children. Second, that she be an active member of a religious body. Third, that she embody those traits highly regarded in mothers: cheerfulness, courage, patience, affection, kindness, understanding, a good homemaking ability. Fourth, that she exemplify in her life and her conduct the precepts of the golden rule. Fifth, that she have a sense of responsibility in civic affairs and that she be active in service for public benefit. Sixth, that

From *Quest* 3, no. 4 (spring 1977). Reprinted by permission.

she be qualified to represent the Mother of America in all responsibilities attached to her role as national mother, if selected."

Where did they find this yardstick for measuring a woman's worth? From the same measure that has always stipulated that this be a one-culture country, and either you assimilate or you pay the consequences. Why must *everything* be based on white, middle-class standards? I keep asking myself these questions, but apparently there are no simple answers. All I know for sure is that we as a people no longer wish to deny our Native American background—not when we see the alternatives that serve as its replacement. Not being able to enter my mother in this contest may seem of small importance, but it's just another in a long list of ways to discriminate. Therefore, I would like to give another version of what is and what isn't important in a mother.

First, that she be a successful mother, as evidenced by the character and the achievements of her children. I can only presume this means college-educated or outstanding in some other "reputable" field of endeavor. This first qualification alone is wrong for many reasons. The sole responsibility for the character and achievement of the children is placed on the mother. The role of the father is of no apparent significance and outside influences are totally ignored. What bothers me most is that it's only the finished product that counts. What the mother may have had to sacrifice in raising her children is of no relevance. She can only attain the status of Successful Mother through the achievements of *others*.

Suppose, in your culture, that the emphasis was placed on your ability to live off the land. Just surviving would be a great achievement. Anyone who is aware of the socioeconomic condition of native Americans could attest to this; we have it the worst of any race. In my family we are all highly skilled in ways pertaining to our natural background. I am proud to be considered an expert markswoman. I also fish and hunt as good, or better, than anyone I know. These I consider achievements. Society does not. They are at best considered leisure activities or, at worst, barbaric practices. It is not taken into account that a segment of this society still lives off the land. Fishing and hunting are natural means of survival, although man's continued interference with the environment will soon destroy even this option. What is so wrong in preferring meat that has not been shot full of hormones? Or what is so cruel about giving a wild animal an even chance when you are hunting? Are either of these things taken into consideration in your slaughterhouses? We have a natural respect for all living things. It is wrong to misuse anything the Earth Mother has provided for you. These things, I believe, constitute character. Would a contest judge agree?

Second, that she be an active member of a religious body. At face value, this would seem to mean your standard organized church. Possibly just serving as a Sunday school teacher would constitute being an "active member."

Culture aside, we all know what role we as women have been allowed to play in any church. This country has always been big on pushing Christianity. It has gotten us a foothold in just about every other country. There has always been this overwhelming project to Americanize and Christianize. The terrible thing is that it works so well. You are given religion, and in turn you lose your identity in your own culture. What it gives you is a false sense of being accepted by this all-encompassing religion. In reality, it is only another ploy on your road to assimilation. Therefore, it would not be enough to just be in awe of the moon, the sun, the earth, and all of its elements. Nor would the Earth Mother, or any other deity, be acceptable in this land where a white, male God reigns supreme.

Third, that she embody those traits highly regarded in mothers: cheerfulness, courage, patience, affection, kindness, understanding, a good homemaking ability. These are highly commendable traits, but they won't "put meat on the table." My memories are of a woman carrying water from a creek to wash clothes by hand; a woman constantly in search of dead trees to chop up for firewood; a woman wise in the use of teas and herbs, because unless it was an emergency, doctors were an unaffordable luxury. Superstition played a large part in some of the cures. Two examples: If you stepped on a nail, you greased it and put it above the door. Then if the evil spirits came in, they would slip back out. The wound was also treated with poultices so you were doubly protected. Another cure was for whooping cough. When my mother was a baby, her brother came down with it, and the were afraid if she caught it she would die. So they had a neighbor bring his black stallion over, and had it blow its breath in her face. She's never had the disease, and I have no explanation why it worked. I also know willow bark is good for curing headaches. I know society sneers at cures like these. Well, when we see things like DES and Flagyl and many other things, we can't help but wonder if our ways really are uncivilized.

I would say she had most of the traits mentioned earlier—courage, patience, and so on. However, if you can raise six children to adulthood under the worst of conditions, whether you did it cheerfully or not is of little importance. When you don't have running water or electricity in your house, you can bet you don't have much else either. So being a good homemaker in the shacks we grew up in would have been some neat trick!

Fourth, that she exemplify in her life and her conduct the precepts of the golden rule: "Do unto others as you have them do unto you." Here she would definitely qualify. She would never deliberately hurt anyone, even when it was over some things we considered justifiable. She can make any number of excuses to explain why someone acted a certain way. Maybe her pride won't allow her to admit that such things as racism and classism do exist.

Even the destruction of a family home didn't harden her. A small fire had started in the house, and the fire department was called. The firemen came in, and with their hatchets set about destroying everything in the house. Only two rooms had partially burned, and we decided to clean out what the firemen had destroyed, and build back. No sooner had this been completed and we were ready for rebuilding when someone else came in with gasoline and burned the house to the ground. This list could go on forever, because every day some sort of harassment or discrimination occurs.

The older people like my mother may accept it as the natural order of things, unlike this generation, which is learning to question every aspect of this society. So much for the "golden role."

Fifth, that she have a sense of responsibility in civic affairs and that she be active in service for public benefit. These two are really hilarious. If you are hungry and in rags, civic or public services will not be high on your list of "things to do." Anyway, your race alone might exclude you from "responsibility in civic affairs." It still happens. Having a poor woman volunteering her services would upset the "natural order" even though she would be able to say where those services could really be used. So a working woman is really discriminated against: she can't afford to volunteer, but she won't get paid either.

Sixth, that she be qualified to represent the Mother of America in all responsibilities attached to her role as national mother, if selected. How could anyone not tamed and trained in this society's ways ever hope to qualify? I wouldn't want to qualify. It seems to me everyone is too hung up on certificates and stuff like that. Sure, I would have liked it for my mother; that is, I would have, until I gave it some thought. There is no way I would expose her to so much phoniness. She may have been unacceptable in this contest, but in *my* world she is without comparison.

Maybe I haven't expressed all of her attributes properly. Maybe no one else would see them as such. But this business of accepting only one life-style as proper is unreal. Somewhere along the way, the true values in life have been lost.

Chapter 25

"I Am This Child's Mother": A Feminist Perspective on Mothering with a Disability

CLAIRE REINELT AND MINDY FRIED

Many women take their right to have a child for granted. For women with disabilities, having a child is an act of resistance to the dominant social norms that exclude them from motherhood. When a disabled woman decides to have a child she is affirming her right to be sexually active, to be involved in intimate relationships, and to have and raise a child. This chapter explores the experiences of mothering with a disability. We focus on the choice to become a mother, on the impact of a mother's disability on her children, and on the division of labor between partners in the home.[1]

Sexuality and family life are among the areas of human experience that are most shrouded in secrecy. U.S. society severely limits collective opportunities for discussing and exploring sexualities that affirm our sexual identities in healthy ways. This lack of openness has ramifications for all people, but it can

be particularly severe for women with disabilities. Silence about the sexuality of women with disabilities means that many disabled girls—from early adolescence to adulthood—grow up thinking of themselves as asexual beings (Waxman and Finger 1989). When they do become sexually active, they often lack basic knowledge about how to protect themselves from disease and pregnancy.

Unlike sexuality, motherhood is praised in public discourse. All mothers, however, find little public support for the work they do; mothers with disabilities are likely to find even less. All mothers are adversely affected by the lack of public investment in affordable, high-quality child care; mobility-impaired mothers, however, face the additional task of finding day care that is accessible. Another critical need for mothers with disabilities is baby equipment that is adapted to their disabilities. Very little public or private investment has been made in designing and manufacturing cribs, changing tables, and baby carriers accessible for parents with disabilities.[2] There is also a need to rethink the

From Mark Nagler, ed., *Perspectives on Disability*, 2d ed. (Palo Alto, Calif.: Health Markets Research, 1993), with revisions by the authors. Reprinted by permission.

guidelines for personal care attendants. Most states do not allow mothers with disabilities to use state-supported attendant services to assist them in caring for their children. Attendant services are designed to support a disabled woman's right to work at a job outside the home, not the right to have and raise a child. In addition to their unmet physical needs, mothers with disabilities continually have to defend their ability to be good mothers. While all mothers experience criticism about how they mother, mothers with disabilities endure surprise and disbelief from people who cannot imagine that they are mothers at all.

Like sexuality, family life in the United States has been privatized. Policy makers, judges, and others in positions of power are reluctant to intervene in private family matters. If we look deeper we realize that the reluctance to intervene refers mainly to able-bodied, heterosexual, nuclear families with adequate financial means. There is considerable intervention for single mothers on welfare, mothers with disabilities, lesbian mothers, and others who are considered unfit or undesirable parents. Very little, if any, of this intervention comes in the form of financial or social support; instead, it is punitive, judgmental, and often an attempt to control behavior considered "deviant."

During the 1960s and 1970s, personal and private issues were moved onto the public agenda by feminist and lesbian and gay activists. Reproductive rights, violence against women, and the right to claim one's sexuality without being discriminated against have all been given public attention. The rights and needs of disabled women have not been visible in these movements. There has been a pervasive silence on issues of disability that excludes women with disabilities from comfortably participating in these movements. According to Michelle Fine and Adrienne

Asch (1988), nondisabled feminists have been reluctant to work with disabled women because they perceive them as dependent, passive, and needy. They have sought instead to advance more powerful, competent, and appealing female icons. This same attitude reflects the ambivalence that feminists have historically felt towards the institution of motherhood. Mothers have been perceived as dependent, passive, and needy, while career women have been perceived as independent and powerful. Only recently have white, able-bodied, middle-class feminists begun to reclaim motherhood—defining it as a meaningful personal choice, not a female obligation (Rossiter 1988; McMahon 1995).

Women with disabilities have also begun to claim motherhood. Their struggle, while linked in some ways to the efforts by able-bodied women to alter and improve the conditions under which they mother, must be understood in a different historical context. Women with disabilities have never been expected to be mothers. Their struggle, therefore, has been fundamentally different. It is about claiming the right to be a mother—a struggle that in many ways is more closely linked to the movement of people with disabilities who have sought access to, and participation in, economic and social life. Even the disability rights movement, however, has not made family issues a political priority. The same political forces that have kept family issues off the wider public agenda have kept these issues off the agenda of the disability rights movement as well. Family issues remain privatized and relegated to women.

Recently, disabled women have been raising these and other women's issues at conferences convened by people with disabilities. Despite some increased visibility, their issues are still being marginalized.[3] Moving the issues raised by women with disabilities to the center of the political agenda has not yet occurred. Even in the area of access to employment, housing, and transportation, which have been at the top of the disability rights movement's agenda, very little attention has been given to exploring whether women's access issues are different from men's access issues. For mothers with disabilities, access to day care centers, to schools, to public playgrounds, and to low-income family housing are all fundamental access issues that are not widely addressed by the disability movement.[4]

Disabled feminists are developing their own political agenda. In the area of reproductive rights, they have challenged the presumption that women carrying fetuses with disabilities should unquestionably terminate their pregnancies (see Finger 1984; Saxton 1984; Asch 1988). They have also sought to raise awareness about the inadequacy of reproductive health care services for women with disabilities (Waxman 1994). They are discussing issues of violence against disabled women, as well as aging, self-image, sexuality, and discrimination within the disability rights movement and within the women's movement (Fine and Asch 1988). There are an increasing number of books, articles, and conference workshops that are devoted specifically to disabled women's issues (see, for instance, Browne, Connors, and Stern 1985; Deegan and Brooks 1985; Saxton and Howe 1987; Fine and Asch 1988; Lonsdale 1990; and Morris 1991). Some of these writings have addressed mothering issues, but the experience of mothering with a disability has been explored very little.[5] This chapter is an effort to add to the available information. We address the choices women make to become mothers and what it means to them, how women perceive the impact their disabilities have on their children, and the effect of their disabilities on their relationships with their partners.

Study Participants

This chapter is based on nine interviews conducted in New England (see Table 1). Six of the nine women interviewed were participants in a support group for parents with disabilities; three were not. We are not prepared to conclude, based on this small sample, that support groups improve women's ability to be good parents, but we believe that such groups provide valuable opportunities for women to reduce their isolation and find others who share similar experiences, which may be conducive to a sense of well-being and improved parenting skills.

TABLE 1. Study Participants

Participant	Nature of Disability	Child's Name/Age	Support Group	Partner or Spouse
Mary	polio	Janelle/5	facilitator	Tim (visually impaired)
Allison	multiple sclerosis	7 children (Sarah/10 interviewed)	no	Rajan
Amanda	blind	Alan/3	yes	John
Lisa	multiple sclerosis	Camille/4	yes	Steve
Barbara	polio	Addy/13	no	–
Debra	speech impairment	Michael/6	yes	–
Nicole	paraplegia	Nancy & Eve/4 (twins)	no	Stan
RaeLynn	quadriplegia	Laura/8	yes	Rick
Catherine	arthritic wrists	Joe/12	yes	divorced

The women we interviewed had a variety of disabilities, although the majority were mobility-impaired. Two of the women had multiple sclerosis (MS) and were in wheelchairs; two others were in wheelchairs from spinal cord injuries; two others had post-polio syndrome; one woman had a severe speech impairment; and another woman had been blind since birth. Eight of the women were white; one was black. One woman was upper class, because of her family's finances; the others were working class and middle class. All of the women were heterosexual. Six were married, two were single, and one was divorced. One woman had seven children; the rest had one each at the time of their interview. Two of the women have since had a second child.

Choosing Motherhood

In many ways, women with disabilities are no different than other women; many of them desire to have and raise a child. What is different is that women with disabilities are not expected to have children; in fact, they are often actively discouraged from even considering the possibility. Amanda, who has been blind since birth, said:

> When I was a child, there was a definite subliminal message that I was not supposed to have children. I was the youngest child in the family and I had very little experience caring for children. The blindness was definitely part of the reason I took so long to have a child. . . . Whenever I was around young children, my mother would get tense and give me more instruction.

Mary talks about having to come to terms with relationships and intimacy before being able to have a child with her husband, Tim. Tim is visually limited and Mary has post-polio syndrome. She said:

> Both of us had major relationship things to work through in our twenties and thirties. We're just going to have a child late, and that's better than not doing it at all. . . . I'm forty-four and he's thirty-seven. From the age of twenty he thought he would never have a child because he didn't want to pass on his disability. He changed his mind real quick when it was clear that I was open to having a child if he wanted one. He hadn't realized how much he was saying that because he knew that none of the women he went out with would want to have a blind child. For both of us the timing of this child has been very influenced by disability. This is a first marriage for both of us and that is clearly disability, totally. I had real similar things about men wanting to go out with me but I thought they would never want to marry me. So it took us a long time.

Most disabled women report that their parents encouraged them to have careers, but not to form intimate relationships. While parents often demand equity for their disabled daughters in educational and vocational arenas, they are much more ambivalent about their daughters' sexual lives (Harris and Wideman 1988; Rousso 1988).

When disabled women become pregnant the may initially face disapproval from their family. Amanda said:

> My family was shocked that I was going to have a child. I'm a renegade in my family. They often say, "You can do anything," and then they are indirect about their disapproval of my actions. That's how they were at first, but once they saw that [Alan] is doing well, I think they are more accepting.

Disabled women also encounter disapproval from the medical profession. RaeLynn, who has quadriplegia, tried to see a doctor at a local hospital when she suspected she was pregnant.

> I told her I was sleeping a lot. I said, "I think I should come in. . . . I think I'm going to have a

child." She said, "Oh, you probably just have a bad cold." Finally, I was five months pregnant and she agreed to see me. She was telling my husband that he should be ashamed of himself for making me pregnant. She asked me how I was going to be a good mother and then she ended by saying that I should have an abortion. I said, "Well, I anticipated something like this so this afternoon I'm going to see another doctor."

Most doctors are not so overtly insensitive as RaeLynn's doctor. Far more common is a doctor's inability to answer a disabled woman's questions about how her pregnancy will affect her disability or how her disability will affect her pregnancy. Mary said:

I felt bad that [the doctors] weren't taking my concerns seriously about the post-polio syndrome and how it might affect me later [in pregnancy]. So I sent letters out to people that I knew and asked them if they knew any post-polio syndrome mothers who went though delivery and what happened. I didn't know if my respiratory system would be overstressed. [The doctors] finally did send me in to see how to use a respirator if I needed that. I didn't feel like I was getting the attention I wanted.

Lack of both sensitivity and knowledge continues to create problems for women with disabilities even when they are at the hospital giving birth to their children. Amanda remembers trying to claim her baby before leaving the hospital. As she was preparing to leave, after five days in the hospital, a nurse came by to have the release forms signed verifying that Alan was indeed her child.

Initially, the hospital personnel refused to allow me to sign the form and to identify Alan as my child. I took the paper and said, "I am going to sign this paper," and they said, "Oh no wait until your husband gets the car, he can sign the paper." And I said, "I am this child's mother, you have had him twice in the nursery in the entire five days he's been alive, this is my child. I gave birth to him, I will sign the paper."

As these stories make clear, disabled women spend a lot of time advocating for themselves and claiming what is rightfully theirs. While many disabled women are well prepared to confront discrimination and insensitivity after years of experience, their anger and pain stands as a reminder that no woman should be subjected to this kind of treatment.

Amanda's story has a postscript. She recently had her second baby at the same hospital. This time her experience was completely different. The nurses were comfortable and friendly with her and she felt supported by them. The nurses had not changed, Amanda claims; she had. Her own confidence and knowledge about her ability to be a mother transformed how the nurses related to her. What this story points out is the importance of women like Amanda sharing their knowledge and experience with disabled women who are pregnant for the first time, so that they will not have to go through what she did the first time around.

Raising Children

The experience of raising a child varied tremendously for the women we interviewed. Some had more support than others; some were more comfortable with their disability than others; and some had better parenting skills. All of the women had to devise ways to parent their children that recognized and respected their disability. Barbara learned to change her daughter's diaper using her mouth. Women with wheelchairs designed carriers so their babies could ride with them. Amanda attached a beeper to her son, Alan, when they went out so she could keep track of him. Nicole was very firm with her twins about holding on to her wheelchair whenever they were out in public. Mary built in rest times during her day that Janelle, her daughter, learned to accept. Mothers with physical disabilities teach us that good mothering takes many different forms.

There were several adjectives that mothers used frequently when they described their children: independent, self-sufficient, empathetic, sensitive, and helpful. While these adjectives reveal maternal pride, they also are qualities that mothers have nurtured in their children out of necessity.

Mothers emphasized that their children learned from a young age to be independent and self-sufficient. Allison, who uses a wheelchair, does not have access to her kitchen. Her children have learned to get themselves what they need from the kitchen. For instance, Allison's youngest daughter has gotten her own glass of milk since she was three. Allison said of her children:

> I can talk them through a lot of things. If you take the time and the trouble to give step-by-step instructions you'll find that even a small kid can really be quite helpful. You give them praise afterward and they are quite happy.

Allison does not see her disability as a burden for her children; she sees it as an opportunity to build their self-esteem and confidence.

In addition to being independent and self-sufficient, Allison's ten-year old, Sarah, reported that she liked being helpful.

> I don't know what it would be like to have a mother who could walk, I don't think that would be right for me because I am so used to having a mother that I can help out, I mean really, really help out; most kids don't feel that, you just feel more confident with yourself when you are helping someone in your family.

Allison nurtures this feeling in her children, while at the same time being careful not to overburden them with responsibilities or expect more from them than they are capable of handling.

There is a fine line to walk between asking

too much of a child and helping her to be self-sufficient and self-confident. Barbara acknowledged that Addy got tired of helping her so much.

> She carried bags when she was so little, my mother used to say, "You're going to go to jail, you're having that little girl do so much for you."

Barbara realized that she needed to hire a personal care attendant in order to maintain an appropriate mother-daughter relationship with Addy.

Many mothers reported that their children expressed a unique sense of empathy and sensitivity to others who were disabled. In one instance, Allison's daughter, Sarah, commented about her own ability to empathize with others because her mother had a disability.

> I think I understand when other people have different diseases when I know that my mom has a disease too. I know that they are real people and they are not weird. Others may stare and think, "Oh my god, what are those creatures?" I think I am more understanding because I know my mom has MS; she has a disease, I know she's alive, she's living, and she's happy, and she has children and everything and I really think that I look at different people, like who have AIDS or handicaps, and I know I'm more secure with them than most other people would be.

Sensitivity manifested itself in other ways as well. Whenever Barbara's daughter, Addy, encounters someone with a disability who appears to need help, she always asks, "Would you like me to help you?" She never begins helping someone without asking first.

One of the most frustrating experiences for the women we interviewed was being treated as though they were incompetent. Lisa feels that it has been hard to establish her competence with her daughter, Camille, because there is so much she cannot do with her. One day, however, Camille came into the room while Lisa was tutoring a student (she used to be a teacher) and said, "Mom, you're a teacher." "And that," Lisa beamed, "was one of the first times she was really looking up to me."

Parental competence is often undermined in public interactions. Amanda spoke about how frustrated she gets when she is asking for directions and the adult turns and tells Alan, who is three, the directions.

> When we're in public . . . there have been times that I ask for directions and the person will tell Alan. With Alan this is more upsetting. I'm trying to field his questions, his needs, trying to get us out of being lost. I also don't want him to think I'm incompetent.

Rather than hold in her reaction, Amanda uses this opportunity to teach Alan about discrimination as well as to share her own feelings about the way she has been treated. "I'll say to Alan that these people are silly, or these people are stupid, or some people don't understand, or that makes mommy angry."

A mother's disability can be a burden or a source of pain for her children, but it can also be a source of personal strength and learning. The mothers we interviewed took great care to emphasize that their children were happy and well-adjusted. Disability is simply one aspect of who these mothers are in relation to their children, not the defining characteristic.

Caregiving and the Division of Labor Between Partners

Traditionally women are expected to assume the family caregiving role. What happens when the woman is disabled? How does this affect the division of labor between partners?

Two of the women we interviewed had husbands who were full-time caregivers. Rae-Lynn's husband, Rick, cared for both Rae-Lynn and their daughter, Laura. RaeLynn says that Rick would like to work but there is a financial disincentive for him to do so because she receives medical benefits totaling thirty thousand dollars a year. Without Medicaid, she and Rick would have a difficult time paying for her medical expenses. Consequently, they had to make sure that they kept their income below the benefit threshold. RaeLynn commented, "It's not a good system they have set up. I don't understand why the husband and wife can't both work. If we were divorced we could get a lot more benefits than if we were married; it's crazy." RaeLynn thinks that the divorce rate is so high among couples with disabilities because of the financial disincentive of the marriage relationship.

It is often difficult for husbands to assume a caregiving role because of society's attitudes toward male caregiving. RaeLynn said:

> What I don't like is the attitudes of society towards my husband, that the man should be the financial earner the old-fashioned way, and the wife stays home. Who could ask for anything more rewarding than taking care of wife and child, rather than going out and rushing around. People don't realize the work involved; it's more than a full-time job. People look at him like he's a bum. I hate that. If you had to pay him for all the work he does it would be $60,000."

Whether it is men or women who perform caregiving work, this work is undervalued. Male caregivers face the additional disapproval of not providing financially for their families.

Allison's husband, Rajan, was also a full-time caregiver. They arrived at their arrangement not out of financial necessity but through deliberate planning and choice. During the early stages of Allison's multiple sclerosis she and Rajan began to plan for the day when she would no longer be able to care for the children. He switched jobs and worked overtime in order to make more money. They invested the money in the stock market until they had a nest egg that allowed Rajan to retire. When Allison's last child—her seventh—was born, she was at the end of being able to consider having and raising a child.

> I had her and gave her to my husband and said, "She's yours." He changed every diaper. We divide the family into two families, actually. My family is the first four when he was working and I was raising the kids and managing alright. The last three are his family, where he has been more or less the mother and I've been the father, sort of watching and supporting, but he's doing the work. So we've kind of switched our roles halfway through. So, if you want to have a lot of kids with MS, you probably will run into that time when you have to switch your roles around, but if you are good and flexible you can do it.

Not all of the women were interviewed had switched roles with their husbands. Nicole felt that it was primarily the mother's responsibility to stay home with the children and the father's responsibility to work to support them. Nicole was able to do much of the caregiving work herself, especially now that her daughters were older. In addition, she had a personal care attendant who helped her with caregiving responsibilities. Despite Nicole's commitment to staying home with her children, she did work part-time. Working was a source of self-fulfillment for her, as well as a financial contribution to the family. Nicole's embrace of traditional gender roles affirmed for her the normalcy of her family situation.

Unlike Nicole, Lisa acquired her disability after she and Steve were married. Part of the stress in their relationship came from coping with the disease because it was not a "given" at the start of their relationship.

> It's a bitch of a disease. It's so unrelenting. You just get on top of it. You feel like you're riding the wave and then you're under again. It's really,

really hard. And I feel sympathy for [Steve], which I think is part of what therapy has done for me. I used to feel really angry at him, and I started to realize that I had it first and now I feel like he has the disease. As long as he's connected to me, he has this disease too.

Recognizing that the whole family was affected by her multiple sclerosis was a positive step for Lisa and has helped her feel more sympathy for Steve. Nevertheless, her increasing disability has taken a toll on their relationship.

Steve wanted to be a traditional husband. He wanted to come home from work, put his feet up, and have his wife prepare and serve him dinner. Lisa said that he does more caregiving than the average husband, but he clearly resents having to do it. In their case, negotiating who does how much housework and child care (an issue that every couple deals with) has been complicated by the fact that she has multiple sclerosis. She is very conscious of how tired she gets, and she works hard to stay within her limits. While she needs to do this for herself, Steve has not always been understanding.

Lisa does not have a personal care attendant. Having an attendant means moving daily caregiving responsibilities from partners and children to a paid caregiver—a move that often improves the quality of family relationships. Barbara, a single parent, believes that her relationship with her child's father might have been different if she had had a personal care attendant.

> He used to do everything for me. We never used to argue about it or anything, but it could have been something that he wasn't hot about. It could have played a big role in our breaking up.

Making attendant care more available to women with disabilities enables them not only to work in the productive sphere but also to establish relationships with their partners and children based on mutuality, not dependency.

Conclusion

The disabled women we talked to are asserting their right to have and raise children. They are discovering how to parent in ways that accommodate their disabilities and meet the needs of their children. They are learning how to confront the attitudes of doctors and social workers who continue to perceive disability as a problem rather than as part of who someone is.

Parenting is never easy work, and in some ways it is particularly difficult for people with disabilities, but most of the women we spoke with were very happy to be parents. One of the biggest challenges continues to be confronting the skepticism and disapproval of people who believe that disabled women cannot be good mothers. To combat this, we need more education for professionals, the general public, and for disabled people themselves on parenting with a disability. The disability rights and independent living movements need to place sexuality and family issues squarely on the movement's agenda.

With the passage of the Americans with Disabilities Act in 1990, Americans have a unique opportunity to move disability issues into the public consciousness. It would be a serious oversight for both women and men with disabilities if sexuality and family issues were excluded from this agenda. We need to make sure that the needs of men and women with disabilities are included in public policies that address child care, family and medical leave, sexuality, family planning, and AIDS. When the sexuality and family needs of people with disabilities are addressed in public forums, disability will cease to be a source of stigma and will become instead one identity, among many, that defines a person's life.

NOTES

1. For a more detailed discussion of motherhood and disability see Reinelt (1996).

2. Megan Kirshbaum at Through the Looking Glass in Berkeley, California, recently received a three-year grant to develop and design adaptive equipment for disabled parents and their babies.

3. This problem was raised by Corbett O'Toole at a workshop on Women and Disabilities held during the 1991 Independent Living Movement conference in Oakland, California.

4. At the 1991 Independent Living Movement conference, the World Institute on Disability handed out a lengthy Accessibility Survey that did not include any questions designed to determine accessibility to day care, schools, and low-income housing for parents with disabilities.

5. For recent discussions of mothering with a disability see Killoran (1994), Kocher (1994), and Mathews (1992).

REFERENCES

Asch, Adrienne. 1988. "Reproductive Technology and Disability." In *Reproductive Laws for the 1990s: A Briefing Handbook,* edited by Nadine Taub and Sheril Cohen, 59–101. Newark, N.J.: Rutgers University Press.

Browne, Susan E., Debra Connors, and Nanci Stern. 1985. *With the Power of Each Breath: A Disabled Women's Anthology.* Pittsburgh, Pa.: Cleis Press.

Deegan, Mary Jo, and Nancy Brooks. 1985. *Women and Disability: The Double Handicap.* New Brunswick, N.J.: Transaction Books.

Fine, Michelle, and Adrienne Asch. 1988. *Women with Disabilities: Essays in Psychology, Culture, and Politics.* Philadelphia: Temple University Press.

Finger, Anne. 1984. "Claiming *All* of Our Bodies: Reproductive Rights and Disability." (Chapter 61, this volume.)

Harris, Adrienne, and Dana Wideman. 1988. "The Construction of Gender and Disability in Early Attachment." In *Women with Disabilities: Essays in Psychology, Culture, and Politics,* 115–38, edited by Michelle Fine and Adrienne Asch. Philadelphia: Temple University Press.

Killoran, Carrie. 1994. "Women with Disabilities Having Children: It's Our Right Too." *Sexuality and Disability* 12 (2): 121–26.

Kocher, Meg. 1994. "Mothers with Disabilities." *Sexuality and Disability* 12 (2): 127–33.

Lonsdale, Susan. 1990. *Women and Disability: The Experience of Physical Disability Among Women.* New York: St. Martin's Press.

McMahon, Martha. 1995. *Engendering Motherhood: Identity and Self-Transformation in Women's Lives.* New York: Guilford Press.

Mathews, Jay. 1992. *A Mother's Touch: The Tiffany Callo Story.* New York: Henry Holt and Company.

Morris, Jenny. 1991. *Pride Against Prejudice: A Personal Politics of Disability.* London: Women's Press.

Reinelt, Claire, 1996. "Motherhood and Disability in the Twentieth Century: Historical Constructions and Contemporary Experiences." Ph.D. diss., Department of Sociology, Brandeis University, Waltham, Mass.

Rossiter, Amy. 1988. *From Private to Public: A Feminist Exploration of Early Mothering.* Toronto, Ontario: Women's Press.

Rousso, Harilyn. 1988. "Daughters with Disabilities: Defective Women or Minority Women?" In *Women with Disabilities: Essays in Psychology, Culture, and Politics,* 139–71, edited by Michelle Fine and Adrienne Asch. Philadelphia: Temple University Press.

Saxton, Marsha. 1984. "Born and Unborn: The Implications of Reproductive Technologies for People with Disabilities." In *Test-Tube Women: What Future Motherhood?* 298–312, edited by Rita Arditti and Renate Duelli Klein. London: Pandora Press.

Saxton, Marsha, and Florence Howe. 1987. *With Wings: An Anthology of Literature by and About Women with Disabilities.* New York: Feminist Press.

Waxman, Barbara. 1994. "Up Against Eugenics: Disabled Women's Challenge to Receive Reproductive Health Services." *Sexuality and Disability* 12 (2): 155–71.

Waxman, Barbara, and Anne Finger. 1989. "The Politics of Sex and Disability." *Disability Studies Quarterly,* 9 (3): 2–5.

Section B

Fathering, Fatherhood, and Fathers

Chapter 26

American Fathering in Historical Perspective

JOSEPH H. PLECK

In American society, there has been an explosion of interest in fathers and fatherhood today. One can hardly watch television, open a national magazine, or go to a movie without seeing themes of father-child relationships, fatherhood, or fatherlessness—from *Star Wars*'s Luke Skywalker's search for his true father, to a recent cover story in the Sunday supplement *Parade* about the actor James Caan as a father, tellingly titled "The Only Role That Matters." In the last decade and a half, calls for greater father involvement have become increasingly insistent.

Yet, in spite of this contemporary interest, and signs of widespread support for an enlarged father role, the pace of change has been slow. While men are doing more child care and housework than they used to, women still perform the bulk of these activities (Pleck 1985). Beneath the apparent contemporary

support for greater father involvement lies a deep-seated ambivalence about what the role of the father really should be, rooted in the complex historical legacy of American culture's perceptions of fathering. Contradictory images of fatherhood from the past have left their mark on contemporary attitudes. This chapter analyzes the dominant images of fatherhood in earlier periods of U.S. history,[1] and considers their impact today.

Eighteenth and Early Nineteenth Centuries: Father as Moral Overseer

There is no question that colonial mothers, as their counterparts today, provided most of the caretaking that infants and young children received. But fathers were nonetheless thought to have far greater responsibility for, and influence on, their children. Prescriptions for parents were addressed almost entirely to fathers; the responsibilities of mothers were rarely mentioned (Degler 1980).

Fathers were viewed as the family's ultimate

source of moral teaching and worldly judgments. The father was viewed as a moral pedagogue who must instruct children of both sexes what God as well as the world required of them. A diary entry by Cotton Mather when he was still young and in good health provides a perhaps extreme illustration:

> I took my little daughter Katy into my study and there I told my child that I am to die shortly, and she must, when I am dead remember everything that I said unto her. I set before her the sinful and woeful condition of her nature, and I charged her to pray in secret places every day without ceasing that God for the sake of Jesus Christ would give her a new heart. . . . I gave her to understand that when I am taken from her she must look to meet with more humbling afflictions than she does now [when] she has a careful and tender father to provide for her. (in Demos 1982, 426)

When ministers and others wrote about fatherhood, they emphasized a variety of responsibilities. Fathers ought to concern themselves with the moral and religious education of the young. If literate himself, he should teach reading and writing. He was responsible for guiding his sons into a occupational "calling." He played a key role in the courtship and marriage making of both his sons and daughters, by approving a proposed match and allotting family property to the couple.

Notions of the "duty" of fathers to their children, and of children to their fathers, were central to father-child relationships (Rotundo 1982). One expression of the family hierarchy, viewed as ideal during this period, appears in *The Token of Friendship, or Home, The Center of Affections* (1844):

> The father gives his kind command,
> The mother joins, approves;
> The children all attentive stand,
> Then each obedient moves. (in Ewen 1976, 152)

This emphasis on the paternal role was rooted in this period's conception of the differences between the sexes, and the nature of children. Men were thought to have superior reason, which made them less likely than women to be misled by the "passions" and "affections" to which both sexes were subject. Children were viewed as inherently sinful, ruled by powerful impulses as yet ungoverned by intellect. Because of women's weakness of reason and inherent vulnerability to inordinate affections, only men could provide the vigorous supervision needed by children. Fathers had to restrain their children's sinful urges and encourage the development of sound reason. Mothers were less able to provide these needed influences because of their own tendency to "indulge" or be excessively "fond" of their children. Consistent with these conceptions, common law assigned the right and obligation of child custody to the father in cases of marital separation.

Some descriptions of actual father-child interactions appear in diaries, letters, and other personal accounts: a father and his 10-year-old son carting grain to the mill; a father counseling his adult daughter on her impending marriage; a father and son "discoursing" on witchcraft; a son and daughter joining their father in an argument with neighbors. From such records emerges a "picture, above all, of active, encompassing fatherhood, woven into the whole fabric of domestic and productive life. . . . Fathers were a visible presence, year after year, day after day. . . . Fathering was thus an extension, if not a part, of much routine activity" (Demos 1982, 429). This integration of fatherhood in daily life derived in large part from the location of work, whether farming or artisanship and trade, in the family context. It was natural and even necessary for children to be involved.

Relationships between fathers and children, especially sons, often had strong emotional components. Sons were often regarded as extensions of their fathers; young or newly born sons were commonly described by their fathers as "my hope" or "my consolation" (Demos 1982, 428). However, since fathers believed they could and should restrain their emotions, fathers "tended to express approval and disapproval in place of affection and anger" (Rotundo 1985, 9).

Another indicator of the strength of father-son relationships is that boys serving apprenticeships, and young men on their own, maintained contact with their family primarily through letters to and from their fathers. In contrast to the large volume of letters from children to their fathers that have survived, there are few letters written directly to mothers. Sons would often ask to be "remembered" to their mothers, but in terms that seem formal or even perfunctory. For example, a man whose father had just died included the following message for their mother when he wrote home to a brother: "I sincerely condole with her on the loss of her husband; please tender my duty to her" (Demos 1982, 428).

Early Nineteenth to Mid-Twentieth Centuries: Father as Distant Breadwinner

New conceptions of parent-child relationships began to appear during the nineteenth century. A gradual and steady shift toward a greater role for the mother, and a decreased and more indirect role for the father is clear and unmistakable. Whereas in the earlier period fathers were the chief correspondents of their adolescent and adult children, mothers played that role at least as often in the nineteenth century. To the extent that either parent was involved in the marital choices of their children, it was now usually the mother. In contrast to the earlier period when moth-

ers showed little concern with any aspect of their sons' lives after childhood, letters and diaries now indicated they were emotionally entangled with sons well into adulthood. Where it had been common earlier to give blame or credit for how children turned out as adults entirely to their fathers, now the same judgment was made about mothers (Demos 1982).

This shift paralleled a new ideology about gender. While social historians do not agree on its ultimate structural sources, they have documented its centrality to social thought during the nineteenth century. This gender ideology emphasized the purity of the female "sphere" (i.e., the home) and feminine character as unselfish and nurturant. Women's "purity" elevated her above men, making her particularly suited for "rearing" the young. At the same time, infancy and early childhood (as opposed to middle childhood and adolescence) received greater emphasis; mothers were thought to have a special influence in these earlier periods. The belief in maternal influence extended even to the period before birth: the mother's experience during pregnancy, it was thought, might literally shape the destiny of her child (Demos 1982).

This period saw the development of the contemporary presumption of maternal custody following divorce. It is difficult to define with precision when all vestiges of the earlier practice of awarding custody to fathers disappeared. Increasingly, the interests of the child were interpreted as justifying if not requiring maternal custody. In the latter part of the nineteenth century, court decisions more often promulgated the notion that women have a unique right and obligation to take custody (Grossberg 1983).

Consistent with these trends, educators during the nineteenth century came to view children as needing a "feminine" influence in their schooling (Suggs 1977). It is little remembered today that among the foremost "reforms" of nineteenth century educational innovators such as Horace Mann and Ichabod Crane was their introduction of female teachers in the elementary schools.

It took some time for this shift in parental patterns to become fully reflected in all areas of American social thought. Until well into the twentieth century, psychology continued to be dominated by European theorists, grounded in quite different conceptions of family life. To both Jung and the early Freud, the father was unquestionably the towering figure in the life of the child. Freud, it is true, gave a role to the mother, but primarily as the object of the male child's libidinous drives, not as the molder of his character. To the early Freud at least, the mother was psychologically important primarily because the male child's love for her brought him into competition with his father, in an Oedipal drama whose outcome (identification with the father and consolidation of the superego) creates adult male character structure.

Freudian and other psychodynamic theories began to change in the early twentieth century, reflecting an increasing emphasis on the child's primary affectional tie to the mother. Led by Freud himself, psychoanalysis in the 1920s began to focus on pre-Oedipal issues (the psychoanalytic code word for the mother). Central to the many variant formulations was a clear theme: the Oedipal conflict is the key to the clinically less serious neurotic disorders, but the more severe and less treatable forms of psychopathology (the psychoses and personality disorders) result from earlier, more fundamental problems with the mother.

Harry Stack Sullivan, one of the most influential figures in modern clinical psychiatry, also gave almost exclusive attention to the mother: She transmits anxiety and irrational societal expectations to the child, potentially leading to personality "warps" of varying

severity. Sullivan's writings hardly ever mention the father. The same is true for John Watson, the founder of "behaviorism," whose advice to parents not to give too much affection to the child was addressed almost entirely to mothers.

While the elevation of the maternal role was the dominant theme from the mid-nineteenth to mid-twentieth centuries, some observers expressed reservations about it. Bronson Alcott wrote in 1845 that "I cannot believe that God established the relation of father without giving the father something to do" (in Demos 1982, 432). At the turn of the century, cultural critics attacked rising maternal influence, along with urbanization and immigration, as having a feminizing effect on American political, cultural, and religious institutions (Kimmel 1986). In the first decade of the twentieth century, J. McKeen Cattell, an early founder of American psychology, criticized the "vast horde of female teachers" to whom children were exposed (in O'Neil 1967, 81).

A major structural source of the decline in the father's role and increased maternal influence was the emergence of new paternal work patterns away from the family, brought about by industrialization.[2] "For the first time, the central activity of fatherhood was sited outside one's immediate household. Now being fully a father meant being separated from one's children for a considerable part of each working day" (Demos 1982, 434). As geographical distance between the workplace and the home increased, so too did the father's direct involvement with his children. "The suburban husband and father is almost entirely a Sunday institution," noted a writer in *Harper's Bazaar* in 1900 (Demos 1982, 442).

This new kind of father focused entirely on breadwinning was depicted in early-twentieth-century advertisements. Mothers were shown as the general purchasing managers of the household, while fathers were portrayed primarily as breadwinners whose wages made family consumption and security possible. Life insurance promotions reminded fathers of their primary function as breadwinners. A 1925 Prudential ad showed a widowed mother visiting her children in an orphan asylum. The child in the ad says the asylum authorities told him "father didn't keep his life insurance paid up" (Ewen 1976, 153–154). The mark of a good father had become a good insurance policy.

In his new role, father's authority was reduced. In a well-known passage, Alexis de Tocqueville described how weak paternal authority seemed when he visited the United States in the 1830s:

> A species of equality prevails around the domestic hearth. . . . I think that in proportion as manners and laws become more democratic, the relation of father and son becomes more intimate and more affectionate; rules and authority are less talked of, confidence and tenderness are often increased. . . . The father foresees the limits of this authority . . . and surrenders it without a struggle. (in Degler 1980, 75)

The father continued to set the official standard of morality and to be the final arbiter of family discipline, but he did so at more of a remove than before: He stepped in only when the mother's delegated authority failed. "The father . . . was kicked upstairs, as they say in industry, and was made chairman of the board. As such, he did not lose all his power—he still had to be consulted on important decisions—but his wife emerged as the executive director or manager of the enterprise which is called the family" (LeMasters, in Sebald 1976, 19).

A potential consequence of this indirect authority was that fathers lost touch with what was actually going on in the family. Clarence Day's portrayal of a turn-of-the-century middle-class family, *Life with Father* (1935), was a popular comic expression of this

hazard: In spite of his high-status job and the elaborate deference he appears to receive from his wife and children, he is in fact easily manipulated by them. Contemporary concerns about "declining" paternal authority find many of their roots in this period.

Lynd and Lynd's ([1929] 1956) study of Middletown in the 1920s documents the results of these trends. One resident says: "It is much more important for children to have a good mother than it is for them to have a good father because the mother not only establishes their social position, but because her influence is the prepotent one." A business-class mother says: "My husband has to spend time in civic work that my father used to give to us children." Lynd and Lynd observed little difference in the amount of fathers' involvement between the working-class and business-class fathers; however, business-class wives more often accepted the low involvement, while the working-class wives more often expressed resentment about it.

Middletown notes a "busy, wistful uneasiness" about not being a better parent among many elite fathers: "I'm a rotten dad. If our children amount to anything it's their mother who'll get all the credit. I'm so busy I don't see much of them and I don't know how to chum up with them when I do." Another remarked: "You know, I don't know that I spend any time having a good time with my children. . . . And the worst of it is, I don't know how to. I take my children to school in the car each morning; there is some time we could spend together, but I just spend it thinking about my own affairs and never make an effort to do anything with them." This emotional gap led children to long for greater father involvement. Middletown high school students chose "spending time with his children" among a list of 10 possible desirable qualities in a father far more often than any of the others (Lynd and Lynd [1929] 1956, 148–149).

1940–1965: Father as Sex Role Model

During and following World War II, the criticisms that had accompanied the rise of maternal influence in the earlier period became increasingly powerful. At the turn of the century, excessive mothering had been one of a cluster of social transformations creating concern. Now, while other discomfiting trends such as urbanization and immigration had either been accepted or brought under control, mothers stood more alone as objects of social unease (Kimmel 1986). During the postwar years, this heightened critique of mothering helped usher in a new perception of the father's direct importance in child rearing as a sex role model. This new view derived from negative perceptions of mothers, and encouraged paternal participation of only a limited sort. The new conception did not become dominant; the distant father-breadwinner still prevailed. Nonetheless, the sex role model interpretation of fathering is historically important as the first positive image of involved fatherhood to have a significant impact on the culture since the moral overseer model of the colonial period.

The intensified critique of mothers' influence is particularly evident in Philip Wylie's (1942) popular *A Generation of Vipers*:

> Megaloid momworship has got completely out of hand. Our land, subjectively mapped, would have more silver cords and apron strings crisscrossing it than railroads and telephone wires. Mom is everywhere and everything and damned near everybody, and from her depends all the rest of the U.S. Disguised as good old mom, dear old mom, sweet old mom, your loving mom, and so on, she is the bride at every funeral and the corpse at every wedding. (185)

In academic psychology, David Levy's *Maternal Overprotection* argued that contemporary mothers took too dominant a role in the lives of their children because they were not fully satisfied in their relationships with their husbands. "The child must bear the brunt of the unsatisfied love life of the mother" (Levy 1943, 121). Following the war, military psychiatrists blamed the battle breakdowns and other problems of the American fighting man on the American mother (Strecker 1948). Even the early feminist critiques of the traditional housewife role, written during the early 1960s, sounded a similar theme. Betty Friedan's *The Feminine Mystique* prominently features the argument that the housewife-mother has too close a relationship with her sons, resulting in the "rampant homosexuality" which was described as "spreading a murky smog throughout every area of American life, especially the arts" (1963, 265).

New attention to the father's direct role was first manifested not in research on normal father-child relationships but in studies of what happened when the father was absent. The postwar father was seen as a towering figure in the life of his child not so much by his presence as by his absence. Many of the social factors contributing to this enormous postwar interest in father absence directly or indirectly derived from the events of the war. Most obviously, fathers had gone away to the war en masse, and many had not returned. The first studies of the effects of paternal separation were in fact conducted with children of wartime-absent fathers (e.g., Bach 1946). In addition, wartime induced changes in women's roles. Wives entered paid employment on a large scale and learned greater independence from men through having to live without their husbands for the duration. Partly as a result, the divorce rate immediately following demobilization was high. Further, the war's economic boom stimulated an enormous and historically unprecedented migration of rural dwellers, especially blacks, to the older cities of the Northeast and Midwest and the new cities of the West. Traditional family structure broke down, at least among many of these new urban migrants. Rates of father absence rose.

Parallel to the cultural concern about father absence was a more general concern about fathers' weakness and passivity even when they were technically "present." Mass culture expressed it in parody. "The domesticated Dad, who was most entertaining when he tried to be manly and enterprising, was the butt of all the situation comedies. Danny Thomas, Ozzie Nelson, Robert Young, and (though not a father in the role) Jackie Gleason in 'The Honeymooners,' were funny as pint-sized caricatures of the patriarchs, frontiersmen, and adventurers who once defined American manhood" (Ehrenreich and English 1979, 240).

Father absence and father passivity became linked in the public mind with a perceived epidemic of juvenile delinquency in the 1950s. A dramatic expression of this connection occurs in the film *Rebel Without a Cause.* In one the film's most powerful scenes, the delinquent son finally seeks out his father for advice during a crisis. But when he finds his father wearing an apron while washing dishes in the kitchen, the son recoils in disgust.

A new theory about gender came to dominate developmental psychology which theoretically articulated an extremely significant role for the father, particularly with sons. This theory held that boys face a terrible problem in developing male identity: Developing masculinity is absolutely essential to psychological health, but contemporary child-rearing practices make it difficult for boys to do it. Male identity is thwarted by boys' initial identification with their mothers, and by high rates of father absence and the relative unavailability of fathers even when "present." According to the theory, the combination of too much mothering and inadequate father-

ing lead to insecurity in male identity. This insecure masculinity is manifested directly in homosexuality, as well as more indirectly in delinquency and violence, viewed as "overcompensations" or "defenses" against it (Pleck 1981, 1983). As this theory evolved, fathers came to be seen as essential for the sex role development of their daughters as well. This conception of father as sex role model served as the equivalent of the much earlier view of the father as moral pedagogue. Healthy sex role identification replaced salvation as the moral imperative.

This new view of the father's role encouraged paternal involvement with children, but also drew a clear distinction between paternal and maternal roles. "The mother has a primarily expressive relationship with both boys and girls; in contrast, the father rewards his male and female children differently, encouraging instrumental behavior in his son and expressive behavior in his daughter. The father is supposed to be the principal transmitter of culturally based conceptions of masculinity and femininity" (Biller 1971, 107).

This new interpretation of the role of the father gave the father a direct but limited role with his children. Some academic authorities expressed great concern about the father being overinvolved, or having a role too similar to the mother, particularly if combined with the mother taking a "masculine" role. A standard anthology on the family states that "severe personality problems in one spouse may require the wife to become the wage-earner, or may lead the husband to perform most maternal activities." It further suggests that "a child whose father performs the mothering functions both tangibly and emotionally while the mother is preoccupied with her career can easily gain a distorted image of masculinity and femininity" (Bell and Vogel 1968, 32, 586).

Nor was it thought that fathers should be directly involved in the birth of their children.

An obstetrician asserted in 1964 that whether he is "short, thin or fat, of any race, color, or creed," an expectant father "tends to pace, chain smoke, and talk to himself out loud." The doctor went on to observe that "a prospective father behind the wheel is more dangerous than a drunk on the Fourth of July." A guide for the expectant father of the same era suggested that all fathers-to-be learn from the model of an accountant who passed the time in the hospital waiting room by "determining how much tax money would be saved over the years as a result of the new dependency claim that was on the way" (in Gerzon 1982, 203).

Some Implications for the Present

There is no question that the father-breadwinner model established in the nineteenth and early twentieth centuries remains culturally dominant today, both in fathers' actual behavior and its media representation. It is important to recognize that this model has a specific history. To become dominant, it had to supplant an earlier view in which fathers had the ultimate responsibility for, and influence on, their children. The conception of father as moral overseer was promulgated and reinforced by the paramount colonial social institution, the church. It is perhaps difficult for us today to appreciate the power and depth of this past cultural mentality in which fathers' role was considered so important.

As the influence of the church declined, the changing nature and increasing importance of the economy promoted a new model of father as distant breadwinner, paired with a new view of mother's role. Even as this model arose and became dominant, some criticized it or promoted other views. At the turn of the century, their objections appeared to focus at least as much on mothers' influence being too

strong as fathers' being too weak. In the 1950s and 1960s, such reservations attained a new level of cultural influence. In particular, academic psychology absorbed and systematized these criticisms in its sex role theory, and then used its own growing influence to disseminate it throughout the culture. Thus the sex role model of fatherhood became a strong though still secondary counterpoint to the dominant father-breadwinner image.

Today, the critique of the distant father-breadwinner is intensifying further. A new image, summed up in the term "the new father," is clearly on the rise in print and broadcast media. This new father differs from older images of involved fatherhood in several key respects: he is present at the birth; he is involved with his children as infants, not just when they are older; he participates in the actual day-to-day work of child care, and not just play; he is involved with his daughters as much as his sons.

The new father represents the further extension of the sex role model and other counterimages challenging the dominant breadwinner model over the last century. Several other phenomena parallel or contribute to the new father image. The increase in postwar wives' employment, and the postwar feminism associated with it, have been its greatest impetus. These led mothers to demand that fathers become more involved. Further, feminist scholars generated new development theories of gender (Chodorow 1978; Dinnerstein 1976) which support a much broader father role than the older-sex-role-model theory. Some feminist analyses imply or directly hold that men are impoverished by not being more active as fathers. This argument has been adopted and highly elaborated as one of the central ideas of the contemporary men's movement and has diffused through the culture more broadly.

It is important to recognize that alongside

the "new father," the older alternatives to the father-breadwinner model still have considerable cultural force. The theory of paternal sex role modeling remains the most widely expressed formal argument (that is, the one expressed in most college courses, newspaper articles, popular psychology literature) for greater father involvement. (In recent years, I have been asked repeatedly to testify in support of the Boy Scouts' argument to exclude women as scoutmasters because "boys need male models.")

The moral overseer model of fatherhood also continues to influence a large and probably growing number of fathers today. Its earlier decline coincided with the waning of organized religion as a paramount social institution. One component of the fundamentalist Christian resurgence of recent decades is a revival of Christian fatherhood as an ideal. Today's Christian-father movement is accompanied by its own literature of books (see Benson 1977; MacDonald 1977) and periodicals.[3]

The fathers' rights movement is also a significant force on the cultural scene. This movement reflects a complex amalgam of fathers driven by antifeminist backlash (echoing the critics of maternal influence earlier in this century) with other fathers motivated by an actual denial of their genuine desire to remain involved as fathers after divorce. The "new father" coexists somewhat uneasily with this as well as the other profathering ideologies having an impact today. Seifert (1974), for example, describes the problems for men working in child-care centers when some staff and parents want greater male involvement to help break down traditional sex roles, but others want it to help reinforce them.

The discrepancy between the actual pace of change in men and the profusion of profathering imagery has led some to dismiss the image of the new, involved father as only media "hype." While this element clearly exists,

it is also important to recognize that the new father is not *all* hype. This image, like the dominant images of earlier periods, is ultimately rooted in structural forces and structural change. Wives *are* more often employed, and do less in the family when they are; men *are* spending more time in the family, both absolutely and relative to women (husbands' proportion of the total housework and child care rose from 20% to 30% between 1965 and 1981; see Pleck 1985b). If the distant father-breadwinner has a social-structural base, so too does the new father.

The historical legacy of American culture's images of fatherhood includes both the distant father-breadwinner model and a variety of alternatives to it. While the father-breadwinner model is under increasing attack, it is still unquestionably dominant. The tensions among these competing models will continue to be expressed in both American social institutions and in the lives of American fathers. In the future, tension between the breadwinner model and more involved conceptions of fatherhood will continue, if not increase.

Such tensions are reflected directly in the current debate about improving parental leave policies in the workplace, including broadening them to apply to fathers (Pleck 1986). Although the actual cost of offering paternity leave is minimal compared to the cost of parental leave for mothers (simply because fathers use it much less), paternity leave receives a highly disproportionate share of attention as a frivolous and exorbitantly expensive consequence of gender-neutral parental leave policies. (A 1986 national conference on work and family issues [co-sponsored by the U.S. Department of Labor, the AFL-CIO, and the National Association of Manufacturers] at which I was scheduled to speak on paternity leave had to be canceled because labor contract negotiations between the conference vendor and one of its unions had come to an impasse over the issue of paternity leave, and the union threatened to picket the conference!) Paternity leave, and other policies to reduce work-family conflict for fathers, evoke negative responses; not so much because of their actual cost, but because they so directly challenge the father-breadwinner model.

NOTES

Acknowledgments: Research reported in this article was conducted as part of the Fatherhood Project, supported by the Ford, Leví Strauss, Ittelson, and Rockefeller Family Foundations. Earlier versions have benefited from comments by Harris Dienstfrey, Michael Kimmel, Michael Lamb, James Levine, and Elizabeth H. Pleck.

1. My analysis is especially indebted to Demos (1982) and Rotundo (1985). Both of these rely heavily on Rotundo (1982).

2. There was, of course, considerable diversity in the ways in which industrialization affected patterns of work and family life in the United States and Europe, and diversity in work and family patterns both before and after whatever benchmarks are used to date industrialization (Pleck 1976).

3. For example, *For Dads Only: A News and Creative Ideas Resource for Christian Dads and Husbands,* PO Box 340, Julian, CA 92036.

REFERENCES

Bach, G. (1946). Father-fantasies and father typing in father-separated children. *Child Development, 17,* 63–80.

Bell, N., and E. Vogel (Eds.). (1968). *A modern introduction to the family* (rev. ed.). New York: Free Press.

Benson, D. (1977). *The total man.* Wheaton, IL: Tyndale House.

Bernard, J. (1981). The good-provider role: Its rise and fall. *American Psychologist, 36,* 1–12.

Biller, H. (1971). *Father, child, and sex role.* Lexington, MA: Heath.

Bloom-Feshbach, J. (1981). Historical perceptions of the father's role. In M. E. Lamb (Ed.), *The role of the father in child development* (2nd Ed., pp. 71–112). New York: Wiley-Interscience.

Chodorow, N. (1978). *The reproduction of mothering: Psychoanalysis and the sociology of gender.* Berkeley: University of California Press.

Day, C. (1935). *Life with father.* New York: Knopf.

Degler, C. (1980). *At odds: Women and the family in America from the Revolution to the present.* New York: Oxford University Press.

Demos, J. (1982). The changing faces of fatherhood: A new exploration in American family history. In S. Cath, A. Gurwitt, and J. Ross (Eds.), *Father and child: Developmental and clinical perspectives* (pp. 425–450). Boston: Little, Brown.

Dinnerstein, D. (1976). *The mermaid and the minotaur: Sexual arrangements and the human malaise.* New York: Harper & Row.

Ehrenreich, B., and D. English. (1979). *For her own good: 150 years of the experts' advice to women.* Garden City, NY: Anchor/Doubleday.

Ewen, S. (1976). *The feminine consciousness: Advertising and the social roots of the consumer culture.* New York: McGraw-Hill.

Friedan, B. (1963). *The feminine mystique.* New York: Norton (pagination in citations from 1970 Dell paperback edition).

Gerzon, M. (1982). *A choice of heroes.* Boston: Houghton Mifflin.

Grossberg, M. (1983). Who gets the child? Custody, guardianship, and the rise of judicial patriarchy in nineteenth-century America. *Feminist Studies, 9,* 235–260.

Kimmel, M. (1986). *From separate spheres to sexual equity: Men's responses to feminism at the turn of the century.* Working paper #2, Rutgers University, Department of Sociology.

Levy, D. (1943). *Maternal overprotection.* New York: Norton.

Lynd, R., and H. M. Lynd. (1956). *Middletown: A study in modern American culture.* New York: Harcourt, Brace (original work published 1929).

MacDonald, G. (1977). *The effective father.* Wheaton, IL: Tyndale House.

O'Neill, W. (1967). *Divorce in the progressive era.* New Haven, CT: Yale University Press.

Pleck, E. (1976). Two worlds in one: Work and family. *Journal of Social History, 10,* 178–195.

Pleck, J. (1981). *The myth of masculinity.* Cambridge: MIT Press.

———. (1983). The theory of male sex role identity: Its rise and fall, 1936–present. In M. Lewin (Ed.), *In the shadow of the past: Psychology views the sex* (pp. 205–225). New York: Columbia University Press.

———. (1985a). *Working wives, working husbands.* Newbury Park, CA: Sage.

———. (1985b). American fatherhood: A historical perspective. *American Behavioral Scientist, 29* (1), 7–23.

———. (1986). Employment and fatherhood: Issues and innovative policies. In M. E. Lamb (Ed.), *The father's role: Applied perspectives* (pp. 385–412). Boston: Little, Brown.

Rotundo, A. (1982). Manhood in America: The northern middle class, 1770–1920 (Ph.D. diss., Brandeis University). (University Microfilms No. 82–20,111).

Sebald, H. (1976). *Momism: The silent disease of America.* Chicago: Nelson-Hall.

Seifert, K. (1974). Some problems of men in child care center work. In J. Pleck and J. Sawyer (Eds.), *Men and masculinity* (pp. 69–73). Englewood Cliffs, NJ: Prentice-Hall.

Strecker, E. (1946). *Their mothers' sons.* Philadelphia: Lippincott.

Suggs, R. (1978). *Motherteacher: The feminization of American education.* Charlottesville: University of Virginia Press.

Wylie, P. (1942). *A generation of vipers.* New York: Rinehart.

Chapter 27

Fathers and Sons: Men's Experience and the Reproduction of Fatherhood

NICHOLAS W. TOWNSEND

In popular discussions of fathers, we hear a great deal about "deadbeat dads" who do not pay child support, about "distant fathers" who are not emotionally available to their children, and about how little most men do in the way of caring for their children or doing housework. We also hear about the exceptional "new fathers" who are deeply involved with their children. What we hear very little about, however, is what it means to ordinary men to be fathers—what being a father is from the father's point of view.

The Reproduction of Fatherhood

In this chapter I describe how men talk about, and react to, the changes in themselves that occur when they become fathers. Men describe the particular changes of self that they see as the consequence of fatherhood: their new sense of stability and responsibility, a greater sensitivity and capacity for growth, anxieties they had not shared before, and also a capacity for anger and the abuse of power

that may or may not be controlled. In all these ways, fatherhood is equated not so much with adulthood in any narrow or formal sense as with a transformation of the kind of person a man is. The transition to fatherhood can be seen as coincident with the readiness to leave a stage of youthful freedom and irresponsibility. What becoming a father means is not so much discovering the new and unexpected as *re-experiencing*, from a different perspective, being fathered. Because this is the case, men's descriptions of becoming fathers can be seen as specific instances of the reproduction of a general cultural pattern of fatherhood (Townsend 1992).

This is a "reproduction of fatherhood" in a double sense, for it is by reproducing himself in his children that a man becomes a father, and by becoming a father himself he simultaneously carries his own father's reproduction to another stage. Nancy Chodorow describes the "reproduction of mothering" as a process in which little girls develop "mothering capacities and the desire to mother" (1978, 7). That is, according to Chodorow, women do the work of mothering, the care of and emotional involvement with infants and children, because they have come to want to do those things through their experience of their own mothers. My account of fathering does not share Chodorow's concern with the psychodynamics of early experience, but it does share her focus on the reproduction in succeeding generations of deeply seated emotional capacities and desires and her attention to parenting as a way of being.

The Men I Talked to and Their Social Situation

The men I write about in this chapter all graduated in 1972 from Orchardtown High School, a working-class, suburban high school in northern California.[1] The men were born in 1954 or 1955 and were in their late thirties when I talked to them. For the research project of which this is part, I talked to fifty men who had graduated from the school, half of whom had graduated in 1972 (Townsend 1992). I also talked to some of their female classmates and to some of the men's wives, parents, and former teachers. Their fathers had generally had blue-collar jobs in construction and manufacturing and had moved with their new families to the new housing developments of Orchardtown in the 1950s. These men were, in short, born into the new houses and prosperity of the post–World War II "American dream." They were fortunate to have grown up when they did, for when they graduated from high school they were able to find union jobs in construction or entry-level positions in the electronics firms of "Silicon Valley" that allowed them to buy houses in the neighborhoods in which they were raised and to live at a material level higher than that of their parents. They were, in fact, able to realize many

aspects of the "American dream." These men frequently told me that they would never have gotten the jobs they had, or risen as fast, if they had graduated from high school in 1982 or 1992. Men ten years younger than they were in a very different position, for rapid rises in the price of houses, stagnation and decline in real wages, and higher educational requirements for jobs meant that the younger cohort had to move farther from work to afford housing and, in general, had to scale down their dreams.

Although many of the men I talked to told me about their mother's work histories, the normative or cultural picture of parenting when they were young children was of full-time mothers who were exclusively responsible for the care of children and of fathers who were providers and little else. The male concentration on the provider role was given added force by the recent past; the grandparents of the men I talked to had been adults during the Great Depression of the 1930s, and many of the men's own parents had childhood memories of very hard times. Men's dedication to work was motivated by the immediate memory of the consequences of failure as well as by the lure of success. Talcott Parsons, one of the most influential sociologists of the 1950s, expressed and reinforced the cultural rule of the time: "a mature woman can love, sexually, only a man who takes his full place in the masculine world, above all its occupational aspect, and who takes responsibility for a family" (Parsons and Bales 1955, 22). That is to say, according to Parsons and Bales, a woman can love, sexually, only a man who has a job. And if a man has a job, he has done what is required to be a full adult.

When talking to these men, I found the similarities and differences between my life and theirs helped me to understand them and encouraged them to explain themselves to me. In many ways I was both an outsider, looking at their lives from an external position, and an insider, sharing important aspects of their experience.

To begin with, I am a man, and I am only a couple of years older than they. At the time of the interviews, I had lived and worked in northern California for twenty years, so I knew the places and the events the men talked about. I knew, even if I did not always share, their cultural stereotypes. But I was born and raised in England and am obviously British, so it made sense for me to ask some basic questions about life in the United States that would have seemed strange coming from another American. Similarly, I had worked for several years in construction before I went back to college, so the men and I could share an understanding of blue-collar work. But I was now an academic and a researcher, so the professional men in my sample could talk about their work to someone who would know what they were talking about. In addition, I am the parent of two stepsons, so we could talk about our common experience of child raising. But the fact that my children are stepchildren allowed the men who had biological children of their own to explain why they believed this was a special link. At the same time, it gave me something in common with men who did not have, or did not want, children of their own.

Our conversations focused on the topic of children, family, and fatherhood, and I would always ask the men about their reasons for having (or not having) children and about the good and bad things about having them. Since our talks were conversations, not structured interviews, they frequently ventured off into other topics. I encouraged the men to talk about what they found important and interesting in their own lives: "What else would you like someone to know about your life?" I would ask. The resulting conversations all included a certain amount of comparable information on work and family history, but each also contained a unique account of a unique life.

In the following sections, I treat two broad themes of fatherhood. First, I describe how reproduction is a gendered process for these men: being the father of a *son* is highly significant; men reproduce their own concepts of gender in their children, and sports are particularly important to them as an activity and as a metaphor of masculinity. Second, I examine how becoming a father transforms not only a man himself but also how he sees his own father. When a man becomes a father he replaces his own father by making him a grandfather.

Fatherhood as a Gendered Process

Fathers and Sons: Gender and Reproduction

While biological reproduction and the transmission of genetic material proceed through both male and female children, the reproduction of fatherhood is gendered and proceeds only through the male line. Only men are able to become fathers and thus reproduce their own fathers, and only through boy children can they reproduce themselves as fathers and as men.

My concentration on the male line, on the reproduction of fatherhood, of fathers, and of men, is a reflection of the emphasis that men put on both their fathers and their sons. The men I talked to were generally committed to the idea of equal treatment and equal opportunity for their children, regardless of their sex, but those with both sons and daughters talked more about their sons and reported more activities with them. In this, they are typical of the national pattern. Analyzing responses to the *National Survey of Families and Households*, Lye (1991) found that mothers in "intact" families report more participation in their children's lives than fathers report. Given this difference between mothers and fathers, the only thing that made a significant difference is that men with daughters participate less in outings, playing, talking, and eating meals with their children (Lye 1991).

Mark was typical of the men I talked to in that he talked more about his son than his daughter and typical also in that he noticed that he was doing so, commented on it, and continued to do so. Mark, though he denied that he "cared" more about his son, was aware that he gave him pride of place in his account: "this may sound one-sided, I always bring him up first." He was also typical in his sex preferences for his children. Mark had married his high school sweetheart two years after graduation, was still married to her, and had two children, a boy and a girl three years younger. He described them as "the typical Joe American family." When we talked about the decisions his wife and he had made about having children, he said:

> We knew we wanted two. And with the boy the first, that made it a lot easier. You know, chances are if we had had two girls we might have gone for three. Because I'm the only child [and]— I'm the last one to carry the name on in the West half of the States. So the boy was great. And when [my daughter] was born that was, you know, that's perfect.

It is clear that while Mark wanted two children, he particularly wanted a son to carry on his name, and that it was "great" and "easier" *for him* when they had the son first. When I asked him what they would have done if they had had two sons, he replied that his wife would have wanted to try for a girl, that he "would have gone along with it," but that it would have been up to his wife.

Steve shared Mark's normative picture of the family. He and his wife had both been married and divorced before they got together. They both knew they wanted a family and "figured it was about time" (he was 28 and she 26). Their two children were planned in the sense that they knew they wanted to avoid having both children in diapers at the same time, and they wanted at least two. They had thought about having a third child, but their children were now aged eight and five and a half, and they felt it was not practical to have more since the children could now be left with relatives while their parents went out and had time to themselves. "I love the children dearly," Steve said, "but they can be taxing on your patience. If people were trapped for the rest of their lives and could not get away from children it would be very trying on the marriage."

Steve's daughter was born first, and he and his wife faced the decision about having another child and decided to do so: "Male ego, so to speak, that wants to have a son to carry on the family name." His wife had wanted to have a daughter first, but "I, of course, wanted a boy so that way I knew I would have had my son." At the birth of his daughter, he felt "not disappointment, but a little let down." He did not know if they would have tried a third time if they had had two girls. "I still would have had that feeling, well, Jeez, I would really like to have a son." He was relieved that he did not have to go further.

Expressed male preference for sons has its counterpart in male uneasiness at the thought of daughters, but the story is complicated by men's individual preferences and by their reactions to their own circumstances. Men who had sons were, like Steve, pleased and relieved, but men who had daughters, while they were sometimes anxious about them, never said they did not want them. Men who had daughters and no sons frequently said they preferred having only daughters because having boys would be such a source of worry.

Only one man told me of his worry that he might find a daughter sexually attractive. Men's discomfort about having daughters is more usually expressed in terms of their anxiety over their daughters' greater vulnerability. Some of this vulnerability is directly tied to a sexual double standard for boys and girls. Mark's comment, thinking about his nine-year-old daughter's teenage years, was:

I think you tend to be more protective over your daughter, at least the man does, than his son. You know what you did as a teenager, and you don't want that happening to your daughter. Not that I did anything all that bad, but there were times when you went out, you had a one-night stand with a chick after a football game or something. Do you want your daughter in that situation? No.

That men think about their daughters sexually, or at least that they think about their daughters' sexuality, is not surprising given the sexual focus of their attitudes toward women in general. That they do so, however, does create a wariness in their feelings, based on their interpretation of their own and of other males' motivations toward girls, and does contribute to their perception of their daughters as very different from themselves. It was a common theme in many of my conversations that a father, as a man, could understand what his son was going through, could "be there" for him, and could offer appropriate advice, whereas parts of his daughter's experience would be insurmountably alien to him, though comprehensible to his wife.

The men I talked to who were fathers of daughters all had to come to terms with this sense of distance, just as they had to come to terms with the very general male preference for sons. They all claimed that the disappointment they had anticipated had evaporated or was dissipated by the relief they felt at a safe birth and the joy they found in their relationships with their daughters. Those men who had daughters and no sons also minimized the anxiety they felt about the girls and talked instead about the worries they attributed to the fathers of sons. They told me that they were glad not to have to worry about violence, delinquency, risk-taking, and the other dangers they saw threatening boys.

These men not only came to terms with being fathers of daughters but also found joy and satisfaction in their relationships with their daughters. However, fundamental tensions remain in men's fathering of girls that distinguish it from their fathering of boys. One indication of these tensions is the finding that, at the national level, fathers are more involved with the care of their sons than of their daughters and that couples who are parents of daughters are more likely to divorce than are couples who are parents of sons (Morgan, Lye, and Condran 1988). Another indication of these tensions lies in the perpetuation of stereotypical gender roles for children. There is a basic cultural formula that equal love and different treatment are compatible, and that different treatment of boys and girls can be justified through appeals to their essential differences.

The Reproduction of Gender Roles

The appeal to essential sex-linked difference, and the identification of essential difference with socially imposed gender, were summarized in Jim's comments. He told me first about the physical similarities and differences between his five year-old-son and fourteen-month-old daughter, then turned to their behavioral differences.

What is really neat is the way they handle themselves. He never stops, never stops motion, never stops being rambunctious and all boy, and she is the little girl. Everybody says, "He's the little boy that everybody says is rambunctious and all boy and she's the little girl, all girl." She likes to put bracelets and necklaces on.

His daughter, he says, is quieter, more passive, and more interested in pretty things. Jim expressed his surprise at the differences between his children, "even though they have the same parents, a lot of the same genes. We don't know where my son came from."

The gender differences Jim describes are typical for boys and girls in the United States: boys are more exploratory and physically active, girls are quieter and more concerned with personal adornment. What is crucial in this account of gender differences is the invisibility of the processes through which they are perpetuated. A fourteen-month-old baby, boy or girl, likes to wear jewelry only because it has had it put on by adults and has then been praised for looking pretty.

In Jim's case, the gender construction of his son as "all boy" is a pervasive feature of the relationship between father and son. Jim's five-year-old son is well equipped with sports equipment, masculine toys, and especially a three-foot-long car with an electric motor that he drove wildly around the yard, banging into trees, fences, and buildings, while his father encouraged him. Many of Jim's interactions with his son are exuberantly physical; he and his brother throw their children back and forth between them in the house, and when his son was three Jim used to throw him as far as he could above his head. (Jim is a large, physically vigorous man who has done physical work and played sports for many years; he can throw a three-year-old a good number of feet in the air.) "Anything I do he wants to do too, which is neat. And I let him." Jim's son helps him push the lawn mower and uses hedge clippers and pruning shears. He even holds the wedge when his father is splitting firewood and stands with him holding the chain saw. Jim's wife and sister-in-law, both

nurses, would remonstrate with him. Both, he said, had seen too many children in hospital emergency rooms with broken bones and dislocated joints from such roughhousing to find it amusing.

The significant points of Jim's interactions with his son are that they encourage physical activity, exploration of new activities, manipulation of the physical environment, being with and emulating his father, and ignoring, or at least discounting, his mother's "feminine" concerns and reservations. With all this, it is hardly difficult to see where Jim's son gets his "rambunctiousness," but it is important to notice that Jim explicitly denies the causation and wraps the process in mystery— the outcome is attributed to essential differences between males and females.

Jim was more than usually involved with the care of his children, partly because of the relation between his wife's and his own work schedules, partly because he and his wife were separated when I talked to him, and partly because he was a man whose aspiration to be a family man outweighed his interest in having a career. As an artisan, he had been able to adjust his schedule to his wife's shift and on-call work at the hospital, taking sole responsibility for the children for long periods of the day. He was also unusual in the extent to which he talked about including his son in his second job as a self-employed handyman. Men who go to work, whether to an assembly line, construction site, or office, cannot take their children with them, whereas Jim could contemplate taking his son along when he went to mow a lawn or prune a tree.

Jim was not unusual, however, in the gender distinctions he made between his children, or in the emphasis on physical activity, particularly sports, as the most important area of contact between father and son. Both in response to my questions about what they would like to teach their children, and as spontaneous contributions from men on their roles as fathers, the most frequently mentioned subject was not morals or vocation or even schoolwork but "playing ball." The picture of father and son playing ball together is, for these men, the image that defines the relationship.

Sports, Success, and Masculinity

Sports were very important to many of the men I talked to, and they had been even more important to them in their teenage years. Anthropologists have commented on the cultural significance of sports in the adolescence and growth to maturity of men in the United States (Burnett 1975; Fiske 1975; Messner 1992). Many of the men continued to be involved in sports, as participants as well as spectators. My informants reported playing golf, tennis, and racquetball; swimming, jogging, and running; weightlifting at home and at the gym; and playing in softball leagues. Besides the manifest functions of pleasure in physical activity and the maintenance of health, all of these activities serve the more or less latent function of maintaining social relations. Sports also serve as important markers of masculinity, as activities into which to socialize sons, and as experiences for fathers and sons to share.

As domestic life and industrial life have been increasingly separated, socialization of sons to the world of work has been increasingly removed from families. The state and the marketplace have taken over the education and vocational training that were traditionally provided by apprenticeships and families. At the same time, particularly in cultural images, the amount of physical labor in men's work, and hence the essentialist support for a sexual division of labor, has diminished. The stereotype of family life in the decades after World War II was one of strict division between the provider role of the husband and the domestic and child care responsibilities of the mother. But it was also a picture in which the work a father went off to was in an office. It was not clear that the work he did required any of the "masculine" qualities of physical strength, speed, and coordination. In these circumstances, sports (and recreational hunting and fishing) became a bastion and marker of traditional masculinity.

Mark's ambitions for his son, as the ambitions of so many men of his own generation had been for themselves, centered on athletics. I asked whether he had expectations for his children.

> No. I don't— I have always said— Well, I can't say no. I would love [my son] to be a professional athlete, because he's gifted in baseball, and he's never played football but I think he could be good in that. He plays soccer. He's great in soccer. And I just think that— I'm not one of those parents that I'm out there throwing the ball with him twenty days out of the month. I just keep him aware of the fact that if you want to play sports there's certain things you have to do. Being smart is one of them.

In these few words, Mark expressed the common tension between making your children into what you would like them to be and allowing them to develop their own potential. He also expressed the tension of the relation between sports and academics. Notice that he denied his expectations for his son but then admitted them. He also admitted to the encouragement he gives his son but contrasted it with the pressure some parents place on their children. Finally, he made it clear that in his explanations to his son, success in school ("being smart") is not an end in itself or a path to higher education or a qualification for a vocation but a necessary condition for playing sports.

In all aspects of his parental relationship, Mark, like so many of the men I talked to, was steering a course to avoid what he perceived as outmoded, rigid, and authoritarian fathering while not abdicating his parental responsibilities. The delicacy of the distinction came out particularly when Mark was considering whether he wanted his children to look up to him: "Looking up to me is not important. If they respect me, that is important." Mark explained that he did not want fear or obedience just because he was the father, and that he would always try to explain his actions to his children. "I want them to know I gave it some sort of logical thought before I yell." Mark, in fact, wants his children to obey and respect him because of his greater experience and because they think he is right, not simply because he is their father. However, Mark's distinction between the status of father and the successful performance of the role is blurred because it never occurs to Mark that his essential values and orientation could be incorrect.

Mark is convinced that success in school is something that will open opportunities for his children and that doing one's best and fulfilling one's potential are both instrumental goods, and good in themselves. Because of these beliefs, he does not hesitate to demand effort, application, and success from his children. His major concession in this area is that he tries to explain to his children why his demands are reasonable. These explanations, both to his children and to himself, are frequently couched in terms of sports: certain activities are necessary for athletic success; others are damaging.

Transformation Across Generations

Men and Their Own Fathers

Sports are not just something that men do, do with their sons, and use to motivate their sons. More generally, sports are a way of talking about the relationships between fathers and sons, and between fathers and their own fathers. In talking about this activity men also talk about the complex ways they imitate and react against their own fathers.

Sports are at the same time an expression and marker of masculinity and an activity binding together the generations. Young men play sports themselves, and they may continue to play as they get older. They then play with their sons, and they also teach their sons, both formally and informally, and watch their sons play. They also dream athletic futures for their sons. In all of these areas, men are, in their different ways, considering, replicating, or reacting against, the examples of their own fathers.

In discussing his motivations for having children, his anticipation of watching them grow and develop, Mark expressed the gender division of parenting, the male desire for a son, the salience of sports, and the reproduction of fathering.

> To see them grow and to do things that maybe I was not able to do. To be there and help them along the way. That's a very big reason. Because I knew that I— naturally every— I wanted a son. And to watch him play football and to watch him play baseball, and just— Because my father watched me. And I just felt that was something that needed to be done.

Many of the men I talked to wanted to teach their sons, and to watch them play, because their fathers had taught and watched them, but at least as many did these things because their fathers had *not* done them. It is always hard to know the truth about adult memories of childhood, but it is clear that many of the men felt that they had grown up with fathers who had been distant, uninvolved, or physically absent. They felt something was missing in their relationships with their own fathers, and they were now determined to remedy this with their sons.

When men talk about what they do, they are often comparing themselves to what their fathers do. Mark's comments captured the mix of child's and parent's feelings he brings to his own activities with his son.

> I see a lot of kids who just get dropped off at the [baseball] field. I feel sorry for them that their parents aren't involved. A lot of the other kids are jealous of my son for having a father who is involved. They realize, "Hey, this father is out there, where's my dad? How come my dad doesn't come watch the game?"

It is important to remember, of course, that wishes do not necessarily translate into behavior. For instance, one man I interviewed, one of seven sons of an alcoholic father, repeated his hope to spend more time with his young children. Unskilled and uneducated, he believed that he had no choice but to keep working in the family business, then run by his oldest brother. His brother was interested only in the business and worked long hours and weekends, expecting other family members to do the same. The man I talked to felt trapped by his sense of commitment to the provider role and by the dual ties of family benefit and obligation, in a life where the reality was separation from his children.

But the general desire men have to be involved parents does result in an enormous expenditure of time, energy, and financial resources on children's activities. Baseball's little league, but also soccer leagues, swimming teams, gymnastics classes, skating lessons, martial arts classes of all kinds, all involve parents in a great deal of chauffeuring and equipment buying, besides the direct outlays for memberships and tuition. More significantly for the relationship between parents and children, these activities also involve parents as experts and participants. Frequently they master a technical vocabulary, and many of them become actively involved

as coaches, league secretaries, equipment managers, starters, timers, linesmen, and assorted support staff.

The parents' commitment of money and time is complemented by a commitment of thought and emotion, so that their participation in their children's athletic activity is something they do *with* as well as *for* their children. But parental participation was most strongly and widely described as *watching* children's activities. The relationship of adult and child is not one in which the child watches the parent and learns how to perform adult activities but one in which the parent watches the child perform, expressing through watching both approval and encouragement. This focus on watching children play is part of a shift over the past hundred years from seeing children as economically useful to seeing them as expensive but enjoyable sources of personal satisfaction. For contemporary parents, being involved in their children's activities is part of being a good parent, and being a good parent is a major and organizing element in being a good person.

The Succession of Generations

A folktale told in cultures around the world describes a middle-aged man taking his old father into the wilderness, where he will be left to die. As the old man is being given a blanket, he counsels his son to leave only half so that he, the son, will have something to cover himself with when his own son, the old man's grandson, takes him out to die. The moral of the story is that people should care for their old parents, for they, too, will one day be old. From my perspective, the story summarizes the relationship of three generations in the process of reproduction.

I would not want to say, on the strength of my research, that men recognize in their sons the inevitability of their own deaths. But thinking about children does involve men in thinking about their futures and about getting older. During my research, men in their early forties talked to me about their hesitation to have more, or any, children because they would not want their children to have to deal with a father's death before they grow up. Younger men did not speak of their own deaths as a factor influencing their decisions about when, or whether, to have children, but they did talk about aging in these terms. Once again, sports provided the terms for their discussion.

Harold was thirty-six, married for the second time, with a six-year-old son and two stepdaughters. His wife would like to have another child, but he would not.

> You keep thinking of how old you are, and how old your children, your son or daughter, are going to be when you're this age, or this age, because I kept thinking, because I want to involve my kids. One of my fantasies is— I play a lot of sports, mainly softball. I play about four nights a week. I'm really into it. And one of my fantasies is, when my son is old enough to play ball, hopefully I'll still be active to where we can still play. It's a normal fantasy. I'm sure lots of fathers have the same ideas.

Having talked to a number of fathers, I can confirm that Harold's fantasy is normal, at least in the sense that "lots of fathers have the same ideas." It is also true that cultural ideas about age have an impact on decisions about having children. It is not just that highly educated men postpone having children until their education is completed but also that being highly educated equips them for professional careers in which the trajectory of rewards, prestige, and power continues to rise, so that the passage of time is not simply a process of decline. A forty-year-old male attorney, for instance, is a "young" man, an attorney in his fifties is seen as being at the height of his productivity and professional involvement. A

forty-year-old athlete, in contrast, is thought to be at the end of his career, if he has not already been retired for years. To the extent that young men identify with athletics as a mark of their masculinity, and to the extent that they are on career paths that reach a plateau relatively early, they will compare their ages more to the athlete than the attorney.

For a father, playing sports with his son, however, may also be seen as a threatening activity. It is a cliché of U.S. culture that a man will arm wrestle with his son until the son wins and then will stop. The progress of the contest over time is, of course, predictable: when the son is young he will lose in any serious trial of strength with his father, as he gets older the contest becomes more equal. Eventually the son can win, and from then on he will always win. The point of the contest is for the son to aspire to the level of his father. Once he has done so, that point is gone. The message of his victory is one of replacement rather than aspiration.

Having a son, therefore, transforms the young man who has become a father so that like his father before him, or at least like the cultural image of a good father, he becomes responsible, stable, a good provider, and a disciplinarian. Through this transition, men gain a greater sympathy with their own fathers, for they see their fathers in themselves.

Men's accounts of their changed feelings about their fathers were so consistently phrased that they became almost proverbial. There were two basic versions: the first is a realization that a man has become like his father; the second is a reaction against his father and a refusal to follow in his footsteps.

The first version, often given with a wry but fond humor, recounts the things one's father said or did that, to a child or teenager, were exasperating but that now come naturally to the man himself in his interaction with his own children. Some predictable examples are not understanding one's children's taste in music and clothes ("How can you listen to that garbage?"), disapproving of their use of time, insisting that they do their chores and homework, and urging them to be quiet. Hearing himself say to his children, sometimes with exactly the same tone and words, what his father had said to him, and feeling that it is the right thing to say, gives a man a sense of identification with his father. Feeling like his father gives a man the opportunity—or forces him for his own psychic protection—to reinterpret his father's (now his own) behavior. What he once saw as nagging, criticism, and unnecessary worry by his father becomes, when *he* does it, encouragement, setting standards, and realistic concern for the future. Men sympathetically reinterpret not only their fathers' behavior but also their fathers' motivation. This comes about because men know that they themselves are motivated by the best interests of their children and find themselves acting as their fathers did. It follows, for them, that their fathers, who acted the same way, must also have been motivated by their children's best interests. The conclusion of men who gave this first version of the similarities between themselves and their fathers was almost universally that their fathers had done a good enough job and that they themselves would also be better than adequate fathers.

The second version of coming to terms with one's own father denies the direct identification that comes from doing the same thing and stresses the ways that men are struggling to avoid repeating the mistakes of their fathers. But this version often also includes the sons' coming to a kind of understanding of why their fathers did the things they did even while rejecting that as a model. Jim's account, as he responded (notably, by talking about his father only) to my asking whether his parents were encouraging, is typical.

The wrong way. My dad was the type [who would say]: "Oh you can't do that, " and he thought by doing that you'd say: "Oh yes I can" and go out and do it, prove him wrong. I didn't catch on. He says: "Oh you can't do that" and I go: "Huh. My dad says I can't do that." I was kind of frustrated a little bit.

In fact, Jim was more than a "little bit" frustrated with his father. He was bitter when he told me that when he got out of high school, his father criticized him for not going to college and making something good of himself: but when Jim was going to high school, neither his father nor anyone else "helped, or pushed, or talked encouragingly." Because of what Jim saw as a stream of discouragement, he said that he never wanted to talk to his father when he was in junior high and high school. He said that his father was "not there for communication, talking, making you understand something; [he was] always telling you yes or no." If he was to hear that his father had died, Jim said, he would attend the funeral but would be unmoved.

Men who gave the first version, that they had become like their fathers, generally felt content that they were raising their children as they had been raised. The men who gave the second version rejected the pattern of fathering they had experienced. But even when men reject the kind of fathering they received and resolve to do better themselves, there is also a level of understanding of their own fathers that comes with their now being fathers themselves. For Jim it was important to look back on his childhood with the benefit of his own experience of being a father and having someone to worry about and be responsible for. According to Jim, "Now that I can understand [my father] and what happened in my life, I think I got the wrong kind of encouragement." What is crucial is that Jim now feels able to understand his father and to interpret his behavior as encouragement, in the sense that it was intended to motivate him. It was encouragement, but of the wrong kind: his father was mistaken, not malevolent.

Having achieved this profound reinterpretation of this father, Jim said he was also able to appreciate his father's good qualities. His comments reveal the complexity of many men's emotions about their fathers, the tension between resentment and respect, and the contradictory attitudes they hold. Although Jim feels his father was not there to talk to, he acknowledges that "he was always there to get ice cream, to buy a new glove or bat, or for affection." In conclusion on the subject he was able to stress this affection.

> There's a lot of things I do differently from my dad. Almost everything. The only thing I haven't changed is the love that he gave to us. He was the one who always picked us up, always would sit us on his lap, always would hold us all night long. Rubbed us and pat us.

As a result of his having come to terms with his own father's way of doing things, Jim now says that he is able to be a father in his own way. In particular, he says he works hard to keep communication open with his son. He explained to his son, for instance, that as long as his son will tell him if anything bad happens at school then the two of them can do their planned activities, but if Jim hears something upsetting from the principal or his son's teacher, then he will be "too sad and angry" to do things together. To me as an observer, it seemed that while Jim said he wanted communication with his father and his son, what he meant by this was that he wanted them to talk to him and that his response to "failures of communication" with either of them was to withdraw.

Sons, Fathers, Grandfathers

When their sons become fathers, the men of the class of 1972 will themselves become grandfathers. They do not think about this at the moment—they have other issues to contend with—but they are aware of the equivalent transformation of their own fathers into grandfathers. This transformation, like the whole process of reproduction, is double-sided. On one hand, when a man becomes a father it is a critically important stage in his replacement of his own father and moves his father into the category of grandfather, and thus conceptually closer to old age, decline, and death. On the other hand, when a man has children and thus provides his father with grandchildren (especially grandsons) he ensures the continuity of his bloodline and name, binds the family together, and provides his father with an opportunity to display an indulgent and nurturant aspect that is frequently surprising to his son.

While the structural principle of the succession of generations applies to all men, the immediate practical reality differs for individual men according to the survivorship, age, and health of their parents; the number of siblings they have; the number of grandchildren their parents already have; and a host of other idiosyncratic factors. Some men's fathers are healthy, active, and prosperous, are supports to their children, and are hardly to be considered old men; some are retired from work but full of vitality; others are ill, frail, or have died.

Men explicitly deny that either the need or the desire to have someone to care for and support them in old age are motivations for having children; supporting one's self is seen by younger men as an obligation and an expectation. Not to be able to do so would be an admission of failure. However, many men express a sense of responsibility to their parents, and many also describe their recognition that old people with children and grandchildren are less likely to be lonely and deserted.

The emergence of an indulgent and nurturing grandfather is more clearly noticed and associated with the birth of grandchildren than is the promotion of a father to old age. Clearly, grandparents who do not bear the ultimate responsibility for their grandchildren and who do not have to live with their grandchildren are in a position to be indulgent rather than to be disciplinarians. The impact of this structural change on their fathers' personalities was, however, a source of surprise to the men I talked to. Men reported repeatedly that their fathers acted with affection, spontaneity, fun, and generosity toward their grandchildren and that they enjoyed the company of their grandchildren. "He never acted that way towards me," was the refrain of the men's reports. Some of their perceptions are undoubtedly the result of the age differences of the children in question—men may remember their adolescent conflicts with their fathers and compare them to the observed interactions with their own younger children. Some of their perceptions are the result of changed norms for male demonstrativeness—men compare their own behavior toward their children to the more rigid patterns of their fathers. But a great deal is attributable to the different role expectations attached to the structural positions of father and grandfather.

In any event, the transformation of their fathers into grandfathers helped these men come to terms with their fathers and helped them become fathers themselves. The indulgence displayed by grandfathers has helped the men reinterpret their fathers, for it provides new evidence of the good qualities they discover in their fathers' treatment of them.

New Fatherhood? Continuity and Difference

Jim, who spoke so bitterly about his father's lack of real encouragement and did not want to talk to him after he was twelve, had rejected his father's model and is determined to be a new kind of father. In his stress on open communication with his son, Jim is absolutely prototypical of the men I talked to. He is also typical in the twist he has given to his father's form of "encouragement." In both cases, Jim represents as a personal discovery and intention what is at the same time a general social and historical process. When he says, "Kids I don't believe are limited. They're only limited by their parents," he is expressing a historically specific but widespread view that would have been incomprehensible to, for instance, a colonial parent—a view that has faded in and out of fashion during the twentieth century. When he worries about communicating with his son, he is expressing a concern about the meaning of fatherhood that is virtually universal in the expert and popular literature, as well as in the minds of his peers. When he contrasts his father's style of "encouragement" with his own positive attitude, he is the exponent of a more facilitating, less directive approach to child rearing that has expanded its influence and acceptance in the United States since the 1950s.

All of the changes in fathering, both in expression and in action, are modifications of a basic pattern that is being reproduced. Jim and the other fathers of his generation, whether they are conscious of it or not (and sometimes against their will) are not practicing a totally new form of fatherhood. Jim's account of his "totally different" way of encouraging his son illustrates the continuing salience of paternal influence toward achievement, physical activity, and competition.

Jim told me how he had taught his son to ride a two-wheeler when the boy was four years old, and that he had said to his son,

> You're better than daddy, because daddy was five years old when he learned to ride a two-wheeler. His daddy taught— my daddy taught me when I was five, but you learned when you were four. That shows you how much better you are. I'm real proud of you.

When his son heard this, he "got all giggly and smiley and then told Mom: 'Mommy, I'm better than Daddy.'" As outsiders, we may question whether Jim is really applying any less pressure to his son than his father did to him, even though the pressure is of a different kind. We may notice that his son is being encouraged to compete in just those physical activities that define Jim's own masculinity, and we may wonder what his son will have to say about fatherhood in thirty years.

Beneath the language of self-discovery, emotional closeness, and realization of potential, the process of socialization continues to be carried out. The men I talked to wanted their children to follow their own paths, to pursue their own interests, and to excel at the activities they felt suited for, but these fathers also had very clear cultural conceptions of what those paths, interests, and activities should be. This tension between parental expectations and children's self-realization mirrors the tension that lies at the heart of the reproduction of fatherhood. Men become new fathers, and they produce new children, but they also incorporate old patterns of behavior as they reproduce their own fathers.

NOTE

1. Orchardtown is a made up name for a real place. The men's names in this chapter are pseudonyms.

REFERENCES

Burnett, Jacquetta Hill. 1975. "Ceremony, Rites, and Economy in the Student System of an American High School." In *The Nacirema: Readings on American Culture*, 43–54, edited by James P. Spradley and M. A. Rynkiewich. Boston: Little, Brown.

Chodorow, Nancy. 1978. *The Reproduction of Mothering: Psychoanalysis and the Sociology of Gender.* Berkeley: University of California Press.

Fiske, Shirley. 1975. "Pigskin Review: An American Institution." In *The Nacirema: Readings on American Culture*, 55–68, edited by James P. Spradley and M. A. Rynkiewich. Boston: Little, Brown.

Lye, Diane N. 1991. "Where's Daddy? Paternal Participation in Childrearing in Intact Families." Paper presented at the annual meeting of the Population Association of America, Washington, D.C.

Messner, Michael A. 1992. *Power at Play: Sports and the Problem of Masculinity.* Boston: Beacon.

Morgan, S. Philip, Diane N. Lye, and Gretchen Condran. 1988. "Sons, Daughters, and the Risk of Marital Disruption." *American Journal of Sociology* 94:110–129.

Parsons, Talcott, and Robert F. Bales. 1955. *Family, Socialization, and Interaction Process.* New York: Free Press.

Townsend, Nicholas W. 1992. "Paternity Attitudes of a Cohort of Men in the United States: Cultural Values and Demographic Implications." Ph.D. diss., Department of Anthropology, University of California, Berkeley.

~ *Chapter 28*

The Culture and Conduct of Fatherhood

RALPH LAROSSA

. . . The institution of fatherhood includes two related but still distinct elements. There is the *culture of fatherhood* (specifically the shared norms, values, and beliefs surrounding men's parenting), and there is the *conduct of fatherhood* (what fathers do, their paternal behaviors). The distinction between culture and conduct is worth noting because although it is often assumed that the culture and conduct of a society are in sync, the fact is that many times the two are not synchronized at all. Some people make a habit of deliberately operating outside the rules, and others do wrong because they do not know any better (e.g., my 4-year-old son). And in a rapidly changing society like ours, countervailing forces can result in changes in culture but not in conduct, and vice versa. . . .

From *Family Relations* 37, no. 4 (1988): 451–57, abridged by the editors. Copyrighted 1988 by the National Council on Family Relations, 3989 Central Ave. NE, Suite 550, Minneapolis, MN 55421. Reprinted by permission.

The Conduct of Fatherhood Versus the Conduct of Motherhood

. . . Michael Lamb (1987) notes that scholars generally have been ambiguous about what they mean by parental "involvement," with the result that it is difficult to compare one study with the next, and he maintains that if we ever hope to determine whether or not fathers have changed, we must arrive at a definition that is both conceptually clear and comprehensive. The definition which he thinks should be used is one that separates parental involvement into three components: engagement, accessibility, and responsibility. *Engagement* is time spent in one-on-one interaction with a child (whether feeding, helping with homework, or playing catch in the backyard). *Accessibility* is a less intense degree of interaction and is the kind of involvement whereby the parent is doing one thing (cooking, watching television) but is ready or available to do another (respond to the child, if the need arises). *Responsibility* has to do with who is accountable for the child's welfare and care.

Responsibility includes things like making sure that the child has clothes to wear and keeping track of when the child has to go to the pediatrician.

Reviewing studies that allow comparisons to be made between contemporary fathers' involvement with children and contemporary mothers' involvement with children, Lamb (1987) estimates that in two-parent families in which mothers are unemployed, fathers spend about one-fifth to one-quarter as much time as mothers do in an engagement status and about a third as much time as mothers do just being accessible to their children. In two-parent families with employed mothers, fathers spend about 38 percent as much time as mothers do in an engagement status and 65 percent as much time being accessible. As far as responsibility is concerned, mothers appear to carry over 90 percent of the load, regardless of whether they are employed or not. Lamb also notes that observational and survey data indicate that the behavioral styles of fathers and mothers differ. Mother-child interaction is dominated by caretaking whereas father-child interaction is dominated by play.

> Mothers actually play with their children more than fathers do but, as a proportion of the total amount of child-parent interaction, play is a much more prominent component of father-child interaction, whereas caretaking is more salient with mothers. (p. 10)

. . . What about the dads who are seen interacting with their kids in public (see Mackey and Day 1979)? A thoughtful answer to this question also must address how we conceptualize and measure paternal involvement. Does the paternal engagement level of fathers in public square with the paternal engagement level of fathers in private, or are we getting an inflated view of fatherhood from public displays? If we took the time to scrutinize the behavior of fathers and mothers in

public would we find that, upon closer examination, the division of child care is still fairly traditional. When a family with small children goes out to eat, for example, who in the family—mom or dad—is more accessible to the children; that is to say, whose dinner is more likely to be interrupted by the constant demands to "put ketchup on my hamburger, pour my soda, cut my meat"? And how can one look at a family in public and measure who is responsible for the children? How do we know, for instance, who decides whether the kids need clothes; indeed, how do we know who is familiar with the kids' sizes, color preferences, and tolerance levels for trying on clothes? The same applies to studies of paternal involvement in laboratory settings (see Parke 1981). What can a study of father-child interaction in, say, a hospital nursery tell us about father-child interaction in general? The fact that fathers are making their presence known in maternity wards certainly is not sufficient to suggest that the overall conduct of fathers has changed in any significant way. Finally, the fact that fathers can be seen in public with their children may not be as important as the question, How much time do fathers spend *alone* with their children? One recent study found that mothers of young children spent an average of 44.45 hours per week in total child-interaction time (which goes beyond engagement), while fathers spent an average of 29.48 hours per week, a 1.5 to 1 difference. If one looked, however, at time spent alone with children, one discovered that 19.56 hours of mothers' child-interaction time, compared with 5.48 hours of fathers' child-interaction, was solo time, a 3.6 to 1 difference. Moreover, while fathers' total interaction time was positively affected by the number of hours their wives worked, fathers' solo time was not affected at all (Barnett and Baruch 1987). . . .

The Consequences of Asynchronous Social Change

[Forty] years ago E. E. LeMasters (1957) made the point that parenthood (and not marriage, as many believe) is the real "romantic complex" in our society, and that even middle-class couples, who do more than most to plan for children, are caught unprepared for the responsibilities of parenthood. Later on, he and John DeFrain (1983) traced America's tendency to romanticize parenthood to a number of popular folk beliefs or myths, some of which are: raising children is always fun, children are forever sweet and cute, children will invariably turn out well if they have "good" parents, and having children will never disrupt but in fact will always improve marital communication and adjustment. Needless to say, anyone who is a parent probably remembers only too vividly the point at which these folk beliefs began to crumble in her/his mind.

The idea that fathers have radically changed—that they now are intimately involved in raising their children—qualifies also as a folk belief, and it too is having an impact on our lives and that of our children. On the positive side, people are saying that at least we have made a start. Sure, men are not as involved with their children as some of us would like them to be, but, so the argument goes, the fact that we are talking about change represents a step in the right direction. (Folk beliefs, in other words, are not necessarily negative. The myth that children are always fun, for example, does have the positive effect of making children more valued than they would be if we believed the opposite: that they are always a nuisance.) But what about the negative side of the myth of the changing father? Is there a negative side? My objective is to focus here on this question because up to now scholars and the media have tended to overlook the often unintentional but still very real negative consequences that have accompanied asynchronous change in the social institution of fatherhood.

I am not saying that professionals have been oblivious to the potentially negative consequences of "androgynization" on men's lives, for one could point to several articles and chapters which have addressed this issue (e.g., Benokraitis 1985; Berger 1979; Lamb, Pleck and Levine 1987; Lutwin and Siperstein 1985; Pleck 1979; Scanzoni 1979). Rather, the point being made is that scholars and the media, for the most part, have overlooked the difficulties associated with a *specific* social change, namely the asynchronous change in the social institution of fatherhood.

The Technically Present but Functionally Absent Father

The distinction between engagement and accessibility outlined by Lamb (1987) is similar to the distinction between *primary time* and *secondary time* in our study of the transition to parenthood (LaRossa and LaRossa 1981). The social organization of a family with children, especially young children, parallels the social organization of a hospital in that both are *continuous coverage social systems* (Zerubavel 1979). Both are set up to provide direct care to someone (be it children or patients) on a round-the-clock or continuous basis. And both the family and the hospital, in order to give caregivers a break every now and then, will operate according to some formal or informal schedule such that some person or persons will be "primarily" involved with the children or patients (on duty) while others will be "secondarily" involved (on call or accessible).

Like Lamb, we also found that the fathers' levels of engagement, accessibility, and responsibility were only a fraction of the mothers', and that fathers tended to spend a greater part of their care-giving time playing with their children. Moreover, we found that the kinds of play that fathers were likely to be involved in were the kinds of activities that could be carried out at a secondary (semi-involved) level of attention, which is to say that it was not unusual for fathers to be primarily involved in watching television or doing household chores while only secondarily playing with their children.

When asked why they wanted to be with their children, the fathers often would answer along the lines that a father has to "put in some time with his kids" (LaRossa 1983, 585). Like prisoners who "do time" in prison many fathers see themselves as "doing time" with their children. If, on some level of consciousness, fathers have internalized the idea that they should be more involved with their children, but on another level of consciousness they do not find the idea all that attractive, one would expect the emergence of a hybrid style: the technically present but functionally absent father (cf. Feldman and Feldman 1975, cited in Pleck 1983).

The technically present but functionally absent father manifests himself in a variety of ways. One father in our study prided himself on the fact that he and his wife cared for their new baby on an alternating basis, with him "covering" the mornings and his wife "covering" the afternoons. "We could change roles in a night," he said; "it wouldn't affect us." But when this father was asked to describe a typical morning spent alone with his infant son, he gave the distinct impression that he saw fatherhood as a *job* and that while he was "there" in body, he was someplace else in spirit.

> I have the baby to be in charge of, [which has] really been no problem for me at all. But that's because we worked out a schedule where he sleeps a pretty good amount of that time. . . . I generally sort of have to be with him in the sense

of paying attention to his crying or dirty diapers or something like that for any where between 30 to 45 minutes, sometimes an hour, depending. But usually I can have two hours of my own to count on each morning to do my own work, so it's no problem. That's just the breaks that go with it.

Another example: Recently, there appeared an advertisement for one of those minitelevisions, the kind you can carry around in your pocket. Besides promoting the television as an electronic marvel, the man who was doing the selling also lauded how his mini-TV had changed his life: "Now when I go to my son's track meets, I can keep up with other ball games" (Kaplan 1987). The question is: Is this father going to the track meets to see his son race, or is he going simply to get "credit" from his son for being in the stands? One more example: A newspaper story about a father jogging around Golden Gate Park in San Francisco who is so immersed in his running that he fails to notice his 3-year-old daughter—whom he apparently had brought with him—crying "Daddy, Daddy" along the side of the running track. When he finally notices her, he stops only long enough to tell his daughter that it is not his job to watch her, but her job to watch for him (Gustatis 1982).

What will be the impact of the mixed messages that these children—and perhaps countless others—are getting from their fathers? Research capable of measuring and assessing the complexity of these encounters is needed to adequately answer this question (Pleck 1983).

Marital Conflict in Childbearing and Child-Rearing Families

Because our study was longitudinal, we were able to trace changes over time; and we found that from the third, to the sixth, to the ninth month postpartum, couples became more traditional, with fathers doing proportionately less child care (LaRossa and LaRossa 1981). It was this traditionalization process that provided us with a close-up view of what happens when the bubble bursts; that is, what happens when the romanticized vision of dad's involvement starts to break down.

One father, first interviewed around the third month after his daughter's birth, wanted to communicate that he was not going to be an absentee father like some of his friends were:

> I've got a good friend of mine, he's the ultimate male chauvinist pig. He will not change a diaper. . . . [But] I share in changing the diapers, and rocking the baby, and in doing those kinds of things. . . . I love babies.

During the sixth month interview, however, it was revealed that he indeed had become very much the absentee father. In fact, almost every evening since the first interview he had left the house after dinner to play basketball, or participate in an amateur theater group, or sing in the local choir.

Since what he was doing contradicted what he said he would do, he was asked by his wife to "account" for his behavior. *Accounts* are demanded of social actors whose behavior is thought to be out of line. By submitting an account, which in common parlance generally takes the form of an excuse or justification, and having it honored or accepted by the offended party, a person who stands accused can manage to create or salvage a favorable impression (Scott and Lyman 1968). Because the wife did not honor the accounts that her husband offered, the father was put in the position of either admitting he was wrong (i.e., apologizing) or coming up with more accounts. He chose the latter, and in due course offered no fewer than 20 different explanations for his conduct, to include "I help out more than most husbands do" and "I'm not

good at taking care of the baby." At one dramatic point during the second interview, the husband and wife got into a verbal argument over how much of the husband's contribution to child care was "fact" and how much was "fancy." (He, with his head: "I *know* I was [around a lot]." She, with her heart: "[To me] it just doesn't *feel* like he was.")...

Fathers and Guilt

Several years ago, Garry Trudeau (1985), who writes *Doonesbury*, captured to a tee the asynchrony between the culture and conduct of fatherhood when he depicted a journalist-father sitting at his home computer and working on an autobiographical column on "The New Fatherhood" for the Sunday section of the newspaper. "My editor feels there's a lot of interest in the current, more involved generation of fathers," the journalist tells his wife who has just come in the room. "He asked me to keep an account of my experiences." Trudeau's punch line is that when Super Dad is asked by his wife to watch his son because she has to go to a meeting, he says no because if he did, he would not meet his deadline. In the next day's *Doonesbury*, Trudeau fired another volley at the new breed of fathers. Now the son is standing behind his computer-bound father and ostensibly is asking for his father's attention. But again Super Dad is too busy pecking away at his fatherhood diary to even look up: "Not now, son. Daddy's busy."

Trudeau's cartoons, copies of which sit on my wall in both my office and my den, are a reminder to me not to be so caught up in writing about what it means to be a father (thus contributing to the culture of fatherhood) that I fail to *be* a father. The fact, however, that I took the time to cut the cartoons out of the newspaper (and make not one but two copies) and the fact that Trudeau, who is himself a father, penned the cartoons in the first place is indicative of a feeling that many men today experience, namely, ambivalence over their performance as fathers.

To feel "ambivalent" about something is to feel alternately good and bad about it. The plethora of autobiographical books and articles written by fathers . . . conveys the impression that men do feel and, perhaps most importantly, should feel good about their performance as fathers. A lot of men do seem to be proud of their performance, what with all the references to "new" fatherhood and the like. At the same time, however, men are being almost constantly told—and can see for themselves, if they look closely enough—that their behavior does not square with the ideal, which means that they are being reminded on a regular basis that they are *failing* as fathers. Failing not when compared with their own fathers or grandfathers perhaps, but failing when compared with the image of fatherhood which has become part of our culture and which they, on some level of consciousness, believe in.

This is not to suggest that in the past men were totally at ease with their performance as fathers, that they had no doubts about whether they were acting "correctly." For one thing, such an assertion would belie the fact that role playing is, to a large degree, improvisational, that in everyday life (vs. the theater) scripts almost always are ill defined and open to a variety of interpretations (Blumer 1969). Perhaps more importantly, asserting that men in the past were totally at ease with their performance as fathers would ignore the fact that, contrary to what many think, some of our fathers and grandfathers were ambivalent about the kind of job they were doing. In [my] study on the history of fatherhood in America, I [came] across several cases of men in the early 1900s expressing concern over the quality of their paternal involvement. In 1925,

for example, one father wrote to a psychologist to ask whether he was *too involved* with his 2-year-old son. Apparently, he had taught the boy both the alphabet and how to count, and he now wondered whether he had forced his son to learn too much too soon (LaRossa 1988).

So, what *is* the difference between then and now? I would say it is a difference in degree not kind. I would hypothesize that, given the asynchrony between the culture and conduct of fatherhood, the number of fathers who feel ambivalent and, to a certain extent, guilty about their performance as fathers has increased over the past three generations. I would also hypothesize that, given it is the middle class which has been primarily responsible for the changes in the culture of fatherhood, it is the middle-class fathers who are likely to feel the most ambivalent and suffer from the most guilt.

There is a certain amount of irony in the proposition that middle-class men are the ones who are the most likely to experience ambivalence and guilt, in that middle-class men are also the ones who seem to be trying the hardest to act according to the emerging ideal. . . . But it is precisely because these middle-class professionals are trying to conform to the higher standards that one would expect that they would experience the most ambivalence and guilt. Like athletes training for the Olympics, . . . fathers often are consumed with how they are doing as fathers and how they can do better. For example:

> Should I play golf today, or should I spend more time playing with Scott and Julie? Should I stay late in the office to catch up or should I leave early to go home and have dinner with the children? There is an endless supply of these dilemmas each day. (Belsky 1986, p. 64)

Some may argue that the parental anxiety that men are beginning to experience is all for the better, that they now may start feeling bad enough about their performance to really change. This argument does have merit. Yes, one positive outcome of asynchronous social change is that ultimately men may become not only more involved with their children but also more sensitive to what it is like to be a mother. After all, for a long time women have worried about *their* performance as parents. It should not be forgotten, however, that the guilt which many women experience as mothers (and which has been the subject of numerous novels, plays, and films) has not always been healthy for mothers—or families. In sum, when it comes to parenthood, today it would appear that both men and women can be victims as well as benefactors of society's ideals.

Conclusion

. . . The consequences of the asynchrony between the (comparatively speaking) "modern" culture of fatherhood and the "less modern" or "traditional" conduct of fatherhood are (a) the emergence of the technically present but functionally absent father, (b) an increase in marital conflict in childbearing and child-rearing families, and (c) a greater number of fathers, especially in the middle class, who feel ambivalent and guilty about their performance as fathers.

A number of recommendations seem to be in order. First, more people need to be made aware of the fact that the division of child care in America has not significantly changed, that—despite the beliefs that fathers are a lot more involved with their children—mothers remain, far and away, the primary child caregivers. The reason for publicizing this fact is that if our beliefs represent what we want (i.e., more involved fathers) and we mistakenly assume that what we want is what we have, our

complacency will only serve to perpetuate the culture-conduct disjunction. . . .

Second, and in line with the above, men must be held responsible for their actions. In our study of the transition to parenthood (LaRossa and LaRossa 1981), we found that the language that couples use to account for men's lack of involvement in infant care does not simply reflect the division of infant care, it constructs that division of infant care. . . . Thus, when men say things like "I'm not good at taking care of the baby" or "I can't be with Junior now, I have to go to the office, go to the store, go to sleep, mow the lawn, pay the bills, and so forth" the question must be raised, are these reasons genuine (i.e., involving insurmountable role conflicts) or are they nothing more than rationalizations used by men to do one thing (not be with their children) but believe another ("I like to be with my children")? If they are rationalizations, then they should not be honored. Not honoring rationalizations "de-legitimates" actions and, in the process, puts the burden of responsibility for the actions squarely on the person who is carrying out the actions. Only when men are forced to seriously examine their commitment to fatherhood (vs. their commitment to their jobs and avocations) can we hope to bring about the kinds of changes that will be required to alter the division of child care in this country (LaRossa 1983).

. . . If we hope to alter the way men relate to their children, we cannot be satisfied with individualistic solutions which see "the problem" as a private, therapeutic matter best solved through consciousness-raising groups and the like. Rather, we must approach it as a public issue and be prepared to alter the institutional fabric of American society (cf. Mills 1959). For example, the man-as-breadwinner model of fatherhood, a model which emerged in the nineteenth and early twentieth centuries and which portrays fathers primarily as breadwinners whose wages make family consumption and security possible, remains dominant today (Pleck, Chapter 26, this volume). This model creates structural barriers to men's involvement with their children, in that it legitimates inflexible and highly demanding job schedules which, in turn, increase the conflict between market work and family work (Pleck 1985). More flex-time jobs would help to relieve this conflict. So would greater tolerance, on the part of employers, of extended paternity leaves (Levine 1976). I am not suggesting that the only reason that men are not as involved with their children is that their jobs keep them from getting involved. The fact that many women also contend with inflexible and highly demanding job schedules and still are relatively involved with their children would counter such an assertion. Rather, the point is that the level of achievement in market work expected of men in America generally is higher than the level of achievement in market work expected of women and that this socio-historical reality must be entered into any equation which attempts to explain why fathers are not more involved. . . .

REFERENCES

Barnett, R. C., and G. K. Baruch. (1987). Determinants of fathers' participation in family work. *Journal of Marriage and the Family, 49,* 29–40.

Belsky, M. R. (1986). Scott's and Julie's Daddy. In C. Kort and R. Friedland (Eds.), *The father's book: Shared experiences* (pp. 63–65). Boston: G. K. Hall.

Benokraitis, N. (1985). Fathers in the dual-earner family. In S.M.H. Hanson and F. W. Bozett (Eds.), *Dimensions of fatherhood* (pp. 243–268). Beverly Hills, CA: Sage Publications.

Berger, M. (1979). Men's new family roles—Some implications for therapists. *Family Coordinator, 28,* 638–646.

Blumer, H. (1969). *Symbolic interactionism: Perspective and method.* Englewood Cliffs, NJ: Prentice Hall.

Gustatis, R. (1982). Children sit idle while parents pursue leisure. *Atlanta Journal and Constitution.* August 15, pp. 1D, 4D.

Kaplan, D. (1987). The great $39.00 2″ TV catch. *DAK Industries Inc.,* summer, p. 32A.

Lamb, M. E. (1987). Introduction: The emergent American father. In M. E. Lamb (Ed.), *The father's role: Cross-cultural perspectives* (pp. 3–25). Hillsdale, NJ: Lawrence Erlbaum.

Lamb, M. E., J. H. Pleck, and J. A. Levine. (1987). Effects of increased paternal involvement on fathers and mothers. In C. Lewis and M. O'Brien (Eds.), *Reassessing fatherhood: New observations on fathers and the modern family* (pp. 109–125). Beverly Hills, CA: Sage Publications.

LaRossa, R. (1983). The transition to parenthood and the social reality of time. *Journal of Marriage and the Family, 45,* 579–589.

LaRossa, R. (1988). Toward a social history of fatherhood in America. Paper presented at the Theory Construction and Research Methodology Workshop, Annual Meeting of National Council of Family Relations, Philadelphia, PA, November.

LaRossa, R., and M. M. LaRossa. (1981). *Transition to parenthood: How infants change families.* Beverly Hills, CA: Sage Publications.

LeMasters, E. E., (1957). Parenthood as crisis. *Marriage and Family Living, 19,* 352–355.

LeMasters, E. E., and J. DeFrain. (1983). *Parents in contemporary America: A sympathetic view* (4th ed.). Homewood, IL: Dorsey.

Levine, J. A. (1976). *Who will raise the children?* New York: Bantam.

Lutwin, D. R., and G. N. Siperstein (1985). Househusband fathers. In S.M.H. Hanson and F. W. Bozett (Eds.), *Dimensions of fatherhood* (pp. 269–287). Beverly Hills, CA: Sage Publications.

Mackey, W. C., and R. D. Day. (1979). Some indicators of fathering behaviors in the United States: A cross-cultural examination of adult male-child interaction. *Journal of Marriage and the Family, 41,* 287–297.

Parke, R. D. (1981). *Fathers.* Cambridge, MA: Harvard University Press.

Pleck, J. H. (1979). Men's family work: Three perspectives and some data. *Family Coordinator, 28,* 481–488.

Pleck, J. H. (1983). Husbands' paid work and family roles: Current research issues. In H. Z. Lopata & J. H. Pleck (Eds.), *Research in the interweave of social roles, Vol. 3, Families and jobs* (pp. 251–333). Greenwich, CT: JAI Press.

Pleck, J. H. (1985). *Working wives/Working husbands.* Beverly Hills, CA: Sage Publications.

Pleck, J. H. (1987). American fathering in historical perspective. In M. S. Kimmel (Ed.), *Changing men: New directions in research on men and masculinity* (pp. 83–97). Beverly Hills, CA: Sage Publications. (Chapter 26, this volume.)

Scanzoni, J. (1979). Strategies for changing male family roles: Research and practice implications. *Family Coordinator, 28,* 435–442.

Scott, M. B., and S. M. Lyman, (1968). Accounts. *American Sociological Review, 33,* 46–62.

Trudeau, G. B. (1985). *Doonesbury.* United Press Syndicate, March 24, 25.

Zerubavel, E. (1979). *Patterns of time in hospital life: A sociological perspective.* Chicago: University of Chicago Press.

Chapter 29

"Best Case Scenarios": Fathers, Children, and Divorce

TERRY ARENDELL

In-depth interviews conducted in the early 1990s with 75 New York divorced fathers, most of whom were middle class and all of whom had at least one child under the age of 18, found two predominant tales. Overlapping in many respects, the tales diverged along two rather distinct trajectories with respect to respondents' priorities and behaviors regarding fathering. The men's strategies—"the techniques by means of which people manage the situations of their everyday lives" (Lofland 1978, 14; also see Swidler 1980; Hochschild, with Machung 1989)—fell along a continuum that ranged from *traditionalist* to *innovative*; that is, from gender conformity to gender subversion (Bem 1993). There was far more gender conformity than subversion in their postdivorce attitudes and parenting strategies. However, this chapter focuses on the innovative fathers.

The "Majority Story": Traditionalization

Broadly outlined, the story shared by a large majority of these divorced fathers was one of perceived injustice and discrimination, resistance, frustration, and discontent. It was also, paradoxically, a story of self-confidence and certainty. Involving little self-reflection, the "majority story" was one of men preoccupied with asserting their identities as men. These men sought answers, direction, and affirmation in divorce by looking to customary views about masculinity. They acted in largely conventional ways, relying on the practices and tactics of their gender belief system. Not unlike fathers who respond to the stresses and uncertainty of new parenthood after the birth of a first child by assuming a more conventional division of labor (LaRossa and LaRossa 1989), these men engaged primarily in the processes of *traditionalization;* that is, they turned to that which was familiar. Because they were engaged in the processes of traditionalization, each of these divorced men felt antagonism and resentment toward his former wife, which interferred with his concern for his children's well-being and the father-child relationship.

Men engaged in processes of traditionalization embraced two types of fathers: *traditionalist* and *neo-traditionalist* (May and Strikwerda 1992). Traditionalist fathers were generally inflexible in their conduct and views, and had very limited, if any, relationships with their children. Thirty-five fathers fell into this group. In contrast, the neo-tradionalists (the other 31 of the 66 total engaged in the processes of traditionalization) shifted some in their behaviors between active resistance and reluctant adjustment to their new status as divorced men. Like the others, they felt victimized by divorce and were preoccupied with their former wives; however, on occasion, neo-traditionalist fathers instead gave primary consideration to their parental relationships and their children's well-being. Furthermore, whereas the traditionalist fathers were relatively consistent in their actions and perspectives, the neo-traditionalists vacillated: Tension between the determination to oppose their former wives and concerns for parenting their children led them to shift their behavior and parenting ideas. Importantly, these two types of fathers were more similar than different in their overall responses to divorce; it was in their consideration of their children where their actions sometimes diverged from each other.

The "Minority Story": Innovation

In contrast to the majority of fathers, nine participants engaged in the processes of *innovation*. These fathers, caught up in processes of adaptation and creativity, actively rejected what they perceived to be men's standard behaviors in divorce and searched out and de-

veloped strategies more congruent with their objective to parent their children actively. Child-centeredness prevailed in their accounts and actions.

Behaving in innovative ways entailed both choice and opportunity. "'Choice,'" Theodore Cohen (1989, 222) observed in his examination of men's roles as husbands and fathers, "is related to 'role attachment' in that the degree to which men choose to enact a role depends largely upon the degree of role attachment they possess. 'Opportunity,' on the other hand, is dependent largely on the commitments they have made and the consequences of those commitments." Innovation required three conditions. The first was an awareness of options so that conventional practices and definitions could be rejected. The cooperation of each man's former wife, their children's mother, was the second necessity. The third requisite was somewhat flexible work circumstances. Given these three criteria, both the standard familial and gender discourses were eschewed by innovative men.

These nine men were involved, nurturing parents who collaborated with their former spouses. Caring for and rearing their children was a team effort, requiring extensive cooperation: *Together* they created and maintained *parenting partnerships.* Thus, each divorced man's former wife was seen and treated as a close associate, not as an oppositional figure. Mutual concern for their children's well-being enabled them to transcend their differences and residual feelings about each other and about the demise of the marriage. Volunteering the notion of "best case scenario," a father of one child explained:

> I'm sure the system is not fair. I don't think the system is fair in any kind of law. It cannot be perfectly right or wrong, but I think a lot of the tension and a lot of the problems in divorce are caused by the individuals themselves. We de-

cided that we were going to work to have a best case scenario in order to protect our daughter, to keep our daughter the central person in all of this.

In practice, seven of these nine men shared childrearing to varying extents with their former wives. The other two men had primary custody, and, they reported, their former wives were available to and extensively involved with their children. But custody status was not a determining factor in innovative strategies and collaborative parenting partnerships. Only one of the men who was engaged in innovative lines of action had remarried. One of the other eight fathers was considering remarriage. Eight of the nine men or their former spouses or both, had considered reconciliation after separation.

With only one exception, these men and their estranged spouses had negotiated their parenting arrangements privately and then presented them to attorneys for official acceptance. Circumvention of the legal system and its "family experts," such as therapists and social workers, was deliberate: Engaging wholeheartedly in the formal divorce system could only undermine the possibilities of a positive postdivorce outcome. But this avoidance of legal engagement was indicative of the cooperative relationships between each man and his wife and the choices they had made as they entered divorce.

All nine men, in concert with most respondents, believed that fathers are, or can become, victims of divorce, primarily because the legal system favors mothers. But, in contrast to the majority, these men were minimally concerned about protecting their rights, and they made relatively little use of the *rhetoric of rights* to frame their experiences, relations, and feelings. Agreeing that women are favored in divorce, these men nevertheless held more complex views about divorce than the majority of respondents. Each

viewed his former wife's authority in the postdivorce situation as a logical outcome of her usually greater parental activity and responsibility; moreover, it was not only his own desires, actions, or traits, but also her willingness to negotiate a shared parenting arrangement and her support for his extensive involvement that made it possible for him to be an active and nurturing divorced father.

Even the two sole-custodial fathers, whose former wives "visited" their children, without assuming specific and continuous parental responsibilities, relied upon their former spouses not to divert their energies with a custody fight or interfere with the residential and parenting situations. As one said, "She valued my parenting. Otherwise, she'd drag me into court." Further, both men believed that when their respective spouses quit the marriage each woman had left the children with her former husband out of concern for the children. "She left without them because she loved them and thought I was better equipped to care for them then. I've told the kids that, too: 'She left you here with me because she loved you. We both love you.'"

Family was represented by these innovative fathers as being a network of relationships, and the notion of a broken family was only a part of their understanding of family after divorce: They feared that they could yet become marginalized, and the family thus broken. Existing for the time being for these nine fathers, however, was a family consisting of "us" and "them," the father and his children and the children and their mother, respectively, rather than "me and them," as characterized by the majority of participants. Two of the innovative fathers reformed the conventional definition of family to fit the situation of divorce: They, the former wife and children, constituted a single unit that had dual residences. For example, when he was explaining his argument for a continuation of their parenting arrangement in spite of divorce, one informant observed: "[I] was no longer living at home, but the care situation could remain the same; we were still one family. The only thing that has changed is that now mom and dad don't live together. That's all. I'm still here for them. So is she. We're their parents. Not *one* of us, *both* of us."

The contours of the parenting partnerships differed somewhat among the nine fathers. The variations depended upon the particulars of the custody arrangement, especially. But each of the parenting partnerships was a "cooperative" pattern (Maccoby, Depner, and Mnookin 1990). This pattern involved: sharing major, and day-to-day, decisions, child-rearing problems, and coparenting problems; discussing children's personal problems; sharing children's school and medical problems; planning special events in children's lives; discussing children's adjustments to divorce, progress, and accomplishments; and examining and planning child-related finances.

Integral to these men's accounts, and generally absent in the others', was the notion of parental obligation. Child support, for example, a contentious issue brought up repeatedly by most of the others, was discussed by these nine men in terms of children's needs rather than in terms of an antagonistic relationship with each man's former wife. Child support orders were not viewed as violations of their rights. Although some of the innovative men were concerned about competing financial obligations, none of them was resentful about child support. It was a parental responsibility, "whether married or not." One said, "They're my children. Of course I would never deny them economic support."

The goal for these men was "to hold the children at the center," and very little overt antagonism to or tension with their former wives was allowed to erupt. The essence of fostering and protecting a positive, stable, and sustained father-child relationship, regardless of the specific residential arrangements or feelings about the former spouse, was precluding or limiting conflict.

Innovative, Nurturing Fathering

Thus, nine of the 75 participants were nurturing divorced fathers, according to the multiple criteria of *caring for* and *caring about* their children *and* having a parental commitment central to their self-concepts (May and Strikwerda 1992). For these innovative fathers who were integrally involved in all facets of parenting, the predominant concerns were their children's welfare, happiness, and development, and the character of the father-child relationship. Said one co-custodial father, who had declined several desirable promotions in order to remain in close proximity to his children,

> I'm here to help them grow up, to see what life is about, to experience what they are supposed to experience, go to the right schools and to see that they have enough money to do what they need, to have what they want, and have the values that they're supposed to have. I'm very concerned [that] that all happens. It's going to be the values that I believe in, I'm going to help instill those in them. I want to make sure that they have those values. I'm going to be with them as often as I can.

Only two of the nine nurturing fathers had been a primary parent during marriage. The other seven fathers had "made major changes" in order to become, as one said, "really involved and caring" (also see Risman 1989; Coltrane 1989). He continued,

> If it wasn't for the divorce, I wouldn't have changed my priorities. I might have just as well have forgotten I was a parent otherwise. And I

did [make changes]. It has been the pivotal point of my life, my divorce. I took a job that paid considerably less and didn't require travel just so that I would now have time to spend with my child and really become a parent.

In contrast, only six of the other 66 fathers described having made significant adjustments or alterations in order to accommodate the changed family and parenting situation. Describing the crisis that threw him into the primary parent role, in which he cared for the children alone for some months, one father characterized his adjustments in terms of gender roles in marriage and family.

> It was terrifying at first, just terrifying. I remember the night she walked out the door. And I cried at the thought of it: I said to myself, "How in the hell am I going to do this?" I was raised in a stereotypical way, stereotypically male. I did not cook. I did not particularly clean. I was working a lot so it was "come home and play with the baby." The youngest was just a year and a half, the other one was going towards three. So it was like playtime. I didn't have any responsibility for their daily care. I'd hardly changed a diaper before. I didn't know what parenting was about, really. I mean, who teaches us how to parent? I really didn't know how to ask for help. I don't truly remember the first year. It was day by day by day. After about a year, I managed to figure out that I had my act together. But it goes deeper than all of that. I had to learn to relate to them, relate to them as people.

Further reflecting on the changes made, he speculated about his likely family participation had his wife not left:

> I would have probably, I'm forecasting here, I think I would have fallen into the stereotyped dad: I would have come home from work, I wouldn't have worried about what they were doing from morning to night. My ex would've run their daily social life and where they went and what they did. I would have been called upon to be *dad* in the family. It's what we both

knew how to do. To think what I would have missed is staggering.

What he might have added, as well, is that conformity to the conventional role would have been met with general social support.

Women served as the parenting models for most of these men. Three of the nine nurturing fathers observed that their parenting exemplars were their mothers, three noted their former wives, and another credited his sister. The turn to women for parenting role models reinforced their perceptions that, in seeking to be an "alternative divorced father," they were appropriating women's activities and characteristics. The one person who credited his father as being his principle parental role model believed, nevertheless, that he had adopted parental approaches common to women, not men: *Both* he and his father were atypical. Each of these men lamented that they had few or no male role models for parenting, as did many of the participants.

The nurturing fathers, then, very clearly saw their parenting approaches and actions as being "feminine": They had become primary parents by appropriating skills and characteristics typical of mothers and atypical of fathers. That is, in seeking to be "alternative fathers," they drew upon mothering as a model for parenting and adopted behaviors and postures usually associated with the "feminine" or "female." Two described themselves as "closet mothers." One father who shared parenting equally with his former wife characterized his objectives as he sought to adjust to the divorce circumstance: "I have tried to be a mother, tried to be the image of what a mother should be, do with them in given times what a mother would do, provide a lot of the emotions she would give them, etcetera. You know, do what a *good* mother does."

More was involved in the nurturing fathers' accommodations than an expansion of roles—including, combining employment with primary parenting and abandoning the conventional division of family labor based on gender. Interactional and communication styles had to be modified. One man became a co-custodial parent subsequent to his divorce: "One thing [is that] my college or high school friends would never believe that I'm doing this. They would probably say I was the least likely person to be a single parent [in a de facto shared custody arrangement]. I have a sarcastic, dry humor that isn't always conducive [to] emotional relationships. I was a heavy drinker and part[ier] at college. They just wouldn't have expected me to be a single parent, let alone to want it." Most of these fathers observed that they had to learn to listen: "Learn to listen to my children *and* to my wife, my former wife," said a co-custodial father who added: "Strange, isn't it, the timing?" Parenting was enhanced and not diminished by divorce.

Parenting was intensely meaningful to these fathers, "the most significant thing I've ever done or will ever do," as one said. This father tried to explain:

> I can't give an answer to what it means to be a father to me, but I can tell you when I know I'm a father. When it's 3:00 in the morning, when he's awakened, and he reaches up and touches me. Then all the bullshit in between, the worries, the negativity, the anxieties—they're all washed away. It's the moments of the really positive contacts that clean out and make it all seem so worthwhile. Or, he'll walk up behind me while I'm doing something and just pat me, it's the small unexpected touches and moments. I'm getting all teary trying to talk about this. . . . Maybe 20 years from now, if he's all screwed up—I don't know. I hope to be able to say I did everything I could, but of course I won't be able to say that. But I want to be able to. I take this all very seriously. It's important to me to be a good person, I want him to be and become a good person. So far, so good, I think.

Any vestiges or hints of sentimentality about parenting as a divorced father were quickly offset by efforts to deromanticize it. One custodial father of two children, for example, after expounding on the delights of his children, then issued a few cautionary remarks:

> You know, there are very beautiful, precious moments, but you usually only discover them when they're already over with and they have a life span of about five seconds! You know, there's no scene, and by the time you set it up, it's gone. And it's really true. On a daily basis, it's a crummy job but I wouldn't have it any other way. It's probably the most rewarding job you could ever do. . . . What happened by being single is that I was forced into all of this. I've benefited so greatly, I can't even begin to tell you how much.

Assertions of confidence and mastery of parenting were typically qualified with doubts: "I wasn't made for this, you know? I was raised to be man, not a mother or like a mother." Yet prevalent throughout these nine men's accounts was evidence of competent, committed parenting.

Assessments of Children's Development and Well-Being

The nine nurturing fathers were overwhelmingly positive in their assessments of their children: They had adjusted well to divorce and the postdivorce situation, and their relationships with both parents were affectionate and appropriate. These evaluations, like the men's descriptions of their parental relationships and roles, were supported with particular and numerous examples. For instance: "You know, their behavior around me is fine, we have a good time. They are relaxed. They're familiar with all of this. They fight with each other, misbehave. Not the whole time, of course, but they act normal. They don't behave any differently here or there [with their mother] apparently." Another co-custodial father said: "My kids are happy. My kids don't have any real adjustment issues. They never did seem to. They're totally comfortable with this arrangement." This father, having a de facto custody situation in which his children lived primarily with their mother, asserted, "They are all really blossoming, and they've never shown any lasting adjustment problems. And they openly care about each other. It's wonderful to watch, these kids." He continued, describing an incident involving his youngest son.

> This is the only kind of relationship he really knows or remembers so this is kind of what it's like for him. It's really interesting because his kindergarten teacher said, when we went to his parent conference and asked how he was doing, the teacher said, "He really is a terrific little guy." They'd asked the class to draw pictures. Oh, they were making something for Father's Day or something like that, one of those days. One of his little friends got all upset and started to cry. The teacher asked why he was crying. The little boy said, "I have two fathers and one mother." And the teacher was kind of flabbergasted and Daniel put his arm around him and said, "Oh, I have two fathers too, why don't you just make two pictures? That's what I'm doing." It was a message that it's okay, this is the way things are.

These men, although noting that they could support only their own viewpoints, insisted that their former wives shared their positive evaluations. Because jointly assessing their children's development and emotional states was one of the pillars of the parenting partnerships, they frequently discussed their children with each other.

When asserting that their children were developing "normally," the nurturing fathers typically demonstrated some understanding of the stages of child development and growth, and the range of "normal" behaviors. Most attributed this knowledge to their intentional efforts to become informed. All but two of these fathers had sought personal counseling or parenting education courses subsequent to separation and divorce. Five, including this next father, had pursued both.

> My two children are great kids, wonderful people. They're both very smart. They listen to me, not that listening to me is the measure of them being great kids. But they're very responsive and social. How to put this? I have read lots. Supposedly young kids from divorce are very serious and sober, distanced. But they're very touchable, affectionate, funny. They have great senses of humor, especially the younger one. They do and say wonderful things. I guess it's the luck of the draw, they're just great kids. I worry all of the time. Do I give them too much or too little? I took a parenting class. I read a lot, and I'm in therapy. And my parents try to encourage me all they can. They say, "Does it feel like the right thing to do? Then do it!"

Not only were the nurturing fathers' assessments of their children far more positive but their evaluations were more complex and multifaceted than those offered by most participants.

These fathers were emotionally invested in their positive evaluations of their children: Because they were intimately involved in the rearing of their children, their assessments reflected on them as parents. Problems or concerns could not be disowned by being laid at the mothers' doorsteps. Moreover, they wanted to believe that all of them—children, themselves, and their former wives, the children's mothers—were getting on with their lives and doing well. Nonetheless, the men's assessments of their children were not sanguine and categorical, and each carried residual concerns that divorce-related problems could emerge for their children at any point and potentially be long term.

Circumspection about their affirmative assessments was coupled with cautiousness about the possibility of being overly sensitive to the reputed adverse effects of divorce on children. One man had initiated his divorce and accepted less than equal parenting time in order to spare his children the potential trauma of a custody struggle: "One thing we do get into, maybe my former wife more than me, is over-psychologizing about the impact that divorce and separation is having on the kids." Referring to a recent book on the effects of divorce on children, he continued: "Will *my* daughters have 'a difficult time in developing relationships with men of a lasting and meaningful nature because their mother and father got divorced'? That begins to read a little too much into dysfunctions with male and female relationships. Anyway most [men and women] are having difficulties; many are clueless about how to develop meaningful relationships today, period. We all can see that relationship problems aren't limited to families with divorce. Is this just a self-interested interpretation? I don't know. It's something I keep having to ask myself."

Another father felt split. On one hand, he "had to conclude" that his children were well adjusted and relatively unaffected by the divorce. He believed they benefited from no longer being exposed to their parents' arguing and unhappiness. On the other hand, he was convinced that children are invariably harmed by divorce and that his children could be no exception. To believe otherwise, he insisted, "was pure foolhardiness."

The men's lingering concerns that their children were adversely affected by divorce, or "must be," was reinforced by the responses of others. Children of divorce were, at least according to the judgments of some, inevitably damaged and stigmatized by divorce. They complained, as did custodial mothers in an earlier study (Arendell 1986), that their efforts to minimize the trauma of the family

disruptions were undermined by the social climate. For instance, one father, who had not wanted to divorce, had subsequently formed a highly collaborative parenting partnership with his former wife. "Our son [at six years of age] had some problems in school at the beginning of the year, which we talked to the principal about, problems like not being able to sit still, not finishing his work, having difficulty concentrating. The first thing the principal said was, 'It may be because of the *dysfunctionality* of the family.' That's what he said." Despite these parents' many efforts to maintain a loving and stable environment for their children, each of their families was stigmatized by the parents' divorces, labeled for its arrangements, not its functioning.

Another father was "furious" because his children were discriminated against both because their parents were divorced and they were Latino. After struggling with the local school district to have them taken out of the English as a Second Language program—where they were placed, he argued, only because he was an immigrant and divorced parent—he enrolled them in a parochial school, where they were mainstreamed immediately into regular classes. Both were consistently high achievers who regularly earned places on the school's honor roll.

I always make sure that if anybody is going to tell me anything or look down at me for being a single parent, I immediately jump all over them. I hate that kind of an attitude from anybody. I don't care who they are—lawyers, neighbors, teachers. I've had some pretty serious arguments with people who tried to depict me in a particular way because I'm a single parent. I remember at the registration of my kids, one of the teachers, 'Oh, you're a single parent.' 'Well, is there something wrong with it?' Right away she apologized for about 30 minutes. But I'm very defensive when it comes to that. I want my children treated for who they are, not for who is in their home. My opinion is that they go to the school to learn; that is their job. If they aren't learning or there is some problem, tell me. Don't give me some stupid explanation that because the mother isn't there, that the children are learning disabled. It's completely wrong, whether it's the father or mother who is not in the home. It's completely wrong to come up with such a stupid explanation. I don't care if they live in one room, or "the male figure isn't there," or whatever, it's stupid. Stupid explanations: "a child is too active"; "too poor"; "Latino"; "Black"; "lives in the country"; "lives in the city." I'm very opposed to all of that. I'm always on the defensive. When they start [asking], "Is the mother home full-time?" I say, "Wait a minute. What's the problem here? What are you trying to get at?" I don't buy those explanations.

Personal Life Course Developmental Issues

Unlike many of the other men in the study, the primary parent fathers did not eagerly anticipate the time at which their youngest (or only) child would reach age 18 and thus "emancipate" them, "freeing" them of economic responsibility and, "finally," of the former wife. Instead, they lamented the inevitable changes that would come as their children became more mature and autonomous. "I realize that when they're in high school, they will want to do other things on weekends [than spend the time entirely with me], and I know I will have to go through the pain of adjusting. I thought I had this parenting-thing all figured out, but I'm realizing that I have to make major adjustments now that they're getting older. Now I have to figure out how to let go of them."

This next father, talking about the challenges in maintaining his close relationships with his children as they became older, especially since they lived several hundred miles away with their mother much of the year, expressed particular concerns about his rela-

tionship with his oldest daughter, who was now a young teenager:

I want to make sure that she realizes that it's okay to talk about some of these things, and the only way that I know how to do it is by dealing with the issue head-on. Saying, "I haven't seen you in three or four weeks, and I have to tell you that I miss you, but I also want to let you know that it's okay for you to lead your own life. What are we going to do to stay close? What are we going to do? I'm worried that emotionally you're going to be going in a different direction." I understand when she doesn't come. The reasons she has are legitimate. There are things going on in her life and that's okay. We're making some adjustments. But it still worries me.

For these fathers, being divorced and having their children live between two parents' homes accelerated the developmental issues associated with their children's growing up. These issues were entwined with the residual fears that divorce would lead to the "loss of my kids." The "normal" family life cycle, in which children grow and mature over the course of the years and gradually become more autonomous and independent, separating more steadily from dependence on the parents, was disrupted, and separation was occurring "prematurely." These fathers feared that both they and their former wives were kept outside of whole segments of their children's lives, given the amount of time the children were with the other parent. Integral involvement in their children's upbringing and close collaboration with the other parent did not offset these concerns.

A Price Exacted: Work-Family Conflicts

Contented with, though not complacent about their postdivorce situations, particularly their children's general well-being and development, these men confronted unique dilemmas. Role and identity conflicts were ever-present and far more significant than those experienced by most of the other participants. In defying conventional expectations and behaviors, and in spite of their high levels of parental satisfaction, they received little social or institutional support in being caring fathers.

Tensions and conflicts between work and family were standard experiences for these fathers, as they are for many American parents (e.g., Cohen 1989; Coltrane 1989; Hochschild, with Machung 1989; Thompson and Walker 1989; Martin 1991). The institutional context remained unchanged, even in the midst of dramatic family and individual changes. One custodial father, who while married had worked numerous jobs "in pursuit of the American dream," and whose former wife was unavailable to assist in child care or rearing during the initial year or so following divorce, described his adjustments.

I've had jobs: construction, office, insurance companies, investment company. I used to work for Metropolitan, I was what you call an "upper manager." Finally the only way that I could watch my kids and keep my sanity, so to speak, and having the problem you can't find anybody decent to look after your kids—somebody who really cares for them as much as you do; there's nobody but yourself—I quit my job and started by own business. I gave up the idea of becoming a CEO somewhere. I started my own carpentry business. This way, when my kids were in school, I could be working. I could go for an hour, be back an hour, leave for another hour, and not have to punch a clock or answer to anybody. I can set up my own hours, do what I want, and make as much as I want. And I can do some furniture refinishing and building here when they're at home. I could make much more [money,] but I keep time for them. And I made enough so that I bought a house, my own. I have a house. I have a business. I have the

kids. How happy can you be! But still I would like more time with them. It's my constant refrain.

The others, who retained paid salaried or wage work rather than turning to self-employment, were expected by managers and bosses to make private arrangements for family needs: Parenting was not to interfere with work. The men insisted that when employers did recognize conflicts between work and family, accommodations were aimed at mothers, not fathers. As men, if they sought or took temporary relief from employment for family matters, they were "eyed with suspicion." Certain that coworkers and supervisors watched them to see if the managing of parenting impacted their productivity, they were sensitive to others' attitudes and responses. Secretiveness was necessary, concluded this father:

At work, sometimes they look at me as if there's something wrong with me for this. For instance, when I took off to go to the nursery school open house last week, I had the day coming. I wasn't cheating them. But they acted like it was a strange thing for me to do. You know, I have pictures on my desk of my son and people seem to get turned off by it. But women have pictures of their children and everyone seems to accept that. Female employees at my work don't get treated the same way. Now I just won't tell them when I take off for him. If he's sick or something, I'll just tell them I'm sick.

Particularly eroded after divorce was adherence to the conventional definitions of masculine success through occupational or career advancement. One manager of a major national chain store, for example, discussed his deliberate move to shared parenting nearly two years after divorce.

Since the divorce I have had to change priorities. I went from a more than 65-hour-a-week job to just 40 hours and took a major cut in pay. I was constantly moving up to more challenging stores, ones that were in a mess and I was to straighten out. So I went initially from more than 60,000 dollars a year to just 18,000 dollars. . . . I have to admit that sometimes I wonder if I've just bombed out. I mean, look at my [low] salary.

And workplace flexibility held one custodial father in a job that paid less than others he might have secured.

What happened is [that I had] a lot of absences with the kids being sick and one thing and another. Fortunately I worked for a guy who was fairly good about it. I would get pressured from time to time. But I kept my job. My job has never paid well, but it gave me 12 personal days a year and I'm at the point, where I've been for years, that I have four weeks' vacation every year.

Other fathers declined offers of promotion that would have required relocation.

Concerns about having too little time for parenting and supervising their children were common. Most at issue was the family-work nexus. Discussing these worries, one father confided:

I'm not always satisfied with the amount of time I have with [my son]. . . . I worry about all of this, how to make a living and how to be available at the same time. But I have to make a living and I have to have a life. So does his mother. I would like much more time with him. Maybe if I win the Lotto, then I can give him a full-time father. Short of that, I don't see it happening. I worry about it though. But I need to work, of course, and so do the best I can.

Empathy for this man's former wife, with respect to work-family conflicts, was common among this group. She, too, experienced obvious conflicts between work and children. As one father related, for example,

During the summer I was worn out, worn out, by the time she, my daughter, left. But I realized

what her mother goes through. We'd get up, we'd get ready. Rush, rush. I'd take her to day camp. I go do my work, you're here, you're there, you're there, you pick her up, you go home and do this and do that, wash clothes, and so on and on. I enjoyed it, really enjoyed it, don't get me wrong. But it did wear me out. I needed to be able to take more time off but couldn't. I realize this is what her mother goes through most of the year. It's tough, really tough.

The most overextended fathers were those who received little or no assistance from their former spouses or the children's grandparents. The following comments are from a father who was most similar to a majority of custodial mothers in other studies in that he was raising his children basically unaided (see Arendell 1986; Wallerstein, with Blakeslee 1989).

I know a fellah' who has four children, single, and people refer to him the same way I've heard them refer to me: how wonderful he is, as if these were someone else's kids he was raising. And every morning he takes all four kids to his mother's house, drops them off, and then either goes there after work for dinner, or goes home and cleans up and goes out and gets his kids later when he's finished his date. He and I were comparing notes and he thinks he has it just as hard as I do. I kept on trying to say, very tactfully, "How would you like to do this without your mom?" And I really didn't get any response. I guess it's all where you're coming from. Probably not too easy for him either. But I think some people have no idea how it is when you have nobody around to help. This guy irked me a little bit with his complaining about how tough he's had it. I wish to God I had somebody occasionally to leave them with for a few hours, somebody who cares about them.

Support from parents, which was extensive for five fathers, included emotional, child care, financial, and other logistical support. Help ranged from the occasional and supplementary to the regular and essential. One father of three elementary-school-aged children credited his mother with his successful managing of co-parenting and the holding of two jobs: "She's a jewel, she's helped out a lot. See a lot of guys don't have the situation of all the help from their parents. Where would I be without my mother?" And as this next father observed:

> A lot of it [managing successfully] is my parents: They create an environment in which it's possible to be loving and supportive. They're there when I'm feeling down and alone. They support me in every way. They paid for the divorce. I'm now paying them back. They take only 300 dollars a month for the apartment, which is nothing in this country. Stable is the word to describe my family. They make it possible for me to give my children stability; actually, for both their mother and me to give them stability. I'm not fully alone, or I would be in serious trouble.

Two other men turned regularly to their parents for financial assistance. "I mean, I go shopping the day before the kids come, so the refrigerator is full. The cereal boxes are all there. They walk in and just take the food out, but before that I've been at my mother's house eating. My parents know my situation. I've borrowed more money from my mother and father. They have been fantastic people. They've been my major support, even more. I can't describe the support they've been." Relying on support from parents was justified and rationalized by these fathers, even as it was appreciated: Their dependence on parental assistance as an adult was a previously unforeseen development, unique to their divorced situations. Such dependence significantly countered their basic assumptions of successful adult manhood: "Who would have thought this could happen? I'm a grown guy who depends on his parents."

Several noted, however, that they received special treatment because they were men ac-

tively participating in the rearing of their children. Such support came almost always from women (see Arendell 1986).

Although they were relatively better off financially than the vast majority of divorced custodial mothers, as is the case nationally (Holden and Smock 1991; U.S. Bureau of the Census 1991; Burkhauser and Duncan 1989), none of the nine fathers was affluent, and three faced continuing challenges in meeting their basic living and child-rearing expenses. With the exception of one father, who had stopped paying support some six months previously, these men both paid child support and covered numerous child-rearing costs directly, as their children lived with them a sizable proportion of time. Two-thirds of these fathers had little or no discretionary income. For instance, one father was left with little money for covering recreational activities with his youngest child; covering the costs of the divorce, establishing a second home, paying child support, contributing to an older child's college expenses, and adjusting to a decrease in earnings had depleted his resources. "It's a little hard for him now with all the things I'm going through with the economic problems. I can't say, you know, 'Your're staying with me this week. What are we going to do? Go to the movies, go ice skating, go fishing?' I don't have the money to spend on him and he know that and it bothers him a little bit. It bothers me a lot."

Being a primary parent carried opportunity costs as well as immediate financial ones. Each of the nine nurturing fathers believed that his career or occupational advancement had been restrained by his family situation. Offered as evidence were the achievements of brothers or male friends and co-workers who had proceeded more rapidly through the ranks than had they. None of the six fathers who had discussed the need to pursue further formal education in order to better secure his and his children's economic futures had been able to do so. For one man, time and money shortages interferred with his implementing plans, with an eye on the future: "There's so much going on here that it's almost impossible to juggle school responsibilities with family responsibilities with work responsibilities. And where would I find the money? So going back to school remains on the back burner; I need to if I'm going to advance in this work and I would love to have some adult intellectual conversation, but I just can't do it now."

Identity Management

These nurturing fathers, men engaged in innovative lines of action, varied from the other respondents in their definitions and management of self (Goffman 1959; Hochschild 1983, with Machung 1989; Perinbanayagam 1990), as well as in their behavioral styles and objectives. Unlike the majority of divorced fathers in the study, who presented themselves as overwhelmingly confident and certain, the primary parent fathers were openly ambivalent and questioning. On one hand, they were far more satisfied with their postdivorce circumstances, especially their parenting and parental relationships, than the others. But, on the other hand, their "deviancy" exacted a price. Identity questions persistently confronted them. They and others around them defined their actions and perspectives as being appropriations of "women's activities and experiences" or "mothers' lives." Explaining that he had "tried to be a mother, I have tried to be a mother, to . . . do with them in given times what a mother would do," one co-custodial father followed his characterization with the question: "So who, what, does that make me?" And another co-custodial father of a young child, for example, commented: "I just have to keep asking myself: 'Why are you

doing this?' I need to constantly ask myself if I'm doing this for my child or for some other reason. Am I trying to prove something? Who am I hurting in the process?"

Rejecting the constraints and consequences of conventional expectations and seeking alternative lines of action, these men nonetheless used the norms of masculinity as the measure of self (Lyman 1987; Pleck 1992a; Hantover 1978; Kimmel and Messner 1992; Arendell 1992). The person least beset with identity questions was the one remarried father, who had established, together with his former wife as well as with his present one, a parenting coalition. His "deviancy" as a nurturing father engaged in collaboration with his former spouse was actively offset by other phenomena: a successful and satisfying profession, a stable and happy marriage and family life, and a wife who actively encouraged him and validated his efforts.

These divorced fathers live in a society stratified, ideologically and institutionally, by gender. Particular performances of gender carry more status and power than others and, accordingly, these men find themselves wanting. Their self-doubt and reprisals are reinforced by their past inexperience and isolation and by each man's extensive interdependency with his former wife, which counters the cultural paradigm of divorce. Their adopted strategies and attitudes—cooperation and nurturing, for instance—are contrary to the major themes of the gendered divorce discourse. Fathering is not a recognized primary component of these adult men's definitions of self (Chodorow 1978, 1989; Hearn 1987). Identity—the masculine self, battered by the "failure of the marriage"—was not unequivocally shored up by the success of postdivorce parenting. Though workable, successful, and pleasurable, the primary focus on parenting, despite their pride in it, and the interdependency with the former wife were aberrant.

These men encountered both a lack of institutional support for alternative postdivorce behaviors and fathering and a broad failure of the culture. Social arrangements and cultural scripts convey to them a body of expectations that, as men, their ultimate obligation, when all of the other niceties about modern men are stripped away, is personal autonomy intertwined with interpersonal dominance. The one expected, ongoing postdivorce family obligation was economic support. Yet, because the obligation to provide financial resources countered autonomy and the divorce situation undermined the authority typically related to provision, even that responsibility was subject to dispute. Not called for, and largely unsupported, was their steadfast caring for and emotional nurturance of their children. A postdivorce child-centeredness is a poor match for the power and pervasiveness of the system of gender stratification and beliefs. It is the masculine discourse of divorce that was socially assumed and supported: Divorce is war, and men are supposed to be victorious, or, at least, ever-persistent warriors, not compromising caregivers. These men, having actively sought and forged satisfying and workable parental relations and involvement, in conjunction with their former wives as their children's other parent, see themselves and are treated as cultural eccentrics. In sum, the majority of fathers in the study were at odds with the divorce outcome, their former wives, and often, if sometimes only by extension, with their children. But it was the nurturing fathers, engaged in innovative lines of action, who were at odds with the cultural norms and expectations of masculinity.

REFERENCES

Arendell, Terry. 1986. *Mothers and Divorce: Legal, Economic, and Social Dilemmas.* Berkeley: University of California Press.

———. 1992. "Social Self as Gendered: A Masculinist Discourse of Divorce." *Symbolic Interaction* 5 (2): 151–181.

Becker, Howard. 1980. *Sociological Work: Method and Substance.* Chicago: Aldine.

Bem, Sandra Lipsitz. 1993. *The Lenses of Gender: Transforming the Debate on Sexual Inequality.* New Haven, Conn.: Yale University Press.

Burkhauser, Richard, and Greg Duncan. 1989. "Economic Risks of Gender Roles: Income Loss and Life Events over the Life Course." *Social Science Quarterly* 70 (1):3–23.

Chodorow, Nancy. 1978. *The Reproduction of Mothering: Psychoanalysis and the Sociology of Gender.* Berkeley: University of California Press.

———. 1989. *Feminism and Psychoanalytic Theory.* New Haven, Conn.: Yale University Press.

Cohen, Theodore. 1989. "Becoming and Being Husbands and Fathers: Work and Family Conflict for Men." In *Gender in Intimate Relationships: A Microstructural Approach,* edited by Barbara J. Risman and Pepper Schwartz, 220–234. Belmont, Calif.: Wadsworth.

Coltrane, Scott. 1989. "Household Labor and the Routine Production of Gender." *Social Problems* 36:473–490. (Chapter 56, this volume.)

Goffman, Erving. 1959. *Presentation of Self in Everyday Life.* New York: Doubleday.

Hantover, Jeffrey P. 1978. "The Boy Scouts and the Validation of Masculinity." *Journal of Social Issues* 34:184–195.

Hearn, Jeff. 1987. *The Gender of Oppression: Men, Masculinity, and the Critique of Marxism.* New York: St. Martin's Press.

Hochschild, Arlie. 1983. *The Managed Heart: Commercialization of Human Feeling.* Berkeley: University of California Press.

Hochschild, Arlie, with Anne Machung. 1989. *The Second Shift.* New York: Viking Press.

Holden, Karen, and Pamela J. Smock. 1991. "The Economic Costs of Marital Dissolution: Why Do Women Bear a Disproportionate Cost?" *Annual Review of Sociology* 17:51–78.

Kimmel, Michael, and Michael Messner, eds. 1992. *Men's Lives.* 2d ed. New York: Macmillan.

LaRossa, Ralph, and Maureen Mulligan LaRossa. 1989. "Baby Care: Fathers vs. Mothers." In *Gen-*

der in Intimate Relationships: A Microstructural Approach, edited by Barbara J. Risman and Pepper Schwartz, 138–154. Belmont, Calif.: Wadsworth.

Lofland, John. 1978. Interaction in Everyday Life. Beverly Hills, Calif.: Sage.

Lyman, Peter. 1987. "The Fraternal Bond as a Joking Relationship: A Case Study of the Role of Sexist Jokes in Male Group Bonding." In Changing Men, edited by Michael Kimmel, 148–164. Newbury Park, Calif.: Sage.

Maccoby, Eleanor E., Charlene E. Depner, and Robert H. Mnookin. 1990. "Coparenting in the Second Year After Divorce." Journal of Marriage and the Family 52:141–155.

Martin, George. 1991. "Family, Gender, and Social Policy." In The Sociology of Gender: A Text-Reader, edited by Laura Kraemer, 323–345. New York: St. Martin's Press.

May, Larry, and Robert Strikwerda, eds. 1992. "Fatherhood and Nurturance." In Rethinking Masculinity: Philosophical Explorations in Light of Feminism, edited by Larry May and Robert Strikwerda, 75–92. Lanham, Md.: Rowman and Littlefield.

Perinbanayagam, Robert. 1990. "How to Do Self with Things." In Beyond Goffman: Studies on Communication, Institutions, and Social Interaction, edited by Stephen Riggins, 315–340. Berlin: Mouton–de Grueyer.

Pleck, Joseph. 1992a. "Men's Power with Women, Other Men, and Society: A Men's Movement Analysis." In Men's Lives, 2d ed., edited by Michael Kimmel and Michael Messner, 19–27. New York: Macmillan.

———. 1992b. "Prisoners of Masculinity." In Men's Lives, 2d ed., edited by Michael Kimmel and Michael Messner, 98–107. New York: Macmillan.

Risman, Barbara. 1989. "Can Men 'Mother'? Life as a Single Father." In Gender in Intimate Relationships: A Microstructural Approach, edited by Barbara J. Risman and Pepper Schwartz, 155–164. Belmont, Calif.: Wadsworth.

Swidler, Ann. 1980. "Love and Adulthood in American Culture." In Themes of Work and Love in Adulthood, edited by Neil J. Smelser and Erik Erikson, 120–150. Cambridge: Harvard University Press.

Thompson, Linda, and Alexis Walker. 1989. "Gender in Families: Women and Men in Marriage, Work, and Parenthood. Journal of Marriage and the Family 51:845–871.

United States Bureau of the Census. 1991. Current Population Reports, Series P–60, no. 173: "Child Support and Alimony, 1989," 11. Washington, D.C.: Government Printing Office.

Wallerstein, Judith, with Sandra Blakeslee. 1989. Second Chances: Men, Women, and Children a Decade After Divorce. New York: Ticknor and Fields.

 *Section C*

Kin Networks

~ *Chapter 30*

Kinscripts

CAROL B. STACK AND LINDA M. BURTON

People do not necessarily do for kin what they are supposed to do, but they understand *what* they are supposed to do, and *when* they are supposed to do it; and they know their kin *will* summon them someday. Not long ago a friend, a distinguished professor who was one of five children from a Southern sharecropping family, called to say: "Carol, I've been given ten hours notice that my sister's two children are coming on the train to live with me!" She had been drafted by her older sister to care for these children. It did not matter that she was in the process of finishing a book and preparing for a major international conference. She lamented that over her protests her sister said firmly: "It's your turn."

This chapter presents a framework for examining how individuals and families as multigenerational collectives work out family responsibilities. We provide a useful lens for viewing how work and responsibility concerning the care of children is delegated: in

From *Journal of Comparative Family Studies* 24, no. 2 (1993): 157–70. Reprinted by permission.

particular, with respect to children born to young mothers. This chapter draws upon a broad variety of examples from diverse family situations as a way of thinking about multigenerational families and child care across the life span.

We introduce kinscripts, a framework representing the interplay of family ideology, norms, and behaviors over the life course. Kinscripts encompasses three culturally defined family domains: kin-work, which is the labor and the tasks that families need to accomplish to survive from generation to generation; kin-time, which is the temporal and sequential ordering of family transitions; and kin-scription, which is the process of assigning kin-work to family members.

The kinscripts framework is derived in part from the family life course perspective (Aldous 1990; Elder 1987; Hagestad 1990; Hareven 1982, 1986), studies of kinship (Aschenbrenner 1975; di Leonardo 1986; Hinnant 1986; Stack 1974), and literature on family scripts (Byng-Hall 1985, 1988; Steiner 1974). The principal basis of kinscripts, however, is our ethnographic research conducted between 1968 and 1990 with urban and rural, low-income, multigenerational, black, extended families in the northeast, southeast, and midwest portions of the United States. Case history data on families involved in these ethnographic studies are used to illuminate components of the kinscripts framework where appropriate.

The kinscripts framework was developed to organize and interpret qualitative observations of (a) the temporal and interdependent dimensions of family role transitions; (b) the creation and intergenerational transmission of family norms; and (c) the dynamics of negotiation, exchange, and conflict within families as they construct the life course. This framework is based on the premise that families have their own agendas, their own interpretation of cultural norms, and their own histories (Hagestad 1986a; Reiss 1981; Reiss and Oliveri 1983; Tilly 1987). Families assist individual members in constructing their personal life courses, but in the process families as collectives create a life course of their own (Watkins 1980).

The kinscripts framework can be applied across race, ethnicity, social class, and to the range of family forms existing in contemporary American society. Typically, the conceptual frameworks used to interpret the life course of kin are derived from explorations involving white, middle-class families. Kinscripts, in contrast, is an example of a framework that is derived from the study of low-income, black families but offers insights for study of mainstream families as well.

The Conceptual Basis of Kinscripts

Kinscripts is grounded in a theoretical approach that weaves together the sociological perspectives on the life course and studies of

kinship (Aldous 1978; Aschenbrenner 1975; Clausen 1986; Elder 1984; Fry and Keith 1982; Glick 1977; Nydegger 1986a; Plath 1980; Wilson 1986; Zerubavel 1981). Studies of the life course "trace individuals as social personas and their pathways along an age differentiated, socially marked sequence of transitions" (Hagestad 1990, 151). Life course research has traditionally examined the pathways of individuals as inferred from aggregate data on the timing, duration, spacing, and ordering of role transitions in the context of family and work (Hogan 1985; Marini 1985). From this research, we have learned a great deal about trends and patterns in the timing and sequencing of marriage, childbearing, and entries and exits from the labor force. This research, however, tells us very little about how one individual's life course is connected to another's and how that life course, in the context of kin, is negotiated and constructed. Combining a focus on kinship with the life course perspective offers a more comprehensive view of the interlocking pathways of families as members influencing one another's life choices (Elder 1984; Rossi and Rossi 1990).

Two dimensions of life course perspectives and the study of kinship are central to the kinscripts framework: the temporal nature of the life course and interdependent lives. Regarding the temporal nature of the life course, Elder (1984, 1987) notes that there are four dimensions of time that influence the flow of individuals through the life course—lifetime, social time, family time, and historical time. Lifetime is delineated by chronological age and represents an individual's stage in the aging process. According to Clausen (1986) social time defines the set of norms that "specify when particular life transitions or accomplishments are expected to occur in a particular society or social milieu" (p. 2). Family time refers to the ordering of family events and roles by age-linked expectations, sanctions, and options. Historical time anchors an individual or a family in a social and cultural era. The dimension of time most salient to the kinscripts framework is family time.

Family time has been defined by Hareven (1977, 1982) as the "timing of events such as marriage, birth of a child, leaving home, and the transition of individuals into different roles as the family moves through is life course" (1977, 58). Individual progression through these family stages is influenced by historical and social contexts and by the tensions between individual preferences for the timing of these events and familial expectations. Hagestad (1986a) offers an interpretation of family time in which families, as cultural units, devise timetables for the movement of the group through predictable phases of development and changing generational structures. Family timetables are representations of the shared understandings and interdependencies within kinship structures. They are, in essence, scripts that the entire family embraces about the flow of events in the life cycle. The kinscripts framework is built on these premises, with the recognition that norms for transitions reflected in the broader society do not necessarily reveal the norms for timing in individual families.

In our ethnographic research, we have paid close attention to family timetables concerning the timing of childbearing. Specifically, our interests have been in the norms and sanctions families create with respect to age-appropriate (on-time) and age-inappropriate (off-time) childbearing (Burton and Bengston 1985). Aggregate data from existing demographic studies (Hogan 1985; Rindfuss et al. 1988) suggests, in general, that when married couples have their first child during their twenties, it is considered normative, on-time

childbearing behavior. In certain communities, however, families may establish other norms, expecting that designated adolescent females become "early" childbearers. In an ethnographic study conducted by Burton (1990), of a *unique* northeastern black community referred to as Gospel Hill, early childbearing is often considered a necessary activity. It provides grandmothers with children to raise. In these families, parenthood is normally enacted by grandmothers rather than mothers. Consequently, families believe it is important to become grandmothers as young as possible to assure women the energy to "keep up with toddlers." The following comment made by a 35-year-old potential grandmother, illustrates this desire:

> I suspect that my daughter (14 years old) will have a baby soon. If she doesn't, I'll be too old to be a grandmother and to do the things I'm supposed to do, like raise my grandchild.

The second dimension of the life course perspective and studies of kinship integrated in the kinscripts framework concerns interdependent lives. Life course interdependence is described as the ways in which individual transitions and trajectories are affected by or even contingent upon the life stages of others (Elder 1987; Hagestad and Neugarten 1985; Kahn and Antonucci 1980; Riley and Waring 1976). Interdependent goals in families are witnessed in the plans that parents make about their own lives based on their assumptions of the life course progression of their children (Hagestad 1986a). It is also observed in the transition to grandparenthood, where ascension to the role is dependent on the reproductive behaviors of one's offspring (Hagestad and Burton 1986).

In Gospel Hill and in New Jericho, the rural black community in the Southeast studied by Stack (1993), the dynamics of interdependent lives are illustrated in patterns of intergenerational role responsibilities. In both communities, systems of nonadjacent generational caregiving are the norm. The primary responsibility of grandmothers in the families studied in these communities was the care of their grandchildren, and the principal duty for their daughters (the mothers of their grandchildren) was the care of women who raised them—their own grandmothers. Mary, a 19-year-old mother who lives in Gospel Hill, explains how this system of care across generations in a family works:

> My grandmother raised me. Now it's time for me to give her something back. It's O.K. if my mother raises my child for now. If she didn't, I wouldn't be able to take care of my grandmother.

Several aspects of the life course of kin are illustrated in these brief descriptions of family dynamics in Gospel Hill and New Jericho—the timing of family role transitions (Hagestad 1986a; Hareven 1982), the work of kin (Bahr 1976; di Leonardo 1986; Finely 1989; Rosenthal 1985), family rituals (Lindahl and Back 1987; Rosenthal and Marshall 1988) and the negotiations of individual and family needs (Plath 1980).

Building on the temporal and interdependent dimensions of the life course perspective and the study of kin, we propose the kinscripts framework for studying the lives of individuals embedded within the lives of families. The framework is based on three assumptions: (1) The life course of individuals and the life course of families are two interdependent entities; (2) the life course of families and individuals is shaped within social, cultural, and historical contexts; and (3) the life course of families involves blood and non-blood relatives who mutually share a perception of their inclusion in the family and interact accordingly (Dilworth-Anderson et al. 1993; Stack 1974).

Kinscripts

Family Scripts

The concept of scripts as used in the family therapy literature is also an integral part of the kinscripts framework. Family scripts prescribe patterns of family interaction (Byng-Hall 1988; Ferreira 1963). They are mental representations that guide the role performances of family members within and across contexts.

The kinscripts framework extends the notion of scripts to the study of the family life course. Specifically, kinscripts focuses on the tensions that are produced and negotiated between individuals in families in response to scripts. These dynamics are discussed in the context of three culturally defined family domains: kin-work, kin-time, and kinscription.

Kin-Work

Kin-work is the collective labor expected of family centered networks across households and within them (di Leonardo 1986). It defines the work that families need to accomplish to endure over time. The family life course is constructed and maintained through kin-work. Kin-work regenerates families, maintains lifetime continuities, sustains intergenerational responsibilities, and reinforces shared values. It encompasses, for example, all of the following: family labor for reproduction; intergenerational care for children or dependents; economic survival, including wage and nonwage labor; family migration and migratory labor designated to send home remittances; and strategic support for networks of kin extending across regions, state lines, and nations.

Kin-work is distributed in families among men, women, and children. Samuel Jenkins, a 76-year-old widower in Gospel Hill, provided his own interpretation of kin-work. After Samuel's oldest daughter died, his granddaughter Elaine moved in with him, along with her three children: a six-month-old baby, a two-year-old and a three-year-old. Samuel is raising these children. Elaine, he says, is running the streets and not providing care. When asked why he is parenting his grandchildren, he said:

> There ain't no other way. I have to raise these babies else the service people will take 'em away. This is my family. Family has to take care of family else we won't be no more.

Janice Perry, a 13-year-old pregnant woman from Gospel Hill, described her rather unique kin-work assignment. Her contribution to the family, as she understood it, was through reproduction. She states:

> I'm not having this baby for myself. The baby's grandmother wants to be a 'mama' and my great-grandfather wants to see a grandchild before he goes blind from sugar. I'm just giving them something to make them happy."

Janice's mother, Helen, comments further:

> I want this baby. I want it bad. I need it. I need to raise a child. That's my job now. My mama did it. It's my turn now.

Samuel Jenkins, Janice Perry, and Helen Perry have clear notions of kin-work within families. While their individual family circumstances are different, kin-work for each one of them is tied to providing care across generations and maintaining family traditions and continuity.

Kin-work is the consequence of culturally constructed family obligations defined by economic, social, physical, and psychological family needs. Henry Evans, a 38-year-old resident of New Town (Burton and Jarrett 1991), a northeastern black community, provided a very clear profile of his assigned kin-work. He noted that his kin-work emerged from the physical and psychological needs of his family members. Henry was the only surviving son in his family. His mother had given birth to eleven other sons, all of whom were stillborn or died shortly after birth. At the time of his interview, Henry was providing care for his father, who had recently suffered a heart attack; his 36-year-old sister, who was suffering from a chronic neuromuscular disease; and his 40-year-old sister and her four children. When asked about his family duties, he remarked:

> I was designated by my family as a child to provide care for all my family members. My duties read just like a job description. The job description says the following: (1) you will never marry; (2) you will have no children of your own; (3) you will take care of your sisters, their children, your mother and your father in old age; and (4) you will be happy doing it.

Henry went on to discuss how his commitment to the family life course took precedence over his personal life goals:

> Someone in my family must be at the helm. Someone has to be there to make sure that the next generation has a start. Right now, we are a family of co-dependents. We need each other. As individuals, my sisters and father are too weak to stand alone. I could never bring a wife into this. I don't have time. May be when the next generation (his sister's kids) is stronger, no one will have to do my job. We will redefine destiny.

The life situation of Henry Evans is not an unfamiliar one. Hareven (1982), in detailed historical analysis of families who worked for the Amoskeag Company in Manchester, New Hampshire, provides poignant examples of how, for many individuals, the demands of kin-work superseded personal goals (Hareven and Langenbach 1978). Comparable evidence is noted in Plath's (1980) in-depth interview study of contemporary Japanese families. In each cultural context, across historical time, kin-work was described as self-sacrificing hard work—work designed to insure the survival of the collective.

Kin-Time

Kin-time represents the temporal scripts of families. It is the shared understanding among family members of when and in what sequence role transitions and kin-work should occur. Kin-time encompasses family norms concerning the timing of such transitions as marriage, childbearing, and grandparenthood. It includes temporal guides for the assumption of family leadership roles and caregiving responsibilities. The temporal and sequencing norms of kin-time are constructed in the context of family culture. Consequently, for some families, these norms may not be synonymous with the schedules of family life course events inferred from patterns assumed to exist in larger society.

Stack's (1993) ethnographic study of the migration of black families to and from the rural South provides an example of the relationship between kin-time and kin-work. Two aspects of kin-work are highlighted—reproduction and migration. The timing and sequencing of reproduction and migration is such that young adults first have children and then migrate to the North to secure jobs and send money back home. Their young children are left behind in the South to be reared by grandparents or older aunts and uncles. After an extended period of time, the migrating adults return to the South and, for some, their now-young-adult children repeat the cycle— they bear children and migrate north.

The temporal sequencing of reproduction and migration in these families reflects a scripted family life course involving cooperative action among kin. Family members must be willing to assume economic and childcare responsibilities according to schedule. Individuals in families, however, do not always adhere to kin-time. A young adult may choose not to migrate, another may leave home but fail to send remittances, and yet others may return home sooner than expected. These individuals are considered insurgent by kin and may create unexpected burdens that challenge family resilience.

Kin-time also demarcates rites of passage or milestones within families, including the handing down of familial power and tasks following the death of family elders. For example, in the Appalachian mountains in the southeastern United States, older women proclaim those few years after the death of their husbands, when they alone own the family land, as the time they have the most power in their families. The grown children and nearby community members observe, in a timely fashion, the activities of these elderly rural women. It was still common lore in the 1980s that the year in which each of these older widowed women announced plans for planting her last garden is the last year of her life. In that year kin vie for their inheritances. Thus, the life course of families, which involves a scripted cycle of the relegation of power through land ownership, continues to unfold.

Kin-Scription

It is important to understand how power is brought into play within the context of kin-time and kin-work. The question this raises is summed up in the tension reflected in kin-scription. Rather than accept the attempts of individuals to set their own personal agendas, families are continually rounding up, summoning, or recruiting individuals for kin-work. Some kin, namely, women and children, are easily recruited. The importance women place on maintaining kin ties and fostering family continuity has been assiduously documented (Dressel and Clark 1990; Gilligan 1982; Hagestad 1989b). Placing preeminent emphasis on kin-keeping—the undertakings necessary to keep connected and family traditions transmitted—women often find it difficult to refuse kin demands.

The life course of a young woman, Yvonne Carter, who lives in Gospel Hill, offers an example of the interplay of power, kin-scription, and the role of women. When Yvonne's first love died fourteen years ago, she was twenty-one. At thirty-five, she recounted how the years had unfolded:

> When Charlie died, it seemed like everyone said since she's not getting married, we have to keep her busy. Before I knew it, I was raising kids, giving homes to long lost kin, and even helping the friends of my mother. Between doing all of this, I didn't have time to find another man. I bet they wouldn't want me and all my relatives anyway.

How relatives collude to keep particular individuals wedded to family needs—a chosen daughter in Japan (Plath 1980), a chosen son in rural Ireland (Scheper-Hughes 1979)—confirm Yvonne Carter's suspicion: she has been recruited for specific kin-work in her family.

Recruitment for kin-work is one dimension of power in kin-scription. Exclusion from kin-work is another, as this profile of Paul Thomas, a 36-year-old resident of Gospel Hill, illustrates.

Paul Thomas, down on his luck, out of sorts with his girlfriend, and the oldest of seven children, had just moved back in with his mother, Mattie, when he was interviewed. Eleven of Mattie's family members live in her two-bedroom apartment. The family members include Paul's two younger brothers (one who returned home from the service and moved in with his new wife and child), an unmarried sister, a sister and her child, and a pregnant sister with her two children. Paul reported finding his move back home, the result of repeated unemployment, particularly difficult under these living conditions.

After Paul moved back home, Mattie characterized Paul's history within the family as follows:

> Paul left this family when he was thirteen. I don't mean leave, like go away, but leave, like only do the things he wanted to do, but not pay attention to what me or his brothers and sisters wanted or needed. He took and took, and we gave and gave all the time. We never made him given nothing back.

In Mattie's view, her son Paul abandoned the family early on, claiming rights, but not assuming responsibilities. On a later visit to Mattie's apartment, family members gathered in the living room were asked a rather general question about doing things for kin. Paul stood up to speak. Addressing this question, with anger and entitlement in his voice, he said:

> I come back only for a little while. I am the outsider in the family. The black sheep. I belong, but I don't belong. Do you understand what I mean? I am only important because my mother can say, "I have a son," and my sisters can say, "I have a brother." But it doesn't mean anything. I can't do anything around here. I don't do anything. No one makes me. My sisters know what they have to do. They always have. They know their place! Now that I'm getting old I've been thinking that someway I'll make my place here. I want Ann (his sister) to name her baby after me. I'm begging you, Ann. Give this family something to remember that I'm part of it too.

Renegade relatives such as Paul attest to subtle dynamics that challenge their places within families. These relatives may inadvertently play havoc with family processes while simultaneously attempting to attach themselves to family legacies.

When kin act out or resist procedures to be kept in line, families have been known to use heavy-handed pressures to recruit individuals to do kin-work. However, kin may be well aware that family demands criss-cross and that it is impossible for the individual summoned to do kin-work to satisfy everyone. In particular, those family members assigned to do kin-work cannot be in two places at once. Adults, and even children under such circumstances, may be left to choose between conflicting demands. Stack's study of family responsibilities assumed by children in the rural, southeastern community of New Jericho, provides an example of competing demands placed on adolescents as they are recruited for family tasks.

In New Jericho, multiple expectations are transmitted to children whose parents migrated from the rural south to the northeast. It is not unusual for adolescents, skilled at childcare and other domestic activities, to be pulled in a tug-of-war between family households in the North and South. Kin at both locations actively recruit adolescents to move with them or join their households. Parents in the North and grandparents in the South are the main contenders. Children find themselves deeply caught in a web of family obligations. At eleven years of age, Jimmy Williams was asked to move to Brooklyn to help his parents with their new baby. But his grandmother needed his help in rural North Carolina. Jimmy responded by saying:

> I think I should stay with the one that needs my help the most. My grandmother is unable to do for herself, and I should stay with her and let my mother come to see me.

In this example, Jimmy was conscripted by two households within the family network. The decision Jimmy made to remain with his grandmother punctuates the leeway given to the children to make judgments in the context of personal and family interests. In a similar situation young Sarah Boyce said:

> I'll talk to my parents and try to get them to understand that my grandparents cannot get around like they used to. I want to make an agreement to let my brother go to New York and go to school, and I'll go the school down here. In the summer, I will go and be with my parents, and my brother can come down home.

Children are conscripted to perform certain kin tasks that are tied to the survival of families as a whole. Definitions of these tasks are transmitted through direct and indirect cues from family members. Jimmy and Sarah responded to the needs of kin, taking advantage of the flexibility available to them in negotiating the tasks. That same flexibility is not always available for adults. The life situation of Sandra Smith provides an example.

Sandra Smith, married and a mother, found herself pressed between the demands of kin in her family of origin and her in-laws in Gospel Hill. She states:

> I'm always the one everybody comes to take care of children. My mother expects me to raise my sister's three kids. My mother-in-law calls upon me to mind my nieces and nephews while she takes it easy. She expects me to kiss her feet. I won't do it, none of it, everybody can go to hell.

Sandra, in fact, did refuse kin-work. When asked what impact her choice would have on her situation in the family, she said:

> It means I won't have nobody. But so what, they need me more than I need them.

Pressed between opposing set of demands and resentments that build up over the years, refusal to do kin-work is a choice some individuals opt for. Refusal, however, may be costly, particularly for those individuals who are dependent on the economic and emotional resources of kin.

Discussions

The examples of kin-work, kin-time, and kin-scription provided in this discussion are drawn primarily from our ethnographic studies of low-income, multigenerational black families. The examples illuminate extraordinary situations of individuals embedded in families that have scripted life courses. All families, unlike those described here, do not have such well-defined family guidelines. The family guidelines that exist for those who live in Gospel Hill, New Jericho, and New Town emerge out of extreme economic need and an intense commitment by family members to the survival of future generations.

The kinscripts framework is useful for exploring the life course of the families highlighted in this chapter, but it can also be applied to families that construct their life courses under different circumstances. Kinscripts is particularly suited to exploring the effects that certain individuals within families have on the life course of kin. In all families across racial, ethnic, and socioeconomic groups there are individuals who cannot be counted on to carry out kin tasks; who leave the family fold for reasons of personal survival; who remain as dependent insiders within families, making excessive emotional and economic demands on family members; and who return to the bosom of kin because of personal experiences such as unemployment, homelessness, divorce, or widowhood. From each angle, and in a diversity of family systems, the life course of kin through kin-work, kin-time, and kin-scription are affected by the personal agendas of family members.

Consider, for example, how the kinscripts framework might be used in exploring the life course of a kin network in which one of its members is experiencing divorce. Divorce is a fairly common experience in mainstream American families (Anspach 1976; Hagestad

and Smyer 1982; Norton and Moorman 1987). Under such circumstances, an adult child with dependent children may return to the home of his or her parents. The return home may put the scripted life course of kin in disarray, necessitating that collective family notions of kin-work, kin-time, and kin-scription be reconstructed. In terms of kin-work, grandparents, who in the past may have assumed a less active role in the rearing of their grandchildren, may now be expected to take on a more formal surrogate parent role (Johnson 1988). With respect to kin-time, family members may delay certain transitions in response to the divorce. For example, older parents might put off retirement for a few years to generate enough income to help their adult child reestablish themselves financially. Kin-scription may also be revised. The adult child experiencing the divorce may have been the family kin-keeper—that is, the person in the family charged with organizing family reunions, documenting family history, and negotiating conflicts between relatives. Given the change in this kin-keeper's life course, these duties may have to be reassigned to another family member.

Kinscripts can also be applied to explorations of the relationship between broader social conditions, unemployment, and the life course of kin. Under ideal conditions, unemployed family members are absorbed by kin as best they can. Given severe socioeconomic conditions, however, tensions between individual needs and kin-work, kin-time, and kin-scription may emerge. Again, the family life course may have to be redesigned. For example, low-income families attempting to absorb down and out members, or homeless mothers and children, find that sometimes in the face of economic cutbacks and emotional crises they must, however reluctantly, "let go" of family members who cannot pull their own weight. When public welfare support decreased in the 1980s, it produced a remarkable increase in families with these experiences. Stressful economic conditions decrease both individuals' and families' abilities to perform effectively. Certain economic and political changes can disrupt kin-time—delaying family milestones such as childbearing and adding complexity to family timetables—and inhibit kin-work and kin-scription, thereby increasing tensions between the individual and family life course. The kinscripts framework, drawing on the life course perspective, is attentive to exploring these issues in the context of social change.

Another application of the kinscript framework is seen in the study of family members who leave the fold of kin. Under certain circumstances, particularly in the case of a dysfunctional family, an individual may temporarily disassociate himself from kin as a means of personal survival and then return to the fold having learned new family skills. Within the context of the kinscripts framework, several questions might be addressed: (a) What implications does the individual's exit from the family have on kin-work, kin-time, kin-scription? (b) How does the individual negotiate reentry to the kin network? (c) What affect does that individual's reentry have on the family's restructuring of the life course?

In summary, our contention is that kinscripts can be a useful framework for research in which the basic questions concern how families and individuals negotiate, construct, and reconstruct the life course. The utility of this framework is found in observing the interplay of three culturally defined family domains-kin-work, kin-time, and kin-scription.

Conclusion

The purpose of this chapter was to suggest a way of thinking about the life course of individuals embedded within the life course of families. The kinscript framework was proposed. Kinscripts is conceptually grounded in the life course perspective, studies of kinship, and the literature on family scripts. As such, many of the ideas outlined in kinscripts are not new. What is new, however, is the union of these various perspectives in the domains of kin-work, kin-time, and kin-scription.

In addition to describing three domains of the family life course, kinscripts represents an attempt to use knowledge generated from the study of black multigeneration families to formulate a framework that can be useful for the study of families in general. Minority families have historically experienced issues that mainstream families have only recently been attentive to. Examples of issues include: the juggling of work and family roles for women, single parenthood, extended family relationships, and poverty. Important lessons can be learned through exploring these issues in the context of the life course of minority families. These lessons can provide critical insights on the life course of the variety of family forms existing in contemporary of American society.

NOTES

Acknowledgments: The research reported in this chapter was supported by grants from the Rockefeller Foundation to the first author, and by the National Science Foundation (R11-8613960), the Brookdale Foundation, the Center for the Study of Child and Adolescent Development, the Pennsylvania State University, a FIRST Award from the National Institute of Mental Health (No. R29M1146057-01), and a William T. Grant Faculty Scholars Award, to the second author. This chapter was partially prepared while the authors were Fellows at the Center for Advanced Study in the Behavioral Sciences. We are grateful for financial support from the John D. and Catherine T. MacArthur Foundation, the Spencer Foundation, and the Guggenheim Foundation. We also wish to thank Robert Weiss, Gunhild Hagestad, Ann Crouter, Jean Lave, Blanca Silvestrini, Judy Stacey,

Brad Shore, Jane Ifekwunigwe, Cindy Bracho, and Caridad Souza, for the their helpful comments on an earlier draft.

REFERENCES

Aldous, Joan. 1978. *Family Careers: Developmental Change in Families.* New York: Wiley.

———. 1990. "Family Development and the Life Course: Two Perspectives on Family Change." *Journal of Marriage and the Family* 52 (3): 571–583.

Anspach, Donald F. 1976. "Kinship and Divorce." *Journal of Marriage and the Family* 38: 323–335.

Aschenbrenner, Joyce. 1975. *Lifelines: Black Families in Chicago.* New York: Holt, Rinehart, and Winston.

Bahr, Howard M. 1976. "The Kinship Role." Pp. 61–79 in F. Ivan Nye (ed.), *Role Structures and Analysis of Family.* Beverly Hills, CA: Sage.

Beaver, Patricia D. 1986. *Rural Community in the Appalachian South.* Lexington, KY: University Press of Kentucky.

Burton, Linda M. 1990. "Teenage Pregnancy as an Alternative Life-Course Strategy in Multigenerational Black Families." *Human Nature* 1 (2): 123–143.

Burton, Linda M., and Vern L. Bengston. 1985. "Black Grandmothers: Issues of Timing and Meaning in Roles." Pp. 61–77 in Vern L. Bengston and Joan Robertson (eds.), *Grandparenthood: Research and Policy Perspectives.* Beverly Hills, CA: Sage.

Burton, Linda M., and Robin L. Jarrett. 1991. "Studying African-American Family Structure and Process in Underclass Neighborhoods: Conceptual Considerations." Unpublished manuscript. Pennsylvania State University.

Byng-Hall, John. 1985. "The Family Script: A Useful Bridge Between Theory and Practice." *Journal of Family Therapy* 7: 301–305.

———. 1988. "Scripts and Legends in Families and Family Therapy." *Family Process* 27: 167–179.

Clausen, John. 1986. *The Life Course.* Englewood Cliffs, NJ: Prentice Hall.

di Leonardo, Micaela. 1986. "The Female World of Cards and Holidays: Women, Families, and the Work of Kinship." (Chapter 31, this volume.)

Dilworth-Anderson, Peggye, Leanor Boulin-Johnson, and Linda M. Burton. 1993. "Reframing Theories for Understanding Race, Ethnicity, and Families." In Pauline Boss, William Doherty, Ralph La Rossa, Walter Schumm, and Suzanne Steinmetz (eds.), *Sourcebook of Family Theories and Methods: A Contextual Approach.* New York: Plenum Press.

Dressel, Paula L., and Ann Clark. 1990. "A Critical Look at Family Care." *Journal of Marriage and the Family* 52 (3): 769–782.

Elder, Glen H., Jr. 1978. "Family History and the Life Course." Pp. 17–64 in T. Hareven (eds.), *Transitions: The Family and the Life Course in Historical Perspective.* New York: Academic Press.

———. 1984. "Families, Kin, and the Life Course: A Sociological Perspective." Pp. 80–135 in Ross D. Parke (ed.), *Advances in Child Development Research and the Family.* Chicago: University of Chicago Press.

———. 1987. "Families and Lives: Some Developments in Life-Course Studies." *Journal of Family History* 12: 179–199.

Ferreira, A. J. 1963. "Family Myth and Homeostasis." *Archives of General Psychiatry* 9: 457–463.

Finely, Nancy. 1989. "Theories of Family Labor as Applied to Gender Differences in Caregiving for Elderly Parents." *Journal of Marriage and the Family* 51: 79–85.

Fry, Christine L., and Jeannie Keith. 1982. "The Life Course as a Cultural Unit." Pp. 51–70 in Matilda W. Riley, Ron P. Abeles, and Michael S. Teitelbaum (eds.), *Aging from Birth to Death* (Vol. 2), Boulder, CO: Westview.

Gilligan, Carol. 1982. *In a Different Voice.* Cambridge, MA: Harvard University Press.

Glick, Paul. 1977. "Updating the Family Life Cycle." *Journal of Marriage and the Family* 39: 5–13.

Hagestad, Gunhild O. 1986a. "Dimensions of Time and the Family." *American Behavioral Scientist* 29: 679–694.

———. 1986b. "The Aging Society as a Contex for Family Life." *Daedalus* 115: 119–139.

————. 1990. "Social Perspectives on the Life Course." Pp. 151–168 in Robert K. Binstock and Linda K. George (eds.), *Handbook of Aging and the Social Sciences*. 3d ed. New York: Academic Press.

Hagestad, Gunhild O., and Linda Burton. 1986. "Grandparenthood, Life Context, and Family Development." *American Behavioral Scientist* 29 (4): 471–484.

Hagestad, Gunhild O., and Bernice Neugarten. 1985. "Age and the Life Course." Pp. 35–61 in Robert H. Binstock and Ethel Shanas (eds.), *The Handbook of Aging and the Social Sciences*. 2d ed. New York: Von Nostrand and Reinhold.

Hagestad, Gunhild O., and Michael S. Smyer. 1982. "Dissolving Long-Term Relationships: Patterns of Divorcing in Middle Age." Pp. 155–188 in S. Duck (ed.), *Personal Relationships*. Vol. 4, *Dissolving Personal Relationships*. London: Academic Press.

Hareven, Tamara K. 1977. "Family Time and Historical Time." *Daedalus* 107: 57–70.

————. 1982. *Family Time and Industrial Time: The Relationship Between the Family and Work in a New England Industrial Community*. New York: Cambridge University Press.

————. 1986. "Historical Changes in the Social Construction of the Life Course." *Human Development* 29 (3): 171–180.

Hareven, Tamara K., and Randolph Langenbach. 1978. *Amoskeag*. New York: Pantheon.

Hinnant, John. 1986. "Ritualization of the Life Cycle." In C. L. Fry and J. Keith (eds.), *New Methods for Old Age Research*. South Hadley, MA: Bergin and Garvey.

Hogan, Dennis P. 1978. "The Variable Order of Events in the Life Course." *American Sociological Review* 43: 573–586.

————. 1985. "The Demography of Life-Span Transitions: Temporal and Gender Comparisons," Pp. 65–78 in Alice Rossi (ed.), *Gender and the Life Course*. New York: Aldine.

Johnson, Colleen L. 1988. "Active and Latent Functions of Grandparenting During the Divorce Process." *Gerontologist* 28 (2): 185–191.

Kahn, Robert and Toni Antonucci. 1980. "Convoys over the Life Course: Attachment, Roles, and Social Support." Pp. 62–93 in Paul Baltes

and Orville Brim (eds.), *Life-Span Development*. Vol. 3, *Each Behavior*. New York: Academic Press.

Lindahl, M. W., and Kurt Back. 1987. "Lineage Identity and Generational Continuity: Family History and Family Reunions." *Comprehensive Geronotology* 1:30–34.

Marini, Margaret M. 1984. "Age and Sequencing Norms in the Transition to Adulthood." *Social Forces* 63 (1): 229–244.

Neugarten, Bernice L., Joan Moore, and John Lowe. 1965. "Age Norms, Age Constraints, and Adult Socialization." *American Journal of Sociology* 70: 710–717.

Norton, A. J. and J. E. Moorman. 1987. "Current Trends in Marriage and Divorce Among American Women." *Journal of Marriage and the Family* 49: 3–14.

Nydegger, Corinne N. 1986a. "Age and Life-Course Transitions." Pp. 131–161 in C. L. Fry and J. Keith (eds.), *New Methods for Old Age Research*. South Hadley, MA: Bergin and Garvey.

————. 1986b. "Timetables and Implicit Theory." *American Behavioral Scientist* 29 (6): 710–729.

Plath, David. 1980. *Long Engagements*. Stanford, CA: Stanford University Press.

Reiss, David. 1981. *The Family's Construction of Reality*. Cambridge, MA: Harvard University Press.

Reiss, David, and Mary Ellen Oliveri. 1983. "The Family's Construction of Social Reality and Its Ties to Its Kin Network: An Exploration of Causal Direction." *Journal of Marriage and the Family* 45: 81–91.

Riley, Mathilda, and Joan Waring. 1976. "Age and Aging." Pp. 89–101 in R. K. Merton and R. Nisbet (eds.), *Contemporary Social Problems*. New York: Harcourt, Brace, Jovanovich.

Rindfuss, Ronald R., S. Philip Morgan, and C. Gray Swicegood. 1988. *First Births in America: Changes in Timing of Parenthood*. Berkeley: University of California Press.

Rosenthal, Carolyn, and Victor Marshall. 1988. "Generational Transmission of Family Ritual." *American Behavioral Scientist* 31: 669–684.

Rosenthal, Carolyn J. 1985. "Kin-keeping in the Familial Division of Labor." *Journal of Marriage and the Family* 45: 509–521.

Rossi, Alice. 1980. "Aging and Parenthood in the Middle Years." Pp. 137–205 in Paul Baltes and Orville G. Brim (eds.), *Life Span Development and Behavior,* Vol. 3. New York: Academic Press.

Rossi, Alice, and Peter Rossi. 1990. *Of Human Bonding: Parent-Child Relations Across the Life Course.* New York: Aldine De Gruyter.

Scheper-Hughes, Nancy. 1979. *Saints, Scholars and Schizophrenics.* Berkeley, CA: University of California Press.

Steiner, C. M. 1974. *Scripts People Live: Transactional Analysis of Life Scripts.* New York: Grove Press.

Stack, Carol. 1974. *All Our Kin.* New York: Harper & Row.

———. 1993. *Call to Home: African Americans Reclaim the Rural South.* New York: Basic Books.

Tilly, Charles. 1987. "Family History, Social History, and Social Change." *Journal of Family History* 12: 320–329.

Watkins, Susan C. 1980. "On Measuring Transitions and Turning Points." *Historical Methods* 13 (3): 181–186.

Wilson, Melvin. 1986. "The Black Extended Family: An Analytical Consideration." *Developmental Psychology* 22: 246–256.

Zerubavel, E. 1981. *Hidden Rhythms: Schedules and Calendars in Social Life.* Chicago: University of Chicago Press.

Chapter 31

The Female World of Cards and Holidays:
Women, Families, and the Work of Kinship

MICAELA DI LEONARDO

Why is it that the married women of America are supposed to write all the letters and send all the cards to their
husbands' families? My old man is a much better writer
than I am, yet he expects me to correspond with his whole
family. If I asked him to correspond with mine, he would
blow a gasket.
    —Letter to Ann Landers

Women's place in man's life cycle has been that of nurturer, caretaker, and helpmate, the weaver of those networks of relationships on which she in turn relies.
    —Carol Gilligan, *In a Different Voice*

Feminist scholars in the past fifteen years have
made great strides in formulating new understandings of the relations among gender, kinship, and the larger economy. As a result of
this pioneering research, women are newly
visible and audible, no longer submerged
within their families. We see households as
loci of political struggle, inseparable parts of
the larger society and economy, rather than as
havens from the heartless world of industrial

capitalism.[1] And historical and cultural variations in kinship and family forms have become clearer with the maturation of feminist
historical and social-scientific scholarship.

Two theoretical trends have been key to this
reinterpretation of women's work and family
domain. The first is the elevation to visibility of
women's nonmarket activities—housework,
child care, the servicing of men, and the care of
the elderly—and the definition of all these activities as *labor*, to be enumerated alongside
and counted as part of overall social reproduction. The second theoretical trend is the non-
pejorative focus on women's domestic or kin-
centered networks. We now see them as the
products of conscious strategy, as crucial to the
functioning of kinship systems, as sources of
women's autonomous power and possible primary sites of emotional fulfillment, and, at
times, as the vehicles for actual survival and/or
political resistance.[2]

Recently, however, a division has developed between feminist interpreters of the "labor" and the "network" perspectives on
women's lives. Those who focus on women's

work tend to envision women as sentient, goal-oriented actors, while those who concern themselves with women's ties to others tend to perceive women primarily in terms of nurturance, other-orientation—altruism. The most celebrated recent example of this division is the opposing testimony of historians Alice Kessler-Harris and Rosalind Rosenberg in the Equal Employment Opportunity Commission's sex discrimination case against Sears Roebuck and Company. Kessler-Harris argued that American women historically have actively sought higher-paying jobs and have been prevented from gaining them because of sex discrimination by employers. Rosenberg argued that American women in the nineteenth century created among themselves, through their domestic networks, a "women's culture" that emphasized the nurturance of children and others and the maintenance of family life and that discouraged women from competition over or heavy emotional investment in demanding, high-paid employment.[3]

I shall not here address this specific debate but, instead, shall consider its theoretical background and implications. I shall argue that we need to fuse, rather than to oppose, the domestic network and labor perspectives. In what follows, I introduce a new concept, the work of kinship, both to aid empirical feminist research on women, work, and family and to help advance feminist theory in this arena. I believe that the boundary-crossing nature of the concept helps to confound the self-interest/altruism dichotomy, forcing us from an either-or stance to a position that includes both perspectives. I hope in this way to contribute to a more critical feminist vision of women's lives and the meaning of family in the industrial West.

In my field research among Italian-Americans in northern California, I found myself considering the relations between women's kinship and economic lives. As an anthropologist, I was concerned with people's kin lives beyond conventional American nuclear family or household boundaries. To this end, I collected individual and family life histories, asking about all kin and close friends and their activities. I was also very interested in women's labor. As I sat with women and listened to their accounts of their past and present lives, I began to realize that they were involved in three types of work: housework and child care, work in the labor market, and the work of kinship.[4]

By kin work I refer to the conception, maintenance, and ritual celebration of cross-household kin ties, including visits, letters, telephone calls, presents, and cards to kin; the organization of holiday gatherings; the creation and maintenance of quasi-kin relations; decisions to neglect or to intensify particular ties; the mental work of reflection about all these activities; and the creation and communication of altering images of family and kin vis-à-vis the images of others, both folk and mass media. Kin work is a key element that has been missing in the synthesis of the "household labor" and "domestic network" perspectives. In our emphasis on individual women's responsibilities within households and on the job, we reflect the common picture of households as nuclear units, tied perhaps to the larger social and economic system, but not to *each other*. We miss the point of telephone and soft drink advertising, of women's magazines' holiday issues, of commentators' confused nostalgia for the mythical American extended family: it is kinship contact *across households*, as much as women's work within them, that fulfills our cultural expectation of satisfying family life.

Maintaining these contacts, this sense of family, takes time, intention, and skill. We tend to think of human social and kin networks as the epiphenomena of production and reproduction: the social traces created by our material lives. Or, in the neoclassical tradition, we see them as part of leisure activities, outside an economic purview except insofar as they involve consumption behavior. But the creation and maintenance of kin and quasi-kin networks in advanced industrial societies is *work*; and, moreover, it is largely women's work.

The kin-work lens brought into focus new perspectives on my informants' family lives. First, life histories revealed that often the very existence of kin contact and holiday celebration depended on the presence of an adult woman in the household. When couples divorced or mothers died, the work of kinship was left undone; when women entered into sanctioned sexual or marital relationships with men in these situations, they reconstituted the men's kinship networks and organized gatherings and holiday celebrations. Middle-aged businessman Al Bertini, for example, recalled the death of his mother in his early adolescence: "I think that's probably one of the biggest losses in losing a family— yeah, I remember as a child when my Mom was alive . . . the holidays were treated with enthusiasm and love . . . after she died the attempt was there but it just didn't materialize." Later in life, when Al Bertini and his wife separated, his own and his son Jim's participation in extended family contact decreased rapidly. But when Jim began a relationship with Jane Bateman, she and he moved in with Al, and Jim and Jane began to invite his kin over for holidays. Jane single handedly planned and cooked the holiday feasts.

Kin work, then, is like housework and child care: men in the aggregate do not do it. It differs from these forms of labor in that it is harder for men to substitute hired labor to accomplish these tasks in the absence of kinswomen. Second, I found that women, as the workers in this arena, generally had much greater kin knowledge than did their husbands, often including more accurate and extensive knowledge of their husbands' families. This was true both of middle-aged and younger couples and surfaced as a phenomenon in my interviews in the form of humorous arguments and in wives' detailed additions to husbands' narratives. Nick Meraviglia, a middle-aged professional, discussed his Italian antecedents in the presence of his wife, Pina:

Nick: My grandfather was a very outspoken man, and it was reported he took off for the hills when he found out that Mussolini was in power.

Pina: And he was a very tall man; he used to have to bow his head to get inside doors.

Nick: No, that was my uncle.

Pina: Your grandfather too, I've heard your mother say.

Nick: My mother has a sister and a brother.

Pina: Two sisters!

Nick: You're right!

Pina: Maria and Angelina.

Women were also much more willing to discuss family feuds and crises and their own roles in them; men tended to repeat formulaic statements asserting family unity and respectability. (This was much less true for younger men.) Joe and Cetta Longhinotti's statements illustrate these tendencies. Joe responded to my question about kin relations: "We all get along. As a rule, relatives, you got nothing but trouble." Cetta, instead, discussed her relations with each of her grown children, their wives, her in-laws, and her own blood kin in detail. She did not hide the fact that relations were strained in several cases; she was eager to discuss the evolution of problems and to seek my opinions of her actions. Similarly, Pina Meraviglia told the following story of her fight with one of her brothers with hysterical laughter: "There was some biting and hair pulling and choking . . . it was terrible! I shouldn't even tell you. . . ." Nick, meanwhile, was concerned about maintaining an image of family unity and respectability.

Also, men waxed fluent while women were quite inarticulate in discussing their past and present occupations. When asked about their work lives, Joe Longhinotti and Nick Meraviglia, union baker and professional, respectively, gave detailed narratives of their work careers. Cetta Longhinotti and Pina Meraviglia, clerical and former clerical, respectively, offered only short descriptions focusing on factors of ambience, such as the "lovely things" sold by Cetta's firm.

These patterns are not repeated in the younger generation, especially among young women, such as Jane Bateman, who have managed to acquire training and jobs with some prospect of mobility. These younger women, though, have *added* a professional and detailed interest in their jobs to a felt responsibility for the work of kinship.[5]

Although men rarely took on any kin-work tasks, family histories and accounts of contemporary life revealed that kinswomen often negotiated among themselves, alternating hosting, food-preparation, and gift-buying responsibilities—or sometimes ceding entire task clusters to one woman. Taking on or ceding tasks was clearly related to acquiring or divesting oneself of power within kin networks, but women varied in their interpretation of the meaning of this power. Cetta Longhinotti, for example, relied on the "family Christmas dinner" as a symbol of her central kinship role and was involved in painful negotiations with her daughter-in-law over the issue: "Last year she insisted—this is touchy. She doesn't want to spend the holiday dinner together. So last year we went there. But I still had my dinner the next day. . . . I made a big dinner on Christmas Day, regardless of who's coming—

candles on the table, the whole routine. I decorate the house myself too. . . . well, I just feel that the time will come when maybe I won't feel like cooking a big dinner—she should take advantage of the fact that I feel like doing it now." Pina Meraviglia, in contrast, was saddened by the centripetal force of the developmental cycle but was unworried about the power dynamics involved in her negotiations with daughters- and mother-in-law over holiday celebrations.

Kin work is not just a matter of power among women but also of the mediation of power represented by household units.[6] Women often choose to minimize status claims in their kin work and to include numbers of households under the rubric of family. Cetta Longhinotti's sister Anna, for example, is married to a professional man whose parents have considerable economic resources, while Joe and Cetta have low incomes and no other well-off kin. Cetta and Anna remain close, talk on the phone several times a week, and assist their adult children, divided by distance and economic status, in remaining united as cousins.

Finally, women perceived housework, child care, market labor, the care of the elderly, and the work of kinship as competing responsibilities. Kin work was a unique category, however, because it was unlabeled and because women felt they could either cede some tasks to kinswomen and/or could cut them back severely. Women variously cited the pressures of market labor, the needs of the elderly, and their own desires for freedom and job enrichment as reasons for cutting back Christmas card lists, organized holiday gatherings, multifamily dinners, letters, visits, and phone calls. They expressed guilt and defensiveness about this cutback process and, particularly, about their failures to keep families close through constant contact and about their failures to create perfect holiday celebrations. Cetta Longhinotti, during the period when she was visiting her elderly mother every weekend in addition to working a full-time job, said of her grown children, "I'd have the whole gang here once a month, but I've been so busy that I haven't done that for about six months." And Pina Meraviglia lamented her insufficient work on family Christmases, "I wish I had really made it traditional . . . like my sister-in-law has special stories."

Kin work, then, takes place in an arena characterized simultaneously by cooperation and competition, by guilt and gratification. Like housework and child care, it is women's work, with the same lack of clear-cut agreement concerning its proper components: How often should sheets be changed? When should children be toilet trained? Should an aunt send a niece a birthday present? Unlike housework and child care, however, kin work, taking place across the boundaries of normative households, is as yet unlabeled and has no retinue of experts prescribing its correct forms. Neither home economists nor child psychologists have much to say about nieces' birthday presents. Kin work is thus more easily cut back without social interference. On the other hand, the results of kin work—frequent kin contact and feelings of intimacy—are the subject of considerable cultural manipulation as indicators of family happiness. Thus, women in general are subject to the guilt my informants expressed over cutting back kin-work activities.

Although many of my informants referred to the results of women's kin work—cross-household kin contacts and attendant ritual gatherings—as particularly Italian-American, I suggest that in fact this phenomenon is broadly characteristic of American kinship. We think of kin-work tasks such as the preparation of ritual feasts, responsibility for holiday card lists, and gift buying as extensions of women's domestic responsibilities for cooking, consumption, and nurturance. American men in general do not take on these tasks any more than they do housework and child care—and probably less, as these tasks have not yet been the subject of intense public debate. And my informants' gender breakdown in relative articulateness on kinship and workplace themes reflects the still prevalent occupational segregation—most women cannot find jobs that provide enough pay, status, or promotion possibilities to make them worth focusing on —as well as women's perceived power within kinship networks. The common recognition of that power is reflected in Selma Greenberg's book on nonsexist child rearing. Greenberg calls mothers "press agents" who sponsor relations between their own children and other relatives; she advises a mother whose relatives treat her disrespectfully to deny those kin access to her children.[7]

Kin work is a salient concept in other parts of the developed world as well. Larissa Adler Lomnitz and Marisol Pérez Lizaur have found that "centralizing women" are responsible for these tasks and for communicating "family ideology" among upper-class families in Mexico City. Matthews Hamabata, in his study of upper-class families in Japan, has found that women's kin work involves key financial transactions. Sylvia Junko Yanagisako discovered that among rural Japanese migrants to the United States the maintenance of kin networks was assigned to women as the migrants adopted the American ideology of the independent nuclear family household. Maila Stivens notes that urban Australian housewives' kin ties and kin ideology "transcend women's isolation in domestic units."[8]

This is not to say that cultural conceptions of appropriate kin work do not vary, even within the United States. Carol B. Stack documents institutionalized fictive kinship and concomitant reciprocity networks among impoverished black American women. Women in populations characterized by intense feelings of ethnic identity may feel bound to emphasize particular occasions—Saint Patrick's or Columbus Day—with organized family feasts. These constructs may be mediated by religious affiliation, as in the differing emphases on Friday or Sunday family dinners among Jews and Christians. Thus the personnel involved and the amount and kind of labor considered necessary for the satisfactory performance of particular kin-work tasks are likely to be culturally constructed.[9] But while the kin and quasi-kin universes and the ritual calendar may vary among women according to race or ethnicity, their general responsibility for maintaining kin links and ritual observances does not.

As kin work is not an ethnic or racial phenomenon, neither is it linked only to one social class. Some commentators on American family life still reflect the influence of work done in England in the 1950s and 1960s (by Elizabeth Bott and by Peter Willmott and Michael Young) in their assumption that working-class families are close and extended, while the middle class substitutes friends (or anomie) for family. Others reflect the prevalent family pessimism in their presumption that neither working- nor middle-class families have extended kin contact.[10] Insofar as kin contact depends on residential proximity, the larger economy's shifts will influence particular groups' experiences. Factory workers, close to kin or not, are likely to disperse when plants shut down or relocate. Small businesspeople or independent professionals may, however, remain resident in particular areas—and thus maintain proximity to kin—for generations, while professional employees of large firms relocate at their firms' behest. This pattern obtained among my informants.

In any event, cross-household kin contact can be and is affected at long distance through letters, cards, phone calls, and holiday and vacation visits. The form and functions of contact, however, vary according to economic resources. Stack and Brett Williams offer rich accounts of kin networks among poor blacks and migrant Chicano farmworkers functioning to provide emotional support, labor, commodity, and cash exchange—a funeral visit, help with laundry, the gift of a dress or piece of furniture.[11] Far different in degree are exchanges such as the loan of a vacation home, a multifamily boating trip, or the provision of free professional services—examples from the kin networks of my wealthier informants. The point is that households, as labor- and income-pooling units, whatever their relative wealth, are somewhat porous in relation to others with whose members they share kin or quasi-kin ties. We do not really know how class differences operate in this realm; it is possible that they do so largely in terms of ideology. It may be, as David Schneider and Raymond T. Smith suggest, that the affluent and the very poor are more open in recognizing necessary economic ties to kin than are those who identify themselves as middle class.[12]

Recognizing that kin work is gender rather than class based allows us to see women's kin networks among all groups, not just among working-class and impoverished women in industrialized societies. This recognition in turn clarifies our understanding of the privileges and limits of women's varying access to economic resources. Affluent women can "buy out" of housework, child care—and even some kin-work responsibilities. But they, like all women, are ultimately responsible, and subject to both guilt and blame, as the administrators of home, children, and kin network. Even the wealthiest women must negotiate the timing and venue of holidays and other family rituals with their kinswomen. It may be that kin work is the core women's work category in which all women cooperate, while women's perceptions of the appropriateness of cooperation for housework, child care, and the care of the elderly varies by race, class, region, and generation.

But kin work is not necessarily an appropriate category of labor, much less gendered labor, in all societies. In many small-scale societies, kinship is the major organizing principle of all social life, and all contacts are by definition kin contacts.[13] One cannot, therefore, speak of labor that does not involve kin. In the United States, kin work as a separable category of gendered labor perhaps arose historically in concert with the ideological and material constructs of the moral mother/cult of domesticity and the privatized family during the course of industrialization in the eighteenth and nineteenth centuries. These phenomena are connected to the increase in the ubiquity of productive occupations *for men* that are not organized through kinship. This includes the demise of the family farm with the capitalization of agriculture and rural-urban migration; the decline of family recruitment in factories as firms grew, ended child labor, and began to assert bureaucratized forms of control; the decline of artisanal labor and of small entrepreneurial enterprises as large firms took greater and greater shares of the commodity market; the decline of the family firm as corporations—and their managerial workforces—grew beyond the capacities of individual families to provision them; and, finally, the rise of civil service bureaucracies and public pressure against nepotism.[14]

As men increasingly worked alongside of non-kin, and as the ideology of separate spheres was increasingly accepted, perhaps the responsibility for kin maintenance, like for child rearing, became gender-focused. Ryan points out that "built into the updated family economy . . . was a new measure of voluntarism." This voluntarism, though, "per-ceived as the shift from patriarchal authority to domestic affection," also signaled the rise of women's moral responsibility for family life. Just as the "idea of fatherhood itself seemed almost to wither away" so did male involvement in the responsibility for kindred lapse.[15]

With postbellum economic growth and geographic movement, women's new kin burden involved increasing amounts of time and labor. The ubiquity of lengthy visits and of frequent letter-writing among nineteenth-century women attests to this. And for visitors and for those who were residentially proximate, the continuing commonalities of women's domestic labor allowed for kinds of work sharing—nursing, childkeeping, cooking, cleaning—that men, with their increasingly differentiated and controlled activities, probably could not maintain. This is not to say that some kin-related male productive work did not continue; my own data, for instance, show kin involvement among small businessmen in the present. It is, instead, to suggest a general trend in material life and a cultural shift that influenced even those whose productive and kin lives remained commingled. Yanagisako has distinguished between the realms of domestic and public kinship in order to draw attention to anthropology's relatively "thin descriptions" of the domestic (female) domain. Using her typology, we might say that kin work as gendered labor comes into existence within the domestic domain with the relative erasure of the domain of public, male kinship.[16]

Whether or not this proposed historical model bears up under further research, the question remains. Why do women do kin work? However material factors may shape activities, they do not determine how individuals may perceive them. And in considering issues of motivation, of intention, of the cultural construction of kin work, we return to the altruism versus self-interest dichotomy in recent feminist theory. Consider the epigraphs to this article. Are women kin workers the nurturant weavers of the Gilligan quotation, or victims, like the fed-up woman who writes to complain to Ann Landers? That is, are we to see kin work as yet another example of "women's culture" that takes the care of others as its primary desideratum? Or are we to see kin work as another way in which men, the economy, and the state extract labor from women without a fair return? And how do women themselves see their kin work and its place in their lives?

As I have indicated above, I believe that it is the creation of the self-interest/altruism dichotomy that is itself the problem here. My women informants, like most American women, accepted their primary responsibility for housework and the care of dependent children. Despite two major waves of feminist activism in this century, the gendering of certain categories of unpaid labor is still largely unaltered. These work responsibilities clearly interfere with some women's labor force commitments at certain life-cycle stages; but, more important, women are simply discriminated against in the labor market and rarely are able to achieve wage and status parity with men of the same age, race, class, and educational background.[17]

Thus for women informants, as for most American women, the domestic domain is not only an arena in which much unpaid labor must be undertaken but also a realm in which one may attempt to gain human satisfactions—and power—not available in the labor market. Anthropologists Jane Collier and Louise Lamphere have written compellingly on the ways in which varying kinship and economic structures may shape women's competition or cooperation with one another in domestic domains.[18] Feminists considering Western women and families have looked at the issue of power primarily in terms of husband-wife relations or psychological relations between parents and children. If we adopt Collier and Lamphere's broader canvas, though, we see that kin work is not only women's labor from which men and children benefit but also labor that women undertake in order to create obligations in men and children and to gain power over one another. Thus Cetta Longhinotti's struggle with her daughter-in-law over the venue of Christmas dinner is not just about a competition over altruism, it is also about the creation of future obligations. And thus Cetta's and Anna's sponsorship and their children's friendship with each other is both an act of nurturance and a cooperative means of gaining power over those children.

Although this was not a clear-cut distinction, those of my informants who were more explicitly antifeminist tended to be most invested in kin work. Given the overwhelming historical shift toward greater autonomy for younger generations and the withering of children's financial and labor obligations to their parents, this investment was in most cases tragically doomed. Cetta Longhinotti, for example, had repaid her own mother's devotion with extensive home nursing during the mother's last years. Given Cetta's general failure to direct her adult children in work, marital choice, religious worship, or even frequency of visits, she is unlikely to receive such care from them when she is older.

The kin-work lens thus reveals the close relations between altruism and self-interest in women's actions. As economists Nancy Folbre and Heidi Hartmann point out, we have inherited a Western intellectual tradition that both dichotomizes the domestic and public domains and associates them on exclusive axes such that we find it difficult to see self-interest in the home and altruism in the workplace.[19] But why, in fact, have women fought for better jobs if not, in part, to support their children? These dichotomies are Procrustean beds that warp our understanding of women's lives both at home and at work. "Altruism" and "self-interest" are cultural constructions that are not necessarily mutually exclusive, and we forget this to our peril.

The concept of kin work helps to bring into focus a heretofore unacknowledged array of tasks that is culturally assigned to women in industrialized societies. At the same time, this concept, embodying notions of both love and work and crossing the boundaries of households, helps us to reflect on current feminist debates on women's work, family, and community. We newly see both the interrelations of these phenomena and women's roles in creating and maintaining those interrelations. Revealing the actual labor embodied in what we culturally conceive as love and considering the political uses of this labor helps to deconstruct the self-interest/altruism dichotomy and to connect more closely women's domestic and labor-force lives.

The true value of the concept, however, remains to be tested through further historical and contemporary research on gender, kinship, and labor. We need to assess the suggestion that gendered kin work emerges in concert with the capitalist development process; to probe the historical record for women's and men's varying and changing conceptions of it; and to research the current range of its cultural constructions and material realities. We know that household boundaries are more porous than we had thought—but they are undoubtedly differentially porous, and this is what we need to specify. We need, in particular, to assess the relations of changing labor processes, residential patterns, and the use of technology to changing kin work.

Altering the values attached to this particular set of women's tasks will be as difficult as are the housework, child-care, and occupational- segregation struggles. But just as feminist research in these latter areas is complementary and cumulative, so researching kin work should help us to piece together the home, work, and public-life landscape—to see the female world of cards and holidays as it is constructed and lived within the changing political economy. How female that world is to remain, and what it would look like if it were not sex-segregated, are questions we cannot yet answer.

NOTES

Acknowledgments: Many thanks to Cynthia Costello, Rayna Rapp, Roberta Spalter-Roth, John Willoughby, and Barbara Gelpi, Susan Johnson, and Sylvia Yanagisako of *Signs* for their help with this chapter. I wish in particular to acknowledge the influence of Rayna Rapp's work on my ideas. Acknowledgment and gratitude also to Carroll Smith-Rosenberg for my paraphrase of her title, "The Female World of Love and Ritual: Relations Between Women in Nineteenth-Century America," *Signs: Journal of Women in Culture and Society* 1, no. 1 (Autumn 1975): 1–29. The epigraphs are from Ann Landers letter printed in *Washington Post* (April 15, 1983); Carol Gilligan, *In a Different Voice* (Cambridge, Mass.: Harvard University Press, 1982), 17.

1. Heidi I. Hartmann, "The Family as the Locus of Gender, Class, and Political Struggle: The Example of Housework," *Signs* 6, no. 3 (Spring 1981): 366–94; and Christopher Lasch, *Haven in a Heartless World: The Family Besieged* (New York: Basic Books, 1977).

2. Representative examples of the first trend include Joann Vanek, "Time Spent on Housework," *Scientific American* 231 (November 1974): 116–20; Ruth Schwartz Cowan, "A Case Study of Technological and Social Change: The Washing Machine and the Working Wife," in *Clio's Consciousness Raised*, ed. Mary Hartmann and Lois Banner (New York: Harper & Row, 1974), 245–53; Ann Oakley, *Women's Work: The Housewife, Past and Present* (New York: Vintage, 1974); Hartmann; and Susan

Strasser, *Never Done: A History of American Housework* (New York: Pantheon Books, 1982). Key contributions to the second trend include Louise Lamphere, "Strategies, Cooperation and Conflict Among Women in Domestic Groups," in *Women, Culture and Society,* ed. Michelle Zimbalist Rosaldo and Louise Lamphere (Stanford, Calif.: Stanford University Press, 1974), 97–112; Mina Davis Caulfield, "Imperialism, the Family and the Cultures of Resistance," *Socialist Revolution* 20 (October 1974): 67–85; Smith-Rosenberg; Sylvia Junko Yanagisako, "Women-Centered Kin Networks and Urban Bilateral Kinship," *American Ethnologist* 4, no. 2 (1977): 207–26; Jane Humphries, "The Working Class Family, Women's Liberation and Class Struggle: The Case of Nineteenth Century British History," *Review of Radical Political Economics* 9 (Fall 1977): 25–41; Blanche Weisen Cook, "Female Support Networks and Political Activism: Lillian Wald, Crystal Eastman, Emma Goldman," in *A Heritage of Her Own,* ed. Nancy F. Cott and Elizabeth H. Pleck (New York: Simon & Schuster, 1979); Temma Kaplan, "Female Consciousness and Collective Action: The Case of Barcelona, 1910–1918," *Signs* 7, no. 3 (Spring 1982): 545–66.

3. On this debate, see Jon Weiner, "Women's History on Trial," *Nation* 241, no. 6 (September 7, 1985): 161, 176, 178–80; Karen J. Winkler, "Two Scholars' Conflict in Sears Sex-Bias Case Sets Off War in Women's History," *Chronicle of Higher Education* (February 5, 1986), 1, 8; Rosalind Rosenberg, "What Harms Women in the Workplace," *New York Times* (February 27, 1986); Alice Kessler-Harris, "Equal Employment Opportunity Commission vs. Sears Roebuck and Company: A Personal Account," *Radical History Review* 35 (April 1986): 57–79.

4. Portions of the following analysis are reported in Micaela di Leonardo, *The Varieties of Ethnic Experience: Kinship, Class and Gender Among California Italian-Americans* (Ithaca, N.Y.: Cornell University Press, 1984), chap. 6.

5. Clearly, many women do, in fact, discuss their paid labor with willingness and clarity. The point here is that there are opposing gender tendencies in an identical interview situation, tendencies that are explicable in terms of both the material realities and current cultural constructions of gender.

6. Papanek has rightly focused on women's unacknowledged family status production, but what is conceived of as "family" shifts and varies (Hanna Papanek, "Family Status Production: The 'Work' and 'Non-Work' of Women," *Signs* 4, no. 4 [Summer 1979]: 775–81).

7. Selma Greenberg, *Right from the Start: A Guide to Nonsexist Child Rearing* (Boston: Houghton Mifflin Co., 1978), 147. Another example of indirect support for kin work's gendered existence is a recent study of university math students, which found that a major reason for women's failure to pursue careers in mathematics was the pressure of family involvement. Compare David Maines et al., *Social Processes of Sex Differentiation in Mathematics* (Washington, D.C.: National Institute of Education, 1981).

8. Larissa Adler Lomnitz and Marisol Pérez Lizaur, "The History of a Mexican Urban Family," *Journal of Family History* 3, no. 4 (1978): 392–409, esp. 398; Sylvia Junko Yanagisako, "Two Processes of Change in Japanese-American Kinship," *Journal of Anthropological Research* 31 (1975): 196–224; Maila Stivens, "Women and Their Kin: Kin, Class and Solidarity in a Middle-Class Suburb of Sydney, Australia," in *Women United, Women Divided,* ed. Patricia Caplan and Janet M. Bujra (Bloomington: Indiana University Press, 1979), 157–84.

9. Carol B. Stack, *All Our Kin: Strategies for Survival in a Black Community* (New York: Harper & Row, 1974). These cultural constructions may, however, vary within ethnic-racial populations as well.

10. Elizabeth Bott, *Family and Social Network,* 2d ed. (New York: Free Press, 1971); Michael Young and Peter Willmott, *Family and Kinship in East London* (London: Routledge & Kegan Paul, 1957), and *Family and Class in a London Suburb* (London: Routledge & Kegan Paul, 1960). Classic studies that presume this class difference are Herbert Gans, *The Urban Villagers: Group and Class in the Life of Italian-Americans* (New York: Free Press, 1962); and Mirra Komarovsky, *Blue-Collar Marriage* (New York: Random House, 1962). A recent example is Ilene Philipson, "Heterosexual Antagonisms and the Politics of Mothering," *Socialist Review* 12, no. 6 (November–December 1982): 55–77. Edward Shorter, *The Making of the Modern Family* (New York: Basic Books, 1975), epitomizes the pessimism

of the "family sentiments" school. See also Mary Lyndon Shanley, "The History of the Family in Modern England: Review Essay," *Signs* 4, no. 4 (Summer 1979): 740–50.

11. Stack; and Brett Williams, "The Trip Takes Us: Chicano Migrants to the Prairie" (Ph.D. diss., University of Illinois at Urbana-Champaign, 1975).

12. David Schneider and Raymond T. Smith, *Class Differences and Sex Roles in American Kinship and Family Structure* (Englewood Cliffs, N.J.: Prentice-Hall, 1973), esp. 27.

13. See Nelson Graburn, ed., *Readings in Kinship and Social Structure* (New York: Harper & Row, 1971), esp. 3–4.

14. The moral mother/cult of domesticity is analyzed in Barbara Welter, "The Cult of True Womanhood, 1820–1860," *American Quarterly* 18, no. 2 (Summer 1966): 151–74; Nancy Cott, *The Bonds of Womanhood: "Women's Sphere" in New England, 1780–1835* (New Haven, Conn.: Yale University Press, 1977); and Ruth Bloch, "American Feminine Ideals in Transition: The Rise of the Moral Mother, 1785–1815," *Feminist Studies* 4, no. 2 (June 1978): 101–26. The description of the general political-economic shift in the United States is based on Harry Braverman, *Labor and Monopoly Capital: The Degradation of Work in the Twentieth Century* (New York: Monthly Review Press, 1974); Peter Dobkin Hall, "Family Structure and Economic Organization: Massachusetts Merchants, 1700–1850," in *Family and Kin in Urban Communities, 1700–1950*, ed. Tamara K. Hareven (New York: New View-

points, 1977), 38–61; Michael Anderson, "Family, Household and the Industrial Revolution," in *The American Family in Social-Historical Perspective*, ed. Michael Gordon (New York: St. Martin's Press, 1978), 38–50; Tamara K. Hareven, *Amoskeag: Life and Work in an American Factory City* (New York: Pantheon Books, 1978); Richard Edwards, *Contested Terrain: The Transformation of the Workplace in the Twentieth Century* (New York: Basic Books, 1979); Mary Ryan, *The Cradle of the Middle Class: The Family in Oneida County, New York, 1790–1865* (Cambridge: Cambridge University Press, 1981); Alice Kessler-Harris, *Out to Work: A History of Wage-Earning Women in the United States* (New York: Oxford University Press, 1982).

15. Ryan, 231–32.

16. Sylvia Junko Yanagisako, "Family and Household: The Analysis of Domestic Groups," *Annual Review of Anthropology* 8 (1979): 161–205.

17. See Donald J. Treiman and Heidi I. Hartmann, eds., *Women, Work and Wages: Equal Pay for Jobs of Equal Value* (Washington, D.C.: National Academy Press, 1981).

18. Lamphere (n. 2 above); Jane Fishburne Collier, "Women in Politics," in Rosaldo and Lamphere, eds. (n. 2 above), 89–96.

19. Nancy Folbre and Heidi I. Hartmann, "The Rhetoric of Self-Interest: Selfishness, Altruism, and Gender in Economic Theory," in *The Consequences of Economic Rhetoric*, ed. Arjo Klamer, Donald McCloskey, and Robert M. Solow (New York: Cambridge University Press, 1988).

Chapter 32

Fictive Kin, Paper Sons, and *Compadrazgo:* Women of Color and the Struggle for Family Survival

BONNIE THORNTON DILL

Race has been fundamental to the construction of families in the United States since the country was settled. People of color were incorporated into the country and used to meet the need for cheap and exploitable labor. Little attention was given to their family and community life except as it related to their economic productivity. Upon their founding, the various colonies that ultimately formed the United States initiated legal, economic, political, and social practices designed to promote the growth of family life among European colonists. As the primary laborers in the reproduction and maintenance of families, White[1] women settlers were accorded the privileges and protection considered socially appropriate to their family roles. The structure of family life during this era was strongly patriarchal: denying women many rights, constraining their personal autonomy, and making them subject to the almost unfettered will of the male head of the household. Nevertheless, women were rewarded and protected within patriarchal families because their labor was recognized as essential to the maintenance and sustenance of family life.[2] In addition, families were seen as the cornerstone of an incipient nation, and thus their existence was a matter of national interest.

In contrast, women of color experienced the oppression of a patriarchal society but were denied the protection and buffering of a patriarchal family. Although the presence of women of color was equally important to the growth of the nation, their value was based on their potential as workers, breeders, and entertainers of workers, not as family members. In the eighteenth and nineteenth centuries, labor, and not the existence or maintenance of families, was the critical aspect of their role in building the nation. Thus they were denied

From Maxine Baca Zinn and Bonnie Thornton Dill, eds., *Women of Color in U.S. Society* (Philadelphia: Temple University Press, 1994). Portions of this chapter were previously published under the title "Our Mothers' Grief: Racial-Ethnic Women and the Maintenance of Families," pp. 415–31 in *Journal of Family History* 13, no. 4 (1988), copyright © 1988 by Sage Publications. Reprinted by permission of Sage Publications, Inc.

the societal supports necessary to make their families a vital element in the social order. For women of color, family membership was not a key means of access to participation in the wider society. In some instances racial-ethnic families were seen as a threat to the efficiency and exploitability of the workforce and were actively prohibited. In other cases, they were tolerated when it was felt they might help solidify or expand the workforce. The lack of social, legal, and economic support for the family life of people of color intensified and extended women's work, created tensions and strains in family relationships, and set the stage for a variety of creative and adaptive forms of resistance.

African American Slaves

Among students of slavery, there has been considerable debate over the relative "harshness" of American slavery, and the degree to which slaves were permitted or encouraged to form families. It is generally acknowledged that many slave owners found it economically advantageous to encourage family formation as a way of reproducing and perpetuating the slave labor force. This became increasingly true after 1807, when the importation of African slaves was explicitly prohibited. The existence of these families and many aspects of their functioning, however, were directly controlled by the master. Slaves married and formed families, but these groupings were completely subject to the master's decision to let them remain intact. One study has estimated that about 32 percent of all recorded slave marriages were disrupted by sale, about 45 percent by death of a spouse, about 10 percent by choice, and only 13 percent were not disrupted (Blassingame 1972). African slaves thus quickly learned that they had a limited degree of control over the formation and

maintenance of their marriages and could not be assured of keeping their children with them. The threat of disruption was one of the most direct and pervasive assaults on families that slaves encountered. Yet there were a number of other aspects of the slave system that reinforced the precariousness of slave family life.

In contrast to some African traditions and the Euro-American patterns of the period, slave men were not the main providers or authority figures in the family. The mother-child tie was basic and of greatest interest to the slave owner because it was essential to the reproduction of the labor force.

In addition to the lack of authority and economic autonomy experienced by the husband-father in the slave family, use of rape of women slaves as a weapon of terror and control further undermined the integrity of the slave family.

> It would be a mistake to regard the institutionalized pattern of rape during slavery as an expression of white men's sexual urges, otherwise stifled by the spector of the white womanhood's chastity. . . . Rape was a weapon of domination, a weapon of repression, whose covert goal was to extinguish slave women's will to resist, and in the process, to demoralize their men. (Davis 1981, 23–24)

The slave family, therefore, was at the heart of a peculiar tension in the master-slave relationship. On the one hand, slave owners sought to encourage familiarities among slaves because, as Julie Matthaei (1982, 81) states, "These provided the basis of the development of the slave into a self-conscious socialized human being." They also hoped and believed that this socialization process would help children learn to accept their place in society as slaves. Yet the master's need to control and intervene in the family life of the slaves is indicative of the other side of this tension. Family ties had the potential to become a competing and more potent source of allegiance than the master. Also, kin were as likely to socialize children in forms of resistance as in acts of compliance.

It was within this context of surveillance, assault, and ambivalence that slave women's reproductive labor[3] took place. They and their menfolk had the task of preserving the human and family ties that could ultimately give them a reason for living. They had to socialize their children to believe in the possibility of a life in which they were not enslaved. The slave woman's labor on behalf of the family was, as Angela Davis (1971) has pointed out, the only labor in which the slave engaged that could not be directly used by the slave owner for his own profit. Yet, it was crucial to the reproduction of the slave owner's labor force, and thus a source of strong ambivalence for many slave women. Whereas some mothers murdered their babies to keep them from being slaves, many sought autonomy and creativity within the family that was denied them in other realms of the society. The maintenance of a distinct African American culture is testimony to the ways in which slaves maintained a degree of cultural autonomy and resisted the creation of a slave family that only served the needs of the master.

Herbert Gutman (1976) gives evidence of the ways slaves expressed a unique African American culture through their family practices. He provides data on naming patterns and kinship ties among slaves that fly in the face of the dominant ideology of the period, which argued that slaves were immoral and had little concern for or appreciation of family life. Yet Gutman demonstrates that within a system that denied the father authority over his family, slave boys were frequently named after their fathers, and many children were named after blood relatives as a way of maintaining family ties. Gutman also suggests that

after emancipation a number of slaves took the names of former owners in order to reestablish family ties that had been disrupted earlier. On plantation after plantation, Gutman found considerable evidence of the building and maintenance of extensive kinship ties among slaves. In instances where slave families had been disrupted, slaves in new communities reconstituted the kinds of family and kin ties that came to characterize Black family life throughout the South. The patterns included, but were not limited to, a belief in the importance of marriage as a long-term commitment, rules of exogamy that excluded marriage between first cousins, and acceptance of women who had children outside of marriage. Kinship networks were an important source of resistance to the organization of labor that treated the individual slave, and not the family, as the unit of labor (Caulfield 1974).

Another interesting indicator of the slaves' maintenance of some degree of cultural autonomy has been pointed out by Gwendolyn Wright (1981) in her discussion of slave housing. Until the early 1800s, slaves were often permitted to build their housing according to their own design and taste. During that period, housing built in an African style was quite common in the slave quarters. By 1830, however, slave owners had begun to control the design and arrangement of slave housing and had introduced a degree of conformity and regularity to it that left little room for the slaves' personalization of the home. Nevertheless, slaves did use some of their own techniques in construction, often hiding them from their masters.

Even the floors, which usually consisted of only tamped earth, were evidence of a hidden African tradition: slaves cooked clay over a fire, mixing in ox blood or cow dung, and then poured it in place to make hard dirt floors almost like asphalt. . . . In slave houses, in contrast to other crafts, these signs of skill and tradition would then be covered over. (Wright 1981, 48)

Housing is important in discussions of family because its design reflects sociocultural attitudes about family life. The housing that slave owners provided for their slaves reflected a view of Black family life consistent with the stereotypes of the period. While the existence of slave families was acknowledged, they certainly were not nurtured. Thus, cabins were crowded, often containing more than one family, and there were no provisions for privacy. Slaves had to create their own.

> Slave couples hung up old clothes or quilts to establish boundaries; others built more substantial partitions from scrap wood. Parents sought to establish sexual privacy from children. A few ex-slaves described modified trundle beds designed to hide parental lovemaking. . . . Even in one room cabins, sexual segregation was carefully organized. (Wright 1981, 50)

Perhaps most critical in developing an understanding of slave women's reproductive labor is the gender-based division of labor in the domestic sphere. The organization of slave labor enforced considerable equality among men and women. The ways in which equality in the labor force was translated into the family sphere is somewhat speculative. Davis (1981, 18), for example, suggests that egalitarianism between males and females was a direct result of slavery: "Within the confines of their family and community life, therefore, Black people managed to accomplish a magnificent feat. They transformed that negative equality which emanated from the equal oppression they suffered as slaves into a positive quality; the egalitarianism characterizing their social relations."

It is likely, however, that this transformation was far less direct than Davis implies. We know, for example, that slave women experienced what has recently been called the "dou-

ble day" before most other women in this society. Slave narratives (Jones 1985; White 1985; Blassingame 1977) reveal that women had primary responsibility for their family's domestic chores. They cooked (although on some plantations meals were prepared for all the slaves), sewed, cared for their children, and cleaned house after completing a full day of labor for the master. John Blassingame (1972) and others have pointed out that slave men engaged in hunting, trapping, perhaps some gardening, and furniture making as ways of contributing to the maintenance of their families. Clearly, a gender-based division of labor did exist within the family, and it appears that women bore the larger share of the burden for housekeeping and child care.

In contrast to White families of the period, however, the division of labor in the domestic sphere was reinforced neither in the relationship of slave women to work nor in the social institutions of the slave community. The gender-based division of labor among the slaves existed within a social system that treated men and women as almost equal, independent units of labor.[4] Thus Matthaei (1982, 94) is probably correct in concluding that

> whereas . . . the white homemaker interacted with the public sphere through her husband, and had her work life determined by him, the enslaved Afro-American homemaker was directly subordinated to and determined by her owner. . . . The equal enslavement of husband and wife gave the slave marriage a curious kind of equality, an equality of oppression.

Black men were denied the male resources of a patriarchal society and therefore were unable to turn gender distinctions into female subordination, even if that had been their desire. Black women, on the other hand, were denied support and protection for their roles as mothers and wives, and thus had to modify and structure those roles around the demands of their labor. Reproductive labor for slave women was intensified in several ways: by the demands of slave labor that forced them into the double day of work; by the desire and need to maintain family ties in the face of a system that gave them only limited recognition; by the stresses of building a family with men who were denied the standard social privileges of manhood; and by the struggle to raise children who could survive in a hostile environment.

This intensification of reproductive labor made networks of kin and fictive kin important instruments in carrying out the reproductive tasks of the slave community. Given an African cultural heritage where kinship ties formed the basis of social relations, is is not at all surprising that African American slaves developed an extensive system of kinship ties and obligations (Gutman 1976; Sudarkasa 1981). Research on Black families in slavery provides considerable documentation of participation of extended kin in child rearing, childbirth, and other domestic, social, and economic activities (Gutman 1976; Blassingame 1972; Genovese and Miller 1974).

After slavery, these ties continued to be an important factor linking individual household units in a variety of domestic activities. While kinship ties were also important among native-born Whites and European immigrants, Gutman (1976, 213) has suggested that these ties

> were comparatively more important to Afro-Americans than to lower-class native white and immigrant Americans, the result of their distinctive low economic status, a condition that denied them the advantages of an extensive associational life beyond the kin group and the advantages and disadvantages resulting from mobility opportunities.

His argument is reaffirmed by research on African American families after slavery

(Shimkin et al. 1978; Aschenbrenner 1975; Davis 1981; Stack 1974). Niara Sudarkasa (1981) takes this argument one step further, linking this pattern to the African cultural heritage.

> Historical realities require that the derivation of this aspect of Black family organization be traced to its African antecedents. Such a view does not deny the adaptive significance of consanguineal networks. In fact, it helps to clarify why these networks had the flexibility they had and why they, rather than conjugal relationships, came to be the stabilizing factor in Black families.

In individual households, the gender-based division of labor experienced some important shifts during emancipation. In their first real opportunity to establish family life beyond the controls and constraints imposed by a slave master, Black sharecroppers' family life changed radically. Most women, at least those who were wives and daughters of able-bodied men, withdrew from field labor and concentrated on their domestic duties in the home. Husbands took primary responsibility for the fieldwork and for relations with the owners, such as signing contracts on behalf of the family. Black women were severely criticized by Whites for removing themselves from field labor because they were seen to be aspiring to a model of womanhood that was considered inappropriate for them. The reorganization of female labor, however, represented an attempt on the part of Blacks to protect women from some of the abuses of the slave system and to thus secure their family life. It was more likely a response to the particular set of circumstances that the newly freed slaves faced than a reaction to the lives of their former masters. Jacqueline Jones (1985) argues that these patterns were "particularly significant" because at a time when industrial development was introducing a labor system that divided male and female labor, the freed Black family was establishing a pattern of joint work and complementarity of tasks between males and females that was reminiscent of preindustrial American families. Unfortunately, these former slaves had to do this without the institutional supports given white farm families and within a sharecropping system that deprived them of economic independence.

Chinese Sojourners

An increase in the African slave population was a desired goal. Therefore, Africans were permitted and even encouraged at times to form families, as long as they were under the direct control of the slave master. By sharp contrast, Chinese people were explicitly denied the right to form families in the United States through both law and social practice. Although male laborers began coming to the United States in sizable numbers in the middle of the nineteenth century, it was more than a century before an appreciable number of children of Chinese parents were born in America. Tom, a respondent in Victor Nee and Brett de Bary Nee's book, *Longtime Californ'*, says: "One thing about Chinese men in America was you had to be either a merchant or a big gambler, have a lot of side money to have a family here. A working man, an ordinary man, just can't!" (1973, 80).

Working in the United States was a means of gaining support for one's family with an end of obtaining sufficient capital to return to China and purchase land. This practice of sojourning was reinforced by laws preventing Chinese laborers from becoming citizens, and by restrictions on their entry into this country. Chinese laborers who arrived before 1882 could not bring their wives and were prevented by law from marrying Whites. Thus, it

is likely that the number of Chinese American families might have been negligible had it not been for two things: the San Francisco earthquake and fire in 1906, which destroyed all municipal records, and the ingenuity and persistence of the Chinese people, who used the opportunity created by the earthquake to increase their numbers in the United States. Since relatives of citizens were permitted entry, American-born Chinese (real and claimed) would visit China, report the birth of a son, and thus create an entry slot. Years later, since the records were destroyed, the slot could be used by a relative or purchased by someone outside the family. The purchasers were called "paper sons." Paper sons became a major mechanism for increasing the Chinese population, but it was a slow process and the sojourner community remained predominantly male for decades.

The high concentration of males in the Chinese community before 1920 resulted in a split household form of family. As Evelyn Nakano Glenn observes:

> In the split household family, production is separated from other functions and is carried out by a member living far from the rest of the household. The rest—consumption, reproduction and socialization—are carried out by the wife and other relatives from the home village. . . . The split household form makes possible maximum exploitation of the workers. . . . The labor of prime-age male workers can be bought relatively cheaply, since the cost of reproduction and family maintenance is borne partially by unpaid subsistence work of women and old people in the home village. (1983, 38–39)

The Chinese women who were in the United States during this period consisted of a small number who were wives and daughters of merchants and a larger percentage who were prostitutes. Lucia Cheng Hirata (1979) has suggested that Chinese prostitution was an important element in helping to maintain the split household family. In conjunction with laws prohibiting intermarriage, it helped men avoid long-term relationships with women in the United States and ensured that the bulk of their meager earnings would continue to support the family at home.

The reproductive labor of Chinese women, therefore, took on two dimensions primarily because of the split household family. Wives who remained in China were forced to raise children and care for in-laws on the meager remittances of their sojourning husband. Although we know few details about their lives, it is clear that the everyday work of bearing and maintaining children and a household fell entirely on their shoulders. Those women who immigrated and worked as prostitutes performed the more nurturant aspects of reproductive labor, that is, providing emotional and sexual companionship for men who were far from home. Yet their role as prostitutes was more likely a means of supporting their families at home in China than a chosen vocation.

The Chinese family system during the nineteenth century was a patriarchal one and girls had little value. In fact, they were considered temporary members of their father's family because when they married, they became members of their husband's family. They also had little social value; girls were sold by some poor parents to work as prostitutes, concubines, or servants. This saved the family the expense of raising them, and their earnings became a source of family income. For most girls, however, marriages were arranged and families sought useful connections through this process. With the development of a sojourning pattern in the United States, some Chinese women in those regions of China where this pattern was more prevalent would be sold to become prostitutes in the United States. Most, however, were married to men whom they saw only once or twice in the twenty- or thirty-year period during

which he was sojourning in the United States. A woman's status as wife ensured that a portion of the meager wages her husband earned would be returned to his family in China. This arrangement required considerable sacrifice and adjustment by wives who remained in China and those who joined their husbands after a long separation.

Maxine Hong Kingston tells the story of the unhappy meeting of her aunt, Moon Orchid, with her husband, from whom she had been separated for thirty years: "For thirty years she had been receiving money from him from America. But she had never told him that she wanted to come to the United States. She waited for him to suggest it, but he never did" (1977, 144). His response to her when she arrived unexpectedly was to say: " 'Look at her. She'd never fit into an American household. I have important American guests who come inside my house to eat.' He turned to Moon Orchid, 'You can't talk to them. You can barely talk to me.' Moon Orchid was so ashamed, she held her hands over her face" (1977, 178).

Despite these handicaps, Chinese people collaborated to establish the opportunity to form families and settle in the United States. In some cases it took as long as three generations for a child to be born on U.S. soil.

In one typical history, related by a 21 year old college student, great-grandfather arrived in the States in the 1890s as a "paper son" and worked for about 20 years as a laborer. He then sent for the grandfather, who worked alongside great-grandfather in a small business for several years. Great-grandfather subsequently returned to China, leaving grandfather to run the business and send remittance. In the 1940s, grandfather sent for father; up to this point, none of the wives had left China. Finally, in the late 1950s father returned to China and brought his wife back with him. Thus, after nearly 70 years, the first child was born in the United States. (Glenn 1983, 14).

Chicanos

Africans were uprooted from their native lands and encouraged to have families in order to increase the slave labor force. Chinese people were immigrant laborers whose "permanent" presence in the country was denied. By contrast, Mexican Americans were colonized and their traditional family life was disrupted by war and the imposition of a new set of laws and conditions of labor. The hardships faced by Chicano families, therefore, were the results of the U.S. colonization of the indigenous Mexican population, accompanied by the beginnings of industrial development. The treaty of Guadalupe Hidalgo, signed in 1848, granted American citizenship to Mexicans living in what is now called the Southwest. The American takeover, however, resulted in the gradual displacement of Mexicans from the land and their incorporation into a colonial labor force (Barrera 1979). Mexicans who immigrated into the United States after 1848 were also absorbed into that labor force.

Whether natives of northern Mexico (which became part of the United States after 1848) or immigrants from southern Mexico, Chicanos were a largely peasant population whose lives were defined by a feudal economy and a daily struggle on the land for economic survival. Patriarchal families were important instruments of community life, and nuclear family units were linked through an elaborate system of kinship and godparenting. Traditional life was characterized by hard work and a fairly distinct pattern of sex-role segregation.

> Most Mexican women were valued for their household qualities, men by their ability to work and to provide for a family. Children were taught to get up early, to contribute to their family's labor to prepare themselves for adult life. . . . Such a life demanded discipline, authority, defer-

ence—values that cemented the working of a family surrounded and shaped by the requirements of Mexico's distinctive historical pattern of agricultural development, especially its pervasive debt peonage. (Saragoza 1983, 8)

As the primary caretakers of hearth and home in a rural environment, Chicanas' labor made a vital and important contribution to family survival. A description of women's reproductive labor in the early twentieth century may be used to gain insight into the work of the nineteenth-century rural women.

> For country women, work was seldom a salaried job. More often it was the work of growing and preparing food, of making adobes and plastering houses with mud, or making their children's clothes for school and teaching them the hymns and prayers of the church, or delivering babies and treating sickness with herbs and patience. In almost every town there were one or two women who, in addition to working in their own homes, served other families in the community as *curanderas* (healers), *parteras* (midwives), and schoolteachers. (Elasser et al. 1980, 10)

Although some scholars have argued that family rituals and community life showed little change before World War I (Saragoza 1983), the American conquests of Mexican lands, the introduction of a new system of labor, the loss of Mexican-owned land through the inability to document ownership, and the transient nature of most of the jobs in which Chicanos were employed resulted in the gradual erosion of this pastoral way of life. Families were uprooted as the economic basis for family life changed. Some people immigrated from Mexico in search of a better standard of living and worked in the mines and railroads. Others, who were native to the Southwest, faced a job market that no longer required their skills. They moved into mining, railroad, and agricultural labor in search of a means of earning a living. According to Albert Camarillo (1979), the influx of Anglo[5] capital into the pastoral economy of Santa Barbara, California, rendered obsolete the skills of many Chicano males who had worked as ranch hands and farmers prior to the urbanization of that economy. While some women and children accompanied their husbands to the railroad and mining camps, many of these camps discouraged or prohibited family settlement.

The American period (after 1848) was characterized by considerable transiency for the Chicano population. Its impact on families is seen in the growth of female-headed households, reflected in the data as early as 1860. Richard Griswold del Castillo (1979) found a sharp increase in female-headed households in Los Angeles, from a low of 13 percent in 1844 to 31 percent in 1880. Camarillo (1979, 120) documents a similar increase in Santa Barbara, from 15 percent in 1844 to 30 percent by 1880. These increases appear to be due not so much to divorce, which was infrequent in this Catholic population, as to widowhood and temporary abandonment in search of work. Given the hazardous nature of work in the mines and railroad camps, the death of a husband, father, or son who was laboring in these sites was not uncommon. Griswold del Castillo (1979) reports a higher death rate among men than women in Los Angeles. The rise in female-headed households, therefore, reflects the instabilities and insecurities introduced into women's lives as a result of the changing social organization of work.

One outcome, the increasing participation of women and children in the labor force, was primarily a response to economic factors that required the modification of traditional values. According to Louisa Vigil, who was born in 1890, "The women didn't work at that time. The man was supposed to marry that girl and take care of her. . . . Your grandpa never did let me work for nobody. He always had to work, and we never did have really bad times" (Elasser et al. 1980, 14).

Vigil's comments are reinforced in Mario Garcia's (1980) study of El Paso, Texas. In the 393 households he examined in the 1900 census, he found 17.1 percent of the women to be employed. The majority of this group were daughters, mothers with no husbands, and single women. In Los Angeles and Santa Barbara, where there were greater work opportunities for women than in El Paso, wives who were heads of household worked in seasonal and part-time jobs, and lived from the earnings of children and relatives in an effort to maintain traditional females roles.

Slowly, entire families were encouraged to go to railroad work camps and were eventually incorporated into the agricultural labor market. This was a response both to the extremely low wages paid to Chicano laborers and to the preferences of employers, who saw family labor as a way of stabilizing the workforce. For Chicanos, engaging all family members in agricultural work was a means of increasing their earnings to a level close to subsistence for the entire group and of keeping the family unit together. Camarillo provides a picture of the interplay of work, family, and migration in the Santa Barbara area in the following observation:

> The time of year when women and children were employed in the fruit cannery and participated in the almond and olive harvest coincided with the seasons when the men were most likely to be engaged in seasonal migratory work. There were seasons, however, especially in the early summer when the entire family migrated from the city to pick fruit. This type of family seasonal harvest was evident in Santa Barbara by the 1890s. As walnuts replaced almonds and as the fruit industry expanded, Chicano family labor became essential. (1979, 93).

This arrangement, while bringing families together, did not decrease the hardships that Chicanas had to confront in raising their families. We may infer something about the rigors of that life from Jesse Lopez de la Cruz's description of the workday of migrant farm laborers in the 1940s. Work conditions in the 1890s were as difficult, if not worse.

> We always went to where the women and men were going to work, because if it were just the men working it wasn't worth going out there because we wouldn't earn enough to support a family.... We would start around 6:30 a.m. and work for four or five hours, then walk home and eat and rest until about three-thirty in the afternoon when it cooled off. We would go back and work until we couldn't see. Then I'd clean up the kitchen. I was doing the housework and working out in the fields and taking care of two children. (Quoted in Goldman 1981, 119–120)

In the towns, women's reproductive labor was intensified by the congested and unsanitary conditions of the barrios in which they lived. Garcia described the following conditions in El Paso:

> Mexican women had to haul water for washing and cooking from the river or public water pipes. To feed their families, they had to spend time marketing, often in Ciudad Juarez across the border, as well as long, hot hours cooking meals and coping with the burden of desert sand both inside and outside their homes. Besides the problem of raising children, unsanitary living conditions forced Mexican mothers to deal with disease and illness in their families. Diphtheria, tuberculosis, typhus and influenza were never too far away. Some diseases could be directly traced to inferior city services. . . . As a result, Mexican mothers had to devote much energy to caring for sick children, many of whom died. (1980, 320–321)

While the extended family has remained an important element of Chicano life, it was eroded in the American period in several ways. Griswold del Castillo (1979), for example, points out that in 1845 about 71 percent of Angelenos lived in extended families, whereas by 1880, fewer than half did. This decrease in extended families appears to be a response to the changed economic conditions and the instabilities generated by the new sociopolitical structure. Additionally, the imposition of American law and custom ignored, and ultimately undermined, some aspects of the extended family. The extended family in traditional Mexican life consisted of an important set of family, religious, and community obligations. Women, while valued primarily for their domesticity, had certain legal and property rights that acknowledged the importance of their work, their families of origin, and their children. In California, for example,

> equal ownership of property between husband and wife had been one of the mainstays of the Spanish and Mexican family systems. Community-property laws were written into the civil codes with the intention of strengthening the economic controls of the wife and her relatives. The American government incorporated these Mexican laws into the state constitution, but later court decisions interpreted these statutes so as to undermine the wife's economic rights. In 1861, the legislature passed a law that allowed the deceased wife's property to revert to her husband. Previously it had been inherited by her children and relatives if she died without a will. (Griswold del Castillo 1979, 69)

The impact of this and similar court rulings was to "strengthen the property rights of the husband at the expense of his wife and children" (Griswold del Castillo, 1979, 69).

In the face of the legal, social, and economic changes that occurred during the American period, Chicanas were forced to cope with a series of dislocations in traditional life. They were caught between conflicting pressures to maintain traditional women's roles and family customs and the need to participate in the economic support of their families by working outside the home. During this period the preservation of traditional customs—such as languages, celebrations, and healing practices—became an important element in maintaining and supporting familial ties.

According to Alex Saragoza (1983), transiency, the effects of racism and segregation, and proximity to Mexico aided in the maintenance of traditional family practices. Garcia has suggested that women were the guardians of Mexican cultural traditions within the family. He cites the work of anthropologist Manuel Gamio, who identified the retention of many Mexican customs among Chicanos in settlements around the United States in the early 1900s.

> These included folklore, songs, and ballads, birthday celebrations, saints' days, baptisms, weddings, and funerals in the traditional style. Because of poverty, a lack of physicians in the barrios, and adherence to traditional customs, Mexicans continued to use medicinal herbs. Gamio also identified the maintenance of a number of oral traditions, and Mexican style cooking. (Garcia 1980, 322)

Of vital importance to the integrity of traditional culture was the perpetuation of the Spanish language. Factors that aided in the maintenance of other aspects of Mexican culture also helped in sustaining the language. However, entry into English-language public schools introduced the children and their families to systematic efforts to erase their native tongue. Griswold del Castillo reports that in the early 1880s there was considerable pressure against speakers of Spanish in the public schools. He also found that some Chicano parents responded to this kind of discrimination by helping support independent bilingual schools. These efforts, however, were short-lived.

Another key factor in conserving Chicano culture was the extended family network, particularly the system of *compadrazgo* (godparenting). Although the full extent of the impact

of the American period on the Chicano extended family is not known, it is generally acknowledged that this family system, though lacking many legal and social sanctions, played an important role in the preservation of the Mexican community (Camarillo 1979). In Mexican society, godparents were an important way of linking family and community through respected friends or authorities. Participants in the important rites of passage in the child's life, such as baptism, first Communion, confirmation, and marriage, godparents had a moral obligation to act as guardians, to provide financial assistance in times of need, and to substitute in case of the death of a parent. Camarillo (1979) points out that in traditional society these bonds cut across class and racial lines.

The rite of baptism established kinship networks between rich and poor, between Spanish, mestizo and American Indian, and often carried with it political loyalty and economic-occupational ties. The leading California patriarchs in the pueblo played important roles in the *compadrazgo* network. They sponsored dozens of children for their workers or poorer relatives. The kindness of the *padrino* and *madrina* was repaid with respect and support from the *pobladores* (Camarillo 1979, 12–13)

The extended family network, which included godparents, expanded the support groups for women who were widowed or temporarily abandoned and for those who were in seasonal, part- or full-time work. It suggests, therefore, the potential for an exchange of services among poor people whose income did not provide the basis for family subsistence. Griswold del Castillo (1979) argues that family organization influenced literacy rates and socioeconomic mobility among Chicanos in Los Angeles between 1850 and 1880. His data suggest that children in extended families (defined as those with at least one relative living in a nuclear family household) had higher literacy rates than those in nuclear families. He also argues that those in larger families fared better economically and experienced less downward mobility. The data here are too limited to generalize to the Chicano experience as a whole, but they do reinforce the actual and potential importance of this family form to the continued cultural autonomy of the Chicano community.

Conclusion

Reproductive labor for African American, Chinese American, and Mexican American women in the nineteenth century centered on the struggle to maintain family units in the face of a variety of assaults. Treated primarily as workers rather than as members of family groups, these women labored to maintain, sustain, stabilize, and reproduce their families while working in both the public (productive) and private (reproductive) spheres. Thus, the concept of reproductive labor, when applied to women of color, must be modified to account for the fact that labor in the productive sphere was required to achieve even minimal levels of family subsistence. Long after industrialization had begun to reshape family roles among middle-class White families, driving White women into a cult of domesticity, women of color were coping with an extended day. This day included subsistence labor outside the family and domestic labor within the family. For slaves, domestics, migrant farm laborers, seasonal factory workers, and prostitutes, the distinctions between labor that reproduced family life and labor that economically sustained it were minimized. The expanded workday was one of the primary ways in which reproductive labor increased.

Racial-ethnic families were sustained and maintained in the face of various forms of disruption. Yet the women and their families paid a high price in the process. High rates of infant mortality, a shortened life span, and the early onset of crippling and debilitating disease give some insight into the costs of survival.

The poor quality of housing and the neglect of communities further increased reproductive labor. Not only did racial-ethnic women work hard outside the home for mere subsistence, they worked very hard inside the home to achieve even minimal standards of privacy and cleanliness. They were continually faced with disease and illness that resulted directly from the absence of basic sanitation. The fact that some African women murdered their children to prevent them from becoming slaves is an indication of the emotional strain associated with bearing and raising children while participating in the colonial labor system.

We have uncovered little information about the use of birth control, the prevalence of infanticide, or the motivations that may have generated these or other behaviors. We can surmise, however, that no matter how much children were accepted, loved, or valued among any of these groups of people, their futures were precarious. Keeping children alive, helping them to understand and participate in a system that exploited them, and working to ensure a measure—no matter how small—of cultural integrity intensified women's reproductive labor.

Being a woman of color in nineteenth-century American society meant having extra work both inside and outside the home. It meant being defined as outside of or deviant from the norms and values about women that were being generated in the dominant White culture. The notion of separate spheres of male and female labor that developed in the nineteenth century had contradictory outcomes for the Whites. It was the basis for the confinement of upper-middle-class White women to the household and for much of the protective legislation that subsequently developed in the workplace. At the same time, it sustained White families by providing social acknowledgment and support to women in the performance of their family roles. For racial-ethnic women, however, the notion of separate spheres served to reinforce their subordinate status and became, in effect, another assault. As they increased their work outside the home, they were forced into a productive labor sphere that was organized for men and "desperate" women who were so unfortunate or immoral that they could not confine their work to the domestic sphere. In the productive sphere, racial-ethnic women faced exploitative jobs and depressed wages. In the reproductive sphere, they were denied the opportunity to embrace the dominant ideological definition of "good" wife or mother. In essence, they were faced with a double-bind situation, one that required their participation in the labor force to sustain family life but damned them as women, wives, and mothers because they did not confine their labor to the home.

Finally, the struggle of women of color to build and maintain families provides vivid testimony to the role of race in structuring family life in the United States. As Maxine Baca Zinn points out:

> Social categories and groups subordinate in the racial hierarchy are often deprived of access to social institutions that offer supports for family life. Social categories and groups elevated in the racial hierarchy have different and better connections to institutions that can sustain families. Social location and its varied connection with social resources thus have profound consequences for family life. (1990, 74)

From the founding of the United States, and throughout its history, race has been a funda-mental criterion determining the kind of work people do, the wages they receive, and the kind of legal, economic, political, and social support provided for their families. Women of color have faced limited economic resources, inferior living conditions, alien cultures and languages, and overt hostility in their struggle to create a "place" for families of color in the United States. That place, however, has been a precarious one because the society has not provided supports for these families. Today we see the outcomes of that legacy in statistics showing that people of color, compared with Whites, have higher rates of female-headed households, out-of-wedlock births, divorce, and other factors associated with family disruption. Yet the causes of these variations do not lie merely in the higher concentrations of poverty among people of color; they are also due to the ways race has been used as a basis for denying and providing support to families. Women of color have struggled to maintain their families against all of these odds.

NOTES

Acknowledgments: The research in this study was an outgrowth of my participation in a larger collaborative project examining family, community, and work lives of racial-ethnic women in the United States. I am deeply indebted to the scholarship and creativity of members of the group in the development of this study. Appreciation is extended to Elizabeth Higginbotham, Cheryl Townsend Gilkes, Evelyn Nakano Glenn, and Ruth Zambrana (members of the original working group), and to the Ford Foundation for a grant that supported in part of the work of this study.

1. The term "White" is a global construct used to characterize peoples of European descent who migrated to and helped colonize America. In the seventeenth century, most of these immigrants were from the British Isles. However, during the time period covered by this chapter, European im-

migrants became increasingly diverse. It is a limitation of this chapter that time and space do not permit a fuller discussion of the variations in the White European immigrant experience. For the purposes of the argument being made herein and of the contrast it seeks to draw between the experiences of mainstream (European) cultural groups and those of racial-ethnic minorities, the differences among European settlers are joined and the broad similarities emphasized.

2. For a more detailed discussion of this argument and the kinds of social supports provided these families, see an earlier version of this chapter: "Our Mothers' Grief: Racial-Ethnic Women and the Maintenance of Families," *Journal of Family History* 13 (4) (1988): 415–431.

3. The term "reproductive labor" is used to refer to all of the work of women in the home. This includes, but is not limited to, the buying and preparation of food and clothing, provision of emotional support and nurturance for all family members, bearing children, and planning, organizing, and carrying out a wide variety of tasks associated with socialization. All of these activities are necessary for the growth of patriarchal capitalism because they maintain, sustain, stabilize, and reproduce (both biologically and socially) the labor force.

4. Recent research suggests that there were some tasks assigned primarily to males and some others to females. Whereas some gender-role distinctions with regard to work may have existed on some plantations, it is clear that slave women were not exempt from strenuous physical labor.

5. This term is used to refer to White Americans of European ancestry.

REFERENCES

Aschenbrenner, Joyce. 1975. *Lifelines: Black Families in Change.* New York: Holt, Rinehart, and Winston.

Baca Zinn, Maxine. 1990. "Family, Feminism and Race in America." *Gender and Society* 4 (1) (March): 68–82. (Chapter 3, this volume.)

Barrera, Mario. 1979. *Race and Class in the Southwest.* Notre Dame, Ind.: Notre Dame University Press.

Blassingame, John. 1972. *The Slave Community: Plantation Life in the Antebellum South.* New York: Oxford University Press.

———. 1977. *Slave Testimony: Two Centuries of Letters, Speeches, Interviews, and Autobiographies.* Baton Rouge: Louisiana State University Press.

Camarillo, Albert. 1979. *Chicanos in a Changing Society.* Cambridge, Mass.: Harvard University Press.

Caulfield, Mina Davis. 1974. "Imperialism, the Family, and Cultures of Resistance." *Socialist Review* 4 (2) (October): 67–85.

Davis, Angela. 1971. "Reflections on the Black Woman's Role in the Community of Slaves." *Black Scholar* 3 (4) (December): 2–15.

———. 1981. *Women, Race, and Class.* New York: Random House.

Degler, Carl. 1980. *At Odds.* New York: Oxford University Press.

Elasser, Nan, Kyle MacKenzie, and Yvonne Tixier Y. Vigil. 1980. *Las Mujeres.* New York: The Feminist Press.

Garcia, Mario T. 1980. "The Chicano in American History: The Mexican Women of El Paso, 1880–1920—A Case Study." *Pacific Historical Review* 49 (2) (May): 315–358.

Genovese, Eugene D., and Elinor Miller, eds. 1974. *Plantation, Town, and County: Essays on the Local History of American Slave Society.* Urbana: University of Illinois Press.

Glenn, Evelyn Nakano. 1983. "Split Household, Small Producer, and Dual Wage Earner: An Analysis of Chinese-American Family Strategies." *Journal of Marriage and the Family* 45 (1) (February): 35–46.

Goldman, Marion S. 1981. *Gold Diggers and Silver Miners.* Ann Arbor: University of Michigan Press.

Griswold del Castillo, Richard. 1979. *The Los Angeles Barrio: 1850–1890.* Los Angeles: University of California Press.

Gutman, Herbert. 1976. *The Black Family in Slavery and Freedom, 1750–1925.* New York: Pantheon.

Hirata, Lucia Cheng. 1979. "Free, Indentured, Enslaved: Chinese Prostitutes in Nineteenth Century America." *Signs* 5 (Autumn): 3–29.

Jones, Jacqueline. 1985. *Labor of Love, Labor of Sorrow*. New York: Basic Books.

Kennedy, Susan Estabrook. 1979. *If All We Did Was to Weep at Home: A History of White Working-Class Women in America*. Bloomington: Indiana University Press.

Kessler-Harris, Alice. 1981. *Women Have Always Worked*. Old Westbury, N.Y.: The Feminist Press.

———. 1982. *Out to Work*. New York: Oxford University Press.

Kingston, Maxine Hong. 1977. *The Woman Warrior*. New York: Vintage Books.

Matthaei, Julie. 1982. *An Economic History of Women in America*. New York: Schocken Books.

Nee, Victor G., and Brett de Bary Nee. 1973. *Longtime Californ'*. New York: Pantheon Books.

Saragoza, Alex M. 1983. "The Conceptualization of the History of the Chicano Family: Work, Family, and Migration in Chicanos." In *Research Proceedings of the Symposium on Chicano Research and Public Policy*. Stanford, Calif.: Stanford University, Center for Chicano Research.

Shimkin, Demetri, E. M. Shimkin, and D. A. Frate, eds. 1978. *The Extended Family in Black Societies*. The Hague: Mouton.

Spruill, Julia Cherry. 1972. *Women's Life and Work in the Southern Colonies*. New York: W. W. Norton. (First published Chapel Hill: University of North Carolina Press, 1938.)

Stack, Carol S. 1974. *All Our Kin: Strategies for Survival in a Black Community*. New York: Harper & Row.

Sudarkasa, Niara. 1981. "Interpreting the African Heritage in Afro-American Family Organization." In *Black Families*, edited by Harriette Pipes McAdoo, 37–53. Beverly Hills, Calif.: Sage. (Chapter 8, this volume.)

White, Deborah Gray. 1985. *Ar'n't I a Woman? Female Slaves in the Plantation South*. New York: W. W. Norton.

Wright, Gwendolyn. 1981. *Building the Dream: A Social History of Housing in America*. New York: Pantheon.

Zaretsky, Eli. 1978. "The Effects of the Economic Crisis on the Family." In *U.S. Capitalism in Crisis*, edited by Crisis Reader Editorial Collective, 209–218. New York: Union of Radical Political Economists.

Section D

On Marriage and Divorce

⌒ *Chapter 33*

The Two Marriages

JESSIE BERNARD

The Future of Whose Marriage?

Both Uncle Honoré and Gigi's grandmother remembered it well, according to Alan Jay Lerner's lyric. And this is what it had been like according to Uncle Honoré: "It was a lovely moonlit evening in May. You arrived at nine o'clock in your gold dress only a little late for our dinner engagement with friends. After-wards there was that delightful carriage ride when we were so engrossed in one another that we didn't notice you had lost your glove." Ah, yes, Uncle Honoré remembered it well in-deed, down to the last detail.

Or, come to think of it, did he? For Gigi's grandmother remembered it too, but not at all the same way. "There was no moon that rainy June evening. For once I was on time when we met at eight o'clock at the restaurant where we dined alone. You complimented me on my pretty blue dress. Afterwards we took a

From Jessie Bernard, *The Future of Marriage* (New York: World Publishing, 1972), copyright © 1972 by Jessie Bernard. Reprinted by permission of Yale University.

long walk and we were so engrossed in one another that we didn't notice I had lost my comb until my hair came tumbling down."

The Japanese motion picture *Rashomon* was built on the same idea—four different versions of the same events. So, also, was Robert Gover's story of the college boy and the black prostitute in his *One Hundred Dol-lar Misunderstanding.* Also in this category is the old talmudic story of the learned rabbi called upon to render a decision in a marital situation. After listening carefully to the first spouse's story, he shook his head, saying, "You are absolutely right"; and, after listening equally carefully to the other spouse's story, he again shook his head, saying, "You are ab-solutely right."

There is no question in any of these exam-ples of deliberate deceit or prevarication or in-sincerity or dishonesty. Both Uncle Honoré and Grandmamma are equally sincere, equally honest, equally "right." The discrepancies in their stories make a charming duet in *Gigi.* And even the happiest of mates can match such differences in their own memories.

In the case of Uncle Honoré and Grand-mamma, we can explain the differences in the pictures they had in their heads of that evening half a century earlier: memories play strange tricks on all of us. But the same differences in the accounts of what happened show up also among modern couples even immediately after the event. In one study, for example, half of all the partners gave differing replies to questions about what had happened in a laboratory decision-making session they had just left. Other couples give different responses to questions about ordinary day-by-day events like lawn mowing as well as about romantic events. Once our attention has been called to the fact that both mates are equally sincere, equally honest, equally "right," the presence of two marriages in every marital union becomes clear—even obvious, as artists and wise persons have been telling us for so long.

Anyone, therefore, discussing the future of marriage has to specify whose marriage he is talking about: the husband's or the wife's. For there is by now a very considerable body of well-authenticated research to show that there really are two marriages in every marital union, and that they do not always coincide.

"His" and "Her" Marriages

Under the jargon "discrepant responses," the differences in the marriages of husbands and wives have come under the careful scrutiny of a score of researchers. They have found that when they ask husbands and wives identical questions about the union, they often get quite different replies. There is usually agreement on the number of children they have and a few other such verifiable items, although not, for example, on length of premarital acquaintance and of engagement, on age at marriage and interval between mar-

riage and birth of first child. Indeed, with respect to even such basic components of the marriage as frequency of sexual relations, social interaction, household tasks, and decision making, they seem to be reporting on different marriages. As, I think, they are.

In the area of sexual relations, for example, Kinsey and his associates found different responses in from one- to two-thirds of the couples they studied. Kinsey interpreted these differences in terms of selective perception. In the generation he was studying, husbands wanted sexual relations more often than the wives did, thus "the females may be overestimating the actual frequencies" and "the husbands . . . are probably underestimating the frequencies." The differences might also have been vestiges of the probable situation earlier in the marriage when the desired frequency of sexual relations was about six to seven times greater among husbands than among wives. This difference may have become so impressed on the spouses that it remained in their minds even after the difference itself had disappeared or even been reversed. In a sample of happily married, middle-class couples a generation later, Harold Feldman found that both spouses attributed to their mates more influence in the area of sex than they did to themselves.

Companionship, as reflected in talking together, Feldman found, was another area where differences showed up. Replies differed on three-fourths of all the items studied, including the topics talked about, the amount of time spent talking with each other, and which partner initiated conversation. Both partners claimed that whereas they talked more about topics of interest to their mates, their mates initiated conversations about topics primarily of interest to themselves. Feldman concluded that projection in terms of needs was distorting even simple, everyday events, and lack of communication was permitting the distortions to continue. It seemed to him that "if these sex differences can occur so often among these generally well satisfied couples, it would not be surprising to find even less consensus and more distortion in other less satisfied couples."

Although, by and large, husbands and wives tend to become more alike with age, in this study of middle-class couples, differences increased with length of marriage rather than decreased, as one might logically have expected. More couples in the later than in the earlier years, for example, had differing pictures in their heads about how often they laughed together, discussed together, exchanged ideas, or worked together on projects, and about how well things were going between them.

The special nature of sex and the amorphousness of social interaction help to explain why differences in response might occur. But household tasks? They are fairly objective and clear-cut and not all that emotion-laden. Yet even here there are his-and-her versions. Since the division of labor in the household is becoming increasingly an issue in marriage, the uncovering of differing replies in this area is especially relevant. Hard as it is to believe, Granbois and Willett tell us that more than half of the partners in one sample disagreed on who kept track of money and bills. On the question, who mows the lawn? more than a fourth disagreed. Even family income was not universally agreed on.

These differences about sexual relations, companionship, and domestic duties tell us a great deal about the two marriages. But power or decision making can cover all aspects of a relationship. The question of who makes decisions or who exercises power has therefore attracted a great deal of research attention. If we were interested in who really had the power or who really made the decisions, the research would be hopeless. Would it be pos-

sible to draw any conclusion from a situation in which both partners agree that the husband ordered the wife to make all the decisions? Still, an enormous literature documents the quest of researchers for answers to the question of marital power. The major contribution it has made has been to reveal the existence of differences in replies between husbands and wives.

The presence of such inconsistent replies did not at first cause much concern. The researchers apologized for them but interpreted them as due to methodological inadequacies; if only they could find a better way to approach the problem, the differences would disappear. Alternatively, the use of only the wife's responses, which were more easily available, was justified on the grounds that differences in one direction between the partners in one marriage compensated for differences in another direction between the partners in another marriage and thus canceled them out. As, indeed, they did. For when Granbois and Willett, two market researchers, analyzed the replies of husbands and wives separately, the overall picture was in fact the same for both wives and husbands. Such canceling out of differences in the total sample, however, concealed almost as much as it revealed about the individual couples who composed it. Granbois and Willett concluded, as Kinsey had earlier, that the "discrepancies . . . reflect differing perceptions on the part of responding partners." And this was the heart of the matter.

Differing reactions to common situations, it should be noted, are not at all uncommon. They are recognized in the folk wisdom embedded in the story of the blind men all giving different replies to questions on the nature of the elephant. One of the oldest experiments in juridical psychology demonstrates how different the statements of witnesses of the same act can be. Even in laboratory studies, it takes intensive training of raters to make it possible for them to arrive at agreement on the behavior they observe.

It has long been known that people with different backgrounds see things differently. We know, for example, that poor children perceive coins as larger than do children from more affluent homes. Boys and girls perceive differently. A good deal of the foundation for projective tests rests on the different ways in which individuals see identical stimuli. And this perception—or, as the sociologists put it, definition of the situation—is reality for them. In this sense, the realities of the husband's marriage are different from those of the wife's.

Finally, one of the most perceptive of the researchers, Constantina Safilios-Rothschild, asked the crucial question: Was what they were getting, even with the best research techniques, family sociology or wives' family sociology? She answered her own question: What the researchers who relied on wives' replies exclusively were reporting on was the wife's marriage. The husband's was not necessarily the same. There were, in fact, two marriages present:

> One explanation of discrepancies between the responses of husbands and wives may be the possibility of two "realities," the husband's subjective reality and the wife's subjective reality—two perspectives which do not always coincide. Each spouse perceives "facts" and situations differently according to his own needs, values, attitudes, and beliefs. An "objective" reality could possibly exist only in the trained observer's evaluation, if it does exist at all.

Interpreting the different replies of husbands and wives in terms of selective perception, projection of needs, values, attitudes, and beliefs, or different definitions of the situation by no means renders them trivial or incidental or justifies dismissing or ignoring them. They are, rather, fundamental for an understanding of the two marriages, his and hers, and we ignore them at the peril of serious misunderstanding of marriage, present as well as future.

Is There an Objective Reality in Marriage?

Whether or not husbands and wives perceive differently or define situations differently, still, sexual relations are taking place, companionship is or is not occurring, tasks about the house are being performed, and decisions are being made every day by someone. In this sense, some sort of "reality" does exist. David Olson went to the laboratory to see if he could uncover it.

He first asked young couples expecting babies such questions as these: Which one of them would decide whether to buy insurance for the newborn child? Which one would decide the husband's part in diaper changing? Which one would decide whether the new mother would return to work or to school? When there were differences in the answers each gave individually on the questionnaire, he set up a situation in which together they had to arrive at a decision in his laboratory. He could then compare the results of the questionnaire with the results in the simulated situation. He found neither spouse's questionnaire response any more accurate than the other's; that is, neither conformed better to the behavioral "reality" of the laboratory than the other did.

The most interesting thing, however, was that husbands, as shown on their questionnaire response, perceived themselves as having more power than they actually did have in the laboratory "reality," and wives perceived that they has less. Thus, whereas three-fourths (73 percent) of the husbands overestimated their power in decision making, 70 percent of the wives underestimated theirs. Turk and Bell found similar results in Canada. Both spouses tend to attribute decision-making power to the one who has the "right" to make the decision. Their replies, that is, conform to the model of marriage that has characterized civilized mankind for millennia. It is this model rather than their own actual behavior that husbands and wives tend to perceive.

We are now zeroing in on the basic reality. We can remove the quotation marks. For there is, in fact, an objective reality in marriage. It is a reality that resides in the cultural—legal, moral, and conventional—prescriptions and proscriptions and, hence, expectations that constitute marriage. It is the reality that is reflected in the minds of the spouses themselves. The differences between the marriages of husbands and of wives are structural realities, and it is these structural differences that constitute the basis for the different psychological realities.

The Authority Structure of Marriage

Authority is an institutional phenomenon; it is strongly bound up with faith. It must be believed in; it cannot be enforced unless it also has power. Authority resides not in the person on whom it is conferred by the group or society, but in the recognition and acceptance it elicits in others. Power, on the other hand, may dispense with the prop of authority. It may take the form of the ability to coerce or to veto; it is often personal, charismatic, not institutional. This kind of personal power is self-enforcing. It does not require shoring up by access to force. In fact, it may even operate subversively. A woman with this kind of power may or may not know that she possesses it. If she does know she has it, she will probably disguise her exercise of it.

In the West, the institutional structure of marriage has invested the husband with authority and backed it by the power of church and state. The marriages of wives have thus been officially dominated by the husband. Hebrew, Christian, and Islamic versions of deity were in complete accord on this matter. The laws, written or unwritten, religious or civil, which have defined the marital union have been based on male conceptions, and they have undergirded male authority.

Adam cam first. Eve was created to supply him with companionship, not vice versa. And God himself had told her that Adam would rule over her; her wishes had to conform to his. The New Testament authors agreed. Women were created for men, not men for women; women were therefore commanded to be obedient. If they wanted to learn anything, let them ask their husbands in private, for it was shameful for them to talk in the church. They should submit themselves to their husbands, because husbands were superior to wives; and wives should be as subject to their husbands as the church was to Christ. Timothy wrapped it all up: "Let the woman learn in silence with all subjection. But I suffer not a woman to teach, nor to usurp authority over the man, but to be in silence." Male Jews continued for millennia to thank God three times a day that they were not women. And the Koran teaches women that men are naturally their superiors because God made them that way; naturally, their own status is one of subordination.

The state as well as the church had the same conception of marriage, assigning to the husband and father control over his dependents, including his wife. Sometimes this power was well-nigh absolute, as in the case of the Roman patria potestas—or the English common law, which flatly said, "The husband and wife are as one and that one is the husband." There are rules still lingering today with the same, though less extreme, slant. Diane B. Schulder has summarized the legal framework of the wife's marriage as laid down in the common law.

> The legal responsibilities of a wife are to live in the home established by her husband; to perform the domestic chores (cleaning, cooking, washing, etc.) necessary to help maintain that home; to care for her husband and children.... A husband may force his wife to have sexual relations as long as his demands are reasonable and her health is not endangered.... The law allows a wife to take a job if she wishes. However, she must see that her domestic chores are completed, and, if there are children, that they receive proper care during her absence.

A wife is not entitled to payment for household work; and some jurisdictions in the United States expressly deny payment for it. In some states, the wife's earnings are under the control of her husband, and in four, special court approval and in some cases husband's consent are required if a wife wishes to start a business of her own.

The male counterpart to these obligations includes that of supporting his wife. He may not disinherit her. She has a third interest in property owned by him, even if it is held in his name only. Her name is required when he sells property.

Not only divine and civil law but also rules of etiquette have defined authority as a husband's prerogative. One of the first books published in England was a *Boke of Good Manners,* translated from the French of Jacques Le Grand in 1487, which included a chapter on "How Wymmen Ought to Be Gouerned." The thirty-third rule of Plutarch's *Rules for Husbands and Wives* was that women should obey their husbands; if they "try to rule over their husbands they make a worse mistake than the husbands do who let themselves be ruled." The husband's rule should not, of course, be brutal; he should

not rule his wife "as a master does his chattel, but as the soul governs the body, by feeling with her and being linked to her by affection." Wives, according to Richard Baxter, a seventeenth-century English divine, had to obey even a wicked husband, the only exception being that a wife need not obey a husband if he ordered her to change her religion. But, again, like Plutarch, Baxter warned that the husband should love his wife; his authority should not be so coercive or so harsh as to destroy love. Among his twelve rules for carrying out the duties of conjugal love, however, was one to the effect that love must not be so imprudent as to destroy authority.

As late as the nineteenth century, Tocqueville noted that in the United States the ideals of democracy did not apply between husbands and wives.

> Nor have the Americans ever supposed that one consequence of democratic principles is the subversion of marital power, or the confusion of the natural authorities in families. They hold that every association must have a head in order to accomplish its objective, and that the natural head of the conjugal association is man. They do not therefore deny him the right of directing his partner; and they maintain, that in the smaller association of husband and wife, as well as in the great social community, the object of democracy is to regulate and legalize the powers which are necessary, not to subvert all power.
>
> This opinion is not peculiar to men and contested by women; I never observed that the women of America consider conjugal authority as a fortunate usurpation [by men] of their rights, nor that they thought themselves degraded by submitting to it. It appears to me, on the contrary, that they attach a sort of pride to the voluntary surrender of their own will, and make it their boast to bend themselves to the yoke, not to shake it off.

The point here is not to document once more the specific ways (religious, legal, moral, traditional) in which male authority has been built into the marital union—that has been done a great many times—but merely to illustrate how different (structurally or "objectively" as well as perceptually or "subjectively") the wife's marriage has actually been from the husband's throughout history.

The Subversiveness of Nature

The rationale for male authority rested not only on biblical grounds but also on nature or natural law, on the generally accepted natural superiority of men. For nothing could be more self-evident than that the patriarchal conception of marriage, in which the husband was unequivocally the boss, was natural, resting as it did on the unchallenged superiority of males.

Actually, nature, if not deity, is subversive. Power, or the ability to coerce or to veto, is widely distributed in both sexes, among women as well as among men. And whatever the theoretical or conceptual picture may have been, the actual, day-by-day relationships between husbands and wives have been determined by the men and women themselves. All that the institutional machinery could do was to confer authority; it could not create personal power, for such power cannot be conferred, and women can generate it as well as men. Thus, keeping women in their place has been a universal problem, in spite of the fact that almost without exception institutional patterns give men positions of superiority over them.

If the sexes were, in fact, categorically distinct, with no overlapping, so that no man was inferior to any woman or any woman superior to any man, or vice versa, marriage would have been a great deal simpler. But there is no such sharp cleavage between the sexes except with respect to the presence or absence of certain organs. With all the other characteristics

of each sex, there is greater or less overlapping, some men being more "feminine" than the average woman and some women more "masculine" than the average man. The structure of families and societies reflects the positions assigned to men and women. The bottom stratum includes children, slaves, servants, and outcasts of all kinds, males as well as females. As one ascends the structural hierarchy, the proportion of males increases, so that at the apex there are only males.

When societies fall back on the lazy expedient—as all societies everywhere have done—of allocating the rewards and punishments of life on the basis of sex, they are bound to create a host of anomalies, square pegs in round holes, societal misfits. Roles have been allocated on the basis of sex which did not fit a sizable number of both sexes—women, for example, who chafed at subordinate status and men who could not master superordinate status. The history of the relations of the sexes is replete with examples of such misfits. Unless a modus vivendi is arrived at, unhappy marriages are the result.

There is, though, a difference between the exercise of power by husbands and by wives. When women exert power, they are not rewarded; they may even be punished. They are "deviant." Turk and Bell note that "wives who ... have the greater influence in decision making may experience guilt over this fact." They must therefore dissemble to maintain the illusion, even to themselves, that they are subservient. They tend to feel less powerful than they are because they *ought* to be.

When men exert power, on the other hand, they are rewarded; it is the natural expression of authority. They feel no guilt about it. The prestige of authority goes to the husband whether or not he is actually the one who exercises it. It is not often even noticed when the wife does so. She sees to it that it is not.

There are two marriages, then, in every marital union, his and hers. And his is better than hers. The questions, therefore, are these: In what direction will they change in the future? Will one change more than the other? Will they tend to converge or to diverge? Will the future continue to favor the husband's marriage? And if the wife's marriage is improved, will it cost the husband's anything, or will his benefit along with hers?

REFERENCES

Bell, Norman. *See* Turk, James L.

Bernard, Jessie. *American Family Behavior.* New York: Harper, 1942.

———. *Remarriage: A Study of Marriage.* New York: Dryden Press, 1956; New York: Russell and Russell, 1971.

———. *The Sex Game.* Englewood Cliffs, N.J.: Prentice Hall, 1968; New York: Atheneum, 1972.

———. *Women and the Public Interest: An Essay on Policy and Protest.* Chicago, Ill.: Aldine-Atherton, 1971.

Brown, George W., and Ritter, Michael. "The Measurement of Family Activities and Relationships." *Human Relations* 19 (August 1966): 241–63.

Cheraskin, E., and Ringsdorf, W. M. "Familial Factors in Psychic Adjustment," *Journal of the American Geriatric Society* 17 (June 1969): 609–11.

1 Cor. 14:35; 1 Cor. 11:3.

De Tocqueville, Alexis. *Democracy in America.* New York: J. and H. G. Langley, 1840.

Elinson, Jack. *See* Haberman, Paul W.

Eph. 5:22–24.

Feld, Sheila. *See* Veroff, Joseph.

Feldman, Harold. *Development of the Husband-Wife Relationship.* Ithaca, N.Y.: Cornell University Press, 1967.

Feldman, Harold. *See* Rollins, Boyd C.

Ferber, Robert. "On the Reliability of Purchase Influence Studies." *Journal of Marketing* 19 (January 1955): 225–32.

Gen. 1, 2, and 3.

Gover, R. *One Hundred Dollar Misunderstanding.* New York: Grove Press, 1962.

Granbois, Donald H., and Willett, Ronald P. "Equivalence of Family Role Measures Based on Husband and Wife Data." *Journal of Marriage and the Family* 32 (February 1970).

Haberman, Paul W., and Elinson, Jack. "Family Income Reported in Surveys: Husbands Versus Wives." *Journal of Marketing Research* 4 (May 1967): 191–94.

Heer, David M. "Husband and Wife Perceptions of Family Power Structure." *Marriage and Family Living* 24 (February 1962): 67.

Hoffman, Dean K. *See* Kenkel, W. F.

Kenkel, W. F., and Hoffman, Dean K. "Real and Conceived Roles in Family Decision Making." *Marriage and Family Living* 18 (November 1956): 314.

Kinsey, A. C., Pomeroy, Wardell B., and Martin, Clyde E. *Sexual Behavior in the Human Male.* Philadelphia, Pa.: W. B. Saunders, 1948.

Lerner, Alan Jay. "I Remember It Well." From *Gigi.*

Maccoby, Eleanor E. "Woman's Intellect." In *The Potential of Woman,* edited by Seymour M. Farber and Roger H. L. Wilson, 29. New York: McGraw-Hill, 1963.

Michels, Roberto. "Authority." *Encyclopedia of the Social Sciences,* 2:319. New York: Macmillan, 1933.

Morrison, Denton E. *See* Wilkening, E. A.

Olson, David H. "The Measurement of Family Power by Self-Report and Behavioral Methods." *Journal of Marriage and the Family* 31 (August 1969): 549.

Ringsdorf, W. M. *See* Cheraskin, E.

Ritter, Michael. *See* Brown, George W.

Rollins, Boyd C., and Feldman, Harold. "Marital Satisfaction over the Family Life Cycle." *Journal of Marriage and the Family* 32 (February 1970): 24.

Safilios-Rochschild, Constantina. "Family Sociology or Wives' Family Sociology? A Cross-Cultural Examination of Decision-Making." *Journal of Marriage and the Family* 31 (May 1969).

———. "The Study of Family Power Structure: A Review 1960–1969." *Journal of Marriage and the Family* 32 (November 1970): 539–52.

Scanzoni, John. "A Note on the Sufficiency of Wife Responses in Family Research." *Pacific Sociological Review,* fall 1965, 12.

Schulder, Diane B. "Does the Law Oppress Women?" In *Sisterhood Is Powerful,* edited by Robin Morgan, 147. New York: Vintage Books, 1970.

1 Tim. 2:11.

Turk, James L., and Bell, Norman. "The Measurement of Family Behavior: What They Perceive, What They Report, What We Observe." Paper read at meeting of American Sociological Association, September 1970.

Veroff, Joseph, and Feld, Sheila. *Marriage and Work in America,* 120–21. New York: Van Nostrand-Reinhold, 1970.

Wilkening, E. A., and Morrison, Denton E. "A Comparison of Husband-Wife Responses Concerning Who Makes Farm and Home Decisions." *Journal of Marriage and the Family* 25 (August 1963): 351.

Willett, Ronald P. *See* Granbois, Donald H.

Wolgast, Elizabeth. "Do Husbands or Wives Make the Purchasing Decisions?" *Journal of Marketing* 23 (October 1958): 151–58.

Zelditch, Morris. "Family, Marriage, and Kinship." In *Handbook of Modern Sociology,* edited by Robert E. L. Faris. Chicago, Ill.: Rand McNally, 1964.

Chapter 34

Wives' Marital Work in a Culture of Divorce

KARLA B. HACKSTAFF

Ever since Jessie Bernard (1972) discovered that there is a "his" and "her" to every marriage—and that "his" marriage is generally better, researchers have examined inequalities between women's and men's experiences in families. Family scholars have analyzed this inequality, in part, by examining the work that wives and mothers do, beyond paid labor, to sustain marriages and families: kin work, emotion work, reproductive labor, the "second shift," and marriage work (Cancian 1987; DeVault 1987; di Leonardo 1987; Goldscheider and Waite 1991; Hochschild 1983; Hochschild with Machung 1989; Oliker 1989; Thompson 1991). Most researchers have found that women have been responsible for monitoring the emotional quality of marriage—a responsibility deriving from the legacy of "separate spheres" (Kitson with Holmes 1992; Thompson and Walker 1989). Blaisure and Allen (1995) found that beyond sharing housework and paid work, reflective assessment and emotional involvement are crucial to egalitarian marriages. No one, however, has examined how the context of divorce might be influencing women's work as wives (White 1990).

Divorce rates have been relatively stable from the late 1980s into the 1990s; half of all marriages contracted during the 1970s and thereafter are projected to end in divorce (U.S. Bureau of the Census 1992, 5). How has the prevalence of divorce influenced the labor of sustaining marriages? Are women still monitoring the emotional quality of marriages, sharing the work, or falling down on the job? Some scholars imply that wives are becoming less self-sacrificing and increasingly individualistic and that they are abandoning the work of monitoring marriages (Lasch 1979; Glenn 1987; Popenoe 1988; Spanier 1989). But one could argue alternatively that a context of prevalent divorce compels more work to sustain marriages. Indeed, monitoring a marriage may be more demanding than ever because we live in a culture of divorce.[1]

Divorce culture is a cluster of symbols, beliefs, and practices that anticipate and reinforce divorce and, in the process, redefine marriage. Divorce culture is marked by three key premises: marrying is an option, marriage is contingent, and divorce is a gateway. To believe that marriage is optional is to envision adulthood separate from marriage. To believe that marriage is contingent is to dilute the lifetime promise of "till death do us part." To say that divorce is a gateway is to suggest that divorce is not simply an option to be shunned but may be a means to a more fulfilling life. As an incipient cultural construction, divorce culture challenges an older ideology of marriage culture. However, the tenets of marriage culture—that marrying is given, marriage is forever, and divorce is a last resort—endure, even as its hegemony has lapsed.

Today, spouses feel vulnerable to divorce. In the early 1990s I interviewed 17 married couples to find out how they were coping with the rise of divorce and gender equality. I found that couples devise various strategies to cope with divorce and that the "marital work ethic" is the most important of these.[2] Nearly everyone I interviewed referred to the idea of a marital work ethic: the widespread *belief* that marital work is crucial to cope with the option of divorce.[3] "Marital work" is the ongoing work necessary to create, sustain, and reproduce an emotionally gratifying relationship. The marital work ethic expresses divorce culture by assuming that marital endurance is contingent upon a gratifying marriage. Indeed, in their large surveys, Kitson and Holmes found that "relational complaints," such as the absence of communication or affection, are increasingly seen, by divorced and married alike, as legitimate grounds for marital dissolution (1992, 341). Despite spouses' shared beliefs in a marital work ethic, more often than not, the work itself divided by gender. Like the literature documenting women's disproportionate responsibility for family work, my research finds that women are more likely to do or to initiate the work of taking care of the marriage.

Because wives have been responsible for monitoring marriages, they also take responsibility for redistributing marital work. I found that wives try to enlist husbands in the work of monitoring marriage, not to abandon the work, but to share it. However, sometimes the means are paradoxical. For many wives, achieving equality in the relational work of monitoring a marriage requires exercising the power of independence. Divorce threats allow wives to set limits. For example, after one wife threatened her husband with "recovery or the marriage," her drug-dependent husband complied. Her reservations about her ultimatum concerned relationships: "It was very hard; you've got two children who love their father—it's not just me." However, her concern for individual integrity and independence were apparent when she explained that she wanted her daughters to "know that their needs are important and should be honored"—that one needs to learn "to compromise without giving yourself away."

The wives I interviewed are not simply concerned with either their own individual rights or their relational responsibilities but with both.[4] Increasing financial independence, made possible by women's increasing labor force participation, enables wives to take their own needs and rights into account and, in effect, rely upon individualism. Yet, it is "relationality" rather than individualism that motivates wives' desire to share the work of monitoring marriage. In contrast to individualism—a stance that puts the self first—relationality "is a stance which emphasizes expressivity and takes others into account not as 'other' but as important in themselves" (Johnson 1988, 68–69). While relationality informs many a wife's ideal of marriage, individualism can be crucial for wives to produce relational ends. Concerns about divorce that accuse wives of individualism or of a decreasing willingness to sacrifice for families overlook the complexity of wives' emotional desires and interactional limits. Wives may want an equality of sacrifice based on relational connection, yet relationality cannot be forced. Thus, wives may find it easier to secure an individualistic equality in which neither spouse sacrifices.

In this chapter, I document wives' and husbands' belief in a marital work ethic and suggest that this belief has been intensified by widespread divorce. I illustrate that wives are more likely than their husbands to do marital work, and how they attempt to recruit their husbands in the work of monitoring marriages. The dynamics and results of wives' efforts are represented in three case studies.

Research Design and Method

A number of economic, legal, and demographic indicators suggest that the 1970s represent a "tipping point" for the social context of marriage and divorce.[5] These 1970s indicators include such developments as the rise of the two-job couple as the norm among married couples, the institution of no-fault divorce, a projected divorce rate of 50 percent for all marriages contracted after 1970, and a women's movement.[6] Given these indicators, I designed my research to interview heterosexual couples marrying after what I designate as this seventies tipping point.[7] In order to hold age relatively constant, I primarily selected individuals from a twentieth-year high school reunion list.[8] One spouse from each couple was born in 1953, so the average age of respondents was 39. This is basically a quota sample. I aimed to vary race-ethnicity and religion among respondents in order to capture diverse meanings regarding marriage, divorce, and gender.[9] I did not intentionally pursue quotas on religious affiliation, but I obtained variation.[10] The couples were mostly dual-career couples, and all were middle-class, married parents from the San Francisco Bay area.

I interviewed 17 couples (34 individuals) in total in the early 1990s. The average year of marriage was 1979. At the time of the interviews, the mean number of years married was 11; six couples had been married less than 10 years and 11 couples had been married 10 or more years.[11] Of the 34 spouses, 25 were in their first marriage, and the remaining nine were in their second marriage. All couples had children and averaged two children each.

I designed my study to conduct three in-depth interviews with every couple.[12] The wife and husband were first interviewed separately; the individual interviews averaged three hours each. Then a joint interview was scheduled; the joint interviews averaged two and a half hours. The interview tapes were transcribed and the text was coded and analyzed according to grounded theory procedures (Corbin and Strauss 1990). My research aim was to discover how spouses' talked about marriage, divorce, and gender, with the rise of both divorce and gender equality.

The Marital Work Ethic

As Craig Morris[13] pondered changes in marriage and divorce since his parents' marriage in the late 1940s, he articulated a relationship between divorce and work in marriage:

> I guess there were a lot of people who were stuck in marriages, and very unhappy at that time, and didn't feel like they had a way out. And yet, on the other hand, um, you look at today and you say—I think maybe a lot of people are leaving too soon, before they really look for ways to . . . save their marriage. But then again people are working harder today to save their marriages than ever before. Um, because you have to work hard to save it 'cause it's so easy to let it slip away, compared to 30 years ago. (European American, age 45, remarried 5 years)

Craig's discussion reflects two interpretations of divorce. Divorce rates seem to suggest that spouses are "leaving too soon" and not working on marriages. Yet a context of prevalent divorce, alternatively, compels marital work. Indeed, nearly everyone I interviewed confirmed Craig's belief that to maintain a marriage in a context of divorce, spouses are "working harder today."

I found that a majority of spouses believed in a marital work ethic. About 80 percent of this sample (28 of 34 spouses) talked about the need to work on marriage.

> And it was work. That's the other thing. It meant working really hard at what we had, and if we had something. And I think I took it more seriously than he did. (Pamela Jordan, European American, age 38, married 7 years)

> Mostly it involves effort, work, communication, and tolerance. (Naomi Rosenberg, European American, age 42, remarried 9 years)

> To make it work. Maybe that's the largest decision. It's so easy to say, "I quit." It's more difficult to stay and make it work. (Rosemary Gilmore, African American, age 38, married 13 years)

> [To] do custodial things, you know, to keep myself in a sound frame of mind. And not go overboard in voicing my way of doing things. Sometimes, you know, it does go overboard and I have to reel that in. Sometimes she'll point those out to me, and sometimes I'm aware of them. And sometimes the kids bring points and stuff up—it's about my being willing to, you know, make those changes necessary to get back on course. (Bill Gilmore, African American, age 39, married 13 years)

These husbands and wives talk about a work ethic—assuming, implying, or asserting that coping with the divorce option requires periodic effort. It is interesting that the six spouses who did not talk about the marital work ethic consider themselves "traditional"—traditional denoting both a strong belief in "marriage as forever" and in a male-dominant marriage. But for most couples, widespread divorce means husbands are talking about the need to work on marriage fully as much as wives are.

The Work of Marriage

The belief in the marital work ethic is not the same as actually *doing* the work of monitoring a marriage. The work of marriage should be understood as an extension of Hochschild's (1983) concept of "emotion work." Emotion work entails inducing or suppressing "feeling in order to sustain the outward countenance that produces the proper state of mind in others" (Hochschild 1983, 7). As Hochschild observes, "We put emotion to private use. . . . We continually try to put together things that threaten to pull apart—the situation, an appropriate way to see and feel about it, and our own real thoughts and feelings" (1983, 85). Among other private relationships, spouses certainly "try to put together things" within the marital situation—and hold them together despite forces that threaten to pull a marriage apart. Here, I focus on the aspect of emotion work that attempts to induce feelings of intimacy, connection, and attunement. The code words of marital work are: adjusting, adapting, trying, learning, growing, fulfilling needs, caring, and, above all, communicating.

For example, Jane and Gordon Walker's 17-year marriage has not been gratifying throughout, and Jane emphasized communication and sharing feelings as she discussed a marital crisis:

> We weren't communicating. I guess I wasn't really expressing my feelings. He wasn't expressing his. It just seems like the door was closing out, and I realized that—and he realized that as well—but he wouldn't identify it as much as I would. And say something's really wrong here—you have to let me in. (African American, age 39)

As Gordon also attests, Jane initiated the repair work. Although Jane identified the problem, Gordon was willing to reflect, respond, and work.

> I think we both recognize—I'm pretty sure she'd tell you the same thing—we worked at it. We understand that you just don't: "okay, we love each other, we got married, okay, fine that's it, let's go on." Because if you are an individual who is growing, you change. And if you care about the relationship that you're in, you're constantly communicating with your mate so that they adjust with you. Or if the adjustments are uncomfortable, you are aware of those changes, and you make them fit if you're concerned about the relationship. (African American, age 40)

Perhaps reflecting the view of a longstanding tradition of egalitarianism and relationality among African Americans (Collins 1990; Davis 1983; Nobles 1976; Taylor et al. 1990), Gordon was not a resistant recruit to the work of monitoring marriage. For other wives, however, the process of recruiting husbands to marital work has meant more conflict.

When 35-year-old Iris Sutton asserted that the biggest challenge of her 13-year marriage is "probably just staying married" and added "I mean there are so many reasons to get divorced, I mean that are very good reasons," she not only was referring to marital difficulties, but also was implying that marital endurance requires active effort. Under the influence of egalitarian ideals, wives like Iris increasingly attempt to share the work of monitoring marriage. Iris has threatened to divorce her husband, Ben Yoshida because of her frustrations with his lack of emotional attunement. Ben explained that he realized he must pay attention to the marriage.

> I think I realized I'm not dealing with a Japanese woman; in the sense that when Iris was threatening me to break up—at one time or another I really had the realization that she really, really means it—if I don't behave she really would not hesitate to leave me and that really scared the hell out of me. (Japanese, age 40)

"Behaving" in this case means attuning to his wife and his children. For Ben, Iris's European American ethnicity explains her seriousness. But this seriousness appears to be relatively recent for European American women, too. Women's use of divorce threats to produce emotional equality requires them to have financial independence, egalitarian ideals, and accessible divorce.

Wives' efforts to recruit men into the relational work of marriage, in essence, can be understood as efforts to "defeminize" love. By "defeminizing" love, I mean fostering men's valuation of nurturance and expressiveness, rather than Cancian's meaning, for example, which emphasizes redefining love. Cancian (1987) has argued that since the nineteenth century, love has been exceedingly "feminized," in its emphasis on tenderness, nurturance, and the expression of feelings. She emphasizes the need to expand the definition of love to include qualities that have been considered "masculine," not only sex, but the practical giving of help or sharing of activities that are absent from dominant cultural understandings of love in the West. But we may miss a more important point if we simply expand our definition of love rather than redistribute the emotion work of love. My data suggest that it is not wives who undervalue the practical giving of help or the sharing of activities—in fact, they dearly value the sharing of the "second shift" (Hochschild with Machung 1989); rather it is husbands who resist the nurturance and expression of feelings required by marital work.

Like their efforts to redistribute reproductive and productive labor, I found that wives' attempts to get men to do more emotion work in marriage often met with resistance.

The following three case studies reveal this process and the uneven results. One shows cooperation in the work, the second shows a conflicted process, and the third shows a failed attempt. Whether wives' efforts are met with cooperation or resistance, understanding these gendered dynamics is crucial in a culture of divorce. In the past when there was a sense of "no alternative," it may have taken more effort to leave the marriage; today, it may take more effort to stay in the marriage.

The Clement-Leonettis: Cooperation in Marital Work

The Clement-Leonetti marriage illustrates how an active work ethic serves to sustain a gratifying marriage and arises in response to "unexpected divorces." Dana Clement and Robert Leonetti are in a 10-year marriage, the first for both, and have three children. They are struggling to maintain a middle-class lifestyle as Robert works two jobs as a professional policy analyst and a consultant, while Dana works part-time in a biological laboratory and is the primary caretaker of their children. Both spouses are European American, age 32, and are lapsed Catholics.

For Robert, the first unexpected divorce was that of his parents; for Dana, it was that of her best friend from kindergarten. Children, homes, and marital length all figure into the unexpected quality of these divorces for Dana. The topic arises when I open the interview by asking Dana "what's good or happy about your marriage?" She replies by reviewing their brushes with others' divorces:

> I think that Robert and I have certain understandings that--I think a big part of what has shaped our marriage and the reason we're still together and all that is because he comes from a family that is divorced. His parents are divorced. And when my first child was born, my

best friend from kindergarten went through a divorce. And I was totally, you know, unaccustomed to divorces in a family. And one of the things that helped us, I think, is that we both shared our feelings about both of those sets of divorces. For me, it was terribly shocking that my friend who had been married 15 years and had two kids, and a car, and a house, and a yard, and a dog, and you know the whole American picture—to be getting divorced. At that time, this was eight years ago already, we agreed that we would never stay together with one of us unhappy, that if something was going wrong, we would at least have the respect for the other person to tell them what was happening.

Dana assumed that she should give a reason for still being together. When marriage culture prevailed, this kind of explanation was unnecessary except under "last resort" conditions.

As Dana discussed the array of divorces surrounding Robert and herself, she turned a potential vulnerability to divorce on its head. They pledged to share their feelings with one another and to keep one another abreast of encroaching unhappiness or doubts. That the goal of the work ethic is a "gratifying" and not simply an "enduring" marriage is captured in Dana's statement that "we agreed we would never stay together with one of us unhappy." To avert an unhappy marriage and subsequent divorce, they "work" at it. But how exactly do they do this?

Part of the work is managing emotions and their expression. When I asked Robert about how they have changed over the course of their marriage, he explained that in the early years of their relationship their differences were more "pronounced" and that there were many more arguments. When I ask Robert how they had gotten through those years of conflict, he begins by laughingly reporting "years of arguing," and then elaborates.

> And we struggled with it. I don't know maybe we grew up—I grew up, she grew up—together.

. . . And I wasn't, clearly, I really wasn't asking what she was feeling, I was just telling her what she was feeling. And as I watched that in myself, and I had to 'cause she forced me to—and I was also kind of growing . . . I was really forced to deal with it. I either had to deal with it or leave. [A lesson was learned] which is that there are ways that are different than what you want, and that I really wasn't—I was expressing my own disappointment, my own anger in a way that didn't leave enough room for her.

As Robert learned to monitor himself and avoid imposing his "version" of reality—learned to suppress his anger and redefine his disappointment—he also learned to recognize Dana's feelings. He felt forced, as he repeated twice, to adjust. He reiterated later that he had to "let go of his version of resolution as right" and remind himself that "her way of expression was okay and mine was not better." In this way, he feels he has "grown."

In addition to these struggles and their pledge to keep one another informed of their feelings about the marriage, Dana contended that her friend's divorce was "one of the reasons I went to therapy at the time I did." She observed that these divorces were "what I talked about a lot." Both Dana and Robert portray therapy as part of the work they did, not only to deal with the divorces around them, but also to further the relational work in their own marriage. While Robert and Dana simultaneously went to individual, as opposed to couples, therapy, their reliance upon therapy reflected a widespread generation-based pattern.

The number of couples who attend "couples therapy" serves as one indicator of marital monitoring and was prevalent in my sample. Seven of the 17 couples had gone to couples therapy at some point during their relationship—some briefly and some at length. Other research, also, suggests that spouses rely on therapy more often than in the past (Bellah et al. 1985; Philipson 1993, 58).

Therapy helps couples monitor their relationships, but the men's and women's attitudes toward therapy differed. Although some of the wives criticized or resisted therapy, wives were more likely to be dissatisfied with marital communication, to advocate therapy, and to want husbands to go to therapy with them. The wives were more likely to talk the "vocabulary" of therapeutic culture, using such terms as "the inner child" and "codependency." In contrast, husbands were less likely to use such words. They were less likely to express dissatisfaction with communication and more likely to refuse, resist, deride, or downplay the role of therapy in their marriages. Therapists are, in some sense, allies to many women not because they necessarily support their agendas but because they legitimate women's relational concerns, validate women's desires for men to take active responsibility for their marriages, and suggest that men may have to contribute to the "emotion work" of marriage.[14] While some scholars have argued that therapeutic culture has been a vehicle for individualism, it can also serve as a vehicle for relationality. Therapy often requires emotion work that can nurture relationality in marriage.

Robert and Dana's mutual efforts to monitor the marriage are less typical in this sample. However, they illustrate the key facets of marital work by responding to a culture of divorce with the aims of growth, fulfillment, and happiness, and by using therapy. They provide a portrait of a successful redistribution of relationship work in marriage.

The Turners: Conflict over Marital Work

The Turners engaged in a more overt struggle over the marital work. Mina and Nick Turner lived together for three years and have been married for 10. They are one of four interracial couples I interviewed; Mina is Japanese American and Nick is African American. While this is Mina's second, it is Nick's first marriage; she is 41, he is 38. They are currently raising three children. Both Mina and Nick are college-educated, middle class, and full-time workers.

When I opened my interview with Mina, I asked what was good about her marriage. She initially stated: "Everything." She elaborates that it is good "sexually," provides "emotional support as far as career-wise, . . . there's no really set role of who does what, you know, everyone does everything." The latter comment represents their egalitarian marriage; the Turners share work and home responsibilities.

Mina's previous marriage has affected her view of marriage with Nick. When I asked Mina about the biggest surprise of her marriage, she replied in a way that reflects divorce culture.

> One of the surprises is that it's lasted this long. (Laughs.) No really, it's like I feel like "who is gonna put up with me?" You know? Because at this point in my life, it's like, you take me like I am or else forget it, because I'm not going to be in the same situation as I was in my first, where I did everything to please a person and lost myself, you know. So I'm just going to be the bitch I am and you take me, or else you're gone.

As Mina suggested by appropriating the pejorative term "bitch," criticisms of her aggressiveness or selfishness will not sway Mina to cede her independence. Perhaps concluding that "offense is the best defense," she refused to "lose herself" again. Her marriage is undeniably contingent upon her independence. The strength of her independence is verified in a story both Mina and Nick tell of a crisis in their marriage.

Two years ago the Turner's youngest child was hit by a car. While their daughter has gen-

erally recovered, the crisis represented a marital communication problem to both spouses. One evening, during this traumatic period, a new crisis emerged when, as they both attested, he "erupted"—got drunk and violent. When I asked about the biggest surprise of "his" marriage, Nick began to relate his version of the same event. He replied, "I guess the—we're still together after I erupted one evening, you know, I had too much to drink and one thing set me off and I went on a screaming rampage." This "near divorce" was averted because, with some resistance, Nick conformed to Mina's condition. Mina's conditions were, as she stated:

> I go, "Okay," you know, "you go see the therapist or I'm out of here." . . . You know, I wasn't gonna wait around for him to put his mitts on me. That was—that's all it took for me, you know. And uh—but you know, it was just so out of character for him. . . . like I said, I think it was all that internalizing.

Mina went on to frame the "violence" as not only pivotal but also exceptional; it was, as she put it, "Dr. Jeckyl and Mr. Hyde." When Mina demanded that Nick go into therapy, she was trying to share the work of monitoring marriage. Mina not only forged a direct link between Nick's noncommunication and his explosive behavior that night but also she expects Nick to share the emotion work of marriage. She wants Nick to learn the expressive and relational skills for the survival of the marriage. Or else.

Independence empowers Mina to achieve her goal of a relational marriage. She is defining the terms of the marriage contract—and using the option of divorce to redefine the division of emotion work in the marriage. "Communication" and "talk" are marks of her relational criteria of marital happiness. She does not simply want independence, she also wants to feel connected.

A dilemma for many wives is how to procure equality without exercising the power of independence—without, in effect, relying upon individualism. Mina Turner's individualism is apparent in her interview and appears to be a reaction to her first marriage. Women can use their income and occupational status to improve their standing and power in relationships; yet, their desire for independence should not be viewed apart from their relational concerns. Wives like Mina have a second agenda based on relationality; they want to share not only individual rights but also relational responsibilities—including the "emotion work" of monitoring marriage. Although some women are using independence to bring about relational ideals in their marriages, they need husbands who are willing to reciprocate; that is, willing to value and to do the marital work entailed in sustaining heterosexual marriage.

The final case study, the Kason-Morris marriage, suggests that not all husbands are willing to reciprocate—and not all wives are as willing as Mina to exercise their power.

The Kason-Morrises: Failure to Redistribute the Work

Roxanne and Craig have been married for five years and are raising two daughters. They are European American, nonreligious, and are college educated. Craig is an accountant and Roxanne is a part-time word processor. Both have been married before and were wary of remarriage, but they asserted that the theme of their marriage is "practice makes perfect." Still, this marriage is not perfect. While Craig clearly articulated that spouses are "working harder today" because they must if they do not want it to "slip away," he was not as clear about what that "work" entails.

Whether speaking of child care, household,

or market labor, Roxanne did not feel that responsibilities are shared in her marriage. When I ask Roxanne about the biggest compromise of her marriage, she asserted: "Housework. It's my compromise, not his." Later, she described the choice not to work full-time as the biggest "concession" of her marriage: "it's really a powerless situation in a marriage when you're barely working." She explained: "you have no monetary power" and "you're at their beck and call." Finally, when I asked what's not good about the marriage, she stated, "He complains that I strap him with the load of child care when he comes home from work . . . which isn't true, but that's what he thinks."

It might seem that Roxanne's claimed sacrifices, compromises, and concessions are an array of separate issues; however, in many ways her account suggests that productive labor, reproductive labor, and emotion work are all of a piece. Roxanne reports that in her first marriage she was repeatedly venting her anger about the "second shift." In this marriage, she resolved, "I'm not going to do that anymore, I'm not going to lower myself and I'm not going to get that angry." She has learned, as she puts it, to "press down my anger when he won't do the dishes." Roxanne's efforts illustrate Hochschild's point that "across the nation at this particular time in history, this emotion work is often all that stands between the stalled revolution on the one hand, and broken marriages on the other" (with Machung 1989, 56).

In addition to the spouses divergent expectations of marital labors, the Kason-Morris marriage also revealed tension in their visions of what constitutes a fulfilling marriage. Craig wants Roxanne to be more appreciative of things as they are. In contrast, Roxanne perceives "talk" as constituting emotional intimacy and wants more of it. When I ask what's missing in the marriage, Roxanne replies:

"One thing that I would want more of is more intimacy, just on a, on a daily basis. More visiting. More communication. More talking. Sharing." Roxanne, is among a number of wives who feel that their husbands refuse to express thoughts and feelings and do not care about women's emotional lives (Thompson and Walker 1989, 846).

The Kason-Morris marriage reflects conventional gender differences found in heterosexual marriages (Rubin 1983). If these conflicts are not new, the ways in which wives contend with them are: wives are increasingly likely to press for their vision of a fulfilling marriage, a vision that is informed by connection and an increasing awareness that the emotion work of marriage needs to be shared. Wives' desire for relationality have them searching for strategies to recruit husbands into the emotion work of marriage and family and, as I have suggested, couples therapy has become an increasingly common vehicle for sharing this work.

Roxanne has tried to get Craig to go to therapy with her, and she "would still like to," but "he hated it." She reported, "we got in our worst arguments after each session." Most of these arguments concerned family responsibilities, housework, and sharing feelings. She "decided it would be the ruin of our marriage if we continued."[15]

Craig would also like to see improvement in their communication dynamics—not more talk but more understanding. In this way, Craig's view reflects Cancian's (1987) insight that his practical giving of help and sharing of activities go unrecognized as love. For Craig, therapy was not a means to overcome these difficulties but a setting to reenact them. He states that he "doesn't care for" therapy and that he is uncomfortable with a lot of talk.[16] Moreover, Craig felt manipulated into therapy—he felt that Roxanne was hauling him into therapy to focus on his prob-

lems. In ways he was right: Roxanne wants him to take more time and responsibility for the emotional contours of marital and parental relationships. Yet, ultimately, Roxanne is more focused on how the marriage needs change. Craig may be aware that therapy legitimates Roxanne's relational concerns, but his resistance blinds him to Roxanne's larger aims and to therapy's potential for averting a growing breach between himself and Roxanne. Craig's refusal to participate in therapy doesn't change the degree to which therapeutic culture informs Roxanne's vision of marital relationships. What it does change, however, is whether she attends to the vying messages in therapeutic culture of relationality or individualism. Relationality cannot be wrested from another. By choice or default, Roxanne is attuned to the message of individualism. She wants to conquer her "codependency," that is, her tendency to take care of others and neglect herself.

According to Roxanne's talk, her marriage is contingent not only on a sense of autonomy but also on a sense of connection; in actuality, she is neither very autonomous nor connected. Roxanne wanted connection, but I sensed that she might "choose" separation. She asserted that it would be his "moodiness, pouting, and childlike behavior" that would break her marriage. She was tired of Craig's refusal to answer her and she was tired of doing all the emotion work in their marriage. Roxanne's initiation of a divorce could suggest that her individualism split the marriage. Craig's resistance to the emotion work would not be reflected in most statistics; yet, he could become one of those ex-husbands who "didn't know what happened."

Kitson and Holmes discovered a notable gender difference in their research on the marital complaint "not sure what happened": For ex-husbands this complaint ranked third, for ex-wives it ranked twenty-eighth (1992,

123). These results suggest that these husbands were not attuned to the well-being of their wives or their marriages. Other research also finds that "in marriages that eventually ended in separation or divorce, women usually knew the relationship was in trouble long before their partners did" (Thompson and Walker 1989, 848). In short, Craig may be missing the implication of not sharing the marital work with Roxanne. In response, Roxanne gravitates toward the ideal of individualism.

Wives and Marital Work: Individualism or Relationality?

In the past decade, family scholars have debated whether we should be optimistic or pessimistic about family life in the United States (Glenn 1987, 349). Optimistic theorists have argued that the family is not falling apart, but simply changing and adapting (Riley 1991; Scanzoni 1987; Skolnick 1991). These theorists emphasize the oppression that has attended women's self-sacrifices in marriage and point to the potential for greater self-determination and happier relationships today (Cancian 1987; Coontz 1992; Reissman 1990; Skolnick 1991; Stacey 1990). They tend to downplay individualism and troubles in family bonds.

Pessimistic theorists have argued alternatively that the institution of marriage is a cause for concern—that divorce rates signify an unraveling of social bonds (Bellah et al. 1985; Glenn 1987; Lasch 1979; Popenoe 1988; Spanier 1989). Given that marital dissolution by divorce, rather than death, entails individual choice, these theorists focus on the role played by "individualism" in divorce. Pessimists fear we have forsaken nurturance, commitment, and responsibility in our aggregate rush to divorce. And because these are the very virtues that have been traditionally valorized in women, these "divorce debates" are always

implicitly, if not explicitly, about gender. As one scholar has observed, "when commentators lament the collapse of traditional family commitments and values, they almost invariably mean the uniquely female duties associated with the doctrine of separate spheres for men and women" (Coontz 1992, 40).[17]

We know that as heads of the household, even when not primary breadwinners, most husbands, historically, have had greater authority, and therefore greater freedom, to be independent, compared to wives. Women's greater labor force participation, increased activity in the political sphere, and greater initiation of divorces suggest that women are appropriating the masculinist model of individualism. However, if we focus on these social changes, we obscure women's enduring responsibility for family labors—including monitoring marriages.

While marital monitoring was important in the past, when a culture of marriage prevailed, it was more likely to be done by and expected of wives and was more likely to lead to wives' accommodation within the marriage. Economic constraints and cultural disincentives pressed for accommodation. In a culture of divorce, however, marital monitoring by wives in heterosexual marriage takes on new meanings.

In a climate of marital contingency, the work of monitoring marriage demands to be shared. Wives' efforts to redistribute the monitoring of marriage may be successful, as in the Clement-Leonetti case, because of the spouses' shared receptivity to the marital work; or these efforts may be successful, as in the Turner case, because the wife engages the power of independence and the husband responds. However, the wife's efforts to redistribute the monitoring of marriage may falter, as in the Kason-Morris case, because her husband resists and because she hesitates to engage her power. My research leads me to conclude that more wives are less interested in conducting a marriage on old terms, terms that denied their autonomy and devalued their relational concerns.

Women such as Dana, Roxanne, and Mina are alert to the meaning of sacrificing self to others. Given an awareness of the subordinate role of wives and the devaluation of "women's work," they are rightfully suspicious of the wife role. Many refuse to sacrifice themselves.

While women may want an equality of sacrifice based on relational connection, they may have to settle for an equality of nonsacrifice based on individualism. It is easier for women to appropriate the male model of individualism than it is to compel relationality from men. Because relationality cannot be wrested from husbands, wives' individualism is a predictable default in a cultural context that valorizes individual choice.

Optimistic scholars have been quick to deny women's increasing individualism—because it has been used against women. Rather than denying it, women's individualism needs to be understood in a political, structural, and historical context. Because we proceed from a history of male-dominant marriages, individualism does not *mean* the same thing for women as it does for men. Wives who are more individualistic are often trying to counter male-dominance in marriage. As one family scholar succinctly observed about the egalitarian marriage: "What most women seek is not power but the absence of domination" (Johnson 1988, 261). Wives fear being subordinated in a way that husbands do not. Moreover, independence is not just an end but a means for some wives to counter old terms and to secure a relational agenda. Wives are not necessarily forgoing relational responsibilities, but are combining them with individual rights. Yet individualism does mean that a wife can use the lever of the divorce option to secure her marital vision.

In sum, even though wives want a relational marriage, they may need to draw on individualism to secure it; and if secured, they may change the power dynamics of their marriages. If wives are unable to secure their vision of the marriage, they may choose to pass through the gateway called divorce. Yet, ultimately, what many wives want is not freedom from but freedom within a relational marriage.

NOTES

Acknowledgments: I want to thank Arlie Hochschild for her meticulous and insightful feedback on this chapter. I am also grateful for the clear and thoughtful commentary provided by Anita Garey and Karen Pugliesi.

1. I fully address the meaning of a culture of divorce in "Divorce Culture: A Breach in Gender Relations." Ph.D. diss. University of California, Berkeley, 1994.

2. "Strategies" here refers to mental and symbolic actions for coping with perceived realities, in this case, the potential of divorce. I found three other strategies: "passing the test," "hypothetical divorces," and "gender ideology as a shield." Spouses' stories of "passing the test" entailed overcoming a notable hurdle, which comes to signify a resilient marriage. Spouses' recognition of the vulnerability of all married couples is reflected in their references to "hypothetical divorces"; these are the divorces that "could have been" had they married someone else or at a different time. A third strategy relates to gender ideology; wives and husbands account for marital endurance in terms of their adherence to either traditional or egalitarian gender ideologies.

3. The "marital work ethic" is a second-order category that I derived from 1970s spouses' references to work in maintaining marriage. Kerry Daly points out that Alfred Schutz distinguishes between first-order constructs, which are "rooted in the everyday language of families," and second-order constructs, which "arise from the process of analytic induction (1992, 9)." I emphasize that this

is a second- rather than a first-order construct because even though respondents talk about the "work" of marriage in their everyday language, the "marital work ethic" is meant to capture how that belief is widely shared and is consistently linked to the challenge of divorce culture in their talk.

4. These concerns should be seen as an instance of Collins's (1990) important insight that "both/and" is a more illuminating framework than the ever popular "either/or" for understanding peoples' experiences.

5. A "tipping point" means that there were sufficient numbers of people divorcing to designate it as a behavioral norm or standard. Social norms have changed when as many, if not more, marriages dissolve as endure. Bernard (1972/1982) designated 1980 as the "tipping point" for the "two-earner marriage" because at that time the employed wife became the standard.

6. By the 1970s it became more common for an adult to lose a spouse and a child to lose a parent through divorce rather than death (Glick 1979; Sweet and Bumpass 1987). It is predicted that 50 percent of marriages contracted in 1970 will eventually end in divorce. In addition to these demographic developments, the legal regulation of marriage and divorce has changed radically since 1970, when California first introduced "no-fault" divorce, which is now incorporated into the legal systems of all 50 states. The no-fault rule liberalized divorce by abolishing grounds and deeming fault irrelevant. Furthermore, the traditional criteria of "gender" was replaced by the principle of "equality" to determine the distribution of property, support awards, and child custody (Kay 1987; Weitzman 1985). Finally, economic developments have transformed the typical family experience. From 1950 to 1980, working mothers with young children increased over 300 percent (McLaughlin et al. 1988, 120). Today, the two-job couple is the norm among married couples.

7. In my larger project, I investigated how matched wives and husbands are redefining marriage for two generations: couples marrying in the 1950s and couples marrying in the 1970s. For the older generation I analyzed a series of archival longitudinal interviews with twelve couples conducted from 1958 to 1982 (Hackstaff 1994).

8. I also included interviews with seven couples that I conducted for Judith Wallerstein's "Marriage Project," which became her book *The Good Marriage*. I only included couples that met my parameters, such as age, and, therefore, five couples were eliminated. I am indebted to Dr. Wallerstein for allowing me to use these additional interviews for my research.

9. Twenty-one spouses were European American, five were Japanese American, five were African American, and three identified themselves as biracial (including one European-Latino American, one African-European and American Indian, and one African-European American).

10. By adulthood, thirteen of the selected individuals were not religious, ten spouses were Christian, three were Catholic, four were Jewish, and four were Buddhist.

11. The longest marriage was 20 years. The shortest marriage was one year and was only included in the sample because the couple had lived with each other for many years prior to the marriage; also, the husband in this couple was among the nine remarried spouses in the sample.

12. I conducted 34 individual interviews, but only 14 joint interviews because three couples could not arrange time for a joint interview.

13. All interviewees' names used in this chapter are pseudonyms.

14. The agendas themselves are often gendered—particularly regarding the "second shift" as manifested in parenting, homemaking, and other work to sustain a home.

15. Roxanne was not the only wife to say that therapy threatened to dissolve their marriage. The implication is that the husbands felt too threatened, angered, and manipulated by the demands of relationality.

16. Craig was hesitant to participate in my research, he told me, because it resembles therapy. While an in-depth interview does not share the structure or the aims of therapy, Craig is right that the processes are similar insofar as in-depth interviewing asks respondents to "share their inner life." And it is this very aspect, I believe, that made Craig reluctant to participate. He participated for his wife, who loves to "share herself," according to both of their accounts. Although in many couples

the desire to participate was mutual, when it was not mutual, the husband claimed to participate for his wife more often than the reverse.

17. Of course, husbands' individualism has also been a concern among family scholars. Ehrenreich (1984) argues that a "male flight from commitment" started in the 1950s. Stacey points out that if there is a family crisis, it is a male family crisis" (1990, 269). Recent research shows a bifurcation between "good dads" and "bad dads"; efforts to secure child support from the "bad dads" suggests this "male crisis" is being recognized (Furstenberg 1988; Furstenberg and Cherlin 1991).

REFERENCES

Bellah, Robert N., Richard Madsen, William Sullivan, Ann Swidler, and Steven Tipton. 1985. *Habits of the Heart.* Berkeley: University of California Press.

Bernard, Jessie. 1972/1982. *The Future of Marriage.* New Haven, Conn.: Yale University Press.

Blaisure, Karen R., and Katherine R. Allen. 1995. "Feminists and the Ideology and Practice of Marital Equality." *Journal of Marriage and the Family* 57:5–19.

Cancian, Francesca. 1987. *Love in America: Gender and Self-Development.* New York: Cambridge University Press.

Cherlin, Andrew. 1992. *Marriage, Divorce, Remarriage.* Revised and enlarged edition. Cambridge Mass.: Harvard University Press.

Collins, Patricia Hill. 1990. *Black Feminist Thought: Knowledge, Consciousness, and the Politics of Empowerment.* Boston: Unwin Hyman.

Coontz, Stephanie. 1992. *The Way We Never Were: American Families and the Nostalgia Trap.* New York: Basic Books.

Corbin, Juliet, and Anselm Strauss. 1990. "Grounded Theory Research: Procedures, Canons, and Evaluative Criteria." *Qualitative Sociology* 13 (1): 3–21.

Daly, Kerry. 1992. "The Fit Between Qualitative Research and Characteristics of Families." In *Qualitative Methods in Family Research,* edited by Jane Gilgun, Kerry Daly, and Gerald Handel, 3–11. Newbury Park, Calif.: Sage Publications.

Davis, Angela. 1983. *Women, Race, and Class.* New York: Vintage Books.

DeVault, Marjorie. 1987. "Doing Housework: Feeding and Family Life." In *Families and Work,* edited by Naomi Gerstel and Harriet Engle Gross, 178–191. Philadelphia: Temple University Press.

di Leonardo, Micaela. 1987. "The Female World of Cards and Holidays: Women, Families, and the Work of Kinship." *Signs: Journal of Women and Culture in Society* 12 (3): 440–453. (Chapter 31, this volume.)

Ehrenreich, Barbara. 1984. *The Hearts of Men.* Garden City, N.Y.: Anchor Press.

Furstenberg, Frank. 1988. "Good Dads-Bad Dads: Two Faces of Fatherhood." In *Family in Transition,* 8th ed., edited by Arelene S. Skolnick and Jerome H. Skolnick, 348–368. New York: HarperCollins.

Furstenberg, Frank, and Andrew Cherlin. 1991. *Divided Families: What Happens to Children When Parents Part.* Cambridge, Mass.: Harvard University Press.

Glenn, Norval D. 1987. "Continuity Versus Change, Sanguineness Versus Concern." *Journal of Family Issues* 8 (4): 348–354.

Glick, Paul. 1979. "Children of Divorced Parents in Demographic Perspective." *Journal of Social Issues* 35 (4): 170–182.

Goldscheider, Frances K., and Linda J. Waite. 1991. *New Families, No Families?* Berkeley: University of California Press.

Hackstaff, Karla B. 1994. "Divorce Culture: A Breach in Gender Relations." Ph.D. diss., Department of Sociology, University of California, Berkeley.

Hochschild, Arlie R. 1983. *The Managed Heart: The Commercialization of Human Feeling.* Berkeley: University of California Press.

Hochschild, Arlie R., with Anne Machung. 1989. *The Second Shift: Working Parents and the Revolution at Home.* New York: Viking Press.

Johnson, Miriam. 1988. *Strong Mothers, Weak Wives: The Search for Gender Equality.* Berkeley: University of California Press.

Kay, Herma Hill. 1987. "An Appraisal of California's No-Fault Divorce Low." *California Law Review* 75 (29): 291–319.

Kitson, Gay C., with William Holmes. 1992. *Portrait of Divorce: Adjustment to Marital Breakdown.* New York: Guilford Press.

Lasch, Christopher. 1979. *The Culture of Narcissism.* New York: W. W. Norton.

McLaughlin, Steven D., Barbara D. Melber, John O. G. Billy, Denise M. Zimmerle, Linda D. Winges, and Terry R. Johnson. 1988. *The Changing Lives of American Women.* Chapel Hill: University of North Carolina Press.

Nobles, Wade W. 1976. "Extended Self: Rethinking the So-Called Negro Self-Concept." *Journal of Black Psychology.* 2 (2): 15–24.

Oliker, Stacey. 1989. *Best Friends and Marriage.* Berkeley: University of California Press.

Philipson, Ilene. 1993. *On the Shoulders of Women: The Feminization of Psychotherapy.* New York: Guilford Press.

Popenoe, D. 1988. *Disturbing the Nest: Family Change and Decline in Modern Societies.* New York: Aldine De Gruyter.

Riessman, Catherine Kohler. 1990. *Divorce Talk: Women and Men Make Sense of Personal Relationships.* New Brunswick, N.J.: Rutgers University Press.

Riley, Glenda. 1991. *Divorce: An American Tradition.* New York: Oxford University Press.

Rubin, Lillian. 1983. *Intimate Strangers: Men and Women Together.* New York: Harper & Row.

Scanzoni, John. 1987. "Families in the 1980s: Time to Refocus Our Thinking." *Journal of Family Issues* 8 (4): 394–421.

Skolnick, Arlene. 1991. *Embattled Paradise.* New York: Basic Books.

Spanier, Graham B. 1989. "Bequeathing Family Continuity." *Journal of Marriage and the Family* 51:3–13.

Stacey, Judith. 1990. *Brave New Families: Stories of Domestic Upheaval in Late Twentieth Century America.* New York: Basic Books.

Sweet, James A., and Larry L. Bumpass. 1987. *American Families and Households.* Population of the United States in the 1980s, a Census monograph series. New York: Russell Sage Foundation.

Taylor, Robert J., Linda M. Chatters, M. Belinda Tucker, and Edith Lewis, 1990. "Developments in Research on Black Families: A Decade Review." *Journal of Marriage and the Family* 52:993–1014.

Thompson, Linda. 1991. "Family Work: Women's Sense of Fairness." *Journal of Family Issues* 12 (2): 181–196.

Thompson, Linda, and Alexis Walker. 1989. "Gender in Families: Women and Men in Marriage, Work, and Parenthood." *Journal of Marriage and the Family* 51:844–871.

U.S. Bureau of the Census. 1992. *Marriage, Divorce, and Remarriage in the 1990's.* Current Population Reports, Series P23–180. Washington, D.C.: U.S. Government Printing Office.

Walker, Thaii. 1993. "Census Misses the Mark on Race." *San Francisco Chronicle,* July 26, 1993, p. A–1.

Wallerstein, Judith, with Sandra Blakeslee. 1995. *The Good Marriage: How and Why Love Lasts.* Boston: Houghton Mifflin.

Weitzman, Lenore. 1985. *The Divorce Revolution.* New York: Free Press.

White, Lynn. 1990. "Determinants of Divorce: A Review of Research in the Eighties." *Journal of Marriage and the Family* 52:904–912.

Chapter 35

Why Gay People Should Seek the Right to Marry

THOMAS B. STODDARD

Even though, these days, few lesbians and gay men enter into marriages recognized by law, absolutely every gay person has an opinion on marriage as an "institution." (The word "institution" brings to mind, perhaps appropriately, museums.) After all, we all know quite a bit about the subject. Most of us grew up in marital households. Virtually all of us, regardless of race, creed, gender, and culture, have received lectures on the propriety, if not the sanctity, of marriage—which usually suggests that those who choose not to marry are both unhappy and unhealthy. We all have been witnesses, willing or not, to a lifelong parade of other people's marriages, from Uncle Harry and Aunt Bernice to the Prince and Princess of Wales. And at one point or another, some nosy relative has inevitably inquired of every gay person when he or she will finally "tie the knot" (an intriguing and probably apt cliché).

From *Out/look: National Lesbian and Gay Quarterly,* no. 6 (fall 1989): 9–13. Reprinted by permission of Walter Rieman, Executor of the Estate of Thomas B. Stoddard.

I must confess at the outset that I am no fan of the "institution" of marriage as currently constructed and practiced. I may simply be unlucky, but I have seen preciously few marriages over the course of my forty years that invite admiration and emulation. All too often marriage appears to petrify rather than satisfy and enrich, even for couples in their twenties and thirties who have had a chance to learn the lessons of feminism. Almost inevitably, the partners seem to fall into a "husband" role and a "wife" role, with such latter-day modifications as the wife who works in addition to raising the children and managing the household.

Let me be blunt: in its traditional form, marriage has been oppressive, especially (although not entirely) to women. Indeed, until the middle of the last century, marriage was, at its legal and social essence, an extension of the husband and his paternal family. Under the English common law, wives were among the husband's "chattel"—personal property—and could not, among other things, hold property in their own names. The common law crime of adultery demonstrates the unequal treatment accorded to husbands and wives: while a woman who slept with a man who wasn't her husband committed adultery, a man who slept with a woman not his wife committed fornication. A man was legally incapable of committing adultery, except as an accomplice to an errant wife. The underlying offense of adultery was not the sexual betrayal of one partner by the other, but the wife's engaging in conduct capable of tainting the husband's bloodlines. (I swear on my *Black's Law Dictionary* that I have not made this up!)

Nevertheless, despite the oppressive nature of marriage historically, and in spite of the general absence of edifying examples of modern heterosexual marriage, I believe very strongly that every lesbian and gay man should have the right to marry the same-sex partner of his or her choice, and that the gay rights movement should aggressively seek full legal recognition for same-sex marriages. To those who might not agree, I respectively offer three explanations, one practical, one political and one philosophical.

The Practical Explanation

The legal status of marriage rewards the two individuals who travel to the altar (or its secular equivalent) with substantial economic and practical advantages. Married couples may reduce their tax liability by filing a joint return. They are entitled to special government benefits, such as those given surviving spouses and dependents through the Social Security program. They can inherit from one another even when there is no will. They are immune from subpeonas requiring testimony against the other spouse. And marriage to an American citizen gives a foreigner a right to residency in the United States.

Other advantages have arisen not by law but by custom. Most employers offer health insurance to their employees, and many will include an employee's spouse in the benefits package, usually at the employer's expense. Virtually no employer will include a partner who is not married to an employee, whether of the same sex or not. Indeed, very few insurance companies even offer the possibility of a group health plan covering "domestic partners" who are not married to one another. Two years ago, I tried to find such a policy for Lambda, and discovered that not one insurance company authorized to do business in New York—the second-largest state in the country with more than 17 million residents—would accommodate us. (Lambda has tried to make do by paying for individual insurance policies for the same-sex partners of its employees who otherwise would go uninsured, but these individual policies are usually narrower in scope than group policies, often require applicants to furnish individual medical information not required under most group plans, and are typically much more expensive per person.)

In short, the law generally presumes in favor of every marital relationship, and acts to preserve and foster it, and to enhance the rights of the individuals who enter into it. It is usually possible, with enough money and the right advice, to replicate some of the benefits conferred by the legal status of marriage through the use of documents like wills and power of attorney forms, but that protection will inevitably, under current circumstances, be incomplete.

The law still looks upon lesbians and gay men with suspicion, and this suspicion casts a shadow over the documents they execute in recognition of a same-sex relationship. If a lesbian leaves property to her lover, her will may be invalidated on the grounds that it was executed under the "undue influence" of the would-be beneficiary. A property agreement may be denied validity because the underlying relationship is "meretricious"—akin to prostitution. (Astonishly, until the mid-1970s, the law throughout the United States deemed "meretricious" virtually *any* formal economic arrangement between two people not married to one another, on the theory that an exchange of property between them was probably payment for sexual services; the Supreme Court of California helped unravel this quaint legal fantasy in its 1976 ruling in the first famous "palimony" case, *Marvin v. Marvin.*) The law has progressed considerably beyond the uniformly oppressive state of affairs before 1969, but it is still far from enthusiastic about gay people and their relationships—to put it mildly.

Moreover, there are some barriers one simply cannot transcend outside of a formal marriage. When the Internal Revenue Code or the Immigration and Naturalization Act say "married," they mean "married" by definition of state statute. When the employer's group health plan says "spouse," it means "spouse" in the eyes of the law, not the eyes of the loving couple.

But there is another drawback. Couples seeking to protect their relationship through wills and other documents need knowledge, determination and—most importantly—money. No money, no lawyer. And no lawyer, no protection. Those who lack the sophistication or the wherewithal to retain a lawyer are simply stuck in most circumstances. Extending the right to marry to gay couples would assure that those at the bottom of the economic ladder have a chance to secure their relationship rights, too.

The Political Explanation

The claim that gay couples ought to be able to marry is not a new one. In the 1970s, same-sex couples in three states—Minnesota, Ken-

tucky and Washington—brought constitutional challenges to the marriage statutes, and in all three instances they failed. In each of the three, the court offered two basic justifications for limiting marriage to male-female couples: history and procreation. Witness this passage from the Supreme Court of Minnesota's 1971 opinion in *Baker v. Nelson*: "The institution of marriage as a union of man and woman, uniquely involving the procreation and rearing of children within a family, is as old as the book of Genesis. . . . This historic institution manifestly is more deeply founded than the asserted contemporary concept of marriage and societal interests for which petitioners contend."

Today no American jurisdiction recognizes the right of two women or two men to marry one another, although several nations in Northern Europe do.* Even more telling, until earlier this year [1989], there was little discussion within the gay rights movement about whether such a right should exist. As far as I can tell, no gay organization of any size, local or national, has yet declared the right to marry as one of its goals.

With all due respect to my colleagues and friends who take a different view, I believe it is time to renew the effort to overturn the existing marriage laws, and to do so in earnest, with a commitment of money and energy, through both the courts and the state legisla-

----

*In 1993, the Supreme Court of Hawaii ruled that the denial of marriage licenses to same-sex couples violated the Hawaii constitution's equal-rights protections. As of September 1997, this issue was still being debated in the courts. In response to the case in Hawaii, Congress passed the "Defense of Marriage Act," which President Bill Clinton signed into law in September 1996. This act permits states not to recognize same-sex marriages performed in other states or jurisdictions. In other words, even if a state allows same-sex marriages, those marriages will not necessarily be legally recognized in other parts of the United States or by the federal government. *Eds.*

tures. I am not naive about the likelihood of imminent victory. There is none. Nonetheless—and here I will not mince words—I would like to see the issue rise to the top of the agenda of every gay organization, including my own (although that judgment is hardly mine alone).

Why give it such prominence? Why devote resources to such a distant goal? Because marriage is, I believe, the political issue that most fully tests the dedication of people who are *not* gay to full equality for gay people, and also the issue most likely to lead ultimately to a world free from discrimination against lesbians and gay men.

Marriage is much more than a relationship sanctioned by law. It is the centerpiece of our entire social structure, the core of the traditional notion of "family." Even in its present tarnished state, the marital relationship inspires sentiments suggesting that it is something almost suprahuman. The Supreme Court, in striking down an anti-contraception statute in 1965, called marriage "noble" and "intimate to the degree of being sacred." The Roman Catholic Church and the Moral Majority would go—and have gone—considerably further.

Lesbians and gay men are now denied entry to this "noble" and "sacred" institution. The implicit message is this: two men or two women are incapable of achieving such an exalted domestic state. Gay relationships are somehow less significant, less valuable. Such relationships may, from time to time and from couple to couple, give the appearance of a marriage, but they can never be of the same quality or importance.

I resent—indeed, I loathe—that conception of same-sex relationships. And I am convinced that ultimately the only way to overturn it is to remove the barrier to marriage that now limits the freedom of every gay man and lesbian.

That is to not to deny the value of "domestic partnership" ordinances, statutes that prohibit discrimination based on "marital status," and other legal advances that can enhance the rights (as well as the dignity) of gay couples. Without question, such advances move us further along the path to equality. But their value can only be partial. (The recently enacted San Francisco "domestic partnership" ordinance, for example, will have practical value only for gay people who happen to be employed by the City of San Francisco and want to include their non-marital spouses in part of the city's fringe benefit package; the vast majority of gay San Franciscans—those employed by someone other than the city—have only a symbolic victory to savor.) Measures of this kind can never assure full equality. Gay relationships will continue to be accorded a subsidiary status until the day that gay couples have *exactly* the same rights as their heterosexual counterparts. To my mind, that means either that the right to marry be extended to us, or that marriage be abolished in its present form for all couples, presumably to be replaced by some new legal entity—an unlikely alternative.

The Philosophical Explanation

I confessed at the outset that I personally found marriage in its present avatar rather, well, unattractive. Nonetheless, even from a philosophical perspective, I believe the right to marry should become a stated goal of the gay rights movement.

First, and most basically, the issue is not the desirability of marriage, but rather the desirability of the *right* to marry. That I think two lesbians or two gay men should be entitled to a marriage license does not mean that I think all gay people should find appropriate partners and exercise the right, should it eventually exist. I actually rather doubt that I, myself, would want to marry, even though I share a household with another man who is exceedingly dear to me. There are others who feel differently, for economic, symbolic, or romantic reasons. They should, to my mind, unquestionably have the opportunity to marry if they wish and otherwise meet the requirements of the state (such as being old enough).

Furthermore, marriage may be unattractive and even oppressive as it is currently structured and practiced, but enlarging the concept to embrace same-sex couples would necessarily transform it into something new. If two women can marry, or two men, marriage—even for heterosexuals—need not be a union of a "husband" and a "wife." Extending the right to marry to gay people—that is, abolishing the traditional gender requirements of marriage—can be one of the means, perhaps the principal one, through which the institution divests itself of the sexist trappings of the past.

Some of my colleagues disagree with me. I welcome their thoughts and the debates and discussions our different perspectives will trigger. The movement for equality for lesbians and gay men can only be enriched through this collective exploration of the question of marriage. But I do believe many thousands of gay people want the right to marry. And I think, too, they will earn that right for themselves sooner than most of us imagine.

∾ Chapter 36

Since When Is Marriage a Path to Liberation?

PAULA L. ETTELBRICK

"Marriage is a great institution . . . if you like living in institutions," according to a bit of T-shirt philosophy I saw recently. Certainly, marriage is an institution. It is one of the most venerable, impenetrable institutions in modern society. Marriage provides the ultimate form of acceptance for personal intimate relationships in our society, and gives those who marry an insider status of the most powerful kind.

Steeped in a patriarchal system that looks to ownership, property, and dominance of men over women as its basis, the institution of marriage long has been the focus of radical feminist revulsion. Marriage defines certain relationships as more valid than all others. Lesbian and gay relationships, being neither legally sanctioned or commingled by blood, are always at the bottom of the heap of social acceptance and importance.

Given the imprimatur of social and personal approval which marriage provides, it is

not surprising that some lesbians and gay men among us would look to legal marriage for self-affirmation. After all, those who marry can be instantaneously transformed from "outsiders" to "insiders," and we have a desperate need to become insiders.

It could make us feel OK about ourselves, perhaps even relieve some of the internalized homophobia that we all know so well. Society will then celebrate the birth of our children and mourn the death of our spouses. It would be easier to get health insurance for our spouses, family memberships to the local museum, and a right to inherit our spouse's cherished collection of lesbian mystery novels even if she failed to draft a will. Never again would we have to go to a family reunion and debate about the correct term for introducing our lover/partner/significant other to Aunt Flora. Everything would be quite easy and very nice.

So why does this unlikely event so deeply disturb me? For two major reasons. First, marriage will not liberate us as lesbians and gay men. In fact, it will constrain us, make us

From *Out/look: National Lesbian and Gay Quarterly*, no. 6 (fall 1989): 9, 14–17. Reprinted by permission.

more invisible, force our assimilation into the mainstream, and undermine the goals of gay liberation. Second, attaining the right to marry will not transform our society from one that makes narrow, but dramatic, distinctions between those who are married and those who are not married to one that respects and encourages choice of relationships and family diversity. Marriage runs contrary to two of the primary goals of the lesbian and gay movement: the affirmation of gay identity and culture; and the validation of many forms of relationships.

When analyzed from the standpoint of civil rights, certainly lesbians and gay men should have a right to marry. But obtaining a right does not always result in justice. White male firefighters in Birmingham, Alabama, have been fighting for their "rights" to retain their jobs by overturning the city's affirmative action guidelines. If their "rights" prevail, the courts will have failed in rendering justice. The "right" fought for by the white male firefighters, as well as those who advocate strongly for the "rights" to legal marriage for gay people, will result, at best, in limited or narrowed "justice" for those closest to power at the expense of those who have been historically marginalized.

The fight for justice has as its goal the realignment of power imbalances among individuals and classes of people in society. A pure "rights" analysis often fails to incorporate a broader understanding of the underlying inequities that operate to deny justice to a fuller range of people and groups. In setting our priorities as a community, we must combine the concept of both rights and justice. At this point in time, making legal marriage for lesbian and gay couples a priority would set an agenda of gaining rights for a few, but would do nothing to correct the power imbalances between those who are married (whether gay of straight) and those who are not. Thus, justice would not be gained.

Justice for gay men and lesbians will be achieved only when we are accepted and supported in this society *despite* our differences from the dominant culture and the choices we make regarding our relationships. Being queer is more than setting up house, sleeping with a person of the same gender, and seeking state approval for doing so. It is an identity, a culture with many variations. It is a way of dealing with the world by diminishing the constraints of gender roles which have for so long kept women and gay people oppressed and invisible. Being queer means pushing the parameters of sex, sexuality, and family, and in the process transforming the very fabric of society. Gay liberation is inexorably linked to women's liberation. Each is essential to the other.

The moment we argue, as some among us insist on doing, that we should be treated as equals because we are really just like married couples and hold the same values to be true, we undermine the very purpose of our movement and begin the dangerous process of silencing our different voices. As a lesbian, I am fundamentally different from non-lesbian women. That's the point. Marriage, as it exists today, is antithetical to my liberation as a lesbian and as a woman because it mainstreams my life and voice. I do not want to be known as "Mrs. Attached-to-Somebody-Else." Nor do I want to give the state the power to regulate my primary relationship.

Yet, the concept of equality in our legal system does not support differences, it only supports sameness. The very standard for equal protection is that people who are similarly situated must be treated equally. To make an argument for equal protection, we will be required to claim that gay and lesbian relationships are the same as straight relationships. To gain the right, we must compare ourselves to married couples. The law looks to the insiders as the norm, regardless of how flawed or unjust their institutions, and requires that those seeking the law's equal protection situate themselves in a similar posture to those who are already protected. In arguing for the right to legal marriage, lesbians and gay men would be forced to claim that we are just like heterosexual couples, have the same goals and purposes, and vow to structure our lives similarly. The law provides no room to argue that we are different, but are nonetheless entitled to equal protection.

The thought of emphasizing our sameness to married heterosexuals in order to obtain this "right" terrifies me. It rips away the very heart and soul of what I believe it is to be a lesbian in this world. It robs me of the opportunity to make a difference. We end up mimicking all that is bad about the institution of marriage in our effort to appear to be the same as straight couples.

By looking to our sameness and deemphasizing our differences, we don't even place ourselves in a position of power that would allow us to transform marriage from an institution that emphasizes property and state regulation of relationships to an institution which recognizes one of many types of valid and respected relationships. Until the constitution is interpreted to respect and encourage differences, pursuing the legalization of same-sex marriage would be leading our movement into a trap; we would be demanding access to the very institution which, in its current form, would undermine *our* movement to recognize many different kinds of relationships. We would be perpetuating the elevation of married relationships and of "couples" in general, and further eclipsing other relationships of choice.

Ironically, gay marriage, instead of liberating gay sex and sexuality, would further outlaw all gay and lesbian sex not performed in a marital context. Just as sexually active non-married women face stigma and double standards around sex and sexual activity, so too would non-married gay people. The only legitimate gay sex would be that which is cloaked in and regulated by marriage. Its legitimacy would stem not from an acceptance of gay sexuality but because the Supreme Court and society in general fiercely protect the privacy of marital relationships. Lesbians and gay men who do not seek the state's stamp of approval would clearly face increased sexual oppression.

Undoubtedly, whether we admit it or not, we all need to be accepted by the broader society. That motivation fuels our work to eliminate discrimination in the workplace and elsewhere, fight for custody of our children, create our own families, and so on. The growing discussion about the right to marry may be explained in part by this need for acceptance. Those closer to the norm or to power in this country are more likely to see marriage as a principle of freedom and equality. Those who are more acceptable to the mainstream because of race, gender, and economic status are more likely to want the right to marry. It is the final acceptance, the ultimate affirmation of identity.

On the other hand, more marginal members of the lesbian and gay community (women, people of color, working class and poor) are less likely to see marriage as having relevance to our struggles for survival. After all, what good is the affirmation of our relationships (that is, marital relationships) if we are rejected as women, black, or working class?

The path to acceptance is much more complicated for many of us. For instance, if we choose legal marriage, we may enjoy the right to add our spouse to our health insurance policy at work, since most employment policies are defined by one's marital status, not family relationship. However, that choice assumes that we have a job *and* that our employer provides us with health benefits. For women, particularly women of color who tend to occupy the low-paying jobs that do not provide health care benefits at all, it will not matter one bit if they are able to marry their woman partners. The opportunity to marry will neither get them the health benefits nor transform them from outsider to insider.

Of course, a white man who marries another white man who has a full-time job with benefits will certainly be able to share in those benefits and overcome the only obstacle left to full societal assimilation—the goal of many in his class. In other words, gay marriage will not topple the system that allows only the privileged few to obtain decent health care. Nor will it close the privilege gap between those who are married and those who are not.

Marriage creates a two-tier system that allows the state to regulate relationships. It has become a facile mechanism for employers to dole out benefits, for businesses to provide special deals and incentives, and for the law to make distinctions in distributing meager public funds. None of these entities bothers to consider the relationship among people; the love, respect, and need to protect that exists among all kinds of family members. Rather, a simple certificate of the state, regardless of whether the spouses love, respect, or even see each other on a regular basis, dominates and is supported. None of this dynamic will change if gay men and lesbians are given the option of marriage.

Gay marriage will not help us address the systemic abuses inherent in a society that does not provide decent health care to all of its citizens, a right that should not depend on whether the individual (1) has sufficient resources to afford health care or health insurance, (2) is working and receives health insurance as part of compensation, or (3) is married to a partner who is working and has

health coverage which is extended to spouses. It will not address the underlying unfairness that allows businesses to provide discounted services or goods to families and couples— who are defined to include straight, married people and their children, but not domestic partners.

Nor will it address the pain and anguish of the unmarried lesbian who receives word of her partner's accident, rushes to the hospital and is prohibited from entering the intensive care unit or obtaining information about her condition solely because she is not a spouse or family member. Likewise, marriage will not help the gay victim of domestic violence who, because he chose not to marry, finds no protection under the law to keep his violent lover away.

If the laws change tomorrow and lesbians and gay men were allowed to marry, where would we find the incentive to continue the progressive movement we have started that is pushing for societal and legal recognition of all kinds of family relationships? To create other options and alternatives? To find a place in the law for the elderly couple who, for companionship and economic reasons, live together but do not marry? To recognize the right of a long-time, but unmarried, gay partner to stay in his rent-controlled apartment after the death of his lover, the only named tenant on the lease? To recognize the family relationship of the lesbian couple and the two gay men who are jointly sharing child-raising responsibilities? To get the law to acknowledge that we may have more than one relationship worthy of legal protection?

Marriage for lesbians and gay men still will not provide a real choice unless we continue the work our community has begun to spread the privilege around to other relationships. We must first break the tradition of piling benefits and privileges on to those who are married, while ignoring the real life needs of those who are not. Only when we de-institutionalize marriage and bridge the economic and privilege gap between the married and the unmarried will each of us have a true choice. Otherwise, our choice not to marry will continue to lack legal protection and societal respect.

The lesbian and gay community has laid the groundwork for revolutionizing society's views of family. The domestic partnership movement has been an important part of this progress insofar as it validates non-marital relationships. Because it is not limited to sexual or romantic relationships, domestic partnership provides an important opportunity for many who are not related by blood or marriage to claim certain minimal protections.

It is crucial, though, that we avoid the pitfall of framing the push for legal recognition of domestic partners (those who share a primary residence and financial responsibilities for each other) as a stepping stone to marriage. We must keep our eyes on the goals of providing true alternatives to marriage and of radically reordering society's view of family.

The goals of lesbian and gay liberation must simply be broader than the right to marry. Gay and lesbian marriages may minimally transform the institution of marriage by diluting its traditional patriarchal dynamic, but they will not transform society. They will not demolish the two-tier system of the "haves" and the "have nots." We must not fool ourselves into believing that marriage will make it acceptable to be gay or lesbian. We will be liberated only when we are respected and accepted for our differences and the diversity we provide to this society. Marriage is not a path to that liberation.

~ *Chapter 37*

Love Demands Everything

PHYLLIS BURKE

Gilbert Baker, aka Pink Jesus, had attired himself in jeans and a Rolling Stones tour T-shirt. In the basement storage bins in City Hall—or Silly Hall, as Harvey Milk had liked to call it—I helped Gilbert rummage for some banners in red, orange, and pink, which he had originally made for the inauguration of Mayor Art Agnos. This Valentine's Day would be the first day of official domestic partnership, when any committed couple, regardless of sexual preference, could be legally recognized by the City of San Francisco. It was the first time in the country that such a law had been passed by voter approval.

I hated it. As the law was written, there were absolutely no tangible benefits to legally registering. You got a piece of paper that said you were responsible for each other's living expenses, and that was it. Domestic partnership held no legal weight whatsoever in terms of health insurance, child custody, inheritance,

or taxes. I thought it was a marriage sham for the untouchables.

The international press and an army of television cameras and photographers prowled City Hall, anxious to find lesbian and gay couples willing to be photographed. They would not have long to wait. All day, hundreds of couples registered. Ironically, stationed here and there on the galleries in City Hall, framed by blue-and-gold burnished ironwork, were clusters of heterosexuals enacting real marriages. I had not realized that Valentine's Day marriages in City Hall were such a long-standing tradition. I had always looked the other way. Why would lesbian and gay people bother going through with what to me was a charade, especially when it was juxtaposed with these happy, heterosexual couples right in our faces, kissing to applause and blessed by the state.

I began to videotape. With the camera on my shoulder, the images were transmutted into black-and-white, which gave them that comfortable distance and gave me the feeling of being a faux journalist. I stood at the balcony of the second-floor gallery outside the mayor's office. The square rotunda rises four stories, with galleries on each floor. As I scanned the heterosexual couples in the process of taking their marriage vows, my camera caught on the image of Jean Harris, every salt-and-pepper hair in place, forty-seven years old, strong and athletic-looking. She stood directly across from me on the other side of the rotunda, in the shadow just outside the massive carved oak doors to the chambers of the Board of Supervisors. She walked to the top of the thirty-six sweeping marble steps that fan down to the first floor.

Jean was surveying the preparations for the domestic partners' celebration. Chairs were being placed at the base of the steps, flowers were being arranged, a sound system was being set up, and Gilbert was finishing hanging the banners. Jean scanned the rotunda, and her eyes went to the massive dome, which is over a hundred feet wide and weighs ninety thousand tons. When Harvey Milk and George Moscone were assassinated, Gilbert designed a poster of the exterior of City Hall, the spectacular dome lifted from its base at a ninety-degree angle, a wide shaft of light thrusting from inside the building into the sky.*

Jean Harris seemed to be watching the light as it filtered through multipaned windows at the dome's base and flickered across the surfaces of the ornate scrolls, carved heads, and a rather remarkable amount of sculpted fruit. Harvey Milk had loved this building, and he had always encouraged us to take the main staircase.

Jean Harris was working at the time as an aide to Supervisor Harry Britt. Jean Harris can easily be mistaken for a man, which is part of her charm. She is the only complete cross-dresser in the history of City Hall, and I have actually heard her say that heterosexuality is a learned response. It is hard to know if she really believes this or has simply learned the power of hyperbole. Her enemies call her the lesbian Al Sharpton; her friends, the lesbian Harvey Milk. I had sat with her in her City Hall office, the room where Harvey Milk had been murdered. It was his assassin's old office. Dan White had called Harvey into the room to kill him. The last thing Harvey saw was the Opera House across the avenue. There was no plaque, there was nothing to tell you that in that little room the course of history had been changed. I found myself looking for some sign of the brutal assassination—some mark on the rug, on the wall—but the decorators had covered up everything. I could, however, feel something in that room, but it might quite simply have been Jean Harris's rage.

"I wear a necktie because I want every man who sees me to know I got the necktie on, I'm after their power, I want their money, and I want their women. Okay? And I will wear the necktie and wave it in their face," she said. "When I enter their offices, I'm not some girl coming in with sensible pumps on and a nice little dress to be a nice, sweet lady, and just sit down and try to get the boys to be nice to me. They know right up front, I'm a dyke, I'm tough, I'm here, I want to know exactly what's going on, and if you've got the power, I'm gonna try and take it from you."

As a child, she was a ringleader, and her favorite game was "Ditchum." There would be two gangs, and one gang would go off and try to ditch the other gang. The goal was to capture every member of the gang that was trying to ditch you. A game of Ditchum lasted for hours. Jean Harris was still playing this game.

*George Moscone was the mayor of the San Francisco. Harvey Milk, who was elected in November 1977, was the first openly gay person to be elected to the city's Board of Supervisors. Both men were shot to death in City Hall on November 27, 1978, by Dan White, another member of the Board of Supervisors. *Eds.*

Her expertise and tenacity would help to topple the sitting mayor of San Francisco, who did not understand just who Jean was.

In one of the candlelight vigils for Harvey Milk, Jean had been marching, holding her candle. She said, "I was cussing Harvey Milk out: 'I don't have a lesbian leader. Tell me what I'm supposed to be doing.' And I swear he was flying around overhead as we were walking, and he said, 'No one's going to do it for you, Jean. Get into it yourself. Do it. You do it. You have to do it.'" A spiritual giant or séance fanatic Jean Harris was not, but she began to obsessively watch *The Life and Times of Harvey Milk*, the Academy Award–winning documentary about Harvey's life. She had been, in essence, born again queerly. Perhaps my favorite moment with Jean was when she shouted into a microphone at the Harvey Milk Democratic Club, of which she was then president, "We're a kinder, gentler people, goddammit."

I watched from the balcony as Jean leaned against the burnished gold ironwork of the balusters at the top of the marble staircase, her white shirtsleeves rolled up, a tie askew around her neck. Her legs rested against the gold carving of a roaring lion's head, trapped in the metalwork like the beings in the castle of Cocteau's Beast. She was looking at the marriage ceremonies, and then at nothing but the base of the staircase where Harvey Milk's body had lain in state beside George Moscone's, his mahogany casket strewn with white chrysanthemums and red roses.

Harry Britt walked out to the steps behind Jean, said nothing, and returned to his office, which was across the narrow hallway from hers. It was Harvey's old office. Harry had been there for twelve years; he had been appointed by then-mayor Dianne Feinstein. Harry likened Feinstein to the queen of England after World War II, wanting only to do the right thing after the assassinations. Despite the fact that Feinstein and Milk were usually at odds politically, she a classic moderate and he a progressive, she wanted to appoint someone as politically close to Harvey as possible, someone who would carry on Harvey's work—even if that person opposed her policies—so that Dan White's bullets would not have won. Dianne Feinstein had been the president of the Board of Supervisors at the time of the killings, sitting, in fact, in her office beside Milk's (and across from Dan White's) when the five slow shots were fired into him. Her great dignity, strength, and sensitivity at the time of the assassinations held the city together and warded off a chaos of emotion and destruction.

In the tape-recording to be played only in the event of his assassination, Harvey Milk named Harry Britt among those he felt would be acceptable successors to his seat. In accordance with Milk's wishes, Dianne Feinstein appointed Britt. Harvey Milk had thought it would be George Moscone who listened to that tape; he never dreamed that the mayor would be killed along with him.

Harry Britt grew up in Port Arthur, Texas, where his principal role model was Liberace. He was a Methodist, and as a precocious fourteen-year-old he taught the summer vacation Bible school. There was a little girl in his class, seven or eight years old, a visiting Baptist. She was very naughty, and Harry considered her a discipline problem. She grew up to be Janis Joplin. They were probably the two most alienated children in Port Arthur.

The walls of Harry's office were covered with photographs of the first memorial march, of Harvey, of movie stars like Jane Fonda who had lent their star power to fund-raising for gay politicians in the days before all of their energies were recruited for AIDS fund-raising. The day after Harvey was elected, at seven-thirty in the morning, he told Harry that he expected to be killed. "This is the moment in his life of greatest triumph and fulfillment," Harry told me, "and he's thinking about getting killed. It shows you how close he lived to death and anti-gay hatred, and how distrustful he was, and at the very time he's telling gay people with every breath of his life to get involved in mainstream politics, he also understood—like a general sending his troops into war—that they may get killed."

Harry Britt had a deep disregard for those gay people who were "very skilled at ingratiating themselves to the masters." He called them "house faggots" and he felt that many straight liberal politicians kept them around when they wanted to be reassured that going the extra round for gay rights was not wise or possible until after the next election. To Harry Britt, Mayor Art Agnos fell into this category of straights.

It had taken twelve years for Harry to pass the domestic partnership ordinance, which Mayor Agnos did sign. Harry claimed that the mayor had not wanted to sign it if it allowed for nonresidents to register their relationships. The city attorney's office was worried about "lavender chapels" and yet another string of trivializing jokes on the late-night talk shows. Harry accommodated this concern, yet left a loophole. Out-of-towners, and city residents who did not wish to appear on an official list, could get the forms and have them privately notarized. For twelve years, Harry Britt had fought for domestic partnership legislation. He was not interested in marriage for himself, but he knew that there had to be a way legally to prove that we existed, and he vowed to remain in office until that legislation was enacted. For twelve years, he had watched Valentine's Day come and go, and he was finally victorious. Twelve years of hate mail. Twelve years of death threats. Twelve years of pondering, What would Harvey think? At fifty-two years old,

Harry might now find it possible to achieve, with a clear conscience, his wish for anonymous retirement.

When Jean and Harry decided to hold the Valentine's Day celebration in City Hall, it was suggested by the registrar that because of the traditional heterosexual marriages that would be taking place, there would not be enough personnel available to process the forms of the homosexuals and others wishing to become domestic partners. It was suggested that perhaps we should wait for another day, perhaps the day before Valentine's Day. Or the day after. Valentine's Day had already been taken.

Obviously, these people did not know with whom they were dealing. Jean Harris and her protégé, Kurt Barrie, were adamant about our right to Valentine's Day, and they arranged for volunteers, identifiable by rainbow armbands, to work in the registrar's office.

I stood across the street from City Hall and videotaped the affirmation of partnership ceremony taking place on the steps between Doric pillars flanked on either side by colonnades. I happened to be among some straight men who appeared to be homeless as well as alcoholic. They were incensed, infuriated by queers getting married in a public ceremony. One man was particularly angry about a sign that a gay man was holding on the steps. The sign read GOD IS GAY.

"I'm gonna do somethin' about that," he said. His buddies agreed, and I followed them closer to the festivities, watching them through the video lens. The nature of the festivities stopped them, however. It was an interfaith service sponsored by the Lutheran Lesbian and Gay Ministry. Among those listening carefully to the minister's words were a lesbian couple with their two-week-old baby. I was filming them as a carload of adolescent boys and girls drove by behind them, shouting obscenities. They were oblivious to the shouts, listening instead to the Song of Solomon.

Jean Harris appeared on the steps in a black tuxedo. She looked transported, oblivious to anything but the ceremony as she sang along to Cris Williamson's "Song of the Soul."*

Open mine eyes that I may see
Glimpses of truth thou hast for me
Open mine eyes, illumine me
Spirit Divine

I was now on the top of the steps, filming the crowd. They were holding flowers, and twenty feet behind them another truckload passed by, this time packed with white males in their thirties. They slowed down to shout, "Faggots! Dykes!"

Jean Harris looked right at the truck as it raced away but she did not seem to see it—no one did—and they continued to sing, joyful and wondrously oblivious to the catcalls, shouts, and gestures.

"Love of my life," I am crying
I am not dying, I am dancing;
Dancing along in the madness
There is no sadness,
Only a Song of the Soul.

As the song ended, we were asked to link arms for a prayer. I stopped filming and happened to link arms with the man carrying the GOD IS GAY sign. As I looked up and across the crowd, I caught the eye of the man who was "gonna do somethin'" about this. He was seething, and here I was, arm in arm with his target. I was very happy he did not have a gun.

Jean's right, I thought. We're a kinder, gentler people, goddamnit.

I followed a lesbian couple through the process of registering; as they finished, they were exiting the registrar's office, arm-in-arm. They had to pass by three men in their late twenties, street people, who had draped themselves around the perimeter of the exit doors for the sole purpose of snickering at the couples and gesturing at their backs as they passed into the rotunda. Again, the lesbian couple did not see or hear the hecklers. Was it that I was watching everything through the lens of the video camera, and so saw things that I would normally miss? I was beginning to think that a very powerful fairy had sprinkled some sort of magical dust throughout this magnificent building, and that it was protecting our people.

I followed the lesbian couple to the chambers of the Board of Supervisors at the top of the grand staircase on the second-floor gallery. The chambers are a jewel of carved oak; happy couples were seated on the benches, waiting attentively. Their arms were linked, and they appeared nervous and excited. They were of every ethnicity, shape, and age. They were so vulnerable, and I could still not understand why they were doing this. It was just symbolic, which to me was worse than nothing.

I returned to the second-floor gallery outside the mayor's office and focused my camera on the staircase. Gilbert was beside me; he gained the distinction of being the only one in a red ball gown. We stood on either side of a spotlight, which Gilbert carefully focused at the top of the stairs where each couple would stand in the pool of light.

Jean stepped to the microphone at the bottom of the staircase and, as she announced that "Harvey Milk is flying around in this rotunda right now," the doors to the chambers opened. The couples emerged and formed a line as a string-and-keyboard ensemble began to play "The Shadow of Your Smile." Just like a real wedding, I thought, down to the bad music. As they descended the stairs, Kurt and Jean took turns announcing the couples' names.

"Tom Ammiano and Tim Curbo." Tom, the vice president of the school board, and his partner of fourteen years, who was also a schoolteacher, descended the staircase. The cheers from the hundreds gathered at the bottom of the steps to witness the celebration echoed throughout the building. Down they came, the variety of human beings unbelievable, dressed in tuxedoes, dresses, leather, ACT UP and Queer Nation outfits.

I saw Jonathan standing at the foot of the steps, his arms crossed against his gym-toned chest, the words QUEER NATION emblazoned across his shirt. Along with other members of Queer Nation, he had walked dozens of precincts—including those traditionally ignored as being too conservative—on behalf of Proposition K, the domestic partnership ordinance.

One man walked by himself down the thirty-six steps. His lover was dying of AIDS in the hospital, so he was taking the walk for them both. There were six straight couples, and one of these couples made the walk with their nine-year-old daughter. Two bleached-blond boys took the walk hand in hand, each wearing a T-shirt with the words MR. RIGHT. Another male couple descended slowly, arm in arm, one of the men appearing weak as he leaned heavily upon his cane. The applause washed over them, and the dying man smiled with such burning happiness that I was sure he felt no pain.

Two old fellows in their sixties, with rumpled baggy pants and John Deere hats, walked carefully down the stairs, their work-battered hands entwined, their eyes on their feet. They looked like they had just come off the farm. I looked beside me at Gilbert, who was now dramatically dabbing at his eyes with a white handkerchief.

"What's the matter?" I asked.

"Wedding," he said, dabbing away, and although he was camping it up, there were real tears in his eyes. Gilbert liked to pretend that he was solely a political cartoon, above the emotional fray, but that was a lie. I saw it time after time. What was true was what was happening inside City Hall, and the only reminder of the world outside was the words Gilbert had scrawled across a large paper heart that he had pinned to his faux cleavage: "This war is breaking my heart."

The names of the couples continued to reverberate as they descended the marble staircase, which had graced the presentations of kings, queens, and heads of state.

"Simone Dorman, Anne Dorman, and daughter Elizabeth Simone Dorman."

The family stood at the top of the staircase as their names were read. Anne Dorman held their blond three-year-old daughter in one arm, and as they walked down the steps, I was beginning to understand why these families were doing this. At the bottom of the steps, in the quivering light flashes of cameras, Anne took Simone's hand and kissed it. My eyes filled with tears.

"Gail Brown, Lucinda Young, and their daughter, Mara Young." Mara was a teenager. It is difficult for a teenager to be different from her peers in any way, yet she had walked down the stairs with her two mothers.

"Lori Feldman, Marcia Baum, and Baby Maya." Maya was less than two weeks old. The applause and love washed over them as they very carefully made their way down the stairs, and I realized that I was crying. These were not people used to grand entrances, photographic flashes, televisions, and a crush of press. Yet these were people willing to perform this very public act, which had absolutely no material or practical gain attached to it, in order to affirm their love.

Most of the people who descended those

steps never have gone and never will go into the streets. They never have used and never will use the word "queer," or confront the Traditional Values Coalition or a President Bush who called them immoral and unfit to parent. They are our silent majority, and it was only in this way, only to express their love for each other, that they would perform such a public act.

As the last couple descended the steps, Harry Britt stood at the podium, flushed with emotion. "The voters of this city overwhelmingly acknowledged the right of lesbians and gay couples to come out of the shadows and to become publicly recognized as loving, caring, and committed people. What you have done by bringing your love to this place, and walking down these steps together, is truly an important moment in the life of the American family."

Then lesbian and gay leaders took the stage: Supervisor Roberta Achtenberg, Tom Ammiano, and Supervisor Carole Migden. Tom Ammiano announced, "I particularly liked the straight couples that came today. I approve of mixed marriages." Congratulating the community, and also taking the stage, were Supervisors Kevin Shelley and Angela Alioto, both the children of former mayors of San Francisco.

Jean returned to the microphone, dashing in her tuxedo, and introduced Judge Donna Hitchens as if she were the lesbian Socrates.

"I'm now gonna have her come up," said Jean, "and do whatever judges do at these kind of things. So welcome her: Judge Donna Hitchens."

We loved Donna Hitchens, and she could not stop the applause. She could only step from behind the podium briefly and applaud us. Donna Hitchens is a rare public figure, a source of wisdom and unconditional love.

"This isn't quite the intimate wedding our parents planned for us," she said, "but it is truly a joyous occasion. As I watched people come down the steps, there were tears. . . . Today, you signed a declaration that you share an intimate, committed relationship of mutual caring. Today is a day of public celebration of those relationships, and of your personal relationship. It is a day when most of you did not make your first commitments, but have recommitted to that relationship you have shared with each other over the last five, ten, fifteen, thirty, thirty-five years. So I'm here to wish you the best from the city and county of San Francisco, but to also say, May your closeness not diminish, but strengthen your individuality and your wisdom, the gift that you bring to others. Many poets have said that love asks nothing, but I submit to you today that love demands everything."

I bought carnations, roses, and candy, and threw my anger and cynicism in the car trunk for the night. I went home and handed the flowers to Cheryl. She held them in her arms, but she did not move.

"Why are you so far away from me?" she asked.

I told her I didn't know, but that I loved her and needed her to trust me, to know that I would always love her, but that right now, this was the best I could do. The adoption proceedings were cornering me emotionally.

"You're his mom," she said. "Don't you know that? Why do you care what they think?"

"I do."

"I don't understand," she said, but she put her arms around me anyway.

Our child's whisper reached us from the floor near our feet.

"I drank the poison."

Jesse was sprawled upon the rug, arms outstretched, eyes closed.

"What's he doing?" I asked, somewhat alarmed.

"Dying," she said, in a matter-of-fact voice. "He's been doing it all night."

"The poison, I drank the poison," Jesse whispered, pretending to swoon.

"He just watched Mary Martin's *Peter Pan*," said Cheryl. "Captain Hook puts the poison in Peter's milk, but Tinker Bell drinks it and begins to die."

I picked Jesse up, the imaginary poison pulling the life out of him as he sprawled Pietà-style in my arms. This guy is *dramatic*.

"I *do* believe in fairies. I *do* believe in fairies," I repeated again and again, as Cheryl clapped her hands and Jesse miraculously came back to life.

That was my first good night's sleep since the adoption process had begun. That day had been like no other. San Francisco's City Hall is a building filled with magic and history, built on top of a cemetery and fashioned after the Invalides in Paris, which houses the tomb of Napoleon. Given the power of certain places, given the obliviousness of the lovers and families to the taunts and ridicule of the ignorant on Valentine's Day, 1991, I cannot say with absolute certainty that Harvey Milk's ghost was *not* flying around in that rotunda.

Chapter 38

Divorced Parents and the Jewish Community

NATHALIE FRIEDMAN

According to conservative estimates, almost one of every two marriages that took place in the United States in the past 15 years will end in divorce; by 1990 half of all children under 18 will have lived for some time with a single (divorced) parent.

Some sociologists view these projections with relative equanimity as reflections of and necessary adaptations to social change. Others hear the death knell of the family as we have known it and predict increased alienation of youth, more women and children living in poverty, and the loss of the grandparent-grandchild relationship.

Most observers of the Jewish scene agree that the divorce rate among Jews is somewhat below that of the general population.[1] Projections of current rates suggest that at least one in every three or four Jewish couples married over the past 15 years will divorce, leaving an increasing number of Jewish children to grow up in the care of a single parent. The high divorce rate among Jews has triggered a good deal of unease within the Jewish community. The reasons for concern are many. A high Jewish divorce rate threatens the basic family structure, traditionally so essential to Jewish identity. It is likely to mean fewer children being born to Jewish families. And it is seen as raising a number of social, psychological, and economic problems that erode Jewish commitment, participation and involvement.

Little, however, is actually known about the impact of divorce on ties to the Jewish community. Do the social, economic, and psychological problems that often accompany divorce erode Jewish commitment and involvement? Are synagogue affiliation and attendance affected? Does the child's Jewish education continue? Do families turn to the Jewish community, and does that community serve in any way as a support system before, during or after divorce? What about those with only minimal or no Jewish communal involvement prior to divorce—to whom do

From Steven Bayme and Gladys Rosen, eds., *The Jewish Family and Jewish Continuity* (Hoboken, N.J.: KTAV Publishing House, 1994), copyright © 1994, by the American Jewish Committee. Reprinted by permission.

they turn, and how do they cope in the aftermath of divorce?

This study examines these questions from the perspective of the divorced parents.

Through interviews with 40 women and 25 of their former husbands, it explores the nature of the couples' communal ties both before and after their divorces, and inquires particularly into the impact of divorce on their religious affiliations. The study also focuses on the degree of support that Jewish communal institutions provided these couples and suggests how the institutions can become more responsive to the needs of Jewish single-parent families.

The sample selected for study spanned the religious spectrum from ultra-Orthodox to unaffiliated. The research design called for extensive interviews with 40 sets of parents: 10 Orthodox (including two ultra-Orthodox), 10 Conservative, 10 Reform, and 10 unaffiliated—all divorced or separated from one to five years and with at least one child aged three to 16 at the time the marriage was dissolved.

The research design presented several problems when it came to classifying the family's religious orientation. How, for example, would one classify a family where the mother said she was unaffiliated and her ex-spouse called himself Conservative? What about the family in which the mother was affiliated with a Reform temple but identified herself as Conservative? Should a family be classified by its affiliation during the marriage or after the divorce? Since one purpose of the research was to look at Jewish identity and affiliation *after* a divorce, it was decided to classify families on the basis of the temple or synagogue with which the custodial parent was affiliated, unless that parent clearly designated herself or himself otherwise. And, because the religious affiliation of a husband might differ from that of his wife, data were also collected on the current religious status of each parent,

on the family during the marriage, and on each parent at the time he or she was growing up. Thus the religious odysseys of the 40 families could be traced, and Jewish affiliation after the divorce could be compared with that in the immediate and more distant past.

Prospective respondents were located with the help of community workers and of respondents who identified persons they thought it would be informative to interview. Typically, the referral was to the mother, who was usually the custodial parent. At the conclusion of the interview with one parent, permission was sought to contact the other parent so the study could report the perspectives of both.

The final sample consisted of 40 mothers and 25 fathers ranging in age between 31 and 62. All had lived in the New York City metropolitan area during their marriages. Fifteen of the fathers could not be interviewed—four were not living in the United States or their whereabouts were unknown; four were not contacted at the wife's request; and seven refused. Interviews with the mothers were conducted between the fall of 1983 and the summer of 1984, and averaged about two hours in length. Interviews with fathers were somewhat less lengthy, both because the mother had already provided the basic family information and because fathers were less likely to offer details about activities and feelings.

In all but four instances the women were interviewed first. They described their former husbands' Jewish backgrounds and affiliations, if any, both before and during the marriage, and most were able to provide some information about their former husbands' participation in the Jewish community after the marriage ended. Thus, although 15 fathers were not interviewed, considerable background information about them was obtained. When the information provided by the mothers was compared with the self-reports of the 25 fathers who were interviewed, the accounts proved virtually identical.

One note of caution. This research was not designed to permit generalization to the entire population of Jewish divorced persons. Its purpose, rather, was to uncover patterns, relationships, causal links, and critical variables that might provide clues to how communal institutions can better serve that rapidly increasing phenomenon, the Jewish single-parent family.

Profile of the Single Parent

Social Characteristics

Most divorces in the United States take place within the first five years of marriage; but because this study concerned families with school-age children, the couples selected for study had been married an average of 11 years at the time of the separation and had been separated or divorced for an average of four years. The original research plan was to restrict the sample to couples who had been divorced between one and five years, and in fact all but three couples fell into this category. However, the couples who had been divorced somewhat longer were included because their experiences point to some of the long-range effects of divorce on family members.

The steadily decreasing birth rate among Jews is a source of concern in the Jewish community, and the sample suggests that these fears are well founded. In only two families, both ultra-Orthodox, were there four or more children. Six families had three children; 17 had two (among them four sets of twins); and the remaining 15 families had only one child. The average number of children in the sample as a whole was 1.9, a figure well below the zero-population-growth point of 2.1. Had divorce (and perhaps years of unhappiness prior to divorce) not occurred, there might have been more children. Thus a high divorce rate probably compounds the problem of an already low Jewish birth rate.

A number of demographic characteristics are correlated with divorce rates in America. For example, divorce rates are higher among the less educated, the less affluent, those who marry young, and those who intermarry. Except for five intermarried couples, the respondents in this study did not fit this profile of the divorce-prone. While all socioeconomic and educational levels were represented in the sample, the typical respondent was a well-educated, middle- or upper-middle-class Jew living in New York City or a nearby suburb. Sixteen of the men were professionals—lawyers, physicians, social workers, accountants; fourteen were in business or advertising; three were in film, photography, or entertainment; and five worked in blue-collar occupations. The remaining two were unemployed; one of these was occupied in "learning"—that is, studying Torah.

The educational backgrounds of the men paralleled their occupational status. Two had almost no secular education but had "learned" in a yeshiva or *kollel*. Five others had only high-school educations, and 10 had no more than two years of college. Six were college graduates, and the remainder held the professional degrees requisite for their particular occupations.

Most of the women were well educated. Only 11 had less schooling than their husbands; another 11 had about the same amount of schooling; more than half (22) had *more* formal education than their husbands. Even among the professionals, there were wives who had more education than their husbands.

Perhaps because three out of four of the women were at least college graduates, their average age at marriage, 24, was considerably higher than the median age of women at first marriage in the general population (20.6).[2] In fact, only six women were between 18 and 21 when they married.

The men, too, were considerably older at the time they married than their counterparts in the general population. Their average age at marriage was between 27 and 28, compared to the national median of 22.5 for males.

Given their relatively high level of education, it is not surprising that most of the women in the sample had considerable work experience. Most had worked before marriage, and about a third had worked full- or part-time during the marriage. Fourteen women were attorneys, physicians, teachers, or social workers. Thirteen worked in the business world, either as proprietors of their own enterprises or as managers in banks or brokerage firms. The remainder had worked—or were working—in such traditional female occupations as secretaries, personnel assistants, and teaching aides. Ten women, however, had not worked before their divorces, when they became "displaced homemakers."

Recent data released by the National Center for Health Statistics indicate that almost three out of four divorced women, and more than four out of five divorced men, will remarry within several years of the divorce, and about half of these will divorce again. Sociologists, in fact, have begun to speak of "serial monogamy," the pattern in which individuals maintain a commitment to the institution of marriage but not to a particular spouse. For six respondents, the marriage and divorce that provided the focus for this research were neither their first nor their last. Two of the women and four of the men had been previously married and divorced. Neither of the women, but three of the men, had a child from the earlier marriage. In all three cases, the child was in the custody of the mother.

Six women and 13 men had remarried since the divorce about which they were inter-

viewed, and 10 of the 19 had been divorced or separated again. Two men were in their third marriages at the time of the interview.

From a Jewish perspective, divorce and remarriage do not necessarily put an end to the traditional nuclear family but may, in fact, eventuate in two "reconstituted" nuclear families, either or both of which may produce more children and serve as transmitters of Jewish identity. On the other hand, religious affiliation and observance may be disrupted when family ties change. For some of the children in the sample the influence of stepparents as well as natural parents sometimes resulted in conflicting norms about Jewish participation and observance.

Religious Backgrounds and Affiliations

Until recently, Jewish families tended to stress Jewish education more for boys than for girls. That this was the pattern at the time the men and women in the sample were growing up is strikingly evident. Thirty-one of the 37 men raised in Jewish homes had been exposed to some form of Jewish education—ranging from a few months of Bar Mitzvah preparation to several years of intensive "learning" in a *kollel*. All 31 had Bar Mitzvahs. In contrast, only 18 of the 37 women raised in Jewish homes reported that they had attended Sunday school, Hebrew school, or Jewish day school. Six women reported that their brothers had gone to Hebrew school but that no such arrangements had been made for them. Ten women had had Bat Mitzvahs or been confirmed; six others, who had received a Jewish education, said that the Bat Mitzvah was not an institutionalized "rite of passage" in their communities when they were growing up.

The traditional categories of Orthodox, Conservative, Reform, and unaffiliated are too broad to capture the many distinctions respondents made as they talked about what it was like to be Jewish as a child. Thirteen said they came from Orthodox backgrounds, but this meant variously that they grew up in the ultrareligious community of Williamsburg, that their upbringing was "modern Orthodox," that they belonged to an Orthodox synagogue but had little home observance, or that they were observant at home but seldom attended synagogue.

Another 23 respondents said that their parental backgrounds were essentially Conservative. Again, this had varied meanings. Some described their daily lives as "Conservadox," by which they meant affiliation with a Conservative synagogue but strict observance at home; others, though affiliated with Conservative synagogues, lived in homes where observance was minimal.

Seven respondents came from families affiliated with Reform temples. In these homes, observance ranged from moderate ("My mother occasionally lit candles on Friday night, and the family would get together for holiday dinners, but we weren't kosher at all") to minimal ("We really didn't observe anything; it's just that on the High Holidays we went to the Reform temple").

Finally, 22 men and women described their parental homes as unaffiliated. The variations within this category can best be captured through the words of respondents:

Our home was totally American-Jewish, except that my parents forgot the "Jewish."

Said one woman:

I grew up in a left-wing Yiddish, a-religious home. My parents were old-line Communists. But still, my father gave to UJA.

A man put it this way:

Religious background? Zero! The only way I ever knew it was Rosh Hashanah was when I saw that alternate-side-of-the street parking regulations were lifted. On the other hand, I always knew that I was Jewish.

Another man summed up his background as "kitchen-stove Judaism":

My parents felt that Jewish culture was okay, but they saw religion as the opiate of the people. When the holidays came around, my mother would make kugel and things like that, and the family would get together.

Even apart from the five intermarried couples, the religious backgrounds of husband and wife were often quite different. In only 17 of the 40 families did the partners share similar Jewish backgrounds. In 18 families, there were substantial differences in the types of Jewish homes in which the partners had grown up.

In general, couples from dissimilar backgrounds tended to adopt the religious coloration of the less observant partner. In all but two cases where one partner's background included some degree of affiliation and the other's none, the couples were unaffiliated. Similarly, four of the five intermarried couples were unaffiliated even though the non-Jewish partners had converted. In only one instance did a couple adopt a pattern of more traditional religious observance and affiliation than the pattern in which either partner had been reared. Partners from similar backgrounds tended to maintain their premarriage affiliations.

Ties to the Jewish Community During the Marriage

During the years they were married, the patterns of affiliation and observance of these 40 couples varied widely. About half were completely unaffiliated with a synagogue or temple, had minimal or no home observance, and gave their children no Jewish education. For example, only 20 of the 40 couples had actually been members of synagogues or temples in the various communities in which they had lived while married. Among the other 20 couples, four said that they had never joined but had occasionally attended services at neighborhood synagogues or temples; six said they occasionally went to their parents' or in-laws' synagogues for the High Holy Days; 10 couples stated that they had neither belonged to nor attended any house of worship.

It is difficult to attach denominational labels to the 20 couples who were affiliated while married, for some had joined synagogues of different denominations as they moved from one community to another or as their children grew ready for Sunday or Hebrew school. As one mother explained:

First we lived in Queens, and we belonged to a Conservative synagogue there. Then we moved farther out on the Island, and when our son was ready for Sunday school we jointed the Reform temple because that was where most of the Jewish families on our block belonged.

Or another:

In Pennsylvania, where we lived the first five years of our marriage, we belonged to a Conservative synagogue—it was the only one in town. Then when we moved to Manhattan, we joined a modern Orthodox synagogue in the neighborhood.

Just prior to separation, however, eight couples were affiliated with Orthodox and five with Conservative synagogues; seven belonged to Reform temples; and 20 were unaffiliated.

Absence of synagogue affiliation or attendance generally, but not necessarily, precluded some form of Jewish education for the children. In eight instances, the divorce had occurred before the child was old enough for Sunday or Hebrew school, and in eight others, although the children were of age, they

had not received any Jewish education. In 16 families children had attended a Sunday or Hebrew school, and in eight families an Orthodox day school or yeshiva. Observance in the home during the marriage ranged from "zero," as one respondent put it, to strictly Orthodox. For 12 families, observance of the Sabbath and holidays was simply not a part of their lives. As one commented:

Home observance? None. I guess you could say we were borderline Christians because we observed Christmas, but also a little Hanukkah.

Several noted that, although they did not observe at home, they would occasionally go to their parents or in-laws for a Seder or a holiday meal. Ten families characterized their home observance as "minimal." As one explained:

We'd observe the Sabbath and holidays off and on—no regularity. Mostly in an "eating" sense, I guess. You know—a special meal.

This "culinary" theme appeared regularly as these 10 families described home observance:

Matzoh on Passover, but I guess that's about it. The family would get together for dinner on Rosh Hashanah.
A couple of times I made the Seder meal.

If there was any one holiday observed by these families, it tended to be Hanukkah:

We used to light the menorah and give the children gifts.
We thought it was important to celebrate Hanukkah because the children saw so much Christmas around them.

Several of the families said that, although they never attended services and their home observance was at best "limited," they kept their children home from school on Rosh Hashanah and Yom Kippur because "we wanted them to know they were Jewish."

In nine families home observance was

fairly regular, including candles on Friday night and the celebration of such holidays as Passover, Hanukkah, Purim, and Simchat Torah with family meals, a Seder, and special foods. Respondents in this group, however, were quick to add that they did not keep kosher homes. Typical was this woman's response

> We didn't have a kosher home, but we did celebrate all the holidays—Hanukkah, Seders, Purim (I'd get hamantaschen). Friday night was always special—not in a religious sense—but we had chicken and challah, and we tried not to make other plans on Friday nights.

Finally, nine families characterized themselves as "observant," "strictly observant," or "Orthodox." Their homes ranged from "kosher" to "strictly kosher," and all the holidays as well as the Sabbath were observed, with their positive and negative commandments.

The couples' other links to the Jewish community while married were quite limited, even among those with strong synagogue ties. Several used the local Y or Jewish community center for clubs, classes, or gymnastics; a few belonged to Zionist organizations; several were involved with such organizations as B'nai B'rith, Jewish War Veterans and UJA/Federation. However, the majority had no links at all with any Jewish organizations or fraternal groups. As one Orthodox woman explained:

> We were young, busy raising children, and we had very little money. We couldn't afford either the time or the money for anything outside the shul or our son's yeshiva.

Others attributed the absence of Jewish organizational affiliations to lack of interest or simply to the fact that "we're not joiners."

In sum, the ties of these 40 couples to the Jewish community during the marriage varied widely. At the one extreme were about half the families with no synagogue or other Jewish organizational affiliation and minimal or no home observance. About one in four families described strong Jewish institutional ties, regular synagogue attendance, and strict home observance of the Sabbath, holidays, dietary laws, and other religious rituals. In between were some 10 families who were affiliated with a temple or synagogue, attended services frequently, and marked the Sabbath and/or religious holidays with some degree of regularity. Even among those with only the most tenuous institutional connections, however, Jewish education for the children was not necessarily precluded; four of these families sent their children to Sunday or Hebrew schools and one (as long as the grandparents paid for it) to a day school.

The Divorce Experience

Factors Leading to the Divorce

The couples' reasons for ending their marriages probably reflect the experiences of most divorced couples in America. Some attributed the breakup to such unacceptable behavior on the part of their partners as violence or wife abuse (three cases), alcoholism or gambling (two cases), homosexuality (one case), and infidelity (five cases). These reasons were particularly frequent among the Orthodox couples. Although infidelity was cited as a factor in five instances, in only three was it regarded as the determining factor.

The word most frequently used by respondents as they spoke about the factors leading to the divorce was "incompatibility." This word proved to mean different things to different respondents. Some, for example, explained that they had married quite young and had grown apart over the years. In other instances, "incompatibility" referred to temperamental or personality differences. One man, for example, complained about his ex-wife's inability to communicate:

> We weren't on the same wave length. Her tuner is way down while mine tends to be all the way up.

A woman said of her ex-husband:

> He's a very selfish person—totally involved with himself, egocentric. I just needed more love and affection—it was lonely living with him.

A third kind of incompatibility was the couple's disagreement over the woman's role as wife, mother, and employed person. Often, this disagreement arose in the course of the woman's pursuit of personal growth, self-development, and career. One woman said:

> Once I went back to work it became clear that our interests were different. He was opposed to my going back to work. His idea of my role was to bring up the children, entertain, be at home for him. But I felt that I had to develop as a person, find my own identity that was not just a part of him and the children.

A second said that while her husband was still a student he could understand her working, but:

> Then he graduated and got a job, and he woke up to the fact that I was busy working and not home at 4:30 when he got home. I was trying to develop my career as a teacher, but he wanted me to be a "nine-to-three" teacher. I said that if I wanted that kind of job, I would have gone to work at the post office.

Her ex-husband confirmed that his wife's work had been a bone of contention:

> She worked hard all those years supporting us while I was in graduate school. When I finished, however, and began living like a person, I kind of expected that she would go back to being the woman I had married. But she had changed—her job was very important to her. Her career was going gangbusters, and she was loving it.

Two men suggested that the women's movement played a role in their growing incompatibility with their wives. One said:

> I don't know what part this played, but my wife got all wrapped up in the women's movement and with all of her divorced and divorcing friends. She stopped observing our wedding anniversary and said that the wedding ring was a symbol of slavery.

Finally, several respondents suggested that the prevailing social climate, in which divorce carried no stigma, was a factor in the breakup of their marriages. As one said:

> We are probably products of our age—an age of divorce. I think that a lot of divorces that have taken place would not have taken place thirty years ago. People's expectations are higher when it comes to happiness in marriage.

The decision to divorce was generally initiated by the woman and accepted, often reluctantly, by the man. In those few instances where the divorce was initiated by the man, the cause was quite specific: he had met another woman; his wife was an "adulteress"; he couldn't make it financially and felt overwhelmed by marital and parental responsibilities. Only one of the 25 men interviewed attributed the divorce to *his* need for self-fulfillment or personal space.

The Jewish Factor

Was there a Jewish factor in the divorce decision? The answer is "yes and no." On one hand, with only a few exceptions, respondents said that religious or Jewish issues were not precipitating factors. On the other hand, as the marriage bonds weakened, dissension over these issues surfaced in 14 of the 40 couples.

In three of the five interfaith marriages, religious issues were cited by at least one of the partners. In nine other instances, while both partners were Jewish, they came from different religious backgrounds and Jewish issues surfaced. For example:

> First of all, there was another woman, but that was just the straw that broke the camel's back. Basically, we were just not compatible—we had different values about almost everything. And eventually, even our differences over Judaism got to me—he ate nonkosher outside while I was strictly kosher; and he worked on Shabbos while I wanted him to go to shul with me and the boys.

A man from a Conservative background had a similar problem:

> My wife came from a completely assimilated background, but she agreed to keep a kosher home. Then she reneged. Religion was not at all important to her, but it was to me. I felt that there should be at least a minimal observance and understanding, but she had no interest at all—not even for the High Holidays.

In three cases where dissension over religious issues surfaced, both partners came from fairly similar backgrounds. In one instance, where both were from Conservative homes, the wife complained that her husband was too passive about Jewish observance and participation and that she was tired of having to take the lead. In another instance, although both partners had come from Orthodox homes and had attended religious day schools, the wife said:

> He was always less religious than I, and we bickered a lot about it. I wanted to cover my head, and he thought that was silly. I didn't want to eat in a nonkosher restaurant, and he thought it was okay as long as we ate dairy. He opened up the mail and rode up in the elevator on Shabbos, and I wouldn't.

These findings suggest that when husband and wife come from similar religious backgrounds religious issues rarely surface. When the marriage is mixed (and that term is used to denote marriages in which the Jewish backgrounds

are different as well as interfaith marriages) however, religious issues often contribute to the incompatibility of the partners.

Problems Encountered Dissolving the Marriage

Ending a marriage involves more than the decision of one or both partners to go their separate ways. It also means seeing a lawyer and resolving problems over finances, child custody, visitation rights, and, in some instances, the *get*, or religious divorce decree. For 13 couples, things went relatively smoothly, both at the time of the divorce and after.

All six families who agreed upon joint custody arrangements reported relatively amicable divorces, suggesting that only when hostility between the principals is minimal can a joint custody arrangement be agreed upon and successfully implemented.

Sixteen couples reported problems in only one area—15 with finances, one with visitation. The mother who complained that visitation was a problem said:

> The boys seldom see their father—maybe once every three months. He began to live with this woman shortly after the separation, and then he married her. She was always there when they visited. She picked the movie whether they wanted to see it or not. If she wanted to go to the shopping mall and they didn't, everyone went to the mall.

Financial problems ranged from delayed child-support checks to the disappearance of the ex-spouse. Three mothers were receiving welfare, and several others, although employed, were dependent on their parents. Several fathers confirmed that one consequence of divorce was a reduction in their standard of living. Said one:

> After the divorce, money absolutely disappeared. I was living in a seedy hotel with a few boxes and two jammed suitcases. That is all I owned after thirteen years of marriage. Before,

it was two people working and one household, and we were still barely in the black. You can imagine what it was like stretching that money across two households.

One woman noted that finances were a problem not because there wasn't enough money but because:

> It's a thorn in his side to write a check every month. Every month it's a question of "When is it coming?" The anxiety carries over to our nine-year-old son because he's aware of it.

Ten couples experienced multiple problems. In one case where finances were not an issue, custody and visitation rights were. The mother explained:

> I really only wanted a little child support, and he sends four times more than is legally required. But custody arrangements and visitation rights were a problem, largely because of his drinking. He kept moving back and forth between California and New York and in and out of treatment programs. We couldn't draw up a custody agreement, and he couldn't visit our daughter or have her with him in any predictable fashion.

A woman who noted that her ex-husband's lack of responsibility had left her virtually the sole support for herself and her son added that visitation rights was also an acrimonious issue:

> I simply had to limit the visits and arrange that they always be in a supervised setting because of his total lack of responsibility.

The multi-problem couple was usually one whose divorce had been marked by hostility and where anger and bad feelings were still very much in evidence. As a result, every issue that had to be resolved became an occasion for the release of hostility.

The Importance of the Get

Orthodox and Conservative rabbis will not marry a divorced person who has not obtained the religious divorce decree, the *get*. If

a woman without a *get* marries again, any child of the remarriage will be illegitimate in Jewish law. The law imposes no such penalty on a man. Should he remarry without a *get*, a child of that marriage would be legitimate. If a wife refuses to accept the *get* from her husband, Jewish law provides alternative ways for the man to be declared free to remarry. The woman whose husband refuses to provide a *get* has no similar recourse. Thus the law places the obligation to obtain a *get* upon the woman and gives the man a unique advantage in negotiating a divorce settlement.

Ten of the 40 women in the sample had obtained a *get* at the time of, or subsequent to, their divorces. Most were either Orthodox or Conservative. One of two Reform women who had obtained a *get* said:

> The rabbi insisted that I must have it to remarry—if ever I should. My ex paid for it.

The other Reform woman had herself insisted on the *get*:

> I insisted on an Orthodox *get*. I had been married religiously in a Conservative synagogue, and it was important to me to have the most religious divorce I could get. He [the ex] would not pay for it, but at least he went through it. His mother can't understand why I wanted it.

One young woman from the Hasidic community in Flatbush was still trying, after almost five years, to obtain a *get*.

> I've asked, I've tried, but he just won't do it. I've gone to some local rabbis for help but haven't gotten anywhere. Unfortunately, you need money to get them [the rabbis] to help you, and I don't have it.

Then she added with resignation:

> I guess it really doesn't matter because who's going to marry me anyway with my six children?

Eight women said that they would obtain a *get* should they decide to remarry. None of them anticipated any difficulty. Fully half of the women in the sample, however, neither requested a *get* nor had any intention of doing so. Many had never heard of a *get*; it was simply "not an issue," "irrelevant," "nonsense," or "something that would never have occurred to us." From the perspective of the traditional Jewish community, should these women remarry and bear children the absence of a *get* could have serious ramifications when their children, in turn, are ready to marry.[3]

Single-Parent Families in the Jewish Community

The Affiliated

Between the time of the divorce and the time of the interview—an average of four years—changes had occurred in the pattern of Jewish affiliation of the people in the sample. Of the 20 families that had been unaffiliated during the marriage, three became affiliated with a Reform temple or school, three with a Conservative synagogue or school, and four with an Orthodox synagogue and day school.[4] In addition, two families that had been affiliated with an orthodox synagogue during the marriage identified themselves as Conservative at the time of the interview; another moved from Conservative to Reform and still another from Reform to Conservative. Two of these latter changes stemmed from geographic moves and two from dissatisfaction with a particular Sunday or Hebrew school.

More significant is the finding that, after the divorce, 10 previously unaffiliated families had joined the ranks of the affiliated, while none had moved from affiliated to unaffiliated status. This finding appears to run counter to the belief that divorce necessarily erodes Jewish affiliation and identification.

Although the data offered here are too few to refute this belief, these 10 cases suggest factors that may explain the "return" of the unaffiliated. The word "return" is used advisedly because, among the 10 families that had been unaffiliated during the marriage but developed some tie afterward, there were five custodial parents who had grown up in affiliated homes. One woman, for example, who had married a non-Jew against the wishes of her parents, said:

When the girls got to be old enough, I decided that they should have some kind of Jewish education. I guess it's a little strange, because during the marriage we really did nothing Jewish. But I find myself getting more and more conservative with age. Maybe it's that being the child of Holocaust parents, I feel a particular responsibility to pass on a Jewish tradition. So now the girls are in a Reform Hebrew school, and we go to services on Friday night. They love it.

Another woman, also divorced from a non-Jew, had similar sentiments:

The minute my son was old enough, I enrolled him at the nursery school of the Conservative synagogue here. It was highly recommended as a place where there's real Jewish involvement. I wanted him to have this, especially after the absence of all of this with his father. We go to shul all the time, and I'm enrolled in the women's Bat Mitzvah class. When I was young, I never went to Hebrew school—only my brothers did. My son is very close to my parents [Conservative]. We're with them on all the holidays.

And a third:

My ex was a country-club type—golf and cards. He wasn't interested in the synagogue or the community. After the divorce, I decided I wanted my son to have a Jewish upbringing so I enrolled him in the Conservative synagogue nursery school. Now he's in the Hebrew school and will eventually be Bar Mitzvah.

A fourth "returnee" commented:

> We never belonged to anything during the marriage, although occasionally we went to my parents' Conservative synagogue. I put the children in a Conservative Hebrew school just as soon as they were old enough, and we go every Sabbath together. I was brought up in a Conservative synagogue but never went to Hebrew school—although my brother did. I wanted the children to know what it was all about. In fact, at first I had put them in a religious day school, but they had to leave it as part of the divorce settlement. It was important to my ex that they not go, and it didn't matter that much to me.

And finally:

> I Joined a Reform temple after the divorce because I felt it was very important for my son to learn about his Jewish heritage. I myself came from an observant home but didn't have that much of a Jewish education—my brothers did, but the girls, no!

These women had three things in common: a traditional Jewish home background; a husband who wished to have little to do with Jewish communal life; and a child old enough for some form of religious education. It is possible, of course, that had their marriages remained intact, these women would still have seen to it that their children received some form of Jewish education. It appears, however, that the dissolution of their marriages actually removed a barrier to their return to a more traditional Jewish life.

Four women came from completely unaffiliated homes and had been—as one put it—"borderline Christians" while married. Three who lived in the Bronx came under the influence of a rabbi well known for his community activism, his personal warmth and understanding, and his readiness to embrace anyone who expressed a desire to lead a traditional Jewish life. The fourth was referred by a friend to a similarly outgoing rabbi on Manhattan's West Side. All four engaged in religious study, became Sabbath observers, koshered their homes, attended synagogue regularly, and sent their children to religious day schools.

What moved these four women to take on what has been called "the yoke of Orthodoxy"? In each case the key factor was a charismatic rabbi willing to devote considerable time to the family. As one woman remarked:

> The rabbi is one of the most extraordinary human beings I have ever met—generous, warm, giving. He is always "there," and he's willing to accept you "where you're at."

Another commented about the same rabbi:

> Someone had told me about this day school, and I liked the way it looked so I decided my son should go. That's how I met the rabbi. He was the one who arranged for the *get*. I didn't even know such a thing existed. He invited me to come to the shul, and I liked it. He explained to me abut being kosher, and I did the house, little by little.

Of the West Side rabbi, a woman said:

> He was incredible. I was a wreck and a friend suggested him to me. I called and he said to come right over and he didn't even know me. He'll talk to you even at two o'clock in the morning. I had started getting interested in Jewish things even before the divorce. Before that it had always been a great source of pride when people would say "you don't look Jewish." The rabbi got me to take courses at the shul and to send my daughter to a day school.

In all 10 families that moved from unaffiliated to affiliated status, it was the mother who, after the divorce, established the synagogue affiliation, enrolled the children in a religious school, and initiated observance in the home. These women did not have to deal with their ex-husbands about matters of Jewish observance and affiliation. But those fathers who still saw their children regularly did not object to the new patterns of observance and affiliation. One father commented:

> It's true that my ex has become quite involved Jewishly because of the children. But no, it hasn't been a problem for me. I try to encourage the girls. I pick them up from Hebrew school when it's my day. I took them to shul on Purim—I even made their costumes.

One father, whose ex-wife had become increasingly Orthodox, expressed some ambivalence over the fact that she and the children had grown so observant:

> I have no real Jewish ties myself, but I'm very proud of my children. They have strong ties. They speak Hebrew, and they go to a yeshiva. I'm not that involved in their schooling because of the divorce and being an absentee father. The big problem is that I do not have a kosher home and recently their mother made their home 110 percent kosher. Now they won't eat in mine.

A father who had himself grown up in an Orthodox home noted:

> When we got married, I had had my fill of religion, and I moved completely away from it—no synagogue affiliation. But since the divorce, my wife has gotten very involved, and our son is at a yeshiva. The rabbi there is very special—he believes in bringing people back in any way that he can. As a result, I find that I've slowly been moving back to religion over the past few years.

Every family that had been affiliated during the marriage retained an affiliation after the divorce. Children who had been attending Sunday or Hebrew school, day school or yeshiva, continued their Jewish educations at least until their Bar Mitzvahs or Bat Mitzvahs. Since generally it was the mother who had custody, she was the one who met with teachers and attended parent meetings, Hebrew school plays, and special Sabbath programs. In sev-

eral instances, however, the father, rather than the mother, took the lead in ensuring the continued affiliation and participation of the children. For example, one father said:

> During the marriage, I guess you might say we sank to the lower common denominator—hers. Whatever minimal observance there was was because of the children. Now I go to synagogue more than ever, and I'm the one that supervises the children's Jewish education. I spend a lot more time with my parents, and when I have the children on a weekend I take them to my parents' synagogue.

One mother was quite explicit about the fact that she felt that the children's Jewish education was their father's responsibility:

> I occasionally go to the temple on a Sabbath with the children, but I decided that I did not want control over that whole area. As part of the divorce, I gave that responsibility—the kids' Jewish education—to him. I didn't want to have anything to do with it. I felt I had enough responsibility in other areas. I wouldn't say "don't go," but I wanted him to take control. I make my ex drive the car pools for all the kids' Jewish activities.

Her ex-husband confirmed this:

> I live in the city, but I drive out to Long Island four times a week to see the children. Twice a week I pick up my son from Hebrew school at the temple and then take both kids for supper. On Saturdays I participate with them in a special parent-child religious and education program at the temple. Then on Sunday I come out again and pick up my daughter from Sunday school and take the kids for the day.

This father was clearly exerting every possible effort to keep his children identified and affiliated Jewishly. Why did he do it?

> My wife doesn't give a damn about it. But I was brought up with the synagogue playing a very vital role in my life. It was a central focus for my parents—they actually founded this synagogue

in Brooklyn and their lives revolved around it. It was important to me that when I walked in, everyone knew who I was!

Contrary to the belief that divorce is a major factor in the erosion of Jewish affiliation and identity, the sample in this study presented no case of a family *dis*affiliating after the breakup of the marriage. It is true that a number of men and women became synagogue or temple dropouts, particularly after their children passed the age of Bar Mitzvah or Bat Mitzvah. But children who had attended Hebrew or Sunday school before their parents' divorce continued to do so after. And among the previously unaffiliated, fully half moved to affiliated status and provided some form of religious education for their children.

The Unaffiliated

At the time of the interviews, 10 custodial parents classified themselves as unaffiliated. None attended religious services except for an occasional visit to a temple during the High Holy Days, and even that was rare. Nevertheless, several of these parents maintained some institutional ties to the Jewish community. A West Side mother explained:

> The children go to the community Hebrew school. It's good because no one pounds you. Once in a while, they go to services there. I say "Go if you want to." My ex stuck them in this school and then wouldn't pay the tuition. I was ready to take them out, but then they told me they'd take both boys for free. It didn't matter to me—they'll do anything to keep those kids there.

Another unaffiliated mother said:

> Our older son was 11 at the time of the divorce. I wanted to have him Bar Mitzvah for my father's sake, but I couldn't find any place that would condense the preparation time. Our son really wasn't that interested, so the end result was no Bar Mitzvah. When it came to our

younger son, he really wanted it, so we joined a temple just until the Bar Mitzvah. There was no pressure to continue. They were very low-key.

A third unaffiliated mother had a son attending a Hebrew school connected with an Orthodox synagogue. She said:

> I feel anger, fury, and, on the other hand, sheer delight about it. His education is at an Orthodox synagogue. A lot of my son's friends were going there, and he wanted to go, too. It's like a congregation of disaffected Jews. "If you want to come, fine, if not, I wish you would, but no hard feelings." I don't really have much to do with it. The rabbi is an ardent Zionist, and while he's totally accepting of one's own brand of Judaism, he wants you to be a Zionist, and that I'm not.

Several unaffiliated parents noted that they were considering Jewish education for their children. One mother commented:

> Now that she's 10, I think I would like her to have some Jewish education. No Hebrew, and nothing religious—just cultural. The problem is that it would have to be during the week only—no weekends, because we rotate weekends, and I don't think my ex would go for that.

And another:

> My son, nine and a half years old, keeps telling me that he wants to go to Hebrew school. All his peers go, and he wants to "belong." I'm thinking about it. I guess it's important for my son to have a sense of belonging now with his father away and separate from him. Maybe it's particularly important for a boy—Bar Mitzvah represents a turning point in a boy's life.

With a few exceptions, parents who identified themselves as unaffiliated spoke positively about Judaism. A woman put it this way:

> I have a keen emotional sense of being Jewish. It's important for me to be identified as a Jew. So many thousands of years that a people has survived! I have a sympathy and empathy for my people that I want to pass on to my children.

A man who had been married to a non-Jewish woman said:

> Since the divorce, I feel that I've become closer to things Jewish. I've become more cognizant of Jewish tradition and, as a single parent, I feel a responsibility to provide some of this for the kids. For example, I have them every other weekend, and I light candles with them, saying the prayer. Sometimes we do it at my parents; sometimes they each have a friend over; but often it's just the three of us—the kids and me. I also think that as I've gotten a bit older, I've been able to reflect on the traditions and they have become more valuable to me.

Another parent mused:

> I see a change in myself in recent years. I feel intensely, increasingly Jewish. Nothing to do with organized religion, but I tend to think more and more in terms of "is it good or bad for the Jews?"

Thus even among those who were unaffiliated and disinterested in organized religion, there existed a sense of identification as Jews, sympathy for Jewish causes, and attachment to Jewish traditions.

Obstacles to Community Participation

Most families in the sample maintained, and some increased, existing ties to the Jewish community after the divorce. A number reported excellent experiences that illustrate how the Jewish community can reach out to single parents and their children. A majority of the respondents, however, mentioned obstacles to participation in Jewish communal life as a result of their changed marital status. Finances posed one kind of barrier. But equally, if not more, serious were lack of social support and a sense of stigmatization.

Financial Obstacles. Most of the rabbis and school personnel interviewed for *The Jewish Community and Children of Divorce* had insisted that no one was forced to drop out of synagogue or Hebrew or day school for financial reasons. While interviews with parents in this study confirmed that none had *left* because of inability to pay, several respondents—particularly mothers—explained that the synagogue's financial policy had prevented them from joining in the first place. One said:

> I've seen Judaism lose children for financial reasons. At the temple that I first thought I would join after my divorce, I found that they charged the same amount for me as for a couple with several children, so I never joined. Frankly, I could have afforded it, but it was the principle. And there are a lot of people who are embarrassed to ask for special consideration or to say "I can't afford that much."

Another said that lack of money had made it impossible for her to give her son a Jewish education:

> Jewish education for the children is always on my mind. I've asked a lot of people about it. I spoke to someone, and she said it would cost "thus and so." I spoke to a rabbi I happen to know, and he had no suggestions because I simply can't afford the money either for a temple membership or for a Jewish education. Without the money, it just doesn't seem to be possible.

Several were grateful that after the divorce their children were able to continue in the day school on scholarships, but one noted:

> I have a scholarship which gives me one-third off, but every chance that they get, they throw the scholarship in your face. They have bingo, and if you're on scholarship you're supposed to help out, but it's during the day, and I can't go. They said, "It's your obligation; you're on scholarship, you know." I find that very degrading. Do they think I want to be on scholarship?

Another woman stated that after the divorce her daughter was given a scholarship at the day school she had been attending, but:

I find it very hard, and so does my daughter, because we're not in the same "station" as the others. The kids and the parents at the school and the shul can afford things that we just can't. It's not that anyone treats us badly—it's just knowing that we can't do the things that they can do.

These perceptions of second-class status may or may not have been rooted in reality, but they were widely felt and frequently voiced.

Lack of Outreach. More common than financial complaints among respondents were feelings that the synagogue or temple could do far more "reaching out" to the single parent and child, both at the time of the divorce and after. All denominations were criticized in this respect. Said one woman bitterly about the neighborhood Reform temple:

Support from the temple at the time of the divorce? No—it never occurred to the rabbi to call *me*. He spoke with my husband—but, of course, my husband had been a member of the board of directors for 10 years. It certainly would have been nice, considering the fact that I had also been involved in that temple for 10 years, if they had encouraged me to stay on as a member.

Said one woman about the suburban Reform temple that she still attended:

I must say that the temple did not reach out to us at all. When we "fell out," no one followed up. They never tried. I was right there kind of waving for their attention, but they never touched me. It's too bad—they put all their efforts into the strong supporters, the regulars. They should try to reach the hesitants, like us.

Her ex-husband confirmed this:

I used to go regularly to classes at the temple. But after the divorce, they did not reach out in any way, shape, or form—except to ask me to pay the bills. Then when I couldn't pay—no response. Nothing! The rabbi never said a word. He made no overtures, never said "Would you like to come in and talk?" or "How are you doing?" or "My door is open."

Complaints about lack of outreach on the part of Orthodox institutions were expressed less frequently, but they did occur. These words from a successful woman executive echoed some of the comments above:

No, the shul has never reached out to me. As a matter of fact, I'll probably be dropping my membership there because a group of us are starting our own *havurah*-type service—Conservative. It's funny, though—I have so much in the way of business contacts and experience I could have contributed, but they never called on me.

Generally, after a divorce, it is the man who leaves the household and finds housing elsewhere. Several fathers said that they would have appreciated some attempt on the part of the rabbi in the new neighborhood to draw them into the synagogue or temple. One said:

When I first joined the new temple—largely so that my daughter could go to Hebrew school there—I told them my situation and made arrangements about dues, mail, tuition bills, and everything. I go to services regularly, but the rabbi has never approached me.

Another father noted:

I was really surprised that the rabbi did not make any effort at all to draw me in after the divorce. First of all, I hear that he has a degree in psychology so he should know better. And secondly, he himself was divorced so he should understand what it feels like to suddenly find yourself alone.

Stigmatization. Lack of outreach efforts was usually blamed on the rabbi. Many respondents, however, spoke about their general sense of discomfort as single parents in the synagogue or school, of "feeling different," of not being welcomed by the congregation or other parents. As one woman put it:

I'm thinking of dropping my membership. As I see it, the temple [Reform] is regarded as the exclusive province of the family. The widowed or divorced are seen as obstacles—maybe even as threats. At times, I feel almost ostracized. Let me give you just one subtle example. I used to be a frequent reader of the *Haftorah* [weekly reading from the Prophets]; since my divorce almost four years ago, I have not been asked once.

The problem is particularly critical for the Orthodox divorced woman, according to one such respondent:

Divorced fathers get very different treatment than divorced mothers. The whole attitude is different. You should see how respectfully the teachers at the children's yeshiva treat the fathers when they come into the school. Part of it is probably money, but that shouldn't mean that the mother should get less respect. Some of the teachers give you a look as if to say "What more can we expect from these children since their mother is divorced?" That attitude is all wrong.

She went on to note how difficult it is for an Orthodox woman when it comes to observance of the Sabbath and holidays:

The problem is that there is very little place for the Jewish woman in the Jewish community, particularly if you're Orthodox. Orthodoxy is very male-oriented. Comes Shabbos or the holidays and you're alone with your kids. It's no fun trying to make Kiddush and sing *zmirot* [Sabbath songs] or light the menorah by yourself—though I really try to do it. And in shul, the fathers are around with their kids. My nine-year-old son is too old to be sitting with me, but he has no one to sit with so he just runs around the shul and plays.

A woman blamed the rabbi for the problems of single parents at her Reform temple:

Shortly after the divorce, a new rabbi came in. He is a Jackass! He is into religion, but not into people. He has been no help at all. There happens to be a huge singles population at the temple, and several of us tried to put together a singles group, but we got no help from him. That place is for

couples only. It has cliques, too. If you're not married, you can't be comfortable there.

The fathers, too, expressed discomfort as single parents in the synagogue. As one observed:

There seems to be something inherent in Judaism that means a mass denial about divorce. When it happens, it's something shameful, a disgrace. People try to pretend that there's nothing wrong, and as a result they ignore you and the pain you're going through.

As these men and women spoke of the discomfort and aloneness they felt in the synagogue, several acknowledged that the problem was not present only there. One man said:

Sure it's hard. They're all couples at the temple, and it's a lonely feeling. But it's lonely being single in the temple, in the Jewish community, or anywhere I go. It's just lonely being single!

Positive Experiences

Although most respondents had negative feelings about the failure of the synagogue or the community to reach out to them, several had only praise and appreciation for the ways they and their children had been drawn in and made to feel comfortable. Said one about the Reform suburban temple to which she belonged:

The rabbi was extremely supportive of me and the children after the divorce. He tried to pay special attention to the children. He made a point of talking to them about things that interested them—like baseball. I was on the PTA board at the time, and he insisted that I continue. He encouraged me to remain active, to come to services Friday night, [to] work in the PTA. He made me feel that I was as good as everyone else!

Two Orthodox institutions, one in Manhattan and one in the Bronx, were warmly praised. One woman described the atmosphere:

> The shul [in Manhattan] made a real effort to pull me in, as well as to pull in the boys, who were going to Hebrew school there. They have separate fees for single parents that are adjusted according to your ability to pay. They are warm, congenial. They never make you feel pitiable or like a sore thumb. For example, they keep asking my son to usher at the services, and they are always giving him *aliyahs* [blessings over the Torah]. I'm telling you—they never leave us alone. They make sure to keep us involved.

About the synagogue in the Bronx, a mother said:

> I love the shul. It's such a warm place. The men are wonderful to my son. For example, they make sure to put him on their shoulders and carry him around on Simchat Torah. It's little things like that, but they're important. They make him feel so welcome that he really loves going there.

Occasionally, one respondent praised and another criticized the same temple or synagogue. Perceptions vary, of course, and experiences as well. But one factor may be, as some respondents pointed out, the receptivity and behavior of the individual. The suggestion was made, for example, that the single parent has a responsibility to take some initiative. One said:

> There's just so much a synagogue can do for a single parent. As difficult as it is, it's important that we make ourselves get out there and push ourselves a little so we'll get accepted, invited, and involved. I did it, and it worked.

Another suggested:

> I think it has less to do with the synagogue than with the woman herself. You can't sit around and wait for the synagogue to come to you. If you want to be involved, you have to stop kvetching and go out and do it!

These comments underscore the fact that the individual as well as the synagogue has an outreach responsibility. Nevertheless, the extent to which the synagogue or temple reaches out and welcomes the single-parent family will probably determine whether that family will remain involved in the Jewish community.

The Bar Mitzvah and Bat Mitzvah

In *The Jewish Community and Children of Divorce,* rabbis identified a range of problems—financial, ceremonial, social, psychological—that may confront the post-divorce couple at the time of their child's Bar Mitzvah or Bat Mitzvah. In this study, the parents themselves were asked how they had coped with this event if it had occurred after their divorce. Parents with youngsters between nine and 12 were asked if they had given any thought to the event and, if so, what their expectations and plans were.

A total of 15 families had celebrated a Bar Mitzvah or Bat Mitzvah after the parents' divorces. Five felt that things had gone very well. Recalled one mother:

> Our son's Bar Mitzvah went beautifully, largely because of the rabbi's sensitivity. For example, normally the father and the mother sit next to each other on the pulpit, but he arranged for us to sit on opposite sides. It also helped that his father's woman friend did not come. We each invited our own friends, and our son invited the entire religious school class. So there was a head table of fourteen boys, and that made our son feel good.

In another family, while the mother was very pleased about the way things had gone, the father was even more so:

> The Bar Mitzvah was wonderful. Our son was really a delight. He ran the entire ceremony with great dignity. He was obviously on top of it and thoroughly enjoying himself. It was his—a won-

derful event. My mother came, and she loved it. Though she and my ex-wife had never gotten along, they both behaved well toward each other.

In six cases, the parent(s) reported a few problems. One father related:

The Bat Mitzvah took place shortly after the divorce, and I just say that although it went all right, I felt that it was a great source of acrimony in that post-divorce period. Still, we tried not to take our own problems out on our daughter.

A young mother from Borough Park was ambivalent:

Our younger son's Bar Mitzvah was two years ago—after the divorce. It was very difficult. My husband came in from out of town, but he refused to give a cent. My parents and I paid for the whole thing. My son was very tense about how his father would act and what kinds of scenes might occur.

On the other hand, she added:

Around here, people make very fancy Bar Mitzvahs—big parties, lots of flowers, a band. We just made a simple Kiddush and then a party at home for his class. What was beautiful was how supportive the boys in his class were—they kept saying that our Bar Mitzvah was just as nice as all the fancy ones.

In four cases, the Bar Mitzvah or Bat Mitzvah provoked many problems. One mother explained:

The Bar Mitzvah itself didn't go too badly. We divided the *aliyahs* and for our son's sake we tried very hard to behave civilly. But up until the day itself, it was a difficult time. My ex absolutely didn't want a Bar Mitzvah, while my son wanted one like crazy. We had terrible fights over money since my ex thought the whole thing was unnecessary. In the end, he paid for half, but he really gave me a hard time.

The father's side of the story was somewhat different:

It's not that I didn't want a Bar Mitzvah—I just didn't want one of those big, fancy affairs. I wanted to take my son to Israel instead and just have a small affair here. But his mother wouldn't let him go. So in the end, it was the big, fancy affair, and I got stuck paying for half of it.

Eight families with children between nine and 12 contemplated the approaching Bar Mitzvah or Bat Mitzvah with anxiety and concern. The mother of a nine-year-old said:

I worry about everything already. A Bar Mitzvah is usually a big function—100 to 150 people, and I don't know many people. Whom will I invite? I don't have a wide circle of friends anymore. Also, I guess my ex should be there, but I don't think I'd want that. And then, there's the cost—who is going to pay?

In another case, both mother and father were bitter about the forthcoming Bar Mitzvah of their son. Said the mother:

The Bar Mitzvah is next year, and his father will not be there. I won't let him come because I've been left with all the responsibility that should have been his. I resent it terribly. All and any costs relating to a Bar Mitzvah will fall on my shoulders, so why should I let him come?

The father said:

I'm afraid I won't be involved next year when my son's Bar Mitzvah takes place. She wanted me to pay for it, and she wanted it to take place at the Tavern on the Green. I said absolutely not because my whole family is kosher, and I think it would be a slap in the face to them to have it there. So I said "Have it where you want, but pay for it yourself." I'd rather not make a fuss because it's only our son who will suffer.

Five families anticipated the Bar Mitzvah or Bat Mitzvah with pleasure. One father said:

We'll make the Bat Mitzvah a very simple affair, just as our older's was, before the divorce. I'm sure it will go fine.

A mother who looked forward to the Bar Mitzvah of her son in two years said

> My ex and I get along very well. We're very friendly, so I know it won't be a problem.

Several couples reported that at the time of an older child's Bar Mitzvah or Bat Mitzvah they had already decided to separate. These parents postponed their divorces until after the ceremony so as not to mar the occasion for the child or for their respective families, underscoring the fact that many Jews—Orthodox, Conservative, Reform, and even unaffiliated—view the Bar Mitzvah or Bat Mitzvah as a significant event.

The Parents' Recommendations

Respondents were asked what they thought or hoped the Jewish community might do for single-parent families.[5] On the whole, unaffiliated men and women did not see the Jewish community as a source of support for themselves as a single parents, and most had nothing to suggest on that subject.

On the other hand, almost every affiliated respondent had some suggestion regarding the role of the Jewish community vis-à-vis the single parent. Their recommendations fall into three categories: those that address the needs of the child; those that focus on the needs of the single parent; and those that call on the Jewish community to change its values relative to divorce and the single-parent family.

Recommendations Concerning the Child

Ten respondents, nine women and one man, emphasized the need for activities geared toward the children in divorced families. One woman, for example, noted that she wanted to provide some form of Jewish education for her child but had been unable to find a school that had classes only on weekdays:

> That makes it difficult for the divorced parent, because Saturday and Sunday are usually the father's time, and fathers don't want to give this up. Why not provide weekday-only classes?

Another parent emphasized the financial problems involved in providing religious education for the children:

> The Jewish community has to make it easier for a Jewish child to get an education. They must make special provisions for the child from a single-parent family.

An Orthodox woman suggested that synagogues institute Big Brother programs for young boys from divorced homes in the community:

> First of all, there's the problem of my son having someone to sit with in shul. He's too old to sit with me and too young for the Youth Minyan. Perhaps they should have a Big Brother program for shul, and maybe even for after school. I'm not good at things like athletics, and it would be nice if there were someone who could take him to the gym or the park.

At least six parents stressed the importance of activities for single parents, *together with their children,* especially around the holidays. Said one mother:

> The synagogue might organize and sponsor a network of people who could have a Seder together. Since the divorce, my Seder has shrunk to next to nothing, and the children and I feel this. It's particularly difficult around holiday time, and the synagogues could help.

Another mother commented:

> Organized activities for single parents are one thing. But it's very important to have activities which include the children, for example, at Hanukkah time. That way, the children get to celebrate the holidays with others, and you're not alone.

A father had a different idea:

> I would like to see the synagogue arrange for discussion groups for divorced fathers and, at the same time, for the children who are old enough to participate. That way, the children can see that others have similar problems.

The value of activities for single parents together with their children is suggested by the enthusiasm of two parents who had attended a five-day "camp" cosponsored by the American Jewish Committee and B'nai B'rith Camps. Said one mother:

> I can't tell you how significant those five days were in terms of my own and the children's Jewishness. It made me feel that it's okay to be a single parent in the Jewish community, and it was wonderful for the children, sharing experiences with others from divorced homes. We're still friendly with several of the families who were at the camp. I'll tell you, single parents are very hungry to be in a family situation together. I must say that the camp experience really turned me on again to my Jewishness. I've started to go more often to temple.

Another parent who had been at the camp said:

> Federation paid for my daughter and myself to attend this camp. All of us were single parents, men and women, in a very strong Jewish atmosphere. You know, Friday night and Shabbos. I really had never experienced anything like this, and I found it very moving. I've tried to continue it since we got home. And it was wonderful for my daughter. In fact, the most beautiful thing was the children. Somehow, they sensed a bond from the very beginning. From a Jewish point of view, it was an eye-opener for my daughter, and she loved it. As a group we became very close, and we've gotten together four times since the summer. This is the kind of thing we single parents need—opportunities to socialize, with our children, in a Jewish context.

Recommendations Concerning the Single Parent

Parents were quite explicit about what the Jewish community might do to help them deal with their needs and concerns. Several spoke of counseling not only at the time of the divorce but *after* it and suggested that synagogues provide referrals to services such as those available at the Jewish Board of Family and Children's Services.

An Orthodox woman called attention to the need for career and employment counseling to help women like herself who suddenly must go back to work. Other women saw marital counseling as particularly important before marriage. A number of respondents, particularly men, suggested that the Jewish community recognize the need for support groups for single parents. One father put it this way:

> When a former couple is thrust into the singles world, it's the man who loses. It's not as hard for women; they can rap, get emotional, cry. Men aren't allowed to cry. The Jewish community should help men get together to talk, for support. The women at least have the kids, while men have lost their families and have generally had to move. We need supports. The Jewish community should be doing this to help men like myself in these trying times. If they can't, at least *they* should be able to refer us to some programs that can.

An Orthodox father echoed this plea:

> I wish I had had other single-parent men to talk to. You know, men don't talk much, and most of the men I knew were married. I felt lost at the time of the divorce. I couldn't relate to single men, that is, men without children. They're different. At tough times you need someone who can be in your skin. This is what the Jewish community should be doing.

Women, too, spoke of the need for support groups to which the Jewish single parent could turn. An Orthodox woman said:

I wish the Jewish community could help us more. There's a need for support groups, especially for Orthodox women. Maybe something could be done to get Orthodox women from different shuls together since there aren't that many of us at any one shul. We need that kind of thing.

The calls for help from the Jewish community in the form of counseling services and support groups tended to come from those who had been divorced less than three years. Later, priorities change, and most men and women look to single-parent groups for more than support. A number of parents spoke of the need for the Jewish community to provide opportunities for single parents to meet potential marriage partners. About half had tried such groups as Parents Without Partners (PWP), where single parents could meet, discuss common problems, and socialize. Appraisals of these groups were uniformly negative. As one woman explained:

I tried PWP, but it was a shoddy group of people. Then I tried some of the private parties. They have good activities like workshops, cocktail parties, bowling, or picking apples with the children on Sundays. But there's no Jewish orientation—nothing—even though 95 percent of the people who go there are Jewish.

Another woman recalled of PWP:

The men were all over 50, and they looked as though they had been pulled out of institutions. They're all looking for young girls. They have discussions that could be interesting except that they're on a very low level. Besides, there's nothing Jewish about it—no Jewish content

Synagogue-affiliated groups fared little better. A woman said:

I went to one of those things at an Orthodox synagogue. It's just not for me. I know I'm attractive, but I don't like using my looks that

way. It's not that I wouldn't like the kind of men there, because I'd like to meet someone who's observant. But most of the really terrific men, observant or not, don't have to go to singles parties.

A man noted that one of the problems of the singles parties he had attended, whether synagogue-sponsored or not, was that they didn't distinguish between singles and single parents:

There's a big difference. The singles are all very self-centered, part of the "me" generation. And they're usually a lot younger. Single parents are a different breed. We're more seasoned. We've had children. We have responsibilities. I know it's hard because of the numbers, so you probably have to mix the two. But it makes it more difficult to meet the right kind of person.

Recommendations Concerning Community Values

At least one in three respondents, at one point or another during the interview, spoke of the need for the Jewish community, and rabbis in particular, to face the fact that Jewish people divorce and that single-parent families are a constituency of their synagogues. One father, a nonpracticing rabbi himself, said:

Synagogues and schools ought to be changing their assumptions. They still take the intact family for granted and have clearly not adjusted to the fact that, at one and the same time, divorce is shrinking some families and, as single parents remarry, enlarging others. Adjustments have to be made in both cases, and Jewish institutions have not even begun to address this fact.

Another man echoed this:

The issue of divorce is here, unfortunately, and it is not going to go away. It has to be addressed by rabbis in their sermons, by teachers in the Hebrew schools, by Jews everywhere. It can no longer be hidden under the rug.

Summary and Conclusions

Although the sample of 40 divorced couples was too small to permit any generalizations, the study suggests that divorce does not necessarily result in erosion of Jewish identity and community involvement but may, especially for families with young children, open the way for a restoration or strengthening of Jewish affiliation. The determining factor may well be the warmth and sensitivity with which the synagogue, temple, or other Jewish institution welcomes and involves such single-parent families.

In the conference that followed publication of *The Jewish Community and Children of Divorce,* we suggested that some rabbis, particularly among the Orthodox, are concerned that efforts to deal with the single-parent family may be seen as condoning, even encouraging, divorce. Said one rabbi at the conference:

> A problem which emerges from giving special treatment to single parents in relation to institutional activities and fees is the loss of the couple advantage. The subtle indication of approval which emerges from such a response may shift the pro-family balance which is part of the Jewish value system.

While this concern is understandable, it is self-defeating. The divorce rate among Jews has risen, and even among the Orthodox divorced families have become increasingly visible. These families face all the problems associated with the breakup of marriage and, in addition, find, all too often, that the Jewish community is indifferent and unresponsive to their plight. Programs of premarital and marital counseling may help to reduce the incidence of divorce among Jews, but it will not make the problem go away. Single-parent families are a growing segment of the community. Their needs must be recognized, acknowledge and addressed.

NOTES

1. Chaim I. Waxman, *America's Jews in Transition* (Philadelphia: Temple University Press, 1983).

2. Since the average couple in the sample was married in 1972, the median ages at marriage for men and women in the general population were taken for that year.

3. The Jewish community has taken steps to address the problem of the recalcitrant husband. A number of Orthodox rabbis are now asking couples to sign a simple prenuptial agreement stating that, in the event the marriage is dissolved civilly, both parties will agree to give or receive a *get.* The Conservative movement has incorporated a prenuptial agreement in its *ketubah* (marriage contract), and a recent case suggests that the civil courts will enforce such an agreement.

To combat ignorance about the fact that a *get* is necessary for children of subsequent marriages to be legitimate under Jewish law, as well as to address the problem of the recalcitrant husband, an organization called GET (Getting Equitable Treatment) was formed several years ago in New York City. The organization seeks to assist men and women who are involved in battles over the *get,* as well as to forestall such problems through community education.

4. The post-divorce "family" is defined as the custodial parent and child(ren).

5. The comments that follow reveal a tendency on the part of respondents to equate "Jewish community" with the synagogue and/or Hebrew school. This may be a bias of the sample itself, which was largely drawn from New York City. In suburbs and smaller cities, single parents may be more likely to look for support and outreach from the Jewish community center, around which Jewish communal life tends to revolve.

Part IV

Complexities and Contradictions of Family Bonds

In this part, we have put together chapters on caregiving and nurturance with chapters on violence and power. We juxtapose these two groups to call attention to the fact that the family is not universally nurturant, while still recognizing that it is usually as members of families that we care for one another. Caregiving is gendered in both its cultural attribution and its impact on the lives of men and women. In the dominant culture of the United States in the twentieth century, caregiving is considered "women's work" and is associated with characteristics and activities labeled as "feminine." Although some men provide care for others and some women do not, it is predominantly women (in the home, as mothers, daughters, and wives; in the workplace, as nurses and child-care workers) who do the work of caregiving. It is important to understand men's participation in caregiving and how, over time, it has been more or less compatible with cultural notions of "masculinity." In "Masculinity, Caregiving, and Men's Friendship in Antebellum New England," Karen V. Hansen explores men's relationships and caregiving activities in the context of the economic and cultural forces that have shaped social possibilities and ideas of masculinity.

In "Ideals of Care," Arlie Russell Hochschild argues that we are now facing a "crisis in care" because, on one hand, the need for care is increasing as people live longer, as more people are pushed into poverty, and as women, whether married or not, shoulder an unequal share of providing care for children and the elderly. On the other hand, the supply of care is diminishing as family size decreases, the workplace demands more time from family members, and government social services and funds for the poor, the elderly, the ill, the disabled, and children are cut or eliminated. Although caregiving for family members has always been something that most families do, other advanced industrial countries do far more than the United States in providing external sources of care as well as support for family caregiving.

Nina Glick Schiller's chapter, "The Invisible Women," vividly illustrates how community health services rely on and build into their "needs assessments" the invisible caregiving work of family members, usually women and usually the mothers of the ill or disabled persons needing care. By examining how health services planning for the AIDS epidemic relies on the unrecognized work of family members, Schiller draws the connection between a health care system that is based on maximizing profit, a social system that devalues and takes for granted the caregiving work done primarily by women, and the structure and interaction of daily family life. The toll on caregivers is enormous, as both Schiller and Emily K. Abel, in her chapter, "The Ambiguities of Social Support," point out. Abel focuses on adult daughters who are caring for their elderly parents and emphasizes the double-edged nature of caregiving. Caring for the sick, the frail elderly, and the dying is a profound human experience that many people value. At the same time, it is extremely stressful. Abel finds that spouses, children, and friends often create additional stress on the caregiver as well as offering sources of emotional and practical support.

The type of caregiving common to almost all families is the care of young children. Parenting, which includes arranging for the care of children in the parents' absence, is a topic about which volumes could, and have, been written. Chapters on parenting, mothering, fathering, and child care are included throughout this collection because this aspect of families is so central and so connected to a myriad of topics (see Part III, "Webs of Family Relationships," and see also "Guide to Topics"). It is also important to remember that caregiving by parents is not limited to the period when children are very young but may continue into adulthood or, as Schiller's chapter illustrates, may be reactivated when adult children become ill, injured, or disabled. In this part, we have included two chapters that focus on central issues of caregiving for young children. Lynet Uttal examines the child-care concerns of mothers of color in her chapter, "Racial Safety and Cultural Maintenance," and finds that models of child care are not culturally neutral. High quality child care must incorporate the needs of children and parents in all racial-ethnic groups. In "Revolutionary Parenting," bell hooks suggests an ideal of care that includes both women and men in the parenting and care of children, and which asserts that, as a society, we have a group responsibility to the next generation.

Although the family is often portrayed as a buffer against the cruelties of the world, the truth is that families are potential sites of both safety and violence. Much of the research on violence within families has emphasized explanations in terms of the personal characteristics and psychological problems of the perpetrators of violence, and sometimes even of their victims. Analyzing families with a feminist sociological imagination means seeing how such violence is linked to the larger social world. Power and domination within families reflect economic and social patterns of domination and hierarchy in the larger society where women as a group are subordinate to men as a group, and where children are subordinate to adults. These patterns are reinforced and reproduced by certain cultural beliefs about child-rearing practices and about women's and men's appropriate roles. In "Through a Feminist Lens," Kersti A. Yllö reviews the major sociological approaches to understanding the root of the violence that occurs within families and argues that a gendered analysis is a crucial element in understanding, and stopping, this violence.

Two chapters in this part focus specifically on violence toward women by their male spouses, partners, or boyfriends. In "Why Do Men Batter Their Wives?" James Ptacek applies a "critical social psychology" to his interviews with male batterers and finds that the ways in which they report and account for their behavior are linked both to ideas of male entitlement and to culturally sanctioned excuses. Bonnie Zimmer's chapter, "Felicia: Working with a Teen Mother in an Abusive Relationship," provides a personal look at the struggle of one young woman with both the boyfriend who beats her and the social service agencies that are meant to serve her needs. Zimmer addresses the challenges of working with young women who are battered and suggests ways for social workers to help women escape violence from partners.

The other two chapters in this part focus on violence against children. Only since the early 1960s has child abuse been a "public issue," but, as John Demos points out in "Child Abuse in Context," it has a long history. Looking at New England family life in the seventeenth century, Demos poses questions about historical evidence and about whether childhood is becoming better or worse. Looking at the contemporary United States, Murray A. Straus challenges us to think critically about the effects of spanking children. In his book *Beating the Devil Out of Them: Corporal Punishment in American Families* (Lexington Books, 1994), Straus makes a strong case about the negative links between spanking and children's development and well-being. In "Ten Myths That Perpetuate Corporal Punishment," Straus examines the cultural myths that rationalize the use of force in child rearing.

Families are not any *one* thing—they incorporate the best and worst of ourselves and our cultures. But, as John Demos reminds us, only by seeking the truth and by understanding the interconnections of family dynamics and larger social processes can healing and change occur.

 *Section A*

Caregiving

Chapter 39

Ideals of Care: Traditional, Postmodern, Cold-Modern, and Warm-Modern

ARLIE RUSSELL HOCHSCHILD

Among the visual images of care in the modern Western world, a classic view portrays a mother holding a child. Frequently, the mother is seated in a chair at home or in a dreamlike setting, such as her garden. Often found in old-fashioned birthday cards and ads for yarn in women's magazines, the image is a secular, middle-class version of Madonna and child. The caregiver in these images is a woman, not a man. She is at home, not in a public place. Moreover, the caregiving seems natural, effortless. She is sitting, quiescent, not standing or moving—stances associated with "working." She seems to enjoy caring for the child and, as the child's face often suggests, she is good at caring. Thus, the image of care is linked with things feminine, private, natural, and well-functioning: this represents an ideal of care.

Drawn from nineteenth-century, upper-middle-class parlor life, this image has been put to extensive commercial use. Corporate

From *Social Politics*, fall 1995, 311–46. Reprinted by permission of Oxford University Press.

advertisers often juxtapose the mother-and-child image with such products as health insurance, telephone service, Band-Aids, diapers, talcum powder, and a wide variety of foods.[1] Our constant exposure to the commercial image of mother puts us at one remove from it. In a parallel way, the very term "care," at least in the American context, has suffered from commercial over-use, associated as it is with orange juice, milk, frozen pizza, and microwave ovens. Thus, both the image and the word for care have come to seem not only feminine, private, and natural but also emotionally void, bland, dull, even "sappy."

In the small but growing feminist literature on care, scholars have begun to challenge the silence on the issue in much conventional social theory. Such writers as Trudy Knijn, Clare Ungerson, and Kari Waerness note that care is more central in the lives of women than men, since it is more often women who care for children, the sick, and the elderly. While early feminist scholarship focused on the exploitative nature of women's traditional roles, recent feminist writers, as Kari Waerness puts it, "have struggled to redefine the possible grounds of feminist theory" (1987, 229). The quest for new "cultural grounds" coincides with a dilemma that many modern women face (Holter 1984; Waerness 1984; Sassoon 1987; Ungerson 1990; Knijn 1994). Waerness notes that "Women . . . are faced both with the task of caring for children, the ill, the disabled, and the elderly in the private sphere, while at the same time trying to achieve more command over their own lives and a greater measure of economic independence" (1987, 208).

In this chapter, I hope to add to this discussion, first, by describing a growing crisis in care, and second, by analyzing the cultural frameworks through which we see "care." I suggest that recent trends in the United States have expanded the *need* for care while contracting the *supply* of it. This has created a "care deficit" in both private and public life. In private life, the care deficit is most palpable in families where working mothers, married and single, lack sufficient help from partners or kin. (Here I draw illustrations from my research on tensions in American two-job marriages reported in *The Second Shift* [1989].) In public life, the care deficit can be seen in government cuts in funds for services to poor mothers, the disabled, mentally ill, and the elderly. In reducing the financial deficit, legislators add to the "care deficit."

Those on all sides of the care debate use terms and think in images that reflect four models of care.[2] These cultural models set down the basic terms of political debate about care and so deserve a closer look. The first is the *traditional* model represented by the image of the homemaker mother. The second is the *postmodern* model, represented by the working mother who "does it all" with no additional help from any quarter and no adaptation in her work schedule. This image often goes along with a tacit lowering of standards

of care, as well as making those lower standards seem normal. The third is the *cold-modern* model represented by impersonal institutional care in year-round ten-hour day care and old-age homes. The fourth is the *warm-modern* model in which institutions provide some care of the young and elderly, while women and men join equally in providing private care as well. Each model implies a definition of care, an idea about who gives it, and how much of what kind of care is "good enough."

Two Sides of the Care Deficit

First, by the term "care" I refer to an emotional bond, usually mutual, between the caregiver and cared-for, a bond in which the caregiver feels responsible for others' well-being and does mental, emotional, and physical work in the course of fulfilling that responsibility. Thus, care *of* a person implies care *about* him or her. In this chapter, I focus on the care of the very young and old—care we often still think of as "familial" (Abel and Nelson 1990).

Most care requires work so personal, so involved with feeling, that we rarely imagine it to be work. But it would be naive to assume that giving care is completely "natural" or effortless. Care is a result of many small subtle acts, conscious or not (Ruddick 1989). For example, consider a typical case of an elderly woman who becomes sick and despondent. A middle-age daughter visits. She helps her mother acknowledge her illness ("It's worth seeing a doctor") and drives her to the doctor. She lifts her mother's spirits through humor and conversation: she "cheers her up." She hugs her mother, makes her chicken soup, deciphers the intricate insurance forms, pays the doctor, has extra talks with the doctor, buys medicine, and offers long-term care at home. These are some of the many ways to care. In the course of performing these acts, all the moments when we are also trying to get into the task in the right spirit, with the appropriate feeling, can be considered the emotional work of care (Hochschild 1983; Smith 1988). Thus, we put more than "nature" into caring; we put feeling, acting, thought, and time into it.

As the worldwide income gap has widened over the last forty years between the developed and the underdeveloped countries (the oil-rich and the Pacific Rim countries aside), the need for care has expanded in much of the developing world, especially Africa and parts of South America. In this chapter, I focus on the United States, a country that has grown relatively richer during this period. *Within* this declining "core" of capitalism, the class gap has widened, and the care of many dependents seems to have eroded, too. Further research may uncover rough parallels between the American case and that of the countries of Western Europe, Canada, Australia, New Zealand, and Japan.[3] Perhaps these models can sensitize us to the often hidden cultural lining beneath the politics of care in the United States as well as elsewhere in the developed world.

With the exception of Japan, similar conditions seem to prevail in other developed countries: a flight of capital to cheap labor pools in the developing world, the disappearance of well-paid industrial jobs and the rise of poorly paid service jobs, the weakening of labor unions, and the influx of migrant workers, all of which put a squeeze on average blue-collar workers. In addition, the economic recession of the 1980s and cost cutting due to global competition in the 1990s have led to stagnation in the middle class and decline among the poor.

Two additional shifts have affected this growing need and demand for care—changes in the structure of families and at work. In American families over the past forty years,

birth rates have fallen, reducing the demand for care. In the United States, as in Canada, Japan, and the Netherlands, the average number of children born to women (if they lived to the end of their childbearing years) was slightly above 3.0 in 1951 and below 1.9 in 1988. At the same time, the proportions of elderly and single-parent families as well as unwed mothers rose, increasing the need for care.[4] From 1950 to 1990, the proportion of older people (65 and over) in the population rose from 8 to 12 percent.

In most of the advanced industrial world, the divorce rate has also increased. Half of American marriages end in divorce.[5] Often we imagine the single parent to be in a temporary phase before remarriage, but of divorced American women with children, one-third never remarry, and of the two-thirds who do remarry, over half divorce again.

The divorce rate has increased the number of single-parent families. In the United States, of all households with children, the proportion of single-parent homes rose from 9 percent in 1960 to 23 percent in 1988.[6] Since the remarriage rate for women is lower than that for men (because men tend to remarry younger women), and since divorced women are far more likely to gain custody of children, most single parents are women. Divorced men provide relatively less care for their children, and divorced women much more. The rising divorce rate thus creates a care gap.

Further, throughout the developed world, with the exception of Japan, the proportion of all births that occur to unmarried women has risen. For example, in the United States the rate rose from 5 percent in 1960 to 23 percent in 1986 (Sorrentino 1990, 44).[7] Most unwed mothers cohabit with the fathers of their children, but the rate of breakup among cohabiting couples is higher than among married couples. Thus, the single-parent home is the major source of care for many children.

The growing fragility of bonds between women and men has also weakened bonds between men and their children. After divorce, not only are fathers physically absent, but they reduce contact with their children and, over time, give them less money (Arendell 1986; Weitzman 1985). A national study found that, three years after divorce, half of American divorced fathers had not visited their children during the entire previous year and thus did not perform the most basic form of care (Furstenburg and Cherlin 1991; Wallerstein and Blakeslee 1989). After one year, half of divorced fathers were providing no child support at all, and most of the other half paid irregularly or less than the court-designated amounts (Arendell 1986). Wealthy divorced fathers were just as likely to be negligent as poor ones. Thus, recent trends in the class structure, certain demographic shifts, and family decline have all increased the need for care.

The Supply Side of the Care Deficit

As the need for public services has increased, however, American voters have come to favor *reducing* the supply of care that government provides, and many favor turning to the beleaguered family as a main source of care. They fall back on the image of Madonna and child. Despite signs of distress and lower well-being among the growing number of poor children (declining academic performance and high rates of substance abuse, depression, and teen suicide), much of the American middle class responds with "sympathy fatigue," for some of their children are in trouble, too.

While the number of homeless and destitute people rose under the presidencies of Ronald Reagan and George Bush, government services remained static or fell. Both presidents tried to resolve the gap between demand and supply of care by a cultural move—privatizing our idea of care. President Bush cut the national budget for school lunches and Aid to Families with Dependent Children (AFDC), calling instead for volunteers who might model themselves on his nonworking wife, Barbara. In this way, Bush extended a collective, yet private, version of mother and child over a growing array of social ills.

Even under the Democratic administration of President Bill Clinton, the middle-class "sympathy fatigue" has persisted and grown. For example, the Personal Responsibility Act, introduced in January 1995 by Speaker of the House Newt Gingrich, calls for permanent cuts in welfare to unwed mothers under age eighteen, to anyone who has received aid for sixty months, or to anyone who bears a child while on welfare.

If the state refuses to provide a *public* solution to the care gap by funding service programs, can the *private* realm now really serve as the main source of care? Like women in most of the developed world, American women have gone into paid work in extraordinary numbers. In 1960, 28 percent of married women with children under eighteen were in the labor force; by 1992, 68 percent of those mothers were working. More mothers than nonmothers now work. In 1948, 11 percent of married women with children aged six and younger worked outside the home. In 1991, 60 percent did. Today over half of all mothers of children one year and younger are in the labor force.

Working mothers are also working longer hours than they were twenty years ago. In *The Overworked American*, Juliet Schor argues that Americans are working "an extra month" each year compared to twenty years ago. They take shorter vacations, have fewer paid or even unpaid days off, and work longer hours. According to a 1992 national survey, the average worker spends 45 hours a week on the job, including overtime and commuting time (Schor 1991; Galinsky, Bond, and Friedman 1993).

In truth, *the private realm to which conservatives turn for a solution to the care deficit has many problems itself.* Many in need of care are caught between the hardened sensibility of a taxable middle class coping with a recession and government cuts, on the one hand, and fewer helping hands because of overstretched kin networks, on the other.

Care at Home: "Who Will Do What Mother Did?"

Working mothers face the daunting task of balancing work and family life, often in the absence of two things—partners who share work at home and a workplace that offers both parents flexible hours. Such women are caught in what I have called a "stalled gender revolution." It is a revolution because in two decades women have gone from being mainly at home to being mainly at work. It is "stalled" because women have undergone this change in a culture that has neither rewired its notion of manhood to facilitate male worksharing at home, nor restructured the workplace so as to allow more control over and flexibility at work.

Caught in this stall, women have little time to care for their children and elderly parents, much less a sick neighbor. Few can find time to volunteer at a homeless shelter three times a week. The private "supply" with which conservatives would answer the growing needs for care is often made up of women caught in this stalled revolution.

Several points from my recent study reported in the *Second Shift* are relevant here. The study was based on in-depth interviews of fifty two-job couples (who have children six years or younger) and their care-providers in the San Francisco Bay area. I also observed a dozen families in their homes, following workers from home to workplace and back (Hochschild 1989).[8] First, many couples were struggling over who did how much of the "caring" for the home and children. Care for the home was a tension point in their marriage. Frequently, the couple disagreed about how much care each should provide and in what spirit. Often, too, they disagreed about how much each was actually doing. And they disagreed over how much really *needed to be done.* Men who fully shared the "second shift" often wished their wives were more *grateful* to them for being such unusually helpful husbands, especially when they got no praise from the outside world for doing housework. Wives who cut back their work hours to contribute more at home wanted their husbands to appreciate the sacrifices they were making at work. On both sides, hurt feelings over insufficient gratitude were rooted, I argue, in the low value placed on the caregiving work "mother used to do."

Of the husbands I interviewed, one out of five fully shared the care of children and home with their working wives. Of the 80 percent of husbands who did not share—but offered "help" with chores and child care—over half had felt pressure from their wives to do more, but most resisted. Some working-class mothers pressed their husbands by indirect means. They got sick or played helpless at paying bills, shopping, and even cooking and sewing, because, as one wife stated with a wink, "My husband does it so much better." Other women, with traditional viewpoints and working-class backgrounds, became "supermoms" in cycles. They worked hard at the office, raced home to do the chores, went without resting for weeks on end, then collapsed. When they "fell sick" or dropped with exhaustion, their working-class husbands—who otherwise resisted sharing the work at home—took over the cooking and child care. Sometimes women got pneumonia, migraine headaches, a bad cold, or flu. When they recovered, their husbands withdrew and they began the cycle all over again.

Other working mothers used direct means—dramatic confrontations or serious discussions. Met with intransigence, some wives staged "sharing showdowns." They went on "strike." They refused to cook, and they let the laundry pile up. One mother even left a child waiting to be picked up at school, when she knew her husband had forgotten. Another started charging her husband by the hour for work at home beyond her rightful half. In these ways, wives tried to force their husbands to do more but often failed to do so. Neither could afford the emotional "luxury" of a marriage free of a struggle about care. In the absence of wider changes in the culture of manhood and the workplace, two-job couples often suffer a microversion of the care deficit.

Cultural Responses: Traditional, Postmodern, Cold-Modern, and Warm-Modern

To sum it up, the need for care is growing while the supply is declining. While right-wing political forces are cutting off the *public* supply of care, women are moving into the workplace, and a speedup there is straining the *private* sources of care. The present challenge, it seems to me, is to increase the supply of care, while retaining women's hard-won gains in society and the workplace.

To pursue this goal, we must sensitize ourselves to various competing cultural *images* of care, for it is in the persuasive power of these images that an underlying struggle might be won. The couples I studied seemed to reflect four different images of care. For clarity, I shall posit these images as Weberian ideal

types, but the views of any one person are likely to be a blend of several. Moreover, I believe these models are reflected in public discourse about social policy and thus provide a tool for decoding that discourse. Each of the four models—traditional, postmodern, cold-modern, and warm-modern—is a response to the care deficit. Each competes with the others for cultural space in both private and public discourse. Each raises different questions and places a different value on care.

The traditional solution is to retire women to the home where they provide unpaid care. Traditional discourse centers on the topic of where women should and should not be—caretaking is sometimes incidental to the question of proper roles. Proponents include conservative religious figures and right-wing politicians, for this solution basically calls for the wholesale reversal of industrialization and the "de-liberation" of women. Because men are removed from the realm of care, and care is retired to the devalued, pre-monetized realm, those who do care at home (homemakers) become a "colony" within an ever more male, modern state—which has the power to impose its cultural hegemony.

The advantage of the traditional model to men is that women would do the caring work and the care itself would be "personal." The disadvantage is that powerful long-term trends are moving in the opposite direction and the vast majority of women would probably resist. As the economy has grown and families have shrunk, more women want to work outside the home, need the money, desire the security, challenge, and community, and aspire to the identity provided by a job.[9] For women, the question is, "Do I really want to be a housewife?" Even if so, in an era where 50 percent of marriages end in divorce, the second question is, "Do I dare?"

In contrast to the traditional, the postmodern solution is to rid ourselves of the image of mother-and-child, replace it with nothing, and claim that everyone is happy anyway. In this scenario, we leave matters much as they are—with women in the labor force and men doing little at home. We *legitimate* the care deficit by reducing the range of ideas about what a child, wife, husband, aged parent, or home "really needs" to thrive. Indeed, the words "thrive" and "happy" go out of fashion, replaced by thinner, more restrictive notions of human well-being. Popular psychology and advice books provide a fascinating window on the postmodern solution. Most advice books for men concern money and sex and say virtually nothing about caring for their elderly parents or small children. Books for women, such as Helen Gurley Brown's *Having It All* or Sonya Freeman's *Smart Cookies Don't Crumble*, now also glamorize a life for women that is relatively free of the burden of this care.

The culture has produced new images of childhood and old age that pose the corresponding side of this picture. An Orwellian "superkid" language has emerged to normalize what commentators in the recent past labeled as neglect. In a 1985 *New York Times* article on new programs for latchkey children, a child-care professional is quoted making the case for the phrase "children in self-care" rather than "latchkey children," a term coined during World War II when many children (whose mothers were working in defense industries) went home alone wearing a key to the house around their necks. "Children in self-care" suggests that children are being cared for—but by themselves, independently (Hochschild 1989, 231). The popular American film *Home Alone* portrays a boy around eight who is accidentally left behind as his parents set off to a vacation in France. The child breaks open his brother's piggy bank to buy himself frozen pizza and fends off robbers—triumphing happily, independently, without anyone's help.

A recent advice book, *Teaching Your Child to Be Home Alone,* by the psychotherapists Earl A. Grollman and Gerri L. Sweder, tells children, "The end of the workday can be a difficult time for adults. It is natural for them to sometimes be tired and irritable.... Before your parents arrive at the Center, begin to get ready, and be prepared to say good-bye to your friends so that pick-up time is easier for everybody" (1992, 14). Moreover, the psychotherapists advise children, "Don't go to school early just because you don't like staying home alone. Teachers are busy preparing for the day, and they are not expected to care for youngsters until school officially begins" (1992, 4). In another brochure designed for parents who leave their children in "self-care," Work and Family Directions, a nonprofit agency, presents a model "contract"— like a legal document but framed in a lace design—to be signed by parent and child concerning the terms of self-care.

The elderly, too, are increasingly portrayed as "content on their own." An American television advertisement showed how the elderly can "happily" live alone now in the company of a new portable electronic device that they can push to signal an ambulance service in case they suffer a heart attack or fall. Like the term "children in self-care," the image of the "happy" older person also home alone is a disguise of postmodern stoicism.

Pressed for time, many of the two-job couples I studied questioned the need for various kinds of care. One husband said, "We don't really need a hot meal at night because we eat well at lunch." A mother questioned the meaning of cooking green vegetables when her son disliked them. Yet another challenged the need for her children's daily baths or clean cloths: "He loves his brown pants; why shouldn't he just wear them for the week?" Understandable revisions of old-fashioned ideas of "proper care," this line of questioning sometimes led to minimizing children's emotional needs as well. The father of a three-month-old child in nine-hour day care said, "I want him to be independent." In the postmodern model, these reductions raise no eyebrows.

In the public sector, too, some new practices fit the cold-modern model. The current practice in many hospitals of sending new mothers home the day after they give birth or sending patients home soon after serious surgery is cold-modern. Eager to reduce costs, many insurance companies support ten-session psychotherapy instead of the longer time such therapy would need to be truly helpful. Above all, the failure of the American government to create a family policy that protects children and supports women is the ultimate expression of the postmodern model.

Fearful that traditionalists will exploit people's distress in order to return women to the home, some authors argue in part, "Stop feeling a loss. Don't feel nostalgic for the intact homes of the 1950's. You'll never get them back, and they weren't better anyway" (Coontz 1992; Stacy 1990). This critique of nostalgia is needlessly confused, I think, with an implicit postmodern message, "We can make do with less care today."

The advantage of a postmodern solution is that it might seem easy to implement. We only have to continue life as it often is, to make a virtue of current necessity, and say, "I'm fine. I don't need care," or, "They are fine. They don't need care." The crucial disadvantage of the postmodern solution, of course, is that despite the wondrous variety of cultural ideas about "needs," there is a core desire for care. Of the four options, the postmodern requires the most vigorous emotional effort to repress the wish to care or be cared for.

The postmodern model places the least value on care because the very need for care is denied and the problem of making that need

visible is itself erased. Those who have to take care of unsuppressible needs anyway come to feel angry and resentful at the invisibility of their task. The *sociological* context—the care deficit—is culturally transformed into a *psychological* issue: "*Can I manage my emotional needs to match the minimalist norms of care?*"

The cold-modern solution is to institutionalize all forms of human care. How much of a child's day or older person's life is to be spent in institutional care is a matter of degree, but the cold-modern position presses for maximum hours and institutional control. An example is the Soviet model of 7:00 A.M. to 7:00 P.M. day care, with alternative weeklong sleep-over child care available as well. The public debate reflecting this position often centers on what means of care is the most "practical, efficient, and rational," given the realities of modern life.

Advocates of the cold-modern ideal can be found among corporations that want to minimize the familial demands upon their workers so as to maximize workers' devotion to the job. It also includes those managers and proprietors of day care centers, nursing homes, halfway houses, and sick-care programs who want to expand their hours and clientele. Some American companies have expanded day care hours for "weekend workers" and have summer programs that keep children in day care year-round. While such long hours are still uncommon for very young children, Americans, and especially harried professionals and managers, now "working scared" in the wake of layoffs, are tempted to turn to cold-modern solutions.

According to the cold-modern scenario, an increasing amount of life for both women and men goes on within the cash economy, with day care and nursing homes, sick care, and meals-on-wheels programs for invalids. Such programs are taking on more formerly private care. In contrast to the postmodern solution, here we are invited to believe that human beings need care. But in contrast to the traditional solution, mainly public institutions provide that care. There is no "colony of care" entrapping women at home. Men and women do not struggle over who takes care of the children and the elderly or do much care work at all. The tension point in this solution is between would-be and actual providers of care. The basic question for parents who put their children in day care and middle-aged people who put elderly parents in senior citizen homes is: "How genuine or personal is institutional care?"

There is a fourth, warm-modern model of care. It is modern because public institutions have a part in the solution and warm because we do not relinquish all care to them, and because men and women share in what we do not relinquish. In contrast to the postmodern model, notions of need are not reduced or denied, so caring is recognized as important work. In contrast to the cold-modern solution, the warm-modern model calls for fulfilling these needs, in part, personally.

Of the four models, the traditional turns to the past, the two "moderns" turn toward the future, and the postmodern makes a virtue of "grinning and bearing it" in the painful transition between the two. Of the four, only the warm-modern ideal combines characteristics of society that are *both* warm *and* modern. It does so by calling for basic changes in both men and the structure of work. The warm-modern model thus implies three arenas of struggle—male participation at home, time schedules in the workplace, and the value placed on care. While feminists are no less confused than others in their thinking about care, probably most of us advocate a warm-modern ideal, however hard it is to achieve in reality.

Nations, as well as individuals, adopt cultural models of care. Faced with a similar care deficit, developed nations have responded

very differently. Switzerland and Portugal have tended toward the traditional model. The United States is moving steadily toward a synthesis of the post- and cold-modern models, while Sweden and Denmark still lead the world in establishing a warm-modern model (Moen 1989).

What predisposes a society toward a warm-modern model of care? On this we need further research, but three factors are key. The first is an economy that depends on female labor: economic strength in male-dominated industries and alternative sources of cheap labor in female-dominated industries incline a society to retire affluent women to the home and establish the social desirability of this "alternative" for women. The second factor is a public culture of care: a culture of extreme individualism, such as that in the United States, may legitimate individual rights, including the right to care, but discourages collective efforts to help provide it. Third, the stronger and more coordinated the warm-modern model's "interest groups," the better its chances of winning.

Conclusion

Recent trends in the United States have expanded the *need* for care while contracting the *supply* of it, creating a "care deficit" in both private and public life. In the ongoing response to this crisis, I have argued, we are engaging in a cultural politics. To try to clarify the terms of that cultural debate, I have outlined four images of care—the traditional, postmodern, cold-modern, and warm-modern, in an effort to clarify the cultural, and ultimately real, issues at stake.

How we think about care is increasingly a matter of moment. Now armed with a majority in the U.S. Congress, increasingly popular conservative leaders such as Newt Gingrich are proposing to slash the nation's welfare budget and reduce services to poor mothers, the disabled, mentally ill, and the elderly. Gingrich's idea of "care" seems to me to combine the worst and least feasible of the four models of care. He proposed (though he has recently backed down) to place the children of the destitute in orphanages. This is the cold-modern model. Under the mantle of "family values," he proposes to place the care of other children and older people in the hands of women at home. This is the traditional model. The problem, of course, is that most orphanages are "cold" and most women are in paid jobs.

In the end, each model implies a different view of the caregiver and so implies a different emotional "trickle-down effect" to the cared-for.[10] The more helpless a child or frail an older parent, the more keenly they sense the extent to which they are a "burden." The cultural politics of care touch the cared-for most of all. This is a politics, then, on behalf of those most in need. Also at stake, of course, is the value placed on gender equity.

In a warm-modern society, a government would not unload a host of social problems at the doorstep of housewives because that's not fair. At the same time, men would share the care of children and the elderly not simply because "it's fair" but because it's important.

NOTES

Acknowledgments: Many thanks to Adam Hochschild, Ann Swidler, and Sonya Michel for very helpful comments on this chapter. Thanks to Laurie Schaffner for excellent research assistance. In addition, the idea of an increasing need and declining supply of care developed from a conversation with Trudie Knijn.

1. Sometimes this is done by directly applying the same image to a new context and sometimes by posing its negative opposite. Government agencies and voluntary organizations, for example, often exhort citizens to give to the needy by picturing a forlorn child alone in a public place, away from a cozy lap. The picture of need shows nothing feminine, private, natural, or well-functioning.

2. The four models I describe came out in bits and pieces in the interviews with couples described in the *Second Shift.* In that work, I focus on family dynamics, while in this chapter, I focus on the public fate of these four ideals of care.

3. In the developing world, the debt crisis since the 1970s and the rising cost of imports and declining value of exports, in addition to the abiding problems of underdevelopment, have hurt whole populations. But most of the harm passes down to the most vulnerable populations: migrants, refugees, and particularly women and children, among whom rates of sickness and death have risen (Vickers 1991).

4. The proportion of older people has risen in most of Europe. In Sweden, 10 percent of the population was over 65 in 1950 and 18 percent in 1990. In Canada and the United States, the gain was smaller (from 8 to about 12 percent). Most other countries had rates of rise in between those two. To some extent, the declining number of children needing care was replaced by a rising number of older people.

5. In Western Europe, the corresponding ratio is about one divorce for every three or four marriages. Japan has had historically low divorce rates, but since 1960 divorce has been rising in Japan. Divorce statistics also understate the social reality of dissolution, since separations and breakups among cohabiting couples are not counted.

6. In Denmark, a rate already high (17 percent in 1978) rose a bit more (to 20 percent in 1988). Only in Japan, where the rate was initially low (6 percent in 1960), did the rate actually decline (to 5.9 percent in 1985).

7. In this period, the Swedish rate rose from 11 to 48 percent. In the Netherlands, the increase was only from 1 to 9 percent, with Italy and Germany in this more modest range. The rate is now highest in the United States, Denmark, Sweden, France, and the United Kingdom.

8. I drew an initial list of respondents from the personnel roster of a large industrial firm and in this way was able to tap a range of occupations. Since the response rate was lower among unskilled

workers, I "snowballed" out to neighbors and friends of the respondents on the original roster. See Hochschild (1989).

9. Even if women were persuaded to stay home in an era of 50 percent divorce, they would risk "getting caught" with no path to a good job—and be vulnerable to a life of insecurity and poverty. A "divorce culture," such as that permeating much of the developed world, makes lifelong paid work the wise choice for women. (The term "divorce culture" was coined by Karla Hackstaff, Sociology Department, University of Northern Arizona.)

10. The lowest value on care we find is in the postmodern model, in which care is seen as unnecessary because "we don't need it." The next to lowest value we find is in the traditional model: caring for small children and the elderly is honorable only for women, and the very low status of women is itself a statement about the value placed on the work they do. Just above that is the cold-modern model, which proposes upgrading public but not private care. The highest value on care is found in the warm-modern model, which calls for upgrading care in both the public and private realms.

For both the cold- and warm-modern models, the transfer of caring work out of the home to the public realm is viewed as positive (they differ in how much to transfer). But *both* modern models call for upgrading the status of public caregivers.

For advocates of the warm-modern model, there is another task—upgrading the value of care in the *private* realm (Abel and Nelson 1990; Sidel 1990). As the kin system weakens, informal support for careers may wane. From whom does a single mother get thanks for her work at home? Who supports a remarried father for keeping in touch with children by his previous marriage? Does a stepparent get recognized for taking good care of stepchildren or former stepchildren? For the warm-modern model, these questions matter.

REFERENCES

Abel, Emily, and Margery Nelson. 1990. *Circles of Care: Work and Identity in Women's Lives.* Albany: State University of New York Press.

Arendell, Terry. 1986. *Mothers and Divorce: Legal, Economic, and Social Dilemmas.* Berkeley: University of California Press.

Brown, Helen Gurley. 1982. *Having It All.* New York: Pocket Books.

Coontz, Stephanie. 1992. *The Way We Never Were: American Families and the Nostalgia Trap.* New York: Basic Books.

Davis, Kingsley. 1988. "Wives and Work: A Theory of the Sex Role Revolution and Its Consequences." Pp. 67–86 in *Feminism, Children and the New Families,* ed. Sanford M. Dornbusch and Myra Strober. New York and London: Guilford Press.

Ehrenreich, Barbara, and Dierdre English. 1978. *For Her Own Good: 150 Years of the Experts' Advice for Women.* Garden City, N.J.: Anchor Press.

Freeman, Sonya. 1985. *Smart Cookies Don't Crumble: A Modern Woman's Guide to Living and Loving Her Own Life.* New York: Simon and Schuster.

Finch, Janet, and Dulcie Groves, eds. 1983. *A Labour of Love: Women, Work and Caring.* London: Routledge and Kegan Paul.

Furstenburg, Frank, and Andrew Cherlin. 1991. *Divided Families: What Happens to Children When Parents Part.* Cambridge, Mass.: Harvard University.

Galinsky, Ellen, James T. Bond, and Dana E. Friedman. 1993. *The Changing Workplace: Highlights of a National Study.* No. 1. New York: Families and Work Institute.

Grollman, Earl A., and Gerry L. Sweder. 1992. *Teaching Your Child to Be Home Alone.* New York: Lexington Books.

Hochschild, Arlie Russell. 1983. *The Managed Heart: Commercialization of Human Feeling.* Berkeley: University of California Press.

———. 1989. *The Second Shift: Working Couples and the Revolution at Home.* New York: Viking.

———. 1991. "The Fractured Family." *American Prospect* (Summer): 106–15.

Holter, Harriet, ed. 1984. *Patriarchy in a Welfare Society.* Oslo: Norwegian University Press.

Knijn, Trudy. 1994. "Fish Without Bikes: Revisions of the Dutch Welfare State and Its Consequences for the (In)dependence of Single Mothers." *Social Politics* 1:83–105.

Moen, Phyllis. 1989. *Working Parents: Transformations in Gender Roles and Public Policies in Sweden.* Madison: University of Wisconsin Press.

Ruddick, Sara. 1989. *Maternal Thinking: Toward a Politics of Peace.* Boston: Beacon Press.

Sassoon, Anne Showstack, ed. 1987. *Women and the State.* London: Hutchinson.

Schor, Juliet B. 1991. *The Overworked American: The Unexpected Decline in Leisure.* New York: Basic Books.

Sidel, Ruth. 1990. *On Her Own: Growing Up in the Shadow of the American Dream.* New York: Viking Press.

Sivard, Ruth Leger. 1985. *Woman, A World Survey.* Washington, D.C.: World Priorities.

Smith, Pamela. 1988. "The Emotional Labor of Nursing." *Nursing Times* 84:50–51.

Sorrentino, Constance. 1990. "The Changing Family in International Perspective." *Monthly Labor Review* 113:41–58.

Stacey, Judith. 1990. *Brave New Families: Stories of Domestic Upheaval in Late Twentieth-Century America.* New York: Basic Books.

Ungerson, Clare, ed. 1990. *Gender and Caring: Work and Welfare in Britain and Scandinavia.* New York: Wheatsheaf.

Vickers, Jeanne. 1991. *Women and the World Economic Crisis.* London: Zed Books.

Waerness, Kari. 1978. "The Invisible Welfare State: Women's Work at Home." *Acta Sociologica* Supplement 21:193–207.

———. 1984. "Caring as Women's Work in the Welfare State." Pp. 67–88 in *Patriarchy in a Welfare Society,* ed. Holter.

———. 1987. "On the Rationality of Caring." Pp. 206–34 in *Women and the State,* ed. Sassoon.

Wallerstein, Judith, and Sandra Blakeslee. 1989. *Second Chances: Men, Women, and Children a Decade after Divorce.* New York: Tichnor and Fields.

Weitzman, Lenore J. 1985. *The Divorce Revolution.* New York: Free Press.

~ *Chapter 40*

The Invisible Women: Caregiving and AIDS

NINA GLICK SCHILLER

Harry, age 32, lived on a tree-lined street in a predominantly white, working-class city in Northern New Jersey. At the time of the interview Harry was feeling weak, and tired easily but had few other symptoms. After his diagnosis of AIDS, Harry, who had been working in a photo developing firm and living with his mate in New York, lost his job and his partner and moved back to his parents' home.

It was when I began to ask about his experiences with hospitalization that Harry began to talk about his mother. One night, after he had moved in with his parents, something—he said a "tumor"—had burst in the middle of the night and Harry began to bleed profusely. Disregarding the danger to herself of HIV-contaminated blood, Harry's mother had somehow reduced the bleeding and gotten him to the hospital. During the month that he was hospitalized, Harry's mother visited him

in the hospital every day to insure he received adequate attention. She found it necessary to confront the staff at the small hospital, many of whom refused to enter Harry's room to clean or serve meals.

As he told me this story I realized that there was nowhere on the "survey instrument" to record that Harry was alive because of his mother. This kind of information did not fit into the manner in which health services researchers assessed "needs." I was only prepared to "measure" the "level of functioning" of a person with AIDS by determining the degree to which s/he needed help in "activities of daily living" and "instrumental activities of daily living." Questions of assistance from kin were reduced to activities such as "bathing," "toileting," "cooking," and "cleaning."

In the kitchen I could see Harry's mother. She finished cleaning up from lunch, brought Harry a snack, which she put by his chair, and began to do the laundry. At least, I thought, with such an "instrument" we would be able to indicate that Harry did rely on his mother's home-making services on a day-to-day basis.

From *Culture, Medicine and Psychiatry* 17 (1993): 487–512. Copyright © 1993 Kluwer Academic Publishers. Reprinted with kind permission from Kluwer Academic Publishers.

When we reached the measure of functioning Harry reported that, except for making his way outside the house, he needed no help. Harry readily reported the food, clothing, and shelter provided by his family but not the domestic services of his mother. Yet she was clearly making the home that allowed him, in the language of the health services researchers and public health officials, to live "in the community."

I began to see that Harry did not see his mother as helping him but doing what she had always done. But how long, I thought, could he remain living "in the community" without his mother to shop, cook, clean, plan meals, and do the daily work that keeps a household running?

Occasionally Harry's mother would pass through the dining room where we were seated. Each time she went by, some remark would pass between them, generally initiated from Harry. Each time Harry addressed his mother, his voice became taut and the pace of his speech quickened. "What do you want now?" "What's the problem now?" he asked her. Harry's mother, drawing deep breaths, would address me, rather than her son. By the end of the interview it was clear to me that, although or because they were supporting him financially and taking care of him, Harry was furious at his parents, especially his mother. And Harry's mother was so filled with unexpressed rage that it became almost a visible additional presence that filled the small house.

Introduction

In the last two decades, health researchers began to acknowledge the role played by women kin in providing care for family members who are ill, disabled, or elderly (Eisenberg et al. 1984; Gubman and Tessler 1987; Kane and

Kane 1987). One would expect that the advent of a major epidemic such as AIDS would make it even more obvious that women are an essential part of the U.S. health care system. When one reads through nursing journals and handbooks on caregiving that outline the daily routine of people with AIDS, this expectation is met (Richardson 1988; Selenkow 1990). In this realm of the practical, there are matter-of-fact descriptions of women family members providing the majority of the community care. The significance of women kin within the system of AIDS care also can be gleaned from the writings of family counselors (Boyd-Franklin and Aleman 1990), health activists (Caron, Macklin, and Rolland 1988; Younge 1989), obituaries of persons with AIDS (Dunning 1993), and human-interest stories in newspapers (Lawson 1992).

These diverse sources contribute to a portrait of women family members as the major source of care for people with AIDS in the United States. In inner city communities a woman sometimes finds herself responsible for several HIV-infected family members. Moreover, as the prevalence of HIV among women in the United States rises, increasing numbers of women who are themselves infected by the virus also are caregivers for persons with AIDS who are their children, partners, and siblings. Yet in health services research about the utilization and financing of health services by people with AIDS, women kin vanish from sight, as does their daily, onerous labor. How can this be?

In this chapter I ask how and why women can become socially invisible in the discussion of AIDS services. I argue that explanations can be found in the processes by which health services researchers approach the provision of services and debate mechanisms to reduce the cost of services. The growing pressure to reduce health care costs is part of the current effort to make U.S. labor costs competitive in a global economy and yet sustain the health industry. While costly acute care and high priced pharmaceuticals continue to be defined as essential for the health of the nation, it is the unpaid, undocumented health services provided by female kin that allow the health care industry to carry on with business as usual.

I take, as a case in point, the framework within which public health authorities in New Jersey in 1987–90 discussed the provision of health services to people with AIDS in New Jersey. Without making reference to the family caregiving performed by women kin, they spoke of the need to reduce acute care costs by providing community care. I contrast this discourse with the lived experience of women in New Jersey who cared for HIV-infected family members. The labor of these women became evident in the course of a "needs assessment" of people with AIDS commissioned by the New Jersey Department of Health and then disregarded by it (Crystal et al. 1990).

Thinking the Thinkable: Hegemonic Construction and Medical Discourse

Part of the failure by health service researchers to note women's caregiving role within the AIDS epidemic reflects the manner in which people with AIDS have been culturally constructed (Fee and Fox 1988; Schiller 1992; Singer et al. 1990; Treichler 1987) as the "dangerous other" (Clatts and Mutchler 1989). As Treichler (1987) has noted, AIDS is an epidemic of "signification." People with AIDS were first pictured as living in a degenerate gay culture of bath houses and prodigious sexual conquests; they then became drug addicts, living on the streets, immersed in a self-destructive, needle-sharing culture. This construction of difference gains some

of its power from an imagery of persons with AIDS as being without family ties. To be human is to be familiar; that is, to have family (Schiller, Crystal, and Lewellen 1994) By imagining persons with AIDS as people without families, they became unknown entities removed from our empathy. However, there are additional reasons why women family members have been accorded no recognition in health services research or public policy debates about the provision of AIDS services. After several decades in which biomedicine had been assaulted on a number of fronts (Rosenberg 1988), public health authorities have used the occasion of the AIDS epidemic to reconstitute the hegemonic voice and legitimacy of the formal health care system. In this conjuncture, those who give what has been dubbed "informal care" drop out of sight.

In probing the links between the social invisibility of women kin and the legitimization of the health care industry, I am building on Gramsci's concept of hegemony (Gramsci 1971). Gramsci used the term hegemony to refer to the fact that, in addition to coercion, class domination is maintained in capitalist society through the use of cultural processes. "Cultures not only generate meaning, they also produce legitimation for inequality, justification of subordination, denials of exploitation and disguises for oppression" (Frankenberg 1988, 338). Other theorists of hegemony (Williams 1977; Hall 1988; and Comaroff and Comaroff 1991) have gone on to explore the ways in which popular consent is utilized in the maintenance of a social order which perpetuates inequality.

Hegemonic processes create silences so that realms of lived experience remain unvoiced. Without a legitimated voice, these practices and thoughts may only be expressed as unspoken and internalized anger. The concept of hegemony allows us to explore the relationship between the allocation of authority to the representatives of the formal health care system and the bitter, festering, mutual anger that sometimes erupts into outbursts of rage between women and the family members with AIDS for whom they care.

Invisibility of Women's Caregiving in Public Health Policy: A Case Study of New Jersey

By the end of the 1980s, HIV infection was coming to be seen as a chronic disease, and health care planners began to talk about people "living with AIDS." The New Jersey Department of Health became tremendously concerned with the rising cost of health care for persons with AIDS. Infectious disease specialists began to report success in prolonging life through expensive, aggressive acute care for HIV-infected persons and by emphasizing testing, early diagnosis, and prophylaxis with costly drugs such as AZT. New Jersey ranked fifth among states in the cumulative incidence of AIDS, with more than 5,000 cases. While gay men made up the majority of AIDS cases nationwide, New Jersey's pattern of incidence more resembled the changing direction of the national epidemic, with a little more than half of the cases found among intravenous drug users, and a high incidence of cases among minorities and women (Crystal et al. 1990).

Increasingly, following diagnosis, persons with AIDS often were able to live several years more with only intermittent periods of extreme debilitation, which may or may not have required hospitalization. They were often weakened and unable to work or fully care for themselves, however. In 1989 national estimates of the cost of care for each person with AIDS from diagnosis to death ranged from $30,000 to $80,000. Much of this cost resulted from hospitalizations. It was widely believed that both nationally and in New Jersey many

persons with AIDS ended up living in hospitals because no alternative system of care was available to maintain people with AIDS in the community when they no longer were in need of acute care services.

Determined to reduce the cost of hospital care, the Department of Health turned to the development of programs that might assist those with HIV to live in the community. A "key part of New Jersey's strategy to contain hospital costs for the AIDS/ARC population" became the development of "alternative facilities to provide housing or sub-acute care for these who no longer need hospitalization" (Coye et al. 1988, 12). Public reports did not mention that the scale at which the programs were being developed would not begin to meet the needs of the thousands of AIDS cases projected for the 1990s. Nor were financial assistance or other services planned for the families who were providing food, clothing, shelter, and daily care for persons with AIDS living in the community.

In part, the emphasis on the part of New Jersey health officials on the development of "sub-acute" care facilities and the total disregarding of women kin as caregivers can be explained by the widespread belief among health service researchers throughout the United States that people with AIDS don't have families.[1] This belief was reinforced by the popularization of a San Francisco model of volunteer buddy organizations that had been credited in reducing AIDS-related hospitalizations by providing services to gay men living on their own in the community (Hellinger 1991). New Jersey planned to develop buddy programs, but the central concern of the Department of Health was intravenous drug users, whose prolonged hospitalizations were believed to drive up the costs of AIDS health services. For example, the Coordinator for AIDS Health Services for the New Jersey Department of Health stated that the fact that "IV drug users frequently live on the streets . . . complicates their placement from acute care hospitals following episodes of severe illness" (Young 1988, 259).

However, I believe that the willingness of public health authorities and health services researchers to accept the predominant construction of persons with AIDS as without families requires further examination and analysis. Even while speaking of IV drug users "frequently living on the streets," public officials in New Jersey were planning and instituting various programs for HIV-infected people that depended on family caregiving and worked closely with women kin. The New Jersey Department of Human Services, for example, constructed an entire program that relied on the services of female kin of persons with AIDS, including those of intravenous drug users. The AIDS Community Care Program (ACCAP) enabled persons who were diagnosed with AIDS or AIDS-related complex and judged sufficiently disabled to warrant "an institutional level of care" (Coye 1989, 45) to obtain a host of services, including case management, personal care services, and nursing services while living at home. Cost cutting was the motivation behind this program since "community care," even with many costly supported services, was judged less costly to Medicaid than institutionalization in nursing homes.

It was technically possible to be eligible for services from ACCAP and live alone, but this was rare. Most people who had a high enough level of disability to receive ACCAP services needed daily assistance, and they almost always received it from family members. Moreover, in order to be able to obtain skilled nursing care, the person with AIDS had to have a "primary caregiver," who was most often a female relative. Although the women kin who provided homemaking and care for ACCAP clients often developed close relationships with the ACCAP nurse case managers, the Department of Social Services made little official reference to these family members. These family caregivers—wives, mothers, daughters, and sisters—were not asked about their own needs or directly provided with services. Although some of the ACCAP services did function as respite care for families, this aspect of the program was not publicly noted. Beleaguered women caring for family members with AIDS, and sometimes themselves infected with the virus, reported to me that they felt their homes were invaded by an array of health professionals from physical therapists to case managers, but no one wanted to get to the case and pay their overdue bills, fix the furnace, or provide them with an adequate income.

In an evaluation entitled "AIDS Patients Needs: Challenge for the Community-Based Long Term Care System" (Mor, Piette, and Fleishman 1988), health researchers argue the need for case management for persons with AIDS by pointing to the web of bureaucracy so intricate that persons with AIDS trying to access entitlements and benefits cannot broker the system on their own. They concentrated their concern on those who lived alone because, "In the long-term care arena, living alone is one of the most important risk factors for institutional placement" (Mor, Piette, and Fleishman 1989, 9).

Who bears the costs and provides the services for those who live with others was not investigated and became part of the realm of the ordinary and customary on which the system of formal care rested. Yet the data from the evaluation of New Jersey's community-based long term care project indicate that most of the people with AIDS whose cases were reviewed did not live alone. And most of the people who did live "alone" may have done so only because they actually did not yet need help. None of the case management sites had more than 19 percent of the clients who were living alone, were uninsured, and were unemployed; and most of the sites had less than 10 percent in this situation (Mor, Piette, and Fleishman 1988).

Assessing the Needs of People with AIDS: Taking the Study to the People

As part of their efforts to cut the costs of hospitalization by developing community services, in 1988 New Jersey Department of Health officials decided to conduct a "needs assessment" of people with diagnosed AIDS. They wanted to document the degree to which hospitalizations were prolonged because of a lack of "intermediate care facilities." Also of concern was the demand for the community-based long-term care services that New Jersey was developing.

In order to insure that the findings were statistically representative of persons with AIDS in New Jersey, Department of Health officials decided to draw a random sample from the New Jersey "AIDS Registry."[2] The Department contracted with health researchers at Rutgers to conduct the needs assessment, and both the New Jersey Department of Health Institutional Review Board and the legal council agreed to the interpretation that Rutgers researchers would be representing the Department of Health and could have access to confidential material.

I became aware of the planned study, including the proposal to use the "AIDS Registry," when asked to develop a survey instrument, test it among volunteers, and then serve as project director. In four months of preliminary research I engaged in intensive discussions with persons with AIDS, AIDS advocates, including the head of New Jersey Act-Up, and health care providers about the merits of the study and ethical ways of approaching the issue of sampling. Our discussions were within the context that the Department of Health already had access to confidential data, was using them to conduct monthly surveillance, and was determined to use this data to draw names for a sample.

In the end, I decided to direct the needs assessment if I could reach a compromise with the Department of Health as to how respondents would be located. I developed a research protocol that used health service providers who already knew the diagnosis and had a prior relationship to the person with AIDS. These providers contacted people the Department of Health had randomly sampled and obtained their consent to be interviewed. Only at that point would a member of our research team, most of whom had experience as AIDS counselors, make contact with the potential respondent.[3] I felt that the protocol kept potential respondents from experiencing further intrusion into their lives. At the same time, I thought that the survey would allow persons with AIDS to have their voices heard. In the course of testing the questionnaire I became convinced that issues of confidentiality had two sides, both protecting and silencing persons with AIDS. Not every respondent was as eloquent, but the reaction of one Puerto Rican respondent was typical:

> At first I feared the interview because you are a perfect stranger, but its easier than I thought and it helps me to come closer to my own feeling because I don't talk about it enough. This has helped me more than you can imagine. It helps me evaluate what has happened in my life and to realize who is out there for me. If I truly have to die, let me live life to the fullest.

Thus the interview not only provided an outlet for emotions but also conveyed the message that the state of New Jersey was interested in learning from the experiences and suffering of persons with AIDS. This was true despite the two-to-three-hour length of the interview and the intrusive nature of many of the questions. Shaped by the concerns of the diverse body of health researchers who had contributed to the planning of the study, the questions assessed both the physical and mental health status of the respondents and inquired about their experiences utilizing formal services and a variety of informal supports, from mothers to folk practitioners. The interview left respondents with a feeling of empowerment, although as I look back, the strength of the interview lay not in the nature of the questions but in the fact that interviewers were able to sit and listen to the respondents for several hours—often in the course of several visits. However, at the time, both the respondents and I felt that the study would give people struggling to live with HIV, who often are silenced by stigma, an opportunity to speak to health policy makers and to the general public in New Jersey. I hoped that a study that came directly to the HIV-infected persons and asked them about their needs would make it clear that rather than being "the cultural other" people with AIDS have mothers.

I was wrong. By the time the survey was finished, there was very little interest in the New Jersey Department of Health in the needs assessment. It was never publicly released. There were several reasons for this lack of interest. Over the three years it took to conduct the study and analyze the data, much had changed in the political and economic situation in New Jersey. The state economy had faltered and there was a complete shuffling of public health officials. The community services that had been established, some of which had been funded as "demonstration projects" with private grant money, struggled for funding. In part, the findings of the study became lost in the political fallout of the recession. Lack of funds alone could not explain the Department's priorities, however. Even as funds became scarcer and some services were cut back, the Department of Health developed an aggressive campaign of testing, early diagnosis, and treatment with AZT.

There were other, more fundamental, reasons for disregarding the needs assessment. From the point of view of the Department of Health the "Statewide Needs Assessment of People with AIDS in New Jersey" (Crystal et al. 1990), as the final report was entitled, was a failure. Public health authorities wanted documentation that hospitalizations were prolonged unnecessarily and that programs of case management, medical day care, and intermediate care facilities would reduce the length of hospitalizations. The final report provided little insight into these issues, although much of the questionnaire and most of the time spent in data analysis was devoted to investigating these concerns. Our respondents, however, could tell us little about why their hospital stays were long and, if their hospital stays were lengthy or frequent, often could not remember the details.

Rather than succeeding as an instrument of health services research, the statewide needs assessment did succeed in identifying some of the needs of people with AIDS. The final report began by stating:

> A central theme that emerged is the degree of financial privation experienced by PWAs [people with AIDS] in New Jersey and its pervasive influence on their life circumstances. . . . Low income often means that the individual became financially dependent on family or others, adding financial strains to care burdens. Almost half (45 percent) of respondents reported not having enough money even for basic needs. More than a few had no significant income at all. (Crystal et al. 1990, 2)

But the Department of Health wasn't in the business of providing more money for people with AIDS, or better jobs, incomes, or housing for families who were caring for their relatives. We had found that most of the respondents were impoverished, that they were able to live "in the community" because they received various types of assistance from family members, and that women did most of the work that made this community living possible. Such a report did not meet the needs of public health authorities.

Family Support, Women's Work: Unseen Care and Unvoiced Anger

Harry, whose experiences introduced this chapter, was the first person I interviewed. In the course of the research, it became clear that Harry's situation was far from unique.[4] Most of the people with AIDS we interviewed (74 percent), lived with family members, on whom they depended not only for shelter and the basic necessities of life but also for the ongoing work it takes to keep a household up and running. Moreover, most of the people who lived alone were in weekly contact with members of their families, who provided a range of household services. Whether or not they lived in a household with kin, most people we surveyed (73 percent), maintained ties with relatives with whom they did not live. Sisters proved to be especially important.

Our questionnaire did not measure the degree to which persons with AIDS in New Jersey live in the same neighborhoods as their kin, but we observed that family members who lent assistance often lived in close proximity. We found that respondents often lived with kin in two family houses, resided in the same apartment building, or lived on the same street. Having kin as neighbors may well be a widespread residence pattern among the working class of New Jersey, as it is among various strata of the working class in the United States (See, for example, Stack 1975

and Susser 1981). Both Mike and Gerald's experiences are illustrative of our findings.

Mike lived in a basement apartment with his teenage daughter, Maria. His wife had already died from AIDS, and his other child was living with his wife's parents. His parents owned the house and lived upstairs. Maria prepared Mike's daily meals, but in many other ways the households were merged. The phone was upstairs in the apartment of Mike's parents and all utilities and house repairs were done by Mike's parents.

At first, Gerald, interviewed in the hospital after a prolonged stay, appeared isolated from kin. A fairly big time drug dealer, he reported that he lived alone, had no available caregiver, and had not spoken with a relative in the past week. However, the interviewer learned in informal discussion with him after she completed the interview that he lived in the same building as his sister, with whom he did have an ongoing relationship.

When a person with AIDS is removed from the community through imprisonment, family support networks composed primarily of female kin continue. As part of our survey, we interviewed several men in county jails, and, in a subsidiary survey, we interviewed men in a special AIDS unit of the New Jersey prison system. The wives, mothers, or sisters of these men used their own limited budgets to send food packages and to make prison visits. Many of the prisoners who expected to soon be released planned to live with female kin.

Co-residence or close proximity to kin and multiple forms of assistance from them was essential because the daily tasks necessitated by the symptoms that sometimes accompany HIV disease can be overwhelming. This was true even in instances when the person with AIDS would be termed "high functioning" by a standard needs assessment because he or she was able to take care of personal needs. Each person's symptoms fluctuated, but in the bad times, night sweats, incontinence, and bouts of diarrhea led to endless laundry. Mattresses often became hopelessly soiled and needed to be aired or replaced. Money had to be found for new mattresses and they had to be purchased. Many respondents were able to walk about but went through periods of weakness in their legs and needed countless items fetched and carried.

Almost everyone we interviewed had gone through dramatic losses of weight. The struggle to regain pounds lead to constant demands for food to be shopped for, purchased, prepared, served, and cleared. The fluctuations of weight made obtaining adequate clothing a real concern to both people with AIDS and their families. Harry, for example, weighed about 165 pounds before becoming ill. At one point in his illness he weighted scarcely 100 pounds. At the time of the interview he weighted 140. Harry's sister, who lived about an hour away, came to visit several times a week and took him out for an occasional restaurant meal and clothes shopping. She paid for the clothes.

Our study defined couples who lived together "in sickness and health" as conjugal couples so that "lovers" of gay men and common law spouses were counted as conjugal kin. Operationalizing family in this way, consanguineal kin (blood relatives) rather than conjugal kin (spouses) were most often the ones providing the shelter or sharing housing with the respondents. The majority (52 percent) of those who lived with any type of family members lived with at least one parent and this parent was most often the mother. While most respondents reported personal networks that included more than one individual currently giving assistance or available for assistance, half (51 percent) did report that one person was their primary caregiver. Mothers were most frequently designated as primary caregiver. The tendency to live with consan-

guineal kin and be cared for by mothers was true of respondents who were gay as well as those who were heterosexual.[5]

The assumption of the Department of Health officials that intravenous drug users with diagnosed AIDS would be homeless and without families proved wrong on both counts. We found that many intravenous drug users in New Jersey were working-class people, white, Black, and Hispanic, who lived with spouses in small towns and suburbs. They were not street people, and their addiction would not have been public if they had not become HIV infected. Others, whose history of drug use had led them previously to be rejected by their families, and who had been living on the margins of society, were taken back and cared for by kin when they became unable to care for themselves. While drug rehabilitation programs expel residents who do not comply with their mandates, whether or not they have AIDS, it is very difficult for family members to turn away kin when they have a terminal illness. This is especially true for mothers. No matter if you have been robbed, cheated, or abused by your child as part of your child's drug habit, and no matter how angry you are, you don't let your child die in the streets.

Sometimes, as in the case of Leslie, the disease proved an occasion of longtime reconciliation, despite past and continuing behavior that is generally considered socially deviant. Leslie was a transvestite, prostitute, and an intravenous drug user. His lifestyle had kept him apart from his family until he became ill with AIDS. At the time of the interview Leslie was living with a roommate and had case management and home health assistance provided to him. However, his mother, age 62, who also had the responsibility of caring for her daughter's three children, still came to visit Leslie twice a week. She did his grocery shopping and picked up his medication.

548 NINA GLICK SCHILLER

When he was hospitalized, she was the one who visited him. He had lived with his mother for a while after his diagnosis, and he went to stay with her during the Christmas holidays.

In many other cases, the person with AIDS turned his back on his family and returned to the streets once a bout of disability had passed, only to return home again when deathly ill. Russell, age 30, who had been living in the streets, was taken in by his 60-year-old mother when his symptoms became debilitating. After a difficult month in which he was hospitalized twice for phlebitis, Russ's older sister, Carol, who was a registered nurse, took both Russ and her mother into her home. Carol, who was already caring for an elderly relative, helped Russ to regain his strength by feeding him health foods and drink supplements. As soon as Russ started feeling better he went out on the streets, back onto drugs, and landed back in the hospital. His telephone and television bills, while he was in the hospital, were being paid by Carol.

Family support proved to be essential, even when people received formal community services, such as those made available through the ACCAP program. Case management and the wealth of helpful services provided by the Medicaid waiver assisted but did not take the place of a foundation of family support and women's work. In fact, it took the assistance of family for a person with AIDS to survive and to apply for such services. Nor did ACCAP pay for life's necessities.

Laura, for example, had been working as a security guard for a large institution and had benefits and job security before she became ill. She lived with a man she planned to marry, a 12-year-old daughter by a previous relationship, and a toddler, whom she was adopting. After diagnosis, Laura lost her fiancé, her job, and her benefits. She was still responsible for two children. Until she was able to obtain money from Social Security, she survived

with the financial assistance of her mother and brothers and the household assistance of her mother and 12-year-old daughter. Finally, Laura succeeded in obtaining a monthly check of $425, which certainly could not support her household.

At the time I interviewed Laura, she was bedridden, and ACCAP provided her with some home nursing care and an aide who assisted in meal preparation and housework during the day. ACCAP did not pay the bills, however. Nonetheless, Laura's apartment, although it consisted of the compact, ungracious rooms of public housing, had none of the aura of hopelessness and decay I've sometimes witnessed in impoverished households. There were new couches, color-coordinated curtains, and carefully chosen wall decorations. Laura's ability to "live in the community" relied on the fact that her mother, age 58, had moved in and brought to Laura's household both her additional income as well as emotional and physical support.

Laura's mother worked, so the daytime was difficult. The aide came for several hours a day, but this assistance was supplemented during the summer with the services of Laura's daughter age 12 who ran errands and fetched and carried. The toddler was in day care. Summer was ending, however, and it was unclear what Laura would do when her daughter returned to school. If Laura's mother stopped working, the supplemental income that kept Laura from complete impoverishment would be gone. Laura received visits and some assistance from other family members as well. She had daily contact with her father (her parents were divorced) and her two brothers, age 29 and 30.

Even if people with AIDS had a substantial middle-class lifestyle at the time they became ill, we found that often everything that they had achieved was soon at risk. If something of their lifestyle was salvaged, it was with assistance of family members. Sarah, for example, had been employed as a dietician, and on her salary of $25,000 had been buying a house and making payments on a car. She had been living with a 19-year-old daughter, who was going to college. Within a year of diagnosis Sarah was blind, unable to work, and in danger of losing both her home and her car. Her Social Security disability payments could not cover her mortgage and car payments and pay her bills. Sarah's daughter dropped out of school, obtained a secretarial job, and took on the responsibility of caring for her mother and trying to hold on to their housing and transportation.

Although the majority of the people with AIDS we interviewed had been working before becoming ill (71 percent), whatever their "risk" designation or racial or ethnic background, most had only modest incomes, with a mean personal income of $17,500. After becoming ill, most respondents experienced a dramatic reduction in income. Many had lived through a period in which they were too ill to work and had no source of income. Although the majority finally obtained payments from Social Security, these are small so that the median reported income of respondents was only $5,900 a year. Most could not possibly have afforded to live on their own.

The families to whom our respondents turned for assistance were not in much better shape financially. Even if the person with AIDS contributed something to the household, the costs were often being shouldered by family members pushed to their financial, physical, and emotional limits—or beyond. A scarcity of resources was a pervasive theme in the interviews. Often the women who were providing the assistance were also working to support the household, but the incomes they received were small. There was no money for clothing, transportation to the hospital, entertainment, snacks, new bedding, and better housing. In most households, resources,

space, and labor were in short supply. Families were often crowded together, with respondents sleeping on the living room couch or sharing a bedroom with several other people.

Jim contributed to his sister's household and slept on the couch. A former intravenous drug user, Jim had been homeless for two years before he was diagnosed with AIDS. At the time of the interview, he was confined to a wheelchair. He had to have someone attend to his physical needs. "I can't do for myself. I mean if I wanted a glass of water I have to ask someone to get it for me." But he also needed housing and financial assistance. His was able to meet his needs by living with his sister and brother-in-law. He explained that his sister had stopped working to care for him, and he contributed part of his check for household expenses.

> I don't have to worry about food and things like that. I know if I had to do it on my own I'd be on soup lines. And I'd have to try to find a cheap place because I only get $561 a month and I still would have to eat and get around. So I pay my sister $200 a month. And I help buy groceries and little things.

Harry's father had lost his foreman's job when the plant in which he had been working closed, leaving him too old to obtain another job and without a pension. Shortly after that, and about the same time that Harry moved back home without any source of income, Harry's father had cardiac surgery. By the time of the interview, Harry was getting a Social Security disability check, and his parents received Social Security checks totaling $1,100 a month, but the entire household income was less than $18,000 a year. Households headed by single women lived on considerably less.

What life was like beyond the limits of endurance was made apparent when I interviewed Tasha. Tasha lived in a large old house whose crumbling front steps signaled the general disrepair of the entire structure. The house was located in a section of Newark in which the shops stood empty, shattered and burned by the Newark uprising more than two decades before. Unemployed men and women stood outside on street corners, even in winter. Tasha's mother, who owned the house, until recently had been working steady, long hours in a factory, receiving health benefits, and looking forward to retiring in a few years, with the help of a decent pension. When Tasha's sister died and left behind three children, however, Tasha's mother was forced to retire early, without her pension, and live on money from welfare that she received as the guardian of her grandchildren. Tasha was unclear about the cause of her sister's death. It seemed to be hepatitis rather than HIV. After she became ill with AIDS and almost died during a hospitalization, Tasha turned over her own three children, the youngest of whom was HIV infected, to her mother. In Tasha's mother's house lived a third sister who had two children and who lived on welfare. On my first visit with Tasha, her mother let me in. Several children under the age of five were sitting in front of a television, while several others, equally young, were asking their grandmother for something to eat.

Tasha's mother was interested in our survey and told me about how she had been forced to "retire" and how difficult it was to feed and care for eight children with the very small amount of money she received. She said she was always tired, and she looked it. Then Tasha, age twenty-five but looking more like forty, walked into the room. Before she had become ill Tasha had worked sporadically as a waitress, but most of the time she had lived with a series of men, most of whom were intravenous drug users. She sometimes shot up along with her lovers.

It soon became clear that Tasha's mother had taken Tasha in, but not gladly. They exchanged few words and the hostility between the two was visible. Tasha told me that she had no income at all because her mother was getting the welfare money for the children and her Social Security money was caught up in some bureaucratic snag. This meant that Tasha had to beg her mother for money for small and big things. Social Security payments, when they are received, are retroactive to the time of application. Tasha and her mother were fighting about who would get the back check. Her mother wanted to use it to pay the overdue heat and utilities bill and fix the roof that was leaking. Tasha wanted to keep some for herself. She had lost a great deal of weight and her clothes did not fit. The week before, when she couldn't breathe, she had no way to pay for a taxi to the hospital.

Tasha's mother watched her daughters grow up as young women in Newark who saw no future for themselves beyond the short-term diversions provided by men who dealt and used drugs. In the end she was losing her struggle to own a house and carve out a decent retirement for herself. She faced endless child rearing for grandchildren most likely to face the same death sentence as their mothers. Harry's mother saw her husband and herself, after a lifetime of labor, deprived of the assistance of even a pension, and faced with the responsibility of both supporting and caring for a son who, until he needed them, had rejected their lifestyle and values.

Nurses in Newark told me of situations in which family members brought relatives with AIDS to the hospital and then vanished without leaving a "forwarding" address. Such cases, while dramatic, were rare. In general, even when the burden of caregiving was the greatest because of high levels of physical disability, instrumental assistance from family members and daily care from female kin continued to be forthcoming. Our respondents reported, however, that as they became more symptomatic, they received less emotional support. To ward off the hostility that often accompanied the support on which they depended, many people with AIDS reported trying to hide their emotions from their families. Only one-third of the respondents felt that they could confide in family members. Respondents consciously tried to shield family members from the full burden of their fears and anger. "They get tired of it, so I just don't talk about it anymore" was a typical statement.

The level of internal tension within the family sometimes made people with AIDS fearful of retribution. Jim, confined to a wheelchair and constantly dependent on his kin for assistance, voiced the contradiction and the fear. "They never complain and I don't either. Today I can't afford to get mad. . . . They do everything for me, and if I get mad at them, well you never know, . . . these are the people who fix my food. . . . They may just put some poison in it or something." For both people with AIDS and their kin, both support and anger remained buried within the self and encased within the family. Respondents reported that they "just kept it [rage] inside," and the mothers to whom I talked never directly verbalized their bitterness. The hegemonic construction of health care which negated the women's caregiving burdens left the rage of family members silenced and repressed within the realm of the "taken-for-granted."

Discussion

Several broad trends underlie the construction of AIDS health services in ways that permit women's work to disappear into the unremarked categories of "habit and instinct" (Hall 1988, 44). The historical period in which HIV infection took on epidemic proportions in the United States also was the time when HIV infection become increasingly concen-

trated in working-class and minority families and the U.S. industrial base was reconfigured by the pressures of a globalized economy. At first, the failure by health services researchers and sons such as Harry to acknowledge women kin as caregivers for people with AIDS might appear as nothing new, and hardly in need of contextualizing within the current state of the global capitalist system. Although women family members provide the vast majority of the care received by people of all ages in U.S. society who are physically disabled or mentally or chronically ill (Sommers 1985), such care long remained socially invisible. The allocation of women to the role of caregiver has been an expectation to which women are socialized and, as such, structured into the division of labor that underlies the social reproduction of the society.

In certain areas of health service research, however, the past few decades have yielded a voluminous literature on women as caregivers. Particularly in geriatrics, health researchers have explicitly and extensively studied the magnitude and the social implications of the care that women provide (Brody 1978; Doty 1986; Montgomery and Datwyler 1990; Strawbridge and Wallhagen 1992; Walker 1991). Therefore, the absence of a health services literature on women as caregivers for people with AIDS and the lack of interest of public health officials, such as those in New Jersey, in research findings about this topic is significant.

Women as caregivers began to be studied by gerontologists when it was noted that the supply of women available to provide unpaid labor seemed to be threatened by several long-term demographic and social trends (Faulkner and Micchelli 1988). Old people live much longer, in part as a result of the costly high technology of the acute care system. A large amount of resources are made available for extremely expensive hospital care for the elderly through public financing under

Medicare. In contrast, funding for long-term care and nursing home facilities has not been expanded. Public officials and policy makers consider that it would be unacceptable and undesirable for the daily maintenance and care of the elderly to be borne by public funding (Benjamin 1988). However, they find that the traditional source of care for the elderly, female kin, are less available just at a time when the need for their services has increased.

Coincident with the expanded longevity of the population has been the dramatic increase in the numbers of women with elderly relatives engaged in full-time employment (Agency for Health Care Policy and Research 1990; Dusell and Roman 1989). Facing the possibility that women would not be available to care for the frail and ill elderly and that society might soon be faced with a large and enormously expensive demand for nursing homes, researchers began to assess the degree to which women found the care of the elderly onerous and to develop remedial programs to relieve some of the strain of what they labeled "caregiver burden" (Hogan 1990; Parks and Pilisuk 1991; Young and Kahana 1989).

Experts on the financing of health care fear what can be termed the "woodwork effect." They worry that women who silently have been providing care will come out of the woodwork to demand assistance, placing too large a demand on the shrinking public pocketbook. The result may be that patients use community services in addition to institutional ones rather than as substitutes for them (Benjamin 1988, 427). Long-term care specialists have therefore advocated that remedial services such as respite care, home health care, and adult care be limited to those cases in which the absence of services would lead to institutionalization in nursing homes (Weiner 1990; Weissert 1990). Nursing homes have generally been thought to be more costly to the "public" than "community care." Policy makers

don't address what might be called "the rotten wood syndrome" in which millions of dollars are poured into the formal system of care, with large profits going to the health care industry to patch up what is fundamentally a decayed system.

Looking beyond what Hall in his discussion of hegemony labels "the horizon of the taken-for-granted" (1988, 44) that allocates the care of the elderly to women kin, a feminist critique has developed that contests the dominant health services discourse about community care for the elderly. These researchers have estimated the dollar amount contributed by women in unpaid labor, (Ward 1990) as well as the physical and psychic costs of women's caregiving (Parks and Pilisuk 1991). They have argued that the maintenance of the current distribution of power and privilege depends on a societal arrangement in which women in separate households assume primary responsibility, both for the enculturation of children and the provision of care to those who are no longer useful in the labor market—the ill, disabled, or elderly (Sommers 1985). The system rests not only on women's unpaid labor but also on their willingness to sustain the values of the culture, including ideologies of gender and kinship, which underlies the organization of society.

One might have expected that the AIDS epidemic would lead to an expansion of health services research about and debate over women as caregivers. Instead, a conjunction of several factors seems to have produced a profound silence on the topic of women's caregiving. Unlike elder care, which confronted women of all classes and races, a disproportionate amount of AIDS care has become the lot of working-class women and women of color. The inequalities of women's caregiving is being transformed into the unbearable burdens being shouldered by women such as Tasha's mother, Sarah's daughter, or Jim's sister. These are the same women who are facing increasing impoverishment and poor health.

High profit levels for the health care industry were maintained in the 1980s despite (and one could argue in part through) a reallocation of public monies from programs providing housing, food, and income to the bottom strata of U.S. society to the acute care system. However, by the end of the decade, funding for health care became increasingly problematic and pressure to reduce the costs of AIDS care grew. The profits of the health care industry are under pressure from dominant sectors of U.S. society, from the directors of corporations such as General Motors to the President and First Lady (*Time,* February 15, 1993; Norris 1993). U.S. industrial enterprises found that their ability to compete profitably in the global economy is threatened by the high cost of health care (Cassidy 1992).

There is contention within dominant sectors of the society about how the system of health care should be organized and which costs are legitimate. There seems to be agreement, however, on maintaining and reinforcing the long-established formula of disregarding women's caregiving so that tremendous sacrifices by women are turned into the "taken-for-granted." As one of the first acts of his presidency, Clinton took measures to "reduce bureaucratic barriers" such as Medicaid regulations. Heralded as a reform, waivers of Medicaid regulations do provide "community services" for the elderly and severely disabled. However, such "cost-cutting measures" mean shifting a greater burden of unpaid, unacknowledged health care to women kin. Meanwhile, the health care industry will continue to obtain large amounts of resources for providing a smaller percentage of the care.

Looking to the future of the AIDS epidemic from the vantage point of 1993, Albert R. Jonson, the chair of a special study commission of the National Research Council (NRC) observed: "AIDS has devastated the personal lives and social communities it has touched, but the epidemic has had little effect on American society as a whole or its way of doing business." (Previously, health researchers had been concerned that the AIDS epidemic was putting a strain on the delivery and financing of health care.) Nevertheless, the NRC concluded that, with some exceptions, the major institutions in American society have not changed the way they conduct their affairs. The study commission warned that since the epidemic is still largely located in a small number of cities and among people who are considered marginal, it will seem to "disappear" (*New York Times* 1993).

How can it be that several hundred thousand dying people vanish from public view?[6] They disappear not only because they are categorized as poor and powerless but because they are cared for in an unseen system of women's caregiving. They become part of women's work and are absorbed within women's long-smoldering but socially disregarded discontent. People with AIDS are left to receive both home care and the unvoiced anger of the women who care for them. There is a relationship between the legitimization of the costs of the health care industry and the constructed social invisibility of women's caregiving.

For women, the epidemic is not only increasingly a killer in its own right.[7] The manner in which AIDS health services is being represented intensifies the oppressive conditions within which many women live their lives, even as it removes the work of women kin of people with AIDS from public purview. To reveal the unspeakable burdens being shouldered by the women kin who care for family members with AIDS is to challenge the manner in which health services are conceptualized by U.S. health researchers and public officials. It is to oppose the right of the health care industry to continue to profit from large allocations of public funds, while defining as "cost-cutting" programs that place ever-increasing responsibilities for caregiving on the doorsteps of women. By making clear the extent of women's caregiving in the AIDS epidemic, we resist the continuing feminization of poverty (Schaffer 1988) and challenge those who most benefit from the current inequities. Applying this type of critical lens to health care for persons with AIDS forces us to confront the current crisis of U.S. capital that leads political leaders, industrialists, and health policy experts to attempt to shift the burden of profitability to working-class women and women of color in the name of health care reform. As we uncover the unvoiced experiences of women as caregivers in the AIDS epidemic, we simultaneously reveal the structures of domination.

NOTES

Acknowledgments: Many people contributed to this research and I wish to thank them. Among those who can be named are Stephen Crystal, the Principal Investigator of the New Jersey Statewide Needs Assessment, who served as a brilliant and demanding guide and kept encouraging me to write up my field observations; David Mechanic and Allan Horowitz, who provided support and wisdom; John Beals and Ellen Dryer, who shared the wealth of their experience; Denver Lewellen, who shared the pain and the intensity of the study; and Mary Gibbs, who provided technical and moral support. Ron Altman and Sam Costa assisted with AIDS Registry data. Research team members included Gary Branch, Carol Charles, Daniel Fernando, Alma Flores, Israel Lamboy, Docella Lamey, Nettie Nazario, and Sita Venkateswar. Data analysis was done by Donita Devance-Manzini, Sheeram Krishnaswami, and Daniel Karus. The errors and the analysis are mine. I received support during the research from a NIMH postdoctoral grant in Mental Health to the Institute for Health, Health Services, and Aging Research. Many others who lent their voices, hopes, and fears must remain nameless. All names used in the chapter are pseudonyms. I hope that this chapter, at least in part, has served to tell the story, as we promised.

1. I concluded that health researchers did not believe that people with AIDS had families, from discussions of our findings about family support at meetings of the American Public Health Association and International AIDS Conference as well as from the sparsity of literature on the topic.

2. New Jersey regulations mandated physicians to report any of a long list of diseases, including AIDS, and from this data New Jersey reported statistics about the incidence and prevalence in the state of various diseases. Reporting was confidential but not anonymous. New Jersey State Health Department officials and representatives had case reports with the names and addresses of individuals.

3. The procedure had its drawbacks. Sometimes it was months before a health provider again had contact with the sampled person, who, at this time of renewed contact, might be too sick to be interviewed. Of the 361 people who were sampled by the Department of Health and were alive at the time of sampling, we interviewed 107. Only 35 people refused, but 77 people died before we could locate and interview them, 24 were too sick to be interviewed by the time they were finally located, and 72 people were never located by this method.

4. Vignettes in this chapter are based on field observations made during both the pilot study and the survey. The numerical data are from the survey. Most of the statistical analysis is reported in Crystal et al. 1990.

5. Only 22 percent of the gay men surveyed were living in a conjugal relationship. It should be noted that this finding was to some extent shaped by the cross sectional nature of our data. We had some indication that as longtime mates became sick and died, and/or HIV infected gay men became more debilitated, they moved back to their family of origin to be cared for by consanguineal kin. Even respondents who maintained a relationship to their mates sometimes moved in with consanguineal kin. For example, one respondent lived with his mate and his mother and father and a second respondent lived with his mate and his mother.

6. More than one million people in the United

States are probably HIV infected. The Centers for Disease Control projected that 165–215,000 would die between 1991–1993 (Cayton and O'Connell 1991, 2).

7. Only recently, in the light of dramatic increases in the reporting of AIDS incidence among Black and Hispanic women, has there been acknowledgment that in the U.S. AIDS can be a women's disease (Miller, Turner, and Moses 1990).

REFERENCES

Agency for Health Care Policy and Research. 1990. More than 13 Million Persons Have a Disabled Elderly Parent or Spouse. *Research Activities* 130:6.

Benjamin, A. E. 1988. Long Term Care and AIDS: Perspectives from the Experience with the Elderly. *Milbank Quarterly* 66 (3):415–443.

Boyd-Franklin, Nancy, and Julia Aleman. 1990. Black, Inner City Families and Multigenerational Issues: The Impact of AIDS. *New Jersey Psychologist* 40 (3):14–17.

Brody, Elaine. 1978. The Aging of the Family. *Annals of the American Academy of Political and Social Sciences* 438:13–27.

Comaroff, Jean, and John Comaroff. 1991. *Of Revelation and Revolution: Christianity, Colonialism, and Consciousness in South Africa*. Chicago: University of Chicago Press.

Caron, S. E. Macklin, and J. Rolland. 1988. Report on Meeting of the Steering Committee of the National Coalition on AIDS and Families, cited in Elanor Macklin 1988, AIDS: Implications for Families. *Family Relations* 37:141–149.

Cassidy, J., 1992. Global Economy Pressures U.S. Industry, Healthcare. *Health Progress* 73 (6):18–19.

Cayton, Linda, and Carol O'Connell. 1991. Worldwide Projects. CDC HIV/AIDS Prevention Newsletter. February.

Clatts, Michael C., and Kevin M. Mutchler. 1989. AIDS and the Dangerous Other: Metaphors of Sex and Deviance in the Representation of Disease. *Medical Anthropology* 10:105–114.

Coye, Molly. 1989. AIDS. A Report: The Human Immunodeficiency Virus Epidemic in New Jersey. Trenton: Department of Health.

Coye, Molly, Richard Conviser, Howard Berliner, and Christine Grant. 1988. Results of a Statewide Strategy to Contain Hospital Costs of AIDS Patients. Trenton: New Jersey Department of Health.

Crystal, Stephen, Nina Schiller, Denita Devance-Manzini, and Shreeram Krishnaswami. 1990. Statewide Needs Assessment of People with AIDS. Ms on file at Institute for Health, Health Care Policy, and Aging Research. New Brunswick, N.J.: Rutgers University.

Doty, Pamela. 1986. Family Care of the Elderly: The Role of Public Policy. *Millbank Quarterly* 64 (1):34–75.

Dunning, Jennifer. 1993. Huck Snyder, Artist, Dies at 39; Designed Stage Sets For Dancers. *New York Times*, Thursday, January 28, 1993, B7.

Dusell, Christina, and Mary Roman. 1989. Sarah Doesn't Work Here Anymore: The Elder-Care Dilemma. *Generations* 13:30–32.

Eisenberg, Myron, Sutkin LaFaye, and Mary Jansen, eds. 1984. *Chronic Illness and Disability Through the Life Span: Effects on Self and Family*. New York: Springer.

Faulkner, Audrey, and Margaret Micchelli. 1988. The Aging, the Aged, and the Very Old: Women the Policy Makers Forgot. *Women and Health* 14 (3–4):5–19.

Fee, Elizabeth, and Daniel Fox, eds., 1988. *AIDS: The Burden of History*. Berkeley: University of California Press.

Frankenberg, Ronald. 1988. Gramsci, Culture, and Medical Anthropology: Kundry and Parsifal? Or Rat's Tail to Sea Serpent. *Medical Anthropology Quarterly* 4:324–337.

Gramsci, Antonio. 1971. *Selections from the Prison Notebooks*. Quintin Hoare and Geoffrey Nowell Smith ed. and trans. New York: International Publishers.

Gubman, Gayke, and Richard Tessler. 1987. The Impact of Mental Illness on Families. *Journal of Family Issues* 8 (2):226–245.

Hall, Stuart. 1988. The Toad in the Garden: Thatcherism Among the Theorists. In *Marxism and the Interpretation of Culture*. C. Nelson and L. Grossber, eds., pp. 35–37. Urbana: University of Illinois Press.

Hellinger, Fred. 1991. *Forecasting the Personal Medical Care Costs of AIDS from 1988* through 1991. Public Health Reports 103 (3): 309–319.

Hogan, Sharon. 1990. Care for the Caregiver: Social

Policies to Ease Their Burden. *Journal of Geron-tological Nursing* 16 (5):12–17.

Kane, Rosalie A., and Robert L. Kane. 1987. *Long Term Care: Principles, Programs, and Policies*. New York: Springer.

Lawson, Carol. 1992. Parents and AIDS: Rage and Tears. *New York Times,* May 28; C1.

Miller, Heather, Charles Turner, and Lincoln Moses, eds. 1990. AIDS: *The Second Decade*. Washington, D.C.: National Academy Press.

Montgomery, Rhona, and Mary Datwyler. 1990. Women and Men in the Caregiving Role. *Generations* 14:34–38.

Mor, Vincent, John Piette, and John Fleishman. 1988. AIDS Patients' Needs: Challenge for the Community-Based Long-Term Care System. Paper presented at the Fifth Annual Meeting of the Association of Health Services Research, San Francisco, California, 1988.

New York Times. 1993. Research Group Says AIDS Epidemic Will Have Little Effect on U.S. February 5, A12.

Norris, Floyd. 1993. A. G. M. Loss Could Spur Health Reform. *New York Times,* February 7, F1.

Parks, Susan, and Marc Pilisuk. 1991. Caregiver Burden: Gender and the Psychological Costs of Caregiving. *American Journal of Orthopsychiatry* 51(4):501–509.

Richardson, Dianne. 1988. *Women and AIDS*. New York: Methuen.

Rosenberg, Charles. 1988. Disease and Social Order in America: Perceptions and Expectations. In *AIDS: The Burden of History*. Elizabeth Fee and Daniel Fox, eds., pp. 12–32. Berkeley: University of California Press.

Schaffer, Dianne. 1988. The Feminization of Poverty: Prospects for an International Feminist Agenda. In *Women, Power, and Policy: Toward the Year 2000*. E. Bonepart and E. Stopper, eds., pp. 223–246. New York: Pergamon Press.

Schiller, Nina Glick. 1992. What's Wrong With This Picture? The Hegemonic Construction of Culture in AIDS Research in the United States. *Medical Anthropology Quarterly* 6(3):237–254.

Schiller, Nina Glick, Stephen Crystal, Denver Lewellen. 1994. Risky Business: The Cultural Construction of AIDS Risk Groups. *Social Science and Medicine*. 38(10):1337–1346.

Selenkow, Ida. 1990. Enhancing Coping Strategies for PWAs in the Home: Community Health Nursing Implications. *AIDS Patient Care*, April 42–44.

Singer, Merrill, Cundida Flores, Lani Davison, Georgine Burke, Zaida Castillo, Kelly Scanlon, and Migdalia Rivera 1990. SIDA: The Economic, Social and Cultural Context of AIDS Among Latinos. *Medical Anthropology Quarterly* 4:73–114.

Sommers, Tish. 1985. Caregiving: A Woman's Issue. *Generations* 10:9–13.

Stack, Carol. 1975. *All Our Kin: Strategies for Survival in A Black Community*. New York: Harper & Row.

Strawbridge, William, and Margaret Wallhagen. 1992. Is All in the Family Always Best? *Journal of Aging Studies* 5 (1):81–92.

Susser, Ida. 1981. *Norman Street*. New York: Oxford University Press.

Time. 1993. Biting the Bullet, February 15.

Treichler, Paula. 1987. AIDS, Homophobia, and Biomedical Discourse: An Epidemic of Signification. *October* 43:31–70.

Walker, Alan. 1991. The Relationship Between the Family and the State in the Care for Older People. *Canadian Journal on Aging* 10 (2):94–112.

Ward, Debbie. 1990. Gender, Time, and Money in Caregiving. *Scholarly Inquiry for Nursing Practice* 4 (3):223–236.

Weiner, Joshua. 1990. Which Way for Long-Term-Care Financing? *Generations* 14:5–9.

Weissert, William. 1990. Strategies for Reducing Home-Care Expenditures. *Generations* 14:42–44.

Williams, Raymond. 1977. *Marxism and Literature*. Oxford: Oxford University Press.

Wortman, Camille. 1984. Social Support and the Cancer Patient. *Cancer* 53 (May 15 Supplement): 2339–2360.

Young, Rosalie, and Eva Kahana. 1989. Specifying Caregiver Outcomes: Gender and Relationship Aspects of Caregiving Strain. *Gerontologist* 29 (5):660–666.

Young, Steven. 1988. The Impact of AIDS on the Health Care System in New Jersey. *New York State Journal of Medicine*. May: 258–262.

Younge, Richard. 1989. Report from the Frontlines: Unsung Heroines of the AIDS Epidemic. *Health/Pac Bulletin* 19 (4):16–18.

~ *Chapter 41*

The Ambiguities of Social Support:
Adult Daughters Caring for Frail Elderly Parents

EMILY K. ABEL

At a time when pressures to find inexpensive alternatives to public services are overwhelming, many policy makers emphasize informal sources of support. If we can convince more people to look after their own, the argument goes, the demand for publicly funded services will diminish. Because the expense of caring for the burgeoning frail elderly population is expected to be staggering, many policy makers and public officials are especially anxious to encourage family and friends to assume additional responsibility for aging persons.

During the past five years, however, a host of researchers have documented the stresses such caregiving entails. Studies consistently show that families already deliver 70 to 80 percent of all long-term care (Community Council of Greater New York 1978; Comptroller General of the United States 1977; Stone, Cafferata, and Sangl n.d.). Most falls disproportionately on a single individual.

From *Journal of Aging Studies* 3, no. 3 (1989): 211–30, copyright © 1989 by JAI Press, Inc. Reprinted by permission.

Spouses are the most common caregivers, followed by adult children, then other relatives, and finally friends and neighbors (Johnson and Catalano 1983; Kivett 1985; Stephens and Christianson 1986; Stoller 1983; Stone, Cafferata, and Sangl n.d.). Women constitute the great majority of caregivers in all categories (Brody 1981; Cantor 1983; Horowitz 1985a; Stoller 1983). They represent 77 percent of all adult children rendering care and 64 percent of all spousal caregivers (Stone, Cafferata, and Sangl n.d.). Many caregivers experience serious physical and emotional problems. In a study comparing caregivers of memory-impaired adults with age peers who lacked caregiving responsibilities, Linda George and Lisa Gwyther found that the caregivers reported three times as many symptoms of stress (George and Gwyther 1986).

This chapter explores the extent to which family caregivers, in turn, can rely on members of their social networks for help. Although researchers have directed relatively little attention to this issue, the prodigious literature on social support provides a useful framework within which to examine it. Some researchers argue that social ties buffer individuals against stress (Antonovsky 1974, 1979; Caplan 1974; Cassell 1976; Cobb 1976). Others, however, caution us against viewing social relationships as an unambiguous good. Although social support does appear to increase well-being, the extent to which it protects individuals against the harmful effects of stress is by no means clear (see Thoits 1982). Moreover, social networks are not converted automatically into social support. It hardly bears repeating that members of social networks can themselves be a source of stress (Rook and Dooley 1985). When individuals close to us are in trouble, we often experience a "contagion of stress" (Wilkins 1974). In addition, close relationships harbor a range of feelings, including anger and bitterness as well as love and affection. The term "social support" glosses over the complexity of human attachments. It implies that individuals are ensconced in relationships that invariably are warm and harmonious and ignores elements of power and conflict. As statistics about the rising divorce rate and the pervasiveness of family violence remind us, however, intimate relationships can foster tensions and abuse as well as warmth and solicitude.

Then too, even when friends and family act in ways intended to be supportive, they often fail to help. Words of comfort expressed to people who have suffered losses, for example, frequently are misguided. Unemployed women resent family and friends who seek to console them by trivializing their commitment to the workforce (Ratcliff and Bogdan 1988). Parents mourning the death of an infant are offended by well-meaning comments that they are fortunate to have lost the child before they had a chance to grow more attached (Helmrath and Steinitz 1978).

Finally, although we know little about the processes whereby individuals seek help, a variety of objective and subjective barriers constrain people in stress from mobilizing whatever support might be available to them. Potential supporters may live far away or be overburdened with other problems (Eckenrode and Gore 1981). Cancer patients hesitate to call upon potential supporters because they want to shield close relations from the intensity of their feelings (Dunkel-Schetter and Wortman 1982).

Two schools of feminist writing would lead us to expect that support between men and women would be asymmetrical. Some feminist scholars assert that, as members of subordinate groups, women frequently operate from a desire to please people who have power over them; because they tend to submerge their own interests in relationships with men, they might well refrain from asking for the support they need (Hare-Mustin and Marecek 1986). Feminist psychoanalytic theorists argue that women experience themselves as more strongly connected to others than do men. They thus furnish support not only from a sense of obligation and compulsion but also to achieve personal fulfillment. According to Nancy Chodorow (1978), as a result of dominant patterns of mothering, women's sense of identity in this society is affiliational. Recently, Carol Gilligan (1983) has extended this insight by arguing that women judge themselves according to an ethic of responsibility and care.

Although research on gender differences in social support is scanty (Belle 1987), what does exist suggests that social support is unevenly allocated between men and women. Various researchers have found that women seek more help than men throughout the life course, but they also give more support to others than they get in return (e.g., Belle 1982, 1987). Studies of marriage report that men are more likely than women to confide in their spouses, suggesting an imbalance in the amount of emotional sustenance wives and husbands render (see Belle 1987, 264). Women also are called upon to deliver support to a broader array of individuals than are men. Children, for example, are more likely to turn to their mothers than their fathers in difficult times (Belle 1987). Not only are women more likely to be donors than recipients of support, but they also experience more contagion stress. Kessler and McLeod found that men have greater immunity to the problems besetting members of their social networks. When asked to report distressing events, women note more difficulties in the lives of others, and they are more vulnerable to these troubles (Kessler and McLeod, 1984). When women do obtain support, they often receive it from female friends. A range of studies conclude that women have a more extensive web of relationships than men and that their friendships are characterized by greater emotional intensity (see Belle 1987; Rubin 1985).

The few researchers who have explored the effect of social support on caregivers for the frail elderly have concluded that support helps to shield family members from stress and thus reduces the risk of nursing home placement (Morycz 1985; Zarit et al. 1980; see Horowitz 1985b). But these studies fail to provide an adequate conceptualization of social support. Richard K. Morycz (1985), for example, defines social support as caregivers' perceptions that they can rely on others to provide back-up help. As we will see, this definition ignores several critical dimensions of social support. Stephen H. Zarit et al. (1980), measured social support by assessing the frequency of visits by other relatives and friends to the household. Numerous researchers, however, have faulted studies that rely on the quantity rather than the quality of personal interactions (see Rook 1984). In a study based on participant observation of and

focused interviews with a support group of caregivers of Alzheimer's patients, Jaber F. Gubrium found that caregivers occasionally viewed visits by other relatives as intrusive rather than helpful. If some participants in the group bemoaned the absence of friends and family to share the responsibility, others complained that contact with other family members exacerbated the stress they experienced (Gubrium 1988).

A few studies have found that the level of support received by caregivers divides predictably along gender lines. Although daughters who provide care are more likely than sons to live with dependent parents (Wolf and Soldo 1986), perform tasks associated with high levels of stress, and experience caregiving as a boundless, all-encompassing activity (see Abel 1987), they receive less assistance. Daughters-in-law remain an important source of informal care. Sons caring for elderly parents thus obtain more material help and emotional support from their wives than daughters can expect from their husbands (George and Gwyther 1984; Horowitz 1985a; cf. Kleban et al. 1986).

Methods

This chapter is based on an exploratory study of adult daughters caring for frail elderly parents. It examines the women's perceptions of the social support they received. It does not assess the extent to which the women believed that support was adequate or whether it mitigated the stress they experienced. The chapter does, however, examine the types of support the caregivers obtained from various sources, as well as the barriers they encountered in securing additional help.

Respondents were located and recruited through support groups and service agencies. A snow-ball approach was used to obtain additional names. The sample consisted of 40 women. Their median age was 51. One woman was under 40, 14 were between 40 and 49, 23 were between 50 and 59, and two were over 60. To control for variations by race, only Caucasian women were interviewed.

Most of these women were caring for mothers. Twenty seven, or two-thirds, were providing care exclusively for mothers, seven exclusively for fathers, and six for both parents. The women had been providing care for periods ranging from six months to 16 years; the median was four years. Twenty-four women were caring for parents with Alzheimer's disease or related disorders. Eleven were living with their parents at the time of the interviews, and two previously had done so. Thirteen women helped at least one parent with hygiene, 8 assisted with mobility, 13 administered medication, 27 performed household tasks, 37 shopped and/or assisted with transportation, 34 handled finances, and 7 provided economic help.

Most studies of caregivers are based on highly structured interviews, which are analyzed statistically. This type of research is more appropriate for examining the discrete tasks of caregiving than for exploring either the human relationships within which those tasks are embedded or the subjective experiences of the caregivers. The interviews in this study consisted of open-ended as well as structured questions. They lasted an average of 1½ hours and were tape recorded and transcribed. Answers were analyzed using standard techniques for the coding and analysis of qualitative data (Taylor and Bogdan 1984; Glasser and Strauss 1967).

Results

The Costs of Caregiving

In order to understand the need for support, it is important to examine the burden caregiving placed on the women I interviewed. Many claimed that they found caregiving rewarding and fulfilling, but virtually all also insisted that it was a source of strain. Some problems resulted from the particularities of these women's personalities or their relationships with their parents. Nevertheless, a number of patterns can be discerned. I will describe situational factors first and then interpersonal ones.

Very few women anticipated caring for their parents. Some women stated that if they ever had thought about their parents' old age, they simply had assumed that their parents would die quickly. Those who had considered the possibility that parent care would be part of their lives were shocked by the type of disease that struck.

Moreover, many women had little warning that they would be called upon to provide care. Seven had lived far from their parents and had not discovered the extent of their parents' impairments until they went to visit. Four women learned about the one parent's disability only after the death of the other parent, who had shielded them from the initial stages of the disease. Recent writing has emphasized the need for predictability; we can cope better with events that arrive at scheduled times and for which we have prepared (see Pearlin and Aneshensel 1986). But caregiving obligations often occur precipitately, catching family members by surprise.

Most women had little training about how to act. The great majority stated that their parents had not cared for their grandparents. Gunhild Hagestad remarks, "Family members often face each other in relationships for which there is no historical precedent and therefore minimal guidance on which to rely" (Hagestad 1986). Many women in this study complained about being confronted with decisions for which they were unprepared. Some still were pondering decisions they had made months and occasionally years before, and they used the interviews as opportunities to reassess their choices.

Caregiving also competed with work in the lives of many women. Six quit their jobs, at least partly because of caregiving responsibilities. One woman forfeited her chance of a promotion, and three others sought less demanding jobs in order to accommodate their parents' needs. Other women with paid employment complained that phone calls from their parents frequently interrupted their work. These women also took time off from their jobs when their parents became ill, saw doctors, or visited possible residential facilities.

The women I interviewed were even less successful about protecting their leisure from the encroachments of parent care. Like most other caregivers (see Cantor 1983; Horowitz 1985b), the women in this study frequently abandoned vacations and forfeited social activities. Many stated that preoccupation with their parents put a damper on the leisure activities that they did undertake.

Although these women discussed the social and economic disruptions wrought by caregiving, most emphasized emotional dynamics. Caregiving brought women into intimate contact with their parents, often for the first time since they had been adolescents. Issues they assumed had been fully resolved suddenly reemerged. Several women were shocked by the intensity of the feelings this experience provoked. Old resentments suddenly had renewed force. Many women also acknowledged that they found themselves once again looking to their parents for approval and striving to please them. A few expected to receive the approbation and affection that previously had been withheld.

But, if caregiving reawakened childhood feelings, it also compelled these women to acknowledge how much had changed. Many spoke of the difficulties of watching the deterioration of a person to whom they felt intimately bound. Not surprisingly, fears of aging and death also surfaced.

Caregiving itself accentuated the sense of loss. In providing care, daughters must relinquish the illusion that their parents are omnipotent and still can offer protection. Also, caregiving demands that women redefine their roles vis-à-vis their parents. Many women spoke about how difficult it was for them to assume responsibility for their parents' lives. Many were acutely aware that their parents resented their assertions of authority. These caregivers saw themselves wounding their parents further by taking control. Those who still were seeking to please their parents and win their approval felt torn between the need to assume responsibility and the desire to accede to their parents' wishes.

Although these women believed that their parents resisted even essential help, they also saw them as making impossible demands. Many women believed that their parents had boundless expectations about what their daughters could accomplish. Some women interpreted their parents' continuing requests as evidence that they had fallen short as caregivers. They themselves embraced a notion of caregiving that required them to improve the overall quality of their parents' lives. The parents typically had experienced irremediable losses and suffered from physical and mental problems that could not be repaired. Nevertheless, the daughters held themselves accountable for making their parents happy.

In short, parent care involves constant tensions between attachment and loss, pleasing and caring, seeking to preserve an older person's dignity and exerting unaccustomed authority, overcoming resistance to care and fulfilling extravagant demands, reviving a relationship and transforming it.

Defining Social Support

Although researchers have conceptualized social support in a myriad of ways, many agree that it has the following components: instrumental assistance, emotional sustenance, affirmation, and companionship (see House 1981; Wortman 1984). It is important to note that because caregivers exercise some degree of choice over whether or not to render care their situation differs from that of others in which people appear to need support. The women in this study felt compelled to provide care for a variety of reasons: none of their siblings would assume the responsibility, they considered the quality of nursing homes too poor to make institutionalization a viable option, or their parents refused to rely on anyone else. Nevertheless, the intense emotional involvement of the women in this activity suggests that they were not simply responding to external forces. Some took pride in rendering care that was superior to what their parents could receive from other sources. Moreover, although they found it easier to discuss the burdens than the rewards, several did note that they derived emotional benefits from the experience. They grew closer to their parents, acted in accordance with their own values, and provided an essential service. Because caregiving was gratifying as well as burdensome, they wanted friends and other family members to recognize its importance. They were enraged when people belittled their attachment to their parents, trivialized their involvement in caregiving, and failed to acknowledge their parents' unique worth and humanity.

Nevertheless, these women did want assistance with problematic aspects of caregiving. They expressed a need for advice about critical decisions, help in limiting their responsibilities, assistance with concrete chores, and information about available resources. We will see that the women did obtain some of this support from a range of different sources. But a variety of factors prevented them from receiving some of the help they wanted.

Husbands

Of the 27 married women, just three stated unequivocally that their husbands were unsupportive. Although many of the other women noted that their husbands resented the time and energy caregiving consumed and the extent to which it dominated their lives and thoughts, they still characterized their husbands as supportive. When asked how they defined this term, the most common response was that their husbands assumed responsibility for their parents' financial affairs. In addition, some women noted that their husbands sometimes accompanied them when they visited their parents, did assorted chores for their parents, and treated them with consideration. One woman noted that because her husband was unencumbered by the emotional baggage of a lifelong relationship to her mother he could deal with her more effectively:

It's very hard for me to tell her what to do. For years and years and years, doctors have been telling her she should take a daily walk, and she should drink water, and she should do this, but she doesn't do any of these things. It's frustrating. My husband finally spoke up to her the last time she came out of the hospital. He said, "How many more times do you think we can go through this?" He said, "Don't you think it's time for you to take some responsibility?" He said, "There's things you could be doing to help yourself, and we expect you do do them." Somehow, he got the courage to say all that. I have tried to say it, but it doesn't come out quite as well as when he says it. Somehow it comes out kinder, and she accepts it better from him.

But other women indicated that their husbands' participation was far more limited. Three women stated that when they spent joint savings, their husbands did not protest; two women said that their husbands did not complain about the time they devoted to caregiving. How can we explain why women labeled as supportive husbands who did little more than tolerate their own caregiving? One explanation may lie in the fact that women typically hold themselves responsible for their marital relationships (Cancian 1987). The women I interviewed may have felt that any expression of dissatisfaction with their husbands would reflect badly on themselves. An equally compelling explanation is that these women had low expectations about the assistance their husbands would render. Many women insisted that their husbands did not share the responsibility and that they had to be careful not to burden them with requests for aid and comfort. Such women believed that they had an obligation to shield their husbands from the consequences of caregiving. Their first duty, they stressed, was to support their husbands. Because they believed that the care they provided their parents detracted from what they could give their husbands, they felt they should be grateful for the lack of opposition to their involvement in caregiving. Feeling torn between their responsibilities as wives and as daughters, they assumed that they should bear the costs of caregiving alone and thus refrained from asserting their own needs for support.

Children

Twenty-eight women in the study were mothers. When these caregivers spoke about their children, they again emphasized their own obligations, not the support they could elicit. Many women had heard the terms "sandwich generation" and "women in the middle" and believed that these applied to them. Just two women had children under the age of 18 at home. But several had ongoing obligations to older children. Ten had children over 18 who either were living at home or had problems

that required the continuing involvement of their parents.

Although these women welcomed any concern their children demonstrated, they were not surprised when little practical assistance was forthcoming. A common refrain was that their children were young and had their own lives to lead. Many women also absolved their children from responsibility because of the quality of the relationships the children had with their grandparents. Some women stated that their children never had been close to their grandparents and therefore owed them nothing. Other women exonerated their children for the opposite reason—because they had enjoyed a special relationship with their grandparents; these women did not want caregiving to intrude on that relationship. A woman whose mother suffered from Alzheimer's disease explained why her daughter rarely visited the grandmother:

> Our daughter and my mother were very, very close. My mother was probably her very best friend. Our daughter is gay, and my mother was a champion of Joan for a long time and always used to tease us, saying, "Don't knock it till you've tried it." Always was on Joan's side. My mother realized it before she came out of the closet. It's very hard for my daughter to see her now, to be with my mother.

Several women also asserted that their children were too young to have to deal with serious illness and death. One woman sought to protect her children from distressing events by discouraging them from visiting their grandmother in the psychiatric unit of a hospital.

Siblings

Although the women in this study sharply circumscribed the caregiving responsibilities of their husbands and children, they were less willing to let their siblings off the hook. Some did state that their brothers and sisters had legitimate reasons for being less involved; they lived far away, had serious personal problems themselves, or had paid their dues by caring for their parents during an earlier period. But several women, like the ones quoted below, expressed rage at brothers and sisters who evaded the most onerous obligations:

> My sister and I have been having problems around this. We were always very close, and we're not now. I don't think she comes down often enough. She's free to come. She calls, big deal; that's very different from spending three to four hours a day. . . . She does not wheel my mother to the doctor, she does not carry her to the car, she does not oversee the help.

Another woman was distressed that caregiving responsibilities were gender-biased:

> My brother, in the eight years that he's got ahead of me, fell into almost a different generation, and he has a different philosophy. I suppose that a lot of men think that women are the caregivers and men are not. Also, it's easy to take pot shots at me working at home. We're actually a little bit closer now than we had been before, and we are trying to do things for our parents together. We're trying to work on separating their assets now, with these complicated California laws. Both my brother and I seem to be able to share the work that's involved with it. But I think if something were to hit, he would expect me to get in there and find people to hire and all. During the years when we were having disagreements, his answers always were, "Well, I've got a family to support." But are my earnings frivolous? I think he thinks that [caregiving] is something women do primarily.

Even if siblings would not share caregiving responsibilities equitably, they could participate in various ways. Above all, the women in this study wanted their sisters and brothers involved in major decisions because they had an equal stake in the outcome. Those without siblings felt their absence keenly when critical decisions arose. Also, because siblings shared a common family history, they could help to interpret parental behavior and understand the emotional responses of the caregivers. Several women remarked that they found it helpful to recount disturbing incidents to brothers and sisters.

But participation of siblings, even on a limited basis, could bring additional problems. In many cases, this represented the first intimate contact between them in many years. Although two women said that the shared enterprise of caregiving brought them closer to their sisters, most noted that renewed interaction reawakened old feelings of competition and jealousy. Some were painfully aware that their parents reacted more positively to their brothers or sisters. Two women who had given months of sustained care noted bitterly that siblings who made only fleeting appearances elicited more favorable responses from their parents. In a few cases, the women I spoke to felt embarrassed by the greater affection lavished on them. One woman tried to correct the imbalance:

> I have to say I was my father's favorite. He always adored me more than anybody else, and I guess I realized that, and it was special that way, and it still is. He'll always give me credit for everything that's being done for him, even when my brothers will be sitting there. My brother will cook a wonderful meal for my father, and my father will thank me for it. He always thinks in terms of me. I'm the one that's doing everything good. And I feel bad. I keep telling him, "Dad, you know, Jim fixed that wonderful meal," because my older brother was very rejected by my father, so I feel really bad about it, and I try really hard even at this late date to keep reminding my father my brother's doing a huge amount for him.

Moreover, siblings often disagreed about their parents' needs and favored different courses of action. One woman, for example, fought her sister's proposal to place their mother in a nursing home. Another clashed with her sister about more subtle aspects of care. While the latter wanted to encourage their bedridden father to learn to paint by numbers, my informant was convinced that he would consider such an activity demeaning.

And, although some women were buoyed and sustained by siblings who praised the care they provided, many resented unrealistic expectations about what they could accomplish. One woman's sisters repeatedly complained to her about the problems with their mother's housing, implying that she should be able to find a better option. Another woman felt that her brother was saying that she could halt the course of their mother's deterioration. Criticisms from siblings were particularly difficult for women who were struggling with their own feelings of inadequacy as caregivers.

Friends

The women in this study also looked to friends for various kinds of assistance. Several relied on a network of friends for emotional intimacy and assumed as a matter of course that they would discuss feelings abut caregiving with them. Friends also relived the tensions of caregiving by taking women out and diverting them from their troubles at home. In some instances, friends were an important source of advice. One woman, caring for a father with Alzheimer's disease, felt overwhelmed by the need to take control of her father's life. She explained how she was able to do so:

> I would just call my friends up and talk to everybody. I would end up talking about how hard things are for me to everybody, and I'd get a lot of ideas and suggestions and support. And people just kept telling me over and over, my best friends would say, "Look, you have to do this, he's not capable at this point, and to do that, you are taking care of him." And that would give me

the support to go ahead and be a little stronger. . . . I felt real guilt about putting his money into a trust. I thought, "Oh, Susan, you are doing this for yourself, so when he dies, you'll have an inheritance." And they just kept telling me, "No, you are doing it to help him." They pointed out he may need the money in the future for a nursing home and that it wasn't for me, and they were real, real supportive. If I didn't have their feedback, it would have been really bad.

Because the friends of several women in the study were professionals in the fields of gerontology or social welfare, they were able to connect the caregivers to community resources. One woman explained how she was able to find a place for her mother in the one high-quality day care center in her area:

> One friend helped me more than anyone, because she said, "There's a very long line for [the day care center]." But she said, "What are friends for, if not to push everybody else out of line?" And so she made some very necessary calls, and we got mother in, and it was wonderful because there was no place for her.

Other women learned the names of nursing homes and home health aides from friends.

If most of the women acknowledged the critical help of friends, however, these relationships hardly constituted a bulwark against the stresses of providing care. In fact, the constant demands of caregiving made it difficult, if not impossible, for some women to sustain ongoing friendships. One woman was disabled and had lived alone with her father when he was dying of cancer. Interviewed shortly after his death, she commented:

> I was so busy I didn't have time for anyone. You get terribly lonely, which is tough. You just have so much to do that I would look at my friends that I owed telephone calls to, and I would say, "I can never do it."

Women who were employed full time typically shielded their worklives from the impact of caregiving; as a result, they were compelled to sacrifice social activities.

Caregiving fractured friendships for other reasons as well. A few caregivers were hesitant about revealing family problems. A woman who tended her mother suffering from Alzheimer's disease said:

> I'm embarrassed sometimes, because when people hear sometimes about some of the things my mother has done, they say, "Oh, my God." As much as I would like to be able to have someone say, "Oh, that's awful, you poor thing," and to ask me to tell them about it, on the other hand, there's a side of me that's very mistrustful, that if people find out how crazy my mother is that they'll reject me.

Another woman had brought her mother, also suffering from Alzheimer's disease, into her home. She explained her reluctance to invite friends to the house this way:

> I have to say when dealing with someone with Alzheimer's, no one really understands what you are living through, they really don't. An Alzheimer's person is an oddity. Friends would come and my mom would be sitting in the living room with us and she will say things that just really don't make sense and it causes an embarrassment. People are not as sympathetic to someone who has brain damage as to someone who has cancer or a heart ailment. When there is no communication and no understanding of what that person is saying and that they don't understand you. When friends come, some of the time I would ask my mom to come and sit with us. It is embarrassing, I don't want her to be the focus, to be looked at like a freak, and I don't trust that friends understand so I avoid having people over.

In addition, some women who prided themselves on being the more sympathetic and compassionate member of any relationship withdrew from friendships rather than continue to incur additional responsibilities.

Asked whether she turned to her friends for support, one woman said:

> I was always a better listener. I always used to be the one everybody came and told their problems to. When my mother arrived, I pretty much cut that out. I didn't have any room for any more problems.

When friendships persisted, caregivers exercised considerable caution about approaching their friends for help. The few women who asked friends to visit their parents did so only in emergencies or during the rare occasion when they left town. Clinging to an ideology of self-reliance, two women believed that it was inappropriate to turn to others for help with their troubles. Others perceived their friends as unsupportive. When these women first assumed caregiving responsibilities, friends failed to understand that they no longer could accept spur-of-the minute invitations:

> I haven't seen much of my friends. One friend, when she heard what was happening, her response was to call up and say, "We're going out to dinner, do you want to come too?" Now how can I do that?

Nor could they linger over restaurant meals:

> We were just saying today that one of our closest friends is alienated from us. He does not understand that I just don't have the energy anymore to spend three hours dining while he drinks two bottles of wine, and I'm falling asleep in my plate.

Some friends who initially rallied around these women lost interest as caregiving continued to absorb their attention over a period of months and even years:

> Friends don't really want to hear too much about your problems. You can tell them from time to time the status report, but it's not a subject they really want to talk about. They might

ask from time to time how my mom is doing and if I tell them that she's in the hospital, they say, "Isn't there some medication they could find that would fix that?" There's lot of impatience with these chronic things. Nobody wants to deal with chronic anything.

Moreover, some friends who sought to be helpful undermined the caregivers by betraying a lack of sympathy for their undertaking. One woman complained about a friend who counseled her to relinquish her responsibility by institutionalizing her mother; another said that a friend urged her to get a full-time job so that she would have an excuse for limiting her involvement in her mother's care; and a third was offended by a friend's suggestion that she get rid of her mother by putting her on a Greyhound bus. When friends belittled their investment in caregiving, women refrained from revealing their own ambivalent feelings.

Finally, although women in their fifties and sixties said that shared concerns about parents occasionally brought them closer to friends, younger women stated that caregiving responsibilities tended to isolate them. If they were the first members of their group to have to deal with aging parents, they felt out of step with their contemporaries.

Support Groups

Because I located many women through support groups, it was not surprising that a majority (23) of the caregivers in this study participated in them at least sporadically. Some women who considered it inappropriate to burden friends and family members with their troubles viewed caregiving groups as a place to discuss them. But some women claimed that they attended support groups in order to impart wisdom, not to gain it themselves; in the support group, as elsewhere, they obtained satisfaction from giving rather

than getting help. Many women also were happy to discover that they were not singled out for misfortune. As Leonard I. Pearlin and Carol S. Aneshensel comment, "Misery doesn't just love company, misery is in active search of company and is often assuaged by it" (Pearlin and Aneshensel 1986, 423). Several women took comfort in finding out that others were even worse off than themselves—they had less help, more needy parents, or were responsible for other relatives as well.

Support group members also exchanged information about local resources. In some cases, this meant learning how little was available. A few women were shocked to discover that, because there were no good nursing homes in their community, they could not look to institutional placement as a way of shedding caregiving responsibilities. One woman lamented.

> I honestly believed that if you put someone in a nursing home, they got good care. From what I'm finding out, you really have to go everyday and check it. All you're doing is shifting the residence of the person, whereas you really have to be there on a regular basis to make sure they're getting the care that people say they're going to give them. I was totally unaware of that.

Other women felt trapped in the role of caregiver; after listening to discussions about the poor quality of nursing homes, they concluded that they never would be able to bring themselves to institutionalize their parents.

Several women caring for parents with Alzheimer's disease and related dementias attended groups restricted to caregivers of relatives with similar afflictions. Such women traded information about the course of diseases and advice about managing their patients. Some caregivers felt that they could better tolerate troublesome and even frightening behaviors once they understood the genesis of these behaviors and learned techniques for dealing with them.

Most women I spoke to valued the exchange of experiential knowledge more than the acquisition of objective information. Support group members disclosed the rage, guilt, and self-doubt that periodically assailed them. Several women described their enormous relief at finding others who empathized with their plight. As they watched other participants mirror their feelings, their sense of isolation waned. The following comment was typical:

> To go to those meetings and to hear everybody else talk just like me and think just like me and feel like me, it really was just marvelous.

In the light of others' experiences, some women were able to reinterpret their parents' behavior so as to render it less painful. A woman whose father had dementia and continually betrayed his mistrust in her actions remarked:

> The caregivers' group relieved me of a lot of anxiety and guilt that I was carrying. Just showing me that it's not my unique problem, that everybody has basically the same problems. And when I get upset about something, they told me that my father doesn't mean any harm to me. He just doesn't know what he's doing, just that's something that he can't help. It's not himself, it's the aging process that has taken over and diminished his thinking capacities.

The realization that her father's behavior resulted from mental impairment helped to alleviate her overriding sense of personal failure.

If some women asserted that they attended support groups in order to listen to others and respond to their concerns, other acknowledged that listening could be self-serving as well as altruistic. As they heard others narrate personal experiences, they drew comparisons with their own situation and acquired knowledge about themselves. A woman whose mother suffered from recurrent bouts of depression described how she gained critical distance by listening to members of her group and relating their accounts to her own life:

> This caregiver group is the one place that I feel I could go and I could tell whatever was happening and people would really understand. I don't think, unless you're going through it yourself, that you can understand it. So I would say that's my biggest resource, to be able to go every week to that meeting, and even if I don't talk very much about what's going on with me, I'll listen to the other people and I can identify so much with what they're going through, and that helps me.

She explained why much of her earlier rage gradually dissipated:

> I think in the beginning I was totally frustrated and very angry with the medical profession and with my mother for not taking better care of herself and with my father for leaving the scene so soon and not being there for all of us and there was a lot of that built up anger and resentment. At the group, through each of us just listening to one another and sharing what we want to share about what we're going through, I think I've become more peaceful and calmer with the whole problem. I think that I was a lot more angry and a lot more resentful a year ago, and the group has helped me to work through a lot of that.

She attributed her growing acceptance of her mother's illness to the insights she gained from the other group members:

> They helped me in terms of understanding that I need to be letting go, and that I can't control my mother's death. I've just come to realize that whatever will be with my mother is not something that I can really decide. She's not my child. Most of the things that have affected her happened before I could have intervened and done anything. . . .
>
> What was most helpful was watching other people in the group struggling with these same issues. There are several people in earlier stages of

discovery of this than I am, and there are others who are further along and who have graduated from the group and don't come anymore because they have recognized their limitations, and they don't need to keep coming and asking, "Well, am I doing enough," or "Do you think this is O.K.?" or getting permission, they don't need permission from the group anymore. They seem to know that whatever they're doing is the best they can do. And I think that I haven't completely finished that yet, that I'm still needing to know that I'm doing the best I can, and that the group is validating that for me. Whenever I listen to their struggle, then I think, oh, I'm going through that same struggle. And somehow that helps.

Other women similarly reported that support groups helped them to place appropriate limits on their obligations: to hire aides and attendants when the burdens began to seem intolerable, refuse to bring their parents to live with them, ignore requests for help that they considered unreasonable, and readjust their expectations about what they could accomplish. One woman, for example, explained how she was able to contemplate institutionalizing her mother:

They really brought me to the point that I realized I had to do something. They really opened my eyes up to realize that I wasn't a bad person, I wasn't evil because I wasn't dumping my mother.

Q. How did they do that?

Just by listening to them, and the way they felt and what they were going through, and what they were doing, and I thought, "Well, gee, I've done that," and it just really opened up everything for me to realize that I'd done all I could do. I couldn't do anymore.

When she announced to the group that she finally had resolved to find a nursing home for her mother, the other members bolstered her decision:

They were just wonderful, they really were. They were just wonderful. There were only six of us,

you get very close when there's just six. . . . We were all individual, you know, but we were all under the same stresses and I just realized that I really had done all that I could. And they could see it in me. At some of the meetings right towards the end, before I actually said, this is it and I'm going to do it, they could see that I wasn't really there, that I wasn't able to give anything, contribute anything. I felt like I'd said everything there is to say, and I'd done everything there was to do, and I was just under stress. I was deep down inside, torn with the idea that I had to place her and I didn't know how they would take it either, it was like going to confession. But they were wonderful, they were just wonderful.

Because all the members shared her experiences, she invested them with authority and attached enormous significance to their judgment.

This study was biased toward support group participants. Caregivers who were uncomfortable disclosing personal information to strangers or lacked the time to meet regularly thus were underrepresented. Nevertheless, two women had attended caregiving groups just once or twice before concluding that this activity was not for them. Even some who remained members over a substantial period had serious reservations about their usefulness. A few women found fault with the particular groups they attended. One complained that her group was too large to allow each member to speak at every meeting; she often found herself overlooked and thus left feeling even lonelier than before. Two women disapproved of the way other participants treated their relatives; because support groups depend on a basic level of trust, women who judged other members harshly could derive little from the exchange. Others resented spending their few spare hours discussing their parents and learning how to cope better. And two women criticized the entire enterprise. As one exclaimed, "The bottom line is that nobody can help you except yourself." She had joined the group at the behest of her physician but remained a reluctant participant. She felt demeaned by asking others for support and had little faith in her ability to either understand or alleviate her burdens.

Conclusion

This study raises a number of issues that must be explored further before we can understand how social relationships affect the experiences of women caring for frail elderly parents. Previous studies, using quantitative methods, have asserted that social support buffers caregivers from stress. This study suggests that such a conclusion may well be premature. Certainly, caring for elderly parents encroached on various aspects of the lives of the women I interviewed and produced serious emotional difficulties. Nevertheless, it also was a profound human experience which could not be neatly subsumed under the terms stress and burden. These caregivers wanted members of their social networks to affirm the value of their endeavor, not just help them deal with the problems it provoked. Moreover, as other researchers have noted, social support is not a unidimensional entity and therefore is difficult to scale. Then, too, the very name of the concept—support—and the language in which it is commonly described—warmth, affection, solicitude—conceal its inherent contradictions. The women in this study indicated that family and friends could exacerbate distress as well as alleviate it. Some women, for example noted that their husbands resented the time they devoted to caregiving and their emotional investment in it. Children were an important source of "contagion stress" for many women. Renewed contact with brothers and sisters frequently reignited sibling rivalries. Friends who denied

the significance of caregiving and siblings who criticized the type of care that was rendered also undermined the women I interviewed.

These women not only defined social support in diverse and contradictory ways but noted that a variety of factors inhibited them from enlisting greater help: they believed it was improper to rely on others, they thought their friendships were too fragile to withstand repeated requests for assistance, and they lacked the time to visit with friends or attend support groups regularly. Above all, concern for the well-being of others compelled the caregivers to submerge their own needs. Rather then impose on their husbands, they renounced spousal support and attempted to absorb the costs of caregiving themselves. Some sought to shield their children from exposure to illness and death. Women whose parents suffered from severe dementia also were motivated by respect for their parents' dignity. They wanted to preserve their children's image of the grandparents and protect their ailing parents from the scrutiny of unsympathetic outsiders. Future research should explore the extent to which these factors are unique to women.

Despite various obstacles, many women did receive critical help. We have seen that they obtained advice about decisions, information that permitted them to plan ahead, assistance with concrete chores, linkages to community resources, and companionship. Unfortunately, the women spoke most readily about the assistance they received in confronting the practical difficulties of caregiving. They were less forthcoming about the extent to which social relationships enabled them to deal more effectively with the interpersonal and intrapsychic demands. To what extent did social ties bolster the caregivers' sense of personal integrity? Did husbands, children, and friends prevent them from slipping back into childhood relationships with their parents? Future studies should examine this realm of social support in greater depth.

This brings us to two related problems. First, I have stated that researchers who have uncovered the complexity of social support have considerably advanced our understanding of this concept. Nevertheless, by breaking social support into its component parts, we may continue to miss its essential meaning. The social support literature continues to posit unrelated individuals who view each other as instrumental resources for discrete tasks, coming together primarily to exchange specific goods and services. By contrast, feminist writers such as Chodorow and Gilligan argue that women see themselves as embedded in social relationships and derive their sense of identity from such relationships. Studies rooted in women's experiences may have to begin with another set of questions and investigate social support very differently.

Second, although qualitative methods can help to capture the rich detail and personal meaning that quantitative methods ignore, they too may be inadequate. In order to examine social relationships, we must look at more than one individual. Most research strategies, however, focus on the individual as a unit of analysis. I want to suggest that we recognize the equal importance of the dyad or network. In short, we must continue to refine our conceptualization of social support and search for new methods with which to examine it.

NOTES

Acknowledgments: Funded by the Alzheimer's Disease and Related Disorders Association, Inc., and the UCLA Center for the Study of Women.

REFERENCES

Abel, E. K. 1987. *Love Is Not Enough: Family Care of the Frail Elderly.* Washington, D.C.: American Public Health Association.

Antonovsky, A. 1974. "Conceptual and Methodological Problems in the Study of Resistance Resources and Stressful Life Events," in *Stressful Life Events: Their Nature and Effects.* eds. B. S. Dohrenwend and B. P. Dohrenwend, pp. 245–258. New York: Wiley.

——. 1979. *Health, Stress and Coping.* San Francisco: Jossey-Bass.

Belle, D. 1982. "Social Ties and Social Support," pp. 133–143 in *Lives in Stress,* edited by D. Belle. Newbury Park: Sage Publications.

——. 1987. "Gender Differences in the Social Moderators of Stress." Pp. 257–277 in *Gender and Stress,* edited by R. C. Barnett, L. Biener and G. K. Baruch. New York: Free Press.

Brody, E. M. 1981. " 'Women in the Middle' and Family Help to Older People." *Gerontologist* 21:471–80.

Cancian, F. M. 1987. *Love in America: Gender and Self-Development.* Cambridge: Cambridge University Press.

Cantor, M. H. 1983. "Strain Among Caregivers: A Study of Experience in the United States." *Gerontologist* 23:597–603.

Caplan, G. 1974. *Support Systems and Community Mental Health.* New York: Behavioral Publications.

Cassell, J. 1976. "The Contribution of the Social Environment to Host Resistance." *American Journal of Epidemiology* 104:107–22.

Chodorow, N. 1978. *The Reproduction of Mothering.* Berkeley: University of California Press.

Cobb, S. 1976. "Social Support as a Moderator of Life Stress." *Psychosomatic Medicine* 38:300–314.

Community Council of Greater New York. 1978. *Dependency in the Elderly of New York City.* New York.

Comptroller General of the United States. 1977. *The Well-Being of Older People in Cleveland, Ohio.* Washington, D.C.: General Accounting Office.

Dunkel-Schetter, C., and C. B. Wortman. 1982. "The Interpersonal Dynamics of Cancer: Problems of Social Relationships and Their Impact on the Patient." Pp. 69–100 in *Interpersonal Issues in Health Care* edited by H. S. Friedman and M. R. DiMatteo. New York: Academic Press.

Eckenrode, J., and S. Gore. 1981. "Stressful Events and Social Supports: The Significance of Context." Pp. 43–68 in *Social Networks and Social Support,* edited by B. H. Gottlieb. Newbury Park: Sage Publications.

Fitting, M., and P. Rabins. 1985. "Men and Women: Do They Care Differently?" *Generations* 10:23–26.

George, L. K., and L. P. Gwyther. 1984. "The Dynamics of Caregiver Burden: Changes in Caregiver Well-Being over Time." Paper presented at the 34th Annual Scientific Meeting of the Gerontological Society of America, San Antonio, TX.

———. 1986. "Caregiver Well-Being: A Multidimensional Examination of Family Caregivers of Demented Adults." *Gerontologist* 26:253–259.

Gilligan, C. 1983. *In a Different Voice: Psychological Theory and Women's Development.* Cambridge, Mass: Harvard University Press.

Glaser, B. C., and A. L. Strauss. 1967. *The Discovery of Grounded Theory: Strategies for Qualitative Research.* Chicago: Aldine.

Gubrium, J. F. 1988. "Family Responsibility and Caregiving in the Qualitative Analysis of the Alzheimer's Disease Experience." *Journal of Marriage and the Family* 50:197–207.

Hagestad, G. O. 1986. "The Family: Women and Grandparents as Kin-Keepers." Pp. 141–160 in *Our Changing Society: Paradox and Promise,* edited by A. Pifer and L. Bronte, N.Y.: W. W. Norton.

Hare-Musten, R. T. and J. Marecek. 1986. "Autonomy and Gender: Some Questions for Therapists." *Psychotherapy* 23:205–212.

Helmrath, T. H., and E. M. Steinitz. 1978. "Death of an Infant: Parental Grieving and the Failure of Social Support." *Journal of Family Practice* 6:785–90.

Hooyman, N. R., and R. Ryan. 1985. "Women as Caregivers of the Elderly: Catch 22 Dilemmas." Unpublished paper.

Horowitz, A. 1985a. "Sons and Daughters as Caregivers to Older Persons: Differences in Role Performance and Consequences" *Gerontologist* 25: 612–617.

———. 1985b. "Family Caregiving to the Frail Elderly," *Annual Review of Gerontology and Geriatrics:* 194–246.

House, J. S. 1981. *Work, Stress, and Social Support.* Reading, Mass.: Addison-Wesley.

Johnson, C. L., and D. J. Catalano. 1983. "A Longitudinal Study of Family Supports to Impaired Elderly." *Gerontologist* 23:612–628.

Kessler, R. C., and J. D. McLeod. 1984. "Sex Differences in Vulnerability to Undesirable Life Events. *American Sociological Review* 49:620–631.

Kivett, V. R. 1985. "Consanguinity and Kin Level: The Relative Importance to the Helping Networks of Older Adults." *Gerontologist* 40:228–234.

Kleban, M. H., E. M. Brody, C. B. Schoonover, and C. Hoffman. 1986. "Sons'-in-Law Perceptions of Parent Care," Paper presented at the 39th Annual Scientific Meeting of the Gerontological Society of America, Chicago.

Morycz, R. K. 1985. "Caregiving Strain and the Desire to Institutionalize Family Members with Alzheimer's Disease." *Research on Aging* 7:329–361.

Pearlin, L. I., and C. S. Aneshensel. 1986. "Coping and Social Supports: Their Functions and Applications." Pp. 417–438 in *Applications of Social Science to Clinical Medicine and Health Policy,* edited by L. H. Aiken and D. Mechanic, New Brunswick, N.J.: Rugters University Press.

Ratcliff, K. S., and J. Bogdan. 1988. "Unemployed Women: When 'Social Support' Is Not Supportive." *Social Problems* 35:54–63.

Rook, K. S. 1984. "The Negative Side of Social Intervention: The Impact of Psychological Well-Being." *Journal of Personality and Social Psychology* 45:1097–1108.

Rook, K. S., and D. Dooley. 1985. "Applying Social Support Research: Theoretical Problems and Future Directions." *Journal of Social Issues* 41:5–28.

Rubin, L. B. 1985. *Just Friends: The Role of Friendship in Our Lives.* New York: Harper & Row.

Stephens, S. A. and J. B. Christianson. 1986. *Informal Care of the Elderly.* Lexington, Mass.: Lexington Books.

Stoller, E. P. 1983. "Parental Caregiving by Adult Children." *Journal of Marriage and the Family:* 851–858.

Stone, R., G. G. Cafferata, and J. Sangl, n.d. *Caregivers of the Frail Elderly: A National Profile.* Washington, D.C.: DHHS, U.S. Public Health Service.

Taylor, S. J., and R. Bogdan. 1984. *Introduction to Qualitative Research Methods*. New York: John Wiley and Sons.

Thoits, P. A. 1982. "Conceptual, Methodological, and Theoretical Problems in Studying Social Support as a Buffer Against Life Stress." *Journal of Health and Social Behavior* 23:145–159.

Wethington, E., J. D. McLeod, and R. C. Kessler. 1987. "The Importance of Life Events for Explaining Sex Differences in Psychological Distress." Pp. 144–156 in *Gender and Stress*, edited by R. C. Barnett, L. Biener, and G. K. Baruch. New York: Free Press.

Wilkins, W. 1974. "Social Stress and Illness in Industrial Society." In *Life Stress and Illness*, edited by E. Gunderson and R. Rahe. Springfield, IL.: Charles C. Thomas.

Wolf, D. A. and B. J. Soldo. 1986. "The Households of Older Unmarried Women: Microdecision Models of Shared Living Arrangements." Paper presented at the Annual Meeting of the Population Association of America, San Francisco.

Wortman, C. B. 1984. "Social Support and the Cancer Patient: Conceptual and Methodological Issues." *Cancer* 53:2239–2360.

Zarit, S. H., K. E. Reever, and J. Bach-Peterson. 1980. "Relatives of the Impaired Elderly: Correlates of Feelings of Burden." *Gerontologist* 20:649–655.

Chapter 42

Masculinity, Caregiving, and Men's Friendship in Antebellum New England

KAREN V. HANSEN

Farmer John Plummer Foster was extensively involved in nursing his father, who lived and worked with him. In 1851, he wrote in his diary:

> Friday. Fair and cold. I was half sick with a cold, did nothing but the chores, Father was taken in the evening with a slight shock of the palsy. Saturday. Fair and cold. I helped take care of Father.

Each day thereafter Foster gave an account of the weather and the condition of his father's health. The prominence of his father's illness in the diary provides a striking sense of its centrality to John's life. Occasionally, Foster's distress erupted through his rote entries: "It is enough to make one's heart ache to be with him, and see him, when he has his spasms" (Foster Diary, February 7–13, 1851). Gradually, Foster began working again, but

From Karen V. Hansen, *A Very Social Time: Crafting Community in Antebellum New England* (Berkeley and Los Angeles: University of California Press, 1994). Reprinted by permission.

he remained deeply concerned about his father's care. His father died five months later. It is interesting to note that Foster characterized his attendance to his father's needs as "helping"—he saw himself as an assistant rather than a primary care provider. Even so, the number of men caring for other men in this period makes clear that nursing was not exclusively a female vocation.

Illnesses routinely shortened longevity and heightened infant mortality in the nineteenth century. Medicine remained an experimental rather than a scientific practice. Illnesses such as cholera and scarlet fever periodically infested communities, took many lives, and spread rapidly, their causes unknown and their contagion misunderstood. Medicine often treated patients ineffectually and disease frequently brought death. Becoming ill always foretold economic hardship in the form of lost wages or unattended farm chores.

Regardless of the conditions, the sick needed to be tended and "watched." People used whatever means were available—home remedies, herbs, bleeding, water treatments, prayers, doctor visits if the illness was severe—to try to cure their patients. Sometimes nothing could be done, leaving bedside company and hot tea the only comforts. In this context, visiting became central to the treatment of the sick person.

How people responded to the need to care for seriously ill patients, in particular, demonstrated the importance of community responsibility for the sick. When patients had to be watched around the clock, community members would rotate the responsibility. In one example, Samantha Barrett, a farmer, recorded the visitors and watchers at her side for the last twenty-one days of her life. Seventeen neighbors, friends, and kin watched her (in addition to a doctor) during that final period (Barrett diary, October–November 1830). Clearly, caring for the sick was essential to the community as well as to individual households.

Nor was it only women who considered nursing and "watching" a social obligation. While the historical literature identifies nursing as a woman's duty, evidence from my research shows that men, too, often cared for the sick. With their higher wages and greater power, men who were teachers or factory workers typically did not leave their jobs for this purpose. Male farmers and artisans, however, who had greater flexibility in work routines, did take time off to care for sick relatives and friends. In this and other ways, men also participated in the ongoing enterprise of "social work," the web of activities undertaken to activate and sustain social ties.[1] They were part of a more elastic definition of masculinity that embraced male friendship and endorsed caregiving by whomever was available to provide it.

Perhaps unsurprisingly, men's nursing focused almost exclusively on other men and boys—their fathers, male friends, and sons. J.

Foster Beal wrote to Brigham Nims in 1834, indicating the importance of caregiving in their friendship.

> Well Brig:
>
> I suppose you have got to be a school master, since you was in Boston, you need not be so stuck up (as jock Downing says) because you are tucked down in the least post of Nelson, I have been there myself, I guess you have forgot all about you being at Boston last Sept. when you was so sick, and I took care of you, doctored you up, even took you in the bed with myself; you will not do as much, as, to write me. (Correspondence, December 17, 1834)

Sharing a bed in nineteenth-century Boston was not uncommon; with the lack of space in most homes, visitors frequently shared beds with their hosts. What is striking in the above passage, however, is the tender image of Beal nursing Nims. We can imagine Beal sitting beside the bed, mopping Nims's brow, feeding him, and perhaps reading aloud to pass the time. The concept of nursing, historically a female vocation, practiced by Beal challenges our conception of men's relations with one another and of the acceptable boundaries of male behavior in the nineteenth century.

The widespread conformity to the social custom of same-sex caregiving for men reflected a deep-rooted taboo against cross-gender touching and a concern for bodily modesty. The healing arts had long been a primarily female enterprise; and new nineteenth-century concerns about female chastity placed male-female physical intimacy in a particularly delicate situation. The principal exception to same-sex nursing was that married men cared for their ill wives. For example, in August 1854, Sarah Holmes Clark wrote to her friend about the fine nursing skills of her husband, Gilman Holmes. Given her current state of health, she insisted that she could not possibly go north and leave his healing hands.

Gilman has spoiled me since I have been sick so much. I cannot do without him for a nurse when my health is so poor. I depend on him as a child relies on its mother. I believe that no one could nurse me so well as he does, because no one loves me as well as he does. Gilman is the best husband in the world. If you do not believe it come and live with us and judge for yourself. (Holmes Family Papers)

In a second notable exception, two former slaves, James Mars and William Grimes, wrote in their respective autobiographies of their employment and skill in taking care of the sick. James Mars was called to the bedside of his former owner's unmarried adult daughter.

As I had been accustomed to take care of the sick, she asked me to stop with her that night. I did so, and went to my work in the morning. . . . She asked what I thought of her; I told her I feared she would never be any better. She then asked me to stay with her if she did not get any better, while she lived. I told her I would. A cousin of hers, a young lady, was there, and we took care of her for four weeks. (Mars [1864] 1971, 53)

Mars had a long-term acquaintance with this young woman, and she valued the skills and comfort he brought to her bedside. His skin color mitigated the taboo of male nurse to a female patient; race overrode gender concerns. Had Mars not been black, it is highly unlikely that he would have been asked or allowed to care for this sick woman. Because of his subordinate status as a black man however—once slave, now free, but still not a full citizen—he did not pose a sexual threat.[2]

Same-sex nursing was not the only gendered dimension of the caretaking division of labor. Men stayed in their own households most of the time, while women acted as a mobile caretaking force, at times traveling long distances to care for sick relatives and friends and often staying with them. But men typically shouldered the responsibility of going to

get the doctor, nurse, neighbor woman, or midwife. To understand the role of male caregiving, it is important to situate men and women in the context of nineteenth-century notions of masculinity.

Manhood in Historical Context

Industrial development, urbanization, and western expansion began to reorder American society in the pre–Civil War period and resulted in massive shifts in population, as marginal farm workers sought jobs in newly established shoe or textile factories, moved to the city to learn a trade, or migrated west to the ever-expanding frontier to homestead cheap land or to pan for gold. The majority of American citizens lived in rural areas until 1920, but industrialization in particular had a tremendous impact on the organization of social and economic life. It resulted in the movement of production out of the household, theoretically creating a separation between "home life" and "work life." Although most Americans lived in rural areas throughout the nineteenth century (U.S. Bureau of the Census 1975), it was not uncommon for men and women to go back and forth between factory and farm employment and city and country living arrangements.

To what extent either the city or the farm produced a strict separation of work and home is debatable. One school of thought claims that the division of labor into paid production and unpaid reproduction created separate physical, emotional, and cultural spheres of influence and activity for men and women (Degler 1980). The assumption is that men had little to do with the domestic sphere and its activities. The prescriptive cultural manifestation of the separation of home and paid work was the "cult of true womanhood," propagated by middle-class reformers such as

Catherine Beecher (Sklar 1973). The burgeoning domestic advice and religious literature of the 1830s and 1840s encouraged wives and mothers to be "true women." That is, they should guard their sphere and rightful place—the home—with all the virtues imbued in a proper wife and mother: "piety, purity, submissiveness and domesticity" (Welter 1966, 152). While the ideology had a solid audience within the urban middle class, the extent to which it resonated with working-class, poor, and rural women is unclear. The domestic ideology failed to influence some people for economic, cultural, and geographic reasons. This idea was particularly problematic for young farm girls because it was they who populated the first textile factories in New England. They, not their fathers, were the ones to leave the domestic sphere for factory work. At the same time, the message capitalized on the widespread fear and insecurity that resulted from geographic mobility and the shifting modes of production that marginalized large numbers of women workers (Ryan 1981, 118).

Many feminists accept the assumption of the nineteenth-century emergence of separate spheres for men and women (Cott 1977; Halttunen 1982; Smith-Rosenberg 1986). Carroll Smith-Rosenberg (1986), for example, claims that this staunch geographic separation of home and workplace, coupled with a deep cultural division between men and women, led middle-class women to develop emotional relationships with those whom they shared their everyday lives and cares: other women.

What did this separate life mean for men? Men were to be "the movers, the doers, the actors," those who provided for and protected the family (Welter 1966, 159). Ronald Byars (1979, 197), in his study of self-made men, describes the emergent middle-class man as someone who exhibited ambition, courage, and strength, and "who was almost ascetically devoted to the work-related virtues." Nevertheless, the "virtue" required concerted effort because the new man was vulnerable to the lure of vice and evil, particularly under the influence of women. E. Anthony Rotundo (1989, 18) points to the critical transition from youthfulness to middle-class manhood, which involves a strong commitment to a career, marriage, and a house of one's own: "The identity of a middle-class man was founded on independent action, cool detachment, and sober responsibility." And, at least in the advice manuals that Byars (1979, 36, 143–44) studies, "There was a persistent sense that home was an appendage to a man's life. It did not contribute much to his sense of personal identity." Some went so far as to reject those aspects of life that held feminine associations—religion, culture, the home, and women themselves.

Portraits of American working men in the nineteenth century are more rare, but those that do exist attend less frequently to issues of masculinity and men's identity. Peter Stearns (1979) characterizes working-class men as physical, enamored of authority, and somewhat rigid. And John Faragher (1979) describes frontier men as strong, self-indulgent, adventurous, and competitive. Although historical time and geographic location shape these portraits, their development is rooted in laboring activities (e.g., Baron 1989). More positive images have been attributed to the artisan, the "model citizen of the republic" (Clawson 1989, 153), whose power was based on his skilled work and economic self-sufficiency. For men involved in trade associations, masculinity was deeply tied to their work. It was in part a reflection of craft pride, which symbolized independence and adulthood (Wilentz 1984). Even when women entered the paid labor force, masculine identity continued to be defined largely by artisanal identity because, Mary Ann Clawson notes

(1989, 153–154), "apprenticeship was not only an institution for the inculcation and acquisition of craft knowledge; it was a vehicle of masculine socialization."

Friendship and Homoeroticism

Did separate spheres create separate emotional worlds for men and for women? Smith-Rosenberg asserts that nineteenth-century middle-class women had homosocial work lives and emotional circles. Thomas Dublin's (1979) study of New England mill workers before the Civil War demonstrates that women who left the farm to work in factories also existed largely in female worlds because textile factories and boarding houses were segregated by gender.

Smith-Rosenberg argues that explicitly loving relationships between women, as expressed in a literary form, were seen as normal, natural, and acceptable by their families, neighbors, and society. Smith-Rosenberg's research has sparked a debate, however, about the degree to which women's affection for one another expressed the cultural romanticism dominant in the early nineteenth century, reflected a unique women's culture, or revealed a lesbian sexual practice. She recommends that rather than try to label the behavior normal or deviant, we should consider it a part of a sexual continuum ranging from homosexual to heterosexual.

Clawson (1989) and others argue that, like women, men encountered and created opportunities to socialize independent of women, which enabled them to develop relationships with one another, some of them intimate. They point to the all-male worlds of battlefields, the workplace, the wild western frontier and fraternal societies as environments in which men congregated and discovered friendship and the secrets of same-gender intimacy.

Parallel to the experience of women, men's distinct social world allowed them to develop their own culture and, as Elizabeth Pleck and Joseph Pleck (1980, 13) suggest, "encouraged manly intimacy and affection, a love between equals, which was often lacking in sentiments toward the other sex." They point to the men-only spaces that nurtured male culture in the colonial and antebellum periods—lodges, clubs, militias, fire departments, taverns, and voluntary associations. All of these institutions, however, would have encouraged verbal rather than written affection, hence leaving little documentation of the interpersonal dimension of their relationships behind.

The subject of men's friendships with men have only recently been investigated from a feminist perspective. The research on contemporary society shows that male relationships are less personal and less intimate than female ones (Pleck 1975; Rubin 1985; Sherrod 1987). Although men and women have about the same number of friends, women are more self-disclosing and seek friends who feel the same way, while men are more interested in doing things and want companionship and commitment. Drury Sherrod (1987) finds that men reveal more to their female friends than to their male friends. Joseph Pleck (1975) and Lillian Rubin (1985) claim that in contemporary society men's expectations for emotional intimacy focus on women; men need women for emotional expression. Do contemporary forms of male friendship extend back in time? Is this a common male behavior, or is it a phenomenon unique to late-twentieth-century men?

John Crowley (1987) makes a convincing argument that nineteenth-century culture was homosocial and had erotic undercurrents. It associated male homosociality with childishness and powerlessness, but it was not a cause for shame or scorn, and it certainly did not provoke the virulent homophobia evident in the twentieth century. In the mid-nineteenth century, Thoreau wrote that friendship between those of the same sex was easier. In a middle-class world of separate spheres where men had little knowledge of women this seems plausible. Conclusive evidence reveals that in the nineteenth century elite men had romantic correspondences with other men.

In searching archives for evidence of gay relationships throughout history, Jonathan Katz (1976) unearthed a variety of romantic letters written by male political and literary figures to other men. Although the title and content of his book frame the letters as homoerotic, like Smith-Rosenberg, Katz rejects the impulse to label the relationships of these letter writers as homosexual. The term "homosexual," with its emphasis on same-sex genital contact directed toward orgasm, is particularly inadequate as a means of encompassing and understanding the historical variety of same-sex relations. He writes that loving letters between men present the dilemma of interpreting to what extent the writer's epistolary language is a formal literary convention and to what extent it is an honest expression of emotion, referring to some deeply felt, perhaps physical, relation. Katz says that the mere existence of these letters, so causally kept, "suggests more lenient social attitudes toward male-male intimacy" than what we would expect of late-eighteenth or nineteenth-century society or what we find today (Katz 1976, 451). Other historians' assessments of the material range from a conviction that the language reflects only a spiritual love (Richards 1987) to a skeptical ambivalence about the innocence of the erotic messages (D'Emilio and Freedman 1988). There is great difficulty in studying same-sex relationships in our heterosexist and homophobic society because of the tendency to distort innocent relations, to read consummated sexual activity into passionate innuendoes, and because of an inability to put aside twentieth-century biases in order to be sensitive to a pre-Freudian epoch. For these reasons the notion of a sexual continuum is most useful in capturing historical nuance.

Rotundo's (1989) research on nineteenth-century middle-class male friendships shows that men formed friendships throughout their lives but established intimate relationships with other men virtually only in the period between boyhood and manhood. He defines intimacy as "a sharing of innermost thoughts and secret emotions" (Rotundo 1989, 1). During their youth, he asserts, men broke from their families psychologically and sought to establish themselves in the world. It was "a time when a young male had reached physical maturity but had not yet established the two identifying marks of middle-class manhood—a career and marriage" (Rotundo 1989, 13). The casual relationships young men acquired provided companionship for socializing, working, drinking, playing sports, and going to events, but their intimate relationships included sharing secrets and developing serious attachments, which may or may not have included physical intimacy.

Rotundo finds that physical expressions of affection—embracing, sharing a bed—carried no real stigma for men in the nineteenth century and in fact were culturally supported. Rotundo gives an example from the diary of James Blake about Wyck Vanderhoef: "We retired early, but long was the time before our eyes were closed in slumber, for this was the last night we shall be together for the present, and our hearts were full of that true friendship which we could not find utterance by words, we laid our heads upon each other's bosom and wept, it may be unmanly to weep, but I care not, the spirit was touched" (1989, 5). As Rotundo notes, it was not the physical closeness that Blake felt embarrassed about but the fact that he wept.

My own research also shows that emotional self-control was an indication of manhood for working men in the nineteenth century. When Francis Bennett, Jr., son of a fisherman, left his Gloucester, Massachusetts, home in 1854 to work as a clerk in Boston, he wrote in his diary on August 28 of that year: "I found it pretty hard to keep from crying on leaving the home of my childhood. But I had resolved to be as manly as possible about it. Mother would not say goodbye" (Bennett diary).

Rotundo argues that in the nineteenth century manhood was not threatened by physical intimacy because the word "homosexual" was not in the vocabulary of the period. Individuals did not self-consciously worry about their behavior. They did not fear same-sex relationships. In addition, the culture as a whole did not stigmatize the behavior. "The modern terms homosexuality and heterosexuality do not apply to an era that had not yet articulated these distinctions" (D'Emilio and Freedman 1988, 121; see also Katz 1990). Again, the concept of a sexual continuum, ranging from verbal endearment to genital play or intercourse, better explains same-gender friendships than discrete categories.

Rotundo finds middle-class men's friendships similar to the female relationships Smith-Rosenberg describes in their social acceptability, daily content, and physical manifestations. The primary difference he observes is that the male relationships were bound by the life cycle; they did not continue into married life, as did their female equivalents. As I argue elsewhere, there is evidence that what was true of the elite was also true for working men (Hansen 1992, 1994).

Working Men's Friendships

Visiting and Sociability

Working men were firmly ensconced in the prevalent nineteenth-century social ritual of visiting acquaintances, friends, neighbors, and relatives. Men observed visiting conventions (who is supposed to call on whom, how often, and when) and tended to the labor-intensive obligations that they sometimes incurred. Visits were often occasions for the exchange of labor and services—such as making quilts, brewing cider, building barns, or caring for those who were sick—central to rural economic life. One tenant farmer in central Massachusetts, Leonard Stockwell, a failure in most of his ventures, felt pride at being a good host. "He was decidedly a home man and liked to have everything comfortable and make those welcome who came to visit him" (Stockwell memorial ca. 1880, 37). And he found it difficult to forgo visits when he was ill. In sum, men were active as visitors and hosts, laborers and nurses—all central roles in making social ties and building communities in this period. The linchpin of this culture of exchange, reciprocity, and mutual aid was friendship.

Friendship

A case study illuminates the possibilities and range of emotional expression open to nineteenth-century men who worked at different kinds of manual labor. Brigham Nims, the recipient of the letter previously cited, broke many stereotypes of nineteenth-century manhood. He was born in 1811 to farmers Matthew and Lucy Nims, lived and died on the family homestead, and worked seasonally as a teacher over a period of nineteen years. As with most teachers in the 1830s and 1840s, he had other jobs as well because he taught only sixteen weeks of the year and was paid low wages. To supplement his income he was intermittently employed as a clerk in his brother Reuel's store, as an itinerant tailor (living at people's homes while he sewed for them), as a blacksmith and carpenter, as a stone splitter in the farm's rock quarry, as a farm day laborer, and, most important, as a farmer.

When Nims was twenty, he made the acquaintance of Joseph Foster Beal, who became a close confidant. Their friendship may have begun while they both worked in a box factory in Boston or while enmeshed in their overlapping social worlds in Cheshire County, New Hampshire. The few clues to the extent of their relationship exist only in a small collection of letters from Beal to Nims from 1832 to 1834. The letters reveal a vital, loving friendship between the two, which sustained despite geographic distance (Nims was teaching in Nelson and Roxbury, New Hampshire, and Beal was based in Boston) but probably also because of their shared New Hampshire heritage. It is not clear how long the friendship continued. Beal married in 1838, and it appears that he died before 1849.

The earliest letter reveals a rowdy joyfulness in their relationship, with a decidedly masculine physical component.

> Dear friend Sir B Boston March 21st 1832
>
> I received your letter by G Tuffs which I read with the greatest pleasure I rejoice to hear that you are in good health, and the rest of your friends I want to see you very much indeed to have a good box with you which you said you should like to have with me I think if you are as fat as I be we should puff and blow. (Nims correspondence)

In contrast to other men's romantic letters, such as that between Blake and Vanderhoef (see Rotundo 1989), the letter from Beal to Nims does not speak of love. If we compare their exchange to those between middle-class women, we find that theirs is more jovial and less romantic and flowery. Beal's letter reflects a casual friendliness and conveys a sense of delight in the friendship. His teasing seems to ignore Nims's self-portrait—in a letter he wrote to his friend Gould on August 1, 1853—as a man with whom others have difficulty getting along: "I know that my owne temper

and disposition is not so easily governed as I would wish" (Nims correspondence). The physicality embodied in Beal's March letter to Nims—organized play, rambunctiousness, and competitiveness—reflects male expressions of affection (and sometimes attraction).

Their letters were not a literary exercise, as letters often were for elite men who cleverly hinted at romance. They were written by men who were teachers, farmers, and box factory hands, frequently punctuated with misspellings and grammatical errors. And their purpose was not about work but about all matters related to their friendship and community of shared acquaintances. The letters contained a broad range of information and moods. Most included some gossip—news of people, events, greetings from others who knew Nims.

Some passages in Beal's letters read more in the romantic tradition of the 1830s and are similar to the letters exchanged between women who were intimates.

> can not forget those happy hours [th]at we spent at G. Newcombs and the evening walks; but we are deprived of that privilege now we are separated for a time we cannot tell how long perhaps before our eyes behold each other in this world. (Nims correspondence)

It is important to note that, despite what might appear today as deviant behavior, historical records indicate that Nims was not treated as an outcast in his day. There is nothing in any of Nims's correspondence to indicate that Beal or Nims felt secretive or uncomfortable about their relationship or behavior. Nims was a respected member of the community, very active in civic affairs. Over the course of his life he was a town selectman, a representative to the general court, the town treasurer, a member of the school committee, and school superintendent. To put his life in perspective, however, his prominence was limited to a remote geographic area with a population of less than three hundred. Respected citizenship in Roxbury, New Hampshire, meant something quite different than it did in proper Boston. Nims's obituary referred to him as "a man of prominence." "He was interested in every good work, was a man of integrity and industry, possessed a vigorous mind and body, and was strong in his convictions. In politics he was a staunch Republican" (Obituary 1893).

Nevertheless, the Beal-Nims correspondence was the only collection I found in my search for letters between farmers, artisans, and working-class men who were not relatives. The dearth of documents can be interpreted several ways. One interpretation is that the scarcity of such letters reflects the rarity of their friendship. Another is that although working-class men had friendships and although literacy was high for native-born Yankee men, they may have had little occasion to write to one another. Yet another reason researchers do not often find such letters is that the biases inherent in preserving documents of nonelites would render "pedestrian" those letters that might have existed, thus making them not worth preserving and therefore leaving few to be found today, except those between family members.

Class and Gender Implications

The character of contemporary male friendships does not simply extend backward in time. This chapter demonstrates the importance of historically situating men and the range of emotional expression available to them, while investigating the role of the overarching economic and cultural forces that shaped their social possibilities.

The small body of evidence on which this chapter is based tells us not what was typical in antebellum New England but what was possible (see Hansen 1994 for a more elaborate argument). Brigham Nims was not so different from his contemporaries in his work history, his family life, and his place within his community. And although we cannot generalize the experience of Brigham Nims, we can assess reactions to his behavior. He was not regarded as deviant; he was a respected member of his village and region. Neither Nims nor Beal displays any discomfort with their relationship, nor do they express any need for secrecy regarding their claims of affection. This absence of negative reaction suggests that it was acceptable for men to reveal their feelings to one another and to write about them. It also indicates that, unlike in the twentieth century, the suppression of emotion was not required in order to demonstrate manliness. In a similar vein, men took care of sick friends and relatives (largely male). Nonetheless, their behavior breaks the stereotype we hold of nursing as a female task. This chapter raises many more questions than it answers, and in doing so it suggests strategic areas for future research.

The study of historical variation in intimate behavior reveals dramatic fluctuations over the past two centuries. An important message emerges: gender arrangements change historically through the influence of culture, human practices and attitudes, and economic relations. Evidence from this study reveals that the capacity for intimacy in the nineteenth century was not determined by gender or by class. In a culture that broadly defined masculinity and femininity and that accepted fluidity between the categories, rather than imposing rigid boundaries between them, people engaged in an expansive range of feeling, expression, and behavior.

NOTES

1. What I am calling "social work" parallels and extends the concept of "kin-work" used by Micaela di Leonardo (Chapter 31, this volume) to denote

those numerous activities (disproportionately attended to by women) that keep networks of kin in touch with one another—phone calls, cards, letters, holiday celebrations, and the like.

2. The other exceptions to those who were allowed cross-gender contact were doctors and ministers. By professional license, doctors were granted access to women's bedsides, but not without complications (see, for example, Ehrenreich and English 1979). Ministers were also acceptable watchers, visitors, or nurses; indeed, they were expected to call on the sick, regardless of gender.

REFERENCES

Unpublished Sources

Barrett, Samantha. Diary, 1815–1830. Connecticut Historical Society, Hartford, Conn.

Bennett, Francis, Jr. Diary, 1852–1854. American Antiquarian Society, Worcester, Mass.

Clark, Sarah Holmes. *See* Holmes Family Papers.

Foster, John Plummer. Diary, 1848–1888. James Duncan Phillips Library, Peabody and Essex Museum, Salem, Mass.

Holmes Family Papers, Correspondence, 1840–1860. Massachusetts Historical Society, Boston, Mass.

Nims, Brigham. Correspondence, 1830–1860. Roxbury Town Records, New Hampshire State Archives, Concord, N.H., and Historical Society of Cheshire County, Keene, N.H.

Stockwell, Leonard M. Memorial, ca. 1880, American Antiquarian Society, Worcester, Mass.

Published Sources

Baron, Ava. 1989. "Questions of Gender: Deskilling and Demasculinization in the U.S. Printing Industry, 1830–1915." *Gender and History* 1:178–199.

Byars, Ronald Preston. 1979. The Making of the Self-Made Man: The Development of Masculine Roles and Images in Antebellum America." Ph.D. diss. Michigan State University.

Clawson, Mary Ann. 1989. *Constructing Brotherhood: Class, Gender, and Fraternalism.* Princeton: Princeton University Press.

Cott, Nancy. 1977. *Bonds of Womanhood.* New Haven: Yale University Press.

Crowley, John W. 1987. "Howells, Stoddard, and Male Homosocial Attachment in Victorian America." In *The Making of Masculinities: The New Men's Studies,* edited by Harry Brod, 301–24. Boston: Allen & Unwin.

Degler, Carl N. 1980. *At Odds: Women and the Family in America from the Revolution to the Present.* New York: Oxford University Press.

D'Emilio, John, and Estelle B. Freedman. 1988. *Intimate Matters: A History of Sexuality in America.* New York: Harper & Row.

Dublin, Thomas. 1979. *Women at Work: The Transformation of Work and Community in Lowell, Massachusetts, 1826–1860.* New York: Columbia University Press.

Ehrenreich, Barbara, and Deirdre English. 1979. *For Her Own Good: 150 Years of the Experts' Advice to Women.* Garden City, N.Y.: Anchor.

Faragher, John Mack. 1979. *Women and Men on the Overland Trail.* New Haven: Yale University Press.

Halttunen, Karen. 1982. *Confidence Men and Painted Women: A Study of Middle-Class Culture in America, 1830–1870.* New Haven: Yale University Press.

Hansen, Karen V. 1994. *A Very Social Time: Crafting Community in Antebellum New England.* Berkeley and Los Angeles: University of California Press.

———. 1992. " 'Our Eyes Behold Each Other': Masculinity and Intimate Friendship in Antebellum New England," in *Men's Friendships,* edited by Peter Nardi, 35–58. Newbury Park, Calif.: Sage.

Katz, Jonathan Ned. 1976. *Gay American History: Lesbians and Gay Men in the U.S.A.* New York: Harper & Row.

———. "The Invention of Heterosexuality." *Socialist Review* 20:7–34.

Mars, James. [1864] 1971. "Life of James Mars, a Slave Born and Sold in Connecticut." In *Five Black Lives: The Autobiographies of Venture Smith, James Mars, William Grimes, The Rev. G. W. Offley, and James L. Smith,* edited by Arna Bontemps, 35–58. Reprint. Middletown, Conn.: Wesleyan University Press.

Nims, Brigham. 1893. Obituary.

Pleck, Elizabeth H., and Joseph H. Pleck. 1980. *The American Man*. Englewood Cliffs, N.J.: Prentice-Hall.

Pleck, Joseph H. 1975. "Man to Man: Is Brotherhood Possible?" In *Old Family/New Family*, edited by Nona Glazer-Malbin, 229–244. New York: Van Nostrand.

Richards, Jeffrey. 1987. " 'Passing the Love of Women': Manly Love and Victorian Society." In *Manliness and Morality: Middle-Class Masculinity in Britain and America, 1800–1940*, edited by J. A. Mangan and James Walvin, 92–122. New York: St. Martin's Press.

Rotundo, E. Anthony. 1989. "Romantic Friendship: Male Intimacy and Middle-Class Youth in the Northern United States, 1800–1900." *Journal of Social History* 23, no. 1 (Fall): 1–25.

Rubin, Lillian B. 1985. *Just Friends: The Role of Friendship in Our Lives*. New York: Harper & Row.

Ryan, Mary P. 1981. *Cradle of the Middle Class: The Family in Oneida County, New York, 1790–1865*. New York: Cambridge University Press.

Sherrod, Drury. 1987. "The Bonds of Men: Problems and Possibilities in Close Male Relationships." In *The Making of Masculinities: The New Men's Studies*, edited by Harry Brod, 213–239. Boston: Allen & Unwin.

Sklar, Kathryn Kish. 1973. *Catharine Beecher: A Study in American Domesticity*. New York: W. W. Norton.

Smith-Rosenberg, Carroll. 1986. *Disorderly Conduct: Visions of Gender in Victorian America*. New York: Oxford University Press.

Stearns, Peter. 1979. *Be a Man! Males in Modern Society*. New York: Holmes and Meier.

U.S. Bureau of the Census. 1975. *Historical Statistics of the U.S. Colonial Times to 1970*. Washington, D.C.: GPO.

Welter, Barbara. 1966. "The Cult of True Womanhood: 1820–1860." *American Quarterly* 18, no. 2 (Summer): 151–174.

Wilentz, Sean. 1984. *Chants Democratic: New York City and the Rise of the American Working Class, 1788–1850*. New York: Oxford University Press.

~ *Chapter 43*

Revolutionary Parenting

BELL HOOKS

During the early stages of contemporary women's liberation movement, feminist analyses of motherhood reflected the race and class biases of participants. Some white middle-class, college-educated women argued that motherhood was a serious obstacle to women's liberation, a trap confining women to the home, keeping them tied to cleaning, cooking, and child care. Others simply identified motherhood and childrearing as the locus of women's oppression. Had black women voiced their views on motherhood, it would not have been named a serious obstacle to our freedom as women. Racism, availability of jobs, lack of skills or education and a number of other issues would have been at the top of the list—but not motherhood. Black women would not have said motherhood prevented us from entering the world of paid work because we have always worked. From slavery to the present day black

From bell hooks, *Feminist Theory: From Margin to Center* (Boston: South End Press, 1984). Reprinted with permission from the publisher, South End Press, 116 Saint Botolph Street, Boston, MA 02115.

women in the U.S. have worked outside the home, in the fields, in the factories, in the laundries, in the homes of others. That work gave meager financial compensation and often interfered with or prevented effective parenting. Historically, black women have identified work in the context of family as humanizing labor, work that affirms their identity as women, as human beings showing love and care, the very gestures of humanity white supremacist ideology claimed black people were incapable of expressing. In contrast to labor done in a caring environment inside the home, labor outside the home was most often seen as stressful, degrading, and dehumanizing.

These views on motherhood and work outside the home contrasted sharply with those expressed by white women's liberationists. Many black women were saying "we want to have more time to share with family, we want to leave the world of alienated work." Many white women's liberationists were saying "we are tired of the isolation of the home, tired of relating only to children and husband, tired of being emotionally and economically dependent; we want to be liberated to enter the world of work." (These voices were not those of working-class white women who were, like black women workers, tired of alienated labor.) The women's liberationists who wanted to enter the workforce did not see this world as a world of alienated work. They do now. In the last twenty years of feminist movement many middle-class white women have entered the wage-earning workforce and have found that working within a social context where sexism is still the norm, where there is unnecessary competition promoting envy, distrust, antagonism, and malice between individuals, makes work stressful, frustrating, and often totally unsatisfying. Concurrently, many women who like and enjoy the wage work they do feel that it takes too much of their time, leaving little space for other satisfying pursuits. While work may help women gain a degree of financial independence or even financial self-sufficiency, for most women it has not adequately fulfilled human needs. As a consequence, women's search for fulfilling labor done in an environment of care has led to reemphasizing the importance of family and the positive aspects of motherhood. Additionally, the fact that many active feminists are in their mid to late thirties, facing the biological clock, has focussed collective attention on motherhood. This renewed attention has led many women active in the feminist movement who were interested in child rearing to choose to bear children.

Although early feminists demanded respect and acknowledgement for housework and child care, they did not attribute enough significance and value to female parenting, to motherhood. It is a gesture that should have been made at the onset of feminist movement. Early feminist attacks on motherhood alienated masses of women from the movement, especially poor and/or nonwhite women, who find parenting one of the few interpersonal relationships where they are affirmed and appreciated. Unfortunately, recent positive feminist focus on motherhood draws heavily on sexist stereotypes. Motherhood is as romanticized by some feminist activists as it was by the nineteenth-century men and women who extolled the virtues of the "cult of domesticity." The one significant difference in their approach is that motherhood is no longer viewed as taking place primarily within the framework of heterosexual marriage or even heterosexual relationships. More than ever before, women who are not attached to males, who may be heterosexual or lesbian, are choosing to bear children. In spite of the difficulties of single parenting (especially economic) in this society, the focus is on "joys of motherhood," the special intimacy, closeness, and bonding purported to characterize the mother/child relationship. Books like Phyllis Chesler's *With Child: A Diary of Motherhood* rhapsodize over the pleasures and joys of childbirth and child care. Publication of more scholarly and serious works like Jessie Bernard's *The Future of Motherhood*, Elisabeth Badinter's *Mother Love*, Nancy Friday's *My Mother/My Self*, and Nancy Chodorow's *The Reproduction of Mothering* reflect growing concern with motherhood.

This resurgence of interest in motherhood has positive and negative implications for feminist movement. On the positive side there is a continual need for study and research of female parenting, which this interest promotes and encourages. In the foreword to *Of Woman Born*, Adrienne Rich states that she felt it was important to write a book on motherhood because it is "a crucial, still relatively unexplored area for feminist theory." It is also positive that women who choose to bear children need no longer fear that this choice excludes them from recognition by feminist movement, although it may still exclude them from active participation. On the negative side, romanticizing motherhood, employing the same terminology that is used by sexists to suggest that women are inherently life-affirming nurturers, feminist activists reinforce central tenets of male supremacist ideology. They imply that motherhood is a woman's truest vocation; that women who do not mother, whose lives may be focused more exclusively on a career, creative work, or political work are missing out, are doomed to live emotionally unfulfilled lives. While they do not openly attack or denigrate women who do not bear children, they (like the society as a whole) suggest that it is *more* important than women's other labor, and more rewarding. They could simply state that it *is* important and rewarding. Significantly, this perspective is often voiced by many of the white bourgeois women with successful careers who are now choosing to bear children. They seem to be saying to masses of women that careers or work can never be as important, as satisfying, as bearing children.

This is an especially dangerous line of thinking, coming at a time when teenage women who have not realized a number of goals, are bearing children in large numbers rather than postponing parenting; when masses of women are being told by the government that they are destroying family life by not assuming sexist-defined roles. Through mass media and other communication systems, women are currently inundated with material encouraging them to bear children. Newspapers carry headline stories with titles like "motherhood is making a comeback"; women's magazines are flooded with articles on the new motherhood; fashion magazines have special features on designer clothing for the pregnant woman; television talk shows do special features on career women who are now choosing to raise children. Coming at a time when women with children are more

likely to live in poverty, when the number of homeless, parentless children increases by the thousands daily, when women continue to assume sole responsibility for parenting, such propaganda undermines and threatens feminist movement.

To some extent, the romanticization of motherhood by bourgeois white women is an attempt to repair the damage done by past feminist critiques and give women who mother the respect they deserve. It should be noted that even the most outrageous of these criticisms did not compare with sexism as a source of exploitation and humiliation for mothers. Female parenting is significant and valuable work which must be recognized as such by everyone is society, including feminist activists. It should receive deserved recognition, praise, and celebration within a feminist context where there is renewed effort to rethink the nature of motherhood, to make motherhood neither a compulsory experience for women nor an exploitative or oppressive one, to make female parenting good effective parenting whether it is done exclusively by women or in conjunction with men.

In her article, "Bringing Up Baby," Mary Ellen Schoonmaker stressed the often-made point that men do not share equally in parenting:

Since the early days of ambivalence toward motherhood, the overall goal of the women's movement has been a quest for equality—to take the oppression out of mothering, to join "mothering" to "parenting," and for those who choose to have children to share parenting with men and with society in general. Looking back over the past twenty years, it seems as if these goals have been among the hardest for the women's movement to reach.

If men did equally share in parenting, it would mean trading places with women part of the time. Many men have found it easier to share power with women on the job than they have in the home. Even though millions of mothers with infants and toddlers now work outside the home, many women still do the bulk of the housework.

Men will not share equally in parenting until they are taught, ideally from childhood on, that fatherhood has the same meaning and significance as motherhood. As long as women or society as a whole see the mother/child relationship as unique and special because the female carries the child in her body and gives birth, or makes this biological experience synonymous with women having a closer, more significant bond to children than the male parent, responsibility for child care and childrearing will continue to be primarily women's work. Even the childless woman is considered more suited to raise children than the male parent because she is seen as an inherently caring nurturer. The biological experience of pregnancy and childbirth, whether painful or joyful, should not be equated with the idea that women's parenting is necessarily superior to men's.

Dictionary definitions of the word "father" relate its meaning to accepting responsibility, with no mention of words like tenderness and affection, yet these words are used to define what the word mother means. By placing sole responsibility for nurturing onto women, that is to say, for satisfying the emotional and material needs of children, society reinforces the notion that to mother is more important than to father. Structured into the definitions and the very usage of the terms father and mother is the sense that these two words refer to two distinctly different experiences. Women and men must define the work of fathering and mothering in the same way if males and females are to accept equal responsibility in parenting. Even feminist theorists who have emphasized the need for men to share equally in child rearing are reluctant to cease attaching special value to mothering.

This illustrates feminists' willingness to glorify the physiological experience of motherhood as well as unwillingness to concede motherhood as an arena of social life in which women can exert power and control.

Women and society as a whole often consider the father who does equal parenting unique and special rather than as representative of what should be the norm. Such a man may even be seen as assuming a "maternal" role. Describing men who parent in her work *Mother Love*, Elisabeth Badinter comments:

> Under the pressure exerted by women, the new father mothers equally and in the traditional mother's image. He creeps in, like another mother, between the mother and the child, who experiences almost indiscriminately as intimate a contact with the father as with the mother. We have only to notice the increasingly numerous photographs in magazines showing fathers pressing newborns against their bare chests. Their faces reflect a completely motherly tenderness that shocks no one. After centuries of the father's authority or absence, it seems that a new concept has come into existence—father love, the exact equivalent of mother love. While it is obvious that women who parent would necessarily be the models men would strive to emulate, (since women have been doing effective parenting for many more years) these men are becoming parents, effective fathers. They are not becoming mothers.

Another example of this tendency occurs at the end of Sara Ruddick's essay "Maternal Thinking." She envisions a time in which men will share equally in child rearing and writes:

> On that day there will be no more "fathers," no more people of either sex who have power over their children's lives and moral authority in their children's worlds, though they do the work of attentive love. There will be mothers of both sexes who live out a transformed maternal thought in communities that share parental care—practically, emotionally, economically, and socially. Such communities will have

learned from their mothers how to value children's lives.

In this paragraph, as in the entire essay, Ruddick romanticizes the idea of the "maternal" and places emphasis on men becoming maternal, a vision which seems shortsighted. Because the word "maternal" is associated with the behavior of women, men will not identify with it even though they may be behaving in ways that have traditionally been seen as "feminine." Wishful thinking will not alter the concept of the maternal in our society. Rather than changing it, the word "paternal" should share the same meaning. Telling a boy acting out the role of caring parent with his dolls that he is being maternal will not change the idea that women are better suited to parenting; it will reinforce it. Saying to a boy that he is behaving like a good father (in the way that girls are told that they are good mothers when they show attention and care to dolls) would teach him a vision of effective parenting, of fatherhood, that is the same as motherhood.

Seeing men who do effective parenting as "maternal" reinforces the stereotypical sexist notion that women are inherently better suited to parent, that men who parent in the same way as women are imitating the real thing rather than acting as a parent should act. There should be a concept of effective parenting that makes no distinction between maternal and paternal care. The model of effective parenting that includes the kind of attentive love Ruddick describes has been applied only to women and has prevented fathers from learning how to parent. They are allowed to conceive of the father's role solely in terms of exercising authority and providing for material needs. They are taught to think of it as a role secondary to the mother's. Until males are taught how to parent using the same model of effective parenting that has been taught to women, they will not partici-

pate equally in child care. They will even feel that they should not participate because they have been taught to think they are inadequate or ineffective child rearers.

Men are socialized to avoid assuming responsibility for child rearing and that avoidance is supported by women who believe that motherhood is a sphere of power they would lose if men participated equally in parenting. Many of these women do not wish to share parenting equally with men. In feminist circles it is often forgotten that masses of women in the United States still believe that men cannot parent effectively and should not even attempt to parent. Until these women understand that men should and can do primary parenting, they will not expect the men in their lives to share equally in child rearing. Even when they do, it is unlikely that men will respond with enthusiasm. People need to know the negative impact that male non-participation in child rearing has on family relationships and child development.

Feminist efforts to point out to men what they lose when they do not participate in parenting tend to be directed at the bourgeois classes. Little is done to discuss nonsexist parenting or male parenting with poor and working-class women and men. In fact, the kind of maternal care Ruddick evokes in her essay, with its tremendous emphasis on attention given children by parents, especially mothers, is a form of parental care that is difficult for many working-class parents to offer when they return home from work tired and exhausted. It is increasingly difficult for women and men in families struggling to survive economically to give special attention to parenting. Their struggle contrasts sharply with the family structure of bourgeois. Their white women and men who are likely to be better informed about the positive effects of male participation in parenting, who have more time to parent, and who are not perpetually anxious about their material well-being. It is also difficult for women who parent alone to juggle the demands of work and child rearing.

Feminist theorists point to the problems that arise when parenting is done exclusively by an individual or solely by women: female parenting gives children few role models of male parenting, perpetuates the idea that parenting is a woman's vocation, and reinforces male domination and fear of women. Society, however, is not concerned. This information has little impact at a time when men, more than ever before, avoid responsibility for child rearing and when women are parenting less because they work more but are parenting more often alone. These facts raise two issues that must be of central concern for future feminist movement: the right of children to effective child care by parents and other child rearers, the restructuring of society so that women do not exclusively provide that care.

Eliminating sexism is the solution to the problem of men participating unequally or not at all in child care. Therefore, more women and men must recognize the need to support and participate in feminist movement. Masses of women continue to believe that they should be primarily responsible for child care—this point cannot be overemphasized. Feminist efforts to help women unlearn this socialization could lead to greater demands on their part for men to participate equally in parenting. Making and distributing brochures in women's health centers and in other public places that would emphasize the importance of males and females sharing equally in parenting is one way to make more people aware of this need. Seminars on parenting that emphasize nonsexist parenting and joint parenting by women and men in local communities is another way more people could learn about the subject. Before women become pregnant, they need to understand the significance of men sharing equally in par-

enting. Some women in relationships with men who may be considering bearing children do not do so because male partners make it known that they will not assume responsibility for parenting. These women feel their decision not to bear children with men who refuse to share parenting is a political statement reinforcing the importance of equal participation in parenting and the need to end male dominance of women. We need to hear more from these women about the choices they have made. There are also women who bear children in relationships with men who know beforehand that the man will not participate equally in parenting. It is important for future studies of female parenting to understand their choices.

Women need to know that it is important to discuss child care with men before children are conceived or born. There are women and men who have made either legal contracts or simply written agreements that spell out each individual's responsibility. Some women have found that men verbally support the idea of shared parenting before a child is conceived or born and then do not follow through. Written agreements can help clarify the situation by requiring each individual to discuss what they feel about parental care, who should be responsible, etc. Most women and men do not discuss the nature of child rearing before children are born because it is simply assumed that women will be caretakers.

Despite the importance of men sharing equally in parenting, large numbers of women have no relationship to the man with whom they have conceived a child. In some cases, this is a reflection of the man's lack of concern about parenting or the woman's choice. Some women do not feel it is important for their children to experience caring, nurturing parenting from males. In black communities, it is not unusual for a single female parent to rely on male relatives and friends to help with child rearing. As more heterosexual and lesbian women choose to bear children with no firm ties to male parents, there will exist a greater need for community-based child care that would bring children into contact with male child rearers so they will not grow to maturity thinking women are the only group who do or should do child rearing. The child rearer does not have to be a parent. Child rearers in our culture are teachers, librarians, etc. and even though these are occupations which have been dominated by women, this is changing. In these contexts, a child could experience male child rearing. Some female parents who raise their children without the mutual care of fathers feel their own positions are undermined when they meet occasionally with male parents who may provide a good time but be totally unengaged in day-to-day parenting. They sometimes have to cope with children valuing the male parent more because he is male (and sexist ideology teaches them that his attentions are more valuable than female care). These women need to know that teaching their children nonsexist values could help them appreciate female parenting and could eradicate favoritism based solely on sexist standards.

Because women are doing most of the parenting, the need for tax-funded public child care centers with equal numbers of nonsexist male and female workers continues to be a pressing feminist issue. Such centers would relieve individual women of the sole responsibility for child rearing as well as help promote awareness of the necessity for male participation in child raising. Yet this is an issue that has yet to be pushed by masses of people. Future feminist organizing (especially in the interests of building mass-based feminist movement) could use this issue as a platform. Feminist activists have always seen public child care as one solution to the problem of

women being the primary child rearers. Commenting on the need for child care centers in her article "Bringing Up Baby," Mary Ellen Schoonmaker writes;

> As for child care outside the home, the seemingly simple concept envisioned by the women's movement of accessible, reliable, quality day care has proven largely elusive. While private, often overpriced sources of day care have risen to meet middle-class needs, the inadequacy of public day care remains an outrage. The Children's Defense Fund, a child advocacy and lobbying group in Washington, D.C., reports that perhaps six to seven million children, including preschoolers, may be left at home alone while their parents work because they can't afford day care.

Most child care centers, catering either to the needs of the working classes or the bourgeoisie, are not nonsexist. Yet until children begin to learn at a very early age that it is not important to make role distinctions based on sex, they will continue to grow to maturity thinking that women should be the primary child rearers.

Many people oppose the idea of tax-funded public child care because they see it as an attempt by women to avoid parenting. They need to know that the extent to which the isolated parenting that women do in this society is not the best way to raise children or treat women who mother. Elizabeth Janeway makes this point in her book *Cross Sections*, emphasizing that the idea of an individual having sole responsibility for child rearing is the most unusual pattern of parenting in the world, one that has proved to be unsuccessful because it isolates children and parents from society:

> How extreme that family isolation can be today is indicated by these instances listed in a study undertaken for the Massachusetts Advisory Council on Education. . . . This group found:
> 1. Isolation of wage earners from spouses and children, caused by the wage earners' absorption into the world of work.

2. The complementary isolation of young children from the occupational world of parents and other adults.
3. The general isolation of young children from persons of different ages, both adults and other children.
4. The residential isolation of families from persons of different social, ethnic, religious, and racial backgrounds.
5. The isolation of family members from kin and neighbors.

Such isolation means that the role of the family as the agent for socializing children is inadequately fulfilled at present, whether or not mothers are at work outside the home. Children are now growing up without the benefit of a variety of adult role models of both sexes and in ignorance of the world of paid work. Returning women to a life centered in home and family would not solve the fundamental loss of connection between family and community. The effort by the women's movement to see that centers for child care are provided by society is not an attempt to hand over to others the duties of motherhood but to enlist community aid to supplement the proper obligations of parents, as was often the practice in the past.

Ideally, small, community-based, public child care centers would be the best way to overcome this isolation. When parents must drive long distances to take children to day care, dependency on parents is increased and not lessened. Community-based public child care centers would give small children great control over their lives.

Child care is a responsibility that can be shared with other child rearers, with people who do not live with children. This form of parenting is revolutionary in this society because it takes place in opposition to the idea that parents, especially mothers, should be the only child rearers. Many people raised in black communities experienced this type of community-based child care. Black women who had to leave the home and work to help provide for families could not afford to send children to day care centers, and such centers did not always exist. They relied on people in their communities to help. Even in families where the mother stayed home, she could also rely on people in the community to help. She did not need to go with her children every time they walked to the playground to watch them because they would be watched by a number of people living near the playground. People who did not have children often took responsibility for sharing in child rearing. In my own family, there were seven children, and when we were growing up it was not possible for our parents to watch us all the time or even give that extra special individual attention children sometimes desire. Those needs were often met by neighbors and people in the community.

This kind of shared responsibility for child care can happen in small community settings where people know and trust one another. It cannot happen in those setting if parents regard children as their "property," their "possession." Many parents do not want their children to develop caring relationships with others, not even relatives. If there were community-based day care centers, there would be a much greater likelihood that children would develop ongoing friendships and caring relationships with adult people rather than their parents. These types of relationships are not formed in day care centers where one teacher takes care of a large number of students, where one never sees teachers in any context other than school. Any individual who has been raised in an environment of communal child care knows that this happens only if parents can accept other adults assuming parental type care for their children. While it creates a situation where children must respect a number of caretakers, it also gives children resources to rely on if their emotional, intellectual, and material needs are not met solely by parents. Often in black communities where shared child rearing happens elderly women and men participate. Today many children have no contact with the elderly. Another hazard of single parenting or even nuclear family parenting that is avoided when there is community-based child raising is the tendency of parents to over-invest emotion in their children. This is a problem for many people who choose to have children after years of thinking they would not. They may make children into "love objects" and have no interest in teaching them to relate to a wide variety of people. This is as much a problem for feminist women and men who are raising children as it is for other parents.

Initially, women's liberationists felt that the need for population control coupled with awareness of this society's consumption of much of the world's resources were political reasons not to bear children. These reasons have not changed, even though they are now ignored or dismissed. Yet if there were less emphasis on having one's "own" children and more emphasis on having children who are already living and in need of child care, there would be large groups of responsible women and men to share in the process of child rearing. Lucia Valeska supported this position in an essay published in a 1975 issue of *Quest*, "If All Else Fails, I'm Still a Mother":

> To have our own biological children today is personally and politically irresponsible. If you have health, strength, energy, and financial assets to give to children, then do so. Who, then will have children? If the childfree raise existing children, more people than ever will "have" children. The line between biological and non-biological mothers will begin to disappear. Are we in danger of depleting the population? Are you kidding?
>
> Right now in your community there are hundreds of thousands of children and mothers who desperately need individual and community support.

Some people who choose not to bear children make an effort to participate in child rearing. Yet, like many parents, most people without children assume they should be uninterested in child care until they have their "own" children. People without children who try to participate in child rearing must confront the suspicions and resistance of people who do not understand their interest, who assume that all people without children do not like them. People are especially wary of individuals who wish to help in child rearing if they do not ask for pay for their services. At a time in my life when my companion and I were working hard to participate in child rearing, we had children stay with us in our home for short periods of time to give the parent, usually a single mother, a break and to have children in our lives. If we explained the principle behind our actions, people were usually surprised and supportive but wary. I think they were wary because our actions were unusual. The difficulties we faced have led us to accept a life in which we have less interaction with children than we would like, the case for most people who do not have children. This isolation from children has motivated many feminists to bear children.

Before there can be shared responsibility for child rearing that relieves women of the sole responsibility for primary child care, women and men must revolutionize their consciousness. They must be willing to accept that parenting in isolation (irrespective of the sex of the parent) is not the most effective way to raise children or be happy as parents. Since women do most of the parenting in this society and it does not appear that this situation will alter in the coming years, there has to be renewed feminist organizing around the issue of child care. The point is not to stigmatize single parents, but to emphasize the need for collective parenting. Women all over the United Sates must rally together to demand that tax money spent on the arms race and other militaristic goals be spent on improving the quality of parenting and child care in this society. Feminist theorists who emphasize the hazards of single parenting, who outline the need for men to share equally in parenting, often live in families where the male parent is present. This leads them to ignore the fact that this type of parenting is not an option for many women (even though it may be the best social framework in which to raise children). That social framework could be made available in community-based public day care centers with men and women sharing equal responsibility for child care. More than ever before, there is a great need for women and men to organize around the issue of child care to ensure that all children will be raised in the best possible social frameworks; to ensure that women will not be the sole, or primary, child rearers.

Chapter 44

Racial Safety and Cultural Maintenance: The Child Care Concerns of Employed Mothers of Color

LYNET UTTAL

In the 1930s, doctors professed a single model of infant care that was promoted as superior to traditional ethnic infant care practices.[1] A similar movement is currently taking place in the 1990s in the field of paid child care services. Child care advocates are pressing for the professionalization of child care work and the practice of a single model of developmentally appropriate care. Underlying this proposal is the assumption that child rearing can be stripped of cultural values and practices, and that the type of care a child receives can be offered independent of the social and cultural location of the child's family.

This model ignores how membership in historically subordinated racial ethnic groups creates a different experience of child care for people of color than for the White population. Child care research has identified systematic differences in preferences by racial ethnic groups. One difference frequently noted is that African American parents

From *Ethnic Studies Review,* 19, no. 1 (February 1996). Reprinted by permission.

view child care as an educational setting more so than do White parents. White parents, especially middle-class ones, are more likely to view child care as an opportunity for their children to have social interactions with other children.[2] African American parents express a greater preference for child care that provides structured academic programs for preschool-aged children, whereas middle-class White parents prefer loosely structured activities that expose their children to different concepts through play. This high valuation of education is rooted in beliefs that early education will prepare children for kindergarten and create a stronger foundation for social mobility through education.[3]

One study found that African American parents expected the day care center's staff to be aware of and sensitive to racial issues and objected when the day care center's programming violated this expectation.[4] In another study, Chinese American parents expressed concern about the conflicting messages children get when what is taught at home differs from what is taught at their day cares,[5] such as differing beliefs about how to address elders and differing eating practices (e.g., whether picking up a bowl and eating from it is acceptable). These concerns are important to take into account because early childhood education research has shown that presentations of positive ethnic images are important in the formulation of children's self-images and for the transmission of cultural values.[6] Yet, when child care advocates propose a single model of developmentally appropriate child care, they ignore the significance of membership in a historically subordinated racial ethnic group and cultural values in how child care arrangements are viewed.

Racial group membership and cultural practices are important because they create a lens, or historical consciousness, through which child care is assessed. Historical consciousness, according to poet and scholar Janice Gould, is the awareness of one's historical identity.[7] In her discussion of Native American women, Gould states that historical consciousness is the collective awareness of five hundred years of internal colonialism and genocide. Although individual Native American women come from many different tribes and lead very different lives, Gould argues that their historical consciousness informs how individual women live out their lives on a daily basis. Their historical consciousness reflects their social histories as members of particular gender, race, ethnic, and class groups.

The historical consciousness of their status as members of historically subordinated racial ethnic groups informs the types of concerns employed mothers of color have about leaving their children in other people's care. In this chapter, I explore two expressions of this historical consciousness in employed mothers' views of their child care arrangements: racial safety and cultural maintenance. The introduction of these two concepts is central to the understanding of why parents of color seek out child care providers who are members of their own racial ethnic group and of how they view childcare provided by persons who do not share their racial ethnic group membership or knowledge of their racial ethnic histories. Furthermore, this chapter not only identifies child care problems related to overt forms of racism but also discusses the problems that occur when well-intentioned White childcare providers lack experience with caring for children of different racial ethnic groups and with negotiating multicultural interactions.

This chapter is based on in-depth interviews with fifteen women of color (seven Mexican American, seven African American, and one California-born woman of Guamanian descent). The analysis presented here is part of a larger research project that examined how employed mothers of infants, toddlers, and preschool-aged children made, maintained, and changed their child care arrangements. In-depth interviews were conducted with thirty-two employed mothers in a northern California county during 1990–1992. Because this study was exploratory, I used maximum variation sampling to ensure inclusion of a diversity of experiences. This sampling method was used because, unlike snowball sampling, which sometimes produces a tightly networked and homogeneous sample, maximum variation sampling interrupts the social links between respondents and the researcher and diversifies the sample on several different factors. In this study, mother's ethnicity, occupation, and type of child care were the three criteria purposefully diversified. This sampling practice results in an analysis that represents a broad range of experiences, rather than one that is limited to a homogeneous sample. Most mothers were interviewed only once and interviews lasted from two to six hours.

According to the 1990 U.S. Census, the northern California county in which this study was conducted was 85 percent White, 10 percent Hispanic, 4 percent Asian American, and less than 1 percent Black.[8] The child care economy of this county is organized around two sectors: the Formal sector is composed of licensed family day cares and nonprofit (not church-based) and federally funded child care centers, and the informal sector is composed of an underground economy of care provided by relatives and unlicensed individual caregivers, including a labor pool of Mexican and South American immigrant women. The division of the child care economy into two sectors, a formal and an underground one, is a common characteristic nationwide.[9]

The availability of a labor pool of child care providers who are low-paid women of color is also typical; in other parts of the country these women would more likely be African American. The extremely small population of African Americans in this county, however, limited the availability of African American child care providers, and African American mothers reported great difficulty in locating same-race providers. In contrast, due to the sizable population of Mexican Americans and Mexican and South American immigrants in this county, Mexican American mothers, like White mothers, had less difficulty locating a pool of providers of their same racial ethnic group.

The Concern for Racial Safety

According to Harriette Pipes McAdoo, "the 'extreme' difficulties which White society imposes on Black people by denying their identity, their values, and their economic opportunities are not unusual or extreme but 'mundane,' daily pressures for Blacks."[10] McAdoo compares living with racism to living in a harsh physical environment. In order to survive, historically subordinated racial ethnic groups have to adapt to accommodate the daily pervasiveness of this harsh environment. McAdoo identifies how racism affects job opportunities, housing, and health care for African Americans, and we know that these conditions are also imposed upon other historically subordinated racial ethnic groups, such as Latinos, Asian Americans, and Native Americans.[11]

Awareness of racism in U.S. society was a common topic when mothers of color talked about their child care arrangements. Because of their own experiences with racism, they were concerned about how their children would be treated when the child care providers were White. Often times, mothers discovered these problems only after they had established child care arrangements. For example, Gloria Thomas, an African American waitress and mother of two children, observed behaviors that she defined as racist. Gloria said:

> I don't know if she was used to [Black people]. I think she was kind of narrow-minded. I didn't feel comfortable, me being Black. [And] she looked like she put more energy into the White kids than the Black kids. I think she felt that I was on to her, because she said in a couple days, or actually I said, "this isn't going to work," and she pretty much knew also that it wasn't going to work.

Gloria expected White child care providers to have knowledge of how to negotiate cross-racial interactions. She said,

> If you are dealing with my kids, I hope you do have some cultural skills. I don't like prejudiceness at all. . . . You have to be not dumb. Some white people can be really stupid. They say the stupidest things.

When it was clear that child care providers lacked these skills, mothers removed their children from the child care setting. Frances

Trudeau, an African American lawyer and the mother of two children, responded this way when the school's teachers and administrators at her five year old son's school failed to acknowledge and address that the name-calling and chasing of African American children was racism. When she and other parents spoke to the director, they were told that the school could not develop a policy to address the problem because families came from so many different walks of life and the school did not want to tell people how to behave. This response reduced cross-racial interactions to individual interactions and personal disagreements and failed to acknowledge the more systemic nature of racism. Mothers of color found this kind of response inadequate and frustrating. Because they are aware of the pervasiveness of the problem of racism, they do not define unpleasant cross-racial interactions as occasional, individual disagreements even in child care settings.

Mothers of color also experienced racism when they used predominantly White child care settings. Gloria Thomas described one such encounter.

> This one woman was pretty annoying. She asked me this question and to this day I still want to ask her what did she mean by it. She said, "Oh, are you a single parent?" And I said, "yes." And she goes, "Oh, do you live around here?" And I said, "Yes, I live right around the corner." You could tell her mind was [thinking], "she goes to this day care? She's a single parent, Black, and she lives up here. How can she afford it?" It's really weird.

One of the strategies that mothers of color used to protect their children from racism was to find child care within their own racial ethnic communities. The use of kin and community networks protected the children and the mothers from having to deal with cross-racial interactions. When mothers of color were able

to make child care arrangements with child care providers of their same racial ethnic group, the concerns about racial safety and cultural maintenance were eliminated. Yet, care within one's racial ethnic community did not guarantee a fit between the values and child rearing practices of mothers and child care providers. Often times, mothers had several relatives and acquaintances from which to choose. When this was the case, the mothers carefully discriminated between their choices based on what they considered to be a good environment and good care. After insuring their child's racial safety and exposure to traditional cultural practices and values, they invoked additional criteria to decide which child care setting was the best. Sylvia Rodriquez, an office manager and the mother of two children, chose a Mexican immigrant woman over her sister-in-law. She explained:

> It depends on who the relatives are. Like for example, you know, financially [my husband's sister] could have used watch[ing for pay] my son and my daughter at her house. She's real good about feeding them and things like that. But she has a lot of marital problems that I wouldn't want my kids to be around, watching the arguments and fights. I know they use bad language and that's another thing I don't like.

Like Sylvia, Lupe Gonzalez, an administrative assistant and the mother of an eleven-month-old, was discriminating in terms of which relative she chose to watch her young baby. She had two options: an elderly grandmother and an aunt who was the same age as herself. She was pleased that her aunt was available to care for her baby, though she would have left her baby in her grandmother's care if necessary. But her grandmother was elderly and was already watching several other grandchildren. Because of her grandmother's age, Lupe felt that she would not be as attentive or as physically able to pick up her baby. The advantage of care by the aunt was that her infant son would also be the only child for whom the aunt provided care.

Although Gloria Thomas had left a White child care provider because she felt the White provider was unable to negotiate the cross-racial interactions, she found that simply finding an African American child care provider did not necessarily create satisfactory child care arrangements. Gloria had found a family day care run by an African American woman, yet other factors prevented her from feeling comfortable with this arrangement. Gloria rejected high-fat and high-sugar foods in favor of low-fat and low-sugar organic foods. She talked with the African American child care provider about what kinds of foods were provided at the day care, and she expressed her preference that her children be provided with fresh juices instead of sodas or drinks with sugar in them. Despite this initial discussion, it was not unusual for Gloria to come to pick up her kids and find them drinking sugar drinks. Gloria defined what her child care provider was doing as an African American cultural practice.

> Black people are raised different where they can eat the fried foods whatever. But I just wasn't trying to act like my kids were special. I was mainly just concerned about their nutrition, but it wasn't like I was acting they were more special. I was just doing it because I didn't want them to eat any sugar.

Similarly, Gloria and her provider had disagreements about what were appropriate disciplining practices. Gloria talked with her provider about these issues but felt that her preferences were not validated by the child care provider. She said:

> Well, I did, I said, I don't believe in hitting. And she said, "what do you mean by hitting." I said, "just swatting," and she said, "I do, you know, a slap on the hand." And I said, "pretty much

even that, I don't want." But I could feel like that she didn't want to hear that.

Since Gloria also wanted something different from what she perceived as traditional African American child rearing practices, she moved her children into a day care center where she was the only African American parent, as well as of the lowest socioeconomic status and background. She often found herself irritated with what she perceived as a White style of interaction, yet she felt the social, educational, and environmental advantages of the day care center outweighed the need to have her child cared for by her previous African American child care provider.

Young mothers often opposed some of the traditional child rearing practices used by the older and more traditional women in their communities. For example, Maria Hernandez, a Mexican American office manager and the mother of a four year old, expressed dissatisfaction with the care provided by her Mexican American mother-in-law. She said:

> I don't really like the idea of them being yelled at or spanked. I think if there is a behavior problem, they should be able to tell [the parents] and for us to deal with it. Luckily, I have been in the situation where my kids is pretty mellow, but I've seen her spanking her other grandchildren. I wouldn't like that.

Occasionally, Maria would consider moving her child to a day care center. Yet, when Maria weighed out all factors (e.g., convenience, location, flexibility, cost, quality of care, being within the family for child care), she decided that this care by her mother-in-law was the best choice, in spite of the differences about disciplining practices.

One of the formal sources of child care referrals was through the county's child care referral service. This service provided referrals to licensed day care centers, family day cares, and unlicensed individual caregivers. However, given the structure of the childcare market into informal and formal sectors, and the racial demographics of the region, the referral service was often not helpful for African American and Mexican American mothers. Even though the service was provided in both English and Spanish, several Mexican American mothers commented that the service was not a good source for Latino providers. One Mexican American mother pointed out that when she visited the referrals given to her by the county's referral service, she saw only White child care providers and very few non-White children in their care. Mexican American employed mothers reported that they had greater success locating Latino caregivers through informal sources, such as personal referrals and Spanish radio ads. Thus, Mexican American mothers often turned to their social and community-based networks to locate child care instead of using the child care referral service. African American mothers in this study found it difficult to locate African American providers in either the formal or informal sector of the child care market.

Another consideration was that simply being of the same race did not guarantee racial safety. Gloria felt that her African American child care provider was uncomfortable with the fact that her children's father was White. Being biracial located her children in a different category of race than simply "Black." Similarly, other mothers found that their searches for child care were complicated by having mixed-race children. Julie Lopez described how her background complicated her search for child care.

> I'm bilingual, but I'm not bicultural. My father was Black, my mother was White, my husband in Mexican. My child is half Mexican, Chicano. My grandparents are Jewish. We had all these different types of people all there and I picked parts of different cultures. . . . My child is going to get a different concept of different people.

Since within group care was problematic, another strategy that the mothers used to protect their children and themselves against racism was to choose child care settings that were multiracial. Given the very low population of African American mothers in this county, the African American mothers often looked for child care where there were, at least, other children of color, even if they were not African American children. Frances Trudeau said:

> Whenever we look at places for the kids, we always look at what's the number of minority kids, specifically black kids but also minorities. We're also Jewish so what's the make-up in terms of Jews. . . . [He's going] to be spending most of his day with these people, what do they believe in? What is it that he's gonna get either subtle or not so subtle in terms of their teachings?

Several of the middle-class, predominantly White daycares had made a formal commitment to diversify their ethnic composition as well as to developing a multicultural curriculum. They offered full scholarships to children of color in order to diversify race and ethnicity. Yet, even when the daycare center had a formal commitment to a multiculturalism, childcare providers' behaviors and attitudes often demonstrated a lack of cultural competency that resulted in racially unsafe environments for children of color and their mothers. Racism ranged from outright hostile relations with child care staff and other parents at the day care to the interactions with well-intentioned White child care providers who lacked experience with caring for children of color and negotiating cross-cultural interactions. Aurora Garcia, a Mexican American mother, explained how this happens:

> They're all White, and they come from that perspective . . . And they have blind spots. I don't know how else to put it. They're coming from

their perspectives and their reality, their experiences, and so to change that, you have to ask them to. You have to help them do it, too.

And indeed, one of the consequences of being a parent of a child of color in a majority White daycare was the increased need for parental involvement. Aurora negotiated her child's racial safety by becoming, informally, the day care center's multicultural consultant. She intervened when the staff at her daughter's day care center did not interrupt behavior that was racist and stereotypical, such as when a White child pretended to be an Indian and came to school stereotypically dressed in feathers and headbands, wielding a toy tomahawk and whooping war cries. First, she brought to their awareness that certain behaviors and practices were racist and stereotypical. In the case of the White boy who came to school dressed as a stereotypical American Indian, she told them that she objected to the child's practice as well as to the staff's encouragement of it by painting stereotypical American Indian war paint on him. When the day care center was responsive to her concerns and asked her to work with them on it, she talked to the children and staff and recommended multicultural readings. Aurora gave the day care staff credit for trying to improve, but at the same time she was aware that cross-cultural gaffs were going to be a regular part of being in a predominantly White day care. She added:

They are very actively trying to deal with some of these issues, and to me that felt good, culturally, you know. They made some boo-boos. [Like] at one point one of these teachers was talking to one of the [Latino] kids in Spanish, and she said, "She's bilingual, right?" [She wasn't.] Then you have to decode what you are and [let them know that] not all Chicanos speak Spanish. So, on one level, it was like you could ignore it. But I had to talk to her and explain who I am, and this has been my experience, and people assume that if

you're a particular ethnicity then you're going to do what they perceive are the stereotypical things of that ethnicity.

Because of their awareness of racism in U.S. society, mothers of color were acutely aware of whether their children would be racially safe in child care settings. When one is a member of a historically subordinated racial ethnic group, finding child care that provides children with racial safety is an important concern. Yet, the search is complicated by other racial-ethnic factors.

The Search for Cultural Maintenance

Many of the mothers expressed interest in child care by racially and ethnically similar caregivers. For some, this was motivated by the desire to protect their children and have them in racially safe situations. For others, staying within one's own community was an explicit strategy to ensure that their children would learn about their cultural heritage and histories. Many of the mothers had been young adults at a time in history when racial ethnic groups began to take pride in claiming their cultural histories. Prior to the 1960s, historically subordinated racial ethnic groups were expected to socialize their children to the dominant Anglo Saxon Protestant values of U.S. society. As far back as the 1920s, child care services were used to "Americanize" immigrant children and their parents.[12] Mothers were aware of this bias and purposefully sought out culturally similar providers because they saw child care as a site that would influence their children's understandings of their cultural heritage.

Several Mexican American mothers sought Spanish-speaking Mexican or Mexican American caregivers for this reason. For example, when Elena Romero, a Mexican American nutritionist, first needed child care, she used this strategy and found a Spanish speaking Mexican American child care provider. She said:

> We found out about this [family] day care that was run by a preschool teacher that had decided to open up her own day care. And she was Chicana and . . . I really wanted him to know Spanish. Since birth I had [talked] to him [in Spanish] . . . Anyway, so I went to this day care and I really was impressed with the day care center because . . . she was really organized . . . and I liked her right away, you know. Then she had like senoras mexicanas . . . come in and cook for her and like they would make a big ol' pot of albóndigas . . . a meatball soup, you know. So like they would make really good Mexican food.

Similarly, Aurora Garcia said:

> I was hoping that, given that my child would be in the household for a significant number of hours during the day, that there be some [ethnic] similarity, you know, not that I'm traditional, I don't consider myself traditional, but those values I wanted, kind of implanted, you know, issues of discipline, you know, being really caring and nurturing and her being familiar with Spanish.

In describing what she looked for in child care, Julie Lopez, an African American mother whose ex-husband and stepfather are Latino, said:

> There's a cultural thing . . . one of the things for me, and our family, it has been really important to have [my child] in a bilingual place where she can sit down with other kids and speak Spanish and have a teacher that speaks Spanish and they sit down at lunch and they speak Spanish together. And the writing they do is both in English and Spanish and the pictures on the walls and stuff, because that cultural thing to me is really important . . . I'm always more comfortable if they're bicultural as well, versus just being bilingual.

Thus, their concerns were not simply about the skills and types of food that their children would be eating but also addressed a broader understanding that shared cultural practices were expressions of shared cultural values.

Another issue that confronted employed mothers of color was whether to foster cultural maintenance and racial safety at the cost of educational opportunities. In particular, mothers who had been raised working class and were now middle class grappled with this problem. When Aurora Garcia switched her daughter from a family day care home with a Mexican American caregiver to a predominantly White day care center, she felt as if she had to make compromises. She said:

> I'm not getting the ideal. I can't find the ideal . . . there are very few children of color there. I think diversity to them is Jewish. That's being diverse culturally . . . I mean, the ideal to me would be that she be in a school where she would be learning Spanish, she would be learning those things. . . . And that's just a tradeoff for me right now . . . I think of all the skills she's learning right now, but there's a cultural context to them that would be nice to have.

Aurora acknowledged that because she used a predominantly White day care center, she was raising her child in a White environment. However, she pointed out that her daughter was exposed to traditional cultural values because of who her parents were. She said, "I'm very much entrenched in who I am and what my cultural values are and my experience, and my partner is in his." Similarly, Elena Romero reconciled herself to the fact that her children would learn about their culture and their history at home. She said:

> [My husband and I] are both real proud of being Mexicanos, Chicanos, you know. And we're both constantly involved in the Movement kind of things. And we both have friends who are bilingual and that have kids, and, you, our families. If we have a birthday party, we have a piñata and all that stuff. So we decided well, that they would get it from us.

Yet, Aurora and Elena both realized that placing children in White day cares removed them from being fully immersed in their traditional ethnic community. Aurora said:

> It's not the same for a child. I mean, it really is how you play, who you play with, what you play, it's what you eat, it's how people treat you, what they say to you. . . . [Her teachers] are going to present it from a white perspective because they don't have bilingual teachers. They don't have African American teachers. So for me, it's a trade off.

Clearly, choosing to move outside of one's culture into a predominantly White daycare was not an easy decision. When they made the decision to place their children in a predominantly White daycare, they continued to be conflicted about not being able to find a daycare for their children which would provide cultural maintenance and exposure to traditional cultural practices and values. Although on the surface it may appear that mothers of color who place their children in predominantly White daycare settings are rejecting their own cultural practices and turning their back on their racial ethnic group, this was not the case. They were highly self conscious that their children's child care was not fulfilling one of their major criteria for their child care arrangements. By providing their children with the social opportunities and formal education which they had come to expect for any well-educated child of the middle class, they had to work harder at home to ensure that their children learned about their cultures and histories. Furthermore, by placing themselves in predominantly White settings, they more frequently encountered racism and, more frequently and at a younger age, had to explain to their young children about race relations with White society and how to navigate them.

Both of these concerns—racial safety and cultural maintenance—reflect how membership in specific racial ethnic groups influences views of what constitutes appropriate caregiving. The concern of mothers of color for racial safety addresses their awareness that their children can be the targets of racism by a society that has historically devalued their racial ethnic group. The concern for cultural maintenance reflects their preference to retain and/or retrieve traditional cultural practices and values.

Conclusion

Mothers' views challenge the construction of a professional model of developmentally appropriate child care as culturally neutral. The mothers' views do not reflect rigid adherence to traditional cultural practices but rather a recognition of the significance of racism in U.S. society and their desire to have cultural learning be part of the child care curriculum. First, they are concerned about whether the caregivers are culturally competent to negotiate cross-racial and cross-ethnic social relations, and whether their children will be treated with the same respect and positive assumptions as White children. In short, they worried about their children's racial safety. Second, they are concerned about whether the interactions and formal and informal curriculum of the child care setting supports and validates the cultural histories and practices of their racial ethnic group.

Hardly any realm of social life in the United States is not influenced in some way by racial ethnic stratification. Child care choices are another example of how people of color experience the mundane extreme environment of racism.

Like many social experiences in the United States, child care is organized along racial and socioeconomic lines.[13] In areas of the country such as the region where this study was conducted, some families are forced to go outside of their own racial ethnic group for child care either because the racial demographics do not support same race child care or because the new class mobility of many middle-class parents of color encourages them to forgo child care within their own racial ethnic community. Because child care is a racially and class segregated system, a range of choices in types of day cares for parents of color is limited. Mothers of color often must choose between day cares that provide cultural learning without the middle-class opportunities or day cares that provide middle-class educational opportunities without the cultural learning. This study points out the need to train child care providers, especially White caregivers, to effectively negotiate cross-racial interactions and to know about specific racial ethnic histories and cultural practices.

Concerns about racial safety and cultural maintenance call into question the reduction of child care to a single universal model of developmentally appropriate care.

NOTES

1. Jacquelyn Litt, "Mothering, Medicalization, and Jewish Identity, 1928–1940," *Gender & Society* 10, no. 2 (1996): 185–198.

2. Carole E. Joffe, *Friendly Intruders: Childcare Professionals and Family Life* (Berkeley: University of California Press, 1977).

3. Mary Larner and Anne Mitchell, "Meeting the Child Care Needs of Low-Income Families," *Child and Youth Care Forum* 21, no. 5 (1992): 317–334. Katherine Brown Rosier and William A. Corsario, "Competent Parents, Complex Lives: Managing Parenthood in Poverty," *Journal of Contemporary Ethnography* 22, no. 2 (1993): 171–204.

4. Joffe, *Friendly Intruders.*

5. Stevanne Auerbach, "What Parents Want From Day Care," in *Child Care: A Comprehensive Guide: Philosophy, Programs, and Practices for the*

Creation of Quality Services for Children, vol. 1, *Rationale for Child Care Services: Programs vs. Politics,* ed. Stevanne Auerbach with James A. Rivaldo (New York: Human Sciences Press, 1975), 137–152.

6. Janice Hale, "The Transmission of Cultural Values to Young African American Children," *Young Children* (September 1991): 7–14.

7. Janice Gould, "American Indian Women's Poetry: Strategies of Rage and Hope," *Signs* 20, no. 4 (1995): 797–817.

8. U.S. Bureau of the Census, *Summary Population and Housing Characteristics: California.* (Washington, D.C.: GPO, 1990), table 3.

9. Mary Tuominen, "The Hidden Organization of Labor: Gender, Race/Ethnicity, and Child-care Work in the Formal and Informal Economy," *Sociological Perspectives* 37, no. 2 (1994): 229–245.

10. Harriette Pipes McAdoo, "Societal Stress: The Black Family," in *All American Women,* ed. Johnnetta B. Cole. (New York: Free Press, 1986), 189.

11. In this chapter, I use different racial ethnic terms interchangeably. First, I use the terms that were given by the source of information. (E.g., the U.S. Census Bureau uses Hispanic. Different mothers that I interviewed used different terms.) As an analyst, I try to use the most specific racial ethnic label that accurately reflects the group or groups I am referencing. What complicates this decision is whether I am addressing issues that have to do with membership in a particular racial ethnic group or discussing cultural practices and values. Because of the significance of differences in cultural practices between different ethnic groups it is important to refer specifically to them to identify the ethnic group (e.g., Mexican Americans) rather than to use global labels (e.g., Hispanic or Latinos) when speaking about issues of cultural practices and values. When talking about experiences that result from not being white, however, it is appropriate to speak of Latinos as a group, or people of color as a group.

12. Julia Wrigley, "Different Care for Different Kids: Social Class and Child Care Policy," *Educational Policy* 3, no. 4 (1989): 421–439.

13. Wrigley, "Different Care for Different Kids."

Section B

Violence, Power, and Families

Chapter 45

Through a Feminist Lens:
Gender, Power, and Violence

KERSTI A. YLLÖ

Violence within the family is as complex as it is disturbing. Compressed into one assault are out deepest human emotions, our sense of self, our power, and our hopes and fears about love and intimacy, as well as the social construction of marriage and its place within the larger society. Despite this complexity, the most fundamental feminist insight into all of this is quite simple: Domestic violence cannot be adequately understood unless gender and power are taken into account.

Looking at domestic violence through a feminist lens is not a simple matter, however. Developing a theoretical, empirical, political, and personal understanding of violence requires us to analyze its complex gendered nature. This involves the psychologies of perpetrator and victim and their interactions, gendered expectations about family relationships and dynamics, and the patriarchal ideology and structure of society within which individuals and relationships are embedded. Although there is a range of feminist perspectives on each of these dimensions, there is broad consensus that each is profoundly shaped by gender and power.

Social action is the fundamental source of feminist insight into domestic violence. Feminist academic work, theoretical analyses, and methodological debates flow out of feminist practice. The feminist perspective, with its origins in a social movement, is strong on practical programs and critiques of prevailing perspectives. But it is not yet a fully developed, distinctive framework for the explanation of domestic violence, and in this limitation we are in good company, for no single view is complete. I will argue, however, that although a feminist lens may not be sufficient for seeing the full picture of domestic violence, it is a necessary lens without which any other analytic perspective is flawed. Gender and power are key elements of domestic violence, whether one takes a sociological or a psychological perspective.

From Richard J. Gelles and Donileen R. Loseke, eds., *Current Controversies on Family Violence,* pp. 47–62. Copyright © 1993 by Sage Publications, Inc. Reprinted by permission of Sage Publications, Inc.

Focus on Domestic Violence

As social constructionists point out, the phenomena we study (including physical violence) are not simply "out there" to be discovered through direct, objective observation (e.g., empirically). Rather, definitions of problems are socially created through ongoing controversy as well as collaboration. Observation is always theory laden, and this is especially true when the phenomenon under scrutiny is as politically and emotionally fraught as violence (see Yllö 1988).

An important question that has been largely overlooked during the 20-year explosion of the family violence field is whether "family violence" is a unitary phenomenon that requires an overarching theory. I would argue that feminist analysis has made an enormous contribution to our understanding of wife abuse, yet it has produced relatively less insight into child abuse or elder abuse. However, I do not regard this as evidence that feminist theory is constricted. It has made significant contributions to such areas as stranger rape, acquaintance rape, sexual harassment in the workplace, and pornography. Further, this analysis of violence against women (whether in the family or outside it) rests within an even broader feminist analysis of all aspects of women's lives in patriarchal society.

In this sense, the feminist lens is truly a wide-angle lens rather than a telephoto lens. Feminist theory does not regard patriarchy as a discrete, measurable variable (like age, sex, or socioeconomic status). Rather, patriarchy—the system of male power in society—is very complex and multidimensional. Feminist theory is not a narrow theory of one aspect of family violence. It is a very broad analysis of gender and power in society that has been fruitfully applied to domestic violence. I am not arguing that the study of violence against women should supplant the ex-amination of family violence but that we must recognize the distinctions as well as the linkages. The family as a social institution is undeniably a unique context that shapes the nature of the abuse within it. Whether we approach the problem with "gender" or "family" as our primary focus, I believe that we cannot understand one without the other.

Theoretical Lenses (or, What You See Is What You Get)

Over the past two decades, feminist theory and research have developed a picture of the family that reveals that social expectations regarding masculinity and femininity give relationships their shape. Whether it is our attitude toward love and sex, our ability and desire to communicate intimately, our need for connection versus autonomy, our involvement with our children, or our willingness to do the dishes—all of these are influenced (though not determined) by gender (Bernard 1976; Chodorow 1978; Tannen 1990; Thorne and Yalom 1982). However, in contrast to Sigmund Freud, Talcott Parsons, and the generations of psychologists and sociologists who followed them, feminists have argued that these distinctions are neither inherent nor functional. They are socially constructed and they create and maintain male power within the family and society.

Feminist analysis of domestic violence is firmly lodged in this broader theoretical and empirical framework. More than 15 years ago, Del Martin's ground-breaking treatise *Battered Wives* (1976) described violence as husbands' means of maintaining dominance within patriarchal marriage. In conjunction with the battered women's movement, which is built on this insight, feminist analysis grew and gained depth. Male violence was, for the first time, analyzed as a means of social control of women in general (Dobash and Dobash 1979; Schechter 1982).

During this same period, sociologists, led by Murray Straus, discovered family violence and initiated important research into the topic. The field of sociology, and family sociology in particular, was just emerging from functionalism at this point. The events of the day, including the Vietnam War, the civil rights and student movements, and the riots in our cities, called the functionalist model into question. Instead of viewing society and its institutions as consensual systems in equilibrium, sociologists began to focus on inequality, conflict, violence, and change (Collins 1975). Family sociologists, too, began to look beyond the norms and roles of the static consensus model of family relations. Sociological frameworks such as systems theory, resource and exchange theories, and the subculture of violence theory (Gelles 1993) all emerged during this period of theoretical ferment.

"Family violence" became the dominant conceptual rubric in academia because the issue was pioneered by family sociologists (Gelles 1974; Steinmetz & Straus 1974). Up to this point, spouse abuse had been viewed largely in terms of individual psychopathology. This early sociological work was groundbreaking in its emphasis on social forces. However, it was largely gender neutral. The patriarchal nature of these social forces was not adequately incorporated into the theories or empirical measures. The reality that the preponderance of the violence of the period (whether in the home, on the streets, or in the jungle) was perpetrated by men was not central to the analyses.

The sociological theories reviewed by Gelles (1993) illustrate some of the problems of looking at family violence without a feminist lens. Several of the general systems model propositions obscure the importance of gender. For example: "Stereotyped family violence im-

agery is learned in early childhood . . . [and is] continually reaffirmed for adults and children through ordinary social interactions and the mass media." Family violence imagery? The imagery of violence that inundates our culture is of *masculine* violence. Male aggression is the mainstay of our cultural images of violence, whether as fantasy (characters such as the Terminator, Rambo, the Teenage Mutant Ninja Turtles) or in reality (the Persian Gulf War, riots in Los Angeles, Yugoslavia, Father Porter). The exceptions to this taken-for-granted backdrop (e.g., *Thelma and Louise* and female soldiers in the Persian Gulf) get the attention they do because they are exceptional.

Like systems theory, resource exchange/control, and subculture of violence theories ignore gender and are not as fruitful as they might be if a feminist lens sharpened their focus. Resource and exchange frameworks have contributed the important insights that power is based on resources and that violence is the ultimate resource for ensuring compliance. Unfortunately, the structural limits to women's access to key resources (such as income) as well as the cultural ideology of husband dominance are largely overlooked in the neutral/abstract formulation of these theories (Gillespie 1971).

In the subculture of violence picture, men, as gendered human actors, are surprisingly invisible. The proposition that some sectors of society are more violent than others, especially when they have rules that legitimate or even require violence, would seem a useful start toward the analysis of male violence. However, this model is applied to subcultures such as the working class or particular race-ethnic groups. The reality that within these subcultures, as well as in the dominant culture, violence is overwhelmingly a male phenomenon is a nonissue. Is that fact so thoroughly taken for granted that it is not regarded as requiring explanation?

Although the theories outlined have been important in guiding sociological thinking about family violence, I would add conflict theory to the list because of its important influence on how violence is now conceptualized and measured. For the purposes of their research, Murray Straus and Richard Gelles initially conceptualized family violence as a form of conflict, which they regarded as a form of social conflict, more generally. Their theoretical underpinning came from conflict theorists such as Georg Simmel and Lewis Coser, and through this lens they saw the family as a social group in conflict (Sprey 1969). Straus (1990) recently has restated this theoretical position, pointing out that conflict is inherent in families (as in other groups), with individuals "seeking to live out their lives in accordance with personal agendas that inevitably differ" (p. 30). He sees physical assault as a conflict tactic, defined as "the overt actions used by persons in response to a conflict of interests" (e.g., differing "personal agendas") (p. 30).

This conflict perspective offers important insight, but it, too, suffers from its lack of feminist lens. As Dobash, Dobash, Wilson, and Daly (1992) point out, "Such analysis obscures all that is distinctive about violence against wives which occurs in a particular context of perceived entitlement and institutionalized power asymmetry" (p. 83). The conflict perspective (sans feminism) obscures personal interests with gender interests. For example, when a husband forces his wife to have sex because it is her "wifely duty," is this just a conflict of personal interests? Surely we have a better understanding of the assault if we recognize that this "personal agenda" is socially constructed in a way that entitles him as a husband and legitimates his behavior. Conflict and personal interests are not gender neutral.

As Wini Breines and Linda Gordon (1983) emphasize in their review of family violence

research, conflict is a "power struggle for the maintenance of a certain kind of social order" (p. 511). Family conflict occurs between members who hold very different positions in this social order. "Husband," "wife," "parent," and "child" are not neutral statuses whose occupants simply have differing personal agendas. They may all prefer different TV shows, but the conflict that ensues about the matter will likely be structured by expectations of gender and generational entitlement, not just personal preferences. When the issue is more serious (for example, a wife wanting to go back to school or to get a job), the gendered nature of the conflict will be even more salient.

There are many sociologists and psychologists who have contributed to the study of domestic violence. The theoretical assumptions of Straus and Gelles are emphasized here, however, because their impact on the empirical research in this field has been so profound. They developed the Conflict Tactics Scales (CTS), an instrument that dominates the family violence field to an extent rarely matched by other scales in other fields.

A theoretical issue that is rarely raised is: Why begin with the assumption that violence is a conflict tactic? Instead of viewing violence as a conflict tactic, feminists suggest that it is better conceptualized as a tactic of coercive control to maintain the husband's power (Bograd 1988; Hanmer and Maynard 1987; Jones and Schechter 1992; Ptacek 1988). Indeed, Gelles and Straus (1988) themselves recognize that "over and over again, case after case, interview after interview, we hear batterers and victims discuss how *power and control were at the core of events that led up to the use of violence*" (p. 92; emphasis added). Yet these core elements are missing in the "conflict of personal interests" approach to measuring violence.

The CTS is introduced to research subjects with the comment that all couples have disagreements that they try to settle in different ways. CTS questions about violent acts are at the end of a continuum of items such as "discussed an issue calmly," "cried," and "stomped out," about which husbands and wives were asked in parallel fashion. The CTS does not assess the meanings, contexts, or consequences of these individual acts. Further, and more significant in terms of the theoretical question I have raised, the CTS excludes, a priori, information on economic deprivation, sexual abuse, intimidation, isolation, stalking, and terrorizing—all common elements of wife battering and all rarely perpetrated by women. Through the conflict theory lens, gendered dimensions of violence are not seen, not measured, and (not surprisingly) not found.

The theories of violence discussed above are not inherently incompatible with feminist theory. In fact, they offer valuable insights (for example, regarding the relations among resources, power, and violence). Because these theories lack a feminist lens, however, they miss a crucial part of the domestic violence picture.

In the following section, I will discuss some of the important feminist work on domestic violence that is grounded in the empirically well-supported proposition that family relationships are profoundly shaped by gender and power—both interpersonal and institutional (for thorough reviews of feminist family scholarship, see Ferree 1990; Sollie and Leslie 1994; Thompson and Walker 1989).

A Close-Up of Control, Intimacy, and Violence

To say, simply, that domestic violence is about gender and power may seem like nothing more than a sound bite. But it is far more than that—it is a concise expression of a complex body of feminist theory and research. A full discussion of this work would fill volumes; in this chapter I can only outline the coercive control view of domestic violence, consider some of its limitations, and suggest possible directions for fruitful development.

Feminist work in family violence explores and articulates the ways in which violence against women in the home is a critical component of the system of male power. Violence grows out of inequality within marriage (and other intimate relations that are modeled on marriage) and reinforces male dominance and female subordination within the home and outside it (Schechter with Gary 1988). In other words, violence against women (whether in the form of sexual harassment at work, rape by a date, or a beating at home) is a tactic of male control (Hanmer and Maynard 1987). It is not gender neutral any more than the economic division of labor or the institution of marriage is gender neutral.

The conceptualization of violence as coercive control was not deduced from an abstract theoretical model and quantified. Rather, it grew inductively out of the day-to-day work of battered women/activists who struggled to make sense of the victimization they saw. As the shelter movement grew and survivors and activists joined together to discuss their experiences, a clearer vision of what domestic violence is and how to challenge it emerged (Schechter 1982).

A control model of domestic violence, known as the "power and control wheel," developed by the Domestic Abuse Intervention Project in Duluth, Minnesota, is shown in Figure 1. This model has been used across the country in batterers' groups, support groups, and training groups (as well as in empirical studies). It provides a valuable, concise framework for seeing the interconnections between violence and other forms of coercive control, which I will refer to as *control tactics*.

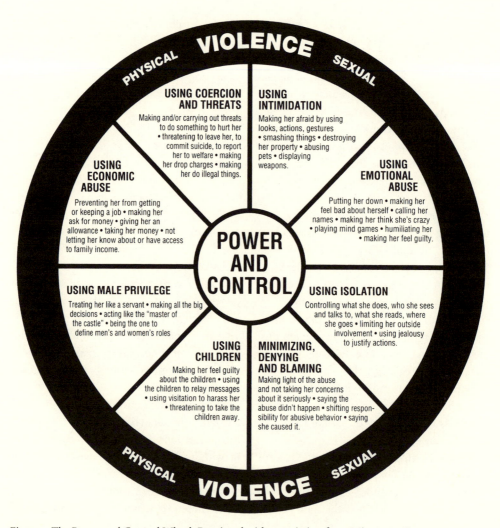

Figure 1. The Power and Control Wheel. Reprinted with permission from Minnesota Program Development, Inc., Domestic Abuse Intervention Project, 206 W. 4th Street, Duluth, MN 55806.

The wheel connects physical and sexual violence to the hub of power and control with a number of "spokes": minimization and denial, intimidation, isolation, emotional abuse, economic abuse, use of children, threats, and assertion of male privilege.

When one looks at these control tactics in a bit more detail, through research based on extensive interviews with battered women and batterers (Jones and Schechter 1992; Ptacek 1988; Yllö et al. 1992), the close-up picture of domestic violence that develops is one of domination rather than one of conflict of interest. The following is an interview excerpt from a study of women who were physically abused during their pregnancies (Yllö et al. 1992). It offers a view of events leading up to violence that differs markedly from the mutuality of the conflict tactics scenario. S., a thirty-one-year-old white woman, describes the control and violence in her marriage that eventually resulted in a miscarriage:

I didn't even realize he was gaining control and I was too dumb to know any better. . . . He was gaining control bit by bit until he was checking my pantyhose when I'd come home from the supermarket to see if they were inside out. . . . He'd time me. He'd check the mileage on the car. . . . I was living like a prisoner. . . . One day I was at Zayers with him . . . and I was looking at a sweater. He insisted I was looking at a guy. I didn't even know there was a guy in the area, because it got to the point that I, I had to walk like I had horse-blinders on. . . . You don't look anybody in the eye. You don't look up because you are afraid.

At one point, S. was insulted by a friend of her husband's and she was furious. She recalls:

I told him, who the hell was he? And I threw a glass of root beer in his face. My husband gave me a back hand, so I just went upstairs to the bedroom and got into a nightgown. And he kept telling me to come downstairs and I said "No— just leave me alone." . . . He come up and went right through the door. Knocked the whole top panel off of the door and got into the room. Ripped the nightgown right off my back, just bounced me off every wall in that bedroom. Then he threw me down the stairs and . . . outside in the snow and just kept kicking me and saying it was too soon for me to be pregnant. . . . His friend was almost rooting him on.

What S. describes is far more than a conflict of personal agendas. The acts of physical abuse against S. are located in a context of male entitlement, control, intimidation, isolation, and emotional abuse. The violence enforces her subjection. As Schechter (with Gary 1988) writes:

Battering is a *pattern* of coercive control. . . . When a woman is battered, there is a pattern of unfair and unwarranted control being exercised over her life. Even as she resists her abuser's efforts, he continues to use coercion to dominate her. It is essential to understand this dynamic in order to understand why violence against women is so pervasive and powerful. (p. 243).

Schechter goes on to point out that when a batterer enforces his entitlement physically, he experiences a number of gains in the relationship. He gets his way, feels strong and manly, and has a partner catering to him in hopes of avoiding further violence (p. 244).

The coercive control model of domestic violence is an important theoretical alternative to the conflict tactics model. It identifies violence as a tactic of entitlement and power that is deeply gendered, rather than as a conflict tactic that is personal and gender neutral. It has deepened our understanding of family violence in substantial and significant ways. However, it is not the final analysis. Although it provides a potent description of violence and its context, it falls short of explaining it fully.

The coercive control model has rested on simple tenets of behavioral psychology and social exchange theory (a charge that has also been leveled at mainstream sociological approaches; see Breines and Gordon 1983). As noted above, feminists have argued that men batter because they have much to gain through violence (Jones and Schehter 1992; Schechter 1988). This analysis parallels Gelles's (1983) exchange view, that "people hit and abuse other family members because they can. . . . People will use violence in the family if the costs of being violent do not out outweigh the rewards" (p. 157). The similarity in psychological assumptions here is apparent, even though Gelles writes in gender-neutral terms.

My purpose is not to undermine the feminist paradigm, but rather to challenge us to develop it further. I agree that men do gain from violence, and in doing so they reinforce inequality within the home and beyond. What we are missing is an explanation of why a relatively small percentage of men batter, given the advantages to be gained. (And, by extension, we lack adequate intervention strategies to deal with those who do batter.)

We have some answers in an empirical smorgasbord of variables (unemployment, stress, alcohol use, child abuse, and so on), yet we have little sense of the psychological dynamics leading to the decision to use violence. The rewards violence brings are, at least in part, subjectively determined. Why is a subordinate, cowering wife pleasing to some men, but not to others?

One intriguing effort to address these questions is the "feminist relational view of battering" developed by feminist therapists[1] at the Ackerman Institute (Goldner et al. 1990). These researchers are trying to explore the full subjective experience of batterers and the women they abuse without losing sight of male dominance in relationships and in society. Their work is not fully developed, but I want to highlight a few of their ideas that, I am sure, will be the subject of further debate. Goldner et al. (1990) argue that it is useful to

> understand male violence as simultaneously an instrumental and expressive act. Its instrumentality rests on the fact that it is a powerful method of social control, . . . a strategy that a man consciously "chooses." At another level violence can be understood as an impulsive, expressive act. . . . [Male violence] represents a conscious strategy of control, and a frightening disorienting loss of control. (p. 346)

In searching for the meaning of expressive violence, Goldner et al. don't rely on narrow, intrapsychic constructs. Instead, they follow recent gender theory, with its emphasis on the social construction of gender. This view holds that because "gender is relational and not essential, creating and recreating ourselves as gendered persons involves not a little struggle and ambivalence" (Hess; quoted in Ferree 1990, p. 869). In sum, "the fundamental question is how the illusion of a gender dichotomy is constructed and maintained in the face of between-sex similarity and within-sex difference, and the

answer is to be found in the constant and contentious process of en-gendering behavior as separate and unequal" (Ferree 1990, p. 869).

Goldner at al. (1990) argue that this contentious process is a key to understanding intimate relationships, particularly violent ones. They have come to see battering as "a man's attempt to reassert gender difference and gender dominance, when his terror of not being different enough from 'his' woman threatens to overtake him" (p. 348). Although the gender struggle is central to masculine identity generally, Goldner et al. suggest that the fear takes extreme form in batterers and that it is grounded in families of origin in which gendered premises about masculinity and femininity are rigidly adhered to, especially by fathers (p. 351). Further, they suggest that these gender premises also shed light on the bond or alliance many battered women have with their abusers. We must not negate the importance of economic dependency and out-and-out terror that entrap so many battered women. However, we can do more, as feminists, to understand the bond that is separate from the bondage.

Caveats and Conclusions

There is, obviously, much more to be said about developing a full understanding of the dynamics of battering, and I believe that feminist work that incorporates coercive control and goes beyond it is very promising. As I challenge our thinking on this issue, I do want to state two important caveats. First, it is crucial that psychological *explanations* of battering not serve as *excuses* for battering. Too often, factors such as a man's low self-esteem, poor impulse control, alcoholism, and traumatic childhood, or a couple's "mutual circular process," have served to relieve batterers of their responsibility for criminally assaulting their partners. Ironically, women's psychological problems have been seen as the cause of their victimization. Feminists charge that such analyses and the interventions based on them, "*collude* with batterers by not making violence the primary issue or by implicitly legitimizing men's excuses for violence" (Adams 1988, p. 177; see also Ptacek 1988). As Goldner et al. (1990) write:

> Our attempt to discern and construct meaning in acts of violence does not overrule or substitute for our clear moral position regarding the acts themselves. Violence may be "explainable," but it is not excusable, and it may or may not be forgivable. That is up to the victim. (p. 345)

The second caveat is that in developing a deeper insight into the subjective meaning of violence, we must not lose sight of the big picture that feminism has so clearly developed: Domestic violence is not just an individual problem, but a social and political one (Dobash and Dobash 1992; Hanmer and Maynard 1987). Violence is a means of social control of women that is at once personal and institutional, symbolic and material. The restrictions on women's psychic and physical freedom created by the fear and reality of male violence are inescapable. Efforts to understand more fully the psychology of violence are important and will, no doubt, contribute to our intervention efforts. However, they will do little to stanch the flow of violence in the absence of wider social action and fundamental social change on behalf of women. And in creating that social change, I believe, feminism makes its greatest contribution.

If our mutual goal is to understand the violence in order to stop it, then we must welcome the challenges other viewpoints pose and give them respectful consideration. My point that feminism is a necessary, but not sufficient, lens for understanding violence is a challenge to all of us to deepen our views.

NOTE

1. Although this theory is intriguing, I am concerned about its application in the context of conjoint treatment. Although Goldner et al. (1990) make reference to the criticisms leveled at couples therapy for domestic violence, they do not take the warnings seriously enough. Their commitment to a systemic approach overrides their safety concerns. See Bograd (1984, 1992), Dell (1989), and Willbach (1989) for fuller critiques of family systems' treatment of battering.

REFERENCES

Adams, D. (1988). Treatment models of men who batter: A profeminist analysis. In K. Yllö and M. Bograd (Eds.), *Feminist perspectives on wife abuse* (pp. 176–199). Newbury Park, CA: Sage.

Bernard, J. (1976). *The future of marriage.* New York: Bantam.

Bograd, M. (1984). Family systems' approaches to wife battering: A feminist critique. *American Journal of Orthopsychiatry* 54:558–568.

———. (1988). Feminist perspectives on wife abuse: An introduction. In K. Yllö and M. Bograd (Eds.), *Feminist perspectives on wife abuse* (pp. 11–26). Newbury Park, CA: Sage.

———. (1992). Values in conflict: Challenges to family therapists' thinking. *Journal of Marital and Family Therapy* 18:245–256.

Breines, W., and L. Gordon (1983). The new scholarship on family violence. *Signs* 8:490–531.

Chodorow, N. (1978). *The reproduction of mothering.* Berkeley: University of California Press.

Collins, R. (1975). *Conflict sociology.* New York: Academic Press.

Dell, P. (1989). Violence and the systemic view: The problem of power. *Family Process* 28:1–14.

Dobash, R. E., and R. P. Dobash (1979). *Violence against wives: A case against the patriarchy.* New York: Free Press.

Dobash, R. P., and R. E. Dobash. (1992). *Women, violence, and social change.* New York: Routledge.

Dobash, R. P., R. E. Dobash, M. Wilson, and M. Daly. (1992). The myth of sexual symmetry in marital violence. *Social Problems* 39:71–91.

Ferree, M. M. (1990). Beyond separate spheres: Feminism and family research. *Journal of Marriage and the Family* 52:866–884.

Gelles, R. J. (1974). *The violent home: A study of physical aggression between husbands and wives.* Beverly Hills, CA: Sage.

———. (1983). An exchange/social control theory. In D. Finkelhor, R. J. Gelles, G. T. Hotaling, and M. A. Straus (Eds.), *The dark side of families: Current family violence research* (pp. 151–165). Beverly Hills, CA: Sage.

———. (1993). Through a sociological lens: social structure and family violence. In R. J. Gelles and D. R. Loseke (Eds.), *Current Controversies on Family Violence.* Newbury Park, CA: Sage.

Gelles, R. J., and Straus, M. A. (1988). *Intimate violence: The causes and consequences of abuse in the American family.* New York: Simon and Schuster.

Gillespie, D. (1971). Who has the power? The marital struggle. *Journal of Marriage and the Family* 33:445–458.

Goldner, V., P. Penn, M. Sheinberg, and G. Walker. (1990). Love and violence: Gender paradoxes in volatile attachments. *Family Process* 29:343–364.

Hanmer, J. and M. Maynard (1987). *Women, violence, and social control.* Atlantic Highlands, NJ: Humanities.

Jones, A., and S. Schechter. (1992). *When love goes wrong.* New York: HarperCollins.

Martin, D. (1976). *Battered wives.* New York: Pocket Books.

Ptacek, J. (1988). Why do men batter their wives? In K. Yllö and M. Bograd (Eds.), *Feminist perspectives on wife abuse* (pp. 133–157). Newbury Park, CA: Sage. (Chapter 46, this volume.)

Schechter, S. (1982). *Women and male violence: The visions and struggles of the battered women's movement.* Boston: South End.

Schechter, S., with L. Gary (1988). A framework for understanding and empowering battered women. In M. Straus (Ed.), *Abuse and victim-* *ization across the life span* (pp. 240–253). Baltimore: Johns Hopkins University Press.

Sollie, D., and L. Leslie (1994). *Genders, families, and close relationships: Feminist research journeys.* Newbury Park, CA: Sage.

Sprey, J. (1969). The family as a system in conflict. *Journal of Marriage and the Family* 31: 699–706.

Steinmetz, S. K., and M. A. Straus (Eds.). (1974). *Violence in the family.* New York: Harper & Row.

Straus, M. A., (1990). The Conflict Tactics Scales and its critics: An evaluation and new data on validity and reliability. In M. A. Straus and R. J. Gelles (Eds.), *Physical violence in American families: Risk factors and adaptations to violence in 8,145 families* (pp. 49–73). New Brunswick, NJ: Transaction.

Straus, M. A. and R. J. Gelles (Eds.). (1990). *Physical violence in American families: Risk factors and adaptations to violence in 8,145 families.* New Brunswick, NJ: Transaction.

Tannen, D. (1990). *You just don't understand: Women and men in conversation.* New York: William Morrow.

Thompson, L., and A. Walker (1989). Gender in families: Women and men in marriage, work, and parenthood. *Journal of Marriage and the Family* 51:845–871.

Thorne, B., and M. Yalom (1982). *Rethinking the family: Some feminist questions.* New York: Longman.

Willbach, D. (1989). Ethics and family therapy: The case management of family violence. *Journal of Marital and Family Therapy* 15:43–52.

Yllö, K. (1988). Political and methodological debates in wife abuse research. In K. Yllö and M. Bograd (Eds.), *Feminist perspectives on wife abuse* (pp. 28–50). Newbury Park, CA: Sage.

Yllö, K., L. Gary, E. H. Newberger, J. Pandolfino, and S. Schechter (1992, October 18). Pregnant woman abuse and adverse birth outcomes. Paper presented at the annual meeting of the Society for Applied Sociology, Cleveland, OH.

Chapter 46

Why Do Men Batter Their Wives?

JAMES PTACEK

Throughout the past decade of feminist work on violence against women, the testimony of battered women has been indispensable in making public the oppression that had long been hidden from view. With the growth in social services for men who batter, researchers and activists have recently had the opportunity to talk with batterers about their perspective on violence against wives. What can we learn about wife beating from men who batter? Surely, the testimony of batterers cannot be taken at face value. Nevertheless, when placed in the context of a feminist analysis of women's oppression, men who batter have a good deal to contribute. Not only is their discussion richer than what is found in clinical interpretations of their behavior but, unwittingly, their testimony also presents its own critique far more powerfully than what is contained in most psychological

and sociological treatments. That is, not only do they present their violence in a light that illuminates its intentionality and cruelty but their words also reveal the blind spots in the dominant clinical perspectives. From the unlikeliest of sources, then, comes a challenge to the narrow psychological explanation of wife beating so popular today.

In this chapter I will present transcripts of how men who batter talk about their violence. For this study I conducted interviews with 18 abusive men. Small as this sample is, this study represents one of only a few successful attempts to gather evidence systemically of batterers' perspectives on wife beating. In order to make sense of the accounts presented here, at least three levels of analysis are necessary. First, there is the issue of methods, in other words, the relationship between the researcher (myself) and the men in the study. Questions of what my motivation was in doing this research, how I collected the data, and how I dealt with conflicts that arose during the process of interviewing will be addressed. By providing this background I seek to sort out the problem of bias and its effect on the content of the interviews.

The second level of analysis involves examining some relationships within the batterers' testimony, that is, the patterns and contradictions that are found in the accounts. The question of the role that batterers' rationalizations play in the progression of the violence and abusiveness can then be investigated.

Finally, the third level of investigation concerns the relationship between the batterers' explanations for their violence and those explanations prevalent in the wider society. I shall compare the batterers' accounts with the analysis offered in the clinical literature on wife beating. In addition, some attention will be given to the discourse on battering encountered in the criminal justice system. With this threefold analysis, I hope to provide a proper context for understanding what batterers have to say.

The Study

In order to examine the ways batterers perceive their violence, I conducted in-depth interviews with 18 male clients I recruited through my work with Emerge, a Boston organization that offers counseling for wife beaters. The men's involvement in counseling ranged from a single intake session to 24 weeks in the group counseling program. Only 33 percent of the sample had completed the full six months of group counseling; 39 percent had attended three or fewer counseling sessions. While their experiences at Emerge likely affected how they viewed their actions, it is important to note that contact with Emerge was rather limited for a good portion of the men. None of the men was in counseling at the time of the interviews; most had been out of contact with Emerge for over a

year. In all but two cases, the man's violence had allegedly stopped.

While this is clearly not a representative sample of batterers in any scientific sense, this group of men is quite diverse as far as demographic data and levels of violence are concerned. The age range is broad, from 22 to 53 years, although most of the men are in their thirties. All but two of the men are white. Only half of the men were officially married during the period of the violence; three men had not even been sharing a common residence with their partner during the time of the abusiveness. The data on education, occupation, and income indicate that the proportion of working-class and middle-class men is about equal. Seven men held at least a college degree; professional, technical, and social service categories account for the employment of eight of the men. One man was unemployed; two men reported income of less than $5,000 for the previous year.

In half the relationships, the men became violent less than a year after the relationship began. Based on their own testimony, the violence involved shoving, slapping, dragging by the hair, throwing objects—such as a plate or an ashtray—punching, kicking, bodily throwing, choking, "beating up," threatening with a knife, and rape. One-third of the men reported that their partners sustained broken bones or other substantial physical injuries as a result of the violence. It is my opinion that this is at best a conservative estimate of the violence these men inflicted; underreporting by batterers is frequently noted in the clinical literature (Adams and Penn 1981; Bograd 1983; Brisson 1982; Lund, Larsen, and Schultz 1982). There was, unfortunately, no way of corroborating the batterers' reports short of calling up the battered women and asking them to talk about the abuse, which in most cases occurred some years ago.

All the interviews were conducted in the

Emerge offices. The men were offered eight dollars for their participation. This indicated that they would be doing something for Emerge's benefit and established that the interview was not formally a counseling session. Half of the men declined the money, usually with the statement that they were happy to give something back to Emerge, since Emerge had helped them. The interviews followed an open-ended, semistructured format. The men were asked to describe the first, last, and most violent episodes; to talk about what happened before, during, and after the episode; and to explain what they were thinking and feeling during all of this.

The value in using the in-depth personal interview to study wife beating lies in its potential for comprehending the batterer's perspective. However, this very virtue raises the possibility of bias, a problem that requires serious attention.

Bias in Field Research

While national surveys and other more "quantitative" methods may not be any less susceptible to bias (Becker 1970), the in-depth interview and more "qualitative" methods pose particular problems for the interpretation and evaluation of research. The major advantage of this approach is the possibility of developing trust and exploring the respondent's perceptions, feelings, and rationalizations through dialogue. The limitations result from the reliance of the research on one unique "instrument"—the field researcher— who often simultaneously acts as theorist, provocateur, observer, recorder, and interpreter. Because of this singularly personal involvement with the phenomenon being studied, a number of field researchers have emphasized the importance of accounting for the motivation and self-presentation of the

researcher in the write-up of the study. This is important in order to enable the reader to gauge the impact of the researcher on the subject of the research. For example, Reinharz (1979, 10–11) states that the process and the biases of the researcher should be made clear.

> Since research is a personal activity, research reports should contain a vivid description of the experience of the researching. In these reports the value positions of the researcher should be faced squarely and addressed fully.

In light of these considerations, I would like to make explicit my motivations for conducting research.

Motivation of the Researcher

I came to study wife beating as a way of contributing to social action against men's domination of women. Prior to entering graduate school, I became involved with Emerge in Boston. I have continued my affiliation with Emerge while in school, working as a group counselor, public speaker, trainer, and researcher for the organization. As Emerge defines wife beating in political terms and draws its analysis from the women's movement, I am both an activist and a researcher on the issue of violence against wives. As the Dobashes point out, there are not many clear models for how to operate in this nexus.

> Despite all protestation to the contrary, social research and political issues are inevitably related. Yet, social science is largely lacking in models of how to develop scientific work within this context, how to analyze the social and political consequences of the messages inherent in research and how to participate with community groups and social agencies in the collective creation of social change. (Dobash and Dobash 1981, 7)

The point is that each orientation on the issue of wife beating carries its own limitations and potential for bias, whether one is an activist or an academic, a man or a woman. If the researcher's motivation is clearly stated, the reader will have a fuller context within which to evaluate the research enterprise.

Presentation of Self in the Research Setting

I presented myself to the 18 respondents as an Emerge counselor, as a researcher, and as a graduate student, in that order of emphasis. Having employed these institutional affiliations in order to secure an interview, it was nonetheless incumbent upon me to minimize my impact on the respondent as much as possible during the interview itself. Leading questions were eliminated from the interview guide. For example, rather than asking directly, "Do you think the violence was justifiable," I assumed that excuses and justifications would arise spontaneously under direct questioning about the violence.

During the interviews, I tried to limit my emotional responses and judgmental affect as much as I could. My intent was to facilitate a narrative rather than continually challenge the men. This interviewing style contrasts with the much more confrontative counseling approach used at Emerge. While the confrontative approach can be an effective strategy in bringing about change in a batterer's behavior, I felt that as an interviewing style this would result in a collection of the most defensive, superficial, and dishonset responses from the men. Such an interviewing posture would maximize my impact on the batterers' testimony, and would minimize their own contributions.

It is nevertheless important to recognize that there are moral and political dimensions to this type of "impartial" approach. As Alan Stone says:

> Human problems do not come packaged in psychiatric bits and moral bits. It seems that there

may be a moral cost even in nonjudgmental listening (1984, 231).

For *psychiatric* one could easily substitute *sociological*. Does it not, at some level, reaffirm a lack of moral seriousness concerning wife beating to listen to a man describe a bloody assault on a woman, and remain dispassionately composed? Does it not, at some level, reinforce male entitlement to hear a man explain how he broke a woman's ribs because she wasn't sexually "motivated," and then continue questioning as though this account was reasonable?

In all but two of the 18 cases, the respondent's physical abusiveness had allegedly stopped. In these two cases, and in a third case involving a child, the men reported ongoing if sporadic violence: pushing, restraining, slapping, hair-pulling. During these three interviews, I switched from an interviewer role to a confrontative counselor role after the formal questions had been completed. On one occasion, this led to a heated argument about the "justifications" for assaulting someone; in another case, the respondent's vengeful intent to hurt and the resulting fear in his wife and children were discussed; and in a third instance, the batterer was encouraged to return to Emerge for help (after a four-year lapse). This third individual did contact the Emerge office and was called by the counseling coordinator but subsequently failed to reenter counseling.

This more confrontative stance followed the collection of the interview data, and therefore did not "contaminate" the interview. While a brief confrontation will likely have little or no immediate effect on an individual's behavior, it must be remembered that a pattern of tolerance of or indifference toward wife beating is implicated by most sociological theories as a reason for its persistence. At the very least, such confrontation ensures that among these batterers' contacts with various professionals there is at least one place where the violence, in and of itself, is made a serious matter.

Regarding those cases where the violence had allegedly stopped, and where this type of confrontation did not take place, I don't feel I resolved the issue of nonjudgmental listening satisfactorily. In retrospect, a frank, confrontational debriefing could have been structured into the interview format.

The Findings: Batterers' Excuses and Justifications

The 18 men interviewed for the study all came for help to Emerge, a counseling program for batterers. Whether they defined the "problem" as their violence or, as is more likely, saving their relationships, the very existence of a program for men who batter established the sense that their violence was wrong. And once they arrived, this sense of wrongness was made explicit by the counselors. On an average of 1.8 years later, these men returned and talked with a man, identified as both an Emerge counselor and a researcher, about their violence. The sense that the violence is wrong is institutionalized in the very setting of the interviews. In this context, and to this interviewer, how do these men talk about their abusiveness?

When an individual whose behavior is regarded as socially unacceptable is questioned about such behavior, the individual's response may be called an account (Scott and Lyman 1968). Accounts represent a complex of anticipated judgment, face-saving, and status negotiation. Scott and Lyman distinguish two types of accounts that serve to neutralize socially disapproved behavior: excuses and justifications. Excuses are those accounts in which the abuser denies full responsibility for his actions. Justifications are those accounts in which the batterer may accept

some responsibility but denies or trivializes the wrongness of his violence. These descriptive categorizations will become clearer in their application to the batterers' testimony. In making excuses and justifications, the deviant individual employs "socially approved vocabularies" that are routinized within cultures (Scott and Lyman 1968, 46, 52). The batterer appeals to standard rationalizations in an attempt to make sense of or to normalize his behavior.

While on the whole, the batterers' accounts consist of more excuses than justifications, most men use both verbal strategies in an attempt to neutralize their behavior. They tend to excuse themselves of full responsibility, and at the same time, they offer justifications for their abusiveness. As a result, their accounts are often internally inconsistent. This suggests that over the course of a two-hour interview, a variety of strategies were employed to neutralize the violence, regardless of whether they conflicted with one another. This lack of integration will be discussed further as the validity of the batterers' explanations is addressed.

Excuses: Denial of Responsibility

Perhaps the most common way that batterers attempt to excuse their violent behavior is by an appeal to loss of control. Such appeals to a diminished capacity to control their actions take several forms. Partial or complete loss of control is usually spoken of as resulting either from alcohol or drug use or from a buildup of frustrations. The sense here is that physiological or psychological factors lead to a state where awareness or will is impaired, thus diminishing responsibility. Of the 18 men interviewed, 94 percent (N = 17) employed an account that falls into one or more subcategories: appeals to alcohol or drugs, frustration, and complete loss of control.

Of the sample of 18 batterers, 33 percent (N = 6) maintain that their self-control was diminished by alcohol or drugs.

> It's taken the edge off my self-control. That's what I will call it, being intoxicated. It's taken my limits off me and let me do things and become disruptive in a way I would not become. I can get angry with people, really violent, stone sober. But the more I was drinking on a day-to-day basis, the more easy that was to come across.

> I've been involved with A. A., and that's why I'm much better. And a lot of—my problems—not all of them, but most of my problems at the time were due to that. And it's just amazing to know that there was a reason for the way I acted.

Asked whether they thought they would be violent with a woman again, it was common for these men to say no, as long as they were able to remain free of alcohol or drug dependency. (Most of them said they had successfully quit.)

To what extent does alcohol cause loss of control over one's behavior? In a study of family violence, Gelles (1974) cites anthropological data that establishes drunken behavior as learned (rather than purely chemically induced) behavior. Drunken comportment varies widely from culture to culture, according to Gelles. Because it is believed to lead to loss of control, people behave as though it actually has that property, and use this "loss of control" to disavow or neutralize deviant behavior such as wife beating. As shall be shown, the contradictions in the batterers' own testimony supports this argument.

A frustration-aggression description of violence is present in the accounts of 67 percent (N = 12) of the men. As in a previous study (Bograd 1983), these accounts present temporary loss of control as resulting from an accumulation of internal pressure. This pressure is often described as building with a hydraulic type of inevitability.

I think I reach a point where I can't tolerate anything anymore, and it's at that time where whatever it is that shouldn't be tolerated in the first place now is a major issue in my life. I do better now. I used to come out at one thing. It didn't matter what it was. It just, you know—I couldn't hold it back anymore. It just came out in a tirade.

> We used to argue about picayune-ass things anyway. And a lot of this was building and building. And I was keeping it all inside. All of the frustration and anger. You're supposed to sit there and take this stuff from your wife. And, like I say, I'd take it for awhile, but then I'd lose my head.

But as Bandura (1973) argues regarding the frustration-aggression hypothesis, aggression is only one of a number of responses to frustration. Other possible responses include dependency, achievement, withdrawal and resignation, psychosomatic illness, drug or alcohol use, and constructive problem-solving. Most of the men in this sample must have responded to frustration in ways other than violence, for they indicate that their violence is very selective. For 39 percent (N = 7) of these men, their frustration led to violence only in the presence of their wives or lovers; for 33 percent (N = 66), their frustration led to violence only when they were in the presence of their partners, children, and mothers. In only 28 percent (N = 5) of these cases were the men violent both within and outside the family.

In the accounts of 56 percent (N = 10) of the batterers, descriptions of the violence are presented in terms of being completely out of control.

> When I got violent, it was not because I really wanted to get violent. It was just because it was like an outburst of rage.

> I was a real jerk for almost a year. And anything would set off. Anything. I was like uncontrollably violent. I would slap her, knock her down, choke her, and call her a slut and a whore.

I struck her once before, and I guess it made me see something of myself that I didn't like to see, the way I had no control over myself. And I knew that the anger that I had inside me was very hard to control.

I'd grab, you know, and squeeze a lot. I grabbed her around the neck one time and I think I almost strangled her. But I finally let go, you know. I realized that—I got a hold of myself, realized what I was doing.

A blowout is where I lose, I just lose everything. I would just blank out, more or less. You know, like there would be a gap in between where I wouldn't actually remember. You know, like all I could remember seeing is like white, little twinkled white, red, like lights. That's all I can remember. That's a blowout.

It was all booze. I didn't think. I didn't think at all. It was just like a madman. It was temporary insanity. I really, all's I really wanted to do was crush her. There was nothing there but—I wanted to cause pain and mess her looks up.

Of the 10 men claiming such total loss of control, only three of them blamed this on alcohol. Blackouts or partial memory losses were reported by two of the men who claimed they had been intoxicated, but such memory losses were also reported by two men who allegedly had not been drinking.

The second main category of excuses is victim-blaming. As in the case of the loss of control excuses, the wrongness of the violence is more or less accepted; but here, the men deny responsibility by claiming they were "provoked." In a few isolated incidents, the batterers presented their violence as a response to the woman's physical aggressiveness.

She slapped me across the face hard. It hurt. . . . And that did it. Then I slapped her, and punched her, and kicked her, and knocked her down. I mean, I just let her have it.

More commonly, the batterers assert that their violence was a response to the woman's verbal aggressiveness. Some 44 percent (N = 8) of the sample blamed the victim in this fashion.

She was trying to tell me, you know, I'm no fucking good and this and that . . . and she just kept at me, you know. And I couldn't believe it. And finally, I just got real pissed and I said wow, you know. I used to think, you're going to treat me like this? You're going to show me that I'm the scumb bag? Whack. Take that. And that was my psychology.

Women can verbally abuse you. They can rip your clothes off, without even touching you, the way women know how to talk, converse. But men don't. Well, they weren't brought up to talk as much as women do, converse as well as women do. So it was a resort to violence, if I couldn't get through to her by words.

It wasn't right for me to slap her. It wasn't unprovoked, you know what I mean? It was almost like she was being an asshole at that particular time. I think for once in her life she realized that, you know, it was her fault.

On some occasions she was the provoker. It didn't call for physical abuse. I was wrong in that. But it did call for something. . . . You know, you're married for that long, if somebody gets antagonistic, you want to defend yourself.

These men seem to regard verbal aggressiveness as equivalent to physical aggressiveness, as if a woman's verbal behavior somehow excuses them of responsibility for their violence. There are serious deficiencies in the men's perspective (Dobash and Dobash 1979). Even if one takes the extreme position that verbal aggressiveness warrants a physical response, the question becomes: who "provoked" the verbal aggressiveness? Furthermore, the "provocation" argument implies that there is a proper way a wife can address her husband that the husband is empowered to maintain. The above accounts reveal just such a male arrogance: While this retaliatory behavior is acceptable, her verbal excesses are not. The "provocation" excuse solidifies male dominance (Dobash and Dobash 1979).

Justifications: Denial of Wrongness

Appeals to loss of control and victim-blaming are common ways by which these men excuse their violence. While excuses represent denial of responsibility, justifications are denials of wrongdoing on the part of the offender.

The first of two categories of justifications is *denial of injury*. According to some clinicians who have worked with men who batter, many batterers neutralize the unacceptability of their behavior by denying or minimizing the injuries battered women suffer (Adams and Penn 1981; Brisson 1982; Star 1983). With this sample, it was not possible to obtain reports from the abused women in order to determine the full extent of minimization. Nonetheless, trivialization of the woman's injuries is apparent in the accounts of 44 percent (N = 8) of the men. With some men, this takes the form of a denial that the behavior was violent. With others, the abusers maintain that the woman's fears were exaggerated. And a number of men minimize the nature of the injuries.

A euphemistic redefinition of violent behavior is presented in the accounts of two men.

> I never beat my wife. I responded physically to her.

> Yes, I do believe my physical punishment as a child can contribute to me having a tendency to react violently and think nothing of it. When I say violent, "physically," I think, would be a much more appropriate term.

Looking at the behavior these men report, the first admitted he pushed, grabbed, and slapped his wife, and that she received bruises and injured her knee as a result. The second man admitted to slapping, punching, and grabbing a woman by the hair and dragging her across the floor. One of the many women with whom this second individual was "physical" received a black eye. He was arrested five or six times for assault and battery on men.

Other men claimed that women exaggerated the severity of the violence. This respondent's account is representative.

> These people told her that she had to get all of these orders of protection and stuff like that because I was going to kill her, you know. Well, I wasn't going to kill her. I mean, I'd yell at her, and scream, and stuff like that, and maybe I'd whack her once or twice, you know, but I wasn't going to kill her. That's for sure.

This individual did admit to slapping and punching his wife, giving her a black eye, and throwing and breaking furniture. During one episode, he stated his wife fled the house screaming. Yet when asked if she was frightened of him, he said, "no."

A number of men minimized the extent of the women's injuries by attributing black and blue marks to the ease with which women bruise. This is how three men responded to the question of whether the woman was injured:

> Not really. Pinching does leave bruises. And, I guess, slapping. I guess women bruise easily, too. They bump into a door and they'll bruise.

> Not injured. She bruises easily.

> Yeah, she bruised. Yeah, she bruises easily anyway. If I just squeeze like that, you know, next day she'll get a mark.

The statement that "women bruise easily" goes beyond an observation of comparative anatomy. By admitting that they have bruised a woman, and yet denying that this is very significant, the more internal nonphysical injuries are also denied: the instilling of fear, the humiliation, the degradation, the assault on her identity as a woman.

These other kinds of injury become more visible in this last category of justification. Among the reasons for the violence given by men who batter, there is a pattern of finding fault with the woman for not being good at cooking, for not being sexually responsive, for not being deferential enough to her husband, for not knowing when she is "supposed" to be silent, and for not being faithful. In short, for not being a "good wife." One batterer reported that he threatened his partner with these words: "I should just smack you for the lousy wife you've been." This is the rationale that underlies the explanations in this category. Bograd (1983) titles this category of justifications *failure to fulfill obligations of a good wife.*

Of the 18 men interviewed, 78 percent (N = 14) gave accounts falling into this category. These accounts came from both married and unmarried men. On cooking:

> Until we were married 10 years or so there was no violence or anything. But then after a while, it just became, it just became too much. . . . I don't know if I demanded respect as a person or a husband or anything like that, but I certainly, you know, didn't think I was wrong in asking not to be filled up with fatty foods.

On availability of sex:

> A couple more incidents happened over the next year . . . where I did strike her, and for basically the same reason. I just tried making love, and making love, and she couldn't do it.

> It was over sex, and it happened I guess because I was trying to motivate her. And she didn't seem too motivated.

On not being deferential enough:

> I think a lot of it had to do with my frustration of not being able to handle children. You know, they'd tell me to shut up. "You're not going to tell me to shut up." And then [my wife] would tell me, you know, "Let me handle this." I said, "I'm the man of the house." Then we'd start arguing. That's basically how they used to happen.

The intent is to have her see it my way. You know, "There's no need for you to think the way you're thinking. And you should see it my way, there's something wrong with you. You're being abusive to me by not seeing it my way."

> That was a way I could win. She would know that she had gone too far in asking me something, in constantly probing, requiring me to answer. So that would let her know how hurt or angry I was feeling.

On not knowing when she is "supposed" to be silent:

> I don't think I used to like to be confronted about being high [on heroin], even though I was high. And it would bother me. It bothered me to a point where I would strike out. I was working, but wasn't making any money. . . . "The baby needs this, and the baby needs that." Jesus Christ what do you want me to do, you know? We were at the table. . . . I just picked my plate up and threw it at her.

On not being faithful:

> I walked right over and slapped her right across the face. . . . I think it was probably around the time when she was telling me she wanted to see other guys, you know. She was too young to get involved with me or one guy. And I didn't want to hear that.

> I was eighteen. And I was going to be true to somebody, for once, to see what it's like. And it turned out two years later, two and a half years later, she was going out on me. And it totalled me. Because I had made that commitment. It was like a big deal, the first time I was acting like a man and I got it. I got betrayed. And I almost killed her.

These accounts illustrate more than just the way that individual men seek to control individual women. As in the example of "provocation," there is a theme of self-righteousness about the violence that pervades these accounts: "I didn't think that I was wrong"; "she couldn't do it"; "she didn't seem too motivated"; "she had gone too far"; "I got betrayed." But here the sense is not that "she provoked me"; rather, it is a sense that the privileges of male entitlement have been unjustly denied. This is evident in the gendered terms used to express this self-righteousness: "I should just smack you for the *lousy wife* you've been"; "I don't know if I demanded respect as a person or a *husband* or anything like that, but . . . "; "I'm the *man of the house*"; "the first time I was *acting like a man* and I got it." There is sentiment here about the way that women should behave when they're sexually involved with a man, whether married or unmarried.

Adrienne Rich speaks to this sense of male entitlement, or, to use her term, "husband-right" as

> one specific form of the rights men are presumed to enjoy simply because of their gender: the "right" to the priority of male over female needs, to sexual and emotional services from women, to women's undivided attention in any and all situations. (Rich 1979, 219–220)

With this assumption of male entitlement, the wrongness of the violence is denied; the batterer sees himself as punishing the woman for her failure to be a good wife. Other investigations have found a similar pattern in the batterer's violence (Bograd 1983; Coleman 1980; Dobash and Dobash 1979; Elbow 1977; Gelles 1974). But this assumption of male privilege is not limited to the expectations of men who batter. Feminists have been pointing out for years that this vocabulary of male entitlement has been routinized within the culture at large.

Patterns and Contradictions in the Batterers' Testimony

The definitions of excuses and justifications turn on the denial (or acceptance) of responsibility and wrongness. Most of the men made statements falling into both categories. Within the context of individual interviews, this presented a great deal of inconsistency. For example, one individual who grabbed his wife around the neck said of his violence:

> It's a condition of being out of control.
>
> She's going on and on about how much money we need. . . . I'll listen to it for a while, but then, you know, you gotta get up and do something, you know. That's the way I felt, the way to do it was go over and try to shut her up physically.
>
> I'd lose my head.

In the space of a few minutes, this man seems to go from *denying* responsibility, to seemingly *accepting* responsibility while minimizing the wrongness, to *denying* responsibility again. How can this be accounted for? Earlier I discussed the jockeying for power I perceived during the interviews. Scott and Lyman (1968) see accounts as attempts at face-saving or avoiding judgment. In this analysis, the conflicting statements result from the batterers' willingness to apply any number of verbal strategies to the task of making the violence appear normal, regardless of whether the accounts have any internal consistency.

But there is more here than inconsistency: there is contradiction. The batterers' excuses of "loss of control" and "provocation" are undercut by the callousness they displayed about their partners' injuries, and by the goal orientation that appeared in their own words. The above transcripts reveal that these men were motivated by a desire to silence their partners; to punish them for their failure as "good wives"; and to achieve and maintain dominance over these women. Their objectives were accomplished, according to the men: The women fell silent; they were taught a lesson; and they were shown who was in control of the relationship and to what length the batterer would go in maintaining control.

Other goals of the violence are acknowledged as well. Asked directly whether they intended to hurt their wives or lovers when they assaulted them, five men admitted such an intent.

I wanted to hurt somebody. She was the best person, the closest one to me. Nobody else really made any difference.

There are times that I really wanted to kill her.

Yeah. Yeah. Because I didn't stop. I mean I wasn't—she slapped me once, and I hit her. I don't know, maybe 10 to 15 times there, and quite a few times at home.

I think I was trying to hurt her.

I just kept beating her. The police arrested me. I would have killed her. . . . Yeah. I wanted to kill her.

And beyond an intent to hurt, frightening their wives or lovers was a goal for 67 percent (N = 12) of the men, at this testimony demonstrates:

A lot of my verbal abuse, in thinking about it now . . . the verbal abuse would be a threat. A threat of violence.

I grabbed her, and said, "I'm going to fucking kill you if you do this again to me."

I put her up against the wall one night and held my fist up cocked and said, I just said, you know, I said, "I'd love to just knock your fucking head off."

There's another form of violence I also remember. Once we had an argument .. . we were in a car . . . I sped up . . . made a quick U-turn, drove recklessly . . . She was terrified. She was terrified, and angry, and really scared. . . . She wanted to get out of the car and walk.

These last three examples are from men who explain their violence by appealing to complete loss of control. However, the hostile manner with which these men terrorized their partners and the warnings of future violence seem more indicative of a deliberate strategy than of an inability to control one's actions.

The batterers' denials of responsibility are further contradicted by other evidence they provided about their behavior. In none of these relationships was the violence completely anomalous to the batterers' other actions toward his wife or lover. In every case, the men's testimony offered other examples of behavior directed at achieving or maintaining dominance. This does not refer merely to subtle controlling behaviors, but to such things as writing threatening letters to the woman, driving her back to her mother's house to make her learn how to cook, forcing sex, threatening the woman if she talks about leaving, tearing the phone off the wall to prevent her from calling the police, and spying on the woman's house and lying in wait to assault her new boyfriend.

Thus a pattern of intentional, goal-oriented violence is established by the batterers' testimony, despite the contradictory denials of responsibility. "Loss of control" and "provocation" cannot explain the violence; they merely serve as excuses, as rationalizations, and as ways of obscuring the benefits (however temporary or enduring) that the violence provides.

Socially Approved Rationalizations for Violence

Scott and Lyman (1968, 46) insist that excuses and justifications are "standardized within cultures," that they are "socially approved vocabularies" for avoiding blame. To complete the analysis of the batterers' accounts, then, it will be necessary to trace the extent to which these rationalizations represent culturally sanctioned strategies for minimizing and denying violence against women.

Appeals to loss of control and victim-blaming are the most common ways that these men sought to escape responsibility for their violence. Having challenged the credibility of these defenses with the batterers' own testimony, the question can be posed: To what degree does the larger society accept these excuses at face value? Evidence from the clinical literature on men who batter and a recent study of battered women and the criminal justice system suggest an answer to this question.

The Clinical Literature on Men Who Batter

An examination of the books and articles written by social workers, psychologists, psychiatrists, and others working directly with batterers reveals that a good portion of the clinical literature appears to take the excuses of "loss of control" and "provocation" at face value.

Most striking is that batterers and clinicians use similar language to characterize "loss of control." The batterers speak in terms of irrational attacks ("I went berserk"; "I wasn't sane"; "temporary insanity"); uncontrollable aggression ("I had no control over myself"; "it's a condition of being out of control"; "uncontrollably violent"); and explosion metaphors ("I just blew up"; "blowout"; "walking time bomb"; "outburst of rage"; "eruptions"). Like the batterers, many clinicians also describe the violence as irrational or psychopathological. There is reference in clinical discussion of batterers to "paroxysmal rage attacks" and the "pathologies of both partners" (Lion 1977); "psychiatric abnormality" and the "mentally disturbed nature of the population" (Faulk 1977); and "irrational aggressive actions" among males who are "passively aggressive," "obsessive-compulsive," "sadistic," "paranoid," and "borderline" (Shainess 1977). Many of the more recent articles and books are less dramatic in their language, but nonetheless assume irra-

tionality with terms such as "aggressive impulses"; "poor impulse control"; or "impulse to batter" (Deschner 1984; Garnet and Moss 1982; Geller 1982; Geller and Walsh 1978; Goffman 1984; Star 1983).

Like the abusers interviewed for this study, many clinicians also explicitly state that the violence represents "uncontrollable rage" or "uncontrollable aggression" (Deschner 1984; Geller 1982; Goffman 1984; Walker 1979). And finally, like the batterers, clinicians frequently use explosion metaphors, such as "violent eruption"; "temper outbursts"; or "explosive rage" (Coleman 1980; Deschner 1984; Goffman 1984; Pagelow 1981; Walker 1979; Weitzman and Dreen 1982).

Despite the variety of theoretical perspectives that inform these works, all assume that the batterer loses control over his behavior. This notion—that the batterer's will is somehow overpowered, that his violence lies outside of the realm of choice, that battering occurs doing brief irrational episodes—constructs a contemporary profile of the batterer as one who is not necessarily *sick*, but who is rather just *temporarily insane*. Seen from this perspective, the batterer is not abnormal enough to be considered a psychopath and not responsible enough to be considered a criminal. But this notion of loss of control is substantially contradicted by the batterers' own testimony. While the men claim that their violence is beyond rational control, they simultaneously acknowledge that the violence is deliberate and warranted.

Concerning victim-blaming, there is also evidence that clinicians accept batterers' rationalizations for the violence. Despite the tireless efforts of feminists in educating the public on this issue, victim-blaming continues in the clinical literature. It is not uncommon to find wife beating treated as a phenomenon no worse than women's "verbal aggressiveness." For example, Deschner

(1984) draws a parallel between a man's physical abuse and what she calls a woman's "verbal persecutions (nagging)" (p. 19). Deschner (p. 20) claims that husbands and wives often

> alternate between giving and getting punishment. After a period of abuse the wife rises up and scolds her husband or else withdraws from him. After tolerating her negatives for a period, he rises up again in another act of violence. . . . Such marriages, though not enjoyable, can be stable over a long period of time because each partner periodically enjoys the rewards of being on top.

Confusing verbal scolding with violence trivializes physical assault and suggests that wife beating is caused by "nagging," redefined by Dobash and Dobash (1979, 133) as "continued discussion once the husband had made up his mind." Another example of equating verbal and physical assaults is:

> Careful exploration of a couple's history with violence may reveal that both spouses have contributed to the escalation of anger with one spouse being the more verbally assaultive while the other is the more physically abusive. This places each partner in the role of both abuser and victim. (Margolin 1979, 16)

In clinical publications, there are additional ways that women are seen as creating their own victimization. For instance, Lion (1977, 127) speaks of the battered woman's "provocation" and states that "the victim may evoke violence in a vulnerable person." Faulk (1977, 121) describes one type of battered woman as "querulous and demanding." And notions of female masochism are still prevalent (Shainess 1977).

It appears that a good number of clinicians accept and legitimate the batterers's excuses. Fortunately, there is a growing number of authors who reject the above excuses and justifications for wife beating. For a more detailed review of this literature, see Ptacek (1984) and Adams (1988).

The Response of the Criminal Justice System

Before concluding this analysis of the batterers' accounts, a few remarks are in order about the prevalence of these excuses and justifications among the police and in the courts. I have shown how men who batter deny responsibility for their violence by claiming they were provoked by their wives. Similar discussions were found in the clinical literature on batterers. This notion that women who are battered must be guilty of wrongdoing can also be found among court clerks, police officers, and judges. A 1985 study of criminal justice responses to battered women in Massachusetts found numerous cases of such victim-blaming. Developed for the governor's anticrime council, this monitoring report detailed such cases as a police officer calling a battered woman a "bitch"; a police officer saying to a woman of color, "you people get what you deserve"; a judge saying to a woman, "most people get married and do not have illegitimate children. These things don't happen to them"; and a court clerk asking a woman what she did to provoke the abuse (Governor's Battered Women's Working Group 1985, 1–2).

These incidents cannot be dismissed as merely anecdotal: They were witnessed and documented by shelter workers, victim/witness advocates, lawyers, and other service providers. In a six-month period in 1985, some 250 such complaints were reported, 79 of which were classified as involving biased or racist attitudes toward battered women on the part of the police, judges, or court clerks. One can only suppose that battered women confronting the system without such witnesses often suffer even worse treatment.

The batterers' accounts detailed previously revealed ways that the men denied or minimized the injuries they caused. Such trivialization of the violence is also evident in this criminal justice report. For example, one judge reproached a woman by saying, "There is nothing wrong with you—you're not bruised or hysterical"; on another occasion, a judge suggested to a woman that if her husband didn't drink, gamble, or run around with other women, she had no reason to be in court; a police officer, refusing to hold a batterer in custody, told the abused woman that she was "only given a whack"; and in a different case, police joked around with a batterer with whom they were friends, despite the fact that he had just injured his wife severely enough to require hospitalization (Governor's Battered Women's Working Group 1985, 8–9).

Such failure to treat violence against women as a crime must be understood as a structural aspect of the criminal justice system (Bowker 1982; Lerman 1981; Tong 1984; U.S. Commission on Civil Rights 1982). On the basis of these case studies, it is reasonable to suspect that when these police officers and judges encounter batterers, a mutual validation of victim-blaming and minimization occurs. While reform is proceeding among the various levels of the criminal justice system, an acceptance of batterers' rationalizations for their violence remains commonplace.

Conclusion

Jürgen Habermas (1971, 311) speaks to the relationship between individual rationalizations and collective interests:

> From everyday experience we know that ideas serve often enough to furnish our actions with justifying motives in place of the real ones. What is called rationalization at this level is called ideology at the level of collective action.

The excuses and justifications I have detailed are ideological constructs: At the individual level, they obscure the batterer's self-interest in acting violently; at the societal level, they mask the male domination under-

lying violence against women. Clinical and criminal justice responses to battering are revealed as ideological in the light of their collusion with batterers' rationalizations.

This study of what batterers have to say about wife beating suggests a context in which to pursue further research on this issue. The interrelationship between private rationalizations and public responses recommends using a critical social psychology framework to examine men's violence against women. Such a theoretical framework could place wife beating, rape, incest, and the sexual harassment of women in relation to one another, which offers fertile ground for addressing class-specific forms of male entitlement, male anger, male subjectivity, and misogyny. A critical social psychology could develop and interrelate sociological and psychological analyses without reducing one to the other. By combining what is generally approached in a piecemeal fragmented fashion, the resulting portrait of male domination becomes more difficult to deny.

REFERENCES

Adams, D. (1988). Treatment models of men who batter. In K. A. Yllö and M. Bograd (Eds.), *Feminist perspectives on wife abuse*. Newbury Park, CA: Sage.

Adams, D. C., and I. Penn. (1981, April). Men in groups: The socialization and resocialization of men who batter. Paper presented at the annual meeting of the American Orthopsychiatric Association, Boston. (Available from Emerge, 25 Huntington Avenue, Room 323, Boston, MA 02116.)

Bandura, A. (1973). *Aggression: A social learning analysis*. Englewood Cliffs, NJ: Prentice Hall.

Becker, H. S. (1970). *Sociological work*. Chicago: Aldine.

Bograd, M. (1983). Domestic violence: Perceptions of battered women, abusive men, and non-violent men and women. Ph.D. diss. University of Chicago.

Bowker, L. H. (1982). Police services to battered

women: Bad or not so bad? *Criminal Justice and Behavior* 9:476–494.

Brisson, N. (1982). Helping men who batter women. *Public Welfare* 40:28–34.

Coleman, K. H. (1980). Conjugal violence: What 33 men report. *Journal of Marital and Family Therapy* 6:107–213.

Deschner, J. P. (1984). *The hitting habit: Anger control for battering couples*. New York: Free Press.

Dobash, R. E., and R. Dobash (1979). *Violence against wives: A case against the patriarchy*. New York: Free Press.

Dobash, R. E., and R. Dobash (1981). Social work and social action: The case of wifebattering. *Journal of Family Issues* 2:439–470.

Elbow, M. (1977). Theoretical considerations of violent marriages. *Social Casework* 58:515–526.

Faulk, M. (1977). Men who assault their wives. In M. Roy (Ed.), *Battered women: Psychosociological study of domestic violence*. New York: Van Nostrand Reinhold.

Garnet, S., and D. Moss (1982). How to set up a counseling program for self-referred batterers: The AWAIC model. In M. Roy (Ed.), *The abusive partner: An analysis of domestic battering*. New York: Van Nostrand Reinhold.

Geller, J. A. (1982). Conjoint therapy: Staff training and treatment of the abuser and the abused. In M. Roy (Ed.), *The abusive partner: An analysis of domestic battering*. New York: Van Nostrand Reinhold.

Geller, J. A., and J. C. Walsh (1978). A treatment model for the abused spouse. *Victimology* 2:627–632.

Gelles, R. J. (1974) *The violent home: A study of physical aggression between husbands and wives*. Newbury Park, CA: Sage.

Goffman, J. M. (1984). *Batterers anonymous: Self-help counseling for men who batter women*. San Bernardino, CA: B. A. Press.

Governor's Battered Women's Working Group (1985). Violent crime in the family: Enforcement of the Massachusetts Abuse Prevention Law. Unpublished monograph.

Habermas, J. (1971). *Knowledge and human interests*. Boston: Beacon Press.

Lerman, L. G. (1981). Criminal prosecution of wife beaters. *Response to Violence in the Family* 4:1–19.

Lion, J. R. (1977). Clinical aspects of wifebattering. In M. Roy (Ed.), *Battered women: A psychosociological study of domestic violence*. New York: Van Nostrand Reinhold.

Lund, S. H., N. E. Larsen, and S. K. Schultz (1982). *Exploratory evaluation of the Domestic Abuse Project*. (Available from the Domestic Abuse Project, 2445 Park Avenue South, Minneapolis, MN 55404.)

Margolin, G. (1979). Conjoint marital therapy to enhance anger management and reduce spouse abuse. *American Journal of Family Therapy* 7:13–23.

Pagelow, M. D. (1981). *Woman-battering: Victims and their experiences*. Newbury Park, CA: Sage.

Ptacek, J. (1984, August). The clinical literature on men who batter: A review and critique. Paper presented at the second national conference for Family Violence Researchers, Durham, NH. (Available from Emerge, 280 Green Street, Cambridge, MA 02139.)

Reinharz S. (1979). *On becoming a social scientist*. San Francisco: Jossey-Bass.

Rich, A. (1979). *On lies, secrets, and silence: Selected prose 1966–1979*. New York: Norton.

Scott, M. B., and S. M. Lyman (1968). Accounts. *American Sociological Review* 33:46–62.

Shainess, N. (1977). Psychological aspects of wifebattering. In M. Roy (Ed.), *Battered women: A psychosociological study of domestic violence*. New York: Van Nostrand Reinhold.

Star, B. (1983). *Helping the abuser: Intervening effectively in family violence*. New York: Family Service Association of America.

Stone, A. (1984). *Law, psychiatry, and morality: Essays and analysis*. Washington, DC: American Psychiatric Press.

Tong, Rosemarie (1984). *Women, sex, and the law*. Totowa, NJ: Rowman and Allanheld.

U.S. Commission on Civil Rights (1982). *Under the rule of thumb: Battered women and the administration of justice*. Washington, DC: U.S. Government Printing Office.

Walker, L. E. (1979). *The battered woman*. New York: Harper & Row.

Weitzman, J., and K. Dreen (1982). Wifebeating: A view of the marital dyad. *Social Casework* 63:259–265.

Chapter 47

Felicia: Working with a Teen Mother in an Abusive Relationship

BONNIE ZIMMER

Felicia[1] and I met at the prenatal clinic of a hospital in a white working-class community in July 1987. It was my first day on a new job, and she was my first client. I introduced myself and asked if she'd ever spoken with a social worker before. She laughed at me. "You're number twenty-three," she reported as her eyes finally met mine in a challenging stare. Our relationship had begun.

Over the next few months, Felicia and I were to develop a close, even intimate, working alliance. We visited several times a week at my office, her home or the local donut shop. We spent time at the welfare office, the bank and the prenatal clinic. We would talk about fashion, hairstyles, soap operas, our favorite foods. I would lecture her about the importance of using birth control, and she would lecture me about keeping my notoriously cluttered and filthy car clean. Eventually, Felicia told me

about her thirteen years as a foster child and her history of school failure, physical and emotional abuse and attempted rape. We discussed intimate details of her life: her pregnancy decision-making (she was keeping her baby), her contraceptive decisions, her feelings about her changing body as the pregnancy progressed. We developed so much trust that Felicia asked me to be her labor coach and I was an honored guest at the birth of her daughter.

What Felicia didn't (or couldn't) tell me until six months after we'd met was that she was being battered. Two years later, Felicia agreed to collaborate with me on this chapter. We met in our kitchens and talked about our work together and about Felicia's experiences with abuse. Ours is a story of a "professional" and a "client" working together to help one woman and child escape from the violence in their lives. We hope that it may speak to other workers and young mothers as well.

Felicia feels it is important for readers to know something about her past, in order to understand the context of her life at the time the violence occurred.

My real mother was an alcoholic, heavy on drinking, doing drugs, not responsible enough to be on birth control. She had ten kids. Her first child was at the age of sixteen. Her sixth child, being me, was at the age of twenty-three. My oldest sister, who's twenty-seven now, took care of me and my sisters. . . . she brought us up until we were put into foster homes. I have no memories at all of ages one to five. I hear stories . . . that I used to get locked in the closest . . . that I used to get beat on . . . things like that I do not remember . . . who knows, maybe in time I will remember . . . Anyway, they put me in a foster home for what was supposed to be three months . . . and that became six months, nine months, all the way up to thirteen years. I got pregnant in February 1987 and I threw my past up into my own face. . . . My exact words were, "I'm being just like my mother. I'm young, I'm unmarried. I'm on welfare. I'm heading right in the same direction as her."

The Legacy of Victim-Blaming

Felicia learned early that people would blame her for her misfortunes. Here, she describes her experiences in school in which she was blamed for things that were beyond her control.

> I was probably one of . . . ten foster kids in the whole school, so I would be more or less . . . picked on . . . ruled out. It was like, it was my fault that I was put somewhere. They'd say . . . if you can't stay with your family you must be no good, a nothing. I was picked on, and it made me feel like a little, small person. And I was held back, too, on account of I couldn't read. But my counselors told me that was because my mother drank when she was pregnant with me, so I had a learning disability.

Felicia claims that her involvement with protective service and mental health professionals replicated her schoolyard experiences of victim-blaming and added to her sense of personal responsibility for her problems.

> I was constantly in counseling, 'cause that's what everyone said was good for me, which I really resented them for. . . . I hated going to counseling. . . . I felt I was being picked on . . . AS AN INDIVIDUAL . . . people prying into my business . . . it was like it was my fault again . . . I'd say, "Why are they ruling me out? Why don't they go talk to my mother." She's the one who needed counseling.

> The social workers wanted to know everything—when you breathed, when you went to the bathroom, everything. They just wanted to know your whole life story. It was just their attitude, that since you're in foster care we can lay anything we want on you, make you feel guilty. We were considered to be state children, so the state, they'd say, had every right to know what was going on.

Repeatedly asked questions about her sex life, the status of her relationship with her partner, the quality of her family life, Felicia felt that these questions never had her best interests in mind. As a child, she had learned not to reveal much about herself for fear of losing even more than she had already lost. Now, as a teenage mother herself, she depended upon the very systems that had failed her as a child. She developed a stony stance toward social workers in general.

> There were several opportunities for me to personally witness the angry, judgmental treatment by her caseworker when I accompanied Felicia to the welfare office. After her worker told her she was a liar, we agreed that she would attend her required meetings only when I could accompany her because Felicia said she was treated more respectfully when I was with her.

Felicia explains the impact of her lifelong involvement with social service providers on her self-image and her growing feelings of helplessness. Felicia's depression began to escalate during her junior year in high school.

> I sometimes thought about killing myself because I felt like such an outsider, and I couldn't

talk about my problems. I couldn't do anything. I was slow in school, and I just began to think "What am I doing here?" My foster parents brought us up that God put us here for some reason: some to succeed and some to fail . . . I figured I was going to fail.

And then, in her senior year of high school, Felicia was kicked out of her foster parents' home following an argument at a family party. She felt desperate.

Like many of the young women I met during my years working with pregnant and parenting teens, Felicia opted out of suicide. She found what she considered to be a more positive solution to her desperate situation. Felicia met a new boyfriend. Within a few short months, she was pregnant.

I got pregnant in February 1987 because I wasn't careful and one thing led to another . . . and in my head I think I wanted to get pregnant. Probably to spite what happened in my family [getting kicked out]. I guess I could have given up the baby, either with abortion or adoption, and I thought about it, being eighteen and not having anyone there for me, like a mother or father. But I decided to keep the baby. I told my boyfriend, and things went . . . [Felicia whistles] whew!!! just right downhill.

During the sixth month of her pregnancy, when she finally began to show, the abuse began.

At the age of eighteen, when I was pregnant, it was pretty much when I started experiencing it . . . being verbally and physically abused . . . He told me I was a bitch. Then he started beating on me, telling me I'm not allowed to leave the house, being pushed, strangled, just a lot of stuff. But you know it was more or less the verbal abuse that killed me most. I just felt like I was no good, I was trash, the things he used to say to me . . . that I would never get another boyfriend in my life, that I'm a bitch, a whore. And then things got even worse. I started getting hurt. I put my hand through two windows when he

was beating on me. He wasn't letting me out the door, and he punched me in the nose. My nose was bleeding, and I put my hand right through the windows to try to get out. I split it right open. So here he was beating on a seven-month pregnant girl, and I thought to myself that if anyone was mentally disturbed at the time it was him.

Felicia tells us what feminist writers have emphasized in recent literature: that physical violence, while terrifying and dangerous, is also only one dimension of the complex pattern of control and domination that we call battering.

We have used the terms *battered* and *abused* interchangeably. Felicia, in fact, prefers the term *abused* since she says that *battered* is not a word she attributes to her own experiences. However, many services remain titled "battered women's services." We agreed, therefore, to refer to Felicia's personal experiences as abuse and to apply the term *battered* to more general references.

Attempts to Seek Help

Felicia was beginning to consider that perhaps her boyfriend, not she, might be responsible for the violence. But several failed attempts at getting help led her back to the victim-blaming that helps to trap so many battered women in self-hatred. I asked her about her attempts to seek help and escape from the violence.

I tried telling his parents. His father said I was lying, that his son couldn't be hitting me.

Another time his mother was right there [during a beating]. The only way I could get her to help was . . . I picked up a bottle of aspirin, and I threatened her that I would take them all. . . . I had them right there in my hand. Then she called the hospital, but all they were worried about was whether I'd hurt the baby. They thought I was crazy, and they didn't talk about that he had been beating on me. They were worried . . . would I abuse the baby?

Once though, when that guy tried to rape me when I was twelve years old, I told my parents, and my father was going to kill the guy. [At the age of twelve, Felicia, while bicycling home from school, was stopped by a man posing as a policeman. He lured her into his car and attempted to rape her. She was able to escape.] There was something clearer cut about that. You can't blame a twelve-year-old girl for riding her bike home.

Though no one could "blame a twelve-year-old girl for riding her bike home," she knew all too well that many would blame a pregnant eighteen-year-old woman for being involved with a violent partner. Felicia began to see that she was no longer seen as a "worthy" victim.

Felicia also tried therapy. Her boyfriend was in counseling, and she was asked to come to a couple's session.

She [the therapist] was more or less shocked when I told her that it was happening. So she asked me if I nagged him too much. I told her I did everything in the world for him. And then I just shut my mouth because she was saying it was my fault.

Building Trust with Teen Mothers Who Are Abused

I wondered why Felicia had decided to tell me about the violence at all? Why would she risk disclosure after so many disappointments throughout her life with twenty-two previous social workers?

You told me you weren't from DSS and that helped. [The Department of Social Services is the child protective agency in Massachusetts.] But even so, when I first met you I was afraid that if I did something wrong my baby would be taken away. Because that's what the state does. I

got over being afraid, though, after about six months . . . actually less, 'cause I asked you to come in and help me deliver my baby so I guess I trusted you then.

You were the first person I told. 'Cause you weren't like a social worker. You always listened. [She laughs.] You know, it's supposed to be that the social worker listens and the client talks, but I would find it would usually be the other way around, with social workers talking and talking at me. But you really listened. And if I needed you, you'd come right over. And you wouldn't blame me . . . for being pregnant or for him beating on me . . . My foster parents would say, "One night in the sack, and this is what happens; it's your fault." You didn't do that.

I asked Felicia what it was like to finally tell me about the violence and to share her feelings about it with a social worker.

It was . . . a relief . . . to let it go, because no one else believed it was happening. But I knew it was happening because I was the victim. I told you because I was sick of it, and I found I could talk to you about it.

But it was also hard. It hurt a lot to talk about it with you. It made it . . . that it was really happening. That someone I had a kid with was doing this to me . . . talking to you was different. I had thought, more or less, "No, it's not real, it's just my imagination." I thought I was too happy of a person for this to be going on. But deep down inside, I was really a miserable person . . . a really hurt person. And when I told you, I believed it.

As professionals we need to remind ourselves of how much courage it takes to reveal one's pain to another human being. And being in an abusive relationship is a profoundly painful experience. In addition to finding the inner strength to face her own pain, Felicia needed outer reassurance that, unlike the others, I would not hurt her with the knowledge of how wounded she felt, inside and out.

She also touched on some issues that I found to be common among the teen mothers I knew. For battered women in Massachusetts, the fear of losing one's baby is very real. Too often when women go for help, protective workers fail to see the woman as being in need of services. Instead, they focus exclusively on the protective concern for the child. The assumption they make is if the woman can't protect herself from violence, she won't be able to protect her child. They often decide to remove children from the home. As a result, younger women, already scrutinized because of their age, retreat from services in an effort to keep their families intact.[2]

The other common thread in Felicia's account is the disbelief that "someone I had a kid with" could be a batterer. Like their adult counterparts, teens who become parents often embrace dreams of escape into a "happy family" of their own creation that may heal the injuries of their often painful personal histories. To admit that their baby's father is battering them means relinquishing the dream that sustained them through pregnancy, childbirth and the difficult adjustment to parenting. Further, beyond the psychological resistance lies the reality of welfare dependence and poor future employability owing to limited educational opportunities and lack of adequate child care, job training and flexible work schedules, which make up the real worlds of most single teen mothers.

Despite this, Felicia decided to tell her twenty-third social worker about the abuse. She struggled with her boyfriend for many more months as the violence escalated. She eventually ended up at the emergency room of the local hospital with a leg injury. She didn't tell the hospital personnel how she sustained the injury for fear of losing her baby. She did, however, call me. We discussed all her options, including leaving him, seeking shelter with the local battered women's group, obtaining a restraining order and changing her telephone number and the locks on her doors.

Through many months I listened as Felicia struggled to accept the reality of her boyfriend's violence. They were reunited several times.

During this same time period, Felicia also began working on some long-range goals for herself and her baby. She enrolled in a state-funded job-training program that provided child care. She studied hard and prepared for her high school General Equivalency Degree (GED) exam while pursuing a training program in automated bookkeeping. Her learning disability has made the GED exam a difficult task, but Felicia has taken the exam repeatedly and increased her score steadily each time. Though she is still falling short of a passing grade, she is confident that she will someday receive her equivalency certificate.

As professionals working with young mothers who may be abused, what can we do to encourage trust, to empower women and to help them escape violence? My work with Felicia and other abused teens was difficult work. I had to be available for crises (which were many). I had to educate myself about the services to battered women in my area, become familiar with the courts and learn how to walk a woman through the process of obtaining a restraining order or pressing criminal charges. I also sat in on an open support and education group at the local shelter.

Having supportive supervision and peer support is also essential. Working with abused women can evoke feelings of helplessness at times, and it is this sense of helplessness that too often leads to victim blaming by well-meaning professionals. Working with teen mothers can present difficult ethical dilemmas stemming from our role as both advocate for the young abused women and mandated reporter in cases of suspected child abuse or neglect. Skilled supervision and close consultation with battered women's advocates can help ensure a balanced response that does not ignore women's needs in favor of children's.

I asked Felicia what had made the difference for her.

> A lot of counseling and a lot of friends telling me I was not a bad person. I had to hear it a lot of times, lots of times, QUITE A FEW TIMES, but then I heard it. And graduating from my book-keeping course and working on my GED.
>
> I have more confidence in myself that I can do anything I want to do. Being able to talk to people, open up, show my expressions, not to hide them . . . just being able to be myself, not

try to be somebody else . . . Now I'm able to be honest with myself and who I am and what I can do to change myself, not have people change me. Because that's the way life is.

NOTES

1. "Felicia" is a pseudonym chosen to protect the client's confidentiality.

2. A unique alternative to traditional social service models can be found in the AWAKE program at Children's Hospital in Boston. Founded by battered women's advocates, the program provides advocacy for the mothers of abused children.

∽ *Chapter 48*

Ten Myths That Perpetuate Corporal Punishment

MURRAY A. STRAUS

Hitting children is legal in every state of the United States and 84 percent of a survey of Americans agreed that it is sometimes necessary to give a child a good hard spanking. Study after study shows that almost 100 percent of parents with toddlers hit their children. There are many reasons for the strong support of spanking. Most of them are myths.

Myth 1: Spanking Works Better

There has been a huge amount of research on the effectiveness of corporal punishment of animals, but remarkably little on the effectiveness of spanking children. That may be because almost no one, including psychologists, feels a need to study it because it is assumed that spanking is effective. In fact, what

From Murray A. Straus, *Beating the Devil Out of Them: Corporal Punishment in American Families.* Copyright © 1994 by Jossey-Bass Inc., Publishers. First published by Lexington Books. All rights reserved. Reprinted by permission.

little research there is on the effectiveness of corporal punishment of children agrees with the research on animals. Studies of both animals and children show that punishment is *not* more effective than other methods of teaching and controlling behavior. Some studies show it is less effective.

Ellen Cohn and I asked 270 students at two New England colleges to tell us about the year they experienced the most corporal punishment. Their average age that year was eight, and they recalled having been hit an average of six times that year. We also asked them what percentage of time they thought the corporal punishment was effective. It averaged a little more than half (53 percent). Of course, 53 percent also means that corporal punishment was *not* perceived as effective about half the time it was used.

LaVoie (1974) compared the use of a loud noise (in place of corporal punishment) with withdrawal of affection and verbal explanation in a study of first- and second-grade children. He wanted to find out which was more effective in getting the children to stop touching certain prohibited toys. Although the loud noise was more effective initially, there was no difference over a longer period of time. Just explaining was as effective as the other methods.

A problem with LaVoie's study is that it used a loud noise rather than actual corporal punishment. That problem does not apply to an experiment by Day and Roberts (1983). They studied three-year-old children who had been given "time out" (sitting in a corner). Half of the mothers were assigned to use spanking as the mode of correction if their child did not comply and left the corner. The other half put their non-complying child behind a low plywood barrier and physically enforced the child staying there. Keeping the child behind the barrier was just as effective as the spanking in correcting the misbehavior that led to the time out.

A study by Larzelere also found that a combination of *non*-corporal punishment and reasoning was as effective as corporal punishment and reasoning in correcting disobedience.

Crozier and Katz (1979), Patterson (1982), Webster-Stratton (1990), and Webster-Stratton et al. (1988) all studied children with serious conduct problems. Part of the treatment used in all three experiments was to get parents to stop spanking. In all three, the behavior of the children improved after spanking ended. Of course, many other things in addition to no spanking were part of the intervention. But, as you will see, parents who on their own accord to do not spank also do many other things to manage their children's behavior. It is these other things, such a setting clear standards for what is expected, providing lots of love and affection, explaining things to the child, and recognizing and rewarding good behavior, that account for why children of non-spanking parents tend to be easy to manage and well-behaved. What about parents who do these things and also spank? Their children also tend

to be well-behaved, but it is illogical to attribute that to spanking since the same or better results are achieved without spanking, and also without adverse side effects.

Such experiments are extremely important, but more experiments are needed to really understand what is going on when parents spank. Still, what Day and Roberts found can be observed in almost any household. Let's look at two examples.

In a typical American family there are many instances when a parent might say, "Mary! You did that again! I'm going to have to send you to your room again." This is just one example of a non-spanking method that did *not* work.

The second example is similar: A parent might say, "Mary! You did that again! I'm going to have to spank you again." This is an example of spanking that did *not* work.

The difference between these two examples is that when spanking does not work, parents tend to forget the incident because it contradicts the almost-universal American belief that spanking is something that works when all else fails. On the other hand, they tend to remember when a *non*-spanking method did not work. The reality is that nothing works all the time with a toddler. Parents think that spanking is a magic charm that will cure the child's misbehavior. It is not. There is no magic charm. It takes many interactions and many repetitions to bring up children. Some things work better with some children than with others.

Parents who favor spanking can turn this around and ask, If spanking doesn't work any better, isn't that the same as saying that it works just as well? So what's wrong with a quick slap on the wrist or bottom? There are at least three things that are wrong:

- Spanking becomes less and less effective over time, and when children get bigger, it becomes difficult or impossible.

- For some children, the lessons learned through spanking include the idea that they only need to be good if Mommy or Daddy is watching or will know about it.
- There are a number of very harmful side effects, such as a greater chance that the child will grow up to be depressed or violent. Parents don't perceive these side effects because they usually show up only in the long run.

Myth 2: Spanking Is Needed as a Last Resort

Even parents and social scientists who are opposed to spanking tend to think that it may be needed when all else fails. There is no scientific evidence supporting this belief, however. It is a myth that grows out of our cultural and psychological commitment to corporal punishment. You can prove this to yourself by a simple exercise with two other people. Each of the three should, in turn, think of the most extreme situation where spanking is necessary. The other two should try to think of alternatives. Experience has shown that it is very difficult to come up with a situation for which the alternatives are not as good as spanking. In fact, they are usually better.

Take the example of a child running out into the street. Almost everyone thinks that spanking is appropriate then because of the extreme danger. Although spanking in that situation may help *parents* relieve their own tension and anxiety, it is not necessary or appropriate for teaching the child. It is not necessary because spanking does not work better than other methods, and it is not appropriate because of the harmful side effects of spanking. The only physical force needed is to pick up the child and get him or her out of danger, and, while hugging the child, explain the danger.

Ironically, if spanking is to be done at all, the "last resort" may be the worst. The problem is that parents are usually very angry by that time and act impulsively. Because of their anger, if the child rebels and calls the parent a name or kicks the parent, the episode can escalate into physical abuse. Indeed, most episodes of physical abuse started as physical punishment and got out of hand (Straus 1994; Kadushin and Martin 1981). Of course, the reverse is not true, that is, most instances of spanking do not escalate into abuse. Still, the danger of abuse is there, and so is the risk of psychological harm.

The second problem with spanking as a last resort is that, in addition to teaching that hitting is the way to correct wrongs, hitting a child impulsively teaches another incorrect lesson—that being extremely angry justifies hitting.

Myth 3: Spanking Is Harmless

When someone says, I was spanked and I'm OK, he or she is arguing that spanking does no harm. This is contrary to almost all the available research. One reason the harmful effects are ignored is because many of us (including those of us who are social scientists) are reluctant to admit that their own parents did something wrong and even more reluctant to admit that we have been doing something wrong with our own children. But the most important reason may be that it is difficult to see the harm. Most of the harmful effects do not become visible right away, often not for years. In addition, only a relatively small percentage of spanked children experience obviously harmful effects.

The delayed reaction and the small proportion seriously hurt are the same reasons the harmful effects of smoking were not perceived for so long. In the case of smoking, the research shows that one-third of very heavy smokers die of lung cancer or some other smoking-induced disease. That, of course, means that two-thirds of heavy smokers do *not* die of these diseases (Mattson et al. 1987). So, most heavy smokers can say, "I've smoked more than a pack a day for 30 years and I'm OK." Similarly, most people who were spanked can say, "My parents spanked me, and I'm not a wife beater or depressed."

Another argument in defense of spanking is that it is not harmful if the parents are loving and explain why they are spanking. The research does show that the harmful effects of spanking are reduced if it is done by loving parents who explain their actions. However, a study by Larzelere (1986) shows that although the harmful effects are reduced, they are not eliminated. The harmful side effects include an increased risk of delinquency as a child and crime as an adult, wife beating, depression, masochistic sex, and lowered earnings (Straus 1994).

In addition to having harmful psychological effects on children, hitting children also makes life more difficult for parents. Hitting a child to stop misbehavior may be the easy way in the short run, but in the slightly longer run, it makes the job of being a parent more difficult. This is because spanking reduces the ability of parents to influence their children, especially in adolescence when they are too big to control by physical force. Children are more likely to do what the parents want if there is a strong bond of affection with the parent. In short, being able to influence a child depends in considerable part on the bond between parent and child (Hirschi 1969). An experiment by Redd, Morris, and Martin (1975) shows that children tend to avoid caretaking adults who use punishment. In the natural setting, of course, there are many things that tie children to their parents. I suggest that each spanking chips away at the bond between parent and child.

Part of the process by which corporal pun-

ishment eats away at the parent-child bond is shown in the study of 270 students mentioned earlier. We asked the students for their reactions to "the first time you can remember being hit by one of your parents" and the most recent instance. We used a check list of 33 items, one of which was "hated him or her." That item was checked by 42 percent for both the first and the most recent instance of corporal punishment they could remember. The large percentage who hated their parents for hitting them is important because it is evidence that corporal punishment does chip away at the bond between child and parent.

Contrary to the "spoiled child" myth, children of non-spanking parents are likely to be easier to manage and better behaved than the children of parents who spank. This is partly because they tend to control their own behavior on the basis of what their own conscience tells them is right and wrong rather than to avoid being hit. This is ironic because almost everyone thinks that spanking "when necessary" makes for better behavior.

Myth 4: One or Two Times Won't Cause Any Damage

The evidence indicates that the greatest risk of harmful effects occurs when spanking is very frequent. However, that does not necessarily mean that spanking just once or twice is harmless. Unfortunately, the connection between spanking once or twice and psychological damage has not been addressed by most of the available research. This is because the studies seem to be based on this myth. They generally cluster children into "low" and "high" groups in terms of the frequency they were hit. This prevents the "once or twice is harmless" myth from being tested scientifically because the low group may include parents who spank once a year or as often as once a month. Studies show that even one or two instances of corporal punishment are associated with a slightly higher probability of later physically abusing your own child, slightly more depressive symptoms, and a greater probability of violence and other crime later in life (Straus 1994). The increase in these harmful side effects when parents use only moderate corporal punishment (hit only occasionally) may be small, but why run even that small risk when the evidence shows that corporal punishment is no more effective than other forms of discipline in the short run, and less effective in the long run?

Myth 5: Parents Can't Stop Without Training

Although everyone can use additional skills in child management, there is no evidence that it takes some extraordinary training to be able to stop spanking. The most basic step in eliminating corporal punishment is for parent educators, psychologists, and pediatricians to make a simple and unambiguous statement that hitting a child is wrong and that a child *never*, ever, under any circumstances except literal physical self-defense should be hit.

That idea has been rejected almost without exception everytime I suggest it to parent educators or social scientists. They believe it would turn off parents and it could even be harmful because parents don't know what else to do. I think that belief is an unconscious defense of corporal punishment. I say that because I have never heard a parent educator say that before we can tell parents to never *verbally* attack a child, parents need training in alternatives. Some do need training, but everyone agrees that parents who use *psychological* pain as a method of discipline, such as insulting or demeaning the child, should stop immediately. But when it comes to causing

physical pain by spanking, all but a small minority of parent educators say that before parents are told to stop spanking, they need to learn alternative modes of discipline. I believe they should come right out, as they do for verbal attacks, and say without qualification that a child should *never* be hit.

This is not to say that parent education programs are unnecessary, just that they should not be a precondition for ending corporal punishment. Most parents can benefit from parent education programs such as The Nurturing Program (Bavolek et al. 1983 to 1992), STEP (Dinkmeyer and McKay 1989), Parent Effectiveness Training (Gordon 1975), Effective Black Parenting (Alvy and Marigna 1987), and Los Niños Bien Educado Program (Tannatt and Alvy 1989). However, even without such programs, most parents already use a wide range of non-spanking methods, such as explaining, reasoning, and rewarding. The problem is that they also spank. Given the fact that parents already know and use many methods of teaching and controlling, the solution is amazingly simple. In most cases, parents only need the patience to keep on doing what they were doing to correct misbehavior. Just leave out the spanking! Rather than arguing that parents need to learn certain skills *before* they can stop using corporal punishment, I believe that parents are more likely to use and cultivate those skills if they decide or are required to stop spanking.

This can be illustrated by looking at one situation that almost everyone thinks calls for spanking: when a toddler runs out into the street. A typical parent will scream in terror, rush out and grab the child, and run to safety, telling the child, No! No! and explaining the danger—all of this accompanied by one or more slaps to the legs or behind.

The same sequence is as effective or more effective *without the spanking*. The spanking is not needed because even tiny children can sense the terror in the parent and understand, No! No! Newborn infants can tell the difference between when a mother is relaxed and when she is tense (Stern 1977). Nevertheless, the fact that a child understands that something is wrong does not guarantee never again running into the street; just as spanking does not guarantee the child will not run into the street again.

If the child runs out again, non-spanking parents should use one of the same strategies as spanking parents—repetition. Just as spanking parents will spank as many times as necessary until the child learns, parents who don't spank should continue to monitor the child, hold the child's hand, and take whatever other means are needed to protect the child until the lesson is learned. Unfortunately, when non-spanking methods do not work, some parents quickly turn to spanking because they lose patience and believe it is more effective. But spanking parents seldom question its effectiveness, they just keep on spanking.

Of course, when the child misbehaves again, most spanking parents do more than just repeat the spanking or spank harder. They usually also do things such as explain the danger to the child before letting the child go out again or warn the child that if it happens again, he or she will have to stay in the house for the afternoon, and so on. The irony is that when the child finally does learn, the parent attributes the success to the spanking, not the explanation.

Myth 6: If You Don't Spank, Your Children Will Be Spoiled or Run Wild

It is true that some non-spanked children run wild. But when that happens it is not because the parent didn't spank. It is because some parents think the alternative to spanking is to ignore a child's misbehavior or to replace spanking with verbal attacks such as, "Only a dummy like you can't learn to keep your toys where I won't trip over them." The best alternative is to take firm action to correct the misbehavior without hitting. Firmly condemning what the child has done and explaining why it is wrong are usually enough. When they are not, there are a host of other things to do, such as requiring a time out or depriving the child of a privilege, neither of which involves hitting the child.

Suppose the child hits another child. Parents need to express outrage at this or the child may think it is acceptable behavior. The expression of outrage and a clear statement explaining why the child should never hit another person, except in self-defense, will do the trick in most cases. That does not mean one such warning will do the trick, any more than a single spanking will do the trick. It takes most children a while to learn such things, whatever methods the parents use.

The importance of how parents go about teaching children is clear from a classic study of American parenting—*Patterns of Child Rearing* by Sears, Maccoby, and Levin (1957). This study found two actions by parents that are linked to a high level of aggression by the child: permissiveness of the child's aggression, namely ignoring it when the child hits them or another child, and spanking to correct misbehavior. The most aggressive children are children of parents who permitted aggression by the child and who also hit them for a variety of misbehavior. The least aggressive children are children of parents who clearly condemned acts of aggression and who, by not spanking, acted in a way that demonstrated the principle that hitting is wrong.

There are other reasons why, on the average, the children of parents who do not spank are better behaved than children of parents who spank:

- Non-spanking parents pay more attention to their children's behavior, both good and bad, than parents who spank. Consequently, they are more likely to reward good behavior and less likely to ignore misbehavior.
- Their children have fewer opportunities to get into trouble because they are more likely to child-proof the home. For older children, they have clear rules about where they can go and who they can be with.
- Non-spanking parents tend to do more explaining and reasoning. This teaches the child how to use these essential tools to monitor his or her own behavior, whereas children who are spanked get less training in thinking things through.
- Non-spanking parents treat the child in ways that tend to bond the child to them and avoid acts that weaken the bond. They tend to use more rewards for good behavior, greater warmth and affection, and fewer verbal assaults on the child (see Myth 9). By not spanking, they avoid anger and resentment over spanking. When there is a strong bond, children identify with the parent and want to avoid doing things the parent says are wrong. The child develops a conscience and lets that direct his or her behavior.

Myth 7: Parents Spank Rarely or Only for Serious Problems

Contrary to this myth, parents who spank tend to use this method of discipline for almost any misbehavior. Many do not even give the child a warning. They spank before trying other things. Some advocates of spanking even recommend this. At any supermarket or other public place, you can see examples of a child doing something wrong, such as taking a can of food off the shelf. The parent then slaps the child's hand and puts back the can, sometimes without saying a word to the child. John Rosemond, the author of *Parent Power* (1981), says, "For me, spanking is a first resort. I seldom spank, but when I decide . . . I do it, and that's the end of it."

The high frequency of spanking also shows up among the parents. The typical parent of a toddler told us of about 15 instances in which he or she had hit the child during the previous 12 months. That is surely a minimum estimate because spanking a child is generally such a routine and unremarkable event that most instances are forgotten. Other studies, such as that of Newson and Newson (1963), report much more chronic hitting of children. My tabulations for mothers of three- to five-year-old children in the National Longitudinal Study of Youth found that almost two-thirds hit their children during the week of the interview, and they did it more than three times in just that one week. As high as that figure may seem, I think that daily spanking is not at all uncommon. It has been documented because the parents who do it usually don't realize how often they are hitting their children.

Myth 8: By the Time a Child Is a Teenager, Parents Have Stopped Spanking

Parents of children in their early teens are also heavy users of corporal punishment, although at that age it is more likely to be a slap on the face than on the behind. More than half of the parents of 13- to 14-year-old children in our two national surveys hit their children in the previous 12 months. The percentage drops each year as children get older, but even at age 17, one out of five parents is still hitting. To make matters worse, these are minimum estimates.

Of the parents of teenagers who told us about using corporal punishment, 84 percent did it more than once in the previous 12 months. For boys, the average was seven times and for girls, five times. These are minimum figures because we interviewed the mother in half the families and the father in the other half. The number of times would be greater if we had information on what the parent who was not interviewed did.

Myth 9: If Parents Don't Spank, They will Verbally Abuse Their Child

The scientific evidence is exactly the opposite. Among nationally representative samples of parents, those who did the least spanking also engaged in the least verbal aggression.

It must be pointed out that non-spanking parents are an exceptional minority. They are defying the cultural prescription that says a good parent should spank if necessary. The depth of their involvement with their children probably results from the same underlying characteristics that led them to reject spanking. There is a danger that if more ordinary parents are told to never spank, they might replace spanking by ignoring misbehavior or by verbal attacks. Consequently, a campaign to end spanking must also stress the importance of avoiding verbal attacks as well as physical attacks, and also the importance of paying attention to misbehavior.

Myth 10: It Is Unrealistic to Expect Parents to Never Spank

It is no more unrealistic to expect parents to never hit a child than to expect that husbands should never hit their wives, or that no one should go through a stop sign, or that a supervisor should never hit an employee. De-

spite the legal prohibition, some husbands hit their wives, just as some drivers go through stop signs, and a supervisor occasionally may hit an employee.

If we were to prohibit spanking, as is the law in Sweden (Deley 1988; Haeuser 1990), there still would be parents who would continue to spank. But that is not a reason to avoid passing such a law here. Some people kill, even though murder has been a crime since the dawn of history. Some husbands continue to hit their wives even though it has been more than a century since the courts stopped recognizing the common law right of a husband to "physically chastise an errant wife" (Calvert 1974).

A law prohibiting spanking is unrealistic only because spanking is such an accepted part of American culture. That also was true of smoking. Yet in less than a generation we have made tremendous progress toward eliminating smoking. We can make similar progress toward eliminating spanking by showing parents that spanking is dangerous, that their children will be easier to bring up if they do not spank, and by clearly saying that a child should *never*, under any circumstances, be spanked.

REFERENCES

Alvy, Kirby T., and Marilyn Marigna. 1987. *Effective Black Parenting*. Studio City, CA: Center for the Improvement of Child Caring.

Bavolek, Stephen J., et al. 1983 to 1992. *The Nurturing Programs*. Park City, Utah: Family Development Resources.

Calvert, Robert. 1974. "Criminal and Civil Liability in Husband-Wife Assaults." Chapter 9 in *Violence in the Family*, ed. Suzanne K. Steinmetz and Murray A. Straus. NY: Harper & Row.

Crozier, Jill, and Roger C. Katz. 1979. "Social Learning Treatment of Child Abuse." *Journal of Behavioral Therapy and Psychiatry* 10: 213–220.

Day, Dan E., and Mark W. Roberts. 1983. "An Analysis of the Physical Punishment Component of a Parent Training Program." *Journal of Abnormal Child Psychology* 11(1):141–152.

Deley, W. (1988). Physical Punishment of Children: Sweden and the USA. *Journal of Comparative Family Studies* 19(3):419–431.

Dinkmeyer, Don, Sr., and Gary D. McKay. 1989. *Systematic Training for Effective Parenting.* Circle Pines, MN: American Guidance Service.

Gelles, Richard J., and Murray A. Straus. 1988. *Intimate Violence.* New York: Simon & Schuster.

Gordon, T. 1975. *Parent Effectiveness Training.* New York: New American Library.

Haeuser, Adrienne Ahlgren. 1990. "Banning Parental Use of Physical Punishment: Success in Sweden." Presented at 8th International Congress on Child Abuse and Neglect, Hamburg, Federal Republic of Germany, September 2–6, 1990.

Hirschi, Travis. 1969. *The Causes of Delinquency.* Berkeley and Los Angeles: University of California Press.

Kadushin, Alfred, and Judith A. Martin. 1981. *Child Abuse: An Interactional Event.* New York: Columbia University Press.

Larzelere, Robert E. 1986. "Moderate Spanking: Model or Deterrent of Children's Aggression in the Family?" *Journal of Family Violence* 1(1):27–36.

——. 1993. "Response to Oosterhuis: Empirically Justified Uses of Spanking: Toward a Discriminating View of Corporal Punishment." *Journal of Psychology and Theory* 21:142–147.

——. 1993. "Should Corporal Punishment by Parents Be Considered Abusive—No" In Eileen Gambrill and Mary Ann Mason, eds. *Children and Adolescents: Controversial Issues.* Newbury Park, CA: Sage.

LaVoie, Joseph C. 1974. "Type of Punishment as a Determination of Resistance to Deviation." *Developmental Psychology* 10:181–189.

Mattson, Margaret E., Earl S. Pollack, and Joseph W. Cullen. 1987. "What Are the Odds That Smoking Will Kill You?" *American Journal of Public Health* 77(4):425–431.

Newson, John, and Elizabeth Newson. 1963. *Patterns of Infant Care in an Urban Community.* Baltimore: Penguin Books.

Patterson, Gerald R. 1982. *A Social Learning Approach to Family Intervention: III. Coercive Family Process.* Eugene, OR: Castalia.

Redd, William H., Edward K. Morris, and Jerry A. Martin. 1975. "Effects of positive and negative adult-child interactions on children's social preferences." *Journal of Experimental Child Psychology* 19:153–164.

Rosemond, John K. 1981. *Parent Power: A Common Sense Approach to Raising Your Children in the 80s.* Charlotte, NC: East Woods Press.

Sears, Robert R., Eleanor C. Maccoby, and Harry Levin. 1957. *Patterns of Child Rearing.* Evanston, IL: Row, Peterson, and Company.

Stern, Daniel. 1977. *The First Relationship: Mother and Infant.* Cambridge, MA: Harvard University Press.

Straus, Murray A. 1991. "Discipline and Deviance: Physical Punishment of Children and Violence and Other Crime in Adulthood." *Social Problems* 38(2):101–123.

——. 1993. "Corporal Punishment of Children and Depression and Suicide in Adulthood." In Joan McCord, ed., *Coercion and Punishment in Long-Term Perspective.* New York: Cambridge University Press.

Straus, Murray A., with Denise A. Donnelly. 1994. *Beating the Devil Out of Them: Corporal Punishment in American Families.* New York: Macmillan.

Straus, Murray A., and Richard J. Gelles. 1990. *Physical Violence in American Families: Risk Factors and Adaptations to Violence in 8,145 Families.* New Brunswick, NJ: Transaction.

Straus, Murray A., and Holley S. Gimpel. 1992. "Corporal Punishment by Parents and Economic Achievement: A Theoretical Model and Some Preliminary Empirical Data." Paper presented at the 1992 meeting of the American Sociological Association. Durham, NH: Family Research Laboratory, University of New Hampshire.

Straus, Murray A., Richard J. Gelles, and Suzanne K. Steinmetz. 1980. *Behind Closed Doors: Violence in the American Family.* New York: Doubleday/Anchor.

Tannatt, Lupita Montoya, and Kirby T. Alvy. 1989. *Los Niños Bien Educados Program.* Studio City,

CA: Center for the Improvement of Child Caring.

Webster-Stratton, Carolyn. 1990. "Enhancing the Effectiveness of Self-Administered Videotape Parent Training for Families with Conduct-Problem Children." *Journal of Abnormal Child Psychology* 18(5):479–492.

Webster-Stratton, Carolyn, Mary Kolpacoff, and Terri Hollinsworth. 1988. "Self-Administered Videotape Therapy for Families with Conduct-Problem Children: Comparison with Two Cost-Effective Treatments and a Control Group." *Journal of Consulting and Clinical Psychology* 56(4):558–566.

Chapter 49

Child Abuse in Context: An Historian's Perspective

JOHN DEMOS

Child abuse—as a public issue—has a very short history. A single event marks its beginning: the publication in 1962 of an article entitled "The Battered Child Syndrome" in the *Journal of the American Medical Association*.[1] The impact of this article owed something to authorship (five highly respected physicians headed by C. Henry Kempe of the University of Colorado Medical Center), something to provenance (one of the leading medical journals in the country), and not a little to rhetorical inventiveness (e.g., the term "battered child," which soon gained wide currency among professionals and lay persons alike).

There was, in addition, the intrinsic power of the issue itself. Child abuse evoked an immediate and complex mix of emotions: horror, shame, fascination, disgust. Dr. Kempe and his co-authors noted that physicians themselves experienced "great difficulty . . . in believing that parents could have attacked

their children" and often attempted "to obliterate such suspicions from their minds, even in the face of obvious circumstantial evidence." In a sense the problem had long been consigned to a netherworld of things felt but not seen, known but not acknowledged. The "Battered Child" essay was like a shroud torn suddenly aside. Onlookers reacted with shock, but also perhaps with a kind of relief. The horror was in the open now, and it would not easily be shut up again.

From the pages of professional journals discussion of child abuse spread quickly to numerous public settings. There was strong response from the news media, from charitable organizations, and from government at every level. Research monies poured forth to a variety of individual investigators; the resultant reports and recommendations soon amounted to a huge scientific literature. Elected officials in state after state rushed to create legislation that would strengthen protective services to children. Legal proceedings were undertaken, and judicial decisions rendered, with the aim of clarifying both public

From John Demos, *Past, Present, and Personal: The Family and the Life Course in American History* (New York: Oxford University Press, 1986). Reprinted by permission.

and private responsibilities in this area. The energies of the federal government were also enlisted in the cause: a Child Abuse Prevention and Treatment Act emerged (in 1973) as a direct result, as did a new National Center on Child Abuse and Neglect.[2]

Of course, the long-term outcome of these activities remains uncertain. Does society have the will and the means to eradicate child abuse, or at least to reduce its incidence? What substantive strategies show the greatest prospect of success? What indeed is the most appropriate framework for *understanding* the problem—and for taking effective remedial measures? Such questions are still well short of resolution.

In the meantime a second group of questions, different in character but not unrelated, reach out from the fact of child abuse to its cultural and historical context. Is there something inevitable and irreducible about all this, regardless of particular social settings? Must we assume a certain *residuum* of abusive impulse—and behavior—in any given human population? Does the incidence of such behavior vary significantly when measured across a range of human cultures? And, within the history of our own culture, do we find child abuse as a continuous presence or a variable one (depending, in short, on time and place)?

This chapter addresses the last of the above questions. This will be an historical inquiry, framed by explicit comparisons of our present with our past. Unfortunately, no systematic research on the history of child abuse is currently available in print (though this has not stopped some writers from pronouncing strong and sweeping opinions on the subject). Hence the ensuing pages unfold an argument that is necessarily tentative and incomplete. The conclusions proposed here would need careful testing, by many hands, in order to become solidly persuasive. Yet all historical inquiry is incremental, and every scholarly project must begin from "inadequate data." Indeed, as we struggle by various routes toward a reckoning with child abuse, history has strong claims on our attention. For history, however imperfectly understood, is one of our best aids in discovering what kind of a people we are.

I

While the aforementioned article by Dr. Kempe and his colleagues produced a first dramatic surge of public recognition, we should not assume that child abuse had no importance before 1962. Recognition and reality (i.e., *what* is recognized) rarely march in lockstep; indeed, it is the task of this chapter to analyze points of disjunction between the two.

It seems clear in retrospect that the battered child was "discovered" by a series of sequential steps. Of great importance, for example, was the perfection of scientific technique in the medical subspecialty of pediatric radiology. This enabled investigators such as John Caffey (of the College of Physicians and Surgeons at Columbia University) and F. N. Silverman (of the University of Cincinnati College of Medicine) to analyze with new evidence a puzzling "syndrome" of "infant trauma"; their findings were published in several technical articles beginning in the late 1940s. In fact, physicians had observed some elements of this pattern as long as a hundred years ago: swellings, bruises, and fractures, in various forms and combinations. They had not, however, managed to pinpoint its source; rickets was their usual diagnosis— "in the absence," noted one commentator, "of any other assignable cause."[3]

The earliest of these medical descriptions date from the closing decades of the last century. Meanwhile churches and charitable organizations had begun to move on a parallel track. A New York girl named Mary Ellen, discovered savagely beaten by her (adoptive) parents in the year 1874, is often cited as the "first recorded case" of child abuse. Mary Ellen was removed from her home following a lawsuit brought by the American Society for the Prevention of Cruelty to Animals. (The law of this era afforded more in the way of formal protection to animals than to children as such.) Succeeding years brought the establishment of various Societies for the Prevention of Cruelty to Children, whose self-defined concerns included child abuse (roughly as we would understand the matter today).[4]

But this is about as far as we can follow the historical trail of child abuse, on the basis of clearly identified markings. Before the middle of the nineteenth century, the evidence is thin and vague and very scattered. Fictional writings, such as the novels of Charles Dickens, are sometimes cited in this connection, but their relation to social reality is inherently problematic. (And they would, in any case, push the story no more than a few decades further back.)

So what are we to conclude about child abuse in all the years before, let us say, 1800? "Recorded cases" are not to be found; shall we therefore assume an absence of actual *behavior*? To this, question most investigators return a negative answer. The change, they assert, lies not with the behavior but with the records—and with the social responses which record-keeping reflects. In brief, their argument goes as follows. Children have always been abused (and perhaps more widely abused, the further one looks back in time). What history has added, over roughly the past century, is a new sensibility—a feeling of outrage that things should be so. The various behaviors which we now designate as child abuse were widely prevalent, were taken for granted, and were scarcely (if ever) discoun-

tenanced, by countless generations of our forebears.

This way of thinking is apparently common among the various professionals active in the child abuse "field" today. One such person, a physician and author of numerous books and articles, writes flatly: "The neglect and abuse of children has been evidenced since the beginning of time. The natural animalistic instincts of the human race have not changed with the passing of the centuries." Another declares that "maltreatment of children has been justified for many centuries by the belief that severe physical punishment was necessary . . . to maintain discipline, to transmit educational ideas, to please certain gods, or to expel spirits." Still another notes "a discrepancy between the magnitude. . . . of child abuse in history and its documentation," but then proceeds, undeterred, to paint a particularly grisly picture of his subject.[5] In fact, academic historians have been no less inclined to these same assumptions. "Of course," writes one scholar, "a great deal of casual wife-beating and child-battering, which today would end up in the courts, simply went unrecorded in medieval and early modern times." And a second declares his firm belief that "a very large percentage of the children born prior to the eighteenth century were what would today be termed 'battered children.'"[6]

In turning to the historians, we enter a very broad area of inquiry—where child abuse as such occupies only a small corner. Historical research has recently broached the subject of family life in a massive way, and the outlines of a "consensus view" are becoming increasingly clear. According to this view, the history of family life in general, and of childhood in particular, has a markedly progressive cast. Change runs from "the Bad Old Days" (as one scholar has chosen to call them) toward something substantially better: from indifference and brutality and emotional constriction toward kindliness and closeness and a burgeoning spirit of "affective individualism." Here is the old "whig interpretation of history" in a new guise; here, in short, is an (ultimately) happy story.[7]

But wherever it focuses on premodern childhood, the story is anything *but* happy; a recent and influential statement begins as follows. "The history of childhood is a nightmare from which we have only recently begun to awaken. The further back in history one goes, the lower the level of child care, and the more likely the children are to be killed, abandoned, beaten, terrorized, and sexually abused." Subsequent parts of the same essay unfold a theory of "parent-child relations" through history, based on a sequence of characteristic "modes." The gist can be grasped quite readily from the labels themselves: (1) Infanticidal Mode (antiquity to fourth century A.D.); (2) Abandonment Mode (fourth to thirteenth century A.D.); (3) Ambivalent Mode (fourteenth to seventeenth centuries); (4) Intrusive Mode (eighteenth century); (5) Socialization Mode (nineteenth to mid-twentieth century); (6) Helping Mode (begins mid-twentieth century).[8]

There is insufficient space here to examine this construction at length (or, indeed, the constructions of other like-minded investigators). However, it may be worthwhile to cite a few particular specimens of evidence and inference, if only to exemplify the larger corpus to which they belong.

Item: Parental reference to children in diaries, correspondence, and other personal documents from premodern times was sparse, brief, sometimes laconic. Evidently this reflected an attitude of profound indifference to the fate of one's own offspring.

Item: Two children, within a single family, were sometimes given the same name (usually after the older one had died). This implies a lack of individualized attachments to either one.

Item: Premodern child rearing included, among its favored techniques of discipline, whipping, threats of death and damnation, innovation of ghosts, goblins, witches, and the like. There was, then, no appreciation of the tender sensibilities of the young.

Item: A reliance on "child labor" (most shockingly, during the early phases of the Industrial Revolution) was well nigh ubiquitous. Here we observe an attitude not just of indifference but also of rank exploitation.

Item: In at least some places, at some points in history, infanticide seems to have been practiced—even "accepted"—on a fairly broad scale. This evinces callousness of the most extreme sort.

Item: In certain premodern settings—those associated with "Puritanism," for example—infants were viewed as inherently corrupt and depraved; and parental duties were framed in terms such as "breaking the [child's] will." Hence the underlying *disposition* toward children was unfriendly, to say the least.

II

Such numerous and varied materials seem at first glance to offer powerful support for the "nightmare" view of the history of childhood. Yet a second (longer) look gives reason for pause. Personal documents, for example, are probably the wrong place to search for signs of affect toward children, for premodern diarists and correspondents did not often write about *any* sector of their affective experience. The practice of naming new born children for deceased siblings may have reflected a deep sense of loss, and a corresponding wish for "replacement." Much of premodern child rearing does indeed seem harsh by our standards, but it was not incongruous, and certainly not capricious, given then-prevalent views of human nature and society. (Moreover, the chill undercurrents in traditional fairy tales may serve the most basic developmental needs of children; such at least is the argument of the psychologist Bruno Bettelheim in his fascinating study *The Uses of Enchantment.*)[9] Child labor was, before the Industrial Revolution, a relatively benign affair. Admittedly, the development of the factory system introduced new and dangerous elements, but the involvement there of children was, historically speaking, of limited duration. Infanticide appears to have been closely associated with illegitimacy; in some (most?) of the documented cases, it was the desperate recourse of unmarried mothers faced with both material privation and social stigma. Finally, the beliefs which emphasized the inborn wickedness of children also furnished hope for their redemption; in a sense, parental repressiveness would redound to the eternal benefit of the "little sinners."

Taken together, these considerations underscore the importance of *context* in the evaluation of any given piece of social behavior. The overall demographic regime, the material basis of life, the prevailing system of beliefs and values, the intrinsic limitations of the evidence itself: all this, and more, must be carefully weighted in the interpretive balance. Of course, no less applies in the evaluation of variant practice in our own time; what seems "deviant" or downright "abusive" from one vantage point may appear innocent, or at least of good intent, from another. The situation of a child left unattended along a busy city street cannot be equated with that of his age-mates turned loose in a suburban patio or rural barnyard. The ostensible reasons for the parental behavior may be the same in each case—say, a trip to the supermarket—but the *meaning* depends on the total configuration of circumstance. Similarly, the use of physical force (e.g., spanking) in disciplining children yields to no single standard of judgment. Is

such practice routine in the family (and community) of the children involved? What is the prevalent pattern of physical expressiveness generally? And (most obviously) how severe, or possibly injurious, are these disciplinary techniques in their actual application?

Clearly, the task of identifying child abuse must be approached with caution. And in the remainder of this chapter we must accept a rather minimal—that is, narrowly circumscribed—definition of terms. In this way we may hope to reduce the uncertainties relating to contextual influence. We seek, in short, a baseline definition of child abuse to which most, if not all, observers could give assent. Four elements seem essential: (1) *physical force*, applied (2) *intentionally*, so as (3) to inflict *substantial, even life-threatening injury* on the body of the child, by (4) *his/her own parents.*[10] In asserting these criteria, we exclude other possibilities. The large and varied area of "neglect"—the failure to provide for the central needs of the child—is left aside, for neglect seems a particularly elastic and elusive category, permeable by all manner of cultural influence. Harsh discipline (which falls short of causing injury) and a seeming lack of empathy for childhood also fall outside our definitional boundaries. Finally, we exclude the abusive treatment of children by persons other than their own parents. This last may seem somewhat arbitrary, yet it does correspond with common usage. The particular horror of modern-day child abuse is its association with adults who might otherwise be seen as the chief protectors of the victims. And the particular shadow which it casts on the contemporary social order is the rending of these most necessary and "natural" of all human ties.

But in order to make a fresh start in the historical study of child abuse, we need not only a clear understanding of terms but a new research strategy as well. Prior comment on this

subject has been muddled by a certain loose-
ness of time perspective—a tendency to lump
together disparate fragments from many
epochs and cultures. Generalizations fashioned by such means are inherently suspect.
Hence in the pages that follow we shall assay
a radically different approach. We shall focus
on a single historical setting, sacrificing
breadth for depth in the development of a
"case study." This will enable us to control
more effectively for context (as previously
discussed) and for the inherent vagaries of the
evidence itself. Our conclusions will express
obvious limitations of time and place, but
within those limitations should attain defini-
tive shape. Moreover, they will not lack *implications* of a broader sort, and may eventually
lend themselves to useful comparison with
other historical "cases."

The particular focus to be developed here is
the culture of early America—more specifically, of early New England—a culture distinctly "premodern" yet related to our own by
an obvious historical chain. Briefly, we shall
ask: what were the central features of experience for children in early New England? In
what particular ways were children at risk, and
how was risk modified or minimized on their
behalf? To what extent is there evidence of actual child abuse in that setting (as we have
chosen to define the terms)? And how, at last,
are we to assess such evidence so as to yield a
more general conclusion to our inquiry?

III

Family life in early New England has been the
subject of considerable study in recent years;
hence we have a relatively firm backdrop to
use as our starting point. The children of this
particular time and place were, first of all, *numerous*. On average, a married couple had 8 to
10 children, and at any given time children

were likely to comprise fully half the population (if we use the term children to mean anyone between the ages 0–16). Then as now,
children's experiences were centered in families—although then, rather *more* than now,
they moved easily and informally into activities beyond the home. They faced considerable threats to life and health, though popular
lore has exaggerated the sum total of their
mortality. Recent investigations show that
some 70 to 80 percent of all infants safely born
could expect to survive to adulthood.[11]

Unlike the pattern of our own day, children
in early New England did not form a sharply
delineated age group. For most, schooling
was a sometime thing (limited to a few years
or seasons), and there was little else in the organized life of the community to set them
apart. They joined their elders in the work of
fields and farm, in the pleasures of the hearth,
in the social round of village and neighborhood, in the devotions of the local church.
They were, in effect, "apprenticed" for adult
life from an early age, and their growth proceeded along a relatively smooth and seamless
track. It has become fashionable to characterize premodern children as "miniature
adults," and—for little New Englanders at
least—this term does come near the mark.[12]

Was there less feeling invested in them than
in children nowadays? Historical evidence of
feeling seems always to come in short supply,
but what we have suggests strong and enduring ties. A country poet (and wife of a farmer
and local magistrate) wrote movingly of the
deaths of various infant grandchildren: "No
sooner came but gone, and fallen asleep/Ac-
quaintance short, yet parting caused us
weep." A village yeoman remembered that
"when his child was sick, and like to die, he
ran barefoot and barelegged, and with tears"
through the night to find assistance. A local
goodwife described the funeral of her cousin,
and the plight of "a poor babe" left mother-

less: "I then did say to some of my friends that . . . I could be very willing to take my cousin's little one and nurse it." Similar expressions could be assembled in large amounts, but the drift is immediately clear.[13]

Of course, the presence in individual instances of tender feeling toward children would not by itself guarantee their immunity from harm—or even from "abuse." Hence we must try to envision them in the social situations which chiefly framed their lives. This aim directs us, in turn, to one particular category of source materials: the records of the legal system. New England courts were notoriously active in all phases of social experience. There, if anywhere, we might expect to find a mirror for the experience of individual children.

Our expectations are not ill-founded. From time to time the records perserve a case such as the following: "Alexander Edwards complains against Thomas Merrick in an action of the case, for abusing his child named Samuel Edwards, being about 5 or 6 years old, the 14th of April last . . . The witnesses: John Mathews, Nathaniel Bliss. They proved 3 batteries besides villifying words [such] as 'hang him; better kill him than he kill my child.'"[14] Such notations show how young children might become implicated in neighborhood squabbles. But they are not very numerous (when the records are considered as a whole), nor, in the average case, do they indicate much real harm to the young "victims."

There were, in addition, particular cases of violence used (or threatened) against children in their own homes. These are obviously pertinent to our inquiry, and they deserve a more extended review. Some—perhaps the largest number—involved an assault on a young bond-servant by his (or her) master. A tragic instance came to light in 1655 in the Plymouth Colony. A boy of thirteen was found dead, his body discolored, "his skin broken in diverse places . . . [and] all his back [covered] with

stripes given him by his master." Further investigation disclosed a sequence of antecedent cruelties: frequent and unreasonable whippings, demands for heavy work far beyond the boy's capacity, periodic deprivation of food and clothing. The master was eventually tried and convicted on a charge of manslaughter, and sentenced to be "burned in the hand, . . . and . . . all his goods confiscated."[15]

This was an extreme case. In other instances servants had received "hard usage" which, however, stopped short of a fatal result. They ranged from one child allegedly assaulted by her master's own children to another "found . . . beaten black and blue, with many marks on her body, so that some doctors despaired of her life."[16] The issue was usually *physical* beating, and the point for the court to decide was whether such practice had exceeded "reasonable" bounds. We must understand that the right (and duty) to administer physical "correction" underlay many forms of authority in this culture. Parents would "chastize" their own children in this way—no less than their servants. And the courts of law regularly prescribed whipping as punishment for adult offenders of many kinds.

Occasionally the courts heard charges of abusive conduct toward children by stepparents. Thus, for example: "Henry Merry, of Woburn, . . . [was called] to answer for the cruel beating [of] John Wallis, his wife's child, about 4 years old."[17] But these cases amount to a mere handful overall. Last—and apparently least, in a quantitative sense—are the cases that involved parents and their own children. Here is a modest example, drawn from the records of the Essex County Court in Massachusetts: "Michael Emerson, for cruel and excessive beating of his daughter with a flail swingle and for kicking her, was fined and bound to good behavior."[18] And here is a much more affecting instance, as described in John Winthrop's journal:

A cooper's wife of Hingham, having been long in a sad, melancholy distemper near to frenzy, and having formerly attempted to drown her child, but prevented by God's gracious providence, did now again take an opportunity, being alone, to carry her child, aged three years, to a creek near her house, and stripping it of the clothes, threw it into the water and mud. But the tide being low, the little child scrambled out, and taking up his clothes, came to its mother who was set down not far off. She carried the child again, and threw it in so far as it could not get out; but then it pleased God that a young man coming that way saved it. She would give no other reason for it, but that she did it to save it from misery, and withal that she was assured she had sinned against the Holy Ghost. . . . Thus doth Satan work by the advantage of our infirmities.[19]

A similar case (but with fatal result) is reported elsewhere in the same document. In 1638 one Dorothy Talbie "was hanged at Boston for murdering her own daughter, a child of three years old." She had previously attempted the lives of her husband, her other children, and her own self. According to Winthrop she was moved to all this "through melancholy and spiritual delusions"—and, in the killing of her daughter, was led by impulses from the Devil which she mistook "as revelations from God."[20]

These two cases require special comment. The principals seem to have been profoundly disturbed—"distempered" and "deluded" by the lights of their own time, and probably "psychotic" by ours. No other instance of plainly murderous intent, on the part of a parent toward a child, appears within the entire range of early New England source materials. Perhaps, therefore, the actions of Dorothy Talbie and the Hingham cooper's wife should be assigned to a small residual category of quite extreme psychopathology. The latter *may* be transhistorical, but would, in any culture, account for only an outer

fringe of abusive behavior. Most such behavior in our own society cannot be associated with full-blown psychosis.

The total of the evidence to this point seems modest indeed. The occasional cases in which children suffered abuse from "masters" or neighbors do not fall within our definitional boundaries as outlined above. And the instances involving parents or stepparents are very few in number and highly exceptional in circumstance. Yet there remains one further possibility: perhaps some portion of parental abuse could have been disguised as accidental injury (evidently a common occurrence today). In this connection we may profitably examine the records of inquest in cases of sudden death (where cause was not immediately ascertainable). Local magistrates regularly empanelled special juries to investigate such cases, at least a portion of which involved children. The resultant reports were entered in the files of the courts; here is a typical specimen:

We whose names are underwritten, being warned to serve on a jury of inquest, have made search on the corpse of Thomas Evans, aged about ten years. [We] do find that his father and he coming from the brook commonly called Griffin's Brook with a barrel of water in a horse cart, and he sitting in the cart behind the barrel, as they were coming up the hill the mare gave a stop. And suddenly moving again, the barrel rolled out and drive the child before it, and pitched [him] on his forehead. And there [he] lay until his father took it from him. And we find that this skull was very much broken, which was the cause of his death.[21]

Other young victims of fatal accidents included "a child of between 3 and 4 years old" crushed by a log which "rolled down" from a sled he was "endeavoring to get up upon;" a boy of four run over by his father's cart ("no person knowing it, it being in the dark of the evening"); still another boy thrown from a cart, "and the wheel, as we conceive, went over his head;" and a child "found dead in the brook ... drowned ... through its own weakness, without the hand of any other person being any occasion or cause thereof."[22]

The court reports on such cases can be supplemented by occasional comments in personal documents. Thus Winthrop's journal describes "a very sad accident at Weymouth" in which a five-year-old was fatally wounded while playing with his father's gun:

He ... took it, and laid it upon a stool, as he had seen his father do, and pulled up the cock (the spring being weak), and put down the hammer, [and] then went to the other end and blowed in the mouth of the piece, as he had seen his father also do; and with that stirring [and] the piece being charged, it went off and shot the child into the mouth and through his head.[23]

In another instance an infant died in a fire started by an older sibling. (The latter had inadvertently "burned a clot, and fearing its mother should see it, thrust it into a haystack by the door, . . . the fire not being quite out.")[24] The particulars on this list make painful reading, yet they convey no hint of parental abuse—and little enough of parental neglect. Over-running by carts, drownings, houses fires, gun mishaps: these form an expectable range of accidental outcomes in a premodern village setting.

The judicial inquests into childhood death belonged to a larger pattern of oversight and protection. Local officials stood ready to intervene whenever the care of particular children seemed imperiled by the wants and failings of their parents. In March 1680, for example, the selectmen of Northampton, Massachusetts, obtained a court order to remove three children from their own home and place them "to service as apprentices" in other households. The parents, it seems, were "in a very low condition . . . and [lacked]

things necessary for supplies and bringing up of [their] children." The same court imposed similar orders on a second family in which the children's "education" was neglected—"it appearing that the father of them is very vicious and rather [is] learning them irreligion than any good literature."[25] These measures (and a host of others like them) reflected official concern with the bodily and spiritual "estate" of young persons thought to be at risk.

In most instances, court action was itself the result of intervention by others with personal knowledge of the key circumstances. For example, an elderly Massachusetts woman brought suit against her son-in-law for neglecting his children (who were also *her* grandchildren), and neighbors volunteered testimony as to their "suffering condition."[26] Probate records supply convergent evidence in large quantities. A man writing a will would create specific lines of responsibility for the welfare of his underage children. Thus, in one case: "My will and mind is that if my wife Edna Bailey marries again, and her husband prove unloving to the child ... I give power to my brother James Bailey and [to] Michael Hopkinson, with my wife's consent, to remove the child, with his portion [i.e., of inheritance] from him, and so to dispose of it for the best behoof of the child." And again, in another case: "I appoint these five Christian dear loving friends ... to be my executors and administrators of this my last will and testament, as also to be the overseers of my wife and children in a friendly Christian way toward them, and [I direct] that you five should take the advice of our [church] elders."[27] Here, in sum, was a web of responsibility for children extending from parents and stepparents to relatives, friends, estate executors, religious leaders—and, as the final resort, civil authorities.

The details of all this demand our attention because the issue at hand is a tricky one. We are trying to understand *an absence of evidence* (e.g., of behavior which might qualify as child abuse). And the outcome depends on careful evaluation of other material with implicitly related meaning; in short, we need to use what *is* in the record to interpret what *does not* appear there. In such cases one must always recognize the possibility that the designated behavior was present, and perhaps even widely so, in reality, but without leaving traces for the historian to follow. (Perhaps it was taken so much for granted by contemporaries that it would not attract notice—and thus not enter the historical record. Or perhaps the evidence it generated has not survived the passage of time.) In the current instance, however, this possibility cannot be fitted to the known facts. Consider the following, by way of summary of the substantive materials reviewed in the preceding pages.

1. Had individual children suffered severe abuse at the hands of their parents in early New England, other adults would have been disposed to respond. The culture, in general, seems to have sponsored a solicitous attitude toward the young. We know, moreover, that in the (relatively infrequent) cases where *servant*-children were brutalized by masters, public sympathy was directly engaged. Hence, we may reasonably infer a *motive* to prevent child abuse.

2. The powers of local magistrates, and the procedures of the courts, would readily have invited action against child abuse. In our own time such action is sometimes inhibited by a distaste for intruding into another family's affairs; indeed, the abuse itself may be long concealed within the private space to which all families feel entitled. But in early New England little value attached to personal and domestic privacy. Elected officials were empowered to over-

see family life, no less than other aspects of life. Neighbors, in fact, accepted informal oversight and responsibility for one another as part of their "Christian duty." In short, there were *means* to discover child abuse (if it should occur) and to take the necessary remedial steps.

3. Had the courts and/or other official bodies been obliged to deal with child abuse, there would now be sufficient *evidence* to alert us to the fact. The early New Englanders kept elaborate records of their various doings—records which have, for the most part, been preserved with loving care by successive generations of their descendants.

These considerations of motive, means, and evidence allow us to interpret the absence of records of child abuse as an absence of the behavior itself. Our "case study" of early New England is now concluded. And it throws a long shadow of doubt on the "consensus view" of this subject.

IV

While we have no other historical "cases" to set alongside the material from early New England, there is interesting and convergent evidence in recent work in anthropology. There, too, the question of child abuse can be put to premodern conditions; the results so far fall into two parts. On one hand, anthropologists feel constrained to underscore the range of culturally normative standards in child rearing; thus one society's abuse may be another's common practice. But on the other hand, the "classic child abuse complex" of the modern West (as one writer has called it) is not found in traditional non-Western societies. (This "complex" conforms roughly to the definition formulated earlier in our discussion.) Moreover, where the old order breaks down in the face of incipient modernization (e.g., urbanization, industrial development, etc.), child abuse begins to appear in its "classic" form.[28]

These findings from a variety of cultures around the contemporary world return us by a natural route to the evolution of our own society. We are confronted, finally, with an historical *conundrum* of large and unsettling proportions. If child abuse is far more prevalent now than two or three centuries ago, the question arises—*why*? What factors, which processes, unraveling through the course of time, account for the change? It is obviously impossible to canvass all the relevant possibilities here, but perhaps we can trace at least the outline of an answer, if only to invite further thought and discussion.

The scientific literature on present-day child abuse provides a good point of entry. Briefly summarized, this literature presents a three-part model of the key "predisposing influences": (1) environmental ones (social and cultural forces, in general); (2) situational ones (pressure-points within abusing families, in particular); (3) psychological ones (the character of abusing parents as individuals).[29] Each of these can be stretched out along the frame of time and joined to other elements in our historical past.

Environmental interpretations of child abuse invariably highlight a pair of central tendencies in modern American society. One is the fact of endemic violence, and a climate of values that condones violence under at least some circumstances. The other is the condition of social isolation in which many individuals and families find themselves obliged to live. Both these tendencies may be considered as historical growths, the second perhaps more strikingly so than the first. Premodern society was, if nothing else, quite fully integrative of the lives of its constituent members. The traditional village setting—for example, in early New England—offered to each person and every family a density of human contact that is hard even to imagine today. The marketplace, the church, the court, the broad spectrum of local routine and custom made a tight web of social experience, allowing few possibilities of escape or exclusion. Premodern communities had their share of nonconformists, eccentrics, and criminals—but no isolates, no habitual "strangers." The shape of life from day to day expressed the twin principles of mutual support and mutual surveillance. It is in just this regard that the situation of our own abusing parents seems most sadly deficient. Study after study finds them rootless, friendless, virtually unknown even to next-door neighbors.[30] Are they overwhelmed by real or imagined adversities? There is no one else to share the load. Do they lash out at the nearest available human targets? There is no one to see the hand rise, and to stay its swift descent.

Other features of contemporary society must also be mentioned here. Unemployment appears to correlate with child abuse (and with wife-beating as well). And there is a reason to think that on-the-job alienation (boredom, frustration, a sense of "depersonalization") may show a similar link.[31] These *residua* of our modern economy find no parallel in premodern times. Work could be—often was—hard and very meager in its rewards, but it was not simply *denied* to some considerable portion of the available hands. Moreover, there was no equivalent to the numbing routines of production in the mass—the assembly line, the secretarial pool, the shapeless ranks of white-collar bureaucracy.

One more part of this environmental matrix is the pace and power of change itself. According to a recent quantitative study, "abusing parents" have a disproportionate experience of "crisis," as measured on a "social readadjustment scale" of "life change units." The details need not concern us; suffice it to say that the scale in question includes many items hard to associate with a premodern setting (e.g., mortgage foreclosure, job change, retirement, "business readjustment," divorce).[32] It is arguable, in short, that change is now a more frequent and disruptive life-presence than was the case a few generations ago. It also seems likely that for many of us the capacity to accept and absorb change is less. We have no clear equivalent to the "providential" worldview of our forebears—their belief that all things, no matter how surprising and inscrutable, must be attributed to God's overarching will.

We turn next to the "situational" factors most often adduced with respect to child abuse. "In abusing families," notes one authority, "there is a constant competition over who will be taken care of." The parents themselves enter this competition with great intensity; they seek, in effect, a "role reversal" in which the children will become their caretakers. Life in such households is characterized by mutual overinvolvement, amounting in some cases to "emotional fusing"; there is a pervasive quality of "stuck-togetherness."[33] Described in more formal terms, these people are poorly differentiated from one another; hence they fall easily into scapegoating, schemes of manipulation, and all manner of misunderstanding.

Here situational elements merge with psychological ones—the third part of our explanatory model—and the personality of the abusing parent comes fully into view. Again, there is a clear thematic center common to all recent studies: "low self-esteem," and feelings of emptiness, worthlessness, and helplessness.[34] Viewed from the standpoint of current psychoanalytic psychology, child abusers suffer from severe deficits in basic "narcissim."[35] Their inner lives are organized around archaic

(and largely unconscious) "grandiose fantasies" for themselves and literally heroic (or "idealized") expectations of others. They are unable to make consistent self/other distinctions; indeed, they characteristically approach others as extensions of their own selves.

The connection to child abuse goes roughly as follows. The parent is unable to recognize the child as a separate individual with needs and aims in his or her own right. When the child, inevitably and appropriately, asserts his or her independent self, the parent is surprised, disoriented, even infuriated. So it is that a mere cry at an inopportune time (inopportune, that is, from the parent's standpoint) can be experienced as a deep flaw in a narcissitically perceived world—indeed, as an outright affront to that world. Like such affronts it threatens inner "fragmentation" (for the parent), and the likely response is that special form of uncompromising anger known to clinicians as "narcissitic rage."[36]

This excursion into clinical theory, brief and oversimplified though it is, will have to serve as the basis for one final group of historical speculations. We have tried to underscore the particular "family constellation" and the (related) psychological set which appear most conducive to child abuse. But, again, we wish to explore the contrast between *then* and *now*. That contrast can be followed through several different, though apparently overlapping, historical dimensions.

1. The *demographic* dimension: We start from the fact that families in early America were characteristically *large*. As previously noted, eight to ten children per married couple was typical. We may infer that in households of this size and shape the emotional exchange between parents and children was necessarily diffused. For one thing, a certain portion of "parenting" was carried on by older children (vis-à-vis younger ones); for another,

there were kin and neighbors nearby who would enter the family circle on a fairly regular basis. By contrast, the modern American family includes significantly fewer persons, and its style of interaction seems far more intense. The element of psychic involvement—specifically including "narcissistic" involvement—is correspondingly deepened.[37]

2. The *structural* dimension: It hardly needs saying that the place of children in the productive sector of family life was greatly diminished over the past several generations. Time was when the young performed valuable service as part of a "working household" (e.g., the farm family of early New England, described above); now, of course, they constitute a substantial drain on family resources.[38] This makes them *vulnerable* in ways both new and profound.

3. The *normative* dimension: In premodern times, the fate of each individual was related, by prevalent custom and belief, to forces well beyond his or her human surroundings: to inherited status in a traditional community, to the "accidents" of Nature, and, above all, to the ultimate purposes of God. But, beginning in the nineteenth century, this view was replaced by a new ethos of "individualism." From henceforth, personal destiny was seen, in part, as something self-determined—and, in equal part, as dependent on one's immediate family. Parents, in particular, were charged with profound responsibility for the life and prospects of their children; little people could be "set on a true course," or ruined for life, by the influence of their home environment. (Conversely, parents near the end of their lives could be vindicated, or destroyed, by the performance of their grown children.) As part of this new belief-set there developed the implicit notion that young children are

somehow the *property* of their parents—part of the larger armamentarium with which a family faces the "outside world." This idea of children-as-property has been deeply consequential in several directions; not least, it has validated new concepts of parental "rights" and prerogatives.

Moreover, ours is a culture which accords an almost unique significance to measures of individual "success" and "failure." These measures are, in the first instance, economic and occupational ones, but they reach out in other directions as well (e.g., good looks, good "personality," etc.). There is room enough here for the cultivation of self-doubt—and the lessening of healthy "narcissim"—in persons of every type and background. Once again, it was not always so. When individuals measured their worth in terms of prescribed position in a given community and presumed status in the eyes of God, their experience of "self" was in some ways easier.

V

The thread of this discussion, now at an end, has been long and somewhat tortuous. We began by considering the current consensus-view that the history of childhood—and, more particularly, of child abuse—is essentially "progressive." We found reason to question this view and the scattershot evidence on which it depends. Next, we developed a "case study" of our subject, from materials on one particular historical setting. The outcome cast further doubt on progressive interpretations. We noticed, in passing, the convergent findings of anthropologists concerned with premodern culture. And we concluded with some broad hypotheses as to why child abuse may have become more prevalent, and more severe, within the past two or three centuries.

There is danger always, when refuting one historical judgment, of rushing to the opposite extreme. We must not resurrect an older, plainly romanticized notion of the past with its down-on-the-farm sentimentality about families, neighborhoods, and life in general. Most childhoods in premodern society knew their own forms of severity. But they seem *not* to have known the particular sufferings which the term "child abuse" now calls so vividly and painfully to mind.

The pain is, of course, a crucial point. Open any casebook, examine any photographic file on battered children—and the impulse to look away is overwhelming. Dr. Kempe has noted the contorted efforts of physicians, in the face of "obvious" signs, to "obliterate such suspicions [of child abuse] from their minds." If we are not careful, history may lend itself to similar stratagems. It is easier to think that this problem, however terrible today, must have been far worse in the past. In such historical comparisons we seek a measure of comfort— not to say, a defense against truth.

And there are other truths with which this one makes a disconcerting fit. The society that finds within itself the malignancy of child abuse is the same society which has, over a few short generations, experienced assassinations of public figures, racial repressions, bitterly divisive wars, and ever-rising levels of street violence.

These are grievous wounds, and they call for massive projects of healing. Historians are not healers, but they can and must contribute to the process of truth-seeking, of diagnosis, of *understanding*—from which alone the healing may come.

NOTES

1. C. Henry Kempe, F. N. Silverman, B. F. Steele, William Droegmueller, and Henry K. Silver, "The Battered Child Syndrome," *Journal of the American Medical Association* 181 (1962), 17–24.

2. The legal and legislative aspects of all this are summarized in Monrad G. Paulsen, "The Law and Abused Children," in *The Battered Child,* Ray E. Helfer and C. Henry Kempe, eds., 2d ed. (Chicago, 1974), 153–78. See also "Appendix B: A Summary of Child Abuse Legislation, 1973," in ibid., 203–27; Vincent DeFrancis, *Child Abuse Legislation: Analysis and Study of Mandatory Reporting Laws in the United States* (Denver, 1966); Joseph J. Costa and Gordon K. Nelson, *Child Abuse and Neglect: Legislation, Reporting, and Prevention* (Lexington, Mass., 1978); Jean M. Giovannoni and Rosina M. Becarra, *Defining Child Abuse* (New York, 1979); and Barbara J. Nelson, *Making An Issue of Child Abuse: Political Agenda-Setting for Social Problems* (Chicago, 1984).

3. The history of medicine, in relation to child abuse, is summarized in David Bakan, *Slaughter of the Innocents* (San Francisco, 1971), 44–54. On the development, specifically, of pediatric radiology, see F. N. Silverman, "Radiologic Aspects of the Battered-Child Syndrome," in Helfer and Kempe, *Battered Child,* 41–60.

4. The "Mary Ellen case" is described in Vincent J. Fontana, *The Maltreated Child* (Springfield, Ill., 1964), 9. Developments subsequent to that case are described and discussed in Samuel X. Radbill, "Children in a World of Violence: A History of Child Abuse," in C. Henry Kempe and Ray E. Helfer, eds., *The Battered Child,* 3d ed. (Chicago, 1980), 3–20; Mason P. Thomas, "Child Abuse and Neglect: Historical Overview, Legal Matrix, and Social Perspective," *North Carolina Law Review, 50* (1972), 293–349; and Catherine J. Ross, "The Lessons of the Past: Defining and Controlling Child Abuse in the United States," in George Gerbner, Catherine J. Ross, and Edward Zigler, eds., *Child Abuse: An Agenda for Action* (New York, 1980), 63–81. For an excellent treatment of parallel developments in England, see George R. Behlmer, *Child Abuse and Moral Reform in England 1870–1908* (Stanford, Calif., 1982); on the situation in France, see Rachel Fuchs, "Crimes Against Children in Nineteenth-Century France: Child Abuse," *Law and Human Behavior 6* (1983), 237–259. For important new work on child abuse in American history see Elizabeth H. Pleck, *Domestic Tyranny: The Process of Reform Against Family Violence* (New York, 1986).

5. Fontana, *The Maltreated Child* 3; Radbill, "Children in a World of Violence," 3; Bakan, *Slaughter of the Innocents*, 25.

6. Lawrence Stone, *The Family, Sex, and Marriage in England, 1500–1800* (New York, 1977), 95; Lloyd deMause, "The Evolution of Childhood," in deMause, ed., *The History of Childhood* (New York, 1974), 40.

7. This viewpoint is found, for example, in Stone, *Family, Sex, and Marriage in England*, in deMause, "Evolution of Childhood," and in Edward Shorter, *The Making of the Modern Family* (New York, 1975).

8. deMause, "Evolution of Childhood," 51–54 and *passim*.

9. Bruno Bettelheim, *The Uses of Enchantment: The Meaning and Importance of Fairy Tales* (New York, 1975).

10. For a discussion of problems in the definition of child abuse see David G. Gil, *Violence Against Children: Physical Child Abuse in the United States* (Cambridge, Mass., 1970), 5–8. The same problems are addressed from a legal standpoint in Giovannoni and Becarra, *Defining Child Abuse*, and from an anthropological standpoint in Jill Korbin, "The Cross-Cultural Context of Child Abuse and Neglect," in Kempe and Helfer, *Battered Child*, 3d ed., 21–35.

11. On childhood in early New England, see John Demos, *A Little Commonwealth: Family Life in Plymouth Colony* (New York, 1970), chs. 4, 9, 10; Edmund S. Morgan, *The Puritan Family: Religion and Domestic Relations in Seventeenth-Century New England*, rev. ed. (New York, 1966), chs. 3–5; Joseph Illick, "Child-Rearing in Seventeenth-Century England and America," in deMause, *History of Childhood*, 303–50; and Philip J. Greven, Jr., *The Protestant Temperament: Patterns of Child-Rearing, Religious Experience, and the Self in Early America* (New York, 1977).

12. The image of children as "little adults" was investigated at length by the French cultural historian Philippe Ariès in his path-breaking study published in English under the title *Centuries of Childhood*, Robert Baldick, trans. (New York, 1962). See also J. H. Plumb, "The New World of Children in Eighteenth-Century England," *Past and Present* 67 (1975), 70–85, and Demos, *A Little Commonwealth*,

ch. 9. For a somewhat different viewpoint, see Ross Beales, "In Search of the Historical Child," *American Quarterly* 27 (1975), 379–98.

13. Anne Bradstreet, "On my Dear Grandchild, Simon Bradstreet, Who Died on 16 November 1669, Being But a Month and One Day Old," in *The Works of Anne Bradstreet*, Jeannine Hensley, ed. (Cambridge, Mass., 1967), 237; "Examination of Hugh Parsons, of Springfield, on a Charge of Witchcraft . . . Before Mr. William Pynchon, at Springfield, 1951," printed in Samuel G. Drake, *Annals of Witchcraft in New England* (New York, 1869), 239; "Bethiah Lothrop's Statement," given to the Essex County Quarterly Court, 27 June 1676, printed in *The Probate Records of Essex County* (Salem, Mass., 1916–20), 3:28. In general, such evidence of emotional experience is located in the depositional statements presented in numerous civil actions before local courts. Since this is largely manuscript material, it is not well-known even to professional historians.

14. From the records of the Hampshire County (Mass.) Court, 21 April 1648, as kept by William and John Pynchon, and published in James M. Smith, ed., *Colonial Justice in Western Massachusetts* (Cambridge, Mass., 1961), 216.

15. Nathaniel B. Shurtleff and David Pulsifer, eds., *Records of the Colony of New Plymouth, in New England*, 6 vols. (1855–61), 3:71–73.

16. Case of William Holdred vs. John Ilsly, Salem Quarterly Court, 17 October 1666, published in *Records and Files of the Quarterly Courts of Essex County Massachusetts*, 8 vols. (1911–21), 3:365; petition of Henry and Jane Stacy, Salem Quarterly Court, 29 June 1680, in the former, 7:421.

17. Case heard by the Middlesex County (Mass.) Court, 18 April 1662, in Middlesex County Court Records, vol. 1, leaf 105 (manuscript volume, Clerk's Office, Middlesex County Courthouse, East Cambridge, Mass.).

18. Case heard by the Ipswich Quarterly Court, 23 May 1676, published in *Records and Files of the Quarterly Courts of Essex County, Massachusetts*, 6:141.

19. *Winthrop's Journal*, James Kendall Hosmer, ed. (New York, 1908), 2:60.

20. *Ibid.*, 1:282.

21. Records of the County Court of Hartford

(Conn.), 29 October 1683, in Hartford Probate Records, vol 4, leaf 74 (manuscript volume, Connecticut State Library, Hartford).

22. Records of the Hampshire County (Mass.) Court, as kept by William and John Pynchon, 27 December 1674, in Smith, ed., *Colonial Justice in Western Massachusetts,* 282; records of the Hampshire County (Mass.) Court, 25 September 1660, in the former 248; records of the Essex County (Mass.) Court, 29 September 1676, in *Records and Files of the Quarterly Courts of Essex County, Massachusetts* 6:234; records of the Hampshire County (Mass.) Court, in Smith, ed., *Colonial Justice in Western Massachusetts,* 245–46.

23. *Winthrop's Journal,* Hosmer, 2:72.

24. *Ibid.,* 2:30.

25. Records of the Hampshire County (Mass.) Court, 30 March 1680, in Hampshire County (Mass.) Probate Records, vol 1, leaf 205 (manuscript volume, Registry of Probates, Northampton, Mass.).

26. Mrs. Elizabeth King vs. John Blano, Salem Quarterly Court, 29 June 1677 in *Records and Files of the Quarterly Courts of Essex County, Massachusetts* 6:299–300. See also some later proceedings in this case, Salem Quarterly Court, 12 November 1677, in the former, 6:359–61.

27. Will of Richard Bailey of Rowley (Mass.), 15 February 1647, in *Probate Records of Essex County* 1:92; will of John Lowell, of Newbury (Mass.), 29 June 1647, in the former, 1:67.

28. See Jill Korbin, "Anthropological Contributions to the Study of Child Abuse," *Child Abuse and Neglect: The International Journal* 1 (1977), 7–24. Korbin has also edited an excellent anthology of essays on the treatment (and maltreatment) of children in a variety of cultures around the world: *Child Abuse and Neglect: Cross-Cultural Perspectives* (Berkeley, Calif., 1981). In many respects the settings described there differ drastically from one another. However, they all support the general proposition stated in a Foreword by Robert B. Edgerton: "Child abuse . . . has become a serious social problem in the United States and in some other industrialized societies, yet it occurs infrequently or not at all in many of the world's [non-industrialized] societies" (ix).

29. On "casual models" in the study of child abuse, a fine summary can be found in R. D. Parke and C. W. Collmer, "Child Abuse: An Interdisciplinary Analysis," in E. M. Heatherington, ed., *Review of Child Development Research* 5 (Chicago, 1975), 509–90. See also Blair Justice and Rita Justice, *The Abusing Family* (New York, 1976), 37–54, and Mildred Daley Pagelow, *Family Violence* (New York, 1984), 74–143.

30. See, for example, Leontine Young, *Wednesday's Children: A Study of Child Neglect and Abuse* (New York, 1964), 37ff.; Justice and Justice, *Abusing Family,* 94; and Brandt F. Steele and Carl B. Pollock, "A Psychiatric Study of Parents Who Abuse Infants and Small Children," in Helfer and Kempe, *Battered Child,* 2d ed., 106.

31. Justice and Justice, *Abusing Family,* 255–57; Leroy H. Pelton, ed., *The Social Context of Child Abuse* (New York, 1981); James Garbarino and Gwen Gilliam, *Understanding Abusive Families* (Lexington, Mass., 1980). The "ecological" approach to the child abuse problem has assumed major importance in recent years, and the literature exemplifying this approach is enormous. For additional authors and titles, see Elizabeth Kemmer, *Violence in the Family: An Annotated Bibliography* (New York, 1984).

32. See Murray A. Straus, "Stress and Child Abuse," in Kempe and Helfer, *Battered Child,* 3d ed. (Chicago, 1980), 86–103; Murray A. Straus, Richard J. Gelles, and Suzanne K. Steinmetz, *Behind Closed Doors: Violence in the American Family* (New York, 1980), esp. ch. 8; Justice and Justice, *Abusing Family,* 25–34.

33. *Ibid.,* 61ff. See also M. Bowen, "The Use of Family Theory in Clinical Practice," *Comprehensive Psychiatry* 7 (1966), 345–74; Murray A. Straus, "A General Systems Theory Approach to a Theory of Violence Between Family Members, *Social Science Information* 12 (1973), 105–25; and Susan K. Steinmetz, *The Cycle of Violence: Assertive, Aggressive, and Abusive Family Interaction* (New York, 1977).

34. A good general survey of the psychiatric literature on child abuse can be found in Brandt Steele, "Psychodynamic Factors in Child Abuse," in Kempe and Helfer, *Battered Child,* 3d ed., 49–85. See also Parke and Collmer, "Child Abuse: An In-

terdisciplinary Analysis," and Gerbner et al., *Child Abuse*, chs. 2–3.

35. The best recent work in the clinical theory of narcissim is that of Heinz Kohut and his colleagues at the Institute of Psychoanalysis in Chicago. See, for example, Kohut, *The Psychology of the Self* (New York, 1970) and *The Restoration of the Self* (New York, 1977).

36. This paragraph is a summary of studies currently in progress, under the direction of Gustavo Lage, M.D., of the Institute of Psychoanalysis in Chicago. I am much indebted to Dr. Lage for various professional communication on the subject.

37. On the issue of "narcissistic" involvement, in modern American families, see Kohut, *Restoration of the Self*, 269–270. See also John Demos, "Oedipus and America: Notes on the Reception of Psychoanalysis in the United States," *The Annual of Psychoanalysis* 6 (1978), 23–39.

38. "The total costs of housing, feeding, and clothing one child, as well as educating him or her through high school, now add up to more than $35,000 by very conservative estimates for a family living at a very modest level." See Kenneth Keniston and the Carnegie Council on Children, *All Our Children: The American Family Under Pressure* (New York, 1977). More recent estimates run over $100,000. For a particularly sensitive treatment of all the issues surrounding the "costs" of raising children, see Viviana A. Zelizer, *Pricing the Priceless Child: The Changing Social Value of Children* (New York, 1985).

Part V

Labor and Family Intersections

In the section "Mediating Work and Family," we have assembled chapters that examine the ways in which labor and family responsibilities are intertwined. Because it is predominantly women, whether they work outside the home or not, who have had daily responsibility for home and children, the chapters in this section concentrate on the relationship between women's labor force participation and family life.

Contemporary discussions of work and family often treat these areas of relationships and activities as "separate spheres," in which families are considered the "private" area of life, and work the "public" area. Until recently, this separation of work and family was also portrayed as a separation of men, who were seen as belonging to the public world of work, and women, who were relegated to the private world of the home. This is an inaccurate portrayal of the historical relationship between work and family in the United States, as well as an incomplete picture of the activities of men and women that misses the intimate connection between employment and family life.

In colonial America, Euro-American mothers, fathers, and children worked together on farms or in family industries, producing in a "family economy" what they needed for subsistence and for trade, and providing children with the daily presence of both mothers and fathers. For most people of African descent in North America, colonial America and the first seven decades of the United States meant slavery.[1] In "'My Mother Was Much of a Woman,'" Jacqueline Jones describes how coercive labor and living conditions combined with a West African cultural heritage resulted in a division of labor that was imposed by white slave masters and a different sexual division of labor that was observed by African Americans in their private lives. Clearly, the social location of families in the broader economic, political, and legal context determines how "work" and "family" intersect.

In the nineteenth and early twentieth centuries, industrialization pulled some family members out of the home to become wage laborers, but it was not only men who took factory jobs or who toiled for wages. Although men became identified as the primary wage earners in families, the labor force participation of women, as wives or as daughters, varied by social class and racial-ethnic group. The family economy gave way to men's wage labor in industries and businesses, and middle-class women were relegated to homes that were now separated from economic production. For white middle-class women, a "cult of domesticity" emerged in the 1820s as a response to the changing economic landscape (Welter 1973), and a wife's employment was interpreted as a sign of her husband's failure to support a family. Although by the end of the nineteenth century, 19 percent of women were in the labor force, this was the case for only 5 percent of married women (U.S. Bureau of the Census 1975, 133). But the proportion of married women workers was not distributed equally across all groups: a larger percentage of married women among women of color, widows, women whose husbands had deserted them, recent immigrants, and other working-class wives worked for wages. Most women workers, and particularly recent immigrant women and women of color, found employment in the secondary labor sector where wages are low and work is often irregular. In "The Dialectics of Wage Work," Evelyn Nakano Glenn traces the work and family experiences of first generation (Issei) Japanese American women from 1905 to 1940; analyzes that experience in terms of race, class, and gender; and illustrates the interconnectedness of paid and unpaid work.

In the twentieth century, women's participation in the formal labor force has risen steadily, particularly among mothers of young children. By 1994, 62 percent of all married women with children under six years old were in the labor force (the figure is similar for mothers who are widowed, divorced, or separated), and 76 percent of all married women with school-age children (6–17 years old) were in the labor force (U.S. Bureau of the Census 1995, 406). As more mothers enter the work force and as more women continue to be employed through pregnancy and after the birth of children, how does this historical shift affect family dynamics? Does it alter our definitions of motherhood and fatherhood? Does it result in new forms of child rearing and child care?

In "Constructing Motherhood on the Night Shift," Anita Ilta Garey examines how some mothers (night-shift nurses) mediate work and family by arranging their work schedules not only so that they are available to their children during the day but also so that they can present themselves to others as "full-time moms" who stay home in the daytime. Their definitions of being a good mother thus intersect with the structure of their employment. Denise A. Segura's chapter, "Working at Motherhood," continues the focus on definitions of motherhood at the intersection of work and family by comparing Chicana mothers' and Mexican immigrant mothers' views on motherhood and employment. Segura finds that Mexican immigrants are more likely to define motherhood to include participation in the labor force, whereas Chicanas are more likely to define motherhood in opposition to employment and are more likely to feel "guilty" when they work outside the home. Her research underscores the fact that definitions of motherhood and the concept of "separate spheres" are rooted in particular economic, social, and cultural contexts.

One of the most important issues in mediating work and family is how to care for children while parents work. Rosanna Hertz observes that people base their choice of child care arrangements on a combination of their beliefs and their economic resources. In "The Parenting Approach to the Work-Family Dilemma," Hertz discusses dual-earner couples who share child care and suggests that this approach challenges the gendered division of labor within families and reshapes our approach to job and career.

In the section "Household Division of Labor," chapters on the contested terrain of housework point to even deeper interconnections between the economy and the family. Historically, while there has always been some kind of gendered division of labor, the specific content of that labor has varied. So, for example, in some regions of the country, milking cows is women's work, while in other areas it has been exclusively men's work. With this in mind, Grey Osterud's discovery of men going to quilting bees and doing "inside" domestic chores in late nineteenth century, rural upstate New York, comes as little surprise. In "'She Helped Me Hay It as Good as a Man'" she finds that men's and women's work lives were so intertwined, their social lives were similarly integrated.

In analyzing the economic transition from the rural producing household unit that Osterud describes, to an urban, primarily consuming one, Arlie Russell Hochschild and Anne Machung explore the attendant dislocations of ideology in "The Working Wife as Urbanizing Peasant." During the nineteenth century, as men increased their ability to earn a wage sufficient to support an entire family, they claimed domestic privileges associated with money and power, privileges such as exemption from household work and child care.

The parallel economic revolution in the twentieth century pulled women, including mothers of young children, into the paid labor force with equivalent disruption to kinship systems and the nuclear family way of life. In the 1900s, very few families can afford to have one parent at home full-time, and most women want to combine participation in the work force and family life. Family arrangements must therefore be rethought and the division of labor renegotiated. With the decline of the male wage in the past twenty-five years, men as a group no longer "earn" the privileges that previously excused them from housework and child rearing.

In a large quantitative study, Frances K. Goldscheider and Linda J. Waite find that the amount of household tasks done by children varies according to number, age, and sex of children. In "Children's Share in Household Tasks," the authors find that families with teenage girls share tasks with children far more than do families with teenage boys. But family form also makes a difference, and children in single female-headed households share more in the amount and kinds of household work than do children in two-parent households. While this finding does not signal a return to the family as an economic entity that counts children as economic assets, it does indicate a redistribution of work and leisure among members of the household. Interestingly, if female heads of households remarry, children once again cease to be fuller partners in household work.

There are men who buck the system of privilege, however, and share the "second shift." In interviews with couples who intentionally share child care and housework, Scott Coltrane found that both men and women struggled to shape their everyday practices with the ideal of equal partnership. He demonstrates, however, that large social and economic constraints affect the implementation of these ideas in "Household Labor and the Routine Production of Gender." Although men and women bring contrasting agendas and strengths to parenting, their involvement in co-parenting prompts them to try to redefine work obligations, and it increases men's commitment to their marital relationships and to housework. The chapters in this section explore how household labor *constructs* gender as well as reflects it.

NOTE

1. In 1790, 8 percent (60,000) of African Americans were not enslaved, but they did not have many of the rights held by white Euro-Americans (Amott and Matthaei 1991, 149).

REFERENCES

Amott, Teresa L., and Julie A. Matthaei. 1991. *Race, Gender, and Work.* Boston: South End Press.
U.S. Bureau of the Census. 1975. *Historical Statistics of the United States: Colonial Times to 1970.* Bicentennial edition, pt. 1. Washington, D.C.: GPO.
————. 1995. *Statistical Abstract of the United States: 1995.* 115th edition. Washington, D.C.: GPO.
Welter, Barbara. 1973. "The Cult of True Womanhood: 1820–1860." In *The American Family in Social-Historical Perspective,* ed. Michael Gordon. New York: St. Martin's Press.

 *Section A*

Mediating Work and Family

∾ *Chapter 50*

"My Mother Was Much of a Woman": Slavery

JACQUELINE JONES

Ah was born back due in slavery," says Nanny to her granddaughter in Zora Neale Hurston's novel *Their Eyes Were Watching God*, "so it wasn't for me to fulfill my dreams of whut a woman oughta be and to do." Nanny had never confused the degrading regimen of slavery with her own desires as they related to work, love, and motherhood: "Ah didn't want to be used for a work-ox and a brood-sow and Ah didn't want mah daughter used dat way neither. It sho wasn't mah will for things to happen lak they did." Throughout her life she had sustained a silent faith in herself and her sisters that was permitted no expression within the spiritual void of bondage: "Ah wanted to preach a great sermon about colored women sittin' on high, but they wasn't no pulpit for me," she grieved.[1]

Although largely ignored by historians over the years, Nanny's lament captures the essence of the antebellum South's dual caste system based on race and sex.[2] A compact, volatile, and somewhat isolated society, the slaveholder's estate represented, in microcosm, a larger drama in which physical force combined with the coercion embedded in the region's political economy to sustain the power of whites over blacks and men over women. Here, then, without pretense or apology were racial and patriarchal ideologies wedded to the pursuit of profit. As blacks, slave women were exploited for their skills and physical strength in the production of staple crops; as women, they performed a reproductive function vital to individual slaveholders' financial interests and to the inherently expansive system of slavery in general. Yet slave women's unfulfilled dreams for their children helped to inspire resistance against "the ruling race" and its attempts to subordinate the integrity of black family life to its own economic and political interests.[3]

The peculiar configuration of enforced labor and sexual relations under slavery converged most dramatically where the two forms of social domination overlapped—that is, in the experiences of slave women—and reflected traditional white notions of womanhood combined with profit-making considerations that were in some sense unique to the plantation economy. In the context of the sexual division of labor in early rural America, the work of black men and white women conformed to certain patterns not limited to the slaveholding South. For example, despite the rhetorical glorification of the slaveholder's wife as the embodiment of various otherworldly virtues, she remained responsible for conventional womanly duties in the mundane realm of household management.[4] Likewise, slave men performed duties similar to those of New England and southern yeomen farmers. They planted, weeded, and harvested crops, and during the winter months they burned brush, cleared pasture, mended fences, and repaired equipment. A few received special training and labored as skilled artisans or mechanics. Clearly, the size, spatial arrangement, commercial orientation, and free use of physical punishment set the southern plantation apart from northern and midwestern family farms. Still, the definition of men's work did not differ substantially within any of these settings.[5]

However, the master took a more crudely opportunistic approach toward the labor of slave women, revealing the interaction (and at times conflict) between notions of women *qua* "equal" black workers and women *qua* unequal reproducers; hence a slaveowner just as "naturally" put his bondswomen to work chopping cotton as washing, ironing, or cooking. Furthermore, in seeking to maximize the productivity of his entire labor force while reserving certain tasks for women exclusively, the master demonstrated how patriarchal and capitalist assumptions concerning women's work could reinforce each other.[6]

However, slave women also worked on be-

half of their own families, and herein lies a central irony in the history of their labor. Under slavery, blacks' attempts to sustain their family life amounted to a political act of protest against the callousness of owners, mistresses, and overseers. In defiance of the slaveholders' tendencies to ignore gender differences in making assignments in the fields, the slaves whenever possible adhered to a strict division of labor within their own households and communities. Consequently, the family played a key role in their struggle to combat oppression, for black women's attention to the duties of motherhood deprived whites of full control over them as field laborers, domestic servants, and "brood-sows." Indeed, the persistence with which slaves sought to define on their own terms "what a woman ought to be and to do" would ultimately have a profound impact on Afro-American history long after the formal institution of bondage had ceased to exist.

Working for Whites: Female Slave Labor as a Problem of Plantation Management

Interviewed by a Federal Writers Project (FWP) worker in 1937, Hannah Davidson spoke reluctantly of her experiences as a slave in Kentucky: "The things that my sister May and I suffered were so terrible. . . . It is best not to have such things in our memory." During the course of the interview she stressed that unremitting toil had been the hallmark of her life under bondage. "Work, work, work," she said; it had consumed all her days (from dawn until midnight) and all her years (she was only eight when she began minding her master's children and helping the older women with their spinning). "I been so exhausted working, I was like an inchworm crawling along a roof. I worked till I thought another lick would kill me." On Sundays, "the only time they [the slaves] had to themselves," she recalled, women washed clothes and some of the men tended their small tobacco patches. As a child she loved to play in the haystack, but that was possible only on "Sunday evening, after work."[7]

American slavery was an economic and political system by which a group of whites extracted as much labor as possible from blacks (defined as the offspring of black or mulatto mothers) through the use or threat of force. A slaveowner thus replaced any traditional division of labor that might have existed among blacks before enslavement with a work structure of his own choosing. All slaves were barred by law from owning property or acquiring literacy skills, and although the system played favorites with a few, black males and females were equal in the sense that neither sex wielded economic power over the other. Hence property relations—"the basic determinant of the sexual division of labor and of the sexual order" within most societies[8]—did not affect male-female interaction among the slaves themselves. To a considerable extent, the types of jobs slaves did, and the amount and regularity of labor they were forced to devote to such jobs, were all dictated by the master.

For these reasons, the definition of slave women's work is problematical. If work is any activity that leads either directly or indirectly to the production of marketable goods, then slave women did nothing *but* work.[9] Even their efforts to care for themselves and their families helped to maintain the owner's workforce and to enhance its overall productivity. Tasks performed within the family context—childcare, cooking, and washing clothes, for example—were distinct from labor carried out under the lash in the field or under the mistress's watchful eye in the Big House. Still, these forms of nurture contributed to the health and welfare of the slave population,

thereby increasing the actual value of the master's property (that is, slaves as both strong workers and "marketable commodities"). White men warned prospective mothers that they wanted neither "runts" nor girls born on their plantations, and slave women understood that their owner's economic self-interest affected even the most intimate family ties. Of the pregnant bondswomen on her husband's large Butlers Island (Georgia) rice plantation, Fanny Kemble observed, "They have all of them a most distinct and perfect knowledge of their value to their owners as property," and she recoiled at their obsequious profession, obviously intended to delight her: "Missus, tho' we no able to work, we make little niggers for Massa." One North Carolina slave woman, the mother of fifteen children, used to carry her youngest with her to the field each day, and "When it get hungry she just slip it around in front and feed it and go right on picking or hoeing..." symbolizing in one deft motion the equal significance of her productive and reproductive functions to her owner.[10]

The rhythm of the planting-weeding-harvesting cycle shaped the lives of almost all American slaves, 95 percent of whom lived in rural areas. This cycle dictated a common work routine (gang labor) for slaves who cultivated the king of all agricultural products, cotton, in the broad swath of the Black Belt that dominated the whole region. Patterns of labor organization varied somewhat in the other staple crop economies—tobacco in the upper South, rice along the coast of Georgia and South Carolina, and sugar in Louisiana. (For example, the task system characteristic of low-country rice cultivation granted slave women and men an exceptional degree of control over the completion of their daily assignments.) Of almost four million slaves, about half labored on farms with holdings of twenty slaves or more; one-quarter endured bondage with at least fifty other people on the same plantation. In its most basic form, a life of slavery meant working the soil with other blacks at a pace calculated to reap the largest harvest for a white master.[11]

In his efforts to wrench as much field labor as possible from female slaves without injuring their capacity to bear children, the master made "a noble admission of female equality," observed Kemble, an abolitionist sympathizer, with bitter irony. Slaveholders had little use for sentimental platitudes about the delicacy of the female constitution when it came to grading their "hands" according to physical strength and endurance. Judged on the basis of a standard set by a healthy adult man, most women probably ranked as three-quarter hands; yet there were enough women like Susan Mabry of Virginia, who could pick 400 or 500 pounds of cotton a day (150 to 200 pounds was considered respectable for an average worker), to remove from a master's mind all doubts about the ability of a strong, healthy woman field worker. As a result, he conveniently discarded his time-honored Anglo-Saxon notions about the types of work best suited for women, thereby producing many a "very dreary scene" like the one described by northern journalist Frederick Law Olmsted: During winter preparation of rice fields on a Sea Island plantation, he saw a group of black women, "armed with axes, shovels and hoes . . . all slopping about in the black, unctuous mire at the bottom of the ditches." In essence, the quest for an "efficient" agricultural work force led slaveowners to downplay gender differences in assigning adults to field labor.[12]

Dressed in coarse osnaburg gowns; their skirts "reefed up with a cord drawn tightly around the body, a little above the hips" (the traditional "second belt"); long sleeves pushed above the elbows and kerchiefs on their heads, female field hands were a common sight throughout the antebellum South. Together with their fathers, husbands, brothers, and sons, black women spent up to fourteen hours a day toiling out of doors, often under a blazing sun. In the Cotton Belt they plowed fields; dropped seed; and hoed, picked, ginned, sorted, and moted cotton. On farms in Virginia, North Carolina, Kentucky, and Tennessee, women hoed tobacco; laid worm fences; and threshed, raked, and bound wheat. For those on the Sea Islands and in coastal areas, rice culture included raking and burning the stubble from the previous year's crop; ditching; sowing seed; plowing, listing, and hoeing fields; and harvesting, stacking, and threshing the rice. In the bayou region of Louisiana, women planted sugar cane cuttings, plowed, and helped to harvest and gin the cane. During the winter, they performed a myriad of tasks necessary on nineteenth-century farms: repairing roads, pitching hay, burning brush, and setting up post and rail fences. Like Sara Colquitt of Alabama, most adult females "worked in de fields every day from 'fore daylight to almost plumb dark." During the busy harvest season, everyone was forced to labor up to sixteen hours at a time—after sunset by the light of candles or burning pine knots. Miscellaneous chores regularly occupied men and women around outbuildings and indoors on rainy days. Slaves of both sexes watered the horses, fed the chickens, and slopped the hogs. Together they ginned cotton, ground hominy, shelled corn and peas, and milled flour.[13]

Work assignments for men and women differed according to the size of a plantation and its degree of specialization. For example, on one Virginia wheat farm, the men scythed and cradled the grain, women raked and bound it into sheaves, which children then gathered and stacked. Thomas Couper, a wealthy Sea Island planter, divided his slaves according to sex and employed men exclusively in ditching and women in moting and sorting cotton. Within the two gender groups, he further classified hands according to individual strength so that during the sugar cane harvest three "gangs" of women stripped blades (medium-level task), cut them (hardest), and bound and carried them (easiest). However, since cotton served as the basis of the southern agricultural system, general patterns of female work usually overshadowed local and regional differences in labor-force management. Stated simply, most women spent a good deal of their lives plowing, hoeing, and picking cotton. In the fields the notion of a distinctive "women's work" vanished as slaveholders realized that "women can do plowing very well & full well with the hoes and [are] equal to men at picking."[14]

To harness a double team of mules or oxen and steer a heavy wooden plow was no mean feat for a strong man, and yet a "substantial minority" of slave women mastered these rigorous activities. White men and women from the North and South marveled at the skill and strength of female plow hands. Emily Burke of eastern Georgia saw men and women "promiscuously run their ploughs side by side, and day after day . . . and as far as I was able to learn, the part the women sustained in this masculine employment, was quite as efficient as that of the more athletic sex." In his travels through Mississippi, Frederick Law Olmsted watched as women "twitched their plows around on the head-land, jerking their reins, and yelling to their mules, with apparent ease, energy, and rapidity." He failed to see "any indication that their sex unfitted them for the occupation."[15]

On another estate in the Mississippi Valley, Olmsted observed forty of the "largest and strongest" women he had ever seen; they "carried themselves loftily, each having a hoe over the shoulder, and walking with a free, powerful swing, like *chasseurs* on the march." In

preparing fields for planting and in keeping grass from strangling the crop, women as well as men blistered their hands with the clumsy hoe characteristic of southern agriculture. "Hammered out of pig iron, broad like a shovel," these "slave-time hoes" withstood most forms of abuse (destruction of farm implements constituted an integral part of resistance to forced labor). Recalled one former slave of the tool that also served as a pick, spade, and gravedigger: "Dey make 'em heavy so dey fall hard, but de bigges' trouble was liftin' dem up." Hoeing was backbreaking labor, but the versatility of the tool and its importance to cotton cultivation meant that the majority of female hands used it a good part of the year.[16]

The cotton-picking season usually began in late July or early August and continued without interruption until the end of December. Thus for up to five months annually, every available man, woman, and child was engaged in a type of work that was strenuous and "tedious from its sameness." Each woman carried a bag fastened by a strap around her neck and deposited the cotton in it as she made her way down the row, at the end of which she emptied the bag's contents into a basket. Picking cotton required endurance and agility as much as physical strength, and women frequently won regional and interfarm competitions conducted during the year. Pregnant and nursing women usually ranked as half hands and were required to pick an amount less than the "average" 150 or so pounds per day.[17]

Slaveholders often reserved the tasks that demanded sheer muscle power for men exclusively. These included clearing the land of trees, rolling logs, and chopping and hauling wood. However, plantation exigencies sometimes mandated women's labor in this area too; in general, the smaller the farm, the more arduous and varied was women's field work. Lizzie Atkins, who lived on a twenty-five-acre

Texas plantation with only three other slaves, remembered working "until slam dark"; she helped to clear land, cut wood, and tend the livestock in addition to her other duties of hoeing corn, spinning thread, sewing clothes, cooking, washing dishes, and grinding corn. One Texas farmer, who had his female slaves haul logs and plow with oxen, even made them wear breeches, thus minimizing outward differences between the sexes. Still, FWP interviews with former slaves indicate that blacks considered certain jobs uncharacteristic of bondswomen. Recalled Louise Terrell of her days on a farm near Jackson, Mississippi: "The women had to split rails all day long, just like the men." Nancy Boudry of Georgia said she used to "split wood jus' like a man." Elderly women reminisced about their mothers and grandmothers with a mixture of pride and wonder. Mary Frances Webb declared of her slave grandmother, "In the winter she sawed and cut cord wood just like a man. She said it didn't hurt her as she was strong as an ox." Janie Scott's description of her mother implied the extent of the older woman's emotional as well as physical strength: She was "strong and could roll and cut logs like a man, and was much of a woman."[18]

Very few women served as skilled artisans or mechanics; on large estates men invariably filled the positions of carpenter, cooper, wheelwright, tanner, blacksmith, and shoemaker. At first it seems ironic that masters would utilize women fully as field laborers, but reserve most of the skilled occupations that required manual dexterity for men. Here the high cost of specialized and extensive training proved crucial in determining the division of labor. Although women were capable of learning these skills, their work lives were frequently interrupted by childbearing and nursing; a female blacksmith might not be able to provide the regular service required on a plantation. Too, masters frequently "hired out" mechanics and artisans to work for other employers during the winter, and women's domestic responsibilities were deemed too important to permit protracted absences from their quarters. However, many young girls learned to spin thread and weave cloth because these tasks could occupy them immediately before and after childbirth.[19]

The drive for cotton profits induced slaveowners to squeeze every bit of strength from black women as a group. According to some estimates, in the 1850s at least 90 percent of all female slaves over sixteen years of age labored more than 261 days per year, eleven to thirteen hours each day. Few overseers or masters had any patience with women whose movements in the field were persistently "clumsy, awkward, gross, [and] elephantine" for whatever reasons—malnutrition, exhaustion, recalcitrance. As Hannah Davidson said: "If you had something to do, you did it or got whipped." The enforced pace of work more nearly resembled that of a factory than a farm; Kemble referred to female field hands as "human hoeing machines." The bitter memories of former slaves merely suggest the extent to which the physical strength of women was exploited. Eliza Scantling of South Carolina, only sixteen years old at the end of the Civil War, plowed with a mule during the coldest months of the year: "Sometimes me hands get so cold I jes' cry." Matilda Perry of Virginia "use to wuk fum sun to sun in dat ole terbaccy field. Wuk till my back felt lak it ready to pop in two.[20]

Although pregnant and nursing women suffered from temporary lapses in productivity, most slaveholders apparently agreed with the (in Olmsted's words) "well-known, intelligent and benevolent" Mississippi planter who declared that "labor is conducive to health; a healthy woman will rear most children." (They obviously did not have the benefit of modern medical knowledge that links the overwork of pregnant mothers not only with a consequent decline in their reproductive capacity but also with Sudden Infant Death Syndrome, affecting primarily children under six months of age.) Still, slaveowners faced a real dilemma when it came to making use of the physical strength of women as field workers and at the same time protecting their investment in women as childbearers. These two objectives—one focused on immediate profit returns and the other on long-term economic considerations—at times clashed, as women who spent long hours picking cotton, toiling in the fields with heavy iron hoes, and walking several miles a day sustained damage to their reproductive systems immediately before and after giving birth. At the regional level, a decline in slave fertility and increase in miscarriage rates during the cotton boom years of 1830 to 1860 reveals the heightened demands made upon women, both in terms of increased workloads in the fields and family breakups associated with the massive, forced migration of slaves from the upper to the lower south.[21]

On individual plantations, for financial reasons, slaveholders might have "regarded pregnancy as almost holy," in the words of one medical historian. But they frequently suspected bondswomen, whether pregnant or not, of shamming illness and fatigue— "play[ing] the lady at your expense," as one Virginia planter put it. These fears help to account for the reckless brutality with which owners forced women to work in the fields during and after their "confinement"—a period of time that might last as long as four to six weeks, or might be considerably shortened by masters who had women deliver their children between the cotton rows. Indeed, in the severity of punishment meted out to slaves, little distinction was made between the sexes. Black women attained parity with black men in terms of their productive abilities in the cotton fields; as a result they often received a proportionate share of the whippings. In response to an interviewer's inquiry, a former Virginia slave declared, "Beat women! Why sure he [master] beat women. Beat women jes lak men. Beat women naked an' wash 'em down in brine."[22]

Moreover, it is significant that overseers ordered and supervised much of the punishment in the field, for their disciplinary techniques were calculated to "get as much work out of the slaves as they can possibly perform." Agricultural journalists, travelers in the South, and planters themselves loudly condemned overseers—usually illiterate men of the landless class—for their excessive use of violence. Yet despite the inevitable depletion of their workforce from illness and high mortality rates, slaveholders continued to search for overseers who could make the biggest crop. Consequently many slave women were driven and beaten mercilessly, and some achieved respite only in return for sexual submission. To a white man, a black woman was not only a worker who needed prodding, but also a female capable of fulfilling his sexual or aggressive desires. For this reason, a fine line existed between work-related punishment and rape, and an overseer's lust might yield to sadistic rage. For example, the mother of Minnie Fulkes was suspended from a barn rafter and beaten with a horsewhip "nekkid 'till the blood run down her back to her heels" for fending off the advances of an overseer on a Virginia plantation.[23]

The whipping of pregnant and nursing mothers—"so that blood and milk flew mingled from their breasts"—revealed the myriad impulses that conjoined to make women especially susceptible to physical abuse. The pregnant woman represented the sexuality of the slave community in general, and that of her husband and herself in particular; she thus symbolized a life in the quarters carried on apart from white interference. One particular method of whipping pregnant slaves was used throughout the South; "they were made to lie face down in a specially dug depression in the ground," a practice that provided simultaneously for the protection of the fetus and the abuse of its mother. Slave women's roles as workers and as childbearers came together in these trenches, these graves for the living, in southern cottonfields. The uniformity of procedure suggests that the terrorizing of pregnant women was not uncommon.[24]

Impatient with slow workers and determined to discipline women whom they suspected of feigning illness, masters and overseers at times indulged in rampages of violence that led to the victim's death. Former Mississippi slave Clara Young told of her seventeen-year-old cousin "in de fambly way fer de fust time" who "couldn' work as hard as de rest." The driver whipped her until she bled; she died the next morning. He had told the other slaves, "if dey said anything 'bout it to de marster, he'd beat them to death, too, so ever'body kep' quiet an de marster neber knowed." Thus cruelty derived not only from the pathological impulses of a few individuals, but also from a basic premise of the slave system itself: the use of violence to achieve a productive labor force.[25]

Upon first consideration, the frequency with which small boys and girls, pregnant women, mothers of as many as ten children, and grandmothers were beaten bloody seems to indicate that an inexplicable sadism pervaded the Old South. In fact, whites often displaced their anger at particularly unruly blacks onto the most vulnerable members of the slave community. Frederick Douglass, a former slave, argued that "the doctrine that submission to violence is the best cure for violence did not hold good as between slaves and overseers. He was whipped oftener who was whipped easiest." Like the mistress who was "afraid of the

grown Negroes" and beat the children "all the time" instead, many whites feared the strong men and women who could defend themselves—or retaliate. Primary sources contain innumerable examples of slaves who overpowered a tormenter and beat him senseless or killed him with his own whip. Referring to a powerful slave who "wouldin' 'low nobody ter whip 'in," one plantation owner told his overseer, "let 'im 'lone[;] he's too strong ter be whup'd." The overseer's hatred of this slave was bound to find some other form of release; by abusing a weaker person, he could unleash his aggression and indirectly punish the menacing relative or friend of his victim.[26]

At times, a woman would rebel in a manner commensurate with the work demands imposed upon her. "She'd git stubborn like a mule and quit." Or she took her hoe and knocked the overseer "plum down" and "chopped him right across his head." When masters and drivers "got rough on her, she got rough on them, and ran away in the woods." She cursed the man who insisted he "owned" her so that he beat her "till she fell" and left her broken body to serve as a warning to others: "Dat's what you git effen you sass me." Nevertheless, a systematic survey of the FWP slave narrative collection reveals that women were more likely than men to engage in "verbal confrontations and striking the master but not running away," probably because of their family responsibilities. A case study of a Georgia plantation indicates that, when women did run away, they usually accompanied or followed spouses already in hiding.[27]

Family members who perceived their mothers or sisters as particularly susceptible to abuse in the fields conspired to lessen their workload. Frank Bell and his four brothers, slaves on a Virginia wheat farm, followed his parents down the long rows of grain during the harvest season. "In dat way one could help de other when dey got behind. All of us would pitch in and help Momma who warn't very strong." The overseer discouraged families from working together because he believed "dey ain't gonna work as fast as when dey all mixed up," but the black driver, Bell's uncle, "always looked out for his kinfolk, especially my mother." James Taliaferro told of his father, who counted the corn rows marked out for Aunt Rebecca, "a short-talking woman that ole Marsa didn't like" and alerted her to the fact that her assignment was almost double that given to the other women. Rebecca indignantly confronted the master, who relented by reducing her task, but not before he threatened to sell James's father for his meddling. On another plantation, the hands surreptitiously added handfuls of cotton to the basket of a young woman who "was small and just couldn't get her proper amount."[28]

No slave woman exercised authority over slave men as part of their work routine, but it is uncertain whether this practice reflected the sensibilities of the slaveowners or of the slaves themselves. Women were assigned to teach children simple tasks in the house and field and to supervise other women in various facets of household industry. A master might "let [a woman] off fo' de buryings' cause she know how to manage de other niggahs and keep dem quiet at de funerals," but he would not install her as a driver over people in the field. Many strong-willed women demonstrated that they commanded respect among males as well as females, but more often than not masters perceived this as a negative quality to be suppressed. One Louisiana slaveholder complained bitterly about a particularly "rascally set of old negroes"—"the better you treat them the worse they are." He had no difficulty pinpointing the cause of the trouble, for "Big Lucy, the leader, corrupts every young negro in her power." On other plantations women were held responsible for instigating all sorts of undesirable behavior

among their husbands and brothers and sisters. On Charles Colcock Jones's Georgia plantation, the slave Cash gave up going to prayer meeting and started swearing as soon as he married Phoebe, well-known for her truculence. Apparently few masters attempted to co-opt high-spirited women by offering them positions of formal power over black men.[29]

Work in the soil thus represented the chief lot of all slaves, female and male. In the Big House, a division of labor based on both sex and age became more apparent. Although women predominated as household workers, few devoted their energies full time to this kind of labor; the size of the plantation determined the degree to which the tasks of cleaning, laundering, caring for the master's children, cooking, and ironing were specialized. According to Eugene Genovese, as few as 5 percent of all antebellum adult slaves served in the elite corps of house servants trained for specific duties. Of course, during the harvest season all slaves, including those in the house, went to the fields to make obeisance to King Cotton. Thus the lines between domestic service and field work blurred during the day and during the lives of slave women. Many continued to live in the slave quarters but rose early in the morning to perform various chores for the mistress—"up wid de fust light to draw water and help as house girl"—before heading for the field. James Claiborne's mother "wuked in de fiel' some, an' aroun' de house sometimes." Young girls tended babies and waited on tables until they were sent outside—"mos' soon's" they could work—and returned to the house years later, too frail to hoe weeds but still able to cook and sew. The circle of women's domestic work went unbroken from day to day and from generation to generation.[30]

Just as southern white men scorned manual labor as the proper sphere of slaves, so their wives strove, often unsuccessfully, to lead a life of leisure within their own homes. Those duties necessary to maintain the health, comfort, and daily welfare of white slaveholders were considered less women's work than black women's and black children's work. Slave mistresses supervised the whole operation, but the sheer magnitude of labor involved in keeping all slaves and whites fed and clothed meant that black women had to supply the elbow grease. For most slaves, housework involved hard, steady, often strenuous labor as they juggled the demands made by the mistress and other members of the master's family. Mingo White of Alabama never forgot that his slave mother had shouldered a workload "too heavy for any one person." She served as personal maid to the master's daughter, cooked for all the hands on the plantation, carded cotton, spun a daily quota of thread, and wove and dyed cloth. Every Wednesday she carried the white family's laundry three-quarters of a mile to a creek, where she beat each garment with a wooden paddle. Ironing consumed the rest of her day. Like the lowliest field hand, she felt the lash if any tasks went undone.[31]

Though mistresses found that their husbands commandeered most bondswomen for field work during the better part of the day, they discovered in black children an acceptable alternative source of labor. Girls were favored for domestic service, but a child's sex played only a secondary role in determining household assignments. On smaller holdings especially, the demands of housework, like cotton cultivation, admitted no finely honed division of labor. Indeed, until puberty, boys and girls shared a great deal in terms of dress and work. All children wore a "split-tail shirt," a knee-length smock slit up the sides: "Boys and gals all dress jes' alike. . . . They call it a shirt iffen a boy wear it and call it a dress iffen the gal wear it." At the age of six or so,

many received assignments around the barnyard or in the Big House from one or more members of the master's family. Mr. and Mrs. Alex Smith, who grew up together, remembered performing different tasks. As a girl, she helped to spin thread and pick seed from cotton and cockleburs from wool. He had chopped wood, carried water, hoed weeds, tended the cows, and picked bugs from tobacco plants. However, slave narratives contain descriptions of both boys and girls elsewhere doing each of these things.[32]

Between the ages of six and twelve, black girls and boys followed the mistress's directions in filling woodboxes with kindling, lighting fires in chilly bedrooms in the morning and evening, making beds, washing and ironing clothes, parching coffee, polishing shoes, and stoking fires while the white family slept at night. They fetched water and milk from the springhouse and meat from the smokehouse. Three times a day they set the table, helped to prepare and serve meals, "minded flies" with peacock-feather brushes, passed the salt and pepper on command, and washed the dishes. They swept, polished, and dusted, served drinks and fanned overheated visitors. Mistresses entrusted to the care of those who were little more than babies themselves the bathing, diapering, dressing, grooming, and entertaining of white infants. (One slave girl, introduced to her new "young mistress," looked at the child in her mistress's arms and replied in disbelief, "No, I don't see no young mistress, that's a baby.") In the barnyard black children gathered eggs, plucked chickens, drove cows to and from the stable, and "tended the gaps" (opened and closed gates). It was no wonder that Mary Ella Grandberry, a slave child grown old, "disremember[ed] ever playin' lack chilluns do today."[33]

In only a few tasks did a sexual division of labor exist among children. In the fields both boys and girls acted as human scarecrows, toted water to the hands, and hauled shocks of corn together. Masters always chose boys to accompany them on hunting trips and to serve as their personal valets. Little girls learned how to sew, milk cows, churn butter, and attend to the personal needs of their mistresses. As tiny ladies-in-waiting they did the bidding of fastidious white women and of girls not much older than themselves. Cicely Cawthon, age six when the Civil War began, called herself the mistress's "little keeper"; "I stayed around, and waited on her, handed her water, fanned her, kept the flies off her, pulled up her pillow, and done anything she'd tell me to do." Martha Showvely recounted a nightly ritual with her Virginia mistress. After she finished her regular work around the house, the young girl would go to the woman's bedroom, bow to her, wait for acknowledgment, and then scurry around as ordered, lowering the shades, filling the water pitcher, arranging towels on the washstand, or "anything else" that struck the woman's fancy. Mary Woodward, only eleven in 1865, was taught to comb her mistress's hair, lace her corset, and arrange her hoop skirts. At the end of the toilet Mary was supposed to say "You is served, mistress!" Recalled the former slave, "Her lak them little words at de last."[34]

The privileged status of slave mistresses rested squarely on the backs of their female slaves. Nevertheless, the system of bondage ultimately involved the subordination of all women, both black and white, to masters-husbands whose behavior ranged from benevolent to tyrannical, but always within a patriarchal context. In Bertram Wyatt-Brown's words, when it came to patriarchs, southern white men were the "genuine article." Mary Boykin Chesnut believed that slave mistresses were "abolitionists in their hearts and hot ones too." But if women's resentment toward slavery found only indirect, or private, expression, the causes for that resentment are readily apparent. The slaveholders' insatiable quest for more and better cotton lands mocked their wives' desire for a more settled, orderly existence. On a more immediate level, slavery rubbed raw the wounds of white women's grievances in two specific ways—first, it added greatly to their household responsibilities, and second, it often injected irreconcilable conflicts into the husband-wife relationship.[35]

As they went about their daily chores, mistresses repeatedly complained about the burdens imposed on them; they were, they felt, "slaves of slaves." To instruct youthful servants in the mysteries of table-setting, fire-stoking, and child care; to cajole and threaten sullen maids who persisted in sewing too slowly or carelessly; to keep track of those women assigned to duties in the yard, garden, or chicken house taxed the patience of even generous-hearted white housewives. Impudence and recalcitrance among black women were recurring problems, but even more significantly, slaves could make a mistress's life miserable by literally doing nothing. A white woman might banish a particularly stubborn cook to the fields (indeed, some slave women calculated upon that response in order to be near their families), only to find herself faced with an even more contentious replacement. Obviously, in these cases lines of dependency blurred; a mistress might have served in a managerial capacity, but she relied on slaves to perform a tremendous amount of work that she was unwilling or unable to do herself.[36]

In their role as labor managers, mistresses lashed out at slave women not only to punish them but also to vent their anger on victims even more wronged than themselves. We may speculate that in the female slave the white woman saw the source of her own misery, but she also saw herself—a woman without rights or recourse, subject to the whims of an egotistical man. These tensions frequently spilled over into acts of violence. Severe chastisement did not necessarily guarantee the repentance of the offender. However, patterns of mistress-initiated violence toward black women suggest that such acts were just as often spontaneous outbursts of rage as they were deliberate measures to reform behavior. When punishing slave women for minor offenses, mistresses were likely to attack with any weapon available—knitting needles, tongs, a fork, butcher knife, ironing board, or pan of boiling water. In the heat of the moment, white women devised barbaric forms of punishment that resulted in the mutilation or permanent scarring of their female servants.[37]

Predictably, jealousy over their spouse's real or suspected infidelity led many white wives to openly express their anger and shame. Husbands who flaunted their activities in the slave quarters essentially dared their wives to attack a specific woman or her offspring. Some promiscuous husbands made no attempts at gentlemanly discretion (or "transcendent silence") within their own households, but rather actively sought to antagonize their wives. For example, Sarah Wilson, the daughter of a slave and her white master, remembered that as a child she was "picked on" by the mistress. The white woman chafed under her husband's taunts; he would order her to "'let [Sarah] alone, she got big, big blood in her,' and then laugh."[38]

Divorce petitions provide one of the few sources that reveal white wives' outrage in response to their husbands' provocative behavior. For example, a witness in a Virginia divorce case in 1848 offered the following testimony: A master one morning told his favorite slave to sit down at the breakfast table "to which Mrs. N [his wife] objected, saying . . . that she (Mrs. N) would have her severely punished." The husband then replied "that in that event he would visit her (Mrs. N) with a like punishment. Mrs. N then burst into tears

and asked if it was not too much for her to stand." Like at least some other masters, Mr. N freely admitted that his initial attraction to his future wife stemmed from her "large Estate of land and negroes." (Thus a favorable marriage became one more consideration for the ambitious slaveholder.) However, this particular husband went out of his way to demonstrate his "strong dislike and aversion to the company" of his bride by sleeping with the slave woman "on a pallet in his wife's room" and by frequently embracing her in the presence of his wife. Mrs. N's first response was to lay "her hands in an angry manner on the said servant." Her husband, besides threatening his wife with bodily harm, "told her if she did not like his course, to leave his house and take herself to some place she liked better." Although the outcome of this case is not known, the patriarchalism of the southern legal system dictated that the odds would be against the humiliated Mrs. N. In any case, the considerable dowry she brought to the marriage would remain in the hands of her spouse.[39]

Scattered evidence from other sources also indicates that slaveholders at times physically abused their wives. While this was hardly normative behavior, it appears to have been a natural by-product of a violent culture. Men who drank freely and whipped their slaves could hardly have been expected to respect even the frail flower of white womanhood at all times.[40] But again, the denigration of white women, whether manifested through physical force or in a more subtle, though no less painful, way was part and parcel of slavery. By directing their anger toward slave women, white wives achieved a fleeting moment of catharsis. Rarely in American history is there a more striking example of the way in which the patriarchal imperative could turn woman against woman, white against black.

In sum, interviews with former slaves suggest that the advantages of domestic service over field work for women have been exaggerated in accounts written by whites. Fetching wood and water, preparing three full meals a day over a smoky fireplace, or pressing damp clothes with a hot iron rivaled cotton picking as back-breaking labor. Always "on call," women servants often had to snatch a bite to eat whenever they could, remain standing in the presence of whites, and sleep on the floor at the foot of a mistress's bed (increasing the chances that they would sooner or later be bribed, seduced, or forced into sexual relations with the master). Peeling potatoes with a sharp knife, building a fire, or carrying a heavy load of laundry down a steep flight of stairs required skills and dexterity not always possessed by little boys and girls, and injuries were common. Chastisement for minor infractions came with swift severity; cooks who burned the bread and children who stole cookies or fell asleep while singing to the baby suffered all kinds of abuse, from jabs with pins to beatings that left them disfigured for life. The master's house offered no shelter from the most brutal manifestations of slavery.[41]

For any one or all of these reasons, black women might prefer field work to housework. During his visit to a rice plantation in 1853, Olmsted noted that hands "accustomed to the comparatively unconstrained life of the negro-settlement detest the close control and careful movements required of the house servants." Marriage could be both a means and an incentive to escape a willful mistress. Jessie Sparrow's mother wed at age thirteen in order "to ge' outer de big house. Dat how come she to marry so soon." Claude Wilson recalled many years later that "his mother was very rebellious toward her duties and constantly harassed the 'Missus' about letting her work in the fields with her husband until finally she was permitted to make the change from the house to the fields to be near her man." Other women, denied an alternative, explored the range of their own emotional resources in attempting to resist petty tyranny; their defiance rubbed raw the nerves of mistresses already harried and high-strung. A few servants simply withdrew into a shell of "melancholy and timidity."[42]

The dual status of a bondswoman—a slave and a female—afforded her master a certain degree of flexibility in formulating her work assignments. When he needed a field hand, her status as an able-bodied slave took precedence over gender considerations, and she was forced to toil alongside her menfolk. At the same time, the master's belief that most forms of domestic service required the attentions of a female reinforced the traditional role of woman as household worker. The authority of the master in enforcing a sexual division of labor was absolute, but at times individual women could influence his decisions to some extent. In certain cases, a woman's preference for either field work or domestic service worked to her advantage. For example, the rebelliousness of Claude Wilson's mother prompted her removal from the Big House to the field, a change she desired. Similarly, masters might promise a woman an opportunity to do a kind of work she preferred as a reward for her cooperation and diligence. On the other hand, a slave's misbehavior might cause her to lose a position she had come to value; more than one prized cook or maid was exiled to the fields for "sassing" the mistress or stealing. A system of rewards and punishments thus depended on the preferences of individual slaves, and a servant determined to make life miserable for the family in the Big House might get her way in any case.[43]

The allocation of slave women's labor by white men and women was based on three different considerations—the whites' desire to increase staple-crop production, enlarge their workforce, and provide for the daily sustenance of their own households. As if it were not difficult enough to balance these three competing objectives, the master often found that he and his overseer and wife were operating at cross purposes when it came to exploiting the labor of black women. Profit-making was a "rational" basis upon which to set female slaves to work in the fields, but long-term interests related to women's child-bearing capacity at times yielded to the demands of the harvest at hand. Owners and overseers alike might easily cross the boundary between chastising black women for work-related offenses and terrorizing them as a means of asserting control over the entire slave labor force. Moreover, the sexual exploitation of a black woman could produce concentric rings of bitterness that engulfed the white mistress, resulting in further (though economically "irrational") abuse of the victim herself. The slave master, armed with both a whip and legal authority over all plantation residents, was able to shield himself from the wellspring of hate that sprang from these peculiarly southern forms of inequality. Yet the slave community too had a claim on the energies of black women, and its own sexual division of labor helped to subvert the authority of the slaveowner in ways that he only dimly understood.

Working for Each Other:
The Sexual Division of Labor
in the Slave Quarters

In the field and the Big House, black women worked under the close supervision of white men and women at a forced pace. The slaves derived few, if any, tangible benefits from their labor to increase staple-crop profits and to render the white family comfortable (at least in physical terms). However, their efforts on behalf of their own health and welfare often took place apart from whites, with a rhythm more in tune with community and

family life. For slave women, these responsibilities, though physically arduous, offered a degree of personal fulfillment. As Martha Colquitt remarked of her slave grandmother and mother who stayed up late to knit and sew clothes "for us chillun": "Dey done it 'cause dey wanted to. Dey wuz workin' for deyselves den." Slave women deprived of the ability to cook for their own kinfolk or discipline their own children felt a keen sense of loss; family responsibilities revealed the limited extent to which black women (and men) could control their own lives. Furthermore, a strict sexual division of labor in the quarters openly challenged the master's gender-blind approach to slave women's field work.[44]

A number of activities were carried out either communally or centrally for the whole plantation by older women. On smaller farms, for example, a cook and her assistants might prepare one or all of the meals for the other slaves each day except Sunday. Likewise, an elderly woman, with the help of children too young to work in the fields, often was assigned charge of a nursery in the quarters, where mothers left their babies during the day. To keep any number of little ones happy and out of trouble for up to twelve to fourteen hours at a time taxed the patience of the most kindly souls. Slave children grew up with a mixed affection and fear for the grandmothers who had dished out the licks along with the cornbread and clabber. Other "grannies" usurped the position of the white physician (he rarely appeared in any case); they "brewed medicines for every ailment," gave cloves and whiskey to ease the pain of childbirth, and prescribed potions for the lovesick. Even a child forced to partake of "Stinkin' Jacob tea" or a concoction of "turpentine an' castor oil an' Jerusalem oak" (for worms) could assert years later that "Gran'-mammy was a great doctor," surely a testimony to her respected position within the slave community if not to the delectability of her remedies.[45]

On many plantations it was the custom to release adult women from field work early on Saturday so that they could do the week's washing. Whether laundering was done in old wooden tubs, iron pots, or a nearby creek, with batten sticks, wooden paddles, or washboards, it was a time-consuming and difficult chore. Yet this ancient form of women's work provided opportunities for socializing "whilst de 'omans leaned over de tubs washin' and a-singin' dem old songs." Mary Frances Webb remembered wash day—"a regular picnic"—with some fondness; it was a time for women "to spend the day together," out of the sight and earshot of whites.[46]

Much of the work black women did for the slave community resembled the colonial system of household industry. Well into the nineteenth century throughout the South, slave women continued to spin thread, weave and dye cloth, sew clothes, make soap and candles, prepare and preserve foods, churn butter, and grow food for the family table. Slave women mastered all these tasks with the aid of primitive equipment and skills passed on from grandmothers. Many years later, blacks of both sexes exclaimed over their slave mothers' ability to prepare clothes dye from various combinations of tree bark and leaves, soil and berries; make soap out of ashes and animal skins; and fashion bottle lamps from string and tallow. Because of their lack of time and materials, black women only rarely found in these activities an outlet for creative expression, but they did take pride in their resourcefulness, and they produced articles of value to the community as a whole.[47]

Black women's work in home textile production illustrates the ironies of community labor under slavery, for the threads of cotton and wool bound them together in both bondage and sisterhood. Masters (or mis-

tresses) imposed rigid spinning and weaving quotas on women who worked in the fields all day. For example, many were forced to spin one "cut" (about three hundred yards) of thread nightly, or four to five cuts during rainy days or in the winter. Women of all ages worked together, and children of both sexes helped to tease and card wool, pick up the loom shuttles, and knit. In the flickering candlelight, the whir of the spinning wheel and the clickety-clack of the loom played a seductive lullaby, drawing those who were already "mighty tired" away from their assigned tasks.[48]

As the "head spinner" on a Virginia plantation, Bob Ellis's mother was often sent home from field work early to prepare materials for the night's work: "She had to portion out de cotton dey was gonna spin an' see dat each got a fair share." Later that evening, after supper, as she moved around the dusty loom room to check on the progress of the other women, she would sing:

> Keep yo' eye on de sun,
> See how she run,
> Don't let her catch you with your work
>   undone,
> I'm a trouble, I'm a trouble,
> Trouble don' las' always.

With her song of urgency and promise she coaxed her sisters to finish their work so they could return home by sundown: "Dat made de women all speed up so dey could finish fo' dark catch 'em, 'cause it mighty hard handlin' dat cotton thread by fire-light."[49]

Slave women's work for other community members challenged the master's authority in direct ways. As the persons in charge of food preparation for both whites and their own families, women at times clandestinely fed runaways in an effort to keep them out of harm's way for as long as possible. One elderly black man recalled that it was not uncommon on his master's plantation for slaves to go and hide after they were punished, and added, "I've known my mother to help them the best she could; they would stay in the woods and come in at night, and mother would give them something to eat." While the act of cooking might not differ in a technical sense when performed for blacks as opposed to whites, it certainly assumed heightened emotional significance for the black women involved, and, when carried out in such subversive ways, political significance for social relations on the plantation.[50]

In the quarters, the communal spirit was but an enlarged manifestation of kin relationships. Indeed, family, kin, and community blended into one another, for blood ties were often supplemented by "fictive kin" when the slaves defined patterns of mutual obligations among themselves. Moreover, depending upon the size and age of the plantation, slave fertility and mortality rates, and the incidence of "abroad" marriages (characterized by spouses who belonged to different masters), kinship might encompass a significant percentage of the slaves at any one time. For example, during the twenty-year period before the Civil War, the bondsmen and bondswomen on the Good Hope, South Carolina, plantation were related to three out of ten of their fellows. When calculated on the basis of household linkages, the average individual could find that fully 75 percent of all residences in the quarters "house[d] kin, or the kin of those kin." These linkages were often more numerous for women than for men, simply because "abroad" marriages, combined with masters' buying and selling practices, reinforced the matrilocality of family structure (that is, children more often remained with their mother than with their father). In any case, a woman's sense of responsibility for her own blood relations often found expression through her service to the slave community.[51]

However, the significance of the nuclear family in relation to the sexual division of labor under slavery cannot be overestimated; out of the father-mother, husband-wife nexus sprang the slaves' beliefs about what men and women should be and do. Ultimately, the practical application of those beliefs, "provided a weapon for joint resistance to dehumanization," according to Eugene Genovese. The two-parent, nuclear family was the typical form of slave cohabitation regardless of the location, size, or economy of a plantation, the nature of its ownership, or the age of its slave community. Because of the omnipresent threat of forced separation by sale, gift, or bequest, the family was not "stable." Yet, as Herbert Gutman found, in the absence of such separations, unions between husbands and wives and parents and children often endured for many years. Households tended to be large; families with eight living children were not uncommon.[52]

Within the quarters, the process of child socialization reflected both the demands made upon the slaves by whites and the values of an emerging Afro-American culture. For most young slave women, sexual maturity marked a crucial turning point, a time when their life experiences diverged quite explicitly from those of their brothers. Until that point, boys and girls shared a great deal in terms of dress, play, and work. In early adolescence (ages ten to fourteen), a child would normally join the regular workforce as a half hand. At that time (or perhaps before), he or she received adult clothing. This rite of passage apparently made more of an impression on boys than girls, probably because pants offered more of a contrast to the infant's smock than did a dress. Willis Cofer attested to the significance of the change: "Boys jes' wore shirts what looked lak dresses 'till dey wuz 12 years old and big enough to wuk in de field . . . and all de boys wuz mighty proud when dey got big enough to wear pants and go to wuk in de fields wid grown folkses. When a boy got to be man enough to wear pants, he drawed rations and quit eatin' out of de trough [in the nursery]."[53]

Whether or not slave girls received any advance warning from female relatives about menarche and its consequences is unknown. Despite the crowding of large families into small cabins, at least some parents managed to maintain a degree of privacy in their own relations and keep a daughter innocent until she acquired firsthand experience. Gutman suggests that a "sizable minority" of girls became sexually active soon after they began to menstruate, though other scholars have argued that the average age of a slave woman at the time of the birth of her first child was twenty or twenty-one, four years after menarche and probably two years after the onset of fertility. The quality of that first sexual experience of course depended upon a number of personal factors, but all of these were overshadowed by the fact that slave women were always vulnerable to rape by white men.[54]

For young black people of both sexes, courtship was both a diversion and a delight. The ritual itself appears to have been intensely romantic with compatibility and physical attraction the primary considerations. A person's status (house or field slave) played a role in mate selection only insofar as it affected contact between the two groups. There is no evidence that parents arranged these liaisons for their children, although in at least some cases the girl's parents expected to be consulted before any wedding plans were made.[55]

Slave men formally initiated the courting process. When a young man saw "a likely looking gal," he found the opportunity to woo her on the way to and from work, in the field behind the overseer's back (George Taylor was "too crazy 'bout de girls" to keep his mind on cotton chopping), or at Saturday night dances in the quarters. Chivalry covered a broad spectrum of behavior, from refraining from chewing tobacco in the presence of a sweetheart to protecting her from the lash. At times it was difficult for the two to slip away by themselves, and flirting was carried on by pairs in a group setting. Della Harris remembered a teasing song sung by the young men on the Virginia plantation where she lived. They began with "Hi, Ho, Johnson gal . . . Johnson gal is de gal fo' me" even though there was no such person; "De boys jus' start dat way to git all de gals to perkin' up." Then each youth proceeded to call the name of a favorite, and if any girl was left out she was bound to feel "mighty po'ly 'bout it, too." Rivalry among suitors—"setting up to a gal and [finding] there was another fellow setting up to her too"—prompted some to obtain magic potions from conjurers and herb doctors. And girls would encourage attention in all the familiar ways. "Gals always tried to fix up fo' partyin', even ef dey ain't got nothin' but a piece of ribbon to tie in dey hair." They played coy and "hard to get."[56]

When this process proceeded naturally and freely, the couple might eventually have a child, or if the girl had already had her first baby (perhaps by a different man), they might marry and settle into a long-lasting monogamous union. (Husbands and wives expected each other to be faithful, and the slave community frowned on adultery.) But on individual plantations, demographic conditions and cultural traditions could interfere with this romantic ideal. An unbalanced sex ratio, in addition to the slaves' exogamous customs, often limited the number of available partners. Moreover, many, like the two Mississippi slaves married in the field between the handles of a plow, were reminded in no uncertain terms that their master considered them primarily as workers, not as lovers or husband and wife. An owner might prohibit a marriage for any reason, and he might forbid a male slave to seek a wife elsewhere, since the children of their marriage would belong not to him but to the wife's owner. Andy Marion insisted that black men "had a hell of a time gittin' a wife durin' slavery. If you didn't see one on de place to suit you and chances was you didn't suit them, why what could you do?" He listed the options and stressed that the preferences of a number of parties had to be taken into consideration: "Couldn't spring up, grab a mule and ride to de next plantation widout a written pass. S'pose you gits your marster's consent to go? Look here, de gal's marster got to consent, de gal got to consent, de gal's daddy got to consent, de gal's mammy got to consent. It was a hell of a way!"[57]

Whites often intervened in more direct ways to upset the sexual order that black men and women created for themselves, thereby obliterating otherwise viable courtship and marriage practices. The issue of slave "breeding" has evoked considerable controversy among historians. The suggestion that masters failed to engage in systematic or widespread breeding (as evidenced by the relatively late age at which slave women bore their first child, for example) does not negate the obvious conclusions to be drawn from the slave narratives—that white men and women at times seized the opportunity to manipulate slave marital choices, for economic reasons on the one hand, out of seemingly sheer high-handedness on the other.[58]

At times, mistresses and their daughters took an unsolicited interest in a slave woman's love life. "Don't you ever let me see you with that ape again," one South Carolina mistress would say to young girls with contempt. "If you cannot pick a mate better than that I'll do the picking for you." Masters frequently practiced a form of eugenics by withholding their permission for certain marriages and arranging others. Some slaves bitterly rejected the proposed spouse. Rose Williams, forced to live with a man named Rufus because the master wanted them "to bring forth portly chillen," warned the slave to stay away from her "'fore I busts yous brains out and stomp on dem." Threatened with a whipping, she finally relented, but never married. Many years later Rose Williams explained, "After what I does for de massa, I's never wants no truck with any man. De Lawd forgive dis cullud woman, but he have to 'scuse men and look for some others for to 'plenish de earth." Some masters followed a policy of separating quarreling spouses and then "bestow[ing] them in 'marriage' on other parties, whether they chose it or not." These slaves often distinguished between their current mate and "real" husband or wife, who had been taken from them.[59]

The economic significance of the American slave population's natural increase over the years obscures the centrality of children to the slave woman's physical, emotional, and social existence. Each new birth represented a financial gain for the slaveholder, but it was welcomed in the quarters as a "social and familial" fact. Some young girls had their first child out of wedlock, an event that was socially acceptable to the slave community. It also proved functional to a girl's family since masters were less likely to sell a woman who early demonstrated her fecundity; young people in their late teens and early twenties were prime candidates for sale if an owner needed the cash. A long-lasting marriage (though not necessarily to the first child's father) often followed within a couple of years. After that, more children came with sustained regularity. Early in the nineteenth century, in areas of the upper South, fertility levels among slave women neared human capacity. A woman whose fertile years spanned the ages of eighteen to forty-five, for example, might conceive thirteen children and spend ten years of her life pregnant and almost the whole period nursing one child after another.[60]

Children were a source of a mother's suffering as well as her joy. Extraordinary rates of slave infant mortality (twice that of whites in 1850) meant that many women regularly suffered the loss of a baby before or after its birth. If slaveholders faced a dilemma when they tried to maximize women's productive and reproductive abilities simultaneously, mothers suffered the emotional and physical consequences. New mothers had to walk long distances from field to nursery to feed their infants, and their overheated milk provided inadequate and unhealthy nourishment. For these and other reasons, fewer than two out of three black children survived to the age of ten in the years between 1850 and 1860; the life expectancy at birth for males and females was only 32.6 and 33.6 years, respectively. (Mortality rates were especially high on large plantations and those that specialized in rice cultivation.) Excessive childbearing, malnutrition, and heavy manual labor left many women weak and susceptible to illness. A slave mother's love protected her children only up to a point: "Many a day my ole mama has stood by an' watched massa beat her chillun 'till dey bled an' she couldn' open her mouf." The reality or threat of separation from their families (a fact of slave life that became even more frequent during the late antebellum period) caused some women to descend into madness, the cries of "Take me wid you, mammy" echoing in their ears, while others donned a mask of stoicism to conceal their inner pain.[61]

As Angela Davis has pointed out, female slaves, like women in all cultures, had a social "destiny" that was intimately related to their biological capacity to bear children and centered within their own families.[62] They assumed primary responsibility for child care and for operations involved in daily household maintenance—cooking, cleaning, tending fires, and sewing and patching clothes.

Wives and mothers completed these tasks either very early in the morning, before the start of the "regular" work day on the plantation, or at night, after other family members had gone to sleep.

Fathers shared the obligations of family life with their wives. In denying slaves the right to own property, make a living for themselves, participate in public life, or protect their children, the institution of bondage deprived black men of access to the patriarchy in the larger economic and political sense. But at home, men and women worked together to support the father's role as provider and protector. In the evenings and on Sundays, men collected firewood; made shoes; wove baskets; constructed beds, tables, chairs, and animal traps; and carved butter paddles and ax handles. Other family members appreciated a father's skills; recalled Molly Ammonds, "My pappy made all de furniture dat went in our house an' it were might' good furniture too," and Pauline Johnson echoed, "De furn'chure was ho-mek, but my daddy mek it good an' stout." Husbands provided necessary supplements to the family diet by hunting and trapping quails, possums, turkeys, rabbits, squirrels, and raccoons, and by fishing. They often assumed responsibility for cultivating the tiny household garden plots allotted to families by the master. Some craftsmen, like Bill Austin's father, received goods or small sums of money in return for their work on nearby estates; Jack Austin, "regarded as a fairly good carpenter, mason, and bricklayer," was paid in "hams, bits of cornmeal, cloth for dresses for his wife and children, and other small gifts; these he either used for his small family or bartered with other slaves."[63]

These familial duties also applied to men who lived apart from their wives and children, even though they were usually allowed to visit only on Saturday night and Sunday. Lucinda Miller's family "never had any sugar, and only got coffee when her father would bring it to her mother" during his visits. The father of Hannah Chapman was sold to a nearby planter when she was very small. Because "he missed us and us longed for him," she said many years later, he tried to visit his family under the cover of darkness whenever possible. She noted, "Us would gather 'round him an' crawl up in his lap, tickled slap to death, but he give us dese pleasures at a painful risk." If the master should happen to discover him, "us would track him de nex' day by de blood stains," she remembered.[64]

Hannah McFarland of South Carolina recounted the time when the local slave patrol attempted to whip her mother, "but my papa sho' stopped dat," she said proudly. Whether or not he was made to suffer for his courage is unknown; however, the primary literature of slavery is replete with accounts of slave husbands who intervened, at the risk of their own lives, to save wives and children from violence at the hands of whites. But in a more general sense, the sexual violation of black women by white men rivaled the separation of families as the foremost provocation injected into black family life by slaveholders in general. It is impossible to document with any precision the frequency of these encounters; the 10 percent of the slave population classified as "mulatto" in 1860 of course provides a very conservative estimate of the incidence of interracial rape or concubinage on southern plantations. The pervasive resentment on the part of black women, as well as men, who knew that such assaults were always a possibility cannot be quantified in any meaningful way. A women's acquiescence in the sexual advances of an overseer or owner might offer a modicum of protection for herself or her family—especially when a master vowed to "put her in his pocket" (that is, sell her) or whip her if the protested. Nevertheless, black women often

struggled to resist, and their fathers, sons, and husbands often struggled to protect them.[65]

Regardless of the circumstances under which their womenfolk were sexually abused, black men reacted with deep humiliation and outrage, a reaction that at least some slaveholders intended to provoke. One Louisiana white man would enter a slave cabin and tell the husband "to go outside and wait 'til he do what he want to do." The black man "had to do it and he couldn't do nothing 'bout it." (This master "had chillen by his own chillen.") Other husbands ran away rather than witness such horrors. Recalled one elderly former slave, "What we saw, couldn't do nothing 'bout it. My blood is bilin' now at the thoughts of dem times." It would be naive to assume that the rape of a black wife by a white man did not adversely affect the woman's relationship with her husband; her innocence in initiating or sustaining a sexual encounter might not have shielded her from her husband's wrath. The fact that in some slave quarters mulatto children were scorned as the master's offspring indicates that the community in general hardly regarded this form of abuse with equanimity; hence the desperation of the young slave wife described by an FWP interviewee who feared that her husband would eventually learn of her ordeal with the master.[66]

The black man's role as protector of his family would find explicit expression in postemancipation patterns of work and family life. Until that time, the more freedom the slaves had in determining their own activities, the more clearly emerged a distinct division of labor between the sexes. During community festivities like log rollings, rail splittings, wood choppings, and corn shuckings, men performed the prescribed labor while women cooked the meals. At times, male participants willingly "worked all night," for, in the words of one, "we had the 'Heavenly Banners' (women and whiskey) by us." A limited amount of primary evidence indicates that men actively scorned women's work, especially cooking, house cleaning, sewing, washing clothes, and intimate forms of child care (like bathing children and picking lice out of their hair). Some slaveholders devised forms of public humiliation that capitalized on men's attempts to avoid these tasks. One Louisiana cotton planter punished slave men by forcing them to wash clothes; he also made chronic offenders wear women's dresses. In *This Species of Property,* Leslie Owens remarks of men so treated, "So great was their shame before their fellows that many ran off and suffered the lash on their backs rather than submit to the discipline. Men clearly viewed certain chores as women's tasks, and female slaves largely respected the distinction."[67]

The values and customs of the slave community played a predominant role in structuring work patterns among men and women within the quarters in general and the family in particular. Yet slaveholders affected the division of labor in the quarters in several ways; for example, they took women and girls out of the fields early on Saturdays to wash the clothes, and they enforced certain task assignments related to the production of household goods. An understanding of the social significance of the sexual division of labor requires at least a brief mention of West African cultural preferences and the ways in which the American system of slavery disrupted or sustained traditional African patterns of women's work. Here it is important to keep in mind two points: First, cotton did not emerge as the South's primary staple crop until the late-eighteenth century (the first slaves on the North American continent toiled in tobacco, rice, indigo, and corn fields); and second, regardless of the system of task assignments imposed upon antebellum blacks, the grueling pace of forced labor represented a cruel break from the past for people who had followed

age-old customs related to subsistence agriculture.[68]

Though dimmed by time and necessity, the outlines of African work patterns endured among the slaves. As members of traditional agricultural societies, African women played a major role in the production of the family's food as well as in providing basic household services. The sexual division of labor was more often determined by a woman's child care and domestic responsibilities than by any presumed physical weakness. In some tribes she might engage in heavy, monotonous field work as long as she could make provisions for nursing her baby; that often meant keeping an infant with her in the field. She cultivated a kitchen garden that yielded a variety of vegetables consumed by the family or sold at market, and she usually milked the cows and churned butter.[69]

West Africans brought with them competencies and knowledge that slaveowners readily exploited. Certain tribes were familiar with rice, cotton, and indigo cultivation. Many black women had had experience spinning thread, weaving cloth, and sewing clothes. Moreover, slaves often used techniques and tools handed down from their ancestors—in the method of planting, hoeing, and pounding rice, for example. Whites frequently commented on the ability of slave women to balance heavy and unwieldy loads on their heads, an African custom.[70]

The primary difficulty in generalizing about African women's part in agriculture stems from the fact that members of West African tribes captured for the North American slave trade came from different hoe-culture economies. Within the geographically limited Niger Delta region, for example, men and women of the Ibo tribe worked together in planting, weeding, and harvesting, while female members of another prominent group, the Yoruba, helped only with the harvest. Throughout most of sub-Saharan Africa (and particularly on the west coast), women had primary responsibility for tilling (though not clearing) the soil and cultivating the crops; perhaps this tradition, combined with work patterns established by white masters in this country, reinforced the blacks' beliefs that cutting trees and rolling logs was "men's work." In any case, it is clear that African women often did field work. But since the sexual division of labor varied according to tribe, it is impossible to state with any precision the effect of the African heritage on the slaves' perceptions of women's agriculture work.[71]

The West African tradition of respect for one's elders found new meaning among American slaves; for most women, old age brought increased influence within the slave community, even as their economic value to the master declined. Owners, fearful lest women escape from "earning their salt" once they became too infirm to go to the field, set them to work at other tasks—knitting, cooking, spinning, weaving, dairying, washing, ironing, caring for the children. (Elderly men served as gardeners, wagoners, carters, and stock tenders.) But the imperatives of the southern economic system sometimes compelled slaveowners to extract from feeble women what field labor they could. In other cases they reduced the material provisions of the elderly—housing and allowances of food and clothing—in proportion to their decreased productivity.[72]

The overwhelming youth of the general slave population between 1830 and 1860 (more than half of all slaves were under twenty years of age) meant that most plantations had only a few old persons—the 10 percent over fifty years of age considered elderly. These slaves served as a repository of history and folklore for the others. Harriet Ware, a northern teacher assigned to the South Car-

olina Sea Islands, reported in 1862, "'Learning' with these people I find means a knowledge of medicine, and a person is valued accordingly." Many older women practiced the healing arts in their combined role of midwife, root doctor, healer, and conjurer. They guarded ancient secrets about herbs and other forms of plant life. In their interpretation of dreams and strange occurrences, they brought the real world closer to the supernatural realm and offered spiritual guidance to the ill, the troubled, and the lovelorn.[73]

For slaves in the late antebellum period, these revered (and sometimes feared) women served as a tangible link with the African past. Interviewed by a Federal Writers Project worker in 1937, a Mississippi-born former slave, James Brittian, recalled his own "grandma Aunt Mary" who had lived for 110 years. A "Molly Gasca [Madagascar?] negro," she was plagued by a jealous mistress because of her striking physical appearance; "Her hair it was fine as silk and hung down below her waist." Ned Chaney's African-born Granny Silla (she was the oldest person anyone knew, he thought) commanded respect among the other slaves by virtue of her advanced age and her remarkable healing powers: "Ever'body set a heap of sto' by her. I reckon, because she done 'cumullated so much knowledge an' because her head were so white." When Granny Silla died, her "little bags" of mysterious substances were buried with her because no one else knew how to use them. Yet Chaney's description of his own mother, a midwife and herb doctor, indicates that she too eventually assumed a position of authority within the community.[74]

As a little girl in Georgia, Mary Colbert adored her grandmother, a strong field hand, "smart as a whip." "I used to tell my mother that I wished I was named Hannah for her, and so Mother called me Mary Hannah," she recalled. Amanda Harris, interviewed in Virginia when she was ninety years old, looked back to the decade before the war when her grandmother was still alive: "Used to see her puffin' on dat ole pipe o' her'n, an' one day I ast her what fun she got outen it. "'Tain't no fun, chile,' she tole me. 'But it's a pow'ful lot o' easment. Smoke away trouble, darter. Blow ole trouble an' worry 'way in smoke." Amanda started smoking a pipe shortly before her grandmother died, and in 1937 she declared, "Now dat I'm as ole as she was I know what she mean." In the quiet dignity of their own lives, these grandmothers preserved the past for future generations of Afro-American women.[75]

The honored place held by elderly women in the quarters serves as a useful example of the ways in which the slaves constructed their own social hierarchy (based on individuals' skills and values to the community), in opposition to the master's exclusive concern for the productive capacity of his "hands." Moreover, older female slaves in particular often rivaled the preacher—widely acknowledged as the preeminent leader among slaves—in terms of the respect they commanded for their knowledge of medicine (especially midwifery). In his examination of "Status and Social Structure in the Slave Community," John Blassingame notes that "slaves reserved the top rungs of the social ladder for those blacks who performed services for other slaves rather than for whites." Although he specifically mentions male craftsmen, it is clear that laundresses, seamstresses, cooks, and child rearers—as well as female conjurers, fortunetellers, and herbalists—played important leadership roles often expressed through informal, everyday means.[76]

Within well-defined limits, the slaves created—or preserved—an explicit sexual division of labor based on their own preferences. Husbands and wives and fathers and mothers had reciprocal obligations toward one an-

other. Together they worked to preserve the integrity of the family. Having laid to rest once and for all the myth of the slave matriarchy, some historians suggest that relations between the sexes approximated "a healthy sexual equality."[77] Without private property, slave men lacked the means to achieve economic superiority over their wives, one of the major sources of inequality in the ("free") sexual order. But if male and female slaves shared duties related to household maintenance and community survival, they were nonetheless reduced to a state of powerlessness that rendered virtually meaningless the concept of equality as it applies to marital relations, especially since black women were so vulnerable to attacks by white men.

Moreover, task allocation among the slaves themselves revealed a tension between two different attitudes toward "women's work." The first involved a profound respect for the labor that women did and their ability to meet the demands imposed upon them by so many different people of both races. For example, in an 1840 speech before a northern audience, John Curry, a former slave who grew up in North Carolina, recalled, "My mother's labor was very hard." He then went on to outline her daily responsibilities in the cow pen (she milked fourteen cows) in addition to caring for the children of mothers who worked in the fields. She also cooked for the slaves on the plantation, and did all the ironing and washing for the master's household as well as for her own husband and seven children (including three orphans she had adopted). At night, she "would find one boy with his knee out, a patch wanting here, and a stitch there, and she would sit down by her lightwood fire, and sew and sleep alternately." Echoes of this type of appreciation for slave women's work are found throughout the narratives and interviews, work recounted in loving detail by both sons and daughters.[78]

On the other hand, though men might regard women's domestic labor as intrinsically valuable, this type of activity was nevertheless labeled "women's work" on the assumption that it was the special province of females. In this sense, black women and men performed complementary functions whenever possible within their own "sphere" of socially defined responsibilities. Yet a husband was not "equally" willing to wash clothes compared to a mother's "willingness" to gather firewood in the absence of her spouse. In addition, the formal task of spiritual leader remained a man's job; although women exercised power through a variety of channels, they could not aspire to the title or recognition that accompanied the preacher's role. This twin impulse to honor the hardworking wife and mother on one hand and relegate "grannies" to positions of informal influence exclusively on the other would help to shape the internal structure of the freed community after the Civil War.

The sexual division of labor under slavery actually assumed two forms—one system of work forced upon slaves by masters who valued women only as work-oxen and broodsows and the other initiated by the slaves themselves in the quarters. Only the profit motive accorded a measure of consistency to the slaveholder's decisions concerning female work assignments; he sought to exploit his "hands" efficiently, and either invoked or repudiated traditional notions of women's work to suit his own purposes. In this respect, his decision-making process mirrored the shifting priorities of the larger society, wherein different groups of women were alternately defined primarily as producers or as reproducers according to the fluctuating labor demands of the capitalist economy.

Because slaveholders valued the reproduction of the plantation workforce just as highly as increases in their annual crop (in fact, the two objectives were inseparable), it would be difficult to argue that racial prejudice superseded sexual prejudice as an ordering principle for this peculiar society. Rather than attempt to determine which was more oppressive, we would do well to remember that the two systems shared a dense, common tangle of roots, and that together they yielded bitter fruit in the antebellum South. Black women bore witness to that bitterness in ways different from those of black men on one hand and white women on the other.

In their devotion to family ties—a devotion that encompassed kin and ultimately the whole slave community—black women and men affirmed the value of group survival over the slaveholders' base financial and political considerations. Slave family life, as the cornerstone of Afro-American culture, combined an African heritage with American exigencies, and within the network of kin relations black women and men sought to express their respect for each other even as they resisted the intrusiveness of whites. Thus when it emerged from bondage, the black family had a highly developed sense of itself as an institution protective of the community at large.

The work of black women helped to preserve that community. Janie Scott's admiration for her mother, who was "much of a women," would help to sustain her through the conflagration of civil war, for freedom demanded of black women the same kind of strength and resourcefulness they and their mothers had demonstrated under slavery. As workers, many freed women would still have to pick cotton and wash dishes for whites. But as family members, they would help to define the priorities of a freed people—or rather, affirm the priorities they had developed under slavery—and thereby participate in the transformation of southern society and economy during the postbellum years.

NOTES

1. Zora Hurston, *Their Eyes Were Watching God* (London: J. M. Dent and Sons, 1938), pp. 31–32. Novelist, folklorist, and anthropologist, Hurston (b. 1901, d. 1960) had collected a massive amount of primary data on the culture and folklore of Afro-Americans before she began work on *Their Eyes Were Watching God*. In 1938 she served as supervisor of the Negro Unit of the Florida Federal Writers Project, which compiled interviews with former slaves. Her various writings are finally receiving long-overdue literary attention and critical acclaim. See Robert E. Hemenway, *Zora Neale Hurston: A Literary Biography* (Urbana, IL: University of Illinois Press, 1977) and a recent anthology: Zora N. Hurston, *I Love Myself When I Am Laughing . . . And Then Again When I Am Looking Mean and Impressive*, ed. Alice Walker (Old Westbury, NY: Feminist Press, 1979).

2. For works that focus on slave women in particular, see Angela Davis, "Reflections on the Black Woman's Role in the Community of Slaves," *The Black Scholar* 3 (December 1971):2–15; Mary Ellen Obtiko, "'Custodians of a House of Resistance': Black Women Respond to Slavery," in *Women and Men: The Consequences of Power*, ed. Dana V. Hiller and Robin Ann Sheets (Cincinnati, OH: Office of Women's Studies, University of Cincinnati, 1977), pp. 256–59; Darlene Clark Hine and Kate Wittenstein, "Female Slave Resistance: The Economics of Sex," in *The Black Woman Cross-Culturally*, ed. Filomina Chioma Steady (Cambridge, MA: Schenkman, 1981), pp. 289–300; bell hooks, *Ain't I a Woman: Black Women and Feminism* (Boston, MA: South End Press, 1981), pp. 15–49; Deborah G. White, "Ain't I a Woman? Female Slaves in the Antebellum South" (Ph.D. diss., University of Illinois-Chicago Circle, 1979). White summarizes her major points in "Female Slaves: Sex Roles and Status in the Antebellum Plantation South," *Journal of Family History* 8 (Fall 1983):248–61. The volumes edited by Gerda Lerner, *Black Women in White America: A Documentary History* (New York: Random House, 1972) and Dorothy Sterling, *We Are Your Sisters: Black Women in the Nineteenth Century* (New York: W. W. Norton, 1984) include material on the history of slave women.

3. General works on slavery include James Oakes, *The Ruling Race: A History of American Slaveholders* (New York: Alfred A. Knopf, 1982); Herbert G. Gutman, *The Black Family in Slavery and Freedom, 1750–1925* (New York: Pantheon, 1976); Eugene D. Genovese, *Roll, Jordan, Roll: The World the Slaves Made* (New York: Random House, 1974); Leslie Howard Owens, *This Species of Property: Slave Life and Culture in the Old South* (New York: Oxford University Press, 1976); John W. Blassingame, *The Slave Community: Plantation Life in the Antebellum South* (New York: Oxford University Press, 1972); Paul A. David et al., *Reckoning With Slavery: A Critical Study in the Quantitative History of American Negro Slavery* (New York: Oxford University Press, 1976); Paul D. Escott, *Slavery Remembered: A Record of Twentieth-Century Slave Narratives* (Chapel Hill, NC: University of North Carolina Press, 1979); Thomas L. Webber, *Deep Like the Rivers: Education in the Slave Quarter Community, 1831–1865* (New York: W. W. Norton, 1978).

In some specialized studies women are largely excluded from the general analysis and discussed only in brief sections under the heading "Women and Children." See, for example, Robert S. Starobin, *Industrial Slavery in the Old South* (New York: Oxford University Press, 1970) and Todd L. Savitt, *Medicine and Slavery: The Diseases and Health Care of Blacks in Antebellum Virginia* (Urbana, IL: University of Illinois Press, 1978).

4. Catherine Clinton, *The Plantation Mistress: Women's World in the Old South* (New York: Pantheon, 1982); Anne Firor Scott, *The Southern Lady: From Pedestal to Politics, 1830–1930* (Chicago: University of Chicago Press, 1970), pp. 22–24; Bertram Wyatt-Brown, *Southern Honor: Ethics and Behavior in the Old South* (New York: Oxford University Press, 1982).

5. Owens, *This Species of Property*, pp. 19–49; Genovese, *Roll, Jordan, Roll*, pp. 285–324; Paul W. Gates, *The Farmer's Age: Agriculture, 1815–1860* (New York: Holt, Rinehart, Winston, 1960).

6. On women's "productive-reproductive" functions and the relationship between patriarchy and capitalism, see Joan Kelly, "The Doubled Vision of Feminist Theory: A Postscript to the 'Women and Power' Conference," *Feminist Stud-*

ies 5 (Spring 1979): 216–27; Heidi Hartman, "Capitalism, Patriarchy, and Job Segregation by Sex"; Zillah Eisenstein, "Developing a Theory of Capitalist Patriarchy and Socialist Feminism" and "Some Notes on the Relations of Capitalist Patriarchy" in *Capitalist Patriarchy and the Case for Socialist Feminism,* ed. Zillah R. Eisenstein (New York: Monthly Review Press, 1979); Annette Kuhn and Annmarie Wolpe, "Feminism and Materialism"; Veronica Beechey, "Women and Production: A Critical Analysis of Some Sociological Theories of Women's Work," in *Feminism and Materialism: Women and Modes of Production,* ed. Annette Kuhn and Annmarie Wolpe (London: Routledge and Kegan Paul, 1978).

7. Interviews with former slaves have been published in various forms, including George P. Rawick, ed., *The American Slave: A Composite Autobiography,* 41 vols., Series 1, Supplement Series 1 and 2 (Westport, CT: Greenwood Press, 1972, 1978, 1979); Social Science Institute, Fisk University, *Unwritten History of Slavery: Autobiographical Accounts of Negro Ex-Slaves* (Nashville, TN: Social Science Institute, 1945); Charles L. Perdue, Jr., Thomas E. Borden, and Robert K. Phillips, *Weevils in the Wheat: Interviews With Virginia Ex-Slaves* (Charlottesville, VA: University Press of Virginia, 1976); John B. Cade, "Out of the Mouths of Ex-Slaves," *Journal of Negro History* 20 (July 1935):294–337; John W. Blassingame, ed., *Slave Testimony: Two Centuries of Letters, Speeches, and Autobiographies* (Baton Rouge, LA: Louisiana State University Press, 1977).

The narratives as a historical source are evaluated in Escott, *Slavery Remembered,* pp. 3–18 ("The slave narratives offer the best evidence we will ever have on the feelings and attitudes of America's slaves"); Martia Graham Goodson, "An Introductory Essay and Subject Index to Selected Interviews from the Slave Narrative Collection" (Ph.D. diss., Union Graduate School, 1977); C. Vann Woodward, "History from Slave Sources," *American Historical Review* 79 (April 1974): 470–81; David T. Bailey, "A Divided Prism: Two Sources of Black Testimony on Slavery," *Journal of Southern History* 46 (August 1980):381–404; John Sekora and Darwin T. Turner, eds., *The Art of Slave Narrative: Original Essays in Criticism and Theory* (Macomb, IL: W. Illinois University, 1982).

The Davidson quotation is from Rawick, ed., *American Slave,* Series 1, *Ohio Narratives,* vol. 16, pp. 26–29. Hereafter all references will include the series number, name of the state, and volume and page numbers. The other major source of slave interview material taken from the Federal Writers Project (FWP) collection for this chapter—Perdue et al.—will be referred to as *Weevils in the Wheat.* The Fisk University study is listed as *Unwritten History of Slavery.*

Donald M. Jacobs has compiled a useful index to the FWP narratives: *Index to the American Slave* (Westport, CT: Greenwood Press, 1981).

8. Joan Kelly-Gadol, "The Social Relations of the Sexes: Methodological Implications of Women's History," *Signs* 1 (Summer 1976): 809–10, 819.

9. For discussions of women's work and the inadequacy of traditional economic and social-scientific theory to define and analyze it see Joan Acker, "Issues in the Sociological Study of Women's Work," in *Women Working: Theories and Facts in Perspective,* ed. Ann H. Stromberg and Shirley Harkess (Palo Alto, CA: Mayfield Publishing Company, 1978), pp. 134–61; Judith K. Brown, "A Note on the Division of Labor by Sex," *American Anthropologist* 72 (October 1970): 1073–78.

10. Supp. Series 1, *Mississippi Narratives,* Pt. II, vol. 7, p. 350; Supp. Series 1, *Oklahoma Narratives,* vol. 12, p. 110; Davis, "Reflections," p. 8; Frances Anne Kemble, *Journal of a Residence on a Georgian Plantation in 1838–1839* (London: Longman, Green, 1863), pp. 60, 92. See also *Unwritten History of Slavery,* p. 286.

11. Owens, *This Species of Property,* pp. 8–20; Stanley L. Engerman, "The Southern Slave Economy," in *Perspectives and Irony in American Slavery,* ed. Harry P. Owens (Jackson, MS: University Press of Mississippi, 1976), pp. 71–102. On the task system, see Ira Berlin, "Time, Space, and the Evolution of Afro-American Society on British Mainland North America," *American Historical Review* 85 (February 1980):66; and Philip D. Morgan, "Work and Culture: The Task System and the World of Lowcountry Blacks, 1700 to 1880," *William and Mary Quarterly* 39 (October 1982): 563–99.

12. Kemble, *Journal,* p. 28; Lewis Cecil Gray, *History of Agriculture in the Southern United States*

to 1860, vol. 1 (Washington, D.C.: Carnegie Institution, 1933), pp. 533–548; *Weevils in the Wheat*, p. 199; Series 1, *Florida Narratives*, vol. 17, p. 305; Charles S. Sydnor, *Slavery in Mississippi* (Gloucester, MA: P. Smith, 1933), p. 20; Frederick Law Olmsted, *A Journey in the Seaboard Slave States* (New York: Dix and Edwards, 1856), p. 470. See also Larry Rivers, "'Dignity and Importance': Slavery in Jefferson County, Florida—1827 to 1860," *Florida Historical Quarterly* 61 (April 1983):422–23; Sterling, ed., *We Are Your Sisters*, pp. 13–17.

13. Olmsted, *Slave States*, p. 387; Series 1, *Alabama Narratives*, vol. 6, p. 87. Work descriptions were gleaned from the Federal Writers Project slave narrative collection (Rawick, ed., *American Slave*, and Perdue, Borden, and Phillips, *Weevils in the Wheat*) and Gray, *History of Agriculture*. Goodson ("Introductory Essay") has indexed a sample of the interviews with women by subject (for example, candlemaking, carding wool, field work, splitting rails.)

For pictures of early twentieth-century black women of St. Helena's Islands, South Carolina, wearing the second belt, see photographs in Edith M. Dabbs, *Face of an Island: Leigh Richmond Miner's Photographs of St. Helena's Island* (New York: Grossman Publishers, 1971). The caption of one photo entitled "Woman with Hoe" reads: "Adelaide Washington sets off for her day's work in the field. The second belt or cord tied around the hips lifted all her garments a little and protected the long skirts from both early morning dew and contact with the dirt. . . .[according to] an African superstition . . . the second cord also gave the wearer extra strength" (no pp.). Olmsted, *Slave States*, p. 387, includes a sketch of this form of dress.

14. *Weevils in the Wheat*, p. 26; Gray, *History of Agriculture*, vol. 1, p. 251; planter quoted in Owens, *This Species of Property*, p. 39.

15. Genovese, *Roll, Jordan, Roll*, p. 495; Burke quoted in Gray, *History of Agriculture*, p. 549; Frederick Law Olmsted, *A Journey in the Back Country in the Winter of 1853–1854* (New York: Mason Brothers, 1860), p. 81. For former slaves' descriptions of women who plowed, see Series 1, *Oklahoma Narratives*, vol. 7, p. 314; Series 1, *Florida Narratives*, vol. 17, p. 33.

16. Olmsted quoted in Sydnor, *Slavery in Mississippi*, p. 68; *Weevils in the Wheat*, p. 77. Of the women who worked in the South Carolina Sea Islands cotton fields, Harriet Ware (a northern teacher) wrote, "they walked off with their heavy hoes on their shoulders, as free, strong, and graceful as possible." Elizabeth Ware Pearson, ed., *Letters from Port Royal, 1862–1868* (New York: Arno Press, 1969; orig. pub. 1906), p. 52

17. Stuart Bruchey, ed., *Cotton and the Growth of the American Economy: 1790–1860* (New York: Harcourt, Brace, and World, 1967), p. 174. See the documents under the heading "Making Cotton" and "The Routine of the Cotton Year," pp. 171–80. For examples of outstanding female pickers see Series 1, *Alabama Narratives*, vol. 6, p. 275 ("Oncet I won a contest wid a man an' made 480 pounds"); *Weevils in the Wheat*, p. 199.

18. Supp. Series 2, *Texas Narratives*, Pt. 1, vol. 2, pp. 93–96; Supp. Series 1, *Mississippi Narratives*, Pt. I, vol. 6, pp. 235–36, and Pt. II, vol. 7, p. 404; Series 1, *Texas Narratives*, Pt. III, vol. 5, p. 231; Series 1, *Indiana Narratives*, vol. 6, p. 25; Series 1, *Georgia Narratives*, Pt. 1, vol. 12, p. 113; Series 1, *Oklahoma Narratives*, vol. 7, p. 314; Series 1, *Alabama Narratives*, vol. 6, p. 338. For additional examples, see *Unwritten History of Slavery*, pp. 203, 217, 241.

19. For a general discussion of slave artisans in the South, see Gray, *History of Agriculture*, vol. 1, pp. 548, 565–67; Sydnor, *Slavery in Mississippi*, p. 9; James E. Newton and Ronald L. Lewis, eds., *The Other Slaves: Mechanics, Artisans, and Craftsmen* (Boston, MA: G. K. Hall, 1978). Roger L. Ransom and Richard Sutch, in *One Kind of Freedom: The Economic Consequences of Emancipation* (New York: Cambridge University Press, 1977) discuss "Occupational Distribution of Southern Blacks: 1860, 1870, 1890" in Appendix B, pp. 220–31. The works of Starobin (*Industrial Slavery*) and James H. Brewer, *The Confederate Negro: Virginia's Craftsmen and Military Laborers, 1861–1865* (Durham, NC: Duke University Press, 1969) focus almost exclusively on male slaves. See also Herbert Gutman and Richard Sutch, "Victorians All? The Sexual Mores and Conduct of Slaves and Their Masters," in David et al., *Reckoning With Slavery*, p. 160; Gutman, *Black Family*, pp. 599–600. The "hiring out" of men and children frequently disrupted family life.

20. Ransom and Sutch, *One Kind of Freedom,* p. 233; Olmsted, *Slave States,* p. 388; Series 1, *Ohio Narratives,* vol. 16, p. 28; Kemble, *Journal,* p. 121; Series 1, *South Carolina Narratives,* Pt. IV, vol. 3, p. 78; *Weevils in the Wheat,* pp. 223–24. Genovese describes the plantation system as a "halfway house between peasant and factory cultures" (*Roll, Jordan, Roll,* p. 286). For further discussion of the grueling pace of field work, see Herbert G. Gutman and Richard Sutch, "Sambo Makes Good, or Were Slaves Imbued with the Protestant Work Ethic?" in David et al., *Reckoning With Slavery,* pp. 55–93.

21. Olmsted, *Back Country,* pp. 58–59; Michael P. Johnson, "Smothered Slave Infants: Were Slave Mothers at Fault?" *Journal of Southern History* 47 (November 1981):493–520. See Herbert Gutman and Richard Sutch, "The Slave Family: Protected Agent of Capitalist Masters or Victim of the Slave Trade?" in David et al., *Reckoning With Slavery,* pp. 94–133; Jack Ericson Eblen, "New Estimates of the Vital Rates of the United States Black Population During the Nineteenth Century," *Demography* 11 (May 1974):307–19; Lewis Cecil Gray, *History of Agriculture in the Southern United States to 1860,* vol. 2 (Washington, D.C.: Carnegie Institution, 1933), pp. 888–907, 562.

22. Savitt, *Medicine and Slavery,* pp. 115–20; planter quoted in Olmsted, *Slave States,* p. 190; Gutman and Sutch, "Sambo Makes Good," p. 67; Series 1, *Virginia Narratives,* vol. 16, p. 51. See also Owens, *This Species of Property,* pp. 38–40.

23. Oakes, *Ruling Race,* pp. 24, 156, 174–75; Olmsted, *Back Country,* p. 61; Series 1, *Virginia Narratives,* vol. 16, p. 11. See also Kemble, *Journal,* p. 121. For other descriptions of overseers and their treatment of slaves, see Frederick Douglass, *Life and Times of Frederick Douglass, Written by Himself* (Hartford, CT: Park Publishing Company, 1882), p. 34; Olmsted, *Back Country,* pp. 56–61, 81–82, 207, and *Slave States,* pp. 438–39; Gray, *History of Agriculture,* vol. 1, pp. 245–46; Escott, *Slavery Remembered,* pp. 87–89. Slaves recall overseers (among them, "the meanest men that ever walked the earth") and their disciplinary techniques in Series 1, *Oklahoma Narratives,* vol. 7, p. 146; *Florida Narratives,* vol. 17, pp. 88, 118; *Texas Narratives,* Pt. IV, vol. 5, p. 210.

24. Moses Grandy, *Narrative of the Life of Moses Grandy, Late a Slave in the United States of America* (Boston: Oliver Johnson, 1844), p. 18; Series 1, *Alabama Narratives,* vol. 6, p. 66; Series 1, *Indiana Narratives,* vol. 6, p. 200. See also Supp. Series 2, *Louisiana Narratives,* vol. 6, pp. 1939–43, 2025, 2299. I wish to acknowledge Prof. Michael P. Johnson for bringing to my attention additional examples of this practice.

25. Series 1, *Mississippi Narratives,* vol. 7, p. 171.

26. Douglass, *Life and Times,* p. 52; Owens, *This Species of Property,* pp. 218–19; Series 1, *Oklahoma Narratives,* vol. 7, p. 347; *Tennessee Narratives,* vol. 16, p. 9.

27. Series 1, *Alabama Narratives,* vol. 6, p. 46; Series 1, *Florida Narratives,* vol. 17, p. 185; *Weevils in the Wheat,* pp. 259, 216; Series 1, *Virginia Narratives,* vol. 16, p. 51; Escott, *Slavery Remembered,* pp. 86–93; Drew Gilpin Faust, "Culture, Conflict and Community: The Meaning of Power on an Antebellum Plantation," *Journal of Social History* 14 (Fall 1980):90. Escott includes an extensive discussion of resistance as revealed in the FWP slave narrative collection and provides data on the age, sex, and marital status of resisters and the purposes and forms of resistance. Gutman argues that the "typical runaway" was a male, aged sixteen to thirty-five years (*Black Family,* pp. 264–65). See also Obitko, "'Custodians'"; Owens, *This Species of Property,* pp. 38, 88, 95; Sterling, ed., *We Are Your Sisters,* pp. 56–84.

28. *Weevils in the Wheat,* pp. 26, 282, 157. According to Gutman, plantation work patterns "apparently failed to take into account enlarged slave kin groups, and further study may show that a central tension between slaves and their owners had its origins in the separation of work and kinship obligations" (*Black Family,* p. 209). See also Webber, *Deep Like the Rivers,* p. 230; Faust, "Culture, Conflict, and Community," p. 87.

In his study, *The Slave Drivers: Black Agricultural Labor Supervisors in the Antebellum South* (Westport, CT: Greenwood Press, 1979), William L. Van Deburg examines the anomalous position of black (male) drivers in relation to the rest of the slave community.

29. Series 1, *Florida Narratives,* vol. 17, p. 191; slaveholder quoted in Gutman, *Black Family,* p. 263; Robert S. Starobin, ed., *Blacks in Bondage: Let-*

ters of American Slaves (New York: New Viewpoints, 1974), p. 54.

30. Genovese, *Roll, Jordan, Roll*, pp. 328, 340; Series 1, *Alabama Narratives*, vol. 6, p. 273; Supp. Series 1, *Mississippi Narratives*, Pt. II, vol. 7, p. 400; Series 1, *Texas Narratives*, Pt. III, vol. 5, p. 45; *Unwritten History of Slavery*, p. 51. Recent historians have emphasized that the distinction between house and field work was not always meaningful in terms of shaping a slave's personality and self-perception or defining his or her status. See Owens, *This Species of Property*, p. 113; Escott, *Slavery Remembered*, pp. 59–60.

31. Series 1, *Alabama Narratives*, vol. 6, pp. 416–17.

32. Series 1, *Texas Narratives*, Pt. IV, vol. 5, p. 11; Series 1, *Indiana Narratives*, vol. 6, p. 183. See also Supp. Series 1, *Mississippi Narratives*, Pt. 1, vol. 6, pp. 54–55, 216, 257, 365, 380–81; *Unwritten History of Slavery*, pp. 56, 60.

33. The FWP slave narrative collection and *Unwritten History of Slavery* provide these examples of children's work and many more. Series 1, *Alabama Narratives*, vol. 6, p. 157; *Unwritten History of Slavery*, p. 263; Genovese, *Roll, Jordan, Roll*, pp. 502–19; Owens, *This Species of Property*, p. 202.

34. Supp. Series 1, *Georgia Narratives*, Pt. I, vol. 3, p. 185; *Weevils in the Wheat*, pp. 264–65; Series 1, *South Carolina Narratives*, Pt. IV, vol. 3, p. 257.

35. Wyatt-Brown, *Southern Honor*, p. 226; C. Vann Woodward, ed., *Mary Chesnut's Civil War* (New Haven, CT: Yale University Press, 1981), p. 255.

36. Clinton, *Plantation Mistress*, pp. 16–35; Genovese, *Roll, Jordan, Roll*, pp. 333–38; Olmsted, *Slave States*, p. 421; Series 1, *South Carolina Narratives*, Pt. IV, vol. 3, p. 126; *Florida Narratives*, vol. 17, p. 356.

37. For specific incidents illustrating these points, see Series 1, *Oklahoma Narratives*, vol. 7, pp. 135; 165–66; *Tennessee Narratives*, vol. 16, p. 14; *Weevils in the Wheat*, pp. 63, 199; Blassingame, ed., *Slave Testimony*, pp. 160–61, 131, 149. See also "A Seamstress Is Punished," in Lerner, ed., *Black Women in White America*, pp. 18–19.

38. Wyatt-Brown, *Southern Honor*, pp. 285, 288–91, 321, 308; Series 1, *Oklahoma Narratives*, vol. 7, p. 347. See also *Unwritten History of Slavery*, p. 261; Linda Brent (Harriet Jacobs), *Incidents in the Life of a Slave Girl, Written by Herself* (Boston, MA: Lydia Maria Child, 1861).

39. James Hugo Johnston, *Race Relations in Virginia and Miscegenation in the South, 1776–1860* (Amherst, MA: University of Massachusetts Press, 1970), pp. 246–47.

40. Wyatt-Brown, *Southern Honor*, pp. 281–83; Clinton, *Plantation Mistress*, pp. 80–81.

41. See, for example, Blassingame, ed., *Slave Testimony*, p. 132.

42. Olmsted, *Slave States*, p. 421; Series 1, *South Carolina Narratives*, Pt. IV, vol. 3, p. 126; Series 1, *Florida Narratives*, vol. 17, p. 356; Escott, *Slavery Remembered*, p. 64; Kemble, *Journal*, p. 98; Genovese, *Roll, Jordan, Roll*, pp. 346–47; *Unwritten History of Slavery*, p. 201.

43. Series 1, *Florida Narratives*, vol. 17, p. 356; Gutman and Sutch, "Sambo Makes Good," p. 74; Kemble, *Journal*, p. 153; Gray, *History of Agriculture*, Vol. 1, p. 553; Owens, *This Species of Property*, p. 113; Faust, "Culture, Conflict, and Community," p. 86.

44. Series 1, *Georgia Narratives*, Pt. I, vol. 12, p. 243; Davis, "Reflections," pp. 4–7. For general discussions of women's work as it related to slave communal life, see also Owens, *This Species of Property*, pp. 23, 225; White, "Ain't I a Woman?" Polly Cancer recalled that, when she was growing up on a Mississippi plantation, the master "wudn't let de mammies whip dey own chillun [or "do dey own cookin"] . . . ef he cum 'cross a 'oman whuppin' her chile he'd say, 'Git 'way 'oman; dats my bizness.'" Supp. Series 1, *Mississippi Narratives*, Pt. II, vol. 7, pp. 340–41.

45. Gray, *History of Agriculture*, Vol. 1, p. 563; Olmsted, *Slave States*, pp. 424–25, 697–98; Owens, *This Species of Property*, p. 47; Series 1, *Florida Narratives*, vol. 17, p. 175; Series 1. *Alabama Narratives*, vol. 6, p. 216; Supp. Series 1 *Mississippi Narratives*, Pt. 1, vol. 6, pp. 10, 23, 25, 123; Supp. Series 1, *Georgia Narratives*, Pt. I, vol. 3, p. 27. Savitt (*Slavery and Medicine*) includes a section on black medicine (pp. 171–84) and confirms Rebecca Hooks's recollection that "on the plantation, the doctor was not nearly as popular as the 'granny' or midwife."

46. Series 1, *Florida Narratives*, vol. 17, p. 175. *Georgia Narratives*, Pt. I, vol. 12, p. 70; *Oklahoma Narratives*, vol. 7, pp. 314–15; White, "Ain't I a

Woman?" pp. 22–23; Supp. Series 1, *Texas Narratives*, Pt. I, vol. 2, p. 98. Group quilting projects served the same functions for women. See Webber, *Deep Like the Rivers*, p. 236.

47. The FWP slave narrative collection contains many descriptions of slaves engaged in household industry. Alice Morse Earle details comparable techniques used by white women in colonial New England in *Home Life in Colonial Days* (New York: Macmillan, 1935).

48. See, for example, Series 1, *South Carolina Narratives*, Pt. III, vol. 3, pp. 15, 218, 236; *Texas Narratives*, Pt. III, vol. 5, pp. 20, 89, 108, 114, 171, 188, 220; Supp. Series 1, *Mississippi Narratives*, Pt. I, vol. 6, p. 36; *Unwritten History of Slavery*, p. 56.

49. *Weevils in the Wheat*, pp. 88–89. George White of Lynchburg reported that his mother sang a similar version of this song to women while they were spinning. See p. 309.

50. *Unwritten History of Slavery*, p. 53. See also Faust, "Culture, Conflict, and Community," p. 91.

51. Gutman, *Black Family*, pp. 220–27; Charles Wetherell, "Slave Kinship: A Case Study of the South Carolina Good Hope Plantation, 1835–1856," *Journal of Family History* 6 (Fall 1982): 294–308.

52. Genovese, *Roll, Jordan, Roll*, p. 319; Gutman, *Black Family*.

53. Series 1, *Georgia Narratives*, Pt. 1, vol. 12, p. 203. For other examples of change from children's to adults' clothing, see Series 1, *Texas Narratives*, Pt. III, vol. 5, pp. 211, 275; Pt. IV, vol. 5, pp. 109–110; *Georgia Narratives*, Pt. 1, vol. 12, p. 277; Genovese, *Roll, Jordan, Roll*, p. 505. On childhood in the quarters, see also the references in Webber, *Deep Like the Rivers*; David K. Wiggins, "The Play of Slave Children in the Plantation Communities of the Old South, 1820–1860," *Journal of Sport History* 7 (Summer 1980): 21–39.

54. Gutman and Sutch, "Victorians All?" p. 146; Gutman, *Black Family*, pp. 61–67, pp. 75–80; Escott, *Slavery Remembered*, pp. 52–53; Genovese, *Roll, Jordan, Roll*, pp. 415, 459, 465–67; James Trussell and Richard Steckel, "The Age of Slaves at Menarche and their First Birth," *Journal of Interdisciplinary History* 8 (Winter 1978):477–505.

55. Owens, *This Species of Property*, p. 126; Escott, *Slavery Remembered*, pp. 59–65; Genovese, *Roll, Jordan, Roll*, p. 339.

56. Series 1, *Oklahoma Narratives*, vol. 7, p. 322; *Alabama Narratives*, vol. 6, p. 370; *Weevils in the Wheat*, pp. 49, 131–32; Series 1, *South Carolina Narratives*, Pt. III, vol. 3, p. 106. For examples of courting practices, see Owens, *This Species of Property*, pp. 195–96; Series 1, *South Carolina Narratives*, Pt. III, vol. 3, pp. 78, 106, 167; Pt. IV, p. 249; *Texas Narratives*, Pt. III, vol. 5, p. 15; *Indiana Narratives*, vol. 6, pp. 139–40; *Oklahoma Narratives*, vol. 7, p. 264; *Mississippi Narratives*, vol. 7, p. 87; *Georgia Narratives*, Pt. I, vol. 12, p. 164; *Weevils in the Wheat*, p. 122; Sterling, ed., *We Are Your Sisters*, pp. 31–43.

57. Gutman, *Black Family*, pp. 50, 67–68; Gutman and Sutch, "Victorians All?" pp. 139–42; Genovese, *Roll, Jordan, Roll*, pp. 466–67; Series 1, *South Carolina Narratives*, Pt. III, vol. 3, pp. 167–68. In *Black Family*, Gutman points out that "violence, even murder, sometimes followed suspected or actual infidelity" (p. 67). The aggrieved husband was almost always the aggressor. Webber suggests that "more community disfavor probably fell upon female than male adulterers," *Deep Like the Rivers*, p. 149.

The marriage ceremony in the fields is described in Sydnor, *Slavery in Mississippi*, p. 63.

58. Richard Sutch argues in "The Breeding of Slaves for Sale and the Westward Expansion of Slavery, 1850–1860," in *Race and Slavery in the Western Hemisphere: Quantitative Studies*, eds. Stanley L. Engerman and Eugene D. Genovese (Princeton, NJ: Princeton University Press, 1975), that slaveowners in the breeding states "fostered polygamy and promiscuity among their slaves" and sold the children ("predominantly as young adults") to planters in the southwestern slave states (p. 198). Cf. Trussell and Steckel, "Age of Slaves"; Robert William Fogel and Stanley L. Engerman, *Time on the Cross: The Economics of American Negro Slavery* (Boston, MA: Little, Brown, 1974), pp. 78–86.

59. Series 1, *South Carolina Narratives*, Pt. IV, vol. 3, p. 53; *Texas Narratives*, Pt. IV, vol. 5, pp. 176–78; Kemble, *Journal*, pp. 167, 205. See also Elizabeth Hyde Botume, *First Days Amongst the Contrabands* (New York: Arno Press, 1968; orig. pub. 1893), pp. 161–63; Escott, *Slavery Remembered*, pp. 43–44; Series 1, *Texas Narratives*, Pt. IV, vol. 5, p. 189; *Alabama Narratives*, vol. 6, pp. 134, 221; *Mississippi Narratives*, vol. 7, p. 4; *Florida Narratives*, vol. 17, p. 167.

60. Gutman, *Black Family*, p. 75; Richard Sutch, "The Care and Feeding of Slaves," and Gutman and Sutch, "Victorians All?" in David et al., *Reckoning With Slavery*, pp. 231–301 and 134–62; Owens, *This Species of Property*, p. 38.

61. Owens, *This Species of Property*, pp. 40–41; Eblen, "New Estimates," pp. 301–19; Richard Steckel, "Slave Mortality: Analysis of Evidence from Plantation Records," *Social Science History* 3 (October 1979):86–114; Kenneth F. Kiple and Virginia H. Kiple, "Slave Child Mortality: Some Nutritional Answers to a Perennial Puzzle," *Journal of Social History* 10 (March 1977):284–309. Kiple and Kiple attribute the high rates of slave infant mortality to "a conspiracy of nutrition, African environmental heritage, and North American climatic circumstances rather than planter mistreatment" (p. 299). But see also Johnson, "Smothered Slave Infants."

On the high fertility rates of slave women in the upper South, see Sutch, "Breeding of Slaves," pp. 173–210.

Quotations from *Weevils in the Wheat*, p. 150; Botume, *First Days*, p. 164. For discussions of the demographic effects of the cotton boom, see Owens, *This Species of Property*, p. 38; Paul A. David, "Time on the Cross and the Burden of Quantitative History," in David et al., *Reckoning with Slavery*, pp. 339–57; Eblen, "New Estimates," p. 312.

62. Davis, "Reflections," p. 7.

63. Series 1, *Alabama Narratives*, vol. 6, p. 9; Supp. Series 2, *Texas Narratives*, Pt. V, vol. 6, pp. 2036–37; Series 1, *Florida Narratives*, vol. 17, pp. 22–23; White, "Ain't I a Woman?" pp. 30–31; Webber, *Deep Like the Rivers*, pp. 112–13; 167–71; *Unwritten History of Slavery*, p. 251. On naming practices in the quarters, one scholar observes, "one function of naming a child for his father or paternal kin was to assert the child's place in slave society." See Cheryll Ann Cody, "Naming, Kinship, and Estate Dispersal: Notes on Slave Family Life on a South Carolina Plantation, 1786 to 1833," *William and Mary Quarterly* 39 (January 1982): 203.

64. Gutman, *Black Family*, pp. 142, 67–68, 267–68; Genovese, *Roll, Jordan, Roll*, pp. 318, 482–94; Series 1, *South Carolina Narratives*, Pt. III, vol. 3, p. 192; Supp. Series 1, *Mississippi Narratives*, Pt. II, vol. 7, p. 382.

65. Series 1, *Oklahoma Narratives*, vol. 7, p. 210; Escott, *Slavery Remembered*, pp. 49–57, 87; Owens, *This Species of Property*, p. 201; Supp. Series 2, *Texas Narratives*, vol. 8, p. 3100; Genovese, *Roll, Jordan, Roll*, p. 512; Gutman and Sutch, "Victorians All? p. 152; Richard H. Steckel, "Miscegenation and the American Slave Schedules," *Journal of Interdisciplinary History* 11 (Autumn 1980):251–63. For accounts of the rape of slave women, see Supp. Series 2, *Mississippi Narratives*, vol. 7, p. 2531, *Louisiana Narratives*, vol. 4, pp. 1238–40. See also Joel Williamson, *New People: Miscegenation and Mulattoes in the United States* (New York: Free Press, 1980).

66. Supp. Series 2, *Texas Narratives*, Pt. II, vol. 2, pp. 23–24; *Weevils in the Wheat*, p. 207; Steckel, "Miscegenation," p. 251; Steven E. Brown, "Sexuality and the Slave Community," *Phylon* 42 (Spring 1981):8; Series 1, *Florida Narratives*, vol. 17, pp. 89–90. See also *Unwritten History of Slavery*, p. 44; Olmsted, *Slave States*, pp. 619, 622; *Weevils in the Wheat*, pp. 202, 207–8; Kemble, *Journal*, pp. 141, 210.

The social-scientific literature on rape reveals the antipathy toward the victim on the part of husbands or lovers who feel personally humiliated by the incident. See, for example, Malkah T. Notman and Carol C. Nadelson, "The Rape Victim: Psychodynamic Considerations," *American Journal of Psychiatry* 133 (April 1976):408–13.

This issue is complicated by the fact that the rape of slave women by black drivers did occur on occasion. As the supervisor of a gang of field workers (sometimes of women exclusively), the driver had temptations and opportunities similar to those of white overseers, and not all of them showed the respect toward their fellow slaves that Frank Bell's uncle did. Some apparently harbored feelings of resentment that found at least partial release in attacks upon women of their own race. See Kemble, *Journal*, p. 228; Series 1, *Mississippi Narratives*, vol. 7, p. 13; Gutman, *Black Family*, pp. 83–84; Olmsted, *Slave States*, pp. 430, 436–38, 470, and *Back Country*, p. 81; Series 1, *Oklahoma Narratives*, vol. 7, p. 50; *Mississippi Narratives*, vol. 7, p. 171; Owens, *This Species of Property*, pp. 123–25.

67. Gutman and Sutch, "Sambo Makes Good," p. 63; Owens, *This Species of Property*, p. 195; Supp. Series 1, *Mississippi Narratives*, Pt. 1, vol. 6, pp. 59–60. For mention of corn shuckings in particular, see Genovese, *Roll, Jordan, Roll*, p. 318; Series 1,

Mississippi Narratives, vol. 7, p. 6; Series 1, *Oklahoma Narratives*, vol. 7, p. 230. In the context of traditional male-female roles, what Genovese calls the "curious sexual division of labor" that marked these festivities was not "curious" at all (p. 318).

68. Unfortunately, much of the data about precolonial African work patterns must be extrapolated from recent findings of anthropologists. I benefited from conversations with Dr. M. Jean Hay of the Boston University African Studies Center concerning women's work in precolonial Africa and methodological problems in studying this subject.

69. For a theoretical formulation of the sexual division of labor in preindustrial societies, see Brown, "A Note on the Division of Labor by Sex."

70. Peter Wood, *Black Majority: Negroes in Colonial South Carolina from 1670 Through the Stono Rebellion* (New York: Alfred A. Knopf, 1974), pp. 59–62; P. C. Lloyd, "Osi fakunde of Ijebu," in *Africa Remembered: Narratives by West Africans from the Era of the Slave Trade*, ed. Philip D. Curtin (Madison, WI: University of Wisconsin Press, 1967), p. 263; Marguerite Dupire, "The Position of Women in a Pastoral Society," in *Women of Tropical Africa*, ed. Denise Paulme (Berkeley, CA: University of California Press, 1963), pp. 76–80; "The Life of Olaudah Equiano or Gustavus Vassa the African Written By Himself," in *Great Slave Narratives*, ed. Arna Bontemps (Boston, MA: Beacon Press, 1969), pp. 7–10; Kemble, *Journal*, p. 42; Pearson, ed., *Letters From Port Royal*, pp. 58, 106.

71. Melville J. Herskovits, *The Myth of the Negro Past* (New York: Harper and Brothers, 1941), pp. 33–85; Wood, *Black Majority*, pp. 179, 250; Hermann Baumann, "The Division of Work According to Sex in African Hoe Culture," *Africa* 1 (July 1928): 289–319.

On the role of women in hoe agriculture, see also Leith Mullings, "Women and Economic Change in Africa," in *Women in Africa: Studies in Social and Economic Change*, eds. Nancy J. Hafkin and Edna G. Bay (Stanford, CA: Stanford University Press, 1976), pp. 239–64; Sylvia Leith-Ross, *African Women: A Study of the Ibo of Nigeria* (New York: Frederick A. Praeger, 1965), pp. 84–91; Ester Boserup, *Woman's Role in Economic Development* (New York: St. Martin's Press, 1974), pp. 15–36; Jack Goody and Joan Buckley, "Inheritance and

Women's Labour in Africa," *Africa* 63 (April 1973): 108–21. No tribes in precolonial Africa used the plow. See also Jean Thomas Griffin, "West African and Black Working Women: Historical and Contemporary Comparisons," *Journal of Black Psychology* 8 (February 1982):55–74.

72. Olmsted, *Slave States*, p. 433; Gray, *History of Agriculture*, p. 548; Kemble, *Journal*, pp. 164, 247; Douglass, *Narrative*, pp. 76–78. According to Genovese, the ability of these elderly slaves "to live decently and with self-respect depended primarily on the support of their younger fellow slaves" (*Roll, Jordan, Roll*, p. 523). See also White, "Ain't I a Woman?" p. 49; Supp. Series 1 *Mississippi Narratives*, Pt. I, vol. 6, p. 242; Leslie J. Pollard, "Aging and Slavery: A Gerontological Perspective," *Journal of Negro History* 66 (Fall 1981):228–34.

73. Eblen, "New Estimates," p. 306; Pearson, ed., *Letters from Port Royal*, p. 25; Genovese, *Roll, Jordan, Roll*, pp. 522–23; Eliza F. Andrews, *The War-Time Journal of a Georgia Girl, 1864–1865* (New York: D. Appleton and Co., 1908), p. 101. Escott, *Slavery Remembered*, pp. 108–9; Owens, *This Species of Property*, p. 140; Gutman, *Black Family*, p. 218. For specific examples, see Series 1, *Alabama Narratives*, vol. 6, pp. 216, 256, 334; Supp. Series 2, *Nebraska Narratives*, vol. 1, pp. 319–20.

74. Supp. Series 1, *Mississippi Narratives*, Pt. I, vol. 6, p. 217; Pt. II, vol. 7, pp. 369–73. See also White, "Ain't I a Woman?" pp. 107–112; Webber, *Deep Like the Rivers*, pp. 175–76.

75. Series 1, *Georgia Narratives*, Pt. 1, vol. 12, p. 214; *Weevils in the Wheat*, p. 128.

76. John W. Blassingame, "Status and Social Structure in the Slave Community: Evidence from New Sources," in Harry P. Owens, ed. *Perspectives and Irony in American Slavery*, p. 142. Blassingame, however, does not take this observation to its logical conclusion in regard to the status of women. See also Albert Raboteau, *Slave Religion: The "Invisible Institution" in the Antebellum South* (New York: Oxford University Press, 1978), pp. 238, 275; Webber, *Deep Like the Rivers*, p. 226; Genovese, *Roll, Jordan, Roll*, pp. 225–27.

77. Genovese, *Roll, Jordan, Roll*, p. 500. See also White, "Ain't I a Woman?" pp. 3–20, 51–54; and Davis, "Reflections," p.7.

78. Blassingame, ed., *Slave Testimony*, p. 133.

Chapter 51

Constructing Motherhood on the Night Shift: "Working Mothers" as "Stay-at-Home Moms"

ANITA ILTA GAREY

Cultural definitions of a good mother typically conflict with cultural definitions of a good worker, and images of motherhood and job or career are constructed in opposition to each other (Collier, Rosaldo, and Yanagisako 1982, 34–36; Coser 1991, 123; Etaugh and Study 1989; Gerson 1985; Moen 1992, 6). This conflict of images continues despite the fact that more than half of women in the United States with children under six years of age are in the labor force (U.S. Bureau of the Census 1990, 385). While the popular literature uses such terms as "balancing" or "juggling" to describe the way in which working mothers structure their time, the scholarly literature talks about the "role strain" experienced by employed women with children and focuses on the stress created by the oppositional demands of work and family. Coser (1991) argues that the demands underlying work roles and family roles are different for men and for women and that these respective demands represent

From *Qualitative Sociology* 18, no. 4 (1995): 415–37. Reprinted by permission.

different, and contradictory, value systems. "Professional women are expected to be committed to their work 'just like men' at the same time that they are normatively required to give priority to their families" (Coser 1991, 114). Research on people's perceptions of mothers found that "employed mothers were seen as simultaneously less dedicated to their families and more dedicated to their careers, as well as more selfish and less sensitive to the needs of others" (Etaugh and Study 1989, 67). The inability to conceptualize *for women* the integration of a commitment to work and a commitment to family means that employed women with children are seen both as less committed to work and as less than fully committed mothers. Because the individual concepts that are fused in the term "working mother" encompass images of "worker" and "mother" that are defined in opposition to each other, "working mothers" face the dilemma of reconciling this conceptual incompatibility, both internally and in their presentation of self.

This chapter is based on a larger study of

how employed women with children construct themselves as "working mothers" (Garey 1993). The women I interviewed talk about their employment as an essential part of their lives and identities. Accomplishment, self-sufficiency, dignity, self-worth, and the notion of "doing something" are the concepts invoked by the working mothers I interviewed to explain the meaning of their employment. Numerous studies have documented the noneconomic rewards of employment cited by working mothers, from Mirra Komarovsky's study of 1950s blue-collar marriages to contemporary studies of women in both working-class and professional employment (Komarovsky 1967; Rollins 1985; Walker 1990; Zavella 1987). In this chapter, however, I focus on the way in which these employed women construct themselves as mothers.

Motherhood is historically and culturally constructued, and therefore variable. However, there were common themes that emerged repeatedly in the interviews. This similarity in expressed values about motherhood and parenting among working mothers is something that other studies have also found (Lamphere et al. 1993; Segura 1994; Walker 1990). These shared themes became signposts in my interviews to hegemonic cultural norms about motherhood. Women confront these cultural norms from varying social locations, and they respond by adopting, modifying, or reinterpreting them. In other words, people are "doing motherhood" in the same way that West and Zimmerman (1987) argue that people are "doing gender"— they are managing their conduct in interaction with dominant-culture conceptions of mother-appropriate attitudes and activities. Differences in resources, however, lead to differences in the strategies used to actualize or represent these norms (Garey 1993; Walker 1990).

The women hospital workers I interviewed used various strategies to integrate their identities as workers as workers and their identities as mothers into a construction of "working mother" that valorized their relation to work while preserving cultural norms about their role as mothers (Garey 1994). In this chapter, however, I am not comparing types of behavioral responses or types of identity constructions. I am taking a close look at *the process by which* one group, night-shift nurses, uses the night shift both to implement certain concrete actions associated with the work of mothering and to invoke particular symbols associated with the institution of motherhood.

Working the night shift allows employed women with children to construct a definition of "working mother" that preserves the dominant cultural ideal[1] of a "traditional" family form in which the mother is at home during the day. What I refer to as the cultural ideal of the *traditional* family form is the family form that Judith Stacey refers to as the modern family: "an intact nuclear household unit composed of a male breadwinner, his fulltime homemaker wife, and their dependent children" (Stacey 1990, 5). In historical terms, Stacy is correct; the prevalence of such families was historically recent, culturally specific, and short-lived. However, in the dominant culture and for the women I interviewed, this family form is conceptualized as the *traditional* family form. If not a common family form in *their modern world*, it is still an ideal by which they measure themselves. The term "traditional family form" best represents the concept that my informants were trying to convey.

Working the night shift can be seen as an attempt to reconcile both the structural and conceptual incompatibilities of being a "working mother." Although there are economic reasons for working a night shift,[2] I focus here on the *symbolic importance* of being a mother who is at home during the day. The importance of this dimension is highlighted by examining the sacrifice of sleep that my respondents are willing to make in their construction of themselves as "traditional" mothers. I argue that while working the night shift addresses some of these women's child care needs and provides a way for spouses or other family members to share work and family responsibilities, the women I interviewed are also using the night shift to deemphasize their employment status and to make more highly visible their identities as mothers. The night shift allows "working mothers" to *appear* to be "stay-at-home moms."

Method

In the years 1991–92, I conducted in-depth open-ended interviews with forty-two women hospital workers from two wards of a large private hospital in California; thirty-five of these women were mothers. I collected employment and family histories and asked respondents about issues relating to their jobs, their children, their daily schedules, child care, and future plans. In addition, I spent time observing hospital workers on the ward. While the hospital ward represents only one of the settings in which working mothers construct the meanings that frame their actions, it is the one setting that my interviewees share in common. By observing people in their work environment I was better able to contextualize the data from the interviews. My interviews with hospital workers invariably contained references by them to others with whom they worked. By interviewing people who share a work setting, conversation about their interactions with other workers and about the meaning given to the actions of oth-

ers is transformed from the level of individual interpretation into a network of meaning and interactions.

I selected a hospital site because hospital employment is typical of the kind of female-dominated occupations that account for most of women's employment in the United States.[3] The health service industry employs more women than any other U.S. service industry, and it is the largest area of female-dominated employment that is still growing (Bennett and Alexander 1987, 226). In the future, an even higher percentage of employed women will work in the health industry, and the overwhelming preponderance of women in the service sector of that industry will be maintained (U.S. Bureau of the Census 1990, 392, 389–391). A further reason for conducting research on hospital employees is that hospitals offer scheduling options that have been characteristic of women's labor force participation: shift work and part-time employment.

I interviewed women hospital workers from a variety of job categories (hospital administrators, registered nurses, nurses' aides, clerical workers, and janitorial service workers). Of the 35 women hospital workers who had children, 18 were registered nurses in nonsupervisory positions, 12 were in nonprofessional positions (2 nurses' aides, 6 clerical workers, and 4 janitorial service workers), and 5, of whom 3 were nursing directors, were in administrative positions. The ethnic and racial composition of this group reflects the ethnic and racial composition of the wards themselves, as well as the existing occupational segregation within the hospital. I interviewed 13 European-Americans, 13 African Americans, 5 Filipina first-generation immigrants, 3 Mexican Americans, one Chinese American, and one African Caribbean immigrant; of the women I interviewed, all of the administrators were European American and all of the janitorial service workers were African American. The nursing staff was more ethnically and racially diverse.

The selection of two wards provides a natural setting for ethnographic investigation. Explicit comparison between ethnic or racial groups was not the intention of this project, nor can that type of comparison be accomplished with this research design. The number of people interviewed is too small and the number of possibly relevant variables too large to make such comparison meaningful. In addition, the occupational segregation within the wards, reflected in the demographic profile of the interviewees, confounds race and class, a problem common in attempts at comparison between ethnic and racial groups (Marshall and Barnett 1990). Rather than making comparisons between ethnic or racial groups based on my interviews, I discuss the processes of self-definition occurring in a shared setting. Where appropriate, I draw on studies of work and family that address differences by race, ethnicity, and class.

The intention in this study was to discover the strategies that employed hospital workers with children use to construct themselves as working mothers. I therefore focused on work schedules and on resources as variable elements, and on the use of symbols and meanings as active management in the process of social construction. In the case of registered nurses, whose work setting, benefits, and salary are similar, differential resources outside of their jobs shape their abilities to actualize norms about motherhood. Marital status, spouse's occupation and income, and presence of children are the major differences between those nurses who worked full-time night shifts, those who worked full-time day shifts, and those who worked part-time schedules (Garey 1993).[4] In each group, women with children represent their reasons

for working their respective schedules in terms of the way those schedules successfully enable them to combine their employment with their motherhood.

This chapter draws on my interviews with registered nurses who work full-time fixed night-shift schedules.[5] Of the eighteen non-supervisory registered nurses with children, six worked the night shift; the others worked either full time on the day shift (six nurses)[6] or part-time on the day or evening shift (six nurses). My interviews with other hospital workers on the night shift, with hospital employees who had previously worked night shifts, and with day-shift registered nurses and nursing supervisors support my analysis of the way in which working the night shift enables these workers to maintain and reproduce a particular construction of motherhood.

The Night Shift as a Child Care Solution

In her research on shift work and dual-earner spouses with children, Harriet Presser found that non-day shifts were more common among couples with children under fourteen years of age than among couples with no children under age fourteen (1980 data) (Presser 1987, 108), and that "one-third (33.8 percent) of dual-earner couples with children under the age of six include at least one spouse who works a non-day shift" (1985 data) (Presser 1989, 530). In addition, Presser shows that there is a high positive correlation between non-day shifts and rates of child care performed by family members, including fathers (Presser 1988).[7] In the case of employed married mothers, fathers provide 19 percent of primary care for children under five years of age (1985 data) (Presser 1989, 529).

The husbands of the married night-shift nurses do a significant part of the child care, and, in most cases, it was they who got their children up and off to school or child care in the morning. However, while not intending to diminish the importance of fathers' contributions to the care of their children while their wives are working, it is nevertheless crucial to remember that most of this care occurs between 10:00 P.M. and 8:00 A.M. It does not occur during the hours children are doing their homework, going to after-school or weekend activities, having their dinner, taking their baths, being read to, or getting tucked in for the night. The nighttime care of children does not occur when children have appointments with doctors and dentists, during parent-teacher conferences, during friends' birthday parties, or when the stores are open so that one can buy school supplies, clothes, Halloween costumes, sports equipment, dancing shoes, and the present for the friend who is having the birthday party. When fathers care for children while their wives are working night shifts, most of the care occurs while the children, and the fathers, are sleeping.

This arrangement should not necessarily be construed as one in which fathers are trying to escape parenting work. There is a need for research on the care fathers provide for their children while mothers are at work as well as on the care fathers provide when both parents are home. Men's resistance to sharing the second shift has been documented (Hochschild 1989) and is clearly a major problem for employed women. Some women, however, may be reluctant to surrender symbolically key activities, especially those connected to their children and to their identities as mothers. In a study of how dual-earner couples talk about child care and housework, Scott Coltrane (1989) notes that "the routine care of home and children are seen to provide opportunities for women to express and reaffirm their gendered relation to men and to the world." In addition,

Coltrane found that fathers who perform activities normatively assigned to mothers often face negative reactions from male coworkers. Men may refuse to take on these responsibilities for the same reason that many women are reluctant to relinquish them: the performance of these activities is symbolically linked to constructions of gender.

The use of shift work by couples with young children is clearly a way of solving child care problems of availability, quality, and expense, but hospital nurses who choose the night shift do more than solve their child care problems. The women I interviewed are using the night shift to make their identities as mothers more highly visible. By working nights they actively construct themselves as mothers who are home during the day. The night shift allows these "working mothers" to appear to be "stay-at-home moms."

The Night Shift and Daily Routine

The night-shift nurses I interviewed work 8-hour shifts, which begin at 11:00 P.M. and end at 7:30 A.M. Many of these nurses live outside the city where the hospital is located and have commutes of up to an hour each way. Most of them reported getting home at about 8:30 in the morning. This schedule enables night-shift nurses to leave for work after their children are in bed for the night and to arrive back home after their children have left for school or day care. During the night, children have been with fathers or other relatives, and it is predominantly the fathers who get the children off to school in the morning. The night-shift schedule means that mothers avoid the rushed morning routine. Nurses who work day shifts, which begin at 7:30 A.M., have to get both themselves and their children up and out the door at a very early hour. The morning is not only rushed and tense but also the mother's work schedule and her children's needs and wants are brought into head-on collisions on a daily basis. Night-shift nurses, tiptoeing out after the children are asleep, avoid the conflicts of a frantic morning exit.

The choice of the night shift by many nurses illustrates the way in which one group of working mothers attempts to reconcile the contradictions and conflicts in both the concrete activities of their daily lives and in their images of themselves as mothers and as workers. The distinction between concrete activities and symbolic gestures is central to understanding the social construction of motherhood. However, it is sometimes difficult to perceive this distinction because of the taken-for-granted assumptions about what should be done for children and about who should do it. Working a night shift enables parents to attend a daytime function at their children's school without taking time off work—a concrete activity. This activity, however, may also act as a symbol that represents cultural meanings about the value of that activity and about the identity and worth of the person performing it. For example, *for mothers*, accompanying children on school field trips has a symbolic function, even though there may be practical reasons that a mother would want to go along. While the mother on the field trip may, for instance, be acting to keep her child safe, she is also, by her action, indicating that she is the kind of mother who acts to keep her child safe, or the kind of mother who is involved in her child's education, or the kind of mother who is not too busy to do her part to support school activities. The women I interviewed told me about their actions in order to show me their mother-ness. To explain who they are, they talk about what they do.

Being at home during the day enables mothers to do some things that otherwise would not be done or that could be done only with complex or expensive arrangements, such as chauffeuring children to dance lessons, sports training, scouts, or other extracurricular activities. It also enables them to *be mothers* by doing things that are, culturally, only appropriate to do because one is the parent: volunteering at their children's school, attending the school's spring pageant, going on field trips, being available if the school calls with a problem, or participating in preschool-age playgroups. Several day-shift workers told me that the play groups in their neighborhoods were restricted to children accompanied by their *mothers*; children accompanied by nannies, au pairs, or other child care workers were not welcome. Certain activities are seen as not only appropriate for mothers to do but also as less as appropriate for other family members, and as clearly inappropriate for nonfamily child care providers. While it is becoming more common for fathers to do some of these things, such as staying home with a child who is ill or meeting with a child's teacher, it is deemed unusual and less acceptable if mothers don't act in these ways. Performing mother-appropriate activities is similar to the concept of "family work" described by DeVault as work that is done within the family that "actually constitutes a social group as 'family' from day to day" (1991, 30). Similarly, mother-appropriate activities are not simply practices performed by women who have children, but are actions that, *in the doing*, constitute women with children *as mothers*.

Mothers who work the night shift are able to emulate nonemployed mothers in their availability to participate in children's school and extracurricular activities. One night-shift nurse told me that she prefers the night shift because

> I get [my twelve-year-old daughter] involved in things. So she's at karate and she's got the different dance things. So if I work nights, then she

can go and I can take her. But if I work daytime . . . she'd have to miss out because I wouldn't be here to take her. [a 53-year old African American nurse]

Because nurses at the hospital work every other weekend, regardless of shift, night-shift nurses avoid the problem of being unavailable to facilitate children's daytime activities on the weekends they work. Another night-shift nurse said:

If I see a field trip coming up I—you could say I'm a little protective—not overly so—but I like to be there, if they're going to go on a bus trip or something, I want to be one of the ones on the bus. . . . And that is one of the reasons I do like working nights. [a 34-year old Mexican American nurse]

Day-shift nurses told me that children's extracurricular activities are a difficult issue for them and are a point of contention between them and nonemployed mothers. A *Newsweek* article focusing on the antagonism between "at-home mothers" and "working mothers" noted that nonemployed mothers complain that "it's the stay-at-home moms who keep the schools going . . . They drive to soccer practice, chaperone class trips, [and] act as class mothers" (Darnton 1990, 66). Several respondents told me that they had experienced this attitude on the part of nonemployed mothers. Activities such as dancing lessons and sports become markers that indicate both how much one is providing for one's child and how a mother's work is not interferring with her children's activities or ability to participate. These activities are highly visible symbols of motherhood that are associated with nonemployed mothers. Mothers who perform these activities are therefore downplaying the incompatibilities between the structure of employment and cultural definitions of good mothering.

Constructing Motherhood

One way that people reconcile incompatibilities is through the construction of meaning (Berger and Luckmann 1966; Blumer 1969). If being a good mother is defined, in part, as performing certain activities or as behaving in certain ways, then the performance of those activities or the expression of that behavior by employed women serves to prove that their employment is not incompatible with their mothering. It also serves a symbolic function because the action embodies a value—it represents "good mothering." The night-shift workers that I interviewed structure their time so that they can do particular things with or for their children. They also structure their lives in ways that preserve certain symbols that are central to their definitions of motherhood.[8] The activities they engage in are symbolic as well as instrumental. Among my respondents, these symbolic activities include such things as being home when their children returned from school or accompanying their children on school field trips. The most salient symbol for the night-shift respondents was their location in the house during the daytime hours. Night-shift nurses talk about themselves as mothers in terms of these symbols, which do the work of constructing an image of the working mother that deemphasizes the points of conflict between being employed and being a mother at home.

Hospital nurses Janice Ho, Doris Chavez, and Julia Ginzburg[9] each have one child in elementary school and a child under five years old in some form of day dare. Their differences in ethnicity, age, and seniority at the hospital notwithstanding, their stated reasons for working the night shift are remarkably similar. Janice, a 30-year-old Filipina registered nurse, told me:

I was always working nights. Cause it's easier to work nights with my young children. I like to be home with them, even [if] I'm sleeping, I like to be, you know, around.

Doris, a 34-year-old Mexican American[10] registered nurse, immediately mentioned being home during the day in response to my request that she "tell me about working and having children." Doris replied,

> It's hard, real hard. I want my kids to go to college; we bought a house. I want them to have a house. And that's one of the reasons I work night shift. I feel more comfortable being at home in the daytime while they're—well, they go to day care. So my husband takes them to day care and then I get home in the morning and sleep. And I know that I'm home by the phone in case something happens to them.

For Doris, being available to her children means being by the telephone, at home, close to her children's school, in case the school needs to reach her. Julia Ginzburg, a 43-year-old Jewish American registered nurse, gave a similar response to my question about her reasons for working the night shift.

> For me, it allows—I mean—I'm available. There's always a parent at home. If there's anything that comes up; if the kid is sick, it's no big deal, I'm here. Like now, during the summer, when my son is finished with his program at noon he comes home. I'm here. He can handle himself around the house. My small one (one year old) I have in child care, but the big one (nine years old) comes home and can go and play with friends, he can go to the library himself, but—I'm here. Whereas, if I were working in the daytime, I wouldn't be comfortable with him coming home to an empty house. I don't want him to be—I don't feel like he's a latchkey kid. I'm here. I'm asleep! But I'm here. If something comes up, I'm available.

"I'm here," "I'm home," "I'm around," "I'm available" are striking refrains in two ways. First, they are coupled with the statement "I'm asleep." Second, for a large part of the time that these women are home their children are not. Notice that both Doris and Julia use the word "comfortable" to describe their reasons for wanting to be home during the daytime. Being at home during the day, evne if they are alseep and even if their children are at school or in child care, "fits" with their construction of motherhood. It not only enables them to respond instrumentally to daytime child-related needs and emergencies and to be home when children return from school but it also places them in the symbolically appropriate place for mothers: in the home. A look at how they each organize their daily schedule illustrates this.

Janice Ho gets home from the hospital at about 8:30 A.M. Her husband has already gotten their older child off to school, taken the baby to the neighbor who does child care for them, and left for work. Janice returns to an empty house and immediately goes to sleep. At 1:30 P.M., she wakes up, picks the baby up from the neighbor's house, and meets her son at the bus stop. She spends the next few hours feeding the children, playing with the baby, and helping her son with his homework. When her husband returns from work in the evening, Janice goes back to bed and gets a few more hours of sleep until it is time to wake up to get ready to leave the house at 10:00 P.M. for another night shift. The routine that Janice reports is in some ways an exception to the reported routines of the other night-shift nurses in that she goes back to bed after her husband returns from work. Her intended routine gives her more sleep than the other nurses I interviewed, and her husband does more of the care when she is home than do the husbands of the other night-shift nurses. However, my interview with Janice indicated that things were rarely routine in her household and that she averages far less sleep than claimed in her report of a "typical" day.

Except for her two days off each week, Janice reports spending about three hours a day with her children. The rest of the time they are either at school or child care, or she is sleeping. For Janice, working nights is not a way of spending more time with her children, since day-shift workers would have about as many child contact hours as Janice does. But, as Janice says, working nights allows her to "be around" during the day: "I like to be home with them, even [if] I'm sleeping, I like to be, you know, around."

Doris Chavez lives over an hour from the hospital and usually doesn't get home until 9:00 A.M. Her husband, who has a 2-hour commute to work, gets the children up at 5:00 A.M., leaves the house by 5:30 A.M. to drop them at the child care center, and then continues on his way to work. Doris's oldest child will then be bussed from the child care center to his elementary school. Unlike Janice, Doris doesn't immediately go to sleep when she gets home; she does some housework, starts dinner preparations, and unwinds a bit. She averages four hours of sleep on the days she works. She wakes about 3:00 P.M. to welcome her son home from school and goes to pick up her youngest child from the child care center. Doris spends the rest of the afternoon preparing dinner, helping her son with his homework, and caring for the children. When her husband comes home from work, they all have dinner together. She leaves the house at 9:30 P.M. to drive back to the hospital for another night shift.

Doris reports spending about twice as much contact time with her children as Janice but, for both of them, what is most salient is *which hours* they are home. As Doris said, "I know that I'm home by the phone in case something happens to them," and she adds,

But I'm usually home by 9 A.M., and I have been called [by the school] before . . . I get that straight with the teacher right off the bat. You know "I work nights, I'm home."

Doris lets her children's teachers know, and she emphasizes the importance that they know, that she is a mother at home during the day. In a discussion on "ideology and work in the experience of a single parent," Smith argues that the concept of "single parenthood" provides the school with a way of analyzing and connecting children's problems at school with their family situations. In addition, it provides a mother with a "procedure for analyzing her own work practices as a mother in terms of how their defects produce the child's problem in the school setting" (Smith 1987, 168). I would argue that the concept of "working mothers" is treated similarly. The night-shift nurses are consciously presenting themselves to the school as at-home mothers rather than as working mothers.

The work of making her presence at home *visible* to her children's teachers illuminates the symbolic nature of Doris's behavior. She, and the other night-shift nurses, are gesturing to themselves, to their children, and to relevant others that they are good mothers (Berger and Luckmann 1966, 150–151; Mead 1962). Doris is "more comfortable being at home in the daytime," even though she's home alone and the children are in school, because the night shift allows her to normalize her family life to look and feel more like the cultural ideal of a "traditional" family: a father who goes to work in the morning, a mother who is home during the day, who welcomes her children home from school, who has dinner on the table for her returning husband, and who tucks the children into bed at night.

Julia Ginzburg's schedule is similar to the others. When I interviewed Julia, she was trying to implement and maintain a healthier sleep schedule than had been the case for the previous three years. On her current schedule, she gets home by 9:00 A.M., after her husband has taken the children to school and to child care. She sleeps until about 3:00 P.M., when her 9-year-old son comes home from school. Although Julia is asleep when her son returns from school, the fact that she is in the house is important to her not only in terms of being physcially present in case of an emergency but also in terms of symbolizing to herself and others that her son does not return to an empty house.

Patricia Anderson, a 53-year-old African American registered nurse who works the night shift and has a 12-year-old daughter, expressed a similar sentiment when I asked her if working nights was her choice.

> I rather because—since I'm divorced . . . to make sure that no one ever has an excuse for saying "Well, my mommy wasn't home and I hit the streets."

There are two concerns being conveyed in these explanations: one is with the immediate safety of the child, and the second is with possible future problems that might be *said to be* caused by the mother's behavior. Patricia wants to be home during the day to keep her child out of trouble, and to be able to facilitate her supervised extracurricular activities, but she also wants to be home during the day so that any problems her child may have in the future will not be blamed retrospectively on the fact that "mommy wasn't home."

In Doris's, Julia's, and Patricia's narratives, there is an emphasis not only on the importance of being at home during the day but also on the importance of being *seen* as mothers who are home. This concern with accountability with respect to cultural norms of good mothering was expressed by many of the mothers I interviewed. The work of presenting oneself as an at-home mother underscores the social or interactional aspect of the construction of motherhood.

> Actions are often designed with an eye to their accountability, that is, how they might look and how they might be characterized. The notion of

accountability also encompasses those actions undertaken so that they are specifically unremarkable and thus not worthy of more than a passing remark, because they are seen to be in accord with culturally approved standards. (West and Zimmerman 1987, 136)

Doris emphasizes that her children's teachers know that she is home during the day and available to be called; Julia stresses that her son is not a "latchkey kid"; and Patricia says that she works nights in part so that no one can say she neglected her daughter because she was away at work during the day.

What explains this commonality of concern with being seen as "at-home moms?" It is not, in any case, a commonality of background. Doris is the daughter of Mexican immigrant working-class parents who both worked while Doris was growing up. Julia came from an upper-middle-class Jewish home; her father was a physician and her mother a homemaker. Patricia's parents were middle-class African Americans who both held professional positions. Janice immigrated to the United States from the Philippines with her parents after she graduated from college. What they all face, however, are similar hegemonic cultural norms about motherhood. From their different backgrounds, they are interacting with prevailing constructions of motherhood; they are not creating motherhood from scratch. What they have in common are constellations of resources that make night-shift work a sensible strategy for negotiating these norms in their constructions of themselves as mothers.

Constellations of resources include, among other things, educational, economic, and family support resources. Unlike the clerical workers and housekeepers at the hospital, the nurses possessed skills and credentials that were currently in demand and, therefore, they had some leverage in choice of shift and weekly number of work hours.[11] The nurses who chose the night shift had patterns of economic and family support resources that differentiated them from full-time day-shift and part-time nurses.[12] The night-shift nurses did not have the economic resources that would have enabled them to work a part-time schedule, which many said they would prefer to working full time. They were, however, able to draw on family resources for night-time child care. In most cases, this care was provided by husbands who worked day shifts. Julia and Patricia are the only night-shift nurses I interviewed who were not living with spouses or partners. Julia was, however, living with her husband when she began working nights, and it was her husband who provided the nighttime care for their children then and who continues to provide that care now that they are separated; Julia's husband comes to her house and spends the night on the nights that she works. Patricia relies on her adult son, who comes to her house on the nights that she works, and on her cousin, to whose house Patricia takes her daughter when her son isn't available.[13] Thus the necessity of working full time, the access to well-paying night-shift work, and the availability of nighttime spousal or family child care are constellations of resources that these women have in common.

We would expect, however, that these similar constellations are experienced differently by women in differing social locations. What it means, for example, to need to work fulltime will be different for Julia, whose parents have economic resources she can call on in an emergency, than for Patricia, who is estranged from her parents and has grown children who will turn to her in times of need. Similarly, we would expect the meaning and construction of motherhood to reflect differences in social location and experience (Cole 1986; Segura 1994). But such differences reflect overlapping distributions, not sharp categorical divisions.

We share some characteristics and not others with a variety of groups, and there is diversity within all groups. Women night-shift nurses, whether African American, Mexican American, European American, or immigrants, whether in their thirties, forties, or fifties, whether married or single, may represent a self-selected group who, in response to hegemonic cultural norms, are constructing motherhood, *in this instance*, along similar lines. They may have traveled different paths to this construction (Cole 1986), but they talk in remarkably similar ways about the way in which working the night shift enables them to be at-home mothers.

Denormalizing Sleep Norms

It might appear that the night-shift workers I interviewed have found the solution to the dilemma of the "working mother," but clearly this solution entails sacrifices in their occupational, marital, and personal lives. In terms of occupational disadvantages, night-shift nurses were more removed from the professional aspects of their positions than were either part-time or full-time day-shift nurses; they interacted far less with other health professionals (physicians, physical therapists, social workers) and did not feel that they were as likely to be promoted or to have opportunities for specialization while they remained on a night shift. Married night-shift nurses may have more "family time" with their children, but they have less "couple time" with their spouses, and they don't sleep with their spouses on the nights they work. Similar patterns were found by Hertz and Charlton (1989) in their study of the impact of shiftwork on the family life of couples in which the husband worked a rotating shift. The diminishment of "couple time" may contribute to the higher divorce rate among couples in which one spouse works a nonday shift (White and Keith 1990). However, while some respondents did express regret at not having more time with their husbands, the primary focus of their accounts was on shift work as a family strategy.

What night-shift nurses did mention, in every case and repeatedly, is the toll that is exacted from sleep. The attempt to normalize family life results in a denormalization of sleep (for example, when one sleeps, how much one sleeps, sleeping with one's spouse). All of the night-shift nurses I interviewed consider themselves to be sleep-deprived; and, in general, employed women with children report inadequate sleep and frequent fatigue (Hochschild 1989; Moen 1989, 47–51). But for night-shift nurses, the sacrifice of sleep and of sleep norms is built into the structure of their work and family lives. They report a schedule in which they get between four and five hours of sleep on the days following a night shift. They actually get less than this, as they admit when asked about any particular day.

When I arrived at Patricia Anderson's house for our scheduled interview at 3:00 P.M., she told me that she hadn't slept since she had gotten home from work that morning; she had been trying to match the color of her daughter's dance costume so that she could dye the skirt to match the headpiece. Patricia is directly giving up sleep in order to do somethimg that symbolizes, to herself and to others, that she is a good mother. What became clear in our conversation was that giving up sleep to perform such activities was not an unusual event. When Patricia gets home between 8:30 and 9:00 A.M. on Saturday mornings, she sleeps for about 30 to 45 minutes and then gets up to take her daughter to karate, and then to dance class. She tells me that when she's working at the hospital, "I go to the bathroom—there's no lounge—I put my head in my lap and I sleep for five minutes sometimes," and later she adds:

> Or sometimes I just drive and I get half way home and I just have to sit in the car and I go to sleep—I can't go any further. I just, my mind, it's like—brain is dead. You know, and the older I get, it seems like I'm having psychological problems. I'm just getting older and falling apart.

Julia Ginzburg, ten years younger than Patricia Anderson, talks about her sleep deprivation in similar terms:

> Until I took ten days off a month ago, I was burning the candle at both ends. I was getting out of work late . . . and I wouldn't get to bed until 11:00 [A.M.]. I was just—I was a mess! . . . About March I was really, God, I just had to have a break. . . . March I was about ready to have a nervous breakdown. I've never been like that but virtually ready to crack up, but I had to keep going because [my husband] wasn't going to be finished with school until [May]. . . . Finally I took ten days the end of June or something. Spent two days on my own and left the kids with him and the child care, you know made everything out so it would work of course. You know . . . I'd made all the plans, of course as we [women] do. And I just went up and visited my sister for two days without any kids and I came back and . . . got sleep. Slept and slept and slept and slept and slept and slept.

Janice Ho gets about five hours of sleep on the days following a night shift. At the age of 30, the youngest of the group, she feels she can manage on this much sleep, making up sleep on her days off. Janice, however, has a chronically ill sixteen-month-old baby, and things are seldom routine. I ask her if the night shift is tiring, and she tells me that

> sometimes it's tiring when I don't get sleep. Like when—like what happened yesterday. I got home in the morning and my husband told me [the baby] had a bad night; she was up most of the night coughing and she has her asthma attack, so

first thing in the morning when I got home I called her pulmonologist . . . and he said, "'Bring her over, I have to evaluate her.'" So meantime I didn't get any sleep at all and I had to bring her over [to the hospital,] so I was there by 9:00 in the morning . . . I got off work at 7:30, got home here by about 8:15, and I had to turn around and go back [to the hospital] by myself to bring [the baby . . . I didn't get any sleep at all until, gosh, until 4:30 [P.M.], till my husband came home. I was up for already twenty-four hours.

Doris reports getting about four hours of sleep on the days after she works a night shift. I ask her how it works to get that much sleep and she replies,

You know, I joke around and say "I'm only 34, but I feel like I'm 50" (laughs). Cause my body feels it. . . . I try to get about a half-hour nap— usually on the couch in front of the t.v., but it works—just that little bit really helps. I can't do it if the kids are up and running around "Mommy I need this." You know, and I say, "Go ask your daddy" (laughs). And so they do, and he's pretty good about that.

Angela Cordova, a 43-year-old Filipina registered nurse, is married and has two children, ages six and nine. She works the night shift and averages about four hours of sleep a day. Arriving home from work about 8:30 A.M., she goes to bed about 10:00 A.M. Her son is in kindergarten at the local school, and his schoolday ends at 11:00 A.M. Angela explains in a matter-of-fact manner:

I hired a lady to pick [my son] up. I just pay her a dollar, but I still have to wake up to get him in [the house] and that breaks my sleep already, and I try to go back to sleep but then you cannot really go to sleep because leaving a five-year-old alone (laughs)—you don't know what he's getting into.

Angela leaves to pick her daughter up from school at 2:00 P.M. and says that

after I get them and tell them to do their homework and all those things, and then I try to get some sleep,

but it doesn't work anymore. So almost every night I have only four hours of sleep every day.

I tell Angela that I don't think I would be able to function well on four hours of sleep, and she replies,

You know, that's what I thought, but (pause) I guess the sign that there is really God. Because I always, I say, "Look God, I can't do this anymore, so you have to give me the strength and the grace that I'll be able to take care of these people," and I regard my children as, they're entrusted to me, they're not mine. He just entrusted to me—And so with my patients. "Look, I'm just weak and you entrusted these people in my hands, I can't do it alone without you." That's all my daily prayer.

When I asked her what were the hardest parts of working and being a mother, Angela didn't mention lack of sleep; instead she said:

Oh, it's like you don't give your whole self as a mother, which I would like to do. I want to be a good, ideal mother, like (pause) everything is right for my children. Like the house is clean and everything; I just want to be that way, you know.

The night-shift nurses I interviewed are "denormalizing" sleep norms in order to absorb the contradictions of working away from home while trying to construct themselves as mothers who stay at home. Fatigue and lack of sleep notwithstanding, night-shift "working mother" nurses feel that they have made the best possible choice of work schedule given the circumstances of their lives: their need for income, their identity as workers, their nursing qualifications and skills, and their desire to be mothers in a very particular way.

Conclusion

One of the most powerful images in modern theatre is the door shutting as Nora Helmer, in Ibsen's *A Doll's House*, leaves her husband

and children. This image, rendered in an off-stage direction: "The sound of a door shutting is heard from below" (Ibsen 1958 [1879], 68), juxtaposes the physical boundary of the house with its symbolic importance in the definition of "family." Houses, the spaces within which homes are made, are important symbols in the construction of meanings about family. Ibsen represents the moment Nora leaves her family with the sound of a closing door, by which the audience knows that she has crossed the threshold and is outside the physical space of the house. By removing the woman from the house, definitions of home and family are called into question and must be reconstructed to account for or to conceal the fact of their missing central element.

Being at home during the day is related to concepts of both what a mother *does* and what a mother *is*, to both *doing* and *being*. To be at home during the day is to emulate nonemployed mothers, who are sometimes referred to as "full-time mothers." I borrow the term "full-time mothers" to point out that this term, used in popular discourse as synonymous with "nonemployed mothers," captures the idea that to be employed lessens the fullness or completeness of one's mothering. It is in response to this concept that the night-shift workers are constructing a "working mother" who is a "full-time mother" because she does what "full-time" (nonemployed) mothers do: she is at home during the day. Even if her husband and children are not at home, the woman *of* the house is the woman *in* the house.

Many dual-earner couples share the care of their children and solve the problem of child care by working different shifts (Hertz and Ferguson 1996). When it is the woman who works a night shift, the solution resolves more than the provision of child care. While the practicalities of providing child care are certainly a central issue for employed women with children, I found that when women

talked about child care they also revealed deeply rooted concerns about their identities as mothers.

Night-shift nurses do not deny the fact of their employment, but they do try to minimize the negative impact of their labor market participation on their ability to activate the symbols from which they construct definitions of themselves as mothers. Mothers who are employed at night simulate a "traditional" family form in which the mother is available to her children during the day, both as the person who performs symbolically invested acitivities, such as volunteering at her child's school, *and* as the person whose very being is symbolically invested—the woman in the house, the mother at home.

The night-shift nurses are working mothers who construct themselves as "stay-at-home moms" in three major ways: (1) they limit the visibility of their labor force participation to their children and in the public sphere of their children's lives; (2) they make themselves available to involve their children in symbolically invested extracurricular activities and available to involve themselves in their children's activities outside the home; and (3) they position themselves in the culturally appropriate place and time: at home, during the day. All three of these strategies work to highlight their visibility as mothers.

The women discussed in this chpater embrace the behaviorally outdated norm of the at-home mother, sacrificing and denormalizing their sleep in the process. Theirs is an individual solution, and one that has both individual and social costs. Looking at individual solutions can tell us something about the force of social norms and about what people feel they need. What are working mothers willing to sacrifice? What do they maintain in spite of difficulties? In terms of work and family policy, the night-shift solution speaks loudly about the concerns that these working mothers have about the shape and content of their mothering.

As sociologists, in order both to understand the situations of employed women with children and to inform policies that address the needs of families, the work of motherhood cannot be subsumed conceptually under the category of "child care." In such a conceptualization, care of children by someone other than the mother becomes the solution and corollary to mothers' participation in the labor force. While the availability of stable, quality child care is an absolute necessity, it does not address a crucial area of concern to the women I interviewed: the flexibility to themselves fulfill certain components of the work of mothering.

The women I interviewed want to *combine* employment and motherhood; but approaches that aim at enabling mothers to participate more fully in their spheres of employment *solely* by freeing them from child care responsibilities are unlikely to be successful. In addition to the provision of adequate child care, social and workplace policies must address the needs of families for flexible work schedules and for part-time work with benefits, security, and the possibility of advancement.

Many women are not looking for ways to mother less but are searching for work structures that will enable them to be employed and personally to implement practices that, in their symbolic universe, represent "good mothering." That women adopt the night shift and sacrifice sleep as a way of combining motherhood and employment is a testament to the force and tenacity of the cultural ideal of "the at-home mother" in an era of "working mothers."

NOTES

Acknowledgments: An earlier version of this chapter was presented at the American Sociological Association Annual Meeting, August 13–17, 1993, Miami Beach, Florida. Funds for this research were provided in part by the University of California and by the National Institute of Child Health and Human Development. I wish to thank Nancy Chodorow, Karla Hackstaff, Eugene Hammel, Arlie Hochschild, Kristin Luker, Harriet Presser, Laura Sanchez, Arlene Stein, and Eleanor Townsley for their helpful comments on earlier drafts of this chapter. I am particularly grateful to Lynn Davidman, Frances K. Goldscheider, Karen V. Hansen, and Nicholas Townsend for their constructive comments on later versions.

1. I use "dominant culture" to convey the idea of hegemony, which includes both concepts of "culture" and "ideology," and which encompasses both the expression of particular meanings and the embeddedness of those meanings in institutions (Ortner 1990).

2. There are two main economic reasons for working a night shift. Child care costs are reduced if other family members are providing some of the child care, and night-shift nurses receive a pay differential for working nights. Economic advantages, however, are part of a matrix of reasons for choosing a night shift, and are not the sole determining factor. I found that the nurses I interviewed, across shifts, explained their choice of shift and the weekly number of hours they worked in terms of their relationship to the profession, their children's needs, their definition of successful mothering, their husbands' schedule, and hospital policies, as well as their economic needs. Several nurses reported turning down opportunities for promotion, and higher pay, if they felt it meant spending more time at the hospital or being responsible to the hospital during their hours at home.

3. In 1988, 68 percent of employed women in the United States were in nonsupervisory positions in sales, services, and secretarial occupations. The 25 percent of employed women in the category of managerial and professional occuaptions were concentrated in female-dominated professional occupations such as elementary and secondary teaching and nondiagnostic health care, the category that includes registered nurses (U.S. Bureau of the Census 1990, 389–391).

4. Of the seven hospital workers who did not have children, all were registered nurses, of whom two were nursing directors, a very prestigious and demanding position within the hospital. All seven of these nurses worked a full-time day shift.

5. Almost all of the hospital workers who work a fixed full-time night-shift schedule are registered nurses; very few people in other occupational categories within the hospital work a night shift.

6. Four of these women worked 12-hour shifts, a full-time schedule in which they work only three days a week. If child care needs can be met, this schedule is a strategy which mothers use to increase the number of days they are at home.

7. Data from the 1984 Youth Cohort (ages 19–26) of the National Longitudinal Survey of Labor Market Experience, indicates that 28 percent of fathers provide primary child care and 40.3 percent of fathers provide primary or secondary child care when their wives work full-time, fixed non-day shifts (Presser 1988, 139). Secondary child care is child care by someone who is not the principal child care provider, measured in hours. A school or child care center may therefore be the primary child care provider and the father the secondary child care provider during the mother's hours of employment.

8. They have also constructed definitions of themselves as nurses and as workers (Garey 1993), but in this chapter I am not treating the night-shift nurses' construction of meaning around employment and professions. Here, their conditions of employment and their occupation as nurses are the backdrop against which I explore their construction of motherhood.

9. I have used fictitious names for all of the women I interviewed.

10. Both of Doris's parents were born in Mexico; "Mexican American" was her self-described ethnic designation. Respondents of Mexican heritage referred to themselves either as "Mexican American" or as "Chicana."

11. A study concerned with finding ways to increase nurses' labor force participation found a negative relationship between presence in the home of children under six years of age and the number of hours worked by registered nurses, and suggests that hospitals offer "subsidized child care facilities and flexibility in scheduling" to "increase the number of hours a nurse is willing and able to engage in market activities" (Bahrami 1988).

12. The nurses who worked part-time day and evening shifts were all married, and their husbands all had college degrees and worked in professional or managerial positions. This pattern is consistent with Moen's (1985) study of women's labor force activity, which found that, over a five-year period, women who were continuously employed in part-time jobs were likely to have husbands in professional or managerial occupations and to have the husbands with the highest salaries. Most of the night-shift nurses I interviewed were married, but their husbands were not employed in the professions and had lower-paying and less secure jobs than the husbands of the part-time nurses. In addition, wives' full-time employment at the hospital often provided the medical insurance coverage and other benefits the family needed.

13. Without a spouse or partner to provide night-time child care. Patricia reaches out to other family members. Collins (1990) states that in the African American community, grandmothers, sisters, aunts, cousins, or fictive kin (Stack 1974) help biological mothers care for their children. I found the reliance on kin for help in caring for children to be common among the African American hospital workers I interviewed; however, I did not find this type of reliance on kin to be restricted to African Americans (Garey 1993). What distinguishes the involvement of kin in caring for children within the African American community, and among the women I interviewed, is the history and pattern of such networks (Collins 1990, 119–123). Shared child care was something they had experienced growing up, used with their own children, and provided for others; there was a matter-of-factness in their telling of these arrangements. The European-American hospital workers I interviewed did not share this history or discourse, even though many of them relied on family members other than husbands for child care.

REFERENCES

Bahrami, B. (1988). Hours of Work Offered by Nurses. *Social Science Journal* 25:325–335.

Bennett, S. K., and L. B. Alexander (1987). The

Mythology of Part-time Work: Empirical Evidence from a Study of Working Mothers. In L. Beneria and C. R. Stimpson (Eds.), *Women, Households, and the Economy* (pp. 225–41). New Brunswick, N.J.: Rutgers University Press.

Berger, P. L., and T. Luckmann (1966). *The Social Construction of Reality*. Garden City, New York: Doubleday.

Blumer, H. (1969). *Symbolic Interactionism: Perspective and Method*. Englewood Cliffs, N.J.: Prentice-Hall.

Collier, J., M. Z. Rosaldo, and S. Yanagisako. (1982). Is There a Family? New Anthropological Views. In B. Thorne and M. Yalom (Eds). *Rethinking the Family: Some Feminist Questions* (pp. 25–39). New York: Longman.

Cole, J. B. (1986). Commonalities and Differences. In *All American Women: Lines That Divide, Ties That Bind* (pp. 1–30). New York: Free Press.

Collins, P. H. (1990). *Black Feminist Thought: Knowledge, Consciousness, and the Politics of Empowerment*. Boston: Unwin-Hyman.

Coltrane, S. (1989). Household Labor and the Routine Production of Gender. *Social Problems* 36: 473–490. (Chapter 56, this volume.)

Coser, R. L. (1991). *In Defense of Modernity: Role Complexity and Individual Autonomy*. Stanford: Stanford University Press.

Darnton, N. (1990). Mommy vs. Mommy. *Newsweek*, June 4, 64–7.

DeVault, M. L. (1991). *Feeding the Family: The Social Organization of Caring as Gendered Work*. Chicago: University of Chicago Press.

Etaugh, C., and G. G. Study (1989). Perceptions of Mothers: Effects of Employment Status, Marital Status, and Age of Child. *Sex Roles* 20:59–70.

Garey, A. I. (1993). Constructing Identities as Working Mothers: Time, Space, and Family in a Study of Women Hospital Workers. Ph.D. diss., University of California, Berkeley.

———. (1994). Employment, Motherhood, and the Concept of "Career": Resolving Conflicting Vocabularies of Motive. Paper presented at the Annual Meetings of the American Sociological Association, 5–9 August.

Gerson, K. (1985). *Hard Choices: How Women Decide About Work, Career, and Motherhood*. Berkeley: University of California Press.

Hertz, R., and J. Charlton (1989). Making Family Under a Shiftwork Schedule: Air Force Security Guards, and Their Wives. *Social Problems* 36:491–507.

Hertz, R., and F. Ferguson (1996). Childcare Choices and Constraints in the United States: Social Class, Race and the Influence of Family Views. *Journal of Comparative Family Studies* 27:249–80.

Hochschild, A. (1989). *The Second Shift: Working Parents and the Revolution at Home*. New York: Viking.

Ibsen, H. (1958 [1879]). A Doll's House. In R. F. Sharp (trans.), *Four Great Plays by Ibsen*. New York: Bantam.

Komarovsky, M. (1967 [1962]). *Blue-Collar Marriage*. New York: Vintage Books.

Lamphere, L., P. Zavella, F. Gonzales, with P. B. Evans (1993). *Sunbelt Working Mothers: Reconciling Family and Factory*. Ithaca, N.Y.: Cornell University Press.

Marshall, N. L., and R. Barnett (1990). Race and Class in the Intersection of Work and Family Among Women Employed in the Service Sector. Wellesley College, *Working Paper #208*.

Mead, George H. (1962). *Mind, Self, and Society: From the Standpoint of a Social Behaviorist*, edited by Charles W. Morris. Chicago: University of Chicago Press.

Moen, P. (1985). Continuities and Discontinuities in Women's Labor Force Activity. In G. H. Elder, Jr. (Ed.), *Life Course Dynamics: Trajectories and Transitions, 1968–1980* (pp. 113–155). Ithaca: Cornell University Press.

———. (1989). *Working Parents: Transformations in Gender Roles and Public Policies in Sweden*. Madison: University of Wisconsin Press.

———. (1992). *Women's Two Roles: A Contemporary Dilemma*. New York: Auburn House.

Ortner, S. B. (1990). Gender Hegemonies. *Cultural Critique* 14:35–80.

Presser, H. B. (1987). Work Shifts of Full-Time Dual-Earner Couples: Patterns and Contrasts by Sex of Spouse. *Demography* 24:99–112.

———. (1988). Shift Work and Child Care among Young Dual-Earner American Parents. *Journal of Marriage and the Family* 50:133–148.

———. (1989). Can We Make Time for Children?

The Economy, Work Schedules, and Child Care. *Demography* 26:523–543.

Rollins, J. (1985). *Between Women: Domestics and Their Employers*. Philadelphia: Temple University Press.

Segura, D. A. (1994). Working at Motherhood: Chicana and Mexican Immigrant Mothers and Employment. In E. N. Glenn, G. Chang and L. R. Forcey (Eds.), *Mothering: Ideology, Experience, and Agency* (pp. 211–233). New York: Routledge.

Smith, D. E. (1987). *The Everyday World as Problematic: A Feminist Sociology*. Boston: Northeastern University Press.

Stacey, J. (1990). *Brave New Families*. New York: Basic Books.

Stack, C. B. (1974). *All Our Kin: Strategies for Sur-vival in a Black Community*. New York: Harper & Row.

U.S. Bureau of the Census (1990). *Statistical Abstract of the United States: 1990*. Washington, D.C.: U.S.G.P.O.

Walker, K. (1990): Class, Work, and Family in Women's Lives. *Qualitative Sociology* 13:297–320.

West, C., and D. Zimmerman (1987). Doing Gender. *Gender & Society* 1:125–151.

White, L., and B. Keith (1990). The Effect of Shift Work on the Quality and Stability of Marital Relations. *Journal of Marriage and the Family* 52:453–462.

Zavella, P. (1987). *Women's Work and Chicano Families: Cannery Workers of the Santa Clara Valley*. Ithaca, N.Y.: Cornell University Press.

Chapter 52

Working at Motherhood: Chicana and Mexican Immigrant Mothers and Employment

DENISE A. SEGURA

In North American society, women are expected to bear and assume primary responsibility for raising their children. This socially constructed form of motherhood encourages women to stay at home during their children's early or formative years and asserts activities that take married mothers out of the home (for instance, paid employment) are less important or "secondary" to their domestic duties.[1] Motherhood as a social construction rests on the ideological position that women's biological abilities to bear and suckle children are "natural," and therefore fundamental to women's "fulfillment." This position, however, fails to appreciate that motherhood is a culturally formed structure whose meanings can vary and are subject to change.

Despite the ideological impetus to mother at home, over half of all women with children

From Evelyn Nakano Glenn, Grace Chang, and Frida Rennie Forcey, eds., *Mothering: Ideology, Experience, and Agency* (New York and London: Routledge, 1994). Reprinted by permission.

work for wages.[2] The growing incongruence between social ideology and individual behaviors has prompted some researchers to suggest that traditional gender role expectations are changing (for example, greater acceptance of women working outside the home).[3] The profuse literature on the "ambivalence" and "guilt" employed mothers often feel when they work outside the home, however, reminds us that changes in expectations are neither absolute nor uncontested.

Some analysts argue that the ambivalence felt by many employed mothers stems from their discomfort in deviating from a socially constructed "idealized mother," who stays home to care for her family. This image of motherhood, popularized in the media, schoolbooks, and public policy, implies that the family and the economy constitute two separate spheres, private and public. However, the notion of a private-public dichotomy largely rests on the experiences of white, leisured women and lacks immediate relevance to less privileged women (for instance, immigrant women, women of color), who have historically been important economic actors both inside and outside the home.[4] The view that the relationship between motherhood and employment varies by class, race, and/or culture raises several important questions. Do the ideology of motherhood and the "ambivalence" of employed mothers depicted within American sociology and feminist scholarship pertain to women of Mexican descent in the United States? Among these women, what is the relation between the ideological constructions of motherhood and employment? Is motherhood mutually exclusive from employment among Mexican-heritage women from different social locations?

In this chapter I explore these questions using qualitative data gathered from thirty women of Mexican descent in the United States—both native-born Chicanas (including two Mexico-born women raised since preschool years in the United States) and resident immigrant Mexicanas.[5] I illustrate that notions of motherhood for Chicanas and Mexicanas are embedded in different ideological constructs operating within two systems of patriarchy. Contrary to the expectations of acculturation models, I find that Mexicanas frame motherhood in ways that foster a more consistent labor market presence than do Chicanas. I argue that this distinction—typically bypassed in the sociological literature on motherhood, women and work, or Chicano Studies—is rooted in their dissimilar social locations—that is, the "social spaces" they engage within the social structure created by the intersection of class, race, gender, and culture.[6]

I propose that Mexicanas, raised in a world where economic and household work often merged, do not dichotomize social life into public and private spheres, but appear to view employment as one workable domain of motherhood. Hence, the more recent the time of emigration, the less ambivalence Mexicanas

express regarding employment. Chicanas, on the other hand, raised in a society that celebrates the expressive functions of the family and obscures its productive economic functions, express higher adherence to the ideology of stay-at-home motherhood, and correspondingly more ambivalence toward full-time employment—even when they work.

These differences between Mexicanas and Chicanas challenge current research on Mexican-origin women that treats them as a single analytic category (for instance, "Hispanic") as well as research on contemporary views of motherhood that fails to appreciate diversity among women. My examination of the intersection of motherhood and employment among Mexican immigrant women also reinforces emerging research focusing on women's own economic and social motivations to emigrate to the United States (rather than the behest of husbands and/or fathers).[7]

My analysis begins with a brief review of relevant research on the relationship between motherhood and employment. Then I explore this relationship in greater detail, using in-depth interview data. I conclude by discussing the need to recast current conceptualizations of the dilemma between motherhood and employment to reflect women's different social locations.

Theoretical Concerns

The theoretical concerns that inform this research on Chicana/Mexicana employment integrate feminist analyses of the hegemonic power of patriarchy over work and motherhood with a critique of rational choice models and other models that overemphasize modernity and acculturation. In much of the literature on women and work, familial roles tend to be portrayed as important constraints on both women's labor market entry and mobility. Differences among women related to immigrant status, however, challenge this view.

Within rational choice models, motherhood represents a prominent social force behind women's job decisions. Becker and Polachek, for example, argue that women's "preference" to mother is maximized in jobs that exact fewer penalties for interrupted employment, such as part-time, seasonal, or clerical work.[8] According to this view, women's pursuit of their rational self-interest reinforces their occupational segregation within low-paying jobs (for example, clerical work) and underrepresentation in higher-paying, male-dominated jobs that typically require significant employer investments (for example, specialized training). Employers may be reluctant to "invest" in or train women workers who, they perceive, may leave a job at any time for familial reasons.[9] This perspective views motherhood as a major impediment to employment and mobility. But it fails to consider that the organization of production had developed in ways that make motherhood an impediment. Many feminist scholars view this particular development as consistent with the hegemonic power of patriarchy.

Distinct from rational choice models, feminist scholarship directs attention away from individual preferences to consider how patriarchy (male domination/female subordination) shapes the organization of production resulting in the economic, political, and social subordination of women to men.[10] While many economists fail to consider the power of ideological constructs such as "family" and "motherhood" in shaping behavior among women, employers, and the organization of production itself, many feminist scholars focus on these power dynamics.

Within feminist analyses, motherhood as an ideology obscures and legitimizes women's social subordination because it conceals particular interests within the rubric of a universal prerogative (reproduction). The social construction of motherhood serves the interest of capital by providing essential childbearing, child care, and housework at a minimal cost to the state, and sustains women as a potential reservoir of labor power, or a "reserve army of labor."[11] The strength of the ideology of motherhood is such that women continue to try to reconcile the "competing urgencies"[12] of motherhood and employment despite the lack of supportive structures at work or within the family.

Because employers view women as mothers (or future mothers), women encounter discrimination in job entry and advancement. Because women are viewed as mothers, they also work a "second shift" at home.[13] The conflict between market work and family work has caused considerable ambivalence within women. Berg, for example, notes that one of the dominant themes in analyzing women and work is the "guilt" of employed mothers based on "espousing something different" from their own mothers.[14]

The notion Berg describes of "conflict" or "guilt" rests on several suppositions. The first assumption is that motherhood is a unilaterally oppressive state; the second, that employed mothers feel guilt; and the third, that today's employed mothers do not have working mothers (which partially explains their "guilt feelings"). Inasmuch as large numbers of working-class, immigrant, and racial ethnic women have long traditions of working in the formal and informal economic sectors, such assumptions are suspect.

Research on women of Mexican descent and employment indicates their labor force participation is lower than that of other women when they have young children.[15] Moreover, Chicanas and Mexicanas are occupationally segregated in the lowest-paying of female-dominated jobs.[16] Explanations for their unique employment situation range from analyses of labor market structures and employer discrimination[17] to deficient individual characteristics (for instance, education, job skills)[18] and cultural differences.[19]

Analyses of Chicana/Mexicana employment that utilize a cultural framework typically explain the women's lower labor force participation, higher fertility, lower levels of education, and higher levels of unemployment as part of an ethnic or cultural tradition.[20] That is, as this line of argument goes, Chicano/Mexican culture emphasizes a strong allegiance to an idealized form of motherhood and a patriarchal ideology that frowns upon working wives and mothers and does not encourage girls to pursue higher education or employment options. These attitudes are supposed to vary by generation, with immigrant women (from Mexico) holding the most conservative attitudes.[21]

There are two major flaws in the research on Chicana/Mexicana employment, however. First, inconsistency in distinguishing between native-born and resident immigrant women characterizes much of this literature. Second, overreliance on linear acculturation persists. Both procedures imply either that Chicanas and Mexicanas are very similar, or that they lie on a sort of "cultural continuum," with Mexican immigrants at one end holding more conservative behaviors and attitudes grounded in traditional (often rural) Mexican culture, and U.S.-born Chicanos holding an amalgamation of cultural traditions from Mexico and the United States.[22] In terms of motherhood and employment, therefore, Mexicanas should have more "traditional" ideas about motherhood than U.S.-born Chicanas. Since the traditional ideology of motherhood typically refers to women staying home to "mother" children rather than going outside the home

to work, Mexicanas theoretically should not be as willing to work as Chicanas or North American women in general—unless there is severe economic need. This formulation, while logical, reflects an underlying emphasis on modernity—or the view that "traditional" Mexican culture lags behind North American culture in developing behaviors and attitudes conducive to participating fully in modern society.[23] Inasmuch as conventional North American views of motherhood typically idealize labor market exit to care for children, embracing this prototype may be more conducive to maintaining patriarchal privilege (female economic subordination to men) than facilitating economic progress generally. In this sense, conceptualizations of motherhood that affirm its economic character may be better accommodating to women's market participation in the United States.

The following section discusses the distinct views of motherhood articulated by Chicanas and Mexicanas and their impact on employment attitudes and behaviors. In contrast to the notion that exposure to North American values enhances women's incentives to work, proportionately more Chicanas than Mexicanas express ambivalence toward paid employment when they have children at home. I analyze these differences among a selected sample of clerical, service, and operative workers.

Method and Sample

This chapter is based on in-depth interviews with thirty Mexican origin women—thirteen Chicanas and seventeen Mexicanas—who had participated in the 1978 to 1979 or 1980 to 1981 cohorts of an adult education and employment training program in the greater San Francisco Bay area.[24] All thirty respondents had been involved in a conjugal relationship (either legal marriage or informal cohabitation with a male partner) at some point in their lives before I interviewed them in 1985 and had at least one child under eighteen years of age. At the time of their interviews, six Chicanas and fourteen Mexicans were married; seven Chicanas and three Mexicanas were single parents.

On the average, the married Chicanas have 1.2 children at home; the Mexicanas report 3.5 children. Both Chicana and Mexicana single mothers average 1.6 children. The children of the Chicanas tend to be preschool age or in elementary school. The children of the Mexicanas exhibit a greater age range (from infant to late adolescence), reflecting Mexicanas earlier marriages and slightly older average age.

With respect to other relevant characteristics, all but two Mexicanas and five Chicanas had either a high school diploma or its equivalent (GED). The average age was 27.4 years for the Chicanas and 33 years for the Mexicanas.[25] Upon leaving the employment training program, all the women secured employment. At the time of their interviews, about half of the Chicanas (n = 7); and three-fourths of the Mexicanas were employed (n = 12). Only two out of the seven (28 percent) employed Chicanas worked full-time (35 or more hours per week) whereas nine out of the twelve (75 percent) employed Mexicanas worked full-time. Most of the Chicanas found clerical or service jobs (for example, teacher assistants); most of the Mexicanas labored in operative jobs or in the service sector (for example, hotel maids), with a small minority employed as clerical workers.

I gathered in-depth life and work histories from the women to ascertain

1. what factors motivated them to enter, exit, and stay employed in their specific occupations;

2. whether familial roles or ideology influenced their employment consistency; and
3. whether other barriers limited their job attachment and mobility.

My examination of the relationship between motherhood and employment forms part of a larger study of labor market stratification and occupational mobility among Chicana and Mexican immigrant women.

Motherhood and Employment

Nearly all of the respondents, both Chicana and Mexicana, employed and nonemployed, speak of motherhood as their most important social role. They differ sharply in their employment behaviors and views regarding the relationship between motherhood and market work. The women in this study fall into four major groups. The first group consists of five *Involuntary Nonemployed Mothers* who are not employed but care full time for their children. All of these women want to be employed at least part-time. They either cannot secure the job they want and/or they feel pressured to be at home mothering full-time.

The second group consist of six *Voluntary Nonemployed Mothers* who are not employed but remain out of the labor force by *choice*. They feel committed to staying at home to care for preschool and/or elementary school age children.

The third category, *Ambivalent Employed Mothers,* includes eleven employed women. They have either preschool or elementary school age children. Women in this group believe that employment interferes with motherhood and feel "guilty" when they work outside the home. Despite these feelings, they are employed at least part-time.

The fourth group, *Nomambivalent Employed Mothers* includes eight employed women. What distinguishes these women from the previous group is their view that employment and motherhood seem compatible social dynamics, irrespective of the age of their children. All eight women are Mexicanas. Some of these women believe employment could be problematic, however, *if* a family member could not care for their children or be at home for the children when they arrived from school.

Chicanas tend to fall in the second and third categories, whereas Mexicanas predominate in the first and fourth groups. Three reasons emerged as critical in explaining this difference:

1. the economic situations of their families;
2. labor market structure (four-fifths of the nonemployed Mexicanas were involuntarily unemployed); and
3. women's conceptualizations of motherhood, in particular, their expressed *need* to mother

Age of the women and number of children did not fall into any discernible pattern, therefore I did not engage these factors in depth within my analysis.

First, I consider the situation of the *Voluntary Nonemployed Mothers,* including three married Chicanas, one single-parent Mexicana, and one single-parent Chicana. All but one woman exited the labor market involuntarily (for reasons such as layoffs or disability). All five women remain out of the labor force by choice. Among them, the expressed need to mother appears strong—overriding all other concerns. They view motherhood as mutually exclusive from employment. Lydia, a married Chicana with a small toddler, articulates this perspective:

> Right now, since we've had the baby, I feel, well he [her husband] feels the same way, that I want to spend this time with her and watch her grow

up. See, because when I was small my grandmother raised me so I felt this *loss* [her emphasis] when my grandmother died. And I've never gotten that *real love*, that mother love from my mother. We have a friendship, but we don't have that "motherly love." I want my daughter to know that I'm here, especially at her age, it's very important for them to know that when they cry that mama's there. Even if it's not a painful cry, it's still important for them to know that mommy's there. She's my number one—she's all my attention . . . so working-wise, it's up to [her husband] right now.

Susana, a Chicana single parent with a five-year-old child said:

> I'm the type of person that has always wanted to have a family. I think it was more like I didn't have a family-type home when I was growing up. I didn't have a mother and a father and the kids all together in the same household all happy. I didn't have that. And that's what I want more than anything! I want to be different from my mother, who has worked hard and is successful in her job. I don't want to be successful in the same way.

Lydia, Susana, and the other voluntarily unemployed Chicanas adamantly assert that motherhood requires staying home with their children. Susana said, "A good mother is there for her children all the time when they are little and when they come home from school." All the Chicanas in this category believe that motherhood means staying home with children—even if it means going on welfare (AFDC). This finding is similar to other accounts of working-class women.[26]

The sense shared among this group of women that motherhood and employment are irreconcilable, especially when children are of preschool age, is related to their social locations. A small minority of the Chicanas had been raised by nonemployed mothers (n = 3). They feel they should stay at home with their children as long as it's economically feasible.

Most of the Chicanas, however, resemble Lydia and Susana, who had been raised by employed mothers. Although these women recognize that their mothers had worked out of economic need, they believe they did not receive sufficient love and care from their mothers. Throughout their interviews, this group of Chicanas expressed hostility and resentment against their employed mothers for leaving them with other caretakers. These feelings contribute to their decisions to stay at home with their children, and/or their sense of "guilt" when they are employed. Their hostility and guilt defies psychoanalytic theories that speculate that the cycle of gender construction locking women into "exclusive mothering" roles can be broken if the primary caretaker (the mother) undertakes more diverse roles.[27] Rather, Chicanas appear to value current conceptionalizations of motherhood that prioritize the expressive work of the mother as distinct from her economic activities.

This group of Chicanas seems to be pursuing the social construction of motherhood that is idealized within their ethnic community, their churches, and society at large.[28] Among Chicanos and Mexicanos the image of *la madre* as self-sacrificing and holy is a powerful standard against which women often compare themselves.[29] The Chicana informants also seem to accept the notion that women's primary duty is to provide for the emotional welfare of the children and that economic activities which take them outside the home are secondary. These women's desires to enact the socially constructed motherhood ideal was further strengthened by their conviction that many of their current problems (for instance, low levels of education, feelings of inadequacy, single parenthood) are related to growing up in families that did not conform to the stay-at-home mother/father-as-provider configuration. Their evaluation of the close relationship between motherhood and economic or emo-

tional well-being of offspring parallels popular emphasis on the primacy of individual efforts and the family environment to emotional vigor and achievement.[30]

Informants in this group speak to a complex dimension of mothering and gender construction in the Chicano/Mexicano communities. These women reject their employed mothers' organization of family life. As children, most had been cared for by other family members and now feel closer to their grandmothers or other female relatives than to their own biological mothers. This causes them considerable pain—pain they want to spare their own children. Many, like Susana, do not want to be "successful" in the tradition of their own employed mothers. Insofar as "success" means leaving their children with other caretakers, it contradicts their conceptualization of motherhood. Rather, they frame "success" in more affective terms: having children who are happy and doing well in school. This does not suggest that Chicanas disagree with the notion that having a good job or a lucrative career denotes "success." They simply feel that successful careers could and should be deferred until their children are older (for instance, in the upper grades of elementary school) and doing well academically and emotionally.

Only one married Mexicana, Belen, articulated views similar to those of the Chicanas. Belen left the labor market in 1979 to give birth and to care for her newborn child. It is important to note that she has a gainfully employed husband who does not believe mothers should work outside the home. Belen, who has two children and was expecting a third when I interviewed her, said,

> I wanted to work or go back to school after having my first son, but my husband didn't want me to. He said, "No one can take care of your child the way you can." He did not want me to work. And I did not feel right having someone

else care for my son. So I decided to wait until my children were older.

Belens' words underscore an important dynamic that impacted on both Mexicana and Chicana conceptualizations of motherhood: spousal employment and private patriarchy. Specifically, husbands working in full-time, year-round jobs, with earnings greater than those of their wives, tended to pressure women to mother full-time. Women who succumb to this pressure become economically dependent on their husbands and reaffirm male authority in the organization of the family. These particular women tend to consider motherhood and employment in similar ways. This suggests that the form the social construction of motherhood takes involves women's economic relationship to men as well as length of time in the United States.

Four Mexicanas and one Chicana were involuntarily nonemployed. They had been laid off from their jobs or were on temporary disability leave. Three women (two Mexicanas/one Chicana) were seeking employment; the other two were in the last stages of pregnancy but intended to look for a job as soon as possible after their child's birth. All five women reported feeling "good" about being home with their children, but wanted to rejoin the labor force as soon as possible. Ideologically, these women view motherhood and employment as reconcilable social dynamics. As Isabel, an unemployed production worker, married with eight children, said:

> I believe that women always work more. We who are mothers work to maintain the family by working outside, but also inside the house caring for the children.

Isabel voiced a sentiment held by all of the informants—that women work hard at motherhood. Since emigrating to the United States about a decade ago, Isabel had been employed nearly continuously, with only short leaves for childbearing. Isabel and nearly all of the Mexicanas described growing up in environments where women, men, and children were important economic actors. In this regard they are similar to the *Nonambivalent Employed Mothers*—all of whom are also Mexicanas. They tended not to dichotomize social life in the same way as the *Voluntary Nonemployed Chicanas* and *Ambivalent Employed* informants.

Although all of the Chicanas interviewed believe that staying home best fulfills their mother roles, slightly fewer than half actually stay out of the labor market to care for their young children. The rest of the Chicanas are employed and struggling to reconcile motherhood with employment. I refer to these women as *Ambivalent Employed Mothers*. They express guilt about working and assert they *would not work* if they did not have to for economic reasons. Seven of these women are Chicanas; four are Mexicanas.

To try to alleviate their guilt and help meet their families' economic goals, most of these Chicanas work in part-time jobs. This option permits them to be home when their children arrive from school. Despite this, they feel guilty and unhappy about working. As Jenny, a married Chicana with two children, ages two and four, who is employed part-time, said,

> Sure, I feel guilty. I *should* [her emphasis] be with them [her children] while they're little. He [her husband] really feels that I should be with my kids all the time. And it's true.

Despite their guilt, most of the women in this group remain employed because their jobs offer them the means to provide for family economic betterment—a goal that transcends staying home with their children. However, these women's utilization of economic rationales for working sometimes served as a smoke screen for individualistic desires to "do something outside the home" and to establish a degree of autonomy. Several of the women, for example, stated that they enjoyed having their "own money." When I asked these women to elaborate, they typically retreated to a familistic stance. That is, much of *her* money is used *for the family* (for example, child care, family presents, clothing). When money is used *for the woman* (makeup, going out with the girls) it is often justified as necessary for her emotional well-being, which in turn helps her to be a good wife and mother.

The Mexicana mothers who are employed express their ambivalence somewhat differently from the Chicanas. One Mexicana works full-time; the other three are employed part-time. Angela, a Mexicana, married with one child and employed full-time as a seamstress, told me with glistening eyes:

> Always I have had to work. I had to leave my son with the baby-sitter since he was six months old. It was difficult. Each baby-sitter has her own way of caring for children which isn't like yours. I know the baby-sitter wouldn't give him the food I left. He always had on dirty diapers and was starving when I would pick him up. But there wasn't any other recourse. I had to work. I would just clean him and feed him when I got home.

Angela's "guilt" stemmed from her inability to find good, affordable child care. Unlike most of the Mexicanas, who had extensive family networks, Angela and her husband had few relatives to rely on in the United States. Unlike the Chicana informants, Angela did not want to exit the labor market to care for her child. Her desire is reinforced by economic need; her husband is irregularly employed.[31]

For the other three Mexicanas in this group, guilt as an employed mother appears to have developed with stable spousal employment. That is, the idea of feeling guilty about full-time employment emerged *after*

husbands became employed in secure, well-paying jobs and "reminded" them of the importance of stay-at-home, full-time motherhood. Lourdes, who was married with eight children and working as a part-time hotel maid said:

> I was offered a job at a—factory, working from eleven at night to seven in the morning. But I had a baby and so I wasn't able to work. I would have liked to take the job because it paid $8.25 an hour. I couldn't though, because of my baby. And my husband didn't want me to work at night. He said, "If we both work at night, who will take care of the children?" So I didn't take the job.

To thwart potential guilt over full-time employment and to ease marital tension (if she had taken this job she would have earned more money than her husband), Lourdes declined this high-paying job. When her child turned two, she opted to work part-time as a hotel maid. Lourdes, and the other Mexicanas employed part-time, told me that they *would* work full-time *if* their husbands supported their preferences. Mexicanas' ambivalence, then, is related to unease about their children's child care situations, as well as to anger at being held accountable to a narrow construction of motherhood enforced by their husbands.

All *Ambivalent Employed Mothers* report worrying about their children while at work. While this does not necessarily impair their job performance, it adds another psychological or emotional burden on their shoulders. This burden affects their ability to work full-time (over time is especially problematic) or seek the means (especially schooling) to advance in their jobs.

Women seem particularly troubled when they have to work on weekends. This robs them of precious family time. As Elena, a Chicana single parent with two children, ages nine and three, who works part-time as a hotel maid, said,

Yes, I work on weekends. And my kids, you know how kids are—they don't like it. And it's hard. But I hope to find a job soon where the schedule is fixed and I won't have to work on weekends—because that time should be for my kids.

There is a clear sense among the women I interviewed that a boundary between *time for the family* and *market time* should exist. During times when this boundary folds, women experience both internal conflict (within the woman herself) and external conflict (among family members). They regard jobs that overlap on family time with disfavor and unhappiness. When economic reasons compel woman to work during what they view as family time, they usually try to find as quickly as possible a different job that allows them to better meet their mother roles.

Interestingly, the Chicanas appear less flexible in reconciling the boundaries of family time and market time than the Mexicanas. That is, Chicanas overwhelmingly "choose" part-time employment to limit the amount of spillover time from employment on motherhood and family activities. Mexicanas, on the other hand, overwhelmingly work full-time (n = 9) and attempt to do both familial caretaking and market work as completely as possible.

This leads us to consider the fourth category, which I call *Nonambivalent Employed Mothers.* This category consists of Mexicana immigrants, both married and single-parent (six and two women, respectively). Mexicanas in this group do not describe motherhood as a *need*, requiring a separate sphere for optimal realization. Rather, they refer to motherhood as one function of womanhood that is compatible with employment insofar as employment allows them to provide for their family's economic subsistence or betterment. As Pilar, a married Mexicana with four children, employed full-time as a line supervisor in a factory, said, "I work to help my

children. That's what a mother should do." This group of Mexicanas does not express *guilt* over leaving their children in the care of others so much as *regret* over the limited amount of time they could spend with them. As Norma, a Mexicana full-time clerical worker, who is married with two children ages three and five, said,

> I don't feel guilty for leaving my children because if I didn't work they might not have the things they have now. . . . Perhaps if I had to stay at home I would feel guilty and frustrated. I'm not the type that can stay home twenty-four hours a day. I don't think that would help my children any because I would feel pressured at being cooped up [*encerrada*] at home. And that way I wouldn't have the same desire to play with my daughters. But now, with the time we have together, we do things that we want to, like run in the park, because there's so little time.

All of the Mexicanas in this group articulate views similar to Norma's. Their greater comfort with the demands of market and family work emanates from their social locations. All of the Mexicanas come from poor or working-class families, where motherhood embraced both economic and affective features. Their activities were not viewed as equal to those of men, however, and, ideologically, women saw themselves as *helping* the family rather than *providing* for it.

Few Mexicanas reported that their mothers were wage-laborers (n = 3), but rather described a range of economic activities they remembered women doing "for the family." Mexicanas from rural villages (n = 7) recounted how their mothers had worked on the land and made assorted products or food to sell in local marketplaces. Mexicanas from urban areas (n = 5) also discussed how their mothers had been economically active. Whether rural or urban, Mexicanas averred that their mothers had taught them to "help" the family as soon as possible. As Norma said,

My mother said, "It's one thing for a woman to lie around the house but it's a different thing for the work that needs to be done." As the saying goes, work is never done; the work does you in [*el trabajo acaba con uno; uno nunca acaba con el trabajo*].

Lourdes and two other Mexicanas cleaned houses with their mothers after school. Other mothers sold clothes to neighbors, cooked and sold food, or did assorted services for pay (for example, giving penicillin shots to neighbors). The Mexicanas do not view these activities as "separate" or less important than the emotional nurturing of children and family. Rather, they appreciate both the economic and the expressive as important facets of motherhood.

Although the Mexicanas had been raised in worlds where women were important economic actors, this did not signify gender equality. On the contrary, male privilege, or patriarchy, characterizes the organization of the family, the economy, and the polity in both rural and urban Mexican society.[32] In this study, Mexicanas indicated that men wield greater authority in the family, the community, and the state than do women. Mexicanas also tended to uphold male privilege in the family by viewing both domestic work and women's employment as "less important" than the work done by men. As Adela, a married Mexicana with four children, said, "Men are much stronger and do much more difficult work than women." Mexicanas also tended to defer to husbands as the "head" of the family—a position they told me was both "natural" and "holy."[33]

Working at Motherhood

The differences presented here between the Chicanas and Mexicanas regarding motherhood and employment stem from their distinct social locations. Raised in rural or working-class families in Mexico, the Mexicanas described childhoods where they and their mothers actively contributed to the economic subsistence of their families by planting crops, harvesting, selling homemade goods, and cleaning houses. Their situations resonate with what some researchers term a "family economy," where all family members work at productive tasks differentiated mainly by age and sex.[34] In this type of structure, there is less distinction between economic life and domestic life. Motherhood in this context is both economic and expressive, embracing employment as well as childrearing.

The family economy the Mexicanas experienced differs from the family organization that characterizes most of the Chicanas' childhoods. The Chicanas come from a world that idealizes a male wage earner as the main economic "provider," with women primarily as consumers, and only secondarily as economic actors. Women in this context are mothers first, wage earners second. Families that challenge this structure are often discredited or perceived as dysfunctional and the source of many social problems. The ambivalence Chicanas recurrently voice stems from their belief in what Kanter calls "the myth of separate worlds."[35] They seek to realize the popular notion or stereotype that family is a separate structure—a haven in a heartless world. Their attachment to this ideal is underscored by a harsh critique of their own employed mothers and themselves *when* they work full-time. Motherhood framed within this context appears irreconcilable with employment.

There are other facets to the differences between Chicanas and Mexicanas. The Mexicanas, as immigrant women, came to the United States with a vision of improving the life chances of their families and themselves. This finding intersects with research on "selective immigration." That is, that Mexican immigrants tend to possess higher levels of education than the national average in Mexico and a wide range of behavioral characteristics (for instance, high achievement orientation) conducive to success in the United States.[36]

The Mexicanas emigrated hoping to work—hence their high attachment to employment, even in physically demanding, often demeaning, jobs. Mexican and Chicano husbands support their wives' desires to work *so long as* this employment does not challenge the patriarchal structure of the family. In other words, so long as the Mexicanas: (1) articulate high attachment to motherhood *and* family caretaker roles, (2) frame their employment in terms of family economic goals, and (3) do not ask men to do equal amounts of housework or childcare, they encounter little resistance from husbands or other male family members.

When Mexican and Chicano husbands secure good jobs, however, they begin pressuring wives to quit working or to work only part-time. In this way, Mexican and Chicano men actively pursue continuity of their superordinate position within the family. This suggests that the way motherhood is conceptualized in both the Mexican and Chicano communities, particularly with respect to employment, is wedded to male privilege, or patriarchy. Ironically then, Mexicanas' sense of employment's continuity with motherhood enhances their job attachment but does not challenge a patriarchal family structure or ethos.

Similarly, Chicanas' preference for an idealized form of motherhood does not challenge male privilege in their community. Their desire to stay at home to mother exercised a particularly strong influence on the employment behavior of single-parent Chicanas and women with husbands employed in relatively good jobs. This preference reflects an adherence both to an idealized, middle-class lifestyle that glorifies women's domestic roles as well as to maintenance of a patriarchal family order. Chicanas feel they should stay at home to try and provide their children with the mothering they believe children should have—mothering that many of them had not experienced. Chicanas also feel compelled by husbands and the larger community to maintain the status of men as "good providers." Men earning wages adequate to provide for their families' needs usually urged their wives to leave the labor market. While the concept of the good provider continues to be highly valued in our society, it also serves as a rationale that upholds male privilege ideologically and materially and reinforces the myth of separate spheres that emanates from the organization of the family and the economy.

Conclusion

By illustrating how Chicanas and Mexicanas differ in their conceptualizations and organization of the motherhood and employment nexus, this study demonstrates how motherhood is a culturally formed structure with various meanings and subtexts. The vitality of these differences among members of a group who share a common historical origin and many cultural attributes underscores the need for frameworks that analyze diversity among all groups of women. Most essential to such an undertaking is a critique of the privileging of the "separate spheres" concept in analyses of women and work.

This study provides additional coherence to recent contentions that the private-public dichotomy lacks immediate relevance to less-privileged women (for instance, Chicana and Mexican immigrant women). In the process of illustrating how Chicanas and Mexicanas organized the interplay between motherhood and employment, it became clear that a more useful way of understanding this intersection might be to problematize motherhood itself. Considering motherhood from the vantage point of women's diverse social locations revealed considerable heterogeneity in how one might speak of it. For example, motherhood has an economic component for both groups of women, but it is most strongly expressed by Mexicana immigrants. The flavor of the expressive, however, flows easily across both groups of women, and for the Mexicanas embraces the economic. What this suggests is that the dichotomy of the separate spheres lacks relevance to Chicanas and Mexicanas and other women whose social origins make economic work necessary for survival.

This leads us to consider the relative place and function of the ideology of motherhood that is prevalent in our society. Motherhood that is constructed to privilege the woman who stays at home serves myriad functions. It pushes women to dichotomize their lives rather than to develop a sense of fluidity across roles, responsibilities, and preferences. Idealized, stay-at-home motherhood eludes most American women with children. As an ideology, however, it tells them what "should be," rendering them failures *as women* when they enter the labor market. Hence the feelings of ambivalence that characterized employed mother's lives, for the most part—except for those who had not yet internalized these standards. This research provides examples of such women, along with the understanding that other women from different social locations may demonstrate distinct ways of organizing the motherhood-employment nexus as well.

Feminist analyses of women and work emphasize the role of patriarchy to maintain male privilege and domination economically and ideologically. It is important to recognize that male privilege is not experienced equally by all men and that patriarchy itself can be ex-

pressed in different ways. The present study found that notions of motherhood among Mexicanas and Chicanas are embedded in different ideological constructs, operating within two systems of patriarchy. For Mexicanas, patriarchy takes the form of a corporate family model, with all members contributing to the common good. For Chicanas, the patriarchal structure centers more closely around a public-private dichotomy that idealizes men as economic providers and women primarily as caretakers-consumers.

The finding that women from more "traditional" backgrounds (such as rural Mexico) are likely to approach full-time employment with less ambivalence than more "American" women (such as the Chicanas) rebuts linear acculturation models that assume a negative relationship between ideologies (such as motherhood) constructed within "traditional" Mexican society and employment. It also complements findings on the negative relationship between greater length of time in the United States and high aspirations among Mexicans.[37] This suggests that employment problems (for example, underemployment, unemployment) are related less to "traditional" cultural configurations than to labor market structure and employment policies. Understanding the intersections between employment policy, social ideology, and private need is a necessary step toward expanding possibilities for women in our society.

NOTES

Acknowledgments: This chapter is a revised version of "Ambivalence or Continuity? Motherhood and Employment Among Chicanas and Mexican Immigrant Women," *AZTLAN, International Journal of Chicano Studies Research* (1992). I would like to thank Maxine Baca Zinn, Evelyn Nakano Glenn, Arlie Hochschild, Beatriz Pesquera, and Vicki Ruiz for their constructive feedback and criticism of earlier drafts of this chapter. A special thanks goes to Jon Cruz for his assistance in titling this chapter. Any remaining errors or inconsistencies are my own responsibility. This research was supported in part by a 1986–87 University of California President's Postdoctoral Fellowship.

1. Betsy Wearing, *The Ideology of Motherhood: A Study of Sydney Suburban Mothers* (Sydney: George Allen and Unwin, 1984); Barbara J. Berg, *The Crisis of the Working Mother: Resolving the Conflict Between Family and Work* (New York: Summit Books, 1986); Nancy Folbre, "The Pauperization of Motherhood: Patriarchy and Public Policy in the United States," *Review of Radical Political Economics* 16 (1984). The view that mothers should not work outside the home typically pertains to married women. Current state welfare policies (e.g., Aid to Families with Dependent Children [AFDC], workfare) indicate that single, unmarried mothers belong in the labor force, not at home caring for their children full time. See Naomi Gerstel and Harriet Engel Gross, "Introduction," in N. Gerstel and H. E. Gross, eds., *Families and Work* (Philadelphia: Temple University Press, 1987), pp. 1–12; Deborah K. Zinn and Rosemary C. Sarri, "Turning Back the Clock on Public Welfare," *Signs: Journal of Women in Culture and Society* 10 (1984), pp. 355–370; Nancy Folbre, "The Pauperization of Motherhood"; Nancy A. Naples, "A Socialist Feminist Analysis of the Family Support Act of 1988," *AFFILIA* 6 (1991), pp. 23–38.

2. In June 1990, over half (53.1 percent) of women between the ages of 18 and 44 who had had a child in the last year were in the labor force. This proportion varied by race: 54.9 percent of white women, 46.9 percent of Black women, and 44.4 percent of Latinas were in the labor force. See U.S. Bureau of the Census (1991), p. 5.

3. Simon and Landis report that a 1986 Gallup Poll indicates that support for married women to work outside the home is considerably greater than 1938 levels: 76 percent of women and 78 percent of men approve (1989, 270). Comparable 1938 levels are 25 percent and 19 percent, respectively of women and men. The 1985 Roper Poll finds the American public adhering to the view that a husband's career supersedes that of his wife: 72 percent of women and 62 percent of men agree that a wife

should quit her job and relocate if her husband is offered a good job in another city (1989, 272). In the reverse situation, 20 percent of women and 22 percent of men believe a husband should quit his job and relocate with his wife (1989, 272). Simon and Landis conclude: "The Women's Movement has not radicalized the American woman: she is still prepared to put marriage and children ahead of her career and to allow her husband's status to determine the family's position in society" (1989, 269). Rita J. Simon and Jean M. Landis, "Women's and Men's Attitudes About a Woman's Place and Role," *Public Opinion Quarterly* 53 (1989), pp. 265–276.

4. Hood argues that the "ideal" of stay-at-home motherhood and male provider has historically been an unrealistic standard for families outside the middle and upper classes. She points out that early surveys of urban workers indicate between 40 percent and 50 percent of all families supplemented their income with the earnings of wives and children. See Jane C. Hood, "The Provider Role: Its Meaning and Measurement," *Journal of Marriage and the Family* 48 (May 1986), pp. 349–359.

5. It should be noted that native-born status is not an essential requirement for the ethnic label, "Chicana/o." There are numerous identifiers used by people of Mexican descent, including: Chicana/o, Mexican, Mexican-American, Mexicana/o, Latina/o, and Hispanic. Often, people of Mexican descent use two or three of the above labels, depending on the social situation (e.g., "Mexican-American" in the family or "Chicana/o" at school). See John A. Garcia, "Yo Soy Mexicano . . . : Self-identity and Sociodemographic Correlates," *Social Science Quarterly* 62 (March 1981), pp. 88–98; Susan E. Keefe and Amado M. Padilla, *Chicano Ethnicity* (Albuquerque: University of New Mexico Press, 1987). My designation of study informants as either "Chicana" or "Mexicana" represents an analytic separation that facilitates demonstrating the heterogeneity among this group.

6. Patricia Zavella, "Reflections on Diversity among Chicanos," *Frontiers* 2 (1991), p. 75.

7. See Rosalia Solorzano-Torres, "Female Mexican Immigrants in San Diego County," in V. L. Ruiz and S. Tiano, eds., *Women on the U.S.-Mexico Border: Responses to Change* (Boston: Allen and

Unwin, 1987), pp. 41–59; Reynaldo Baca and Bryan Dexter, "Mexican Women, Migration and Sex Roles," *Migration Today* 13 (1985), pp. 14–18; Sylvia Guendelman and Auristela Perez-Itriago, "Double Lives: The Changing Role of Women in Seasonal Migration," *Women's Studies* 13 (1987), pp. 249–271.

8. Gary S. Becker, "Human Capital, Effort, and the Sexual Division of Labor," *Journal of Labor Economics* 3 (1985 Supplement), pp. S33–S58; Gary S. Becker, *A Treatise on the Family* (Cambridge, MA: Harvard University Press, 1981); Solomon W. Polachek, "Occupational Self-Selection: A Human Capital Approach to Sex Differences in Occupational Structure," *Review of Economics and Statistics* 63 (1981), pp. 60–69; S. Polachek, "Occupational Segregation Among Women: Theory, Evidence, and a Prognosis," in C. B. Lloyd, E. S. Andrews, and C. L. Gilroy, eds., *Women in the Labor Market* (New York: Columbia University Press, 1981), pp. 137–157; S. Polachek, "Discontinuous Labor Force Participation and Its Effect on Women's Market Earnings," in C. Lloyd, ed., *Sex Discrimination and the Division of Labor* (New York: Columbia University Press, 1975), pp. 90–122. Becker's classic treatise, *Human Capital,* uses the following example borrowed from G. Stigler, "The Economics of Information," *Journal of Political Economy* (June 1961): "Women spend less time in the labor force than men and, therefore, have less incentive to invest in market skills; tourists spend little time in any one area and have less incentive than residents of the area to invest in knowledge of specific consumption activities." See Gary S. Becker, *Human Capital* (Chicago: University of Chicago Press, 1975), p. 74.

9. Some institutional economists argue that "statistical discrimination" is one critical labor market dynamic that often impedes women and minorities. See Kenneth Arrow, "Economic Dimensions of Occupational Segregation: Comment I," *Signs: Journal of Women in Culture and Society* 1 (1987), pp. 233–237; Edmund Phelps, "The Statistical Theory of Racism and Sexism," in A. H. Amsden, ed., *The Economics of Women and Work* (New York: St. Martin's Press, 1980), pp. 206–210. This perspective suggests that prospective employers often lack detailed information about individual applicants and therefore utilize statistical averages and normative views of the relevant group(s) to which the applicant belongs in their hiring decisions (e.g., college-educated men tend to be successful and committed employees; all women are potential mothers; or women tend to exit the labor force for childbearing).

Bielby and Baron pose an important critique to the underlying rationale of statistical discrimination. They argue that utilizing perceptions of group differences between the sexes is "neither as rational nor as efficient as the economists believe." That is, utilizing stereotypical notions of "men's work" and "women's work" is often costly to employers and therefore irrational. This suggests that sex segregation is imbedded in organizational policies which reflect and reinforce "belief systems that are also rather inert." See William T. Bielby and James N. Baron, "Undoing Discrimination: Job Integration and Comparable Worth," in C. Bose and G. Spitze, eds., *Ingredients for Women's Employment Policy* (New York: State University of New York Press, 1987), p. 216, pp. 221–222.

10. Annette Kuhn, "Structure of Patriarchy and Capital in the Family," in A. Kuhn and Annemarie Wolfe, eds., *Feminism and Materialism: Women and Modes of Production* (London: Routledge & Kegan Paul, 1978); Heidi Hartmann, "Capitalism, Patriarchy, and Job Segregation by Sex," in Martha Blaxall and Barbara Reagan, eds., *Women and the Work Place* (Chicago: University of Chicago Press, 1976), pp. 137–169; H. Hartmann, "The Family as the Locus of Gender, Class, and Political Struggle: The Example of Housework," *Signs: Journal of Women in Culture and Society* 6 (1981), pp. 366–394; Michèle Barrett, *Women's Oppression Today: Problems in Marxist Feminist Analysis* (London: Verso Press, 1980).

11. Lourdes Beneria and Martha Roldan, *The Crossroads of Class and Gender: Industrial Homework, Subcontracting, and Household Dynamics in Mexico City* (Chicago: University of Chicago Press, 1987); L. Beneria and Gita Sen, "Accumulation, Reproduction, and Women's role in Economic Development: Boserup Revisited," in E. Leacock and H. I. Safa, eds., *Women's Work: Development and Division of Labor by Gender* (Westport, CT: Bergin & Garvey Publishers, 1986), pp. 141–157; Dorothy

Smith, "Women's Inequality and the Family," in N. Gerstel and H. E. Gross, eds., *Families and Work* (Philadelphia: Temple University Press, 1987), pp. 23–54.

12. This phrase was coined by Arlie R. Hochschild and quoted in Lillian B. Rubin, *Intimate Strangers, Men and Women Together* (New York: Harper & Row, 1983).

13. Arlie Hochschild, with Anne Machung, *The Second Shift, Working Parents and the Revolution at Home* (New York: Viking Penguin Books, 1989).

14. Barbara J. Berg, *The Crisis of the Working Mother: Resolving the Conflict Between Family and Work* (New York: Summit Books, 1986), p. 42.

15. Howard Hayghe, "Working Mothers Reach Record Number in 1984," *Monthly Labor Review* 107 (December, 1984), pp. 31–34; U.S. Bureau of the Census, "Fertility of American Women: June 1990," in *Current Population Report,* Series P–20, no. 454 (Washington, D.C.: U.S. GPO, 1991); U.S. Bureau of Census Report, "Fertility of American Women: June 1986" in *Current Population Report,* Series P–20, no. 421 (Washington D.C.: U.S. GPO). In June 1986 (the year closest to the year I interviewed the respondents where I found relevant data), 49.8 percent of all women with newborn children were in the labor force. Women demonstrated differences in this behavior: 49.7 percent of white women, 51.1 percent of Black women, and 40.6 percent of Latinas with newborn children were in the labor force. See U.S. Bureau of the Census, "Fertility of American Women: June 1986" (1987), p. 5.

16. Bonnie Thornton Dill, Lynn Weber Cannon, and Reeve Vanneman, "Pay Equity: An Issue of Race, Ethnicity and Sex" (Washington D.C.: National Commission on Pay Equity, February, 1987); Julianne Malveaux and Phyllis Wallace, "Minority Women in the Workplace," in K. S. Koziara, M. Moskow, and L. Dewey Tanner, eds., *Women and Work: Industrial Relations Research Association Research Volume* (Washington, DC: Bureau of National Affairs, 1987), pp. 265–298; Vicki L. Ruiz, " 'And Miles to go.': Mexican Women and Work, 1930–1985," in L. Schlissel, V. L. Ruiz, and J. Monk, eds., *Western Women, Their Land, Their Lives* (Albuquerque: University of New Mexico Press, 1988), pp. 117–136.

17. Mario Barrera, *Race and Class in the Southwest: A Theory of Racial Inequality* (Notre Dame, IN: University of Notre Dame Press, 1979); Tomas Almaguer, "Class, Race, and Chicano Oppression," *Socialist Revolution* 5 (1975), pp. 71–99; Denise Segura, "Labor Market Stratification: The Chicana Experience," *Berkeley Journal of Sociology* 29 (1984), pp. 57–91.

18. Marta Tienda and P. Guhleman, "The Occupational Position of Employed Hispanic Women," in G. J. Borjas and M. Tienda, eds., *Hispanics in the U.S. Economy* (New York: Academic Press, 1985), pp. 243–273.

19. Edgar J. Kranau, Vicki Green, and Gloria Valencia-Weber, "Acculturation and the Hispanic Woman: Attitudes Towards Women, Sex-Role Attribution, Sex-Role Behavior, and Demographics," *Hispanic Journal of Behavioral Sciences* 4 (1982), pp. 21–40; Alfredo Mirande and Evangelina Enriquez, *La Chicana: The Mexican American Woman* (Chicago: University of Chicago Press, 1979).

20. Kranau, Green, and Valencia-Weber, "Acculturation and the Hispanic Woman," pp. 21–40; Alfredo Mirande, *The Chicano Experience: An Alternative Perspective* (Notre Dame, IN: University of Notre Dame Press, 1985).

21. Vilma Ortiz and Rosemary Santana Cooney, "Sex-Role Attitudes and Labor Force Participation Among Young Hispanic Females and Non-Hispanic White Females," *Social Science Quarterly* 65 (June, 1984), pp. 392–400.

22. Susan E. Keefe and Amado M. Padilla, *Chicano Ethnicity* (Albuquerque: University of New Mexico Press, 1987); Richard H. Mendoza, "Acculturation and Sociocultural Variability," in J. L. Martinez, Jr., and R. H. Mendoza, eds., *Chicano Psychology,* 2d ed. (New York: Academic Press, 1984), pp. 61–75.

23. Maxine Baca Zinn, "Mexican-American Women in the Social Sciences," *Signs: Journal of Women in Culture and Society* 8 (1982), pp. 259–272. M. Baca Zinn, "Employment and Education of Mexican-American Women: The Interplay of Modernity and Ethnicity in Eight Families," *Harvard Educational Review* 50 (February 1980), pp. 47–62. M. Baca Zinn, "Chicano Family Research: Conceptual Distortions and Alternative Directions," *Journal of Ethnic Studies* 7 (1979) pp. 59–71.

24. For additional information on the methods and sample selection, I refer the reader to Denise A. Segura, "Chicanas and Mexican Immigrant Women in the Labor Market: A Study of Occupational Mobility and Stratification," Ph.D. diss., Department of Sociology, University of California, Berkeley (1986).

25. The ages of the Chicanas range from 23 to 42 years. The Mexicanas reported ages from 24 to 45. The age profile indicates that most of the women were in peak childbearing years.

26. For an example, see Betsy Wearing, *The Ideology of Motherhood: A Study of Sydney Suburban Mothers* (Sydney: George Allen & Unwin, 1984).

27. For an example, see Nancy Chodorow, *The Reproduction of Mothering* (Berkeley: University of California Press, 1979).

28. Manuel Ramirez III and Alfredo Castaneda, *Cultural Democracy, Bicognitive Development, and Education* (New York: Academic Press, 1974); Robert F. Peck and Rogelio Diaz-Guerrero, "Two Core-Culture Patterns and the Diffusion of Values Across Their Borders," *International Journal of Psychology* 2 (1967), pp. 272–282; Javier I. Escobat and E. T. Randolph, "The Hispanic and Social Networks," in R. M. Becerra, M. Karno, and J. I. Escobar, eds., *Mental Health and Hispanic Americans: Clinical Perspectives* (New York: Grune and Stratton, 1982).

29. Alfredo Mirande and Evangelina Enriquez, *La Chicana, The Mexican American Woman* (Chicago: University of Chicago Press, 1979); Margarita Melville, "Introduction" and "Matrascence," in M. B. Melville, ed., *Twice a Minority: Mexican American Women* (St. Louis: C. V. Mosby, 1980), pp. 1–16; Gloria Anzaldua, *Borderlands, La Frontera: The New Mestiza* (San Francisco: Spinsters/Aunt Lute, 1987); Linda C. Fox, "Obedience and Rebellion: Re-Vision of Chicana Myths of Motherhood," *Women's Studies Quarterly* (Winter, 1983), pp. 20–22.

30. Talcott Parsons and Robert Bales, *Family, Socialization, and Interaction Process* (New York: Free Press, 1955); Robert H. Bradley and Bettye M. Caldwell, "The Relation of Infants' Home Environments to Achievement Test Performance in First Grade: A Follow-up Study," *Child Development* 55 (1984), pp. 803–809; Toby L. Parcel and Elizabeth G. Menaghan, "Maternal Working Conditions and Child Verbal Facility: Studying the Intergenerational Transmission of Inequality from Mothers to Young Children," *Social Psychology Quarterly* 53 (1990), pp. 132–147; Avshalom Caspi and Glen H. Elder, "Emergent Family Patterns: The Intergenerational Construction of Problem Behavior and Relationships," in R. Hinde and J. Stevenson Hinde, eds., *Understanding Family Dynamics* (New York: Oxford University Press, 1988).

31. For a full discussion of the interplay between economic goals and economic status of the respondents and their employment decisions, I refer the reader to Denise Segura, "The Interplay of Familism and Patriarchy on Employment Among Chicana and Mexican Immigrant Women," in the *Renato Rosaldo Lecture Series Monograph* 5 (Tucson: University of Arizona, Center for Mexican American Studies, 1989), pp. 35–53.

32. Patricia M. Fernandez-Kelly, "Mexican Border Industrialization, Female Labor Force Participation and Migration," in J. Nash and M. P. Fernandez-Kelly, eds., *Women, Men, and the International Division of Labor* (Albany: State University of New York Press, 1983), pp. 205–223; Sylvia Guendelman and Auristela Perez-Itriago, "Double Lives: The Changing Role of Women in Seasonal Migration," *Women's Studies* 13 (1987), pp. 249–271; Reynaldo Baca and Dexter Bryan, "Mexican Women, Migration and Sex Roles," *Migration Today* 13 (1985), pp. 14–18.

33. Research indicates that religious involvement plays an important role in gender beliefs. See Ross K. Baker, Laurily K. Epstein, and Rodney O. Forth, "Matters of Life and Death: Social, Political, Religious Correlates of Attitudes on Abortion," *American Politics Quarterly* 9 (1981), pp. 89–102; Charles E. Peek and Sharon Brown, "Sex Prejudice Among White Protestants: Like or Unlike Ethnic Prejudice?" *Social Forces* 59 (1980), pp. 169–185. Of particular interest for this study is that involvement in fundamentalist Christian churches is positively related to adherence to traditional gender role ideology. See Clyde Wilcox and Elizabeth Adell Cook, "Evangelical Women and Feminism: Some Additional Evidence," *Women and Politics* 9 (1989), pp. 27–49; Clyde Wilcox, "Religious Attitudes and Anti-Feminism:

An Analysis of the Ohio Moral Majority," *Women and Politics* 48 (1987), pp. 1041–1051. Half of the Mexicanas (and all but two Chicanas) adhered to the Roman Catholic religion; half belonged to various fundamentalist Christian churches (e.g., Assembly of God). Two Chicanas belonged to other Protestant denominations. I noticed that the women who belonged to the Assembly of God tended both to work full-time in the labor market and to voice the strongest convictions of male authority in the family. During their interviews many of the women brought out the Bible and showed me the biblical passages that authorized husbands to "rule" the family. Catholic women also voiced traditional beliefs regarding family structure but did not invoke God.

34. Frances Rothstein, "Women and Men in the Family Economy: An Analysis of the Relations Between the Sexes in Three Peasant Communities," *Anthropological Quarterly* 56 (1983), pp. 10–23. Ruth Schwartz Cowan, "Women's Work, Housework, and History: The Historical Roots of Inequality in Work Force Participation," in N. Gerstel and H. E. Gross, eds., *Families and Work* (Philadelphia: Temple University Press, 1987), pp. 164–177. Louise A. Tilly and Joan W. Scott, *Women, Work, and Family* (New York: Holt, Rinehart, & Winston, 1978).

35. Rosabeth Moss Kanter, *Men and Women of the Corporation* (New York: Basic Books, 1977).

36. John M. Chavez and Raymond Buriel, "Reinforcing Children's Effort: A Comparison of Immigrant, Native-Born Mexican American and Euro-American Mothers," *Hispanic Journal of Behavioral Sciences* 8 (1986), pp. 127–142. Raymond Buriel, "Integration with Traditional Mexican-American Culture and Sociocultural Adjustment," in J. L. Martinez, Jr., and R. H. Mendoza, eds., *Chicano Psychology*, 2d ed. (New York: Academic Press, 1984), pp. 94–130; Leo R. Chavez, "Households, Migration and Labor Market Participation:

The Adaptation of Mexicans to Life in the United States," *Urban Anthropology* 14 (1985), pp. 301–346.

37. Raymond Buriel, "Integration with Traditional Mexican-American Culture and Sociocultural Adjustment," in J. L. Martinez, Jr., and R. H. Mendoza, eds., *Chicano Psychology* 2d ed. (New York: Academic Press, 1984), pp. 95–130. In their analysis of differences in educational goals among Mexican-Americans, Buriel and his associates found that "third generation Mexican Americans felt less capable of fulfilling their educational objectives." See Raymond Buriel, Silverio Caldaza, and Richard Vasquez, "The Relationship of Traditional Mexican American Culture to Adjustment and Delinquency Among Three Generations of Mexican American Adolescents," *Hispanic Journal of Behavioral Sciences* 4 (1982), p. 50. Similar findings were reported by Nielsen and Fernandez: "We find that students whose families have been in the U.S. longer have *lower* [their emphasis] aspirations than recent immigrants." See Francois Nielsen and Roberto M. Fernandez, *Hispanic Students in American High Schools: Background Characteristics and Achievement* (Washington, D.C.: U.S. GPO, 1981), p. 76.

In their analysis of Hispanic employment, Bean and his associates reported an unexpected finding—that English-proficient Mexican women exhibit a greater "constraining influence of fertility" on their employment vis-à-vis Spanish-speaking women. They speculate that more acculturated Mexican women may have "a greater desire for children of higher quality," and therefore they may "be more likely to devote time to the informal socialization and education of young children." They wonder "why this should hold true for English-speaking but not Spanish-speaking women." See Frank D. Bean, C. Gray Swicegood, and Allan G. King, "Role Incompatibility and the Relationship Between Fertility and Labor Supply Among Hispanic Women," in G. J. Borjas and M. Tienda, eds., *Hispanics in the U.S. Economy* (New York: Academic Press, 1985), p. 241.

Chapter 53

The Dialectics of Wage Work: Japanese-American Women and Domestic Service, 1905–1940

EVELYN NAKANO GLENN

The work of women has been a much-neglected topic in the economic and social history of Japanese Americans in the United States. Yet, from the moment they arrived, Japanese-American women labored alongside the men to secure their own and their families' livelihood.[1] Although much of their work took the form of unpaid labor on family farms and businesses, many women turned to wage work to supplement family income. Until World War II, the most common form of nonagricultural employment for the immigrant women (*issei*) and their American-born daughters (*nisei*) was domestic service.

As was true for immigrant women from other rural societies, domestic work served as a port of entry into the urban labor force.[2] The demand for domestic help among urban middle-class families ensured a constant pool of jobs, but the occupation's low status and unfavorable working conditions made it unattractive to those who could secure other kinds of jobs. Thus, the field was left open to the newcomer and the minority woman.[3]

For European immigrants, domestic service was a temporary way station. By the second generation, they had moved into the expanding white-collar clerical and sales occupations.[4] The Japanese, however, like blacks and other minorities, were barred from most industrial and office settings.[5] Thus, Japanese women remained heavily concentrated in domestic work even into the second generation. Only after World War II did institutional racism diminish sufficiently to enable the *nisei* and their children to move into other occupations. Involvement in domestic service was thus an important shared experience for Japanese women in the prewar years, serving as one basis for ethnic and gender solidarity.[6]

This chapter examines that experience, using the case of *issei* women in the San Francisco Bay Area in the period from 1905 to 1940. The account is based primarily on interviews with domestic workers and community informants.[7]

This article is an abridged version of "The Dialectics of Wage Work: Japanese-American Women and Domestic Service, 1905–1940," *Feminist Studies* 6, no. 3 (fall 1980): 432–71. Reprinted by permission.

What is highlighted in this account is the contradiction between the multiple forms of oppression to which the women were subjected and the resilience that they developed.[8] *Issei* domestic workers were subjugated by institutional racism, by conditions of work in domestic employment, and by the structure of *issei* family life; yet, they were not passive victims but active participants, shaping their own lives. Faced with oppression, *issei* women strived, often in covert and indirect ways, to gain control over their work and other aspects of their lives. Out of this effort, I argue, grew a sense of autonomy and self-reliance that enabled them to transcend the limitations of their circumstances and gain a measure of satisfaction from essentially menial work.

History of Bay Area Japanese Communities

We begin by examining the historical context in which Japanese women's involvement in domestic work developed. The pre–World War II history of Japanese communities in the San Francisco Bay Area can be divided into three periods: frontier, settlement, and stabilization, each demarcated by specific historical events that shaped the immigrants' lives.[9]

The "frontier" period, roughly 1890 to 1910, was when the first wave of immigrants arrived. The *issei* were remarkably homogeneous, and most of the immigrants were young single males from rural villages in southern Japan, with an average of eight years of education.[10] They came as sojourners, expecting to work a few years to mass sufficient capital to establish themselves in Japan. They started out as unskilled wage laborers in agriculture, railroading, mining, and lumbering, or in domestic service.[11] Later, as they accumulated capital and know-how, many launched small enterprises, usually laundries or stores. In place of their old kin ties, the *issei* men formed mutual aid associations with those from the same prefecture (*kenjinkai*) and organized rotating credit associations (*tanomoshi*) to raise capital.[12]

Until 1907, San Francisco, as a port city, was one of three main centers of Japanese population.[13] The Japanese congregated in a section of the Western Addition, a district of low-rent, rundown housing that became known as Little Osaka. From San Francisco, the *issei* spread to other cities in the East Bay. By 1910, the Japanese populations of the four main cities were: San Francisco, 4,518; Oakland, 1,520; Berkeley, 710; and Alameda, 499.[14]

Growing anti-Japanese agitation led to a series of legal measures designed to reduce immigration and to discourage permanent settlement. The 1907 "Gentlemen's Agreement" between Japan and the United States closed entry to laborers. Between 1910 and 1929, more men returned to Japan than entered.[15] However, those who remained began to think in terms of a longer stay. The "Gentlemen's Agreement" contained a loophole: it permitted the entry of wives and relatives. The *issei* began returning to Japan to marry and bring back wives or began sending for picture brides.

The arrival of *issei* women marks the beginning of the "settlement" period. Between 1909 and 1923, over 33,000 *issei* wives immigrated.[16] During this period of family and community building, the sex ratio became less skewed, and the population came to include children as well as adults. Extensive infrastructures developed with the establishment of ethnic churches, newspapers, language schools, and business and service establishments.[17] Ethnic enclaves formed in San Francisco's Western Addition, on the borders of Chinatown in downtown Oakland, and around City Hall in Alameda. Except for jobs, the *issei* could fulfill most of their social and material wants within the ethnic community. According to one observer, "Very few Japanese ventured beyond those comfortable environs."[18]

Meanwhile, partly in response to more permanent settlement, anti-Japanese sentiment grew. The Alien Land Law was passed in California in 1913, prohibiting the *issei*, who were ineligible for citizenship, from owning land or leasing it for more than three years. Finally, the Immigration Act of 1924 cut off all further immigration from Asia.[19]

The end of immigration marks the start of the "stabilization" period, 1924 to 1940. Henceforth, the growth of population depended entirely on births. There was little room for expansion of ethnic enterprises serving a largely Japanese clientele. Thus, the *issei* found their opportunities shrinking and began to pin their hopes for the future on their children, who by virtue of American citizenship had rights denied their parents.[20]

The restriction on immigration also created distinct generational cohorts. The majority of *issei* were born between 1870 and 1900, and their children, the *nisei*, were born mainly between 1910 and 1940. By the mid-1930s, the *issei* were primarily middle-aged, while the eldest *nisei* were just reaching maturity and entering the labor force. Despite American citizenship and education, the *nisei* confronted the same racist restrictions as their parents; they were still barred from union jobs and employment in white-run offices and stores. It is unclear what course ethnic assimilation would have taken over the next decade under normal circumstances, for the Japanese community was shattered almost overnight by the commencement of World War II. The Japanese were evacuated and incarcerated in concentration camps. Those who returned to the Bay Area after the war settled in scattered areas, rather than concentrating in the old enclaves, so the old physical communities were never fully reconstituted.

Issei Women

Most of the *issei* women who arrived in the United States between 1907 and 1924 were from the same southern rural backgrounds as the male immigrants. They had levels of education comparable to the men: the fifteen *issei* domestics in the study averaged six years of education, with two having no schooling and two having completed ten years, the equivalent of high school. The typical *issei* woman was in her early twenties and was married to a man ten years her senior who had lived for some years in the United States, working as a wage laborer or small entrepreneur.[21]

Following Japanese custom, the marriages were arranged by the families of the bride and groom through a go-between (*baishakunin*). Many *issei* men managed to save or borrow money to return to Japan to meet their prospective brides and to get married. Many others, for financial or other reasons, could not return. In such cases, the match was arranged by the go-between through an exchange of photographs, hence the term "picture marriage." The union was legalized by registering it in the husband's home prefecture.

For the most part, the women felt they had little say in the selection of a husband; daughters were expected to go along with their parents' judgment. Yet, the extent to which women felt forced or manipulated by their parents and by circumstances varied.[22]

At one extreme is Mrs. Takagi,[23] who recalls that her father tricked her into going to stay with her adopted grandfather on the pretext that she would receive training to become a midwife:

> Otherwise, I wouldn't have gone, you see. I knew my mother needed help. . . . I stayed one week and helped my uncle [a doctor]. I was thinking I would stay to help him. Pretty soon, they took me to see this man. I'd never seen or heard of him. He was my second cousin. You

don't know the Japanese system: they just pick out your husband and tell you what to do. So, I just did it, that's all. . . . I never gave my parents a fight.

Another *issei*, Mrs. Nishimura, falls somewhere in the middle of the continuum. She was only fifteen when she was persuaded by her father to marry Mr. Nishimura:

In the Japanese style, we used a go-between and the husband would come to Japan to pick up his bride. My father was rather new in his thinking, so he told me that rather than stay in Japan to attend school, I should come to the U.S. My mother told me even then that I was too young. But, it's something that had to be done so . . . I was rather big for my age, and . . . but I cried at the time, and I'll always remember that. My parents felt a little guilty about it, almost as if they had forced me to come, and apparently they kept asking about me, about how I was doing, until they died.

At the other extreme, we have Mrs. Shinoda who claims she dreamed of going to the United States even as a child:

I told my father that I wouldn't get married, unless I could come to the United States. [Did your parents oppose you?] Yes, they were all against me. [How did you know you wanted to come to the United States?] I don't know. When I was small, in elementary school, we had to write an essay on "What I Wish For." I wrote in that essay that I'd like to go to America. My friends read it and told what I had written. That's funny, huh?

Mrs. Shinoda was stubborn enough to hold out until her father gave in. She didn't marry until she was twenty-eight, but she got her way.

In leaving their families and going to the United States, the *issei* women were following usual Japanese practice. Custom dictated that a woman leave her parents' household or village to live in her husband's home. The *issei*

were simply traveling a much greater geographic and cultural distance.[24] Despite the pain of separation and fear of the unknown, the majority of the women said they left Japan with positive expectations. Just as the men came to the United States to better their lot, *issei* women came with their own hopes: to further their educations, to help their families economically, to seek a happier homelife, and to experience new adventures.

The boat trip to the United States, usually from Yokohama to Seattle or San Francisco, normally took over a month. The women report feelings of homesickness and physical illness, although they also recall fondly the friendships they developed with other women during the voyage. Upon arrival, the women confronted many new and strange experiences. The first shock for the picture brides was meeting their new spouses. Mrs. Yoshida, who traveled with a number of other picture brides, recalls the responses of some of her companions upon catching glimpses of their husbands:

A lot of people that I came together with said: "I'm going back on this very boat." I told them, "You can't do that; you should go ashore once. If you really don't like him, and you feel like going back, then you have to have a meeting and then go back." Many times, the picture was taken twenty years earlier and they had changed. Many of the husbands had gone to the country to work as farmers, so they had aged and became quite wrinkled. And very young girls came expecting more and it was natural.

As for herself, Mrs. Yoshida says she was disappointed that her husband (sixteen years her senior) looked much older than a neighbor at home the same age. However, many people from her village in Hiroshima had traveled to Hawaii and to the mainland United States, and she wanted to go too: "I didn't care what the man looked like."

The second shock was having to discard the

comfort of kimonos and slippers for constricting dresses and shoes. The women were generally taken straight off after clearing immigration to be completely outfitted. Mrs. Nomura, who arrived in Seattle in 1919, said,

> At that time, ships were coming into Seattle every week from Japan, carrying one or two hundred Japanese brides. So, there was a store set up especially for these new arrivals. There was a hotel run by a Japanese and also Japanese food available. The Japanese wouldn't go to the stores run by Whites, so there there were stores run by Japanese to deal with Japanese customers. We did all of our shopping there. The lady there would show us how to use a corset— since we had never used one in Japan. And how to wear stockings and shoes.

Mrs. Okamura, who came in 1917, laughs when she remembers her first dress:

> It felt very tight. I couldn't even move my arms. That was the first time I had ever worn Western clothes, so I thought they were supposed to be like that. . . . Later, Mrs. S. taught me to sew my own clothes. She had a pattern that we all used to make the same dress in different materials. So I found out that first dress was too small.

As Mrs. Okamura's account indicates, earlier immigrants taught new arrivals "the ropes," and living quarters were usually secured within the ghetto. Many couples rented rooms in a house and shared kitchen and bathroom facilities with several other Japanese families. Thus, help and comfort were close at hand. Mrs. Horiuchi says the best time in her life was when she was a new bride, just after arriving in the United States. All her husband's friends dropped in to welcome her and bring gifts. Sometimes, husbands who had worked as "schoolboys" or domestics, taught their wives how to shop, cook, and clean. Community agencies such as the YWCA, and the public schools, sponsored housekeeping and English courses for new-comers. Most of the women in the study took some of these classes, but claimed that they were unable to continue their studies once children arrived. Partly for this reason, most never fully mastered English. Another reason was that the women rarely ventured outside the confines of their ethnic community, except to do domestic work for wages. The ethnic community provided for most of their needs and insulated them from the hostility of the larger society.

The *issei* women arrived at a time of accelerating anti-Japanese agitation. Their arrival was itself a focus of attack because it signaled an intention on the part of the *issei* to settle on a long-term basis. Anti-Japanese propaganda depicted the practice of picture marriages as immoral and a ruse to contravene the Gentlemen's Agreement. As a result of mounting pressure, the Japanese government stopped issuing passports to picture brides in 1921.[25]

Mrs. Takagi was outspoken about the racism of the period, saying,

> I think all the [Japanese] people at that age had a real hard time. [They had to work hard, you mean?] Not only that, they were all thinking we were slaves, you know, sleeping in the stable upstairs. And even when we'd get on a streetcar, they'd say, "Jap, get away," Even me, they always threw stuff from up above. [They did? What do you mean?] I don't know why they did that. I was so scared. . . . One man, he was going on a bicycle and someone threw cement. That night he lost an eye. But they never sued, they never reported it because they didn't speak English. . . . I don't know what other people think, but we didn't have very much fun. We didn't have very many jobs. A lot of people graduated from college and still no job, before the war.

The *issei* downplay personal difficulties they encountered as a result of racism. Although they were able to avoid hostile encounters by remaining within their own world, nevertheless, it is clear that their lives were affected in a variety of ways, especially economically. Furthermore, discrimination reinforced the *issei*'s sojourner orientation. Mrs. Adachi notes that because of discrimination, her husband always opposed putting down permanent roots, and they always rented apartments, rather than buying a house, even after they could afford to do so. Her husband also became increasingly nationalistic, keenly following the political and military developments in Japan.

Economic Activities of *Issei* Women

Issei women had little time to brood about their situations. Whether rural or urban, they found they were expected to be full economic contributors almost immediately upon arrival. Like other working-class women of that era, they were manufacturing many basic household necessities, such as foodstuffs and clothing, as well as performing the maintenance and child care tasks.[26] In addition, according to an early observer of the *issei*,

> The great majority of wives of farmers, barbers and small shopkeepers take a more or less regular place in the fields or shops of their husbands, while a smaller number accept places in domestic service, or in laundries or other places of employment. Thus, a larger percentage of those admitted find a place in the "labor supply."[27]

According to U.S. Census figures, 20.8 percent of all Japanese women over age fifteen were gainfully employed in 1920. This proportion is similar to the proportion of women employed in the overall population (23.3 percent). However, because virtually all Japanese women over fifteen were married, the *issei* rate of employment was remarkably high. In the population at large, only 9.0 percent of all married women were in the labor force.[28] Also, because Japanese men were concen-

trated in agriculture and small businesses, which relied on wives' unpaid help, the extent of *issei* women's gainful activity is probably underestimated.

It is difficulty to specify the occupational distribution of *issei* women, for the women frequently divided their time between housework, unpaid work in family farms and businesses, and paid employment. In these cases, the main occupation cannot be pinpointed. However, there are data that indicate the range of their activities. Edward K. Strong surveyed 1,716 *issei* women in a 1933 study of Japanese-American occupations. He classified 998 (58 percent) as housewives, 438 (26 percent) as part-time assistants to their husbands, 53 (3 percent) as full-time assistants, and 227 (13 percent) as engaged in independent occupations. He noted, however, that

> undoubtedly, the last two figures are too low and the first figures too high. Accuracy in this connection was very difficult to secure because many of these women speak very little English and are unaccustomed to talk to strangers, and in some cases the Japanese men prevented or interfered in the interviewing of their wives.[29]

There are similar limitations in the U.S. Census data.[30] Agricultural work, including work in plant nurseries (which was an early Japanese specialty), was the largest field of employment.[31] Domestic service was by far the most common form of nonagricultural employment. In 1900, over one-half of all women were so employed; however, the numbers are so small as to make the data inconclusive. By 1920, domestic service accounted for 40.3 percent of all women engaged in nonagricultural occupations. Overall, there seems to have been a trend away from concentration in domestic work between 1920 and 1940.[32]

During this period, there was increased employment in personal service (which in the

Bay Area was primarily laundry work) and in retail trade. The growth of employment in service and trade reflects the move of Japanese men away from wage labor into small enterprises, which employed women as paid and unpaid sales, service, and clerical workers. A small but steady percentage of women found work in manufacturing, primarily in food processing and garment manufacturing. With the establishment of ethnic community institutions, there was a small demand for professionals, such as teachers in Japanese-language schools.

The occupations in which Japanese women specialized shared several characteristics. The work could be fit in around family responsibilities (for example, children could be taken to work, or the hours were flexible); they were an extension of women's work in the home (such as food preparation, laundry, and sewing); they were in low-technology, labor-intensive fields in which low wages and long hours reduced competition from white women; and they took place in family owned or ethnic enterprises in which language or racial discrimination did not constitute barriers to employment. Domestic service included the first three characteristics and was, therefore, consistent with the general run of occupations open to Japanese women. Because of the common characteristics of the occupations, one would expect the jobs to be highly substitutable.

The job histories of the women support this expectation, for the women in the study moved easily between these occupations, although never outside them. The eleven women with experience in nondomestic employment had worked in one or more of the following fields: farming, hand laundry at home, embroidery at home, midwifery, assisting in a family owned cleaning store, or hotel or nursery work. Domestic service, thus, can be seen as belonging to a set of occupations that constitute a distinct and narrow labor market for Japanese women.

Evidence from the 1940 census indicates that the labor market in the Bay Area was particularly restricted. A comparison of the proportion of *issei* women engaged in domestic work in four cities with substantial Japanese populations shows that domestic work was a specialty among *issei* women only in the Bay Area. Over one-fourth (26.8 percent) of all employed *issei* women in Oakland and over one-half (50.4 percent) in San Francisco were found in domestic work. By contrast, only 6.4 percent of *issei* women in Los Angeles and 3.3 percent in Seattle were so employed. A comparison of the occupational distributions for women in Seattle and San Francisco, cities with comparable Japanese populations, is instructive. Nearly two-thirds of Seattle women were employed as proprietors, service, and clerical workers. These figures reflect the opportunities for small entrepreneurs in Seattle, where the *issei* ran hotels, restaurants, and shops catering to transient male laborers in lumbering and canning. Such opportunities were more limited in the Bay Area, leaving domestic work as the main employment for women and gardening as the main occupation for men.

Issei Women's Entry into Domestic Work

I now turn to an analysis of the circumstances that came together in the lives of *issei* women to lead them into domestic service.

Unlike other immigrant groups that specialized in domestic service, these women did not have a prior tradition of service in their homelands. Generally, only indigent and unattached women became servants in Japan. Most of the immigrants who came to California were better off economically than the average rural peasant. They had sufficient resources to pay their fares and as much cash on hand as immigrants from Northern Europe.[33] Thus, becoming a domestic worker meant a drop in status, as well as a break with tradition. Given the lack of previous experience in wage labor generally, and a cultural prejudice against domestic service, the explanation for *issei* women's involvement in domestic work must lie in the situations they confronted in the United States.

One unusual historical circumstance was that the path into domestic work was paved by *issei* men, starting in the early days of immigration. Many had gained their first footholds in the United States as "Japanese Schoolboys." This designation was reportedly coined in the 1880s by a Mrs. Reid, who enrolled a few Japanese students in her boarding school in Belmont, California. These students earned their tuition and board by doing chores and kitchen work.[34] The term came to refer to any Japanese apprentice servant, whether or not he had any involvement in formal schooling. The job itself was the education: it provided the new immigrant with an opportunity to learn English and become familiar with American customs. In return for his services, the Schoolboy received token wages of about $1.50 a week in 1900 ($2.00 a week by 1909), in addition to room and board, compared with the $15.00 to $40.00 a month earned by trained servants. It has been estimated that at the height of male immigration (1904 to 1907), over 4,000 Japanese were employed as Schoolboys in San Francisco.[35]

Still other immigrants earned their first wages in the United States as dayworkers; they hired out to do yard chores and housecleaning on a daily or hourly basis. Groups of men from the same prefecture sometimes took lodgings together and advertised their services. Newcomers were invited to join the household and were quickly initiated into the work.

Both forms of domestic service were temporary stopgaps. Schoolboy jobs and daywork were frequently first occupations for new arrivals; after a short time, the *issei* moved on to agricultural or city trades.[36] In the Bay Area, many dayworkers graduated into a specialized branch of domestic service—gardening. The Japanese gardener became a status symbol, but the indoor male domestic had largely disappeared by 1930. The early association of men with domestic service, however, established the stereotype of the Japanese domestic—a stereotype inherited by the *issei* women when they arrived. The situations wanted columns in Bay Area newspapers, which prior to 1908 had been dominated by ads for Japanese Schoolboys now began to include ads for women, such as "Japanese girl wants situation to assist in general housework and taking care of baby. Address, Japanese Girl, 1973 P . . . Street."

The path into domestic service was, thus, clearly marked. The issue remains, what were the personal circumstances that launched many *issei* women on the journey?

The case of Mrs. Yoshida is a good place to begin. Ninety-one-years old at the time of the interview, she arrived in 1909 as a picture bride. Her husband, sixteen years her senior, had lived in the United States for almost twenty years and had managed to acquire a laundry in Alameda, which the couple ran together. Because they had one of the few telephones in the Japanese community, they began acting as agents for dayworkers. Employers called to request help for cleaning, or other jobs, and the Yoshidas referred the requests to the *issei* men who dropped by. By 1912, Mrs. Yoshida had two small children, and she felt that her family needed extra income. She explains:

> I started to work because everyone went on vacation and the summer was very hard for us. The cleaning business declined during the sum-

mer. . . . I bought a second-hand bicycle from a friend who had used it for five years. I paid $3 for it. So, at night I went to the beach and practiced on that bicycle. At night nobody was at the beach, so even if I fell down, I didn't feel embarrassed. And then I went to work. I worked half a day and was paid $1. . . . We didn't know the first thing about housework, but the ladies of the house didn't mind. They taught us how at the beginning: "This is a broom; this is a dustpan." And we worked hard for them. We always thought America was a wonderful country. At the time, we were thinking of working three years in America and then going back to Japan to help our parents lead a comfortable life. . . . But, we had babies almost every year, and so we had to give up that idea. [She had 10 children between 1910 and 1923.]

Although the specific details are unique, Mrs. Yoshida's account reveals several common elements which came together in the lives of *issei* women who entered domestic work. First, the Yoshidas' intention of accumulating a nest egg and returning to Japan was shared by other immigrants during this period. The women in the study all claimed that they expected to return to Japan eventually. Many were sending remittances to support parents or other relatives in Japan. Because the sacrifice was seen as short term, the immigrants were willing to work long hours and in menial jobs. In this context, wage work could be viewed as a temporary expedient which, therefore, did not reflect on the family's social standing.

A second common element was the economic squeeze experienced by many *issei* families, especially after children arrived. Some families managed to accumulate enough capital to return to Japan.[37] Those who were less well off postponed their return and continued to struggle for day-to-day survival. The majority of women in the study were married to gardeners, whose earnings fluctuated. As Mrs Yoshida's case illustrates,

even those who owned small businesses found their marginal enterprises did not generate sufficient income to support a family. Some women were in even more dire straits: a husband who was ill, who refused to turn over his earnings, or who died and left children to support. Three women, facing this situation, took or sent their children to Japan to be cared for by relatives, so they could work full-time.

Mrs. Shinoda was part of this group. Her husband, a college graduate, was killed in an accident in 1928. She was thirty-nine and had two young sons.

> I started work after my husband died. I went to Japan to take my children to my mother. Then, I came back alone and started to work. . . . My sons were ten and eight . . . and I worked in a family. At that time, I stayed in the home of a professor at the University of California as a live-in maid. . . . I got the job through another Japanese person. She was going back to Japan, so I took her place. [What kind of things did you do?] Cleaned house, and cooking, and serving food. [Did you know how to cook and things like that?] No, I didn't, at first. The lady told me.

Given the factors pushing the *issei* to seek wage work, what factors drew them particularly into domestic work? The basic limiting factor was the labor market situation described earlier. Race segregation, family responsibilities, and the lack of English and job skills severely limited job options. Given limited choices, domestic work offered some desirable features. Its main attraction was flexibility; those with heavy family responsibilities could work part-time, yet during times of financial pressure, they could work extra days or hours, as needed. A further pull was the demand for domestic labor. Dayworkers were sought by the growing number of middle-class urban families who could not afford regular servants. The demand was great enough so that, as Mrs. Yoshida and Mrs. Shinoda noted, employers were willing to take on someone with no experience and provide on-the-job training.

Conditions of Work

Domestic service encompasses a variety of specific situations. The jobs that the *issei* women entered were of three types: live-in service, full-time nonresidential jobs, and daywork.

For most of its history, domestic service was a live-in occupation, and up until World War I, this was the most common pattern in the United States. This merging of residence and workplace stood as a marked exception to the increasing separation of production from the household and the accompanying segregation of work and nonwork life brought about by industrialization. For the live-in domestic, there was no clear delineation between work and nonwork time. Work hours were open-ended, with the domestic "on call" most of her waking hours, and with little time to devote to family and outside social relationships. As other forms of wage work which gave workers greater autonomy expanded, the confinement and isolation of domestic service grew more onerous. Observers noted that women preferred factory or shop employment, even though wages and physical amenities were frequently inferior.[38] Two *issei* in the study had worked as live-in servants; a widow who needed a home as well as a job, and a woman who arrived as an adolescent with her parents and worked as a live-in Schoolgirl before marriage.[39]

Their situations were unusual for *issei* women. Unlike European immigrant domestics, who were primarily young and single, almost all *issei* domestics were married and had children. Their circumstances were similar to those of black women in the South, and like

them, the *issei* turned to nonresidential work. Until the 1930s, full-time positions with one employer were fairly common. Some *issei* women worked as general household help for middle-class families, performing a wide range of tasks from laundry to cooking to cleaning. Other *issei* worked as "second girls" in multiservant households, where they carried out a variety of tasks under the direction of a paid housekeeper.

The nonresidential jobs gave workers stable employment, set hours, and a chance for a private life. However, for the worker to provide all-around services, she had to put in an extended day, which typically began with breakfast cleanup and ended only after supper cleanup. The day was broken up by an afternoon break of one to three hours, during which the women returned home to prepare meals or do chores. Mrs. Kayahara described her workday, which began at 6:30 in the morning when she left home to catch a trolley. She arrived at work before 8:00. Then: "Wash the breakfast dishes, clean the rooms, make lunch and clean up. Go home. Back at 5:00 to help with cooking dinner and then do the dishes. Come, go, and back again. It was very hard. I had to take the trolley four times."

Partly because of the extended hours in full-time domestic jobs and partly because of the greater availability of day jobs, all the women in the study eventually turned to daywork. They worked in several different households for a day or half-day each week and were paid on an hourly or daily basis. The workday ended before dinner, and schedules could be fitted around family responsibilities. Many women worked part-time, but some women pieced together a forty- or forty-eight-hour week out of a combination of full and half-day jobs.

The duties of the dayworker generally consisted of housecleaning and laundry. Sometimes the worker did both, but many employers hired different workers for the two sets of tasks. Laundry was viewed as less skilled and more menial, and was often assigned to minority women, such as the Japanese.[40] Both cleaning and laundry were physically demanding, because of low-level household technology. Ruth Cowan suggests that the availability of household help slowed the adoption of labor-saving appliances by middle-class housewives.[41] Moreover, employers felt that hand labor created superior results. Workers were expected to scrub floors on hands and knees and to apply a lot of elbow grease to waxing and polishing. Some sense of the work is conveyed by Mrs. Tanabe's description of her routine, when she began work in 1921.[42]

> When we first started, people wanted you to boil the white clothes. They had a gas burner in the laundry room. I guess you don't see those things any more—an oval shaped boiler. When you did daywork, you did the washing first. And, if you were there 8 hours, you dried and then brought them in and ironed them. In between, you cleaned the house from top to bottom. But, when you go to two places, one in the morning and one in the afternoon, you do the ironing and a little housework.

The *issei* express contradictory attitudes toward the demands of the work. On one hand, they acknowledge that the work was menial, that it consisted largely of unskilled physical labor. As one put it, "You use your body, not your mind." The women also say that the reason they were satisfied with the work is that they lacked qualifications; for example, "I'm just a country person." Yet, one is also aware that the women are telling stories of their own prowess when they describe the arduousness of the work. What emerges out of their descriptions is a sense of pride in their physical strength and endurance, a determination to accomplish whatever was asked, and a devotion to doing a good job. Mrs. Yoshida explains that she never found housework difficult; even today she can work for hours in her garden without being aware of it, because

> from the time I was a little girl, I was used to working hard. I was born a farmer and did farm work all along. Farm work is very hard. My body was trained so nothing was hard for me. If you take work at a hakujin [caucasian] place, you have to work hard. There was a place where the lady asked me to wash the ceilings. So I took a table and stood up on it. It was strenuous, but I washed the whole ceiling. So the lady said: "That was hard work, but next time it won't be so hard." She gave me vegetables, fruits, and extra money and I went home.

This kind of pride in physical strength is talked about in relation to men in manual occupations, but is rarely seen as relevant to women. Similarly, an orientation toward completing a task is seen as more evident among skilled craftsworkers than among those engaged in devalued work. Yet, we find evidence of both among this group of older women engaged in what has been called "the lowest rung of legitimate employment."[43]

The evolution from live-in service to non-residential jobs to daywork can be viewed as a modernizing trend that has brought domestic work closer to industrialized wage work. First, work and nonwork life became clearly separated. Second, the basis for employment became more clearly contractual; that is, the worker sold a given amount of labor time for an agreed-upon wage. Yet, as long as the work took place in the household, it remained fundamentally preindustrial. While industrial workers produced surplus value that was taken as profit by the employer, the domestic workers produced only simple use value.[44] In a society based on a market economy, work that produces no exchange value is devalued.[45] Whereas the work process in socially organized production is subjected to division of labor, task specialization, and standardization of output, domestic labor remained diffuse and nonspecialized. The work consisted essentially of whatever tasks were assigned by the employer. While industrial workers were integrated into a socially organized system of production, the domestic worker remained atomized. Each domestic performed her tasks in isolation, and her work was unrelated to the activities of other workers.

Because of its atomization, domestic work remained invisible and was not subject to regulation. Domestic workers were excluded from protections won by industrial workers in the 1930s, such as Social Security and minimum wages.[46] Although sporadic attempts to organize domestics were made in large cities, such efforts rarely succeeded in reaching more than a small minority. The *issei* in the study appear never to have been included in organizing efforts. Thus, there was no collectivity representing their interests, and, of course, the *issei* received none of the benefits accorded more privileged workers, such as sick days or paid vacations. In fact, when the employer went out of town, the worker was put on unpaid leave. The *issei* claimed, in any case, that they never took vacations before World War II.

Work and Family Life

Issei women's experiences in domestic employment cannot be understood without also considering the relationship between wage work and family roles.

To do so, we must refer back to the family system of the society from which the immigrants came. In late nineteenth- and early twentieth-century southern, rural Japan, the basic social and economic unit was the *ie* (household), which typically included husband, wife, unmarried children, and in the case of an eldest son, the husband's parents. The *ie* served as the basic unit of production

and as a corporate economic body. Ownership and authority were vested in the male head of household. Members were graded by gender, age, and insider-outsider.[47]

Most households were engaged in small-scale farming and petty manufacturing and trade, the economy of which relied on the unpaid labor of all members, including women and children.[48] Most of what was produced was directly consumed, and any income generated was corporate, rather than individual. There was no separation of work and family life because production, consumption, maintenance, and child care were carried on more or less simultaneously. Women's work was thus incorporated into the overall work of the household and did not differ organizationally from men's work. There was, of course, a clear division of labor by sex. Women were assigned most domestic chores, as well as certain female-typed agricultural and manufacturing tasks; men supervised the household work and represented the family in relation to the larger community.

When they came to the United States, the *issei* were entering an industrialized economy in which wage labor was becoming the predominant mode. The majority of *issei* families found "preindustrial" niches in farming and small business enterprises. In these families, the traditional system of household labor, as well as the old role relationships, were transplanted, more or less intact.[49] Many *issei* families, however—especially those in Bay Area cities—adapted to the urban economy by turning to multiple wage earning. Husband and wife and older children were individually employed, mostly in marginal, low-paying jobs. Each worker's earnings were small, but the pooled income was sufficient to support a household and to generate some surplus for savings, remittances, and consumer goods.

This strategy was in many ways consistent with the values of the *ie* system. Because multiple wages were needed, the economic inter-dependence of family members was preserved. Moreover, the employment of women was consistent with the assumption that women were full economic contributors. In other ways, however, the strategy was inconsistent with the traditional *ie* structure. Wage work represented a form of economic organization in which the individual, rather than the family, was the unit of production, and in which work and family life were separated, rather than integrated. Women working outside the home violated the principle that men had exclusive rights to, and control over, their wives' labor.

Perhaps because of this duality, *issei* men were divided in their attitudes toward their wives' participation in the labor force. Some men opposed their wives' employment on the grounds that their services were needed at home. In contrast, other men expected their wives to pull their full weight by being employed, regardless of the women's own inclinations. Thus, while Mrs. Adachi said she was defying her husband's wishes by going out to work, Mrs. Uematsu indicated that she felt compelled to seek wage work:

My husband didn't bring in enough money, so I went out to work. I didn't even think twice about it. If I didn't take a job, people would have started to call me "Madam" [i.e., accusing her of thinking she was too much of a lady to work]. . . . It was like a race; we all had to work as hard as possible.

The duality is further mirrored in the contradictory impacts of wage work on women's position in the family. On one hand, to the extent that the traditional division of labor and the structure of male privilege persisted, wage work added to the burdens and difficulties experienced by women. On the other hand, to the extent that wage work reduced women's economic dependence and male control over their labor, it helped the women transcend

the limitations of traditional role relationships. Evidence of both tendencies emerge from the women's accounts; the increased burdens are greater and more obvious.

Among the women in the study, the major share of housework and child care remained with them even if they were employed. All but two women claimed their husbands did no work "inside" the house. Mrs. Nishimura explained:

No, my husband was like a child. He couldn't even make tea. He couldn't do anything by himself. He was really Japan-style. Sometimes, I had too much to do, so although I would always iron his shirts, I might ask him to wait a while on the underwear, but he'd say no. He'd wait there until I would iron them. People used to say he was spoiled. He was completely a Japanese man. Some people divorce their husbands for not helping around the house, but that never entered my mind. I thought it was natural for a Japanese.

Although Mr. Nishimura might be viewed as extreme, even by other *issei*, there was unanimous agreement among the women that Japanese men expected to be waited upon by their wives.

The result was that the women experienced considerable overload. The men worked long hours, often at physically exhausting jobs, but the women's days were longer. Their days began earlier than other members of the household with the preparation of a morning meal and ended later with the preparation and cleanup of the evening meal; in between, they had to fit in laundry and cleaning. Some women were endowed with natural vitality. They could maintain an immaculate household and do extras, such as making clothes for children. Mrs. Nishimura described her schedule during the years she was doing seasonal garment work.

Since I had so many children, I asked my mother-in-law to take care of the children. I would get up at 5 o'clock and do the laundry. In those days—we'd do it by hand—hang up the laundry, than go to Oakland. I would come home and since my husband didn't have much work then, he'd get drunk and bring the children home. I would cook and eat, and then go to sleep. They all asked me how long I slept at night. But, since I was in my twenties, it didn't affect me too much.

Others, like Mrs. Uematsu, were exhausted at the end of the day and had to let things slide. She exclaimed, "My house was a mess. I went to work in the morning and when I came back from work, I'd cook a little and then go to sleep and that's about all."

As Mrs. Nishimura's account indicates, an additional problem was created by wage work that did not exist under the family work system—the need for separate child care. Employers sometimes allowed domestics to bring a young child to work, but as more children arrived, other arrangements had to be made. Friends, neighbors, older children, and husbands were recruited to baby-sit. Women with older children often set their work hours to correspond to school schedules. When no other means were available, and employment was a necessity, the *issei* sometimes resorted to sending their children to Japan to be raised by relatives, as three of the women in the study did. They planned to return to Japan and rejoin their children. In all three cases, the women stayed in the United States, and the children returned as adolescents or adults.[50]

Despite the prevalence of male privilege, role relationships sometimes underwent change in response to new circumstances. The most common adjustment was for husbands to take on some child care responsibilities. Even Mr. Nishimura, the "completely Japanese man," took on transporting and minding children when he was out of work. One woman, Mrs. Nomura, claimed that her husband did quite a lot around the house, including drying dishes. She explained:

He was considerably Americanized. He was young when he came over and he was a Schoolboy, so he was used to the American way of doing things. Even when we quarreled, he wouldn't hit me, saying it's bad in this country for a man to hit a woman, unlike Japan. In Japan, the man would be head of the family without any question. "Japan is a man's country; America is a woman's country," he often used to say.

Some respondents and informants reported cases of role reversal between husband and wife (although not among the women in the study). Role reversals occurred most often when the husband was considerably older than the wife. Because many *issei* men married late in life to much younger women, they were in their fifties by the time their children reached school age. As laborers, their employment prospects were poor, while their wives could easily find domestic jobs. Mrs. Tanabe, a *nisei* raised in Alameda, recalls that her husband was "retired" while she was still a young girl:

The Hiroshima men in Alameda were the laziest men. Their wives did all the work. My dad raised me while my mother went out and did domestic work. He did the cooking and kept house and did the shopping and took me when I went to work. So, he didn't do much really. But, in Alameda, they're known for being the lazy ones—most Hiroshima men are—so no one's rich.

One reason for this pattern may be that domesticity was considered appropriate for older men. Mrs. Yamashita, another *nisei*, reported that her father, a widower, acted as a housekeeper and baby-sitter while she and her husband both went out to work.

In addition to the division of labor by sex, the traditional Japanese family was characterized by what Elizabeth Bott[51] has called segregated conjugal role relationships; that is, husband and wife had a considerable number of separate interests and activities. This pattern seems to have been maintained by the *issei* to a marked degree. Leisure time was rarely spent in joint activities. The women's orbit was restricted to the home and the domestic world of women; men engaged in a wider range of formal church and community activities. Informal socializing, including drinking and gambling, were common male activities. The men's drinking seems to have been a source of conflict in many families. Two women's lives were tragically affected by their husband's drinking. Mrs. Takagi's husband got into frequent accidents, and spent much of his earnings on alcohol. Mrs. Shinoda's husband was killed in a judo mishap that occurred while he was intoxicated. The extent of drinking among *issei* men can be gauged by the fact that women whose husbands did not drink thought it worthy of comment. Mrs. Nomura feels her life was much easier than other women's because her husband was straitlaced:

> Yes I've been lucky. I worked, of course, and encountered social problems [discrimination], but . . . I didn't suffer at all with regard to my husband. He didn't smoke, drink or gamble . . . Very serious Christian with no faults. Everyone else was drinking and gambling. Park Street was full of liquor stores, and so they'd all go there; but my husband led such a clean life, so I was lucky.

Overwork and poverty exacerbated conflicts generated by gender division in the family: the discrepancy in power and privilege, the unequal division of household labor, and the separation of female and male emotional spheres. Far from being passive, the women actively fought with their husbands. Mrs. Nakashima had to send her three children back to Japan and work in a laundry to support herself because her husband was sickly. She reports: "My life in the U.S. was very hard in the beginning because my husband was ill so much and we had such totally different personalities. We were both selfish so we had many problems. But, after I started going to church, I became more gentle. So we had fewer quarrels. I think that is a gift from God." Mrs. Nishimura also reported that she and her husband quarreled a great deal. She explained: "Well, he was rather short-tempered . . . there were times when I thought he was stubborn, but we were far apart in age, so I would attribute our differences to that. Being apart in age does create quite a lot of differences. . . . But, I bore it all." Thus, while the *issei* women express the traditional Japanese attitude that women must bear up under hardship, it is evident that they did not always do so quietly!

Given these additional strains imposed by employment, what did the women gain in the family through domestic employment? There was, of course, the tangible benefit of income, part of which could be retained for individual saving or spending. A less tangible, but perhaps more significant, gain was increased control over their economic circumstances. In Japan, women were ultimately at the mercy of their husband's ability or willingness to provide support. Mrs. Takagi's mother suffered extreme poverty as a result of her father's irresponsibility and drinking. He ran up debts that led to the loss of their farm in Japan. Her own husband proved to be similarly unreliable. However, Mrs. Takagi felt less victimized than her mother because she could work to support herself and her children. As she put it, "I killed myself, but did it all, myself." The sense of self-sufficiency is clearly important to the women, for they maintain an independence, even in later life, from their children. About one-half the women worked into their seventies and even eighties, and all the women worked into their sixties.

In addition to working for their own independence, the *issei* worked for their children. They gained a sense of purpose by seeing their work as contributing to their children's futures. Although most women agreed that the present was the best (that is, easiest) period of their lives, many looked back nostalgically to the days when their children were growing up. Mrs. Nishimura spoke for this group when she said, "This is my best time, but my happiest time was then, when my children were small. I was poor and busy then, but that might have been the best time. It was good to think about my children—how they'd go through high school and college and afterwards."

It is difficult to document the extent of special consideration or deference the women received as a result of their sacrifices. However, the long-term respect they earned is strikingly evident. The daughters and sons of these women were uniform in their expressions of respect toward their mothers. They were eager to do whatever possible to make life comfortable for them. A few spoke ruefully about their mother's "stubbornness" or "independence," which prevented them from doing more.

The very difficulty of the *issei*'s circumstances and their ability to "bear it all" gave them added respect. Looking back, the women expressed amazement at their own capacities: Mrs. Nishimura concluded it was because she was young, while Mrs. Yoshida cited her early conditioning in farm work. The hard work of the *issei* women has become legendary within the Japanese community. Several *nisei* domestics claimed that even now they are unable to match the endurance of *issei* women in their seventies.

The good opinion of others was important in the close-knit Japanese community. The comradery and common frame of reference eased some of the hardships and counteracted the isolating conditions of their work. Sharing their experiences with others in the same situation, they found sympathy and understanding. Mrs. Kayahara recalled:

> In Alameda, the Japanese were living in five or six houses near the City Hall—all of them from Fukuoka were living together. That was so enjoyable. Myself, I never thought to be ashamed of doing domestic work. We had to do any sort of work that was available. Also our friends were doing the same sort of work, and we used to talk about it. . . . Sometimes, things that were worrying us, we'd talk about it. That helped us. If you don't talk to anyone, your heart gets heavy. So we told each other things right away.

Conclusion

This chapter has analyzed the contradictions in *issei* women's involvement in domestic work in the pre–World War II period. The approach taken here has highlighted several aspects of these contradictions.

First, it draws attention to conflict as an underlying dynamic in women's relationship to paid and unpaid work. The attention to conflict makes it possible to see *issei* women as actors striving to gain control and self-respect, rather than as passive targets of oppression. The contest was obviously uneven: *issei* women had few resources for direct resistance, and they lacked collective strength in the form of worker organization or female kin networks. Thus, there is no evidence that they directly confronted their employers or their husbands, that they were militant, or that they engaged in collected action. If these are the criteria, it is easy to overlook the woman's resistance to control by employers and husbands. The strategies the *issei* adopted reflected their relative lack of power; they engaged in indirect forms of resistance, such as evasion. The *issei* maximized autonomy in employment by choosing work situations in which employers were absent or inactive. In the family, they went out to work secretly or withheld part of their wages as a means of gaining control over disposable income. Another strategy women used in both employment and family life was to define their own standards and goals. The *issei* had internalized criteria for what constituted a good day's work; some women defined their jobs in terms of tasks accomplished, rather than hours, for example. They also set their own priorities in relation to housekeeping, education for their children, and the family's standard of living. There is evidence that the women gained satisfaction from meeting their own standards, irrespective of the employers' or their husbands' evaluations.

Second, as the previous discussion indicates, the analysis highlights the interconnectedness of different aspects of the women's experiences, particularly between paid and unpaid work. In both employment and family life, women were in a subordinate position in which their role was defined as service to another. The content of activities in both spheres was also similar, and the structures of employment and family life were, therefore, mutually reinforcing. The parallel structures in turn contributed to a similarity in the strategies used to cope with subordination. The reliance on indirect strategies in conflicts with employers, for example, can be related in part to *issei* women's experience of subordination in the household and the community and their inability to directly confront their husbands' authority. In contrast, black women domestics resisted or defied their employers more openly and were also less subordinate in the family.[52]

Coping strategies are usually conceptualized as situationally specific; that is, as growing out of and being confined to a particular setting.[53] In this case, at least, the strategies appear to form a coherent whole. This is to be expected in part because of structural parallels in women's positions in work, family, and community life and in part because of internalized cultural attitudes, such as the value of hard work, which carried across situations. Perhaps, more important, the process of striving in one area developed orientations that carried over into other arenas. Thus, the theme of self-sufficiency pervaded all aspects of the women's life and has persisted over time.

Finally, the analysis points to the contradictory implications of employment for *issei* women's status. The issue has often been framed in either/or terms. Some theorists, including some Marxists, have viewed employment as a liberating force, arguing that women would gain status in society by becoming producers in the market economy, rather than remaining nonproductive household workers. By contributing to family income and by gaining a role outside the family, women would increase their power in the family. More recently, analysts have argued that employment, far from contributing to equality, actually reinforces women's oppression. They point out that women are relegated to low-status, routine, and low-paying jobs; that women remain responsible for unpaid domestic work and are, thereby, saddled with a double burden; that in both realms, women are subjugated by male authority.[54] Although this account shares this recent perspective and documents the multiple forms of oppression faced by *issei* domestic workers, the focus on contradictions makes it possible to see oppressive and liberating consequences as interrelated. *Issei* women were constrained by the larger economic and political system that forced them to seek employment, but limited them to the most marginal jobs. The conditions of domestic work subjected them to further oppression. But, out of these conditions, *issei* women gained advantages that enabled them to achieve certain goals (such as helping their families in Japan and providing extras for their children), to become less dependent on the ability or willingness of husbands to provide support, and to form ties outside the immediate family group. And, despite the menial nature of employment, the *issei* achieved a sense of their own strength, and in some cases, superiority to employer and husband within their own area of competence.

NOTES

Acknowledgments: The research for this chapter was supported in part by a faculty grant from the Graduate School, Boston University. The author is grateful to Jean Twomey for assistance in organizing the data, Haru Nakano for help in arranging interviews, Peter Langer for detailed suggestions during writing, Murray Melbin for clarifying issues in an earlier version, and Edna Bonacich and Lucie Cheng Hirata for encouraging me to explore the topic. Special thanks are also owed to the Women and Work Group, Chris Bose, Carol Brown, Peggy Crull, Roz Feldberg, Myra Ferree, Heidi Hartmann, Alice Kessler-Harris, Dorothy Remy, Natalie Sokoloff, and Carole Turbin. Our meetings were supported by a grant from the Problems of the Discipline Programs, American Sociological Association; and our discussions helped crystallize some key conceptual issues.

1. H. A. Millis, *The Japanese Problem in the United States* (New York: Macmillan, 1915); and Edward K. Strong, *Japanese in California* (Stanford, Calif.: Stanford University Press, 1933).

2. David Chaplin, "Domestic Service and Industrialization," *Comparative Studies in Sociology* 1 (1978): 98–127; and U.S. Department of Labor, Women's Bureau, *Women's Occupations Through Seven Decades,* by Janet M. Hooks, Bulletin no. 218 (Washington, D.C., 1947).

3. Lewis Coser, "Domestic Servants: The Obsolescence of a Social Role," *Social Forces* 52 (1973): 31–40.

4. George J. Stigler, *Domestic Servants in the United States, 1900–1940* (New York: National Bureau of Economic Research, 1946).

5. C.f. Gerda Lerner, *Black Women in White America: A Documentary History* (New York: Vintage Books, 1973).

6. William L. Yancey, Eugene P. Ericksen, and Richard N. Julian, "Emergent Ethnicity: A Review and Reformulation," *American Sociological Review* 41 (June 1976): 391–403.

7. The material for this chapter is drawn from several sources. Information on the economic context and historical background was obtained from census material, a few early surveys, and secondary accounts. Newspaper files and documents furnished by community members provided valuable details; these sources included the files of the *Alameda Daily Argus* from the 1880s to 1920; surviving copies of the *Nichi-Bei Times* annual directories, 1910, 1914, and 1941; and privately printed church histories, *Eighty-Fifth Anniversary of Protestant Work Among Japanese in North America* (1975) and *Buddhist Churches of America* (1976), which included the chronologies of individual churches and temples in the Bay Area. Overall, however, documentary evidence was scanty. Japanese community directories, organizational records, and newspaper files were lost during World War II, or they were destroyed by their owners prior to evacuation because they feared the material would be used as evidence of subversive activities.

The heart of the data for this chapter was derived from in-depth interviews of fifteen *issei* women who worked as domestics, and for comparison, twelve *nisei* (American-born) and seven *kibei* (American-born, Japan-educated) domestics. These interviews were supplemented by informant interviews of thirty older *issei* and *nisei* who had lived in the prewar communities of San Francisco, Oakland, Alameda, Berkeley, and San Leandro.

8. Cf. Bonnie Dill, "The Dialectics of Black Womanhood," *Signs* 4 (Spring 1979): 543–55, for a similar argument regarding black women.

9. Frank Miyamoto, "Social Solidarity Among the Japanese in Seattle," *University of Washington Publications in the Social Sciences* 11 (1939): 57–130, first designated these three time periods in his study of the prewar Seattle, Washington, Japanese community. I have adopted his chronology, sub-

stituting the term "stabilization period" to designate the third period, which Miyamoto called the "second generation period." For a discussion of the social characteristics of frontier situations, for example, the preponderance of males, see Murray Melbin, "Night as Frontier," *American Sociological Review* 43 (1978): 3–22.

10. Edward K. Strong, *The Second-Generation Japanese Problem* (Stanford, Calif.: Stanford University Press, 1934).

11. See Yamato Ichihashi, *Japanese Immigration* (San Francisco: Marshall Press, 1915) and his more detailed *Japanese in the United States* (Stanford, Calif.: Stanford University Press, 1932); also Roger Daniels, *The Politics of Prejudice* (New York: Atheneum, 1973).

12. For an account of the immigrant associations, see Ivan H. Light, *Ethnic Enterprise in America* (Berkeley and Los Angeles: University of California Press, 1972).

13. The other areas of concentration were around Sacramento and the upper San Joaquin Valley (Daniels, *Politics of Prejudice*).

14. Strong, *Second-Generation Japanese Problem.*

15. Ichihashi, *Japanese in the United States.*

16. Census figures for 1900 show only 985 Japanese women over age fifteen. By 1910, the number had jumped to 9,087. Sydney Gulik compiled data showing that 45,706 Japanese females were admitted to the continental United States between 1909 and 1923, of whom 33,628 were listed as wives (reprinted in Ichihashi, *Japanese in the United States,* as appendix C).

17. *1914 Yearbook of the Nichi-Bei Times* is a directory of residents, associations, and businesses in the Bay Area. Most Christian churches were founded in the 1890s with the aid of white Protestant churches. The Buddhist churches, which were ethnically supported, were founded and developed between 1900 and 1915.

18. Harry H. L. Kitano, "Housing of Japanese Americans in the San Francisco Bay Area," in *Studies in Housing and Minority Groups,* ed. Nathan Glazer and D. McEntire (Berkeley and Los Angeles: University of California Press, 1960), pp. 178–97.

19. Daniels, *Politics of Prejudice.*

20. Miyamoto, "Social Solidarity."

21. Strong, *Japanese in California.*

22. Although the women spoke of the decision as their parents', it appears to be the father as head of the household who had the power. See beginning of section on the Japanese family. The full range of attitudes among the women did not necessarily fall in one dimension; however, roughly scaling the women's attitudes from "most reluctant" to "most eager," the following attitudes can be identified: (1) felt tricked, went reluctantly; (2) persuaded, inveigled by promises for the future by parents; (3) "carefree," thought it would be a new experience; (4) felt that this mate or going to the United States was better than another alternative; (5) aspired to come to the United States, parents concurred; and (6) aspired to come to the United States, had to overcome parents' opposition.

23. This and all other names in the text are pseudonyms. Other identifying details have been disguised to ensure anonymity.

24. During this period, many Japanese women had to marry men who were emigrating for demographic reasons. This was a time of Japanese expansionism. Young men were colonizing Manchuria and Korea, as well as seeking their fortunes in Hawaii and the mainland United States. Among the various destinations, the United States was viewed as offering the easiest situation for women.

25. Ichihashi, *Japanese in the United States.*

26. Robert W. Smuts, *Women and Work in America* (New York: Columbia University Press, 1959).

27. Millis, *Japanese Problem,* p. 27.

28. U.S. Department of Commerce, Bureau of the Census, *Fourteenth Census of the United States Taken in the Year 1920,* vol. 4, *Population, Occupations* (Washington, D.C.: Government Printing Office, 1923), and U.S. Department of Commerce, Bureau of the Census, *Women in Gainful Occupations, 1870 to 1920,* by Joseph A. Hill, Census Monographs 9 (Washington, D.C.: Government Printing Office, 1929).

29. Strong, *Japanese in California,* p. 109.

30. Unless special instructions were given to enumerators (as occurred in 1910) to count the unpaid work of women and children, such labor was

likely to be overlooked. (See Hill, *Women in Gainful Occupations.*) Because the Japanese faced legal harassment, they were suspicious of outsiders and feared giving out personal information. Finally, the women's inability to communicate in English undoubtedly hampered accuracy in reporting. Despite these shortcomings, the census remains the best source of detailed occupational information.

31. This figure is lower than would be expected from geographic distributions. During the period between 1900 and 1930, slightly more than one-half of the Japanese (56 percent) lived in rural areas, according to a survey conducted by the Japanese consulate (Strong, *Japanese in California*). There appears to have been an undercount of unpaid agricultural labor among women.

32. If data for *issei* and *nisei* are combined, however, the percentage in domestic work actually goes up slightly in 1940. This is because the *nisei* were even more heavily concentrated in domestic work than the *issei*.

33. Ichihashi, *Japanese in the United States.*

34. Ibid.

35. Daniels, *Politics of Prejudice.*

36. Strong, *Japanese in California.*

37. An old-time resident of Alameda recalled that the early stores and businesses were owned by a succession of different families. The owners sold their businesses to other families and returned to Japan.

38. Lucy M. Salmon, *Domestic Service* (New York: Macmillan, 1897); and Amy Watson, "Domestic Service," in *Encyclopedia of the Social Sciences* 5 (New York: Macmillan, 1937), pp. 198–206.

39. Some other women later worked as live-in help right after World War II in order to have a place to live after returning from internment camp.

40. Cf. Lerner, *Black Women in White America;* and David M. Katzman, *Seven Days a Week: Women and Domestic Service in Industrializing America* (New York: Oxford University Press, 1978).

41. Ruth S. Cowan, "The Industrial Revolution in the Home: Household Technology and Social Change in the Twentieth Century," *Technology and Culture* 17 (January 1976): 1–23.

42. Mrs. Tanabe is counted as one of the *nisei*, even though she is technically an *issei*, having arrived in Hawaii as an infant and later coming to California when she was five. She is one of the oldest *nisei*, however, having been born in 1898, and her work experience overlaps with those of the *issei*.

43. Theodore Caplow, *The Sociology of Work* (New York: McGraw-Hill, 1954), p. 233.

44. Perhaps, the point is made clearer by Braverman's remark that although the work of a cleaner employed by a firm that sells cleaning services generates profit and thereby increases the employer's capital, the work of the private domestic actually reduces the wealth of the employer. Harry Braverman, *Labor and Monopoly Capital* (New York and London: Monthly Review Press, 1974).

45. Margaret Benston, "The Political Economy of Women's Liberation," in *From Feminism to Liberation,* ed. Edith H. Altbach (Cambridge, Mass., and London: Shenkman, 1971), pp. 199–210.

46. Social Security coverage was extended to domestics in the 1950s and federal minimum wage laws in the 1970s. See U.S. Department of Labor, Women's Bureau, *Handbook of Women Workers* (Washington, D.C.: Government Printing Office, 1975); and David M. Katzman, "Domestic Service: Women's Work," in *Women Working,* ed. Ann H. Stromberg and Shirley Harkess (Palo Alto, Calif.: Mayfield, 1978), pp. 377–91.

47. Chie Nakane, *Kinship and Economic Organization in Rural Japan,* London School of Economics Monographs on Social Anthropology, no. 32 (London: Athlone Press, 1967).

48. Sylvia J. Yanagisako, "Two Processes of Change in Japanese-American Kinship," *Journal of Anthropological Research* 31 (175): 196–224.

49. Ibid.

50. These *kibei* children (American born, Japanese educated) frequently encountered the same difficulties as their parents. Language and cultural barriers handicapped them in the labor market. Mrs. Nishimura's three older children, raised in Japan, for example, ended up in farming and domestic work, and the three younger children became white-collar workers.

51. Elizabeth Bott, *Family and Social Network: Roles, Norms and External Relationships in Ordinary Urban Families* (London: Tavistock, 1957).

52. See Dill, "Dialectics of Black Womanhood"; and Lerner, *Black Women in White America.*

53. For example, Erving Goffman, in *Asylums* (Garden City, New York: Anchor Books, 1961) identifies several situationally specific strategies that patients develop for coping with conditions in total institutions.

54. Heidi Hartmann, "Capitalism, Patriarchy, and Job Segregation by Sex," *Signs* 1 (Spring 1976): 137–69; and Natalie Sokoloff, "A Theoretical Analysis of Women in the Labor Market," paper presented at the meetings of the Society for the Study of Social Problems, San Francisco, 1978.

Chapter 54

The Parenting Approach
to the Work-Family Dilemma

ROSANNA HERTZ

Child rearing tends to be regarded as an individualistic concern for parents in the United States. Society may purport to be "pro-family" but, judging by the small number of policies and programs that pertain to child care, society largely ignores how young children spend their days, despite widespread recognition that women's labor force participation has increased dramatically over the past several decades.[1] Indeed, it has become quite popular for political contenders to "support" family values but to sidestep the sticky questions about how children are being cared for when mothers (and fathers) must work for pay outside the home.

Child care should be a leading social issue, addressed at workplaces, in communities,

This chapter is excerpted from "A Typology of Approaches to Childcare: The Centerpiece of Organizing Family Life for Dual-Earner Couples," *Journal of Family Issues* 18, no. 4 (1997): 355–85, copyright © 1997 by Sage Publications, Inc. Reprinted by permission of Sage Publications, Inc. A version of that article was presented at the British Psychological Society, London, 1996.

and at the state and federal levels of government. But without an array of good solutions to preschool child care (e.g., quality, affordability, and certification), couples attempt to resolve this work-family dilemma through individual solutions.

My research suggests that a combination of a priori beliefs and economic resources explains the choice of child care practice. However, in the absence of strong evidence regarding the relationship between beliefs and economic resources, I propose a typology of approaches to child care that reflects the interaction of ideology and economic factors. From a study of dual-earner couples I suggest that there are three general approaches to child care: the mothering approach, the market approach, and the parenting approach. The mothering approach assumes that the person best suited to raise the couple's children is the wife, who should be with them at home. The "market" approach to caring for children involves hiring other people to care for one's own children. Both wife and husband are career-oriented and they emphasize the use of professional caregivers. These couples' children spend their days with adults caregivers who are not family members. In the "parenting" approach, both parents are full participants in child care. This chapter focuses on the parenting approach as the approach that most strongly challenges both the traditional division of labor within families and the traditional definition of job and career.

The Study and the Interview Sample

This chapter is part of an in-depth study of ninety-five dual-earner couples in eastern Massachusetts, with the majority (eighty-eight couples) having at least one child still living in the home. Husbands and wives were interviewed separately; the majority of couples were also interviewed simultaneously (Hertz 1995). I used a stratified quota sample. Different strategies were used to find different segments of the study's population. In general, access to individual couples was either through other professionals who identified couples who fit the study's parameters or through mailings to day care parents in several communities.

Thirty-six percent of the couples are working class; the other three-fifths are middle and upper middle class.[2] Within the working class, thirty couples are White and four couples are of other races. Within the middle and upper middle class, thirty-five couples are White and twenty-one couples are of other races. In an additional five couples, the spouses are of different races; these couples are all middle- and upper-middle-class couples. There are no "cross-class" couples (husbands and wives who differ in occupational prestige). Racial differences in the three approaches to mothering appear not to be as important for this typology as social class.[3]

At the time of the interview each spouse within a couple had a minimum of one job.

This does not mean, however, that they held two full-time jobs at the time of having young children (preschool or elementary age). In most cases, women did not leave the labor force for more than one year, but in a small number of cases women were not employed in the labor force when their children were preschool age or younger. At the time of the interviews just over 60 percent of the couples were between their late thirties and middle forties. But there is great variation among this group in the age at which they had their first children. For those couples who had children in early decades, there may have been a greater economic ability for the wife to stay at home. For those couples who have had children in the last five years, most remain in the paid labor force with wives typically taking only brief maternity leaves. At the time of the interview sixty-three couples (66 percent) had at least one child age 5 or under. An additional twenty-five couples (26 percent had children over age 5 living at home.

The couples most likely to adopt the parenting approach were from two distinct social classes. One was the working-class underemployed who had held blue-collar jobs before those jobs were eliminated by downsizing, the other was couples with middle-range managerial and professional jobs that allowed them to request more flexible worktime or fewer workdays. Those at the top of their organizations, who had the most authority and responsibility for lower-level employees, were the least likely to restructure their work in order to adopt the parenting approach. It is possible that those at the top could have chosen to seek alternative employment, but they would have had to give up salient parts of their careers and to redefine their work and family goals. The couples least likely to adopt a parenting approach to child care are those who work in organizations or work settings that are highly structured or highly demanding of their time.

The Parenting Approach

The parenting approach is exemplified in the belief that the family ought to be organized around caring for the children—with the critical distinction that *both* parents are full participants. Couples who adopt the parenting approach create new ways of combining family and work by seeking less demanding jobs or by negotiating more flexible arrangements with present employers (at least during the early years of their children's lives). Some couples, particularly those who have middle-class occupations, are choosing to push employment in new directions. But for others, particularly those with working-class occupations, underemployment becomes a catalyst for rethinking traditional gender-based divisions of labor. These couples are crafting strategic responses to a shrinking labor market.

Regardless of how they came to share parenting, at the time of the interviews these couples do not essentialize the mother as the only parent capable of nurturing children. Couples who chose to modify rigid work structures out of a belief that the responsibility for child rearing should be shared between mother and father talk about parenting with expectations that both parents are essential as nurturers and providers, though parents are not androgynous. Among those couples where the men have lost full-time jobs and are now doing less challenging work or are working part-time or both, the realization that men can care for children throws into question prior ideological beliefs about the dichotomy that conflates manhood and fatherhood with economic provision, and womanhood and motherhood with nurturing activities. (Even though new practices of work and family divisions emerge it does not necessarily follow that underemployed men view caring for their children as a substitute for their present employment situations.)

Emphasizing the sharing of child rearing between parents limits the need to use external child care providers. When they are used, parents attempt to control the kind of child care that supplements their own involvement with children prior to their children's entry into the public schools. Some use only a few hours a week of day care or babysitters; others find cooperative exchanges between families with young children.

Restructuring Employment to Maximize Parenting

This group of parents shares a belief about *parental* superiority in raising children. They believe that men and women should work outside and inside the home *and* share responsibility for child rearing. Individuals attempt to modify their jobs and employment commitments in order to regulate on their own terms the demands that paid work makes and thus restore some semblance of control even if it means loss of income (Hertz and Ferguson 1996).

Couples emphasize that men have historically been short-changed as nurturers and they are seeking parity with wives in their desire to experience fatherhood (see Coltrane, Chapter 56, this volume). Men explained their efforts to modify their work schedules in order to be actively involved in child care. One man, age 37, employed in a social service agency, explains why he decided to reorganize his work schedule to have one day a week at home when his first child was born. He was able to reorganize which forty hours he worked in order to not cut back on his pay, to have one day a week at home, and occasionally to hold staff meetings in his home with his infant daughter present.

> Why did I do it? I think I was a new father, I wanted to spend time with my child, first year of life. I also sort of figured I might not have this

opportunity again. I thought this was unique. I knew I wasn't going to forever stay at this job and I just had immense flexibility. I still was working very hard, but I had immense flexibility and control since I was the director, so I could really set the policy, and I did. But it was just important to me to spend some time and not have either a professional caregiver or have it so my wife had some time. It also worked in terms of our hours. Partly there was some pragmatism here in terms of—we wanted to minimize the day care she was in, maximize our time with her, certainly in that first year.

Another unusual arrangement which highlights the prioritizing of family togetherness over full-time work is a middle-class couple who each work part-time day hours; she as a social worker and he as a patient advocate. The wife, age 33, explains that initially she thought she would remain at home, but they each negotiated part-time work hours in their respective jobs in order to share child rearing. Understanding her husband's desire to be with their child, she reported that they figured out the following solution:

> I had negotiated, at my job, to go back part-time after my maternity leave, but I thought in my heart that I might not go back at all. Then when Andy went back to work, he missed Sam so much that he felt like he really wanted to be home more. And what we were able to figure out was that if I went back part-time, and he cut back his hours—so he decided he'd work thirty hours and I'd work twenty hours. And we could always be home with him. So that was what we did, and that's what we've done. . . . He worked three mornings and two afternoons and I worked three afternoons and two mornings. He worked six hours a day and I worked four hours a day.

She explains why parental child rearing and part-time jobs better matched their desires:

> I don't have criticisms of people who use day care. I just couldn't bear the thought. But it just

felt, for me, that I really wanted to be with Sam and I wanted Andy to be with Sam and I feel like I got the absolute best of all possible worlds. Because I think it would have been really hard for me to be home full-time and have Andy work full-time. And working part-time is just the perfect balance. So to be able to work, and to have Sam home with Andy, we just couldn't ask for more. . . . I thought it was better for him to be with one of his parents.

The husband, age 39, explains the price he has paid and the confusion this arrangement has caused at the agency where he is employed:

> I felt really stressed out initially. When I started working part-time, it was incredibly difficult, because the expectations of myself were that I could do what I used to do just in less time. . . . I think more than anybody else at my office, I have had to scale back my expectations of myself. And I feel like people have been very supportive. . . . But it was frustrating. I'd post my schedule for everybody and give them a list. We'd try to set up a staff meeting and if we're going to do it on a Tuesday, do we do it in the morning or the afternoon? . . . And initially I'd have to scratch my own head and wonder when I was going to be in.

Some middle-class couples find a way to implement even more atypical arrangements such as "mutual exchanges" where families swap child care and keep track of hours. Administering part-time two different social services, the couple quoted below, ages 47 and 42, are making ends meet, are placing themselves at the economic fringes of the middle class, and are conscious of their own downward mobility relative to their own parents. They know they could earn more money but as she put it:

> We want to maximize as much as possible these first five years of being with him. So I would say the first thing is values about the amount of day care. It is also more expensive and it makes you work more. . . . I would say the driving factor

was about values. We didn't want him to be in a lot of day care. I figured the longer he had more intimate settings, the better.

She describes their present arrangements in the following manner:

And now what we do is on Mondays I take care of a little girl in the morning and then her mom takes care of Mark in the afternoon. On Tuesday and Thursdays, I bring Mark to a friend's house and that little girl's dad take care of Mark and walks him to preschool with his little daughter. And then picks them up and takes care of him. Then on Wednesdays, I take care of both little girls: the little girl whose mom takes care of Mark on Monday, and the little girl whose dad takes care of Mark on Tuesdays and Thursdays. Then on Fridays, I take care of the little girl whose dad walked Mark to preschool. I take care of her on Friday mornings. So that evens out that because we get two afternoons and we give a day in the mornings. And then Friday afternoon, I pay the little girl's mother twenty dollars to take care of him.

It is more common in this study sample for women to be the part-time worker or ask for special arrangements in order for them to combine motherhood and work, trading a solid middle-class standard of living for a more modest one. One woman, age 36, found a job working part-time as a lawyer. She explains why:

I've seen the way other people's lives had been crazy and I wanted to have a good time with my kids. I just kept hearing from people all the time: "These are the most precious years, don't give them up, hold onto them." . . . There's some truth to that and I really wanted to cherish the time I had with them. . . . I wanted to go back to work because I needed the intellectual stimulation and the respect.

But, in many ways, the couples quoted above are labor-force elites: They can shift the number of hours they work or change jobs with-

out facing permanent career penalties. Eventually, the men and some of the women in these families shifted back to full-time work when their children entered preschool or grade school. But at least during the early years they restructured the gender system to make fathering and mothering essential to childhood socialization.

Underemployment as a Route to Shared Parenting

For others the downward economy and downsizing by corporations beginning in the 1980s (Hodson and Sullivan 1990) led couples to piece together new work arrangements with active fathering a by-product. These couples did not make conscious choices to work less (and earn less) in order to do more for their children directly. They worry about spiraling downward even further. One father, who is age 39 with two children and at present works part-time as a home health aid, explains how this employment history has devolved:

I think like MANY of the long-term unemployed, people like me who don't show up in the statistics, life goes on. So you do other things; you work part-time, either delivering pizza, which I did for three years, or bunking mail for the post office, whatever. But life goes on, so you have to adjust yourself because, first of all, no one's gonna hire you. Once you're over 30, no one's gonna hire you for any real job. So what's the sense? . . . Your buddy who mows lawns for a living is offering you ten dollars an hour. So you do what you have to do. And you just fall into a whole other world that you forget exists when you worked for a large company, working nine to five for six years.

The wife, age 35, a nurse who typically works the 7 P.M. to 7 A.M. night shift worries that if she loses her overtime she will have to find a second nursing job. She added to her husband's comments her thoughts on how underemployment has affected her husband's sense of masculinity:

> And of course his ego was all shot to hell. He's not the family provider he wants to be and he's not doing exactly what he wanted, what he set in his mind. All his goals are rearranged.

Couples in which the wife was working full-time and the husband part-time often wished that the wife could opt to work fewer hours. While middle-class white women continue to think about their lives as having the option of staying at home or working full-time, ideological and structural barriers prevent men from having similar choices (Gerson 1993). Another mother, age 40, an office manager with two children ages 9 and 5, assumed that there would be two full-time paychecks. She now carries the economic burden and wishes she could have a more flexible work schedule.

> When I decided I would have children, I knew I would always be working, but I thought there would be more flexibility in my work schedule which would allow me to take extended vacations with my children, sometimes come home, be available after school to go to a school function with my son, sometimes be able to go to a soccer practice in the afternoon on a Thursday, be able to go to my daughter's ballet classes with her, that kind of thing. I don't feel like I have that kind of flexibility in my life. . . . In the nicer part of the year, I'll arrive home at six-thirty and they've just come from a baseball practice and they're rosy-cheeked and they're laughing about what happened, and I'm not a part of that. So I guess over a period of time you do build up a little resentment. It goes away. But that's what I'm missing.

Another man who now works part-time as a postal worker, age 37, was laid off from a factory job after a dozen years at his company. His inability to find a full-time job for the past

several years made it necessary for his wife to remain employed full-time. Since she is the carrier of the medical benefits, they feel unable to reduce her work to part-time because they would lose these benefits. Despite his positive experiences caring for his three-year-old son since he was an infant, this father describes the deep ambivalence he feels about contributing in atypical ways to family life:

> I was sort of thrust into the role. Thrust into it by job circumstances. . . . Sometimes it does bother me [not to be the main breadwinner]. . . . I just don't feel like I'm with the crowd. Not that I have to be with the crowd. . . . I realize that most men my age are probably established in careers now and I'm not. . . . But, I just have that vague sense that ah . . . like the world is going on out there and I'm here. I know it's more accept now in society, but still I feel like I'm in the vast minority when it comes to my role. . . . I've more or less settled into the routine of taking care of my son. At first, it was quite an adjustment. . . . It's been kind of a metamorphosis for me. I've gone from being scared to death of it, to ah, being actually quite comfortable now. Maybe that's why I stopping looking for full-time work, I don't know.

His wife, age 31, explains how her fantasies of the kind of family life she thought about have not materialized:

> It's funny because I guess we all have an idea of what's going happen when you get married and all this. All my friends had it easy, you know, got married and then they did have the kids and then they stayed home. So I figured that would just happen to me too. But it was tough. The first year that I was at work it was hard. I think we had a lot of arguments. And I didn't think he could do anything right. When we were both with him it was like, "What we DOING now? There was no set of instructions or anything that come with a baby. I always felt I was better with him. As an infant he felt very awkward with him. And actually, he's done very well with him. I can't, you know, knock him now. But you know, at that time I was very resentful. VERY re-

sentful. And the thing is I had a job I didn't like and I had a manager I didn't like, he was terrible to me, very demanding, and he was very chauvinistic about women.

The last woman quoted admits that mothering does not come "naturally" and it is only through practice that we learn how to do it (Ruddick 1980). She concedes that her husband has mastered maternal practice. That is, he is engaged in sharing the work of parental love, a kind of work he never imagined himself doing. It is ironic that the couples who are on the cutting-edge of transforming maternal thinking are doing so, not because of an ideological belief, but because of the structural constraints of a shrinking labor force that catapult men to learn the work of child rearing. In the process, couples rethink family life, particularly caring for children, as they cobble together identities that are no longer unidimensional. Underemployed couples continue to wish their home and work time could be more evenly divided, but not because they wish wives would become full-time mothers.

The Rise of Fathering

Fathering emerges but without a separate language from mothering, although the practice of it is markedly different from that of the white middle-class breadwinning fathers of a past generation (Bernard 1981; Goode 1982). Regardless of the route to sharing child care, the practice of fathering transformed these men into more nurturing and sensitive caregivers who are teaching their young children how to navigate the world (Coltrane, Chapter 56, this volume). These men report wanting to be different from their own fathers. The husband of the couple who swap child care put it this way:

I didn't want to be the same kind of father my father had been. I wanted to be a more involved father. So, it seemed to me the way to do that was that I would work less and spend more time with [my child].

The patient advocate quoted earlier talked about what he feels he has gained by taking care of his child:

When James was born, I was smitten, I was blown away by the strong feelings I had toward him. It was kind of like falling in love with a lover for me. I was really—I was shocked by that feeling, by how strong my feelings are and were. . . . But I also feel that I really—it's been a window for me, it's been watching him learn about the world and how much the influence I have over that. I feel a tremendous amount of responsibility and I feel really eager to help him explore the world. I want him to do it on his own, but I know that I also have a lot of say in how things get set up, presentations which are made. But it's exciting to be part of that and I really love his discovery of things.

Even though the home health worker quoted above wishes he could return to full-time work to take some of the work pressure off his wife, he also was very eloquent about what it meant to be a father. The detailed response he gives about infants was once reserved for mothers.

Let's see. I don't think it's that different than being a mother. It's very stressful, very, at the same time it's very rewarding. An . . . but I think to have a lot of your father's influence is a good experience for a lot of children. Because I would take her places that my wife normally wouldn't take her. Like down to the auto parts store. . . . It got a lot harder when my second was born. It's twice as hard, ya. Especially right now, he is cutting teeth. He can't walk and he can't talk and so he can't TELL you anything. And he's at that time when he's trying to rearrange his clock to sleep at night so he's up, like last night he was up at midnight. So I brought him to bed with me. And I put him back to bed around two and he was up at four, so like three or four times a night. And lack of sleep more than anything else gets you. Then the older one wakes up. Sometimes ARGGGGHHHH. I feel like a lioness with cubs crawling all around. . . . Fatherhood, it's a lot of hard work but it can also be a lot of fun too. . . . As they get older, you can play more and you can put them in a car and go for a ride and it's a lot easier once they're older.

The father who now works part-time as a postal worker explains that what he feels is most important is making a difference in his child's life:

> Mr. Mom? Um . . . it's frus— . . . it's rewarding, but it's also very frustrating. It's, it's ah . . . it seems like after a day of being with my son all day, it's fun and all that, but sometimes, some days it just wears thin, and I need some adult interaction if you know what I mean? . . . But I feel like I'm in the role of teacher and ah . . . which is I think the most fun part. And just watching him develop and learn new things . . . to see the difference that I can sort of shape and mold my son's life, it gives me some personal satisfaction. Nobody told me that.

The people who use the parenting approach to child care are testing and contesting the limits of their work environments. While there are certainly career costs and unwanted underemployment, these couples are altering the landscape of traditional ways that couples have attempted to integrate work and family and, in the process, are altering the gender system that locates women according to a primary identity as mother and men as economic providers. Men's caring work undermines the belief that mothering comes "naturally" to women. Further, caring for children elevates the status of parenting as a source of primary identity for both mothers and fathers; it even takes priority over workplace goals and job advancement. In short, changing labor force patterns and creating flexible jobs forced new family practices and in the process altered beliefs about child care and nurturing.

Conclusion

Couples who adopt the parenting approach come to reorganize their work in response to placing family first. They are challenging and restructuring the workplace even if it is only temporary. These couples attempt to restructure work in order to accommodate their family needs by making demands on employers. Both women and men are restructuring their work in order to be active parents at the expense of job mobility, career success, and economic sacrifice. In the process they are altering the organization of gender in ways that challenge "mothering" as the exclusive territory of women. In short, they are crafting new ways of parental thinking about child rearing. These couples personify "family values" as they attempt to push workplaces to care about families as much as they care about organizational goals.

A smaller group of couples back into the parental approach—forced into this reorganization of family and jobs by economic constraints. Decreasing jobs will lead more men to rethink their contributions to family life and to adapt to a shrinking economy by staying home and sharing child care. While the circumstances of their "fathering" may not be based on their own choice, these men are potential models for a future in which job uncertainty is likely to increase. On one hand, structural workforce constraints for men may alter motherhood ideals, giving rise to equally compelling arguments for men's greater involvement in sharing the work of child care. But, on the other hand, this data suggests that gender ideology is a powerful countervailing force to a shrinking labor market. Husbands and wives are not willing to agree that parenting is a substitute for men's paychecks. These couples craft shared parenting models but hope that this is a temporary family/work arrangement.

When we look at different approaches to child care, it is not surprising that in many respects the "parenting" approach appears the most novel. Husbands' involvement consciously challenges a traditional familial division of labor and a traditional definition of job and career.

NOTES

Acknowledgments: I thank Faith I. T. Ferguson, who helped me interview some of the couples; Wellesley College, for a faculty award for tape transcriptions; and Robert J. Thomas for helpful comments.

1. In 1993, fully 60 percent of all women with children under 6 years old were in the paid labor force. For those with children 6 to 17 years old, 75 percent of all women were employed, a marked increase from 1966 when 44 percent of women with children this age were employed (Hayghe and Bianchi 1994). For women between 15 and 44 who have had a child for the year 1994, 53 percent were in the labor force (Bachu 1995).

2. I used a combination of factors to decide who belongs in each social class stratum; these included the combined incomes of both spouses. Families in the upper middle class had a combined income of at least $100,000 annually and held professional or managerial occupations; middle-class couples had a combined income of between $40,000 and $100,000, and most were in white-collar jobs in service professions or middle-management occupations; and working-class couples had incomes that overlapped those earned by the middle class, but these couples were distinguished by their occupations. I tried to locate couples for this segment who were employed in traditional working-class occupations or trades, such as, painter, police officer, nurse, waitress, and factory worker.

3. For instance, upper-middle-class African American families were as likely to have a professional approach to child rearing as their White counterparts. Racial differences are relevant when it comes to deciding between types of non-kin care and selecting between settings (see Hertz and Ferguson 1996).

REFERENCES

Bachu, Amara. 1995. *Fertility of American Women: June 1994.* U.S. Bureau of the Census. Washington, D.C.: GPO. P20–482, p. xvii.

Bernard, Jessie. 1981. "The Good-Provider Role: Its Rise and Fall." *American Psychologist* 36(1):1–12.

Coltrane, Scott. "Household Labor and the Routine Production of Gender." (Chapter 56, this volume.)

Goode, William J. 1982. "Why Men Resist," in *Rethinking the Family: Some Feminist Questions,* 131–150, ed. Barrie Thorne, with Marilyn Yalom. New York: Longman.

Gerson, Kathleen. 1993. *No Man's Land: Men's Changing Commitments to Family and Work.* New York: Basic Books.

Hayghe, Howard V., and Suzanne M. Bianchi. 1994. "Married Mothers' Work Patterns: The Job-Family Compromise." *U.S. Department of Labor, Bureau of Labor Statistics, Monthly Labor Review* 117 (6) (January): 24–30.

Hertz, Rosanna. 1995. "Separate But Simultaneous Interviewing of Husbands and Wives: Making Sense of Their Stories." *Qualitative Inquiry* 1(4): 429–451.

Hertz, Rosanna, and Faith I. T. Ferguson. 1996. "Childcare Choices and Constraints in the United States: Social Class, Race, and the Influence of Family Views." *Journal of Comparative Family Studies* 27 (2): 249–280.

Hodson, Randy, and Teresa Sullivan. 1990. *The Social Organization of Work.* Belmont, Calif.: Wadsworth.

Ruddick, Sara. 1980. "Maternal Thinking." *Feminist Studies* 6(3): 343–367.

 *Section B*

Household Division of Labor

~ *Chapter 55*

The Working Wife as Urbanizing Peasant

ARLIE RUSSELL HOCHSCHILD

WITH ANNE MACHUNG

Women's move into the economy is the basic social revolution of our time. It embraces the lifetimes of Nancy Holt, Nina Tanagawa, Anita Judson, their mothers and grandmothers. Nancy Holt is a social worker and mother of two. Her mother was a Nebraska housewife and mother of four, and her grandmother raised five children on a wheat farm. Nina Tanagawa is an executive and mother of two. Her mother ran the house, raised three children, and helped keep the books in her father's hardware store. Her grandmother raised chickens and cows on a farm. Anita Judson is a billing clerk, mother of three. Her mother worked two jobs as a domestic and raised four children. Her grandmother worked a farm in Louisiana. Working from the present generation back, there is often this pattern of working mother now, urban housewife thirty years ago, farm woman fifty

From Arlie Russell Hochschild with Anne Machung, *The Second Shift: Working Couples and the Revolution at Home* (New York: Viking, 1989). Reprinted by kind permission of the author.

years ago. Sometimes two generations of urban housewives precede the farm woman, sometimes none. All these women worked. What's new is that, in taking paid work outside the home, masses of women live a life divided between two competing urgency systems, two clashing rhythms of living, that of the family and the workplace. What's new, in scale at least, is child care for pay, the massive spread of the double day, and the struggle within marriage to equalize the load at home. What's new is the pervasive *effect* of the struggle on the rest of family life.

The recent change is an extension of an earlier industrial revolution. Before the industrial revolution in America, most men and women lived out their lives on the private family farm—where crops were grown and craft work done mainly for domestic consumption. With industrialization, more crops and goods were produced and distributed to wider markets for money. But industrialization did not affect men and women at the same time or in the same way. It has affected men and women at different times and in different ways. In a sense, there is a "his" and a "hers" to the history of industrialization in America.

Painting the picture in broad strokes, the growth of factories, trades, and businesses in early American cities first began to draw substantial numbers of men and women away from farm life around the 1830s. Many single girls worked in the early New England textile mills for four and five years until they married, but mill girls represented a tiny fraction of all women and less than 10 percent of all those who worked for wages.[1] In 1860, most industrial workers were men. Only 15 percent of women worked for pay, most of them as domestic servants. As men entered factory work, they gradually changed their basic way of life; they moved from open spaces to closed-in rooms, from loose seasonal time to fixed industrial time, from life among a tight circle of kinsfolk and neighbors to a life of more varied groups of kin and neighbors. At first, we might say, men did something like trying to "have it all." In the early New England rural factories, for example, men would work in these factories during the day and go home in the evenings to work in the fields. Or they moved in and out of factory work, depending on the season and the crop ready for harvest. But over time, the farmer became an urban worker.

On the whole, the early effects of industrial employment probably altered the lives of men in a more dramatic and immediate way than it altered the lives of women, most of whom maintained a primary identity at home. To be sure, life changed for women, too. Earlier in the century, a young mother might churn butter and raise chickens and hogs. Later in the century, a young mother was more likely to live in the city, but her butter and eggs at the grocery store, take in boarders, be active in the church, and subscribe to what the historian Barbara Welter (1966), has called a

"cult of true womanhood" centered in the home and based on the special moral sensibility of women. Through this period, most women who married and raised children based their role and identity at home. "Home" changed. But, as the historian Nancy Cott (1977) argues in *Bonds of Womanhood*, throughout the nineteenth century, compared to men, women maintained an orientation toward life that was closer to what had been. Thus, if we compare the overall change in the lives of married women to the overall change in the lives of married men, we might conclude that during this period men changed more.

Today, it is women whose lives are changing faster. The expansion of service jobs has opened opportunities for women. Given that women have fewer children now (in 1800 they gave birth to about eight and raised five or six to adulthood; in 1988, they averaged less than two) and given that their wage has been increasingly needed at home, it has become "the woman's turn" to move into the industrial economy. It is now women who are wrenched out of a former domestic way of life. If earlier it was men who tried to combine an old way of life with a new one, now it is women who are, by trying to combine the duties of the housewife and full-time mother with an eight-hour day at the office.

In the early nineteenth century, it was men who began to replace an older basis of power—land—with a new one—money. It was men who began to identify their "manhood" with having money in a ways they had never done before. Through the great value on a man's purchasing power, the modern worship of goods—or what Karl Marx criticized as a "commodity fetishism"—became associated with "being a man."

Today, it is women who are establishing a new basis of power and identity. If women previously based their power mainly on attractiveness to men or influence over children and kin, now they base their power more on wages or authority on the job. As Anita Judson, the billing clerk married to a forklift driver, commented, "After I started earning money, my husband showed me more respect." Given the wage gap, and given the greater effect of divorce on women, the modern woman may not have a great deal more power than before, but what power she has is *based* differently.

Altering her source of power by earning money also gives some women, like Carol Alston, a new basis of identity. Carol, a systems analyst whose husband does carpentry around the house and helps a lot in a "male" way, described her reaction to quitting work after the birth of her first child, "I really discovered how important it was to my identity to earn money." While earning money didn't make Carol feel more like a woman in the same sense that earning money made Ray Judson feel more like a man, earning money was more important to her identity than it had been to her mother's. Furthermore, the great autonomy that often comes with working outside the home has probably changed the identity of women such as Carol to the same extent that it earlier changed that of men.

Housewives who go out to paid work are like the male farmers who, in an earlier era, left the country for the city, farm for factory. They've made an exodus "for the city." If earlier it was men who changed the social patterns of their fathers faster than women changed those of their mothers, today it is women who are changing these faster.

Paid work has come to seem exciting, life at home dull. Although the most acceptable motive for a woman to work is still "because I have to," most of the working mothers I talked to didn't work just for the money. In this way they have begun to participate in a value system once exclusively male and have developed motivations more like those of men. Many women volunteered to me that they would be "bored" or would "go bananas just staying home all day," that they were not, on any permanent basis, the "domestic type." This feeling held true even among women in low-level clerical jobs. A nationwide Harris poll taken in 1980 asked women: "If you had enough money to live as comfortably as you'd like, would you prefer to work full-time, work part-time, do volunteer-type work, or work at home caring for the family?" Among working women, 28 percent wanted to stay home. Of all the women in the study, including housewives, only 39 percent wanted to stay home—even if they had enough money to live as comfortably as they liked. When asked if each of the following is an important reason for working or not, 87 percent of working women responded "yes" to "providing you with a sense of accomplishment and personal satisfaction," 84 percent to "helping ends meet," and 81 percent to "improving your family's standard of living."[2] Women want paying jobs, part-time jobs, interesting jobs—but they want jobs, I believe, for roughly the same complex set of reasons peasants in modernizing economies move to the cities. (In the United States we speak of farmers, not "peasants." The term *farmer* connotes free ownership of land, and a certain pride, while the term *peasant* suggests the humility of a feudal serf. I draw the analogy between modern American women and the modernizing peasantry because women's inferior social, legal, educational, and economic position had until recently been like that of peasants.)

In many ways, the twentieth-century influx of married women into an industrial economy differs from the earlier influx of men. For one thing, through the latter half of the nineteenth century up until the present, women's tasks at home have been reduced.

Store-bought goods gradually replaced homespun cloth, homemade soap and candles, home-cured meats, and home-baked bread. More recently, women have been able to buy an array of prepared meals, or buy "carry-out," or, if they can afford it, to eat out. Some send out clothes to a "wash and fold" laundry, and pay for mending and alterations. Other tasks women used to do at home have also gradually come to be done elsewhere for pay. Day care for children, retirement homes for the elderly, homes for delinquent children, mental hospitals, and even psychotherapy are, in a way, commercial substitutes for jobs a mother once did at home.

To some extent, new services and goods have come to be preferred over the older domestic ones. Products and services of the "native" housewife have given way to mass production outside the home. Store-bought clothes, utensils, and foods have come to seem just as good if not better. In the two-job couple this trend moves even faster; working couples do less at home and buy more goods and services instead. A woman's skills at home are then perhaps also less valued. One working mother remarked: "Sometimes when I get upset and want to make a point, I refuse to cook. But it doesn't work. My husband just goes and picks up some Colonel Sanders fried chicken; the kids love it." Another mother said, "When I told my husband I wanted him to share the laundry, he just said, 'Let's take it to a laundry.'" The modern industrial versions of many goods and services come to be preferred over the old-fashioned domestic ones, even as colonial cultures came to prevail over old-fashioned "native ways." Just as the First World has raised its culture over the Third World's indigenous culture, so too the store-bought goods and services have marginalized the "local crafts" of the housewife.

The Two Cultures: The Housewife and the Working Woman

Not only are many of the products and services of the home available and cheap elsewhere, the status of the full-time housewife has been eroded. As the role of housewife has lost its allure, the wives who "just" stay home have developed the defensiveness of the downwardly mobile. Facing the prospect of becoming a housewife after quitting her job, Ann Myerson said, "If you want to know what shunning feels like, go to a cocktail party, and when they ask you what you do, say 'I'm a housewife.'" One illustration in the November 1970 issue of *True* magazine sums up the housewife's predicament: a commuter train is filled with businessmen reading morning newspapers and office memos. A bewildered middle-aged housewife in bathrobe and furry slippers, hair in curlers, searches the aisles for her husband, his forgotten briefcase in hand. Her husband is hiding behind his seat, embarrassed that his wife looks so ridiculous, so out of place. In their suits, holding their memo pads, reading their newspapers, the men of the commuter care determine what is ridiculous. They represent the ways of the city; the housewife represents those of the peasant.

Working mothers often feel poised between the cultures of the housewife and the working man. On one hand, many middle-class women feel severely criticized by relatives or neighbors who stay home, and who, feeling increasingly threatened and militant about their own declining position, inspect working mothers with critical eye. Nina Tanagawa felt the critical eye of the nonworking mothers of her daughter's friends. Another woman said that she felt it from affluent neighbors. Nancy Holt felt scrutinized by her mother-in-law. Some of these watchful relatives and neighbors cross over the big divide themselves. When Ann Myerson's mother was a housewife, she criticized Ann for her overzealous careerism, but when her mother got a job herself, she questioned Ann's decision to quit.

At the same time, many working mothers seemed to feel both superior to housewives they know and envious of them. Having struggled hard to achieve her position as a systems analyst, Carol Alston didn't want to be confused with "ordinary" women who had not. Whenever she saw a housewife with a child, Carol recalled thinking, Why isn't she doing something *productive*? But seeing housewives slowly pushing their carts down the aisle at the Safeway at midday, she also questioned her own hectic life. When she dropped out of her "real" job to consult part-time and care for her two children—and crossed the deepening rift—she began to sympathize with housewives.

Women who've remained back in the "village" as housewives have been burdened with extra tasks—collecting delivered parcels, letting in repairman, or keeping afternoon company with the children of neighborhood mothers who work. Their working neighbors seldom have time to stop and chat or, sometimes, to fully return favors.

Their traditional source of honor, like the peasant's, has been threatened. In a preindustrial setting, a woman's claim to honor was based primarily on her relation to her husband, her children, her home. As the cash economy spread, money has become the dominant symbol of honor and worth. Unpaid work, like that of housewives, came to seem like not "real" work. The housewife became "just a housewife," her work became "just housework." In their book *For Her Own Good*, Barbara Ehrenreich and Deirdre English (1978) have described how, at the turn of the century, the Home Economics Movement struggled against the social decline of the housewife by trying to systematize and upgrade the role into a profession. Women, its leaders claimed, could be dignified "professionals" in their own homes. Ironically, the leaders of the Home Economics Movement thought housework was honorable—not because it was *intrinsically* valuable—but because it was just as real as *paid* work, a concession revealing how much moral ground had been lost already.

Class Differences

If working wives are the modern-day urbanizing peasant, then there are important differences between some "peasants" and others. In addition to the split between housewives and working women, this social revolution also widens a second split among women—between the women who do jobs that pay enough to pay a babysitter and the women who babysit or tend to other home needs. Carmen Delacorte, who sat for the children of two other families I talked to; Consuela Sanchez, a Nicaraguan woman who babysat for another family's daughter and whose mother was raising Consuela's child back in Nicaragua, and the Myersons' Filipino babysitter, who had an eight-year-old daughter in the Philippines are part of a growing number of workers forming an ever-broadening lower tier of women doing bits and pieces of housewife's role for pay. Most likely, three generations back, the grandmothers of all of these women—professional women, baby-sitters, housekeepers—were housewives, though perhaps from different social classes. Since class has a remarkable sticking power, it may be that the granddaughters of working-class housewives moved into the economy mainly as maids, day care workers, and laundry and other service workers—doing low-paid "female" worker—while the granddaughters of upper-middle-class and upper-class housewives tended to move in as lawyers, doctors, professors, and executives—doing mainly high-status "male" (and some "female") professional work. The granddaughters of the middle class may have tended to move into the expanding world of clerical jobs "in between." There is an important class difference between Carmen Delacorte and Ann Myerson: both from part of the new "peasantry," but as in the industrial revolution of the nineteenth century, some newcomers to the city found it much tougher going than others, and were more tempted to go home.

Preserving a Domestic Tradition?

But many women of every social class and in every kind of job are faced with a common problem: how shall I preserve the domestic culture of my mother and grandmother in the age of the nine-to-five or eight-to-six job? In some ways, the experience of Chicana women condenses the experience of all working women. Many Chicanas have experienced the strains of three movements—that from rural to urban life, from Mexican to American life, and from domestic work to paid employment. In her research on Chicana working women, the sociologist Beatrice Pesquera (1986) discovered that many conceived it to be their job as women to keep alive la cultura, to teach their children Spanish songs, stories, religious rituals; to teach their daughters to cook tortillas and chile verde. Their task is to maintain an ethnic culture eroded by television and ignored by schools in America. The Chicana considers herself a cultural bridge between present and past, and this poses yet another takes in her second shift. When they don't have time to be the bridge themselves, Chicana working mothers often seek a "tortilla grandma" to babysit and provide la cultura. Many white working mothers have

fought a similar—and often, losing—battle to carry forward a domestic culture—a culture of homemade apple pie, home-sewn Halloween costumes, hand-ironed shirts. On weekends and holidays most working women revert to being housewives.

Many traditional women such as Carmen Delacorte and Nina Tanagawa feel they should carry on all of the domestic tradition. To them, the female role isn't simply a female role; it is part of a cultural tradition, like a rural or ethnic tradition. To the traditional, it seems that only women can carry on this tradition. Having secured a base in the industrial economy, having forged a male identity through their position in that economy, men have then relied on women to connect them back to a life outside it. In The Remembered Gate, Barbara Berg (1978) argues that as Americans moved off the land, the values of farm life moved into the home. The woman at home became the urban agrarian, the one who preserved the values of a bygone rural way of life while living in the city. By "staying back" in this sense, she eased the difficult transition for the men who moved ahead. Who is easing the transition for women now?

Although traditional women want to preserve the "domestic heritage" their mothers passed on, most working mothers I talked to felt ambivalent about it. "Do I really need to cook an elaborate meal every night?" they ask themselves. Cutting back on tasks at home often means working mothers are not living up to their mothers' standards of care for home or child, nor to the collective female tradition of the recent past. One woman summed up the feelings of many others: "I'm not the type that has to see my face in the kitchen floor. That part of my mother's cleaning routine I can let go, no problem. But I don't give my child as much as my mother gave me. That's why I want my husband involved—to make up for that."

Some men have responded to the declining domestic culture, much as colonizers once responded to the marginalization of traditional peasant life. Secure in their own modern culture, the colonizers could collect peasant rugs, jewelry, or songs, or cultivate a taste for the indigenous cuisine. Today, some successful professional men, secure in their own modern careers, embrace a few tokens of the traditional female culture. They bake bread or pies on Saturdays, or fix a gourmet meal once a month. But very few men go completely "native."

Unequal Wages and Fragile Marriages: The Counter-Tendency

Women's move into the economy, as a new urban peasantry, is the basic social revolution of our time. On the whole, it has increased the power of women. But at the same time, other realities lower women's power. If women's work outside the home increases their need for male help inside it, two facts—that women earn less and that marriages have become less stable—inhibit many women from pressing men to help more.

Today, women's average earnings are only a bit higher, relative to men's, than they were a hundred years ago; for the past hundred years women have earned 60 percent of what men earn; today it's 70 percent. Given this difference, women still have more of an economic need for marriage than men do.

Meanwhile, what has changed is the extent to which a woman can depend on marriage. The divorce rate has risen steadily through the century, and between 1970 and 1980 it actually doubled. Experts estimate that 49 percent of all men and women who marry today are likely to divorce sometime before they die. Whatever causes divorce, as the sociologist Terry Arendell (1986) points out in *Divorce: Women and Children Last*, the effect of it is much harder on women. Divorce usually pushes women down the class ladder—sometimes way down. According to Lenore Weitzmann's *The Divorce Revolution* (1985) in the first year after divorce women experience a 73 percent loss in their standard of living, whereas men experience a 42 percent gain. Most divorced men provide surprisingly little financial support for their children. According to the Bureau of the Census in 1985, 81 percent of divorced fathers and 66 percent of separated fathers have court orders to pay child support. Twenty percent of these fathers fully comply with the court order; 15 percent pay irregularly. (And how much child support a father pays is not related to his capacity to pay.)[3]

Most divorced fathers have distressingly little emotional contact with their children as well. According to the National Children's Survey conducted in 1976 and 1981 and analyzed by sociologist Frank Furstenberg et al. (1983), 23 percent of all divorced fathers had no contact with their children during the past five years. Another 20 percent had no contact with their children in the past one year. Only 26 percent had seen their children for a total of three weeks in the past year. Two-thirds of fathers divorced for over ten years had not had any contact with their children in more than a year. In line with this finding, in her study of divorced women, sociologist Terry Arendell (1986) found that over half of the children of divorced women had not received a visit or a call from their father in the past year; 35 percent of these children had not seen their fathers in the past five years. Whatever jobs they took; these women would also have to be the most important person in their children lives.

Arendell also found that many middle-class divorced women didn't feel they could turn to their parents or other family members for help. Thus, divorced women are often left in charge of the children, are relatively poorer—often just plain poor—and often lack social and emotional support. The frightening truth is that once pushed down the class ladder, many divorced women and their children get stuck there. This is because they have difficulty finding jobs with adequate pay and because most of them have primary responsibility for the children. Also, fewer divorced women than men remarry, especially older women with children.

While women's entrance into the economy has increased women's power, the growing instability of marriage creates an anonymous, individualistic "modern" form of oppression. In the nineteenth century, before a woman could own property in her own name, get a higher education, enter a profession, or vote, she might have been trapped in a marriage to an overbearing husband and have had nowhere else to go. Now we call that women "oppressed." Yet today, when a woman can legally own property, vote, get an education, work at a job, and leave an oppressive marriage, she walks out into an apparently "autonomous" and "free" form of inequality.

Divorce is an undoing of an economic arrangement between men and women. Reduced to its economic bare bones, traditional marriage has been what the economist, Heidi Hartmann (1981) calls a "mechanism of redistribution": in a sense, men have "paid" women to rear their children and tend their homes. In the late nineteenth and early twentieth centuries, unions fought for and won a higher "family wage" for male workers, on the grounds that men needed the money more than women in order to support wives and children. At that time it seemed reasonable that men should get first crack at the better-paying jobs, and even earn more than women for doing the same work because "women didn't support a family." Since this arrangement put men and women in vastly unequal financial positions, the way most women got a living wage was to marry. In the job market,

the relation between men and women was as the upper to the lower class in society. Marriage was the economic equalizer.

But as marriage—this "mechanism of redistribution"—has grown more fragile, most divorced men still earn a "family wage" but no longer "redistribute" it to their children or the ex-wife who cares for them. The media stress how man and women both have the freedom to choose divorce, and surely this choice is an important advance. But at the same time, the more men and women live outside marriage, the more they divide into separate classes. Three factors—the belief that child care is female work, the failure of ex-husbands to support their children, and higher male wages at work—have taken the economic rug from under that half of married women who divorce.

Formerly, many men dominated women within marriage. Now, despite a much wider acceptance of women as workers, men dominate women anonymously outside of marriage. Patriarchy has not disappeared; it has changed form. In the old form, women were forced to obey an overbearing husband in the privacy of an unjust marriage. In the new form, the working single mother is economically abandoned by her former husband and ignored by a patriarchal society at large. In the old form, women were limited to the home but were economically maintained there. In the new form, the divorced woman does the work of the home but isn't paid for it.

The "modern" oppression of women outside of marriage has also reduced the power of women *inside* marriage as well. Married women are becoming more cautious, more like Nina Tanagawa or Nancy Holt, who look at their divorcing friends and say to themselves, "Put up with the extra month a year or divorce? I'll put up with it."

The influx of women into paid work and their increased power raise a woman's aspirations and hopes for equal treatment at home. Her lower wage and status at work and the threat of divorce reduce what she presses for and actually expects.

The "new" oppression outside marriage thus creates a tacit threat to women inside marriage. Married women say to themselves, "I don't want what happened to her to happen to me." Among the working parents I talked with in this study, both men and women expressed sympathy for the emotional pain of divorcing friends. But women told these stories with more anxious interest, and more empathy for the plight of the divorced woman. For example, one evening at the dinner table, a mother of two who worked at word processing had this exchange with her husband, a store manager, and her former boss, as they were telling me about the divorce of a friend:

A good friend of mine worked as a secretary for six years, putting her husband through dental school. She worked like a dog, did all the housework, and they had a child too. She didn't really worry about getting ahead at the job because she figured they would rely on his work and she would stop working as soon as he set up practice. Well, he went and fell in love with another woman and divorced his wife. Now she's still working as a secretary and raising their little boy. Now he's got two other children by the other woman.

Her husband commented: "That's true, but she was hard to get along with, and she had a drinking problem. She complained a lot. I'm not saying it wasn't hard for her, but there's another side to the story."

The wife answered, surprised, "Yeah, but she was had! Don't you think?"

Her husband said, "Oh, I don't know. They both have a case."

Earlier in our century, the most important cautionary tale for women was of a woman who "fell" from chastity before marriage and came to a bad end because no man would have her. Among working mothers of small children, and especially the more traditional of them, the modern version of the "fallen woman" is the divorcée. Of course, not all women fear the prospect of divorce: for example, not Anita Judson. But the cases of Nancy Holt and Nina Tanagawa are telling because their fear of divorce led them to stop asking for more held in the second shift. When life is made to seem so cold "out there," a woman may try to get warm inside an unequal marriage.

All in all, then, two forces are at work: new economic opportunities and needs, which draw women to paid work and which put pressure on men to share the second shift. These forces lend appeal to an egalitarian gender ideology to strategies of renegotiating the division of labor at home. But other forces—the wage gap between men and women, and the effect on women of the rising rate of divorce—work in the opposite direction. These forces lend appeal to a traditional gender ideology and to the female strategy of the supermom and to the male strategy of resistance to sharing. All of the couples I studied were exposed to both sets of forces, though they differed in their degree of exposure: some women were more economically dependent than others; some were in more precarious marriages. It is the background of this "modern" oppression that made many women, like Carol Alston or Ann Myerson, feel very grateful for the men they had, even when they didn't share the whole strain of the second shift.

The Haves and Have-Nots of Backstage Support for Work

The trends I have described constitute the stall in the revolution and stack the cards in favor of husbands not sharing the second shift with their working wives. Once all these forces are set in motion, one final pattern keeps men doing less: women's lack of "backstage support" for their paid jobs.

It sets up a cycle that works like this: because men put more of their "male" identity into work, their work time is worth more than female work time—to the man and to the family. The greater worth of male work times makes his leisure more valuable, because it is his leisure that enables him to refuel his energy, strengthen his ambition, and move ahead at work. By doing less at home, he can work longer hours, prove his loyalty to his company, and get promoted faster. His aspirations expand. So does his pay. So does his exemption from the second shift.

The female side of the cycle runs parallel. The woman's identity is less in her job. Since her work comes second, she carries more of the second shift, thus providing backstage support for her husband's work. Because she supports her husband's efforts at work more than he supports hers, her personal ambitions contract, and her earnings, already lower, rise more slowly. The extra month a year that she works* contributes not only to her husband's success but to the expanding wage gap between them, and keeps the cycle spinning.

More than wages, what affects a man's contribution at home is the value a couple puts on the husband's or wife's job. That judgment depends on the investment in education, the occupational status, and the future expectations each partner has with regard to the other. In general, the more important a man's job the more backstage support he receives, and the less backstage support for her job a woman receives the less important her job becomes.

---

*Adding together the time it takes to do a paid job and to do housework and childcare, women work an extra month of twenty-four-hour days a year. *Ed.*

The inequality in backstage support has received little notice because most of it is hidden from view. One cannot tell from sheer workplace appearance who goes home to be served dinner and who goes home to cook. Any more than we can tell rich from poor these days just by how people dress. Both male and female workers come to work looking the same. Yet one is "poorer" in backstage support than the other. One irons a spouse's uniform, fixes a lunch, washes clothes, types a résumé, edits an office memo, takes a phone calls, or entertains clients. The other has a uniform ironed, a lunch fixed, clothes washed, a résumé typed, an office memo edited, phone calls taken, and clients entertained.

Women (with traditional or transitional ideologies) believe they ought to give more backstage support than they get. Career-centered egalitarian women gunning for promotion feel they deserve to receive as much as they give. But family oriented egalitarians—men and women alike—aren't eager to clear the decks at home for more time at the office. They consider the home as their front stage. The rise of the two-job family has reduced the supply of housewives, thus increased the demand for backstage support, and finally somewhat redistributed the supply of that support.

There is a curious hierarchy of backstage "wealth." The richest is the high-level executive with an unemployed wife who entertains his clients and runs his household and a secretary who handles his appointments, makes his travel arrangements, and orders anniversary flowers for his wife. The poorest in backstage support is the single mother who works full-time and rears her children with no help from anyone. Between these two extremes lie the two-job couples. Among them, the husbands of working wives enjoy less support than husbands of housewives, and the men whose working wives do all the second shift enjoy more support than men who share. In general, men enjoy more support than women, and the rich enjoy more of it than the poor.

In a study I did of the family life of workers in a large corporation, I discovered that the higher up the corporate ladder the more home support a worker had. Top executives were likely to be married to housewives. Middle managers were likely to be married to a working spouse who does some or most of the housework and child care. And the clerical worker, if she is a woman, is likely to be single or a single mother and does the work at home herself.[4] At each of these three levels in this company, men and women fared differently. Among the female top executives, 95 percent were married to men who also worked and 5 percent were single or single parents. Among male top executives, 64 percent were married to housewives, 23 percent were married to working wives, and 5 percent were single or single parents. So compared to men, female top executives worked in a disadvantageous environment of backstage support. As one female manager remarked: "It's all men at my level in the company and most of them are married to housewives. But even the ones whose wives work seem to have more time at the office than I do." As women executives at this company often quipped, "What I really need is a wife."

In the middle ranks, a quarter of the men were married to housewives, nearly half were married to working wives, and about a third were single. Among women in the middle ranks, half were part of two-job couples and carried most of the second shift. The other half were single or single parents. Among lower-level clerical workers, most were single or single mothers.

Being "rich" or "poor" in backstage support probably influences what traits people develop. Men who have risen to the top with great support come to be seen and to actually be "hard driving," ambitious, and "committed" to their careers. Women who have had little support are vulnerable to the charge of being "uncommitted." Sometimes, they do become less committed: Nancy Holt and Nina Tanagawa withdrew their attention to work in order to take care of "everything else." These women did not lack ambition; their work felt very real to them. They did not suffer from what psychologist Matina Horner (1970) calls a "fear of success." Rather, their "backstage poverty" raised the emotional price of success impossibly high.

In an earlier economic era, when men entered industrial life, their wives preserved for them—through the home—a link to a life they had known before. By "staying back" such wives eased a difficult transition for the men who were moving into the industrial age. In a sense, Nancy Holt is like a peasant new to a factory job in the city; she is part of a larger social trend, doing what others like her are doing. In the nineteenth century, men had women to ease the transition for them, but in the twentieth century, no one is easing the transition for women like Nancy Holt.

NOTES

1. Alice Kessler-Harris, *Out to Work* (New York: Oxford University Press, 1982). Also see Julie A. Matthaie, *An Economic History of Women in America* (New York: Schocken Books, 1982).

2. Louis Harris and Associates, "Families at Work," General Mills American Family Report, 1980–81. Other research also shows that even working-class women who do not have access to rewarding jobs prefer to work. See Myra Ferree, "Sacrifice, Satisfaction and Social Change: Employment and the Family," in Karen Sacks and Dorothy Remy, eds., *My Troubles Are Going to Have Trouble with Me* (New Brunswick, N.J.: Rutgers University Press, 1984), 61–79. Women's paid work leads to their personal satisfaction (Charles Weaver and Sandra Holmes, "A Comparative Study of the Work Satisfaction of Females with

| | Family Type | | | |
Level in Company	Traditional Family	Dual Work	Single/ Single Parent	Total
Top executive	54%	39%	8%	101%*
Middle manager	13%	50%	37%	100%
Clerical worker	—	50%	50%	100%

*This adds up to 101 because of rounding.

Full-Time Employment and Full-Time House-keeping," *Journal of Applied Psychology* 60 [1975]: 117–28) and—if a woman has the freedom to choose to work or not—it leads to marital happiness. See Susan Orden and N. Bradburn, "Working Wives and Marriage Happiness, "*American Journal of Sociology* 74 (1969): 107–123.

3. See U.S., Bureau of the Census, *Current Population Reports: Households, Families, Marital Status, and Living Arrangements,* series P–20, no. 382 (Washington, D.C.: U.S. GPO, 1985). Also see *Statistical Abstracts of the U.S. National Data Book, Guide to Sources* (Washington, D.C.: U.S. GPO, 1985). Spousal support is awarded in less than 14 percent of all divorces, and in less than 7 percent of cases do women actually receive it. See Lenore Weitzman, *The Divorce Revolution* (New York: Free Press; London: Collier Macmillan, 1985).

4. These findings are based on questionnaires I passed out to every thirteenth name on the personnel roster of a large manufacturing company. Of those contacted, 53 percent replied. The results show that the typical form of a worker's family life differs at different levels of the corporate hierarchy. The traditional family prevails at the top. Dual-work families prevail in the middle, and single-parent families and singles prevail at the bottom, as the accompanying table shows.

REFERENCES

Arendell, Terry. 1986. *Divorce: Women and Children Last.* Berkeley: University of California Press.

Berg, Barbara. 1978. *The Remembered Gate: Origins of American Feminism.* New York: Oxford University Press.

Cott, Nancy. 1977. *The Bonds of Womanhood.* New Haven: Yale University Press.

Ehrenreich, Barbara, and Deirdre English. 1978. *For Her Own Good: One Hundred Fifty Years of the Experts' Advice to Women.* Garden City, N.Y.: Anchor Press.

Furstenberg, Frank, C. Nord, James Peterson, and Nicholas Zill. 1983. "The Life Course of Children of Divorce, Marital Disruption, and Parental Contact." *American Sociological Review* 48:656–68.

Hartmann, Heidi. 1981. "The Family as the Locus of Gender, Class, and Political Struggle: The Example of Housework." *Signs* 6:366–94.

Horner, Matina S. 1970. "Femininity and Successful Achievement: A Basic Inconsistency." In *Feminine Personality and Conflict,* edited by Judith Barwick, Elizabeth Douvan, Matina S. Horner, and David Gutmann, pp. 45–74. Belmont, Calif.: Brooks/Cole.

Pesquera, Beatrice. 1986. "Work and Family: A Comparative Analysis of Professional, Clerical, and Blue Collar Chicana Workers." Ph.D. diss., University of California, Berkeley.

Weitzman, Lenore. 1985. *The Divorce Revolution.* New York: Free Press.

Welter, Barbara. 1966. "The Cult of True Womanhood." *American Quarterly* 18:151–74.

Chapter 56

Household Labor and the Routine Production of Gender

SCOTT COLTRANE

Motherhood is often perceived as the quintessence of womanhood. The everyday tasks of mothering are taken to be "natural" expressions of femininity, and the routine care of home and children are seen to provide opportunities for women to express and reaffirm their gendered relation to men and to the world. The traditional tasks of fatherhood, in contrast, are limited to begetting, protecting, and providing for children. While fathers typically derive a gendered sense of self from these activities, their masculinity is even more dependent on *not* doing the things that mothers do. What happens, then, when fathers share with mothers those tasks that we define as expressing the true nature of womanhood?

This chapter describes how a sample of twenty dual-earner couples talk about sharing housework and child care. Since marriage is one of the least scripted (Goffman 1959) or most undefined (Blumer 1962) interaction

From *Social Problems* 36 no. 5 (December 1989): 473–90, copyright © 1989 by the Society for the Study of Social Problems, Inc. Reprinted by permission.

situations, the marital conversation (Berger and Kellner 1964) is particularly important to a couple's shared sense of reality. I investigate these parents' construction of gender by examining their talk about negotiations over who does what around the house; how these divisions of labor influence their perceptions of self and other; how they conceive of gender-appropriate behavior; and how they handle inconsistencies between their own views and those of the people around them. Drawing on the parents' accounts of the planning, allocation, and performance of child care and housework, I illustrate how gender is produced through everyday practices and how adults are socialized by routine activity.

Gender as an Accomplishment

Candace West and Don Zimmerman (1987, 126) suggest that gender is a routine, methodical, and recurring accomplishment. "Doing gender" involves a complex of socially guided perceptual, interactional, and micropolitical activities that cast particular pursuits as expressions of masculine and feminine "natures." Rather than viewing gender as a property of individuals, West and Zimmerman conceive of it as an emergent feature of social situations that results from and legitimates gender inequality. Similarly, Sarah Fenstermaker Berk (1985, 204, emphasis in original) suggests that housework and child care

> can become the occasion for producing commodities (e.g., clean children, clean laundry, and new light switches) and a reaffirmation of one's *gendered* relation to the work and to the world. In short, the "shoulds" of gender ideals are fused with the "musts" of efficient household production. The result may be something resembling a "gendered" household-production function.

If appropriately doing gender serves to sustain and legitimate existing gender relations, would inappropriate gender activity challenge that legitimacy? Or, as West and Zimmerman (1987, 146) suggest, when people fail to do gender appropriately, are their individual characters, motives, and predispositions called into question? If doing gender is unavoidable and people are held accountable for its production, how might people initiate and sustain atypical gender behaviors?

By investigating how couples share child care and housework, I explore (1) the sorts of dyadic and group interactions that facilitate the sharing of household labor; (2) how couples describe the requirements of parenting and how they evaluate men's developing capacities for nurturing; and (3) the impact of sharing domestic labor on conceptions of gender.

The Sample

To find couples who shared child care, I initially contacted schools and day care centers in several suburban California communities. Using snowball sampling techniques (Bier-

nacki and Waldorf 1981), I selected twenty moderate-to middle-income dual-earner couples with children. To compensate for gaps in the existing literature and to enhance comparisons between sample families, I included couples if they were the biological parents of at least two school-aged children, they were both employed at least half time, and both identified the father as assuming significant responsibility for routine child care. I observed families in their homes and interviewed fathers and mothers separately at least once and as many as five times. I recorded the interviews and transcribed them for coding and constant comparative analysis (Glaser and Strauss 1967).

The parents were primarily in their late thirties and had been living together for an average of ten years. All wives and 17 of 20 husbands attended some college and most couples married later and had children later than others in their birth cohort. The median age at marriage for the mothers was 23; for fathers, 26. Median age at first birth for mothers was 27; for fathers, 30. Fifteen of 20 fathers were at least one year older than their wives. Median gross annual income was $40,000, with three families under $25,000 and three over $65,000. Sixteen of the couples had two children and four had three children. Over two-thirds of the families had both sons and daughters, but four families had two sons and no daughters, and two families had two daughters and no sons. The children's ages ranged from four to fourteen, with 80 percent between the ages of five and eleven and with a median age of seven.

Mothers were more likely than fathers to hold professional or technical jobs, although most were employed in female-dominated occupations with relatively limited upward mobility and moderate pay. Over three-quarters held jobs in the "helping" professions: seven mothers were nurses, five were teachers, and four were social workers or counselors. Other occupations for the mothers were administrator, laboratory technician, filmmaker, and bookbinder. Sample fathers held both blue-collar and white collar jobs, with concentrations in construction (3), maintenance (2), sales (3), business (3), teaching (3), delivery (4), and computers (2). Like most dual-earner wives, sample mothers earned, on average, less than half of what their husband's did, and worked an average of eight fewer hours per week. Eleven mothers (55 percent), but only five fathers (25 percent) were employed less than 40 hours per week. In nine of twenty families, mothers were employed at least as many hours as fathers, but in only four families did the mother's earnings approach or exceed those of her husband. (For a more complete description of the sample, see Coltrane 1988.)

Developing Shared Parenting

Two-thirds of the parents indicated that current divisions of labor were accomplished by making minor practical adjustments to what they perceived as an already fairly equal division of labor. A common sentiment was expressed by one father who commented.

> Since we've both always been working since we've been married, we've typically shared everything as far as all the working—I mean all the housework responsibilities as well as child care responsibilities. So it's a pattern that was set up before the kids were even thought of.

Nevertheless, a full three-quarters of the couples reported that the mother performed much more of the early infant care. All of the mothers and only about half of the fathers reported that they initially reduced their hours of employment after having children. About a third of the fathers said they increased their employment hours to compensate for the loss

of income that resulted from their wives taking time off work before or after the births of their children.

In talking about becoming parents, most of the fathers stressed the importance of their involvement in conception decisions, the birth process, and early infant care to later assumption of child care duties. Most couples planned the births of their children jointly and intentionally. Eighty percent reported that they mutually decided to have children, with two couples reporting that the wife desired children more than the husband and two reporting that the husband was more eager than the wife to become a parent. For many families, the husband's commitment to participate fully in childrearing was a precondition of the birth decision. One mother described how she and her husband decided to have children.

> Shared parenting was sort of part of the decision. When we decided to have children, we realized that we were both going to be involved with our work, so it was part of the plan from the very beginning. As a matter of fact, I thought that we only could have the one and he convinced me that we could handle two and promised to really help (laughs), which he really has, but two children is a lot more work than you realize (laughs).

By promising to assume partial responsibility for childrearing, most husbands influenced their wives' initial decision to have children, the subsequent decision to have another child, and the decision of whether and when to return to work. Almost all of the mothers indicated that they had always assumed that they would have children, and most also assumed that they would return to paid employment before the children were in school. Half of the mothers did return to work within six months of the birth of their first child.

All but one of the fathers were present at the births of their children and most talked about the importance of the birth experience, using terms like "incredible," "magical," "moving," "wonderful," and "exciting." While most claimed that they played an important part in the birth process by providing emotional support to their wives or acting as labor coaches, a few considered their involvement to be inconsequential. Comments included, "I felt a little bit necessary and a lot unnecessary," and "I didn't bug her too much and I might have helped a little." Three quarters of the fathers reported that they were "very involved" with their newborns, even though the mother provided most of the daily care for the first few months. Over two-thirds of the mothers breastfed their infants. Half of the fathers reported that they got up in the night to soothe their babies, and many described their early infant care experience in terms that mothers typically use to describe "bonding" with newborns. The intensity of father-infant interaction was discussed by fathers as enabling them to experience a new and different level of intimacy and was depicted as "deep emotional trust," "very interior," "drawing me in," and "making it difficult to deal with the outside world."

About half of the fathers referred to the experience of being involved in the delivery and in early infant care as a necessary part of their assuming responsibility for later child care. Many described a process in which the actual performance of caretaking duties provided them with the self-confidence and skills to feel that they knew what they were doing. They described their time alone with the baby as especially helpful in building their sense of competence as a shared primary caretaker. One man said,

I felt I needed to start from the beginning. Then I learned how to walk them at night and not be totally p.o'ed at them and not feel that it was an infringement. It was something I *got* to do in some sense, along with changing diapers and all these things. I was certainly not repulsive and in some

ways I really liked it a lot. It was not something innate, it was something to be learned. I managed to start at the beginning. If you *don't* start at the beginning then you're sort of left behind.

This father, like almost all of the others, talked about having to learn how to nurture and care for his children. He also stressed how important it was to "start at the beginning." While all fathers intentionally shared routine child care as the children approached school age, only half of the fathers attempted to assume a major share of daily infant care, and only five couples described the father as an equal caregiver for children under one year old. These early caregiving fathers described their involvement in infant care as explicitly planned:

She nursed both of them completely, for at least five or six months. So, my role was—we agreed on this—my role was the other direct intervention, like changing, and getting them up and walking them, and putting them back to sleep. For instance, she would nurse them but I would bring them to the bed afterward and change them if necessary, and get them back to sleep. . . . I really initiated those other kinds of care aspects so that I could be involved. I continued that on through infant and toddler and preschool classes that we would go to, even though I would usually be the only father there.

This man's wife offered a similar account, commenting that "except for breastfeeding, he always provided the same things that I did—the emotional closeness and the attention."

Another early caregiving father described how he and his wife "very consciously" attempted to equalize the amount of time they spent with their children when they were infants: "In both cases we very consciously made the decision that we wanted it to be a mutual process, so that from the start we shared, and all I didn't do was breastfeed. And I really would say that was the only distinction." His wife also described their infant care arrangements as "equal," and commented that other people did not comprehend the extent of his participation:

> I think that nobody really understood that Jennifer had two mothers. The burden of proof was always on me that he was literally being a mother. He wasn't nursing, but he was getting up in the night to bring her to me, to change her poop, which is a lot more energy than nursing in the middle of the night. You have to get up and do all that, I mean get awake. So his sleep was interrupted, and yet within a week or two, at this work situation, it was expected that he was back to normal, and he never went back to normal. He was part of the same family that I was.

This was the only couple who talked about instituting, for a limited time, an explicit record-keeping system to ensure that they shared child care equally.

> [Father]: We were committed to the principle of sharing and we would have schedules, keep hours, so that we had a pretty good sense that we were even, both in terms of the commitment to the principle as well as we wanted to in fact be equal. We would keep records in a log—one might say in a real compulsive way—so that we know what had happened when the other person was on.
> [Mother]: When the second one came we tried to keep to the log of hours and very quickly we threw it out completely. It was too complex.

Practicality and Flexibility

Both early- and later-sharing families identified practical considerations and flexibility as keys to equitable divisions of household labor. Most did not have explicit records or schedules for child care or housework. For example, one early involved father reported that practical divisions of labor evolved "naturally":

> Whoever cooks doesn't have to do the dishes. If for some reason she cooks and I don't do the dishes, she'll say something about it, certainly. Even though we never explicitly agreed that's how we do it, that's how we do it. The person who doesn't cook does the dishes. We don't even know who's going to cook a lot of the time. We just get it that we can do it. We act in good faith.

Couples who did not begin sharing routine child care until after infancy were even more likely to describe their division of labor as practical solutions so shortages of time. For example, one mother described sharing household tasks as "the only logical thing to do," and her husband said, "It's the only practical way we could do it." Other fathers describe practical and flexible arrangements based on the constraints of employment scheduling:

> Her work schedule is more demanding and takes up a lot of evening time, so I think I do a lot of the every day routines, and she does a lot of the less frequent things. Like I might do more of the cooking and meal preparation, but she is the one that does the grocery shopping. An awful lot of what gets done gets done because the person is home first. That's been our standing rule for who fixes dinner. Typically, I get home before she does so I fix dinner, but that isn't a fixed rule. She gets home first, then she fixes dinner. Making the beds and doing the laundry just falls on me because I've got more time during the day to do it. And the yardwork and cuttin' all the wood, I do that. And so I'm endin' up doin' more around here than her just because I think I've got more time.

While mothers were more likely than fathers to report that talk was an important part of sharing household labor, most couples reported that they spent little time planning or arguing about who was going to do what around the house. Typical procedures for allocating domestic chores were described as "ad hoc," illustrated by one mother's discussion of cooking:

Things with us have happened pretty easily as far as what gets done by who. It happened without having to have a schedule or deciding—you know—like cooking. We never decided that he would do all the cooking; it just kind of ended up that way. Every once in a while when he doesn't feel like cooking he'll say, "Would you cook tonight?" "Sure, fine." but normally I don't offer to cook. I say, "What are we having for dinner?"

In general, divisions of labor in sample families were described as flexible and changing. One mother talked about how routine adjustments in task allocation were satisfying to her: "Once you're comfortable in your roles and division of tasks for a few months then it seems like the needs change a little bit and you have to change a little bit and you have to regroup. That's what keeps it interesting. I think that's why it's satisfying."

Underlying Ideology

While ad hoc divisions of labor were described as being practical solutions to time shortages, there were two major ideological underpinnings to the sharing of housework and child care: child-centeredness and equity ideals. While those who attempted to share infant care tended to have more elaborate vocabularies for talking about these issues, later sharing couples also referred to them. For instance, all couples provided accounts that focused on the sanctity of childhood and most stressed the impossibility of mothers "doing it all."

Couples were child-centered in that they placed a high value on their children's well-being, defined parenting as an important and serious undertaking, and organized most of their nonemployed hours around their children. For instance, one father described how his social life revolved around his children:

Basically if the other people don't have kids and if they aren't involved with the kids, then we aren't involved with them. It's as simple as that. The guys I know at work that are single or don't have children my age don't come over because then we have nothing in common. They're kind of the central driving force in my life.

While about half of the couples (11 of 20) had paid for ongoing out-of-home child care, and three-quarters had regularly used some form of paid child care, most of the parents said that they spent more time with their children than the other dual-earner parents in their neighborhoods. One father commented that he and his wife had structured their lives around personally taking care of their children:

An awful lot of the way we've structured our lives has been based around our reluctance to have someone else raise our children. We just really didn't want the kids to be raised from 7:30 in the morning 'till 4:30 or 5:00 in the afternoon by somebody else. So we've structured the last ten years around that issue.

Many parents also advocated treating children as inexperienced equals or "little people," rather than as inferior beings in need of authoritarian training. For examples, an ex-military father employed in computer research stated, "We don't discipline much. Generally the way it works is kind of like bargaining. They know that there are consequences to whatever actions they take, and we try and make sure they know what the consequences are before they have a chance to take the action." Another father described his moral stance concerning children's rights:

I'm not assuming—when I'm talking about parent-child stuff—that there's an inequality. Yes, there are a lot of differences in terms of time spent in this world, but our assumption has been, with both children, that we're peers. And so that's how we are with them. So, if they say something and they're holding fast to some position, we do not say, "You do this because we're the parent and you're the child."

About half of the parents talked directly about such equity ideals as applied to children.

Concerning women's rights, 80 percent of fathers and 90 percent of mothers agreed that women were disadvantaged in our society, but only two mothers and one father mentioned equal rights or the women's movement as motivators for sharing household labor. Most did not identify themselves as feminists, and a few offered derogatory comments about "those women's libbers." Nevertheless, almost all parents indicated that no one should be forced to perform a specific task because they were a man or a woman. This implicit equity ideal was evidenced by mothers and fathers using time availability, rather than gender, to assign most household tasks.

Divisions of Household Labor

Contributions to 64 household tasks were assessed by having fathers and mothers each sort cards on a five-point scale to indicate who most often performed them (see Table 1). Frequently performed tasks, such as meal preparation, laundry, sweeping, or putting children to bed, were judged for the two weeks preceding the interviews. Less frequently performed tasks, such as window washing, tax preparation, or car repair, were judged as to who typically performed them.

Some differences occurred between mothers' and fathers' accounts of household task allocation, but there was general agreement on who did what.

Table 1 shows that in the majority of families, most household tasks were seen as shared. Thirty-seven of 64 tasks (58 percent), including all direct child care, most household business, meal preparation, kitchen clean-up, and about

half of other housecleaning tasks were reported to be shared about equally by fathers and mothers. Nevertheless, almost a quarter (15) of the tasks were performed principally by the mothers, including most clothes care, meal planning, kin-keeping, and some of the more onerous repetitive housecleaning. Just under one-fifty (12) of the tasks were performed principally by the fathers. These included the majority of the occasional outside chores such as home repair, car maintenance, lawn care, and taking out the trash. As a group, sample couples can thus be characterized as sharing an unusually high proportion of housework and child care, but still partially conforming to a traditional division of household labor. The fathers and mothers in this study are pioneers in that they divided household tasks differently than their parents did, differently from most others in their age cohort, and from most families studied in time-use research (e.g., Berk 1985; Coverman and Sheley 1986; Geerken and Gove 1983; Hiller and Philliber 1986; Nickols and Metzen 1982; Walker and Woods 1976).

Managing Versus Helping

Household divisions of labor in these families also can be described in terms of who takes responsibility for planning and initiating various tasks. In every family there were at least six frequently performed household chores over which the mother retained almost exclusive managerial control. That is, mothers noticed when the chore needed doing and made sure that someone adequately performed it. In general, mothers were more likely than fathers to act as managers for cooking, cleaning, and child care, but over half of the couples shared responsibility in these areas. In all households the father was responsible for initiating and managing at least a few chores traditionally performed by mothers.

TABLE 1. Household Tasks by Person Most Often Performing Them

Mother More	Fathers and Mother Equally	Father More
Cleaning		
Mopping	Vacuuming	Taking out trash
Sweeping	Cleaning tub/shower	Cleaning porch
Dusting	Making beds	
Cleaning bathroom sink	Picking up toys	
Cleaning toilet	Tidying living room	
	Hanging up clothes	
	Washing windows	
	Spring cleaning	
Cooking		
Planning menus	Preparing lunch	Preparing breakfast
Grocery shopping	Cooking dinner	
Baking	Making snacks	
	Washing dishes	
	Putting dishes away	
	Wiping kitchen counters	
	Putting food away	
Clothes		
Laundry	Shoe care	
Hand laundry		
Ironing		
Sewing		
Buying clothes		
Household		
	Running errands	Household repairs
	Decorating	Exterior painting
	Interior painting	Car maintenance
	General yardwork	Car repair
	Gardening	Washing car
		Watering lawn
		Mowing lawn
		Cleaning rain gutters
Finance, Social		
Writing or phoning	Deciding major purchases	Investments
Relatives/friends	Paying bills	
	Preparing taxes	
	Handling insurance	
	Planning couple dates	
Children		
Arranging baby-Sitters	Waking children	
	Helping children dress	
	Helping children bathe	
	Putting children to bed	
	Supervising children	
	Disciplining children	
	Driving children	
	Taking children to doctor	
	Caring for sick children	
	Playing with children	
	Planning outings	

Note: Tasks were sorted separately by fathers and mothers according to relative frequency of performance: (1) Mother mostly or always, (2) Mother more than father, (3) Father and mother about equal, (4) Father more than mother, (5) Father mostly or always. For each task a mean ranking by couple was computed with 1.00–2.49 = Mother, 2.50–3.50 = Shared, 3.51–5.0 = Father. If over 50 percent of families ranked a task as performed by one spouse more than the other, the task is listed under that spouse, otherwise tasks are listed as shared. N = 20 couples.

Based on participants' accounts of strategies for allocating household labor, I classified twelve couples as sharing responsibility for household labor and eight couples as reflecting manager-helper dynamics. Helper husbands often waited to be told what to do, when to do it, and how it should be done. While they invariably expressed a desire to perform their "fair share" of housekeeping and childrearing, they were less likely than the other fathers to assume responsibility for anticipating and planning these activities. Manager-helper couples sometimes referred to the fathers' contributions as "helping" the mother.

When asked what they liked most about their husband's housework, about half of the mothers focused on their husband's self-responsibility: voluntarily doing work without being prodded. They commented, "He does the everyday stuff" and "I don't have to ask him." The other mothers praised their husbands for particular skills with comments such as "I love his spaghetti" or "He's great at cleaning the bathroom." In spite of such praise, three-fourths of the mothers said that what bothered them most about their husband's housework was the need to remind him to perform certain tasks, and some complained of having to "train him" to correctly perform the chores. About a third of the fathers complained that their wives either didn't notice when things should be done or that *their* standards were too low. Although the extent of domestic task sharing varied considerably among couples, 90 percent of both mothers and fathers independently reported that their divisions of labor were "fair."

Some mothers found it difficult to share authority for household management. For instance, one mother said, "There's a certain control you have when you do the shopping and the cooking and I don't know if I'm ready to relinquish that control." Another mother who shares most child care and housework with her husband admitted that "in general, household organization is something that I think I take over." In discussing how they divide housework, she commented on how she notices more than her husband does:

> He does what he sees needs to be done. That would include basic cleaning kinds of things. However, there are some detailed kinds of things that he doesn't see that I feel need to be done, and in those cases I have to ask him to do things. He thinks some of the details are less important and I'm not sure, that might be a difference between men and women.

Like many of the mothers who maintained a managerial position in the household, this mother attributed an observed difference in domestic perceptiveness to an essential difference between women and men. By contrast, mothers who did not act as household managers were unlikely to link housecleaning styles to essential gender differences.

Many mothers talked about adjusting their housecleaning standards over the course of their marriage and trying to feel less responsible for being "the perfect homemaker." By partially relinquishing managerial duties and accepting their husband's housecleaning standards, some mothers reported that they were able to do less daily housework and focus more on occasional thorough cleaning or adding "finishing touches." A mother with two nursing jobs whose husband delivered newspapers commented:

> He'll handle the surface things no problem, and I get down and do the nitty gritty. And I do it when it bugs me or when I have the time. It's not anything that we talk about usually. Sometimes if I feel like things are piling up, he'll say "Well, make me a list," and I will. And he'll do it. There are some things that he just doesn't notice and that's fine: he handles the day-to-day stuff. He'll do things, like for me cleaning off the table—for him it's getting everything off it; for me it's putting the tablecloth on, putting the flowers

on, putting the candles on. That's the kind of stuff I do and I like that; it's not that I want him to start.

This list-making mother illustrates that responsibility for managing housework sometimes remained in the mother's domain, even if the father performed more of the actual tasks.

Responsibility for managing child care, on the other hand, was more likely to be shared. Planning and initiating "direct" child care, including supervision, discipline and play, was typically an equal enterprise. Sharing responsibility for "indirect" child care, including clothing, cleaning, and feeding, was less common, but was still shared in over half of the families. When they cooked, cleaned, or tended to the children, fathers in these families did not talk of "helping" the mother; they spoke of fulfilling their responsibilities as equal partners and parents. For example, one father described how he and his wife divided both direct and indirect child care:

> My philosophy is that they are my children and everything is my responsibility, and I think she approaches it the same way too. So when something needs to be done, it's whoever is close does it . . . whoever it is convenient for. And we do keep a sense of what the other's recent efforts are, and try to provide some balance, but without actually counting how many times you've done this and I've done that.

In spite of reported efforts to relinquish total control over managing home and children, mothers were more likely than fathers to report that they would be embarrassed if unexpected company came over and the house was a mess (80 percent vs. 60 percent). When asked to compare themselves directly to their spouse, almost two-thirds of both mothers and fathers reported that the mother would be more embarrassed than the father. Some mothers reported emotional reactions to the house being a mess that were similar to those they experienced when their husbands "dressed the kids funny." The women were more likely to focus on the children "looking nice," particularly when they were going to be seen in public. Mothers' greater embarrassment over the kemptness of home or children might reflect their sense of mothering as part of women's essential nature.

Adult Socialization Through Childrearing

Parents shared in creating and sustaining a worldview through the performance and evaluation of childrearing. Most reported that parenting was their primary topic of conversation, exemplified by one father's comment: "That's what we mostly discuss when we're not with our kids—either when we're going to sleep or when we have time alone—is how we feel about how we're taking care of them." Others commented that their spouse helped them to recognize unwanted patterns of interaction by focusing on parenting practices. For instance, one father remarked,

> I'm not sure I could do it as a one-parent family, 'cause I wouldn't have the person, the other person saying, "Hey, look at that, that's so much like what you do with your own family." In a one-parent family, you don't have that, you don't have the other person putting out that stuff, you have to find it all out on your own, and I'm not sure you can.

Usually the father was described as being transformed by the parenting experience and developing increased sensitivity. This was especially true of discourse between parents who were trying to convert a more traditional division of family labor into a more egalitarian one. A self-employed construction worker said his level of concern for child safety was heightened after he rearranged his work to do half of the parenting:

> There's a difference in being at the park with the kids since we went on the schedule. Before it was, like, "Sure, jump off the jungle bars." But when you're totally responsible for them, and you know that if they sprained an ankle or something you have to pick up the slack, it's like you have more investment in the kid and you don't want to see them hurt and you don't want to see them crying. I find myself being a lot more cautious.

Mothers also reported that their husbands began to notice subtle cues from the children as a result of being with them on a regular basis. The wife of the construction worker quoted above commented that she had not anticipated many of the changes that emerged from sharing routine child care.

> I used to worry about the kids a lot more. I would say in the last year it's evened itself out quite a bit. That was an interesting kind of thing in sharing that started to happen that I hadn't anticipated. I suppose when you go into this your expectations about what will happen— that you won't take your kids to day care, that they'll be with their dad, and they'll get certain things from their dad and won't that be nice, and he won't have to worry about his hours— but then it starts creeping into other areas that you didn't have any way of knowing it was going to have an impact. When he began to raise issues about the kids or check in on them at school when they were sick, I thought, "Well, that's my job, what are you talking about that for?" or, "Oh my god. I didn't notice that!" Where did he get the intuitive sense to know what needed to be done? It wasn't there before. A whole lot of visible things happened.

Increased sensitivity on the part of the fathers, and their enhanced competence as parents, was typically evaluated by adopting a vocabulary of motives and feelings similar to the mothers', created and sustained through an ongoing dialogue about the children: a dialogue that grew out of the routine child care practices. Another mother described how her husband had "the right temperament" for parenting, but had to learn how to notice the little things that she felt her daughters needed:

> When it comes to the two of us as parents, I feel that my husband's parenting skills are probably superior to mine, just because of his calm rationale. But maybe that's not what little girls need all the time. He doesn't tend to be the one that tells them how gorgeous they look when they dress up, which they really like, and I see these things, I see when they're putting in a little extra effort. He's getting better as we grow in our relationship, as the kids grow in their relationship with him.

Like many fathers in this study, this one was characterized as developing sensitivity to the children by relying on interactions with his wife. She "sees things" which he has to learn to recognize. Thus, while he may have "superior" parenting skills, he must learn something subtle from her. His reliance on her expertise suggests that his "calm rationale" is insufficient to make him "maternal" in the way that she is. Her ability to notice things, and his inattention to them, serves to render them both accountable: parenting remains an essential part of her nature, but is a learned capacity for him. Couples talked about fathers being socialized, as adults, to become nurturing parents. This talking with their wives about child care helped husbands construct and sustain images of themselves as competent fathers.

Greater paternal competence was also reported to enhance marital interaction. Fathers were often characterized as paying increased attention to emotional cues from their wives and engaging in more reciprocal communication. Taking responsibility for routine household labor offered some men the opportunity to better understand their mothers' lives as well. For instance, one involved father who did most of the housework suggested that he could sometimes derive pleasure from cleaning the bathroom or picking up a sock if he looked at it as an act of caring for his family:

> It makes it a different job, to place it in a context of being an expression of caring about a collective life together. It's at that moment that I'm maybe closest to understanding what my mother and other women of my mother's generation, and other women now, have felt about being housewives and being at home, being themselves. I think I emotionally understand the satisfaction and the gratification of being a homemaker.

More frequently, however, sharing child care and housework helped fathers understand its drudgery. One father who is employed as a carpenter explained how assuming more responsibility for housework motivated him to encourage his wife to buy whatever she needs to make housework easier.

> It was real interesting when I started doing more housework. Being in construction, when I needed a tool, I bought the tool. And when I vacuum floors, I look at this piece of shit, I mean I can't vacuum the floor with this and feel good about it, it's not doing a good job. So I get a *good* vacuum system. So I have more appreciation for housecleaning. When I clean the tubs, I want something that is going to clean the tubs; I don't want to work extra hard. You know I have a kind of sponge to use for cleaning the tubs. So I have more of an appreciation for what she had to do. I tell her "If you know of something that's going to make it easier, let's get it."

Most sample fathers reported that performance of child care, in and of itself, increased their commitment to both parenting and housework. All of the fathers had been involved in some housework before the birth of their children, but many indicated that their awareness and performance of housework in-

creased in conjunction with their involvement in parenting. They reported that as they spent more time in the house alone with their children, they assumed more responsibility for cooking and cleaning. Fathers also noted that as they became more involved in the daily aspects of parenting, and in the face of their wives' absence and relinquishment of total responsibility for housekeeping, they became more aware that certain tasks needed doing and they were more likely to perform them. This was conditioned by the amount of time fathers spent on the job, but more than half reported that they increased their contributions to household labor when their children were under ten years old. This did not always mean that fathers' relative proportion of household tasks increased, because mothers were also doing more in response to an expanding total household workload.

Gender Attributions

Approximately half of both mothers and fathers volunteered that men and women brought something unique to child care, and many stressed that they did not consider their own parenting skills to be identical to those of their spouse. One mother whose husband had recently increased the amount of time he spent their school-aged children commented: "Anybody can slap together a cream cheese and cucumber sandwich and a glass of milk and a few chips and call it lunch, but the ability to see that your child is troubled about something, or to be able to help them work through a conflict with a friend, that is really much different." A list-making mother who provided less child care and did less housework than her husband described herself as "more intimate and gentle," and her husband as "rough and out there." Like many others, she emphasized that mothers and fathers provide "a balance" for their children. She described how she had to come to terms with her expectations that her husband would "mother" the way that she did:

One of the things that I found I was expecting from him when he started doing so much here and I was gone so much, I was expecting him to mother the kids. And you know, I had to get over that one pretty quick and really accept him doing the things the way he did them as his way, and that being just fine with me. He wasn't mothering the kids, he was fathering the kids. It was just that he was the role of the mother as far as the chores and all that stuff.

A mother who managed and performed most of the housework and child care used different reasoning to make similar claims about essential differences between women and men. In contrast to the mothers quoted above, this mother suggested that men could nurture, but not perform daily child care:

Nurturance is one thing, actual care is another thing. I think if a father had to—like all of a sudden the wife was gone, he could nurture it with the love that it needed. But he might not change the diapers often enough, or he might not give 'em a bath often enough and he might not think of the perfect food to feed. But as far as nurturing, I think he's capable of caring . . . If the situation is the mother is there and he didn't have to, then he would trust the woman to.

This mother concluded, "The women has it more in her genes to be more equipped for nurturing." Thus, many of the manager-helper couples legitimated their divisions of labor and reaffirmed the "naturalness" of essential gender differences.

Parents who equally shared the responsibility for direct and indirect child care, on the other hand, were more likely to see similarities in their relationships with their children. They all reported that their children were emotionally "close" to both parents. When

asked who his children went to when they were hurt or upset, one early- and equal-sharing father commented: "They'll go to either of us, that is pretty indistinguishable." Mothers and fathers who equally shared most direct child care reported that their children typically called for the parent with whom they had most recently spent time, and frequently called her mother "daddy" or the father "mommy," using the gendered form to signify "parent." Most often, parents indicated that their children would turn to "whoever's closest" or "whoever they've been with," thus linking physical closeness with emotional closeness. In-home observations of family interactions confirmed such reports.

The central feature of these and other parental accounts is that shared activities formed an emotional connection between parent and child. Shared activities were also instrumental in constructing images of fathers as competent, nurturing care givers. Two-thirds of both mothers and fathers expressed the belief that men could care for children's emotional needs as well as women. When asked whether men, in general, could nurture like women, mothers used their husbands as examples. One said, "I don't necessarily think that that skill comes with a sex-type. Some women nurture better than others, some men nurture better than other men. I think that those skills can come when either person is willing to have the confidence and commitment to prioritize them."

However, the parents who were the most successful at sharing child care were the most likely to claim that men could nurture like women. Those who sustained manager-helper dynamics in child care tended to invoke the images of "maternal instincts" and alluded to natural differences between men and women. In contrast, more equal divisions of household labor were typically accompanied by an ideology of gender *similarity* rather than gender difference. The direction of causality is twofold: (1) those who believed that men could nurture like women seriously attempted to share all aspects of child care, and (2) the successful practice of sharing child care facilitated the development of beliefs that men could nurture like women.

Normalizing Atypical Behavior

Mothers and fathers reported that women friends, most of whom were in more traditional marriages or were single, idealized their shared-parenting arrangements. About two-thirds of sample mothers reported that their women friends told them that they were extremely fortunate, and labeled their husbands "wonderful," "fantastic," "incredible," or otherwise out of the ordinary. Some mothers said that women friends were "jealous," "envious," or "amazed," and that they "admired" and "supported" their efforts at sharing domestic chores.

Both mothers and fathers said that the father received more credit for his family involvement than the mother did, because it was expected that she would perform child care and housework. Since parenting is assumed to be "only natural" for women, fathers were frequently praised for performing a task that would go unnoticed if a mother had performed it:

> I think I get less praise because people automatically assume that, you know, the mother's *supposed* to do the child care. And he gets a lot of praise because he's the visible one. Oh, I think that he gets far more praise. I can bust my butt at that school and all he has to do is show up in the parking lot and everybody's all *gah gah* over him. I don't get resentful about that—I think it's funny and I think it's sad.

While the fathers admitted that they enjoyed such praise, many indicated that they did not

take these direct or implied compliments very seriously.

> I get more credit than she does, because it's so unusual that the father's at home and involved in the family. I realize what it is: it's prejudice. The strokes feel real nice, but I don't take them too seriously. I'm sort of proud of it in a way that I don't really like. It's nothing to be proud of, except that I'm glad to be doing it and I think it's kind of neat because it hasn't been the style traditionally. I kind of like that, but I know that it means nothing.

These comments reveal that fathers appreciated praise, but actively discounted compliments received from those in dissimilar situations. The fathers's everyday parenting experiences led them to view parenthood as drudgery as well as fulfillment. They described their sense of parental responsibility as taken-for-granted and did not consider it to be out of the ordinary or something worthy of special praise. Fathers sometimes reported being puzzled by compliments from their wives' acquaintances and judged them to be inappropriate. When I asked one what kinds of reactions he received when his children were infants, he said,

> They all thought it was really wonderful. They thought she'd really appreciate how wonderful it was and how different that was from her father. They'd say, "You ought to know how lucky you are, he's doing so much." I just felt like I'm doing what any person should do. Just like, shouldn't anybody be this interested in their child? No big deal.

Another father said he resented all the special attention he received when he was out with his infant son:

> Constant going shopping and having women stop me and say "Oh it's so good to see you fathers." I was no longer an individual: I was this generic father who was now a liberated father who could take care of his child. I actually didn't

like it. I felt after a while that I wanted the time and the quality of my relationship with my child at that point, what was visible in public, to simply be accepted as what you do. It didn't strike me as worthy of recognition, and it pissed me off a lot that women in particular would show this sort of appreciation, which I think is well-intentioned, but which also tended to put a frame around the whole thing as though somehow this was an experience that could be extracted from one's regular life. It wasn't. It was going shopping with my son in a snuggly or on the backpack was what I was doing. It wasn't somehow this event that always had to be called attention to.

Thus fathers discounted and normalized extreme reactions to their divisions of labor and interpreted them in a way that supported the "natural" character of what they were doing.

One mother commented on a pattern that was typically mentioned by both parents: domestic divisions of labor were "normal" to those who were attempting something similar, and "amazing" to those who were not: "All the local friends here think it's amazing. They call him 'Mr. Mom' and tell me how lucky I am. I'm waiting for someone to tell him how lucky *he* is. I have several friends at work who have very similar arrangements and they just feel that it's normal."

Because fathers assumed traditional mothering functions, they often had more social contact with mothers than with other fathers. They talked about being the only fathers at children's lessons, parent classes and meetings, at the laundromat, or in the market. One father said it took mothers there a while before they believed he really shared a range of household tasks.

At first they ask me, "Is this your day off?" And I say, "If it's the day off for me, why isn't it the day off for you?" 'Well, I work 24 hours a day!' And I say, "Yeah, right. I got my wash done and hung out and the beds made." It takes the mother a couple of times to realize that I really do that stuff.

In general, fathers resisted attempts by other people to compare them to traditional fathers, and often compared themselves directly to their wives, or to other mothers.

Fathers tended to be employed in occupations predominantly composed of men, and in those settings were often discouraged from talking about family or children. Several fathers reported that people at their place of employment could not understand why they did "women's work," and a few mentioned that coworkers would be disappointed when they would repeatedly turn down invitations to go out "with the boys" for a drink. One of three self-employed carpenters in the study said that he would sometimes conceal that he was leaving work to do something with his children because he worried about negative reactions from employers or coworkers:

I would say reactions that we've got—in business, like if I leave a job somewhere that I'm on and mention that I'm going to coach soccer, my son's soccer game, yeah. I have felt people kind of stiffen, like, I was more shirking my job, you know, such a small thing to leave work for, getting home, racing home for. I got to the point with some people where I didn't necessarily mention what I was leaving for, just because I didn't need for them to think that I was being irresponsible about their work, I mean, I just decided it wasn't their business. If I didn't know them well enough to feel that they were supportive. I would just say, "I have to leave early today"—never lie, if they asked me a question. I'd tell them the answer—but not volunteer it. And, maybe in some cases, I feel like, you know, you really have to be a little careful about being too *groovy* too, that what it is that you're doing is just so wonderful. "I'm a father, I'm going to go be with my children." It isn't like that, you know. I don't do it for what people think of me: I do it because I enjoy it.

Some fathers said their talk of spending time with their children was perceived by coworkers as indicating they were not "serious" about their work. They reported receiving indirect messages that *providing for* the family was primary and *being with* the family was secondary. Fathers avoided negative workplace sanctions by selectively revealing the extent of their family involvement.

Many fathers selected their current jobs because the work schedule was flexible, or so they could take time off to care for their children. For instance, even though most fathers worked full-time, two-thirds had some daytime hours off, as exemplified by teachers, mail carriers, and self-employed carpenters. Similarly, most fathers avoided extra, work-related tasks or overtime hours in order to maximize time spent with their children. One computer technician said that he was prepared to accept possible imputations of nonseriousness:

> I kind of tend to choose my jobs. When I go to a job interview, I explain to people that I have a family and the family's very important to me. Some companies expect you to work a lot of overtime or work weekends, and I told them that I don't have to accept that sort of thing. I may not have gotten all the jobs I ever might have had because of it, but it's something that I bring up at the job interview and let them know that my family comes first.

The same father admitted that it is sometimes a "blessing" that his wife works evenings at a local hospital, because it allows him to justify leaving his job on time:

> At five o'clock or five thirty at night, when there are a lot of people that are still going to be at work for an hour or two more. I go "Adios!" [laughs]. I mean, I *can't* stay. I've gotta pick up the kids. And there are times when I feel real guilty about leaving my fellow workers behind when I know they're gonna be there for another hour or so. About a block from work I go "God, this is great!" [laughs].

Over half of the study participants also indicated that their own mothers or fathers re-

acted negatively to their divisions of labor. Parents were described as "confused," "bemused," and "befuddled," and it was said that they "lack understanding" or "think it's a little strange." One mother reported that her parents and in-laws wouldn't "dare to criticize" their situation because "times have changed," but she sensed their underlying worry and concern:

> I think both sides of the family think it's fine because it's popular now. They don't dare—I mean if we were doing this thirty years ago, they would dare to criticize. In a way, now they don't. I think both sides feel it's a little strange. I thought my mom was totally sympathetic and no problem, but when I was going to go away for a week and my husband was going to take care of the kids, she said something to my sister about how she didn't think I should do it. There's a little underlying tension about it, I think.

Other study participants reported that disagreements with parents were common, particularly if they revolved around trying to change childrearing practices their own parents had used.

Many couples reported that initial negative reactions from parents turned more positive over time as they saw that the children were "turning out all right," that the couple was still together after an average of ten years, and that the men were still employed. This last point, that parents were primarily concerned with their son's or son-in-law's provider responsibilities, highlights how observers typically evaluated the couple's task sharing. A number of study participants mentioned that they thought their parents wanted the wife to quit work and stay home with the children and that the husband should "make up the difference." Most mentioned, however, that parents were more concerned that the husband continue to be the provider than they were that the wife made "extra money" or that the husband "helped out" at home.

In the beginning there was a real strong sense that I was in the space of my husband's duty. That came from his parents pretty strongly. The only way that they have been able to come to grips with this in any fashion is because he has also been financially successful. If he had decided, you know, "Outside work is not for me, I'm going to stay home with the kids and she's going to work." I think there would have been a whole lot more talk than there was. I think it's because he did both and was successful that it was okay.

Another mother noted that parental acceptance of shared parenting did not necessarily entail acceptance of the woman as provider:

There is a funny dynamic that happens. It's not really about child care, where I don't think in our families—with our parents—I don't get enough credit for being the breadwinner. Well they're still critical of him for not earning as much money as I do. In a way they've accepted him as being an active parenting father more than they've accepted me being a breadwinner.

Here again, the "essential nature" of men is taken to be that of provider. If the men remain providers, they are still accountable as men, even if they take an active part in child care.

Discussion

This brief exploration into the social construction of shared parenting in twenty dual-earner families illustrates how more equal domestic gender relations arise and under what conditions they flourish. All couples described flexible and practical task-allocation procedures that were responses to shortages of time. All families were child-centered in that they placed a high value on their children's well-being, defined parenting as an important and serious undertaking, and organized most of their nonemployed time around their children. Besides being well-

educated and delaying childbearing until their late twenties or early thirties, couples who shared most of the responsibility for household labor tended to involve the father in routine child care from the children's early infancy. As Sara Rudduck (1982) has noted, the everyday aspects of child care and housework help share ways of thinking, feeling, and acting that become associated with what it means to be a mother. My findings suggest that when domestic activities are equally shared, "maternal thinking" develops in fathers, too, and the social meaning of gender begins to change. This deemphasizes notions of gender as personality and locates it in social interaction.

To treat gender as the "cause" of household division of labor overlooks its emergent character and fails to acknowledge how it is in fact implicated in precisely such routine practices.

NOTES

Acknowledgments: For a more complete discussion of study results, see *Family Man: Fatherhood Housework, and Gender Equity* (New York: Oxford University Press, 1996). Funds for this research were provided by the University of California and the Business and Professional Women's Foundation, Wasington, D.C. I thank Candace West and the anonymous reviewers of *Social Problems* for their helpful comments on earlier drafts.

REFERENCES

Berger, Peter, and Hansfried Kellner. 1964. "Marriage and the construction of reality." *Diogenes* 46:1–23.
Berheide, Catherine. 1984. "Women's work in the home." *Marriage and Family Review* 7:37–55.
Berk, Sarah Fenstermaker. 1985. *The Gender Factory.* New York: Plenum.
Biernacki, Patrick, and Dan Waldorf. 1981. "Snowball sampling." *Sociological Methods and Research* 10:141–63.

Blumer, Herbert. 1962. "Society as symbolic interaction." In *Human Behavior and Social Processes*, ed. Arnold Rose, 179–92. Boston: Houghton Mifflin.

Coltrane, Scott. 1988. "Role sharing in dual-earner families." Ph.D. diss., University of California, Santa Cruz.

Coverman, Shelly, and Joseph Sheley. 1986. "Change in men's housework and child-care time, 1965–1975." *Journal of Marriage and the Family* 48:413–22.

Geerken, Michael, and Walter Gove. 1983. *At Home and at Work*. Beverly Hills, Calif.: Sage.

Glaser, Barney, and Anselm Strauss. 1967. *The Discovery of Grounded Theory*. New York: Aldine.

Goffman, Erving. 1959. *The Presentation of Self in Everyday Life*. New York: Doubleday/Anchor.

Hiller, Dana, and William Philliber. 1986. "The division of labor in contemporary marriage." *Social Problems* 33:191–201.

Nickols, Sharon, and Edward Metzen. 1982. "Impact of wife's employment upon husband's housework." *Journal of Family Issues* 3: 199–216.

Ruddick, Sara. 1982. "Maternal thinking." In *Rethinking the Family*, ed. Barrie Thorne and Marilyn Yalom, 76–94. New York: Longman.

Walker, Kathryn E., and Margaret E. Woods. 1976. *Time Use: A Measure of Household Production of Family Goods and Services*. Washington, D.C.: American Home Economics Association.

West, Candace, and Don H. Zimmerman. 1987. "Doing gender." *Gender and Society* 1:125–51.

~ *Chapter 57*

Children's Share in Household Tasks

FRANCES K. GOLDSCHEIDER AND

LINDA J. WAITE

Children growing up in America learn early that the home is not a very egalitarian place, far less even than the world of work. The roles of males and females in the home differ sharply. Although most mothers are working, like fathers, it is mothers who are primarily responsible for running the household, with few fathers taking more than a secondary role. Further, the tasks children do are still rigidly divided by gender in most families, with girls doing different and *more* tasks around the house than boys.

Sex typing of children's household tasks begins very early, so sharp differences have crystalized by adolescence. Girls tend to spend about twice as much time on housework as their brothers, mirroring the different levels of contribution by their mothers and fathers (Thrall 1978; White and Brinkerhoff 1981). However, their schools have rela-

From Frances K. Goldscheider and Linda J. Waite, *New Families, No Families?* (Berkeley: University of California Press, 1991). Reprinted by permission of Rand Corporation, 1700 Main Street, Santa Monica, Calif.

tively gender-free curricula (at least in theory) and they have working-mother role models, so most girls are being prepared for adult roles both in the workplace and in the home. In contrast, boys in most families receive almost no preparation for competence in any aspect of making a home.

It is often the case, however, that neither boys nor girls gain much experience doing household tasks, because in many families their mothers do almost all of them. As men's productive efforts were being withdrawn from the home with the growth of new urban, industrial jobs, children were also increasingly diverted from home tasks by a new definition of childhood that emphasized the importance of preparation for adult roles only in the workplace, not in the home. The old view that children should help their parents (and eventually support them in their old age) has given way to an expectation that parents must exert themselves to the utmost to ensure that their children grow up to be successes. As a result, the ideal American child has been transformed from a "useful child" to a "useless child" (Zelizer 1985). Few children would agree that their childhoods totally fit this new stereotype, thinking of the many onerous and resented tasks that diverted them from play; in fact, children do almost as much household work as their fathers. But young people learn early that claiming heavy school assignments will nearly always serve as an adequate excuse for the room uncleaned or the lawn unmowed. What has happened?

Children's Work in the Household

When mothers and fathers are asked *why* they expect their children to share some responsibility for household tasks, they give a variety of reasons, revealing the strong ambivalence parents in the United States feel about children's role in the household economy. Most parents respond that performing household work builds character and develops a sense of responsibility. Only a few report that they require the child's labor in running the house, and even fewer indicate that they view "chores" as a way to prepare the child for the performance of household tasks they will need as adults—learning to cook, do laundry, and clean up one's room—and this answer is most often given by families with daughters. Another minority response, most commonly given in large families, is that parents want children to feel they have a responsibility to participate in the work of the household enterprise. (Of course, since more than a third of parents *pay* children for work around the house, they are really reinforcing a view that such work is optional.)

Our premise in this study is that the experiences children have in childhood and early adulthood are extremely important for the families they later form. And it is clear that the experiences children have even in relatively modern families reinforce a traditional division of labor in the next generation. If children, particularly boys, have little experience with the tasks associated with maintaining a home, it is difficult to expect them to feel comfortable taking them on as adults.

This is a critical area for our understanding of future family trends: Will egalitarian roles be achieved only through a complete abandonment of family-centered activities, or can men and women achieve a redefined and more egalitarian combination of work and family life? However, systematic research on children's roles in the family that would help us understand how children are being prepared for future family roles is even more dramatically lacking than it is for men. For example, although we have learned in the last decade or so that married men are increasing their contribution to domestic tasks, we have no direct evidence for trends in the extent to which children have participated in household tasks, or trends in the proportions of boys and girls performing these tasks. There have been studies showing that youths growing up on farms have numerous duties that often require substantial numbers of hours (Light, Hertsgaard, and Martin 1985). We have also learned that families in urban areas depend less on their children's labor than those in more rural areas (Straus 1962; Lawrence, Tasker, and Babcock 1983). These findings imply that as families became increasingly urbanized and as fewer grew up on farms, children were involved less in family tasks. But we do not know how much change is really involved, or which children have participated most in it. And it has now been decades—even generations—since urban life came to dominate American society.

What is happening to the roles of children in homemaking? Under what circumstances, if any, are children more involved in household tasks and in which families are children's tasks becoming more egalitarian? Have *parents'* experiences of nontraditional family forms in childhood and young adulthood influenced the way they share with their own children? And are divorce and remarriage changing the involvement of children in household tasks? To answer these questions, we will examine how much, and under what circumstances, children share in household work, taking into consideration the nature and amount of work needed to be done and the parents' attitudes and values, particularly those resulting from experience with nontraditional families in their own lives.

Measuring Children's Share in the Division of Household Labor

The women included in the National Longitudinal Studies (NLS) of Young Women and Mature Women answered a series of questions about a variety of household chores, including cooking, cleaning, laundry, child care, dishes, yard work, grocery shopping and paperwork. From the answers to these questions, we created a detailed scale of how much responsibility children took for seven of these tasks. (Children's share of family paperwork is not included.) In brief, the scale takes on a higher value the more tasks children do and the more responsibility they take for them, from a value of zero if children do no tasks at all to a high of 28 if children do all tasks completely by themselves.

In order to interpret the answers women gave, we translate them into percentage terms. So the range of answers (0–4) given for each task can be interpreted to mean that women who said that children did not share in a given task share none of that task with children; women who said their children shared "some but less than half" share about 25 percent; women who said they shared "about half" a

task with children share 50 percent of that task with their children; and so on.

In our analysis, we consider only families with at least one child between the ages of six and eighteen, although they could have younger and older children, too.

How Much Do These Children Share?

Children take relatively little responsibility for most household tasks, although the list of tasks we consider includes some that are often shared with children as well as some that are virtually never shared. Overall (averaging children's sharing across the set of seven tasks), children contribute a relatively small proportion of total household labor—15 percent; but their share is quite substantial for some tasks. Mothers report that their children take a good deal of responsibility for washing dishes and for cleaning the house, taking more than a quarter of the responsibility for these tasks (and more than their fathers do). Equally clearly, most families do not give children any responsibility for paperwork, or much responsibility for grocery shopping or child care. Laundry, cooking, and yard work fall in between, with children doing 12 to 15 percent of these tasks. Thus, children's participation in household tasks depends very much on *which* task.

Which Children Share?

The NLS questions on household labor allow a woman to report that her children share some responsibility for various household tasks, but they do not provide information on which of her children are actually sharing in these tasks. So two women could report identically that children have sole responsibility for the dishes and for the yard, but in one family, one of the children always does the dishes and the other always cuts the grass, and in the other family, the two children share equally in both tasks. The questions do not allow us to distinguish easily between these two women and their children.

But we want to know whether there are differences in the involvement of children, between younger and older children, and particularly between boys and girls. Previous research and common sense suggest that the age and sex composition of the children in the household will affect whether a woman shares tasks with any of her offspring.

These distinctions—male/female, preteen/teen—seem straightforward. However, the role of children who have reached adulthood in household tasks is less obvious. On one hand, they are adults, and might be expected to take an adult's share of responsibilities. On the other hand, simply by reaching this age, the common justification for sharing—as a mechanism for character development—becomes inappropriate. Further to the extent that grown children spend more time at work than they did at school, they are less available for household chores. Many parents may continue to feel responsibility for investing their own time (and money) in their child's future as long as he or she remains at home. They may reason that in early adulthood, even more than during high school, a social life is necessary to get married and starting careers is stressful; as a result, they may be unwilling to make demands on their grown children for help. So we need to examine sharing tasks with children in families with children of different ages and sexes, even adult "children."

What we found is that even though we cannot know exactly which children are actually sharing a given task with the mother, the pattern of sharing duties in families is responsive both to the number and type of children present. The more children in the family the more the mother reports sharing housework with

children as a group. This is sensible, since the more potential workers there are the more likely some of them will be to pitch in.

The children's age and gender also influence the amount of task sharing, sometimes very clearly, sometimes not so clearly. Considering the younger children (under twelve), there are few differences among families that have only preteen children. It doesn't matter whether all children are ages six to eleven or whether some are younger. Based on our results that husbands share more tasks when there are toddlers in the household than when there are only older children, we had expected that the presence of very young children might increase sharing with older children. Babies and toddlers require extra work, and harassed mothers might press their older children into service (since each family in our analysis has at least one child between the ages of six and eighteen in the household).

Since it is families with children ages four to six who share tasks least of all, we infer that older children are helping a little with the toddlers, help that is not as necessary for somewhat older children. But the differences are small, in part because the level of sharing with children is low across all families that only have children in these ages.

As children get older, they clearly become more involved in household chores, indoors and outdoors. Families with teenage children share substantially more housework with their children than families with only preteens. Teenage children are most particularly helpful with yard work, with about equal amounts of task sharing from teenage boys and girls. But the biggest differences by age and sex are in "female" chores.

Families with teenage girls report sharing *five times more* of these other tasks with children than do families with boys of the same age. In fact, girls ages twelve to eighteen seem to carry the largest share of housework of all children. Mothers with a daughter age twelve to eighteen delegate essentially three-quarters of an entire task (most of the laundry, say, or most of the dishes) compared to mothers with children ages six to eleven. Although teenage girls do more of all household tasks (except paperwork) than their younger brothers and sisters, they seem to contribute especially large amounts toward doing dishes and cleaning the house, and to share substantially in cooking and laundry. Their teenage brothers, in contrast, share more than younger siblings overall, but only because they do significantly more yard work.

Turning to adult sons and daughters, girls seem to continue their contributions to the household economy as they reach young adulthood, sharing only slightly less after age eighteen than before. Older daughters shift their contributions to grocery shopping, child care, and laundry and away from dishes and cleaning, and they drop their share of yard work substantially. However, young adult males contribute no more to housework than do preteen children, and substantially less than their sisters of the same age. In fact, grown sons do significantly less cooking and child care than children six to twelve years old. It is not that these young men contribute financially to the family, since most evidence suggests that adult children living at home keep their earnings (Goldscheider and Goldscheider 1988). Hence, grown sons are being subsidized by their parents both financially and in terms of household services, since although they certainly eat and require clean clothes, they rarely contribute to the performance of these tasks; yet someone has to provide these services to them. Unless grown daughters contribute even less of their earnings to the family than grown sons, staying at home after age eighteen seems to provide much less benefit for daughters than for sons. While sons provide virtually no help in

housework (even in yard and home maintenance), daughters continue to contribute at a very high level after age eighteen.

These basic results show that families raising children in the early 1980s shared household tasks with them in very traditional ways, giving older children more responsibility than younger ones, girls more than boys, and dividing tasks up so that what are considered female adult tasks are shared with daughters and what are considered male adult tasks are primarily shared with sons. But what factors influence this division by gender? Are there any that increase young males' sharing in the central tasks involved in making a home?

New Family Experiences and Sharing with Children

Children perform sex-traditional tasks, learning to do—and to like—the tasks usually assigned to adults of their gender. Boys mostly help around the house by cutting the lawn or doing repairs, while watching their sisters cook meals and clean the house. This childhood socialization helps to reproduce the sex segregation of household labor found among husbands and wives. The family is a "gender factory," (Berk 1985) serving as a focal point where the importance—especially the symbolic importance—of the division of labor between the sexes is most strongly reinforced.

But for many families, "reproducing" the parental division of labor is not possible, since the traditional parental structure does not exist. The rise in divorce, together with the increase in out-of-wedlock parenthood, means that unmarried women are increasingly heading families with children. How might this influence the children's role in household tasks?

Women who head families alone face enormous pressures with relatively few resources. In many ways, they are the new "farms" in which the labor of children is once again a dire necessity. These families lack two elements generally available in married-couple families: the earning capacity and labor power of an adult male. So female-headed families tend to have much lower incomes than do families headed by married couples. Moreover, women who head families show higher rates of labor force participation than do married women, because these unmarried women are almost always responsible for their own support and that of their children (U.S. Bureau of the Census 1989). Families headed by unmarried women, then, have both less money and less of the mother's time at home than do families headed by couples; they are in effect squeezed in both directions. Under these circumstances, families may feel more need to turn to the labor power of the children, both in the home and in the market (Tilly and Scott 1978; Greif 1985; Sanik and Mauldin 1986).

The family's need for the children's contribution suggests that women who head families alone will share more tasks with children. In fact, many such mothers say they cannot function without the children's labor (Peters and Haldeman 1987). But this reasoning does not tell us *which* children will take on extra tasks. Perhaps teenage or young adult males take over only the household duties of the absent male head, increasing sharing in such traditionally male tasks as yard work, leaving girls to take over traditionally female tasks such as cooking, cleaning, and child care. This could lead to more task sharing in female-headed families, but no change in the traditional allocation of tasks between boys and girls. However, boys are the obvious candidates for extra responsibilities, even those normally done by females, since the household duties of the absent male head are usually not very onerous, and even in two-parent families, girls do much more work than boys.

This situation provides the potential for a less-traditional allocation of household tasks among children in mother-only rather than in married-couple families.

If mother-only families are more egalitarian, it is also likely that children who spend some time in such a situation may become socialized to greater sharing and to exchanging tasks between the sexes. Even if their mother remarries, the recent experience that the mother and children had as a single-parent family may affect their division of household labor in the new blended family. The effect might extend even further, into the next generation of the children of divorce. Those who spend at least part of their childhood in a female-headed household may have received different training and socialization in the levels and nature of children's participation in household tasks. If female-headed families share more with children than do married-couple families, as we expect, than those raised in such families may transfer this pattern of greater participation by children to their own families. This effect should appear regardless of the structure of the current family.

Mother-Only Families

Children who live in a mother-only family play a key role in the household economy: they share more overall and they share more in every single task. Comparing the children's share of household responsibilities in intact families and in mother-only families shows that children in mother-only families take nearly twice as much responsibility for households tasks as those in standard nuclear (non-blended) families.

Children are drawn into the pool of family labor far more intensively in mother-only families than in any other type of family. This effect takes into account differences in the mother's hours of employment and family income, and so goes beyond the obvious stress that these two "shortages" tend to put on mother-only families. Clearly, children are central to the family economy in these households in a way that they are not in other families, and as a result, they are likely to feel needed and more responsible. Weiss (1979) speculates that single parents develop a very different relationship with their children than do married couples, essentially forming partnerships in which children share responsibility with the parent for decision making and for getting tasks done.

Do all children do much more housework in mother-only than in intact families, or does the burden fall disproportionately on some? We find that both sons and daughters are drawn into more household chores in mother-only as compared to married couple families. Figure 1 shows that boys in mother-only families—both teenagers and young adults—take *much* more responsibility for housework than do sons in otherwise comparable families headed by two parents. Teenage boys only contribute more than younger children if they live in mother-only families.

We considered the argument that this increased participation results only from the greater involvement of these young men in traditionally male tasks, so that in some sense sons take over the chores that were the province of the absent father. This is the case, but it is not the whole story. Although teenage boys do about twice as much yard work and home maintenance in families headed by their mother only than they do in two-parent families, they also do more grocery shopping, more cooking, and more cleaning if they live with their unmarried mother (and the same result applies to dishes, child care, and paperwork). Similarly, young adult sons share more in every household task except yard work.

What about daughters in mother-only families? We find that teenage girls take more responsibility for housework when they live with a single mother than they do in two-parent families. But the difference between the amount of housework done by children in mother-only and two-parent families is actually larger for teenage boys than for teenage girls, perhaps because girls do so much in all families, whereas boys in two-parent families

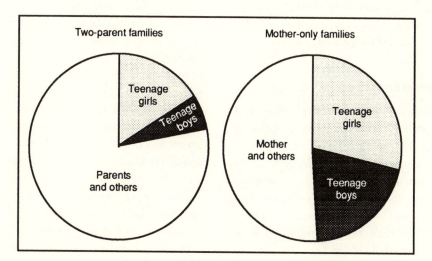

Figure 1. Effect of Living in a Mother-Only Family on Sharing Housework with Teenage Sons and Daughters

do very little. As with boys, girls share significantly more of nearly every task when they live in a family headed by their mother alone than if they live with two parents. Indeed, teenage boys in mother-only families share considerably more housework than do teenage girls in two-parent families.

We found another surprise in our results: adult daughters are the workhorses in mother-only families. These young women take twice as much responsibility for housework as do girls their age in two-parent families, including more of every household task but laundry and yard work. Mother-only families with young adult daughters allocate more to children by assigning complete responsibility for entire tasks—for example dishes and cooking.

These results show very clearly that mothers heading families do not maintain the traditional segregation of household tasks by sex. Daughters in these families participate much more than girls the same age living with two parents, including greater participation in the two traditionally male tasks in our scale, yard work and paperwork. But these mothers also incorporate teenage boys into virtually all traditionally female household tasks, whereas boys participate very little in families headed by married couples.

Stepparent Families

Children who live with their mother and a stepfather take a greater role in household chores than do children who live with both their biological parents, primarily because they wash more dishes and do more child care. However, the differences between stepparent families and other two-parent families are much less than between mother-only and never-disrupted families.

Evidently, the increased involvement the children are likely to have experienced before the remarriage does not carry over very much in the new family constellation; perhaps the stepfather takes over many of their chores. It is likely that part of the difference between the effects of mother-only and stepparent families reflects the fact that most children in these stepparent families experienced a shorter period in a mother-only family, and at a much younger age. Data that allow a detailed breakdown of when and how long children were exposed to a mother-only family are needed to see how much of the experience carries over into stepparent families.

We also examined whether the pattern of increased participation in household tasks by boys, established while they were living in a mother-only household, carried over into remarriage. We saw that children in general share more in such households than those living with their biological parents. It turns out that this is a general pattern, with few differences by age and sex of children. Not only do stepfathers create "Cinderellas," they seem to increase the household contribution of stepsons as well, so that both are involved in the "extra" work. Stepdaughters are significantly more likely to take responsibility for child care, paralleling the finding that stepfathers seem less likely to share in the care of small children, even those likely to be theirs. This results in part because their stepdaughters are helping out more. Boys between the ages of twelve and eighteen share more in household tasks than younger children in stepfamilies, as they did in mother-only families; boys with two natural parents do not assume significantly more responsibility when they reach their teens.

The few stepchildren who remain in the household after they become adults, in contrast, do not help out much at all. Unlike adult daughters in mother-only families, otherwise comparable stepdaughters are particularly unlikely to participate in cooking, dishwashing, or shopping for groceries. This pattern also characterizes young adult stepsons, who pitched in when their family was headed only by their mother, but who are very unlikely to share in many tasks—particularly laundry, dishwashing, or household cleaning—when a stepfather is present.

Comparing these three types of families suggests very strongly that the composition of the household has a considerable influence on the exposure of children, and particularly of sons, to household tasks. It may be that women generally try to establish some feeling of teamwork in their approach to housework, but that they generally "team" with a spouse, when one is available. Perhaps women only feel that it is legitimate to divert children from schoolwork to take responsibility for housework when they *feel* they have no one else to turn to. What is clear at this point is that the current period of family disruption, characterized as it is by high proportions of children living at least for some period in mother-only families, is contributing strongly to household competence in men.

REFERENCES

Berk, Sarah Fenstermaker. *The Gender Factory.* New York: Plenum, 1985.

Goldscheider, Calvin, and Frances K. Goldscheider. "The Intergenerational Flow of Income: Family Structure and the Status of Black Americans." Paper presented at the annual meetings of the Population Association of America, New Orleans, 1988.

Greif, Geoffrey L. "Children and Housework in the Single Father Family." *Family Relations* 34, no. 3 (July 1985): 353–357.

Lawrence, Frances Cogle, Grace E. Tasker, and Deborah K. Babcock. "Time Spent in Housework by Urban Adolescents." *Home Economics Research Journal* 12, no. 2 (December 1983): 199–205.

Light, Harriett K., Doris Hertsgaard, and Ruth E. Martin. "Farm Children's Work in the Family." *Adolescence* 20, no. 78 (Summer 1985): 425–432.

Peters, Jeanne M., and Virginia A. Haldeman. "Time Used for Household Work." *Journal of Family Issues* 8, no. 2 (June 1987): 212–225.

Sanik, Margaret Mietus, and Teresa Mauldin. "Single Versus Two Parent Families: A Comparison of Mothers' Time." *Family Relations* 35, no. 1 (January 1986): 53–56.

Straus, Murray A. "Work Roles and Financial Responsibility in the Socialization of Farm, Fringe, and Town Boys." *Rural Sociology* 27, no. 3 (September 1962): 257–274.

Thrall, Charles A. "Who Does What: Role Stereotype, Children's Work, and Continuity Between Generations in the Household Division of Labor." *Human Relations* 31, no. 3 (March 1978): 249–265.

Tilly, Louise, and Joan Scott. *Women, Work, and Family.* New York: Holt, Rinehart & Winston, 1978.

U.S. Bureau of the Census. "Money Income of Households, Families, and Persons in the United States: 1987." *Current Population Reports,* Series P–60, no. 162. Washington: U.S. Government Printing Office, 1989.

Weiss, Robert S., "Growing Up a Little Faster: The Experience of Growing Up in a Single-Parent Household." *Journal of Social Issues* 35, no. 4 (1979): 97–111.

White, Lynn K., and David B. Brinkerhoff, "The Sexual Division of Labor: Evidence from Childhood." *Social Forces* 60, no. 1 (September 1981): 170–181.

Zelizer, Viviana, *Pricing the Priceless Child: The Changing Social Value of Children.* New York: Basic Books, 1985.

Chapter 58

"She Helped Me Hay It as Good as a Man": Relations Among Women and Men in an Agricultural Community

GREY OSTERUD

On December 31, 1880, George W. Riley wrote in his diary:

> Today ends another year of our lives and this is my sixteenth diary. I am able to give an account of myself every day for the past 16 years or 1840 days. Perhaps I cannot give as good a record as I ought to be able to give, but am glad that things have gone no worse for us than they have, but on the contrary have great reason to praise the giver of all good gifts that our lives have been spared and so many blessings have followed us during the whole time of my diary keeping together with our whole lives. But many has been the changes, with all its disappointments and trials that this world of cares are heir to. During that time our little seven-year-old girl have grown to womanhood, got married, got to be a mother over four years ago. Juddie has been born and grown to be a man in size and is a great help to us. And we

Nancy Grey Osterud, " 'She Helped Me Hay It as Good as a Man': Relations Among Women and Men in an Agricultural Community," in *"To Toil the Livelong Day": America's Women at Work, 1780–1980*, edited by Carol Groneman and Mary Beth Norton, copyright © 1987 by Cornell University. Used by permission of the publisher, Cornell University Press.

> have been able to pay our debts, bought the Frost place, built a new barn on it, got Ida and Bert on it and started. Built our wagon house, an addition on our house, wood mill and shops, cleared and improved a good deal of our place. Helped to build a church at Maine and have tried to do what little I could towards helping the cause of religion along. During the past sixteen years many afflictions have befallen us in the loss of my father, Lucy's father, one of my half brothers and one half sister, together with scores of friends that have gone to their last resting place. But death has not been permitted to enter into our little family, for which we cannot be too thankful, and with all the rest we have had many good times which is pleasant to reflect on. . . . It is a fact ever apparent to me that during all the quarter of a century that has past in my married life the greatest good that this world has afforded me has been my ever true and faithful wife to stand by and help and encourage, doing all in her power to make every thing pleasant to all around. May God bless her, guide and direct and keep and save us all is my earnest and sincere prayer.[1]

This meditation expresses George Riley's sense of what has been most significant and meaningful in his life. Keeping a diary was in itself an important act; George's wish to be able to give an account of himself echoes the Protestant tradition of self-examination, of recording one's conduct and state of mind in order to reflect upon and assess one's spiritual condition. But George Riley's stock-taking was not primarily individual. It begins with George himself but shifts immediately from first person singular to first person plural, from "I" to "we." Although George Riley kept his own diary, he did not think of himself separately from his immediate family.

In describing the changes that had occurred over sixteen years, George began with the growth of his children toward adulthood. The passage of time was marked not by some external chronology but by the family cycle. George and Lucy's daughter, Ida, had become a woman, wife, and mother; their son, Judson, had become able to perform a man's work. During that time the family had accumulated property and improved it. The ideal implicit in George Riley's account is simultaneously economic and familial. The parents secured a farm that was adequate to their family's support, and they helped their daughter and her husband get established on a farm of their own nearby. The losses suffered during those sixteen years—the deaths of relatives and friends—were tempered by the recollection of the good times they had shared with neighbors and kin.

The meditation moves out from the family into the community, from temporal to spiritual concerns. There is no discontinuity in this progression, for Riley saw the ordering of human relationships in spiritual terms. Six years before, he had resolved on New Year's Day: "I hope to cultivate such a disposition that I may be a good father, a good and affectionate husband, and a reliable neighbor and citizen and above all may set such an example before my family and a dying world that I may serve the cause of salvation."[2] His closest companion

and greatest help in this endeavor had been his wife, Lucy Ann. Although George's paean to his wife owes something to the contemporary sentimentalization of woman as the center of family life, "doing all in her power to make everything pleasant to all around," its context is very different from that of the popular magazines. George describes Lucy Ann as a helpmeet, not an idol; she has stood by him in "all the disappointments and trials that this world of cares are heir to."

Lucy Ann Riley's presence pervades George's diary, not only in the relatively few reflective passages but also in the daily entries that record the round of chores, seasonal farm work, and visiting that made up his world. Lucy Ann was there to "help and encourage" him in his struggles with stoney fields, potato bugs, and wet hay. Equally important, he was involved in her regular tasks: carrying water on washday, sewing shirts on the machine, starting dinner while she and the children attended church. He watched over her in sickness and was present when she gave birth. The degree to which they shared farm and household labor was exceeded only by the commonality of their social activities. This was not simply a matter of joint visiting among relatives and friends; it extended into formal organizational activities in the community. George attended meetings as well as socials of the Ladies' Aid Society of the church, and Lucy Ann went to debates sponsored by the Farmers's Jubilee Club.

The Riley diary, along with other personal documents and narratives from the community, raises the question of whether women had a "separate sphere"—a set of activities and experiences not shared with men—or whether they joined with men in family and community affairs. The idea of "separate spheres" appeared during the early nineteenth century and defined the position of women in urban middle-class families. Commercialization and industrialization brought a separation between household and workplace, and between income-producing and non-income-producing labor. Women remained responsible for the home while men assumed the primary responsibility for earning money. This distinction between men's and women's activities was interpreted as a fundamental difference between the male and female character. Women, who nurtured children and mediated family relationships, were described as naturally selfless, sensitive, virtuous, and pious; men, who competed in the rough-and-tumble world of the capitalist marketplace and popular politics, were seen as strong-willed and decisive, practical and rational. Ideally, women's supposed passivity and men's activity balanced each other: women were to be protected by men, while men would be softened and spiritualized by female influence. The private life of the family was deemed responsible for maintaining stability in a time of rapid social change.[3]

Although this ideology did not fit the situations of the majority of American women—including working-class and immigrant women in cities, women living on farms in the Northeast and on the frontier, and both black and white women in the slave South—it became dominant in American culture. Ideologies do not necessarily reflect social experience but rather shape the ways of people interpret their lives and interact with one another. The notion of "separate spheres" implied that women's field of action, although distinct from that of men, was neither incomplete nor secondary; instead of being excluded from critical arenas of social life or subordinated to their husbands, women were seen as having a world of their own in which they enjoyed considerable power and autonomy. The connections between women and men and between the family and capitalism were both obscured by this ideology and fundamental to it.[4]

Studies of the lives of women in nineteenth-century America have been subtly shaped by the ideology of "separate spheres" at the same time that they have subjected it to a feminist critique. In an attempt to see women as historical actors rather than as the passive victims of male domination, historians of women have emphasized the ways in which women created a separate culture within their socially prescribed sphere. Rooted in such experiences as childbirth and enacted primarily in friendship, this "female world of love and ritual" not only functioned as a resource for women within their marriages but also nurtured a distinctively feminine sensibility and form of cultural expression.[5] Although some scholars see the "bonds of womanhood" as providing the social basis for the feminist movement, this line of analysis most often encapsulates women within their "separate sphere," and the ways in which this ideology shaped women's relationships with men in their families and communities remain unexamined. As John Mack Faragher reminds us, the vast majority of women lived in families, and "the cultural expectation was that husbands and wives, despite their differences, would reach some ordered harmony within the bonds of marriage."[6] The feminist insight that the family is not necessarily united by common interests, that husbands and wives occupy fundamentally different positions within as well as outside the family, is crucial to our understanding of women's lives.[7] But we need to locate women within their families, in relation to men, in order to examine the process of conflict and adjustment that defined most women's experiences.

In the Nanticoke Valley, a rural community in upstate New York, women did not occupy a "separate sphere," a gender-defined realm of experiences and activities distinct from that of men. Although women and men were not equal, they were not separate either. Women were assigned to a subordinate position within their families and kin groups, and they engaged in gender-defined and relatively devalued forms of labor in their households. The support of women's mothers, daughters, and sisters was crucial in the predictable crises of family life. But women neither elaborated the experiences they shared into a female-defined subculture nor turned to female networks as an alternative to their relationships with men. Rather, they strove to create mutuality in their marriages, reciprocity in their performance of labor, and integration in their patterns of sociability. Individually and collectively, women in the Nanticoke Valley responded to inequality by actively enlarging the dimensions of sharing in their relationships with men.

In the rural community, the elements of conjunction between women and men outweighed those of disjunction. Socially and culturally, women were defined in direct relation to men rather than in terms of their differences from men. This situation presented women with both a problem and an opportunity. The difficulty was that the possibilities for even a relative autonomy were highly circumscribed, and the resources to which women had independent access were strictly limited. Men controlled the real property upon which rural households were based, and women had few means of support outside of the households in which they lived as daughters, wives, and mothers. Women's interactions with the men in their families and kin groups were immediate and powerful.

Women could, however, try to redefine the terms of those interactions. They could attempt to meet men as much as possible on common ground rather than in situations that were shaped by gender difference; they could focus their energies on those aspects of life in which sharing provided some basis for equality rather than on those that were marked by hierarchical divisions. Thus women emphasized the familial rather than

the feminine dimensions of their lives; for example, they chose to have their husbands present at the births of their children even though midwives and female relatives presided at the delivery. Women actively and for the most part voluntarily participated in the most highly valued and least gender-marked modes of productive labor. Equally important, women could draw upon the resources of social networks beyond their immediate families. The joint patterns of sociability that women sustained in their kin groups and community organizations helped overcome the elements of gender separation that existed within conjugal households. In all these aspects of life, women adopted strategies of mutuality.

These strategies were supported by certain economic and social-structural conditions that served as a basis on which mutuality could be built and provided women with resources on which they could draw. First, there was no separation between household and workplace in this agricultural community, and women's labor was as integral to the production of farm income as it was to family subsistence. Dairy products were the most important marketable commodities produced by Nanticoke Valley farms, and women and men shared responsibility for the dairy process, organizing the work it involved in a variety of ways.

This fact is especially significant in light of the conventional division of labor between women and men in farm households. In the Nanticoke Valley, as in other rural areas, men were responsible for plowing and planting the fields, cultivating and harvesting the field crops, and preparing the hay, grain, and root crops for use as animal and human food. Women were responsible for tending the vegetable garden, processing and preserving the year's supply of vegetables and fruits, and preparing meals. Men were responsible for the construction and maintenance of the house, barn, and outbuildings, for the provision of fuel for heat and cooking, and for the repair of farm and household equipment; women were responsible for cleaning the house, tending the fires, and sewing, mending, and laundering the family's clothing and household textiles.

This allocation of tasks between women and men was somewhat flexible. It varied from one family to another, depending on that mix of choice and necessity we call custom. In some families, women hoed corn and dug potatoes; in others, men cultivated the vegetable garden. Sometimes women did what was generally regarded as men's work because there weren't enough men in the household to complete it, and the family couldn't afford to hire labor. But other families seem to have departed from the conventional pattern simply as a matter of preference. And no matter how strictly some families maintained the gender division of labor, they all were willing to readjust in case of emergency—when frost jeopardized the winter vegetable supply, bugs took over the potato patch, or rain threatened the hay. On those occasions, all available hands would be pressed into service.

On July 21, 1875, George Riley wrote in his diary that his wife "helped me hay it as good as a man."[8] This phrase epitomizes George's attitude toward Lucy Ann's participation in the work of the farm. It assumes a clear division of labor by sex—haying was defined in principle as men's work—but it also asserts that the allocation of tasks between women and men was flexible: in practice, women and men stepped out of their customary work roles when the good of the farm required them to do so. On that summer day, George had been unable to hire any extra male help, so Lucy Ann put aside her usual work to join her husband in the fields, raking and turning the hay, loading it onto the wagon, and drawing it into the barn. In her husband's eyes, she had done that work "as good as a man": the

standard was male, but Lucy Ann had attained it.

The opposite phrase, "she done a good job, for a woman," would have diminished her achievement by maintaining a double standard that presumes that women's work is generally inferior to men's. George Riley's comment, in contrast, is entirely positive. While it assumes a division of labor based on sex, it recognizes that women are fully capable of performing tasks generally assigned to men, even those requiring substantial strength and skill. George Riley recorded the event because he found it remarkable. But his diary is filled with notations of similar occasions: the labor that women performed on family farms was so integral to the agricultural economy that their husbands and fathers had to recognize the reality and significance of their work.

The allocation of tasks between women and men was most flexible in the dairy process, perhaps because it was conducted in a domain between the fields and the house. It was generally accepted that men cared for the cattle and did the barn chores, both men and women milked, and women skimmed the cream and churned the butter.[9] In some families, however, women both milked and helped with barn chores; in others, men did all the work in the barn and also churned the butter. Within families, too, the exchange of roles between women and men was common: the allocation of particular tasks changed from day to day, depending on what else had to be done; from season to season, depending on the amount of milk being produced; and from year to year, depending on the family's available labor supply. Husbands and wives took over each other's usual tasks in the dairy when either of them was ill, away, or too busy to perform them. The flexibility of the gender division of labor in dairying may have resulted in part from the fact that the dairy process involved a chronic emergency: cows had to be milked twice a day, milk had to be skimmed after it had separated but before it had soured, and cream had to be churned within a certain range of temperatures. Few other farm processes involved so many built-in temporal constraints.

Women and men who lived and worked on farms that produced butter for the market engaged in a substantial amount of joint or closely coordinated activity. In a context that devalued women's domestic labor, women's participation in commercial dairying was vital; while women and men shared and exchanged other tasks primarily with members of their own sex, dairying provided a basis for cooperation and mutual respect across gender lines.[10] At the same time, significant differences in the spatial and temporal dimensions of women's and men's working lives arose from the more gender-specific aspects of their labor. Aside from morning and evening chores, men performed fewer distinct tasks each day than women did. Men focused their energies on one major job, while women orchestrated a variety of processes; a man might plow a field while a woman tended fires and children, cooked dinner, baked bread, ironed, and mended. On the other hand, men's work varied more than women's from one season to the next. Women complained that their work was repetitive and monotonous—"the same dull round of chores"—and seasonal tasks were more of a burden than a relief. Part of the monotony came from the fact that women's work confined them to the household and farmstead. While men came into regular contact with men on neighboring farms and in the wider community in the ordinary course of their labor, women had to create occasions for sociability; they shared work not simply to get it done more efficiently but also in order to see other women.

This difference in the temporal and spatial qualities of women's and men's lives could have provided the basis for distinctive modes of socializing: men might have participated in community-wide organizations, while women might have been restricted to more informal contacts with relatives and neighbors. To some degree, husbands and wives might have had separate social networks. They did not do so in the Nanticoke Valley. During the late nineteenth century, formal and informal social activities tended to counteract and overcome, rather than extend and reinforce, the separation between women and men arising from their gender-specific labor. Husbands and wives did not have independent circles of friends; instead, both interacted with the same small group of families in their open-country neighborhood. For every instance in which two men shared work, there was another occasion on which the two women got together, and yet another when the two couples visited. A woman might come over to help Lucy Ann Riley sew in the afternoon, and her husband might join her at the Rileys' place in the evening.

Husbands and wives also attended quilting parties together. Indeed, organized social activities almost always included both sexes, even though they were planned by groups whose membership was formally restricted to a single sex. George Riley attended meetings of the Ladies' Benevolent Society and the Ladies' Improvement Society, for example. The women who planned these gatherings could have excluded men had they chosen to do so. In fact, the women's auxiliaries of the churches were formed because women were excluded from the exercise of power in sexually mixed institutions. But women did not use these auxiliaries to create single-sex enclaves; rather, they drew men into the activities they controlled and used their auxiliary organizations to expand their power in the larger institutions. Similarly, women were not generally excluded from the social activities sponsored by men's organizations. There were women and children in the audience when the men of the Jubilee Club debated the proposition: "Is the influence of women greater than that of men?" No wonder it was "decided in the affirmative."[11]

This pattern of joint rather than segregated sociability was based on the settlement pattern and kinship system of the Nanticoke Valley. The way land was transmitted from one generation to another meant that farm families usually lived near kin, and open-country neighborhoods developed around clusters of related families. While the asymmetries of inheritance meant that the vertical links in such networks generally followed the male line—sons rather than daughters generally were given a share of their parents' land—the horizontal links that resulted from marriage were forged by women: daughters sought to marry into neighboring farm families in order to remain near their kin. Intermarriage among neighbors thus helped to balance the gender bias created by inheritance. Relatives shared resources both within and between households, and across as well as within gender and generational groupings. Women were especially active in providing mutual aid and in turn were able to rely on their families not only as a recourse in case of disaster, desertion, or death but also as a resource within their marriages. Their closeness to fathers, brothers, and cousins protected women from the arbitrary power of their husbands.

Kinship ties served as a model for friendship and legitimated sexually mixed forms of sociability in neighborhood and community. Kinship also served as a model for marriage. Women in particular tried to make their marriages resemble the relationships among kin, which were characterized by reciprocal caregiving on a long-term basis that was not defined by exchange or calculations of advantage. The integration of women and men in

the farm family economy and their participation in social networks that included both sexes, then, supported and reinforced one another. Both involved joint rather than separate modes of activity, and both helped mitigate the hierarchical nature of property and authority relations between husbands and wives. For women in family centered societies characterized by deeply structural asymmetries between women and men, the elaboration of integrated modes of work and sociability could be an effective way of redressing inequality.

Although the nature of the rural economy and its dense, kin-based settlement pattern provided women with the foundation on which they constructed joint modes of work and sociability, these structural factors did not guarantee that such mutuality would automatically emerge. The degree to which husbands and wives, brothers and sisters, and friends and neighbors enjoyed relations of mutual respect and human concern testifies to the achievements of the women of the community. Not all Nanticoke Valley men were like George Riley, with so deeply internalized a sense of their duty to be a "good father, affectionate husband, and reliable neighbor." It was women's active response to the conditions in which they found themselves placed by the gender system that enlarged existing areas of commonality and created new modes of sharing between women and men. In struggling to improve their own lives, women transformed the quality of life for men as well.

NOTES

1. George W. Riley diary, Nanticoke Valley Historical Society, Maine, N.Y.

This chapter is based on Nancy Grey Osterud, "Strategies of Mutuality: Relations Among Women and Men in an Agricultural Community" (Ph.D. diss., Brown University, 1984), a reconstruction of the lives of women and men in one rural community between its settlement in 1790 and World War II. The Nanticoke Valley is located in western Broome County, in south-central New York State; approximately fifteen miles long and five miles wide, it is a sociocultural region defined geographically by the Nanticoke Creek, which flows into the Susquehanna River near Union. The community was settled by families from eastern New York, New England, and the British Isles. By the time of Civil War, its population had stabilized at about 3,000; a slow decline had begun by 1890, but in 1900 there were still 2,200 residents. In addition to studying public records (primarily New York State and federal manuscript censuses), I have analyzed three dozen collections of family papers, and diaries, representing nearly the entire range of the socioeconomic scale and including women at different stages of life and in a variety of family situations. While the only diary quoted here is that of George Riley, his observations are typical of those recorded by other diarists and narrators. Some of these documents are in the library of the Nanticoke Valley Historical Society in Maine, New York.

2. Riley diary.

3. On the ideology of "separate spheres," see Nancy F. Cott, *The Bonds of Womanhood: "Woman's Sphere" in New England, 1780–1835* (New Haven, Conn., 1977); Ann Douglas, *The Feminization of American Culture* (New York, 1977); and Mary P. Ryan, *The Empire of the Mother: American Writing About Domesticity, 1830–1860* (New York, 1982).

4. For a brilliant analysis of the meaning of domestic ideology in the context of changing the class relations, see Mary P. Ryan, *Cradle of the Middle Class: The Family in Oneida County, New York, 1790–1865* (Cambridge, Eng., 1981). Elizabeth Pleck, "Two Worlds in One: Work and Family." *Journal of Social History* 10 (Winter 1976): 178–95, summarizes a number of studies of urban women and points to the complex unity of work and family relations.

5. The classic statement of this perspective is Carroll Smith-Rosenberg, "The Female World of Love and Ritual: Relations Between Women in Nineteenth-Century America," *Signs* 1 (1975): 1–29.

6. John Mack Faragher, *Women and Men on the Overland Trail* (New Haven, Conn., 1979), 2.

Faragher also developed this approach in his review article, "History from the Inside Out: Writing the History of Women in Rural America," *American Quarterly* 33 (Winter 1981): 237–257.

7. Rayna Rapp, Ellen Ross, and Renate Bridenthal, "Examining Family History," *Feminist Studies* 5 (Spring 1977): 174–200.

8. Riley diary.

9. The division of labor by sex was customary in New England and the mid-Atlantic states, and migrants to the Nanticoke Valley probably brought it with them; during the late eighteenth and early nineteenth centuries, even the work of the dairy was as much divided between women and men as shared by them. But men's involvement with churning increased during the nineteenth century as dairying was conducted on a larger scale. Indeed, in New England men eventually took over complete responsibility for milking, and women withdrew (or were pushed) from the barn; this development did not occur in upstate New York. For analyses of women's role in dairying during the late eighteenth and early nineteenth centuries, see Joan M. Jensen, "Cloth, Butter, and Boarders: Women's Household Production for the Market," *Review of Radical Political Economics* 12 (Summer 1980): 14–25; and "Churns and Butter-Making in the Mid-Atlantic Farm Economy, 1750–1850," in *Industrious Women: Home and Work in the Nineteenth Century Mid-Atlantic Region,* ed. Glenn Porter and William H. Mulligan, Jr. (Wilmington, Del., 1982), 61–100. For New England, see Nancy Grey Osterud, *The New England Family, 1790–1840* (Sturbridge, Mass., 1978); and Nancy F. Cott, *The Bonds of Womanhood,* 19–62.

10. See Nancy Grey Osterud, "The Valuation of Women's and Men's Work: Gender, Kinship, and the Market," presented at the national conference on American Farm Women in Historical Perspective, Las Cruces, New Mexico, 1985.

11. Riley diary, 7 January 1868. It should be noted that women remained silent during this debate, in keeping with the unstated assumptions of the ideology of women's "influence." Women did speak at meetings of the Nanticoke Valley Grange, however, and advocated woman suffrage at Grange-sponsored debates in the late nineteenth century.

∼ *Part VI*

Social Policy and Family Values

As the country debates issues so fundamental as what constitutes a family, it is inevitable that government policies have important consequences for families. In an age when family structures have dramatically changed, but work structures and cultural ideologies have not—a situation Arlie Russell Hochschild (1989, 1997) calls the "stalled revolution"—the government becomes an important mediator of the debates. At the same time, it becomes the terrain on which the battles are fought. So, as a society we are asking:

Who can marry whom? Can a man marry another man?

Can a child have two legal mothers at the same time?

Who can stay home and raise children? Does a woman or man have to be wealthy in order to qualify?

Does receiving public assistance automatically disqualify one from being a "good enough" parent?

A key debate raging within the United States at the end of the twentieth century is over what role the government should take in family life. With topics as diverse as welfare "reform," divorce laws, the regulation of child care centers, state support for family and medical leave, and tax breaks for parents, the relationship between government and families is constantly being challenged and negotiated.

The chapters in this part re-examine that relationship from different starting points, each in very creative ways. Anne Finger, in "Claiming *All* of Our Bodies," raises questions about the state's relationship to family life through the issues of disability and reproductive rights. The technological innovations of the past forty years have enabled us as individuals to make choices unthinkable earlier and have encouraged a kind of eugenics thinking even among progressives and feminists. Finger argues that narrowly founding reproductive rights on principles of privacy and bodily integrity relies on individualist thinking and ignores a consideration of the public good.

Nancy Folbre poses a similar issue from a different vantage point in "Children as Public Goods." She asks, What responsibility do we collectively share for children? One question routinely posed by the family courts—What constitutes the "best interests of the child"?—should be posed by our society as a whole. Folbre argues that because children are the future of all society, they should be viewed as a public responsibility, not the private property of individuals.

One way to evaluate how well a society does by its children is to examine its child-rearing practices. In an economy that demands and utilizes the solid majority of all mothers and fathers, the question of how children are cared for in the absence of their parents becomes central. In "The Politics of Child Care," Sonya Michel surveys critical junctures in the past fifty years that have influenced the character and availability of child care. Through comparing state-supported child care, profit-making child care centers, and business-subsidized child care, Michel finds that various administrations have consistently undermined higher standards of care and contracted the availability of services. So, for example, the Reagan administration, which claimed its intentions were to rid family life of the burden of state intervention, created additional hardships on families by deregulating child care centers and simultaneously making child care more expensive and more difficult to arrange. We must ask, Is this in the best interests of children? Is this in the best interests of families?

But even our definition of " the best interests of the child" is politically and culturally imbued, as Judith Stacey so wisely reminds us. In "The Right Family Values," she points to the way that the Christian Right set an agenda for family politics that deeply influenced the Clinton administration and the supposedly neutral academics who study families. In general, the social scientists and the politicians are willing to concede the intractability of women's labor force participation as a necessary economic contribution to family life. But at the same time they are willing to sacrifice women's egalitarian status within the family to "stability," which has become a goal for its own sake.

Through these chapters we can see the many ways that domestic politics—discussions about "the family" both inside the home and in Washington, D.C.—are full-blown debates over our fundamental assumptions about the nature of motherhood, the meaning of kinship, and our collective responsibility to our neighbors and future generations.

REFERENCES

Hochschild, Arlie Russell. 1997. *The Time Bind: When Work Becomes Home and Home Becomes Work.* New York: Metropolitan Books.
————— with Anne Machung. 1989. *The Second Shift: Working Parents and the Revolution at Home.* New York: Viking.

∼ *Chapter 59*

Children as Public Goods

NANCY FOLBRE

Children tumble out of every category econo-mists try to put them in. They have been de-scribed as consumer durables providing a flow of utility to their parents, investment goods providing income, and public goods with both positive and negative externalities. Children are also people, with certain rights to life, liberty, and the pursuit of happiness.

However, we categorize children, we know that the consequences of raising them are changing. Economic development tends to increase their costs to parents in general, and mothers in particular. Yet the growth of transfer payments and taxation of future gen-erations "socialize" many of the benefits of children. All citizens of the United States en-joy significant claims upon the earnings of fu-ture working-age adults through Social Secu-rity and public debt. But not all citizens contribute equally to the care of these future adults. Individuals who devote relatively little

From *American Economic Review* 84, no. 2 (May 1994): 86–90, copyright © 1994 by the American Economics As-sociation. Reprinted by permission.

time or energy to childrearing are free-riding on parental labor.

Parents who derive sufficiently high non-pecuniary benefits from their children may not care. Increases in the private costs of rais-ing children, however, are exerting tremen-dous economic pressure on parents, particu-larly mothers. Economists need to analyze the contributions of nonmarket labor to the de-velopment of human capital: as children be-come increasingly public goods, parenting becomes an increasingly public service.

I. Economic Development and the Costs of Children

Much of the economic literature on families is couched within a neoclassical framework based on individual optimization. This framework treats familial altruism, like other tastes and preferences, as exogenously given and focuses on household responses to changes in prices and incomes. Altruism is considered rare outside the family, where self-interest undermines the potential for collective action (Becker 1991).

An alternative approach, influenced by feminist theory, places more emphasis on self-interest within the home, and group solidarity outside it. Individuals often engage in forms of collective action that shape the social institutions that govern the distribution of the costs of children (Folbre 1994). The effects are visible not only in the history of family property rights and law but also in public policies with disparate impacts on old and young, men and women (as well as upon groups defined by nation, race, and class).

Considerable evidence suggests that parents in the now-developed countries once enjoyed important economic benefits from child-rearing, not only because children began to work at an early age but also because parental control over assets such as family farms gave them leverage over adult children. Restrictions on women's ability to support themselves outside of marriage lowered the opportunity costs of children and limited women's ability to exercise reproductive choice. Similar factors contribute to high fertility in many developing countries today (Caldwell 1982).

The growth of markets for labor, as well as increased geographic mobility, has weakened patriarchal property rights, raised the cost of children, and increased women's economic independence. The imposition of mandatory education and laws restricting child labor has improved children's future productivity but has imposed new costs on parents. Education has become an increasingly important determinant of children's future earnings. In the long run, all these factors have encouraged fertility decline.

However, people do not respond instantly or effortlessly to increases in the cost of children, which are often difficult to anticipate. Furthermore, the motives for raising children are mediated by values, norms, and preferences that are resistant to change. As a result, many families with young children experience prolonged forms of economic stress that result in increased susceptibility to poverty and weakened ability to care for their dependent members.

The growth of labor markets and geographic mobility lowers the cost of defaulting on the implicit contracts of family life. Toward the end of the nineteenth century, policy-makers in both northwestern Europe and the United States expressed fears that adult children were taking less responsibility for the care of their elderly parents. Such fears provided part of the rationale for the collective provision of public old-age insurance.

Increases in the cost of children have also been associated with trends that shift a greater share of the cost to mothers, such as new child-custody laws, growth in the proportion of families maintained by women alone, and poor enforcement of fathers' child-support responsibilities (Folbre 1994). Recognition of the growing economic vulnerability of single mothers played an important role in the development of public assistance programs in the early twentieth century.

However, public policies have provided far greater benefits to the elderly than to mothers and children on their own, particularly in the United States. Social Security expenditures dramatically reduced poverty among elderly men and married couples. Through the end of the 1980s, retirees in this country received between two and four times as much from Social Security as they could have if they had placed their tax contributions in a high-yielding private pension (Hewlett 1991, 140).

Since 1960, public expenditures on adults have risen far more rapidly than expenditures on children (Fuchs and Reklis 1992). Both poor child-support enforcement and the declining adequacy of public transfers have contributed to an increased incidence of poverty.

Income inequality is extreme: among African American and Latino children in the United States, the poverty rate is over 40 percent. Even in northwestern Europe, with more generous family-support programs, single mothers and their children remain more vulnerable to poverty than any other group (Smeeding et al. 1988).

In short, public policies have reinforced and perhaps even augmented income flows from the young to the old, giving the elderly formal claims upon the earnings of the younger generation. At the same time, the share of fathers' income transferred to mothers and children has declined, partly as a result of the growth of families maintained by women alone.

II. Public Finance and Unpaid Labor

The public economy of the state is often conceptualized in terms analogous to the private economy of the family. Therefore, it is hardly surprising that most theories of public finance assume either perfect selfishness or perfect altruism and understate the potential for collective conflict along lines of age, gender, race, and class. This problem is exacerbated by a tendency to underestimate the value of unpaid labor and a reluctance to consider the incentive effects of unequal opportunity.

The assumptions of intergenerational altruism, formalized by Paul Samuelson (1956) and Robert Barro (1974), have recently been challenged by evidence of rent-seeking by the elderly as a group (Preston 1984). Also at stake is the relationship between present and future generations. If current fiscal policies persist, the lifetime net tax burdens of future generations will likely be about 21 percent larger than those of young Americans today (Kotlikoff 1992, 29).

Those who benefit from children's future income do so partly at the expense of present-day parents. Reduction in children's future disposable income may lower future transfers from children to parents, elicit compensating transfers from parents to children, or lower parents' welfare by lowering children's welfare. Moreover, there is no reason to assume that parents are equally affected: mothers often invest more time, energy, and affection in their children than do fathers.

The direction and extent of intergenerational transfers are shaped by many factors other than public transfers and debt, such as the composition of investment, the structure of taxation, and the extent of environmental degradation. Also relevant are private parental inputs into children (including time, expenditures, and bequests) and the value of "social capital" (the benefits of living in a safe, healthy community). Class and race inequalities greatly complicate intergenerational transfers: children from affluent families are far more likely to enjoy net transfers over their lifetime than are children from poor families.

Inputs of parental labor are crucial. Yet estimates of the value of nonmarket work lump child care in with other tasks and value it at close to minimum wage (Eisner 1989). Recent studies of the accumulation of human capital define it entirely in terms of formal schooling (Jorgenson and Fraumeni 1989). Official definitions of the poverty line ignore nonmarket labor, with perverse results such as failing to consider the cost of a paid substitute for a single mother's time when she works outside the home (Renwick and Bergmann 1993).

Many economists seem to believe that time and energy devoted to children reflect an exogenously given preference that provides a compensating differential for costs incurred. For instance, Becker (1991, 375) suggests that divorced fathers pay little child support because they have less contact with their children and therefore derive less pleasure from them. Similarly, Fuchs (1988) argues that women are more susceptible than men to poverty because they derive more utility from children and are therefore more likely to assume responsibility for them.

However, parents act out of a moral commitment and sense of responsibility as well as altruistic feelings toward their offspring. When an infant cries in the middle of the night, why does a mother drag herself out of bed to feed it? If she doesn't act from altruism alone, then the utility gains from children don't fully "compensate" her for the costs she pays (Nelson 1992).

Both moral commitments and social norms are subject to erosion as the price of satisfying them increases, and even altruistic preferences may be endogenous. In the long run, failure to remunerate commitments to parental labor may weaken the values, norms, and preferences that supply it. Most economists ridicule the utopian socialist vision of a society based entirely on altruism. Is a utopian vision of a family sustained by love alone any more realistic?

However significant the disincentives now facing prospective parents, they may exert less influence than disincentives imposed on children who lack anything resembling equal access to education and income. Large per capita differences in public educational investments, social capital, and parental transfers result in very different rates of return to individual children's efforts to develop their own capacities. Those who perceive a very poor chance of success have less incentive to try hard and greater incentive to subvert the rules.

Enormous criticism has been directed toward social programs aimed at indigent families. Yet the Social Security system transfers almost as much money to children of dead or disabled workers as the AFDC program to children of divorced or deserted mothers (U.S. Social Security Administration 1992 p.

57). Average survivors' and disability benefits are more than 2.3 times higher than average AFDC benefits; no work requirements or time limits are imposed. Of course, the assumption is that social insurance against death or disability is unlikely to prompt individuals to murder or maim a spouse, while social insurance against desertion or divorce may create perverse incentives.

While this may be true to some extent, the incidence of desertion and divorce has increased rapidly among all families, partly because men's values and preferences seem to have shifted more rapidly than women's away from family commitments. Many mothers are just as powerless to avoid desertion or divorce as to avoid the death or disability of their childrens' father. Children are certainly not to blame.

Public transfers to children are extremely unequal, as well as small. And public policy literally transfers resources from parents to nonparents by providing social insurance based on participation in paid employment without explicitly valuing time, effort, or money devoted to children. In an economy increasingly based on individual careers, parenthood seems to promise moral and cultural rewards but no economic rewards

III. New Directions for Family Policy

Family policy has important macroeconomic implications. In fiscal terms, children represent a positive externality. There are good reasons to believe that we are currently underinvesting in human capital as well as flouting our collective moral obligation for children's welfare.

Those who believe that commitments to children can be efficiently sustained by pure parental (or maternal) altruism may simply call for the reinforcement of traditional family values (particularly for women). Those with less confidence in altruism may put their faith in immigration: the United States can probably rely on imports of skilled labor from other countries, thus exporting the problem of nonsupport for family labor.

The simplest though most extreme way to remove the externality would be to eliminate all taxation of future generations, out lawing all debt-financing as well as pay-as-you-go Social Security funding. While nonparents would no longer be able to benefit from unpaid parental labor, this would impose stringent and inefficient limits on macroeconomic and social policy.

Another alternative would be "re-privatization" of the economic benefits of children. Shirley Burggraf (1993) proposes converting Social Security to a parents' dividend. Deductions from workers' paychecks could be sent to parents, rather than to the older generation as a whole. This would provide less income security, but would certainly reward parental labor.

The form of the reward, however, might encourage parents to treat their children in instrumental terms. In the United States, as well as in other countries, parental control over adult children's income has been associated with child abuse, forced marriages, and a preference for male children (who tend to earn more). Such personal forms of control are inconsistent with liberal principles of individual autonomy and modern family values. Furthermore, re-privatization ignores the issue of equal opportunity for children.

The same objections apply to a proposal by James Coleman (1993) for an even more incentive-based system, designed less to remunerate parents than to encourage greater private investments in children: the state would pay a "bounty" to anyone who increased children's contributions to society beyond their expected level. It is not clear what

incentives children would have to take responsibility for themselves, particularly if their parents or communities lack the resources necessary to invest in them.

The best alternative is to promote more equal distribution of the costs of children as well as more equal opportunity for children themselves. Improved child-support enforcement would help, as would increased public subsidies for child care. But however necessary, these are not sufficient. Parents should be compensated for their efforts through a greater tax exemption or credit for raising children. And families with children should be guaranteed the means to obtain a minimum income above the poverty line.

While there are good reasons to encourage all capable adults to engage in job training or paid employment, it is important to remember that nonmarket work is still work. In fact, it is probably the most important work we do.

REFERENCES

Barro, Robert. "Are Government Bonds Net Wealth?" *Journal of Political Economy*, November-December 1974, 82 (6):1095–1117.
Becker, Gary. *A Treatise on the Family*. Cambridge, MA: Harvard University Press, 1991.
Burggraf, Shirley. "How Should the Cost of Child Rearing Be Distributed?" *Challenge*, September-October 1993, 37 (5):48–55.
Caldwell, John. *The Theory of Fertility Decline*. New York: Academic Press, 1982.
Coleman, James. "The Rational Reconstruction of Society." *American Sociological Review*, February 1993, 58 (1):1–15.
Eisner, Robert. *The Total Incomes System of Accounts*. Chicago: University of Chicago Press, 1989.
Folbre, Nancy. *Who Pays for the Kids? Gender and the Structures of Constraint*. New York: Routledge, 1994.
Fuchs, Victor. *Women's Quest for Economic Equality*. Cambridge, MA: Harvard University Press, 1988.

Fuchs, Victor, and Diane Reklis. "America's Children: Economic Perspectives and Policy Options." *Science,* 3 January 1992, 255 (5040): 41–46.

Hewlett, Sylvia. *When the Bough Breaks: The Cost of Neglecting Our Children.* New York: Basic Books, 1991.

Kotlikoff, Laurence. *Generational Accounting: Knowing Who Pays and When for What We Spend.* New York: Free Press, 1992.

Jorgenson, Dale, and Barbara Fraumeni. "The Accumulation of Human and Nonhuman Capital, 1948–84," in Robert Lipsey and Helen Stone, eds., *The Measurement of Saving, Investment, and Wealth.* Chicago: University of Chicago Press, 1989, pp. 227–85.

Nelson, Julie. "Towards a Feminist Theory of the Family." Unpublished manuscript presented at the meetings of the American Economics Association, New Orleans, LA, 1992.

Preston, Samuel. "Children and the Elderly: Divergent Paths for America's Dependents," *Demography,* November 1984, 24 (4):435–57.

Renwick, Trudi and Bergmann, Barbara. "A Budget-Based Definition of Poverty, with an Application to Single-Parent Families." *Journal of Human Resources,* Winter 1993, 28 (1):1–24.

Samuelson, Paul. "Social Indifference Curves." *Quarterly Journal of Economics,* February 1956, 70 (1):1–22.

Smeeding, Timothy, Barbara Torrey, and Martin Rein. "Patterns of Income and Poverty: The Economic Status of Children and the Elderly in Eight Countries," in John Palmer, Timothy Smeeding, and Barbara Boyle Torry, eds., *The Vulnerable.* Washington, DC: Urban Institute, 1988, pp. 89–119.

U.S. Social Security Administration. "Security for America's Children: A Report from the Annual Conference of the National Academy of Social Insurance." *Social Security Bulletin,* Spring 1992, 55 (1):57–75.

Chapter 60

The Politics of Child Care in America's Public/Private Welfare State

SONYA MICHEL

In modern industrial societies, child care is an essential element of social citizenship for women. It allows them to participate in the labor force on an equal footing with men.[1] High-quality child care also ensures that children will receive adequate nurturance and developmental stimulation. The United States, unlike a number of other advanced industrial societies, has no system of universal, publicly supported child care. Instead, child care is part of what has been called a "public/private welfare state," that is, one in which social services are provided by both the government and the private sector (Esping-Andersen 1990). Depending on their economic level and type of employment, wage-earning parents may have access to child care through employee benefit programs, they may purchase services on the market, or they may receive them through a government program. There are advantages and disadvantages to each type of arrangement, and the uncertainty and expense involved not only affects the well-being of children and parents but also limits women's mobility in the labor force.

Child Care in the Public Sector

Provision of child care has, throughout American history, been sporadic and inadequate. Until the Great Depression and World War II, most services were offered through the private sector—not by businesses, however, but by philanthropy. Under the New Deal, the federal government sponsored child care through the Emergency Nursery Schools program of the Works Progress Administration (WPA), and during World War II, public child care centers were established under the provisions of the Lanham Act. Wartime brought more mothers into the labor force than ever before in American history and, after a brief postwar dip, the trend continued. The proportion of mothers of children under age 18 who were employed rose from about 10% in 1950 to over 30% by 1962—a total of 9 million women. More than one third of these wage-earning mothers (3.3 million) had children under age 6. One fifth of mothers with children under age 3 were employed and in mother-only households; the proportion was as high as one third (Low 1963, 15; U.S. Congress, House 1994).

Continuing high levels of maternal employment prompted a general discussion about whether mothers should work, which resolved itself in a split based on class and, implicitly, race (Michel, forthcoming). Public opinion condoned employment for middle-class mothers who could find adequate child care or arrange their working hours to coincide with school hours—on the principle that such women were entitled to self-fulfillment but should not permit employment to conflict with or take priority over their responsibilities to their children. Public opinion also condoned employment for working-class mothers, but on distinctly different grounds. These women *needed* to work in order to raise and maintain their families' standard of living and, in extreme cases, keep their families off the welfare rolls. Thus while paid employment was regarded as optional for middle-class mothers, it became virtually mandatory for those who were low-income and working-class, especially women of color.

The class and racial split carried over to discussions of governmental support for child care. While public officials saw no need to provide services for middle-class families, they included child care provisions in a comprehensive program designed to reduce welfare rolls by using employment to rehabilitate recipients and make them financially independent. This program was embodied in two pieces of legislation, the Public Welfare Amendments of 1962 and the Social Security Amendments of 1967. The first of these used child care as an incentive to encourage low-income mothers to enter the labor force, while the second, which established the Work Incentive (WIN) program, made employment mandatory for certain groups of mothers, provided that child care was available.

Some children's and family advocates believed that these pieces of legislation, though limited, were valuable because at least they put child care on the federal agenda and gained public funding for it (U.S. Congress, House 1962). Others, however, feared that the very existence of day care services might be used to pressure mothers receiving Aid to Families with Dependent Children (AFDC) to take jobs when it was not appropriate. Ruth Atkins of the National Council of Negro Women opposed coerced work and predicted that families would be forced into using poor child care arrangements. She pointed to the irony that, under the terms of WIN, a woman who refused to leave her children in unsatisfactory conditions to enter a training program could then be labeled an unfit or unsuitable mother and penalized (U.S. Congress, Senate 1967). According to Congress, however, there were safeguards: The work requirement for mothers was discretionary, and states were prohibited from enforcing it without providing adequate child care (Herk 1993).

Problematic as these bills were, they did, in theory, contain provisions that, properly implemented, might have allowed some AFDC recipients to participate in training and find jobs with the assurance that their children were receiving adequate care. In practice, however, these early workfare programs did not deliver, for both administration and funding were erratic. Many states dragged their feet in setting up training and were even slower in setting up the child care that was necessary so that women could be referred to these programs (Herk 1993). Even when services were in place, local welfare officials often refused to make referrals because they basically disapproved of maternal employment (Handler and Hollingsworth 1970). The combination of the threat of benefit loss on one hand and conservative attitudes on the other left AFDC mothers at the mercy of the government.

The late 1960s and early 1970s did see some political efforts to address the needs of wage-earning mothers in a more positive—and universal—way. In 1968 and 1969, Congress held hearings on the first peacetime legislation to expand and improve child care programs that were *not* coupled to welfare. These measures, which called for federal funding to expand the supply of day care centers and enhance their *educational* benefits, ultimately formed the basis for the Comprehensive Child Development Act (CDA) of 1971, which passed both houses of Congress but was vetoed by President Richard Nixon.

The reasons for Nixon's veto are complex. In the wake of the Supreme Court's decision to require busing to achieve integration in public schools, there was widespread fear about creating a public service that would mix the races at an even earlier age (Morgan 1997). While it sought to appease "the silent majority," Nixon's veto message was not blatantly racist; instead, it drew on more acceptable Cold War rhetoric about the need to preserve the American family, and it fueled latent conservative opposition to increasing government services in general. The conservative mood prevailed throughout the 1970s, barring subsequent efforts to pass modified versions of the CDA.

By contrast, policies linking child care to the poor gained momentum. In 1974 Congress passed Title XX of the Social Security Act, which targeted child care to workfare and "at-risk" populations; and in 1976, through the Aid to Day Care Centers Act, it increased funding in order to raise standards in public day care centers (while deferring implementation of those standards), and encouraged the creation of child care jobs for low-income women. Because of underfunding, severe constraints on eligibility, low quality, and limited choice of service, however, these laws had a ambiguous outcome on the supply of child care and its effects on poverty reduction. Some mothers were reluctant to place their children in the facilities that were available to them, while others could not find slots or became ineligible when their incomes rose above maximum levels.

In the early 1980s, already scarce child care resources for low-income women shrank still further as a result of cuts by Ronald Reagan's administration; and the quality of these provisions was severely compromised. Under the Omnibus Budget Reconciliation Act of 1981, Title XX was transformed into a block grant and funding was cut by 20%. The total amount of public support for child care shrank still further through elimination of the state matching-funds requirement. Between 1980 and 1986, these cuts produced major reductions in almost all categories of federal spending for child care for low-income families (see Table 1). The exceptions were Head Start spending, which increased by about 50%, and the child care food program, which nearly doubled. Neither of these, however, affected the supply of affordable child care.

Transformation of Title XX into a block grant also eliminated the Federal Interagency Day Care Requirements, which set standards for all federally financed services. Coupled with funding decreases, this reduced both the supply and quality of child care for low-income families while raising its cost to all consumers (Blank 1983, 5–7).

The overall impact of Reagan-era cuts in spending for public child care was devastating. For low-income and welfare mothers, inadequate child care, coupled with erratic and poorly paying job opportunities and discrimination in job-training programs, meant that it was extremely difficult to become or remain self-sufficient. This, in turn, caused welfare rolls and expenditures to swell, leading to congressional impatience with the AFDC program.

TABLE 1. Federal Expenditures for Child Care (Fiscal Years 1980 and 1986)

Programs	Expenditure (in Millions of Dollars)	
	1980	1986
Title XX (SSBG)	$600[a]	$387[a]
Head Start	$766[b]	$1,040
AFDC Disregard (Title IV-A)	$120[c]	$35
Child Care Food Program	$239[a]	$501[a]
Title 4–C (WIN)	$115[d]	0
Appalachian Regional Commission (ARC) Child Devel.	$11[b]	$1
Employer-provided child care	0	$110[e]
Dependent care tax credit	$956[a]	$3,410[a]
Total	$2,807	$5,484
Total without tax credit	$1,851	$2,074[f]

Source: Kahn and Kamerman (1987, 19). Copyright © 1987 by Auburn House. Reproduced with permission of Greenwood Publishing Group, Inc., Westport, Conn.

Note: State and local education and social service expenditure not included in table.

[a]Administration of Children, Youth, and Families (ACYF) estimate provided by Patricia Divine Hawkins.

[b]Testimony, Jo Ann Gasper, Deputy Assistant Secretary for Social Services, *Child Care: Beginning a National Initiative* (Washington, D.C.: Government Printing Office, 1984).

[c]E. Duval et al., "AFDC: Characteristics of Recipients in 1979," *Social Security Bulletin* 45, no. 4 (1980): 4–19.

[d]Congressional Budget Office (CBO).

[e]CBO, based on Joint Tax Committee estimates.

[f]Since the inflation rate was 31% between 1980 and 1985, according to the CBO, this total would have had to be $2,425 to sustain the 1980 direct expenditure level.

In 1988 the Family Support Act was passed, renewing the requirement that a proportion of the mothers receiving public assistance enter job-training programs or find employment, provided that child care was available. As with previous measures, this one foundered because few states look the initiative to set up services.

Around the same time, congressional liberals once again attempted to pass universal child care legislation, but they could not overcome conservative opposition. Finally, in 1991, all sides agreed on the Child Care and Devel-

opment Block Grants, which were broader than the welfare-related programs but still primarily targeted low-income families who were "at risk" of becoming welfare-dependent. Five years later, Congress once again narrowed the scope of child care funding by folding it into the Personal Responsibility and Work Opportunity Act of 1996, which mandated employment and placed strict time limits on benefits for nearly all mothers on aid.

Child Care in the Private Sector

Motives for establishing child care in the private sector appear very different. Nonprofit centers were set up to meet community needs, commercial services to profit from as well as satisfy a clientele, and corporate or employer-supported facilities and services to induce certain groups of women to enter the labor force. Yet, though the logic of private-sector child care has been distinct from that of public-sector policy, there is also a conjunction of the two. At points, the state has urged or offered incentives to both nonprofit and commercial providers to offer services that the federal government was not systematically undertaking.

Federal support was especially important in the early development of corporate child care. The government offered businesses several different types of aid. Through Title IV-A of the Social Security Act (the workfare legislation), business firms could obtain funds for child care for employees who were low-income mothers or welfare recipients. This source was quite lucrative, for the government matched employer dollars at a 3:1 ratio. Employers who were not in a position to hire welfare recipients, most of whom were low-skilled, could instead take advantage of a tax write-off for child care expenses. A landmark 1973 Internal Revenue Service ruling stipulated that the expense was justified if the purpose of a center or program was "(1) to provide an employee with a place to send his or her child while at work, knowing that the child is receiving proper care; (2) to reduce absenteeism, increase productivity, and reduce company training costs; and (3) to reduce employee turnover" (quoted in Canon 1978, 85). In addition, the Small Business Administration offered loans to cover start-up costs as well as lease guarantees, and the Department of Agriculture provided funding for lunches (U.S. Department of Labor 1969).

In the early 1970s, the annual cost of full-time center-based care could run from $1,100 to $2,000 per child. Parent fees usually covered only a portion of the cost, with employers absorbing the rest. In making their calculations, employers also figured in other expenses. Where there was heavy investment in plant and equipment as well as tight production schedules, for example, employee turnover could be very costly. A modest investment in child care could lower turnover and increase productivity. Government subsidies could ease the burden considerably. For instance, in 1972, the owner of a million-dollar paper-processing plant in Pennsylvania feared that his new factory would begin to moulder unless his low-wage female workers could locate affordable child care. His on-site child care center proved so successful in lowering absenteeism and turnover that he decided he could provide *free* care for 35 children and still turn a profit (Lorimer 1982, 8-L).

From the 1960s through the 1990s, the number of employer-supported child care programs rose from fewer than 200, serving about 6,000 children, to 5,600, serving perhaps half a million youngsters.[2] It should be noted, however, that the way government aid was set up, the initiative was all on the side of the *employer;* each firm could decide whether it wanted to create some sort of child care program—a decision that was, in turn, based on whether it wanted to attract female employees. Businesses were under no compunction to offer universal care. At the same time, as noted above, with the failure of the 1971 Comprehensive Child Development Act, there was no direct federal support for universal child care that was *not* tied to either welfare or business initiatives.

All told, by the mid-1970s, employer-supported services could account for only a tiny proportion of the child care provisions used by the more than 6 million children who had working mothers. Nearly 1 million children were enrolled in voluntary or commercial (but not employer-sponsored) centers, while the remainder received care at home or in private family-care settings.

From the late 1970s on, corporate child care policy diverged still further from that of the public sector. While federal policy continued to link child care provision with welfare as it sought to move unskilled women from welfare to work, corporate policy increasingly focused on the needs and demands of upper-level employees—management and skilled technicians.

This resurgence of corporate interest in child care had multiple sources. In part it arose from the women's liberation movement, which, more than ever before, framed child care as a feminist issue and claimed to speak for working mothers.[3] Though the women's movement undoubtedly broke the ice, it was *individual* women in high-level positions who ultimately brought the issue home to employers. By 1980, the efforts of the Equal Employment Opportunities Commission were beginning to show results, and the gender profile of the American labor force was changing. Occupational segregation and the concentration of women in the service sector began to decline, however slightly, while the proportion of women in the professions, management, and sales was on the upswing (Goldin 1990, 74–75). Though few women had risen high enough in the corporate ranks to begin worrying about hitting the "glass ceiling," many felt sufficiently confident of their market value to seek accommodations such as maternity leave and child care without fear of being stigmatized, marginalized, or dismissed outright. As one Harvard Business School graduate put it to a recruiter from Corning Glass Works, "What's your company going to do about my two-year-old daughter?" (Gallese 1980, 17).

This woman was not overestimating her worth to the corporate world. In sectors that were suffering from severe labor shortages, such as high technology, employers were more than willing to accommodate women's demands. A spokeperson for Wang Laboratories in Lowell, Massachusetts, conceded, "We have women in highly-skilled positions. These are one-of-a-kind people" (Gallese 1980, 17). To retain such employees, in 1981 Wang invested $150,000 in its on-site child care center—three fifths of the program's annual budget. Parent fees made up the remainder of the cost ($25 per week for Wang employees, $50 for non-Wang personnel). In general, women made the most gains in personnel-intensive industries, particularly where their talents or skills were perceived as unique. On-site child care also continued to be viewed as the best means of retaining nurses.

Employers' renewed interest in sponsoring child care was based on a simple calculation: It was cheaper to support child care than to train fresh cohorts of new employees for high-level managerial and technical positions. In 1979 Union Fidelity Insurance, a Pennsylvania firm, started an on-site child care center when it was threatened with the departure of five key executives who had all become pregnant simultaneously (Lorimer 1982, 1-L).[4] With training for some positions running as high $100,000 per employee, executives readily concluded that it was less ex-

pensive to provide child care and allow innovations such as flexible hours and job sharing than to risk turnover by rigidly adhering to work rules and conditions that had been codified in the days when managers were nearly all male and depended on non-wage-earning wives to shoulder family responsibilities. Employers were also encouraged by the 1981 Economic Recovery Tax Act, which allowed employers to accelerate depreciation for the cost of constructing on-site or nearby child care facilities. By 1986, the annual value of taxes forgone under this provision amounted to $110 million. The proliferation of employer-supported services, combined with their growing popularity, raised employee expectations and consolidated a clientele for what appeared to be an expanded, woman-friendly, privatized welfare state.

A Spur to the Private Sector

Even at its height, however, the supply of employer-sponsored child care was not adequate to meet the need for services, but other forms of privatized child care were also expanding. As with the corporate sector, this component of the privatized welfare state benefited from governmental incentives. Just as President Reagan was slashing support for child care for the poor, federal expenditures for child care for *middle*-class families were being markedly increased (see Table 1). Under the "Dependent Care Assistance Plan" provisions of the Economic Recovery Tax Act, individuals were permitted to exclude the value of employer-provided child care services from their gross income. At the same time, the amount of the child care tax credit was increased (mainly to the advantage of lower-income families), and the Internal Revenue Code was modified to permit taxpayers to shelter pre-tax dollars for child care and other personal and dependent care services in "flexible spending plans" (families had to choose between flexible spending or the tax credit) (Kahn and Kamerman 1987, 19–21, 195–96). By 1986, the total value of these foregone taxes had risen to over $3 billion, more than triple what it had been in 1980, and by far the federal government's greatest single expenditure for child care.

The nature of these policies—tax cuts for individuals and tax breaks for employers—were intended to facilitate parent choice and spur child care initiatives in the private sector. To a large extent, they appear to have achieved the desired effect. A sizable increase in the labor force participation rates of middle-class mothers made such policies especially timely (see Table 2). This group of women needed child care, and they were reasonably well positioned to take advantage of financial assistance in the form of tax credits or flexible spending accounts, which require advance planning and some flexibility in household cash flow.

The relaxation of federal standards also spurred the growth of privatized child care, nowhere more so than in the for-profit sector. Operators of commercial child care centers gravitated toward regions of the country that were underserved by nonprofit centers and states that had looser regulations. From 1980 to 1985, Kinder-Care, the largest chain of proprietary child care centers, more than doubled in size, expanding from 510 centers serving 53,000 children to 1,040 centers, with a capacity for 100,000. Children's World, the third-largest chain, grew from 84 centers in 7 states to 240 centers in 13 states (Kahn and Kamerman 1987; Kagan and Glennon 1982; Hayes, Palmer, and Zaslow 1990).

It would be misleading to suggest that only the for-profit sector of the privatized welfare state expanded during this period; many nonprofit child care facilities were established as well. Among the sponsors were educational institutions and voluntary organizations such as

TABLE 2. Labor Force Participation of Mothers with Young Children in March 1980 and March 1986, by Marital Status

Marital Status of Mother	Percentage in the Labor Force		
	1980	1986	1995
All mothers with children under age 6	47	54	61
Married mothers, husband present	45	54	64
Women heading families alone	55	59	60
All mothers with children under age 3	42	51	n/a
Married mothers, husband present	41	51	61
Women heading families alone	45	49	n/a
All mothers with children under age 1	n/a	n/a	n/a
Married mothers, husband present	39	50	59
Women heading families alone	n/a	n/a	n/a

Source: U.S. Department of Labor, Bureau of Labor Statistics, "Half of Mothers with Children Under Three Now in Labor Force," NEWS, August 20, 1986.

the YWCA and the Salvation Army, which made child care a national priority, as well as hundreds of local groups, both independent and affiliated. Churches and synagogues started child care centers or converted existing part-day nursery schools into all-day programs. The availability of these new services facilitated a shift from family based to center-based care; between 1958 and 1991 the proportion of families using child care centers of all types more than quadrupled (Bergmann 1986).

Family-based child care by both relatives and nonrelatives increased from 1958 through 1982, but fell off somewhat from 1982 to 1994 (Bergmann 1986). Throughout these years, the use of family providers exceeded the use of center-based care, though the margin shrank over time. In 1982, over 46% of wage-earning mothers used family based care (25.5% by nonrelatives, 20.8% by relatives), as opposed to 19.9% who used center-based care. By 1994, those figures had changed markedly: only 33% used family based care (20% nonrelatives, 13% relatives), as opposed to 28% who used centers. Much of the shift appears to have been from care by relatives to center-based care.[5] But a core of families continued to prefer family based care by nonrelatives.

At the same time, the proportion of families with employed mothers using in-home care by nonrelatives declined significantly, though it remained an important source of care for upper-middle-class and upper-income families (Bergmann 1986). For various reasons, many of those in a financial position to do so preferred to avoid group care situations when possible, though for older preschool children they often arranged a combination of part-day nursery school and in-home caregiving. The federal child care tax credit underwrote this choice—another example of the state encouraging the market, in this case, the market for domestic service workers.

As a result of these various arrangements, a multitiered system emerged during the 1980s: publicly funded centers or family caregivers struggling, with declining resources, to provide child care for poor and low-income children; family child care with a primarily working-class and lower-middle-class clientele; voluntary or proprietary centers for middle-class families; and in-home caregiving by nonrelatives, supplemented by nursery schools, for the well-to-do.

Social and Economic Markets

Though providers of all types in the private sector were responding to the same perception of a critical need for child care services, their motivations, goals, and methods—as well as the quality of care offered—differed considerably, particularly when proprietary and voluntary child care were compared. Most observers concurred that, with a few notable exceptions, the level of care in nonprofits generally exceeded that at proprietary centers (Hayes, Palmer, and Zaslow 1990, 160). While Children's World centers were, for example, generally considered high in quality, the majority of for-profits, especially those that belonged to chains, standardized equipment and curricula—to the detriment of accommodating cultural variations and preferences among clienteles (see Uttal, Chapter 44, this volume).

The profit motive clearly affected the atmosphere of child care facilities. While the environments and curricula of voluntary centers took many forms and shapes, often reflecting the countercultural tastes of their founders, for-profits maintained a modicum of quality that tended to remain only at the surface level. As one study put it, "While all [commercial] centers met licensing requirements, none exceeded minimum standards. Centers were clean and bright, but unimaginative" (Kagan and Glennon 1982, 408).

Whether voluntary, independent for-profits, or chains, all child care centers tended to operate with extremely tight budgets. Chains are able to achieve certain economies of scale in purchasing supplies and equipment and through multiple construction projects, but this kind of savings was seldom available to independent centers. The major expense—and therefore the major site for realizing a profit, if that was the goal—was (and is) in salaries. Profits could be made only by maintaining the lowest possible wage scales and caregiver-to-child ratios the local labor market or the law would allow. According to one study done in the mid-1970s, the salary ranges in nonprofits were generally about 5% to 10% higher than those in for-profits, even though caregiver-to-child ratios were higher in the former than in the latter (Travers and Ruopp 1978). Another study done in 1982 found that for-profit centers spent only 63% of their budgets on salaries, while nonprofits spent 73% (Kagan and Glennon 1982, 406). Turnover, not surprisingly, was greater at for-profits than at voluntary centers. To cover the cost of higher salaries and better staffing ratios and to insure continuity, fees at nonprofits sometimes ran higher than at commercial facilities.

Voluntary child care centers struggled to offer the best possible care while still keeping fees as low as possible. In contrast, proprietary child care center operators sought to maintain or, preferably, to raise profit margins by keeping standards and regulation to a minimum, even though this inevitably meant compromising quality.

When legislators and children's advocates called for tougher requirements at both the federal and state levels, the proprietaries rose to challenge them (Muscari 1989).[6] By the early 1980s, the National Association of Child Care Management, with a membership of owners and managers of proprietary centers, had become a vocal force on Capitol Hill (Kagan and Glennon 1982, 410). Their chief concern was to block federal standards that would raise either staffing levels or salary requirements.

Recent research has found a strong relationship between compensation and levels of child care. "The most important predictor of the quality of care children receive, among the adult work environment variables, is staff wages," according to the 1989 National Child Care Staffing Study (*Who Cares?* 1989, 4). The study also found that child care staff salaries were "abysmally low" compared with the pay of other employees with similar levels of education and training; that between 1977 and 1988, "staff turnover has nearly tripled, . . . jumping from 15% . . . to 41%; and that "children attending lower-quality centers [i.e., those with lower staff salaries and provider-to-child ratios] were less competent in language and social development" (*Who Cares?* 1989, 4). While low salaries are endemic throughout the child care field, they have, as noted above, tended to be lower in proprietary than in voluntary child care centers. Thus children attending the for-profits during the 1980s were more likely to suffer the consequences of their caretakers' poor pay.

Outside the Centers

During this same period, more informal arrangements such as family child care and in-home caregiving were also expanding (Bergmann 1986). The proportion of mothers using family care doubled between 1958 and 1982 (Bloom and Steen 1996, 31) with the bulk of the clientele coming from working-class or lower-middle-class backgrounds—much like the providers themselves.

It is difficult to document precisely the patterns of growth in this sector of care because most providers operated independently in a kind of occupational "gray market" (Hayes, Palmer, and Zaslow 1990, 151–56). Somewhat self-effacing, they did not regard themselves as being professional or even employed in any usual sense. Adopting the identifier "babysitter" rather than child care provider or caregiver, they saw their activities as an extension of their domestic duties, requiring no particular training or qualifications other than "a love of children."[7] Some family providers were young mothers who took in a few extra children in order to afford staying home with their own offspring while they were young. In their minds, they were merely "temporary providers" for whom family day care was expedient. This group also tended to eschew professionalism with regard to child care, though they might not have with regard to an occupation outside the home.

It is also difficult to track family care because only a small proportion of the providers were licensed, some because state laws did not require them to be, others because they did not want to report their income, their homes did not meet the standards, or they wished to avoid oversight for other reasons, such as maintaining ethnic or racial homogeneity. Nevertheless, in the 1970s, several organizations of family child care providers emerged, attracting those who wished to enhance their own visibility and status or obtain access to government benefits such as food assistance that might not be available to small-scale providers operating independently. These informal arrangements should definitely be included in any conceptualization of the private sector of the welfare state, for they clearly filled an important gap in child care, particularly for lower-income families who fell through the cracks between public provisions and more expensive market-based services. However, as in other instances, this area of the private sector was not completely autonomous or separate from the public sector—the state. Through regulation, however erratic, and through incentives and supports such as the food program and tax credits, the government, at both state and federal levels, encouraged and sustained the development of family child care as another form of market-based services.

Wage-Earning Mothers in the Public-Private Welfare State

The division of child care services between the public and private sectors has important consequences for wage-earning mothers. In neither sector can mothers rely on a steady supply of high-quality, affordable care. Private-sector services, whether purchased by parents or employer-sponsored, can be expensive, and quality is not always assured. In the case of commercial services, profits are often based on the exploitation of child care workers. Employer-supported services are still rare; as of 1991, they were offered by only 8 percent of medium and large firms and only one percent of small firms (Bloom and Steen 1996, 32). Low-paid, low-skilled mothers, who seldom find jobs with good benefits, such as child care, also find themselves priced out of most other forms of private-sector services.

This group of mothers must turn to the public sector, where provisions are even more uncertain. As we have seen, funding for child care depends on the whims of Washington as well as on local vicissitudes. In the past, gaining eligibility involved a complicated and often humiliating application process; now, under the terms of the Personal Responsibility and Work Opportunity Reconciliation Act of 1996, mothers must subject themselves to harsh work requirements. Though Congress has earmarked funds for child care, there is resistance at the state level to making free or low-cost quality services available. As one Ohio state legislator caustically put it in a recent interview, "Why should we replace one entitlement [i.e., AFDC] with another [i.e., "child care]?" (Lawrence 1997).

Thus in both the private and public sectors—and in the policy space that is governed by their interaction—women lack control over the social provisions that govern their lives. Neither sector offers the type of unconditional, universal entitlement to child care and other family benefits women need to enter the labor force on a sound footing and gain economic independence and personal autonomy.

Moreover, the public-private division of child care provisions is reproduced in the political constituency for child care. Employer-sponsored services have generated an employee elite that serves to hire off an articulate and powerful cohort of women (and men) who might otherwise lend their strength to a lobby for universal child care and other family provisions through the public sector of the welfare state. Consumers of market, non-profit, family, and in-home child care provisions are equally alienated from the political process. Usually ideologically committed to the type of care they have chosen, they are also isolated from one another spatially, socially, and temporally, and thus are also incapable of joining in to form a solid child care lobby. Finally, as the recent welfare debates revealed so tragically, poor and low-income women—though often mobilized—lack the wherewithal to project their voices effectively in policy-making arenas and, without assurance of minimal provisions for themselves, can hardly be expected to push for broader provisions.

Because of the political inertia generated by the public-private welfare state, prospects for universal child care in the United States are currently quite dim. But growing acceptance of maternal employment, coupled with a recognition of the social consequences of inadequate child care provisions, may well lead to a political breakthrough in the decades to come.

NOTES

1. Child care is a necessary but not sufficient condition for economic gender equality. Equal access to education and training, nondiscriminatory hiring and employment conditions, and wage equity are also essential.

2. These programs included child care centers, both on- and off-site; voucher plans; after-school activities; and other schemes whose evolution will be discussed below. Because of the variety of programs, it is difficult to calculate the total number of children being served at any one time. As late as 1990, employer-supported child care served only a small proportion of the 10 million children receiving nonparental care, 38% in child care centers,

27% from relatives, 20% in family day care homes, 5.6% from an unrelated caregiver their own homes, 9.1% in other arrangements (Children's Defense Fund 1992, 17).

3. Feminists addressed demands toward the federal government and also began to criticize labor unions for failing to take up the issue. According to Muriel Tuteur, director of the Amalgamated Clothing and Textile Workers Union ACTWU's Chicago child care center and a member of the Coalition of Labor Union Women (CLUW), child care was not a "gut issue" for male union leaders. "Until women take hold of that issue," Tuteur told a *New York Times* reporter, "we are not going to see a heck of a lot happen" ("Better Child Care Urged . . ." 1979).

4. One Boston bank was not so fortunate: In 1982 it lost eight female vice-presidents who had become pregnant after the bank failed to reach an accommodation with them about working part-time. This bank's experience prompted other banks in the city to quickly reassess their policy on hours (Manuel 1982, 17).

5. In some instances, relatives who were initially willing to care for kin children branched out to take in nonkin children, charging fees for services they had previously provided to kin for nothing (Zinsser 1991).

6. For a discussion of motives from the perspective of the proprietary child care centers, see Muscari 1989. Muscari was affiliated with Kinder-Care.

7. In some cases their self-effacing stance allowed them to avoid the wrath of spouses who oppose employment for women in general, or for their wives in particular.

REFERENCES

Bergmann, Barbara. 1986. *The Economic Emergence of Women.* New York: Basic Books.

"Better Child Care Urged as a Support to Family." 1979. *New York Times,* November 20, 1979, B11.

Blank, Helen. 1983. *Child Care and Federal Child Care Cuts.* Washington, D.C.: Children's Defense Fund. Summarized on p. 22 in Alfred J. Kahn and Sheila Kamerman. *Child Care: Facing the Hard Choices.* Dover, Mass.: Auburn House.

Bloom, David E., and Todd P. Steen. 1996. "Minding the Baby in the United States." In *Who Will Mind the Baby? Geographies of Child Care and Working Mothers*, ed. Kim England, pp. 23–25. London and New York.: Routledge.

Brown, Paul B. 1981. "Band-Aids by the Boxcar." *Forbes* 128, no. 5:88–89.

Canon, Belle. 1978. "Child Care Where You Work." *Ms.* 6, no. 10: 83–86.

Children's Defense Fund. 1992. *The State of America's Children, 1992.* Washington, D.C.: Children's Defense Fund.

Esping-Andersen, Gøsta. 1990. *The Three Worlds of Welfare Capitalism.* Princeton: Princeton University Press.

Gallese, Liz Roman. 1980. "Moms and Pops Get Break as Employers Sponsor Day Care." *Wall Street Journal,* May 9, 1980, 17.

Goldin, Claudia. 1990. *Understanding the Gender Gap: An Economic History of American Women.* New York: Oxford University Press.

Handler, Joel F., and Ellen Jane Hollingsworth. 1970. "Work, Welfare, and the Nixon Reform Proposals." *Stanford Law Review* 22:907–942.

Hayes, Cheryl D., John L. Palmer, and Martha J. Zaslow, eds. 1990. *Who Cares for America's Children? Child Care Policy for the 1990s.* Washington, D.C.: National Academy Press.

Herk, Monica. 1993. "Helping the Hand that Rocks the Cradle." Ph.D. diss., Princeton University, Princeton, N.J.

Kagan, Sharon L., and Theresa Glennon. 1982. "Considering Proprietary Child Care." In *Day Care: Scientific and Social Policy Issues,* ed. Edward F. Zigler and Edmund F. Gordon, 402–412. Boston: Auburn House.

Kahn, Alfred J., and Sheila B. Kamerman. 1987. *Child Care: Facing the Hard Choices.* Dover, Mass.: Auburn House.

Lawrence, Joan (Ohio State Representative). 1997. *The News Hour,* PBS, February 6.

Lorimer, Anne. 1982. "For Companies with Day Care, Big Dividends." *Philadelphia Inquirer,* January 31, 8–L.

Low, Seth. 1963. "Child Welfare Services, 1962—Their Range and Extent." *Welfare in Review* 1, 1:1–5.

Manuel, Diane Casselberry. 1982. "Business Responds to Family Concerns." *Christian Science Monitor,* May 10, 17.

Michel, Sonya. Forthcoming. *Children's Interests/Mothers' Rights: The Shaping of America's Child Care Policy.* New Haven: Yale University Press.

———. 1995. "From Welfare to Workfare: The Paradigm Shifts of the 1960s." Paper presented at the Social Science History Association meetings, Chicago.

Morgan, Kimberly. 1997. "Race and the Politics of American Child Care." Paper presented at the Comparative Research on Welfare States and Gender conference, University of Wisconsin, Madison.

Muscari, Ann. 1989. "Aims, Policies, and Standards of For-Profit Child Care." In *Caring for Children: Challenge to America,* ed. Jeffrey S. Lande, Sandra Scarr, and Nina Gunzenhauser, 233–240. Hillsdale, N.J.: Lawrence Erlbaum Associates.

Travers, J., and R. Ruopp. 1978. *National Day Care Study: Preliminary Findings and Their Implications.* Cambridge, Mass.: Abt Associates.

U.S. Congress. House. Committee on Ways and Means. 1994. *1994 Green Book: Overview of Entitlement Programs.* Washington, D.C.: Government Printing Office.

U.S. Congress. House. Committee on Ways and Means. 1962. Statement of Elinor Guggenheimer. In *Public Welfare Amendments of 1962,* 416–419. Washington, D.C.: Government Printing Office.

U.S. Congress. Senate. Committee on Finance. 1967. *Social Security Amendments of 1967.* Washington, D.C.: Government Printing Office.

U.S. Department of Labor. Women's Bureau. 1969. *Federal Funds for Day Care Projects.* Washington, D.C.: Government Printing Office.

Who Cares? Child Care Teachers and the Quality of Care in America. 1989. Executive Summary of the National Child Care Staffing Study. Oakland, Calif.: Child Care Employee Project.

Zinsser, Caroline. 1991. *Raised in East Urban: Child Care Changes in a Working Class Community.* New York: Teachers College Press.

~ *Chapter 61*

Claiming *All* of Our Bodies: Reproductive Rights and Disability

ANNE FINGER

Just as I can't remember a time of my life when I wasn't a feminist, I can't remember not believing in disability rights. From the time I was a very young child, I understood that I was "more handicapped" by people's perceptions and attitudes toward me than I was by my disability (I had polio shortly before my third birthday). Although as a child I didn't have the word "disability," never mind "oppression" or "attitudinal barriers," to describe my experience, what I *did* have was the example of the black civil rights movement, then beginning in the South. From about the age of five or six, I used to think, "People are prejudiced against me the same way that they are against Negroes."

While increased understanding has led me to see the differences as well as the similarities between Black experiences and my own, my belief that disability in and of itself was much

From Rita Arditti, Renate Duelli Klein, and Shelley Minden, *Test-Tube Women: What Future for Motherhood?* (London: Routledge, 1984). Reprinted by permission of the author.

less of a problem than social structures and attitudes toward disability has never changed. In part because I was exempted from traditional feminine roles—*no one* ever so much as mentioned the possibility of my having babies when I grew up—I was also a feminist, at least in some incipient form, as far back as I can remember.

But it has not always been easy building a politics that connects these two parts of my experience. The feminist movement—the movement which has been my home for most of my adult life—has by and large acted as if disabled women did not exist. For instance, the 1976 edition of *Our Bodies, Our Selves* mentioned disability only twice—both times speaking of fetuses with potentially disabling conditions, not disabled women (Boston Women's Health Book Collective 1976). In the early years of the feminist movement I heard constantly about how women were sex objects—I could see that that was true for a lot of my abled sisters, but there were no voices saying that being stereotyped as asexual was also oppressive—and also was part of our female experience. More recently, the disability rights movement and the women's movement have seemed to be at loggerheads with each other over issues of reproductive technologies, genetics, and fetal and neonatal disabilities. I hope this chapter will be a step toward helping us to claim *all* of ourselves.

Most discussions of disability begin with a laundry list of disabling conditions. Disability, we are told, does not just mean being in a wheelchair. It also includes a variety of conditions, both invisible and visible. These include being deaf or blind, having a heart condition, being developmentally disabled, or being "mentally ill." While this is necessary to an understanding of disability, thinking about disability only in medical or quasi-medical terms limits our understanding: disability is largely a social construct.

Women, like disabled people, can be defined in terms of physical characteristics that make us different from men (only women menstruate; only women get pregnant; women tend to be shorter than men). We can also be defined socially. A social description would include all of the above physical characteristics but would emphasize that, in our society, we are paid far less than men; we are less likely to vote Republican; and we are more likely to be emotional and empathetic.

In the same manner, when we start looking at disability socially, we see not only the medically defined conditions that I have described but the social and economic circumstances that limit the lives of disabled people. We look, for instance at the fact that white disabled women earn twenty-four cents for every dollar that *comparably qualified* nondisabled men earn; for Black disabled women, the figure is 12 cents. (Figures for other racial groups were not reported.) Media images almost always portray us as being either lonely and pitiful or one-dimensional heroes (or, occasionally, heroines) who struggle valiantly to

"overcome our handicaps." Many of us are still being denied the free public education that all American children supposedly receive; and we have a (largely unknown) history of fighting for our rights that stretches back at least to the mid-nineteenth century (and probably further). To understand that disability is socially constructed means understanding that the economic, political, and social forces that now restrict our lives can (and will) change.

The Eugenics Movement and Sterilization Abuse

The reproductive rights movement has, by and large, failed to address the ways that sterilization abuse has affected disabled people. Compulsory and coerced sterilization of the disabled began in the late nineteenth century. The eugenics movement provided the ideological basis for these actions (as well as providing a similar rationale for racist actions). The term "eugenics" was coined by Sir Francis Galton; the *Oxford English Dictionary* defines the word as "pertaining or adapted to the production of fine offspring, esp. in the human race." The aim of this movement was to apply the same principles of improving "stock" that were used for horses and vegetables to human beings. This movement has strong roots in Social Darwinism—the idea that life is a struggle between the fit and the unfit. The unfit—which includes the "feeble minded, insane, epileptic, diseased, blind, deaf, [and] deformed" were to be bred out of existence (Bajema 1976).

Based on the mistaken notion that all disabilities were inherited, there were several factors that contributed to the growth of the eugenics movement in this period. One factor was the prevalent assumption of nineteenth-century science that human perfection could be achieved through a combination of technological and social manipulation, an increased understanding of heredity, and the fact that surgical techniques for sterilization had become available. But any discussion of the eugenics movement that leaves out the changing social role of disabled people in this period fails to grasp the true nature of this movement.

As America industrialized, there was less room for those who had physical or mental limitations to adapt their work environment to their needs. Our history as disabled people has yet to be written. But from what I have been able to glean, I believe that in rural societies disabled people had far more of a social role than they have had in the more urban and industrialized world. The fact that folk tales and rhymes refer to "the simple," that "the village idiot" was a stock figure, that blind and other disabled people appear in the myths and legends of many places, indicate that in the past, disabled people had more of a daily presence in the world.

As work became more structured and formalized, people who "fit" into the standardized factories were needed. Industrializing America not only forbade the immigration of disabled people from abroad, it shut the ones already here away in institutions. The growth of social welfare organizations and charities that "helped" those with disabilities did provide jobs for a certain segment of the middle class; and volunteer charity fit in with the Victorian notion of women's duties and sphere.

This change in attitudes toward disabled people can be traced in language. The word "defective," for instance, was originally an adjective meaning faulty or imperfect: it described one aspect of a person, rather than defining that person totally. By the 1880s, it had become a noun: people were considered not merely to have a defective sense of vision or a defective gait—they had become totally defined by their limitations, and had become

defectives. A similar transformation took place a few decades later with the word "unfit," which also moved from being an adjective to being a noun. The word "normal," which comes from the Latin word *norma,* square, until the 1830s meant standing at a right angle to the ground. During the 1840s it came to designate conformity to a common type. By the 1880s, in America, it had come to apply to people as well as things (Illich 1976).

Close on the heels of the rise of institutions for disabled people was an increase in forced and coerced sterilization. Adele Clarke has pointed out that "the intentional breeding of plants and animals is almost exclusively undertaken to improve the products . . . [to increase] profitability from the products, whether they be Arabian horses or more easily transportable tomatoes or peaches. Eugenics applies, I believe, the same profit motive to the breeding of people" (Clarke n.d.). Since disabled people were of little or no use to the profitmakers, and since they were thought likely to become burdens on the state coffers, they were to be stopped from producing others like themselves.

Compulsory sterilization laws were passed in the early 1900s. By the 1930s, in addition to sterilization laws, forty-one states had laws that prohibited the marriage of the "insane and feeble-minded," seventeen prohibited the marriage of people with epilepsy, and four outlawed marriage for "confirmed drunkards." More than twenty states still have eugenics laws on their books (Clarke n.d.).

Coerced sterilization is still very much a reality, especially among the developmentally disabled. "Voluntary" sterilizations are sometimes a condition for being released from an institution; there has been at least one reported case of a "voluntary" sterilization being performed on a six-year-old boy (Friedman 1976).

It is important to understand the connections between sterilization abuse of disabled people and of Third World people. The U.S.

Senate Committee on Nutrition and Human Needs reported in 1974 that between 75 percent and 85 percent of the "mentally defective and retarded children" who are born each year are born into families with incomes below the poverty line. This means that a large number of those who are labeled as "retards" are people of color. The vast majority of people who get diagnosed as being mentally retarded have no definite, identifiable cause for their retardation: they are called the "mildly retarded," the "educable," and those with "cultural-familial" retardation. The same IQ tests that "prove" that Black people as a whole are less intelligent than whites label a far greater percentage of individual Black children as "retarded" (Chase 1980).

The Model Sterilization Law of Harry Laughlin was never passed in its totality by any state in this country; however a version of it was adopted in Nazi Germany. American eugenicists were often enthusiastic supporters of Hitler's attempt to rid Germany of "defectives."

Nazi ideology stressed purity, fear of disease, and the importance of heredity, intertwining these concepts with racism. In *Mein Kampf*, Hitler calls syphilis "the Jewish disease"; Jewish people (and other "subhumans") are portrayed as being weak, sickly, and degenerate, in contrast with healthy blonde Aryans. Before the start of World War II, Nazi eugenics courts had forced hundreds of thousands of disabled people to be sterilized. This forced sterilization helped to pave the way for the wartime genocide of Germany's disabled population (Chase 1980).

The Reproductive Rights Movement

Many disabled women find involvement in the reproductive rights movement problematic. Not only have many activists in this movement talked about the issues raised by disabled fetuses in ways that are highly exploitative and prey upon fears about disability, the movement also has, by and large, failed to address the denial of reproductive rights to disabled women and men. It has also failed to make itself physically accessible to disabled women.

I often hear an argument in favor of abortion rights that says, "The right-wing would even force us to give birth to a child who was deformed." ("Deformed" is mild in this context. I've heard "defective," "grossly malformed," and "hideously deformed.") This attitude has become so widespread that at a recent conference on reproductive rights I heard disabled infants referred to as "bad babies."

No woman should be forced to bear a child, abled or disabled; and no progressive social movement should exploit an oppressed group to further its end. We do not need, as Michelle Fine and Adrienne Asch (1982) point out, to list conditions—such as the presence of a fetus with a disability—under which abortion is acceptable. The right to abortion is not dependent on certain circumstances: it is our absolute and essential right to have control over our bodies. We do not need to use ableist arguments to bolster our demands. There are racist and classist arguments that can be made for abortion: to argue against them does not compromise our insistence on abortion rights.

Issues Raised by Fetal Diagnosis

When we first fought for and won abortion rights, we focused on the situation of the *woman* herself. Most women who choose abortion do so early on in pregnancy, having made the decision that they do not want a child, any child, at the time. Now, however, the availability of techniques for diagnosis of fetal disabilities (such as amniocentesis, ultrasonography, and fetoscopy) means that women can now choose not to give birth to a *particular* fetus. This is a radical shift, one that raises profound and difficult questions. Perhaps some of the knee-jerk reactions to the issues of disabled fetuses reflect our unwillingness to explore fully these hard issues.

It is a little too pat to say that decisions about whether to have amniocentesis or to abort a disabled fetus are personal ones. Ultimately, of course, they are and must remain so. But we need to have a feminist political language and ways of thinking about this issue to aid us in making those personal decisions and discussing these issues.

As Adrienne Asch has pointed out, discussions about whether to carry to term a pregnancy when the fetus will be born with a disability are clouded when we think in terms of the "severity" of the "defect." Instead, potential parents need to consider who *they* are and what they see as *their* strengths and weaknesses as parents making these decisions.

In choosing to be a parent, none of us knows what we are getting into: prenatal diagnosis may shed a little light, but everyone who becomes a parent takes a giant leap into the unknown. We need to remember that there is no such thing as a "perfect" child; that all children, abled and disabled, are going to experience suffering and joys in this world.

One thing that feminists should push for is good amniocentesis counseling. Unfortunately, despite my attempts, I haven't been able to witness any such counseling firsthand. I was able to interview one disabled woman who had amniocentesis. She was having amnio, not because she intended to abort if her fetus had a potential disability, but because she felt that, given her special needs, she needed to be able to make plans if her child was going to have a disability. She was shocked at the assumptions made by the counselors that any woman who was carrying a fetus with Down's syndrome or spina bifida

would of course abort. After the group counseling session, she called the clinic to voice her objections about their presentation of disability. She was told by counselors at the clinic that they felt they should provide as *negative* a picture as possible.

Much of this stems from medical attitudes toward physical impairment. One woman did an informal survey in which she asked doctors, "What things would be worse than death?" They answered, being paraplegic, or being deaf, or partially sighted or not having both arms (Carleton 1981). I think having attitudes like that is a fate worse than death. Too often, people who see physical and mental limitations as tragedies are counseling women following amniocentesis. Are women who are told they are carrying a Down's fetus told that, because of deinstitutionalization and better educational methods, some people with Down's now go to school in regular classrooms, live in their own apartments and hold jobs? Are they told that 95 percent of Down's people have moderate to mild retardation? Are they told that if they choose to bear their child, but not raise her or him, the child can be adopted immediately—usually within twenty-four hours? (Ganz 1983). Do they have anything more to go on than fear, shame, and their own prejudices, combined with those of the medical profession? Women who are considering aborting a disabled fetus must have the opportunity to talk to disabled people and the parents of disabled children. Anything less is not real reproductive freedom.

Women considering whether or not to give birth to a disabled child have few, if any, positive role models. Mothers who remain the primary caregivers of disabled children are seen as being either self-sacrificing saints or bitter, ruined women. These popular images get carried into the "objective" scientific literature. Wendy Carlton reviewed the studies done of mothers of disabled children: These mothers were seen as either being "rejecting" or "overprotecting"; they denied the child's condition or had unrealistic expectations; they were "unconcerned or overinvolved" (Carlton 1981). No matter what they did, they couldn't seem to get it right.

One in every twenty children is born with some sort of disability—a quarter of a million children a year. In addition, many become disabled during childhood. There are millions of mothers of disabled children in the United States, most of whom, I am sure, manage to do a halfway decent job of childrearing, despite stereotypes, social service cutbacks, and the limitations of the nuclear family.

Dealing with Fears

This chapter grew out of a talk that I gave to a reproductive rights group on this issue. In the discussion that followed, I was very disappointed that women in the audience never once addressed the reproductive rights of disabled women and men, despite extensive presentation of such issues. Instead, the discussion focused on disabled infants and, more specifically, on the women's personal fears of having a disabled child.

The women I talked to are hardly alone. For instance, Sheila Kitzinger (1984), well-regarded in the alternative birth movement has a chapter entitled "The Psychology of Pregnancy" in her book *The Experience of Childbirth*. In the subsection entitled "Fear that the baby will be malformed," she states:

> Any time after about the fifth month of pregnancy, when the child begins to move and becomes a reality to the mother, she may start to think about her baby as possibly deformed . . . What if this thing I am nourishing and cherishing within my own body, around which my whole life is built now, whose pulse beats fast deep within me—what if this child should prove to be *a hideous deformed creature, subhuman, a*

thing I should be able to love, but which I should shudder to see? (emphasis added)

Kitzinger deals with this issue solely on the level of a neurotic fear, never once discussing what happens when a child is actually born with a disability.

The deeply rooted fears that many women have of giving birth to a disabled child extend to our politics. They need to be worked through. But please don't expect disabled women to sit there and listen to you while you do so.

Killing Babies, Left and Right

Infanticide of the disabled has gone on at least as long as history has been recorded. Killing of disabled infants continues today—sometimes through denial of nutrition, more often through withholding of medical treatment. "Baby Doe" is probably the best known case. A Down's syndrome infant, born with a blocked esophagus, his parents and the doctors involved decided to deny him standard lifesaving surgery, resulting in his death by starvation. This happened despite the fact that child welfare workers went to court to try to get an injunction to force the surgery to be performed, and despite the fact that there were twelve families ready to adopt the child, and a surgeon willing to perform the surgery free (Ganz 1983). Nearly all Down's syndrome children, up to about the age of five, are now adoptable—thanks in large part to the baby shortage caused by legal abortion and the increased number of single women who keep their children.

I believe that it is inconsistent with feminism for us to say that human beings should be killed (or allowed to die, if you prefer) because they do not fit into oppressive social structures. "Anatomy is destiny" is a right-wing idea. It is right wing whether it is applied to women or whether it is applied to disabled children by the people I usually think of as my sisters and brothers.

So-called right-to-lifers are among the loudest voices heard in defense of these children's lives, and I have heard the argument made that it is dangerous for us to sound like we are on "their" side. But if we fail to call for full rights for *all* disabled people, we will have allowed right-wing, antifeminist forces to define totally the terrain on which we struggle. And we can distinguish ourselves from the Right on this issue, by standing for full rights for disabled people—not just the right to live so that we can, in the words of antiabortionist Nathanson, "evoke pity and compassion" from the abled.

Sexuality, Birth Control, and Parental Rights

Occasionally, reproductive rights groups make a token mention of disabled women. When we are included, it is usually at the end of a long list. But our particular needs and concerns are rarely addressed, much less fought for. One reproductive rights activist said to me, "We always used to talk about the rights of disabled women, but I was never sure exactly what that meant." Lack of access to offices, newsletters, demonstrations, and meetings remains a barrier, preventing many disabled women from being physically present within the movement to voice their concerns.

Part of this problem lies in the pervasive stereotype of disabled women as being asexual. Disabled women have been asked, "What do you need birth control for?" or "How did *you* get pregnant?" In 1976 the Sex Information and Education Council on the United States (SIECUS), which is quite a respectable organization, prepared a booklet on "Sexuality and the Handicapped," which was sent to the 1976 White House Conference on the Handicapped—and promptly rejected as "inappropriate" (Calderone 1981).

At least some of this prevalent stereotype of asexuality stems from seeing disabled people as eternal children. Telethons and other charitable activities have played a large role in creating this image. They portray us as being wan, pathetic, pitiful. The Jerry Lewis telethon even showed a series of film clips of adult disabled people saying, "I'm forty-seven years old and I'm one of Jerry's kids," "I'm fifty-five years old and I'm one of Jerry's kids." I won't go into the way that children's sexuality is treated in this society.

This asexual image is often prevalent among doctors and counselors as well. Women who have had a spinal cord injury report that when they asked questions about their sexual functioning they were given the information that they could still have children—and nothing more. Or else, they received sexist and heterosexist information, typified by the following:

> A female paraplegic can have intercourse more easily than a male paraplegic, since she does not have to participate actively. Although some such women have no subjective feeling of orgasm [as opposed to an objective feeling of organism?] they are perfectly capable of satisfying their husbands. (Becker 1978)

All human bodies are sexual. People without genital sensation (which is a fairly common occurrence following a spinal cord injury) can have orgasms through the stimulation of other parts of their bodies, such as their breasts, earlobes, or necks. One measure of the rigid structure that the medical profession imposes on our bodies is that these nongenital orgasms are sometimes referred to by clinicians as "phantom orgasms." These are not genuine, medically approved orgasms—they only *feel* like the real thing.

There is an opposite stereotype, in some ways similar to the madonna-whore dichotomy that women face. Disabled people (particularly men, although also women) are sometimes seen as being filled with diseased lusts. Lewis Terman, one of the early authorities on what was then called "feeble-mindedness" said that all developmentally disabled women were "potential prostitutes" since moral values could not "flower" without full intelligence. Media images portray disabled men—whether they are physically disabled or "escaped mental patients"—as rapists and potential rapists. The chilling realities about rape of disabled people, particularly within institutions, has been largely ignored both by the public at large and within the women's movement.

Disabled lesbians are rarely seen as having made a choice about their sexuality. Many people see them as having had to take "second best" because of their disability, or as having relationships that must be asexual. For mentally retarded lesbians the "normalization" that is a part of moving developmentally disabled people into the community holds pitfalls. "Normal" women are supposed to curl their hair, wear makeup and dresses, giggle, and sleep with men. Many who argue for the sexual rights of developmentally disabled people point out that if they aren't allowed to form heterosexual relationships that they will form—horror of horrors—homosexual ones.

Birth Control

The stereotype of asexuality persists in information that comes from the women's health movement. I have never seen a discussion of birth control methods—no matter how extensive—that talks about how a particular method works for a woman who is blind, or has cerebral palsy, or is developmentally disabled. *Our Bodies, Our Selves*, for instance, warns that the pill should not be taken by women who have a "disease or condition associated with poor blood circulation," without mentioning what those diseases or condi-

tions are. Unfortunately, many of us with disabilities are far from fully informed about our medical conditions. I had no idea (and neither, apparently, did any of the gynecologists I saw) that, due to my disability, taking birth control pills put me at great risk of thromboembolism.

When we work for improved birth control, we need to remember that there are many disabled women for whom there is *no* method that comes close to being safe and effective. The pill is contraindicated for most women in wheelchairs because of circulation problems. Many women who have paralysis cannot insert a diaphragm; and these same women may have problems with an IUD, especially if they do not have uterine sensation and cannot be warned by pain and cramping of infection or uterine perforation.

Parenting, Custody Issues, and Adoption

In preparing this chapter, I looked for, but was unable to find, any statistics about the number or percentage of disabled people who have children. I did find lots of anecdotal information about disabled people being told they *shouldn't* have children, and I heard some chilling stories from disabled women about being pressured into having abortions. There is almost no public image of disabled people as parents, and I do not know of a single book about being a disabled parent—although there are probably hundreds about having a disabled child.

There have been two fairly well-known cases in which a disabled parent fought to win or keep custody of a child. One of these concerned a single mother who had been born without arms or legs: welfare workers attempted to take her child away from her. After demonstrating to the judge that she was able to care for her child's needs herself, she won the right to custody. In the second case, a divorced quadraplegic father won custody of his sons.

It is particularly important that we in the women's movement take up these issues, since too often they are ignored when demands for disability rights are raised. The American Civil Liberties Union puts out a handbook called *The Rights of Physically Handicapped People* (Hull 1979) that contains no mention of parental rights, sexual rights, rights to adoption, or rights to safe and effective birth control.

The many political issues around adoption are too complex for me to delve into here. We do need to be sure that people are not denied the right to adopt on the basis of their disability. This has a special importance for two reasons: a small percentage of people with disabilities are unable to become biological parents. In addition, there is a growing tendency for disabled people to adopt children with disabilities, so that they can be raised within our community.

Because both the reproductive rights movement and the disability rights movement are rooted in our rights to control our bodies and our lives, there are strong links between the two. Just as there needs to be a realization within the disabled rights movement that the rights of disabled women must be fought for, so there needs to be an awareness within the reproductive rights movement that those of us who are disabled can no longer be exploited and ignored.

NOTE

Acknowledgements: I would like to thank Adele Clarke, Judy Heumann, Susan Hansell, Jean Miller, Kim Marshall, Carla Schick, Lisa Manning, Susan Dambroff, and Sex Education for Disabled People in Oakland, California, for their assistance in preparing this chapter.

REFERENCES

Bajema, Carl. 1976. *Eugenics Then and Now.* Benchmark Papers in Genetics, 15. Stroudsburg, Pa: Dowden, Hutchinson and Ross.

Becker, Elle F. 1978. *Female Sexuality Following Spinal Cord Injury.* Bloomington, Ind.: Accent Special Publications.

Boston Women's Health Book Collective. 1976. *Our Bodies, Out Selves.* New York: Simon & Schuster.

Calderone, Mary S. 1981. "Sexuality and disability in the United States." In David G. Bullard and Susan E. Knight, eds., *Sexuality and Physical Disability: Personal Perspectives.* St. Louis, Mo.: C.V. Mosby.

Carlton, Wendy. 1981. "Perfectibility and the Neonate: The Burden of Expectations on Mothers and Their Health Providers." In Helen Holmes, Betty Hoskins, and Michael Gross, eds., *The Custom-Made Child? Women-Centered Perspectives.* Clifton, N.J.: Humana Press.

Chase, Allan. 1980. *The Legacy of Malthus.* Urbana: University of Illinois Press.

Clarke, Adele. n.d. "Compulsory sterilization: past, present, and future." Unpublished paper.

———. n.d. "The double-life of eugenics 1900–1930: Pseudo-science and social movement." Unpublished paper.

Fine, Michelle, and Adrienne Asch. 1982. "The question of disability: No easy answers for the women's movement." *Reproductive Rights Newsletter* (Fall).

Friedman, Paul. 1976. *The Rights of the Mentally Retarded: An American Civil Liberties Civil Liberties Union Handbook.* New York: Avon.

Ganz, Mary. 1983. "Retarded boy's right to live: Who decides?" *Sunday San Francisco Examiner and Chronicle,* January 30.

Hull, Kent. 1979. *The Rights of Physically Handicapped People: An American Civil Liberties Union Handbook.* New York: Avon.

Illich, Ivan. 1976. *Medical Nemesis: The Expropriation of Health.* New York: Pantheon.

Kitzinger, Sheila. 1984. *The Experience of Childbirth.* New York: Penguin.

~ Chapter 62

The Right Family Values

JUDITH STACEY

The way a male becomes a man is by supporting his children. . . . What [the Democrats] cannot accept is that government proposals have failed. It is the family that can rebuild America. . . . The dissolution of the family, and in particular, the absence of fathers in the lives of millions of America's children is the single most critical threat [to our future].

— Dan Quayle, September 8, 1994.

That is a disaster. It is wrong. And someone has to say again, "It is simply not right. You shouldn't have a baby before you're ready, and you shouldn't have a baby when you're not married."

— President Clinton, September 9, 1994

In November of 1992, there seemed impeccable cause to imagine that the U.S. family wars were about to abate. The extent and irreversibility of family change, assisted by

This is an updated version of an essay originally published as "Scents, Scholars, and Stigma: The Revisionist Campaign for Family Values," *Social Text* 40 (fall 1994): 51–75. Copyright © by Duke University Press, 1994. Reprinted with permission from Duke University Press. This material also appears as chapter 3 in Judith Stacey, *In the Name of the Family: Rethinking Family Values in a Postmodern Age* (Boston: Beacon Press, 1996).

Murphy Brown, the Republican Convention fiasco, and the Year of the Woman, seemed to have vanquished the family-values brigades, while "the economy, stupid" lured many Reagan Democrats back from their costly supply-side fling. Who would have predicted that even the liberal media would scramble to rehabilitate Dan Quayle's image before Bill and Hillary Clinton had survived their blistering first one hundred days?

Yet that is exactly what happened. "Dan Quayle Was Right," blared the April 1993 cover of the *Atlantic* monthly, a magazine popular with the very "cultural elite" whom the former vice-president had blamed for the decline of Western civilized family life. Far from withering, a revisionist campaign for family values flourished under Democratic skies. While Clinton's job stimulus package suffered a silent demise, pro–family values stories mushroomed in magazines and newspapers, on radio and television talk shows, and in scholarly journals. The *Atlantic* cover story by Barbara Dafoe Whitehead[1] ignited "the single strongest public response" to any issue ever published by the *At-*

lantic since at least 1981 and was recycled from sea to rocky sea.[2] A *New York Times* op-ed, "The Controversial Truth: The Two-Parent Family Is Better," by Rutgers University sociologist David Popenoe, also enjoyed acclaim, with retreads and derivatives appearing from the *Chronicle of Higher Education* to the Santa Rosa, California, *Press Democrat*.[3] In the winter 1993 issue of *American Scholar,* New York Senator Daniel Patrick Moynihan, a Founding Father of post–World War II family crisis discourse in the United States, added to his hefty inventory of family values jeremiads, while James Q. Wilson, the Collins Professor of Management and Public Policy at UCLA, earlier proponent of racial theories of criminality, weighed in with a featured family-values essay in *Commentary*.[4] From "This Week with David Brinkley" to the "MacNeil-Lehrer News Hour" television followed suit, featuring guests, like Popenoe, chanting kaddish over an idealized family past.

Less a revival than a creative remodel job, the 1990s media blitz on "family values," which coincided with the Clinton administration's rapid conversion to its credo, signals the considerable success of a distinctively new political phenomenon. Because the rhetoric of family values discourse seems so numbingly familiar, most progressives have failed to recognize, or to respond appropriately to, what is dangerously novel here. To comprehend the cultural politics of the Clinton administration, one must understand how and why a revival of the family-values campaign coincided with the very changing of the political guard that appeared to spell its decline.

Pseudo-Scholarly Cultural Combat

Old-fashioned family-values warriors, such as Jerry Falwell, Dan Quayle, and Pat Buchanan, are right-wing Republicans and fundamentalist Christians, overtly antifeminist, antihomo-

sexual, and politically reactionary. Their "pro-family" campaign, which provided zeal and zeitgeist for both of Ronald Reagan's presidential victories, enjoyed its heyday in the 1980s and suffered a major setback during the 1992 electoral season—from Quayle's infamous "Murphy Brown" speech, through the ill-advised "family-values" orgy of the Republican Convention, to defeat at the polls. By 1996, this highly mobilized, zealously Christian, pro-family movement had secured such a firm grip on the Republican Party that "moderate" Republican candidates, such as Pennsylvania's Senator Arlen Specter and California's Governor Pete Wilson, who failed its antiabortion or antigay litmus tests, could not seriously contend for their party's presidential nomination. In contrast, the revisionist family-values campaign to which the Clinton administration succumbed has an explicitly centrist politics, rhetoric, and ideology. A product of academicians rather than clerics, it grounds its claims in secular social science instead of religious authority, and it eschews antifeminism for a postfeminist family ethic.

While the right wing may prove the prime beneficiary of current family-values discourse, it is not its primary producer. Instead, an interlocking network of scholarly and policy institutes, think tanks, and commissions began mobilizing during the late 1980s to forge a national "consensus" on family values that soon shaped the family ideology and politics of the Clinton administration and its "new" Democratic Party. Central to this effort are the Institute for American Values, of which David Blankenhorn is president and Barbara Dafoe Whitehead vice-president; and its offshoot, the Council on Families in America, cochaired by Popenoe and Jean Bethke Elshtain. The former, which Popenoe describes as a "nonpartisan public policy organization," sponsors the latter, whose eighteen members depict themselves as "a volunteer, nonpartisan program of scholarly research and interdisciplinary deliberation on the state of families in America. We come from across the human sciences and across the political spectrum."[5]

"This is an attempt to bring people together who could convince the liberal intelligentsia that the family was in trouble and that this was a big problem," Popenoe explained to me in an interview. "Most of us are neoliberal—you know, New Democrats, affiliated with the Progressive Policy Institute. We try to keep to the middle of the road."[6] The political networks and the funding sources of these center-laners merge with those of the "communitarians"—a movement that its founder, sociologist Amitai Etzioni, characterized as "struggling for the soul of the Clinton Administration."[7] They are linked as well with those of the Democratic Leadership Council's Progressive Policy Institute.

These groups share the same benefactors, such as the Randall, Smith Richardson, Scaife and Mott foundations, and the Brookings and American Enterprise Institutes, according to Popenoe, more of which are conservative than liberal, he conceded.[8] With such support, revisionists are self-consciously waging a cultural crusade—one modeled explicitly after the antismoking campaign—to restore the privileged status of lifelong heterosexual marriage. Declaring that "the principal source of family decline over the past three decades has been cultural," Whitehead urged the Institute of American Values readership to join a cultural mobilization to restore nuclear family supremacy.[9] Wilson's *Commentary* essay went further, calling "this raging cultural war" over family values "far more consequential than any of the other cleavages that divide us."[10]

If the effects of this campaign on sexual and conjugal behaviors in the "private" sphere remain to be seen, it quickly achieved an astonishing, and disturbing, impact on the public behavior and policy priorities of the Clinton administration. It took scarcely a year to convert Clinton from representing himself as a proud icon of an independent single mom's glory into a repentant Quayle acolyte. "Hurray for Bill Clinton. What a difference a year makes," Quayle gloated in December 1993, right after *Newsweek* had published the president's revised family credo: "Remember the Dan Quayle speech? There were a lot of very good things in that speech," Clinton acknowledged. "Would we be a better-off society if babies were born to married couples? You bet we would."[11] The rhetorical means through which Clinton's family-values makeover occurred merit close scrutiny.

Feigning Iconoclastic Courage

In one of the more effective rhetorical ploys of the revisionist campaign, these mainstream social scientists, policy lobbyists, and prominent political officeholders and advisers ride the coattails of the antipolitical correctness crusade by positioning themselves as dissident challengers of a formidable, intolerant, ideological establishment. Popenoe, for example, is associate dean of social and behavioral sciences at Rutgers University, as well as cochair of the Council on Families in America. Wilson occupies an endowed professorship of management and public policy at UCLA, and Elshtain an endowed professorship of theology at the University of Chicago. Etzioni was the 1994–95 President of American Sociological Association. And Senator Moynihan, well . . .

Yet Wilson characterizes those scholars who reject a nostalgic view of 1950s families as "policy elites."[12] During a radio debate over the superiority of the two-parent family, Popenoe portrayed me and other feminist sociologists as part of the "liberal social science establishment."[13] Whitehead laments, "It is nearly impossible to discuss changes in family structure without provoking angry protest,"[14] citing as evidence enraged responses in the mid-1960s to Moynihan's *The Negro Family: The Case for National Action,* which had labeled the rising percentages of black single-mother families a "tangle of pathology." Whitehead attributes to ideological pressures some of the "caution" exercised by researchers who do not support the claim that single-parent families are deficient. "Some are fearful that they will be attacked by feminist colleagues," Whitehead claims, "or, more generally, that their comments will be regarded as an effort to turn back the clock to the 1950s—a goal that has almost no constituency in the academy."[15]

Wilson predicted that were President Clinton to exercise leadership in condemning unwed childbearing, he would elicit "dismayed groans from sitcom producers and ideological accusations from sociology professors, but at least the people would know that he is on their side."[16] Exploiting popular resentment against "politically correct" cultural elites builds upon a tradition of disingenuous populism honed by former Republican vice-presidents Spiro Agnew and Dan Quayle. At the same time, it pays tribute to the considerable, albeit precarious, influence over gender and family discourse that feminism has achieved during the past quarter-century. Inside the academy, many centrists probably do feel threatened and displaced by feminist scholars. They are fighting back.

Constructing Social Scientific Stigma

While the right-wing family-values campaign appeals to religious and traditional patriarchal authority for its family vision, centrists are engaged in an active, indeed, an entrepreneurial, process of transmuting into a newly established social scientific "truth" one of the most widely held prejudices about family life in North America—the belief in the superiority of families composed of married heterosexual couples and their biological children. Revisionists argue that the presence or absence of two married biological parents in the household is the central determinant of a child's welfare, and thereby of our society's welfare. They identify fatherless families as the malignant root of escalating violence and social decay, claiming that such families generate the lineage of unemployed, undomesticated, "family-less fathers," as John Gillis aptly puts it,[17] who threatened middle-class tranquility.

Through the sheer force of categorical assertion, repetition, and cross-citation of each other's publications, these social scientists seem to have convinced most of the media, the literate public, and Clinton himself that a fault-free bedrock of social science research validates the particular family values that they and most Americans claim to favor, but fail to practice. "In three decades of work as a social scientist," asserted Popenoe in his *New York Times* op-ed, "I know of few other bodies of data in which the weight of evidence is so decisively on one side of the issue: on the whole for children, two-parent families are preferable to single-parent and stepfamilies."[18] In the *Atlantic* story three months later, Whitehead quoted these very lines as authority for a similar assertion: "The social arrangement that has proved most successful in ensuring the physical survival and promoting the social development of the child is the family unit of the biological mother and father."[19] Whitehead also relied on Moynihan's "Defining Deviancy Down," which blamed "broken families" for almost all of our current social crises. Moynihan, in turn, had quoted an earlier essay by Whitehead in support of a similar argument.[20] Moynihan, Whitehead, and Popenoe all cited the National Commission on Children's *Beyond Rhetoric* (known as the Rockefeller Report), and the commission returned the favor with frequent citations in its report to essays by Popenoe and his associates in the Institute for American Values and the Council on Families in America.[21]

It is not often that the social construction, or more precisely here, the political construction of knowledge is quite so visible or incestuous as in the reciprocal citation practices of these cultural crusaders. Through such means they have convinced President Clinton and most of the public that "it is a confirmed empirical generalization," as Popenoe maintains, that nontraditional families "are not as successful as conventional two-parent families."[22] Yet the current status of social scientific knowledge of the success of diverse family structures is far more complex and the views of family scholars far more heterogeneous than revisionists pretend.

Social scientists continue actively to debate whether family forms or processes determine diverse family outcomes and whether our family or socioeconomic crisis has generated its counterpart.[23] For example, in a judicious, comprehensive review essay of the cumulative research on changing parent-child relations, prominent family sociologist David Demo concluded that "the consequences of maternal employment, divorce, and single-parent family structure have been greatly exaggerated, and . . . researchers need to investigate processes more directly influencing children, notably economic hardship and high levels of marital and family conflict.[24] In fact, according to Demo,

> the accumulated evidence is sufficiently consistent to wonder whether we, as researchers, are asking the most important questions, or whether we, like the families we are trying to study, are more strongly influenced by traditional notions of family formality.[25]

Revisionist social scientists suppress these debates by employing social-scientific sleights-of-hand. For example, they rest their claims on misleading comparison groups and on studies that do not use any comparison groups at all, such as Judith Wallerstein and Joan Kelly's widely cited research on divorcing parents.[26] While it is true that, on average, children whose parents divorce fare slightly worse on several measures than those whose parents remain in intact marriages, this fact reveals little about the impact of divorce on children. To address that question, one must compare children of divorce not with all children of married parents but with those whose unhappily married parents do not divorce. In fact, research indicates that high-conflict marriages harm children more than do low-conflict divorces. "There is abundant evidence," David Demo concludes, "that levels of family conflict are more important than type of family structure for understanding children's adjustment, self-esteem, and other measures of psychological well-being."[27] Unhappily married parents must ask themselves not if divorcing or staying married is worse for children in general but which would be worse for their particular children in their particular unhappy marriage.

Centrists use additional statistical tricks to exaggerate the advantages that some children from two-parent families enjoy over their single-parented peers. For example, they pretend that correlation proves causality, they ignore mediating variables, or they treat small and relative differences as though they were gross and absolute. In fact, most children from both kinds of families turn out reasonably all right, and when other parental resources—such as income, education, self-esteem, and a supportive social environment—are roughly similar, signs of two-parent privilege disappear. Most research indicates that a stable, intimate relationship with one responsible, nurturant adult is a child's surest track to becoming the same kind of adult. In short, the research scale tips handily toward those who stress the quality of family relationships over their form.[28]

Once dissenting scholarly views on the pathology of single-parent families had been muffled or marginalized, only a rhetorical baby step was needed to move from the social to the moral inferiority of such families: ergo, the remarkably respectful public response that American Enterprise Institute scholar Charles Murray received in November 1993 to his overtly punitive quest to restigmatize unwed childbearing via Dickensian welfare policies. "My proposition is that illegitimacy is the single most important social problem of our time—more important than crime, drugs, poverty, illiteracy, welfare or homelessness because it drives everything else," Murray declared in defense of his proposal "to end all economic support for single mothers." Forcing single mothers on welfare to go cold turkey would slash nonmarital childbearing, Murray reasoned, because "the pressure on relatives and communities to pay for the folly of their children will make an illegitimate birth the socially horrific act it used to be, and getting a girl pregnant something boys do at the risk of facing a shotgun."[29]

Instead of receiving timely visits from the Ghosts of Christmases Past, Present, and Future, Murray was soon the featured guest on "This Week with David Brinkley," and even in liberal San Francisco, an op-ed by a supporter of his proposals from the right-wing Hoover Institute upstaged the more charitable Christmas week commentaries that aired on the local affiliate of National Public Radio.[30] By then, revisionists had deftly paved the Yellow Brick Road to Murray's media coronation.

"Bringing a child into the world outside of marriage," Blankenhorn had asserted three years earlier, "is almost always personally and socially harmful."[31] In December 1992, Moynihan had congratulated himself on having predicted nearly thirty years earlier both the epidemic of single-parent families and its calamitous social consequences. "There is one unmistakable lesson in American history," he had written in 1965, "a community that allows a large number of young men to grow up in broken families, dominated by women . . . asks for and gets chaos."[32]

Thus by the time the 1993 holiday season had begun, the ideological mortar had dried firmly enough to encourage *Newsweek* columnist Joe Klein's view that "the issue is so elemental, the question so basic, the answer so obvious" that one should not have to ask a president, as the magazine had just done, whether it is "immoral for people to have children out of wedlock?" Klein applauded when President Clinton—himself possessed of dubious parentage and out-of-wedlock half-siblings who seem to surface intermittently—answered, according to Klein, "Much as Dan Quayle, to whom [the president] gave considerable credit, might have: 'I believe this country would be a lot better off if children were born to married couples.'"[33]

Indeed, by then, the revisionist cultural onslaught had been so effective that even Donna Shalala, the token feminist progressive in Clinton's cabinet, felt politically compelled to recite its moralist mantra: "I don't like to put this in moral terms, but I do believe that having children out of wedlock is just wrong." And, "a dyed-in-the-wool, but curious, White House liberal," confided off the record to *Newsweek*: "I'd like to see the Murray solution tried somewhere—just to see, y'know, what might happen."[34]

In June 1994, *before* the right-wing Republican midterm electoral rout, Clinton sent to Congress a "welfare reform" proposal with caps on childbearing and benefits that threatened to satisfy such liberal curiosity.

The New Postfeminist Familism

Despite inflated claims to iconoclasm, revisionists promote family values that seem, at first glance, tediously familiar. Sounding like card-carrying conservatives in academic drag, they blame "family breakdown" for everything from child poverty, declining educational standards, substance abuse, homicide rates, AIDS, infertility, and teen pregnancy to narcissism and the Los Angeles riots. They attribute family breakdown, in turn, to a generalized decline in family values, which, in its turn, they often associate with feminism, the sexual revolution, gay liberation, excessively generous welfare policies, and escalating demands for social rights.

While orthodox and revisionist family preachers share obvious affinities, centrists take wiser note of present demographic and cultural terrain than do their right-wing counterparts. Because centrists claim to decry rampant individualism, they tend to acknowledge greater public and corporate responsibility for family decline and redress than is palatable to family values hardliners. Many used to claim to support the Progressive Policy Institute's call for a "guaranteed working wage" that would lift families with full-time workers out of poverty. Most also claim to favor family-friendly workplace reforms like flextime, family leaves, and flexible career paths.[35] Disappointingly, however, they and the Clinton administration have devoted much less of their political energies to these more progressive goals than to the cultural campaign that has done much to undermine them.

Perhaps the most significant distinction between the traditional–and the neo–family values campaigns is in gender ideology. Departing from the explicit antifeminism and homophobia of a Jessie Helms or a Pat Buchanan, family centrists accommodate their family values to postindustrial society and postfeminist culture.[36] They temper their palpable nostalgia for Ozzie and Harriet with rhetorical gestures toward gender equality. "The council does not bemoan the loss of 'the traditional nuclear family,' with its strict social roles, distinguishing between male breadwinners and female homemakers," Popenoe maintains. "Recognizing," instead,

the importance of female equality and the changing conditions of modern society, we do not see the previous model of lifelong, separate gender roles within marriage as either desirable or possible on a society-wide scale. But we do believe strongly that the model of the two-parent family, based on a lasting, monogamous marriage, is both possible and desirable.[37]

Revisionists place great emphasis on reviving paternal commitment. Wilson lauds efforts by the National Center for Neighborhood Enterprise "that try to encourage men to take responsibility for their children."[38] Whitehead praises a high-powered Boston attorney who "left his partnership at a law firm and took a judgeship that gave him more manageable hours," so that he could spend more time with his children and his wife, also an attorney, who left trial law for more family-friendly work.[39] Similarly, Galston cited his paternal priorities when he resigned as Clinton's chief domestic-policy adviser to attend to his own domestic concerns and his university professorship in June 1995: "I told the president, 'You can replace me and my son can't.'"[40]

Blankenhorn has turned combating fatherlessness into his overarching mission. Joining forces with Don Eberly, a former aide to Jack Kemp, he formed a national organization of fathers to "restore to fatherhood a sense of pride, duty and reward."[41] Blankenhorn combined a massive promotional tour for his 1995 book, *Fatherless America,* with a campaign for the National Fatherhood Initiative, which he chairs. He is actively crusading to counter "excesses of feminism," like the belief that "men will not become new fathers unless they do half the diaper changes or bottle feedings." Instead, his campaign promotes a neotraditional model of fatherhood in which "the old father, with some updating in the nurturing department, will do just fine."[42]

Such postfeminist ideology appeals to many conservative feminists and to many liberals. It builds upon a body of thought I once labeled "new conservative feminism."[43] One of the defining features of this ideology is its weak stomach for sexual politics. Centrists offer tepid support, at best, for abortion rights, often supporting restrictions like spousal and parental notification, partly with the claim that these could hold men more paternally accountable.[44] And as communitarian founder Etzioni put it: "There are some issues, such as abortion and gay rights, that we know communitarians cannot agree on, so we have completely avoided them."[45]

Rather than confront the internal contradictions, unjust power relations, and economic reorganizations that underlie the decline of lifelong marriage, revisionists promote what Whitehead terms a New Familism, in which postfeminist women willingly, admirably, and self-consciously *choose* to place familial needs above the demands of "a life defined by traditional male models of career and success." "In the period of the New Familism," Whitehead exults, "both parents give up something in their work lives in order to foster their family lives. The woman makes the larger concession, but it is one she actively elects and clearly sees as temporary."[46]

Blankenhorn's bioevolutionary view of parenthood explicitly scorns feminist or androgynous family values: "Ultimately, the division of parental labor is the consequence of our biological embodiment as sexual beings

and of the inherent requirements of effective parenthood."[47]

And Other Euphemisms for Injustice

1. The "Stability" of Gender Inequality

One need hardly be a paranoid feminist to penetrate the shallow veneer of revisionist commitments to gender equality. Defending a lengthy lament by Popenoe about American "family decline," family sociologist Norval Glenn, for example, conceded that there is "a rational basis for concern that attempts to 'put the family back together' may tend to erase recent feminist gains." Likewise, Wilson acknowledged, "What is at stake, of course, is the role of women."[48]

Of course. Few feminists were confused when Quayle lashed out at Murphy Brown. Perhaps a few more will be misled by the higher-toned centrist retread of his views. Yet despite lip-service to gender equality, the revisionist campaign does not redress marital inequities or question that women bear disproportionate responsibility for their children and families. Instead, in the guise of rejecting "male models," it adds to the unjust burden of guilt, anxiety, and marginality that divorced, unmarried, and unhappily married mothers already suffer. That Wilson and Glenn recognize the gender stakes in this discursive game underscores how much more the cummunitarian rhetoric of "family values" impugns the individualism of women than that of men.

Postfeminist familist ideology appropriates feminist critiques of conventionally masculine work priorities while appealing to those conventionally feminine maternalist values that feminist scholars like Carol Gilligan and Deborah Tannen have made popular. This ideology also exploits women's weariness with the incompatibility of postindustrial work and family demands, as well as their anxiety over the asymmetrical terms of the heterosexual courtship and marriage market and of women's vulnerability to divorce-induced poverty.

Centrists often blame excessive divorce rates as well as unwed motherhood on a general rise of selfishness—gender unspecified. To curb such indulgence, they advocate measures to restrict access to divorce, such as mandatory waiting periods and counseling and the reinstatement of "fault" criteria in divorces that involve children. Typically, they present their proposals for these restrictive measures under a child-centered mantle that taps women's all-too-ready reservoirs of guilt about failing to serve "the best interests" of their children. In *It Takes a Village*, Hillary Clinton follows this suit. She supports mandatory "cooling off" periods and counseling for parents considering divorce, explaining, "With divorce as easy as it is, and its consequences so hard, people with children need to ask themselves whether they have given a marriage their best shot and what more than can do to make it work before they call it quits."[49]

The backlash against no-fault divorce is gaining popularity among politicians in both political parties. Republican Governor Terry Brandstad of Iowa denounced no-fault divorce in his 1996 state of the state message. In February 1996, Michigan became the first state to consider a bill to revoke no-fault divorce in cases in which one spouse opposes the divorce; and several other states are considering following Michigan's lead. Arguing that people "must begin to see the connection between divorce and other problems, especially poverty and juvenile delinquency," the Republican sponsor of the Michigan bill augmented the child-protection rationale with a direct appeal to women's fear of impoverishment.[50] Likewise, Dan Jarvis, director of the Michigan Family Forum policy group that has campaigned vigorously for this bill, portrayed it as protecting women: "Let's say a homemaker has a husband who cheats on her. Under the proposed law, she would have the upper hand. She can say: 'All right, you want your divorce? You can have it. But it's going to cost you.' "[51]

Many women—especially homemakers—and their children indeed have been impoverished by the unfair effects of current no-fault divorce property settlements, as feminist scholars and lawyers have documented.[52] The current unjust economic consequences of no-fault divorce laws is a serious problem in need of serious legislative and judicial reforms. It is a postfeminist sleight-of-hand, however, to pretend that repeal of no-fault divorce is the only or best possible remedy, or that it will promote greater gender equality in marriage. The rhetoric against no-fault divorce erroneously implies that men seek a disproportionate number of contemporary divorces and that women have greater interests than men in sustaining their marriages. Unfortunately, the reverse is closer to the truth. Women seek a disproportionate number of contemporary divorces, despite the unjust consequences they risk in doing so, often because they find the injustices and difficulties of their marriages even harder to bear.[53]

Whether revisionist efforts to affix a tepid norm of gender equality to family-values rhetoric are well-intentioned or disingenuous, their marriage seems ill-fated. Principles of egalitarianism and stability frequently collide, and, as in too many traditional marriages, the former are sacrificed to the latter. Revisionists, unlike orthodox family-values advocates and feminists, rarely confront a disturbing contradiction at the heart of the Western ideal of a fully volitional marriage system—historically, stable marriage systems have rested upon coercion, overt or veiled, and on inequality. Proposals to restrict access to divorce implicitly recognize this unpleasant contradiction, one which poses a thorny dilemma for a democracy. If, as many feminists fear, a stable marriage system depends upon systemic forms of inequality, it will take more than moralistic jeremiads bemoaning family decline, or even mandatory waiting and counseling prerequisites to divorce, to stanch our contemporary marital hemorrhage.

This bleaker feminist analysis of contemporary marital fragility, rather than the "family optimism" that revisionists attribute to social scientists, like me, who do not share revisionists' views,[54] explains some of the political passions at stake in our dispute. Without coercion, as Wilson concedes, divorce and single motherhood rates will remain high. Indeed, I agree with Popenoe that women's capacity to survive outside marriage, however meagerly, explains why both rates rose so sharply in recent decades. Marriage became increasingly fragile as it became less economically obligatory, particularly for women. These developments expose the inequity and coercion that always lay at the vortex of the supposedly voluntary "companionate marriage" of the traditional nuclear family. It seems a poignant commentary on the benefits to women of that family system that even in a period when women retain primary responsibility for maintaining children and other kin, when most women continue to earn significantly less than men with equivalent "cultural capital," and when women and their children suffer substantial economic decline after divorce, despite all this, so many regard divorce as the least of evils.

I do not dispute Glenn's judgment that "male-female equality in a society in which the quality of life is mediocre for everyone is hardly anyone's idea of utopia."[55] However, because I am far less willing to sacrifice women's precarious gains on the chimerical altar of social stability, I am more motivated to find alternative social responses to our misdiagnosed familial ills.

2. The "Biology" of Heterosexism

Homophobia also plays a closeted role in the centrist campaign, one that could prove more insidious than right-wing gay-bashing. Wilson includes popular discomfort with same-sex marriage in his sympathetic inventory of the family values of "reasonable people."[56] Popenoe makes one foray at a definition of "the family" broad enough to encompass "homosexual couples, and all other family types in which dependents are involved," only to retreat instantly to the linguistic mantra favoring "two biological parents" that pervades revisionist rhetoric.[57] Moynihan's conviction that children need to grow up in families that provide them with a "stable relationship to male authority" is echoed by Whitehead's undocumented claim that research demonstrates "the importance of both a mother and a father in fostering the emotional well-being of children."[58] Blankenhorn, once again, goes even further by explicitly condemning lesbian childbearing. Indeed, in *Fatherless America* he formally proposes restricting access to donor sperm and alternative insemination services only to married couples with fertility problems. "In a good society," Blankenhorn maintains, "people do not traffic commercially in the production of radically fatherless children."[59]

Elshtain unapologetically concedes that when she and her colleagues affirm a heterosexual family model they "are privileging relations of a particular kind in which certain social goods are at stake."[60] Doing so panders to popular heterosexist prejudice. Despite consistent research findings that lesbians and gays parent at least as successfully as heterosexuals,[61] the Council on Families in America refuses to advocate equal marriage, adoption, or childbearing rights for the former. If neo–family-values fans were faithful to their stated goals of promoting lasting familial bonds and committed two-parent families, they should actively endorse what former *New Republic* editor Andrew Sullivan calls "a conservative case for gay marriage."[62] Yet no such sermons issue from their bully pulpits. Rather, these challengers of "ideological constraints" remain faithful to Etzioni's credo: "There are some issues, such as abortion and gay rights, that we know communitarians cannot agree on, so we have completely avoided them."[63] Similarly, even though First Lady Hillary Clinton claims that she wrote *It Takes a Village* in order to challenge "false nostalgia for family values," the book pursues this centrist strategy of evasion by failing even to mention the subject of gay marriage or gay families, let alone to advocate village rights or resources for children whose parents are gay.[64] Likewise, in the 1995 fall preelection season, when President Clinton sought to shore up his flagging credibility among gays and lesbians by announcing his administration's support of a bill to outlaw employment discrimination against gays, he specifically withheld his support from gay marriage.[65]

This evasion abetted the social agenda and political strategy of organized reactionaries. Homophobia became the latest "wedge issue" of the New Right family warriors and of the 1996 Republican electoral strategy. When Republicans sought to scuttle passage of the Family Leave Act in January 1993—newly inaugurated Clinton's own first family-values offering—they did so by attempting to saddle it with a rider to prevent lifting the ban on gays in the military. Likewise, Falwell seized upon Clinton's nomination of a lesbian, Roberta Achtenberg, to an undersecretary post as an opportunity to flood the coffers of his Liberty Alliance. Urging readers to send donations of $25 with a "Stop the Lesbian Nomination Reply Form," Falwell warned that

> President Clinton's nomination of Roberta Achtenberg, a lesbian, to the Department of Housing and Urban Development is a threat to the American family. . . . Achtenberg has dedicated her life to winning the "rights" of lesbians to adopt little babies. Please help me stop her nomination.[66]

The Traditional Values Coalition, based in Anaheim, California, claims to have sold 45,000 copies of the videotape "Gay Rights, Special Rights" that they designed expressly to mobilize antigay sentiment among African Americans.[67] However, gay marriage, precisely the issue that Clinton and his centrist advisers sought to evade, emerged as the family-values centerfold of the 1996 Republican electoral strategy. At a Saturday night church service and "marriage protection" rally on the eve of the Iowa primary caucuses, "Republican presidential hopefuls declared war on the notion of same-sex marriages."[68] Promising to pursue the culture war he had waged at the 1992 GOP convention, Pat Buchanan declared: "We cannot worship the false god of gay rights. To put that sort of relationship on the same level as marriage is . . . a moral lie." Following the service, candidates Phil Gramm and Alan Keyes joined Buchanan in signing a pledge to oppose same-sex marriage.[69] One month later, Randall Terry, director of Operation Rescue, the extreme right-wing antiabortion group, flew to Hawaii to wage a direct action campaign against the state court's anticipated legalization of gay marriage.

On May 8, 1996, gay marriage galloped onto the nation's center political stage when congressional Republicans introduced the Defense of Marriage Act (DOMA), which defines marriage in exclusively heterosexual terms as "a legal union between one man and one woman as husband and wife." The last legislation that Republican presidential candidate Bob Dole cosponsored before he resigned from the Senate to pursue his White House bid full throttle, DOMA exploited homophobia in order to defeat President Clinton and the Democrats in November 1996. With Clinton severely bruised by the political debacle incited by his support for gay rights in the military when he first took office but still dependent upon the support of his gay constituency, the president indeed found himself "wedged" between a rock and a very hard place. Unsurprisingly, he first tried to waffle. Naming this a "time when we need to do things to strengthen the American family," Clinton publicly opposed same-sex marriage at the same time that he tried to reaffirm support for gay rights and to expose the divisive Republican strategy. However, he also tried to finesse the Republican strategy by quickly promising he would sign the bill if it reached his desk.[70] It did, and Clinton promptly kept his promise.

Ironically, the identification of Republicanism with such intolerance alarms many party moderates. However, a forum they convened in May 1993 to reorient the party foundered on just this faultline, with conservatives supporting Buchanan's view that "traditional values is the last trump card the Republican Party possesses."[71] Clinton's capitulation to the centrist family-values ideology colluded with a homophobic right-wing agenda at a dangerous moment.

3. Making a "Career" of Class Bias

Less obvious than the gender and sexual stakes of family-values rhetoric, perhaps, are ways it also serves as a sanitized decoy for less reputable prejudices of class and race. Having studied working-class families struggling to

sustain body, soul, and kin ties in the economically depressed Silicon Valley during the mid-1980s, I cannot help but wonder what sort of bourgeois bubble world such revisionists as Whitehead, Popenoe, and the communitarians inhabit. Perhaps their moralistic images of selfish, individualistic, hedonistic adults who place their own emotional and sexual pleasures and "career" ambitions above the needs of their vulnerable children derive from observations of some who reside in a professional-corporate social cocoon.

Such caricatures bear little resemblance to twenty-something Carole, a laid off electronics assembler and fotomat envelope stuffer, a wife and mother of four, who left and returned to her abusive husband before she died of cancer. Nor do they apply to Lanny, another twenty-something, laid off drafter, who divorced the substance-abusing father of her young daughter after discovering he had "snorted away" the down payment she had laboriously accumulated to purchase a house. They do not fit Jan, a forty-year-old lesbian social service worker who continues to contribute time, resources, and love to the son of a former lover. They do not adequately depict the tough choices or the family realities that confront any of the women I studied, nor, I would venture, those of the vast majority of citizens. The idiom of "careers" that family-values enthusiasts employ suggests ignorance of how few adults in postindustrial U.S.A. enjoy the luxury of joining "a new familism" by choosing to place their children's needs above the demands of their jobs. They could win much more respect for their cause and enhance its prospects if they would spend nearly as much time badgering public and corporate leaders to provide citizens with the kinds of jobs, incomes, schedules, and working conditions that might make the practice of any reasonable sort of "familism" viable as they have devoted to persuading individuals that "the most important thing to change is our minds."[72] Ironically, it is the failure of the Clinton administration's 1992 employment and health care agenda that fostered its retreat into the rhetorical politics of family values. In June 1996, for example, "seeing no immediate prospect of an agreement with Congress on welfare," as one reporter put it, "President Clinton announced yesterday that we was taking steps on his own to increase child-support collections and track down fathers who violate child-support orders."[73] Yet this in turn buttresses the very assaults on welfare that now threaten to devastate millions of the nation's poorest children and families.

4. *Willie Horton in Whiteface*

Wherever class bias flourishes in the United States, race can seldom be far behind, for, in our society, these two axes of injustice are always already hopelessly entangled. Quayle's 1992 attack on "Murphy Brown" was an ill-fated attempt to play the Willie Horton card in whiteface. Without resorting to overtly racist rhetoric, the image conjured up frightening hordes of African American welfare "queens" rearing infant fodder for sex, drugs, and video-taped uprisings, such as had just erupted in Los Angeles. As Elizabeth Traube points out, "Shadow traces of African-American family practices are inscribed in postfeminist visions of the family," and the *Murphy Brown* program directly exploits semiotic effects of this ancestry with Motown music on its opening theme soundtrack.[74] Lurking in Murphy's shadows were descendents of the pathological "black matriarchs" Moynihan permanently etched into the collective consciousness nearly three decades ago.[75]

In case anyone in fin de siècle U.S.A. remained ignorant of the racial coding of family-values discourse, Charles Murray used a megaphone to teach them a crash course. His *Wall Street Journal* op-ed, reprinted by the *Philadelphia Inquirer* under the title "The Emerging White Underclass and How to Save It," warned whites that their family patterns now resemble that malignant "tangle of pathology" that Moynihan presciently diagnosed in 1965 among African Americans. Displaying greater honesty than most revisionists, Murray concluded by speaking the unspeakable: "The brutal truth is that American society as a whole could survive when illegitimacy became epidemic within a comparatively small ethnic minority. It cannot survive the same epidemic among whites."[76]

Racial anxiety runs as subtext to the entire history of family-crisis discourse in the United States, a history that long predates Moynihan's incendiary 1965 report. It reaches back a century to xenophobic fears that in the face of high fertility among "inferior" eastern and southern European migrants the "selfishness" of native white women, whose birth rates were declining, threatened their tribe with "race suicide." It reaches back much further into the history of colonial settler fears of the diverse sexual and kinship practices of indigenous cultures, as well as to rationales that esteemed white scholars offered for African American slavery—that it helped civilize the heathen by teaching family values to a species that lacked these. Consider that until E. Franklin Frazier published *The Negro Family in the United States* in 1939, most social scientists subscribed to the view of Howard Odum that "in his home life, the Negro is filthy, careless, and indecent, . . . as destitute of morals as many of the lower animals . . . [and with] little knowledge of the sanctity of home or marital relations"[77]: and this about a system that denied slaves the right to legal or permanent conjugal and parental bonds.

If marriage was a form of racial privilege under slavery, it is rapidly becoming so again today. William J. Wilson's chauvinistic but still stunning "marriageable Black male index" graphs the increasing scarcity of African American men who are neither unemployed nor incarcerated. His index indirectly demonstrates that male breadwinning and marriage are becoming interactive badges of race and class status.[78] Indeed, the greatest contrast in family patterns and resources in the United States today is between two steady-earner and single-mother households, and these divide notably along racial lines. No doubt this is why presidential voting patterns in 1992 displayed a "family gap" more pronounced than the gender gap. Married voters heavily favored George Bush, while the unmarried shored Clinton's precarious margin of victory.[79] A campaign that sets couple- and single-parent families at odds has political consequences. During the 1996 campaign, Clinton strategists set out to erode the advantage Republicans enjoy among the largely white, middle-class, heterosexual, two-parent family set. According to Democratic National Committee pollster Stanley Greenberg, by June 1996, married mothers were favoring Clinton over Dole, and Clinton had reduced Dole's strong support from married fathers to a margin of only 5 to 6 percentage points. "It's a very big deal," Greenberg enthused, "that the President is running very well with married mothers and, to some extent, married men."[80] The disproportionately white middle-class character of that constituency appears to have escaped Greenberg's and the public's notice.

The Emerging Conservative Cultural "Consensus"

Whether the centrist family-values strategy successfully enhanced Clinton's reelection prospects, it did succeed in promoting a conservative political agenda. As leaders of the right-wing Christian "profamily" movement

recognize, with delight, family-values ardor furthers their reactionary goals. Gary Bauer, president of the right-wing Family Research Council and editor of the fundamentalist *Focus on the Family Citizen,* gloated over "signs that a pro-family consensus, which has been forming for several years, is continuing to gel," despite the election of Clinton. Identifying the *Atlantic* as the premier organ "of smug, elitist, knee-jerk liberalism," Bauer aptly read Whitehead's vindication of Quayle as the most prominent of increasing "signs that the traditionalist revival among policy experts has not been snuffed out."[81]

Bauer understands the political implications of revisionist discourse better than do its propagators. Despite the collectivist aspirations of communitarian ideology, the political effects of identifying "family breakdown" as crucible of all the social crises that have accompanied U.S. postindustrialization and the globalization of capitalism are privatistic and profoundly conservative. Clinton's own "welfare reform" proposals, which differed from those of the Republican right wing only in their lesser degree of severity rather than in their ideological presumptions about family breakdown and welfare dependency, should be persuasive on this score.

Particularly troubling, and ironic, has been the success of recent appeals to homophobic family values among many African American ministers and the electorate they influence. In November 1993, the religious right succeeded in winning support for repeal of a local gay rights protection ordinance from 56 percent of the voters in traditionally liberal black precincts in Cincinnati, Ohio. Effectively portraying the gay and lesbian movement "as a group of well-off whites fighting for 'special rights,'" their right-wing family-values campaign convinced a majority of African American voters that the interests and constituencies of the two movements are antagonistic.[82]

Similar strategic alliances of right-wing family-values activists and African American clergy had blocked the passage of the first referendum for domestic partners legislation in San Francisco in 1989.

Thus the rush to consensus on family values is not only premature, it is also undemocratic. The idea that we should all subscribe to a unitary ideal of family life is objectionable on social scientific, ethical, and political grounds. I had hoped, and Bauer and his associates had feared, that Clinton's 1992 electoral defeat of the right-wing family-values campaign would signal an opportunity for democratic initiatives on family and social reforms, initiatives that would begin with a recognition of how diverse our families are and will continue to be. Instead, under the Clinton administration, we witnessed the startling resurrection of family-values ideology. Beneath its new velvet gown is an old-fashioned, confining, one-size-fits-all corset. But our nation's families come in many shapes and sizes, and will continue to do so. A democratic family politics must address diverse bodily and spiritual desires in rhetoric people find at least as comfortable as the ever-popular combat uniform of "family values."

Toward Reconfiguring Feminist Family Politics

No sound byte rebuttal can convey the complex, contradictory character of family and social turmoil. Still, we must disrupt the stampede to premature consensus on family values. To wage a viable countercultural campaign for *social* values, progressives need to confront the impoverishment of our national capacity to imagine human bonds beyond familial ones that can harbour individuals from our "heartless world." So atrophied is this cultural muscle that "family" impulses overcom-

pensate, a voracious floating signifier for all manner of social ties, as is "family break-down" for all manner of social disarray.

We cannot counter the flawed reductionist logic of family-values ideology, however, unless we resist using knee-jerk symmetrical responses, such as a feminist bumper sticker Whitehead cited effectively to mock feminism: "Unspoken Traditional Family Values: Abuse, Alcoholism, Incest."[83] Portraying nuclear families primarily as sites of patriarchal violence, as some feminists have done, is inaccurate and impolitic.[84] It reinforces a stereotypical association of feminism with antifamilism, which does not even accurately represent feminist perspectives on the subject. Certainly, protecting women's rights to resist and exit unequal, hostile, dangerous marriages remains a crucial feminist project, but one we cannot advance by denying that many women, many of them feminists, sustain desires for successful and legally protected relationships with men and children. We must steer a tenuous course between cultural warriors who blame public violence on (patriarchal) family decline and those feminists who blame family decline on (patriarchal) domestic violence.

A better strategy is to work to redefine family values democratically by extending full rights, obligations, resources, and legitimacy to a diversity of intimate bonds. We might take our lead, here, from the only partly parodic family-values campaign currently blossoming among gays and lesbians.[85] Progressives could appeal to the rhetoric of the revisionist family-values crusade to advocate full marital, reproductive, and custody rights for gays and lesbians. Such a strategy requires bridging the rift between gays and blacks, first by disputing the erroneous notion that these are distinct communities, and second by addressing racism among white gays and black homophobia at the grass-roots level. African

American heterosexuals and all homosexuals, supported by a full-spectrum "rainbow coalition," must come to recognize mutual interests in democratizing family rhetoric, rights and resources.

Exposing the professional middle-class (PMC) bias of communitarian ideology, as Charles Derber has done, offers another opportunity to identify with the actual family needs of the vast majority of citizens.[86] However, we must first acknowledge that full-time homemaking, like the male family wage on which it depends, has become a form of class privilege in fin de siècle U.S.A. that eludes increasing numbers of women to whom it appears, often legitimately, far preferable to the unsatisfying poorly-paid work to which they are consigned.[87] Until feminism can shed its well-earned reputation for disdain toward the world of the full-time, cookie-baking mom, revisionists will effectively exploit feminist class prejudices.

Another way to reconfigure family values is to up the ante in the revisionist bid to elevate the cultural status and responsibilities of fatherhood. Here, I agree with Blankenhorn that the sort of family values campaign we most urgently need is one to reconfigure popular masculinities. "Family-less fathers," be they married or single, do seem to be disproportionately harmful to women, children, and civil society, as well as to themselves. Normative masculine behavior among the overpaid ranks of greedy, power-hungry, competitive, corrupt, corporate, and professional, absent fathers and also among more overtly macho, underpaid, underemployed, undereducated, volatile "boyz in the hood," can lead women, as well as men like Blankenhorn, to idealize cinematic visions of Victorian patriarchy. We sorely need cultural drives to deglamorize violence, predatory sexuality, and sexism, such as one announced in 1994 by an organization of Black professional women, as well as efforts to combat the destructive androcentric logic behind "the clockwork of male careers."[88] Unfortunately, currently the most prominent initiatives of this sort—the Christian men's movement, Promise Keepers, and the 1995 African American Million Man March called by Louis Farrakhan—seem to share with Blankenhorn a nostalgic affection for a world of *Father Knows Best*. The democratic challenge is to find ways to affirm the laudable sentiments these movements tap while enticing them to follow Patricia Williams's call for a more egalitarian "different drummer marchers, please."[89]

Progressives might try to go further than revisionists in efforts to domesticate men. Why not promote full-time homemaking and child rearing as a dignified alternative to over-, under- and unemployment for men, as well as for women? Although the percentages remain small, increasing numbers of men have begun to find this a rewarding and challenging vocation. Popenoe, citing both James Q. Wilson and George Gilder and echoing even feminist Sherry Ortner, maintains that "men need the moral and emotional instruction of women more than vice versa, and family life, especially having children, is a considerable civilizing force for men."[90] If correct, then giving men full-time domestic obligations should prove a potent curriculum.

Rethinking family values requires dodging ideological corners into which revisionists deftly paint feminists and other progressives. First, we should concede that the best familial interests of women (or men) and children do not always coincide. While research demonstrates that high-conflict marriages are at least as destructive to children as is parental divorce, there *are* some unhappy marriages whose adult dissatisfactions harm children less than do their postdivorce circumstances. Some divorces *are* better for the adults who initiate them than for the children who must adjust to them. Ironically, joint custody arrangements often impose a particularly unfair burden on children of divorce. Joint custody preferences were adopted by many states along with no-fault divorce not only to foster greater gender equality for parenting adults but also to serve children's interests in maintaining intimate relationships with both parents after a divorce. Unfortunately, the consequences have been far less benevolent. At their best, even amicable joint custody arrangements typically force children, rather than parents, to become residential commuters between two different households, neighborhoods, or even communities. At their worst, antagonistic joint custody situations extend indefinitely the exposure of children to the damaging effects of parental hostility and conflict. In consequence, so many women have bargained away economic support in order to retain primary custody of their children that some feminist lawyers are proposing to revise the custody standard applied to divorce custody conflicts. For example, University of California family law professor Carol Bruch is promoting legislation to replace the state's current judicial presumption in favor of joint custody awards, with one that grants primary custody to the parent who actually had served as a child's primary caretaker prior to the divorce.

Likewise, just as there are "his" and "her" marriages, so too, divorce is often better for one spouse (not always the male) than the other, as are many remarriages and the stepfamilies they create. When the best interests of the genders collide, it is not easy to say whose should prevail. However, it is also not easy to say whether the genders actually do have incompatible interests in making all marriages harder to leave. The vast majority of women, men, and their children derive clear benefits from living in loving, harmo-

nious, secure relationships, but men and women in marriages like these rarely choose to divorce. What is really at issue in the great divorce controversy is the extent to which easy access to divorce encourages individuals to indulgently throw in the towel on marriages that are not too wet to be saved. In other words, how many marriages that now end in divorce could have been saved and would have been better off for all parties if they had been?

Research does not, and probably cannot, shed much useful light on this question. No doubt "divorce culture," as critics call it, does foster some undesirable instances of capricious divorce. But, how large is that incidence, and at what cost do we deter it? Contrary to the claims of the antidivorce campaigners, there is little evidence that many parents regard divorce as a casual, impulsive, or easy decision. Nor is there evidence that divorce restrictions are likely to achieve that intended effect of buttressing marital commitment. They are at least as likely to deter people from marrying in the first place, and more likely to encourage unhappily married individuals to resort to extralegal forms of desertion and separation. These practices have become so widespread in Roman Catholic countries that even Ireland has taken measures to legalize divorce. For better and worse, governmental attempts to socially engineer the quality, as opposed to the legal form, of intimate relationships have an abysmal historical track record.

The campaign against single mothers calls for an analogous response. We do not need to defend single mothers from the open season of cultural bounty hunters by denying that two compatible, responsible, committed, loving parents generally *can* offer greater economic, emotional, physical, intellectual, and social resources to their children than can one from a comparable cultural milieu. Of course, if two parents are generally better than one, three or four might prove better yet. A version of Barbara Ehrenreich's Swiftian proposal that to lift their families out of poverty Black women should wed "Two, Three, Many Husbands,"[91] is unlikely to win popular affection. Still, we might draw up communitarian sentiments to foster much more collective responsibility for children. Spontaneously, many childless and childfree adults are choosing to become unofficial "para-parents," by forming nurturant, long-term relationships with the children of overburdened parents (a category from which few parents would exclude themselves). Children's advocates might actively promote and seek social protection for these voluntary extended kin relationships, which, as the *New York Times* put it, treat "children as a collective commitment that is more than biological in its impulse."[92] No doubt such proposals would prove more appealing and constructive than polyandry.

Similarly, we should not feel obliged to reject the claim that in industrial societies teenage motherhood often does not augur well for the offspring. Without disputing the view that most teens today lack the maturity and resources to parent effectively, we might point out that this is at least as true of those whom Murray would shame and starve into shotgun marriages as of those who lack daddies or whose daddies lack shotguns. The rising age of marriage since the 1950s is a positive rather than a negative trend, but one which leads to more nonmarital sexuality and pregnancies. Yet countries like Sweden, which do not stigmatize unwed births but make sex education, contraception, and abortion services widely and cheaply available to all, witness few unwanted births and few births to teen mothers. The misguided drive in the United States to restigmatize "illegitimacy," with which the Clinton administration collaborated, demands renewed struggle to destig-

matize abortion among both the populace and health providers and to increase vastly its accessibility. A reinvigorated campaign for comprehensive reproductive rights, perhaps reviving that old Planned Parenthood slogan "every child a wanted child," should promote a full panoply of contraceptive options, like RU–486. It might include a "take back our bodies" drive to wrest exclusive control over abortion provision from doctors, particularly when so few of these in the United States have proven willing to subject their professional status, personal safety, perhaps even their lives, to the formidable risks that the antiabortion movement imposes on abortion providers. At the same time, we should resist the misrepresentation of feminism as hostile to motherhood or "life" by continuing the struggle for genuine, humane workplace and welfare *reforms* (rather than repeals) that make it possible for women to choose to mother or to reject maternity.

Feminists are well-placed to promote this humane brand of progressive family values. Unlike the centrists, we understand that it is not "the family," but one *historically specific* system of family life (the "modern nuclear family") that has broken down. We understand that this has had diverse effects on people of different genders, races, economic resources, sexual identities, and generations. Some have benefited greatly; others have lost enormously; most have won a few new rights and opportunities and lost several former protections and privileges. The collapse of our former national consensus on family values, like the collapse of our prosperous economy to which it was intricately tied, has not been an "equal opportunity" employer. Indeed, women, especially poor and "minority" women, have been some of the biggest winners, and most of the biggest losers. Those who do not want to count feminism, liberalism, and human compassion casualties of the Clinton administration's conversion to the politics of neo–family values had better disrupt the mesmerizing, but misguided, centrist campaign.

NOTES

1. Barbara Dafoe Whitehead, "Dan Quayle Was Right," *The Atlantic* 271, no. 4 (April 1993): 47–84.

2. Barbara Dafoe Whitehead, "Was Dan Quayle Right?" *Family Affairs* 6 (Winter 1994): 13. For sample retreads, see Mona Charen, "Hey, Murphy, Quayle Was Right," *Orange County Register,* March 29, 1993, B9; and Suzanne Fields, "Murphy's Chorus of Enlightened Celebrities," *Orange County Register,* March 29, 1993, B9.

3. David Popenoe, "The Controversial Truth: The Two-Parent Family Is Better," *New York Times,* December 26, 1992, 13; Popenoe, "Scholars Should Worry About the Disintegration of the American Family," *Chronicle of Higher Education,* April 14, 1993, A48; Joan Beck, "What's Good for Babies: Both Parents," *The Santa Rosa Press Democrat,* March 7, 1993, Gi, G6.

4. Daniel Patrick Moynihan, "Defining Deviancy Down," *American Scholar* (Winter 1993): 17–30; James Q. Wilson, "The Family-Values Debate," *Commentary* 95, no. 4 (1993): 24–31.

5. Popenoe, "Scholars Should Worry," A48. For the statement and list of council members, see "Family and Child Well-Being: Eight Propositions," *Family Affairs* 6, nos. 1–2 (Winter 1994): 11.

6. Personal interview conducted April 6, 1994, Oakland, California.

7. Quoted in Karen Winkler, "Communitarians Move Their Ideas Outside Academic Arena," *Chronicle of Higher Education,* April 21, 1993, A7.

8. Personal interview, April 6, 1994.

9. Barbara Dafoe Whitehead, "A New Familism?" *Family Affairs* 5, nos. 1–2 (Summer 1992): 5.

10. Wilson, "Family-Values Debate," 31.

11. Quoted in Michael Kranish, "In Bully Pulpit, Preaching Values," *Boston Globe,* December 10, 1993, 17.

12. Wilson, "Family-Values Debate," 24.

13. The debate took place on an ABC radio call-in program, "The Gil Gross Show," broadcast on January 18, 1993.

14. Whitehead, "Dan Quayle Was Right," 47.

15. Ibid, 80.

16. Wilson, "Family-Values Debate," 31.

17. Gillis suggested the term during a discussion of an early draft of this chapter with the "family values" seminar at the Center for Advanced Studies in the Social and Behavioral Sciences, Stanford, Calif., November 29, 1993.

18. Popenoe, "Controversial Truth."

19. Whitehead, "Dan Quayle Was Right," 48.

20. Whitehead, "The Expert's Story of Marriage," quoted in Moynihan, "Defining Deviancy Down," 24.

21. National Commission on Children, *Beyond Rhetoric: A New American Agenda for Children and Families* (Washington, D.C.: Government Printing Office, 1991), cites essays by Blankenhorn, Elshtain, Popenoe, Sylvia Hewlett, and other contributors to David Blankenhorn, Jean Bethke Elshtain, and Steven Bayme, eds., *Rebuilding the Nest: A New Commitment to the American Family* (Milwaukee: Family Service America, 1990).

22. Popenoe, "Controversial Truth."

23. To sample the diversity of scholarly views, see a careful evaluation of the inconclusive findings of research on the impact of divorce on children, Frank Furstenberg and Andrew Cherlin, *Divided Families: What Happens to Children When Parents Part?* (Cambridge, Mass: Harvard University Press, 1991). For a review of the research on gay and lesbian parenting, see Charlotte Patterson, "Children of Lesbian and Gay Parents," *Child Development* 63 (1992): 1025–42. Indeed, even Sara McLanahan, who Whitehead's *Atlantic* essay portrayed as recanting her earlier views on the benign effects of single parenting, provides a more nuanced analysis of the sources of whatever disadvantages the children of single-parents experience than Whitehead leads readers to believe. She acknowledges that research does not demonstrate that children of "mother-only" households would have been better off if their two biological parents had married or never divorced. See McLanahan and Karen Booth, "Mother-Only Families: Problems, Prospects, and Politics," *Journal of Marriage and the Family* 51, no. 3 (August 1989): 557–80.

24. David Demo, "Parent-Child Relations: Assessing Recent Changes," *Journal of Marriage and the Family* 54 (February 1992): 104.

25. Ibid., 110.

26. Judith Wallerstein and Joan B. Kelly, *Surviving the Breakup: How Children and Parents Cope with Divorce* (New York: Basic Books, 1980); and Judith Wallerstein and Sandra Blakeslee, *Second Chances: Men, Women, and Children a Decade After Divorce* (New York: Ticknor and Fields, 1989).

27. Demo, "Parent-Child Relations," 110. For an even more comprehensive, balanced survey of research on the impact of divorce on children, see Furstenberg and Cherlin, *Divided Families.*

28. See Furstenberg and Cherlin for a summary of this research.

29. Charles Murray, "The Time Has Come to Put a Stigma Back on Illegitimacy," *Wall Street Journal* 29 (October 1993), Forum.

30. Murray appeared on "This Week with David Brinkley," November 29, 1993. The op-ed by Hoover Institute scholar John Bunzel aired on "Perspective," KQED–FM, San Francisco, December 21, 1993.

31. Blankenhorn et al., *Rebuilding the Nest,* 21.

32. Moynihan, quoting from an essay he wrote in 1965, "Defining Deviancy Down," 26.

33. Klein, "Out-of-Wedlock Question," 37.

34. The quotes from Shalala and the unidentified liberal appear in Klein, "Out-of-Wedlock Question."

35. See Elaine Ciulla Kamarck and William A. Galston, "Putting Children First: A Progressive Family Policy for the 1990s" (Progressive Policy Institute pamphlet, September 27, 1990).

36. Many feminists fear that even employing the concept "postfeminism" cedes important political ground to the backlash. I disagree and use the term to indicate a culture that has both assimilated and tamed many of the basic ideas of second-wave feminism. For a fuller discussion of this use of this term, see Deborah Rosenfelt and Judith Stacey, "Second Thoughts on the Second Wave," *Feminist Studies* 13, no. 2 (Summer 1987): 341–61.

37. Popenoe, "Scholars Should Worry."

38. Wilson, "Family-Values Debate," 31.

39. Whitehead, "A New Familism?" 2.

40. Sue Shellenbanger, "Bill Galston Tells the President: My Son Needs Me More," *Wall Street Journal,* June 21, 1995, B1.

41. Jay Lefkowitz, "Where Dad Belongs," *Wall Street Journal,* June 18, 1993, A12.

42. Susan Chira, "Push to Revamp Ideal for American Fathers," *New York Times,* June 19, 1994, 10. Blankenhorn presents an extended polemical exposition of his neotraditional fatherhood ideology in his *Fatherless America: Confronting Our Most Urgent Social Problem* (New York: Basic Books, 1995).

43. For my earlier critiques of the "new conservative feminism" and its contributions by Elshtain, Friedan, and Hewlett, see Judith Stacey, "The New Conservative Feminism," *Feminist Studies* 9, no. 3 (Fall 1983): 559–83; and Rosenfelt and Stacey, "Second Thoughts on the Second Wave."

44. Blankenhorn, for example, is interpreted approvingly by a *Wall Street Journal* columnist as providing intellectual justification for "laws that mandate spousal notification prior to all abortions. Today laws in most states consider fetuses the property of pregnant women. Unfortunately, this posture leads to the view that children are the sole responsibility of mothers." Lefkowitz, "Where Dad Belongs."

45. Quoted in Winkler, "Communitarians Move Their Ideas Outside Academic Arena," A13.

46. Whitehead, "A New Familism?" 2.

47. Blankenhorn, *Fatherless America,* 122.

48. Norval Glenn, "A Plea for Objective Assessment of the Notion of Family Decline," *Journal of Marriage and the Family* 55, no. 3 (August 1993): 543; Wilson, "Family-Values Debate," 25.

49. Hillary Rodham Clinton, *It Takes a Village: And Other Lessons Children Teach Us* (New York: Simon & Schuster, 1996).

50. Dirk Johnson, "No-Fault Divorce Is Under Attack," *New York Times,* February 12, 1996, A8.

51. Ibid.

52. The most influential treatment of no-fault divorce has been Lenore J. Weitzman, *The Divorce Revolution: The Unexpected Social and Economic Consequences for Women and Children in America* (New York: Free Press, 1985). However, Weitzman's data have since been challenged, and she has acknowledged errors in coding and analysis.

53. Constance R. Ahrons, *The Good Divorce* (New York: HarperCollins, 1994): 35.

54. Popenoe applies this term to me and to other critics of "family-values" ideology in "Scholars Should Worry."

55. Glenn, "Plea for an Objective View," 544.

56. Wilson, "Family-Values Debate," 29.

57. David Popenoe, "American Family Decline, 1960–1990," *Journal of Marriage and the Family* 55, no. 3 (August 1993): 529.

58. Moynihan, "Defining Deviancy Down," 26; Whitehead, "Dan Quayle Was Right," 70.

59. Blankenhorn, *Fatherless America,* 233.

60. Jean Bethke Elshtain, "Family and Civic Life," in *Rebuilding the Nest,* 130.

61. See, for example, Patterson, "Children of Lesbian and Gay Parents," and Joan Laird, "Lesbian and Gay Families," in Froma Walsh, ed., *Normal Family Processes* 2d ed. (New York: Guilford Press, 1993): 282–328.

62. Andrew Sullivan, "Here Comes the Groom: A Conservative Case for Gay Marriage," *New Republic,* August 28, 1989, 10.

63. Moynihan, quoted in Winkler, "Communitarians Move Their Ideas," A13.

64. Clinton, *It Takes a Village,* book jacket copy.

65. Clinton, according to his senior adviser George Stephanopoulos, "thinks the proper role for the government is to work on the fight against discrimination, but he does not believe we should support [gay] marriage." Quoted in Marc Sandalow and David Tuller, "White House Tells Gays It Backs Them," *San Francisco Chronicle,* October 21, 1995, A2.

66. John Batteiger, "Bigotry for Bucks," *San Francisco Bay Guardian,* April 7, 1993, 19. For primary evidence of the prominence of homophobic appeals in right-wing organizing see, for example, James C. Dobson, "1993 in Review," *Focus on the Family Newsletter,* January 1994.

67. Evelyn C. White, "Christian Right Tries to Capitalize on Anti-Gay Views," *San Francisco Chronicle,* January 12, 1994, A6.

68. Susan Yoachum and David Tuller, "Right Makes Might in Iowa," *San Francisco Chronicle,* February 12, 1996, A1.

69. Quoted in Yoachum and Tuller, "Right Makes Might in Iowa," A1, A3.

70. Carolyn Lochhead and David Tuller, "Clinton Attempts to Strike Balance on Gay Marriages," *San Francisco Chronicle,* May 15, 1996, A1, A11.

71. Robin Toner, "Republican Factions Gather Under One Tent, Then Argue," *New York Times,* May 11, 1993.

72. Blankenhorn made these remarks during his presentation to "Safe Communities: A Search For Solutions," a 1995 California Public Affairs forum sponsored by Hitachi, Ltd., which was held at the Sheraton Palace Hotel, San Francisco, September 28, 1995.

73. Chronicle News Services, "Clinton Cracks Down on Deadbeat Dads," *San Francisco Chronicle,* June 19, 1996, A2.

74. Elizabeth Traube, "Family Matters," *Visual Anthropology* 9, no. 1 (1995): 56–73.

75. Daniel Patrick Moynihan, *The Negro Family: The Case for National Action* (Washington, D.C.: U.S. Department of Labor, 1965).

76. Charles Murray, "The Emerging White Underclass and How to Save It," *Philadelphia Inquirer,* November 15, 1993, A15.

77. Howard Odum, *Social and Mental Traits of the Negro* (New York: Columbia University Press, 1910), quoted in Gutman, "Persistent Myths About the Afro-American Family," *Journal of Interdisciplinary History* 6, no. 2 (Autumn 1975): 184.

78. Wilson defines this index as the ratio of employed Black males per one hundred black females in the same age group. He charts a decline in this ratio from 70:100 in 1960 to 40:100 in 1986, and the disparity is reflected in the decline of Black marriage rates. William J. Wilson, *the Truly Disadvantaged: The Inner City, the Underclass, and Public Policy* (Chicago: University of Chicago Press, 1987).

79. Married voters ages 18 to 34 with children voted 48% for Bush, 39% for Clinton, and 22% for Perot; singles (with and without children) in that age group voted 58% for Clinton, 20% for Bush, and 19% for Perot. Poll data were reported in a *Washington Post* story by Barbara Vobejda, reprinted as "'Family Gap' Found in Post-Election Poll," *San Francisco Chronicle,* November 27, 1992, A4.

80. Quoted in Allison Mitchell, "Banking on Family Issues, Clinton Seeks Parents' Votes," *New York Times,* June 25, 1996, C19.

81. Gary L. Bauer, "Family Values Matter!" *Focus on the Family Citizen,* May 17, 1993, 16.

82. Donald Suggs and Mandy Carter, "Cincinnati's Odd Couple," *New York Times,* December 13, 1993, A11.

83. Whitehead, "Dan Quayle Was Right," 55.

84. Some academic feminists indulge this impulse as well. For a recent example, see Elspeth Probyn's otherwise incisive critique of postfeminist TV family fare, "Television's *Unheimlich* Home," in *The Politics of Everyday Fear,* ed. Brian Massumi (Minneapolis: University of Minnesota Press, 1994).

85. I discuss the politics of the gay and lesbian family values campaign at length in chapter five of Judith Stacey, *In the Name of The Family: Rethinking Family Values in a Postmodern Age* (Boston: Beacon Press, 1996).

86. Charles Derber, "Coming Glued: Communitarianism to the Rescue," *Tikkun* 8, no. 4 (July-August 1993): 27–30.

87. For example, in a 1985 Roper poll, 51% of women claimed that, given this choice, they would prefer a paid job to full-time homemaking, but in 1991 only 43% of women expressed that preference, while 53% said they would rather stay home. Nancy Gibbs, "The War Against Feminism," *Time,* March 9, 1992, 55.

88. Arlie Hochschild, "Inside the Clockwork of Male Careers," in *Women and the Power to Change,* ed. Florence Howe (New York: McGraw-Hill, 1975): 47–81.

89. Patricia J. Williams, "Different Drummer Please, Marchers!" *The Nation,* October 30, 1995, 493.

90. David Popenoe, "The Family Condition of America: Cultural Change and Public Policy," in *Values and Public Policy,* ed. Henry J. Aaron, Thomas E. Mann, and Timothy Taylor (Washington, D.C.: Brookings Institute, 1994): 98. See also, Wilson, "Family-Values Debate," 30: "Marriage is in large measure a device for reining in the predatory sexuality of males." While, according to Gilder, "Men without women frequently become the 'single menace,' . . ." often destined to a Hobbsean life—solitary, poor, nasty, brutish, and short." Gilder, *Men and Marriage* (Gretna, La: Pelican, 1986): 6–7, 10. For a feminist reading of the social evolutionary domestication of men, see Sherry Ortner, "The Virgin and the State," *Feminist Studies* 4, no. 3 (October 1978): 19–35.

91. Barbara Ehrenrich, "Two, Three, Many Husbands," in *The Worst Years of Our Lives: Irreverent Notes from a Decade of Greed* (New York: Pantheon, 1990): 183–87.

92. Pepper Schwartz, "Children's New Bonds: Para-Dads, Para-Moms," *New York Times,* November 9, 1995, B1, B4.

∾ Contributors

EMILY K. ABEL is Professor of Health Services and Women's Studies at the University of California, Los Angeles. Her recent books include *Circles of Care: Work and Identity in Women's Lives* (SUNY Press, 1990), coedited with Margaret K. Nelson, and *Who Cares for the Elderly? Public Policy and the Experiences of Adult Daughters* (Temple, 1991). She currently is writing a history of women's care for sick and disabled family members in the United States from 1850 to 1940.

TERRY ARENDELL is Associate Professor and Chair of the Department of Sociology at Colby College. Her interests include interpretive sociology, family, gender, feminist theory, and qualitative research methods. She is the author of *Fathers and Divorce* (Sage, 1996) and *Mothers and Divorce: Legal, Economic, and Social Dilemmas* (California, 1987) and the editor of *Contemporary Parenting: Issues and Challenges* (Sage, 1997). Also, she has been published in various scholarly journals, including *Signs, Gender & Society, Family Science Review,* and *Qualitative Sociology.*

MICHÈLE BARRETT is the coauthor of *The Anti-Social Family* (Verso, 1982), and most recently, the coeditor of *Destabilizing Theory: Contemporary Feminist Debates* (Polity, 1992).

JESSIE BERNARD (1903–1996) was an eminent sociologist and feminist, one of the founders of Sociologists for Women in Society and of the Center for Women's Policy Studies. She was also the author of numerous books and articles, including *The Future of Marriage* (Bantam Books, 1972), *The Future of Motherhood* (Dial Press, 1974), *Women, Wives, Mothers: Values and Options* (Aldine, 1975), *The Female World* (Free Press, 1981), and *The Female World from a Global Perspective* (Indiana, 1987).

PHYLLIS BURKE won the 1994 American Library Association's Gay and Lesbian Book Award for Nonfiction as well as the 1993 PEN Oakland Josephine Miles Award and was nominated for a 1993 Lamda Literary Award for her book *Family Values* (Random House, 1993). She is also the author of the novel *Atomic Candy* and a nonfiction work, *Gender Shock: Exploding the Myths of Male and Female* (Anchor, 1996). She lives in San Francisco with her family and teaches at San Francisco State University.

LINDA M. BURTON is Professor of Human Development and Family Studies and Sociology, and Senior Research Associate at the Population Research Institute at Pennsylvania State University. She recently completed a five-year ethnographic study of the neighborhood contexts and family transitions in four- and five-generation urban African American kin networks with teen parents. She is currently working on a book entitled *Meeting Places,* which chronicles the lives of families involved in this study.

SUZANNE C. CAROTHERS is Professor at the City College of the City University of New York in the Department of Education, the Elementary Education Program. After conducting an ethnographic study for her dissertation, "Generation to Generation: The Transmission of Knowledge Skills and Role Models from Black Working Mothers to Their Daughters in a Southern Community," she earned a Ph.D. from New York University in 1987. She develops programs for parents, children, and child care workers, in collaboration with community agencies. She is author of "Taking Teaching Seriously," in *To Become a Teacher: Making a Difference in Children's Lives* (Teachers College Press, 1995).

NANCY J. CHODOROW is Professor of Sociology at the University of California, Berkeley, a faculty member of the San Francisco Psychoanalytic Institute, and a psychoanalyst in private practice. She is the author of *The Reproduction of Mothering* (California, 1978), *Feminism and Psychanalytic Theory* (Yale, 1989), and *Femininities, Masculinities, and Sexualities: Freud and Beyond* (Kentucky, 1994). She is working on a book, *The Power of Feelings: Personal Meaning in Psychoanalysis, Gender, and Culture* (working title).

SCOTT COLTRANE is Associate Professor of Sociology at the University of California, Riverside. His research on families and gender has appeared in various scholarly journals and books. He is the author of *Family Man: Fatherhood, Housework, and Gender Equity* (Oxford, 1996) and *Gender and Families* (Pine Forge Press, 1997) and coauthor with Randall Collins of *Sociology of Marriage and the Family: Gender, Love, and Property* (Nelson Hall, 1995). Coltrane's current research focuses on families' responses to economic stress, ethnic diversity, and media images of men and masculinity.

JOHN D'EMILIO is Professor of History at the University of North Carolina, Greensboro, and founding director of the Policy Institute of the National Gay and Lesbian Task Force. He is the author of *Sexual Politics, Sexual Communities: The Making of a Homosexual Minority in the United States, 1940–1970* (Chicago, 1983) and coauthor, with Estelle Freedman, of *Intimate Matters: A History of Sexuality in America* (Harper & Row, 1988). He is currently at work on a biography of the civil rights leader and pacifist Bayard Rustin.

JOHN DEMOS was born and raised in Cambridge, Massachusetts, graduated from Harvard College, and received his professional training at Oxford, the University of California at Berkeley, and Harvard. He has taught at Brandeis University and at Yale, where he is currently Samuel Knight Professor of American History. His books include *The Unredeemed Captive: A Family Story from Early America* (Knopf, 1994), *A Little Commonwealth: Family Life in Plymouth Colony* (Oxford, 1970), and *Entertaining Satan: Witchcraft and the Culture of Early New England* (Oxford, 1982), for which he received the 1983 Bancroft Prize.

MARJORIE L. DEVAULT is Associate Professor of Sociology and a member of the Women's Studies Program at Syracuse University. Her book *Feeding the Family: The Social Organization of Caring as Gendered Work* (Chicago, 1991) examines the household work of producing care and sociability. She has also written on feminist research methods, the social organization of interpretation, and the "women's profession" of dietetics and nutrition counseling. She is currently exploring constructionist approaches to family studies.

MICAELA DI LEONARDO has written *The Varieties of Ethnic Experience: Kinship, Class, and Gender Among California Italian-Americans* (Cornell, 1984) and *Exotics at Home: Anthropologies, Others, American*

Modernity (Chicago, 1998). She has edited *Gender at the Crossroads of Knowledge: Feminist Anthropology in the Postmodern Era* (California, 1991) and coedited *The Gender/Sexuality Reader* (Routledge, 1997). She teaches anthropology and women's studies at Northwestern University.

BONNIE THORNTON DILL is Professor of Women's Studies and Affiliate Professor of Sociology at the University of Maryland, College Park. She founded and directed the Center for Research on Women at the University of Memphis, which, under her leadership, gained national prominence for outstanding work on the interconnections of race, class, and gender. Her research focuses on African American women, work, and families; and she is currently conducting a research project on coping and survival strategies of low-income single mothers in rural southern communities.

PAULA L. ETTELBRICK has been an advocate for family definitions that include lesbian and gay families for nearly two decades. Through her legal work, writings, and speaking, she promotes a vision of family that more realistically responds to the needs of all families and is not solely contingent upon marriage or biology. She is the Legislative Counsel for the Empire State Pride Agenda and an Adjunct Lecturer in Law at the University of Michigan Law School.

ANNE FINGER is a Lecturer in the Department of English at Wayne State University, Detroit, where she teaches women's studies and creative writing. Her most recent book is a novel, *Bone Truth* (Coffee House Press, 1994). She has also written an autobiographical essay entitled *Past Due: A Story of Disability, Pregnancy, and Birth* (Seal Press, 1980).

NANCY FOLBRE, Professor of Economics at the University of Massachusetts, Amherst, has served as a consultant on gender and development for the Population Council, the United Nations Human Development Report Office, and the World Bank. Her research explores the interface between feminist theory and political economy in a variety of ways. In addition to numerous articles published in academic journals, she is the author of *Who Pays for the Kids? Gender and the Structures of Constraint* (Routledge, 1994) and an associate editor of the journal *Feminist Economics*.

MINDY FRIED, Ph.D., teaches sociology at Tufts University. Her book about corporate culture and parental leave policy is forthcoming from Temple University Press. Her other books include *Babies and Bargaining*, a book for union activists who want to negotiate family benefits into their contracts, and *How Does Your Community Grow: Planting Seeds for Quality Day Care*. She also has a six-year-old daughter, who has taught her a lot about motherhood.

NATHALIE FRIEDMAN is a Special Research Scholar at Columbia University and Adjunct Professor of Sociology at Barnard College. She is currently conducting a study on religious youth.

ANITA ILTA GAREY is Assistant Professor of Sociology at the University of New Hampshire. Her forthcoming book, *Weaving Work and Family* (working title), focuses on the social construction of motherhood and the interconnection of work and family. During 1997–98 she was a fellow at the Bunting Institute at Radcliffe College, finishing her book and working on a study of kinship in Botswana.

EVELYN NAKANO GLENN is Professor of Women's Studies and Ethnic Studies at the University of California, Berkeley. She has written extensively on work and technology issues, racial-ethnic women, and the political economy of family and household. She is the author of *Issei, Nisei, Warbride* (Temple, 1986) and editor (with Grace Change and Linda Forcey) of *Mothering: Ideology, Experience, and Agency*. Her current research centers on the race-gender construction of labor and citizenship.

FRANCES K. GOLDSCHEIDER is University Professor and Professor of Sociology at Brown University. She has done extensive research on changes in living arrangements (who lives with whom) as well as research on changes in the nature of coresidence, including between men and women, as cohabitation replaces marriage, and between parents and their young adult children living at home.

KARLA B. HACKSTAFF is Assistant Professor of Sociology at Northern Arizona University, Flagstaff. She received her doctorate in 1994 from the University of California, Berkeley. Her areas of expertise include divorce and marriage, family, gender, feminisms, and qualitative research methods. She is interested in politics and processes of constructing knowledge.

KAREN V. HANSEN wrote *A Very Social Time: Crafting Community in Antebellum New England* (California, 1994) and coedited *Women, Class, and the Feminist Imagination* (Temple, 1990). She is the author of numerous articles on nineteenth-century friendship, masculinity, and historical sociology and is currently working on a project that explores the relationships between Native Americans and Norwegian immigrants in turn-of-the-century Dakota. Hansen is Associate Professor of Sociology at Brandeis University, where she teaches feminist theory, sociology of families, and women's biography.

DONALD J. HERNANDEZ, Ph.D., serves as Study Director with the Board on Children, Youth, and Families at the National Academy of Sciences for a study on the health and adjustment of immigrant children and families. He also serves as Senior Subject Matter Expert with the U.S. Bureau of the Census for the Survey of Program Dynamics, which is a ten-year longitudinal study designed to assess the consequences of federal welfare reform for child development and family well-being.

ROSANNA HERTZ, Professor of Sociology and Women's Studies at Wellesley College, is the author of *More Equal Than Others: Women and Men in Dual-Career Marriages* (California, 1986) and the author of the forthcoming *Heart Strings and Purse Strings.* She is the coeditor of *Studying Elites Under Qualitative Methods,* with Jonathan B. Imber (Sage, 1995), and the editor of *Reflexivity and Voice.* She is also the editor of the journal *Qualitative Sociology.* She is currently working on a study of single mothers by choice. During the 1996–97 academic year she was a visiting scholar at the Florence Heller Graduate School for Advanced Studies in Social Welfare at Brandeis University.

ARLIE RUSSELL HOCHSCHILD, Professor of Sociology at the University of California, Berkeley, is the author of *The Managed Heart* (California, 1983), *The Second Shift* (Viking, 1989), and most recently, *The Time Bind: When Work Becomes Home and Home Becomes Work* (Metropolitan, 1977).

LINDA J. HOLTZMAN is a Reconstructionist rabbi who is currently the Director of Practical Rabbinics at the Reconstructionist Rabbinical College. She is also the education director for Congregation Mishkan Shalom. Holtzman is a founding member and organizer of the Reconstructionist Herva Kaddisha of Philadelphia.

BELL HOOKS is a feminist critic and cultural studies scholar who has written fourteen books. Her most recent works are *Bone Black: Memories of Girlhood* (Henry Holt, 1996) and *Reel to Real: Race, Sex, and Class at the Movies* (Routledge, 1996). She writes frequently for such magazines as *Spin, Interview, Paper,* and *Z.* Currently, bell hooks resides in New York.

JACQUELINE JONES is Truman Professor of American Civilization at Brandeis University, where she teaches American social history. Her most recent book is *American Work: Black and White Labor Since 1600* (W. W. Norton, 1998).

NAZLI KIBRIA is Assistant Professor of Sociology and Director of the Women's Studies Program at Boston University. Her research and teaching interests include the comparative study of families, race, and ethnicity. She is currently writing a book, tentatively titled *Becoming Asian American: Race, Identity, and Second-Generation Chinese and Korean Americans.* She is also conducting a longitudinal study on households headed by women in Bangladesh.

RALPH LAROSSA is Professor of Sociology at Georgia State University and the author of a number of books and articles on the culture and conduct of fatherhood in the United States. His most recent work on the subject is *The Modernization of Fatherhood: A Social and Political History* (Chicago, 1997), which recounts how the image of the father as economic provider, pal, and male role model all rolled into one became institutionalized during the Roaring Twenties and the Great Depression.

ANNE MACHUNG is currently a Research Associate at the Institute for the Study of Social Change at the University of California, Berkeley. She collaborated with Arlie Hochschild in writing *The Second Shift* (Viking, 1989) and is currently writing on issues dealing with women and organizational change in today's labor force.

MARY MCINTOSH taught sociology at the University of Essex in England for many years. She has written on a variety of topics: "The Homosexual Role" (1968); *The Organisation of Crime* (1975); "The State and the Oppression of Women" (1978); *The Anti-Social Family* (with Michèle Barrett, 1982), and *Sex Exposed: Sexuality and the Pornography Debate* (edited with Lynne Segal, 1992). She is now retired and living in London.

JULIANNE MALVEAUX is an economist, columnist, and television and radio commentator. She is an independent scholar affiliated with the Center for Women Policy Studies in Washington, D.C., who also owns a production company, "Last Word Productions." Malveaux's research focuses on race, gender, and public policy. She is working on a film on Dr. Martin Luther King Jr.'s economic legacy, and on a series of essays, *Wall Street, Main Street, and the Side Street,* on economic stratification.

MARTHA MAY teaches at Western Connecticut State University. She recently edited *The New Christian Right* (Garland, 1996) with Melvin Urofsky.

SONYA MICHEL is Director of Women's Studies and Associate Professor of History and Women's Studies at the University of Illinois, Urbana-Champaign. She is also coeditor of the journal *Social Politics: International Studies in Gender, State, and Society.* Her book *Children's Interests/Mothers' Rights: The Shaping of America's Child Care Policy* is forthcoming from Yale University Press.

MARTHA MINOW, Professor of Law at Harvard Law School, teaches family law and civil procedure. She is the author of a book entitled *Making All the Difference: Inclusion, Exclusion, and American Law* (Cornell, 1990), and a forthcoming book, *Not Only for Myself: Identity, Politics, and Law* (New Press). She edited *Family Matters: Readings on Family Lives and the Law* (New Press, 1993) and coedited with Gary Bellow *Law Stories* (Michigan, 1996). Her scholarship includes articles about the treatment of women, children, persons with disabilities, and members of ethnic, racial, or religious minorities.

GREY OSTERUD coedits *Gender & History* and teaches American and women's history in the Boston area. The chapter included in this collection draws upon her book *Bonds of Community: The Lives of Farm Women in Nineteenth-Century New York* (Cornell, 1991). Osterud is currently at work on a sequel, *"Putting the Barn Before the House": The Lives of Farm Women in Twentieth-Century New York* (working title).

MARY PARDO teaches in the Department of Chicana/o Studies at California State University, Northridge. She continues to research the links between social change and gender, race, and class identity in Los Angeles. Her forthcoming book, *Mexican American Women Activists: Identity and Resistance in Two Los Angeles Communities* (Temple, 1998), draws a comparative analysis between the activism of the women in the Mothers of East L.A. in an inner-city working-class community and women's activism in a middle-class, ethnically mixed suburb.

JENNIFER L. PIERCE is Associate Professor of Sociology and an affiliate of the Center for Advanced Feminist Studies at the University of Minnesota. She has published *Gender Trials: Emotional Lives in Contemporary*

Law Firms (California, 1995), in addition to articles in the *American Sociological Review, Signs, Explorations in Ethnic Studies, Women's Studies,* and the *Berkeley Journal of Sociology.* She is currently coediting an anthology with the Center for Advanced Studies Book Collective, *Social Justice, Feminism, and the Politics of Location.*

JOSEPH H. PLECK is Professor of Human Development and Family Studies at the University of Illinois, Urbana-Champaign. He is the author of *Men and Masculinity* (Prentice-Hall, 1974), *The American Man* (Prentice-Hall, 1980), *The Myth of Masculinity* (M.I.T., 1981), and *Working Wives, Working Husbands* (Sage, 1985). His research interests include fatherhood and adolescent males' sexual and contraceptive behavior.

JAMES PTACEK is Assistant Professor of Sociology at Suffolk University in Boston, where he is also on the faculty of the master's program in criminal justice. He has worked on the problem of violence against women as a researcher, a batterer's counselor, and a trainer of criminal justice, mental health, and hospital personnel. He is currently writing a book, *Judging Violence: Women, Battering, and the State* (working title). With his partner, Bonnie Zimmer, he has a son, Alex.

CLAIRE REINELT received her Ph.D. in sociology from Brandeis University. Her dissertation, "Motherhood and Disability in the Twentieth Century: Historical Constructions and Contemporary Experiences," explores how women with disabilities are positioned historically in relation to motherhood and how they negotiate their right to mother. She is currently a senior evaluation consultant in Brookline, Massachusetts, working to build the capacity of nonprofit organizations to learn from the work they are doing and share that learning with others.

BARBARA KATZ ROTHMAN is Professor of Sociology at Baruch College and the Graduate School of the City University of New York. In addition to *Recreating Motherhood* (1989), from which the chapter in this volume is excerpted, she is the author of *In Labor: Women and Power in the Birthplace, The Tentative Pregnancy: How Amniocentesis Changes Women's Experience of Pregnancy* (1986; all three published by W. W. Norton), and with Wendy Simonds, *Centuries of Solace: Expressions of Maternal Grief in Popular Literature* (Temple, 1992). She is currently working on a book on genetics.

NINA GLICK SCHILLER is a social and medical anthropologist who has worked with Haitian migrants, the homeless mentally ill, people with AIDS, women on welfare, black and white working women, and convicted arsonists. Her books include *Nations Unbound: Transnational Processes, Postcolonial Predicaments, and the Deterritorialized Nation-State* (Gordon and Breach, 1994) and *Towards a Transnational Perspective on the Study of Migration: Race, Class, Ethnicity, and Nationalism Reconsidered* (New York Academy of Sciences, 1992). She is currently Associate Professor of Anthropology at the University of New Hampshire and editor of the journal *Identities: Global Studies in Culture and Power.*

JULIET B. SCHOR is Director of Studies in the Women's Studies Program at Harvard University, where she has been teaching since 1984. She is also Professor of the Economics of Leisure at Tilburg University in the Netherlands and author of *The Overworked American* (Basic Books, 1991). Schor's new book, which is a critical look at the U.S. consumer system, is scheduled for publication in 1998. Her current research focuses on "downshifting" and an emergent voluntary simplicity movement.

DENISE A. SEGURA is Associate Professor of Sociology and Director of the Center for Chicano Studies at the University of California, Santa Barbara. She has written numerous articles on Chicana/Mexicano immigrant workers, family life, and Chicana political consciousness. Currently she is doing research on adaptation strategies and community construction among Mexican immigrants. She is also working on a coauthored book on Chicana feminism.

JUDITH STACEY, the Streisand Professor of Contemporary Gender Studies and Professor of Sociology at the University of Southern California, has written and lectured extensively on the politics of family change. Her publications include: *In the Name of the Family: Rethinking Family Values in the Postmodern*

Age (Beacon, 1996); *Brave New Families: Stories of Domestic Upheaval in Late-Twentieth-Century America* (Basic Books, 1990); and *Patriarchy and Socialist Revolution in China* (California, 1983). She is a founding member of the Council on Contemporary Families, a group committed to challenging the research and politics behind contemporary campaigns for family values.

CAROL B. STACK, author of *Call to Home* (Basic Books, 1996) and *All Our Kin* (Harper & Row, 1974), is Professor and Chair of Women's Studies and Education at the University of California, Berkeley. She is currently working on a book on youth in the low-wage labor market in Oakland, California. She is the author of numerous articles on family and poverty policy, and on family, generation, and migration within the United States.

THOMAS B. STODDARD (1949–1997) was a lawyer, teacher, writer, and political activist who worked principally on issues concerning civil liberties, the rights of lesbians and gay men, and the rights of persons living with HIV. From 1986 to 1992, he was Executive Director of the Lamda Legal Defense and Education Fund. In 1992 and 1993 he led the Campaign for Military Service, which worked to end the exclusion of lesbians and gay men from the United States military. He was Adjunct Professor of Law at New York University School of Law, where he taught from 1981 to 1996, and Vice Chair of the American Foundation for AIDS Research. Professor Stoddard died from HIV disease on February 12, 1997, at the age of 48.

MURRAY A. STRAUS is founder and codirector of the Family Research Lab at the University of New Hampshire. He is the coauthor of *Intimate Violence* (Simon & Schuster, 1988) and *Behind Closed Doors* (Anchor, 1980). Most recently he is the author of *Beating the Devil Out of Them: Corporal Punishment in American Families* (Lexington, 1994).

NIARA SUDARKASA was appointed as the first woman to head Lincoln University, the formerly all-male institution chartered in 1854 as America's first Black college. Sudarkasa received her undergraduate education as an early entrant at Fisk University and Oberlin College and earned an M.A. and Ph.D. in anthropology from Columbia University. She is a widely published scholar who has received seventeen academic fellowships and awards, thirteen honorary degrees, and over sixty civic and professional honors. She is one of seventy-five women photographed by Brian Lanker for his now famous book and traveling exhibit entitled *I Dream a World: Portraits of Black Women Who Changed America*.

MAURA I. TORO-MORN is Associate Professor in the Department of Sociology and Anthropology at Illinois State University. She is currently working on a book manuscript about the class and gender dimensions of Puerto Rican migration to Chicago.

NICHOLAS W. TOWNSEND is Assistant Professor of Anthropology at Brown University. His research interests are in the varied connections men have to children, families, and households, and in the relationship between social processes and demographic events and structures. He has conducted field work on fatherhood in California and in Botswana.

PETER UHLENBERG is Professor of Sociology and a Fellow of the Carolina Population Center at the University of North Carolina, Chapel Hill. He received his Ph.D. in demography from the University of California, Berkeley, in 1971. His research interests include the demography of aging and intergenerational relationships. Recent publications include "The Burden of Aging: A Theoretical Framework for Understanding the Shifting Balance of Care Giving and Care Receiving as Cohorts Age" (*The Gerontologist*, 1996).

LAUREL THATCHER ULRICH is completing a study of textiles in the social history of early America, a project that relies upon analysis of existing artifacts as well as written documents. She is the Phillips Professor of Early American History and Professor of Women's Studies at Harvard University. She is the author of the Pulitzer Prize–winning book *A Midwife's Tale: The Life of Martha Ballard, Based on Her Diary, 1785–1812* (Knopf, 1990), and *Good Wives: Image and Reality in the Lives of Women in Northern New England, 1650–1750* (Oxford, 1980).

LYNET UTTAL is Assistant Professor in the Department of Child and Family Studies at the University of Wisconsin, Madison. She studies the relationships between employed mothers and child care providers in order to understand how these relationships support employed mothers' efforts simultaneously to manage employment and family life with young children.

LINDA J. WAITE is Professor of Sociology at the University of Chicago, where she directs the Center on Aging. She is a former President of the Population Association of America. Her research focuses primarily on the family, from the youngest to the oldest ages. At the early stages of family life, she has examined the choices families make for child care for preschool children. At the later stages, she has studied intergenerational support and exchange and family structure and living arrangements of older adults. Waite is a coauthor with Frances Goldscheider of *New Families, No Families: The Transformation of the American Home* (California, 1991), which received the Duncan Award from the American Sociological Association.

KATARINA WEGAR is the author of *Adoption, Identity, and Kinship: The Debate over Sealed Birth Records* (Yale, 1997) and has published several articles on adoption. She has also written about the division of labor in medicine and the role of social science in American medical education. She is the coeditor of *Gender, Work, and Medicine: Women and the Medical Division of Labour* (Sage, 1993). She received her Ph.D. from Brandeis University in 1994, and she is currently Assistant Professor of Sociology at Old Dominion University.

BARRY WELLMAN, born in the Bronx, knew that pundits' predictions of the death of community were overly exaggerated. Now Professor of Sociology at the University of Toronto, Wellman's research at the Centre for Urban and Community Studies concerns how social networks function as communities. Wellman is also studying how networks of work and community operate in cyberspace. He is co-editor of *Social Structures: A Network Approach*, 2d ed. (JAI Press, 1997) and of *Networks in the Global Village* (Westview, 1997).

JUDITH K. WITHEROW was born in 1944 in the Pennsylvania Appalachians. A mixed-blood Native American lesbian, she was raised in rural poverty. She resides in Maryland with her partner of twenty years, Sue. Judith struggles with many illnesses including multiple sclerosis and systemic lupus. She is a storyteller, writer, and poet, and the winner of the first annual Audre Lord Memorial Prose Contest for Non-Fiction, April 1994.

KERSTI A. YLLÖ is Professor of Sociology at Wheaton College in Norton, Massachusetts. She received her Ph.D. in sociology from the University of New Hampshire in 1981. She has conducted research in the field of domestic violence for nearly twenty years and is coauthor of *License to Rape: The Sexual Abuse of Wives* (Free Press, 1985) and *Feminist Perspectives on Wife Abuse* (Sage, 1988). She is currently involved in evaluating the U.S. Marine Corps intervention into spouse abuse.

BONNIE ZIMMER is the Director of HAVEN at MGH, a domestic violence advocacy program based at Massachusetts General Hospital. She is the cochair of the Massachusetts chapter of the National Association of Social Workers Committee on Domestic Violence and Sexual Assault. She and her life partner, Jim Ptacek, were the cocreators and instructors of an innovative women's studies course at Brandeis University, "Internship in the Prevention of Violence Against Women and Children," from 1994 to 1996. The chapter in this collection is drawn from several years' work with teen mothers in the Merrimack Valley of Massachusetts.

MAXINE BACA ZINN is Professor of Sociology and Senior Research Associate at the Julian Samora Research Institute at Michigan State University. She has a long-standing interest in unraveling the meanings of race, class, and gender in family settings. She is the coeditor of *Women of Color in U.S. Society* (Temple, 1994) and co-author of *Diversity in Families,* the pioneer textbook in treating family diversity as the norm and showing how public issues shape the private lives of a population varied in race, class, and gender.